UNDERSTANDING AND APPLYING MEDICAL ANTHROPOLOGY

Peter J. Brown

Emory University

Mayfield Publishing Company
Mountain View, California
London • Toronto

Library of Congress Cataloging-in-Publication Data

Understanding and applying medical anthropology / [compiled by] Peter
    J. Brown.
        p.   cm.
    Includes bibliographical references and index.
    ISBN 1-55934-723-6
    1. Medical anthropology—Methodology.   2. Medical anthropology—
Philosophy.   I. Brown, Peter J.
GN296.U54   1998
306.4'61'01—dc21   97-31050
                                                                         CIP

Manufactured in the United States of America
10   9

Mayfield Publishing Company
1280 Villa Street
Mountain View, California 94041

Sponsoring editor, Janet M. Beatty; production, Strawberry Field
Publishing; manuscript editor, Jennifer Gordon; art director, Jeanne M.
Schreiber; text designer, Cynthia Bassett; cover designer, Susan M.
Breitbard; illustrator, Joan Carol; manufacturing manager, Randy Hurst.
The text was set in 10/12 Palatino by Archetype Book Composition and
printed on 45# Baycoat Velvet by the Banta Book Group.

Credits appear at the back of the book on pages 445–446, which constitute
an extension of the copyright page.

For Betsy

To the Instructor

Teaching medical anthropology is both exciting and challenging. Undergraduates are able to relate to sickness and healing because they have had some experience with these central issues and because many are thinking of careers in the health industry. Learning about the multiple causes of disease and the cultural variation in healing practices makes students examine their own lives and culture with a fresh perspective; one of the real satisfactions of being a teacher comes from watching students get excited by such an intellectual journey. At the same time, teaching medical anthropology is challenging due to its amorphous yet undeniably growing body of knowledge. How does a professor organize such a course?

I have divided this book into two main parts: Part I illustrates the variety of theoretical and analytical approaches used by medical anthropologists, and Part II provides examples of those approaches as they are relevant to a variety of health issues and problems; hence, the title of the reader—*Understanding and Applying Medical Anthropology*. From looking at the first part of the book, it should be apparent that I hold a very broad view of the scope of medical anthropology and that I am committed to the traditional four-field approach of general anthropology. I believe that the application of anthropological knowledge—the job of making our research useful—is part of the responsibility of all anthropologists. Aspects of nearly all anthropological work are relevant to the understanding and solution of human problems. That is why I use the term *applying* medical anthropology rather than the narrower and more specific *applied* anthropology. The latter refers to anthropological work done for a client on a problem identified by the client. I think students want to read about anthropological research and analysis on relevant topics, and the second part of the collection provides some good examples of this. At times I have included two or more selections on a similar topic in order to enhance in-class discussions. The organization of this book, I believe, will suit a heterogeneous approach to a medical anthropology course.

As far as I can tell, there is no agreement about how a basic course in medical anthropology should be taught. Almost twenty years ago, the first special publication of the new Society for Medical Anthropology concerned teaching medical anthropology; the volume included nine different model courses (Todd and Ruffini 1979). The diversity of those courses—ranging from ethnomedicine to biomedical anthropology to family structure and health—was impressive. Theoretical diversity has been a continuing hallmark of medical anthropology, and it is reflected in most of the edited textbooks of the field. On the other hand, the relatively few regular textbooks in the field have had, by necessity, a more narrow theoretical focus, like the ecological approach (McElroy and Townsend 1996) or cultural aspects of healing and medicine (Foster and Anderson 1978; Helman 1994). Recently, some new books have provided a synthesis of medical anthropology, even as the discipline has expanded and the theoretical basis of research has become more sophisticated (Anderson 1996; Hahn 1995).

I put together this reader in medical anthropology because there is a need for a book of original research articles to accompany the texts, ethnographies, and case studies that we use in such courses. At first I thought it would be easy to assemble such a reader—after all, I was already using a Xerox collection of about twenty-five articles—but it turned out to be quite a difficult task. This is partially because of the expanding breadth of the field and partially because there are so many fascinating articles available. My first list included more than 220 articles, and when I asked colleagues to help they simply suggested more titles! I eventually pared the list to the current number through a long and painful process. I was at times forced to cut entire articles that I really admired and to edit out portions of articles due to space constraints.

In the end, I selected the readings with five criteria in mind:

- Readability
- A mix of classic articles and more recent contributions
- A range in theoretical orientation
- A range of theoretical difficulty or sophistication
- Ethnographic variation

I expect the reading level to be appropriate for upper-division undergraduates who have already taken a basic anthropology course. Many selections are from the standard professional journals in the field, including *Medical Anthropology Quarterly, Medical Anthropology, Social Science and Medicine, Human Organization,* and *Culture, Medicine and Psychiatry.* Interestingly, there has been no new textbook reader in medical anthropology since the launching of many of these journals. The growth of medical anthropology has been astounding; both the quantity and quality of ethnographic, biocultural, and critical medical anthropological research is impressive.

To add to the pedagogical value of this collection, I have included section and reading introductions. In section introductions, I emphasize the "conceptual tools" that are put to work in each kind of medical anthropology. It is important for students to be reminded of the central concepts before they start reading the details of a particular case. In selection introductions, I describe the context for the problem at hand by raising related issues and by listing some questions for discussion. All the introductions include some bibliographic suggestions for further reading, which are listed at the back of the book. These references might be useful for undergraduates who are writing term papers or for graduate students who are developing a stronger grasp of the field. There are, of course, a great many other resources in medical anthropology, many of which are available through the Society for Medical Anthropology (SMA). Those who are interested may want to consult the SMA's web page: <http://www.people.memphis.edu/~sma>.

I am painfully aware that, due to space constraints, there are many important topics in medical anthropology that are not represented here, including ethnopharmacology, health policy, childbirth, gerontology, and clinical cases. I hope that instructors using this book will feel free to contact me with their opinions about selections that work (or do not work) and with suggestions for future editions; my e-mail address is <antpjb@emory.edu>.

Acknowledgments

There are many people who have helped me in this endeavor. They deserve all of my thanks and none of the blame for the mistakes that are here. Holli Levinson, Rob Goddard, and Erin Finley were terrific advice-givers, permission-seekers, index-makers, and copy editors. I relied heavily on the insightful reading and opinions of two gifted graduate students, Mark Padilla and Ron Barrett. I also wish to thank my colleagues in medical anthropology at Emory, especially Marcia Inhorn, Michelle Lampl, and George Armelagos, as well as Mel Konner, Charles Nuckolls, Claudia Fishman Parvantha, Robert Hahn, Mark Auslander, Bradd Shore, Cory Kratz, Elizabeth Whitaker, Thom McDade, and Carol Worthman. The department at Emory has been a continuing source of intellectual inspiration and dynamic tension. Colleagues at other institutions, such as Alan Goodman, and five reviewers of a draft of the book were also extremely helpful. These five are Mark Cohen, State University of New York at Plattsburgh; Pamela I. Erickson, University of Connecticut; David Kozak, Fort Lewis College; Lynnette E. Leidy, University of Massachusetts; and Joan C. Stevenson, Western Washington University.

I am particularly grateful for the many undergraduate students of medical anthropology whom I have had the pleasure to teach over the past nineteen years. I have learned a great deal from all of them. I have also benefited from the opportunity of editing the journal *Medical Anthropology* over the past seven years, and I want to thank the authors, reviewers, and editorial board members for the great deal that I have learned from them. I want to thank my Mayfield editor, Jan Beatty, for her support, advice, encouragement, and patience. I appreciate your work. During part of the time I worked on this book, I was supported by the Emory University Research Committee, and I gratefully acknowledge that support.

To the Student

I think it is exciting that you have decided to take a course in medical anthropology. What initially sparked your interest? The prospect of studying other medical systems, like shamanism? Discovering what made disease rates increase in ancient societies? Your concern about the serious health problems both in the United States and throughout the world? All these topics—exotic and mundane—are related to medical anthropology. Or maybe your interest is related to your career ambitions or current work in the health care field? Whatever the case, you will find the study of medical anthropology to be intriguing and intellectually rewarding. You will also find the study of medical anthropology to be relevant to your life—if only because disease, illness, healing, and death are universal in the human experience. All cultures have medical systems. Whether you participate in that medical system as a patient or a healer, there is real value in understanding the big picture of how and why that system works. Medical anthropology is an exciting field both for intellectual understanding and for social action.

As you skim through this book, notice the extremely wide variety of topics that are included within medical anthropology. That is because anthropology itself takes a broad, holistic approach to the study of human biology and cultures. In the United States, anthropology traditionally includes four fields: biological or physical anthropology, archaeology, cultural anthropology, and anthropological linguistics. Medical anthropology is *not* one of the four fields; rather, it is the use of anthropological concepts and methods in the study of health, disease, and healing. One of the hallmarks of medical anthropology, therefore, is the theoretical and practical diversity within the field; this is one reason why I refer to "medical anthropologies" in the first selection.

Your course instructor may not cover all of these approaches during your particular course. Most medical anthropologists, like most anthropologists in general, concentrate on the cultural end of the field. Many courses in medical anthropology do not deal with evolutionary or biological questions. Your course instructor will likely pick and choose selections according to his or her orientation to the field. That is as it should be, but I hope that you will also see this book as a resource for independently exploring other approaches.

I have selected the readings here with you, the student, in mind. Primarily, I tried to pick selections that were readable and that contained interesting case studies. Some I picked because they are controversial in order to help spark class discussions. But I also wanted the selections to reflect diversity—in both sophistication as well as in the areas of the world represented. There are quite a few selections based in the United States. Most of these are articles from professional scholarly publications (for example, *Medical Anthropology Quarterly*, *Medical Anthropology*, *Social Science and Medicine*, and *Culture, Medicine and Psychiatry*), and they will, on occasion, require concentrated reading on your part. When reading primary sources, you may want to skim the article first in order to familiarize yourself with the overall structure of the argument. Prereading for the main ideas is not a substitute for the real reading, but it can better prepare you to understand the article.

In the introductions to the sections and to the readings themselves, I have provided an orientation to the general context and framework of the material. Section

introductions provide a thumbnail description of important "conceptual tools." It
will be useful for you to put these concepts and vocabulary into your own personal intellectual toolbox. Each selection introduction includes thought questions
to ponder. My aim is to help you place a particular selection into the larger scheme
of things; so the introductions are designed to get you to think about the broader
(and sometimes unanswerable) questions involved. Finally, the introductions cite
several sources of related work in medical anthropology (found at the back of the
book); these references will be useful if you are doing an independent project like
a term paper or if you would like to do some further reading on the topic.

Because medical anthropology is such a diverse field, I have divided this book
into two main parts. Part I is designed to introduce you to the multiple approaches
used by medical anthropologists in their research and other work. As you can see,
I have identified four major approaches in bio-culturally oriented medical anthropology and five distinct approaches in culturally oriented medical anthropology.

The second part of the book is about applying medical anthropology. In Part
II, I have identified nine different problem areas—from doctor–patient communication to international health programs—and selections that illustrate how anthropological analysis can be *relevant* to the understanding and solution of those
real problems. There is an important field called "applied anthropology" in which
people, including medical anthropologists, do research, program implementation,
and program evaluation for particular clients who hire them to work on particular
problems. The writings of those applied anthropologists are often reports written
for their clients. The selections in Part II do not all fit neatly within the domain of
applied anthropology. Although many discuss the particular solution to a problem—such as the AIDS epidemic or social stigma related to disease—the main
purpose of other selections is to get readers to "re-think" the problem in a new
way. That is what I mean by "applying" medical anthropology (Podolefsky and
Brown 1997).

If you are interested in learning more about medical anthropology, you may
want to consult the "handbook" of the field by Carolyn Sargent and Thomas
Johnson (1996), which includes nineteen review articles about different aspects of
medical anthropology. It also has a terrific bibliography. If you are thinking about
graduate study, you may want to consult the directory, *Graduate Programs in
Medical Anthropology*, produced by the Society for Medical Anthropology (a unit of
the American Anthropological Association [AAA]), or the *Guide to Departments*,
published annually by the AAA. For further information, contact the AAA on the
Internet: <http://www.ameranthassn.org>. The major academic journals in the
field, including *Medical Anthropology Quarterly, Medical Anthropology, Social Science
and Medicine, Culture, Medicine and Psychiatry,* and *Anthropological Medicine,* are
also useful places to look for information.

I hope you enjoy the selections here and that you learn a lot from your study
of medical anthropology. More importantly, I hope that what you learn in this
course will be useful to you in the future, because you were encouraged to think
about disease, healing, and medicine in new ways. I would appreciate your feedback on the selections here (for future editions of this book) so contact me at
<antpjb@emory.edu>.

Contents

Part I

UNDERSTANDING MEDICAL ANTHROPOLOGY
Biocultural and Cultural Approaches

This book is divided into two parts: The first deals with understanding medical anthropology, and the second is devoted to applying medical anthropology. Understanding must come before utilization. But what does it mean to understand something (or somebody)? Of course, understanding requires knowledge, but that is not enough. Four things come to mind. First, understanding means being able to take another point of view or at least imagine another point of view. It follows, then, that understanding also means you have mastered the basic vocabulary and conceptual framework used by another so that you can articulate or communicate that point of view. Understanding means that you have a grasp of the range of interests and abilities of the "other." Finally, understanding requires that you have a basic knowledge of the history and goals of another.

The selections in this first part of the book will acquaint you with the fundamental goals, concepts, and theoretical approaches used by medical anthropologists. You will learn to understand what medical anthropology is all about. As you will learn in the first selection, there is no single field that can be called "medical anthropology." There is so much diversity of theoretical approaches that it is more accurate to think of multiple medical anthropologies. This diversity can be considered in two fundamental areas—biocultural approaches and cultural approaches. In general, anthropologists are very tolerant and encouraging of a multidisciplinary approach to understanding humans. In the simplest sense, medical anthropology refers to an anthropological way of exploring issues of health, disease, healing, and sickness. But what is anthropology?

Anthropology is the holistic and comparative study of people or, more properly, humankind. Obviously, many other disciplines study people: psychology, sociology, medicine, political science, biology, history, and so on. However, to understand ourselves in a complete way, we must join these separate and somewhat narrow views into a single framework. Anthropology attempts to integrate these disparate views by beginning with our biological and evolutionary roots, by exploring the development of culture through prehistoric and historic time, by examining the unique human ability for language, and, finally, by examining the diversity of *present-day* cultures throughout the world.

The effort to integrate these different views has resulted in the four fields that characterize U.S. anthropology: cultural anthropology, biological (or physical) anthropology, archaeology, and anthropological linguistics. These different fields have three basic things in common. First, their approaches are all comparative, although these comparisons may be across cultures, time periods, or species. Second, all four fields emphasize the importance of the concept of culture. Third, they share an interest in understanding humans holistically, within a broader context. However, the four fields differ greatly in the kind of data or information they use and the methods they employ, with some fields borrowing from the biological sciences, some the humanities, and some the social sciences.

Medical anthropology provides a unique way of understanding the human experience. This is because all human beings—irrespective of culture, class, or historical epoch—experience sickness and death. Simultaneously, all cultures—irrespective of technological complexity—have medical systems that help people cope with the inevitability of sickness, just as all cultures have religious systems that deal with the inevitability of death. Medical anthropology tries to understand the causes of health and illness in societies. Our own health is influenced by the environment, our genetic inheritance, and, most importantly, our socioeconomic circumstances; all of these factors interact in complex ways.

In the first half of this book, I have divided medical anthropology into two basic approaches: biocultural and cultural. Although this distinction is a bit artificial, I think it is useful. In my view, the term *biocultural* (or *biosocial*) refers to an anthropological view of the ways in which people adapt to their environment and change that environment that make health conditions better or worse. On the other hand, cultural approaches in medical anthropology emphasize the role of ideas, beliefs, and values in creating systems of illness classification and medical programs for curing illness. In other words, biocultural approaches focus on health, and cultural approaches focus on aspects of medicine or ethnomedicine. There is considerable variation within each of these two basic approaches, as can be seen in this organizational table:

Approaches in Medical Anthropology
I. Biocultural Approaches
    A. Evolution, health, and medicine
    B. Human biological variation
    C. Bioarchaeology and the history of health
    D. Cultural and political ecologies of disease
II. Cultural Approaches
    A. Belief and ethnomedical systems
    B. The social construction of illness and the social production of health
    C. Healers in cross-cultural perspective
    D. Culture, illness, and mental health
    E. Critical medical anthropology

In general, biocultural approaches try to combine the concepts and questions that are common in biological (physical) anthropology, archaeology, and ecology. Cultural approaches are more influenced by ethnography, linguistics, psychology, sociology, and philosophy. All these approaches reflect slightly different theoretical orientations and consequently use slightly different methods for research and analysis.

Why should you learn about the diversity of the theoretical perspectives in medical anthropology? Certainly, it is an important part of the process of understanding a field of study. Knowing about diverse theoretical orientations can help you understand why certain questions about health and illness have been asked in particular ways.

Anthropological research projects usually begin with three elements that, when combined, allow researchers to do their work. First, there is a problem or question that the anthropologist wants to explore. Second, there is an ethnographic site, a particular society, or a historical period that will provide the information and the context for answering the question. Third, the researcher has a theoretical approach that is used to ask questions in a certain way, to pay attention to particular things, or to determine what research methods to use. When a researcher proposes a project, all three factors come into play; in a sense, the researcher focuses on the topic by sharpening each of these dimensions, like triangulating in on a target. In this regard, the theoretical orientation is of primary importance. To a significant extent, the theoretical orientation determines what questions get asked and how they get answered. It is therefore useful to examine the different theoretical orientations of medical anthropology that are illustrated in the different sections in the first part of the book.

BIOCULTURAL APPROACHES IN MEDICAL ANTHROPOLOGY

The first kind of medical anthropological studies we will explore are those that focus on the intersection of human populations, ecology, and evolutionary (including historical) change over time. This intersection involves biological anthropology, archaeology, and ecologically oriented medical anthropology. This general approach might be called *biocultural* because it emphasizes society and patterns of behavior rather than patterns of thought. (Many anthropologists also call this a biosocial approach.) The research examples in this first biocultural section are more data-oriented and analytical of physical evidence (that is, more positivistic). There is a common theoretical paradigm shared in the first eleven selections that involves concepts of biocultural evolution, adaptation (and maladaptation) to disease, and patterns of social organization (including inequality). These selections tend to be focused on disease rather than illness and body rather than mind. But these differences are a matter of emphasis; all anthropological studies recognize the interrelatedness of disease and illness, body and mind. The selections in this part of the book all take human biology quite seriously, and this is an important attribute of medical anthropology in general.

Evolution, Health, and Medicine

Biological anthropology and medical anthropology have important common interests in health and disease. Biological anthropologists are interested in understanding humans as a particular kind of animal: a culture-bearing, bipedal primate (Jurmain, Nelson, and Turnbaugh 1984). Medical anthropologists are interested in aspects of health, disease, and healing practices in those human animals. Some parts of biological anthropology, like the study of fossil hominids (paleoanthropology) or research on nonhuman primate social behavior (primatology) are not directly related to issues of health. On the other hand, questions about the distribution of disease, physiological adaptations to disease, and social factors related to health status—central questions in medical anthropology—all fall within the domain of two areas of biological anthropology. The first biological approach involves the application of evolutionary theory to understanding diseases in the past and to understanding what they may tell us about contemporary health issues. The second biological approach concerns morphological, physiological, and genetic variation among people—modern *Homo sapiens*—living in different kinds of conditions.

The central theoretical concept in all of the life sciences is evolution. Many students misunderstand evolution, thinking that it is just a theory, when in fact a general theory like this is actually a rare and powerful explanatory tool, supported by hundreds of thousands of hard scientific facts (hard as rocks, in the case of fossils). Evolution means that things change over time, including a species changing into another species. It is important to remember that humans have a *dual system of inheritance;* that is, we utilize (or are shaped by) both biological and cultural systems of evolution. We inherit genetic traits from our parents through the process of sexual reproduction, and we inherit our culture (including our society's ideas, beliefs, and values) from our social group (including our parents) through the process of learning. As we discuss in the first selection, culture is a central concept in anthropology, and the existence of culture has played a major role in the success of our species on the planet. Evolutionary pressures have shaped cultures to fit within particular ecological, political, and economic constraints.

This part of the book starts with two selections dealing with evolution, health, and medicine. Human biocultural evolution means that human societies have transformed from small hunting and gathering bands into large, crowded industrialized states; these changes have resulted in different distributions of disease. The genetic makeup of our species, *Homo sapiens,* was largely shaped in the long prehistoric era of hunting and gathering. Today, some medical anthropologists argue, there is a mismatch between modern diet and exercise patterns and our genetic heritage. That mismatch between Paleolithic genes and a postmodern lifestyle is a major reason for serious health problems such as cardiovascular disease (the largest single cause of death in the United States). The application of this type of reasoning is central to a new area of research and thinking called Darwinian medicine. Anthropological research in this area uses evolutionary models to examine both the physiological responses of the human host to a disease organism and the physiological responses to medical therapies, and I think that the results of such Darwinian reasoning are quite thought provoking.

Human Biological Variation

The second section of selections deals with the important issue of understanding and explaining human biological variation, a central topic of biological anthropology (Harrison et al. 1988). Human variation is sometimes a touchy subject, particularly in the United States, because it deals with the question of race. Anthropologists generally agree that race is *not* a useful biological concept, although it is a relevant and powerful sociocultural construct (that is why readings on racial categorization are found in the section on ethnicity in this book). Human biological variation can be either genotypic or phenotypic, that is, in the total genetic makeup (genotype) or in the physiological expression of genes as they are shaped by environment (phenotype). In this regard, we may inherit a gene for a certain height, but whether or not we reach that potential depends on important factors like childhood nutrition. Human biological variation is sometimes explained by evolutionary pressures caused by, for example, a disease like malaria. Human biological variation can also be the result of different access to resources (like food) or exposure to environmental stressors (like lead paint); in this way, human biological variation invariably reflects both genes and culture. Ultimately, however, it is impossible to separate the discussion of human biological variation from the ideas of evolution and adaptation.

There are three selections dealing with human biological variation in this section. The first deals with an issue in nutritional anthropology that has relevance to international health questions. How do we explain the fact that children in most Third World countries are short in stature? In selection 4, Reynaldo Martorell argues against a hypothesis called "small but healthy." Selection 5 deals with an issue in Native American health: the high prevalence of diabetes mellitus in these people. If the distribution of this chronic disease is the result of a genetic predisposition—the so-called thrifty gene—then how can anthropologists explain this? The answer requires a holistic and evolutionary approach. Selection 6 considers the ethical problems associated with genetic screening; it is written by an anthropologist who has studied the social implications of a rare genetic disease in a small island community. In other words, the cultural and personal impact of genetic variation is important to consider.

Medical anthropologists need to take human biology seriously (Johnston and Low 1984; Moore et al. 1980). At the same time we must recognize that biomedical categories and ideas are often oversimplified, like the assumption of a distinction between mind and body. The fact that medical systems are social and cultural constructs, however, should not detract from the fact that we are biological animals. Although many courses in medical anthropology do not begin with a discussion of the biological underpinnings of health and illness, I think that this is the best place to start.

Bioarchaeology and the History of Health

Many people first hearing the word *anthropology* think of archaeology (as well as Indiana Jones, dusty excavations, exotic locales, and the discovery of cool artifacts). Although archaeology is indeed a part of anthropology, most anthropological researchers are in fact cultural anthropologists who study contemporary peoples.

Archaeologists are interested in describing and analyzing the patterns of culture and the processes of cultural change in the past. Of course, the vast majority of the past is *pre*history, that is, from before the invention of written records. Even in more recent periods, the story of regular people without political power is barely reflected in the written historical record. Therefore, archaeologists use the methodology of excavation and the analysis of the remains of *material culture*—mostly, the ancient trash that is left behind. Archaeologists find and analyze this trash because they want to do two things: first, describe prehistoric cultures and lifeways, and second, explain how and why cultural systems change. This second goal is a large task. Archaeologists want to know, for example, how urban-based civilizations evolved, why some ancient state societies collapsed, and who invented agriculture. Archaeologists want to know the causes and consequences of cultural change over substantial periods of time.

One of the most important consequences of cultural change is that it influences health—patterns of disease and mortality. Some cultural inventions (like the Big Mac and the automobile) can influence health through diet and activity patterns. The invention of agriculture has had important ramifications in regard to health too. In fact, Jared Diamond has argued that the invention of agriculture, which brought with it state-level civilizations, was the "worst mistake in the history of the human race" (Diamond 1987). This obviously overstates the case. Important thresholds of cultural change can benefit some people and hurt others—for example, the accomplishments of early civilizations were built on the backs of slaves. Whether complex, urban society reliant on agriculture is an improvement or a mistake compared to the hunting and gathering life of our ancestors depends, in large measure, on whether you are the slave or the pharaoh. In this regard, the system of social stratification or structured inequality must be central in all anthropological analyses.

Bioarchaeologists are interested in measurements of human health in the past. They use methods such as paleopathology—the analysis of skeletal remains of a prehistoric population—to reconstruct patterns of disease and the demographic profile of life and death. Paleopathological analysis complements archaeological explanation. Archaeologists can help in the understanding of food production systems or cycles of warfare, and paleopathologists can demonstrate the biological consequences of those food shortages or warfare.

Bioarchaeological and historical approaches in medical anthropology focus on the process of cultural change over time. Looking at both continuity and change over time is called *diachronic* analysis, as contrasted with *synchronic* ethnographic descriptions that focus on how a cultural system works in a single snapshot of time.

Historical approaches in the study of health are obviously diachronic. But the history of health requires scholars to examine more than the traditional archival sources that document the political accomplishments of great men. Historians of health must use population data to describe important phenomena like the decline of mortality in Europe (as Thomas McKeown [1979] does in selection 8), or the effects of little-documented epidemics that William H. McNeill describes in his book *Plagues and Peoples* (1976). In this regard, historians of health differ in focus from historians of medicine. The traditional saying of historians—those who do not know the past are condemned to repeat it—may be overstated, but it is patently true that important parallels exist between the past and the present. Many of these parallels center on the relationship of social stratification (wealth) and health status. In the past as well as the present, disparities of wealth, power, and access to resources have biological consequences reflected in patterns of morbidity and mortality. In these ways, bioarchaeological and historical approaches within medical anthropology provide an important and enlightening historical perspective for understanding contemporary health problems and policies.

Cultural and Political Ecologies of Disease

This section of the book approaches medical anthropology ecologically. Ecology is the study of the relationship between organisms in an environment. Human societies share their environment with many other organisms, including ones that produce disease. An ecological approach to human health and illness emphasizes the fact that the environment and its health risks are, to a significant extent, created by the culture. When they think of ecology, many students mistakenly narrow their view to clean water, air, endangered animals, and rain forests. It is important to remember that other species, and particularly other human groups, must be considered as part of the environment. As such, ecological understanding must include a component of political analysis.

To a large extent, the ecological approach in medical anthropology fits midway between the biological orientations described previously and the cultural approaches that are described later; the ecological approach is clearly *biocultural*. Because ecology focuses on the relationships between species, there is an inherent emphasis on the study of disease. I believe that the study of disease and human behavior in an ecological setting is a fundamental task for medical anthropology.

Disease is an inevitable part of life, and coping with disease is a universal aspect of the human experience. All humans, during the course of their lives, harbor infections by disease organisms and suffer the consequences of those infections. The experience of disease—by individuals or whole populations—is as inescapable as death itself. Yet the particular diseases that afflict people, as well as the ways in which symptoms are interpreted and acted on, vary greatly from culture to culture.

In many cultures (including our own) people think of themselves as masters of their environment, because, within the food chain they exploit so many plants and animals as sources of energy and nutrients. Yet at the same time humans are being exploited by microorganisms, including those that cause disease, as a source of food and shelter. Disease ecology primarily focuses on the complex interactions of the pathogen, the environment, and the human host. The nutritional, physiological, genetic, and mental condition of the individual human host all play significant, if not completely understood, roles in both infectious and noninfectious disease states. Current international health problems, called emerging infections, provide a good example of how flexible these ecological interactions can be. Often, new disease strains emerge because of the misuse of technologies like antibiotics and because human actions have created ecological imbalance, famine, displacement of refugees, and so forth.

The ecological approach can be applied to anthropological questions concerning the interaction of biology and culture in human evolution. It can help us understand why particular cultural behaviors may make sense and have been retained in an ecological setting. In epidemiology, the contribution of an anthropological focus on human behavioral patterns can help in unraveling fundamental questions of disease causality. Through the study of behavioral patterns related to the social epidemiology of disease, it is possible to design health programs that are both effective and culturally acceptable. Moreover, the ecological approach may help anticipate the health implications

of technological change or new political-economic policies.

The ecological approach in medical anthropology has been a standard paradigm, primarily because of the successful textbook by Ann McElroy and Patricia Townsend (1996), who use the label "medical ecology." This approach has been criticized for ignoring the political-economic dimensions of health and illness and therefore "blaming the victims" of disease (Singer 1997). Such criticisms have a certain validity, just as traditional cultural ecological studies have been criticized for underemphasizing history and power relations, for example, the "revisionist" studies of !Kung history (Lee 1992). Nevertheless, these criticisms have touched off a valuable debate, spearheaded by Andrea Wiley (1992), about the usefulness of biocultural approaches and the concept of adaptation in medical anthropology. One consequence of this debate has been that more medical anthropologists and biological anthropologists have started to incorporate political-economic variables into their ecological models (Goodman and Leatherman [in press]).

The distinction between cultural ecology and political ecology is useful in this regard. The selections in this part of the book are divided into these two categories. Cultural ecology and political ecology are not exclusive categories; they refer, in large measure, to different levels of analysis. Cultural ecology refers to analyses at the level of individuals or human groups interacting with other species (plants, animals, pathogens) within the environment. It therefore looks at individual behaviors and their association with disease rates; this is a *micro*sociological approach. Political ecology refers to historical interactions between human groups (ethnic groups, classes, nations) that affect the ecology through population movements, land use, or differential access to resources. Political ecology often focuses on the stratification caused by political systems and how that is related to the distribution of disease. Because it focuses on the interaction of groups, political ecology calls for a *macro*sociological analysis (Brown, Inhorn, and Smith 1996). It is important to recognize that adding the dimension of political ecology to microsociological studies reveals the "unnatural history" of many diseases (Turshen 1984).

In the three selections in the section on ecology, you will meet (and hopefully not contract) a variety of different infectious diseases: malaria, sleeping sickness (African trypanosomiasis), schistosomiasis, tuberculosis, and AIDS. All these diseases are complicated from a microbiological or parasitological point of view; all these diseases are serious and warrant medical management. But medical anthropologists believe that to really understand the causation of these diseases, it is paramount to take a broader view, one that acknowledges the role of both individual behaviors and political-economic forces.

In summary, the first part of understanding medical anthropology requires us to focus on the biocultural origins of health and disease. The approaches of evolutionary medicine, paleopathology, and health history, as well as cultural and political ecology, all share an emphasis on themes of adaptation, evolution, and the ways that human behaviors shape patterns of disease and death. These are simultaneously biological and cultural themes common to all of anthropology.

CULTURAL APPROACHES IN MEDICAL ANTHROPOLOGY

Cultural approaches form the core of medical anthropological research and theory. Most people who identify themselves as medical anthropologists are trained in cultural anthropology, and most medical anthropological studies utilize some form of ethnographic methodology. There is probably more theoretical diversity in culturally oriented medical anthropology than in the biocultural orientation. Cultural approaches consider the systems of ideas, beliefs, and values of a particular social group. In regard to health and illness, culture provides ways of explaining and combating sickness. Medicine is a cultural system of knowledge and practice.

Culture is the most important concept in anthropology, and most anthropological studies of health, healing, and medicine utilize some type of cultural approach. Ironically, despite the centrality of culture, there is little agreement among cultural anthropologists concerning the exact definition of culture. Philosophers of science say that this means that culture is an orienting concept in anthropology. Culture refers to the learned patterns of thought and behavior characteristic of a social group—but that covers a lot of territory. Anthropologists are interested in culture in a myriad of domains—religion, kinship, economy, art, law, child-rearing practices, markets, and conceptions of the self, just to name a few. Some anthropologists emphasize materialistic aspects of culture like the productive economy; others emphasize social relations and the way that political power is organized in a group; still others are interested in the interpretation of symbols and meaning in a cultural context.

All cultural anthropologists agree, however, that the best way to collect information about culture is through ethnographic fieldwork—living in another society, observing, interviewing, and learning from the local people. Some of the most important cultural anthropological work is ethnographic description of peoples' lives and their cultural beliefs and behaviors. These ethnographic descriptions, typically published in book form, are called ethnographies. Most ethnographies have some description of the local culture's beliefs and practices regarding medicine. This is largely because medicine is not a separate category from religion in many cultures that anthropologists have traditionally studied.

It is impossible to do a pure or complete description of another culture or to do an ethnography that is theory-free. For one thing, despite the goal of holism, it is impossible for a single anthropologist to describe and understand everything in another society. Additionally, the anthropologist's preexisting theoretical orientation determines what that anthropologist finds interesting and pays attention to during field research. Today, nearly all cultural anthropological studies are still ethnographic, but they focus on a particular question in a particular cultural context, and they use an explicit theoretical orientation that informs the analysis of that question. To understand cultural anthropology and culturally oriented medical anthropology, therefore, it is very useful to have some idea of the variety of theoretical orientations that are being used by researchers.

All anthropologists enjoy cross-cultural comparisons. They like to know about a wide variety of customs and practices, some of which seem exotic and extremely different from our own way of doing things. Cross-cultural comparisons tell us about both similarities and differences in customs and ways of thinking. But whether there are more similarities or differences between societies depends on one's point of view. All humans face the problems of getting adequate food and shelter; all humans face a similar life cycle of childhood dependence, growth, reproduction, sickness, and death; all humans live in social groups marked by family ties, conformity, and conflict. The variation in the ways humans solve these problems—not only in behaviors but in ways of thinking—is enormous.

There are very few things that anthropologists regard as cultural universals; the cultural prohibition about incest always comes to mind, even though the definition of incest varies from society to society. Another cultural universal is the fact that all societies have systems of belief and ritual that we can call religion. Similarly, most medical anthropologists would argue that all societies have a cultural system for explaining and struggling against the inevitability of sickness and death. The cultural beliefs and practices that are learned and shared by a group of people can be called a medical system. Most societies have specific people who know about sickness and disease, people who are able to diagnose and treat. These people may be shaman, *curanderos,* "medicine men," folk healers, or physicians. People come to these practitioners in times of difficulty; they are treated with respect and sometimes fear. Curers have special knowledge that gives them power. In general, curers are perceived to have courage that gives them strength in the struggle against sickness and death. All people in all cultures have to cope with sickness in themselves and their loved ones. Cultural systems of belief help people cope with those difficult, inevitable times. Our culture provides explanations for how and why we get sick. Our medical systems, as part of culture, tell us what to do when confronted with illness.

Culturally constructed medical systems are generally called ethnomedicine by anthropologists. People used to think of ethnomedicine as limited to exotic, non-Western systems for healing that medical anthropologists have traditionally described and studied. But over the last two decades, people have come to recognize that Western allopathic or scientific medical practices (the regular medicine at regular doctors' offices and hospitals) are also products of a particular culture. Anthropologists use the label "biomedicine" to refer to this medical system, but what they mean is that scientific Western medicine is actually just another type of ethnomedicine. In other words, biomedicine is based on a set of cultural assumptions about the nature of reality and the nature of health. Most biomedical treatments (especially surgeries) and therapies, in fact, have not been subjected to adequate scientific testing to prove their utility. Most Americans do not know, for example, that the practice of biomedicine in the United States is quite different from medical practice in France, Germany, or England. Lynn Payer (1988) has described U.S. biomedicine as aggressive and based on a metaphor of the body as a machine. It is for this cultural reason that U.S. treatments use heavier dosages of drugs and more frequent and more invasive surgeries. In all likelihood, actual healing in biomedicine depends on dynamic somatic and psychological processes based on beliefs. In other words, belief in the power of the doctor and the medicine creates a placebo effect that is remarkably powerful. The body heals itself most of the time, but we give medicine the credit for the cure.

Most anthropologists are cultural anthropologists, and, similarly, most medical anthropologists have a cultural orientation. But there is so much variation in this part of medical anthropology that I have divided this section into five areas based on theoretical themes. As you will see from the selections, however, there is a

good deal of overlap among these themes, and they all emphasize the social and cultural aspects of medical systems.

Belief and Ethnomedical Systems

These selections revolve around the question of ethnomedical systems and the power of belief. In general, ethnomedical systems provide three elements: a theory of the etiology (causation) of illness, mechanisms for the diagnosis of those causes; and, finally, the prescription of appropriate therapy based on that diagnosis. The practice of medicine depends on the art of diagnosis and the craft of therapy. The theory of the causation of health and illness represents the cultural knowledge based upon which a medical system is built. A theory of health and illness and the medical practices based on it are generally logically coherent: The theory provides the categories and symptomatology of diagnosis, and the therapy is based on the diagnosis. In actual practice, however, things are not that simple. People often use multiple medicine systems (called "medical pluralism") simultaneously. A classic on the topic of ethnomedicine is selection 12 by George Foster, in which he describes the variation in ethnomedical systems across cultures. A more recent case study based in Mexico, by Kaja Finkler (selection 13), compares a medical system based on sacred healing with biomedicine. Both selections are good examples of cross-cultural comparison. The actual phenomenon of healing, however, may be a different story—one linking mind, belief, and body. There are two selections on this theme: Claude Lévi-Strauss analyzes three elements of belief necessary for sorcery as well as curing, and Robert Hahn, an epidemiologist–anthropologist, reviews scientific evidence of the "nocebo" phenomenon—how beliefs can make people sick—which is the analogue to placebo in curing.

The Social Construction of Illness and the Social Production of Health

The second thematic area within cultural anthropological approaches concerns the social construction of illness and the social production of health. A standard conceptual distinction in medical anthropology is the difference between *disease* and *illness.* Although this distinction has been criticized and refined recently (Hahn 1995), the basic difference is between objectively defined disease based on clinical signs and the patient's perception of not being well and having an illness. Many anthropologists and social philosophers think that *all* of reality is socially constructed, that is, based on a culturally learned set of assumptions about how and why the world works. There is little doubt that illness categories are culturally agreed upon and that these categories change over time and through cultural circumstances. One example of an illness that has not always been considered legitimate is chronic fatigue syndrome (Ware 1992). Another example in this section involves the social factors surrounding leprosy (Hansen's disease) as it is experienced in the United States and other cultures (selection 16). Social stigma, classically associated with leprosy but extended to many other social and medical conditions, is an important theme in medical anthropology.

Another important theme in medical social science is the examination of the illness behavior of people as they seek treatment. This approach involves medical decision making: When do people seek help when they are sick, and whom do they go to first? To what extent are gender and poverty influential in people's decisions to seek medical care? Is it possible to identify cognitive rules that help us understand the social organization of health-seeking behavior? This approach involves researching the sick role and the individual's strategies for getting help. A quantitative approach can be applied to study treatment decision making (Weller and Romney 1988); a good example of this is James Young's *Medical Choice in a Mexican Village* (1981). Anthropologists have made an important contribution to this literature by emphasizing the household production of health (Kendall 1990). Ethnography adds an "experience-near" dimension of people's lives to medical social science, as seen in Lauren Clark's study of poor Latina women in the United States (selection 17).

Healers in Cross-Cultural Perspective

The next kind of cultural approach to medical anthropology involves the ethnographic description of the world of healers themselves. Many anthropologists have studied healers in other societies very closely; some anthropologists, in fact, have become shaman. Shamanism has gained popularity with the New Age movement, but anthropologists like Michael Brown (selection 18) remind us of the importance of understanding healers within their wider social and cultural context. In one selection in this section, we see the anthropologist as a participant–observer, for example, when Melvin Konner goes into a trance in the curing ritual of the !Kung San people of Botswana (selection 19). There is also a selection in this section by an anthropologist whose goal is to demonstrate the

shaman's tricks (magical sleight of hand) in a ritual of Filipino "psychic surgery" (selection 20).

Culture, Illness, and Mental Health

These selections deal with mental health in cross-cultural perspective. Issues of mental health and illness entail cultural questions about the definition of normal. How do we presume that we are normal? How do we decide when someone is crazy? Why are there different rates of mental illness in different societies? Is it possible to find cross-culturally valid categories of mental illness? All of these are thorny questions in cross-cultural psychiatry (the topic of selection 21). Also in this section is a classic case study of the epidemiology of a particular folk illness—*susto*, or soul loss illness—in a Latin American context (selection 22); the anthropological analysis of the etic cause of this illness revolves around the concept of social stress.

Critical Medical Anthropology

The final set of selections in Part I illustrates a relatively new area of inquiry called critical medical anthropology (CMA). This approach refers to the application of critical theories in looking at medical systems, particularly biomedicine. Although we have already seen similar critical theories applied to political-ecological studies of disease (selection 11), the first selection in this section—a classic by Nancy Scheper-Hughes and Margaret Lock (selection 23)—questions the underlying cultural assumptions about the nature of mind–body dualism, for example, that permeate biomedicine. This epistemologically different approach to the study of the body applies a critical perspective to biomedicine and the study of emotions, as well as to the politics and social processes linked with health questions. The final selection in Part I (selection 24) is written from a Marxist CMA perspective that is particularly instructive because it illustrates how the general CMA approach might be combined with efforts of applied anthropology.

In all five of these approaches there is an emphasis on social and cultural variables affecting health, illness behavior, medicinal practices, and medical beliefs. I hope that these cultural approaches, particularly because of their cross-cultural comparisons, challenge most students' beliefs about medical systems in the United States and other countries. The selections should also challenge ethnocentric assumptions that the U.S. biomedical system is the correct or the best system. Culture is all around us, like the water in a goldfish bowl. If we were the goldfish in the bowl, it would be hard, if not impossible, for us to be aware of the water. But by taking a step back, often through cross-cultural comparison, we can come to see the wider context and to recognize our own cultural blinders.

In summary, there are two basic approaches within medical anthropology. The biocultural and cultural approaches complement each other, but they do not necessarily share the same epistemological assumptions or research methodologies. Nevertheless, medical anthropologists might use one orientation to discuss one type of problem, like emerging infectious diseases, and a completely different orientation to discuss another phenomenon, like faith healing. One exciting aspect of medical anthropology is that it provides us with multiple ways of examining questions of health and illness. There may be central concepts in medical anthropology, but there is no central dogma.

1

Medical Anthropology: An Introduction to the Fields

Peter J. Brown, Ronald L. Barrett, Mark B. Padilla

WHAT IS MEDICAL ANTHROPOLOGY?

To define medical anthropology, we must first introduce its parent discipline and some of its key concepts. Introductory anthropology courses usually begin with some variation of the short and classic definition, "Anthropology is the study of humankind." Although vague, this definition underscores that anthropology is a holistic and interdisciplinary enterprise that uses many different approaches to important human issues. In the broadest sense, these approaches are usually categorized into four major fields: cultural anthropology, physical or biological anthropology, archaeology, and linguistics.

Today, however, introductory courses are often the first and last place where anyone gives much thought to the relationships between the four fields of anthropology. In recent decades, anthropology has gone the way of many academic disciplines. Its fields and subfields have become increasingly specialized, each with its own lexicon and theoretical orientation. As a result of these increasingly specialized differences, the academic discussions between the fields of anthropology have diminished considerably, especially between many areas of biological and cultural anthropology. Such trends are unfortunate because the compartmentalization of anthropology often undermines the discipline's greatest strengths: its holistic approach and interdisciplinary nature.

Despite their specialized perspectives, cultural and biological anthropologists have a great deal in common. For example, one useful definition of *culture* is learned patterns of thought and behavior shared by a social group. (Anthropologists have many different definitions of *culture,* and the lack of complete agreement about this term might be considered evidence of the concept's centrality within the discipline.) Cultural patterns might be considered to have three basic, interconnected domains: (1) infrastructure—the domain of material and economic culture; (2) structure—the domain of social organization, power, and interpersonal relations; and (3) the belief system or superstructure—the domain of symbols, cognitive models, and ideology. For example, in the traditional culture of a north Indian village, all three levels of the cultural system are important—in agriculture and the economy of the village, in the social organization of the caste system, and in the religious beliefs and rituals of Hinduism. The three domains are closely related, and they all satisfy human needs. Many anthropologists argue that the three domains of culture are influenced by the biological aspects of human experience as a social species living within an ecological setting. The human organism is an open system, highly permeated by cultural influences, many of which can have a profound impact on growth and development. Human biology and culture are intimately related, and it is important to have a holistic perspective on these interrelationships when studying human issues pertaining to health and sickness.

Medical anthropology is a relatively new area of specialization within anthropology. Medical anthropology is not really a subfield (like biological anthropology, archaeology, cultural anthropology, or anthropological linguistics), partly because these subfields generally have a central theoretical paradigm. Medical anthropologists use a wide variety of theoretical perspectives, and they do not agree on which ones are best. Therefore, medical anthropology is simply the application of anthropological theories and methods to questions of health, illness, medicine, and healing. As such, it may be more correct to refer to a variety of medical anthropologies.

Medical anthropologists engage in basic research on issues of health and healing systems as well as applied research aimed at improving therapeutic care in clinical settings or public health programs in community settings. The purpose of basic research is to expand knowledge; the purpose of applied research is to help solve specific human problems. There is a great deal that we do not know about the causes of sickness and the processes of healing, and anthropologists may contribute to the growth of human knowledge in these important areas. The health problems facing people in all parts of the world are overwhelming and complex, and there is good evidence that anthropologists can contribute to the design and implementation of programs to alleviate these problems.

In regard to the four traditional fields of American anthropology, the most common type of anthropologist is a cultural anthropologist. Most practicing medical anthropologists were trained in cultural anthropology. On the other hand, as you will see by the selections in this book, biological anthropologists, archaeologists, and even anthropological linguists may be interested in and may contribute to studies in medical anthropology. Medical anthropology includes any of these subfields as they apply to issues of human health, sickness, and healing.

As is the concept of culture, the notion of health is difficult to define. According to the charter of the World Health Organization, health refers not merely to the absence of disease but to a state of physical, social, and psychological well-being (Dubos 1959). What constitutes well-being in one society, however, may be quite different in another. The ideal lean-figured body may signal health in the West but may indicate sickness and malnutrition in sub-Saharan Africa (Brown 1991). In the fishing villages that line Lake Victoria, the parasitic disease schistosomiasis is so prevalent that the bloody urine of young males is considered a healthy sign of approaching manhood (Desowitz 1981). In the United States, the "elegant pallor" and "hectic flush" of consumption (tuberculosis) were often mimicked at the turn of the century because of their association with famous writers and artists (Sontag 1978). Any conceptualization of health must therefore depend on an understanding of how so-called normal states of well-being are constructed within particular social, cultural, and historical contexts.

Sickness is an inclusive term that includes all unwanted variations in the physical, social, and psychological dimensions of health. Robert Hahn defines sickness as "unwanted conditions of self, or substantial threats of unwanted conditions of self" (Hahn 1995:22). These conditions may include "states of any part of a person—body, mind, experience, or relationships" (Hahn 1995:22). More specifically, the criteria that people use when they assign the term *sickness* to a given state is based on complex interactions between human biology and culture.

Sickness can be further divided into two basic categories: illness and disease. *Disease* refers to the outward, clinical manifestations of altered physical function or infection. It is a clinical phenomenon, defined by the pathophysiology of certain tissues within the human organism. *Illness,* on the other hand, encompasses the human experience and perceptions of alterations in health as informed by their broader social and cultural meanings. The distinction between disease and illness is useful because it helps to explain the phenomenon of patients who seek medical attention in the absence of clinically identifiable symptoms (illness without disease) and those who do not seek medical attention even though they exhibit signs of pathophysiology (disease without illness).

This distinction also explains differences in the quality of communication and therapeutic exchange between patients and healers. For example, a physician using a disease model may see the patient's symptoms as the expression of clinical pathology, a mechanical alteration in bodily processes that can be "fixed" by a prescribed biomedical treatment. From the patient's perspective, however, an illness experience may include social as well as physiological processes. The patient's problem may just as easily be caused by an evil spirit, a germ, or both. The physician's diagnosis may not make sense in terms of the patient's theory of illness, and the "cure" may not take into consideration the patient's family dynamics, the potential for social stigma in the community, or the lack of resources for follow-up visits or long and expensive therapies.

Healing systems often cut across categories of religion, medicine, and social organization. Therapeutic modalities may range from cardiac bypass surgery to amulets to protect against the evil eye to conflict resolution between kin groups. Shaman, priests, university-trained physicians, and family members may assume a healing role at any given time. In recent decades, medical anthropologists have distinguished between biomedical systems of healing based on Western scientific notions of medicine and ethnomedical systems of healing based on all other notions of healing. As we shall see, this distinction may be more a convenience than a reality.

BASIC APPROACHES TO MEDICAL ANTHROPOLOGY

Although the scope of anthropological inquiry into issues of human health, sickness, and healing is very diverse, and the subfields engaged in these inquiries often overlap with one another, we can nevertheless identify five basic approaches to medical anthropology: (1) biological, (2) ecological, (3) ethnomedical, (4) critical, and (5) applied. The first two of these approaches focus on the interaction of humans and their environment from a biosocial perspective, that is, with a focus on the interaction between biological and health questions and socioeconomic and demographic factors. The other three approaches emphasize the influence of culture (the patterns of thought and behavior characteristic of a group).

All five approaches in medical anthropology share four essential premises: first, that illness and healing are basic human experiences that are best understood holistically in the complex and varied interactions between human biology and culture; second, that disease is an aspect of human environments influenced by culturally specific behaviors and sociopolitical circumstances; third, that the human body and symptoms are interpreted through cultural filters of beliefs and epistemological assumptions; and fourth, that cultural aspects of healing systems have important pragmatic consequences for the acceptability, efficacy, and improvement of health care in human societies.

Biological Approaches

Much of the research in biological anthropology concerns important issues of human health and illness and therefore often intersects with the domains of medical anthropology. Many contributions of biological anthropologists help to explain the relationships between evolutionary processes, human genetic variation, and the different ways that humans are sometimes susceptible, and other times resistant, to disease and other environmental stressors. The evolution of disease in ancient human populations helps us to better understand current health trends. For example, the recent global trend of emerging and reemerging infectious diseases, such as tuberculosis and AIDS, is influenced by forces of natural and cultural selection that have been present throughout modern human evolution. During the time of the Paleolithic, early human populations lived in small bands as nomadic hunters and gatherers. The low population densities during this period would not have supported the acute infectious diseases found today (Hart 1983); instead, chronic parasitic and arthropod-borne diseases were more prevalent (Kliks 1983; Lambrecht 1964).

The shift toward sedentary living patterns and subsistence based on plant and animal domestication, sometimes called the Neolithic Revolution, had a profound effect on human health. Skeletal evidence from populations undergoing this transition indicates an overall deterioration in health consistent with the known relationship between infectious disease and malnutrition (Pelletier et al. 1993). These emerging infections have been attributed to increasing population density, social stratification, decreased nutritional variety, water and sanitation problems, and close contact with domesticated animals (Cockburn 1971; Fenner 1970). These changes had a disproportionate impact on women, young children, the elderly, and the emerging underclass, who were most susceptible to infections in socially stratified societies (Cohen and Armelagos 1984).

A more recent threat to human health has come from chronic degenerative conditions. These so-called diseases of civilization—such as heart disease, diabetes, and cancer—are the leading causes of adult mortality throughout the world today. Many of these diseases share common etiological factors related to human adaptation over the last 100,000 years. For example, obesity and high consumption of refined carbohydrates and fats are related to increased incidence of heart disease and diabetes. Human susceptibility to excessive amounts of these substances can be explained by the evolution of human metabolism throughout millions of years of seasonal food shortages and diets low in fat (Eaton, Shostak, and Konner 1988).

A related theory of "thrifty genes" has been proposed to explain relatively shorter term evolutionary changes that account for genetic variation in the susceptibility to chronic diseases among different contemporary populations (Neel 1982). For example, certain Native American and other recently acculturated populations have significantly higher prevalences of adult-onset diabetes and hypertension in comparison to populations that have been subsisting on high calorie and fatty diets for many generations. The thrifty gene hypothesis proposes that the difference in susceptibility to chronic diseases in these populations is related to the degree of genetic adaptiveness to changes in diet and activity that have occurred in recent human history [see selection 5 by Ritenbaugh and Goodby]. In other words, during feast or famine times in the past, genes affecting insulin physiology were selected for, which allowed people to adapt to irregular food supply; some populations may have been forced through an evolutionary bottleneck of natural selection resulting in higher gene frequencies of this particular adaptation. In the context of modern diets, however, these genes add to the burden of chronic disease.

As with infectious disease, variation in human susceptibility to chronic diseases cannot be accounted for by genes alone. Environmental and sociocultural factors play a major role as well. Here, human physiological measurements have demonstrated the impact of sociocultural conditions on human health. For example, a recent anthropological study of African Americans suggests that the psychological stress related to racial discrimination may contribute to higher prevalences of hypertension in these populations (Dressler 1993).

Some biological contributions to medical anthropology actually critique the misapplication of biological concepts. During the late nineteenth century, measurements of cranial size were taken of Jewish and southern European immigrants to the United States and compared with Anglo-American residents. The difference in cranial size between these populations was used to support a theory of racial hierarchy based on hereditary differences in brain size. By careful comparisons between first- and second-generation groups from these immigrant populations, Franz Boas was able to demonstrate that these differences were attributable to environmental influences on body size (Boas 1940). Subsequent analyses have discredited previous studies relating measurements of intelligence to those of cranial capacity (Gould 1981), and categories of human races have been shown to have little validity in the study of human variation.

In 1980, an economist put forward a hypothesis that children suffering from mild to moderate malnutrition (MMM) were positively adapted to their circumstances by conserving growth in order to maintain an equilibrium of body functioning. These children were not considered impaired aside from diminished growth and were therefore "small but healthy." This same paper recommended that aid programs restrict food distribution to children who were actually starving (Seckler 1982). However, anthropological studies have shown that MMM children are not healthy at all. They suffer from increased infections, decreased cognitive development, and decreased fertility later in life (Martorell 1989). This information is very important as it can influence health policy affecting the lives of millions of children.

Finally, biological anthropologists provide important information regarding the ethnopharmacological aspects of traditional medical systems. Nina Etkin defines ethnopharmacology as "the study of indigenous medicines that connects the ethnography of health and healing to the physical composition of medicines and their physiologic actions" (Etkin 1996:151). Eschewing biological reductionism, she asserts that ethnopharmacologists consider not only the physiological properties of plant substances but also issues related to their selection, preparation, and intended uses within particular social settings and broader biocultural frameworks.

Ecological Approaches

Ecology refers to the relationships between organisms and their total environment. Within medical anthropology, the ecological perspective has three major premises. First, the interdependent interactions of plants, animals, and natural resources comprise an "ecosystem" with characteristics that transcend its component parts. Second, the common goal of the species within an ecosystem is homeostasis: a balance between environmental degradation and the survival of living populations. In this homeostatic system, infectious disease agents (pathogens) and their human hosts are understood to exist in a dynamic adaptive tension that strives toward a relatively stable balance between pathogens and human responses. Third, modern human adaptations include cultural and technological innovations that can dramatically alter the homeostatic relationship between host and disease, occasionally creating severe ecological imbalances. In some cases, these imbalances may benefit humans in the short term, decreasing the prevalence of a particular disease in a population and improving human health. In other cases, homeostatic imbalances favor disease agents, providing an opportunity for diseases to reach epidemic proportions and dramatically increase human morbidity and mortality.

Thus, an ecological approach to medical anthropology emphasizes that the total environment of the human species includes the products of large-scale human activity as well as "natural" phenomena and that health is affected by all aspects of human ecology. The term *medical ecology* has been used to describe this approach as the intersection of culture, disease ecology, and medicine in the study of medical issues (McElroy and Townsend 1996). This approach can be further distinguished by two levels of analysis. At the microlevel, *cultural ecology* examines how cultural beliefs and practices shape human behavior, such as sexuality and residence patterns, which in turn alter the ecological relationship between host and pathogen. At the macrolevel, *political ecology* examines the historical interactions of human groups and the effects of political conflicts, migration, and global resource inequality on disease ecology (Brown, Inhorn, and Smith 1996). Many ecological approaches to medical anthropology include some aspects of both cultural and political ecology. We can use malaria and schistosomiasis to explain these approaches.

Malaria is a disease caused by a microscopic plasmodium parasite that is transmitted to human hosts through contact with mosquitoes of the genus anopheles. These mosquitoes breed and multiply in stagnant pools of water in warm climatic regions. Malaria has a long and sordid history in many societies, and it continues to be a major cause of human morbidity and mortality today (Brown 1997). At a cultural-ecological level, adaptations to malaria include the highland Vietnamese building practices, in which stilted houses allowed people to live above the 10-feet mosquito flight ceiling (May 1958). Although malaria has since been eradicated on the southern Italian island of Sardinia, Peter Brown (1981) discovered that, although perhaps unintended, many of the cultural practices that functioned to reduce contact with malaria-carrying mosquitoes continue today (see selection 9). These include settlement and land use patterns, in which nucleated villages are located in highland areas and flocks of sheep are taken to the lowlands in the winter, thus minimizing contact with the mosquitoes during peak malaria seasons.

At a political-ecological level, however, we find that these adaptive cultural practices were probably motivated by historical threats of military raids and expropriation of land by foreigners. Furthermore, wealthy Sardinians had less contact with the mosquitoes because they did not have to leave the safety of the village to work in the fields as did the laborers, nor did they have to stay in the village during peak malaria season when they could afford to take summer vacations abroad. Thus, the example of malaria demonstrates that multiple ecological variables—biological, cultural, political, and economic—interact to influence the prevalence of particular diseases in a given environmental context.

Finally, schistosomiasis, a parasitic disease spread by snails, provides one of the most dramatic examples of the relationship between political ecology and disease. As Donald Heyneman (1974) has described, economic development programs throughout the world have often focused on the building of dams in order to prevent seasonal flooding, improve irrigation, and provide hydroelectric power. Enormous dams, such as the Aswan High Dam on the Nile River, have dramatically altered the ecology of surrounding areas by preventing seasonal flooding and creating some of the world's largest man-made bodies of water. A byproduct of such changes, however, is that they create homeostatic imbalances between human populations and certain water-borne parasitic infections, such as schistosomiasis. The small snails that carry schistosomiasis thrive in the numerous irrigation canals emanating from the dams, increasing human exposure to the parasites. The result has been continual increases in the prevalence of debilitating schistosomiasis, an infection that primarily affects children, in numerous developing countries.

The story of schistosomiasis demonstrates that political-economic forces, such as dam development programs, can dramatically shape the relationship between host and disease in human populations. This, in turn, emphasizes the need for medical ecology to widen its definition of "environment" beyond the purely natural to include the political-economic consequences of collective human activity.

Ethnomedical Approaches

All societies have medical systems that provide a theory of disease etiology, methods for the diagnosis of illness, and prescriptions and practices for curative or palliative treatment. Medical anthropology initially derived from anthropological interests in the healing beliefs and practices of different cultures. These interests stemmed from a growing recognition of the complex relationship between issues of health and sickness, culturally specific beliefs and healing practices, and the opportunities and constraints afforded by larger social forces (Wellin 1978).

Promoting the need for ethnomedical science, Horacio Fabrega defines ethnomedical inquiry as "the study of how members of different cultures think about disease and organize themselves toward medical treatment and the social organization of treatment itself" (Fabrega 1975:969). As a domain of inquiry, ethnomedical research is as broad as the discipline of anthropology. Generally speaking, medical anthropologists studying ethnomedical systems have focused on five major areas of research: (1) ethnographic description of healing practices; (2) comparison of ethnomedical systems; (3) explanatory models of health and sickness; (4) health-seeking behaviors; and (5) the efficacy of ethnomedical systems.

At the beginning of this century, anthropological studies of medical systems were confined to ethnographic descriptions of "exotic" practices within non-Western societies. Many observations about sickness and therapeutic rituals were analyzed from the perspective of underlying cosmological beliefs and cultural values within comparative studies of myth and religion. However, some aspects of these works have been criticized for a tendency to sensationalize the differences of "primitive" people in comparison to those in Western industrialized societies (Rubel and Hass 1996).

In later decades, cultural notions of disease etiology around the world were described, classified, and mapped in order to trace the evolution of cultures. The classification of ethnomedical beliefs and practices continued into the 1960s with projects emphasizing cross-cultural comparisons, such as the Human Relations Area Files (HRAF—a cross-indexed survey of hundreds of world cultures). One question that arose from these comparisons was the relationship between Western and non-Western medical systems. The term *ethnomedicine* was first defined as "beliefs and practices related to disease which are the products of indigenous cultural development and are not explicitly derived from the conceptual framework of modern medicine" (Rubel and Hass 1996).

In the simplest sense, all ethnomedical systems have three interrelated parts: (1) a theory of the etiology (causation) of sickness; (2) a method of diagnosis based on the etiological theory; and (3) the prescription of appropriate therapies based on the diagnosis.

Although this initial definition of ethnomedicine is convenient for many applications, it also forces an arbitrary distinction between so-called indigenous, traditional, and nonscientific medical systems and Western, modern, and scientific medical systems. In India, for example, many Ayurvedic practitioners receive university training, practice in commercial institutions, and supplement their therapies with antibiotics, x-rays, and other tools of biomedicine (Nichter 1992). Likewise, many Indian physicians trained in English medicine use indigenous categories to explain health issues to their patients. Furthermore, in her comparison of biomedical systems in Europe and North America, Lynn Payer (1988) found considerable variability in the health beliefs and practices that constitute biomedicine. Because of this medical pluralism, it may be more useful to consider ethnomedicine as the study of any form of medicine as a cultural system. In other words, biomedicine can be considered as just another ethnomedical system.

In the context of medical pluralism, clinicians can elicit the person's *explanatory model* of his or her sickness rather than memorize the details of a specific ethnomedical belief system (Brown, Gregg, and Ballard 1997). An explanatory model (EM) is a personal interpretation of the etiology, treatment, and outcome of sickness by which a person gives meaning to his or her condition. Although EMs are personal, they are also learned cultural models, so that an EM shared by a group might be considered a folk model of disease. These models constitute health belief systems that, from a cross-cultural perspective, generally fall into two categories: (1) *personalistic belief systems* that explain sickness as the result of supernatural forces directed at a patient, either by a sorcerer or by an angry spirit; and, (2) *naturalistic belief systems* that explain sickness in terms of natural forces, such as the germ theory of contagion in Western biomedicine or the imbalance of humors in many forms of Chinese, Indian, and Mediterranean systems [see selection 12]. There is often disparity between the explanatory models of patients and healers, which may lead to problems of communication and nonadherence to prescribed therapies (Brown, Gregg, and Ballard 1997).

Health-seeking behavior refers to the process whereby people seek medical assistance and select health care practitioners. Information on such behavior is important for public health programs aimed at disease prevention and treatment. Although stated health beliefs may influence treatment decisions, explanatory models alone are not good predictors of people's observed patterns of health-seeking. This is because, as anthropologists have long noted, there is often a significant difference between cultural ideals—what people say they do—and real (observable) behavior. For example, a study of Nepalese patients found that people often sought multiple medical resources for a single illness despite verbal claims to the contrary (Durkin-Longley 1984). Many different factors may affect decisions concerning when and where to seek treatment, such as the influence of family members (Janzen 1978), social networks, and geographic access to health resources (Kunitz 1983). In many cases, economic resources can severely limit treatment options, as in the case of Uganda, where annual per capita health expenditures are less than the cost of a single HIV test.

An emerging area of interest among medical anthropologists is the efficacy of ethnomedical systems in meeting the health needs of patients in particular settings. Yet it is no accident that the criteria of medical efficacy are precisely as problematic as those of health. One solution may be to base the effectiveness of a particular treatment on the patient's own criteria. However, Thomas Csordas and Arthur Kleinman (1996) note that patients often claim satisfaction with their therapies while still retaining symptoms. These same authors suggest a broader set of criteria involving structural, clinical, discursive, persuasive, and social indices for the evaluation of ethnomedical therapies.

Critical Approaches

In recent decades, medical anthropology has witnessed a significant break from its disciplinary past. In the last fifteen years, there have been intense intellectual debates, especially in the humanities, surrounding the "critical theories," which include postmodernism, Marxism, and deconstructionism. In general, these approaches require people to critically examine their own intellectual assumptions about how the world works. The basic idea is that reality is socially constructed and that versions of reality can be used to conceal complex political, economic, and social relationships. These debates have influenced cultural anthropology in general and medical anthropology specifically. An important outcome has been the development of *critical medical anthropology* (CMA), a perspective that coalesced in the 1980s and 1990s (Singer 1989). Although CMA subsumes much theoretical diversity, it expresses at least two broad critiques.

The first critique is that many medical anthropologists have incorrectly attributed regional disparities in health to local sociocultural differences without examining the influence of global political-economic inequality on the distribution of disease. In the past, the intellectual tendency of medical anthropologists has been to view illness only within local cultural systems and to neglect the larger political and economic context within which these cultures are found. Proponents of CMA insist that medical anthropology broaden its explanatory framework to include the macrolevel forces that connect individuals to the larger world system. The discourse about CMA—how it is discussed and written about—has often been emotionally charged and activist-oriented; the questioning of research assumptions (for example, the unarticulated political assumptions of scientific research) has sometimes made anthropologists from other perspectives feel attacked and defensive and led to increased factionalism between disciplinary subfields.

Critical medical anthropologists describe how large-scale political, economic, and cognitive structures constrain individuals' decisions, shape their social behavior, and affect their risk for disease [see selection 11 by Farmer]. For example, in an analysis of the political-economic dimensions of disease in Tanzania, Meredith Turshen has described how a history of colonialism drastically affected the country's nutritional base, altered its kinship structure, and imposed constraints on its health care system. This analysis is specifically designed to question the hidden assumptions behind the ahistoric, scientific, epidemiological, "natural history" approach to understanding disease and international health problems. As such, she questions the epistemology (the way of knowing) of standard studies, and she emphasizes an alternative she calls the "unnatural history of disease" (Turshen 1984). This study exemplifies the CMA approach in two ways: first, it questions the epistemological assumptions in standard analyses and recognizes that those assumptions highlight some causes and obfuscate others; and second, it emphasizes how historical and political factors shape contemporary decision making as well as the distribution of present-day health problems (Turshen 1984). This approach is also called the "political economy of health" (Morsy 1996).

Critical medical anthropologists make similar arguments concerning health disparities *within* industrialized Western societies. Due to their interest in macrolevel forces (such as world capitalism), critical medical anthropologists are generally skeptical of public health policies that propose microlevel solutions. Thus, CMA not only challenges the socioculturalism of traditional medical anthropology but also criticizes the narrow focus of international health

agencies, whose policies and interventions rarely address the large-scale factors influencing disease (Morsy 1996). Recently, Merrill Singer has provided examples of ways that CMA may be merged with applied anthropology [see selection 24].

The second critique offered by CMA emerges from a heated epistemological debate on the nature of biomedicine. Some critical medical anthropologists, influenced by the work of postmodern thinkers such as Michel Foucault (1990), have challenged the medical anthropological presumption that Western biomedicine is an empirical, law governed science that is unbiased by its own cultural premises. They point to the assumptions and generalizations underlying the theory and practice of Western medicine, which have been historically exempt from cultural analysis in medical anthropology. Nancy Scheper-Hughes and Margaret Lock [see selection 23], for example, critically question and analyze ("deconstruct") the mind–body distinction—a fundamental premise of biomedicine that asserts the separation of "mind from body, spirit from matter, and real from unreal"—as a way to gain insight into how health care is planned and delivered in Western societies (1987:6). They suggest that the dominance of science and medicine has made the separation of mind and body so pervasive that people currently lack a precise vocabulary to express the complex interactions of mind, body, and society (Lock and Scheper-Hughes 1996; Scheper-Hughes and Lock 1987). Even within the newly integrated paradigm of health in medicine—the "bio-psycho-social" approach—there is an assumed predominance of biology and a lack of attention to the very important interactions of mind, body, and society (Hahn and Kleinman 1983). Critical medical anthropologists have thus proposed a new paradigm that views sickness not just as an isolated event but as a product of complex interactions involving nature, society, and culture.

Applied Approaches

As its name implies, applied anthropology emphasizes the direct application of anthropological theory and method to particular social problems. Within medical anthropology, applied approaches can be categorized into two general domains: applied anthropology in clinical settings (for example, hospitals) and applied anthropology in public health programs. Clinically applied anthropology focuses on health care within biomedical settings and analyzes the effects of cultural and socioeconomic factors on doctor–patient interaction, adherence to treatment, and the experience of healing. A growing body of literature within clinically applied anthropology demonstrates how knowledge of explanatory models can be used to improve cultural sensitivity in physician–patient communications (Kleinman, Eisenberg, and Good 1978).

Explanatory models may be of particular importance in understanding the relationship between ethnicity and disease (Brown, Gregg, and Ballard 1997; Chrisman and Johnson 1996). For example, Suzanne Heurtin-Roberts and Efrain Reisin [see selection 26] have shown that the explanatory models of "high blood" and "high-pertension" among African American women can cause clinical communication difficulties in the treatment of high blood pressure as well as affecting patient adherence to treatment. Because the explanatory model of "high-pertension" refers to an episodic illness that cannot be treated (except to avoid stressful situations), patients who believe that their illness is "high-pertension" see no point in taking daily medication prescribed by a biomedical doctor; they are "noncompliant." Similar obstacles to clinical treatment have been described in studies of the explanatory models of other ethnic groups, such as the hot–cold theory of disease among Hispanics [see selection 28]. Such studies suggest that greater attention to patients' explanatory models of illness—and the specific ways in which they conflict or conform to biomedical models—can facilitate mutual understanding between physicians and their patients and ultimately improve health outcomes (Csordas and Kleinman 1996; Helman 1994).

The second major branch of applied medical anthropology deals with public health policymaking, program development, and intervention. Medical anthropologists are being called on to consult with international and domestic health agencies in an effort to formulate health programs that are culturally sensitive, applicable to local needs, and effective in obtaining community support. Anthropological perspectives are relevant at all levels of the public health process, from the interpretation of disease trends to the design, implementation, and evaluation of programs.

One of the areas in which anthropologists have contributed their insight to public health is in their collaboration with epidemiologists (Trostle and Sommerfeld 1996). Through ethnography, anthropologists have assisted epidemiologists in identifying some of the specific behaviors that increase risk for disease and the cultural norms or beliefs that promote them (Nations 1986). One classic example is the prominent role of anthropologists in unraveling the social etiology of kuru, an infectious disease found among the South Fore of New Guinea, probably transmitted through funerary practices (Lindenbaum 1979). Thus, although some medical anthropologists have not supported the methods and assumptions of epidemiology itself, applied anthropologists are beginning to bridge what

they view as the complementary strengths of epidemiology and medical anthropology (Inhorn 1995). Other applied anthropologists have focused on creating more effective public health programs by appealing to local cultural values and personnel. For example, in the area of HIV/AIDS, several anthropologists have advocated the use of traditional healers as educators and trusted health advisors in local communities (Green 1994; Schoepf 1992). The use of traditional healers as collaborators in the introduction of health technologies and information avoids many of the problems of distrust, translation, applicability, and sustainability that often plague public health programs.

Finally, some medical anthropologists have examined the cultural dimensions of the public health bureaucracy itself. Similar to studies of biomedicine as a cultural system, applied anthropologists are increasingly turning their attention to the cultural beliefs, norms, and implicit premises on which public health funding and administration are based (Justice 1986). Frequently, such research seeks to expose the cultural and bureaucratic assumptions within public health that create obstacles to the implementation of locally relevant, effective, and culturally sensitive programs.

CONCLUSION

We began this introduction with the assertion that medical anthropology, like its parent discipline, is a holistic and interdisciplinary enterprise. Because there is a remarkable diversity of theories and methods used in this field, it may be more appropriate to refer to medical anthropologies. We have outlined five major approaches that medical anthropologists use in understanding issues of human health, healing, and sickness. When we explore the specific examples, however, it becomes clear the five major categories overlap. The first two parts of this book—the part devoted to understanding medical anthropology—contrast biosocial approaches (using a paradigm of behavior and ecological interaction between diseases and society) with a series of approaches that emphasize culture, including ethnomedical systems.

Despite this diversity, there are essential commonalities in an anthropological study of health and illness. Just as critical medical anthropologists demonstrate the relationships between social inequalities and health today, biological studies of ancient populations similarly demonstrate how these inequalities have affected health throughout modern human evolution. Political economic forces have reshaped the natural waterways of developing nations, which in turn have reshaped human disease ecologies. Studies of ethnomedical systems can bring together ethnopharmacology with personalistic beliefs of sorcery. Additionally, applied medical anthropologists must often find solutions to public health problems in the common ground of all these approaches. Thus, although the subfields within medical anthropology can be conceptually separated into the perspectives outlined above, they necessarily intersect in the multidimensional study of health and disease.

REFERENCES

Boas, Franz. 1940. *Race, Language, Culture*. New York: Macmillan.

Brown, Peter J. 1981. "Cultural Adaptation to Endemic Malaria in Sardinia." *Medical Anthropology* 5(4):311–339.

Brown, Peter J. 1991. "Culture and the Evolution of Obesity." *Human Nature* 2:31–57.

Brown, Peter J. 1997. "Culture and the Global Resurgence of Malaria." In *The Anthropology of Infectious Disease: International Health Perspectives*, edited by Marcia Inhorn and Peter J. Brown, pp. 119–141. Newark, NJ: Gordon and Breach.

Brown, Peter J., Jessica Gregg, and Bruce Ballard. 1997. "Culture, Ethnicity, and the Practice of Medicine." In *Human Behavior for Medical Students*, edited by Alan Stoudemire. New York: Lippincott.

Brown, Peter J., Marcia Inhorn, and Daniel Smith. 1996. "Disease, Ecology, and Human Behavior." In *Medical Anthropology: Contemporary Theory and Method*, edited by Carolyn Sargent and Thomas Johnson, pp. 183–219. Westport, CT: Praeger.

Chrisman, Noel J., and Thomas M. Johnson. 1996. "Clinically Applied Anthropology." In *Medical Anthropology: Contemporary Theory and Method*, edited by Carolyn Sargent and Thomas Johnson, pp. 88–109. Westport, CT: Praeger.

Cockburn, T. A. 1971. "Infectious Disease in Ancient Populations." *Current Anthropology* 12(1):45–62.

Cohen, M. N., and G. J. Armelagos. 1984. *Paleopathology at the Origins of Agriculture*. New York: Academic.

Csordas, Thomas, and Arthur Kleinman. 1996. "The Therapeutic Process." In *Medical Anthropology: Contemporary Theory and Method*, edited by Carolyn Sargent and Thomas Johnson, pp. 3–20. Westport, CT: Praeger.

Desowitz, R. S. 1981. *New Guinea Tapeworms and Jewish Grandmothers: Tales of Parasites and People*. New York: Norton.

Dressler, W. 1993. "Health in the African American Community: Accounting for Health Inequalities." *Medical Anthropology Quarterly* 7(4):325–335.

Dressler, W. H., J. R. Bindon, and M. J. Gilliland. 1996. "Sociocultural and Behavioral Influences on Health Status Among the Mississippi Choctaw." *Medical Anthropology* 17:165–180.

Dubos, Rene. 1959. *The Mirage of Health*. New York: Harper & Row.

Durkin-Longley, Maureen. 1984. "Multiple Therapeutic Use in Urban Nepal." *Social Science and Medicine* 19:867–872.

Eaton, S. B., M. Shostak, and M. Konner. 1988. "Stone Agers in the Fast Lane: Chronic Degenerative Diseases in Evolutionary Perspective." *The American Journal of Medicine* 84:739–749.

Etkin, Nina. 1996. "Ethnopharmacology: The Conjunction of Medical Ethnography and the Biology of Therapeutic Action." In *Medical Anthropology: Contemporary Theory and Method*, edited by Carolyn Sargent and Thomas Johnson. Westport, CT: Praeger.

Fabrega, Horacio. 1975. "The Need for an Ethnomedical Science." *Science* 189:969–975.

Farmer, Paul. 1996. "Social Inequalities and Emerging Infectious Diseases." *Emerging Infectious Diseases* 2(4):259–269.

Fenner, F. 1970. "The Effects of Changing Social Organization on the Infectious Diseases of Man." In *The Impact of Civilization on the Biology of Man*, edited by S. V. Boyden. Canberra: Australia National University Press.

Foucault, Michel. 1990. *The History of Sexuality Volume I: An Introduction*. New York: Vintage.

Gould, Stephen Jay. 1981. *The Mismeasure of Man*. New York: Norton.

Green, Edward C. 1994. *AIDS and STDs in Africa: Bridging the Gap Between Traditional Healing and Modern Medicine*. Boulder, CO: Westview.

Hahn, Robert A. 1995. *Sickness and Healing: An Anthropological Perspective*. New Haven, CT: Yale University Press.

Hahn, Robert A., and Arthur Kleinman. 1983. "Belief as Pathogen, Belief as Medicine: 'Voodoo Death' and the 'Placebo Phenomenon' in Anthropological Perspective." *Medical Anthropology Quarterly* 14(3):3, 16–19.

Hart, G., ed. 1983. *Diseases in Ancient Man*. Toronto: Clarke Irwin.

Harwood, A. 1971. "The Hot-Cold Theory of Disease: Implications for the Treatment of Puerto Rican Patients." *Journal of the American Medical Association* 216:1153–1158.

Heiman, Cecil G. 1994. *Culture, Health, and Illness: An Introduction for Health Professionals*, 3rd ed. Oxford: Butterworth-Heinemann, Ltd.

Heurtin-Roberts, S., and E. Reisin. 1990. "Health Beliefs and Compliance with Prescribed Medication for Hypertension Among Black Women." *Morbidity and Mortality Weekly Report* 39(40):701–703.

Heyneman, Donald. 1974. "Dams and Disease." *Human Nature* 2:50–57.

Inhorn, Marcia C. 1995. "Medical Anthropology and Epidemiology: Divergences or Convergences?" *Social Science and Medicine* 40(3):285–290.

Janzen, John. 1978. *The Quest for Therapy: Medical Pluralism in Lower Zaire*. Berkeley: University of California Press.

Justice, Judith. 1986. *Policies, Plans, and People: Foreign Aid and Health Development*. Berkeley: University of California Press.

Kleinman, Arthur M., L. Eisenberg, and Byron J. Good. 1978. "Culture, Illness and Care: Clinical Lessons from Anthropologic and Cross-Cultural Research." *Annals of Internal Medicine* 88:251–258.

Kliks, M. M. 1983. "Parasitology: On the Origins and Impact of Human-Helminth Relationships." *Human Ecology and*

Infectious Disease, edited by N. A. Croll and J. H. Cross, pp. 291–313. New York: Academic.

Kunitz, Stephen. 1983. *Disease Change and the Role of Medicine: The Navajo Experience*. Berkeley: University of California Press.

Lambrecht, F. L. 1964. "Aspects of Evolution and Ecology of Tsetse Flies and Trypanosomiasis in Prehistoric African Environments." *Journal of African History* 5:1–24.

Lindenbaum, Shirley. 1979. *Kuru Sorcery: Disease and Danger in the New Guinea Highlands*. Mountain View, CA: Mayfield.

Lock, Margaret, and Nancy Scheper-Hughes. 1996. "A Critical-Interpretive Approach in Medical Anthropology: Rituals and Routines of Discipline and Dissent." In *Medical Anthropology: Contemporary Theory and Method*, edited by Carolyn Sargent and Thomas Johnson, pp. 41–70. Westport, CT: Praeger.

Martorell, Reynaldo. 1989. "Body Size, Adaptation and Function." *Human Organization* 48:15–20.

May, J. M. 1958. *The Ecology of Human Disease*. New York: MD Publications.

McElroy, Ann, and Patricia K. Townsend. 1996. *Medical Anthropology in Ecological Perspective*. Boulder, CO: Westview.

Morsy, Soheir A. 1996. "Political Economy in Medical Anthropology." In *Medical Anthropology: Contemporary Theory and Method*, edited by Carolyn Sargent and Thomas Johnson, pp. 21–40. Westport, CT: Praeger.

Nations, Marilyn K. 1986. "Epidemiological Research on Infectious Disease: Quantitative Rigor or Rigormortis? Insights from Ethnomedicine." In *Anthropology and Epidemiology: Interdisciplinary Approaches to the Study of Health and Disease*, edited by C. R. Janes, R. Stall, and S. M. Gifford. Dordrecht: D. Reidel.

Neel, J. V. 1982. "The Thrifty Genotype Revisited." In *Genetics of Diabetes Mellitus*, edited by J. Kobberling and R. Tattersall, pp. 283–293. London: Academic Press.

Nichter, M. 1992. "The Layperson's Perception of Medicine as Perspective into the Utilization of Multiple Therapy Systems in the Indian Context." *Social Science and Medicine 148*:225–233.

Nichter, Mark, and Mimi Nichter. 1996. *Anthropology and International Health: Asian Case Studies*. Newark, NJ: Gordon and Breach.

Payer, Lynn. 1988. *Medicine and Culture*. New York: Penguin.

Pelletier, D. L., E. A. Frongillo, et al. 1993. "Epidemiologic Evidence for a Potentiating Effect of Malnutrition on Child Mortality." *American Journal of Public Health 83*(8): 1130–1133.

Rubel, Arthur J. 1964. "The Epidemiology of a Folk Illness: *Susto* in Hispanic America." *Ethnology* 3:268–283.

Rubel, Arthur J., and Michael R. Hass. 1996. "Ethnomedicine." In *Medical Anthropology: Contemporary Theory and Method*, edited by Carolyn Sargent and Thomas Johnson, pp. 113–130. Westport, CT: Praeger.

Scheper-Hughes, Nancy, and Margaret M. Lock. 1987. "The Mindful Body: A Prolegomenon to Future Work in Medical Anthropology." *Medical Anthropology Quarterly* 1(1):6–41.

Schoepf, Brooke Grundfest. 1992. "AIDS, Sex and Condoms: African Healers and the Reinvention of Tradition in Zaire." *Medical Anthropology* 14:225–242.

Seckler, D. 1982. " 'Small but Healthy': A Basic Hypothesis in the Theory, Measurement, and Policy of Malnutrition." In *Newer Concepts in Nutrition and Their Implications for Policy*, edited by P. V. Sukhatme, pp. 127–137. Pune, India: Maharashtra Association for the Cultivation of Science Research Institute.

Singer, Merrill. 1989. "The Coming of Age of Critical Medical Anthropology." *Social Science and Medicine* 28:193–203.

Sontag, Susan. 1978. *Illness as Metaphor*. New York: Farrar, Straus, & Giroux.

Trostle, J., and J. Sommerfeld. 1996. "Medical Anthropology and Epidemiology." *Annual Review of Anthropology* 25:253–274.

Turshen, Meredith. 1984. *The Political Ecology of Disease in Tanzania*. New Brunswick, NJ: Rutgers University Press.

Wellin, Edward. 1978. "Theoretical Orientations in Medical Anthropology: Change and Continuity over the Past Half-Century." In *Health and the Human Condition*, edited by M. Logan and E. Hunt, pp. 23–39. North Scituate, MA: Duxbury.

Evolution, Health, and Medicine

❦ CONCEPTUAL TOOLS ❦

- *Evolution is the central theoretical concept in all the biological sciences, including anthropology.* Many people misunderstand evolution, thinking that it is just a theory or that it has to do with perfectibility and progress. In fact, evolution is a powerful, awesome idea. Evolutionary theory is able to explain literally millions of biological observations of the natural world. The fact that scientists argue about specific cases or that there are parts of the evolutionary record that we know little about should not detract from our appreciation of this important concept.

- *Evolution means three things: Things change over time, change occurs because of natural forces, and these changes occur in predictable directions.* Evolutionary change includes the possibility that, over generations, a species can change into another species. The primary driving force determining the direction, character, and speed of that change is *natural selection.* Natural selection means that because some inherited traits affect the ability of individuals to survive and reproduce, traits that enhance reproductive fitness will, over generations of individuals living and dying in a particular ecological context, tend to increase. On the other hand, genetic traits that make it more likely that individuals or their offspring will die early will tend to decrease. Evolutionary change, therefore, depends on the interaction of organisms and their environment. That interaction results in differential rates of morbidity (sickness), mortality, and fertility for individuals with different traits. Geographic isolation of a population undergoing selection is necessary for a species to change into another species.

- *There are other forces in evolution besides natural selection.* These include mutation, gene flow or migration, and genetic drift.

- *Humans are special because of our dual system of inheritance.* Humans are unique in that we have a dual system of inheritance—through both genes and culture—and in that we largely depend on culture for

survival. Genetic evolution works through Darwinian principles. That means that, first, there is variation in a population based on inherited characteristics. When that genetic variation affects different individuals' ability to survive and reproduce, then those successful individuals will pass the genes down to the next generation with greater frequency. Darwinian evolution means that individuals with other, less-adapted characteristics will die at greater frequencies, or their offspring will die more often, or they will have fewer offspring. These are the same rules of life that apply to all living things.

- *On the other hand, cultural evolution is a more flexible and potentially faster process.* Cultural systems change as people evaluate the influence of their behavior in interaction with the environment. Simply put, people tend to do things that improve their conditions and avoid things that harm them or make them sick. Cultural evolution is partly related to the processes of problem solving and evaluation and partly related to issues of social power structures that influence behavior. Cultural learning can be based on borrowing ideas from non-kin, so that it doesn't take generations to occur. In many ways, cultural evolution has outstripped biological evolution for humans. Anthropologists often discuss cultural evolution in the sense of patterned changes in economy and social structure (Johnson and Earle 1987). In economic systems, for example, we know that the original human lifestyle was based on hunting and gathering and that this was surpassed (about 10,000 years ago) with the advent of farming. Therefore, an economic typology would include hunting and gathering, pastoralism, horticulture (low-intensity gardening), agriculture, and then industry. A cultural evolutionary typology regarding social forms would include egalitarian bands, tribes, chiefdoms, and state societies. The differences between these social forms involve variation in economic stratification, the relative importance of kinship, and population size.

2

Stone Agers in the Fast Lane: Chronic Degenerative Diseases in Evolutionary Perspective

S. Boyd Eaton
Marjorie Shostak
Melvin Konner

This selection was written for a medical journal by anthropologist–physicians interested in using an evolutionary approach to explain what our diet and exercise patterns should be if we want to prevent chronic degenerative diseases like cardiovascular disease, hypertension, and some cancers. The primary argument here is an important one: There is a "discordance," or biological estrangement, between our genes and contemporary patterns of diet and activity. The result of this discordance is that, in rich countries like the United States, there has been a marked increase in a variety of chronic diseases. These diseases, sometimes called diseases of civilization, are largely preventable. The prescription is a familiar one—a low-fat, high-fiber diet and an increase in exercise—but the reasoning behind it is evolutionary, rather than authoritative moralism. The authors wrote a popular book on this subject (Eaton, Shostak, and Konner 1988), and some cartoonists even poked fun at their work, calling it the "cave man diet." But medical anthropologists would argue that there are a lot of lessons modern people could learn from so-called cave men.

Two of the authors (Shostak and Konner) did anthropological fieldwork among the !Kung San hunter-gatherers who live in the Kalahari Desert in southern Africa. Hunter-gatherers today cannot be thought of as some type of living fossil; these peoples are affected by significant historical and political-economic pressures (Solway and Lee 1990). But on the other hand, their lives more closely resemble those of our remote ancestors (as this selection says, in the "environment of evolutionary adaptedness"). Most anthropologists strongly believe that so-called modern people have a lot to learn from so-called primitive people. Those practical lessons include not only diet and exercise but things like breast-feeding patterns, child-rearing rules, and the organization of schools.

When you read this selection, think about your own health or that of your friends and family. Do you smoke cigarettes or drink alcohol? Do you eat a diet high in saturated fat? Do you get enough exercise? Why is that?

As you read this selection, consider these questions:

- *How can you tell that this selection was written for physicians reading a medical journal? What kind of assumption may be embedded here regarding the nature and causation of health?*
- *If there is a "discordance" in the evolution of our genes and culture, why haven't our genes caught up?*
- *Can you devise an evolutionary explanation for why we like to eat things (say, ice cream or alcohol) that are bad for us?*

From a genetic standpoint, humans living today are Stone Age hunter-gatherers displaced through time to a world that differs from that for which our genetic constitution was selected. Unlike evolutionary maladaption, our current discordance has little effect on reproductive success; rather it acts as a potent promoter of chronic illnesses: atherosclerosis, essential hypertension, many cancers, diabetes mellitus, and obesity among others. These diseases are the results of interaction between genetically controlled biochemical processes and a myriad of biocultural influences—lifestyle factors—that include nutrition, exercise, and exposure to noxious substances. Although our genes have hardly changed, our culture has been transformed almost beyond recognition during the past 10,000 years, especially since the Industrial Revolution. There is increasing evidence that the resulting mismatch fosters "diseases of civilization" that together cause 75 percent of all deaths in Western nations, but that are rare among persons whose lifeways reflect those of our preagricultural ancestors.

In today's Western nations, life expectancy is over 70 years—double what it was in preindustrial times. Infant death rates are lower than ever before and nearly 80 percent of all newborn infants will survive to age 65 or beyond. Such vital statistics certify that the health of current populations, at least in the affluent nations, is superior to that of any prior group of humans. Accordingly, it seems counterintuitive to suggest that, in certain important respects, the collective human genome is poorly designed for modern life. Nevertheless, there is both epidemiologic and pathophysiologic evidence that suggests this may be so.

In industrialized nations, each person's health status is heavily influenced by the interaction between his or her genetically controlled biochemistry and a collection of biobehavioral influences that can be considered lifestyle factors. These include nutrition, exercise, and exposure to harmful substances such as alcohol and tobacco. This report presents evidence that the genetic makeup of humanity has changed little during the past 10,000 years, but that during the same period, our culture has been transformed to the point that there is now a mismatch between our ancient, genetically controlled biology and certain important aspects of our daily lives. This discordance is not genetic maladaptation in the terms of classic evolutionary science—it does not affect differential fertility. Rather, it promotes chronic degenerative diseases that have their main clinical expression in the post-reproductive period, but that together account for nearly 75 percent of the deaths occurring in affluent Western nations.

THE HUMAN GENOME

The gene pool from which current humans derive their individual genotypes was formed during an evolutionary experience lasting over a billion years. The almost inconceivably protracted pace of genetic evolution is indicated by paleontologic findings that reveal that an average species of late cenozoic mammals persisted for more than a million years,[1] by biomolecular evidence indicating that humans and chimpanzees now differ genetically by just 1.6 percent even though the hominid-pongid divergence occurred seven million years ago,[2] and by dentochronologic data showing that current Europeans are genetically more like their Cro-

Magnon ancestors than they are like 20th-century Africans or Asians.[3] Accordingly, it appears that the gene pool has changed little since anatomically modern humans, Homo sapiens sapiens, became widespread about 35,000 years ago and that, from a genetic standpoint, current humans are still late Paleolithic preagricultural hunter-gatherers.

THE IMPACT OF CULTURAL CHANGES

It has been proposed that chronic degenerative disorders, sometimes referred to as the "diseases of civilization," are promoted by discordance between our genetic makeup (which was selected over geologic eras, ultimately to fit the life circumstances of Paleolithic humans) and selected features of our current bioenvironmental milieu. The rapid cultural changes that have occurred during the past 10,000 years have far outpaced any possible genetic adaptation, especially since much of this cultural change has occurred only subsequent to the Industrial Revolution of 200 years ago.

The increasing industrialized affluence of the past two centuries has affected human health both beneficially and adversely. Improved housing, sanitation, and medical care have ameliorated the impact of infection and trauma, the chief causes of mortality from the Paleolithic era until 1900, with the result that average life expectancy is now approximately double what it was for preagricultural humans. The importance of these positive influences can hardly be overstated; their effects have not only increased longevity, but also enhanced the quality of our lives in countless ways. But, on the other hand, the past century has accelerated the biologic estrangement that has increasingly differentiated humans from other mammals over the entire two-million-year period since Homo habilis first appeared. Despite the increasing importance of culture and technology during this time, the basic lifestyle elements of Homo sapiens sapiens were still within the broad continuum of general mammalian experience until recently. However, in today's Western nations, we have so little need for exercise, consume foods so different from those available to other mammals, and expose ourselves to such harmful agents as alcohol and tobacco that we have crossed an epidemiologic boundary and entered a watershed in which disorders such as obesity, diabetes, hypertension, and certain cancers have become common in contrast to their rarity among remaining preagricultural and other traditional humans.

METHODS

Pertinent data on fitness, diet, and disease prevalence in non-industrial societies were reviewed, tabulated, and contrasted with comparable data from industrialized nations. The literature cited is based on studies of varied traditional groups: pastoralists, rudimentary horticulturalists, and simple agriculturalists, as well as technologically primitive hunter-gatherers. We would have preferred to present data derived solely from studies of pure hunter-gatherers, since they are most analogous to Paleolithic humans. Unfortunately, only a few such investigations have been performed, so that inclusion of selected non-foraging populations constitutes a necessary first approximation. However, there is a continuum of human experience with regard to lifestyle factors that now affect disease prevalence, and on this continuum, traditional peoples occupy positions much closer to those of our preagricultural ancestors than to those of affluent Westerners. In each case, the groups analyzed resemble late Paleolithic humans far more than ourselves with respect to factors (such as exercise requirements and dietary levels of fat, sodium, and fiber) considered likely to influence the prevalence of the disease entity under consideration.

THE LATE PALEOLITHIC LIFESTYLE

The Late Paleolithic era, from 35,000 to 20,000 B.P., may be considered the last time period during which the collective human gene pool interacted with bioenvironmental circumstances typical of those for which it had been originally selected. It is because of this that the diet, exercise patterns, and social adaptations of that time have continuing relevance for us today.

Nutrition

The diets of Paleolithic humans must have varied greatly with latitude and season just as do those of recently studied hunter-gatherers; undoubtedly, there were periods of relative plenty and others of shortage; certainly there was no one universal subsistence pattern. However, the dietary requirements of all Stone Age men and women had to be met by uncultivated vegetables and wild game exclusively; from this starting point, a number of logically defensible nutritional generalizations can be extrapolated. (1) The amount of protein, especially animal protein, was very great. The mean, median, and modal protein intake for 58

TABLE I   Late Paleolithic, Contemporary American, and Currently Recommended Dietary Composition

	Late Paleolithic Diet	Contemporary American Diet	Current Recommendations
Total dietary energy (percent)			
Protein	33	12	12
Carbohydrate	46	46	58
Fat	21	42	30
Alcohol	~0	(7–10)*	—
P:S ratio	1.41	0.44	1.00
Cholesterol (mg)	520	300–500	300
Fiber (g)	100–150	19.7	30–60
Sodium (mg)	690	2,300–6,900	1,100–3,300
Calcium (mg)	1,500–2,000	740	800–1,600
Ascorbic acid (mg)	440	87.7	60

Updated from Eaton and Konner, note 4. Data base now includes 43 species of wild game and 153 types of wild plant food.

* Inclusion of calories from alcohol would require concomitant reduction in calories from other nutrients—mainly carbohydrate and fat.

P:S = polyunsaturated-to-saturated fat.

hunter-gatherer groups studied in this century was 34 percent[4] and protein intake in the Late Paleolithic era may have been higher still.[5,6] The current American diet derives 12 percent of its energy from protein (Table I). (2) Because game animals are extremely lean, paleolithic humans ate much less fat than do 20th-century Americans and Europeans, although more than is consumed in most Third-World countries. (3) Stone Age hunter-gatherers generally ate more polyunsaturated than saturated fat. (4) Their cholesterol intake would ordinarily have equaled or exceeded that now common in industrialized nations. (5) The amount of carbohydrate they obtained would have varied inversely with the proportion of meat in their diet, but (6) in almost all cases they would have obtained much more dietary fiber than do most Americans. (7) The availability of simple sugars, especially honey, would have varied seasonally. For a two- to four-month period, their intake could have equaled that of current humans, but for the remainder of the year it would have been minimal. (8) The amounts of ascorbic acid, folate, vitamin B_{12}, and iron available[7,8] to our remote ancestors equaled, and likely exceeded, those consumed by today's Europeans and North Americans; probably this reflects a general abundance of micronutrients (with the possible exception of iodine in inland locations). (9) In striking contrast to the pattern in today's industrialized nations,[9] Paleolithic humans obtained far more potassium than sodium from their food (as do all other mammals). On the average, their total daily sodium intake was less than a gram—barely a quarter of the current American average. (10) Because they had no domesticated animals, they had no dairy foods; despite this, their calcium intake, in most cases, would have far exceeded that generally consumed in the 20th century.

Physical Exercise

The hunter-gatherer way of life generates high levels of physical fitness. Paleontologic investigations and anthropologic observations of recent foragers[10] document that among such people, strength and stamina are characteristic of both sexes at all ages.

Skeletal remains can be used for estimation of strength and muscularity. The prominence of muscular insertion sites, the area of articular surfaces, and the cortical thickness and cross-sectional shape of long bone shafts all reflect the forces exerted by the muscles acting on them. Analyses of these features consistently show that preagricultural humans were more robust than their descendants, including the average inhabitants of today's Western nations. This pattern holds whether the population being studied underwent the shift to agriculture 10,000[11] or only 1,000[12] years ago, so it clearly represents the results of habitual activity rather than genetic evolution. The fact that hunter-gatherers were demonstrably stronger and more muscular than succeeding agriculturalists (who worked much longer hours) suggests that the intensity of intermittent peak demand on the musculoskeletal system is more important than the mere number of hours worked for the development of muscularity.

The endurance activities associated with both hunting and gathering involve considerable heat production. The long-standing importance of such behaviors for humankind is apparently reflected in the unusual mechanisms for heat dissipation with which evolution has endowed us: we are among the very few animal species that can release heat by sweating; also, our hairless, exposed skin allows heat to escape readily, especially during rapid movement, like running, when airflow over the skin is increased. These physiologic adaptations suggest the importance of endurance activities in our evolutionary past,[13] and evaluation of recent preliterate populations confirms that their daily activities develop superior aerobic fitness (Tables II and III). Whereas actual measurements of maximal oxygen uptake capacity have been made almost exclusively on men, anthropologic observations suggest commensurate aerobic fitness for women in traditional cultures as well.[15]

Alcoholic Beverages

Honey and many wild fruits can undergo natural fermentation, so the possibility that some preagricultural persons had alcoholic beverages cannot be excluded. However, widespread regular use of alcohol must have been a very late phenomenon: of 95 preliterate societies studied in this century,[16] fully 46, including the San (Bushmen), Eskimos, and Australian Aborigines, were unable to manufacture such beverages. It is estimated that 7 to 10 percent of the average adult American's daily energy intake is provided by alcohol; such levels are far in excess of what Late Paleolithic humans could have conceivably obtained.

In general, native alcoholic beverages are prepared periodically and drunk immediately.[17] Their availability is subject to seasonal fluctuation, and as

TABLE II   Aerobic Fitness

Subsistence Pattern	Population	Average Age	Maximal Oxygen Uptake (ml/kg/minute)	Fitness Category*
Hunter-gatherers	Canadian Igloolik Eskimos	29.3	56.4	Superior
	Kalahari San (Bushmen)	Young men	47.1	Excellent
Rudimentary horticulturists	Venezuelan Warao Indians	Young men	51.2	Excellent
	New Guinea highland Lufas	25	67.0	Superior
Simple agriculturists	Mexican Tarahumara Indians	29.8	63.0	Superior
Pastoralists	Finnish Kautokeino Lapps	25–35	53.0	Superior
	Tanzanian Masai	32–43	59.1	Superior
Industrialized Westerners	Canadian Caucasians	20–29	40.8	Fair
	Canadian Caucasians	30–39	38.1	Fair
	Canadian Caucasians	40–49	34.9	Fair

* From note 14.

TABLE III   Fitness Classification for American Males*

Age	Maximal Oxygen Uptake (ml/kg/minute)					
	Very Poor	*Poor*	*Fair*	*Good*	*Excellent*	*Superior*
20–29	<33.0	33.0–36.4	36.5–42.4	42.5–46.4	46.5–52.4	>52.5
30–39	<31.5	31.5–35.4	36.5–40.9	41.0–44.9	45.0–49.4	>49.5
40–49	<30.2	30.2–33.5	33.6–38.9	39.0–43.7	43.8–48.0	>48.1

* Data modified from note 14.

products of natural fermentation, their potency is far less than that of distilled liquors. Their consumption is almost invariably subject to strong societal conventions that limit the frequency and place of consumption, degree of permissible intoxication, and types of behavior that will be tolerated. In small-scale preliterate societies, drinking tends to be ritualized and culturally integrated.[18] Solitary, addictive, pathologic drinking behavior does not occur to any significant extent; such behavior appears to be a concomitant of complex, modern, industrialized societies.[17]

Tobacco Abuse

Recent hunter-gatherers such as the San (Bushmen), Aché, and Hadza had no tobacco prior to contact with more technologically advanced cultures, but the Australian Aborigines chew wild tobacco, so seasonal use by Paleolithic humans in geographically limited areas cannot be excluded. However, widespread tobacco usage began only after the appearance of agriculture in the Americas, perhaps 5,000 years ago. With European contact, the practice spread rapidly throughout the world. Pipes and cigars were the only methods employed for smoking until the mid-19th century, when cigarettes first appeared. Cigarettes had three crucial effects: they dramatically increased per capita consumption among men; after World War I, they made smoking socially acceptable for women; and they made inhalation of smoke the rule rather than the exception. Although the hazards of chewing tobacco, snuff, pipes, and cigars are not insignificant, the major impact of tobacco abuse is a post-cigarette phenomenon of this century.

HOW ALTERED LIFESTYLE FACTORS AFFECT DISEASE PREVALENCE

In many, if not most, respects, the health of humans in today's affluent countries must surpass that of typical Stone Agers. Infant mortality, the rate of endemic infectious disease (especially parasitism), and the prevalence of post-traumatic disability were all far higher 25,000 years ago than they are at present. Still, pathophysiologic and epidemiologic research conducted over the past 25 years supports the concept that certain discrepancies between our current lifestyle and that typical of preagricultural humans are important risk factors for the chronic degenerative diseases that account for most mortality in today's Western nations. These "diseases of civilization" are not new: Aretaeus described diabetes 2,000 years ago, atherosclerosis has been found in Egyptian mummies, paleolithic "Venus" statuettes show that Cro-Magnons could be obese, and the remains of 500-year-old Eskimo burials reveal that cancer afflicted hunter-gatherers isolated from contact with more technologically advanced cultures.[19] However, the lifestyle common in 20th-century affluent Western industrialized nations has greatly increased the prevalence of these and other conditions. Before 1940, diabetes was rare in American Indians,[20] but now the Pimas have one of the world's highest rates;[21] hypertension was unknown in East Africans before 1930, but now it is common;[22] and in 1912, primary malignant neoplasms of the lungs were considered "among the rarest forms of disease."[23] It is not only because persons in industrialized countries live longer that these illnesses have assumed new importance. Young persons in the Western world commonly harbor developing asymptomatic atherosclerosis,[24] whereas youths in technologically primitive cultures do not;[25,26] the age-related rise in blood pressure so typical of affluent society is not seen in unacculturated groups;[27] and older members of preliterate cultures remain lean[28–30] in contrast to the increasing proportion of body fat that is almost universal among affluent Westerners.[31]

Obesity

Obesity is many disorders: its "causes"—genetic, neurochemical, and psychologic—interact in a complex fashion to influence body energy regulation. Superimposed upon this underlying etiologic matrix, however, are salient contrasts between the Late Paleolithic era and the 20th century that increase the likelihood of excessive weight gain (Table IV). (1) Most of our food is calorically concentrated in comparison with the wild game and uncultivated fruits and vegetables that constituted the Paleolithic diet.[4] In general, the energy-satiety ratio of our food is unnaturally high: in eating a given volume, enough to create a feeling of fullness, Paleolithic humans were likely to consume fewer calories than we do today.[32] (2) Before the Neolithic Revolution, thirsty humans drank water; most beverages consumed today provide a significant caloric load while they quench our thirst. (3) The low levels of energy expenditure common in today's affluent nations may be more important than excessive energy intake for development and maintenance of obesity.[33] Total food energy intake actually has an *inverse* correlation with adiposity, but obese persons have proportionately even lower levels of energy expenditure—a low "energy throughput" state. Increased levels[33] of physical exercise raise energy expenditure proportionately more than caloric intake[34] and may lower the body weight "set point."

Diabetes Mellitus

Mortality statistics for New York City between 1866 and 1923 show a distinct fall in the overall death rate, but a steady, impressive rise in death rates from diabetes. For the over-45 age group, there was a 10-fold increase in the diabetic death rate during this period.[35] This pattern anticipated the more recent experience of Yemenite Jews moving to Israel,[36] Alaskan Eskimos,[37] Australian Aborigines,[38] American Indians,[39] and Pacific Islanders of Micronesian, Melanesian, and Polynesian stock.[40] In these groups, diabetic prevalence, if not the actual mortality rate, has risen rapidly and it has been observed that obesity and maturity-onset diabetes are among the first disorders to appear when unacculturated persons undergo economic development. At present, the overall prevalence of non-insulin-dependent diabetes among adults in industrialized countries ranges from 3 to 10 percent,[41] but among recently studied, unacculturated native populations that have managed to continue a traditional lifestyle, rates for this disorder range from nil to 2.0 percent (Table V).

Like obesity, diabetes mellitus is a family of related disorders, each of which reflects the interplay of genetic and environmental influences. But again, in comparison with Paleolithic experience, the lifestyle of affluent, industrialized countries potentiates underlying causal factors to promote maturity-onset diabetes by several mechanisms. (1) A 1980 World Health Organization expert committee on diabetes concluded that the most powerful risk factor for type II diabetes is obesity.[42] The obese persons common in Western nations have reduced numbers of cellular insulin receptors. They manifest a relative tissue resistance to insulin,[43] and therefore their blood insulin levels tend to be higher than those of lean persons. (2) Conversely, high-level physical fitness, characteristic of aboriginal persons, is associated with an increased number of insulin receptors and better insulin binding;[44] these effects enhance the body's sensitivity to insulin.[45] Serum insulin levels are typically low in hunter-gatherers[46] and trained athletes;[44] cellular insulin sensitivity can be improved by physical conditioning that increases cardiorespiratory fitness.[47] This effect is independent from,[47] but may be augmented by, an associated effect on body weight and composition.[43] (3) Diets containing ample amounts of non-nutrient fiber and complex carbohydrate have been shown to lower both fasting and post-prandial blood glucose levels.[48] Diets with high intakes of fiber and complex carbohydrates are the rule among technologically primitive societies, but are the exception in Western nations. Their recommendation by the American Diabetes Association underscores the merit of these Paleolithic dietary practices.

Hypertension

Across the globe, there are many cultures whose members do not have essential hypertension nor experience the age-related rise in average blood pressure that characterizes populations living in industrialized Western nations. These persons are not genetically immune from hypertension since, when they adopt a Western style of life, either by migration or acculturation, they develop, first, a tendency for their blood pressure to rise with age and, second, an increasing incidence of clinical hypertension.[27,49] These normotensive cultures exist in varied climatic circumstances—in the arctic, the rain forest, the desert, and the savanna—but they share a number of essential similarities, each of which is the reciprocal of a postulated causal factor for hypertension. These include diets low in sodium and high in potassium.[50] In addition, the pastoralists and those groups still subsisting as hunter-gatherers have diets that provide a high level of calcium.[51] These persons are slender,[52] aerobically fit,[53] and, at least in their unacculturated state, have limited or no access to alcoholic beverages.[54]

More than 90 percent of the hypertension that occurs in the United States and similar nations is idio-

TABLE IV   Triceps Skinfold Measurements in Males*

Subsistence Pattern	Population	Age	Thickness (mm)
Hunter-gatherers	Australian Aborigines	25–29	4.7
	Kalahari San (Bushmen)	Young men	4.6
	Canadian Igloolik Eskimos	20–29	4.4
	Congo Pigmies	20–29	5.5
	Tanzanian Hadza	25–34	4.9
Rudimentary horticulturists	New Guinea Tukisenta	16–37	5.0
	Venezuelan Warao Indians	Young men	5.9
	New Guinea Biak	25	5.3
	Solomon Islanders	19–70	5.4
	New Guinea Lufa	21–35	5.1
	Surinam Trio Indians	21 and over	6.0
Simple agriculturists	Peruvian Quechua Indians	35	4.0
	Japanese Ainu	Young men	5.3
	Tarahumara Indians	21 and over	6.3
	Rural Ethiopian peasants	20–30	5.3
Mean			5.2
Industrialized Westerners	Canadian Caucasians	20–29	11.2
	American Caucasians	18–24	9.0
Mean			10.1

* As initially submitted, the manuscript included 236 supportive references. A copy of the original manuscript can be obtained by sending a stamped ($1.80), addressed envelope (to accommodate 47 8 ½ × 11" pages) to: Eaton/Konner/Shostak, Department of Anthropology, Emory University, Atlanta, Georgia 30322.

pathic or "essential" in nature. Many theories about the origin of this hypertension have been advanced and it may represent a family of conditions that share a final common pathway resulting in blood pressure elevation. Although its "causes" remain obscure, its occurrence in most cases probably reflects the interaction between individual genetic predisposition and pertinent modifiable lifestyle characteristics. Accordingly, a promising approach to its prevention is suggested by the practices of traditional persons who are spared this disorder; the common features they share reflect components of our ancestral lifestyle.

TABLE V   Diabetes Prevalence*

Subsistence Pattern	Population	Prevalence (percent)
Hunter-gatherers	Alaskan Athabaskan Indians	1.3
	Greenland Eskimos	1.2
	Alaskan Eskimos	1.9
Rudimentary horticulturists	Papua, New Guinea Melanesians	0.9
	Loyalty Island Melanesians	2.0
	Rural Malaysians	1.8
Simple agriculturists	Rural villagers, India	1.2
	"New" Yemenite immigrants, Israel	0.1
	Rural Melanesians, New Caledonia	1.5
	Polynesians on Pukapuka	1.0
	Rural Figians	0.6
Pastoralists	Nomadic Broayas, North Africa	0.0
Mean		1.1
Industrialized Westerners	Australia, Canada, Japan, United States	Range 3.0–10.0**

* See footnote to Table IV.

** Data are from note 41.

Atherosclerosis

Clinical and postmortem investigations of arctic Eskimos,[55–57] Kenyan Kikuyu,[58] Solomon Islanders,[59] Navajo Indians,[60] Masai pastoralists,[61] Australian Aborigines,[62] Kalahari San (Bushmen),[30] New Guinea highland natives,[63] Congo Pygmies,[64] and persons from other preliterate societies reveal that, in the recent past, they experienced little or no coronary heart disease. This is presumably because risk factors for development of atherosclerosis were so uncommon in such cultures. Like our Paleolithic ancestors, they traditionally lacked tobacco, rarely had hypertension, and led lives characterized by considerable physical exertion. In addition, their serum cholesterol levels were low (Table VI). The experience of hunter-gatherers is of special interest in this regard: their diets are low in total fat and have more polyunsaturated than saturated fatty acids (a high polyunsaturated-to-saturated fat ratio), but contain an amount of cholesterol similar to that in the current American diet. The low serum cholesterol levels found among them suggest that a low total fat intake together with a high polyunsaturated-to-saturated fat ratio can compensate for relatively high total cholesterol intake.[65] This supposition is supported by the experience of South African egg farm workers. Their diets include a mean habitual cholesterol intake of 1,240 mg per day, but fat (polyunsaturated-to-saturated fat ratio = 0.78) provides only 20 percent of total energy and their serum cholesterol levels average 181.4 mg/dl (with high-density lipoprotein cholesterol = 61.8 mg/dl).[66]

The adverse changes that occur in atherosclerotic risk factors when persons from societies with little such disease become westernized recapitulate the pattern observed for the other diseases of civilization. The experiences of Japanese,[67] Chinese,[68] and Samoans[69] migrating to the United States, of Yemenite Jews to

TABLE VI   Serum Cholesterol Values*

Subsistence Pattern	Population	Gender	Cholesterol Value (mg/dl)
Hunter-gatherers	Tanzanian Hadza	M	114
		F	105
	Kalahari San (Bushmen)		130
	Kalahari San (Bushmen)		109
	Congo Pygmies	M	101
		F	111
	Australian Aborigines	M	146
		F	132
	Canadian Eskimos		141
Rudimentary horticulturists	Palau Micronesians	M	160
		F	170
	New Guinea Chimbu		130
	New Guinea Wabag		144
	Brazilian Xavante Indians	M	107
		F	121
	Brazalian Kren-Akorore Indians		100
	Solomon Islands Aita	M	135
		F	142
	Solomon Islands Kwaio	M	114
		F	125
	New Guinea Bomai	M	130
		F	140
	New Guinea Yongamuggi	M	139
		F	140
Simple agriculturists	Mexican Tarahumara Indians	M	136
		F	139
	Rural Samoans	M	167
		F	180
	Guatemalan Mayan Indians	M	132
		F	143
Pastoralists	Kenyan Samburu	M	166
	Kenyan Masai	F	135

* See footnote to Table IV.

Israel,[70] and of Greenland Eskimos to Denmark[71] parallel those of Kalahari Bushmen,[72] Solomon Islanders,[59] Ethiopian peasants,[73] Canadian Eskimos,[74] Australian Aborigines,[38] and Masai Pastoralists[75] who have become increasingly westernized in their own countries.

Abnormalities of coagulability may contribute to both the development and the acute clinical manifestations of atherosclerosis.[76] Platelet function has received considerable attention in this respect.[77] Fibrinolytic activity is enhanced by physical exercise,[78] but decreased by smoking cigarettes,[79] obesity,[80] and hyperlipoproteinemia,[81] so it is not surprising that preliterate peoples have more such activity than do average Westerners.[82,83] Platelet aggregation is influenced by hypercholesterolemia,[84] by physical exercise,[85] and by blood levels of long-chain polyunsaturated omega-3 class fatty acids.[86] The latter, in turn, are related to dietary intake of fats containing these constituents; fish oils have especially high concentrations of such fatty acids. Meat from domesticated animals is deficient in this regard[87] but the wild game consumed by our ancestors contained a moderate amount,[4,87] possibly enough to induce blood levels comparable to those of the Japanese[88] or Dutch,[89] although almost certainly not those of the Eskimos.[71]

Coronary atherosclerosis was apparently uncommon in the United States before about 1930,[90,91] but its importance thereafter rapidly increased to a peak in the 1960s, then began a gradual decline. Whereas many factors ranging from changes in the diagnostic classification codes to improvements in treatment are involved in these trends, both the "epidemic" and the decline have been linked to alterations in lifestyle—initially away from and subsequently back toward the pattern that prevailed among preagricultural humans.[92]

Cancer

The perception of cancer as a disease primarily related to the environment has been progressively strengthened over the past decade.[93] International studies reveal large differences in cancer incidence rates between countries; for example, age-standardized analyses reveal that Canadian women have seven times more breast cancer than do non-Jewish women in Israel.[94] Genetic variation cannot account for these major differences, since groups migrating from an area with a characteristic pattern of cancer incidence rates acquire different rates typical of their new geographic location within a few generations. Age-standardization data show that Japanese men in Hawaii have 11 times more prostatic cancer than do Japanese men in Japan and

that black Americans have 10 times more colon cancer than do black Nigerians.[94] Also, there have been large changes in incidence rates for many types of cancer within genetically stable populations: in Ireland, lung cancer mortality increased 177 percent between 1950 and 1975.[94] In Canada, acculturation of western and central Arctic Eskimos has led to an increase in overall cancer morbidity together with marked change in the relative frequency of specific tumor types. Between 1950 and 1980, the number of proven salivary gland cancers decreased by two thirds, whereas lung cancers increased 550 percent.[95] Furthermore, tumor incidence in laboratory animals can be readily altered by manipulating external factors ranging from radiation exposure to dietary composition.

On the basis of these observations, epidemiologists have argued that it should be theoretically possible to reduce site-specific incidence for each type of cancer to the lowest rate found in any population.[96] By summing the lowest national or regional rates observed for each cancer site, basal or "naturally occurring" minimal incidence rates can be developed. When these minimal rates are compared with the rates observed in countries where each type of tumor is common, it appears that from 70 to 90 percent of cancers are the result of environmental influences and hence potentially preventable.[94,96]

The factors considered most likely to affect the development of cancer are tobacco abuse[93,97] and nutritional influences.[98] Extensive tobacco usage (and the regular consumption of alcoholic beverages) postdate the Agricultural Revolution, whereas current cancer-preventive nutritional recommendations[99,100]—to avoid obesity, reduce total fat intake, consume a wide variety of fruits and vegetables (including considerable dietary fiber, vitamin C, and vitamin A or beta-carotene), and to drink alcohol only in moderation if at all—are a fairly accurate, if incomplete, summary of Paleolithic nutritional practices.

CONCLUSION

The diseases considered, as well as others ranging from dental caries to diverticulosis, share important features. In each case, the condition is uncommon, rare, or almost unknown in cultures whose pertinent essential features mimic those of our Late Paleolithic ancestors. However, in each instance, the prevalence of disease increases dramatically when the previously unaffected society adopts a Western lifestyle, whether by migration or acculturation. Furthermore, extensive pathophysiologic research has identified bioenvironmental factors that are likely etiologic agents for each condition. Such factors (e.g., caloric concentration, tobacco abuse, sedentary living, diets high in fat and salt, and so on) are pervasive in affluent industrialized society, but not in traditional cultures where the lifestyle is, in important ways, similar to that of preagricultural humans—similar to that for which the current human genome was selected. These considerations are consistent with the hypothesis that discordance between our genes and the affluent 20th-century lifestyle (defined to include diet, exercise, and exposure to harmful substances) accentuates underlying causal factors and thereby promotes the chronic "diseases of civilization."

Of course, cancer, atherosclerosis, non-insulin-dependent diabetes mellitus, and other afflictions of affluence are all disorders whose clinical manifestations become increasingly common with advancing age; might not the prevalence of these conditions in 20th-century Western nations result simply from the unprecedented life expectancy that characterizes these countries? The population's greater age must certainly be a contributing factor, but the failure of young persons in traditional cultures to exhibit the early stages of these chronic diseases [58, 101] contrasts with the experience of youths in Western nations,[24] indicating that age is not the primary determinant. Furthermore, those persons in traditional societies who do reach age 60 and beyond remain lean [28-30] and normotensive,[27] while clinical[57] and postmortem[58] examinations reveal little or no significant coronary atherosclerosis. Findings like these suggest that chronic degenerative diseases need not be the inevitable consequence of advancing years.

Evolution has endowed Homo sapiens with the ability to adapt and thrive under an extraordinary range of conditions, and this adaptability allows us to benefit enormously from the manifold advantages of today's civilization. In 20th-century industrialized nations, parameters such as infant mortality, childhood growth rates, and average life expectancy all indicate a state of public health far exceeding that which was obtained in the Stone Age or at any time thereafter until the current century. Indeed, more than half the persons who have ever lived beyond age 65 are alive today. Nevertheless, we can still profit from the experience of our remote ancestors. We still carry their inheritance—genes selected for their way of life, not ours. Despite the achievements of science and technology, we remain collectively fearful of diseases that available evidence suggests were uncommon, rare, or unknown in the Late Paleolithic era. In order to regain relative freedom from these illnesses, we need to take a step backward in time. For each disorder, we may anticipate increasingly sophisticated and effective treatments, but the crucial corrective measure will almost certainly be prevention. This will entail reintroduction of essential elements from the lifestyle of our Paleolithic ancestors.

REFERENCES

1. Stanley SM: Chronospecies' longevities, the origin of genera, and the punctuational model of evolution. Paleobiology 1978; 4: 26–40.
2. Sibley CG, Ahlquist JE: The phylogeny of the hominoid primates, as indicated by DNA-DNA hybridization. J Mol Evol 1984; 20: 2–15.
3. Turner CG: The dental search for native American origins. In: Kirk R, Szathmary E. eds. Out of Asia: peopling the Americas and the Pacific. Canberra, Australia: Journal of Pacific History, 1985; 31–78.
4. Eaton SB, Konner MJ: Paleolithic nutrition. A consideration of its nature and current implications. N Engl J Med 1985; 312: 283–289.
5. Ember CR: Myths about hunter-gatherers. Ethnology 1978; 17: 439–448.
6. Foley R: A reconsideration of the role of predation on large mammals in tropical hunter-gatherer adaptation. Man 1982; 17: 393–402.
7. Metz J, Hart D, Harpending HC: Iron, folate and vitamin B_{12} nutrition in a hunter-gatherer people: a study of the !Kung Bushman. Am J Clin Nutr 1971; 24: 229–242.
8. Ellestad-Sayed J, Hildes JA, Schaefer O, Lobban MC: Twenty-four hour urinary excretion of vitamins, minerals and nitrogen by Eskimos. Am J Clin Nutr 1975; 28: 1402–1407.
9. Holbrook JT, Patterson KY, Bodner JE, et al: Sodium and potassium intake and balance in adults consuming self-selected diets. Am J Clin Nutr 1984; 40: 786–793.
10. Clastres P: The Guayaki. In: Bicchieri MG. ed. Hunters and gatherers today. New York: Holt, Rinehart and Winston, 1972; 138–174.
11. Smith P, Bloom RA, Berkowitz J: Diachronic trends in humeral cortical thickness of Near Eastern populations. J Hum Evol 1984; 13: 603–611.
12. Larsen CS: Functional implications of post cranial size reduction on the prehistoric Georgia coast, U.S.A. J Hum Evol 1981; 10: 489–502.
13. Carrier DR: The energetic paradox of human running and hominid evolution. Curr Anthropol 1984; 25: 483–495.
14. Cooper KH: The aerobics way. New York: Bantam Books, 1977; 257–266.
15. Macpherson RK: Physiological adaptation, fitness, and nutrition in peoples of the Australian and New Guinea regions. In: Baker PT, Weiner JS, eds. The biology of human adaptability. Oxford: Clarendon Press, 1966; 431–468.
16. Bacon MK, Barry H, Child IL, Snyder CR: A cross-cultural study of drinking. V. Detailed definitions and data. Q J Studies Alcohol 1965; suppl 3: 78–111.

17. Horton D: The functions of alcohol in primitive societies: a cross cultural study. Q J Studies Alcohol 1943; 4: 199–320.

18. Bacon MK, Barry H, Child IL: A cross-cultural study of drinking. II. Relations to other features of culture. Q J Studies Alcohol 1965; suppl 3: 29–48.

19. Hart Hansen JP, Meldgaard J, Nordquist J: The mummies of Qilakitsoq. Natl Geograph 1985; 162: 190–207.

20. West KM: Diabetes in American Indians and other native populations in the new world. Diabetes 1974; 23: 841–855.

21. Bennett PH, LeCompte PM, Miller M, Rushforth NB: Epidemiological studies of diabetes in the Pima Indians. Recent Prog Horm Res 1976; 32: 333–376.

22. Trowell HC: From normotension to hypertension in Kenyans and Ugandans 1928–1978. East Afr Med J 1980; 57: 167–173.

23. Adler I: Primary malignant growths of the lungs and bronchi. New York: Longmans, Green. 1912; 3.

24. Velican D, Velican C: Atherosclerotic involvement of the coronary arteries of adolescents and young adults. Atherosclerosis 1980; 36: 449–460.

25. Schaeffer O: Medical observations and problems in the Canadian arctic. Can Med Assoc J 1959; 81: 386–391.

26. Kennelly BM, Truswell AS, Schrive V: A clinical and electrocardiographic study of !Kung Bushmen. S Afr Med J 1972; 46: 1093–1097.

27. Page LB: Epidemiologic evidence on the etiology of human hypertension and its possible prevention. Am Heart J 1976; 91: 527–534.

28. Glanville EV, Geerdink RA: Skinfold thickness, body measurements and age changes in Trio and Wajana Indians of Surinam. Am J Phys Anthropol 1970; 32: 455–462.

29. Sinnett PF, Keig G, Craig W: Nutrition and age-related changes in body build in adults: studies in a New Guinea highland community. Hum Biol Oceania 1973; 2: 50–62.

30. Truswell AS, Hansen DL: Medical research among the !Kung. In: Lee RB, DeVore I, eds. Kalahari hunter-gatherers. Cambridge, Massachusetts: Harvard University Press 1976; 166–195.

31. Durnin JVGA, Womersley J: Body fat assessed from total body density and its estimation from skinfold thickness: measurements on 481 men and women aged from 16 to 72 years. Br J Nutr 1974; 32: 77–97.

32. Duncan KH, Bacon JA, Weinsier RL: The effects of high and low energy density diets on satiety, energy intake, and eating time of obese and nonobese subjects. Am J Clin Nutr 1983; 37: 763–767.

33. Stern JS: Is obesity a disease of inactivity? In: Stunkard AJ, Stellar E, eds. Eating and its disorders. New York: Raven Press, 1984; 131–139.

34. Woo R, Garrow JS, Pi-Sunyer FX: Effect of exercise on spontaneous calorie intake in obesity. Am J Clin Nutr 1982; 36: 470–477.

35. Emerson H, Larimore LD: Diabetes mellitus. A contribution to its epidemiology based chiefly on mortality statistics. Arch Intern Med 1924; 34: 585–630.

36. Cohen AM, Chen B, Eisenberg S, Fidel J, Furst A: Diabetes, blood lipids, lipoproteins and change of environment. Restudy of the 'new immigrant Yemenites' in Israel. Metabolism 1979; 28: 716–728.

37. Mouratoff GJ, Scott EM: Diabetes mellitus in Eskimos after a decade. JAMA 1973; 226: 1345–1346.

38. O'Dea K, Spargo RM, Nestle PJ: Impact of Westernization on carbohydrate and lipid metabolism in Australian Aborigines. Diabetologia 1982; 22: 148–153.

39. West K: North American Indians. In: Trowell HC, Burkitt DP, eds. Western diseases: their emergence and prevention. Cambridge, Massachusetts: Harvard University Press, 1981; 129–137.

40. Taylor R, Zimmet P: Migrant studies in diabetes epidemiology. In: Mann JI, Pyorala K, Teuscher A. eds. Diabetes in epidemiological perspective. London: Churchill Livingstone, 1983; 58–77.

41. Hamman RF: Diabetes in affluent societies. In: Mann JI, Pyorala K, Teuscher A, eds. Diabetes in epidemiological perspective. London: Churchill Livingstone, 1983; 7–42.

42. Zimmet P: Type 2 (non-insulin-dependent) diabetes—an epidemiological overview. Diabetologia 1982; 22: 399–411.

43. Yki-Jarvinen H, Koivisto VA: Effects of body composition on insulin sensitivity. Diabetes 1983; 32: 965–969.

44. Koivisto VA, Somon V, Conrad P, Hendler R, Nadel E, Felig P: Insulin binding to monocytes in trained athletes. Changes in the resting state and after exercise. J Clin Invest 1979; 64: 1011–1015.

45. Rosenthal M, Haskell WL, Solomon R, Widstrom A, Reaven GM: Demonstration of a relationship between level of physical training and insulin-stimulated glucose utilization in normal humans. Diabetes 1983; 32: 408–411.

46. Merimee J, Rimoin DL, Cavalli-Sforza LL: Metabolic studies in the African Pygmy. J Clin Invest 1972; 51: 395–401.

47. Jennings G, Nelson L, Nestel P, et al: The effects of changes in physical activity on major cardiovascular risk factors, hemodynamics, sympathetic function, and glucose utilization in man: a controlled study of four levels of activity. Circulation 1986; 73: 30–40.

48. Villaume C, Beck B, Gariot P, Desalme A, Debry G: Long term evolution of the effect of bran ingestion on meal-induced glucose and insulin responses in healthy man. Am J Clin Nutr 1984; 40: 1023–1026.

49. Blackburn H, Prineas R: Diet and hypertension: anthropology, epidemiology, and public health implications. Prog Biochem Pharmacol 1983; 19: 31–79.

50. Meneely GR, Battarbee HD: High sodium-low potassium environment and hypertension. Am J Cardiol 1976; 38: 768–785.

51. McCarron DA, Morris CD, Cole C: Dietary calcium in human hypertension. Science 1982; 217: 267–269.

52. Tobian L: Hypertension and obesity. N Engl J Med 1978; 298: 46–48.

53. Nelson L, Jennings GL, Esler MD, Korner PI: Effect of changing levels of physical activity on blood-pressure

and haemodynamics in essential hypertension. Lancet 1986; 11: 473–476.

54. Klatsky AL, Friedman G, Armstrong MA: The relationships between alcoholic beverage use and other traits to blood pressure: a new Kaiser Permanente study. Circulation 1986; 73: 628–636.

55. Gottman AW: A report of one hundred three autopsies on Alaskan natives. Arch Pathol 1960; 70: 117–124.

56. Arthaud JB: Cause of death in 339 Alaskan natives as determined by autopsy. Arch Pathol 1970; 90: 433–438.

57. Kronmann N, Green A: Epidemiological studies in the Upernavik district, Greenland. Incidence of some chronic diseases 1950–1974. Acta Med Scand 1980; 208: 401–406.

58. Vint FW: Post-mortem findings in the natives of Kenya. E Afr Med J 1937; 13: 332–340.

59. Page LB, Danion A, Moellering RD: Antecedents of cardiovascular disease in six Solomon Islands societies. Circulation 1974; 49: 1132–1146.

60. Fulmer HS, Roberts RW: Coronary heart disease among the Navajo Indians. Ann Intern Med 1963; 59: 740–764.

61. Ho K-J, Biss K, Mikkelson B, Lewis LA, Taylor CB: The Masai of East Africa: some unique biological characteristics. Arch Pathol 1971; 91: 387–410.

62. Woods JD: The electrocardiogram of the Australian Aboriginal. Med J Aust 1966; 1: 438–441.

63. Sinnett PF, Whyte HM: Epidemiological studies in a total highland population, Tukisenta, New Guinea. Cardiovascular disease and relevant clinical, electrocardiographic, radiological and biochemical findings. J Chronic Dis 1973; 26: 265–290.

64. Mann GV, Roels OA, Price DL, Merrill JM: Cardiovascular disease in African Pygmies: a survey of the health status, serum lipids and diet of Pygmies in Congo. J Chronic Dis 1962; 15: 341–371.

65. Schonfeld G, Patsch W, Rudel LL, Nelson C, Epstein M, Olson RE: Effects of dietary cholesterol and fatty acids on plasma lipoproteins. J Clin Invest 1982; 69: 1072–1080.

66. Vorster HH, Silvis N, Venter CS, et al: Serum cholesterol, lipoproteins, and plasma coagulation factors in South African blacks on a high-egg but low-fat intake. Am J Clin Nutr 1987; 46: 52–57.

67. Kato H, Tillotson J, Nichaman M, Rhoads GG, Hamilton HB: Epidemiologic studies of coronary heart disease and stroke in Japanese men living in Japan, Hawaii, and California. Serum lipids and diet. Am J Epidemiol 1973; 97: 372–385.

68. Gerber LM, Madhavan S: Epidemiology of coronary heart disease in migrant Chinese populations. Med Anthropol 1980; 4: 307–320.

69. Hornick CA, Hanna JM: Indicators of coronary risk in a migrating Samoan population. Med Anthropol 1982; 6: 71–79.

70. Brunner D, Meshulan N, Altman S, Bearman JE, Loebl K, Wendkos ME: Physiologic and anthropometric parameters related to coronary risk factors in Yemenite Jews living different time spans in Israel. J Chronic Dis 1971; 24: 383–392.

71. Dyerberg J, Bang HO, Hjorne N: Fatty acid composition of the plasma lipids in Greenland Eskimos. Am J Clin Nutr 1975; 28: 958–966.

72. Wilmsen EN: Studies in diet, nutrition, and fertility among a group of Kalahari Bushmen in Botswana. Social Science Information 1982; 21: 95–125.

73. Ostwald R, Gerbre-Medhin M: Westernization of diet and serum lipids in Ethiopians. Am J Clin Nutr 1978; 31: 1028–1040.

74. Schaefer O, Timmermans JFW, Eaton RDP, Matthews AR: General and nutritional health in two Eskimo populations at different stages of acculturation. Can J Public Health 1980; 71: 397–405.

75. Day J, Carruthers M, Bailey A, Robinson D: Anthropometric, physiological, and biochemical differences between urban and rural Masai. Atherosclerosis 1976; 23: 357–361.

76. Kannel WB, Wolf PA, Castelli WP, D'Agostino RB: Fibrinogen and risk of cardiovascular disease. The Framingham study. JAMA 1987; 258: 1183–1186.

77. Rao AK, Mintz PD, Lavine SJ, et al: Coagulant activities of platelets in coronary artery disease. Circulation 1984; 69: 15–21.

78. Khanna PK, Seth HN, Balasubramanian V, Hoon RS: Effects of submaximal exercise on fibrinolytic activity in ischaemic heart disease. Br Heart J 1975; 37: 1273–1276.

79. Fuster V, Cheseboro JH, Frye RL, Elveback LR: Platelet survival and the development of coronary artery disease in the young adult: effects of cigarette smoking, strong family history and medical therapy. Circulation 1981; 633: 546–551.

80. Shaw DA, MacNaughton D: Relationship between blood fibrinolytic activity and body fatness. Lancet 1963; 1: 352–354.

81. Lowe GDO, McArdle BM, Stromberg P, Lorimer AR, Forbes CD, Prentice CRM: Increased blood viscosity and fibrinolytic inhibitor in type II hyperlipoproteinaemia. Lancet 1982; I: 472–475.

82. Goldrick RB, Whyte HM: A study of blood clotting and serum lipids in natives of New Guinea and Australians. Aust Ann Med 1959; 8: 238–244.

83. Gillman T, Naidoo SS, Hathorn M: Fat, fibrinolysis and atherosclerosis in Africans. Lancet 1957; II: 696–697.

84. Stuart MJ, Gerrard JM. White JG: Effect of cholesterol on production of thromboxane B_2 by platelets in vitro. N Engl J Med 1980; 302: 6–10.

85. Rauramaa R, Salonen JT, Seppanen K, et al: Inhibition of platelet aggregability by moderate-intensity physical exercise: a randomized trial in overweight men. Circulation 1986; 74: 939–944.

86. Glomset JA: Fish, fatty acids, and human health. N Engl J Med 1985; 312: 1253–1254.

87. Crawford MA, Gale MM, Woodford MH: Linoleic acid and linolenic acid elongation products in muscle tissue of Syncerus caffer and other ruminant species. Biochem J 1969; 115: 25–27.

88. Hirai A, Hamazaki T, Terano T, et al: Eicosapentaeroic acid and platelet function in Japanese. Lancet 1980; II: 1132–1133.

89. Kromhaut D, Bosschieter EB, DeLezenne Coulander C: The inverse relation between fish consumption and 20-year mortality from coronary heart disease. N Engl J Med 1985; 312: 1205–1269.

90. White PD: The historical background of angina pectoris. Mod Concepts Cardiovasc Dis 1974; 43: 109–112.

91. Perry TM: The new and old diseases: a study of mortality trends in the United States, 1900–1969. Am J Clin Pathol 1975; 63: 453–474.

92. Walker WJ: Changing U.S. lifestyle and declining vascular mortality—a retrospective. N Engl J Med 1983; 308: 649–651.

93. Cairns J: The treatment of diseases and the war against cancer. Sci Am 1985; 253: 51–59.

94. Doll R, Peto R: The causes of cancer: quantitative estimates of avoidable risks of cancer in the United States today. JNCI 1981; 66: 1191–1308.

95. Hildes JA, Schaefer O: The changing picture of neoplastic disease in the western and central Canadian Arctic (1950–1980). Can Med Assoc J 1984; 130: 25–32.

96. Wynder EL, Gori GB: Contribution of the environment to cancer incidence: an epidemiologic exercise. JNCI 1977; 58: 825–832.

97. Public Health Service: The health consequences of smoking—cancer: a report of the Surgeon General (DHHS publication no. [PHS] 82-50179). Washington: Government Printing Office, 1982.

98. Byers T, Graham S: The epidemiology of diet and cancer. Adv Cancer Res 1984; 41: 1–69.

99. National Research Council: Diet, nutrition, and cancer. Washington: National Academy Press, 1982.

100. American Cancer Society: Nutrition and cancer: cause and prevention. CA—A cancer journal for clinicians 1984; 34: 121–128.

101. Oliver WJ, Cohen EL, Neel JV: Blood pressure, sodium intake and sodium related hormones in the Yanamamo Indians, a "no-salt" culture. Circulation 1975; 52: 146–151.

3

Dr. Darwin

Lori Oliwenstein

This selection introduces "Darwinian medicine"—a biological and evolutionary approach to understanding health and illness (Nesse and Williams 1994). As you will read, the goal of this kind of work is to examine the relationship between the host and the pathogen through the lens of natural selection. The author of this summary argues that Darwinian medicine represents a brand-new field, even though biologically oriented medical anthropologists have used evolutionary analyses for decades. What is new is the selfish-gene theory, otherwise known as inclusive fitness theory, sociobiology, or, more broadly, behavioral ecology. The general principle is that the ultimate explanation of any individual's behavior is how that behavior tends to maximize genetic success, passing the individual's genes to the next generation. In this sense, the driving force of change is an evolutionary strategy that gets the greatest reproductive benefit at lowest cost.

Using this kind of reasoning, for example, Paul Ewald explains variations in the reproductive strategies of pathogens as the reason why some diseases are more virulent than others (Ewald 1994). Similarly, the fact that an infected host suffers symptoms like diarrhea may be best understood not as a simple response to the disease but as the disease's attempt to reproduce itself in another host. Fever, in this view, is a host's physiological attempt to kill an invading infection (Whitaker 1996). The recent emergence of strains of pathogens that are resistant to multiple antibiotics is simply the evolutionary consequence of the ongoing struggle between human hosts and their pathogens.

You will probably find that much of the reasoning of Darwinian medicine is either persuasive or commonsensical. Certainly, some of the solutions suggested by this approach—like Boyd Eaton's idea of lowering women's risk of reproductive cancer by using hormones to postpone menarche and to create pseudopregnancies—are obviously controversial. Ultimately, the value of the evolutionary approach will not be its persuasiveness but the quality of the hypotheses it generates for careful scientific research (Armelagos 1997).

As you read this selection, consider these questions:

- *Why do people tend to think that evolution is a process that only happened in the past?*

- *Why does the route of transmission of an infectious pathogen (like the Ebola virus, which is spread directly from person to person) have an effect on the virulence of the disease?*

- *How can some of the ideas of Darwinian medicine be tested scientifically?*

Paul Ewald knew from the beginning that the Ebola virus outbreak in Zaire would fizzle out. On May 26, after eight days in which only six new cases were reported, that fizzle became official. The World Health Organization announced it would no longer need to update the Ebola figures daily (though sporadic cases continued to be reported until June 20).

The virus had held Zaire's Bandundu Province in its deadly grip for weeks, infecting some 300 people and killing 80 percent of them. Most of those infected hailed from the town of Kikwit. It was all just as Ewald predicted. "When the Ebola outbreak occurred," he recalls, "I said, as I have before, these things are going to pop up, they're going to smolder, you'll have a bad outbreak of maybe 100 or 200 people in a hospital, maybe you'll have the outbreak slip into another isolated community, but then it will peter out on its own."

Ewald is no soothsayer. He's an evolutionary biologist at Amherst College in Massachusetts and perhaps the world's leading expert on how infectious diseases—and the organisms that cause them—evolve. He's also a force behind what some are touting as the next great medical revolution: the application of Darwin's theory of natural selection to the understanding of human diseases.

A Darwinian view can shed some light on how Ebola moves from human to human once it has entered the population. (Between human outbreaks, the virus resides in some as yet unknown living reservoir.) A pathogen can survive in a population, explains Ewald, only if it can easily transmit its progeny from one host to another. One way to do this is to take a long time to disable a host, giving him plenty of time to come into contact with other potential victims. Ebola, however, kills quickly, usually in less than a week. Another way is to survive for a long time outside the human body, so that the pathogen can wait for new hosts to find it. But the Ebola strains encountered thus far are destroyed almost at once by sunlight, and even if no rays reach them, they tend to lose their infectiousness outside the human body within a day. "If you look at it from an evolutionary point of view, you can sort out the 95 percent of disease organisms that aren't a major threat from the 5 percent that are," says Ewald. "Ebola really isn't one of those 5 percent."

The earliest suggestion of a Darwinian approach to medicine came in 1980, when George Williams, an evolutionary biologist at the State University of New York at Stony Brook, read an article in which Ewald discussed using Darwinian theory to illuminate the origins of certain symptoms of infectious disease—things like fever, low iron counts, diarrhea. Ewald's approach struck a chord in Williams. Twenty-three years earlier he had written a paper proposing an evolutionary framework for senescence, or aging. "Way back in the 1950s I didn't worry about the practical aspects of senescence, the medical aspects," Williams notes. "I was pretty young then." Now, however, he sat up and took notice.

While Williams was discovering Ewald's work, Randolph Nesse was discovering Williams's. Nesse, a psychiatrist and a founder of the University of Michigan Evolution and Human Behavior Program, was exploring his own interest in the aging process, and he and Williams soon got together. "He had wanted to find a physician to work with on medical problems," says Nesse, "and I had long wanted to find an evolutionary biologist, so it was a very natural match for us." Their collaboration led to a 1991 article that most researchers say signaled the real birth of the field.

Nesse and Williams define Darwinian medicine as the hunt for evolutionary explanations of vulnerabilities to disease. It can, as Ewald noted, be a way to interpret the body's defenses, to try to figure out, say, the reasons we feel pain or get runny noses when we have a cold, and to determine what we should—or shouldn't—be doing about those defenses. For instance, Darwinian researchers like physiologist Matthew Kluger of the Lovelace Institute in Albuquerque now say that a moderate rise in body temperature is more than just a symptom of disease;

it's an evolutionary adaptation the body uses to fight infection by making itself inhospitable to invading microbes. It would seem, then, that if you lower the fever, you may prolong the infection. Yet no one is ready to say whether we should toss out our aspirin bottles. "I would love to see a dozen proper studies of whether it's wise to bring fever down when someone has influenza," says Nesse. "It's never been done, and it's just astounding that it's never been done."

Diarrhea is another common symptom of disease, one that's sometimes the result of a pathogen's manipulating your body for its own good purposes, but it may also be a defense mechanism mounted by your body. Cholera bacteria, for example, once they invade the human body, induce diarrhea by producing toxins that make the intestine's cells leaky. The resultant diarrhea then both flushes competing beneficial bacteria from the gut and gives the cholera bacteria a ride into the world, so that they can find another hapless victim. In the case of cholera, then, it seems clear that stopping the diarrhea can only do good.

But the diarrhea that results from an invasion of shigella bacteria—which cause various forms of dysentery—seems to be more an intestinal defense than a bacterial offense. The infection causes the muscles surrounding the gut to contract more frequently, apparently in an attempt to flush out the bacteria as quickly as possible. Studies done more than a decade ago showed that using drugs like Lomotil to decrease the gut's contractions and cut down the diarrheal output actually prolong infection. On the other hand, the ingredients in over-the-counter preparations like Pepto Bismol, which don't affect how frequently the gut contracts, can be used to stem the diarrheal flow without prolonging infection.

Seattle biologist Margie Profet points to menstruation as another "symptom" that may be more properly viewed as an evolutionary defense. As Profet points out, there must be a good reason for the body to engage in such costly activities as shedding the uterine lining and letting blood flow away. That reason, she claims, is to rid the uterus of any organisms that might arrive with sperm in the seminal fluid. If an egg is fertilized, infection may be worth risking. But if there is no fertilized egg, says Profet, the body defends itself by ejecting the uterine cells, which might have been infected. Similarly, Profet has theorized that morning sickness during pregnancy causes the mother to avoid foods that might contain chemicals harmful to a developing fetus. If she's right, blocking that nausea with drugs could result in higher miscarriage rates or more birth defects.

Darwinian medicine isn't simply about which symptoms to treat and which to ignore. It's a way to understand microbes—which, because they evolve so much more quickly than we do, will probably always beat us unless we figure out how to harness their evolutionary power for our own benefit. It's also a way to realize how disease-causing genes that persist in the population are often selected for, not against, in the long run.

Sickle-cell anemia is a classic case of how evolution tallies costs and benefits. Some years ago, researchers discovered that people with one copy of the sickle-cell gene are better able to resist the protozoans that cause malaria than are people with no copies of the gene. People with two copies of the gene may die, but in malaria-plagued regions such as tropical Africa, their numbers will be more than made up for by the offspring left by disease-resistant kin.

Cystic fibrosis may also persist through such genetic logic. Animal studies indicate that individuals with just one copy of the cystic fibrosis gene may be more resistant to the effects of the cholera bacterium. As is the case with malaria and sickle-cell, cholera is much more prevalent than cystic fibrosis; since there are many more people with a single, resistance-conferring copy of the gene than with a disease-causing double dose, the gene is stably passed from generation to generation.

"With our power to do gene manipulations, there will be temptations to find genes that do things like cause aging, and get rid of them," says Nesse. "If we're sure about everything a gene does, that's fine. But an evolutionary approach cautions us not to go too fast, and to expect that every gene might well have some benefit as well as costs, and maybe some quite unrelated benefit."

Darwinian medicine can also help us understand the problems encountered in the New Age by a body designed for the Stone Age. As evolutionary psychologist Charles Crawford of Simon Fraser University in Burnaby, British Columbia, puts it: "I used to hunt saber-toothed tigers all the time, thousands of years ago. I got lots of exercise and all that sort of stuff. Now I sit in front of a computer, and all I do is play with a mouse, and I don't get exercise. So I've changed my body biochemistry in all sorts of unknown ways, and it could affect me in all sorts of ways, and we have no idea what they are."

Radiologist Boyd Eaton of Emory University and his colleagues believe such biochemical changes are behind today's breast cancer epidemic. While it's impossible to study a Stone Ager's biochemistry, there are still groups of hunter-gatherers around—such as the San of Africa—who make admirable stand-ins. A foraging life-style, notes Eaton, also means a life-style in which menstruation begins later, the first child is born earlier, there are more children altogether, they are breast-fed for years rather than months, and menopause comes somewhat earlier. Overall, he says, American women today probably experience 3.5 times more menstrual cycles than our ancestors did 10,000 years ago. During each cycle a woman's body is flooded with the hormone estrogen, and breast cancer, as research has found, is very much estrogen related. The more frequently the breasts are exposed to the hormone, the greater the chance that a tumor will take seed.

Depending on which data you choose, women today are somewhere between 10 and 100 times more likely to be stricken with breast cancer than our ancestors were. Eaton's proposed solutions are pretty radical, but he hopes people will at least entertain them; they include delaying puberty with hormones and using hormones to create pseudopregnancies, which offer a woman the biochemical advantages of pregnancy at an early age without requiring her to bear a child.

In general, Darwinian medicine tells us that the organs and systems that make up our bodies result not from the pursuit of perfection but from millions of years of evolutionary compromises designed to get the greatest reproductive benefit at the lowest cost. We walk upright with a spine that evolved while we scampered on four limbs; balancing on two legs leaves our hands free, but we'll probably always suffer some back pain as well.

"What's really different is that up to now people have used evolutionary theory to try to explain why things work, why they're normal," explains Nesse. "The twist—and I don't know if it's simple or profound—is to say we're trying to understand the abnormal, the vulnerability to disease. We're trying to understand why natural selection has not made the body better, why natural selection has left the body with vulnerabilities. For every single disease, there is an answer to that question. And for very few of them is the answer very clear yet."

One reason those answers aren't yet clear is that few physicians or medical researchers have done much serious surveying from Darwin's viewpoint. In many cases, that's because evolutionary theories are hard to test. There's no way to watch human evolution in progress—at best it works on a time scale involving hundreds of thousands of years. "Darwinian medicine is mostly a guessing game about how we think evolution worked in the past on humans, what it designed us for," says evolutionary biologist James Bull of the University of Texas at Austin. "It's almost impossible to test ideas that we evolved to respond to this or that kind of environment. You can make educated guesses, but no one's going to go out and do an experiment to

show that yes, in fact humans will evolve this way under these environmental conditions."

Yet some say that these experiments can, should, and will be done. Howard Howland, a sensory physiologist at Cornell, is setting up just such an evolutionary experiment, hoping to interfere with the myopia, or nearsightedness, that afflicts a full quarter of all Americans. Myopia is thought to be the result of a delicate feedback loop that tries to keep images focused on the eye's retina. There's not much room for error: if the length of your eyeball is off by just a tenth of a millimeter, your vision will be blurry. Research has shown that when the eye perceives an image as fuzzy, it compensates by altering its length.

This loop obviously has a genetic component, notes Howland, but what drives it is the environment. During the Stone Age, when we were chasing buffalo in the field, the images we saw were usually sharp and clear. But with modern civilization came a lot of close work. When your eye focuses on something nearby, the lens has to bend, and since bending that lens is hard work, you do as little bending as you can get away with. That's why, whether you're conscious of it or not, near objects tend to be a bit blurry. "Blurry image?" says the eye. "Time to grow." And the more it grows, the fuzzier those buffalo get. Myopia seems to be a disease of industrial society.

To prevent that disease, Howland suggests going back to the Stone Age—or at least convincing people's eyes that that's where they are. If you give folks with normal vision glasses that make their eyes think they're looking at an object in the distance when they're really looking at one nearby, he says, you'll avoid the whole feedback loop in the first place. "The military academies induct young men and women with twenty-twenty vision who then go through four years of college and are trained to fly an airplane or do some difficult visual task. But because they do so much reading, they come out the other end nearsighted, no longer eligible to do what they were hired to do," Howland notes. "I think these folks would very much like not to become nearsighted in the course of their studies." He hopes to be putting glasses on them within a year.

The numbing pace of evolution is a much smaller problem for researchers interested in how the bugs that plague us do their dirty work. Bacteria are present in such large numbers (one person can carry around more pathogens than there are people on the planet) and evolve so quickly (a single bacterium can reproduce a million times in one human lifetime) that experiments we couldn't imagine in humans can be carried out in microbes in mere weeks. We might even, says Ewald, be able to use evolutionary theory to tame the human immunodeficiency virus.

"HIV is mutating so quickly that surely we're going to have plenty of sources of mutants that are mild as well as severe," he notes. "So now the question is, which of the variants will win?" As in the case of Ebola, he says, it will all come down to how well the virus manages to get from one person to another.

"If there's a great potential for sexual transmission to new partners, then the viruses that reproduce quickly will spread," Ewald says. "And since they're reproducing in a cell type that's critical for the well-being of the host—the helper T cell—then that cell type will be decimated, and the host is likely to suffer from it." On the other hand, if you lower the rate of transmission—through abstinence, monogamy, condom use—then the more severe strains might well die out before they have a chance to be passed very far. "The real question," says Ewald, "is, exactly how mild can you make this virus as a result of reducing the rate at which it could be transmitted to new partners, and how long will it take for this change to occur?" There are already strains of HIV in Senegal with such low virulence, he points out, that most people infected will die of old age. "We don't have all the answers. But I think we're going to be living with this virus for a long time, and if we have to live with it, let's live with a really mild virus instead of a severe virus."

Though condoms and monogamy are not a particularly radical treatment, that they might be used not only to stave off the virus but to tame it is a radical notion—and one that some researchers find suspect. "If it becomes too virulent, it will end up cutting off its own transmission by killing its host too quickly," notes James Bull. "But the speculation is that people transmit HIV primarily within one to five months of infection, when they spike a high level of virus in the blood. So with HIV, the main period of transmission occurs a few months into the infection, and yet the virulence—the death from it—occurs years later. The major stage of transmission is decoupled from the virulence." So unless the protective measures are carried out by everyone, all the time, we won't stop most instances of transmission; after all, most people don't even know they're infected when they pass the virus on.

But Ewald thinks these protective measures are worth a shot. After all, he says, pathogen taming has occurred in the past. The forms of dysentery we encounter in the United States are quite mild because our purified water supplies have cut off the main route of transmission for virulent strains of the bacteria. Not only did hygienic changes reduce the number of cases, they selected for the milder shigella organisms, those that leave their victim well enough to get out and about. Diphtheria is another case in point. When the diphtheria vaccine was invented, it targeted only the most severe form of diphtheria toxin, though for economic rather than evolutionary reasons. Over the years, however, that choice has weeded out the most virulent strains of diphtheria, selecting for the ones that cause few or no symptoms. Today those weaker strains act like another level of vaccine to protect us against new, virulent strains.

"You're doing to these organisms what we did to wolves," says Ewald. "Wolves were dangerous to us, we domesticated them into dogs, and then they helped us, they warned us against the wolves that were out there ready to take our babies. And by doing that, we've essentially turned what was a harmful organism into a helpful organism. That's the same thing we did with diphtheria; we took an organism that was causing harm, and without knowing it, we domesticated it into an organism that is protecting us against harmful ones."

Putting together a new scientific discipline—and getting it recognized—is in itself an evolutionary process. Though Williams and Nesse say there are hundreds of researchers working (whether they know it or not) within this newly built framework, they realize the field is still in its infancy. It may take some time before *Darwinian medicine* is a household term. Nesse tells how the editor of a prominent medical journal, when asked about the field, replied, "Darwinian medicine? I haven't heard of it, so it can't be very important."

But Darwinian medicine's critics don't deny the field's legitimacy; they point mostly to its lack of hard-and-fast answers, its lack of clear clinical guidelines. "I think this idea will eventually establish itself as a basic science for medicine," answers Nesse. "What did people say, for instance, to the biochemists back in 1900 as they were playing out the Krebs cycle? People would say, 'So what does biochemistry really have to do with medicine? What can you cure now that you couldn't before you knew about the Krebs cycle?' And the biochemists could only say, 'Well, gee, we're not sure, but we know what we're doing is answering important scientific questions, and eventually this will be useful.' And I think exactly the same applies here."

Human Biological Variation

✤ CONCEPTUAL TOOLS ✤

■ *Human biological variation can be genetic or phenotypic.* Anthropologists study human similarities and differences; the variation from individual to individual and from one human group to another can be both biological and cultural (Lasker 1969). Some biological variation among contemporary humans is related to health—either phenotypic variation is the result of different health and nutritional experiences or genotypic variation affects patterns of morbidity and mortality. Differences in stature (height), for example, may reflect the adequacy of childhood diet whereas genetic differences are involved with predispositions to a wide variety of diseases (Frisancho 1993).

Genetic variation among populations can be measured in the frequency of particular gene forms (alleles). Gene frequency differences usually reflect historical forces of natural selection or migration. Comparative studies of anthropological genetics can help in reconstructing prehistoric patterns of population movement, for example, the movement of Siberian people to the New World. Difference in gene frequencies among populations can also reflect historical exposure to particular factors in natural selection—including diseases and food shortages.

Phenotype refers to expressed biological features resulting from the interaction of genes and environment. People living for a long period at high elevations, for example, can physiologically adapt to the shortage of oxygen by developing greater hemoglobin density as well as greater lung capacity. Babies born in higher altitudes tend to be smaller than babies born at sea level. Probably the most important mechanism for phenotypic variation involves nutrition. Biological anthropologists studying human growth and development have shown that poor growth—stunting and wasting—is a sensitive measure of lack of adequate food in childhood. Other kinds of malnutrition, such as deficiencies in the micronutrients iodine or vitamin A, may have permanent effects on mental capacity. Therefore, observed biological variations among groups often reflect environmental rather than genetic difference.

■ *Race is not a useful biological concept. Ethnicity is a construct of cultural identity.* Race is not a viable biological concept because it cannot be adequately defined either genetically or phenotypically. Most genetic variation can be found within so-called racial groups, whereas the differences among groups are extremely small and have little physiological significance. All humans today are part of the same species. The rule of racial hypodescent found in North America (a "mixed race" child is categorized as African American) strongly supports that race is a concept of folk biology rather than a useful scientific category.

Ethnicity is an important social construction, and ethnic groups are sometimes thought to be recognizably different by phenotype. Nearly all of the difference, however, is in culture—dress, language, religion, and so forth. Ethnicity is related to subcultural differences in a pluralistic society, and there is often an additional overlap with social class.

■ *The study of human biology must be comparative.* Human biology is different from biomedicine in its aims and scope. The explanation of human biological variation is important to biologically oriented medical anthropologists; such variation requires careful documentation and analysis using principles of adaptation and evolution. In biomedicine, such variation is largely considered "noise" that sometimes complicates the identification of a single etiology (cause) of an illness and the prescription of a therapy. In human biology, the history of particular populations is relevant to understanding their characteristic genetic and physiological traits. By doing cross-cultural comparisons, for example, anthropologists find that Western girls are early maturers with regard to menarche, and this physiological trend has both health repercussions and reproductive implications. It is important not to assume that a particular group (say, white Americans) is the "normal" standard for growth patterns, reactions to drugs, and so forth. Comparative medical research, such as that by the National Institutes of Health on women's health, is central to understanding human biological variation.

4

Body Size, Adaptation and Function

Reynaldo Martorell

Some biologically oriented medical anthropologists focus on issues of child growth and development—that is, measuring and explaining patterns of growth through the life cycle. Measurement of the human biology—in stature, weight, fat folds, and so forth—is called **anthropometry**. *In the medical field of pediatrics, a major tool of monitoring a child's health is judging whether the child is growing as expected. An individual child's actual growth rate is plotted along a standardized growth curve. Failure to grow is an indication that something is wrong.*

But does this mean that being short is a sign of unhealthiness? To what extent are anthropometric measurements a reflection of our genes and to what extent does our body size and shape reflect environmental conditions? The most important environmental condition, of course, must be nutrition: Is a child getting enough foods and the right kinds of foods? If children live in poverty, their adult phenotype will be affected (Armelagos 1997).

This is a problem identified by the father of American anthropology, Franz Boas, who compared immigrant populations and their children raised in the United States during the 1920s (Boas 1940). He documented a rapid increase in all anthropometric measurements, including stature and cranial measurement, for the U.S.-raised offspring, even though the genetic composition was identical. Boas used this data to refute the notion of fixed races based on phenotypic characteristics.

In this selection, Reynaldo Martorell argues against an idea called the "small but healthy" hypothesis. He distinguishes between wasting and stunting in growth failure, and he discusses poverty's direct influence on growth. Notice the quantitative orientation of the argument; this is a characteristic of medical anthropological studies of human variation. Also realize that this argument about "small but healthy" has important policy implications.

As you read this selection, consider these questions:

- *What are the policy implications of the "small but healthy" idea? Does it make the worldwide problem of malnutrition larger or smaller?*

- *Is there a difference between malnutrition and just plain old hunger?*

- *Does access to food and social stimulation affect brain development? What does this mean with regard to the genetic potential and the actual achievements of children growing up in poverty?*

An economist by the name of David Seckler proposed the "small but healthy" hypothesis a few years ago (Seckler 1980, 1982). This hypothesis has generated a lively literature (Messer 1986), including heated debates and thoughtful but sometimes emotionally charged rebuttals from nutritionists such as Gopalan (1983) and Latham (1984). Seckler's views have sparked a great deal of interest because they result in policy and programmatic implications which differ markedly from the conventional. The "small but healthy" hypothesis implies a world in which the problem of malnutrition is no longer of massive propor-

tions since most of the world is "small but healthy." In Seckler's world, the only individuals who are "truly" malnourished are those showing clinical signs of malnutrition. The latter, Seckler tells us, should be the first priority of nutrition policy, and nutritional resources should not be squandered on the "small but healthy population." My presentation is not a comprehensive critique of Seckler's ideas nor of the resulting policy implications, but rather it is a selective discussion of issues that seem to have been ignored by Seckler. First allow me to briefly describe some of the principal elements of the "small but healthy" hypothesis.

SECKLER'S "SMALL BUT HEALTHY" HYPOTHESIS

Seckler's "small but healthy" child is the child who is short but not thin. In the Waterlow classification, this refers to children whose heights are two standard deviations below the median of the reference population but whose weight for heights are above this criterion (see Table 1). In the jargon of the day, these children are said to be "stunted but not wasted." This group of children makes up a significant proportion of the population in many Third World countries and is the majority in India, Bangladesh, and some African nations (Martorell 1985). Children who are wasted, on the other hand, are far less common, and rarely exceed 10% of the population, even in areas where nutritional problems are a serious concern (Martorell 1985). Wasting is synonymous with marasmus and Seckler has no objection to classifying these children as unhealthy. To repeat, it is the stunted but not wasted child who Seckler calls "small but healthy."

According to Seckler (1980, 1982), most nutritional scientists believe in what he calls the "Deprivation Theory." This view holds that an individual is healthy and well nourished if he grows along his genetically determined growth curve. On the other hand, growth significantly below this curve indicates that the individual is malnourished and in poor health. Seckler believes that this view is incorrect and instead proposes the "Homeostatic Theory of Growth." In this theory, the single potential growth curve is replaced by the concept of a broad array of potential growth curves. Within the bounds of this potential growth space, the child may move through various paths of size and shape without suffering any functional implications. Seckler tells us that while the *deprivation* theory of nutritionists postulates a continuous functional relationship between small size and impairments, his *homeostatic* theory postulates a threshold relationship. Seckler (1982:129) goes on to tell us that "smallness may not be associated with functional impairments

over a rather large range of variation; but the system explodes into a high incidence of functional impairments at the lower bound of size." The stunted but not wasted child is within this safe zone, or to use his words, "small but healthy."

I am certain that the vast majority of researchers do not agree with the "deprivation theory" as formulated by Seckler. Growth retardation is widely recognized as a response to a limited nutrient supply at the cellular level. The maintenance of basic metabolic functions takes precedence and resources are diverted away from growth and physical activity. The concurrence of growth retardation and functional impairments is the rationale for the use of anthropometric indicators as risk indicators of poor health and as predictors of mortality. It is incorrect to claim that nutritional scientists uniformly hold that growth retardation and functional impairments are linearly related. In fact, much of the research shows curvilinear relationships (see Martorell and Ho 1984 for a review of the literature). Minor and brief interruptions in growth are not likely to be a cause of concern, whereas chronic patterns of growth retardation leading to stunting invariably are.

My remarks are limited to a discussion of four issues. The first issue is that the causes of stunting are unhealthy. Second, I will emphasize that linear growth retardation is a danger signal and not an innocuous adjustment to environmental stimuli. Third, I will discuss the fact that the factors that affect linear growth also affect other functional domains. Finally, I will refer to the fact that stunted adults suffer certain disadvantages.

THE PROCESS OF STUNTING IS UNHEALTHY

First, I would like to underscore that the *process* of stunting is unhealthy. Seckler implies that the child is healthy while he is becoming stunted so long as he avoids wasting, and that stunting has no functional implications once it has occurred. Throughout his writings we are presented with the image of the child who "indifferently" adjusts his growth trajectory in response to environmental stimuli while enjoying perfect health. Moreover, he seems to ascribe only a small role to nutrition and infection factors in causing smallness. Seckler proposes that there are two kinds of smallness. The first, he says, is "smallness due to poverty, and to poor physical and socio-economic environments" (Seckler 1982:134). The second is "smallness due to malnutrition, a pathological state of

TABLE 1   Waterlow's Classification

		Height	
		<2 SD	*≥2 SD*
Weight for height	*<2 SD*	Stunted and wasted	Not stunted but wasted
	≥2 SD	Stunted but not wasted	Normal

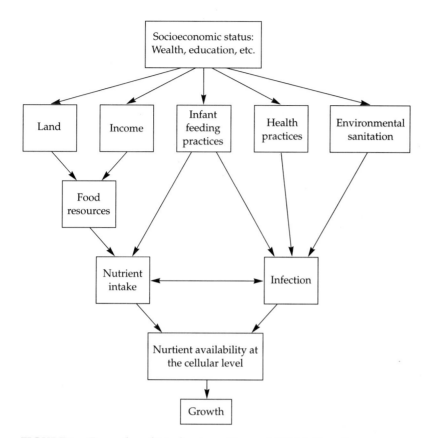

FIGURE 1   Examples of Mechanisms Through Which Poverty Influences Growth in Children

deficiency entailing functional impairment of individuals" (Seckler 1982:134).

There are no known mechanisms through which poverty can affect growth which do not involve nutrition and infection. Examples of mechanisms through which socio-economic factors influence growth in children are shown in Figure 1. The relative importance of the components of poverty will vary from place to place, but these will always lead to low dietary intakes and/or infection which result in decreased nutrient availability at the cellular level and which then gives rise to growth retardation (Chen 1983). The diets of poor children are generally deficient in both quantity and quality and these characteristics are the result of several factors: limited food availability *per se*, inappropriate infant feeding practices and the influence of infections on appetite. Infections will also have direct effects on nutrient metabolism and thus lead to poor nutrient utilization. In short, there are not two kinds of smallness. Rather, the basic cause of stunting is poverty and the effects on size are mediated through poor diets and infection.

We know a great deal about the timing of stunting (see Martorell and Habicht 1986 for a detailed discus-

sion of this subject). One of the best available illustrations of the development of stunting is a figure published in Waterlow and Rutishauser (1974; see Figure 2). By expressing mean growth rates in length in populations of preschool children from developing countries as a percentage of the average velocity in the reference population, one will obtain curves which are similar to the ones shown in Figure 2 for Jamaica, Gambia, and Uganda. The choice of reference population, as noted below, matters little if at all. Growth in length in the first few months of life is generally as fast in Third World children as in reference populations. Growth retardation begins anywhere from the second to the sixth month and continues till about three years of age. Growth rates generally equal those in reference populations after about three years of age.

The period from three months to as long as three years is the period of weaning in traditional societies, which I define as the transition from total dependence on mother's milk to complete reliance on the local diet. Stunting is a phenomenon intimately associated with the perils of this period. Numerous factors play a role in determining nutrient intake and infectious disease patterns, including infant feeding practices, the

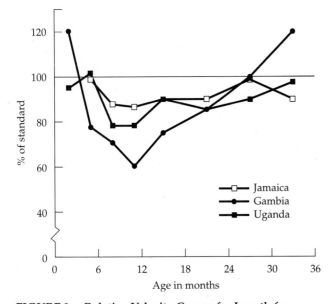

FIGURE 2   Relative Velocity Curves for Length for Young Children from Three Countries *(from Waterlow and Rutishauser 1974)*

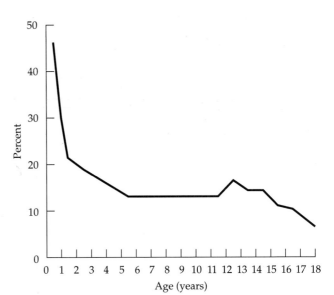

FIGURE 3   Proportion of Protein Requirement Due to Growth Needs at Various Ages in Boys *(from data in FAO/WHO/UNU 1985)*

nature of the local diet and the foods offered to children, environmental sanitation, and the degree of contamination of foods and liquids.

Weaning brings together powerful factors which lead to stunting. The first two years of life is a time when growth is very rapid and therefore a time when adverse factors are going to have a significant and lasting effect. Also, infancy and the second year of life are when nutritional requirements, expressed as energy or as nutrients per kg per day, are greater than at any other subsequent time of life. As shown in Figure 3, a greater proportion of the requirement for protein is due to growth during this critical phase of human development than is the case later. Thus, growth rates are not only fastest during the weaning period, but also account for a greater share of the total nutrient demand than is the case later on in life.

Another feature is that infections, particularly diarrheal diseases, occur most frequently during the first two to three years of life. This is illustrated in Figure 4 which shows the percent of time Guatemalan children are ill with diarrhea from birth to seven years of age. The first two years or so of life is a time when children's immunological systems are maturing rapidly and when they are first coming into contact with disease pathogens. If children survive to four or five years of age, they will be healthier than they were earlier in life.

There is now considerable evidence from a variety of settings showing that almost all of the growth retar-

dation observed in Third World populations has its origin in this stormy period of weaning (Billewicz and McGregor 1982; Hauspie et al. 1980; Dahlmann and Petersen 1977; Satyanarayana et al. 1980, 1981). By the time children in developing countries are three to four

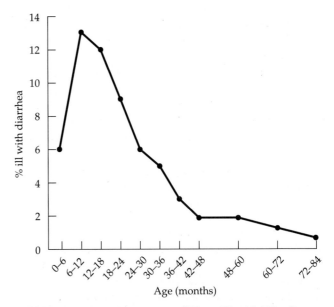

FIGURE 4   Mean Percentage of Time Ill with Diarrhea from Birth to Seven Years of Age in Guatemalan Children *(from Martorell and Habicht 1986)*

years of age, many are already destined to be stunted adults.

Ethnicity or race plays a minor role in determining population differences in length during the weaning period. In fact, it has been rather difficult to show that there are ethnic differences in growth potential in pre-pubescent children. Differences associated with poverty, on the other hand, are easy to demonstrate (Victora et al. 1986) and far overshadow those which might be ascribed to race or ethnicity (see Martorell 1985 for a review of the literature).

GROWTH RETARDATION IS A RISK INDICATOR

The second issue I want to address is that linear growth is our best indicator of child health. *Good growth means good health.* Seckler, you will recall, claims that linear growth retardation has no functional implications. Only wasting implies an impaired state and therefore only wasting represents a nutritional and public health problem. This is a very narrow and out-dated clinical view of the problem of malnutrition.

Seckler's views ignore that there is a continuum of responses as children face nutritional deficits. As indicated in Figure 5, at severe levels of deficiency, linear growth ceases altogether and it becomes necessary to use tissue reserves as an energy and nutrient source to maintain vital functions. However, at less severe stages, normal mass to length dimensions will be maintained as it may be possible to cope with dietary deficits simply by slowing down in growth and by decreasing physical activity. This seems to be the situation in Latin America where moderate linear growth retardation occurs but where wasting is rare. However, in parts of Africa and the Indian subcontinent, the burden is much greater and marked growth retardation prevails and severe wasting is more common (Martorell 1985).

A fundamental principle of pediatrics and of modern public health nutrition is the notion that a child who is growing normally is more likely to be healthy than one who is growing poorly. This is the philosophy behind growth monitoring programs which seek to identify children who are failing to grow adequately in order to intervene with appropriate measures before the situation progresses to wasting and malnutrition (Morley 1976; Rohde et al. 1975).

The rationale for growth monitoring is evidence that children who grow poorly are more likely to be severely ill when infected and more likely to die than

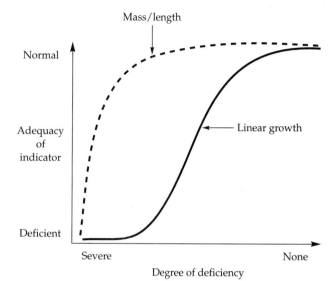

FIGURE 5   Response of Anthropometric Indicators to Varying Degrees of Deficiency

children who grow well. Wasting appears to be a stronger predictor of risk than stunting, as one would expect, but indicators of stunting are definitely important, even after controlling for socio-economic status (Martorell and Ho 1984).

OTHER FUNCTIONAL EFFECTS

A third and related point I would like to make is that the factors which cause growth to be retarded also affect other functional domains as well. One reason growth retardation is predictive of morbidity and mortality is that immunocompetence is impaired, thus rendering the child more vulnerable to infections (Kielmann et al. 1976; McMurray et al. 1981). Physical activity is probably affected even at early stages of energy deficiency but the evidence on this is lacking. This is unfortunate because activity may be an important factor in child development since it is one determinant of the ability of the child to explore the environment and to learn from it.

There are a number of studies showing strong relationships between stunting and poor psychological test performance (Pollitt and Thomson 1977). The relationship is complex and probably due to third factors, such as those related to poverty, which cause both physical and developmental retardation. The point we should remember is that stunting is a marker for poor psychological performance.

FUNCTIONAL IMPLICATIONS OF STUNTING IN ADULTS

So far I have focused on the functional implications of stunting in children. However, is the child who survives to become a stunted adult healthy? In other words, does stunting in adults have any functional implications? This is the fourth and last point of my presentation.

To answer this question, I would like to focus on two aspects: work capacity and productivity in males, and reproductive performance in females.

In discussing the relationship between body size and work, we should distinguish between capacity and productivity. Work capacity is largely a measure of the biological potential to do work and is determined in the laboratory, whereas productivity is an economic term measured in terms of goods produced per unit time. There is overwhelming evidence showing that stunted men have reduced muscle masses and significantly diminished work capacities (Spurr 1983). However, many jobs in agriculture, manufacturing and industry are not that physically demanding. Also, many factors other than work capacity determine productivity, and among these we can include motivation and training. Hence, one would not necessarily expect small body sizes to be a limiting factor for light to moderate activities. As it turns out, current nutritional status—as measured by weight for height, iron status, and energy intakes—seems to be a better predictor of productivity than height for many types of activities (see Martorell and Arroyave 1988 for a review of the literature). There are, of course, physically demanding tasks such as sugarcane cutting where physical size has been found to be related to productivity. This is to be expected since at a strenuous work load, those with a lower work capacity would be closer to a maximal effort and would function at faster heart rates. Such overtaxed individuals may not be able to maintain the work pace for very long and may produce less (Spurr 1983).

Greater height in women in areas where malnutrition is endemic is associated with an enhanced capacity to conceive, and to deliver a baby more likely to survive and to have better growth and development. The results of a study of maternal stature and infant mortality in several hundred Mayan women illustrate this point (Table 2). Variations in socio-economic status were minimal because all families lived and were employed by owners of coffee plantations, and because all received the same low salaries and small amounts of corn in payment for their labor. Mothers were very short; in fact, the population studied appears to be among the shortest in the world. The mean height was 142.4 cm and the tallest woman was only

TABLE 2   Maternal Stature, Infant Mortality, Parity, and Number of Surviving Children in Mayan Women

	Terciles of Height[a]			Analysis of Variance Main Effects	
	Lower (N = 127)	*Middle (N = 124)*	*Upper (N = 129)*	*F*	*p*
Infant mortality[b]	205	150	101	7.9	<.001
Parity[b]	4.75	4.10	4.22	2.1	.12
Surviving children[b]	2.83	3.02	3.15	1.7	.18

[a] Means and ranges for height (cm) for each of the three groups were as follows: Lower (mean 137.7, range 126.3–140.2), middle (mean 142.0, range 140.3–144.7) and upper (mean 148.2, range 144.8–158.6).

[b] Values standardized for age by analyses of covariance. Adjusted to the mean age of 28.4 years.

Data from Martorell et al. 1981.

158.6 cm or 5 ft 2 in. As shown in Table 2, maternal height was significantly associated with infant mortality which was 205 per 1,000 live births for the shortest group, 150 for the middle group, and 101 for the tallest group. This is not a new finding. Low maternal height is widely recognized as a risk indicator of low birth weight and infant mortality.

CONCLUDING REMARKS

It is clear I do not believe small is healthy. This is largely because the process by which children become small is associated with major functional impairment and because its causes are undesirable. I also do not embrace policies which are targeted only at the severely malnourished. Rather, I favor broad public health and nutrition measures which aim to prevent severe malnutrition. Promoting actions which prevent growth failure in young children will reduce the risk of progression to severe malnutrition and death. Throughout my presentation I have emphasized four key points.

First, it is a travesty to call the process of stunting healthy since its causes are deficient diets and infections. To acclaim the end result of the process, small body size, as a desirable attribute of populations is also to affirm that its causes are desirable.

Second, *good growth means good health.* I am not promoting maximal size, but rather insisting that growth retardation is an early warning signal. Linear growth retardation is one of our best indicators that something is going wrong and it should be a call for action.

Third, the stunted child has other unfortunate characteristics such as poor cognitive development. This simply reflects the fact that the harsh conditions which give rise to markedly reduced stature have other undesirable repercussions as well.

And finally, small body size does have functional implications in adults. Productivity may be limited in small individuals engaged in very strenuous activities, and very short stature in mothers is a powerful predictor of low birth weight and infant mortality.

For all these reasons, small is not healthy. Quite the contrary, poor growth in a child is an indicator of major functional impairment. A society in which a major proportion of its children are stunted is one with serious public health problems.

REFERENCES

Billiewicz, W. Z., and I. A. McGregor. 1982. A Birth-to-Maturity Longitudinal Study of Heights and Weights in Two West African (Gambian) Villages, 1951–1975. Annals of Human Biology 9(4):309–320.

Chen, L. C. 1983. Interactions of Diarrhea and Malnutrition: Mechanisms and Interventions. In Diarrhea and Malnutrition: Interactions, Mechanisms, and Interventions. L. C. Chen and N. Scrimshaw, eds. Pp. 3–19. New York: Plenum Press.

Dahlmann, N., and K. Petersen. 1977. Influences of Environmental Conditions During Infancy on Final Body Stature. Pediatric Research 11:695–700.

FAO/WHO/UNU Joint Expert Consultation. 1985. Energy and Protein Requirements. Technical Report Series 724. Geneva, Switzerland: World Health Organization.

Gopalan, C. 1983. Small Is Healthy? For the Poor, Not for the Rich. Nutrition Foundation of India Bulletin, October.

Hauspie, R. C., S. R. Das, M. A. Preece, and J. M. Tanner. 1980. A Longitudinal Study of the Growth in Height of Boys and Girls of West Bengal (India) Aged Six Months to 20 Years. Annals of Human Biology 7:429–441.

Kielmann, A. A., I. S. Uberoi, R. K. Chandra, and V. L. Mehra. 1976. The Effect of Nutritional Status on Immune Capacity and Immune Responses in Preschool Children in a Rural Community in India. Bulletin of the World Health Organization 54:477–483.

Latham, M. C. 1984. Smallness—a Symptom of Deprivation. Nutrition Foundation of India Bulletin 5(6), July.

Martorell, R. 1985. Child Growth Retardation: A Discussion of its Causes and its Relationship to Health. In Nutritional Adaptation in Man. Sir Kenneth Blaxter and J. C. Waterlow, eds. Pp. 13–30. London: John Libbey.

Martorell, R., and G. Arroyave. 1988. Malnutrition, Work Output and Energy Needs. In Capacity for Work in the Tropics. K. J. Collins and D. F. Roberts, eds. Pp. 57–75. Cambridge: Cambridge University Press.

Martorell, R., H. L. Delgado, V. Valverde, and R. E. Klein. 1981. Maternal Stature, Fertility, and Infant Mortality. Human Biology 53(3):303–312.

Martorell, R., and J. P. Habicht. 1986. Growth in Early Childhood in Developing Countries. In Human Growth: A Comprehensive Treatise, 2nd ed. Vol. 3: Methodology: Ecological, Genetic, and Nutritional Effects on Growth. F. Falkner and J. M. Tanner, eds. Pp. 241–262. New York: Plenum Press.

Martorell, R., and T. J. Ho. 1984. Malnutrition, Morbidity, and Mortality. In Child Survival: Strategies for Research. H. Mosley and L. Chen, eds. Pp. 49–68. Supplement to Volume 10 of the Population and Development Review.

McMurray, D. N., S. A. Loomis, L. J. Casazza, H. Rey, and R. Miranda. 1981. Development of Impaired Cell-Mediated Immunity in Mild and Moderate Malnutrition. American Journal of Clinical Nutrition 34:68–77.

Messer, E. 1986. The "Small but Healthy" Hypothesis: Historical, Political, and Ecological Influences on Nutritional Standards. Human Ecology 14(1):57–75.

Morley, D. 1976. Nutritional Surveillance of Young Children in Developing Countries. International Journal of Epidemiology 5(1):51–55.

Pollitt, E., and C. Thomson. 1977. Protein-Calorie Malnutrition and Behavior: A Review from Psychology. In Nutrition and the Brain, Vol. 2. R. J. Wurtman and J. J. Wurtman, eds. Pp. 261–307. New York: Raven Press.

Rohde, J. E., D. Ismail, and R. Sutrisno. 1975. Mothers as Weight Watchers: The Road to Child Health in the Village. Environmental Child Health 21:295–297.

Satyanarayana, K., A. Nadamuni Naidu, M. C. Swaminathan, and B. S. Narasinga Rao. 1980. Adolescent Growth Spurt Among Rural Indian Boys in Relation to Their Nutritional Status in Early Childhood. Annals of Human Biology 7:359–366.

———. 1981. Effect of Nutritional Deprivation in Early Childhood on Later Growth—a Community Study Without Intervention. American Journal of Clinical Nutrition 34(8):1636–1637.

Seckler, D. 1980. Malnutrition: An Intellectual Odyssey. Western Journal of Agricultural Economics 5(2):219–227.

———. 1982. "Small but Healthy": A Basic Hypothesis in the Theory, Measurement, and Policy of Malnutrition. In Newer Concepts in Nutrition and Their Implications for Policy. P. V. Sukhatme, ed. Pp. 127–137. Maharashtra Association for the Cultivation of Science Research Institute. Law College Road, Pune, India.

Spurr, G. B. 1983. Nutritional Status and Physical Work Capacity. Yearbook of Physical Anthropology 26:1–35.

Victora, C. G., J. P. Vaughan, B. R. Kirkwood, J. C. Martines, and L. B. Barcelos. 1986. Risk Factors for Malnutrition in Brazilian Children: The Role of Social and Environmental Variables. Bulletin of the World Health Organization 64(2):299–309.

Waterlow, J. C., and I. H. E. Rutishauser. 1974. Malnutrition in Man. In Early Malnutrition and Mental Development. Symposia of the Swedish Nutrition Foundation XII. J. Cravioto, L. Harnbreaus, and B. Vahlquiest, eds. Pp. 13–26. Uppsala, Sweden: Almquist and Wiksell.

5

Beyond the Thrifty Gene: Metabolic Implications of Prehistoric Migration into the New World

Cheryl Ritenbaugh and Carol-Sue Goodby

The last selection dealt with variation in human morphology—physical shape and appearance—and this selection considers the causes and consequences of physiological variation—the ways that bodies function biochemically. There is a great deal of ethnic variation among the hundreds of tribes of Native Americans (also known as First Nations people). At the same time, archaeological evidence indicates that Native Americans came to the New World from Siberia in two or three migrations, beginning some 20,000 years ago (although anthropologists argue about the precise dates). The culture and biology of Native American peoples are therefore characterized by both similarities and differences. Many of these groups share a common genetic ancestry; at the same time, many also live in conditions of extreme poverty.

About fifty years ago, Western biomedical doctors began to notice unusually high rates of some metabolic diseases like diabetes mellitus among certain Native American groups. Some of the immediate epidemiological questions included the following: How can high rates of a particular disease be explained? Is this "simply" a genetic disease, or is this a genetic predisposition to disease? Do modern living conditions play a role in the causation of the disease? What can this tell us about the nature of human biological variation? What can this tell us about evolutionary pressures in the past?

The most common type of diabetes mellitus—non-insulin dependent diabetes mellitus (NIDDM)—begins in adulthood; it is statistically associated with obesity and tends to run in families. The anthropological geneticist J.V. Neel postulated that NIDDM was caused by a "thrifty gene" that allowed individuals to survive with less nutritional glucose in a "feast or famine" historical context. The disease itself was caused, therefore, by a lack of fit between the "thriftiness" of the glucose metabolism system (the pancreas that produces the insulin needed to break down glucose) and a modern diet characterized by a lot of carbohy-drate sugars. This argument is quite similar to what you read in selection 3 on Stone Agers in the fast lane. Native Americans show a predisposition to a group of adult-onset metabolic diseases that K. M. Weiss has called the New World Syndrome.

The current selection is written by biological anthropologists interested in human biological variation affecting nutritional metabolism and the health consequences of that variation. In other words, they are interested in the intermediate level of analysis between the genes and NIDDM. You will see that they focus on the biochemical patterns of nutritional metabolism. Don't let those details bother you; read on even when you don't completely understand. You will see from this research that studies in biologically oriented medical anthropology require a good deal of knowledge in the natural sciences—in this case, in the biochemistry of nutrition. But you will also notice that the anthropological orientation of these scientific questions is holistic. In this study, it is important to understand how the historical changes in Native American culture affect contemporary diet and exercise patterns. It is not useful to draw a connection between genes and disease without recognizing the intervening level of cultural variables.

As you read this selection, consider these questions:

- *What might be the origins of metabolic variations among people? Why might particular variations become more common in certain ethnic groups?*

- *Is this "thrifty gene" (if it exists) a good thing or a bad thing?*

- *What role do culture and cultural change play in the causation of NIDDM?*

- *Is this selection racist? What does the argument tell us about race and ethnicity?*

Non-insulin dependent diabetes mellitus (NIDDM) (Type II) has been recognized as a growing health problem among American Indians since the early 1960s. Initially, it was thought to be a problem unique to a few tribes. With the passage of time, however, the problem has become increasingly widespread and cross-cuts most major linguistic and genetic boundaries. As early as the 1930s, NIDDM was occasionally

46

reported among Pima Indians in Arizona, who by now have the highest rates known (West 1974, 1981:129; Heaton 1981:47). In the 1970s, however, Navajos and White River Apache continued to have among the lowest rates while San Carlos Apache women, closely related to the Navajo genetically, showed rates almost equal to the Pima (Ritenbaugh 1981:183). Thus it now seems likely that whatever genetic components are responsible are shared among all American Indians.

Neel was the first to argue for a "thrifty genotype" (Neel 1962, 1982), hypothesizing that adaptations to store energy in a feast or famine lifestyle such as experienced by Southwestern desert dwellers would predispose to NIDDM in the present time. His concept continues to be discussed and evaluated today, but it remains a general one without clear linkages to particular genetic or metabolic mechanisms. More recently, Weiss (Weiss, Ferrell, and Hanis 1984) reviewed health data on American Indians of both North and South America as well as Mexicans and Mexican-Americans, who genetically are a mixture of European and American Indian alleles. He identified a "New World Syndrome," highly prevalent among Indians and of intermediate prevalence among Mexican-Americans, which includes obesity, NIDDM, gallstones, gallbladder cancer, and abnormalities of cholesterol metabolism. In light of this combination, cardiovascular disease, hypertension and stroke are conspicuously absent. He argues that the genetic difference or "thrifty gene" must represent some form of altered lipid metabolism.

Szathmary (1986) has approached the study of American Indian NIDDM from a slightly different perspective. She has worked since 1979 with the Dogrib, an Athapaskan-speaking tribe of the Canadian NWT, performing two glucose tolerance test surveys in 1979 and 1985 (Szathmary and Holt 1983; Szathmary, Ritenbaugh, and Goodby 1987; Ritenbaugh et al. 1987). In both, the Dogrib showed little hyperglycemia, and by 1985 had only four confirmed cases of NIDDM in a population of more than 1,700 (Szathmary, Ritenbaugh, and Goodby 1987; DIAND 1977). Her studies have been designed to follow the impact of continuing acculturation on this group. She argues that a group such as this is of particular interest since most theories of prehistoric migration into the New World assume passage from Asia across the Beringia land bridge, an environment not unlike the Canadian NWT. In surviving such an environment, populations would have passed through a "genetic filter" requiring the ability to survive on a diet high in protein, moderate in fat, and very low in glucose. The genetic adaptation would proceed in the direction of coping with very small glucose supply via a "glucose-sparing" genotype (Schae-

fer, Crockford, and Romanowski 1972). This is a more specific focus than the "thrifty genotype," and a northern hunting adaptation filter can provide a basis for developing metabolic hypotheses.

Recent advances in unraveling the interrelationships among food intake, human fuel (energy) metabolism, and activity patterns allow a more specific description of the metabolic consequences of a northern hunting adaptation than was previously possible. A wide range of older and newer studies of fuel metabolism among northern peoples, carbohydrate and lipid metabolism among diabetic and nondiabetic American Indians and Anglos, and animal and human studies of fuel metabolism during exercise and rest can be brought together to elaborate Szathmary's model. The following pages describe the dietary and lifestyle changes that American Indians may have faced in their New World experience and relate these to selective pressures on metabolic pathways. With northern hunting adaptations, rapid changes in lifestyles among this group could lead to the NIDDM seen in present day American Indians and other New World populations. Detailed biochemical evidence is presented elsewhere (Randle et al. 1963) on the glucose fatty acid cycle interactions which serve as the basis for this model.

NORTHERN HUNTERS

Life in the far northern latitudes presents a series of major challenges for survival. The most viable initial problem is the cold, which requires cultural responses (clothing, housing, gloves, heating fuel) as well as metabolic ones (production of body heat, and continuing blood flow to extremities or "the hunting response" [Steegman 1977]). The cold and dark produces a secondary problem of food base, since plant foods are limited in their growing season, and most available ones are not suited to human consumption. Some berries, bark, roots and tubers, and a few greens are edible, but quantities are limited and availability seasonal. Thus marine and land animals are relied upon as the primary food base because they can convert the indigestible plant material into edible flesh. The most dependable source of animal products is the marine environment; on land the only nearly equivalent resource is herd ungulates. Alternative models for New World entry cite exploitation of coastal resources or the following of inland animal herds. While these may be distinct cultural traditions, their physiologic impacts are similar (Table I).

A significant aspect of both of these animal-based adaptations is the irregularity of food availability.

TABLE I   Northern Hunting Lifestyle

Diet based on animal sources:
    Low in carbohydrate
    Low in dietary fiber
    Moderate in fat
    High in protein
High energy demands for:
    Activity
    Warmth
Seasonal macronutrient shortages

While we assume that both land and marine environments would have been far more abundantly supplied with animals in the late Pleistocene than today, vagaries of weather and season would demand cultural mechanisms of food preservation (beyond the world's largest freezer) to help through times of food shortages. Seasonal and other environmental changes also would result in nutrient variations and deficiencies within the animals, which would be passed along to their human predators. Speth and Spielman (1983) described the depletion of fat stores which occurs in most land and marine animals by spring. Thus, the total nutrient content of the animal declines as it uses its own body fat stores for survival; this leads to periodic shortages of non-protein sources of energy, since the sole dietary source of fat is depleted (Speth 1987).

Low carbohydrate availability, intermittent lipid shortage, protein sufficiency, and high energy demands for activity and body warmth in this environment present a complex set of environmental pressures with specific physiologic consequences. Those requirements are listed below.

1.   Carbohydrate Requirements. Humans require carbohydrate for maintenance of normal function in several key organs including the brain, kidney medulla and red blood cells (Tepperman 1980). Blood glucose levels of less than 50 gm/dl are detrimental to the overall functioning of the human body, and are associated with confused mental states. The minimum amount of glucose necessary to maintain this level is estimated to be 80 gms/day. If food sources ("exogenous glucose") are not available, the body's first response is to release glucose stored as glycogen in the liver and muscles; however, this source of glucose is limited. The almost inexhaustible source of glucose is the body's protein stores, ranging from albumin in the blood to muscle tissue. Fatty acids, in contrast, cannot be converted into glucose, although the glycerol backbone of triglyceride can provide minimal amounts of glucose metabolites. Manufacture of glucose from glucogenic amino acids takes place in the liver and

kidney cortex through a process called gluconeogenesis. Amino acids available from protein in food can provide this substrate; if not, body proteins will be broken down to be transformed into glucose metabolites. However, the ability to convert glucogenic amino acids to glucose metabolites to meet both energy and glucose requirements is limited.

2.   Detrimental Effects of Excessive Protein Ingestion. Nutritional complications are associated with diets that are excessively high in protein without the benefit of additional carbohydrate and/or fat. Historic reports of plains Indians going without food rather than eating rabbit ("rabbit hunger") provide vivid testimony to this problem in humans (Speth and Spielman 1983; Speth 1987). When only lean meat (like rabbit) is available for food, consumption initially will be enormous (3 to 5 pounds) because hunger continues; however, over several weeks, intake decreases to zero. Symptoms of delirium, diarrhea, weakness and finally death are associated with continued high protein intakes after only three weeks. Laboratory rats will not consume enough food to meet their energy requirements when the protein level of the diet is above 75%, presumably related in some way to these detrimental effects. Whether these effects arise from a build-up of nitrogenous waste products in the blood, potassium and/or sodium depletion, or from some other metabolic process remains unknown.

3.   Fatty Acids as Fuel. Body heat is produced as a consequence of metabolic processes; when extra body heat is needed, it can be produced through muscle activity (including shivering) or by the brown fat cells. Both processes can use fatty acids for fuel. Protein can only be converted to fatty acids via pathways related to those used for glucose production, and nitrogen is excreted in this process as well. Most body tissues—muscle, liver and heart—can use glucose or fatty acids as fuel. In fact, in certain tissues (liver and heart) fatty acids are the preferred fuel (Montague 1983:116). When adequate dietary fat or carbohydrate is not available, fat stores will be converted to fatty acids and used to provide needed energy. Fatty acids are not converted to glucose. Fat stores provide a protein sparing effect by limiting the need for dietary or body protein to be used for energy. In this context, preferential storage of fat would provide a distinct survival advantage.

4.   Insulin. Insulin is a hormone which allows glucose and neutral amino acids to be transported into muscle and adipose cells (Montague 1983). Insulin levels rise when blood glucose rises, leading to lowering of blood glucose to "normal." When an animal exercises, glucose initially diffuses freely into muscles without insulin, although some insulin is still required for maintaining the infusion of glucose as exercise contin-

ues (Björntorp et al. 1972; Holloszy 1973:45; Heath et al. 1983; Holloszy and Coyle 1984). This serves as a shunt to remove glucose from the blood for use as fuel, or to be converted to glycogen for storage. Insulin also stops gluconeogenesis, glycogenolysis (degradation of glycogen to glucose), and the breakdown of stored fats for use as fuel (Randle et al. 1963). In the northern hunter environment insulin requirements would be relatively low; excess glucose is rare, exercise is common, gluconeogenesis is needed to maintain glucose levels, and fatty acids are typically used for fuel.

5. Glucagon. Glucagon is a hormone produced by the pancreas when blood sugar is low. Its actions are the opposite of insulin; its main action is to increase the level of blood glucose, primarily through the conversion of glucogenic amino acids to glucose metabolizable substances in the liver. Glucagon acts to increase the uptake of amino acids, and to increase the enzymes necessary for both glucose and urea synthesis. Glucagon is secreted by the pancreas in response to low blood glucose levels and also to ingestion of a high protein, low carbohydrate meal (with cholecystokinin [CCK] as a messenger), which apparently signals the body that glucose sources are limited (Randle et al. 1963; Montague 1983:116). Glucagon would be instrumental in the maintenance of blood glucose levels for the northern hunter.

EARLY AGRICULTURE

As the northern hunters migrated south and a greater supply of plant foods became available, severe carbohydrate shortages probably became more limited in duration. Finally, the advent of agriculture brought with it a new dietary complex including large amounts of carbohydrates from corn, beans and squash diets (Table II). It is clear from several studies of prehistoric Indian populations across this transition that agriculture did *not* result in an improvement in nutritional status (Buikstra 1976; Cassidy 1980:117). This period in Amerindian prehistory was characterized by high energy demands met by a high carbohydrate diet with moderate protein and lower fat content than that of their ancestors. The glucose readily available from this diet would have easily been used for fuel in most body tissues and would have limited the need for gluconeogenesis. The increased work load apparently associated with an agricultural subsistence system would have been associated with high energy demands; glucose would provide the ideal fuel for muscles in this context. The high activity levels would minimize (although not eliminate) the need for insulin to facilitate movement of glucose into

TABLE II   Agricultural Lifestyle

Diet based on agricultural production:
    High in carbohydrate
    High in dietary fiber
    Moderate in protein
    Low in fat
High energy demands for:
    Work
Seasonal macronutrient shortages

muscle cells (Björntorp et al. 1972; Holloszy 1973:45; Heath et al. 1983; Holloszy and Coyle 1984). In addition, the traditional diet was high in soluble and insoluble dietary fiber, slowing the absorption rate of glucose from the intestine, and further minimizing insulin demands. Fat would not be necessary as a fuel source, except in times of famine. Therefore, fat could preferentially be stored. As in Neel's "Thrifty Gene" hypothesis, this preferential fat storage would continue as a survival factor during this period.

MODERN ACCULTURATION OF AMERINDIANS

Amerindians of today vary greatly in their degree of acculturation to Western lifestyles, including both diet and activity patterns. The most acculturated Indians (e.g., Pima) have diets that are similar in composition to the average U.S. diet although total intakes may well be higher (Bell and Heller 1978:145; Knowler et al. 1981). These diets are higher in fat and carbohydrate and much lower in protein than those currently consumed among the northern hunters such as the Dogrib (Szathmary, Ritenbaugh, and Goodby 1987; Ritenbaugh et al. 1987), but they are higher in protein, fat and simple sugars and lower in complex carbohydrates and fiber than those probably consumed in the earlier agricultural periods. Food is now available continuously; the famine periods previously evident are no longer inevitable. However, feasting is still a common and frequent practice; in the present it is no longer necessary or even desirable for survival (Table III). Lifestyles are also radically different. For many American Indians, especially in the U.S., the energy intensive agricultural or pastoral activities of the past have been reduced or eliminated by the labor-saving devices of today (running water, electricity, cars, etc.). Television is available to most modern Indians; in many places this has lead to a decrease in voluntary or leisure activity as well.

TABLE III   Modern Lifestyle

Diet based on grocery stores and modern food technology:
    High in carbohydrate
    Moderate in fat
    Moderate in protein
    Low in dietary fiber
Low energy demands for:
    Work
    Sedentary leisure time activities (TV)
No macronutrient shortages

If we compare diabetes and obesity rates among tribes to lifestyle factors, supporting patterns emerge. Among the Dogrib Indians, we (Szathmary and Holt 1983; Szathmary, Ritenbaugh, and Goodby 1987) have reported a low prevalence of both obesity and hyperglycemia in a population which still includes many active fishers, hunters and trappers, as well as individuals active in traditional practices of preserving fish, hauling wood, walking long distances, etc. For many of these people, diets remain closer to the traditional hunting diet than to modern western patterns (Szathmary, Ritenbaugh, and Goodby 1987; Ritenbaugh et al. 1987). The Navajo, a tribe with the lowest prevalence of obesity and diabetes in the Southwest, continue a tradition of scattered housing on a large and remote reservation. Accepted aspects of life for many still include hauling water and fuel, splitting wood, herding sheep and goats, small scale agriculture, and weaving. Among the Hopi, it is reported anecdotally that the least obese and most healthy elders are those pursuing a traditional lifestyle, including intensive farming and walking, hauling water and wood and a traditional diet (Ritenbaugh 1981:183). Movement into the "modern" lifestyle is associated with creeping obesity and failing health (Schaefer 1974; Knowler et al. 1981; King et al. 1984; Mohs, Leonard, and Watson 1985; Taylor 1985).

RELATING RESEARCH OBSERVATIONS TO PREHISTORIC AND MODERN LIFESTYLES

The most frequently encountered explanation for the increased incidence of NIDDM is that obesity increases insulin resistance which results in high circulating levels of glucose. However, obesity is not the only cause of insulin resistance and abnormalities of high insulin output have been studied among nondiabetic Pima (Howard et al. 1979; Knowler et al. 1981;

Nagulesparan et al. 1982). Continued high output of insulin may exceed the threshold level necessary to produce down-regulation of insulin receptors in muscle and/or adipose tissue, leading to the observed insulin resistance and excess circulating glucose. Insulin retains the ability to decrease fatty acid output from adipose cells in even the very obese Pima (Howard et al. 1979). Neutral amino acids are also cleared by insulin, yet no information has been reported on whether insulin resistance alters the capacity to clear neutral amino acids. The mechanism through which insulin resistance occurs is still unclear. The roles of reduced insulin receptors, reduced uptake of glucose, altered handling of glucose by the adipose cells, and the specific effects of obesity remain important research questions in this area.

Other metabolic alterations are also likely possibilities. At least two intestinal hormones stimulate insulin secretion by the pancreas. Protein and fat in the intestinal track stimulate CCK secretion which in turn stimulates not only insulin but glucagon as well. Gastric Inhibiting Polypeptide (GIP) secretion is stimulated by carbohydrate ingestion, and it stimulates the release of insulin only. Any adaptations to a hunting-based diet among these hormones would have emphasized reliance on CCK. Metabolic alterations may still be evident today in modern Amerindians in these systems which could lead to alterations in pancreatic function. This may help to explain the observations of Schaefer et al. (1972) that oral glucose tolerance test glucose curves in Eskimos were normalized by preceding the test with a protein meal. A protein meal would stimulate the release of CCK and hence insulin. This insulin release would occur prior to the intake of glucose and thus increase glucose disposal during the test. Schaefer also reported normal glucose curves when glucose was administered intravenously rather than by mouth. This test bypassed the gut and the associated hormone stimulating system within it. His results are consistent with alterations in gut hormone response in this group of Amerindians which would be expected with a hunting adaptation.

Cholesterol saturated bile and increased risk of gall bladder disease is a common finding in Amerindians, and part of the New World Syndrome described by Weiss, Ferrell, and Hanis (1984). Gallstone disease is usually associated with a decrease in bile acids and an increase in cholesterol saturation of the bile. Insulin and CCK may both be implicated in this process (Jazrawi and Northfield 1986). Insulin acts on the cells of the intestine to stimulate cholesterol synthesis, resulting in increased cholesterol saturation of the bile. CCK increases cycling of the bile which decreases the liver's production of bile salts and increases intestinal loss.

Another unexpected metabolic pattern among Amerindians is a low blood lipid profile. Caucasian subjects with NIDDM display high circulating blood lipids (cholesterol and triglycerides); these are uncommon in Amerindians, as is cardiovascular disease. A primary mechanism to store glucose is to transform it into lipids for adipose tissue storage. In a glucose poor, but fatty acid rich environment this would be disadvantageous since glucose would be the limiting nutrient. Several enzyme systems could have altered kinetics which would reduce the ability to store glucose as fat, but little research has been done in this area.

CONCLUSIONS

Feasting without fasting, decreased energy requirements and a change in dietary constituents and availability have lead to increasing obesity in many New World populations. Previously uncommon diseases, to which American Indians were once thought to be immune, are on the rise with uncommonly high prevalence in many populations. The increased availability of carbohydrate and fats in the diet, along with the decreased dietary fiber and a more sedentary lifestyle, have lead to several metabolic consequences. Insulin secretion has increased due both to the greater quantities of dietary glucose and to the inactivity-induced requirement of muscle for insulin to take in, use and store glucose for energy. Examination of the metabolic consequences of the northern hunting adaptation in the contemporary setting provides new directions for research into the physiologic bases for the New World Syndrome among American Indians.

REFERENCES

Bell, R. R., and C. A. Heller. 1978. Nutritional Studies: An Appraisal of the Modern North Alaskan Eskimo Diet. *In* Eskimos of Northwestern Alaska: A Biological Perspective. P. L. Jamison et al., eds. Pp. 145–156. Stroudsburg, PA: Dowden, Hutchinson and Ross.

Björntorp , P., M. Fahlén, G. Grimby, A. Gustafson, J. Holm, P Renström, and T. Scherstén. 1972. Carbohydrate and Lipid Metabolism in Middle-aged, Physically Well-trained Men. Metabolism 21(11):1037–1044.

Buikstra, J. E. 1976. The Caribou Eskimo: General and Specific Disease. American Journal of Physical Anthropology 45(3, part 1):351–368.

Cassidy, C. M. 1980. Nutrition and Health in Agriculturalists and Hunter-Gatherers: A Case Study of Two Prehistoric Populations. *In* Nutritional Anthropology: Contemporary Approaches to Diet and Culture. N. W. Jerome, R. F. Kendal, and G. H. Pelto, eds. Pp. 117–146. Bedford Hills, NY: Redgrave.

DIAND (Department of Indian Affairs and Northern Development). 1977. Band List, Yellowknife, N.W.T., Mimeograph.

Heath, G. W., J. R. Gavin III, J. M. Hinderliter, J. M. Hegberg, S. A. Bloomfield, and J. O. Holloszy. 1983. Effects of Exercise and Lack of Exercise on Glucose Tolerance and Insulin Sensitivity. Journal of Applied Physiology 55(2):512–517.

Heaton, K. 1981. Gallstones. *In* Western Diseases: Their Emergence and Prevention. H. C. Trowell and D. D. Burkitt, eds. Pp. 47–59. Cambridge, Mass: Harvard University Press.

Holloszy, J. O. 1973. Biochemical Adaptations to Exercise: Aerobic Metabolism. *In* Exercise and Sports Science Review. J. Wilmore, ed. Pp. 45–71. New York: Academic Press.

Holloszy, J. O., and E. F. Coyle. 1984. Adaptations of Skeletal Muscle to Endurance Exercise and Their Metabolic Consequences. Journal of Applied Physiology 56:831–838.

Howard, B. V., P. J. Savage, M. Nagulesparan, L. J. Bennion, R. J. Unger, and P. H. Bennett. 1979. Evidence for Marked Sensitivity to the Antilipolytic Action of Insulin in Obese Maturity-Onset Diabetics. Metabolism 28(7):744–750.

Jazrawi, R. P., and T. C. Northfield. 1986. Effects of a Pharmacological Dose of Cholecystokinin on Bile Acid Kinetics and Biliary Cholesterol Saturation in Man. Gut 27: 355–362.

King, H., P. Zimmet, P. Bennett, R. Taylor, and L. R. Raper. 1984. Glucose Tolerance and Ancestral Genetic Admixture in Six Semitraditional Pacific Populations. Genetic Epidemiology 1:315–328.

Knowler, W. C., D. J. Pettitt, P. J. Savage, and P. H. Bennett. 1981. Diabetes Incidence in Pima Indians: Contributions of Obesity and Parental Diabetes. American Journal of Epidemiology 113(2):114–156.

Mohs, M. E., T. K. Leonard, and R. R. Watson. 1985. Selected Risk Factors for Diabetes in Native Americans. Nutritional Research 5:1035–1045.

Montague, W. 1983. Function of the Islets of Langerhans. *In* Diabetes and the Endocrine Pancreas. W. Montague, ed. Pp. 116–131. New York: Oxford University Press.

Nagulesparan, M., P. J. Savage, W. C. Knowler, G. C. Johnson, and P. H. Bennett. 1982. Increased In Vivo Insulin Resistance in Nondiabetic Pima Indians Compared with Caucasians. Diabetes 31:952–956.

Neel, J. V. 1962. Diabetes Mellitus: A "Thrifty" Genotype Rendered Detrimental by "Progress." American Journal of Human Genetics 14:353–362.

———. 1982. The Thrifty Genotype Revisited. *In* The Genetics of Diabetes Mellitus. Serono Symposium, No. 47. J. Kobberling and R. Tattersall, eds. Pp. 283–293. New York: Academic Press.

Randle, P. M., P. B. Garland, C. N. Hales, and E. A. Newsholme. 1963. The Glucose Fatty-Acid Cycle: Its Role in Insulin Sensitivity and the Metabolic Disturbances of Diabetes Mellitus. Lancet i:785–789.

Ritenbaugh, C. 1981. Uses of Clines in the Analysis of Diabetes Mellitus. *In* The Perception of Evolution. Essays

Honoring Joseph B. Birdsell. L. L. Mai, E. Shanklin, and W. Sussman, eds. Pp. 183–188. Los Angeles: UCLA Publications.

Ritenbaugh, C., E. J. E. Szathmary, C. S. Goodby, and C. Feldman. 1987. Dietary Acculturation among the Dogrib Indians of the Canadian Northwest Territories. Unpublished manuscript.

Schaefer, O. 1974. The Relative Roles of Diet and Physical Activity on Blood Lipids and Obesity. American Heart Journal 88(5):673–674.

Schaefer, O., P. M. Crockford, and B. Romanowski. 1972. Normalization Effect of Preceding Protein Meals on "Diabetic" Oral Glucose Tolerance in Eskimos. Canadian Medical Association Journal 107:733–738.

Speth, J. D. 1987. Early Hominid Subsistence Strategies in Seasonal Habitats. Journal of Archaeological Science 14(l):13–29.

Speth, J. D., and K. A. Spielman. 1983. Energy Source, Protein Metabolism, and Hunter-Gatherer Subsistence Strategies. Journal of Anthropological Archaeology 2(1):1–31.

Steegman, A. J., Jr. 1977. The Finger Temperature During Work in Natural Cold: The Northern Ojibwa. Human Biology 49(3):349–362.

Szathmary, E. J. E. 1986. Diabetes in Arctic and Subarctic Populations Undergoing Acculturation. Collegium Anthropologicum 10(2):145–158.

———. In Press. Diabetes in Amerindian Populations: The Dogrib Studies. In Epidemological Perspectives on Populations in Transition. G. Armelagos and A. Swedlund, eds. New York: Bergin and Garvey.

Szathmary, E. J. E., and N. Holt. 1983. Hyperglycemia in Dogrib Indians of the Northwest Territories, Canada: Association with Age and a Centripetal Distribution of Body Fat. Human Biology 55:493–515.

Szathmary, E. J. E., C. Ritenbaugh, and C. S. Goodby. 1987. Diet Change and Plasma Glucose Levels in an Amerindian Population Undergoing Cultural Transition. Social Science and Medicine 24(10):791–804.

Taylor, R., P. Bennett, R. Uli, R. Germain, S. Levy, and P. Zimmet. 1985. Diabetes in Wallis Polynesians: A Comparison of Residents of Wallis Island and First Generation Migrants to Noumea, New Caledonia. Diabetes Research and Clinical Practice 1:169–178.

Tepperman, J. 1980. Metabolic and Endocrine Physiology. Chicago, Ill.: Yearbook Medical Publishers.

Weiss, K. M., R. E. Ferrell, and C. L. Hanis. 1984. A New World Syndrome of Metabolic Diseases with a Genetic and Evolutionary Basis. Yearbook of Physical Anthropology 27:153–178.

West, K. M. 1974. Diabetes in American Indians and Other Native Populations of the New World. Diabetes 23: 841–855.

———. 1981. North American Indians. In Western Diseases: Their Emergence and Prevention. H. C. Trowell and D. D. Burkitt, eds. Pp. 129–137. Cambridge, Mass: Harvard University Press.

 6

Genetic Prophecy: Promises and Perils for Late-Onset Diseases

Marie I. Boutté

One of the most important and controversial projects being conducted in human biology and genetics today is a large-scale endeavor called the Human Genome Initiative *(HGI). HGI is an ambitious project with the aim of mapping the entire human genome: the hundreds of thousands of genes on human chromosomes and the variants at each genetic address. The project is huge, involving thousands of biological investigators (funded by the Department of Energy) who are decoding the human DNA sequence, one*

base pair at a time. Even though computers have accelerated this scientific process considerably, the HGI will probably take another decade to complete.

How will genetics and medicine be changed by the completion of the HGI? How will the HGI deal with the complexities of human biological variation? What will be done to prevent ethical abuses of genetic information?

Clearly, medical science is able to screen for more and more inherited traits, both from adults and fetuses. Today, amniocentesis allows identification of fetuses with genetic diseases like Down's syndrome (see selection 40 by Rayna Rapp) and therefore gives parents the option of terminating the pregnancy. On the other hand, in Rajastan in northwest India, for example, amniocentesis has been used to ensure the birth of a son by terminating female fetuses. The ethical dilemmas of cross-cultural relativism are certainly apparent.

In the near future, genetic screening may be able to identify hereditary predispositions to conditions like alcoholism or homosexuality. It also may be useful for identifying which individuals will develop late-onset diseases like multiple sclerosis or Huntington's disease. Certainly, genetic screening can be used in prevention—that is, in identifying the carriers of certain traits and counseling parents about the likelihood of having a child with a severe genetic disease. But what about confidentiality? Will employers or insurance companies have access to our genetic profiles? Do people really want to know about the genes that they carry and what that means for their personal future? Do they have a right to know, or not to know?

In this selection, medical anthropologist Marie Boutté discusses these issues of genetic prophecy, based in large measure on her research in the biocultural dynamics of genetic screening for a rare condition called Machado-Joseph disease, which is found in the greatest concentrations among a small group of people in the Azore's Islands.

Human biological variation involves genetic differences. Geneticists have clearly demonstrated that the vast majority of genetic variation is found within so-called racial or ethnic populations. This fact does little to stem the terrible tide of discrimination and mistreatment of people based on archaic notions of folk biology, like race. In the future we will all have more genetic information about human variation. Some of that information will help in the prevention of suffering. But there is little doubt that the same information also has the potential to create even more suffering.

As you read this selection, consider these questions:

- *If you had the opportunity, would you want to know everything about your genetic potentials and predispositions? Even if it meant finding out something terrible? Even if you knew that all tests carry probabilities of false negatives and false positives?*

- *What does the huge complexity of the human genome tell us about the problems and utility of anachronistic concepts like race?*

- *The HGI research agenda sets aside a small amount of funds for examination of ethical issues related to genetic screening and prognosis. What do you think may be anthropological contributions to this discussion in regard to cross-cultural variation in beliefs and values?*

In 1975 an unusual family reunion was held at Children's Hospital in Oakland, California. The large Joseph family had gathered for the first time. One of their members had finally taken the family secret to the National Genetics Foundation and asked for help with the unique disease that for many years had been passed in their family from one generation to the next. The National Genetics Foundation sent a team of neurologists and geneticists to the reunion and held the first screening clinic for what became known as Joseph's Disease, and later as Machado-Joseph disease (MJD). Diagnosis of those afflicted with the disease was made from neurological examinations, and at-risk status was determined from family history and genealogical analysis.

Preliminary findings indicated that Machado-Joseph disease is a late-onset, neurologically degenerative disorder which is inherited as a dominant trait. Those who had a parent with the disease were told they each had a 50 percent chance of inheriting this disorder. For many individuals the diagnosis and naming of the malady corrected what they had been erroneously told in the past—namely, that they suffered from syphilis, multiple sclerosis, Parkinson's disease, or some other form of spinocerebellar degeneration. For others, especially those who were un-

aware they exhibited signs of the disease, the diagnosis was extremely distressing. One young man walked away from the hospital and said, "I couldn't come back, I had to leave and just walk. It was heavy. It really was."

For those who were told they had a 50 percent chance of inheriting the disease, life became one of waiting, and for many the waiting continues because there are as yet no predictive tests to clarify their ambiguous state. The development of such a test is the primary focus of several international teams of biomedical scientists.

As a medical anthropologist, my interest in MJD was stimulated several years ago when a woman of Azorean-Portuguese descent, speaking generally of health problems within her particular ethnic group, stated, "We have this thing called Joseph's Disease but no one seems to know much about it and no one wants to talk about it." This statement led me initially to an investigation of the stigma that has historically been associated with MJD, both in the United States and in the Azores Islands. Later work focused on the subjective experiences of being at risk for the disease.

During the course of my research on MJD, I have become closely acquainted with the biomedical scientists who are tracking the genetic marker for the disease. In the summer of 1990 I had the opportunity to visit and observe in their research laboratories. Through interviews with these scientists, with genetic counselors, and with individuals both afflicted and at risk for MJD, I have begun to think about questions and issues that might be addressed by anthropologists concerning genetic prediction and the role anthropologists might play in the new genetic frontier. In this brief article I explore the promises and perils of a predictive test for late-onset, dominantly inherited disorders such as MJD.

GENETIC IDENTIFICATION

Genetic screening began in the United States in the early 1960s with programs to test for metabolic disorders among newborns, in particular phenylketonuria (PKU). In 1966, when the technique of amniocentesis was developed, prenatal screening for certain genetic disorders and congenital defects became possible. It was in the early 1970s, however, that carrier screening of selected populations began. For example, screening was carried out for Tay-Sachs disease among the Jewish population and for sickle-cell among African-Americans. There is a large literature comparing and contrasting these two screening programs, with the screening program for Tay-Sachs generally considered a successful endeavor and possibly a model for future programs, and the program for sickle-cell a failure—a model of what not to do.

Since the 1970s, partly as a result of these particular screening programs, there has been a shift from mass, adult, public screening programs targeting certain genetic diseases to the screening of families at special genetic disease clinics usually associated directly or indirectly with a major university or with a disease "foundation." The International Joseph Disease Foundation (IJDF), for example, periodically holds screening clinics in California and New England, specifically targeting individuals and families with Azorean Portuguese heritage. The majority of cases of MJD have, to date, been identified among this population.

The primary language used to examine and justify genetic screening is the language of potential benefits. It is argued by people in the field of genetics that screening individuals at risk for inherited disease, especially those of child-bearing age, provides these individuals with information that they can take into account when making decisions about procreation.

The literature on this issue strongly suggests that most couples who are screened do consider this information in making reproductive decisions. However, they may not base their decision exclusively on being identified as a carrier. Other primary factors considered by carriers in their reproductive decisions include the pattern of transmission and nature of the disease. That is, it makes a difference whether the disease is recessive or dominant and whether the mother or father will remain healthy carriers or eventually manifest the disease.

In the unique case of MJD, the individual will most likely remain a healthy carrier until the age of twenty to forty. Since the disease does not generally manifest until child-bearing age, the majority of my informants had started their families before supposedly learning of the genetic nature of MJD and before manifesting signs of the disease. All suggested that had they known they were at risk and that the disease could be passed from one generation to the next, they probably would not have had children. There were indications, however, that several individuals knew at some level, because of family history, that the disease was hereditary before their first child was born. When I queried a young man in his early twenties who had been diagnosed with MJD about having children, he said that of course he wanted a family. "I know that I have the disease and what the chances are for my children but I've lived a good life until now and expect to have some more good years. I'm sure glad my mother didn't decide not to have children."

Arlo Guthrie, son of Woody Guthrie who died as a result of Huntington's disease (HD), another late-onset, dominantly inherited neurological disease, recently expressed somewhat the same sentiment on an *ABC News Special* (July 18, 1990) entitled "The Perfect Baby." Arlo, now at risk for the disease, said,

> There were doctors who yelled at us and said, "How could you be having kids? How could you be bringing them into the world, knowing that you're risking this and this?" And you don't have to be a big expert to know that kids are wonderful or that life is wonderful. No matter how long or short it is, no matter how big or small it is, it's always wonderful, you know.

In regards to living life at risk for HD, Arlo Guthrie went on to say,

> I can tell you, it's worth it. It's worth having the risk, I know that, 'cause I got it and I know it's worth it. And you asked my dad, he had it. It wasn't a risk for him. And still, he wrote great songs and still he made a difference in the world. The world is different because of my dad, to a lot of people.

The severity of the disease and available treatment are also factors considered in reproductive decisions. Although MJD generally manifests in the second to fourth decades and runs a progressively degenerative course over a period of fifteen to twenty years, there is some variation among individuals and families in the severity of the course. For example, debilitation may be less acute if onset occurs in the fifth to the seventh decades of life. However, subjective perception by those at risk for potential disability is based on other family members' disabilities, as well as what is seen at the IJDF-sponsored clinics. Several informants said that they quit attending the IJDF screening clinics because it was too painful to see the disease in its varying stages all at one time.

Biomedical scientists suggest that when a predictive test is developed, the vast majority of individuals at risk for MJD will seek such a test in order to clarify their present ambiguous situation. However, my research on this disorder over the past four years indicates that far fewer will come forward than biomedical scientists predict.

Many at risk already refuse the annual screening exam for fear of being told the dreaded news that they too are now showing signs of the disease. As one informant said,

> If you want to, you can develop ways to help you deny the disease. But if you go to the clinic and see all those people with canes, walkers, and in wheelchairs, there's no way you can get away from it. I used to get nightmares after going to the clinic, so I just quit going. I know my risks and I won't need a doctor to tell me when I have it. I'll know because my mother died with the disease.

A positive, predictive test for this particular young man could mean a perpetual nightmare.

A comparison in this regard can again be drawn between MJD and Huntington's disease (HD). In 1983 a genetic marker was found for HD that is 96 percent accurate. Surveys taken before the test became available indicated that between 60 and 80 percent of those at risk would want the test. Since 1986, however, when the Johns Hopkins Hospital in Baltimore and the Massachusetts General Hospital in Boston began offering the test, most have changed their mind. According to Denise Grady in her *Discover* article "The Ticking of a Time Bomb in the Genes" (June 1987), of fifteen hundred persons at risk for the disease in New England (many of whom heard about the test through local chapters of the Huntington's Disease Society of America) only thirty-two had gone in for preliminary counseling by June of 1987. And at Johns Hopkins, which notified 350 at-risk individuals of the availability of the test, only about 70 had signed up by June 1987. David Beers, in his article "The Gene Screen" (*Vogue Magazine*, June 1990) quotes Stephen Bajardi, executive director of the New York-based Huntington's Disease Society of America, as saying that only

about four hundred individuals have taken the test for HD in the past four years.

My research suggests that the majority of individuals would like to know that they are *not* carrying the gene for MJD because it would free them and their children from uncertainty. Many, however, are fearful of a test that will tell them, while they are healthy, that they are destined sometime in the future to suffer and die like many of their family members. This same sentiment is expressed by Alice Wexler, who is at risk for Huntington's Disease. She and her sister Nancy Wexler, who is also at risk and who was instrumental in helping to locate a genetic marker for HD, now have great reservations about taking the predictive test. As Alice said on *60 Minutes* (June 28, 1987), "I would like to know that I don't have it, but I do, absolutely do, not want to know if I do have it." Alice, in imagining the unimaginable, thinking about the unthinkable, says,

> Now as I start to do that and try to really imagine, well, really, how would I feel sitting down at my desk in front of the computer knowing that I have this gene. Would I go on? And sometimes, some days I think, "Well no, I couldn't do that. I really couldn't do that."

At present there is no treatment or cure for either HD or MJD. Biomedical scientists predict that a treatment or cure is on the horizon for HD because the marker has been located. They also anticipate that a treatment or cure will follow once a predictive test for MJD is developed. Many of my informants participate in the on-going research endeavor to find a marker for MJD because they hope that such research will lead to a treatment or cure, especially for coming generations. Many also noted, however, that they themselves will wait until a treatment or cure is available before asking for the results of their own tests.

There is stigma associated with being at risk for MJD, and a predictive test could potentially free from stigma those who test negative for the gene. However, it could permanently label with stigma those who test positive. Historically, such labeling has occurred in the case of other diseases. For example, there was labeling and discrimination in employment and insurance benefits of healthy individuals who were identified as being carriers of the sickle-cell trait in the 1970s in the United States. Similarly, in the small Greek village of Orchemenos where such carriers were also identified in the 1970s, there was discrimination and stigmatization, especially in terms of selection of marriage partners.

There is no evidence to suggest that the situation would be any different for those healthy individuals identified as carriers of MJD. In fact, the discrimination and stigma would most likely be much more severe because, unlike those who may only "carry" sickle-cell trait, those with the gene for MJD manifest the disease at some point in time. This discrimination would be based on the disabled status expected to occur several years down the road. New labeling categories for at-risk individuals are already emerging, labels such as the "asymptomatic ill" and the "biological underclass."

There is also the dilemma that a positive test for an incurable disease like MJD could lead to suicide. This is such a concern in the testing for HD that at Hopkins therapists do psychological follow-ups for three years after the test. At Massachusetts General Hospital at-risk individuals are psychologically profiled before, during, and after the genetic testing procedure.

There is some indication in my data that a number of individuals at risk for MJD, especially young males in their late teens to late twenties, engage in high risk recreational activities such as driving at excessive speeds and frequent use of illicit drugs and alcohol. A positive, presymptomatic test has the potential for exacerbating these behaviors.

ISSUES FOR FUTURE STUDY

There is a vast literature from a multitude of disciplines on the topic of genetic prediction, but social scientists, especially anthropologists, have come rather late to the study of genetic issues. A beginning literature treats features associated with specific genetic conditions, such as stigmatization, but there are relatively few published works on other aspects of genetic prediction.

Some areas of investigation for anthropologists, especially medical anthropologists, might include:

1. *The social and cultural construction of risk.* Until now most of the work in this area has focused either on subjective or objective risk. The subjectivist seeks explanation in the individual, in universal psychic laws of cognition, or in personality traits, while the objectivist looks to statistical modeling. However, culture gives rise to risk as a collective construct. *Practicing Anthropology* (10[3–4],1989) provided insight by anthropologists into the social contexts of particular environmental risks. The social and cultural construction of genetic risk could be viewed in much the same way.

For example, how does the community perceive genetic risk? Does "type" of community influence perceptions? Are risk perceptions different in face-to-face communities versus communities where anonymity is the general rule? What in our own society has led us to

put vast sums of money and scientific energy into such endeavors as the Human Genome Project, supported and supervised by the Department of Energy and the National Institutes of Health at a cost of three billion dollars? Why have hereditary diseases been selected for this massive project over other types of disorders? In other words, why is there such a focus on "doctoring the genes"? What is the social distribution of genetic disease knowledge and what factors act to shape the distribution of such knowledge? What are the issues of social control with this new technology?

2. *The language and metaphors of genetics and genetic prediction and popular images of genetics.* An advertisement in the *San Francisco Chronicle* of October 1988 showed a woman struggling to zip her jeans with the caption "Are your genes filling your jeans?" This was advertising the latest biochemical scientific testing, with the idea that a person's unique metabolic chemistry could be identified and such knowledge used to reduce pounds and inches and restore energy. How are the new technologies being marketed? What are the cultural images and symbolic meanings and metaphors adhering to genetic disease in general and to specific inherited disorders? What role does the public media play in creating and maintaining particular cultural images? How does the language of genetic counseling shape knowledge and mold patterns of utilization of genetic services?

3. *The industry of genetic prediction.* There are now thousands of biotechnology companies spread throughout the United States, including many located in Montgomery County, Maryland, where they take advantage of their proximity to the National Institutes of Health. A significant number of these biotechnology companies are involved in various aspects of genetic prediction. In addition, major university laboratories are affiliated with the genetic prediction industry.

Some research has begun on the discourse of genetic counseling, but these companies and laboratories are another arena in which a number of research questions can be addressed. For example, how will genetic information be used? What are the safeguards, if any, to protect the privacy of the consumer who has been identified as carrying a disease-causing gene or genes? In other words, how can the optimal use of genetic data be coupled with the maintenance of privacy?

4. *Labeling and stigmatization.* This is the one area in which social scientists have done some excellent research, but much more needs to be done. What are the cultural attitudes toward technology utilization? If a test for a particular disorder is available or becomes available and individuals elect *not* to take the test, what are the consequences, if any? Will these individ-

uals suffer social ostracism? And, what if an individual tests positive for a disease and yet chooses to bear offspring who are also at risk? Do they, or will they, too suffer social ostracism or be labeled social liabilities? What are the dynamics within families when some members elect to be tested and others do not, especially when test results reveal information about untested family members?

CONCLUSION

One of our best contributions to the discourse of genetic prediction is as ethnographers, providing thick descriptions of what is happening and analyzing and interpreting these descriptions. As Marc Lappe notes in his book *Broken Code: The Exploitation of DNA* (San Francisco: Sierra Club Books, 1984),

> In an ideal world, those who ultimately benefit or suffer from a new technology would have some say in its evolution. With the present system of proprietary secrets and patentable inventions, it is the venture capitalists and their corporate partners who control a technology's evolution.

Through our research efforts we as anthropologists can help bring the voices of those who will either benefit or suffer the perils of the new technology to the arena of genetic prediction. In the vast literature on this topic, it is the voices of individuals with genetic disorders and those who are at risk that are currently missing from the record.

Bioarchaeology and the History of Health

✤ CONCEPTUAL TOOLS ✤

- *The importance of the Neolithic Revolution and other epidemiological transitions must be stressed.* The Neolithic Revolution refers to the domestication of plants and animals, a process that began about 10,000 years ago. The invention and spread of agriculture and pastoralism was a process that probably took several thousand years to complete, but there is no doubt that the social and cultural implications of this economic transformation were revolutionary. Agriculture meant that there was a fundamentally different relationship between humans and their environment than was the case with hunter-gatherers. Agriculture both allowed and required local populations to grow: It *allowed* population growth because it provided a more predictable source of carbohydrate foods and because people settled in permanent villages; it *required* growth because more people were necessary to labor in the fields and to process food (Cohen and Armelagos 1984). A denser population and permanent ties to the land resulted in concentrated power in the hands of fewer people and the creation of systems of social stratification (Armelagos and Dewey 1970).

- *Paleopathologists have documented the negative effect of the Neolithic Revolution on health status.* One excellent source of epidemiological, paleopathological, and ethnographic information on this topic is Mark Cohen's *Health and the Rise of Civilization* (1989). Another edited volume, *Paleopathology at the Origins of Agriculture* (Cohen and Armelagos 1984), provides seventeen specific case studies of health at this important historical juncture and demonstrates the controversy surrounding this issue; twelve cases show definite negative health effects, whereas five cases do not.

- *Historians of health have documented how the spread of epidemic diseases, and the mortality caused by them, influenced larger historical processes.* One classic example is the spread of the Spanish empire into the New World, particularly in Cortez's conquest of Mexico. William H. McNeill (1976) has shown how Cortez's party (inadvertently) introduced infectious diseases to the Amerindian population and how these diseases caused massive mortality because the local populations lacked childhood immunities to European diseases. Massive die-offs caused economic collapse, famine, and social unrest. European conquest was greatly aided by this native die-off and cultural collapse. In this regard, McNeill has described world history as the "confluence of disease pools," in which populations with a larger number of childhood endemic diseases historically win out over more isolated populations. Recently, Stephen Kunitz (1994) has disputed the universality of such a historical law by demonstrating that the health consequences of initial interactions between aboriginal populations and European colonizers shows much more variation. Finally, epidemics have historically brought social and ethnic tensions to the forefront of social interaction.

- *The modern decline in mortality and increase in population growth is primarily the result of socioeconomic changes (affecting hygiene, nutrition, and so forth) and not because of therapeutic inventions of biomedicine.* Health historians using demographic data have documented a decline in mortality in Europe primarily during the 19th century. The reasons for this improved health are not completely known, but Thomas McKeown (1979) provides convincing evidence that these health improvements historically preceded the development of scientific therapies in modern medicine (see selection 8). He credits public health interventions affecting hygiene, nutrition, and birth spacing as the primary reasons for these improvements. Demographic historians have made significant progress in understanding the role of breast-feeding and birth-spacing patterns on total fertility that also play an important role in population change—most strikingly in the demographic transition from large completed families to small completed families (and the zero population growth that characterized some of the richest countries of the world) (Caldwell 1982).

7

Health and Disease in Prehistoric Populations in Transition

George J. Armelagos

It is hard for people to know if things are getting better or worse. On the one hand there is the myth of progress, which claims that technological innovation makes our lives less grueling, healthier, more productive, and happier. On the other hand, there is the myth of the good old days, with people bemoaning crumbling morality, increased misery throughout the world, and backlashes from progress, such as antibiotic-resistant diseases. I guess it's a question of personal optimism and pessimism—our individual perception. But aren't there historical facts about this? Isn't it the case that, given the choice to live in the prehistoric past, everyone would choose the comforts of today?

This selection is about the health of populations who undergo rapid historical change, particularly with the domestication of plants and animals during the Neolithic Revolution. The author reviews paleopathological research methods to examine skeletal remains uncovered in archaeological excavations. A variety of infectious diseases leave definitive traces on the bones; some conditions, such as porotic hyperostosis, reflect nutritional anemias in childhood; other markers, such as Harris lines and enamel hypoplasia, resemble the rings in tree trunks that reflect the availability of adequate nutrition in the past.

A large area of concern in bioarchaeology is the cause of population growth. In this selection, George Armelagos considers the effects of sedentary village life on fertility and child mortality.

As you read this selection, consider these questions:

- *In what ways can the domestication of plants and animals be considered the worst mistake or the most important event in human history?*

- *Why is it important for bioarchaeologists and paleopathologists to study disease history and biochemistry as well as anatomy?*

- *Why do you think that family size and fertility would increase when humans changed from hunter-gatherers to farmers?*

The study of disease in prehistory offers a unique opportunity for the anthropologist. Paleopathologists have contributed significantly to our knowledge about the history and geography of numerous pathological conditions. While there is still a vigorous debate concerning the chronology and geographic distribution of diseases such as syphilis, tuberculosis, and rheumatoid arthritis, we know a great deal about their occurrence in many regions. However, paleopathology can potentially provide a broader understanding of the relationship between disease and human populations. For example, the interaction between human populations and the disease process provides information about biocultural adaptation. The cultural system can dramatically influence the disease process, and disease can significantly alter the cultural adaptation.

Populations in transition often experience change in ecological relationships that alter their disease patterns. The paleopathology of prehistoric populations provides a means for examining these changes from an evolutionary perspective. While early human populations subsisted primarily as gatherer-hunters, there was a dramatic shift to primary food production about 10,000 years ago. I will discuss the impact of this shift and subsequent changes on the disease profile of populations undergoing these major transitions.

During the last four million years human disease ecology has changed significantly as a function of changes in the environment, evolution of the species, and cultural adaptation. These processes created different environments for the pathogens and altered their interaction with human populations. There is a substantial literature that describes the evolutionary impact of disease on human populations. These studies (Armelagos 1967; Armelagos and Dewey 1970; Armelagos and McArdle 1975; Cockburn 1971;

Boyden 1970; Fenner 1970; Polgar 1964) agree that there has been dramatic change in the pattern of disease and the human response, especially within the last 10,000 years. When gathering and hunting were the sole means of human subsistence (a period lasting from 4,000,000 years ago to the beginning of the Neolithic), population size was small, and density was quite low.

Human population size and density presumably remained quite low throughout the Paleolithic. It is assumed that fertility and mortality rates in these small gathering-hunting populations were balanced and that population growth was low and stable. Controversy continues as to the demographic factors which created this stability. Some demographers argue that gatherer-hunters were at their maximum natural fertility and this was balanced by high mortality. Other demographers argue that gatherer-hunters maintained a stable population with controlled moderate fertility balanced by moderate mortality.

A critical key to resolving this controversy is to understand the demographic changes that occurred during the Neolithic period. The Neolithic not only heralded a major shift in subsistence, it also resulted in a dramatic increase in population size and density. The reasons for this increase are complex. There are those who have argued that the Neolithic economy generated food surpluses which provided the key to population growth. The abundance of food would have led to a better nourished and healthier population with a reduced rate of mortality. Since populations were at their natural maximum fertility, there would have been a rapid increase in population.

While this scenario is appealing in its simplicity, the empirical evidence paints a different picture. The biological consequence of the shift from gathering and hunting to agriculture presents a much bleaker picture of health and disease. Instead of experiencing improved health, there is evidence of an increase in infectious and nutritional disease.

DISEASE IN GATHERER-HUNTERS

A consideration of the disease ecology of contemporary gatherer-hunters provides insights into the types of disease that would have affected our gatherer-hunter ancestors. Polgar (1964) suggests that gatherer-hunters would have two types of disease to contend with in their adaptation to their environment. One class of disease would be those organisms that had adapted to prehominid ancestors and persisted with

them as they evolved into hominids. Head and body lice (*Pediculus humanus*), pinworms, yaws, and possibly malaria would be included in this group. Cockburn (1967b) adds to this list most of the internal protozoa found in modern humans and such bacteria as salmonella, typhi and staphylococci.

Livingstone (1958) dismisses the potential of malaria in early hominids because of the small population size and an adaptation to the savannah, which would not have been within the range of the mosquitos that carry the malaria plasmodium. The second class of diseases is the zoonotics, which have nonhuman animals as their primary host and only incidentally infect humans. Humans can be infected by zoonoses through insect bites, by preparing and eating contaminated flesh, and from wounds inflicted by animals. Sleeping sickness, tetanus, scrub typhus, relapsing fever, trichinosis, tularemia, leptospirosis, and schistosomiasis are among the zoonotic diseases which could have afflicted earlier gatherers and hunters.

The range of the earliest hominids was probably restricted to the tropical savannah. This would have limited the pathogens that were potential disease agents. During the course of human evolution there was eventually an expansion of habitat into the temperate and eventually the tundra zones. As Lambrecht (1964, 1985) points out, the hominids would have avoided large areas of the African landscape because of tsetse flies and thus avoided the trypanosomes they carried. The evolution of the human species and its expansion into new ecological niches would have led to a change in the pattern of trypanosome infection. While this list of diseases that plagued our gathering-hunting ancestors is informative, those diseases that would have been absent are also of interest. The contagious community diseases such as influenza, measles, mumps, and smallpox would have been missing. Burnet (1962) states that there would have been few viruses infecting these early hominids. On the other hand, Cockburn (1967b), in a well-reasoned argument, suggests that the viral diseases found in nonhuman primates would have been easily transmitted to humans.

DISEASE IN AGRICULTURAL POPULATIONS IN TRANSITION

Given the limited list of diseases found in gatherer-hunters, it should not have been surprising that a shift to primary food production (agriculture) would increase the number and the impact of disease in sedentary populations. Sedentism would undoubtedly increase parasitic disease spread by contact with human waste. In gathering-hunting groups, the frequent movement of the base camp and frequent forays away from base camp by men and women would decrease their contact with human wastes. In sedentary populations the proximity of habitation area and their waste deposit sites to the water supply would be a source of contamination. While sedentism could and did occur prior to the Neolithic period in those areas with abundant resources (acorns in California and marine resources in the Northwest Coast), the shift to agriculture would necessitate sedentary living.

The herding of animals would also increase the frequency of contact with zoonotic diseases. The domestication of animals in the Neolithic would have provided a steady supply of disease vectors. The zoonotic infections would likely increase because of domesticated animals, such as goats, sheep, cattle, pigs, and fowl. Products of domesticated animals such as milk, hair, and skin, as well as the dust raised by the animals, could transmit anthrax, Q fever, brucellosis, and tuberculosis (Polgar 1964). Breaking the sod during cultivation exposes workers to insect bites and diseases such as scrub typhus (Audy 1961). Livingstone (1958) showed that slash-and-burn agriculture in west Africa exposed populations to *Anopheles gambiae,* a mosquito which is the vector for *Plasmodium falciparum,* which causes malaria.

The development of urban centers is a recent event in human history. In the Near East, cities as large as 50,000 people were established by 3000 B.C. In the New World, urban settlements of half a million were in existence by 5000 B.C. Settlements of this size increase the already difficult problem of removing human wastes and delivering uncontaminated water to the people. Cholera, which is transmitted by contaminated water, was a potential problem. Diseases such as typhus (carried by lice) and the plague bacillus (transmitted by fleas or by the respiratory route), could be spread from person to person. Viral diseases such as measles, mumps, chicken pox, and smallpox could be spread in a similar fashion. We had, for the first time, populations which were large enough to maintain disease in an endemic form. Cockburn (1967b) estimates that populations of one million would be necessary to maintain measles as an endemic disease.

There were also social changes and social upheavals, which resulted in a different mode of disease transmission; for example, the crowding of urban centers, changes in sexual practices, such as prostitution, and an increase in sexual promiscuity may have been factors in the venereal transmission of the treponema, the pathogen which causes syphilis (Hudson 1965). The period of urban development can also be characterized by the exploration and expansion into new areas which would result in the introduction of novel diseases to populations that had little resistance to them (McNeill 1976).

The evolutionary picture of infectious disease suggests that agriculturalists faced considerable difficulties. However, there exists a possible paradox that deserves further consideration. Zoonotic diseases in gatherer-hunters would likely have the greatest impact on the segment of the society that contains the producers (those between age 20 and 40). This segment, in its daily rounds, is more likely to come into contact with the animals that are the vector of disease. As Lambrecht (1985: 642) points out, exposure to fly bites is unavoidable in tsetse fly country. The degree of exposure to fly bites is influenced by the choice of habitat and the behavior of the potential host. He writes, "In many areas, Rhodesian sleeping sickness is significantly higher in men than women. This is related to men's activity such as hunting and honey collecting which brings them in close contact with *morsitans* savanna flies, major vector of *T. b. rhodesiense.*" The infection is called "honey collector's disease" by the native groups.

The occurrence of endemic diseases in larger urban agriculturalist areas would most likely kill the very young infants, young children, and the very old adults. In this situation, the predictability of mortality allows them to reduce birth spacing to meet the increase in mortality. Sedentary societies can wean infants earlier, allowing the women to become pregnant again. The social costs of disruption from this pattern of endemic disease mortality may not be as great as the impact of zoonotic diseases on the gatherer-hunters. Even the energetic costs of endemic diseases that are fatal would not be as great. Infants require relatively little energetic investment when compared to older children and young adults. Those who do survive (because of acquired immunity) will be protected from these pathogens. The protected producers segment would be able to reproduce and continue to extract the resources essential for survival.

The process of industrialization, which began a little over 200 years ago, would lead to an even greater environmental and social transformation. City dwellers would have to contend with industrial wastes and polluted water and air. Slums that rise in industrial cities become the focal point for poverty and the spread of disease. Epidemics of smallpox, typhus, typhoid, diphtheria, measles, and yellow fever in urban settings are well documented (Polgar 1964). Tuberculosis and respiratory diseases such as pneumonia and bronchitis are even more serious problems with harsh working situations and crowded living conditions.

In the modern era, there are organized public health and medical practices to control infectious diseases in many western societies. Yet, in many of the developing nations, infectious diseases still extract a great toll of human life. Even with public health and medical advances, nations such as the United States experience new outbreaks of infectious disease which they find very threatening. The current AIDS epidemic generates great fear among the public.

The above discussion has focused our concerns on the ecology of disease in these populations in transition. The issue of the biological response of the host and pathogen remains. It has been assumed that the pathogen-host interaction would result in a decrease in the virulence of the pathogen and an increase in the resistance of the host. The short generation time of the pathogens makes it possible for them to evolve mechanisms which decrease their pathogenicity. This evolutionary strategy would be effective if the virulence of the pathogen threatened the extinction of the host. A dead host is of little value in maintaining the reproductive potential of the pathogen.

The potential response of the human host is still an open question. It is often assumed that human populations have developed genetic resistance to disease. For example, generalized host factors and highly specific genetically determined resistance factors (r) would have evolved (Motulsky 1963). The development of resistance factors (r) is assumed but difficult to demonstrate. Since the interaction of the endemic pathogen and the human host is quite recent in evolutionary terms, there is a question of the potential for a human genetic response to have evolved. The 5,000 years since the development of large urban centers may not have been an adequate time for evolution to occur. However, according to Lederberg (1963), it is possible that the human host-pathogen contact may have preceded the Neolithic period. He suggests that during the Paleolithic period, animals may have acted as a reservoir for diseases. If there had been intense and continuing contact between the human population and the animals, then a potential for humans to develop a genetic response to diseases would have existed.

NUTRITIONAL DEFICIENCY AND THE ORIGIN OF AGRICULTURE

The evidence suggesting that nutritional problems plagued Neolithic groups is more surprising. It would seem that agriculturalists could control their food supply by generating surpluses. Even though there is the potential of periodic famines and blight, the surpluses should be theoretically able to buffer the society through these critical periods.

The nutritional difficulties of agriculturalists may be more problematical. Periodic famines have been and remain a problem. Hollingsworth (1973) has documented thousands of famines that occurred during the historical period. Presently, vast areas of Africa are experiencing famines that are extracting a toll on the populations. It is estimated that a million people will die during a single year.

Even without the occurrence of famine or blight nutritional deficiencies can result from the intensification of agricultural production. The intensification of agriculture through irrigation often leads to a reliance on cereal grains. Diets which rely on cereal grains can be deficient in essential nutrients. Maize, for example, is deficient in the essential amino acid lysine. Other cereal grains contain phytates which combine with important minerals decreasing their bioavailablility.

The development of social classes within Neolithic societies also has nutritional implications. Since class, by definition, reflects differences in the access to resources, there is the probability that there will be individuals within the society who are not receiving adequate nutrition.

THE EVIDENCE FROM SKELETAL REMAINS: DEAD MEN (AND WOMEN) DO TELL TALES

The response of the human skeleton to normal and abnormal growth is deceptively simple. Bone is limited to a process by which osteons (the building unit of bone) can be deposited or they can be resorbed—or they can combine these processes in response to a stimulus.

An individual who weighs 160 pounds will have a skeleton comprised of 206 bones the sum weighing about thirty pounds. These thirty pounds of bones, which are composed of about fifteen pounds of calcium, seven pounds of water and a few ounces of major, minor, and trace minerals, are responsible for supporting our muscle structure, protecting vital organs such as the brain and the eyes, producing red blood cells, and maintaining chemical balance in the body.

Many diseases leave their mark on bone, and these marks can be used to diagnose disease occurrence. Tuberculosis, syphilis, and leprosy have skeletal "signatures" which aid in their diagnosis. In severe cases of tuberculosis, for example, there is often a collapse of the vertebral body and frequently resorptive lesions in other parts of the skeleton which are diagnostic.

Many pathogens leave only generalized changes in the skeleton. For example, we often find a periosteal reaction that reflects a pathogenic change to a number of organisms. These nonspecific lesions (periosteal reactions) are confined to the outer layer of bone and show a roughened appearance caused by the inflammatory process. The periosteal reaction occurs when the fibrous outer layer is stretched and subperiosteal hemorrhages occur. Micro-organisms such as staphylococcus and streptococcus and other pathogens can cause these changes. Unfortunately, there are many pathogens (viruses) that leave no evidence on bone. These viruses can cause an illness and even death without any skeletal response.

Nutritional deficiencies can also leave specific lesions which are easily diagnosed from bone. Deficiencies of vitamin D (rickets) result in a constellation of characteristics that are very distinct. Similarly, vitamin C deficiency (scurvy) leaves unique changes but these are more difficult to diagnose in prehistoric remains.

A major breakthrough in analyzing nutritional disease resulted from a movement away from using single indicators of stress to an approach that considers multiple indicators which are systematically analyzed to provide an understanding of nutritional disease stress. For example, there are a number of lesions such as porotic hyperostosis, defects in enamel development, and premature bone loss that, when coupled with evidence of growth retardation, can provide clues to a pattern of nutritional deficiency.

Porotic hyperostosis, which potentially occurs on the cranium and the roof of the eye orbits, can be used to diagnose iron deficiency anemia. The lesion, as the name implies, has a very porous, coral like appearance, which develops when diploe (the trabecular portion of the cranial bone that separates the inner and outer surfaces) expands. Then the outer layer of bone becomes thinner and may eventually disappear, exposing the trabecular bone (diploe) which is quite porous. The expansion of the diploe can be caused by any anemia that stimulates red blood cell production. While there are a number of anemias (sickle cell anemia, thalassemia, iron deficiency) that can cause these changes, the relatively minor manifestation of the lesion on the cranial surface and roof of the orbits and its high frequency in children between ages one and three and in young adult females would suggest iron deficiency anemia as the most likely cause.

In conjunction with the analysis of porotic hyperostosis, other stress indicators such as a decrease in long bone growth may provide information about the individual's physiological state. Since we are by necessity using cross-sectional data, comparison with longitudinal growth studies are very difficult. Growth patterns are determined by averaging long bone lengths of individuals whose developmental age is determined by tooth eruption patterns. These lengths are then compared to standards that exist for living populations. There are few growth standards from peasant agriculturalists, and it is often necessary to use growth standards developed from well-nourished children from the United States. Even with these difficulties, we can often see indications of growth retardation. However, internal comparison of populations experiencing shifts in subsistence may be the most useful method for understanding the impact of these changes on growth.

Recently, histological techniques have provided additional tools for analyzing the impact of nutritional deficiencies on bone growth and maintenance. Microscopic analysis of cross-sections of femora reveal that some children have very thin cortical bone. By examining the percentage of cortical bone for each individual and comparing it with an age-matched sample, we can determine those individuals experiencing nutritional difficulties. It is even possible to ascertain if the bone loss is the result of a lack of osteonal deposition or an increase in bone resorption.

Finally, two additional methods can be used to determine disruption of normal growth and development. Harris lines (lines of increased radiopaque density) found by radiographic analysis have been used as an indicator of growth arresting and recovery. Recent research suggests that Harris lines are more likely to be evidence of recovery and therefore can be used to assess the ability of the individual to respond to stress.

The Harris lines can also be used to assess the age at which an individual experienced growth disruption and subsequent recovery. Since growth occurs at both ends of a long bone, the Harris lines will maintain their relative position to the midshaft. If a researcher knows the relative growth rates of the proximal and distal portion of the long bone, then the age at which a line developed can be estimated.

The analysis of defects in dental enamel is another measure of growth disruption. Dental enamel hypoplasia is a deficiency in enamel thickness that results from a disruption in the formation of the matrix. Enamel defects can result from systemic disruption, hereditary conditions, or localized trauma. Since systemic disruption is likely to affect more than one tooth, we use the occurrence on multiple teeth as the criteria for assessing a systemic cause. Unlike bone, once enamel matures it can not be remodeled. Enamel is secreted in a regular ringlike pattern, and the crown development provides a permanent chronological record of any physiological disruption. An understanding of rates of enamel formation allows one to define the time in development at which the metabolic disruption occurred.

There are two ways in which the chronological distribution can be used. First, we can examine the chronological pattern of hypoplasia in adults to see the age at which they were exposed to physiological disruption. Second, we can evaluate the impact of this disruption on other aspects of their morbidity and mortality. Do adults who were stressed as children suffer from other insults, and do they live as long as those who were not stressed?

Trauma is another insult that provides information on the adaptation of the group. The location of the callus formation which results from the healing of the fracture provides clues to their cause. For example, fractures of the bones of the forearm (the radius and ulna) at the midshaft usually result from raising the arm to parry or ward off a blow. These fractures, called "parry fractures," are a good index of strife in a population. When individuals extend an arm to break a fall, however, they frequently fracture the bones of the forearm at the wrist. These fractures, "Colles and Potts" fractures, are indices of klutziness.

DICKSON MOUNDS: A PREHISTORIC POPULATION IN TRANSITION

The change in subsistence from ?900 to 1250 A.D. at the Dickson Mounds, Illinois, was profound. In the period from ?900 A.D. to 1175 A.D., there was a shift from a late woodland adaptation, which can be characterized as a general gathering-hunting strategy, to one which emphasized agriculture. The latter phase of this development (Mississippian Acculturated Late Woodland) was a period in which maize agriculture became established at Dickson Mounds.

From 1175 to 1250 A.D. there was an intensification of agriculture in what has been called the Middle Mississippian period. When these earlier groups from Dickson Mounds are compared to the Middle Mississippian people, there is evidence of a remarkable deterioration of health. In this short period there was a fourfold increase in iron deficiency anemia (porotic hyperostosis) and a threefold increase in infectious disease (periosteal reaction) (see Table 1). The frequency of individuals with both iron deficiency and infectious lesions increases from 6 percent in the Late Woodland period to 40 percent in the Middle Mississippian period. Furthermore, individuals with both conditions display a synergistic disease interaction (Lallo et al. 1977; Lallo et al. 1978), that is, they experience more severe manifestation of each condition.

The relationship of infection and anemia in children can be ascertained by examining the age of onset and distribution of the lesions by age. The infectious lesion in children under ten years of age peaks during the first year while the anemia shows its highest frequency during the second and third year. This pattern suggests that individuals who do survive the infectious pathogen may have problems in maintaining adequate iron reserves. The exposure to the pathogens that are the consumers of iron and iron deficiencies due to nutritional intake are the most likely explanation of this pattern. The biological cost of infection and anemia can be determined from an analysis of a life expectancy constructed for individuals who died before their tenth year (Figure 1). It is apparent that individuals with infections show a dramatic decrease in life expectancy. Those children in the group with periosteal lesions at birth can be expected to live less

TABLE 1   Frequency of Infectious Lesions (Periostitis and Osteomyelitis) and Porotic Hyperostosis

Dickson Population	N	Postcranial Infectious Lesions		Porotic Hyperostosis		Porotic Hyperostosis and Infectious Lesions	
		N	%	N	%	N	%
Late Woodland	44	9	20.5	6	13.6	3	6.5
Mississippian Acculturated Late Woodland	93	45	48.4	29	31.2	20	21.5
Middle Mississippian	101	74	73.3	52	51.5	41	40.6
Total	238	128	53.8	87	36.5	64	26.9

Source: Huss-Ashmore, Goodman, and Armelagos (1982).

than a year. Even those suffering from iron deficiency display a decrease in life expectancy of up to six months at each age group.

The impact of the shift to agriculture at Dickson Mounds can be seen in other aspects of growth and development. There is evidence of delayed growth in the long bone length and circumference of Mississippian children from their fifth through fifteenth year (Goodman et al. 1984).

The frequency and the chronology of hypoplastic defects in the dental enamel of the Dickson Mounds population supports the argument that the shift to agriculture had deleterious effects on the health of the group. There is an increase in hypoplasia from 0.90 defects per individual (Late Woodland) to 1.61 per individual in the Middle Mississippian period. The proportion of individuals with one or more hypoplasias increases from 45 percent to 80 percent during the same period (Goodman et al. 1984). Since the chronological development of the enamel is well understood, it is possible to determine the age at which the hypoplasias occurred during the life of the individual. The hypoplastic lines in adults provide "metabolic memory" of events which occurred during their childhood.

The chronology of enamel hypoplasia shows that the Dickson Mounds population experienced peak stress between the ages of two and four, which corresponds to the period of weaning. The pattern of porotic hyperostosis in this population occurs at about the same phase of development. The comparison of the chronology between the earlier groups and the intensive agriculturalists at Dickson Mounds (Figure 2) shows an earlier age of onset of hypoplasia, suggesting an earlier age of weaning.

Enamel hypoplasia is considered a relatively benign pathology. However, Goodman and Armelagos (1988) have calculated the mean age at death for those with and without hypoplasias and find significant differences. Individuals with no lesions have a mean age at death five years greater than individuals with one hypoplasia and nine years greater than individuals with two or more hypoplastic episodes (Figure 3).

Two hypotheses have been proposed to explain the difference in mean age at death. The first suggests that those with hypoplasia represent a group of individuals who were challenged by the insult early in their lifetime and continued to be subjected to insults during the rest of their lives. This increased "wear-and-tear" throughout their lives leads to an earlier death. Another hypothesis suggests that major insults occur at a critical period of immunological development. Individuals experiencing severe stress during the development of their immunological system may

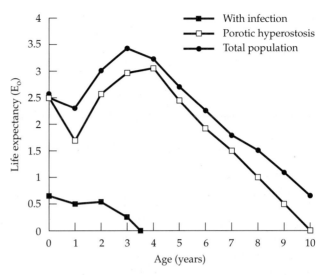

FIGURE 1   Life Expectancy for the Dickson Mounds Population for Those Dying Within the First Ten Years.
(Source: Huss-Ashmore, Goodman, and Armelagos [1982].)

irreparably damage their ability to fight infection throughout their lifetime. The "damaged goods" hypothesis suggests that significant thymolymphatic growth, which is essential for developing effective immunological competence, occurs prenatally, in infancy and early childhood.

Clark (1985) and co-workers (Clark et al. 1986) use the growth of the vertebral column to offer support to

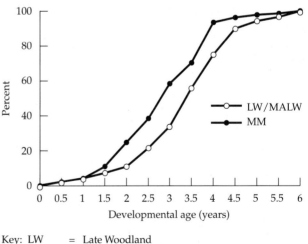

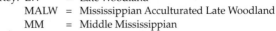

Key: LW   = Late Woodland
MALW = Mississippian Acculturated Late Woodland
MM   = Middle Mississippian

FIGURE 2   The Cumulative Frequency of Enamal Hypoplasias in Two Dickson Mounds Populations.
(Source: Goodman, and Armelagos, and Rose [1984].)

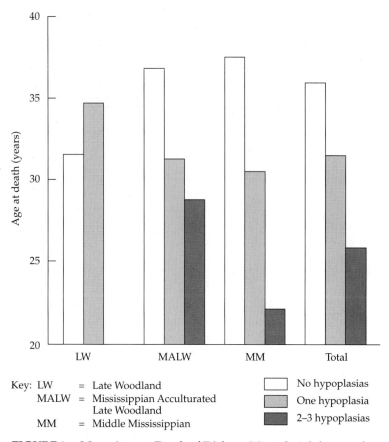

FIGURE 3   Mean Ages at Death of Dickson Mounds Adolescents/ Adults by Number of Hypoplasias-Stress Periods Between 3.5–7.0 Years Development Age. *(Source: Goodman and Armelagos [1988].)*

the "damaged goods" hypothesis. The size of the vertebral neural canal (VNC) is a good measure of childhood growth. The VNC is completed in childhood and is not subjected to catch-up growth. Since the VNC is growing during the phase of the neurological (of which it is a part) and the thymolymphatic development, it may reflect disruptions that occur during this period which affect immunological development. Multivariate, bivariate, and nonparemetric analyses show that small VCN are associated with greater vertebral wedging (a measure of morbidity) and decreased mean age at death (Clark et al. 1986).

The impact of multiple stressors affected the mortality pattern of the Dickson Mounds population. Change in the mortality profile is the final measure of the biological cost of the shift to agriculture at Dickson Mounds. A comparison of life expectancy (Figure 4) shows a decrease in life expectancy at all ages for the intensive agriculturalists.

In summary, the population at Dickson Mounds suffered biologically from the shift to intensive agriculture. The success of the cultural system occurred at the expense of individuals and the population. The ability to reduce birth spacing allowed the population not only to meet the increase in mortality but also to meet the increased labor needs for intensifying agriculture. But there was an increase in nutritional and infectious disease load that affected all segments of the population but especially women, infants, and children.

SUDANESE NUBIA: AGRICULTURAL INTENSIFICATION AND DISEASE

The archaeological record for the Wadi Halfa area of Sudanese Nubia is remarkably complete. There are bi-

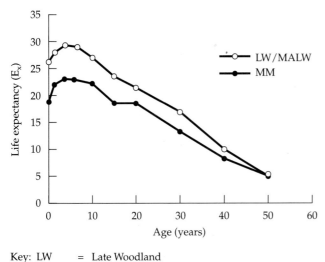

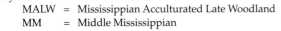

Key: LW   = Late Woodland
     MALW = Mississippian Acculturated Late Woodland
     MM   = Middle Mississippian

FIGURE 4   Comparison of Life Expectancies for Two Dickson Mounds Populations. *(Source: Goodman et al. [1984]. Reprinted by permission.)*

ological remains which date back to the Mesolithic period. Although the critical material from the earliest agriculturalists is not available, there are two series of populations which reflect a less intensive (A-Group and G-Group) and a more intensive agricultural adaptation (Meroitic, X-Group, and Christians). These samples provide a wealth of data for understanding the impact of change in subsistence.

Populations from the Meriotic (350 A.D.), X-Group (350–550 A.D.) and Christian (550–1300 A.D.) periods show a pattern of pathology similar to that at the Dickson Mounds. There is, for example, similarity in the distribution of porotic hyperostosis (iron deficiency anemia) in which the children between two and six years of age and young adult females are affected. A significant difference did exist in frequency of infectious disease in the Nubian population. The frequency of periosteal reaction was much lower. This surprising finding can be explained by the consumption of a broad spectrum antibiotic. The Nubians ingested tetracycline (Basset et al. 1981) produced by mold-like bacteria (*Streptomycetes*) which contaminated the grain. The contaminated grain may have been brewed into beer that provided them with therapeutic doses of the antibiotic, a serendipitous factor in controlling infectious diseases which affect bones.

Growth retardation in the Nubians is extremely difficult to demonstrate from the cross-sectional data (Armelagos et al. 1972). Since we are not able to follow the growth of individuals during the various phases of their lifetime, we rely on averaging the long bone lengths for the various developmental ages and infer

growth pattern from these data. Long bone length and widths fail to show any definitive evidence of growth retardation. The comparison with standards developed from United States data shows that the Nubians are smaller but are experiencing similar patterns of growth. However, when the long bone lengths and widths are compared with the thickness of cortical bone, problems in growth become evident. The cortices are very thin and are equivalent to the thicknesses found in two-year-old children. Microscopic analysis confirms this observation. Huss-Ashmore (1981) finds that the premature osteoporosis results from an increase in intercortical resorption. Martin and Armelagos (1979) show that young adult women (ages 19–25) from this same population also have problems maintaining cortical bone. There is a significant increase in rates of endosteal resorption (when compared to males of the same age).While these women are able to form osteons on their periosteal surface, there is no indication that these osteons are being mineralized. Instead, the resorption of osteons from the endosteal surface is the source for calcium for the lactating women.

THE TEST: PREHISTORIC POPULATIONS IN TRANSITION

These two case studies do not prove that a shift to agriculture will always result in a deterioration of health. There is other evidence that provides information to further test this hypothesis. In *Paleopathology at the Origins of Agriculture* (Cohen and Armelagos 1984a), there are seventeen case studies (in addition to the Nubian and Dickson Mounds examples) that examine the impact of subsistence change on the health of both New World and Old World populations. In general, the shift to a sedentary habitation pattern (with or without agriculture) may have triggered the most significant changes in disease profile. As expected, the sedentary populations show a dramatic shift in infectious diseases. The increased contact between individuals and close contact with human wastes which contaminate the environment are undoubtedly the major causes of this change in disease pattern.

Twelve of the case studies published in *Paleopathology at the Origins of Agriculture* (Cohen and Armelagos 1984a), for which observations on the pattern of infectious disease were available, show an increase in infections in the agricultural groups when compared with the gatherer-hunters. This increase is due to the increase in sedentism, the increase in population size, and the synergism between malnutrition and infection (Cohen and Armelagos 1984b). One study records a decrease in infections from the gathering-hunting to the early farming period, with an increase as agriculture became intensified (Norr 1984).

The same sample demonstrates that the intensification of agriculture consistently led to poorer nutrition as evidenced by the occurrence of porotic hyperostosis (an indicator of iron deficiency anemia). In sixteen groups where data are available, twelve show an increase with the intensification of agriculture.

CONCLUSIONS

1. The small population size of paleolithic gatherer-hunters made contagious or infectious disease a relatively minor problem for these earlier groups.

2. The impact of zoonotic diseases may have presented more of a problem to gatherer-hunters because of the greater impact of disease on the producer segment of the population. In small populations an increase in mortality among the producers would be potentially more socially and economically disruptive.

3. The transition to sedentism among gatherer-hunters with a stable and abundant food supply and among early agriculturalists potentially represents a new ecological setting. Population and pathogens are placed in new relationships that can result in an increase in parasitic and infectious diseases.

4. Beyond the problems associated with sedentism, the transition to agriculture increases the potential problems with infectious diseases. The increase in population size and density will increase the possibility of infectious disease transmission.

5. Although primary food production can generate surpluses, there is a potential for nutritional deficiencies from blight, drought, and the reliance on single crops which may be deficient in essential nutrients.

6. Agricultural populations which experienced an increase in nutritional and infectious disease were able to increase their population size. The predictability of mortality in these sedentary populations (deaths of the very young and very old) and a producer segment of the population with acquired immunity to disease may have been able to respond to the increase in mortality. The population size can be maintained or increased by decreasing the birth spacing. Furthermore, the acquired immunity of those who survive these childhood diseases may act to protect the producer segment of the population and thus make infectious disease socially less disruptive.

7. The rise of population in urban centers was relatively late in human history. In the Old World, preindustrial urban centers developed only 5,000 years ago and 2,400 years ago in the New World. This suggests that human populations have been exposed to endemic diseases for a relatively short time in evolutionary terms. For this reason, specific genetic adaptation to specific pathogens is unlikely. The development of a generalized physiological response is more likely than the evolution of a specific genetic response.

8. Lederberg (1963) argues that a genetic response may have occurred earlier than the post-Neolithic period. He claims that a specific genetic response may have evolved in situations in which humans and animals develop an intense and long-term interaction. In that situation the animals could act as reservoirs for pathogens and repeatedly infect humans.

9. In the last 10,000 years, Homo sapiens has experienced a number of periods of rapid transition that have had a dramatic impact on health and disease patterns. The shift to a Neolithic economy that relied on primary food production, the development of urban centers, the Industrial Revolution, and the development of rapid long distance travel changed the pattern of disease in human population. The interaction of pathogens and people has been influential in shaping our biology and culture.

REFERENCES

Armelagos, G. J. 1967. Man's changing environment. In *Infectious Diseases: Their Evolution and Eradication*. T. A. Cockburn, ed. Springfield, Ill.: Charles C. Thomas.

Armelagos, G. J., and J. Dewey. 1970. Evolutionary response to human infectious disease. *Bioscience* 20(5):271–75.

Armelagos, G. J., and A. McArdle. 1975. Population, disease, and evolution. In *Population Studies in Archaeology and Biological Anthropology: A Symposium*. A. C. Swedlund, ed. *Memoir of the Society of American Archaeology*, No. 30.

Armelagos, G. J., J. H. Mielke, K. H. Owen, D. P. Van Gerven, J. R. Dewey, and P. E. Mahler. 1972. Bone growth and development in prehistoric populations from Sudanese Nubia. *Journal of Human Evolution* 1:89–119.

Audy, J. R. 1961. The ecology of scrub typhus. In *Studies in Disease Ecology*. J. M. May, ed. New York: Hafner.

Basset, E., Margaret Keith, George J. Armelagos, Debra L. Martin, and A. Villanueva. 1981. Tetracycline-labeled human bone from prehistoric Sudanese Nubia (A.D. 350). *Science* 209:1532–34.

Boyden, S. V. 1970. *The Impact of Civilization on the Biology of Man*. Toronto: University of Toronto Press.

Burnet, F. M. 1962. *Natural History of Infectious Disease*. Cambridge: Cambridge University Press.

Clark, G. A. 1985. Hetrochrony, allometry and canalization in the human vertebral column: Examples from prehistoric American populations. Ph.D diss., University of Massachusetts, Amherst.

Clark, G. A., N. R. Hall, G. J. Armelagos, G. A. Borkan, M. M. Panjabi, and G. T Wetzel. 1986. Poor growth prior to early childhood: Decreased health and life-span in the adult. *American Journal of Physical Anthropology* 70:145–60.

Cockburn, T. A. 1971. Infectious disease in ancient populations. *Current Anthropology* 12(1):45–62.

———. 1967a. Infections of the order primates. In *Infectious Diseases: Their Evolution and Eradication*. T. A. Cockburn, ed. Springfield, Ill.: Charles C. Thomas.

———. 1967b. The evolution of human infectious diseases. In *Infectious Diseases: Their Evolution and Eradication*. T. A. Cockburn, ed. Springfield, Ill.: Charles C. Thomas.

Cohen, M. N., and G. J. Armelagos, eds. 1984a. *Paleopathology at the Origins of Agriculture*. Orlando: Academic Press.

———. 1984b. Paleopathology at the origins of agriculture: Editors' summation. In *Paleopathology at the Origins of Agriculture*. M. N. Cohen and G. J. Armelagos, eds. Orlando: Academic Press.

Fenner, F. 1970. The effects of changing social organization on the infectious diseases of man. In *The Impact of Civilization on the Biology of Man*. S. V. Boyden, ed. Canberra: Australia National University Press.

Goodman, A. H., and G. J. Armelagos. 1988. Childhood stress, cultural buffering, and decreased longevity in a prehistoric population. *American Anthropologist* 90:936–44.

Goodman, A. H., G. J. Armelagos, and J. C. Rose. 1984. The chronological distribution of enamel hypoplasia from prehistoric Dickson Mounds. *American Journal of Physical Anthropology* 65:259–266.

Goodman, A. H., J. Lallo, G. J. Armelagos, and J. Rose. 1984. Health changes at Dickson Mounds, Illinois (A.D. 950–1300). In *Paleopathology at the Origins of Agriculture*. M. N. Cohen and G. J. Armelagos, eds. Orlando: Academic Press.

Goodman, A. H., D. L. Martin, and G. J. Armelagos. 1984. Indications of stress from bone and teeth. In *Paleopathology at the Origins of Agriculture*. M. N. Cohen and G. J. Armelagos, eds. Orlando: Academic Press.

Haldane, J. B. S. 1949. Disease and evolution. Supplement to *La Ricerca Scientifica* 19:68–76.

Hollingsworth, T. H. 1973. Population crises in the past. In *Resources and Population*. B. Cox and J. Peel, eds. New York: Academic.

Hudson, E. H. 1965. Treponematosis and man's social evolution. *American Anthropologist* 67:885–901.

Huss-Ashmore, R. 1981. Bone growth and remodeling as a measure of nutritional stress. In *Biocultural Adaptation: Comprehensive Approaches to Skeletal Analysis*. University of Massachusetts, Department of Anthropology, Research Reports No. 20, pp. 84–95.

Huss-Ashmore, R., A. H. Goodman, and G. J. Armelagos. 1982. *Advances in Archaeological Method and Theory*, vol. 5. Orlando, Fla.: Academic Press.

Lallo, J., G. J. Armelagos, and R. P. Mensforth. 1977. The role of diet, disease and physiology in the origin of porotic hyperostosis. *Human Biology* 40:471–83.

Lallo, J., G. J. Armelagos, and J. C. Rose. 1978. Paleoepidemiology of infectious disease in the Dickson Mounds population. *Medical College of Virginia Quarterly* 14:17–23.

Lambrecht, F. L. 1985. Trypanosomes and hominid evolution. *Bioscience* 35(10):640–46.

———. 1964. Aspects of evolution and ecology of tsetse flies and trypanosomiasis in prehistoric African environments. *Journal of African History* 5:1–24.

Lederberg, J. 1963. Comments on A. Motulsky's "Genetic systems in disease susceptibility in mammals." In *Genetic Selection in Man*. W. J. Schull, ed. Ann Arbor: University of Michigan Press (Comments are interspersed with the Motulsky text).

Livingstone, F. B. 1958. Anthropological implications of sickle-cell gene distribution in West Africa. *American Anthropologist* 60:533–62.

McNeill, W. H. 1976. *Plagues and People*. Garden City: Anchor/Doubleday.

Martin, D. L., and G. J. Armelagos. 1979. Morphometrics of compact bone: An example from Sudanese Nubia. *American Journal of Physical Anthropology* 51:57 l–78.

Motulsky, A. G. 1963. Genetic systems involved in disease susceptibility in mammals. In *Genetic Selection in Man*. W J. Schull, ed. Ann Arbor: University of Michigan Press.

Norr, L. 1984. Prehistoric subsistence and health status of the Coastal peoples from the Panamanian Isthmus of Lower Central America. In *Paleopathology at the Origins of Agriculture*. M. N. Cohen and G. J. Armelagos, eds. Orlando: Academic Press.

Polgar, S. 1964. Evolution and the ills of mankind. In *Horizons of Anthropology*. S. Tax, ed. Chicago: Aldine.

8

Determinants of Health

Thomas McKeown

The question of what determines health is very important. If we, as a society, can agree about what causes health, then we should be able to agree on where our financial resources should be placed in order to get the best results from our investment. If there is a single most important lesson to be obtained from studying the history of health, it must be this one.

It turns out, of course, that defining "health" is not as simple as it might first appear. The World Health Organization says that health is not merely the absence of disease but an overall state of physical, mental, and social well-being. You may think such a definition seems utopian. Most scientists and scholars would agree, however, that levels of disease in a population (morbidity) and the frequency of death at particular ages in a population (mortality) represent essential, if gross, measures of health. In other words, improved health is reflected in the decline of mortality.

We can ask this historical question more specifically: What is the role of medicine in the improvement of health? If by "medicine" we mean biomedical clinical care including modern inventions like x-rays, antibiotics, and immunizations, then it is possible to compare mortality rates before and after significant medical interventions were introduced. This is exactly the topic of Thomas McKeown's famous book, The Role of Medicine: Dream, Mirage, or Nemesis? *(1979), as well as this selection. McKeown demonstrates that the biggest advancements in health occurred after specific medical interventions became available. He suggests (but he doesn't have the data to prove this) that more significant factors regarding health improvement involved sanitation, better food, and birth spacing. This argument has been controversial, largely because there is a widespread presumption in our society that improved health in developed*

countries is due to advances in medical knowledge and the technological and scientific breakthroughs in biomedical science. McKeown disputes this premise.

Medical anthropologist Stephen Kunitz has done a similar, focused study of historical changes in health status on the Navajo reservation and the impact of improved medical care because of Indian Health Service facilities (1983). His findings suggest that the determinants of health are more complicated than McKeown suggests and that access to medical facilities (in this case, a free health care system) has a measurable although rather small effect. Other influences of the dominant white society—for example, drinking and automobile accidents—are also important factors.

In the end, the study of health history does not hinge on an either/or decision. I believe that solutions to health problems are going to be found not in technology but in bringing about the more equitable distribution of adequate food, sanitation, housing, health information, **and** *medical care services.*

As you read this selection, consider these questions:

- *In the United States today, we spend about 15 percent of our gross national product on health care. What do you think McKeown would say about this expenditure?*

- *Do many people actually believe the presumption that McKeown is arguing against—that modern health improvements are caused by modern medicine? What do your friends think are the determinants of health?*

- *What implications does McKeown's discussion have for combating infectious diseases in the Third World, where they are still a very significant cause of morbidity and mortality?*

Modern medicine is not nearly as effective as most people believe. It has not been effective because medical science and service are misdirected and society's investment in health is misused. At the base of this misdirection is a false assumption about human health. Physicians, biochemists, and the general public assume that the body is a machine that can be protected from disease primarily by physical and chemical intervention. This approach, rooted in 17th Century science, has led to widespread indifference to the influence of the primary determinants of human health—environment and personal behavior—and emphasizes the role of medical treatment, which is actually less important than either of the others. It has also resulted in the neglect of sick people whose ailments are not within the scope of the sort of therapy that interests the medical professions.

An appraisal of influences on health in the past suggests that the contribution of modern medicine to the increase of life expectancy has been much smaller than most people believe. Health improved, not because of steps taken when we are ill, but because we become ill less often. We remain well, less because of specific measures such as vaccination and immunization than because we enjoy a higher standard of nutrition, we live in a healthier environment, and we have fewer children.

For some 300 years an engineering approach has been dominant in biology and medicine and has provided the basis for the treatment of the sick. A mechanistic concept of nature developed in the 17th Century led to the idea that a living organism, like a machine, might be taken apart and reassembled if its structure and function were sufficiently understood. Applied to medicine, this concept meant that understanding the body's response to disease would allow physicians to intervene in the course of disease. The consequences of the engineering approach to medicine are more conspicuous today than they were in the 17th Century largely because the resources of the physical and chemical sciences are so much greater. Medical education begins with the study of the structure and function of the body, continues with examination of disease processes, and ends with clinical instruction on selected sick people. Medical service is dominated by the image of the hospital for the acutely ill, where technological resources are concentrated. Medical research also reflects the mechanistic approach, concerning itself with problems such as the chemical basis of inheritance and the immunological response to transplanted tissues.

No one disputes the predominance of the engineering approach in medicine, but we must now ask whether it is seriously deficient as a conceptualization of the problems of human health. To answer this question, we must examine the determinants of human health. We must first discover why health improved in the past and then go on to ascertain the important influences on health today, in the light of the change in health problems that has resulted from the decline of infectious diseases.

It is no exaggeration to say that health, especially the health of infants and young children, has been transformed since the 18th Century. For the first time in history, a mother knows it is likely that all her children will live to maturity. Before the 19th Century, only about three out of every 10 newborn infants lived beyond the age of 25. Of the seven who died, two or

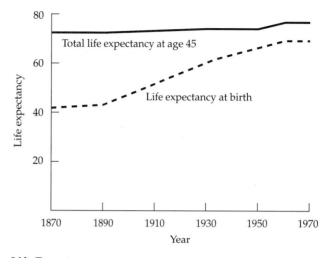

Life Expectancy

three never reached their first birthday, and five or six died before they were six. Today, in developed countries fewer than one in 20 children die before they reach adulthood.

The increased life expectancy, most evident for young children, is due predominantly to a reduction of deaths from infectious diseases. Records from England and Wales (the earliest national statistics available) show that this reduction was the reason for the improvement in health before 1900 and it remains the main influence to the present day.

But when we try to account for the decline of infections, significant differences of opinion appear. The conventional view attributes the change to an increased understanding of the nature of infectious disease and to the application of that knowledge through better hygiene, immunization, and treatment. This interpretation places particular emphasis on immunization against diseases like smallpox and polio, and on the use of drugs for the treatment of other diseases, such as tuberculosis, meningitis, and pneumonia. These measures, in fact, contributed relatively little to the total reduction of mortality; the main explanation for the dramatic fall in the number of deaths lies not in medical intervention, but elsewhere.

Deaths from the common infections were declining long before effective medical intervention was possible. By 1900, the total death rate had dropped substantially, and over 90 percent of the reduction was due to a decrease of deaths from infectious diseases. The relative importance of the major influences can be illustrated by reference to tuberculosis. Although respiratory tuberculosis was the single largest cause of death in the mid-19th Century, mortality from the

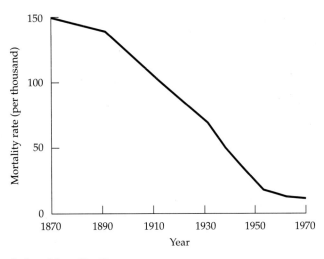

Infant Mortality Rate

disease declined continuously after 1838, when it was first registered in England and Wales as a cause of death.

Robert Koch identified the tubercle bacillus in 1882, but none of the treatments used in the 19th or early 20th Centuries significantly influenced the course of the disease. The many drugs that were tried were worthless; so, too, was the practice of surgically collapsing an infected lung, a treatment introduced about 1920. Streptomycin, developed in 1947, was the first effective treatment, but by this time mortality from the disease had fallen to a small fraction of its level during 1848 to 1854. Streptomycin lowered the death rate from tuberculosis in England and Wales by about 50 percent, but its contribution to the decrease in the death rate since the early 19th Century was only about 3 percent.

Deaths from bronchitis, pneumonia, and influenza also began to decline before medical science provided an effective treatment for these illnesses. Although the death rate in England and Wales increased in the second half of the 19th Century, it has fallen continuously since the beginning of the 20th. There is still no effective immunization against bronchitis or pneumonia, and influenza vaccines have had no effect on deaths. The first successful treatment for these respiratory diseases was a sulfa drug introduced in 1938, but mortality attributed to the lung infections was declining from the beginning of the 20th Century. There is no reason to doubt that the decline would have continued without effective therapeutic measures, if at a slower rate.

In the United States, the story was similar; Thomas Magill noted that "the rapid decline of pneumonia death rates began in New York State before the turn of the century and many years before the 'miracle drugs' were known." Obviously, drug therapy was not re-

sponsible for the total decrease in deaths that occurred since 1938, and it could have had no influence on the substantial reduction that occurred before then.

The histories of most other common infections, such as whooping cough, measles, and scarlet fever, are similar. In each of these diseases, mortality had fallen to a low level before effective immunization or therapy became available.

In some infections, medical intervention *was* valuable before sulfa drugs and antibiotics became available. Immunization protected people against smallpox and tetanus; antitoxin treatment limited deaths from diphtheria; appendicitis, peritonitis, and ear infections responded to surgery; Salvarsan was a long-sought "magic bullet" against syphilis; intravenous therapy saved people with severe diarrheas; and improved obstetric care prevented childbed fever.

But even if such medical measures had been responsible for the whole decline of mortality from these particular conditions after 1900 (and clearly they were not), they would account for only a small part of the decrease in deaths attributed to all infectious diseases before 1935. From that time, powerful drugs came into use and they were supplemented by improved vaccines. But mortality would have continued to fall even without the presence of these agents; and over the whole period since cause of death was first recorded, immunization and treatment have contributed much less than other influences.

The substantial fall in mortality was due in part to reduced contact with microorganisms. In developed countries an individual no longer encounters the cholera bacillus, he is rarely exposed to the typhoid organism, and his contact with the tubercle bacillus is infrequent. The death rate from these infections fell continuously from the second half of the 19th Century when basic hygienic measures were introduced: purification of water; efficient sewage disposal; and improved food hygiene, particularly the pasteurization of milk, the item in the diet most likely to spread disease.

Pasteurization was probably the main reason for the decrease in deaths from gastroenteritis and for the decline in infant mortality from about 1900. In the 20th Century, these essential hygienic measures were supported by improved conditions in the home, the work place, and the general environment. Over the entire period for which records exist, better hygiene accounts for approximately a fifth of the total reduction of mortality.

But the decline of mortality caused by infections began long before the introduction of sanitary measures. It had already begun in England and Wales by 1838, and statistics from Scandinavia suggest that the death rate had been decreasing there since the first half of the 18th Century.

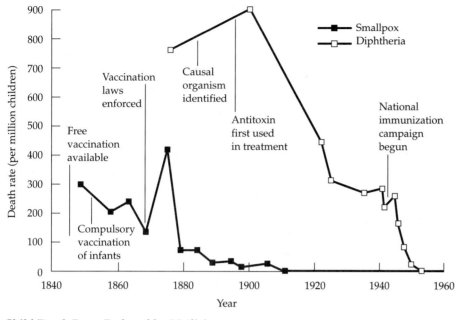

Child Death Rates Reduced by Medicine

A review of English experience makes it unlikely that reduced exposure to microorganisms contributed significantly to the falling death rate in this earlier period. In England and Wales that was the time of industrialization, characterized by rapid population growth and shifts of people from farms into towns, where living and working conditions were uncontrolled. The crowding and poor hygiene that resulted provided ideal conditions for the multiplication and spread of microorganisms, and the situation improved little before sanitary measures were introduced in the last third of the century.

Another possible explanation for the fall in mortality is that the character of infectious diseases changed because the virulence of microorganisms decreased. This change has been suggested in diseases as different as typhus, tuberculosis, and measles. There is no infection of which it can be said confidently that the relationship between host and parasite has not varied over a specified period. But for the decline of all infections, this explanation is obviously inadequate because it implies that the modern improvement in health was due essentially to a fortuitous change in the nature of the infections, independent of medical and other identifiable influences.

A further explanation for the falling death rate is that an improvement in nutrition led to an increase in resistance to infectious diseases. This is, I believe, the most credible reason for the decline of the infections, at least until the late 19th Century, and also explains

why deaths from airborne diseases like scarlet fever and measles have decreased even when exposure to the organisms that cause them remains almost unchanged. The evidence demonstrating the impact of improved nutrition is indirect, but it is still impressive.

Lack of food, and the resulting malnutrition were largely responsible for the predominance of the infectious diseases, from the time when men first aggregated in large population groups about 10,000 years ago. In these conditions an improvement in nutrition was necessary for a substantial and prolonged decline in mortality.

Experience in developing countries today leaves no doubt that nutritional state is a critical factor in a person's response to infectious disease, particularly in young children. Malnourished people contract infections more often than those who are well fed and they suffer more when they become infected. According to a recent World Health Organization report on nutrition in developing countries, the best vaccine against common infectious diseases is an adequate diet.

In the 18th and 19th Centuries, food production increased greatly throughout the Western world. The number of people in England and Wales tripled between 1700 and 1850 and they were fed on home-grown food.

In summary: The death rate from infectious diseases fell because an increase in food supplies led to better nutrition. From the second half of the 19th Century this advance was strongly supported by

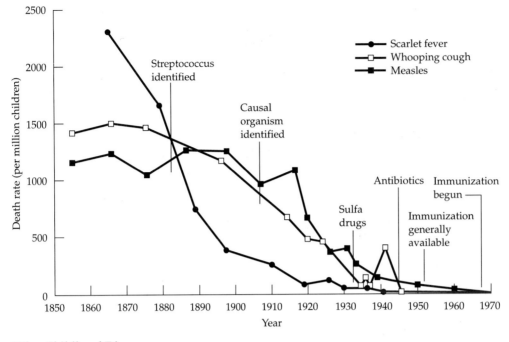

Other Childhood Diseases

improved hygiene and safer food and water, which reduced exposure to infection. With the exception of smallpox vaccination, which played a small part in the total decline of mortality, medical procedures such as immunization and therapy had little impact on human health until the 20th Century.

One other influence needs to be considered: a change in reproductive behavior, which caused the birth rate to decline. The significance of this change can hardly be exaggerated, for without it the other advances would soon have been overtaken by the increasing population. We can attribute the modern improvement in health to food, hygiene, and medical intervention—in that order of time and importance—but we must recognize that it is to a modification of behavior that we owe the permanence of this improvement.

But it does not follow that these influences have the same relative importance today as in the past. In technologically advanced countries, the decline of infectious diseases was followed by a vast change in health problems, and even in developing countries advances in medical science and technology may have modified the effects of nutrition, sanitation, and contraception. In order to predict the factors likely to affect our health in the future, we need to examine the nature of the problems in health that exist today.

Because today's problems are mainly with noncommunicable diseases, physicians have shifted their approach. In the case of infections, interest centers on

the organisms that cause them and on the conditions under which they spread. In noninfective conditions, the engineering approach established in the 17th Century remains predominant and attention is focused on how a disease develops rather than on why it begins. Perhaps the most important question now confronting medicine is whether the commonest health problems—heart disease, cancer, rheumatoid arthritis, cerebrovascular disease—are essentially different from health problems of the past or whether, like infections, they can be prevented by modifying the conditions that lead to them.

To answer this question, we must distinguish between genetic and chromosomal diseases determined at the moment of fertilization and all other diseases, which are attributable in greater or lesser degree to the influence of the environment. Most diseases, including the common noninfectious ones, appear to fall into the second category. Whether these diseases can be prevented is likely to be determined by the practicability of controlling the environmental influences that lead to them.

The change in the character of health problems that followed the decline of infections in developed countries has not invalidated the conclusion that most diseases, both physical and mental, are associated with influences that might be controlled. Among such influences, those which the individual determines by his own behavior (smoking, eating, exercise, and the like) are now more important for his health than those

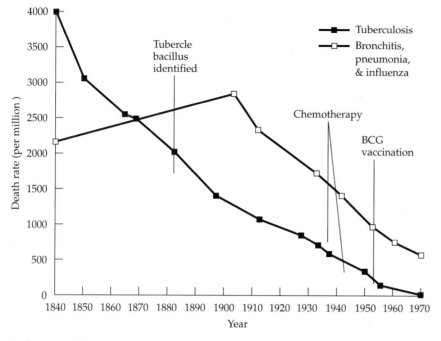

Pulmonary Diseases

that depend mainly on society's actions (provision of essential food and protection from hazards). And both behavioral and environmental influences are more significant than medical care.

The role of individual medical care in preventing sickness and premature death is secondary to that of other influences; yet society's investment in health care is based on the premise that it is the major determinant. It is assumed that we are ill and are made well, but it is nearer the truth to say that we are well and are made ill. Few people think of themselves as having the major responsibility for their own health, and the enormous resources that advanced countries assign to the health field are used mainly to treat disease or, to a lesser extent, to prevent it by personal measures such as immunization.

The revised concept of human health cannot provide immediate solutions for the many complex problems facing society: limiting population growth and providing adequate food in developing countries, changing personal behavior and striking a new balance between technology and care in developed nations. Instead, the enlarged understanding of health and disease should be regarded as a conceptual base with implications for services, education, and research that will take years to develop.

The most immediate requirement in the health services is to give sufficient attention to behavioral influences that are now the main determinants of health.

The public believes that health depends primarily on intervention by the doctor and that the essential requirement for health is the early discovery of disease. This concept should be replaced by recognition that disease often cannot be treated effectively, and that health is determined predominantly by the way of life individuals choose to follow. Among the important influences on health are the use of tobacco, the misuse of alcohol and drugs, excessive or unbalanced diets, and lack of exercise. With research, the list of significant behavioral influences will undoubtedly increase, particularly in relation to the prevention of mental illness.

Although the influences of personal behavior are the main determinants of health in developed countries, public action can still accomplish a great deal in the environmental field. Internationally, malnutrition probably remains the most important cause of ill health, and even in affluent societies sections of the population are inadequately, as distinct from unwisely, fed. The malnourished vary in proportion and composition from one country to another, but in the developed world they are mainly the younger children of large families and elderly people who live alone. In light of the importance of food for good health, governments might use supplements and subsidies to put essential foods within the reach of everyone, and provide inducements for people to select beneficial in place of harmful foods. Of course these aims cannot exclude other considerations such as international agreements and the solvency of farmers who have been encouraged to produce meat and dairy products rather than grains. Nevertheless, in future evaluations of agricultural and related economic policies, health implications deserve a primary place.

Perhaps the most sensitive area for consideration is the funding of the health services. Although the contribution of medical intervention to prevention of sickness and premature death can be expected to remain small in relation to behavioral and environmental influences, surgery and drugs are widely regarded as the basis of health and the essence of medical care, and society invests the money it sets aside for health mainly in treatment for acute diseases and particularly in hospitals for the acutely ill. Does it follow from our appraisal that resources should be transferred from acute care to chronic care and to preventive measures?

Restricting the discussion to personal medical care, I believe that neglected areas, such as mental illness, mental retardation, and geriatric care need greatly increased attention. But to suggest that this can be achieved merely by direct transfer of resources is an oversimplification. The designation "acute care" comprises a wide range of activities that differ profoundly in their effectiveness and efficiency. Some, like surgery for accidents and the treatment of acute emergencies, are among the most important services that medicine can offer and any reduction of their support would be disastrous. Others, however, like coronary care units and iron treatment of some anemias are not shown to be effective, while still others—most tonsillectomies and routine check-ups—are quite useless and should be abandoned. A critical appraisal of medical services for acute illnesses would result in more efficient use of available resources and would free some of them for preventive measures.

What health services need in general is an adjustment in the distribution of interest and resources between prevention of disease, care of the sick who require investigation and treatment, and care of the sick who do not need active intervention. Such an adjustment must pay considerable attention to the major determinants of health: to food and the environment, which will be mainly in the hands of specialists, and to personal behavior, which should be the concern of every practicing doctor.

REFERENCES

Burnet, Macfarlane. *Genes, Dreams and Realities.* Basic Books, 1971.

Cochrane, A. L. *Effectiveness and Efficiency.* Nuffield Provincial Hospitals Trust, 1972.

Dubos, René. *Mirage of Health.* Harper & Row, Publishers, 1971.

McKeown, Thomas. *The Modern Rise of Population.* Academic Press, 1977.

McKeown, Thomas. *The Role of Medicine: Dream, Mirage or Nemesis?* Nuffield Provincial Hospitals Trust, 1976.

Thomas, Lewis. *The Lives of a Cell: Notes of a Biology Watcher.* Viking Press, 1974.

Cultural and Political Ecologies of Disease

✤ CONCEPTUAL TOOLS ✤

■ **What is disease?** From an ecological perspective, disease does not exist as a thing in and of itself. *Disease* is a process that is triggered by the interaction between a host and an environmental insult, often a pathogenic organism or germ. Disease is one possible outcome of the relationship between the host and the potential pathogen. Since the advent of bacteriology and germ theory, it has been recognized that infection is a necessary but not sufficient condition for disease to occur. For tuberculosis, for example, this principle has been recognized since the work of the turn-of-the-century bacteriologist, Robert Koch. Normal, healthy individuals typically harbor many different colonies of viruses and bacteria that are not pathogenic (that is, disease-producing) primarily because these agents are held in check by the human immune system. Indeed, individuals are constantly being challenged by microorganisms in their environment (Burnet and White 1978). Disease only occurs when the host's immunological system is unable to keep pace with the reproduction of the pathogen—a process that is affected by age and that can be accelerated through malnutrition, co-infection, or immunosuppression.

■ **What is ecology?** *Ecology* is the study of the relationship between a species and its total environment. Most often considered a subfield of biology, ecology deals with the interactions of organisms and their environments with the population, community, and ecosystem levels of organization (Moran 1990). Integral to most ecological studies is the idea that the complex set of interactions among organisms in an ecological niche (territory) makes up a system. This ecosystem includes not only natural resources (for example, water, minerals) but also plants, animals, and humans. Two of the assumptions of this model are that the ecosystem is maintained through mutually dependent interactions among members of the system and that the common goal of the various species in the system is homeostasis. The primary benefit of homeostatic balance is the prevention of environmental degradation and thus mutual survival. In this view, human activities, such as agriculture, create imbalances in natural ecosystems.

Humans are capable not only of ecological change but also of ecological destruction. There is no doubt that humans have often been responsible for radical changes in their environment and that such ecological changes have had negative effects on health (for example, the impact of the construction of dams on the prevalence of schistosomiasis).

■ **What are adaptation and maladaptation?** Adaptation is an important concept in biology and in ecologically oriented medical anthropology. *Adaptation* refers to a general process through which either genes or cultural traits are shaped (that is, selected for) to fit a particular environment. The term comes from the Latin *ad aptus*, meaning "toward a fit," and it refers to the relative direction of change in the evolutionary process. It is important to remember, however, that the mechanisms of biological adaptation and cultural adaptation are quite different (Durham 1991; Wiley 1992). *Maladaptation* refers to a trait or process that results in decreased chances of survival and reproduction. Contrary to what a naïve interpretation of the theories of ecology and evolution might suggest, there are an amazing number of examples of maladaptive behaviors in the anthropological record (Edgerton 1992). Some maladaptations exist because of unequal power relationships between groups. Other maladaptations persist because of the inertia of culture and the fact that the linkage of cause and effect might be obscured by time or complexity. Poor states of health may be, in a general sense, a reflection of maladaptation, but more often they reflect political-economic inequities or other pressures limiting people's choices.

■ **What is the political ecology of disease?** *Political ecology* is a relatively new term referring to a theoretical orientation emphasizing political-economic factors—such as the history of colonialism—and macrosociological factors—such as social stratification, ethnic conflicts, and migration—within a general ecological framework. Political ecology contrasts with the more traditional anthropological approach of cultural ecology (associated with theorists like Julian Steward and Roy Rappaport) and with the medical anthropological orientation attempting to link biological and cultural anthropology (associated with the work of Alexander Alland [1970]). The primary difference is in the recognition and emphasis of higher levels of analysis than a singular culture—for example, the nation-state, colonial powers, or multinational corporations. In other words, it combines political economy with ecology. Within medical anthropology, Meredith Turshen was one of the first to use this term in *Political Ecology of Disease in Tanzania,* as she emphasized the German colonial policies regarding labor reserves, plantation agriculture, and colonial medicine that together shaped the social epidemiological distribution of disease (Trostle and Sommerfeld 1996). More recently, Hans Baer, arguing that "political ecology" is a useful label related to "green politics," has provided an excellent review of current work and ongoing challenges (1996).

■ *The "natural history" of disease refers to the study of disease transmissions and disease processes within an ecological setting.* The term itself refers to the approach used by scientists Macfarlane Burnet and David White in their textbook *The Natural History of Infectious Disease* (1978), which examines diseases and disease rates "in the wild," as naturalists would. The problem is that many naturalists, in describing the interaction of species in an ecosystem, neglect to recognize that the larger ecological context has been shaped by political forces; in other words, they tend to see external conditions as natural when in fact they are the result of cultural activities or political policies.

The approach to understanding disease that "naturalizes" the context is limited. The term *unnatural*

history encapsulates this political-ecological critique of the limitations of a traditional ecological or epidemiological analysis. Scholars who use this term argue that it is dangerous to assume that the underlying ecological context is a given or natural. They argue that by focusing on the microbiological or individual behavioral levels of analysis, people are not only ignoring but also reinforcing the larger political-economic systems of inequality. Scholars who defend traditional ecology and epidemiology respond that they recognize the limitations of their approach and the importance of the larger political context but that the traditional scientific approaches can yield tangible applications to combat disease.

■ *Colonialism and so-called tropical diseases are found most often in the poorer countries of the "developing" world and are encountered by citizens of rich developed countries through international travel.* The main problem with the term *tropical diseases* is that it implies that the prevalence of diseases is somehow rooted in the climate and geography of a region. In fact, many so-called tropical diseases like malaria used to be common in the American Midwest and southern England. In modern world history, most of the industrialized countries that became colonial powers were located in temperate climates, and most of the colonies were located in warmer tropical environments. The two kinds of countries had, and continue to have, substantially different epidemiological profiles. But these differences are not the result of temperature and humidity. Rather, there is clear evidence that the primary factor involved in the transmission of so-called tropical diseases is simply poverty. Thomas McKeown (1988) suggests that scientists rename these diseases "diseases of poverty." A history of colonialism and, more importantly, postcolonial patterns of economic inequity, play a central role in the creation of poverty and therefore the continuation of "tropical" disease.

9

Cultural Adaptations to Endemic Malaria in Sardinia

Peter J. Brown

The sickle-cell trait in West Africa is the textbook example of a genetic trait that has increased in frequency because it confers selective advantage to individuals in the context of a particular disease. The sickle-cell trait, in its heterozygous form, protects people who have the gene from P. falciparum malaria, which is fatal. Sickle cell is a very expensive adaptation, however, because in its homozygous form it causes a painful and deadly condition called sickle-cell anemia. For people of African descent in the United States, for example, sickle cell can be a serious worry—a "birth defect" that serves no obvious purpose. For people living in West Africa today, where up to one-quarter of the population can carry the gene, the sickle-cell trait is less of a problem than malaria. Therefore, the protection against malaria made possible by this "'birth defect" is very valuable indeed, as malaria is a serious and growing problem throughout the world today. Estimates are that of the 30 million people who get malaria each year, 3 million of them—most often small children in Africa and Asia—will die from the disease (Oaks et al. 1991).

Malaria is a very old disease, but there is little mystery surrounding it. Scientists have known the basic cycle of transmission (through anopheles mosquitoes) for a hundred years, and medical doctors have had effective medicines for prevention and treatment for fifty years. Right after World War II, a new residual insecticide (DDT) was used to kill malarial mosquitoes and stop the disease; this strategy was effective in Europe and the United States. Given that we have the scientific knowledge and technology, why does malaria continue to be such a problem? There are some new problems of insecticide resistance in the mosquitoes and chemical resistance in the malaria parasite, but the largest obstacles continue to be money and political will (Brown 1997).

This selection is a case study analyzing cultural adaptations to malaria on the island of Sardinia, Italy. In doing this work, I wanted to understand the role of traditional Sardinian economy, social organization, and folk medical beliefs in protecting certain groups from malaria. To do this, I first needed to understand the particular disease ecology (in this case, temperate climate malaria is different from malaria in Africa) and to describe the social epidemiological distribution of the disease. Then I could examine the microsociological behaviors that helped explain the distribution of the disease. Note that this analysis of cultural traits as having an adaptive function in the context of malaria does not *imply that malaria is the reason for the origins of the cultural traits.*

Malaria no longer exists in Sardinia, thanks, in small part, to a U.S.-funded malaria eradication project. People used their cultural technology to change their ecology and stop the transmission of malaria. That is a good example of an ecologically adaptive change. At the same time, the sudden conquest of malaria might be seen as a natural experiment for understanding the relationship between improved health, economic development, and population change (Brown 1986).

As you read this selection, consider these questions:

- *How is it that people can culturally adapt to a disease without being aware that they are doing so?*
- *If malaria is such a problem in the world today, why don't cultural systems adapt to solve the problem? Has cultural evolution stopped working?*
- *What is* ecological *about this case study?*
- *If malaria did not cause these cultural traits to exist, might the disease have played a role in maintaining the cultural traits?*

The analysis of how human populations adapt to specific disease entities in their environment is an important goal of medical anthropology (Alland 1966). It may be argued that humans are unique because they rely on culture as the primary mechanism for adaptation and hence survival. Diseases act as agents of natural selection and therefore affect human evolution, both biological and cultural (Alland 1970). As such, the study of the interaction between disease and the persistence of particular cultural patterns is an important area for study in medical anthropology. This paper examines some basic features of traditional Sardinian culture and economy for possible adaptive features of traditional Sardinian culture and economy for possible adaptive functions in the context of endemic malaria. These cultural adaptations to malaria are found at three levels of traditional Sardinian culture: economic production, social organization, and folk medical beliefs.

The importance of malaria as a force in human evolution has been well documented by Livingstone (1958, 1964, 1971) and others (Motulsky 1960; Wiesenfeld 1967). Often called the "queen of diseases," malaria has historically been the largest single cause of human mortality (Bruce-Chwatt 1979). Anthropologists have made major contributions to the understanding of the interaction between agricultural change, increased malaria prevalence, and the processes of genetic selection for abnormal hemoglobins. The study of cultural adaptations to malaria in Sardinia is of particular interest because the island has been a classic case study in population genetics (Mourant et al. 1978), and there is extensive data linking the geographical distribution of malaria with thalassemia and G-6-PD deficiency (Bernini et al. 1960; Siniscalco et al. 1966; Brown 1981). Nevertheless, there is very little understanding of how traditional behavior and beliefs may have affected malaria prevalence, or conversely, how the ecological variable of malaria may have influenced the persistence of cultural traits.

Some of the cultural elements discussed here in the Sardinian context are relatively common in the ethnographic literature of southern European societies. The analysis of these elements in relation to malaria, however, can provide a new, ecologically oriented interpretation of such features. Cultural adaptations to malaria in Sardinia either limited exposure to anopheles mosquitoes, or prescribed behaviors which decreased the probability of malaria relapses. From the native viewpoint, these traditions reflected rational choices based upon an ethnomedical theory in which malaria was caused by "bad air." Nevertheless, such traditions did function to interrupt the transmission of malaria through anopheles mosquitoes; they had positive preventive functions despite being founded on an erroneous supposition.

This paper will first discuss the concept of cultural adaptation and its importance in medical anthropology. It will then describe the ecology and epidemiology of malaria in Sardinia, including the geographic and socioecological distribution of the disease. This background information is necessary for understanding the mechanisms of cultural adaptation to malaria. The core of the paper involves an analysis of cultural

traits, characteristic of lowland zones, which had adaptive functions in the context of malaria. The findings of this paper are the result of field and archival research on the socioeconomic effects of malaria and its eradication, conducted in a lowland district of northwestern Sardinia during 1976 and 1977.[1]

THE CONCEPT OF CULTURAL ADAPTATION

The concept of adaptation refers to the fundamental process of evolution in which particular traits are selected in a given environment because they increase an organism's chances for survival and reproduction. While primarily used in evolutionary biology, the concept of adaptation has been central to anthropological discussions of cultural evolution and cultural ecology (Alland 1966, 1970; Alland and McCay 1973; Netting 1964; Rappaport 1979). Adaptation implies that the environment sets certain "problems" which organisms need to "solve," and that natural selection is the mechanism by which such solutions are found. In this regard, it is obvious that diseases are primary environmental "problems" and agents of natural selection; anthropologists therefore expect that diseases shape both biological and cultural evolution (Alland 1970). The concept of adaptation does not imply that the resulting biological or cultural traits are the *only* solution to a specific environmental problem, nor does it imply that they are the optimal solutions. Rather, adaptation means that the biological or cultural traits are tolerable or have minimally sufficient positive consequences to improve an organism's chances for survival in a particular environment. Some of the confusion which surrounds the use of the concept of adaptation (Alland and McCay 1973; Lewontin 1978) stems from the fact that the single term is sometimes used to describe the basic evolutionary process (i.e. adaptation used as a verb), while in other contexts the term is used as an identification of traits which have "adaptive value" in a particular environment (i.e. adaptation used as a noun).

In this paper, the concept of cultural adaptations refers to certain culture traits or social institutions which function to increase the chances of survival for a society in a particular ecological context. This sweeping definition implies that many culture traits are adaptations, but one cannot assume that all culture traits have adaptive value. To avoid this type of tautology, this paper is concerned with a single important environmental "problem," endemic malaria. In the analysis of cultural adaptations, the question of ultimate causation for the traits described here is irrelevant (Alland 1966:41). I do not argue that endemic malaria caused Sardinian culture to develop in a certain way, but rather that particular traits functioned to limit malaria prevalence and malaria mortality. The practice of such traits therefore increased the fitness, or probability of survival, for the Sardinian population. As such, the analysis of cultural adaptations is not concerned with the origin of cultural features, but with the explanation of the persistence of such traits over time. None of the traits described here exclusively functioned to limit malaria, since they also satisfied more directly functional needs.

Cultural adaptations differ from biological ones, not only due to diverse mechanisms of transmission, but also because human cultural behavior can be volitional and maintained by choice. Cultural adaptations need not be the result of conscious processes; indeed, many of the adaptations discussed in this paper occurred without subjective awareness. However, some cultural adaptations are the result of cultural theories and willful behavior. As described by Alland and McCay, cultural adaptation is both a functional and volitional concept, since "humans, because they think, can be stimulated to think about environmental prob-

lems" (1973:172). Cultural theories designed to solve environmental "problems" can in fact retard adaptation if they block other solutions; Alland (1970) has made this argument in reference to ethnomedical curative practices. In the case of cultural adaptations to malaria in the Sardinian context, many practices function adaptively despite being based on a faulty epidemiological model.

THE ECOLOGIC AND ETHNOGRAPHIC SETTING

Sardinia, an autonomous region of the Italian Republic, is located near the center of the western Mediterranean basin. The island is roughly rectangular in shape, with an approximate length of 270 kilometers and a width of 100 kilometers. Though only slightly smaller than Sicily in territory, the Sardinian population historically totaled fewer than one-third of the neighboring island. The single most important historical cause of this low population density has been endemic malaria (Brown 1979). Certain elements of

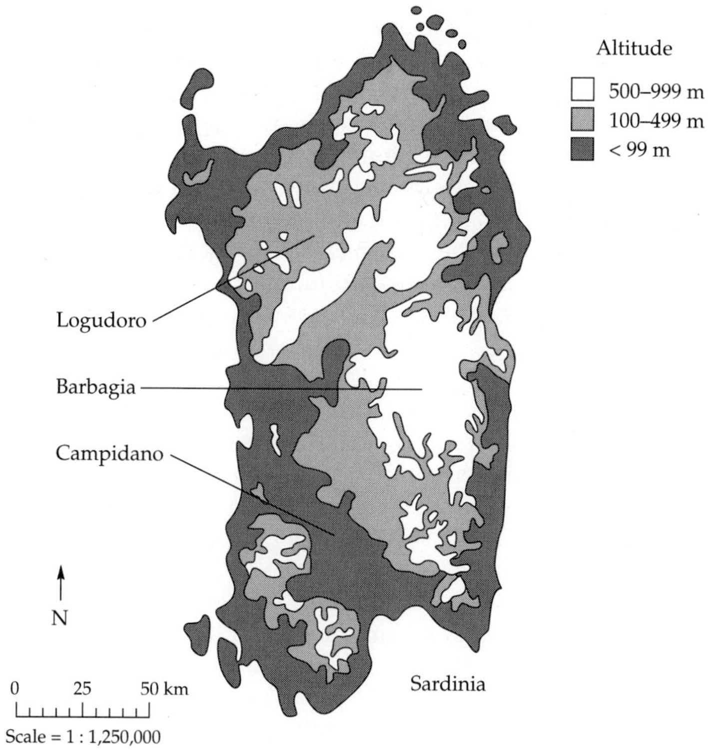

FIGURE 1   Map of Altitude and Major Geographical Zones of Sardinia

Sardinian geography may also have contributed to this low population density.

For over two thousand years, Sardinia was the most malaria-ridden territory of the western Mediterranean. The disease was hyperendemic and comprised the major cause of mortality on the island. The annual incidence and case-mortality rates for Sardinia rivaled those of many tropical zones. Italian scholars have long noted the importance of endemic malaria as a limiting factor in the economic history of Sardinia and the rest of the Italian *Mezzogiorno* (Celli 1933; Carta-Raspi 1971; Boscolo et al. 1962; Braudel 1972). In fact, in the first half of this century, a large body of public health literature argued that malaria was the underlying cause of economic underdevelopment in many areas of the world, including Sardinia (re: Tornu 1907; Jones 1908; Conti 1910; Dettori 1911; Brambilla 1912; Fermi 1925; Brotzu 1934; Hackett 1937).

Due to the high prevalence of malaria on the island, Sardinia was selected as the site of a pioneering malaria eradication project conducted by the Rockefeller International Health Foundation between 1947 and 1951. This project, labeled ERLAAS (*Ente Regionale per la Lotta Anti Anofelica in Sardegna*), marked the first use of DDT attempting species eradication of an indigenous anopheline vector (Logan 1953). Because of the ERLAAS campaign, there are detailed data available concerning the epidemiology of malaria in Sardinia and the entomology of the malaria vector, *Anopheles labranchiae*.[2]

THE EPIDEMIOLOGY OF MALARIA IN SARDINIA

The discovery of cultural adaptations to any disease requires information on disease ecology, the social and geographic distribution of the disease, and ethnographic details concerning the organization of daily life. The central question in such a study is whether culturally prescribed behavior patterns affect the mechanisms of disease transmission. In relation to malaria, one must ask whether certain behaviors functioned to reduce the probability of being bitten by an infected anopheles mosquito. Endemic malaria in Sardinia was characterized by two epidemiological factors which are of critical importance: first, the seasonal cycle of malaria prevalence; and secondly, the sylvatic, or nonanthrophilic nature of the principal vector, *A. labranchiae*. These ecological variables directly affected the pattern of malaria transmission in Sardinia, and the analysis of cultural adaptations must take them into account.

Different anopheline populations show remarkable variability in breeding habits and feeding preferences; this variability has compounded the difficulties of malaria control programs worldwide (Harrison 1978:228). Obviously, precise entomological information is crucial for a successful malaria eradication effort. The lack of such data was probably a critical factor in the failure of the ERLAAS project, since differences in the behavior of the Sardinian population of *A. labranchiae* from their mainland con-specifics were not anticipated by program malariologists (Aitken 1953:303).

The single most important behavioral difference was the *sylvatic* nature of the Sardinian population of *A. labranchiae*. This meant that the mosquitoes did not regularly rest or hibernate in human habitations, nor were they totally dependent on humans as a source of blood feasts. An important discovery of the ERLAAS campaign was that the spraying of interior house walls with a residual insecticide, which is a successful strategy against domestic anopheline vectors, was totally ineffective against a sylvatic species. The sylvatic nature of *A. labranchiae* is evidence that it is a well-adapted indigenous species, which possibly predated human occupation of the island (Trapido 1953:369).

In addition to the sylvatic nature, several other features of the behavior of the Sardinian *A. labranchiae* are important to recognize. First, the vector preferred fresh water to brackish water for breeding. Second, the mosquitoes were found in all ecological zones of the island, including highland regions, but predominated in low elevation zones with fresh water suitable for breeding. In this regard, the highest concentrations of *A. labranchiae* were found in areas immediately surrounding human settlements. Finally, like most anophelines, the Sardinian vector is an active feeder primarily in the hours around dawn and dusk (Aitken 1953:329). Because of the marked variation in breeding and feeding habits of different anopheline species, it should be remembered that the cultural adaptations to malaria described here may not always be applicable to ecological zones where *A. labranchiae* is not the primary malaria vector.

The epidemiology of malaria in temperate climates like Sardinia is very different from that of tropical zones because of a characteristic seasonal, or epidemic, cycle (Hackett 1937; Logan 1953:181). The seasonal cycle of malaria in Sardinia is graphically depicted in figure 2 (. . .); this cycle is often labeled *estivo-autumnal*. The fact of a "malarial season" in Sardinia is of critical importance for understanding cultural adaptations. The incidence of primary malaria transmission reaches an epidemic peak during the months of August, September, and October. The epidemic peak is contrasted with a hiatus of primary infections during the

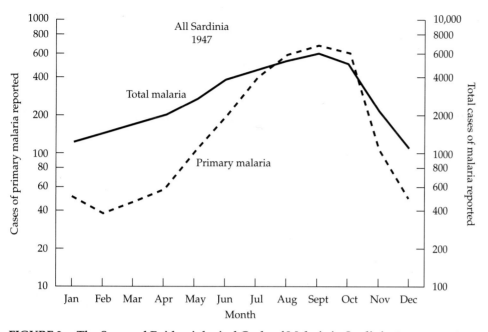

FIGURE 2   The Seasonal Epidemiological Cycle of Malaria in Sardinia *(based on data for 1947 reported in Logan [1953])*

winter and early spring. It is important to recognize, however, that malaria relapses can occur at any time during the year, and for this reason the incidence of total malaria cases remains at constantly high endemic levels. The epidemic cycle of malaria is causally related to the ecological parameter of temperature which affects both larval development of the *A. labranchiae* and the extrinsic reproductive cycle of the malaria protozoa, *Plasmodium* (Aitken 1953:313). Because of this seasonal cycle, adults cannot gain immunity to malaria as they do in tropical zones, since acquired immunity is possible only from constant exposure to the disease.

The epidemiology of malaria in Sardinia is rather complex because both *Plasmodium vivax* and *P. falciparum* coexisted, and neither strain was predominant. In this regard, multiple infections were not uncommon (Hackett 1937:167). In general, *P. vivax* had a consistently high annual incidence which accounted for the stable, endemic nature of malaria on the island; this can be seen in the curve for "total malaria" in figure 2. *P. vivax* mainly affected children, and was characterized by high morbidity but low mortality rates. On the other hand, *P. falciparum*, the more deadly strain, had an unstable annual incidence (also shown in figure 2). *P. falciparum* had a more seasonal nature and accounts for the annual epidemic during late summer and early fall; the size of this annual epidemic primarily depended upon variable ecological conditions, such as the amount of summer precipitation (Aitken 1953:312).

THE GEOGRAPHIC AND SOCIAL DISTRIBUTION OF MALARIA

There are difficulties in reconstructing the geographic and social distribution of malaria in Sardinia because of the variability of the annual incidence of the disease and certain weaknesses inherent in the historical health statistics. Nevertheless, in comparison with most parts of the world, the specificity of the historical epidemiological data for Sardinia is unique. This is primarily because of the work of the malariologist Claudio Fermi, who conducted an island-wide village survey for malaria prevalence between 1933 and 1937 (Fermi 1937, 1939). The magnitude of Fermi's survey is impressive—the final publication totals more than 2,000 pages and includes analyses of forty-one variables, for each of the island's 337 settlements. Fermi's database incorporates a number of measures in malaria morbidity, including physicians' records, quinine consumption, and site visits; although unsophisticated by modern standards, the Fermi survey is an impressive and important database. Before this survey, the traditional interpretation of the geographic distribution of malaria on the island was that certain subregions, like the Campidano plain in the southern sector of the island, and all coastal zones were characterized by the most malaria. Conversely, the central highlands of the Barbagia were generally thought to be malaria-free. However, by mapping the malaria morbidity prevalence data from Fermi's survey, one

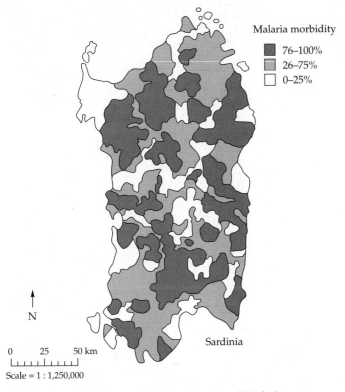

Malaria morbidity

■ 76–100%
▨ 26–75%
□ 0–25%

N

0   25   50 km

Scale = 1 : 1,250,000

Sardinia

FIGURE 3   The Geographic Distribution of Malaria Morbidity *(based on the malaria survey by Fermi [1934, 1938])*

must recognize a more complex geographical distribution. The geographic distribution of malaria on the island is shown in figure 3 (. . .); this distribution can be compared with the pattern of elevation depicted in figure 1. It must be understood that although under-populated coastal zones may have developed strong historical reputations for malaria, the data show that no ecological zone, including the mountainous highlands, was totally impervious to the disease.

The geographic distribution of malaria in Sardinia can be predicted by two primary ecological variables: elevation and settlement size. Fermi's malaria survey data reveal a relatively weak, but statistically significant, inverse correlation between malaria morbidity and settlement size ($r = -0.203$, $p \leq .001$). This inverse correlation means that urban centers, with populations greater than 10,000, had relatively low malaria rates; conversely, the smallest agricultural communities, with populations less than 1,500, generally had the highest malaria rates. Malaria was a *rural* disease. The rationale for this ecological distribution is obvious when one remembers the sylvatic nature of the Sardinian malaria vector. In general, the ecological settings of cities are inhospitable to anopheles mosquitoes, and consequently the probability of malaria

transmission in cities is low. Urban inhabitants may have low risks of exposure to infected anophelines during most of the year; however, this situation is sometimes reversed during the peak of the seasonal epidemic cycle.

The map of malaria morbidity in figure 3 (. . .) is relatively complex, and yields no striking geographical pattern. The highland Barbagia is definitely not malaria-free; the Logudoro plateaus have some of the island's highest malaria rates; and the distribution within the Campidano plain is mixed. The complexity of this geographic distribution makes one question the simple assumption that malaria morbidity rates can be considered a direct function of altitude (cf. Brown 1981). Nevertheless, Fermi's survey data indicate a statistically significant inverse correlation between malaria prevalence and altitude ($r = -0.223$, $p \leq .001$). Altitude is inversely correlated with malaria prevalence because of its relationship to two ecological parameters—temperature and standing water (Brown 1979:113). These parameters directly affect the size and life span of the Anopheline population; as such, altitude has only an *indirect* relation to malaria transmission. Temperature affects the length of the malaria epidemic season since the Plasmodium lifecycle is interrupted at low temperatures. For this reason, there is a longer season of possible malaria transmission in lowland zones where average temperatures are higher. Because of a history of deforestation beginning with the Carthaginian epoch, many highland zones have been severely eroded and lowland areas are characterized by poor drainage and inland swamps (*stagni*). Because they provided good breeding conditions for *A. labranchiae*, lower elevation zones had higher densities of the malaria vector. As such, elevation provides a gross measure of local ecological conditions and can be used as an adequate predictor of malaria prevalence.

The sociological distribution of malaria in Sardinia is difficult to reconstruct, particularly for the small rural villages characteristic of the island. In these rural areas, there was never an adequate system for accurate recording of malaria cases. However, three available data sources permit a general understanding of social epidemiological patterns. These sources include: ERLAAS data from a sample of fifty-two Sardinian communities (Logan 1953); historical records of rural physicians in malarious communities (for example, Martinelli 1883); and interviews with older residents of ex-malarious communities (Brown 1979). Despite the lack of standardized prevalence data, these sources allow one to make generalizations of malaria morbidity prevalence based upon age, sex, and occupation categories. Similar social epidemiological distributions of malaria based upon prevalence survey data have been reported for other parts of the world (Hackett 1937; Russell 1955). Four generalizations concerning the social distribution of malaria in Sardinia can be supported:

1. Children experience more malaria than adults.
2. Among adults, men experience more malaria than women.
3. Among men, agro-pastoral workers experience more malaria than professionals, artisans, and merchants.
4. Among agro-pastoral workers, peasants experience more malaria than shepherds.

If standardized social epidemiological data were available, these basic generalizations would probably be found island-wide, despite local variations in malaria prevalence. The first generalization, relating age to malaria morbidity, is characteristic of any endemic disease. Higher rates for children probably reflect more *P. vivax* to which adults have possibly acquired a mild immunity (Hackett 1937:167). In general, the portion of the Sardinian population which ex-

perienced the highest rates of malaria infection were rural-dwelling, male agriculturalists. Conversely, the portion of the population with lowest malaria prevalence were urban-dwelling, upper-class adult females. It is important to understand how culturally prescribed behavior patterns for these groups may help account for this social epidemiological pattern.

CULTURAL ADAPTATIONS TO MALARIA

Having described the basic ecological and epidemiological context, the present analysis will examine cultural adaptations to malaria in reference to three levels of a single cultural system: human ecology; social organization; and ethnomedicine. On the level of human ecology, the cultural adaptations to malaria included characteristic settlement patterns, and the traditional land utilization of inverse transhumance. Although the ultimate causation of these traits can be traced to other factors, the settlement and land usage patterns had important adaptive value because they reduced exposure to the malaria vector. On the level of social organization, the analysis will focus on two aspects: first, cultural rules limiting the geographical mobility for particular social groups; and secondly, class related behaviors which limited malaria exposure for the landed elite. This second adaptation is illustrated in the ethnographic example of the social organization of one of the grape harvests in Bosa, a town on the western coast of the island. Finally, cultural adaptations on the ideological level of ethnomedicine are considered. Traditional Sardinian folk-medical theories of fever causation and preventive medicine are examined in relation to the concept of *buon aria* (good air). This ethnomedical theory reinforced all three levels of cultural adaptations, and it is hypothesized that behaviors prescribed by this belief system reduced the probability of malaria relapses.

The cultural adaptations discussed here were predominant in *traditional* Sardinia, which for present purposes can be considered as before 1947. Contemporary Sardinian society is undergoing rapid change (Weingrod and Morin 1971), but it is important to note that most of the fundamental aspects of these cultural adaptations have persisted into the post-eradication epoch. However, not all of the cultural traits described here, particularly those of traditional ethnomedicine, are important or elaborated features of modern Sardinian culture. For this reason, the methodology used in this research combined historical analysis with traditional ethnographic techniques.

NUCLEATED SETTLEMENT PATTERN AND INVERSE TRANSHUMANCE

Both the formation and distribution of settlements in Sardinia have been influenced by the ecological restrictions of malaria. The settlement pattern found in all ecological zones of the island is characterized by extreme nucleation and a clear preference for "high ground" locations, specifically hilltops, precipices, and foothills (Pinna and Corda 1956; Alivia 1954; Anfossi 1915). This settlement pattern is not unique to Sardinia, and can be found in many non-malarious parts of Europe. However, the pattern has been particularly characteristic for the Italian *Mezzogiorno*, where it has affected both the political economy and history (Schneider and Schneider 1976). To a visitor on the island, this settlement pattern appears picturesque but irrational, since it requires rigorous daily commutes to agricultural fields. The adaptive value of the nucleated settlement pattern is linked to the sylvatic behavior of *A. labranchiae*. The man-made environment of nucleated settlements decreases anopheles densities and therefore the probability of anopheles-human contact. It therefore lowers the prevalence of malaria. Anthropological discussions of this Mediterranean settlement pattern (Blok 1969) have been correct in not viewing the ecological threat of malaria as a primary, causal variable. More direct factors, such as the historical threat of pirate raids, military conquests, and the expropriation of land by foreigners, were probably more important than malaria in driving people from coastal plains to hilltop settlement sites. It was malaria, however, which made the resettlement of abandoned lands extremely difficult, if not impossible, because it threatened the health of individuals in isolated farmsteads. The constant threat of malaria transmitted by a sylvatic vector gave an advantage to relatively large, densely populated communities. It also made the formation of new settlements a risky venture at best. The historical disappearance of 300 hamlets in the Campidano plain during the fifteenth century (Loddo-Canepa 1932) may be taken as evidence of the insuitability of a dispersed settlement pattern in a malarious environment. The disastrous failure of agricultural development schemes to repopulate low-lying plains in Sardinia (Tyndale 1849 III:28), as well as malarious areas of mainland Italy (Celli 1933), further document this point. Although it cannot be claimed to have originally caused the nucleated hilltop settlement pattern, malaria may help to explain its persistence long after historical periods of political insecurity.

In the native ideology, the most important quality for a settlement site is buon-aria, which means that a hilltop village is subjected to healthful, cleansing breezes. The location of nucleated settlements in sites with buon-aria, yet also within walking distance to agricultural flatlands, is an important modal pattern. The settlement pattern reflects an essential compromise between health and economic productivity since it allows the agricultural exploitation of malarial flatlands without the habitation of them. This appears to be an example of cultural adaptations following a minimax strategy, as suggested by Alland (1970:184). It is possible to view the nucleated hilltop settlement pattern as minimizing the malaria-related costs associated with agriculture in low elevation zones of the island.

The practice of inverse transhumance in the traditional pastoral economy in Sardinia is a clear example of the unconscious, adaptive value of settlement pattern in land utilization. The concept of transhumance refers to the seasonal movement of flocks to higher and lower elevation zones corresponding to the seasonal availability of pasture and water. As used by human geographers, the distinction between normal and inverse transhumance centers on the location of permanent settlements, since pasture utilization is nearly identical (LeLannou 1941:171). In normal transhumance, settlements are located at lower elevations and flocks are taken up to mountain pastures for the summer. In inverse transhumance, permanent settlements are located in the mountains and flocks travel down to the lowlands for winter. Figure 4 (. . .) diagrams the pattern of inverse transhumance which has been prevalent in Sardinia, particularly for the central highlands (LeLannou 1941; Berger 1981). However, this inverse pattern is problematic because it creates hardships for the pastoral population, since shepherds spend the greater part of the year (approximately from November to June) in winter pastures, far from their hometown and family. Inverse transhumance has disadvantages, not only because isolation in winter pastures compounds the difficulty in protecting sheep from theft, but also because the winter is the most important economic season in pastoral production. Lambing, milking, cheese making, and shearing must all be accomplished in isolated winter pastures, and this is associated with significant problems of labor recruitment.

The adaptive value of the inverse transhumance pattern rests on the coinciding seasonality of flock movements and the annual malaria cycle. In short, this land use pattern allows for the exploitation of fertile but malarial lowland pastures during the "safe" season of November to May, while it also permits shepherds to escape those high risk zones during the peak of the malarial cycle. This may be an efficient solution to the problem of malaria seasonality in the plains, but it is also an economic necessity for the maintenance of relatively large settlements in mountainous districts. Women and children, as year-round inhabitants of mountainous communities, enjoyed greatly reduced chances of contracting malaria. As shepherds transferred flocks from burnt-out lowland pastures to more lush mountain zones, they unconsciously reduced their exposure to malaria. In contrast to the pastoral pattern, the labor demands of agricultural production are greatest during the late summer harvest which corresponds directly with the peak of the seasonal malaria epidemic. Since fertile agricultural districts were also characterized by the greatest densities of anopheles, the increased incidence of malaria during the late summer often resulted in labor shortages for the harvest. The land use pattern of inverse transhumance resulted in greater risk of exposure for peasants than shepherds, and this differential risk has been borne out in social epidemiological data.

ADAPTIVE ASPECTS OF SOCIAL ORGANIZATION

Analysis of traditional Sardinian social organization may enhance the understanding of the observed social distribution of malaria. Since culture determines the daily behavior patterns for different social groups, it also influences the risk of exposure to anopheles and hence malaria rates. Lower malaria prevalence for adult women and upper class individuals may be understood in this manner. It is also important to recognize that patterns of social organization vary between ecological zones of the island, particularly the agricultural lowlands and the pastoral highlands. This significant intracultural variation may be related to the differential influence of malaria as a factor shaping cultural behavior. In this regard, the adaptive aspects of social organization analyzed here are characteristic of the culture of lowland Sardinia, and not the pastoral highlands.

Traditional cultural rules restricted the geographical mobility of women, and these rules were given particular emphasis in the case of pregnant women. In general, women were expected not to leave the confines of the *paese*, or nucleated settlement, during most of their lives. Limited geographical mobility for women is a cultural ideal which corresponds to a pattern of sexual segregation wherein men operate in the public sphere and women control the domestic sphere. The woman's world centers on her house and the immediate neighborhood setting. Except in limited circumstances, women are *not* expected to do

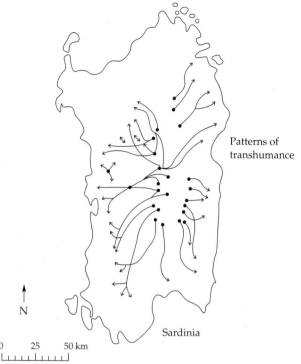

Patterns of transhumance

N

0   25   50 km

Scale = 1 : 1,250,000

Sardinia

FIGURE 4   Flock Movements in the Traditional Pattern of Inverse Transhumance *(after LeLannou [1941])*

agricultural labor, since, from an emic viewpoint, such work would reduce the social prestige of a family. Because of these rules of social organization, women were generally able to stay within the confines of the nucleated settlement, and therefore had limited exposure to the malaria vector. As such, the lower malaria prevalence rates for women are predicated on the adaptive value of the settlement pattern.

Restrictions on mobility were even more rigorously applied during pregnancy and the immediate postpartum period. During this time, the ideal behavior was for women to remain within the house itself. The adaptive value of such a restriction becomes important and obvious when one remembers that a malaria attack during pregnancy carries a high risk of spontaneous abortion. From the Sardinian viewpoint, pregnancy (*gravidanza*) is perceived as a seriously dangerous state, and this certainly was the case with the constant threat of malaria. A famous Sardinian novel begins with the statement, "The pregnancy went well, she did not contract malaria . . ." (Dessí 1951:3). It is clear that the threat of malaria-induced spontaneous abortions may have increased the adaptive value of cultural restrictions on the geographical mobility of females. Evidence of this includes the historical fact that with the eradication of malaria, there has been a significant increase in Sardinian fecundity rates (Brown 1979:351).

The traditional behavior of Sardinian upper classes, particularly large land holders, can be seen to have similar adaptive value. The social organization of production in the agricultural lowlands meant that, like women, the traditional elites did not regularly commute to the fields, and therefore had low exposure to the malaria vector. Members of the upper classes usually remained within the safe confines of the nucleated settlement. This principle was often extended when upper class families took up permanent residence in malaria-free urban areas and appointed intermediaries to handle agricultural affairs on the village level. This social organization of production has been described for many southern European societies (Davis 1970; Schneider and Schneider 1976). This strategy, which was predominant for most small villages in the Campidano, allowed absentee landlords to escape the threat of endemic rural diseases. Obviously, the better health of the upper class was not simply the result of limited contact with the malaria vector, but also due to better living conditions and medical care. By virtue of their access to capital, however, the upper classes were able to escape from the epidemic peak of the malaria cycle during the summer. The "summer vacation" is a European aristocratic tradition which historically may have had important health implications.

An example of a behavioral adaptation by elites who lived in a highly malarial community is illustrated by the traditional social organization of the grape harvest (*vendemmia*) in the community of Bosa, in western Sardinia. This specific ethnographic example cannot be generalized for all Sardinia because, unlike most settlements, this town had a markedly high concentration of land ownership and a small number of aristocratic families. It is, however, a possible example of intracultural variation partly shaped by the ecological threat of malaria. The aristocratic tradition of Bosa is symbolically represented by a particular precious wine, *La Malvasia*, which was produced solely by these few families. Near the La Malvasia vineyards, the elites built houses (*case coloniche*) on sites which they considered to have the healthful characteristic of buon aria. Every year the upper class of Bosa transferred their residence from town to country for a period from August 15 to approximately the middle of October; ostensibly, this transfer was necessary for the supervision of the vendemmia. Yet this is inadequate as a final explanation for the residence change.

It is important to recognize the seasonal coincidence between the grape harvest and the annual epidemic cycle of malaria. This traditional residence

movement allowed the elite to be absent from the nucleated settlement during the height of the malaria epidemic (see figure 2). Based upon fieldwork interviews, it seems clear that many upper class members were aware of the antimalaria function of this movement to their summer houses. Within the traditional ethnomedical model, low rates of malaria in the upper-class children of Bosa were considered to be due to their increased exposure to buon-aria; however, there is also an epidemiological rationale for the observed lower rates of malaria for individuals absent from the nucleated settlement during the late summer. It has been argued above that remaining within the nucleated settlement during most of the year is adaptive against endemic, or stable, malaria because of decreased risk of exposure to the anopheles vector. But the adaptive value of remaining within the nucleated settlement is insignificant during the peak of the epidemic cycle despite the relative paucity of mosquitoes, because there is a greater chance that any *A. labranchiae* within the settlement has been infected by the malaria protozoa. While the overall vector populations may have been larger in the countryside, the greatest concentration of infected anopheles were located on the fringes of the nucleated settlement (Aitken 1953). Only during this epidemic peak period was the probable exposure to an *infected* anopheles lower in the countryside than in the village.

While the social organization of the vendemmia allowed the upper class families to escape the summer epidemic of malaria, this was not true of the laboring classes who actually did the work of the harvest. In the traditional pattern, workers commuted to the Malvasia vineyards around dawn and dusk. Since the paths to the vineyards passed by a large fresh water swamp, these workers were subjected to the prime feeding periods of *A. labranchiae*. This behavioral adaptation by the elite of Bosa seems to reflect a conscious decision to escape from the malaria epidemic of the town to the buon aria of hillside vineyards. Such behavioral adaptations may have been "right for the wrong reason," but in the study of cultural adaptations, it is the ultimate function of a particular trait which is most significant (Netting 1974:46).

ETHNOMEDICINE AND MALARIA RELAPSE RATES

On the level of cultural ideology, one can raise the hypothesis that traditional Sardinian folk theories of fever causation had adaptive value by reducing malaria relapse rates. In this regard, two folk theories are discussed here, *Intemperie* and *Colpo d'Aria*. These elements of the traditional ethnomedical system are concerned with rules of general health, and have particular attention to the etiology of fevers. These theories are associated with a variety of behavioral prescriptions and admonitions which comprise the nucleus of traditional folk preventive medicine. These prescriptions stress the necessity of moderation in daily life and the danger of sudden mixtures of hot and cold elements which may cause physiological shock and bring on fevers. In Sardinia, these folk theories predated the miasmic theory of malaria causation (Brown 1979:244). Today, the concept of Colpo d'Aria is used regularly in lowland communities, but particular details concerning Intemperie can be found only in archival sources. Although the importance of both theories may have dwindled in recent years, the behavioral prescriptions for health maintenance based upon them have persisted in contemporary Sardinian society. The adaptive value of these folk theories involves the prevention of spontaneous malaria relapses rather than primary transmission. In a population with endemic, temperate-climate malaria, relapses regularly account for more attacks than primary transmission. The present goal is to examine how culturally prescribed behaviors may be related to the mechanisms of malaria relapses.

Before the twentieth century and the discovery of the relationship between malaria, anopheles, and plasmodium protozoa, there was no standardization of the name "Malaria," nor was there a consistent method of diagnosis or treatment of the disease (Russell 1955; Harrison 1978). Endemic intermittent fevers had a variety of names because they were thought to be geographically specific; for example, in nineteenth century Sardinia, malaria was called *Intemperie Sarda.* Archival sources emphasize the irregular spacing of fevers and chills as unequivocal evidence of the unique character of the Sardinian fevers (Aquenza-Mossa 1702; Leo 1801; Tendas 1881; Sachero 1833). This symptomological irregularity, however, was actually the result of the coexistence and multiple infections of vivax and falciparum strains of malaria.

The emic term Intemperie referred to both this specific illness of malaria and its etiology. The ethnomedical theory of Intemperie is analogous to the hot-cold theory of illness prevalent in many parts of the world, but they are clearly not identical. With Intemperie, illness is thought to be caused by a sudden and dangerous shift from hot to cold, or from dry to wet. An important distinction is that the external environment, not internal equilibrium, is implicated as a causal element. There is a meteorological analogy throughout this literature, and the earliest source (Aquenza-Mossa 1702) argues that climatic conditions which cause sudden storms also cause human fevers.

Nineteenth century Sardinian physicians (Sachero 1833; Tendas 1881) adapted the folk theory to the then-scientific theory of *miasma* by arguing that *intemperosi* climatic conditions created miasmic reactions in lowland areas which in turn caused malaria. But the underlying concept is that for individual health, like weather, abrupt changes in temperature cause violent reactions.

It is probable that the ethnomedical theory of Intemperie relates seasonal climatic changes with the seasonal epidemic cycle of malaria. The concept of Intemperie finds a correlate in contemporary Sardinia with a pervasive idea that the *cambiamento delle stagione* (change of seasons) is a dangerous period for personal health. In Sardinia's climate, the "change of seasons" refers to two periods—the increasing temperatures of the spring and decreasing temperature of the fall. In this regard, it is significant that in temperate climate malaria, relapse rates sharply increase during the spring; these seasonally-related relapses function as an infection pool which is a prerequisite for the late summer epidemic (Hackett 1937:165).

The health danger of a change in temperature is also a central theme to the ethnomedical concept of *Colpo d'Aria,* which means "blast of air." An individual exposed to a Colpo d'Aria is prone to a variety of minor illnesses, such as the common cold or flare-ups of chronic pains. In everyday life, the concept of Colpo d'Aria is reflected in precautions and concern about drafts. The Sardinians' belief is that an individual with a warm physiological equilibrium is at a great health risk when "shocked" by a sudden blast of cold. A sudden change in an individual's internal temperature equilibrium results in an unhealthy physiological shock and possibly illness; the principle holds true for a drafty room in winter, or drinking a cold beer in summer. As such, a fever represents the body's efforts for renewed equilibrium after being exposed to cold. The chills and fevers characteristic of malaria, therefore, are thought to be analogous to a pendulum, swinging back and forth between hot and cold.

The adaptive value of the folk theories of both Intemperie and Colpo d'Aria depends upon how they shape daily behavior. Both theories aim at a similar strategy of preventive medicine: the avoidance of conditions where a sudden mixing of hot and cold would upset the temperature equilibrium. Both archival sources and contemporary informants produce similar lists of behavioral restrictions which, it is argued, will, if followed, reduce the risk of temperature imbalance and illness. Such a list of Sardinian folk-medical recommendations based on both ethnomedical theories would include: avoiding drafts and dampness; avoiding overexertion; keeping one's stomach full; drinking spirits regularly, but not to excess; wearing hats and layers of clothing; avoiding cold beverages when hot; not sleeping outside without shelter; closing shutters at dusk; never getting overly hot or cold; special care when bathing; and general moderation in all things. Such suggestions should not appear exotic, since they are very similar to "common sense" guidelines for good health in our own culture. It is generally accepted that such recommendations concerning diet, rest, and clothing are important for personal health maintenance and guarding against the common cold.

. . .

When one thinks of malaria causation only in terms of the mosquito vector and primary transmissions, then the folk theories of Intemperie and Colpo d'Aria appear to be nothing but quaint, yet interesting customs. However, by remembering the unique ability of malaria to relapse long after the initial infection, and that certain behaviors can provoke such relapses, then the traditional folk theories of fever causation may have had significant adaptive value.

CONCLUSIONS

This paper has examined particular traits of traditional Sardinian culture in relation to the epidemiology of malaria. It has been suggested that cultural adaptations to the disease can be found at three levels of behavior: human ecology, social organization, and ideology. Cultural traits based on the folk concept of buon aria (good air) have been seen to have adaptive value because they tend to reduce exposure to the malaria vector. Behaviors associated with traditional ethnomedical theories possibly lowered the probability of spontaneous malaria relapses. On the level of human ecology, the nucleated hilltop settlement pattern and the pastoral land use system of inverse transhumance have the function of allowing the exploitation of malaria lowlands without habitation of them. On the level of social organization, it has been argued that lower malaria prevalences for women are the result of cultural rules restricting their mobility outside of the nucleated settlement. Such rules are most important for pregnant women, since reduced exposure to the malaria vector would decrease the risk of spontaneous abortions. Although there was considerable intracultural variation for all Sardinia, the elite classes of Bosa were able to escape the annual summer epidemic of malaria by transferring their residences during the grape harvest. Finally, on the level of ideology, the folk medical theories of Intemperie and Colpo d'Aria provide a functional explanation of the seasonality of malaria. More importantly, culturally prescribed behaviors associated with those theories may have reduced the probability of malaria relapses.

The analysis of cultural adaptations to specific diseases stems directly from cultural evolution theory and can lead to a more thorough understanding of the interaction of biological and cultural evolution. Since diseases directly affect survival rates, they function as selective agents for biological characteristics and, more importantly, cultural traits. The analysis of how cultural behaviors reduce disease prevalence provides examples of cultural systems evolving to meet the demands of specific environmental conditions. In the case of malaria in Sardinia, this search for cultural adaptations has emphasized the intersection between the behavior to the malaria vector, *Anopheles labranchiae,* and the daily activities of particular social groups. Endemic malaria did not cause these cultural traits to first appear, but the fact that they functioned to protect the population from malaria may help explain their persistence over time. The cultural elements discussed here in the Sardinian context are relatively common in the ethnographic literature of southern European societies. This paper, hopefully, provides a new, ecologically-oriented interpretation of those cultural features.

REFERENCES

Aitken, T. 1953. The Anopheline Fauna of Sardinia. *In* The Sardinian Project. J. Logan, ed. Baltimore: Johns Hopkins Press.

Alivia, G. 1954. Poplazione ed Economia: il Problema della Sardegna. Milano: Iglesias.

Alland, A. 1966. Medical Anthropology and the Study of Biological and Cultural Adaptation. American Anthropologist 68:40–50.

———. 1969. Ecology and Adaptation to Parasitic Diseases. *In* Environment and Cultural Behavior. A. Vayda, ed. New York: Natural History Press.

———. 1970. Adaptation in Cultural Evolution: An Approach to Medical Anthropology. New York: Columbia University Press.

Alland, A. and B. McCay. 1973. The Concept of Adaptation in Biological and Cultural Evolution. *In* Handbook of Social and Cultural Anthropology. J. Honigmann, ed. Chicago: Rand McNally.

Anfossi, G. 1915. Ricerche sulla Distribuzione della Popolazione in Sardegna. Sassari: Galizzi.

Aquenza et Mossa, P. 1702. Tractus de Febre Intemperie. Typographia Emmanuelis Ruiz de Murgia. Barcelona.

Belgind, G. 1942. Textbook of Clinical Parasitology. New York: Holmes and Meier.

Berger, A. 1981. The Effects of Capitalism on the Social Structure of Pastoral Villages in Highland Sardinia. Michigan: Discussions in Anthropology.

Bernini, L., V. Carcassi, B. Latte, A. G. Motulsky, M. Siniscalco, G. Montalenti. 1960. Indagini Genetiche Sulla Predispozione al Favismo—III. Distribuzione della Frequenze Geniche per il Locus Gd. in Sardegna: Interazione con la Malaria e la Talassemia al Livello Popolazionistico. Accademia Nazionale dei Lincei (Roma) 29:115–125.

Blok, A. 1969. South Italian Agro-Towns. Comparative Studies in Society and History 11:121–135.

Boscolo, A., L. Bulferetti, L. Delpiano. 1962. Profilo Storico Economico della Sardegna dal Riformismo Sette-Centesco al Piano di Rinascita. Padova: CEDAM.

Brambilla, G. 1912. La Malaria Sotto L'Aspetto Economico-Sociale. Milano: Gorlini.

Braudel, F. 1972. The Mediterranean and the Mediterranean World in the Age of Phillip II. New York: Harper and Row.

Brotzu, G. 1934. La Malaria nella Storia della Sardegna. Mediterranea 8:3–10.

Brown, P. J. 1979. Cultural Adaptations to Endemic Malaria and the Socioeconomic Effects of Malaria Eradication in Sardinia. Ph.D. Dissertation. S.U.N.Y. Stony Brook.

———. 1981. New Considerations on the Distribution of Malaria, Thalassemia, and Glucose-6-Phosphate Dehydrogenase in Sardinia. Human Biology (in press).

Bruce-Chwatt, L. J. 1979. Man against Malaria: Conquest or Defeat. Transactions of the Royal Society of Tropical Medicine and Hygiene 73:605–617.

Carta-Raspi, R. 1971. Storia della Sardegna. Milano: Mursia.

Celli, A. 1933. The History of Malaria in the Roman Campagna. London: John Bale and Sons.

Coggeshall, L. T. 1963. Malaria. In Cecil-Loeb Textbook of Medicine. P. B. Beeson and W. McDermott, eds. St. Louis: C. V. Mosby.

Conti, A. 1910. La Malaria con Rilevi Fatti in Sardegna. Sassari: Gallizzi.

Davis, J. 1970. Land and Family in a South Italian Town. London: Athlone.

Dessí, G. 1951. Forests of Norbio. New York: Harcourt.

Dettori, G. 1911. La Malaria in Sardegna. Cagliari: Giva-Falconi.

Fermi, C. 1925. La Malaria e la Decadenze della Civilia. Grottaferrla: San Nilo.

———. 1937. Regioni Malariche, Decadenze, Risanamento e Spesa. "Sardegna" Vol. 1—Sassari Province. Rome: Tipografia dello Stato.

———. 1939. Regioni Malariche, Decadenza, Risanamento e Spesa. "Sardegna" Vol. 2—Nuoro Province, Vol. 3—Caligari Province. Rome: Tipografia dello Stato.

Hackett, L. W. 1937. Malaria in Europe: An Ecological Study. Cambridge: Oxford University Press.

Hackett, L. W. and A. Missiroli. 1935. The Varieties of Anopheles Maculipennis and Their Relation to the Distribution of Malaria in Europe. Rivista di Malariologia 14:45–109.

Harrison, G. 1978. Mosquitoes, Malaria, and Man: A History of the Hostilities Since 1880. New York: E. P. Dutton.

Jones, W., R. Ross, R. Ellet. 1908. Malaria: A Neglected Factor in the History of Greece and Rome. Naples: Dethen and Rocholl.

Katz, S. H. and J. Schall. 1979. Fava Bean Consumption and Biocultural Evolution. Medical Anthropology 3:459–76.

LeLannou, M. 1941. Patres et Paysans de la Sardaigne. Tours: Arrault.

Leo, P. A. 1801. Di Alcuni Antichi Pregiudizi sulla Cosi-detta Sarda Intemperie, e sulla Malattia Conosciuta con Questo Nome: Lezione Fisico-Medica. Cagliari: Reale Stamperia.

Lewontin, R. C. 1978. Adaptation. Scientific American 239:212–30.

Livingstone, F. B. 1958. Anthropological Implications of Sickle Cell Gene Distribution in West Africa. American Anthropologist 60:533–62.

———. 1964. The Distribution of the Abnormal Hemoglobin Genes and Their Significance for Human Evolution. Evolution 18:685–99.

———. 1971. Malaria and Human Polymorphisms. Annual Review of Genetics 5:33–64.

Loddo-Canepa, M. 1932. Lo Spopolamento della Sardegna durante le Dominazione Aragonese e Spagnuola. Roma: Comitato Italiano per lo Studio dei Problema della Popolazione.

Logan, J. A. 1953. The Sardinian Project. Baltimore: Johns Hopkins Press.

Martinelli, G. 1883. Relazione del Medico Chirugico Giuseppe Martinelli nelle sue Qualita de Medico Condotto e Necroscopico Medico della Sanità Maritima de Commune di Bosa dall'Anno 1852 al 1881. Sassari: Tipografia Chiarella.

Motulsky, A. 1960. Metabolic Polymorphisms and the Role to Infectious Diseases in Human Evolution. Human Biology 32:28–62.

Mourant, A. E., A. C. Kopéc, and K. Domiewska-Sobczak. 1978. Blood Groups and Diseases. Oxford: Oxford University Press.

Netting, R. Mc. 1974. Agrarian Ecology. Annual Review of Anthropology 3:21–56.

Pinna, M. and L. Corda. 1957. La Distribuzione della Popolazione e i Centri Abitati della Sardegna. Pisa: Libreria Goliardica.

Rappaport, R. A. 1979. Ecology, Meaning and Religion. Richmond, California: North Atlantic.

Russell, P. F. 1955. Man's Mastery of Malaria. London: Oxford University Press.

Sachero, C. G. 1833. Dell'Intemperie di Sardegna e delle Febbri Periodiche Perniciose Torino: Tipografia Fodratti.

Schneider, J. and P. Schneider. 1976. Culture and Political Economy in Western Sicily. New York: Academic Press.

Silverman, S. 1968. Agricultural Organization, Social Structure, and Values in Italy: Amoral Familism Reconsidered. American Anthropologist 70:1–20.

Siniscalco, M. L., L. Bernini, G. Filippi, B. Latte, P. Merra Khan, and S. Piomelli. 1966. Population Genetics of Haemoglobin Variants, Thalassemia and Glucose-6-Phosphate Dehydrogenase Deficiency, with Particular Reference to the Malaria Hypothesis. Bulletin of the World Health Organization 34:379–93.

Tendas, D. A. 1881. La Sardegna e le Sue Febbri Telluriche—Riflessioni Fiolosofico, Scientifico, Critiche. Cagliari: Tipografia di Alagna.

Tornu, A. 1907. Lo Stato Attuale del Problema Malarico e i Suoi Rapporti con Agricolura. Iglesias: Canelles.

Trapido, H. 1953. Biological Considerations in the ERLAAS Project. *In* The Sardinian Project. J. Logan, ed. Baltimore: Johns Hopkins Press.

Tyndale, J. W. 1849. The Island of Sardinia. London: Richard Bently.

Weingrod, A. and E. Morin. 1971. Post Peasants: The Character of Contemporary Sardinian Society. Comparative Studies in Society and History 13:301–324.

Wiesenfeld, S. L. 1967. Sickle-cell Trait in Human Biological and Cultural Evolution. Science 157:1134–38.

 10

The Fly That Would Be King

Robert S. Desowitz

The author of this selection is a medical parasitologist, but he has an anthropologist's eye for exploring the cultural-ecological context and has a wonderful knack for story-telling. This is a story of the tsetse fly, the disease called trypanosomiasis or sleeping sickness, and a cultural-ecological system centered on cattle herding. The central character in the story is a small brown fly, the tsetse, that carries a trypanosome disease not only to people but also (and possibly more importantly) to cattle. In what way would this unlikely pair— a fly and a microscopic organism—be trying to be king of a large territory?

As a parasitologist, Robert Desowitz does describe the two bugs (the fly and the trypanosome) in considerable detail, especially in regard to the species variations across the region. Don't let this bother you. The fundamental argument is found in the bigger picture.

This is a case study of the ecology of a disease that was thought to be a block to economic development. It is certainly the case that endemic sleeping sickness made economic development—at least in the form of colonial agribusiness—impossible. The tsetse fly came to be seen as the enemy of progress, and public health campaigns were implemented to stop the disease by destroying the fly (much as in the case of malaria). The fight against the fly involved some drastic measures, such as killing off large mammals from which the fly fed and removing huge tracts of scrub vegetation where the fly rested and reproduced. In other words, humans were changing the ecology in order to eliminate the disease.

As you will see, these anti-tsetse interventions had some unexpected and rather severe consequences. With the original animals gone and territories cleared for pasture, a new type of cattle was introduced, and these cattle prospered. The ecology was out of balance, and the cattle got to be too much of a good thing. They overgrazed the land in what was already a fragile environment, and consequently the Sahara Desert expanded southward. In fact, a geographer named Walter Ormerod (1976) has presented evidence that the expansion of cattle herds, made possible by tsetse fly control, has actually changed the climate in this region, adding to the severe problem of drought.

Since this article was written, there have been new technologies developed for the control of African trypanosomiasis; these new programs are not ecologically invasive like the ones described here. I believe the lesson from this case study is the danger of ecological arrogance and ignorance.

As you read this selection, consider these questions:

- *To what extent might a disease affect the course of history?*

- *Why do you think people proposed tsetse fly control programs without realizing that they would fundamentally change a fragile ecology?*

- *Is it correct to think of a disease like sleeping sickness as an economic disease? In what way?*

- *What makes this analysis ecological?*

One African tyrant does not attend political councils, is not a member of the Organization of African Unity, and has not palavered with roving diplomats, and does have a personal air-transport system—the tsetse. Holding Africa in thralldom since ancient times, this parasite, known as a trypanosome, is only six ten-thousandths of an inch long, but it has affected the economy, social institutions, and even the religious complexion of the continent.

During the mid-nineteenth century, Muslim Fulani cavalry swept from their near-desert West African Sahel kingdom into the savanna to the south and east, conquering and converting the animist tribes with whom they came into contact. But in their progress through woodlands and rain forests they encountered a formidable adversary, the tsetse. Swarms of these flies attacked and bit the horses, transmitting the parasite to them. It caused a lethal form of animal trypanosomiasis, and in rapid order the cavalry became a disarrayed infantry. On foot, the Fulani were virtually powerless; their invasion was halted before it could reach the great population centers of the Benue and Niger river valleys. Thus was Islam, with its concomitant sociopolitical influences, prevented from infiltrating this vast densely peopled region of Africa for more than half a century.

The popular notion of trypanosomiasis is represented by the image of a lethargic human suffering from the "sleeping distemper," to use the words of an English observer some two hundred years ago. Not a form of distemper at all, the infection is caused in man by one of two closely related parasitic organisms, *Trypanosoma gambiense* and *T. rhodesiense*, and in animals by *T. brucei, T. congolense,* and *T. vivax.* (*T. gambiense* was thought to be restricted to man, but researchers have recently implicated the pig as a reservoir host.) Both animal and human trypanosomes are transmitted by the tsetse, a bloodsucking fly of the genus *Glossina.* Tsetse flies inhabit Africa only south of the Sahara, from approximately fifteen degrees north to twenty degrees south latitude, although they once had wider distribution, as evidenced by the discovery of a fossilized tsetse in the Oligocene shales of Colorado. While human trypanosomiasis continues to be a public-health problem, being responsible for some seven thousand deaths each year, it is the infection in domestic animals that has had the greatest impact on African development.

The tsetse belt encompasses more than six million square miles of land denied to livestock production, mixed farming, and in some regions, human settlement. It is an area that could potentially provide 125 million head of cattle to the protein-starved continent.

The disease has forced herdsmen to concentrate their stock on the limited amount of fly-free pasturage, and this practice has led to overgrazing and attendant soil erosion. When cattle are trekked to distant markets through fly-infested country, some 25 percent may die before reaching their destination. And yet, a less anthropocentric view might hold that by preventing overexploitation of this enormous area, the tsetse and the trypanosome are the most stalwart guardians of the African ecosystem and its magnificent wild fauna.

The manner and degree of transmission of trypanosomes involves complex interactions of parasite, host and fly vector. With this in mind, let us consider the scenario and dramatis personae of *The Fly That Would Be King,* an African spectacular with a cast of millions.

Act 1 is set in a forest in Africa. On stage is the host—a man, a cow, or an antelope. A closer, microscopic examination reveals the second character, the trypanosome, swimming about in the blood of the host by means of an undulating membrane and a lashing flagellum. A sound of angry buzzing comes from off stage. Enter a tsetse, a brown insect not much larger than a housefly. The tsetse smells and sights the host, then strikes and bites, sucking in its trypanosome-containing blood.

Act 2 takes place inside the tsetse's gut, where the trypanosome elongates and multiplies by simple asexual division. After about four days it migrates to the fly's salivary glands; there, over the next fifteen days, further transformation takes place, until it assumes the short, stumpy appearance of the metacyclic stage—the terminal developmental form, in which it is capable of infecting a new host.

Act 3 opens in the forest twenty days after act I. The original host lies obviously ill on the stage floor. Enter another host. The infected tsetse strikes, delivering the metacyclic parasites to the blood stream of the new host and completing the cycle. Curtain.

While this plot is essentially the same for all African trypanosomes, the details for each species differ in important respects. In man, the disease caused by *T. gambiense* is chronic and malignant, and gives rise to the torpor and eventual coma and death classically associated with sleeping sickness.

The pathology of the disease is largely unknown. Over the course of time, the trypanosomes tend to leave the blood and enter, first, the lymphatics, and later, the spinal fluid and the tissues of the central nervous system. The patient becomes comatose during this latter phase, and dies after several years if he has not received chemotherapeutic treatment.

Whereas Gambian sleeping sickness results in a slow death, that caused by *T. rhodesiense* kills within weeks or months. The two infections differ not only in degree of virulence but in other respects as well. Gambian trypanosomiasis is essentially a human disease, cycled from person to person, while the transmission cycle of Rhodesian trypanosomiasis includes a third host—the wild antelope—which acts as a reservoir of infection. By all biological criteria, *T. rhodesiense* is a parasite of the wild ungulates, rather than man. Evolution has resulted in a state of equilibrium in which the parasite produces no overt disease in the animal host. Man, for the most part an accidental host, has not attained this accommodation, as the intense virulence of the human disease indicates. The manner by which the antelope modulates the infection remains a mystery; its elucidation might aid in devising a means of similarly stimulating a protective state in man.

The ecological setting—the landscape epidemiology—is different for each of these disease varieties. Gambian sleeping sickness is generally restricted to the humid forests bordering the lakes and rivers of West and Central Africa, the obligatory habitat of *G. palpalis*, the tsetse species that transmits this form of the disease.

Because rural African populations rarely have the means to obtain water from distant sources, communities tend to form along the banks of rivers and lakes, and village activities—bathing, washing, drawing water, and fishing—take place at the water's edge, making for intense man–fly contact. Epidemics flare from time to time, but generally the disease level is low because this tsetse is, biologically, a relatively inefficient vector. Trypanosomes can readily multiply in *G. palpalis* only shortly after the fly emerges from the pupal stage. Very few older flies are able to act as vectors after feeding upon infected humans.

Sleeping sickness caused by *Trypanosoma rhodesiense* is endemic to the dry savanna woodlands of East and Central Africa, the habitat of both the *G. morsitans* vector and the great herds of antelope that serve as reservoir hosts. Human infections occur when people settle in the savanna or intrude to hunt, gather wood, or graze cattle. The species of vector that transmits this form of the disease is not an equal-opportunity biter; and it prefers to take a blood meal from mammals other than humans. When game becomes scarce, however, the fly will feed on humans. Apparently attracted to large, slow-moving objects, it becomes confused when these sometimes turn out to be vehicles rather than antelope, and it will feed on the passengers. In this curious way, a package tour of East African game parks occasionally includes trypanosomiasis.

There is, then, an intimate relationship between the nature of the ecosystem and the epidemiology of trypanosomiasis. The history of Africa, however, is characterized by continuous ecological change—with felled rain forests succeeded by grasslands and savanna woodlands, an advancing or retreating desert, and shifting distribution or concentration of human inhabitants and wild fauna. These environmental changes have played a crucial role in the epidemiological patterns of the Gambian and Rhodesian forms of trypanosomiasis, particularly where their ranges overlap in east-central Africa.

The activities and diseases of both Africans and colonial expatriates have also contributed to the epidemiological status of trypanosomiasis. Before the nineteenth-century colonial period, trypanosomiasis was confined to a relatively few smoldering foci. Internecine warfare and lack of roads restricted communication and prevented the spread of the infection. The rapid dissemination of sleeping sickness can be traced to the opening up of Africa by the colonial powers. It was the *Pax Britannica* as much as the tsetse that was responsible for the broadcast of infection. How this complex of changing environmental and human factors has influenced epidemicity of the two types of human trypanosomiasis is illustrated, par excellence, by the events that have occurred along the Kenya and Uganda shores of Lake Victoria.

Prior to human settlement, the lake was surrounded by a tropical high forest. Primitive farmers migrated to the lake's shores and felled forest tracts for their shifting agriculture. Forest-inhabiting tsetse were present, but human trypanosomiasis was absent. Eventually, deforestation progressed to such a degree that grassland replaced large areas of forest. The grassland then attracted a second wave of migration—Nilotic pastoralists (that is, herders who originated in the Nile basin) and Bantu cultivators. The combined pressures of grazing and agriculture suppressed forest regeneration and thus maintained a fly-free area beyond the forest that fringed the lake.

In the nineteenth century the society along the lake was devastated by the twin pestilences of smallpox and rinderpest, and agricultural activity diminished. Before the population had time to recover, savanna woodland succeeded the grassland. At the close of the nineteenth century the ecological stage was set for sleeping sickness. The shores of the lake were bordered by a rain forest infested with *G. palpalis*, the tsetse vector of *T. gambiense*. Beyond the forest *G. morsitans*, the vector of *T. rhodesiense*, inhabited the savanna woodland. Still the trypanosome had not made its debut.

The parasite is thought to have been introduced when Sir Henry Morton Stanley, employed at that time in the Congo by the Belgians, mounted an expedition in 1887 to the area of Lake Victoria. Natives in Stanley's retinue, probably infected with *T. gambiense*, may have carried the seeds of the epidemic that was to decimate the population for the next ten years.

By 1910, when the Gambian sleeping sickness began to burn itself out, the number of inhabitants in the area had declined from 300,000 to 100,000. Before the epidemic, the large size and number of human settlements had had the effect of suppressing the faunal population; but as people died of the disease or fled the stricken area, the game reservoirs of *T. rhodesiense* increased and moved into the adjacent savanna woodland. The final epidemiological link in the chain of Rhodesian sleeping sickness—from game to man through woodland-dwelling fly—was now present, to complete the cycle. When government-inspired resettlement was attempted in the 1940s, the migrants rapidly became infected with this highly lethal disease, and once again the inhabitants deserted the land. Today, this potentially rich region is virtually abandoned, occupied only by a few fishermen who are at high risk of contracting the infection.

When I joined the West African Institute for Trypanosomiasis Research in 1951, the entire infected population of Nigeria lay, so to speak, before me, but I was to be introduced to the human disease in a much more personal way and under circumstances that gave me a first glimpse into the meshing of the fly, the trypanosome, the ecosystem, and human behavior.

My friend Dan Quaddo, a Rukuba and in the epithets of that unregenerate colonial era, a pagan (being neither Christian nor Muslim) was the household "small boy" (the domestic of all work, age notwithstanding). He was a small, cheerful, but unbeautiful man; his name meant Son of the Frog, and West African "village" names are bestowed with deadly accuracy. The only maggot in Dan Quaddo's otherwise optimistic disposition was his unfathomable terror of "teef men" (pidgin for burglars, not dentists), and even during the hottest nights of the hot season he would barricade himself within his quarters. I once tried to reason with him: "Dan Quaddo, why do you do this? You are so poor and have so little, why would anyone want to teef you?" I vividly recall his reply, in which he explained with the patience of someone describing an immutable law to a small, rather dense child: "Suh, anyone who teef me be so bad he not need a reason."

A short time after this illuminating conversation he returned to his nearby village, on the slopes of the Bauchi Plateau, and spent several weeks there attending to "family affairs." A few weeks after returning he once again locked, bolted, and shuttered himself within his house, this time complaining not of "teef men," but of devils of fever and headache. The American reaction would be to exorcise these with aspirin, but in Africa, where malaria is commoner than the common cold, the first resort is routinely to the magic of antimalarial drugs. After a time the fever abated, but the headache persisted and Dan Quaddo became uncharacteristically eccentric and surly. He took to putting nonperishables in the refrigerator— theater tickets, tennis balls, my wife's brassière (the "small, small vest for chest"). There was no disputing that what ailed Dan Quaddo was not malaria and that he needed medical attention. In the tropics the microscopic examination of the blood takes pride of diagnostic precedence, and I remember peering into the microscope and seeing, for the first time outside a laboratory classroom, the trypanosomes of a human swimming in the microscopic field and the dancing movement of the red blood cells as they were disturbed by the thrashing parasites. We later found that Dan Quaddo's infection had progressed to the stage where his lymph glands had also been invaded by the Gambian trypanosomes, but fortunately the disease was caught before the central nervous system became involved. He was successfully treated and made an uneventful recovery. However, I was curious about how he had contracted the infection, since we were supposed to be outside the tsetse belt. Inquiry revealed that Dan Quaddo was actually one of the last victims of a cataclysmic sleeping-sickness epidemic, beginning some ten years earlier, that had brought his tribe to the verge of extinction.

In former times the outliers of the typical high forests bordering streams and rivers had penetrated the dry savanna, and these outliers had provided a suitable ecological niche for the tsetse vector. The Rukubas had cut down most of the outliers, but each tribe preserved near its village a small area of forest that was sacred, the *tsafi* grove. The flies had retreated to these groves and were concentrated there in great numbers. Every seven years the elders and the young boys went to their sacred grove for a religious retreat, during which the youngsters were initiated into manhood. The secrets and mysteries of the Rukubas were passed from the old to the young, and the genealogy of the tribe was recounted. Circumcision rites were performed, and the elders harangued the initiates about morality. During these religious retreats man and fly were in close contact, but until the early 1940s the trypanosome was absent. The infection is believed to have originated with a farmer who, taking advantage of the relatively new state of intertribal tranquillity imposed by the colonial government, traveled to the south of the plateau, an area of endemic trypanosomiasis. On his return, this farmer participated in a manhood initiation rite and was a source of infection to the fly and consequently to his coreligionists. The human infection slowly built in intensity, and by the mid-1940s one-fourth of some village populations had been stricken. When the first medical teams were sent to the area, the Rukubas either fled or hostilely ejected them from the villages. In 1944 they were finally convinced of their plight and accepted mass drug treatment and tsetse-eradication campaigns. By the early 1950s the epidemic, except for a trickle of infection, had been brought to a halt. My unfortunate friend Dan Quaddo, whose "family affairs" had really been a *tsafi*-grove ritual, was one of the last to become infected, and he had almost been "teefed" of his life. The trypanosome was indeed, so bad it didn't need a reason to rob him.

The trypanosomes that infect domestic animals are not restricted to any particular forest ecosystem; animal trypanosomiasis exists wherever there are tsetse flies of any species. The presence of wild-game reservoirs—along with the fact that the flies, in all probability, carry the trypanosomes (*T. brucei, T. congolense,* and *T. vivax*)—contributes to a level of transmission so intense and ubiquitous as to effectively preclude stock production in one-fourth of Africa. Nomadic and semisettled cattle-owning tribes have been forced to pasture their animals in the fly-free zones in and near the arid Sahel. As the dry season approaches, the Sahel is no longer able to sustain the herds and the annual trek into the fly-infested Guinea savanna begins. Losses to trypanosomiasis always occur, but where nutrition is adequate and the density of flies not too great, the stock may manage to survive, if not flourish.

The breed of cattle favored by the African pastoralist is the zebu, a large, humpbacked longhorn, well adapted to semiarid conditions. Although it produces relatively high yields of milk and meat, the zebu has the unfortunate disadvantage of being susceptible to trypanosomiasis. There are smaller, even dwarf, breeds of cattle, such as the N'dama and Muturu, that possess remarkably high resistance to or tolerance of the trypanosome. Studies carried out at the Nigerian Institute for Trypanosomiasis Research have proved that the resistance of these breeds is due to a highly efficient immune response. Two conditions are necessary for the attainment of this level of protective immunity. First, the animals must be born of a hyperimmune dam, and second, they must receive an early and continuous infection of trypanosomes, so that they produce a protective antibody.

These tolerant breeds have not as yet been economically exploited, probably because of their small size, although the N'dama is large enough to be used for meat. Crossbreeding with zebu or European breeds does not result in offspring capable of developing hyperimmunity.

Combating trypanosomiasis calls for heroic measures, but because of the severity of the side effects, the remedies may not be practicable. The battle against the disease has included massive alteration of the environment, social dislocation, wholesale slaughter of wild fauna, and the mass administration of toxic drugs. A commonly employed means of control has been to deny the tsetse its required habitat by selective or large-scale deforestation. Fly-free zones can only be maintained by intensive land use, brought about by the collectivization of the population into large agricultural villages and townships. This forced dislocation from the traditional, stable life in small, scattered tribal groups has resulted in a disturbing upheaval of the social order.

Perhaps the most controversial control measure was the game-destruction program carried out in East Africa during the 1950s. Designed to open up land to human settlement, this scheme was faultless in its logic. Game animals harbor *T. rhodesiense* and are the main source of blood for the tsetse; therefore, destroying the large fauna means good riddance to both trypanosome and fly. After the campaign, however, small mammals survived in sufficient numbers to support the fly population. Also, as the game was decimated, herdsmen moved their cattle into the cleared areas, the fly began to feed on the livestock and pastoralists, and the result was continued and intensified transmission of both animal and human trypanosomes. Finally, revulsion against the studied slaughter brought the program to a halt.

Another possibility is to control the spread of the disease by means of insecticides. Ironically, one researcher, Dr. Walter Ormerod, has proposed that the use of insecticides was a major, if not prime, contributor to the great drought that recently ravaged sub-Saharan Africa. The reasoning of this hypothesis is as follows: Increasing urbanization and prosperity in West Africa precipitated a demand for meat. Traditional cattle-owning tribes increased the size of their herds to match the market. Widespread, government-sponsored aerial spraying of insecticides, in conjunction with mass chemoprophylactic injections of cattle, followed, permitting growth of herds not only in the Sahel but also in the adjacent Guinea savanna. The large numbers of cattle overgrazed the meager stands of grass and other plant life in this fragile ecosystem, resulting in a higher reflectance of sunlight from the denuded land. There is good evidence that such a situation causes a decrease in rainfall, and in this region matters did indeed proceed to a point where the result was climatic havoc.

Despite more than seventy years of research and effort, the freeing of Africa from trypanosomiasis has not been realized. The effective, practicable means of control now available are too harsh. Except for limited areas, insecticide spraying is too costly. Governments of the new African nations are often too poor in economic and technical resources to maintain the anti-trypanosome and anti-tsetse programs begun during the colonial era.

Drug treatment of infected people has brought about a decline in human trypanosomiasis but the trypanosomes can develop resistance. Confronted with this impasse, scientists have long sought the biological "magic bullet"—immunization—as a solution of the problem. Vaccination has brought many of the great scourges of mankind, such as smallpox and yellow fever, under control without necessitating changes in the environment or turmoil in the socioeconomic order. But unlike the immunologically amenable bacterial and viral pathogens, the trypanosome has confounded all attempts to induce protective immunity. The reason for this failure stems from the parasite's ability to elude the host's immune defense by a process known as antigenic variation.

There is currently great concern over the antigenic shift of the influenza virus, a phenomenon that seems to occur about every ten years. A trypanosome undergoes the same process, but a new antigenic variant arises every five to ten days. This is tantamount to the host's being assaulted by a new, personal epidemic each and every week.

During the course of a trypanosomal infection the host may develop an antibody that eliminates most, but not all, of the trypanosomes. The survivors are of a different antigenic character from the others, so the antibody fails to recognize them. The variant trypanosomes then begin to proliferate in the blood stream. The host responds by producing a new specific antibody. The process is repeated over and over, for the trypanosome possesses the remarkable ability of producing a large, probably infinite, number of antigenic variants.

The underlying mechanism responsible for antigenic variation has been the subject of a long controversy between those who hold it to be a selective process, which presupposes a starting parasite population of one predominant and many minor variants, and those who believe that antigenic variants arise by mutation. There are difficulties in supporting either of these explanations by experimental evidence. Electron microscopy and immunochemical analysis suggest that the trypanosome antigen—the face the parasite

presents to its world—is a glycoprotein coat, or pellicle, situated outside the trypanosome's limiting plasma membrane. Apparently this coat is periodically shed, and the parasite, acting as its own couturier, designs and makes a new antigenic garment.

T. vivax, the important pathogen of livestock, seems to have developed still another maneuver to survive in the immunized host—antigenic mimicry. This trypanosome may be able to absorb a coat of host serum protein that disguises its alien status and also acts as a protective shield against any antibody that the host may produce. A similar phenomenon, the absorption of host substances to the external parasite surface, occurs in the schistosome blood flukes of man. Antigenic disguise may thus be another important adaptive evolutionary strategy that permits some parasites to exist in the immunized host.

New methods for dealing with human and animal trypanosomiasis are urgently needed. However, the extent of research and the amount of resources invested are minuscule compared to the magnitude of the problem. A new trypanocidal drug has not been added to the chemotherapeutic armamentarium for twenty years. Pharmaceutical companies candidly admit that the high cost of development and the potentially poor profits from selling to the generally impoverished underdeveloped nations have virtually taken them out of tropical-disease research. I feel confident, however, that improved means of combating the infections will eventually be forthcoming. A quality of biomedical science is its incurable optimism that all things are possible, given time and support.

But it may well be that Africa's real problems will commence with the effective control of trypanosomiasis. Scientists and the administrators carrying out the practical applications of research often fail to recognize that they are engaged in a gigantic chess game. As one enemy piece is captured, other pieces move to threaten. As trypanosomiasis is conquered, overgrazing, soil erosion, social disruption, and faunal extinction may result. Until the time comes when scientists and their technical-administrative partners appreciate the grand strategy of acting sanely and effectively to protect the well-being of all Africa's citizens, both two-legged and four-legged, we may applaud the cosmic wisdom that has made the tsetse, rather than man, Africa's custodian.

REFERENCES

Desowitz, R. S. 1959. Studies on immunity and host-parasite relationships. I, The immune response of resistant and susceptible breeds of cattle to trypanosomal challenge. *Annals of Tropical Medicine and Parasitology* 53:293–313.

Duggan, A. J. 1962. The occurrence of human trypanosomiasis among the Rukuba tribe of northern Nigeria. *Journal of Tropical Medicine and Hygiene* 65:151–63.

Edge, P. G. 1938. The incidence and distribution of human trypanosomiasis in British tropical Africa. *Tropical Diseases Bulletin*, November 1938, pp. 3–18.

Ford, J. 1971. *The role of trypanosomiases in African ecology.* Oxford: Clarendon Press.

McKelvey, J. J., Jr. 1973. *Man against tsetse: struggle for Africa.* Ithaca, Cornell University Press.

Morris, K. R. S. 1960. Studies on the epidemiology of sleeping sickness in east Africa. III, The endemic area of Lakes

Edward and George in Uganda. *Transactions of the Royal Society of Tropical Medicine and Hygiene* 54:212–24.

Mulligan, H. W. 1970. *The African trypanosomiases.* New York: Halsted Press.

Ormerod, W. E. 1976. Ecological effect of the control of African trypanosomiasis. *Science* 191:815–21.

Terry, R. J. 1976. Immunity to African trypanosomiasis. In *Immunology of parasitic infections.* ed. S. Cohen and E. H. Sadun. Oxford: Blackwell Scientific Publications.

Vickerman, K. 1974. Antigenic variation in African trypanosomes. In *Parasites in the immunized host: mechanisms of survival.* Ciba Foundation Symposium 25 (new series). Amsterdam: Associated Scientific Publishers.

✤ 11

Social Inequalities and Emerging Infectious Diseases

Paul Farmer

Emerging diseases are thought of as "new" diseases that are a threat to the health of people in the United States. The movie Outbreak *and the best-seller* The Hot Zone—*both scary stories about strange hemorraghic fevers like Ebola—represent popularizations of the topic of emerging infectious disease. But emerging disease also refers to old diseases, such as malaria or tuberculosis, that may have evolved chemotherapy-resistant strains. The evolution of antibiotic resistance, as we saw in the selections on Darwinian medicine, is certainly the result of humans changing the environment in which pathogens reproduce. But how do we define the environment? The epidemiological study of emerging infectious diseases generally recognizes the importance of human factors in disease transmission. Things like ecological disruption from the building of roads, overuse of agricultural pesticides, or rapid spread of infections by air travel are often pointed out. These are thought to reflect environmental influences.*

Anthropologists believe that it is also important to recognize what is not *pointed out or discussed when it comes to these new public health threats. One issue that seems left out of discussions of disease ecology is a simple and obvious one: the role of poverty and social inequalities. The goal of this selection, published for an audience of researchers in emerging infectious diseases, is to ask some difficult questions about what is not currently being investigated. This*

"critical" approach fits into the area of political ecology. As the author says, the questions are less about pig–duck agriculture (the Asian ecological setting that is thought to play a key role in the continuation of annual influenza epidemics) and more about the influence of World Bank policies on the spread of infectious disease. The political dimensions of his argument for diseases such as Ebola, TB, and AIDS, or the idea of the unnatural history of disease, is clear in this selection. The political-ecological approach is still young, but the author prescribes some key areas for more research.

Political ecology challenges some of the standard presuppositions that are used in defining health problems. In many ways, this selection announces a research agenda rather than demonstrating ecological research results. The challenge to political-ecological medical anthropology will be to demonstrate the causal chain at different levels of reality—the microbe, the individual, the society, the nation, and the World Bank.

Paul Farmer, the author of this selection, is an anthropologist and practicing physician who has done important research on the social dimensions of AIDS in Haiti. Through a nonprofit organization called Partners in Health he plays a role in community-oriented clinics in U.S. inner cities and in Haiti, Peru, and other parts of the underdeveloped world. His most recent book is called Women, Poverty, and AIDS.

As you read this selection, consider these questions:

- *If the political-ecological argument is true, what are the implications for the distribution of resources to deal with emerging infectious diseases?*

- *Why do many people (including physicians and epidemiologists) feel uncomfortable when an ecological analysis is expanded to the world of politics? Are political dimensions so complicated and thorny that they make solutions seem less imaginable?*

- *How accurate is the metaphor of semipermeable national borders that allow diseases to pass freely but bureaucratically restrict the flow of cures?*

The past decade has been one of the most eventful in the long history of infectious diseases. There are multiple indexes of these events and of the rate at which our knowledge base has grown. The sheer number of relevant publications indicates explosive growth; moreover, new means of monitoring antimicrobial resistance patterns are being used along with the rapid sharing of information (as well as speculation and misinformation) through means that did not exist even 10 years ago. Then there are the microbes themselves. One of the explosions in question—perhaps the most remarked upon—is that of "emerging infectious diseases." Among the diseases considered "emerging," some are regarded as genuinely new; AIDS and Brazilian purpuric fever are examples. Others have newly identified etiologic agents or have again burst dramatically onto the scene. For example, the syndromes caused by Hantaan virus have been known in Asia for centuries but now seem to be spreading beyond Asia because of ecologic and economic transformations that increase contact between humans and rodents.

Neuroborreliosis was studied long before the monikers Lyme disease and *Borrelia burgdorferi* were coined, and before suburban reforestation and golf courses complicated the equation by creating an environment agreeable to both ticks and affluent humans. Hemorrhagic fevers, including Ebola, were described long ago, and their etiologic agents were in many cases identified in previous decades. Still other diseases grouped under the "emerging" rubric are ancient and well-known foes that have somehow changed, in pathogenicity or distribution. Multidrug-resistant tuberculosis (TB) and invasive or necrotizing Group A streptococcal infection are cases in point.

Like all new categories, "emerging infectious diseases" has benefits and limitations. The former are well known: a sense of urgency, notoriously difficult to arouse in large bureaucracies, has been marshaled, funds have been channeled, conferences convened, articles written, and a journal dedicated to the study of these diseases has been founded. The research and action agendas elaborated in response to the perceived emergence of new infections have been, by and large, sound. But the concept, like some of the diseases associated with it, is complex. Its complexity has, in some instances, hampered the learning process. A richly textured understanding of emerging infections will be grounded in critical and reflexive study of how learning occurs. Units of analysis and key terms will be scrutinized and defined more than once. This process will include regular rethinking not only of methods and study design, but also of the validity of causal inference and reflection on the limits of human knowledge. This study of the process, loosely known as epistemology, often happens in retrospect, but many of the chief contributors to the growing research in emerging infectious diseases have examined the epistemologic issues surrounding their work and are familiar with the multifactorial nature of disease emergence: "Responsible factors include ecological changes, such as those due to agricultural or economic development or to anomalies in the climate; human demographic changes and behavior; travel and commerce; technology and industry; microbial adaptation and change; and breakdown of public health measures."[1] A recent Institute of Medicine report on emerging infections does not even categorize microbial threats by type of agent, but rather according to factors held to be related to their emergence.[2]

In studying emerging infectious diseases, many thus make a distinction between a host of phenomena directly related to human actions—from improved laboratory techniques and scientific discovery to economic "development," global warming, and failures of public health—and another set of phenomena much less common and related to changes in the microbes themselves. Close examination of microbial mutations often shows that, again, human actions have played a large role in enhancing pathogenicity or increasing resistance to antimicrobial agents. In one long list of emerging viral infections, for example, only the emergence of Rift Valley fever is attributed to a possible change in virulence or pathogenicity, and this only after other, social factors for which there is better evidence.[1] No need, then, to call for a heightened awareness of the sociogenesis, or "anthropogenesis," of emerging infections. Some bench scientists in the field are more likely to refer to social factors and less likely to make immodest claims of causality about them than are behavioral scientists who study disease. Yet a critical epistemology of emerging infectious diseases is still in its early stages of development; a key task of such a critical approach would be to take existing conceptual frameworks, including that of disease emergence, and ask, What is obscured in this way of conceptualizing disease? What is brought into relief? A first step in understanding the "epistemological dimension" of disease emergence, notes Eckardt, involves developing "a certain sensitivity to the terms we are used to."[3]

A heightened sensitivity to other common rubrics and terms shows that certain aspects of disease emergence are brought into relief while others are obscured. When we think of "tropical diseases," malaria comes quickly to mind. But not too long ago, malaria was an important problem in areas far from the tropics. Although there is imperfect overlap between malaria as currently defined and the malaria of the mid-19th century, some U.S. medical historians agree with contemporary assessments: malaria "was the most important disease in the country at the time." In the Ohio River Valley, according to Daniel Drake's 1850 study, thousands died in seasonal epidemics. During the second decade of the 20th century, when the population of 12 southern states was approximately 25 million, an estimated million cases of malaria occurred each year. Malaria's decline in this country was "due only in small part to measures aimed directly against it, but more to agricultural development and other factors some of which are still not clear."[4] These factors include poverty and social inequalities, which led, increasingly, to differential morbidity with the development of improved housing, land drainage, mosquito repellents, nets, and electric fans—all well beyond the reach of those most at risk for malaria. In fact, many "tropical" diseases predominantly affect the poor; the groups at risk for these diseases are often bounded more by socioeconomic status than by latitude.

Similarly, the concept of "health transitions" is influential in what some have termed "the new public health" and in the international financial institutions that so often direct development efforts.[5] The model of health transitions suggests that nation-states, as they develop, go through predictable epidemiologic transformations. Death due to infectious causes is supplanted by death due to malignancies and to complications of coronary artery disease, which occur at a more advanced age, reflecting progress. Although it describes broad patterns now found throughout the world, the concept of national health transitions also

masks other realities, including intranational illness and death differentials that are more tightly linked to local inequalities than to nationality. For example, how do the variables of class and race fit into such paradigms? In Harlem, where the age-specific death rate in several groups is higher than in Bangladesh, leading causes of death are infectious diseases and violence.[6]

Units of analysis are similarly up for grabs. When David Satcher, director of the Centers for Disease Control and Prevention (CDC), writing of emerging infectious diseases, reminds us that "the health of the individual is best ensured by maintaining or improving the health of the entire community,"[7] we should applaud his clearsighted-ness but go on to ask, What constitutes "the entire community"? In the 1994 outbreak of cryptosporidiosis in Milwaukee, for example, the answer might be "part of a city."[8] In other instances, community means a village or the passengers on an airplane. But the most common unit of analysis in public health, the nation-state, is not all that relevant to organisms such as dengue virus, *Vibrio cholerae* O139, human immunodeficiency virus (HIV), penicillinase-producing *Neisseria gonorrhoeae*, and hepatitis B virus. Such organisms have often ignored political boundaries, even though their presence may cause a certain degree of turbulence at national borders. The dynamics of emerging infections will not be captured in national analyses any more than the diseases are contained by national boundaries, which are themselves emerging entities—most of the world's nations are, after all, 20th-century creations.

Here I have discussed the limitations of three important ways of viewing the health of populations—tropical medicine, "the" epidemiologic transition, and nation health profiles—because models and even assumptions about infectious diseases need to be dynamic, systemic, and critical. That is, models with explanatory power must be able to track rapidly changing clinical, even molecular, phenomena and link them to the large-scale (sometimes transnational) social forces that manifestly shape the contours of disease emergence. I refer, here, to questions less on the order of how pig–duck agriculture might be related to the antigenic shifts central to influenza pandemics, and more on the order of the following: Are World Bank policies related to the spread of HIV, as has recently been claimed?[9] What is the relationship between international shipping practices and the spread of cholera from Asia to South America and elsewhere in the Western Hemisphere?[10,11] How is genocide in Rwanda related to cholera in Zaire?[12]

The study of anything said to be emerging tends to be dynamic. But the very notion of emergence in heterogeneous populations poses questions of analysis that are rarely tackled, even in modern epidemiology, which, as McMichael has recently noted, "assigns a primary importance to studying interindividual variations in risk. By concentrating on these specific and presumed free-range individual behaviors, we thereby pay less attention to the underlying social-historical influences on behavioral choices, patterns, and population health."[13] A critical (and self-critical) approach would ask how existing frameworks might limit our ability to discern trends that can be linked to the emergence of diseases. Not all social-production-of-disease theories are equally alive to the importance of how relative social and economic positioning—inequality—affects risk for infection. In its report on emerging infections, the Institute of Medicine lists neither poverty nor inequality as "causes of emergence."[2]

A critical approach pushes the limits of existing academic politesse to ask harder and rarely raised questions: What are the mechanisms by which changes in agriculture have led to outbreaks of Argentine and Bolivian hemorrhagic fever, and how might these mechanisms be related to international trade agreements, such as the General Agreement on Tariffs and Trade and the North American Free Trade Agreement? How might institutional racism be related to urban crime and the outbreaks of multidrug-resistant TB in New York prisons? Does the privatization of health services buttress social inequalities, increasing risk for certain infections—and death—among the poor of sub-Saharan Africa and Latin America? How do the colonial histories of Belgium and Germany and the neocolonial histories of France and the United States tie in to genocide and a subsequent epidemic of cholera among Rwandan refugees? Similar questions may be productively posed in regard to many diseases now held to be emerging.

EMERGING HOW AND TO WHAT EXTENT? THE CASE OF EBOLA

Hemorrhagic fevers have been known in Africa since well before the continent was dubbed "the white man's grave," an expression that, when deployed in reference to a region with high rates of premature death, speaks volumes about the differential valuation of human lives. Ebola itself was isolated fully two decades ago.[14] Its appearance in human hosts has at times been insidious but more often takes the form of explosive eruptions. In accounting for recent outbreaks, it is unnecessary to postulate a change in filovirus virulence through mutation. The Institute of

Medicine lists a single "factor facilitating emergence" for filoviruses: "virus-infected monkeys shipped from developing countries via air."[2]

Other factors are easily identified. Like that of many infectious diseases, the distribution of Ebola outbreaks is tied to regional trade networks and other evolving social systems. And, like those of most infectious diseases, Ebola explosions affect, researchers aside, certain groups (people living in poverty, health care workers who serve the poor) but not others in close physical proximity. Take, for example, the 1976 outbreak in Zaire, which affected 318 persons. Although respiratory spread was speculated, it has not been conclusively demonstrated as a cause of human cases. Most expert observers thought that the cases could be traced to failure to follow contact precautions, as well as to improper sterilization of syringes and other paraphernalia, measures that in fact, once taken, terminated the outbreak.[15] On closer scrutiny, such an explanation suggests that Ebola does not emerge randomly: in Mobutu's Zaire, one's likelihood of coming into contact with unsterile syringes is inversely proportional to one's social status. Local élites and sectors of the expatriate community with access to high-quality biomedical services (viz., the European and American communities and not the Rwandan refugees) are unlikely to contract such a disease.

The changes involved in the disease's visibility are equally embedded in social context. The emergence of Ebola has also been a question of our consciousness. Modern communications, including print and broadcast media, have been crucial in the construction of Ebola—a minor player, statistically speaking, in Zaire's long list of fatal infections—as an emerging infectious disease.[16] Through Cable News Network (CNN) and other television stations, Kikwit became, however briefly, a household word in parts of Europe and North America. Journalists and novelists wrote best-selling books about small but horrific plagues, which in turn became profitable cinema. Thus, symbolically and proverbially, Ebola spread like wildfire—as a danger potentially without limit. It emerged.

EMERGING FROM WHERE? THE CASE OF TB

TB is said to be another emerging disease, in which case, emerging is synonymous with reemerging. Its recrudescence is often attributed to the advent of HIV—the institute of Medicine lists "an increase in immunosuppressed populations" as the sole factor facilitating the resurgence of TB[2]—and the emergence of drug resistance. A recent book on TB, subtitled "How the battle against tuberculosis was won—and lost," argues that "Throughout the developed world, with the successful application of triple therapy and the enthusiastic promotion of prevention, the death rate from tuberculosis came tumbling down."[17] But was this claim ever documented? Granted, the discovery of effective anti-TB therapies has saved the lives of hundreds of thousands of TB patients, many in industrialized countries. But TB—once the leading cause of death among young adults in the industrialized world—was already declining there well before the 1943 discovery of streptomycin. In the rest of the world, and in pockets of the United States, TB remains undaunted by ostensibly effective drugs, which are used too late, inappropriately, or not at all: "It is sufficiently shameful," notes one of the world's leading authorities on TB, "that 30 years after recognition of the capacity of triple-therapy . . . to elicit 95%+ cure rates, tuberculosis prevalence rates for *many* nations remain unchanged."[18] Some estimate that more than 1.7 billion persons are infected with quiescent, but viable, *Mycobacterium tuberculosis* and, dramatic shifts in local epidemiology aside, a global analysis does not suggest major decreases in the importance of TB as a cause of death. TB has retreated in certain populations, maintained a steady state in others, and surged forth in still others, remaining, at this writing, the world's leading infectious cause of adult deaths.[19]

At mid-century, TB was still acknowledged as the "great white plague." What explains the invisibility of this killer by the 1970s and 1980s? Again, one must turn to the study of disease awareness, that is, of consciousness and publicity, and their relation to power and wealth. "The neglect of tuberculosis as a major public health priority over the past two decades is simply extraordinary," wrote Murray in 1991. "Perhaps the most important contributor to this state of ignorance was the greatly reduced clinical and epidemiologic importance of tuberculosis in the wealthy nations."[20] Thus TB has not really emerged so much as emerged from the ranks of the poor.[21,22] An implication, clearly, is that one place for diseases to hide is among poor people, especially when the poor are socially and medically segregated from those whose deaths might be considered more important.

When complex forces move more poor people into the United States, an increase in TB incidence is inevitable. In a recent study of the disease among foreign-born persons in the United States, immigration is essentially credited with the increased incidence of TB-related disease.[23] The authors note that in some of the immigrants' countries of origin the annual rate of infection is up to 200 times that registered in the United States; moreover, many persons with TB in the United States live in homeless shelters, correctional facilities, and camps for migrant workers. But there is no discussion of poverty or inequality, even though these are, along with war, leading reasons for both the high rates of TB and for immigration to the United States. "The major determinants of risk in the foreign-born population," conclude the authors, "were the region of the world from which the person emigrated and the number of years in the United States."

GOING WHERE? THE CASE OF HIV

To understand the complexity of the issues—medical, social, and communicational—that surround the emergence of a disease into public view, consider AIDS. In the early 1980s, the public was informed by health officials that AIDS had probably emerged from Haiti. In December 1982, for example, a physician affiliated with the National Cancer Institute was widely quoted in the popular press stating that "We suspect that this may be an epidemic Haitian virus that was brought back to the homosexual population in the United States."[24] This proved incorrect, but not before damage to Haitian tourism had been done. Result: more poverty, a yet steeper slope of inequality and vulnerability to disease, including AIDS. The label "AIDS vector" was also damaging to the million or so Haitians living elsewhere in the Americas and certainly hampered public health efforts among them.[25]

HIV disease has since become the most extensively studied infection in human history. But some questions are much better studied than are others. And error is worth studying, too. Careful investigation of the mechanisms by which immodest claims are propagated (as regards Haiti and AIDS, these mechanisms included "exoticization" of Haiti, racism, the existence of influential folk models about Haitians and Africans, and the conflation of poverty and cultural difference) is an important yet neglected part of a critical epistemology of emerging infectious diseases. Also underinvestigated are considerations of the pandemic's dynamic. HIV may not have come from Haiti, but it was going to Haiti. Critical reexamination of the Caribbean AIDS pandemic showed that the distribution of HIV does not follow national borders, but rather the contours of a transnational socioeconomic order. Furthermore, much of the spread of HIV in the 1970s and 1980s moved along international "fault lines," tracking along steep gradients of inequality, which are also paths of migrant labor and sexual commerce.[26]

In an important overview of the pandemic's first decade, Mann and co-workers observe that its course "within and through global society is not being affected—in any serious manner—by the actions taken at the national or international level."[27] HIV has emerged but is going where? Why? And how fast? The Institute of Medicine lists several factors facilitating the emergence of HIV: "urbanization; changes in lifestyles/mores; increased intravenous drug abuse; international travel; medical technology."[2] Much more could be said. HIV has spread across the globe, often wildly, but rarely randomly. Like TB, HIV infection is entrenching itself in the ranks of the poor or otherwise disempowered. Take, as an example, the rapid increase in AIDS incidence among women. In a 1992 report, the United Nations observed that "for most women, the major risk factor for HIV infection is being married. Each day a further three thousand women become infected, and five hundred infected women die."[28] It is not marriage per se, however, that places young women at risk. Throughout the world, most women with HIV infection, married or not, are living in poverty. The means by which confluent social forces, such as gender inequality and poverty, come to be embodied as risk for infection with this emerging pathogen have been neglected in biomedical, epidemiologic, and even social science studies on AIDS. As recently as October 1994—15 years into an ever-emerging pandemic—a *Lancet* editorial could comment, "We are not aware of other investigators who have considered the influence of socioeconomic status on mortality in HIV-infected individuals."[29] Thus, in AIDS, the general rule that the effects of certain types of social forces on health are unlikely to be studied applies in spite of widespread impressions to the contrary.

AIDS has always been a strikingly patterned pandemic. Regardless of the message of public health slogans—"AIDS is for Everyone"—some are at high risk for HIV infection, while others, clearly, are at lower risk. Furthermore, although AIDS eventually causes death in almost all HIV-infected patients, the course of HIV disease varies. Disparities in the course of the disease have sparked the search for hundreds of cofactors, from *Mycoplasma* and ulcerating genital lesions to voodoo rites and psychological predisposition. However, not a single association has been compellingly shown to explain disparities in distribution or outcome of HIV disease. The only well-demonstrated cofactors are social inequalities, which have structured not only the contours of the AIDS pandemic, but also the course of the disease once a patient is infected.[30-33] The advent of more effective antiviral agents promises to heighten those disparities even further: a three-drug regimen that includes a protease inhibitor will cost $12,000 to $16,000 a year.[34]

QUESTIONS FOR A CRITICAL EPISTEMOLOGY OF EMERGING INFECTIOUS DISEASES

Ebola, TB, and HIV infection are in no way unique in demanding contextualization through social science approaches. These approaches include the grounding of case histories and local epidemics in the larger biosocial systems in which they take shape and demand exploration of social inequalities. Why, for example, were there 10,000 cases of diphtheria in Russia from 1990 to 1993? It is easy enough to argue that the excess cases were due to a failure to vaccinate.[35] But only in linking this distal (and, in sum, technical) cause to the much more complex socioeconomic transformations altering the region's illness and death patterns will compelling explanations emerge.[36,37]

Standard epidemiology, narrowly focused on individual risk and short on critical theory, will not reveal these deep socioeconomic transformations, nor will it connect them to disease emergence. "Modern epidemiology," observes one of its leading contributors, is "oriented to explaining and quantifying the bobbing of corks on the surface waters, while largely disregarding the stronger undercurrents that determine where, on average, the cluster of corks ends up along the shoreline of risk."[13] Neither will standard journalistic approaches add much: "Amidst a flood of information," notes the chief journalistic chronicler of disease emergence, "analysis and context are evaporating . . . Outbreaks of flesh eating bacteria may command headlines, but local failures to fully vaccinate preschool children garner little attention unless there is an epidemic."[38]

Research questions identified by various blue-ribbon panels are important for the understanding and eventual control of emerging infectious diseases.[39,40] Yet both the diseases and popular and scientific commentary on them pose a series of corollary questions, which, in turn, demand research that is the exclusive province of neither social scientists nor bench scientists, clinicians, or epidemiologists. Indeed, genuinely transdisciplinary collaboration will be necessary to tackle the problems posed by emerging infectious diseases. As prolegomena, four areas of corollary research are easily identified. In each is heard the recurrent leitmotiv of inequality:

Social Inequalities

Study of the reticulated links between social inequalities and emerging disease would not construe the poor simply as "sentinel chickens," but instead would ask, What are the precise mechanisms by which these diseases come to have their effects in some bodies but not in others? What propagative effects might social inequalities per se contribute?[41] Such queries were once major research questions for epidemiol and social medicine but have fallen out of favor, leaving a vacuum in which immodest claims of causality are easily staked. "To date," note Krieger and co-workers in a recent, magisterial review, "only a small fraction of epidemiological research in the United States has investigated the effects of racism on health."[42] They join others in noting a similar dearth of attention to the effects of sexism and class differences; studies that examine the conjoint influence of these social forces are virtually nonexistent.[43,44]

And yet social inequalities have sculpted not only the distribution of emerging diseases, but also the course of disease in those affected by them, a fact that is often downplayed: "Although there are many similarities between our vulnerability to infectious diseases and that of our ancestors, there is one distinct difference: we have the benefit of extensive scientific knowledge."[7] True enough, but Who are "we"? Those most at risk for emerging infectious diseases generally do not, in fact, have the benefit of cutting-edge scientific knowledge. We live in a world where infections pass easily across borders—social and geographic—while resources, including cumulative scientific knowledge, are blocked at customs.

Transnational Forces

"Travel is a potent force in disease emergence and spread," as Wilson has reminded us, and the "current volume, speed, and reach of travel are unprecedented."[45] Although the smallpox and measles epidemics following the European colonization of the Americas were early, deadly reminders of the need for systemic understandings of microbial traffic, there has been, in recent decades, a certain reification of the notion of the "catchment area." A useful means of delimiting a sphere of action—a district, a county, a country—is erroneously elevated to the status of explanatory principle whenever the geographic unit of analysis is other than that defined by the disease itself. Almost all diseases held to be emerging—from the increasing number of drug-resistant diseases to the great pandemics of HIV infection and cholera—stand as

modern rebukes to the parochialism of this and other public health constructs.[46] And yet a critical sociology of liminality of both the advancing, transnational edges of pandemics and also the impress of human-made administrative and political boundaries on disease emergence has yet to be attempted.

The study of borders qua borders means, increasingly, the study of social inequalities. Many political borders serve as semipermeable membranes, often quite open to diseases and yet closed to the free movement of cures. Thus may inequalities of access be created or buttressed at borders, even when pathogens cannot be so contained. Research questions might include, for example, What effects might the interface between two very different types of health care systems have on the rate of advance of an emerging disease? What turbulence is introduced when the border in question is between a rich and a poor nation? Writing of health issues at the U.S.-Mexican border, Warner notes that "It is unlikely that any other binational border has such variety in health status, entitlements, and utilization."[47] Among the infectious diseases registered at this border are multidrug-resistant TB, rabies, dengue, and sexually transmitted diseases including HIV infection (said to be due, in part, to "cross-border use of 'red-light' districts").

Methods and theories relevant to the study of borders and emerging infections would come from disciplines ranging from the social sciences to molecular biology: mapping the emergence of diseases is now more feasible with the use of restriction fragment length polymorphism and other new technologies.[48] Again, such investigations will pose difficult questions in a world where plasmids can move, but compassion is often grounded.

The Dynamics of Change

Can we elaborate lists of the differentially weighted factors that promote or retard the emergence or reemergence of infectious diseases? It has been argued that such analyses will perforce be historically deep and geographically broad, and they will at the same time be processual, incorporating concepts of change. Above all, they will seek to incorporate complexity rather than to merely dissect it. As Levins has recently noted, "effective analysis of emerging diseases must recognize the study of complexity as perhaps the central general scientific problem of our time."[49] Can integrated mathematical modeling be linked to new ways of configuring systems, avoiding outmoded units of analyses, such as the nation-state, in favor of the more fluid biosocial networks through which most pathogens clearly move? Can our embrace of complexity also include social complexity and the unequal positioning of groups within larger populations? Such perspectives could be directed towards mapping the progress of diseases from cholera to AIDS, and would permit us to take up more unorthodox research subjects—for example, the effects of World Bank projects and policies on diseases from onchocerciasis to plague.

Critical Epistemology

Many have already asked, What qualifies as an emerging infectious disease? More critical questions might include, Why do some persons constitute "risk groups," while others are "individuals at risk"? These are not merely nosologic questions; they are canonical ones. Why are some approaches and subjects considered appropriate for publication in influential journals, while others are dismissed out of hand? A critical epistemology would explore the boundaries of polite and impolite discussion in science. A trove of complex, affect-laden issues—attribution of blame to perceived vectors of infection, identification of scapegoats and victims, the role of stigma—are rarely discussed in academic medicine, although they are manifestly part and parcel of many epidemics.

Finally, why are some epidemics visible to those who fund research and services, while others are invisible? In its recent statements on TB and emerging infections, for example, the World Health Organization uses the threat of contagion to motivate wealthy nations to invest in disease surveillance and control out of self-interest—an age-old public health approach acknowledged in the Institute of Medicine's report on emerging infections: "Diseases that appear not to threaten the United States directly rarely elicit the political support necessary to maintain control efforts."[2] If related to a study under consideration, questions of power and control over funds, must be discussed. That they are not is more a marker of analytic failures than of editorial standards.

Ten years ago, the sociologist of science Bruno Latour reviewed hundreds of articles appearing in several Pasteur-era French scientific reviews to constitute what he called an "anthropology of the sciences" (he objected to the term epistemology). Latour cast his net widely. "There is no essential difference between the human and social sciences and the exact or natural sciences," he wrote, "because there is no more science than there is society. I have spoken of the Pasteurians as they spoke of their microbes"[50] (Here, perhaps, is

another reason to engage in a "proactive" effort to explore themes usually relegated to the margins of scientific inquiry: those of us who describe the comings and goings of microbes—feints, parries, emergences, retreats—may one day be subjected to the scrutiny of future students of the subject.)

Microbes remain the world's leading causes of death.[51] In "The conquest of infectious diseases: who are we kidding?" the authors argue that "clinicians, microbiologists, and public health professionals must work together to prevent infectious diseases and to detect emerging diseases quickly."[52] But past experience with epidemics suggests that other voices and perspectives could productively complicate the discussion. In every major retrospective study of infectious disease outbreaks, the historical regard has shown us that what was not examined during an epidemic is often as important as what was[53,54] and that social inequalities were important in the contours of past disease emergence. The facts have taught us that our approach must be dynamic, systemic, and critical. In addition to historians, then, anthropologists and sociologists accountable to history and political economy have much to add, as do the critical epidemiologists mentioned above.[55–58]

My intention, here, is ecumenical and complementary. A critical framework would not aspire to supplant the methods of the many disciplines, from virology to molecular epidemiology, which now concern themselves with emerging diseases. "The key task for medicine," argued the pioneers Eisenberg and Kleinman some 15 years ago, "is not to diminish the role of the biomedical sciences in the theory and practice of medicine but to supplement them with an equal application of the social sciences in order to provide both a more comprehensive understanding of disease and better care of the patient. The problem is not 'too much science,' but too narrow a view of the sciences relevant to medicine."[59]

A critical anthropology of emerging infections is young, but it is not embryonic. At any rate, much remains to be done and the tasks themselves are less clear perhaps than their inherent difficulties. The philosopher Michel Serres once observed that the border between the natural and the human sciences was not to be traced by clean, sharp lines. Instead, this border recalled the Northwest Passage: long and perilously complicated, its currents and inlets often leading nowhere, dotted with innumerable islands and occasional floes.[60] Serres' metaphor reminds us that a sea change is occurring in the study of infectious disease even as it grows, responding, often, to new challenges—and sometimes to old challenges newly perceived.

REFERENCES

1. Morse S. Factors in the emergence of infectious diseases. Emerging Infectious Diseases 1995;1:7–15.
2. Lederberg J, Shope RE, Oaks SC. Emerging infections: microbial threats to health in the United States. Washington, D.C.: National Academy Press, 1992.
3. Eckardt I. Challenging complexity: conceptual issues in an approach to new disease. Ann New York Acad Sci 1994;740:408–17.
4. Levine N. Editor's preface to selections from Drake D. Malaria in the interior valley of North America. Urbana: University of Illinois Press, 1964 (1850).
5. Frenk J, Chacon F. Bases conceptuales de la nueva salud internacional. Salud Pública Méx 1991;33:307–13.
6. McCord C, Freeman H. Excess mortality in Harlem. N Engl J Med, 1990;322:173–7.
7. Satcher D. Emerging infections: getting ahead of the curve. Emerging Infectious Diseases 1995;1:1–6.
8. MacKenzie W, Hoxie N, Proctor M, Gradus MS, Blair KA, Peterson DE, et al. A massive outbreak in Milwaukee of Cryptosporidium infection transmitted through the water supply. N Engl J Med 1994;331:161–7.
9. Lurie P, Hintzen P, Lowe RA. Socioeconomic obstacles to HIV prevention and treatment in developing countries: the roles of the International Monetary Fund and the World Bank. AIDS 1995;9:539–46.
10. World Health Organization. Cholera in the Americas. Weekly Epidemiol Rec. 1992;67:33–9.
11. McCarthy S, McPhearson R, Guarino A. Toxigenic Vibrio cholera O1 and cargo ships entering the Gulf of Mexico. Lancet 1992;339:624.
12. Goma Epidemiology Group. Public health impact of Rwandan refugee crisis: what happened in Goma, Zaire, in July, 1994? Lancet 1995;345:339–44.
13. McMichael A. The health of persons, populations and planets: epidemiology comes full circle. Epidemiology 1995;6:633–6.
14. Johnson KM, Webb PA, Lange JV, Murphy FA. Isolation and partial characterization of a new virus causing acute hemorrhagic fever in Zaire. Lancet 1977;1:569–71.
15. World Health Organization. Ebola haemorrhagic fever in Zaire, 1976. Report of an international commission. Bull WHO 1978;56:271–93.
16. Garrett L. The Coming Plague. New York: Farrar, Straus and Giroux, 1995.
17. Ryan F. The forgotten plague: how the battle against tuberculosis was won and lost. Boston: Little, Brown, 1993.
18. Iseman M. Tailoring a time-bomb. Am Rev Respir Dis 1985;132:735–6.
19. Bloom B, Murray C. Tuberculosis: commentary on a resurgent killer. Science 1992;257:1055–63.
20. Murray C. Social, economic and operational research on tuberculosis: recent studies and some priority questions. Bull Int Union Tuberc Lung Dis 1991;66:149–56.
21. Farmer P, Robin S, Ramilus St-L, Kim J. Tuberculosis and "compliance": lessons from rural Haiti. Seminars in Respiratory Infections 1991;6:373–9.
22. Spence D, Hotchkiss J, Williams C, Davies P. Tuberculosis and poverty. British Medical Journal 1993;307:759–61.
23. McKenna MT, McCray E, Onorato I. The epidemiology of tuberculosis among foreign-born persons in the United States, 1986 to 1993. N Engl J Med 1995; 332: 1071–6.
24. Chabner B. Cited in the Miami News, December 2, 1982;8A.
25. Farmer P. AIDS and Accusation: Haiti and the Geography of Blame. University of California Press, Berkeley, 1992.
26. Farmer P. The exotic and the mundane: human immunodeficiency virus in the Caribbean. Human Nature 1990;1:415–45.
27. Mann J, Tarantola D, Netter T. AIDS in the world. Cambridge, MA: Harvard University Press, 1992.
28. United Nations Development Program. Young women: silence, susceptibility and the HIV epidemic. New York, UNDP, 1992.
29. Sampson J, Neaton J. On being poor with HIV. Lancet 1994;344:1100–1.
30. Chaisson RE, Keruly JC, Moore RD. Race, sex, drug use, and progression of human immunodeficiency virus disease. N Engl J Med 1995;333:751–6.
31. Farmer P, Connors M, and Simmons J, eds. Women, poverty, and AIDS: sex, drugs, and structural violence. Monroe, ME: Common Courage Press, 1996.
32. Fife E, Mode C. AIDS incidence and income. JAIDS 1992;5:1105–10.
33. Wallace R, Fullilove M, Fullilove R, Gould P, Wallace D. Will AIDS be contained within U.S. minority populations? Soc Sci Med 1994;39:1051–62.
34. Waldholz M. Precious pills: new AIDS treatment raises tough question of who will get it. Wall Street Journal, July 3, 1996, p. 1.
35. Centers for Disease Control and Prevention. Diphtheria outbreak—Russian Federation, 1990–1993. MMWR 1993;42:840–1,847.
36. Field M. The health crisis in the former Soviet Union: a report from the 'post-war' zone. Soc Sci Med 1995;1469–78.
37. Patz J, Epstein P, Burke T, Balbus J. Global climate change and emerging infectious diseases. JAMA 1996; 275:217–33.
38. Garrett L. Public health and the mass media. Current Issues in Public Health 1995;1:147–50.
39. Centers for Disease Control and Prevention. Addressing emerging infectious disease threats: a prevention strategy for the United States. Atlanta, USA. Department of Health and Human Services, 1994.
40. Roizman B, ed. Infectious diseases in an age of change: the impact of human ecology and behavior on disease transmission. Washington, D.C.: National Academy Press, 1995.
41. Farmer P. On suffering and structural violence: a view from below. Daedalus 1996;125:261–83.
42. Krieger N, Rowley D, Herman A, Avery B, Phillips M. Racism, sexism, and social class: implications for studies

of health, disease, and well-being. Am J Prev Med 1993; (Supplement)9:82–122.

43. Navarro V. Race or class versus race and class: mortality differentials in the United States. Lancet 1990;336: 1238–40.

44. Marmot M. Social differentials in health within and between populations. Daedalus 1994;123:197–216.

45. Wilson M. Travel and the emergence of infectious diseases. Emerging Infectious Diseases 1995;1:39–46.

46. Haggett P. Geographical aspects of the emergence of infectious diseases. Geogr Ann 1994;76:91–104.

47. Warner DC. Health issues at the US-Mexican border. JAMA 1991;265:242–7.

48. Small P, Moss A. Molecular epidemiology and the new tuberculosis. Infect Agents Dis 1993;2:132–8.

49. Levins R. Preparing for Uncertainty. Ecosystem Health 1995;1:47–57.

50. Latour B. The pasteurization of France. Sheridan A, Law J, trans. Cambridge, MA: Harvard University Press, 1988.

51. Global Health Situation and Projections. Geneva: World Health Organization, 1992.

52. Berkelman RL, Hughes JM. The conquest of infectious diseases: who are we kidding? Ann Int Med 1993;119: 426–8.

53. Epstein PR. Pestilence and poverty—historical transitions and the great pandemics. Am J Prev Med 1992;8: 263–78.

54. Packard R. White plague, black labor: tuberculosis and the political economy of health and disease in South Africa. Berkeley: University of California Press.

55. Aïach P, Carr-Hill R, Curtis S, Illsley R. Les inégalités sociales de santé en France et en Grande-Bretagne. Paris: INSERM, 1987.

56. Fassin D. Exclusion, underclass, marginalidad. Revue Française de Sociologie 1996;37:37–75.

57. Inhorn M, Brown P, eds. The anthropology of infectious diseases. New York: Gordon and Breach, 1996.

58. Krieger N, Zierler S. What explains the public's health? A call for epidemiologic theory. Epidemiology 1996;7: 107–9.

59. Eisenberg L, Kleinman A. The relevance of social science to medicine. Dordrecht: Reidel, 1981.

60. Serres M. Le passage du nord-ouest. Paris: Editions de Minuit, 1980.

Belief and Ethnomedical Systems

✤ CONCEPTUAL TOOLS ✤

■ *The distinction between disease and illness has had central importance.* Disease refers to outward, objective clinical manifestations of abnormality of physical function or infection by a pathogen in an individual or host. The concept of disease is fundamental to biomedicine; the official listing of disease categories, grouped by causal agents, is found in the *International Classification of Diseases,* currently in its ninth edition (the analogous reference for mental disorders is the *Diagnostic and Statistical Manual of Mental Disorders,* fourth edition). Disease refers to observable, organic, and pathological abnormalities in organs and organ systems, whether or not they are culturally recognized. On the other hand, illness refers to a person's perceptions and lived experience of being sick or "diseased"—that is, socially disvalued states including (but not limited to) disease. The study of illness involves cognitive and social psychological issues like stigma.

Disease is considered a biological phenomenon, whereas illness includes psychological and social dimensions as well. Within a population, the distribution of disease and illness do not completely overlap: There are people with diagnosable disease (for example, hypertension) who do not know or think of themselves as ill; correspondingly, a significant percentage of patients visiting physicians are ill but do not have an identifiable disease. In biomedicine, the illness of a patient with symptoms but no diagnosable disease can be referred to as psychosomatic, referring to a psychological etiology. Although this term is infrequently used today, the negative implication of the "psychosomatic" label was that the illness was not real because the patient's "abnormal" mind caused the abnormalities of the body. The patient, therefore, could be blamed as the cause of her or his own symptoms. The traditional biomedical logic subsumed under the concept of psychosomatic illness (and the disease–illness distinction) has been a central target of analysis in critical medical anthropology.

In recent years, the disease–illness distinction has been criticized because the separation of biological facts from cultural constructions falsely suggests the superiority of a "culture-free" biomedical model. The disease–illness distinction was first described in a seminal article by Leon Eisenberg (1977) who argued that the disease–illness distinction reflected differences between professional and popular ideas of sickness. In a sense, this meant that disease was real but illness was not. The concept was modified in the work of Arthur Kleinman (1980) and, more recently, considered in detail in an important book, *Sickness and Healing,* by Robert Hahn (1995) and a review article by Thomas Csordas and Arthur Kleinman (1996).

■ *All cultures have medical systems comprised of both cognitive and behavioral components.* The cognitive component of a medical system centers on theories of etiology, or causation, of illness. It usually involves a taxonomy of disease categories grouped by causal agent. The study of cultural knowledge about illness and its linkages to differential diagnosis and curative actions is called ethnomedicine. The behavioral component of medical systems concerns the social interactions of healers and their patients in a cultural and economic context. Social mechanisms through which healers are trained, division of labor among healers, and organization of the institutions through which medical services are delivered to a population are all important parts of medical systems.

In technologically simple societies like bands and tribes, with shaman as the principal healers, the medical system is integrated and often indistinguishable from the local religion. In technologically complex societies, the primary medical system is more likely to be secular; complex societies also are often characterized by the simultaneous practice of multiple medical systems or traditions, a situation called medical pluralism.

■ *Biomedicine is an ethnomedicine of Western culture.* In a cultural sense, a medical system is an organized set of ideas referring to a particular healing tradition (for example, Chinese, Ayurvedic, homeopathic, biomedical). Medical anthropologists use the term *biomedicine* to refer to the tradition of scientific, biologically oriented methods of diagnosis and cure.

Biomedicine is a relatively recent tradition that is technologically sophisticated and often extremely successful in curing. Historically known as allopathic medicine, the knowledge and technology of biomedicine has grown extremely fast, and with it the prestige and professionalization of biomedical practitioners. The scientific medical system is international, cosmopolitan, dominant, and hegemonic. It is not, however, culture-free. The cultural and epistemological assumptions of biomedicine have been studied by medical anthropologists (Rhodes 1996); researchers have also studied the significant and fascinating national and regional differences in the practice of biomedicine, especially between European countries and the United States (for example, differences in the interpretation of schizophrenia or low blood pressure and rates and styles of surgery) (Payer 1988).

When viewed as a cultural system, biomedicine becomes one ethnomedicine among many others. All ethnomedicines are rooted in cultural presuppositions and values, associated with rules of conduct, and embedded in a larger context (Hahn 1995). There is little doubt that *belief* in the healer and the power of the medicine by a patient and family plays a fundamental role in the process of healing. All medical systems manipulate symbols to invoke and enhance belief; in this regard, all medical systems involve symbolic healing processes (sometimes labeled the "placebo effect").

12

Disease Etiologies in Non-Western Medical Systems

George M. Foster

If every culture in the world has a medical system, or, more properly, an ethnomedical system, then how is it possible to talk about this great variation? How is it possible to compare medical systems that are based on completely different ideas of what causes illness—from spirits to germs? The first thing that social scientists do when faced with such a problem is to survey the range of variation and then construct a system of categorization, also called a typology. This is a comparative method in which like is grouped with like. The next step is to define these groups with descriptive labels using what the famous sociologist Max Weber called "ideal types."

In this classic article, George Foster surveys the range of variation in medical systems and focuses on an essential aspect of such systems: the etiology or theory of disease causation. This is a good place to start, because medical systems must have three basic components: a theory of etiology, a system of diagnosis, and techniques of appropriate therapy. Theories of causation are actually cognitive blueprints, something that medical anthropologists often refer to as explanatory models.

The distinction between naturalistic and personalistic ethnomedical systems is quite useful. Naturalistic systems tend to have etiologic explanations that are restricted to the disease symptomatology and a single level of causality. In contrast, personalistic explanations extend to the domains of social relations—with living people, ancestors, and other spiritual entities. Naturalistic cures tend to be oriented toward the physical body; personalistic cures must not only deal with immediate causes for an illness (like witchcraft) but also the underlying social rifts that have provoked the witchcraft.

One of the most interesting aspects of this distinction is that personalistic and naturalistic systems have completely different attitudes about the sharing of medical knowledge.

In a personalistic system, a shaman gains prestige as a healer in part because he jealously guards his personal ethnomedical knowledge. In a naturalistic system, a healer gains prestige by producing and giving away medical knowledge—by teaching it to others. The more open information system has adaptive advantages because therapies can be openly compared and evaluated. Naturalistic systems are associated with the great traditions of complex civilizations; medical knowledge becomes codified and taught as a profession.

Notice that the author doesn't clearly come out and say that scientific biomedicine is a naturalistic ethnomedical system. But a careful reading will reveal that biomedicine has more of the attributes of the naturalistic ideal type. Also notice that these ideal types do not really work as a clean and neat categorization scheme. There are two reasons for this: First, many ethnomedical systems have attributes of both naturalistic and personalistic etiologies (the Navajo medical system is an example of one that doesn't fit the typology); second, many societies have multiple medical systems operating simultaneously or medical pluralism.

As you read this selection, consider these questions:

- *Why is it that the author believes that personalistic systems are evolutionarily older than naturalistic ethnomedical systems?*

- *Are personalistic ethnomedical systems kinder to the victim of the disease because they do not blame a person for getting sick? Or is a person really responsible for keeping peaceable social relations to prevent spiritual attacks?*

- *What is the logical connection between etiologic theories and therapeutic practices?*

Impressive in ethnographic accounts of non-Western medicine is the tendency of authors to generalize from the particulars of the system(s) within which they have worked. Subconsciously, at least, anthropologists filter the data of all exotic systems through the lens of belief and practice of the people they know best. Whether it be causality, diagnosis, the nature and role of the curer, or the perception of illness within the wider supernatural and social universe, general statements seem strongly influenced by the writers' personal experiences. Glick, for example, in one of the most interesting of recent general essays, notes that in many cultures religion and medical practices are almost inseparable, and he adds that "We must think about how and where 'medicine' fits into 'religion'. . . . In an ethnography of a religious system, where does the description of the medical system belong; and how does it relate to the remainder?" (Glick 1967:33).

Yet in many medical systems, as, for example, those characterizing mestizo villagers and urbanites in Latin America, medicine would have the most minimal role in an ethnography of religious beliefs and practices. Illness and curing are dealt with largely in nonreligious terms. In Tzintzuntzan, for example, in many hours of recording ideas about origins and cures of illness, not once has religion been mentioned—even though most villagers, if asked, would certainly agree that illness ultimately comes from God.

The ethnologist analyzing medical beliefs and practices in an African community can scarcely avoid dealing with witchcraft, oracles, magic, divining, and propitiation, all of which are categories of only modest concern to the student of Indian Ayurvedic medicine. In short, there has been all too little dialogue between anthropologists who have studied dramatically different non-Western medical systems. So striking is the parochialism at times that one is tempted to agree with the medical sociologist Freidson who notes the existence of a "very large body of sociological and anthropological information" about popular knowledge of and attitudes toward health and disease, but finds most of it to be "grossly descriptive." "Aside from cultural designations like Mexican, Subanun, and Mashona," he writes, "there is no method by which the material is ordered save for focusing on knowledge about *particular* illnesses. Such studies are essentially catalogues, often without a classified index" (Freidson 1970:10).

Yet if we can successfully classify kinship, political and economic systems, and witchcraft and sorcery beliefs, and find the significant behavioral correlates associated with each, then certainly we can do the same with medical systems. We are, after all, dealing with limited possibilities in each of these cases. In this paper I am concerned with the cross-cultural patterning that underlies non-Western medical systems, and with identifying and explicating the primary independent variable—disease etiology—around which orbit such dependent variables as types of curers, the nature of diagnosis, the roles of religion and magic, and the like. This is, then, an essay on comparative ethnomedicine, a term Hughes aptly defines as "those beliefs and practices relating to disease which are the products of indigenous cultural development and are not explicitly derived from the conceptual framework of modern medicine" (Hughes 1968:99).

THE PROBLEMS OF TERMINOLOGY

Throughout most of anthropology's brief history ethnologists have labeled the institutions of the peoples they have studied as "primitive," "peasant," or "folk," depending on the basic societal type concerned. Until relatively recently we investigated primitive religion, primitive economics, primitive art—and, of course, primitive medicine. The seminal writings of the ethnologist-physician Ackerknecht during the 1940s display no uncertainty as to what interested him: it was "primitive medicine," a pair of words that appeared in the title of nearly every article he published (Ackerknecht 1971). Caudill, too, in the first survey of the new field of medical anthropology spoke unashamedly of "primitive medicine" (Caudill 1953).

When, following World War II, studies of peasant communities became fashionable, these peoples were described as possessing a "folk culture." Not surprisingly their medical beliefs and practices were labeled "folk medicine," a frequent source of confusion since the popular medicine of technologically complex societies also often was, and is, so described.

In recent years, however, this traditional terminology has come to embarrass us. In a rapidly changing world, where yesterday's nonliterate villagers may be today's cabinet ministers in newly independent countries, the word "primitive"—initially a polite euphemism for "savage"—is increasingly outmoded. Ackerknecht himself recognizes this change, for in the 1971 collection of his classic essays most titles have been edited to eliminate the word "primitive." "Peasant" and "folk" are less sensitive words, but they too are being replaced by "rural," "agrarian," or something of the kind. The extent to which we have been troubled by terminology is illustrated by the circumlocutions and quotation marks found in the major review articles of recent years: "popular health culture," "indigenous or folk medical roles," "nonscientific health practices," "native conceptual traditions about illness," "culture specific illness," "the vocabulary of Western scientific medicine," "indigenous medical systems," and the like (e.g., Polgar 1962; Scotch 1963; Fabrega 1972; Lieban 1973).

ETIOLOGY: THE INDEPENDENT VARIABLE

Yet the greatest shortcoming of our traditional medical terminology—at least within the profession itself—is not that it may denigrate non-Western people, but rather that, by focusing on societal types it has blinded us to the basic characteristics of the medical systems themselves. There is more than a grain of truth in Freidson's comments, for many accounts *are* "grossly descriptive," with lists of illnesses and treatments taking precedence over interpretation and synthesis. So where do we start to rectify the situation? Glick (1967:36), I believe, gives us the critical lead when he writes that "the most important fact about an illness in most medical systems is not the underlying pathological process but *the underlying cause*. This is such a central consideration that most diagnoses prove to be statements about causation, and most treatments, responses directed against particular causal agents" (emphasis added).

A casual survey of the ethnomedical literature tends to confirm Glick's statement. In account after account we find that the kinds of curers, the mode of diagnosis, curing techniques, preventive acts, and the relationship of all these variables to the wider society of which they are a part, derive from beliefs about illness causality. It is not going too far to say that, if we are given a clear description of what a people believe to be the causes of illness, we can in broad outline fill in the other elements in that medical system. It therefore logically follows that the first task of the anthropologist concerned with medical systems is to find the simplest taxonomy for causality beliefs. Two basic principles, which I call *personalistic and naturalistic,* seem to me to account for most (but not all) of the etiologies that characterize non-Western medical systems. While the terms refer specifically to causality concepts, I believe they can conveniently be used to speak of entire systems, i.e., not only causes, but all of the associated behavior that follows from these views.

A personalistic medical system is one in which disease is explained as due to the *active, purposeful intervention* of an *agent,* who may be human (a witch or sorcerer), nonhuman (a ghost, an ancestor, an evil spirit), or supernatural (a deity or other very powerful being). The sick person literally is a victim, the object of aggression or punishment directed specifically against him, for reasons that concern him alone. Personalistic causality allows little room for accident or chance; in fact, for some peoples the statement is made by anthropologists who have studied them that *all* illness and death are believed to stem from the acts of the agent.

Personalistic etiologies are illustrated by beliefs found among the Mano of Liberia, recorded by the physician Harley, who practiced medicine among them for 15 years. "Death is unnatural," he writes, "resulting from the intrusion of an outside force," usually directed by some magical means (Harley 1941:7). Similarly, among the Abron of the Ivory Coast,

"People sicken and die because some power, good or evil, has acted against them. . . . Abron disease theory contains a host of agents which may be responsible for a specific condition. . . . These agents cut across the natural and supernatural world. Ordinary people, equipped with the proper technical skills, sorcerers, various supernatural entities, such as ghosts, bush devils, and witches, or the supreme god *Nyame,* acting alone or through lesser gods, all cause disease" (Alland 1964:714–715).

In contrast to personalistic systems, naturalistic systems explain illness in impersonal, systemic terms. Disease is thought to stem, not from the machinations of an angry being, but rather from such *natural forces or conditions* as cold, heat, winds, dampness, and, above all, by an upset in the balance of the basic body elements. In naturalistic systems, health conforms to an *equilibrium* model: when the humors, the yin and yang, or the Ayurvedic *dosha* are in the balance appropriate to the age and condition of the individual, in his natural and social environment, health results. Causality concepts explain or account for the upsets in this balance that trigger illness.

Contemporary naturalistic systems resemble each other in an important historical sense: the bulk of their explanations and practices represent simplified and popularized legacies from the "great tradition" medicine of ancient classical civilizations, particularly those of Greece and Rome, India, and China. Although equilibrium is expressed in many ways in classical accounts, contemporary descriptions most frequently deal with the "hot-cold dichotomy" which explains illness as due to excessive heat or cold entering the body. Treatment, logically, attempts to restore the proper balance through "hot" and "cold" foods and herbs, and other treatments such as poultices that are thought to withdraw excess heat or cold from the body.

In suggesting that most non-Western etiologies can be described as personalistic or naturalistic I am, of course, painting with a broad brush. Every anthropologist will immediately think of examples from his research that appear not to conform to this classification. Most troublesome, at least at first glance, are those illnesses believed caused by emotional disturbances such as fright, jealousy, envy, shame, anger, or grief. Fright, or *susto,* widespread in Latin America, can be caused by a ghost, a spirit, or an encounter with the devil; if the agent *intended* harm to the victim, the etiology is certainly personalistic. But often accounts of such encounters suggest chance or accident rather than purposive action. And, when an individual slips beside a stream, and fears he is about to fall into the water and drown, the etiology is certainly naturalistic.

The Latin American *muina,* an indisposition resulting from anger, may reflect a disagreeable interpersonal episode, but it is unlikely that the event was staged by an evil doer to bring illness to a victim. In Mexico and Central America the knee child's envy and resentment of its new sibling-to-be, still in the mother's womb, gives rise to *chipil,* the symptoms of which are apathy, whining, and a desire to cling to the mother's skirt. The foetus can be said, in a narrow sense, to be the cause of the illness, but it is certainly not an active agent, nor is it blamed for the result. Since in a majority of emotionally explained illnesses it is hard to identify purposive action on the part of an agent intent upon causing sickness, I am inclined to view emotional etiologies as more nearly conforming to the naturalistic than to the personalistic principle. Obviously, a dual taxonomy for phenomena as complex as worldwide beliefs about causes of illness leaves many loose ends. But it must be remembered that a taxonomy is not an end in itself, something to be polished and admired; its value lies rather in the understanding of relationships between apparently diverse phenomena that it makes possible. I hope that the following pages will illustrate how the personalistic-naturalistic classification, for all its loose ends, throws into sharp perspective correlations in health institutions and health behavior that tend to be overlooked in descriptive accounts.

Before proceeding, a word of caution is necessary: *the two etiologies are rarely if ever mutually exclusive* as far as their presence or absence in a particular society is concerned. Peoples who invoke personalistic causes to explain most illness usually recognize some natural, or chance, causes. And peoples for whom naturalistic causes predominate almost invariably explain some illness as due to witchcraft or the evil eye. But in spite of obvious overlapping, the literature suggests that many, if not most, peoples are committed to one or the other of these explanatory principles to account for a majority of illness. When, for example, we read that in the Venezuelan peasant village of El Morro 89% of a sample of reported illnesses are "natural" in origin, whereas only 11% are attributed to magical or supernatural causes (Suárez 1974), it seems reasonable to say that the indigenous causation system of this group is naturalistic and not personalistic. And, in contrast, when we read of the Melanesian Dobuans that all illness and disease are attributed to envy, and that "Death is caused by witchcraft, sorcery, poisoning, suicide, or actual assault" (Fortune 1932:135, 150), it is clear that personalistic causality predominates.

Although in the present context I am not concerned with problems of evolution, I believe the personalistic etiology is the more ancient of the two. At the dawn of human history it seems highly likely that *all* illness, as well as other forms of misfortune, was explained in personalistic terms. I see man's ability to depersonalize causality, in all spheres of thought, including illness, as a major step forward in the evolution of culture.

ETIOLOGIES: COMPREHENSIVE AND RESTRICTED

We now turn to the principal dependent variables in medical institutions and health behavior that correlate with personalistic and naturalistic etiologies. The first thing we note is that personalistic medical etiologies are parts of more comprehensive, or general, explanatory systems, while naturalistic etiologies are largely restricted to illness. In other words, in personalistic systems *illness is but a special case in the explanation of all misfortune.* Some societies, to quote Horton (1967) have adopted a "personal idiom" as the basis of their attempt to understand the world, to account for almost everything that happens in the world, only incidentally including illness. In such societies the same deities, ghosts, witches, and sorcerers that send illness may blight crops, cause financial reverses, sour husband-wife relationships, and produce all manner of other misfortune. To illustrate, Price-Williams states "The general feature of illness among the Tiv is that it is interpreted in a framework of witchcraft and malevolent forces" (1962:123). "In common with a great many other people, Tiv do not regard 'illness' or 'disease' as a completely separate category distinct from misfortunes to compound and farm, from relationships between kin, and from complicated matters relating to the control of land" (1962:125).

Similarly, the Kaguru of Taznazia "believe most misfortunes, however small, are due to witchcraft. Most illness, death, miscarriages, sterility, difficult childbirths, poor crops, sickly livestock and poultry, loss of articles, bad luck in hunting, and sometimes even lack of rain are caused by witches" (Beidelman 1963:63–64).

In contrast, naturalistic etiologies are restricted to disease as such. Although a "systemic idiom" may prevail to account for much of what happens in the world, a humoral or a yin-yang imbalance which explains an illness is not invoked to explain crop failure, disputes over land, or kin quarreling. In fact, the striking thing is that while in naturalistic systems disease etiologies are disease specific, other areas of misfortune, such as personal quarrels are, not surprisingly, explained in personalistic terms. In Tzintzuntzan, for example, misunderstandings between friends may be due to natural-born trouble makers, who delight in spreading rumors and falsehoods. Financial reverses, too, may be accounted for by bad luck, or dishonesty and deceit on the part of false friends. But these explanations are quite divorced from illness etiology, which has its own framework, exclusive to it.

DISEASE, RELIGION, AND MAGIC

When Glick (1967:32) writes that "it is common knowledge that in many cultures, ideas and practices relating to illness are for the most part inseparable from the domain of religious beliefs and practices," he is speaking only of those systems with personalistic etiologies. Jansen (1973:34) makes this clear in writing of the Bomvana (Xhosa) that "religion, medicine and magic are closely interwoven, . . . being parts of a complex whole which finds its religious destination in the well-being of the tribe. . . . The Bomvana himself does not distinguish between his religion, magic and medicine." When curers are described as "priests" and "priestesses," as is often the case in Africa (e.g., Warren 1974–75:27), we are clearly in the domain of religion.

In contrast, in naturalistic systems religion and magic play only the most limited roles *insofar as we are dealing with etiology,* and to the extent that religious rituals are found, they are significantly different in form and concept from religious rituals in personalistic systems. For example, in those Latin American societies whose etiological systems are largely naturalistic, victims of illness sometimes place votive offerings on or near "miraculous" images of Christ, the Virgin Mary, or powerful saints, or light votive candles for these supernatural beings, asking for help. These are certainly religious acts. But it is important to note that in personalistic systems the beings supplicated, and to whom propitiatory offerings are made, are themselves held responsible for the illness. It is to appease their anger or ill will that such offerings are made. In contrast, in Catholic countries the beings to whom prayers are raised and offerings made *are not* viewed as causes of the illness. They are seen as merciful advocates who, if moved, can intervene to help a human sufferer. It should be noted, too, that most of these acts conform to a general pattern in which aid of supernaturals is sought for any kind of misfortune, such as financial reverses or the release of a son from jail, as well as illness or accident.

Thus, there is a significant contrast in structure and style between the two systems. In societies where personalistic etiologies predominate, all causality is general and comprehensive, and not specific to illness; but paradoxically, when ritual supplications and sacrifices are made, usually they are narrowly limited in scope, specific to a particular illness, or to prevent feared illness. In contrast, in societies where naturalistic etiologies predominate, illness causality is specific to illness alone, and does not apply to other kinds of misfortune. But, insofar as religion is a part of curing, it is comprehensive or general, conforming to the same patterns that characterize a pious person in the face of any misfortune.

LEVELS OF CAUSALITY

Personalistic and naturalistic etiologies further differ importantly in that, for the former, it is necessary to postulate at least two levels of causality: the deity, ghost, witch, or other being on whom ultimate responsibility for illness rests, and the instrument or technique used by this being, such as intrusion of a disease object, theft of the soul, possession, or witchcraft. In the literature on ethnomedicine the first level—the being—is often referred to as the *efficient* cause, while the second level—the instrument or technique—is referred to as the *instrumental,* or *immediate* cause. A few anthropologists recognize three levels of causation. Goody (1962:209–210), for example, describes both efficient and immediate causes, to which he adds a final cause, an ancestor or earth shrine that withdraws its protection from a person so that he falls victim to a sorcerer. In Honduras Peck (1968:78) recognizes essentially the same three levels: an instrumental cause ("i.e., what has been done to the patient, or what is used"), an efficient cause ("i.e., who or what has done it to the patient"), and a final, or ultimate, cause ("i.e., an attempt to answer the question, 'why did *this* happen to *me* at *this time*?' ").

Naturalistic etiologies differ significantly in that levels of causation are much less apparent; in most cases they tend to be collapsed. Although it can be argued that a person who willfully or through carelessness engages in activities known to upset his bodily equilibrium is the efficient cause of his illness, in practice this line of argument has little analytical value.

It was failure to recognize levels of causality that limited the value of Clements' pioneering study of disease etiology (1932), a defect first pointed out by Hallowell (1935). This distinction, as we are about to see, is critical to an understanding of basic differences in curing strategies found in the two systems.

SHAMANS AND OTHER CURERS

The kinds of curers found in a particular society, and the curing acts in which they engage, stem logically from the etiologies that are recognized. Personalistic systems, with multiple levels of causation, logically require curers with supernatural and/or magical skills, for the primary concern of the patient and his family is not the immediate cause of illness, but rather "Who?" and "Why?" Among the Bomvana (Xhosa) Jansen (1973:39) puts it this way: "They are less interested to know: *How* did it happen? rather than: *Who* is responsible?" Similarly, in Mali we read that "In general the Bambara want to know *why* they are ill and not how they got ill" (Imperato 1974–75:44). And in the Indian village studied by Dube the Brahmin or a local seer is essential to find out what ancestor spirit is angry, and why (Dube 1955:128).

The shaman, with his supernatural powers, and direct contact with the spirit world, and the "witch doctor" (to use an outmoded term from the African literature), with his magical powers, both of whom are primarily concerned with finding out who, and why, are the logical responses in personalistic, multiple causality, etiological systems. After the who and why have been determined, treatment for the immediate cause may be administered by the same person, or the task may be turned over to a lesser curer, perhaps an herbalist. Thus, among the Nyima of the Kordofan mountains in the Sudan, the shaman goes into a trance and discovers the cause and cure of the disease. But he himself performs no therapeutic acts; this is the field of other healing experts, to whom the patient will be referred (Nadel 1946:26).

Naturalistic etiological systems, with single levels of causation, logically require a very different type of curer, a "doctor" in the full sense of the word, a specialist in symptomatic treatment who knows the appropriate herbs, food restrictions, and other forms of treatment such as cupping, massage, poultices, enemas, and the like. The curandero or the Ayurvedic specialist is not primarily concerned with the who or why, for he and the patient both usually are in complete agreement as to what has happened.

DIAGNOSIS

Personalistic and naturalistic etiological systems divide along still another axis, the nature of diagnosis. In personalistic systems, as we have just seen, the shaman or witch doctor diagnoses by means of trance, or other divinatory techniques. Diagnosis—to find out who and why—is the primary skill that the patient seeks from his curer. Treatment of the instrumental cause, while important, is of secondary concern.

In contrast, in naturalistic systems diagnosis is of very minor importance, as far as the curer is con-

cerned. Diagnosis usually is made, not by the curer, but by the patient or members of his family. When the patient ceases treatment with home remedies and turns to a professional, he believes he knows what afflicts him. His primary concern is treatment to cure him. And how is diagnosis done by the layman? The answer is simple, pointed out many years ago by Erasmus (1952:414), specifically for Ecuador. When an individual whose disease etiology is largely naturalistic feels unwell, he thinks back to an earlier experience, in the night, the day before, or even a month or a year earlier, to an event that transpired, or a situation in which he found himself, that is known to cause illness. Did the patient awaken in the morning with swollen tonsils? He remembers that on going to bed the night before he carelessly stepped on the cold tile floor of his bedroom in his bare feet. This, he knows, causes cold to enter his feet and compress the normal heat of his body into the upper chest and head. He suffers from "risen heat." *He* tells the doctor what is wrong, and merely asks for an appropriate remedy.

Does a woman suffer an attack of painful rheumatism? She remembers that she had been ironing, thereby heating her hands and arms, and that without thinking she had washed them in cold water. The cold, to her vulnerable superheated arms and hands, caused her discomfort. She needs no diviner or shaman to tell her what is wrong. The striking thing about a naturalistic system is that, in theory at least, the patient can, upon reflection, identify *every* cause of illness that may afflict him. So powerful is this pattern today in Tzintzuntzan that when people consult medical doctors, their standard opening statement is "Doctor, please give me something for ————," whatever their diagnosis may be. Doctors, traditional or modern, are viewed as curers, not diagnosticians.

To summarize, we may say that in personalistic systems the primary role of the shaman or witch doctor is *diagnostic,* while in naturalistic systems it is *therapeutic.*

PREVENTIVE MEASURES

Preventive medicine, insofar as it refers to individual health-oriented behavior, can be thought of as a series of "dos" and "don'ts," or "shoulds" and "shouldn'ts." In contemporary America we "should" get an annual physical examination, our eyes and teeth checked regularly, and make sure our immunizations are up to date when we travel abroad. We "should not" smoke cigarettes, consume alcohol to excess, breathe polluted air, or engage in a series of other activities known or believed to be inimical to health. Our personal preventive measures are, perhaps, about equally divided between the "dos" and "don'ts."

In all other societies similar "shoulds" and "shouldn'ts" can be identified. Although my grounds are highly impressionistic, I rather have the feeling that naturalistic etiologies correlate predominantly with "don'ts," while personalistic etiologies correlate with "dos." In naturalistic systems a personal health strategy seems to consist of avoiding those situations or not engaging in behavior, known to produce illness. In Tzintzuntzan, and many other Latin American communities, the prudent person doesn't stand on a cold floor in bare feet, doesn't wash hands after whitewashing a wall, doesn't go out into the night air immediately after using the eyes, and a host of other things. In theory, at least, a hypercautious individual should be able to avoid almost all illness *by not doing certain things.*

In contrast, in personalistic systems the basic personal health strategy seems to emphasize the "dos," and especially the need to make sure that one's social networks, with fellow human beings, with ancestors, and with deities, are maintained in good working order. Although this means avoiding those acts known to arouse resentment—"don'ts"—it particularly means careful attention being paid to the propitiatory rituals that are a god's due, to positive demonstrations to ancestors that they have not been forgotten, and to friendly acts to neighbors and fellow villagers that remind them that their good will is valued. In short, recognizing major overlapping, the primary strategies to maintain health in the two systems are significantly different. Both require thought. But in one—the personalistic—time and money are essential ingredients in the maintenance of health. In the other—the naturalistic—knowledge of how the system works, and the will to live according to its dictates, is the essential thing; this costs very little, in either time or money.

THE LOCUS OF RESPONSIBILITY

With respect to personal responsibility for falling ill, do the two etiological systems differ? To some extent I think they do. In Tzintzuntzan, as pointed out, the exercise of absolute care in avoiding disease-producing situations should, in theory, keep one healthy. Hence, illness is *prima facie* evidence that the patient has been guilty of lack of care. Although illness is as frightening as in any other society, and family members do their best to help a sick member, there is often an ambivalent feeling that includes anger at the patient for having fallen ill. I have seen worried grown daughters

losing a night's sleep as they sought medical care for a mother they feared was suffering a heart attack. When the mother confessed that she had not taken her daily pill to keep her blood pressure down (and after she was back to normal, the crisis past), the daughters became highly indignant and angry at her for causing them to lose sleep.

In personalistic systems people also know the kinds of behavior—sins of commission and omission—that may lead to retaliation by a deity, spirit, or witch. To the extent they can lead blameless lives they should avoid sickness. But personalistic causality is far more complex than naturalistic causality, since there are no absolute rules to avoid arousing the envy of others, for doing just the right amount of ritual to satisfy an ancestor, for knowing how far one can shade a taboo without actually breaching it. Consequently, in such systems one has less control over the conditions that lead to illness than in the other, where the rules are clearly stated. Spiro (1967:4) makes this contrast clear among the Burmese. Since suffering (including illness) is the "karmic" consequence of one's demerits accumulated in earlier incarnations, the responsibility for suffering rests on the shoulders of the sufferer himself. But, says Spiro, to accept this responsibility is emotionally unsatisfying. On the other hand, if one subscribes to a supernatural-magical explanatory system, in which all suffering comes from ghosts, demons, witches, and *nats*, in at least some cases the sufferer is entirely blameless. He simply happens to be the victim of a witch who, from malice, chooses him as victim. "In other cases he is only inadvertently responsible—he has unwittingly offended or neglected a nat who, annoyed by his behavior, punishes him." Spiro sees this reasoning as underlying the juxtaposition of Buddhism and supernaturalism—of personalistic and naturalistic etiologies—in Burma.

SUMMARY

By way of summary the two systems of disease etiology and their correlates may be tabularized as follows:

System:	Personalistic	Naturalistic
Causation:	Active agent	Equilibrium loss
Illness:	Special case of misfortune	Unrelated to other misfortune
Religion, Magic:	Intimately tied to illness	Largely unrelated to illness
Causality:	Multiple levels	Single level
Prevention:	Positive action	Avoidance
Responsibility:	Beyond patient control	Resides with patient

REFERENCES

Ackerknecht, Erwin H. 1971. Medicine and Ethnology: Selected Essays. Baltimore: Johns Hopkins Press.

Alland, Alexander, Jr. 1964. Native Therapists and Western Medical Practitioners among the Abron of the Ivory Coast. Transactions of the New York Academy of Sciences. Vol. 26. Pp. 714–725.

Beidelman, T. O. 1963. Witchcraft in Ukaguru. *In* Witchcraft and Sorcery in East Africa. J. Middleton and E. H. Winter, eds. Pp. 57–98. London: Routledge and Kegan Paul.

Caudill, William. 1953. Applied Anthropology in Medicine. *In* Anthropology Today. A. L. Kroeber, ed. Pp. 771–806. Chicago: University of Chicago Press.

Clements, Forrest E. 1932. Primitive Concepts of Disease. University of California Publications in American Archaeology and Ethnology, Vol. 32, Part 2. Pp. 185–252.

Dube, S. C. 1955. Indian Village. London: Routledge and Kegan Paul.

Erasmus, Charles J. 1952. Changing Folk Beliefs and the Relativity of Empirical Knowledge. Southwestern Journal of Anthropology 8:411–428.

Fabrega, Horacio, Jr. 1972. Medical Anthropology. *In* Biennial Review of Anthropology: 1971. Bernard J. Siegel, ed. Pp. 167–229. Stanford: Stanford University Press.

Fortune, Reo F. 1932. Sorcerers of Dobu: The Social Anthropology of the Dobu Islanders of the Western Pacific. London: George Routledge.

Freidson, Eliot. 1970. Professional Dominance: The Social Structure of Medical Care. New York: Atherton.

Glick, Leonard B. 1967. Medicine as an Ethnographic Category: The Gimi of the New Guinea Highlands. Ethnology 6:31–56.

Goody, Jack. 1962. Death, Property and the Ancestors: A Study of the Mortuary Customs of the Lodagas of West Africa. Stanford: Stanford University Press.

Hallowell, A. Irving. 1935. Primitive Concepts of Disease. American Anthropologist 37:365–368.

Harley, George Way. 1941. Native African Medicine: With Special Reference to Its Practice in the Mano Tribe of Liberia. Cambridge: Harvard University Press.

Horton, Robin. 1967. African Traditional Thought and Western Science. Africa 37:50–71, 155–187.

Hughes, Charles C. 1968. Ethnomedicine. *In* International Encyclopedia of the Social Sciences. Vol. 10. Pp. 87–93. New York: Free Press/Macmillan.

Imperato, Pascual James. 1974–75. Traditional Medical Practitioners among the Bambara of Mali and their Role in the Modern Health-Care-Delivery System. *In* Traditional Healers: Use and Non-Use in Health Care Delivery. I. E. Harrison and D. W. Dunlop, eds. Rural Africana 26:41–53.

Jansen, G. 1973. The Doctor-Patient Relationship in an African Tribal Society. Assen, The Netherlands: Van Goreum.

Lieban, Richard W. 1973. Medical Anthropology. *In* Handbook of Social and Cultural Anthropology. John J. Honigmann, ed. Pp. 1031–1072. Chicago: Rand McNally.

Nadel, S. F. 1946. A Study of Shamanism in the Nuba Mountains. Journal of the Royal Anthropological Institute 76:25–37.

Peck, John G. 1968. Doctor Medicine and Bush Medicine in Kaukira, Honduras. *In* Essays on Medical Anthropology. Thomas Weaver, ed. Pp. 78–87. Southern Anthropological Society Proceedings, Vol. 1.

Polgar, Steven. 1962. Health and Human Behavior: Areas of Interest Common to the Social and Medical Sciences. Current Anthropology 3:159–205.

Price-Williams, D. R. 1962. A Case Study of Ideas Concerning Disease among the Tiv. Africa 32:123–131.

Scotch, Norman A. 1963. Medical Anthropology. *In* Biennial Review of Anthropology. Bernard J. Siegel, ed. Pp. 30–68. Stanford: Stanford University Press.

Spiro, Melford E. 1967. Burmese Supernaturalism: A Study in the Explanation and Reduction of Suffering. Englewood Cliffs: Prentice-Hall.

Suárez, María Matilde. 1974. Etiology, Hunger, and Folk Diseases in the Venezualan Andes. Journal of Anthropological Research 30:41–54.

Warren, Dennis M. 1974–75. Bono Traditional Healers. *In* Traditional Healers: Use and Non-Use in Health Care Delivery. I. E. Harrison and D. W. Dunlop, eds. Rural Africana 26:25–39.

13

Sacred Healing and Biomedicine Compared

Kaja Finkler

In the last selection, Foster outlined two general "ideal types" of ethnomedical systems: personalistic and naturalistic. Although there are some problems with that typology, it is a valuable tool for cross-cultural comparison. The epistemologies—the ways of knowing and explaining things—are radically different in these two kinds of medical systems. But does that matter to the patients who seek relief from their symptoms? Do epistemological differences affect the quality of the interaction between healers and their patients?

This selection provides a direct comparison of the theory and practice of healing for two medical systems—Spiritualism and biomedicine—within the single context of urban Mexico. Kaja Finkler has done extensive fieldwork, first studying a Spiritualist temple and then a biomedical hospital. She observed and took notes on thousands of interactions between healers and patients; she did follow-up interviews with patients at their homes in barrios all around Mexico City. Her study of this biomedical system is extremely interesting because its practice is rather different from the way biomedicine is practiced in the United States. Some of this difference is probably attributable to the fact that biomedicine was imported to Mexico from France, and French biomedicine is significantly different from biomedicine in Britain, Germany, and the United States (Payer 1988).

Finkler describes a clear case of medical pluralism. Patients do not seem to be bothered by the fundamental epistemological differences between Spiritualism and biomedicine. They are pragmatic; they want relief from their pain. Many patients come to the Spiritualist temple after disappointing encounters or results at the hospital. Spiritualist healers cultivate their "gift" after they have been cured

themselves. As you will see, there are several aspects of Spiritualist healing that are attractive to patients, and there are characteristics of the biomedical system that are discouraging to patients. From the viewpoint of the patients' subjective experience, the contrast is very real.

The National Institutes of Health—the central facility for funding biomedical research in the United States—has recently set up an office of Alternative and Complementary Medicine to study the wide variety of medical systems in our own medically pluralistic system. Alternative medicine is very popular (and big business) and covers the gamut from New Age Spiritualism to homeopathy to massage therapy to macrobiotic diets. The demand for alternative medicine may stem, at least in part, from the characteristics of the social encounter between the healer and the patient. However, both biomedicine and alternative therapies seem to require belief as part of the cure.

As you read this selection, consider these questions:

- Spiritualist healers seldom talk to or even have eye contact with their patients. Why is this? Why don't their patients feel alienated?

- Do the kinds of questions that biomedical practitioners ask conflict with the cultural sensibilities of the Mexican patients? Why might the encounter feel uncomfortable?

- In what ways does Foster's naturalistic–personalistic typology fit the comparison of biomedicine and Spiritualism? Are there ways it doesn't work?

- What does the author mean when she claims that biomedicine relies on the placebo effect?

INTRODUCTION

In this article, I compare two systems of healing—Spiritualist and biomedicine—as practiced in Mexico. The comparison addresses several dimensions, including the physical setting, etiological concepts, diagnoses, the practitioner–patient relationship, recruitment into the healing role, and treatment repertoires,

as well as issues relevant to the patients' perceptions of their bodies and their existences. My extensive research on Spiritualist healing transformed my understanding of biomedical practice in Mexico and, in turn, my studies of biomedical practice in Mexico furnished me with fresh insights into Spiritualist healing in ways that I had not anticipated. While my specific focus is on Spiritualist healing in Mexico and biomedicine practiced there, the comparison illuminates broader issues relevant to sacred and biomedical treatment regimens cross-culturally.

As a participant and observer of both healing regimes and their patients, I noted similarities and dissimilarities between secular and sacred healing that broaden the grasp of the two medical systems and result in different impacts on patients. The comparison sheds light on the nature of medical regimes embedded in dissimilar systems of knowledge and divergent experiences. In practical terms, the comparison brings into relief the strengths and weaknesses of both.[1]

With its origins in the 19th century,[2] Spiritualism (*Espiritualismo*) in Mexico is both a dissident religious movement and a health care delivery system (Finkler 1981, 1983, 1985a, 1986a). Spiritualist temples, frequently headed by women, are widespread in Mexico and in the border states of the United States. Spiritualism provides its followers with a clearly defined cosmology, ethics, and liturgical order, transmitted orally to its adherents through a medium in trance during weekly rituals consisting chiefly of sermons (Finkler 1983, 1985a). While Spiritualism incorporates an anti-Catholic stance (Finkler 1983), it is firmly rooted in Judeo-Christian teachings.

As a healing system, Spiritualism ministers to hundreds of patients.[3] The majority of those coming to Spiritualist temples for the first time seek treatment from the healers for self-assessed, nongrave ailments. During the period of my study, about 10 percent of first-time patients became temple regulars and participants in the movement (Finkler 1985a).

The French model of scientific medicine was introduced into Mexico in the 19th century.[4] At that time, French texts replaced the classical medieval ones upon which Spanish Colonial medicine was based, and Mexican physicians studied in France. Following World War II, the French influence waned, and the U.S. medical model came to dominate Mexican biomedical practice and continues to do so (Finkler 1991). However, while biomedicine has been transported from the United States to Mexico, it has also been culturally reshaped in its day-to-day practice.[5]

Even a synoptic view of Spiritualist healing reveals that Spiritualism and biomedicine diverge along many dimensions. Spiritualism is embedded in a sacred world while biomedicine is sanctioned by secular science. Using Kleinman's typology (Kleinman 1978), biomedicine is a professional system staffed by professionals with many years of formal training and legitimated by the state. Spiritualist healers are practitioners, lacking formal academics, academic preparation, and state legitimation. And, although the two systems of healing may have developed in Mexico during the same historical period, they are rooted

in disparate realities and distinct epistemologies. Nevertheless, they become unified in day-to-day life by the people who resort to them, a phenomenon that has been recognized cross-culturally.[6] Unlike academicians, who regard the two healing regimens as diametrically opposed and in competition, the people who seek treatment do not distinguish the profound epistemological differences between sacred healing, such as Spiritualism, and biomedicine. In the search for the alleviation of pain, pragmatism prevails; people judge the treatments they are given by their effects. They look toward those who provide them with the best medicine for a given sickness episode.

By and large, people the world over, including those in the United States and Mexico, have assumed at least two distinctive postures regarding alternative healing, of which Spiritualist healing is one variant. On the one hand, folk healers are romanticized and idealized, especially when they are compared to physicians. In this camp, folk healers are usually regarded as enjoying an idyllic relationship with their patients. On the other hand, folk healers, including Spiritualists, are simply dismissed as quacks and charlatans, impeding the work of physicians. The argument is made, usually by local physicians, that patients stubbornly cling to traditional healers and by the time they seek out physicians to treat them, they are too sick to benefit from medical care. Physicians, then, are constantly compared to folk healers,[7] but such comparisons normally lack an empirical grounding in both systems of healing. The comparison presented in these pages emerges out of my research on Spiritualist and biomedical practice in Mexico (Finkler 1985a, 1991).

During my initial research on Spiritualist healing, I found that patients seeking treatment from Spiritualist healers usually did so after unsuccessful treatment by several physicians. Generally, people were referred to the healers by friends, neighbors, or acquaintances (Finkler 1985a), people whose pains had been alleviated by Spiritualist ministrations. This finding led me to carry out my study of biomedical practice in Mexico and to question what propelled people to seek alternative healing and why biomedical treatment failed to alleviate their non-life-threatening conditions.

METHODS

During two separate research periods, I studied Spiritualist and biomedical healing and their respective patients.[8] I spent two years in a Spiritualist temple in a rural region in Mexico where I investigated healers and patients and also trained as a Spiritualist healer (Finkler 1985a). Subsequently, I spent two years in a large urban hospital in Mexico City where I studied biomedical practice and patients' responses (Finkler 1991).

In the Spiritualist temple, I observed 1,212 healer-patient interactions, and in the hospital, I sat in on 800 medical consultations. Subsequently, I followed up on the patients in both studies[9] to assess their responses to treatment at each research site. I studied the healing practices of 10 healers and 17 physicians.

The patients at both research sites were from the lower echelons of Mexican society and had similar non-life-threatening complaints, including headaches, back pain, chest pain, abdominal pains, and general musculoskeletal discomfort.

HEALERS

Mexican Spiritualist healers are primarily women.[10] They are usually recruited as a result of having themselves had an affliction unsuccessfully treated by physicians. Healers minister to the sick through spirit protectors who possess their bodies when they enter a trance. Mexican Spiritualists tame the spirits of the dead that roam the universe and harness them for the good of humankind, that is, for healing the sick. The spirits possess the bodies of the healers—individuals chosen to treat the afflicted. Spiritualist curers resort to a wide variety of healing techniques, including the use of an extensive pharmacopoeia, ritual cleansing, purgatives, massages, baths, spiritual surgeries, religious ritual, pharmaceuticals,[11] and, what I call "passive catharsis," when a patient experiences a sense of release and relief without having said anything (Finkler 1985a).

In general, Spiritualist healers do not provide the patient with a definitive diagnosis, and when they do, it usually consists of informing the person either that he or she possesses a gift (*don*) that requires cultivation or that the person is possessed by an obscure spirit that requires extrication. Normally, people whose illnesses were not readily alleviated by standard Spiritualist procedures were given these types of diagnoses. In either instance, the patient is required to enter training to develop the gift for healing or to expel the evil spirit. A person who does so becomes what I call a regular, an adherent of Spiritualism, and can become a healer or another type of temple functionary. When a healer declares that the patient is possessed of the gift of healing or by an evil spirit, it is a sure way of recruiting the patient into the ranks of Spiritualism. Spiritualist healers and those who be-

come regulars are ordinary people whose lives become restructured by their participation in a community of persons immersed in weekly and monthly religious rituals and by new networks of associations.

While Spiritualist healing and its practices may be alien to many readers, Mexican biomedical practice, on first glance, will be familiar in its overall form. The 17 physicians I studied, two of whom were women, employ similar technological accoutrements (for example, stethoscopes, sphygmomanometers, scales, X-ray machines) and the international vocabulary of disease entities familiar to physicians the world over. The government hospital in which I carried out the study was poorly funded, and its impoverished state was reflected in the conditions under which the physicians performed their medical activities. They received patients in small cubicles furnished only with a desk and a cot, and they shared stethoscopes, blood pressure monitors, and other basic medical tools. The majority of the diagnoses physicians gave to patients were related to nonspecific etiologies, followed by conditions associated with infections and parasites associated with digestive, genitourinary, and respiratory problems (Finkler 1991).

Before turning to the comparison between Spiritualist and biomedical practices, I must emphasize that my discussion attends to the general similarities and dissimilarities between the two regimes. It must be kept in mind also that individual differences exist among Spiritualist healers and among physicians in the ways each type of practitioner exercises healing activities, including the advice a healer or a physician may give to patients concerning life's problems.[12]

SIMILARITIES BETWEEN SPIRITUALISM AND BIOMEDICINE

The disparities between Spiritualist and biomedical therapeutics and the ways in which patients perceive each of the two healing systems unquestionably outweigh the similarities, but the similarities between the two regimes are intriguing. For example, as biomedicine focuses on the body (Pellegrino and Thomasma 1981), so too Spiritualist healers address their ministrations to bodily discomforts. It is important to stress that patients sought, first and foremost, symptom alleviation from Spiritualist healers in much the same way as they did from physicians. In fact, as I noted earlier, the overwhelming majority of first-time patients in a Spiritualist temple arrive with bodily pains of some duration (Finkler 1985a) and after having been unsuccessfully treated by physicians.

Both physicians and Spiritualist healers adhere to a dualistic view of the body and its attendant disturbances. Biomedicine has been criticized for its mind-body dualism (Engel 1977), but it is frequently overlooked that a similar dualism prevails in sacred healing such as Spiritualism. Spiritualists clearly and forcefully distinguish between the corporeal, or in their terminology "material," and "spiritual" disturbances in much the same way that physicians distinguish between organic and psychological sickness. This dualism is contrary to the more characteristic Mexican holistic concepts of the body and sickness in which sickness is normally regarded by both sexes as an extension of day-to-day adverse experience or emotional discharges, especially anger.[13] Thus, both Spiritualist healers and physicians impose a mind-body dualism on their patients.

There are structural, if not contextual, similarities between Spiritualist healers and physicians in their encounters with patients. In both regimens, the patient takes the role of a passive recipient of the practitioner's ministrations, and in both regimens, the practitioners require their patients' compliance.[14] In both settings, I witnessed practitioners reprimanding patients for not having followed the prescribed treatments.

. . .

As I noted previously, while academicians see profound epistemological differences between biomedical practitioners and alternative healers, such as Spiritualists, from the patient's perspective, biomedicine and Spiritualism accomplish similar ends. For example, in their desire to know what is wrong with them, patients expect to have their bodies examined and their "insides" seen. Both physicians and healers attempt to peer inside the patient's body, the former with technological apparatus and the latter with the gaze of the spirits. According to Spiritualist healers and their patients, the healing spirits penetrate the bodies of patients to ascertain their malady. The spiritual gaze exerted by the healers' spirits parallels patients' expectations for technological management that enables physicians, in the words of one patient, "to look inside my body" to make a correct diagnosis. Ironically, while physicians must juggle available resources and struggle with the decision whether to use contemporary technology (Finkler 1991) to make their diagnoses, the spirits' gaze is routine and intrinsic to Spiritualistic healing. The spirits continuously proclaim their omniscience, and patients are not even required to say much, often to the patients' relief. In this way, patients undergo what I have called "passive catharsis" (Finkler 1985a) when the healer tells the patient what the patient is experiencing, eliminating the need for patients' active verbalization of their discomfort.

DIFFERENCES BETWEEN SPIRITUALIST AND BIOMEDICAL PRACTICE

The dissimilarities between the two regimes exist along several dimensions of contrast, including the physical setting, etiological beliefs, diagnosis and treatment repertoire, reorientation of the patient's body, recruitment into practice, and most importantly the practitioner-patient relationship.

The Physical Setting

The physical setting of the healing encounter reflects broad prevailing themes in the respective societies in which each of the two healing regimes is embedded. Mexican Spiritualism evolved out of Mexican culture, and the spatial setting in which the healing takes place reflects Mexican cultural sensibilities. The physical context in which healers discharge their ministrations mirrors the Mexican culture's concern with family and community and its lack of concern with privacy. Not unsurprisingly, in Spiritualist temples, the healing experience is communal. Healers sit in one room, receiving patients separately. Consequently, there is a cacophony in Spiritualist healing rooms that imparts a sense of a collective experience, very unlike the physician-patient encounter that takes place in isolation in a cubicle, occasionally in the presence of onlookers such as students, nurses, and occasional visitors. The relatively private surroundings of biomedical consultations reflect the individualist cast of biomedicine. As I noted earlier, biomedicine was transplanted into Mexico from Europe and the United States, and the spatial structure of the physician-patient encounter as we know it today and as it takes place in Mexico mimics Western industrialized society's emphasis on privacy and individualism. This model conceives of the person as an autonomous unit, independent of and isolated from other individuals and from social and cultural contexts, as the patient is when he or she enters the physician's cubicle for a consultation.

Etiological Beliefs and Diagnoses

The common pool of etiological beliefs[15] in Mexico contains notions about environmental assaults such as climate (cold, wet), inappropriate diet and lack of vitamins, and hard work. Emotional discharges, associated with adverse life events, and day-to-day experience are regarded as sickness producing. Most important, anger, usually associated with moral evaluations and conflicting social relations and frequently allied with nerves (nervios), is a singularly important etiological explanation of a sickness episode. Susto, or sudden fright, is considered to produce various maladies, but especially diabetes. Spiritualist healers subscribe to the ideas held by most Mexicans about sickness causality with one notable exception: belief in witchcraft.

If biomedical treatment fails, many people assume that the infirmity is produced by witchcraft. Patients seeking treatment from Spiritualist healers usually arrive at a Spiritualist temple believing that witchcraft has been worked on them. The Spiritualist healers I studied categorically deny this possibility. Spiritualists' denial of the existence of witchcraft removes the blame for the patient's disorder from a neighbor, relative, or other person with whom the patient interacts. Spiritualists fix culpability squarely on impersonal spirits for which neither the patient nor his or her social circle can be blamed. By doing so, they restore order in the person's disrupted social relations and thereby possibly avoid future anger resulting in illness.

In day-to-day practice, Spiritualist healers, unlike physicians, are not concerned with etiological explanations. Such etiologies as they do offer, however, are relatively limited and unchanging compared with those of biomedicine. Spiritualist healers confer a coherent system of explanation usually reduced to assaults by evil spirits. For example, Spiritualists believe that afflictions that stubbornly resist both biomedical and Spiritualist ministrations must have been caused by the intrusion of a recalcitrant spirit that requires taming in the service of healing and removal from the body.

Mexican physicians combine biomedical and traditional folk understandings to explain sickness.[16] In the majority of cases that I studied, the physicians' causal explanations included biomedical understandings of the breaking down of the bodily machine, invasion by pathogens, stress, and obesity, coupled with folk understandings such as anger, nerves and fright and, to a lesser extent, environmental and social causes, or diet. The emphasis, however, is on the individual's behavior and never on impersonal spirits or witchcraft. Most important, unlike the Spiritualist healer, the physician may provide more than one explanation, or may change explanations, especially if he changes the diagnosis.

Unlike physicians, Spiritualists draw on a limited diagnostic repertoire and eschew multiple diagnoses.

There is usually consistency among different Spiritualist healers regarding etiology, as well as diagnosis and treatment.[17] In fact, Spiritualists rarely furnish patients with a diagnosis, nor do patients expect to receive one, because they usually agree that the spirits are all knowing and know the patient's affliction. On the other hand, patients do expect to be given a diagnosis by physicians. In my studies, whether or not a patient received a diagnosis was an important variable influencing the perceived successful outcome of a physician's treatment (Finkler 1991). Theoretically, at least, physicians made their diagnosis on the basis of patients' presenting symptoms, medical history, and a physical examination. In my study of physicians' clinical judgments, I found that, in the last analysis, diagnoses were based on physicians' stereotypic epidemiological understandings of the patient population, individual physicians' training and experience, and moral values regarding, for example, sexual behavior. In other words, physicians often based diagnoses on understandings unrelated to patients' symptomatic presentations and medical histories.[18] For example, the majority of the physicians in the study diagnosed parasitosis in their poor patients regardless of the presenting symptoms (Finkler 1991).[19] When the initial diagnosis failed, physicians established diagnostic validity on the basis of symptom alleviation. A patient's report of feeling better as a result of the drug the physician had prescribed validated the diagnosis for the physician.

From the standpoint of good medical practice, a physician is required to test hypotheses and revise diagnoses according to empirical observations and the patient's response to the prescribed treatment, but from the patient's perspective, diagnostic revisions were distressing. For example, a physician would change the diagnosis if a patient's complaints were not alleviated by the prescribed treatment. A modification of the diagnosis suggested to the patient that the doctor lacked the certainty and knowledge to cure the illness. Moreover, when patients sought quick relief from pain by consulting various doctors, they often ended up with several different diagnoses for the same symptoms. Patients who were given different diagnoses by the same physician or by several physicians (Finkler 1991; Helman 1985; Koran 1975) became confused and befuddled about the nature of their disturbances and wondered which physician's diagnosis was correct. Interestingly, patients would occasionally ask Spiritualist healers to verify a physician's diagnosis as a way of making sense out of the diverse diagnoses they had been given by other physicians.

Adding to this confusion, physicians reorient the patient's view of his or her own body and the minutiae of its functioning when they explore with the patient the nature of his or her bowel movements and excreta, or when they dwell on issues relating to the patient's sexuality. Biomedical consultations frequently focused on matters related to sexuality, a subject normally not broached by Spiritualist healers, except when women patients reported vaginal discharges or delayed menstruation. Whereas patients confronting Spiritualist healers discussed male-female relations in terms of rights and obligations, within the medical consultation physicians called attention to the individual's sexuality in ways that Spiritualist healers never did. In the medical setting, marital relations became expressed in frequency of sexual intercourse or other issues concerning sexuality.

The focus on an individual's sexuality was inherent to the medical consultation when physicians questioned women (Finkler 1994a) about the frequency of sexual intercourse, menstruation, contraceptive use, and number of births and abortions.

. . .

In addition, women were required to change their concept of the shape of their bodies when physicians diagnosed patients as obese and prescribed special diets. In the impoverished social classes, women are rarely concerned with their weight, and they adhere to a traditional Mexican diet of tortillas, salsa, and beans out of economic necessity and cultural commitment. Unlike Spiritualist healers, who never imposed an esthetic model of the body on their patients, physicians would frequently do so to the consternation of the patients.[20]

The Practitioner–Patient Encounter

The doctor-patient encounter has become a central concern in the study of biomedical activities, given the widespread notion that the doctor-patient relationship provides the key to good medical practice. In this regard, alternative healers, including Spiritualists, are often held up as examples to show what the physician-patient relationship lacks. Numerous assertions have been made about folk healers' personal ties to the patient. It is commonly held, for example, that the folk healer-patient relationship, in contrast to that of the doctor and patient, is based on shared etiological understandings and congruent explanatory models and that traditional healers care more about and are more attentive to patients. Such attentiveness is often measured in terms of healers' having more eye contact with patients, more time with patients, and more empathy and compassion. It is also widely held that traditional healers, unlike physicians, have a holistic view of the patient.[21]

My observations, however, are that Spiritualist healers, unlike physicians, lack eye contact with their patients and ostensibly fail to recognize the individual standing before them. They sit in trance with expressionless faces, eyes closed, holding or stroking the patient, who briefly murmurs a description of the disorder. Being in the trance state precludes the healers' displaying any kind of affect for their patients. By contrast, during the medical consultations in the present study, the physician and patient sit facing each other; their physical contact is limited to the physician's physical explorations by palpation and auscultation. Physicians' affective expressions vary, however. Some constantly smile at the patient, while others maintain a serious demeanor.

Furthermore, in the consultations, physicians spend about 21 minutes on average with a first-time patient (Finkler 1991), whereas the Spiritualist healer-patient interaction usually lasts less than half that time (Finkler 1985a).[22] The affective content of the interaction varies among both physicians and Spiritualist healers. Some Spiritualist healers and physicians are relatively brusque and indifferent to a patient's suffering, while some Spiritualist healers console their patients by reminding them that God and the spirits know their pain and some physicians demonstrate concern for a patient's suffering.

The differing physical postures of the physicians and Spiritualist healers, the time they each spend with their patients, and the requirement that patients reorient their view of their own bodies highlight the dramaturgical nature of the physician-patient consultation in contrast to the Spiritualist healer-patient encounter.

. . .

The patient's major concern is that the healer or physician know his or her pain. When the patient confronts a Spiritualist healer, he or she need not tell the healer very much for the healer to know everything. In fact, the spirit constantly reminds the patient "I know everything." In this way, the healer reassures the patient and also establishes legitimacy in the healing role. The physician, though, must question the patient and anchor the condition and locate it in chronological time and in a specific part of the body in order to make an accurate diagnosis.

While patients' expectations of Spiritualist healers are that the spirits know everything, patients expect the physician to question them (Finkler 1991). In this way, they are assured that the physician will learn about their malady, a knowledge the spirit occupying the healer's body already possesses. Most important, patients are also assured that the Spiritualist healer knows their pain because they know that Spiritualist healers too have suffered afflictions before becoming healers. This brings us to the important difference of recruitment of healers and physicians.

Recruitment into the Healing Role

The different ways in which Spiritualist healers and physicians are recruited into their respective roles have different effects on patients. Whereas those recruited into the medical profession are usually healthy individuals, as we saw earlier, those recruited into Spiritualist healing usually experienced an affliction themselves before becoming healers. As formerly sick people who have become health providers, Spiritualist healers are themselves examples of the potential for recovery through Spiritualist ministrations. Importantly, they convey to the patient that they have grasped the patient's anguish through their personal experience. They experienced the pain in the past in the same way as the patient is experiencing it in the present. The doctor cannot provide the patient with experiential evidence, as Spiritualist healers proudly do, that his ministrations induce a transformation from having been sick to healing others. The potential conversion of a patient to a health practitioner, or other functionary serving God and the spirit world, forms part of the Spiritualist therapeutic repertoire, a technique that the biomedical therapeutic kit lacks.

Treatment Repertoires

As noted earlier, Spiritualist healers' diagnoses are relatively simple, but their treatment repertoires are relatively complex. By contrast, the physicians' diagnoses are complex, but the cure repertoire is limited. The physicians' treatments are chiefly medication or, in extreme cases, surgery. On the other hand, the Spiritualist healers treatment kit contains a large array of treatment options, which also involve a patient's participation in various treatment activities. These include the use of pharmaceuticals or herbs and other botanicals that rural patients are often required to collect in the open fields, getting massages, taking baths that require preparation by the patient, and other activities (for example, placing crosses under the bed), as well as participation in Spiritualist rituals. These activities, in effect, engage patients in their recovery. In keeping with this point, physicians take full responsibility for the patient's successful cure, if not for their failure to heal, whereas Spiritualist healers assign responsibility to patients for their cure by constantly reminding them that they must have unrelenting faith in the Spiritualist God and His benevolence, further involving them in their own therapy.

Furthermore, while the biomedical technological management for which patients clamor carries a heavy symbolic load and no doubt aids in perceived recovery, the cleansing that Spiritualist healers supply embodies powerful symbols that address the profound contradictions in which the patient's illness may be embedded. Not surprisingly, of those patients who perceived themselves as recovered through Spiritualist healing, most attributed the recovery to the cleansing they had received (Finkler 1985a). Whereas patients may have disagreed with the treatment course proposed by physicians, patients always agreed with the Spiritualist treatment, especially when it involved ritual cleansing, coupled with herbal remedies. With these cleansings, the healers symbolically removed evil that may have befallen the patient, and thereby resolved the disorder in the patient's life, even if only temporarily.

CONCLUSION

To summarize the dissimilarities, perhaps the most crucial difference between biomedicine and sacred healing of the Spiritualist variety is this: healers resolve contradictions for patients that physicians cannot because the biomedical script requires physicians to focus on discrete physical pains while the patient is experiencing a timeless and overbearing pain that is not necessarily localized in chronological time or confined to a specific part of the body.

Moreover, physicians do not address the contradictions in which patients are enmeshed. To explain sickness, the biomedical model may blame impersonal pathogens that attack the body, explaining the sickness in generalized terms rather than in terms of the patient's personal suffering. Or, it blames the patient, especially his or her poor habits (McKeown 1979).

Biomedicine often requires patients to alter customary behavior such as diet, work, or drinking habits, as well as to alter profound notions of their bodies. It does not, however, attempt to transform the circumstances of a patient's life in the way Spiritualists do for those who become regulars. Spiritualist healing can gradually transform the person's existence by incorporating him or her, and sometimes the entire family, into a religious community. Over the long term, Spiritualist healing provides new interpersonal networks and also places the person in a new relationship with God. In the latter instance, relationships with other human beings become subsumed within the interaction with God. This process is further facilitated by Spiritualist insistence that witchcraft lacks any reality, that human beings cannot harm one another.

By denying the existence of witchcraft and evil machinated by other humans, Spiritualists facilitate smoother social interactions, militating against anger and future illness episodes.

Spiritualist healing progressively reorders the existence of those patients who eventually become regulars by incorporating them into a community of sufferers who share a satisfying religious reality and symbolic meanings, by God appointing them to become functionaries in their movement, or by His having chosen them to become healers because they possess the gift. As I have emphasized elsewhere, Spiritualist healers do not produce miraculous cures. All transformations are achieved gradually, and some patients even experience great pain in the process (cf. Finkler 1985a).

It is noteworthy, however, that Spiritualist healing differentially reorders men's and women's lives; it reorders men's lives to the ostensible advantage of women. Spiritualists preach against machismo in men, leading them to cease drinking heavily and womanizing. The men tend to spend their leisure time with their wives and families rather than with their former friends or other women. By restructuring men's lives, Spiritualists promote smoother marital relationships (Finkler 1981), a change women recognize as salutary and healthful. As I explain elsewhere, adverse social relations, especially marital discord, can be as pathogenic as any virus, and women's health in Mexico specifically is greatly influenced by their relations with their mates (Finkler 1994a). In the measure that Spiritualist healers succeed in easing the marital relationship, they are also promoting a woman's health.

While biomedicine attempts to refashion the patient's view of his or her body, Spiritualism alters the person's experience of his or her body. On an existential level, healers embody a spirit through trance and, in so doing, experience their bodies in a new and sacred way. Uniformly, all healers and functionaries who entered trance to fulfill their healing roles reported that they have experienced a tingling effect in their bodies, a heightening of the senses, and a vision of extraordinary colors. Additionally, trancing may have physiological correlates that influence the healing process (Finkler 1985a). Clearly, biomedicine does not incorporate trancing into its treatment repertoire, nor does it address the existential dilemmas, reinterpret them, give them new meanings, or change the social relationships in which the patient is embedded, including those between husband and wife (Finkler 1981).

. . .

In the final analysis, Spiritualist healers, like physicians, fail to heal their patients when they fail to attend to the patient's world, with its attendant contradictions and requisite transformations (Finkler 1985a, 1991). To succeed in resolving non-life-threatening, subacute conditions, a healing system must address patients' bodily ills and concurrently transform their perceived existence (Finkler 1991, 1994a). Importantly, the process of transformation, in and of itself, alters the patients' lives and, in the process, their state of health.[23]

One final point merits consideration. This comparison suggests that folk healers, such as Spiritualists, depend on their healing techniques rather than on their persona to effect a cure. Yet, as I noted at the outset of this discussion, great emphasis has been given to the relationship between the healer and patient in the same way as to the doctor-patient relationship in biomedical practice (see also West 1984). In fact, the doctor-patient interaction has formed a focal point of study, and it has become axiomatic that the doctor-patient relationship is a determining factor in successful primary health care delivery and by extension in the healing process (cf. Brody 1992). It has been asserted that a proper doctor-patient relationship, regarded as crucial in biomedicine, produces a placebo effect (Brody 1988), and that treatment outcomes depend on it. It is widely assumed that the relationship between patient and sacred healer has a similar effect.

My findings are (Finkler 1991) that only certain aspects of the doctor-patient relationship tend to influence the healing process in biomedical practice for patients with self-limiting conditions, revolving around the physician's explanations of the patient's condition, the patient's agreement with the physician's diagnosis, and whether or not patients participated in the encounter,[24] reemphasizing the role of patient participation in cures that, as I noted, are incorporated in Spiritualist treatment techniques.

. . .

My argument is that biomedical practice relies greatly on patient management during the therapeutic encounter because its healing techniques lack certainties; in Fox's words, "the development of scientific medicine, then, has both uncovered and created uncertainties and risk that were not previously known or experienced" (1980:19). As I observed earlier, the physician's therapeutic kit lacks certainty and means to resolve the contradictions by which the patient is encompassed, to deal with patients' subjective experiences and the certainties of pain, or to reorder their lives. For this reason, treatment hinges not only on healing techniques, as it does in sacred healing, but also on the encounter itself, including the time it lasts, and the physician's persona becomes part of the physician's tool kit. Significantly, Spiritualists insist that there are no differences among individual healers.

I assert that this is because in Spiritualist healing, the healer-patient encounter is secondary to the healer's techniques, in which the person of the healer is submerged. The treatment techniques involve the patient in the cure rather than the healer's manner or personality itself and aid patients in restructuring the conflicts in which they may be entangled.

The emphasis on the role of the individual healer effecting the cure of the individual patient reflects Western industrialized society's bias, wherein the person has become an atomistic unit. The fostering of the drama in the consultation is based on the model of the doctor-patient relationship that mirrors the prevailing ethos of the abstract, independent individual confronting a self-interested, autonomous physician during the encounter. The individual in Mexico is not solitary; he or she is embedded in a family that encompasses his or her life, and each looks to the physician for alleviation of pain. Spiritualist healing addresses issues of culpability, evil, and witchcraft, and reorders social relationships, especially those with one's mate (Finkler 1981), which biomedicine fails to do.

. . .

Paradoxically, as a folk healing movement, Spiritualist beliefs exert little hegemonic force in Mexico on a national scale, but by transforming patients' existence through incorporation into a community of persons healed spiritually, they have created a religious movement comprising thousands of people. In so doing, Spiritualist ministrations have promoted, on an aggregate level, religious pluralism in Mexico. Spiritualism thereby contributes to advancing social change by mobilizing a sizable population and fomenting a growing movement that furnishes Mexicans with new options for religious participation. While Spiritualist healing may change a couple's day-to-day interaction, on an aggregate level the movement fails to restructure Mexican society in ways that could benefit its participants economically or politically (Finkler 1986a). On the other hand, biomedicine, by treating individual bodies without transforming people's lives, fails to contribute to new social forms for the collectivity. It succeeds only in maintaining its hegemony as the major authorized provider of health care legitimated by the state.

NOTES

1. There has been a surge of interest in alternative healing in the U.S. medical community, as evidenced by the fact that the National Institutes of Health have opened the Office of Alternative Medicine in 1993 to promote stud-

ies of alternative medical practices and their efficacy (see also Eisenberg et al. 1993).

2. The Spiritualist movement in Mexico was founded as a religious movement in 1861 by a recalcitrant priest named Roque Rojas, whose portrait hangs at the altar of every Spiritualist temple. (For a historical overview, see Finkler 1983, 1985a; also see Lagarriga 1991; Ortiz Echániz 1977, 1989.)

3. Sylvia Echániz Ortiz (personal communication) reported that in one Mexico City Spiritualist temple that she had studied for over 20 years, she counted as many as 5,000 patients in one day. In the rural area where I carried out my research on Mexican Spiritualist healing, I counted as many as 125 patients in a day (Finkler 1985a). There are hundreds of Spiritualist temples in Mexico, as well as in certain parts of the United States (Finkler 1983, 1985a).

4. In October 23, 1833, Valentin Gomez Farias instituted the Establecimiento de Ciencias Médicas and established French medicine in Mexico. (See Finkler 1991 for a discussion of the history of medicine in Mexico.)

5. See chapters 5 through 8 in Finkler 1991 for the specific cultural influences on Mexican biomedical practice.

6. This has often been discussed under the rubric of medical pluralism (see, for example, Bastien 1992; Cosminsky 1983; Crandon-Malamud 1991; Janzen 1978).

7. See bibliographies in Finkler 1985a, 1986b, 1986c. Also, see a formal economic analysis done by Lenihan (1990). She compares the cost effectiveness of Spiritualist healers and physicians, using the data reported in Finkler 1985a and 1991.

8. I employed the same method in both studies. Because of space limitations, I refer the reader to Finkler 1985a and 1991 for a detailed description of the method. There I discuss with great specificity sampling techniques and selection, recruitment of patients into the study, instruments used in each study, and interviewing techniques at each research site. In both studies, patients were interviewed before they saw the healers and the physicians, and I observed the healer and physician consultations.

9. I followed up at their homes 125 patients in the rural region seeking treatment from the Spiritualist temple and 205 patients in Mexico City who were initially interviewed at the hospital (see Finkler 1985a, 1991).

10. The fact that the majority of the healers are recruited as a consequence of affliction and that they are also women raises the important question of differential morbidity along gender lines. I initially addressed this issue in Finkler 1985b and more recently in Finkler 1994a where I explore in great detail and in new ways why more women experience sickness than men and I offer a new theory to explain the phenomenon.

11. Many pharmaceuticals have now become part of folk medicine and have been incorporated into folk practitioners' pharmacopoeia, including Spiritualist healers. These may include terramycin, Enterovioforma, Dramamine, and others. Generally speaking, the pharmaceuticals prescribed by a spirit possessing the healer's body reflect the healer's experiences in a waking state. For example, the spirit of a woman healer who had worked

as a nurse assistant tended to prescribe patent medicines, while others who lacked similar exposure prescribed only the standard massages, baths, and teas that are regarded as the most pure type of Spiritualist healing (see Finkler 1985a.)

12. See Finkler 1985a:chapter 7 and Finkler 1991:chapter 7 for a detailed discussion of the variations in practice among Spiritualist healers and among physicians respectively.

13. See Finkler 1985a and 1991 for discussion of etiological beliefs in Mexico. It could, of course, be argued that Spiritualists concretize a holistic view of the body when they literally incorporate the spirits into their bodies during possession trance; nevertheless, they profess a dualistic perspective as do physicians.

14. It is possible that the Spiritualist healers' encounters with their patients mimic in a religious idiom biomedicine's secular practices, given their exposure as patients to biomedicine and its procedures. Spiritualist healers also wear white coats during healing sessions, as do physicians.

15. See Finkler 1991 where I introduce and discuss the notion of a cultural pool of etiological understandings, upon which men and women draw differentially when they are struck by a sickness (see Finkler 1994a).

16. The exact nature of Mexican physicians' etiological explanations is highly complex. For a discussion of their beliefs and clinical judgment, see Finkler 1991:chapter 6.

17. For a detailed comparison of agreements among Spiritualist healers and among healers and patients regarding etiology and treatment, see Finkler 1984.

18. For a similar finding on psychiatric practice in the United States, see Gaines 1979.

19. It is common knowledge that parasitic infections are endemic across Mexico, although it is disputed to what degree people simply carry rather than experience parasitic disease, especially amebiasis (Gutierrez 1986). According to Gutierrez, "The fundamental problem consists of a tendency to erroneously diagnose amebiasis in cases of diarrhea and dysentery due to the difficulty in practicing laboratory examinations" (1986:375).

20. In fact, some physicians would claim that a patient was obese when they lacked a diagnosis for a woman's condition. See Finkler 1994a, especially the case of Josefina who, like other women, was distressed by the physician's suggestion that her body was abnormal. Also, see for example, the case of Nomi in Finkler 1991, where the physician prescribed a diet for the patient that was impossible for her to follow because of economic constraints and work routines.

21. Numerous anthropologists have written on the importance of the folk healer-patient relationship, including Clark 1973; Dobkin de Rios 1981; Fabrega and Silver 1973; Foster and Anderson 1978; Gould 1977; Kinzie 1976; Kleinman 1980; Landy 1977; Peters 1978.

22. In fact, when the head of the temple noticed that a healer spent a relatively long time with a patient, she would reprimand the spirit that it was spending too much time with one patient. This usually occurred when there were many people waiting for a consulta-

tion. During my initial study of Spiritualist healing, I counted as many as 125 patients seeking treatment from the healers in one day. On my subsequent visits, and as recently as the summer of 1993, I observed many more patients than the 125 I noted in my study in 1977–79; and the number of healers grew from 8 to 24, working two shifts, in this temple alone during a span of 14 years.

23. See Finkler 1994a for the case of Margarita. She provides an excellent example of how a woman changed from a sickly to a healthy individual in the process of becoming a Karate champion. Her case emphasizes that it is the *process* of transformation itself that heals.

24. Other variables include: the physician's giving the patient a diagnosis; whether or not physicians explained to the patients what was wrong; whether or not patients agreed with the physician's diagnosis; and whether or not patients posed questions to the physician, meaning they participated in the consultation (see Finkler 1991; for a multivariate analysis of these findings showing the types of patients most responsive to these aspects of the physician-patient encounter, see Finkler 1994b).

REFERENCES

Armstrong, David. 1983. The Political Anatomy of the Body. Cambridge: Cambridge University Press.

Bastien, Joseph W. 1992. Drum and Stethoscope. Salt Lake City: University of Utah Press.

Berger, Peter, et al. 1974. The Homeless Mind. New York: Vintage Books.

Brody, Howard. 1988. The Symbolic Power of the Modern Personal Physician: The Placebo Response under Challenge. Journal of Drug Issues 18:149–161.

———. 1992. The Healer's Power. New Haven, CT: Yale University Press.

Clark, Margaret. 1973. Health in the Mexican American Culture. Berkeley: University of California Press.

Cosminsky, Sheila. 1983. Medical Pluralism in Mesoamerica. *In* Heritage of Conquest. Thirty Years Later. Carl Kendall, John Hawkins, and Laurel Bossen, eds. Pp. 159–174. Albuquerque: University of New Mexico Press.

Crandon-Malamud, Libbet. 1991. From the Fat of Our Souls. Berkeley: University of California Press.

Dobkin de Rios, Marlene D. 1981. Socio-Economic Characteristics of an Amazon Urban Healer's Clientele. Social Science & Medicine 15B:51–63.

Eisenberg, David M., et al. 1993. The Unconventional Medicine in the United States. New England Journal of Medicine 328:246–252.

Engel, George L. 1977. The Need for a New Medical Model: A Challenge for Biomedicine. Science 196:129–136.

Fabrega, Horacio, Jr., and Daniel B. Silver. 1973. Illness and Shamanistic Curing in Zinacantan. Stanford, CA: Stanford University Press.

Finkler, Kaja. 1981. Dissident Religious Movements in the Service of Women's Power. Sex Roles 7(5):481–495.

———. 1983. Dissident Sectarian Movements, the Catholic Church, and Social Class in Mexico. Comparative Studies in Society and History 25(2):277–305.

———. 1984. The Nonsharing of Medical Knowledge among Spiritualist Healers and Their Patients: A Contribution to the Study of Intra-Cultural Diversity and Practitioner-Patient Relationship. Medical Anthropology 8(3): 195–209.

———. 1985a. Spiritualist Healers in Mexico. South Hadley, MA: Praeger, Bergin and Garvey Publishers.

———. 1985b. Symptomatic Differences between the Sexes in Rural Mexico. Culture, Medicine and Psychiatry 9:27–57.

———. 1986a. The Social Consequence of Wellness: A View of Healing Outcomes from Micro and Macro Perspectives. International Journal of Health Services 16(4):627–642.

———. 1986b. The Westernization of the Therapeutic Encounter. Paper prepared for the Joint Conference of British Medical Anthropology Society and the Society for Medical Anthropology, Cambridge.

———. 1986c. The Healer-Patient Relationship in Sacred and Medical Contexts. Paper presented at the Annual Meeting of the American Anthropological Association, Philadelphia.

———. 1991. Physicians at Work, Patients in Pain: Biomedical Practice and Patient Response in Mexico. Boulder, CO: Westview Press.

———. 1994a. Women in Pain. Philadelphia: University of Pennsylvania Press.

———. 1994b. Factors Influencing Patient Perceived Recovery in Biomedical Practice. Unpublished manuscript.

Foster, George M., and Barbara Anderson. 1978. Medical Anthropology. New York: John Wiley and Sons.

Foucault, Michel. 1975. The Birth of the Clinic. New York: Vintage Books.

Fox, Renée C. 1980. The Evolution of Medical Uncertainty. Milbank Memorial Fund Quarterly/Health and Society 58(1):1–49.

Gaines, Atwood. 1979. Definitions and Diagnoses. Culture, Medicine and Psychiatry 3:381–418.

Gould, Harold A. 1977. Modern Medicine and Folk Cognition in Rural India. In Culture, Disease and Healing. David Landy, ed. Pp. 249–305. New York: Macmillan.

Gutierrez, Gonzalo. 1986. Epidemiologia y control de la amibiasis en México. Archivos De Investigación Médica (Mexico) 17(Suppl. 1):375–383.

Helman, Cecil G. 1985. Communication in Primary Care: The Role of Patient and Practitioner Explanatory Models. Social Science & Medicine 29(9):923–931.

Janzen, John. 1978. The Quest for Therapy in Lower Zaire. Berkeley: University of California Press.

Kinzie, David, et al. 1976. Native Healers in Malaysia. In Culture Bound Syndromes, Ethnopsychiatry and Alternate Therapies. William P. Lebra, ed. Honolulu: The University Press of Hawaii.

Kleinman, Arthur. 1978. Concepts and Models for the Comparison of Medical Systems as Cultural Systems. Social Science & Medicine 12:85–93.

———. 1980. Patients and Healers in the Context of Culture. Berkeley: University of California Press.

Koran, Lorrin. 1975. The Reliability of Clinical Methods, Data and Judgements. New England Journal of Medicine 293(13):642–646.

Lagarriga, Isabel Attias. 1991. Espiritualismo Trinitario Mariano nuevas perspectivas de análisis. Xalapa, Mexico: Universidad Veracruzana.

Landy, David. 1977. Role Adaptation: Traditional Curers under the Impact of Western Medicine. In Culture, Disease and Healing. David Landy, ed. Pp. 468–480. New York: Macmillan.

Lenihan, Bonnie. 1990. The Economic Development and Implications of Informal Sector Health Care. Ph.D. dissertation, University of Tennessee, Knoxville.

McKeown, Thomas. 1979. The Role of Medicine. Princeton, NJ: Princeton University Press.

Ortiz Echániz, Silvia. 1977. Espiritualismo en México. Cuadernos DEAS, 20. Mexico: Instituto Nacional de Antropologia e Historia.

———. 1989. Una religiosidad popular en México: El espiritualismo Trinitario Mariano. México: Instituto Nacional de Antropologia e Historia.

Pellegrino, Edmund D., and David C. Thomasma. 1981. A Philosophical Basis of Medical Practice. New York: Oxford University Press.

Peters, Larry. 1978. Psychotherapy in Tamang Shamanism. Ethos 6(2):63–91.

Torgovnick, Marianna. 1990. Gone Primitive. Chicago: University of Chicago Press.

Turner, Bryan S. 1984. The Body and Society. New York: Basil Blackwell.

West, Candace. 1984. Routine Complications. Bloomington, IN: Indiana University Press.

Wilson, Robert N. 1963. Patient-Practitioner Relationships. In Handbook of Medical Sociology. Howard E. Greenman et al. eds. Pp. 273–298. Englewood, NJ: Prentice-Hall.

14

The Sorcerer and His Magic

Claude Lévi-Strauss

This selection, foundational in medical anthropology, is about the role of belief in both healing and harm—what are today called the placebo and nocebo effects. Written by the famous French anthropologist who pioneered the study of structuralism and the analysis of myth, this selection may be a little difficult, but it is well worth the effort. Claude Lévi-Strauss uses four compelling stories: "voodoo death" among Australian aborigines; a Nambicuara shaman and political leader from the Amazonian rain forest; a teenage boy accused of witchcraft among the Zuni, a Pueblo people of New Mexico; and Quesalid, a Kwakiutl shaman from the Pacific Northwest coastal tribe studied by Franz Boas. Each story illustrates Lévi-Strauss's argument that there are three levels of belief involved in a shamanistic cure. These beliefs in the power of the sorcerer are socially constructed and socially maintained. Belief is enhanced by the manipulation of symbols in a ritual setting.

The interaction of belief and experience is very important. As we saw in selection 13, being cured by a Spiritualist healer can be a life-altering experience. The story of Quesalid in this selection by Lévi-Strauss is a powerful and poignant story; it is a story of knowledge, power, a "trick," and ultimately the transformation of an individual's life. Lévi-Strauss comments that Quesalid "did not become a great shaman because he cured his patients; he cured his patients because he had become a great shaman." This delineates precisely the relationship between belief and healing. Belief plays a central role in the "shamanistic complex." It provides the mechanism for the "fabulation" of an unknown reality— the cultural process of controlling something by naming and telling a story about it.

The use of symbols, like the doctor's white coat, plays an important role in reinforcing the patient's beliefs; these symbols can be objects or words, but they have special meaning to participants. Participants do not often see the symbolic dimension to their activities; anthropologists tend to see them, partly because that is a benefit of being an outsider looking in. The bone pointed at the sorcerer's victim, in the voodoo death case described at the beginning of this selection, is a good example of a powerful object–symbol. Quesalid's scrap of bloody feather is another.

The manipulation of symbols, however, is only a means to an end. Its purpose is to bring a cure. That is done, psychosomatic research tells us, by harnessing the power of the mind and the body's own ability to heal itself. The exact mechanisms for this process remain unknown. Lévi-Strauss uses the idea of "abreaction" (a powerful turning point of reliving an event), borrowed from psychoanalytic theory, to explain this mechanism. Although this part of the analysis generally has not been accepted by anthropologists, recent theories about symbolic healing by James Dow (1986), Daniel Moerman (1991), and Robert Hahn (1995) should be of interest to advanced students.

As you read this selection, consider these questions:

- *What are the three levels of belief that Lévi-Strauss thinks form the core of the "shamanistic complex"? Which of these beliefs do you think is the most important?*

- *Why does Quesalid change from a nonbeliever to a believer? How does he get incorporated into the system? Why doesn't he tell the truth at the end of his life?*

- *To what extent do patients expect that their biomedical doctor act like a shaman?*

- *How does the use of symbols facilitate belief?*

Since the pioneering work of Cannon, we understand more clearly the psycho-physiological mechanisms underlying the instances reported from many parts of the world of death by exorcism and the casting of spells.[1] An individual who is aware that he is the object of sorcery is thoroughly convinced that he is doomed according to the most solemn traditions of his group. His friends and relatives share this certainty.

From then on the community withdraws. Standing aloof from the accursed, it treats him not only as though he were already dead but as though he were a source of danger to the entire group. On every occasion and by every action, the social body suggests death to the unfortunate victim, who no longer hopes to escape what he considers to be his ineluctable fate. Shortly thereafter, sacred rites are held to dispatch him to the realm of shadows. First brutally torn from all of his family and social ties and excluded from all functions and activities through which he experienced self-awareness, then banished by the same forces from the world of the living, the victim yields to the combined effect of intense terror, the sudden total withdrawal of the multiple reference systems provided by the support of the group, and, finally, to the group's decisive reversal in proclaiming him—once a living man, with rights and obligations—dead and an object of fear, ritual, and taboo. Physical integrity cannot withstand the dissolution of the social personality.[2]

How are these complex phenomena expressed on the physiological level? Cannon showed that fear, like rage, is associated with a particularly intense activity of the sympathetic nervous system. This activity is ordinarily useful, involving organic modifications which enable the individual to adapt himself to a new situation. But if the individual cannot avail himself of any instinctive or acquired response to an extraordinary situation (or to one which he conceives of as such), the activity of the sympathetic nervous system becomes intensified and disorganized; it may, sometimes within a few hours, lead to a decrease in the volume of blood and a concomitant drop in blood pressure, which result in irreparable damage to the circulatory organs. The rejection of food and drink, frequent among patients in the throes of intense anxiety, precipitates this process; dehydration acts as a stimulus to the sympathetic nervous system, and the decrease in blood volume is accentuated by the growing permeability of the capillary vessels. These hypotheses were confirmed by the study of several cases of trauma resulting from bombings, battle shock, and even surgical operations; death results, yet the autopsy reveals no lesions.

There is, therefore, no reason to doubt the efficacy of certain magical practices. But at the same time we see that the efficacy of magic implies a belief in magic. The latter has three complementary aspects: first, the sorcerer's belief in the effectiveness of his techniques; second, the patient's or victim's belief in the sorcerer's power; and, finally, the faith and expectations of the group, which constantly act as a sort of gravitational field within which the relationship between sorcerer and bewitched is located and defined.[3] Obviously, none of the three parties is capable of forming a clear picture of the sympathetic nervous system's activity or of the disturbances which Cannon called homeostatic. When the sorcerer claims to suck out of the patient's body a foreign object whose presence would explain the illness and produces a stone which he had previously hidden in his mouth, how does he justify this procedure in his own eyes? How can an innocent person accused of sorcery prove his

innocence if the accusation is unanimous—since the magical situation is a consensual phenomenon? And, finally, how much credulity and how much skepticism are involved in the attitude of the group toward those in whom it recognizes extraordinary powers, to whom it accords corresponding privileges, but from whom it also requires adequate satisfaction? Let us begin by examining this last point.

It was in September, 1938. For several weeks we had been camping with a small band of Nambicuara Indians near the headwaters of the Tapajoz, in those desolate savannas of central Brazil where the natives wander during the greater part of the year, collecting seeds and wild fruits, hunting small mammals, insects, and reptiles, and whatever else might prevent them from dying of starvation. Thirty of them were camped together there, quite by chance. They were grouped in families under frail lean-tos of branches, which give scant protection from the scorching sun, nocturnal chill, rain, and wind. Like most bands, this one had both a secular chief and a sorcerer; the latter's daily activities—hunting, fishing, and handicrafts—were in no way different from those of the other men of the group. He was a robust man, about forty-five years old, and a *bon vivant*.

One evening, however, he did not return to camp at the usual time. Night fell and fires were lit; the natives were visibly worried. Countless perils lurk in the bush: torrential rivers, the somewhat improbable danger of encountering a large wild beast—jaguar or anteater—or, more readily pictured by the Nambicuara, an apparently harmless animal which is the incarnation of an evil spirit of the waters or forest. And above all, each night for the past week we had seen mysterious campfires, which sometimes approached and sometimes receded from our own. Any unknown band is always potentially hostile. After a two-hour wait, the natives were convinced that their companion had been killed in ambush and, while his two young wives and his son wept noisily in mourning for their dead husband and father, the other natives discussed the tragic consequences foreshadowed by the disappearance of their sorcerer.

Toward ten that evening, the anguished anticipation of imminent disaster, the lamentations in which the other women began to join, and the agitation of the men had created an intolerable atmosphere, and we decided to reconnoiter with several natives who had remained relatively calm. We had not gone two hundred yards when we stumbled upon a motionless figure. It was our man, crouching silently, shivering in the chilly night air, disheveled and without his belt, necklaces, and arm-bands (the Nambicuara wear nothing else). He allowed us to lead him back to the camp site without resistance, but only after long exhortations by his group and pleading by his family was he persuaded to talk. Finally, bit by bit, we extracted the details of his story. A thunderstorm, the first of the season, had burst during the afternoon, and the thunder had carried him off to a site several miles distant, which he named, and then, after stripping him completely, had brought him back to the spot where we found him. Everyone went off to sleep commenting on the event. The next day the thunder victim had recovered his joviality and, what is more, all his ornaments. This last detail did not appear to surprise anyone, and life resumed its normal course.

A few days later, however, another version of these prodigious events began to be circulated by certain natives. We must note that this band was actually composed of individuals of different origins and had been fused into a new social entity as a result of unknown circumstances. One of the groups had been decimated by an epidemic several years before and was no longer sufficiently large to lead an independent life; the other had seceded from its original tribe and found itself in the same straits. When and under what circumstances the two groups met and decided to unite their efforts, we could not discover. The secular leader of the new band came from one group and the sorcerer, or religious leader, from the other. The fusion was obviously recent, for no marriage had yet taken place between the two groups when we met them, although the children of one were usually betrothed to the children of the other; each group had retained its own dialect, and their members could communicate only through two or three bilingual natives.

This is the rumor that was spread. There was good reason to suppose that the unknown bands crossing the savanna belonged to the tribe of the seceded group of which the sorcerer was a member. The sorcerer, impinging on the functions of his colleague the political chief, had doubtless wanted to contact his former tribesmen, perhaps to ask to return to the fold, or to provoke an attack upon his new companions, or perhaps even to reassure them of the friendly intentions of the latter. In any case, the sorcerer had needed a pretext for his absence, and his kidnapping by thunder and its subsequent staging were invented toward this end. It was, of course, the natives of the other group who spread this interpretation, which they secretly believed and which filled them with apprehension. But the official version was never publicly disputed, and until we left, shortly after the incident, it remained ostensibly accepted by all.[4]

Although the skeptics had analyzed the sorcerer's motives with great psychological finesse and political acumen, they would have been greatly astonished had someone suggested (quite plausibly) that the incident

was a hoax which cast doubt upon the sorcerer's good faith and competence. He had probably not flown on the wings of thunder to the Rio Ananaz and had only staged an act. But these things might have happened, they had certainly happened in other circumstances, and they belonged to the realm of real experience. Certainly the sorcerer maintains an intimate relationship with the forces of the supernatural. The idea that in a particular case he had used his power to conceal a secular activity belongs to the realm of conjecture and provides an opportunity for critical judgment. The important point is that these two possibilities were not mutually exclusive; no more than are, for us, the alternate interpretations of war as the dying gasp of national independence or as the result of the schemes of munitions manufacturers. The two explanations are logically incompatible, but we admit that one or the other may be true; since they are equally plausible, we easily make the transition from one to the other, depending on the occasion and the moment. Many people have both explanations in the back of their minds.

Whatever their true origin, these divergent interpretations come from individual consciousness not as the result of objective analysis but rather as complementary ideas resulting from hazy and unelaborated attitudes which have an experiential character for each of us. These experiences, however, remain intellectually diffuse and emotionally intolerable unless they incorporate one or another of the patterns present in the group's culture. The assimilation of such patterns is the only means of objectivizing subjective states, of formulating inexpressible feelings, and of integrating inarticulated experiences into a system.

These mechanisms become clearer in the light of some observations made many years ago among the Zuni of New Mexico by an admirable field-worker, M. C. Stevenson.[5] A twelve-year-old girl was stricken with a nervous seizure directly after an adolescent boy had seized her hands. The youth was accused of sorcery and dragged before the court of the Bow priesthood. For an hour he denied having any knowledge of occult power, but this defense proved futile. Because the crime of sorcery was at that time still punished by death among the Zuni, the accused changed his tactics. He improvised a tale explaining the circumstances by which he had been initiated into sorcery. He said he had received two substances from his teachers, one which drove girls insane and another which cured them. This point constituted an ingenious precaution against later developments. Having been ordered to produce his medicines, he went home under guard and came back with two roots, which he proceeded to use in a complicated ritual. He simulated a trance after taking one of the drugs, and after taking the other he pretended to return to his normal state. Then he administered the remedy to the sick girl and declared her cured. The session was adjourned until the following day, but during the night the alleged sorcerer escaped. He was soon captured, and the girl's family set itself up as a court and continued the trial. Faced with the reluctance of his new judges to accept his first story, the boy then invented a new one. He told them that all his relatives and ancestors had been witches and that he had received marvellous powers from them. He claimed that he could assume the form of a cat, fill his mouth with cactus needles, and kill his victims—infants, three girls, and two boys—by shooting the needles into them. These feats, he claimed, were due to the magical powers of certain plumes which were used to change him and his family into shapes other than human. This last detail was a tactical error, for the judges called upon him to produce the plumes as proof of his new story. He gave various excuses which were rejected one after another, and he was forced to take his judges to his house. He began by declaring that the plumes were secreted in a wall that he could not destroy. He was commanded to go to work. After breaking down a section of the wall and carefully examining the plaster, he tried to excuse himself by declaring that the plumes had been hidden two years before and that he could not remember their exact location. Forced to search again, he tried another wall, and after another hour's work, an old plume appeared in the plaster. He grabbed it eagerly and presented it to his persecutors as the magic device of which he had spoken. He was then made to explain the details of its use. Finally, dragged into the public plaza, he had to repeat his entire story (to which he added a wealth of new detail). He finished it with a pathetic speech in which he lamented the loss of his supernatural power. Thus reassured, his listeners agreed to free him.

This narrative, which we unfortunately had to abridge and strip of all its psychological nuances, is still instructive in many respects. First of all, we see that the boy tried for witchcraft, for which he risks the death penalty, wins his acquittal not by denying but by admitting his alleged crime. Moreover, he furthers his cause by presenting successive versions, each richer in detail (and thus, in theory, more persuasive of guilt) than the preceding one. The debate does not proceed, as do debates among us, by accusations and denials, but rather by allegations and specifications. The judges do not expect the accused to challenge their theory, much less to refute the facts. Rather, they require him to validate a system of which they possess only a fragment; he must reconstruct it as a whole in an appropriate way. As the field-worker noted in relation to a phase of the trial, "The warriors had become so absorbed by their interest in the narrative of the boy

that they seemed entirely to have forgotten the cause of his appearance before them."[6] And when the magic plume was finally uncovered, the author remarks with great insight, "There was consternation among the warriors, who exclaimed in one voice: 'What does this mean?' Now they felt assured that the youth had spoken the truth."[7] Consternation, and not triumph at finding a tangible proof of the crime—for the judges had sought to bear witness to the reality of the system which had made the crime possible (by validating its objective basis through an appropriate emotional expression), rather than simply to punish a crime. By his confession, the defendant is transformed into a witness for the prosecution, with the participation (and even the complicity) of his judges. Through the defendant, witchcraft and the ideas associated with it cease to exist as a diffuse complex of poorly formulated sentiments and representations and become embodied in real experience. The defendant, who serves as a witness, gives the group the satisfaction of truth, which is infinitely greater and richer than the satisfaction of justice that would have been achieved by his execution. And finally, by his ingenious defense which makes his hearers progressively aware of the vitality offered by his corroboration of their system (especially since the choice is not between this system and another, but between the magical system and no system at all—that is, chaos), the youth, who at first was a threat to the physical security of his group, became the guardian of its spiritual coherence.

But is his defense merely ingenious? Everything leads us to believe that after groping for a subterfuge, the defendant participates with sincerity and—the word is not too strong—fervor in the drama enacted between him and his judges. He is proclaimed a sorcerer; since sorcerers do exist, he might well be one. And how would he know beforehand the signs which might reveal his calling to him? Perhaps the signs are there, present in this ordeal and in the convulsions of the little girl brought before the court. For the boy, too, the coherence of the system and the role assigned to him in preserving it are values no less essential than the personal security which he risks in the venture. Thus we see him, with a mixture of cunning and good faith, progressively construct the impersonation which is thrust upon him—chiefly by drawing on his knowledge and his memories, improvising somewhat, but above all living his role and seeking, through his manipulations and the ritual he builds from bits and pieces, the experience of a calling which is, at least theoretically, open to all. At the end of the adventure, what remains of his earlier hoaxes? To what extent has the hero become the dupe of his own impersonation? What is more, has he not truly become a sorcerer? We are told that in his final confession, "The longer the boy talked the more absorbed he became in his subject. . . . At times his face became radiant with satisfaction at his power over his listeners."[8] The girl recovers after he performs his curing ritual. The boy's experiences during the extraordinary ordeal become elaborated and structured. Little more is needed than for the innocent boy finally to confess to the possession of supernatural powers that are already recognized by the group.

We must consider at greater length another especially valuable document, which until now seems to have been valued solely for its linguistic interest. I refer to a fragment of the autobiography of a Kwakiutl Indian from the Vancouver region of Canada, obtained by Franz Boas.[9]

Quesalid (for this was the name he received when he became a sorcerer) did not believe in the power of the sorcerers—or, more accurately, shamans, since this is a better term for their specific type of activity in certain regions of the world. Driven by curiosity about their tricks and by the desire to expose them, he began to associate with the shamans until one of them offered to make him a member of their group. Quesalid did not wait to be asked twice, and his narrative recounts the details of his first lessons, a curious mixture of pantomime, prestidigitation, and empirical knowledge, including the art of simulating fainting and nervous fits, the learning of sacred songs, the technique for inducing vomiting, rather precise notions of auscultation and obstetrics, and the use of "dreamers," that is, spies who listen to private conversations and secretly convey to the shaman bits of information concerning the origins and symptoms of the ills suffered by different people. Above all, he learned the *ars magna* of one of the shamanistic schools of the Northwest Coast: The shaman hides a little tuft of down in a corner of his mouth, and he throws it up, covered with blood, at the proper moment—after having bitten his tongue or made his gums bleed—and solemnly presents it to his patient and the onlookers as the pathological foreign body extracted as a result of his sucking and manipulations.

His worst suspicions confirmed, Quesalid wanted to continue his inquiry. But he was no longer free. His apprenticeship among the shamans began to be noised about, and one day he was summoned by the family of a sick person who had dreamed of Quesalid as his healer. This first treatment (for which he received no payment, any more than he did for those which followed, since he had not completed the required four years of apprenticeship) was an outstanding success. Although Quesalid came to be known from that moment on as a "great shaman," he did not lose his critical faculties. He interpreted his success in psychological

terms—it was successful "because he [the sick person] believed strongly in his dream about me."[10] A more complex adventure made him, in his own words, "hesitant and thinking about many things."[11] Here he encountered several varieties of a "false supernatural," and was led to conclude that some forms were less false than others—those, of course, in which he had a personal stake and whose system he was, at the same time, surreptitiously building up in his mind. A summary of the adventure follows.

While visiting the neighboring Koskimo Indians, Quesalid attends a curing ceremony of his illustrious colleagues of the other tribe. To his great astonishment he observes a difference in their technique. Instead of spitting out the illness in the form of a "bloody worm" (the concealed down), the Koskimo shamans merely spit a little saliva into their hands, and they dare to claim that this is "the sickness." What is the value of this method? What is the theory behind it? In order to find out "the strength of the shamans, whether it was real or whether they only pretended to be shamans" like his fellow tribesmen,[12] Quesalid requests and obtains permission to try his method in an instance where the Koskimo method has failed. The sick woman then declares herself cured.

And here our hero vacillates for the first time. Though he had few illusions about his own technique, he has now found one which is more false, more mystifying, and more dishonest than his own. For he at least gives his clients something. He presents them with their sickness in a visible and tangible form, while his foreign colleagues show nothing at all and only claim to have captured the sickness. Moreover, Quesalid's method gets results, while the other is futile. Thus our hero grapples with a problem which perhaps has its parallel in the development of modern science. Two systems which we know to be inadequate present (with respect to each other) a differential validity, from both a logical and an empirical perspective. From which frame of reference shall we judge them? On the level of fact, where they merge, or on their own level, where they take on different values, both theoretically and empirically?

Meanwhile, the Koskimo shamans, "ashamed" and discredited before their tribesmen, are also plunged into doubt. Their colleague has produced, in the form of a material object, the illness which they had always considered as spiritual in nature and had thus never dreamed of rendering visible. They send Quesalid an emissary to invite him to a secret meeting in a cave. Quesalid goes and his foreign colleagues expound their system to him: "Every sickness is a man: boils and swellings, and itch and scabs, and pimples and coughs and consumption and scrofula; and also this, stricture of the bladder and stomach aches. . . . As soon as we get the soul of the sickness which is a man, then dies the sickness which is a man. Its body just disappears in our insides."[13] If this theory is correct, what is there to show? And why, when Quesalid operates, does "the sickness stick to his hand"? But Quesalid takes refuge behind professional rules which forbid him to teach before completing four years of apprenticeship, and refuses to speak. He maintains his silence even when the Koskimo shamans send him their allegedly virgin daughters to try to seduce him and discover his secret.

Thereupon Quesalid returns to his village at Fort Rupert. He learns that the most reputed shaman of a neighboring clan, worried about Quesalid's growing renown, has challenged all his colleagues, inviting them to compete with him in curing several patients. Quesalid comes to the contest and observes the cures of his elder. Like the Koskimo, this shaman does not show the illness. He simply incorporates an invisible object, "what he called the sickness" into his head-ring, made of bark, or into his bird-shaped ritual rattle.[14] These objects can hang suspended in mid-air, owing to the power of the illness which "bites" the house-posts or the shaman's hand. The usual drama unfolds. Quesalid is asked to intervene in cases judged hopeless by his predecessor, and he triumphs with his technique of the bloody worm.

Here we come to the truly pathetic part of the story. The old shaman, ashamed and despairing because of the ill-repute into which he has fallen and by the collapse of his therapeutic technique, sends his daughter to Quesalid to beg him for an interview. The latter finds his colleague sitting under a tree and the old shaman begins thus: "It won't be bad what we say to each other, friend, but only I wish you to try and save my life for me, so that I may not die of shame, for I am a plaything of our people on account of what you did last night. I pray you to have mercy and tell me what stuck on the palm of your hand last night. Was it the true sickness or was it only made up? For I beg you have mercy and tell me about the way you did it so that I can initiate you. Pity me, friend."[15]

Silent at first, Quesalid begins by calling for explanations about the feats of the head-ring and the rattle. His colleague shows him the nail hidden in the head-ring which he can press at right angles into the post, and the way in which he tucks the head of his rattle between his finger joints to make it look as if the bird were hanging by its beak from his hand. He himself probably does nothing but lie and fake, simulating shamanism for material gain, for he admits to being "covetous for the property of the sick men." He knows that shamans cannot catch souls, "for . . . we all own a soul"; so he resorts to using tallow and pretends that

"it is a soul . . . that white thing . . . sitting on my hand." The daughter then adds her entreaties to those of her father: "Do have mercy that he may live." But Quesalid remains silent. That very night, following this tragic conversation, the shaman disappears with his entire family, heartsick and feared by the community, who think that he may be tempted to take revenge. Needless fears: He returned a year later, but both he and his daughter had gone mad. Three years later, he died.

And Quesalid, rich in secrets, pursued his career, exposing the impostors and full of contempt for the profession. "Only one shaman was seen by me, who sucked at a sick man and I never found out whether he was a real shaman or only made up. Only for this reason I believe that he is a shaman; he does not allow those who are made well to pay him. I truly never once saw him laugh."[16] Thus his original attitude has changed considerably. The radical negativism of the free thinker has given way to more moderate feelings. Real shamans do exist. And what about him? At the end of the narrative we cannot tell, but it is evident that he carries on his craft conscientiously, takes pride in his achievements, and warmly defends the technique of the bloody down against all rival schools. He seems to have completely lost sight of the fallaciousness of the technique which he had so disparaged at the beginning.

We see that the psychology of the sorcerer is not simple. In order to analyze it, we shall first examine the case of the old shaman who begs his young rival to tell him the truth—whether the illness glued in the palm of his hand like a sticky red worm is real or made up—and who goes mad when he receives no answer. Before the tragedy, he was fully convinced of two things—first, that pathological conditions have a cause which may be discovered and second, that a system of interpretation in which personal inventiveness is important structures the phases of the illness, from the diagnosis to the cure. This fabulation of a reality unknown in itself—a fabulation consisting of procedures and representations—is founded on a threefold experience: first, that of the shaman himself, who, if his calling is a true one (and even if it is not, simply by virtue of his practicing it), undergoes specific states of a psychosomatic nature; second, that of the sick person, who may or may not experience an improvement of his condition; and, finally, that of the public, who also participate in the cure, experiencing an enthusiasm and an intellectual and emotional satisfaction which produce collective support, which in turn inaugurates a new cycle.

These three elements of what we might call the "shamanistic complex" cannot be separated. But they are clustered around two poles, one formed by the intimate experience of the shaman and the other by group consensus. There is no reason to doubt that sorcerers, or at least the more sincere among them, believe in their calling and that this belief is founded on the experiencing of specific states. The hardships and privations which they undergo would often be sufficient in themselves to provoke these states, even if we refuse to admit them as proof of a serious and fervent calling. But there is also linguistic evidence which, because it is indirect, is more convincing. In the Wintu dialect of California, there are five verbal classes which correspond to knowledge by sight, by bodily experience, by inference, by reasoning, and by hearsay. All five make up the category of knowledge as opposed to conjecture, which is differently expressed. Curiously enough, relationships with the supernatural world are expressed by means of the modes of knowledge—by bodily impression (that is, the most intuitive kind of experience), by inference, and by reasoning. Thus the native who becomes a shaman after a spiritual crisis conceives of his state grammatically, as a consequence to be inferred from the fact—formulated as real experience—that he has received divine guidance. From the latter he concludes deductively that he must have been on a journey to the beyond, at the end of which he found himself—again, an immediate experience—once more among his people.[17]

The experiences of the sick person represent the least important aspect of the system, except for the fact that a patient successfully treated by a shaman is in an especially good position to become a shaman in his own right, as we see today in the case of psychoanalysis. In any event, we must remember that the shaman does not completely lack empirical knowledge and experimental techniques, which may in part explain his success. Furthermore, disorders of the type currently termed psychosomatic, which constitute a large part of the illnesses prevalent in societies with a low degree of security, probably often yield to psychotherapy. At any rate, it seems probable that medicine men, like their civilized colleagues, cure at least some of the cases they treat and that without this relative success magical practices could not have been so widely diffused in time and space. But this point is not fundamental; it is subordinate to the other two. Quesalid did not become a great shaman because he cured his patients; he cured his patients because he had become a great shaman. Thus we have reached the other—that is, the collective—pole of our system.

The true reason for the defeat of Quesalid's rivals must then be sought in the attitude of the group rather than in the pattern of the rivals' successes and failures.

The rivals themselves emphasize this when they confess their shame at having become the laughingstock of the group; this is a social sentiment *par excellence*. Failure is secondary, and we see in all their statements that they consider it a function of another phenomenon, which is the disappearance of the *social consensus*, re-created at their expense around another practitioner and another system of curing. Consequently, the fundamental problem revolves around the relationship between the individual and the group, or, more accurately, the relationship between a specific category of individuals and specific expectations of the group.

In treating his patient the shaman also offers his audience a performance. What is this performance? Risking a rash generalization on the basis of a few observations, we shall say that it always involves the shaman's enactment of the "call," or the initial crisis which brought him the revelation of his condition. But we must not be deceived by the word *performance*. The shaman does not limit himself to reproducing or miming certain events. He actually relives them in all their vividness, originality, and violence. And since he returns to his normal state at the end of the seance, we may say, borrowing a key term from psychoanalysis, that he *abreacts*. In psychoanalysis, abreaction refers to the decisive moment in the treatment when the patient intensively relives the initial situation from which his disturbance stems, before he ultimately overcomes it. In this sense, the shaman is a professional abreactor.

We have set forth elsewhere the theoretical hypotheses that might be formulated in order for us to accept the idea that the type of abreaction specific to each shaman—or, at any rate, to each shamanistic school—might symbolically induce an abreaction of his own disturbance in each patient. In any case, if the essential relationship is that between the shaman and the group, we must also state the question from another point of view—that of the relationship between normal and pathological thinking. From any non-scientific perspective (and here we can exclude no society), pathological and normal thought processes are complimentary rather than opposed. In a universe which it strives to understand but whose dynamics it cannot fully control, normal thought continually seeks the meaning of things which refuse to reveal their significance. So-called pathological thought, on the other hand, overflows with emotional interpretations and overtones, in order to supplement an otherwise deficient reality. For normal thinking there exists something which cannot be empirically verified and is, therefore, "claimable." For pathological thinking there exists experiences without object, or something "available." We might borrow from linguistics and say that so-called normal thought always suffers from a deficit of meaning, whereas so-called pathological thought (in at least some of its manifestations) disposes of a plethora of meaning. Through collective participation in shamanistic curing, a balance is established between these two complementary situations. Normal thought cannot fathom the problem of illness, and so the group calls upon the neurotic to furnish a wealth of emotion heretofore lacking a focus.

An equilibrium is reached between what might be called supply and demand on the psychic level—but only on two conditions. First, a structure must be elaborated and continually modified through the interaction of group tradition and individual invention. This structure is a system of oppositions and correlations, integrating all the elements of a total situation, in which sorcerer, patient, and audience, as well as representations and procedures, all play their parts. Furthermore, the public must participate in the abreaction, to a certain extent at least, along with the patient and the sorcerer. It is this vital experience of a universe of symbolic effusions which the patient, because he is ill, and the sorcerer, because he is neurotic—in other words, both having types of experience which cannot otherwise be integrated—allow the public to glimpse as "fireworks" from a safe distance. In the absence of any experimental control, which is indeed unnecessary, it is this experience alone, and its relative richness in each case, which makes possible a choice between several systems and elicits adherence to a particular school or practitioner.[18]

In contrast with scientific explanation, the problem here is not to attribute confused and disorganized states, emotions, or representations to an objective cause, but rather to articulate them into a whole or system. The system is valid precisely to the extent that it allows the coalescence or precipitation of these diffuse states, whose discontinuity also makes them painful. To the conscious mind, this last phenomenon constitutes an original experience which cannot be grasped from without. Because of their complementary disorders, the sorcerer-patient dyad incarnates for the group, in vivid and concrete fashion, an antagonism that is inherent in all thought but that normally remains vague and imprecise. The patient is all passivity and self-alienation, just as inexpressibility is the disease of the mind. The sorcerer is activity and self-projection, just as affectivity is the source of symbolism. The cure interrelates these opposite poles, facilitating the transition from one to the other, and demonstrates, within a total experience, the coherence of the psychic universe, itself a projection of the social universe.

Thus it is necessary to extend the notion of abreaction by examining the meanings it acquires in psychotherapies other than psychoanalysis, although the latter deserves the credit for rediscovering and insisting upon its fundamental validity. It may be objected that in psychoanalysis there is only one abreaction, the patient's, rather than three. We are not so sure of this. It is true that in the shamanistic cure the sorcerer speaks and abreacts *for* the silent patient, while in psychoanalysis it is the patient who talks and abreacts *against* the listening therapist. But the therapist's abreaction, while not concomitant with the patient's, is nonetheless required, since he must be analyzed before he himself can become an analyst. It is more difficult to define the role ascribed to the group by each technique. Magic readapts the group to predefined problems through the patient, while psychoanalysis readapts the patient to the group by means of the solutions reached. But the distressing trend which, for several years, has tended to transform the psychoanalytic system from a body of scientific hypotheses that are experimentally verifiable in certain specific and limited cases into a kind of diffuse mythology interpenetrating the consciousness of the group, could rapidly bring about a parallelism. (This group consciousness is an objective phenomenon, which the psychologist expresses through a subjective tendency to extend to normal thought a system of interpretations conceived for pathological thought and to apply to facts of collective psychology a method adapted solely to the study of individual psychology.) When this happens—and perhaps it already has in certain countries—the value of the system will no longer be based upon real cures from which certain individuals can benefit, but on the sense of security that the group receives from the myth underlying the cure and from the popular system upon which the group's universe is reconstructed.

Even at the present time, the comparison between psychoanalysis and older and more widespread psychological therapies can encourage the former to reexamine its principles and methods. By continuously expanding the recruitment of its patients, who begin as clearly characterized abnormal individuals and gradually become representative of the group, psychoanalysis transforms its treatments into conversions. For only a patient can emerge cured; an unstable or maladjusted individual can only be persuaded. A considerable danger thus arises: The treatment (unbeknown to the therapist, naturally), far from leading to the resolution of a specific disturbance within its own context, is reduced to the reorganization of the patient's universe in terms of psychoanalytic interpretations. This means that we would finally arrive at precisely that situation which furnishes the point of departure as well as the theoretical validity of the magico-social system that we have analyzed.

If this analysis is correct, we must see magical behavior as the response to a situation which is revealed to the mind through emotional manifestations, but whose essence is intellectual. For only the history of the symbolic function can allow us to understand the intellectual condition of man, in which the universe is never charged with sufficient meaning and in which the mind always has more meanings available than there are objects to which to relate them. Torn between these two systems of reference—the signifying and the signified—man asks magical thinking to provide him with a new system of reference, within which the thus-far contradictory elements can be integrated. But we know that this system is built at the expense of the progress of knowledge, which would have required us to retain only one of the two previous systems and to refine it to the point where it absorbed the other. This point is still far off. We must not permit the individual, whether normal or neurotic, to repeat this collective misadventure. The study of the mentally sick individual has shown us that all persons are more or less oriented toward contradictory systems and suffer from the resulting conflict; but the fact that a certain form of integration is possible and effective practically is not enough to make it true, or to make us certain that the adaptation thus achieved does not constitute an absolute regression in relation to the previous conflict situation.

The reabsorption of a deviant specific synthesis, through its integration with the normal syntheses, into a general but arbitrary synthesis (aside from critical cases where action is required) would represent a loss on all fronts. A body of elementary hypotheses can have a certain instrumental value for the practitioner without necessarily being recognized, in theoretical analysis, as the final image of reality and without necessarily linking the patient and the therapist in a kind of mystical communion which does not have the same meaning for both parties and which only ends by reducing the treatment to a fabulation.

In the final analysis we could only expect this fabulation to be a language, whose function is to provide a socially authorized translation of phenomena whose deeper nature would become once again equally impenetrable to the group, the patient, and the healer.

NOTES

1. W. B. Cannon, "'Voodoo' Death," *American Anthropologist*, n.s., XLIV (1942).
2. An Australian aborigine was brought to the Darwin hospital in April 1956, apparently dying of this type of sorcery. He was placed in an oxygen tent and fed intravenously. He gradually recovered, convinced that the white man's magic was the stronger. See Arthur Morley in the *London Sunday Times*, April 22, 1956, p. 11.
3. In this study, whose aim is more psychological than sociological, we feel justified in neglecting the finer distinctions between the several modes of magical operations and different types of sorcerers when these are not absolutely necessary.
4. C. Lévi-Strauss, *Tristes Tropiques* (Paris: 1955), Chapter XXIX.
5. M. C. Stevenson, *The Zuni Indians*, 23rd Annual Report of the Bureau of American Ethnology (Washington, D.C.: Smithsonian Institution, 1905).
6. *Ibid.*, p. 401.
7. *Ibid.*, p. 404.
8. *Ibid.*, p. 406.
9. Franz Boas, *The Religion of the Kwakiutl*, Columbia University Contributions to Anthropology, Vol. X (New York: 1930), Part II, pp. 1–41.
10. *Ibid.*, p. 13.
11. *Ibid.*, p. 19.
12. *Ibid.*, p. 17.
13. *Ibid.*, pp. 20–21.
14. *Ibid.*, p. 27.
15. *Ibid.*, p. 31.
16. *Ibid.*, pp. 40–41.
17. D. D. Lee, "Some Indian Texts Dealing with the Supernatural," *The Review of Religion* (May, 1941).
18. This oversimplified equation of sorcerer and neurotic was justly criticized by Michel Leiris. I subsequently refined this concept in my "Introduction à l'oeuvre de Marcel Mauss," in M. Mauss, *Sociologie et Anthropologie* (Paris: 1950), pp. xviii–xxiii.

15

The Nocebo Phenomenon: Concept, Evidence, and Implications for Public Health

Robert A. Hahn

This selection is about the flip side of the placebo effect. The nocebo phenomenon refers to the process by which negative expectations result in negative effects. In one hospital-based study reported here, 80 percent of patients who were given a glass of sugar water and told that it would make them vomit actually did vomit. Is "power of suggestion" this powerful? Certainly this is a central theme in the previous selection by Lévi-Strauss, but surprisingly this topic has not been systematically evaluated in biomedicine. In general, the placebo and nocebo phenomena seem to be viewed by biomedical scientists as a type of "noise" that contaminates the "real" interactions of cause and effect. It would be worthwhile to change this conception—to see the placebo effect instead as something to be understood and as power to be harnessed in order to improve medical care.

This selection was written by an anthropologist for biomedical scientists in the field of preventive medicine. Robert Hahn suggests that the nocebo phenomenon should be considered in health education programs. He suggests that the creation of medical categories of disease may be a double-edged sword: "Categories of an ethnomedicine may not only describe conditions of sickness, but may also foster those conditions by establishing expectations that may occur" (p. 12). A similar point is made in a recent book by Lynn Payer, The Disease Mongers *(1994), in which she argues that the explosion of medical testing for risk factors like cholesterol may actually do patients more harm than good, although they generate enormous revenue for biomedical corporations.*

The value of looking at the nocebo phenomenon is not merely that we will remember the possible harm of engendering negative expectations. It is also important to think about the power of belief in all types of medical treatments. In what ways do ethnomedical treatments function by providing patients and their families with hope and by distracting everyone while the body heals itself? In this regard, if ethnomedical treatments are to be effective, they must follow the first rule of Hippocrates: "First do no harm." The value of examining the nocebo phenomenon is that it provides an important insight into the placebo effect, something that typically plays a role in the healing process.

This selection was written for a public health–oriented audience, so it offers many specific case studies as evidence. Readers interested in medical anthropological studies of the placebo effect may want to look at the work of Daniel Moerman (1991), James Dow (1986), or earlier work by Robert Hahn and Arthur Kleinman (1983).

As you read this selection, consider these questions:

- *What is the relationship between nocebos and placebos? Why do you think beliefs or expectations can be so powerful? Or do you?*

- *Is a person more suggestible to the nocebo effect as a member or a group (for example, children in a cafeteria)? What role does social context play?*

- *Many cultures have a custom of not talking specifically about a disease, for example, not using the term* cancer *to the patient. What do you think about this custom in relation to the nocebo effect as well as the principle of informed consent in doctor–patient communication?*

The nocebo hypothesis proposes that expectations of sickness and the affective states associated with such expectations cause sickness in the expectant. Resultant pathology may be subjective as well as objective conditions. Some nocebo effects may be transient; others may be chronic or fatal. An extreme form of the nocebo phenomenon was described in Cannon's classic paper (1942) as "voodoo death." Because expectations are largely learned from the cultural environment, nocebo effects are likely to vary from place to place.

The nocebo phenomenon, first named by Kennedy (1961) and then elaborated by Kissel and Barrucand (1964), has not been systematically assessed. In this review, I formulate a working definition of the nocebo phenomenon that relates nocebos and placebos; present a range of examples of nocebo phenomena; and draw several implications for public health.

A. A WORKING DEFINITION OF THE NOCEBO PHENOMENON

The nocebo effect is the causation of sickness (or death) by expectations of sickness (or death) and by associated emotional states. Two forms of the nocebo effect should be recognized: In the *specific* form, the subject expects a particular negative outcome and that outcome consequently occurs; for example, a surgical patient expects to die on the operating table and does die—not from the surgery itself, but from the expectation and associated affect (Weisman and Hackett 1961; Cannon 1942). In the *generic* form, subjects have vague negative expectations—for example, they are diffusely pessimistic—and their expectations are realized in terms of symptoms, sickness, or death—none of which was specifically expected. Again, expectation plays a causal role.

The nocebo phenomenon considered in this review is distinct from placebo side-effects (Figure 1). Placebo side-effects occur when expectations of healing produce sickness, i.e., a positive expectation has a negative outcome. For example, a rash that occurs following administration of a placebo remedy may be a placebo side-effect. Diverse placebo side-effects have been documented; one review reports an incidence of 19% in the subjects of pharmacologic studies (Rosenzweig, Brohier, and Zipfel 1993). In the nocebo phenomenon, however, the subject expects sickness to be the outcome, i.e., the expectation is a negative one. Nocebos may also have side-effects, i.e., when negative expectations produce positive outcomes or outcomes other than those expected.

When Kennedy (1961) and Kissel and Barrucand (1964) first referred to the nocebo phenomenon, they did not distinguish placebo side-effects from the effects of negative expectations. However, reference to voodoo death, for example, as an instance of the placebo phenomenon is etymologically inappropriate. Kennedy and Kissel and Barrucand distinguished placebos from nocebos only in terms of positive and negative *outcomes*, not *also* in terms of expectations. Kennedy's examples are all placebo side-effects, and Kissel and Barrucand did not separate examples of placebo side-effects from an example of nocebo in the sense proposed here: 80% of hospitalized patients given sugar water and told that it was an emetic subsequently vomited. What distinguishes nocebos is that the subject has negative expectations and experiences a negative outcome. Schweiger and Parducci (1981) refer to nocebos as "negative placebos."

Nocebos are causal in the same way that commonly recognized pathogens are, e.g., cigarette smoke of lung cancer, the tubercular bacillus of tuberculosis

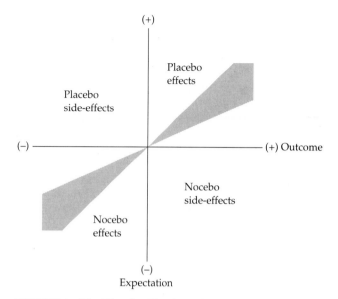

FIGURE 1   The Placebo Thesis: Relations Between Expectation and Outcome *(From R. Hahn,* Sickness and Healing: An Anthropological Perspective, *New Haven, CT: Yale University Press, 1995)*

(Surgeon General 1989; Harris and McClement 1983). That is, nocebos increase the likelihood that the sickness they refer to will occur, and this effect is not the result of confounding, i.e., the empirical association of the hypothesized nocebo with another cause of the condition. None of these exposures is a necessary or a sufficient cause of the given outcome.

B. EVIDENCE OF NOCEBO PHENOMENA

This review of evidence is divided according to the source or manner of acquisition of expectations. It begins with (1) the effects of inner, mental worlds, moves to (2) the effects of nosological categories and self scrutiny, (3) sociogenic illness, or mass hysteria, and (4) the deliberate induction of sickness or symptoms.

Inner, Mental World

Mood, affect, and some psychiatric conditions are often associated with negative expectations (American Psychiatric Association 1980). For example, hopelessness is a prominent component of diverse forms of depression. Somatoform disorders such as hypochondriasis and conversion disorder may also be associated with expectations of pathology. And some anxiety disorders, too, may be associated with expectations of pathology. Panic disorder, for example, may involve a sense of "impending doom" and a fear of death (American Psychiatric Association 1980).

Although several studies indicate an association of negative expectations and affect associated with psychiatric conditions and pathological outcomes (Black et al. 1985a, 1985b; Newman and Bland 1991; Bruce et al. 1994; Weissman et al. 1990; Reich 1985; Friedman and Booth Kewley 1987; Wells, Stewart, Hays et al. 1989), only the study by Anda and colleagues (1993) uses epidemiologic methods to control for the confounding effects of other risk factors. Anda and colleagues examined the effects of depression on ischemic heart disease (IHD) incidence and mortality in a sample of U.S. adults. They examined persons who were free from heart disease at the outset of the study and excluded subjects whose initial depressed affect might have been the *consequence* of chronic disease. Depression was assessed from the General Well-Being Schedule (Dupuy 1977). Anda and colleagues found that persons with depressive affect were 1.6 times more likely to have nonfatal IHD and 1.5 times more likely to have fatal IHD than persons who did not have depressive affect, independent of other known risk factors for ischemic heart disease. These researchers also examined the effects of hopelessness on heart disease incidence and mortality, and found a dose response—a critical criterion in the inference of causality. Greater hopelessness was associated with greater incidence and mortality.

Considering that an 11.1% prevalence of depressed affect was assessed in the study cohort—a sample of U.S. adults—it can be estimated (as the "population attributable risk") that approximately 26,000 deaths a year (i.e., more than 5% of U.S. IHD mortality and more than 1% of all U.S. deaths) may be attributable to depression, independent of other risk factors. Mortality associated with depressive expectations is an example of the generic form of the nocebo phenomenon. The other examples in this review are of specific nocebo phenomena.

Nosological Categories and Self-Scrutiny

In one specific form, cardiac neurosis or cardiophobia, patients are persistently fearful of heart attacks or other cardiac symptoms, and report chest pain, described by physicians as "non-specific." Although these patients may not manifest recognized cardiac symptoms, there is evidence that belief that one is susceptible to heart attacks is itself a risk factor for coronary death. Eaker examined women, 45 to 64 years of age, in the Framingham study for the 20-year incidence of myocardial infarction and coronary death (Eaker 1992). Women who believed they were more likely than others to suffer a heart attack were 3.7 times as likely to die of coronary conditions as were women who believed they were less likely to die of such symptoms, independent of commonly recognized risk factors for coronary death (e.g., smoking, systolic blood pressure, and the ratio of total to high density lipoprotein cholesterol).

Sociogenic Illness

Sickness or symptoms may also occur when one person observes or learns of the sickness or symptoms in others. Knowledge of sickness in others fosters an expectation that one may also be subject to the same condition. Perhaps the best recognized form of contagion by observation are epidemics referred to as "sociogenic," "psychogenic illness," "mass hysteria," or, in the workplace, "assembly line hysteria" (Colligan and Stockton 1978).

Sirois (1974) reviewed 78 documented outbreaks of "epidemic hysteria" reported between 1872 and 1972. Of these, 44% occurred in schools, 22% in towns, and 10% in factories. Twenty-eight percent involved fewer than 10 persons, 32% involved 10–30 persons, and 19% more than 30 persons; 5% were of unreported magnitude. (Whereas the largest outbreak noted by Sirois involved approximately 200 persons, an outbreak has been described that involved 949 persons [Modan, Tirosh, Weissenberg et al. 1983].) Only females were involved in 74% of the outbreaks, only males in 4% (Sirois 1974). Outbreaks occurred more commonly among persons from lower socioeconomic classes and in periods of uncertainty and social stress. Convulsions were reported in 24% of outbreaks, abnormal movements in 18%, and fainting, globus/cough/laryngismus, and loss of sensation in 11.5% each. Symptomatology changed over the 100 years surveyed, from more globus/cough/laryngismus and abnormal movements to more fainting, nausea, abdominal malaise, and headaches.

Colligan and Murphy (1979) point out that sociogenic outbreaks are commonly associated with a source believed to be related to the symptoms, e.g., a strange odor or gas, new solvent, or an insect bite. However, sometimes reported symptoms do not fit biomedical knowledge of associations between potential toxins or pathogens and pathophysiology. Persons affected often have repetitive jobs, are under unusual stress, and/or have poor relations with superiors. They may be in poorer general health and have been absent more often than persons who are not affected. Colligan and Murphy indicate that sociogenic outbreaks in workplace settings are substantially underreported.

Sirois (1975) estimates that sociogenic outbreaks occur in approximately one out of every 1,000 schools per year in the province of Quebec. A review of recent school outbreaks in diverse countries indicates attack rates (i.e., the proportion of persons exposed who experience the condition) of 6%—48% (Arcidiacono, Brand, Coppenger, and Calder 1990).

The study of Kerckhoff and Back (1968) of the 1962 "June Bug" outbreak in a Montana mill is one of the few to carefully reconstruct social patterns of the spread of a sociogenic condition. In the June Bug event, those affected fainted or complained of pain, nausea, or disorientation. Sixty-two (6.4%) of 965 workers were affected, 59 (95.2%) of them women; all those affected worked in dressmaking departments. Persons affected were 70% more likely than controls to believe that the cause of the outbreak was an insect or other physical object. Persons affected were 62% more likely to have worked overtime at least two or three times a week than those not affected. Persons affected were less likely to go to a supervisor with a complaint or to be members of the union. They were 2.2 times as likely to be sole breadwinners, 5.6 times as likely to be divorced, and 30% more likely to have a child under 6 years of age. The outbreak began among women who were socially isolated, subsequently spread among women connected by links of close social relations, and finally diffused among women less closely connected. The phenomenon analyzed by Kerckhoff and Back might be described as "mass somatization."

The effects of a person's social environment on sickness or illness behavior need not involve direct personal contact. An association has been found between traumatic death or violence in the community environment and subsequent suicide or suicide-like behavior (Phillips 1974, 1977; Phillips and Carstenen 1986). In this instance, the first victim serves as a model with whom others may "identify." For example, when newspaper or television stories about a suicide are released, the rate of suicide may increase in the following week; the greater the circulation of the newspaper, the greater the increase (Phillips 1974). After Marilyn Monroe's suicide in 1962, 197 suicides occurred in the United States during the following week—12% more than the number expected on the basis of past suicide patterns (Phillips 1974). A recent study indicates that teenagers are more susceptible to televised publicity about suicide and that increases in suicides are greater for girls than boys (Phillips and Carstensen 1986).

Motor-vehicle fatalities also follow newspaper stories of suicide. Phillips (1977) calculates that, on average, motor vehicle fatalities increase 9% above the expected rate in the week following front-page reporting of suicides in newspaper stories, and that, reporting in newspapers with greater than average circulation, the increase is 19%.

Sickness/Symptoms Induced

Social psychologists have conducted diverse experiments that demonstrate the effects of negative suggestion on the experience of negative symptoms (Schachter and Singer 1962; Lancman et al. 1994; Jewett, Fein, and Greenberg 1990; Sternbach 1964; Schweiger and Parducci 1981). In one experiment, 47.5% of asthmatics who were exposed to (normally innocuous) nebulized saline solution and told they were inhaling irritants or allergens experienced substantially increased airway resistance and changes in airway resistance and thoracic gas volume (Luparello, Lyons, Bleecker, and McFadden 1968). Controls who did not have asthma were unaffected by exposure to the same stimulus. Twelve asthmatic subjects developed full-blown attacks that were relieved by the same saline solution presented therapeutically. (The researchers also refer to an asthmatic patient in another study whose allergy to roses was induced by plastic as well as natural roses, indicating that the effect of the rose did not result entirely from its botanical properties.)

In a follow-up, double-blind experiment, Luparello, Leist, Lourie, and Sweet (1968) randomized asthmatic patients to four conditions: Two groups were given a bronchodilator, the other two a bronchoconstrictor; half of the group given each substance was told they were being given a bronchodilator, the other half that they were being given a bronchoconstrictor. For each substance administered, expectations induced by misinformation about the substance reduced its physiologic effectiveness by 43% (for the bronchoconstrictor) and 49% (for the bronchodilator).

Another study was designed to evaluate a method for the diagnosis of psychogenic seizures, reported to account for as many as 20% of "refractory epilepsy" (Lancman et al. 1994). Lancman and colleagues compared the effect of suggestion on the induction of seizure behavior in patients with psychogenic seizures and others with known epilepsy. Patients were told that a medicine administered through a skin patch would induce seizures within 30 seconds, and that removal of the patch would end the seizure. Of patients with psychogenic seizures, 77% manifested seizures when the patch was applied, with symptoms such as nonresponsiveness, generalized violent thrashing, and uncoordinated movements; 19% of these patients reported auras, and 44% showed postictal confusion and/or sleepiness. None of the patients with diagnosed epilepsy manifested seizures.

Finally, another study (Jewett, Fein, and Greenberg 1990), designed to evaluate a controversial method of food allergy testing, compared the effect of injecting the food substances—the test to be evaluated—with the effect of injecting saline diluent without the substance in question on symptoms that included itching of the nose, watering or burning eyes, plugged ears, tight or scratchy throat, nausea, dizziness, sleepiness, and depression. (Patients with a history of anaphylactic reactions or documented cardiac irregularity, or other severe reactions to their allergies were excluded.) In this double-blind study, the proportion of patients who experienced symptoms was not statistically different in patients given test (27%) and *nocebo* diluent injections (24%). "Neutralizing" injections, given to eliminate the reactions, were also equally effective whether they contained the food substance or—in this case—the diluent *placebo*. An injection becomes a nocebo (or placebo) not because of its contents, but because of the pessimistic (or optimistic) expectations of its consumer.

C. DISCUSSION

I have reviewed a range of studies indicating that socially given negative expectations and their emotional associations facilitate their own realization. Beliefs can make us sick as well as healthy. The nocebo phenomenon is a little-recognized facet of culture that may be responsible for a substantial variety of pathology throughout the world. However, the extent of the phenomenon is not yet known, and evidence is piecemeal and ambiguous. There is evidence that inner, mental states affect pathological outcomes, independent of other risk factors; that symptoms may spread in communities by being witnessed; and that symptoms may be caused by experimentally induced expectations. Further investigations should explore the ways in which, like the placebo phenomenon, the expectations of the nocebo phenomenon translate diverse cultural beliefs into physiological process.

I conclude with two implications of the nocebo phenomenon for public health.

First, the nocebo phenomenon is a side-effect of human culture. A society's culture tells its members how the world is divided, inter-connected, and known; it specifies what is valued and what is not, what is good, beautiful, right, wrong, and indifferent; it provides rules of conduct whereby the society's members know how to behave and how to judge the behavior of others (Hahn 1995). One element of cultures has been referred to as an "ethnomedicine." A society's ethnomedicine tells societal members what sicknesses there are, how they are acquired, how manifested, how treated. The nocebo phenomenon suggests that the categories of an ethnomedicine may not only describe conditions of sickness, but may also foster those conditions by establishing expectations that they may occur. Thus, a cultural system commonly thought to serve a healing function may also have a contrary outcome, fostering the same pathologies intended to be healed. The assessment of the extent of this noxious facet of ethnomedicines, including our own system of biomedicine, is an important public health challenge.

Second, and more immediately practical, if communication about pathological conditions may serve not only to describe, but, in a sense, also to foster sickness by creating expectations, then we must be cautious in both public health communications and in clinical medicine. We need to know more about how health messages affect their audience. Such knowledge may enhance our ability to minimize the pathological consequences of negative messages. The placebo/nocebo phenomenon suggests that it may be healthier to err on the side of optimism than on the side of pessimism.

REFERENCES

American Psychiatric Association. 1980. *Diagnostic and Statistical Manual of Mental Disorders*, 3rd ed. Washington, D.C.: American Psychiatric Association.

Anda, R., D. Williamson, D. Jones, C. Macera, E. Eaker, A. Glassman, and J. Marks. 1993. "Depressed Affect, Hopelessness, and the Risk of Ischemic Heart Disease in a Cohort of U.S. Adults." *Epidemiol* 4(4):285–294.

Arcidiacono, S., J. I. Brand, W. Coppenger, and R. A. Calder. 1990. "Mass Sociogenic Illness in a Day-care Center—Florida." *MMWR* 31(18):301–304.

Black, D. W. G. Warrack, and G. Winokur. 1985a. "Excess Mortality among Psychiatric Patients." *JAMA* 253(1):58–61.

———. 1985b. "The Iowa Record-Linkage Study: II. Excess Mortality among Patients with 'Functional' Disorders." *Arch Gen Psychiatry* 42:82–88.

Bruce, M. L., P. J. Leaf, G. P. M. Rozal et al. 1994. Psychiatric Status and 9 Year Mortality Data in the New Haven Epidemiologic Catchment Area Study." *Am J Psychiatry* 151(5):716–721.

Cannon, W. B. 1942. "Voodoo Death." *American Anthropologist* 44(2):169–181.

Colligan, M. J., and L. R. Murphy. 1979. "Mass Psychogenic Illness in Organizations: An Overview." *Journal of Occupational Psychology* 52:77–90.

Colligan, M. J., and W. Stockton. 1976. "The Mystery of Assembly-line Hysteria." *Psychology Today* 12:93–116.

Conti, S., G. Savron, G. Bartolucci et al. 1989. "Cardiac Neurosis and Psychopathology." *Psychother Psychosom* 52:88–91.

Dupuy, H. J. 1977. "A Concurrent Validational Study of the NCHS General Well-Being Schedule." *Vital and Health Statistics*, Series 2, No. 73. DHEW Pub. No. (HRA)78–1347. Washington, D.C.: U.S. Government Printing Office.

Eaker, E., J. Pinsky, and W. P. Castelli. 1992. "Myocardial Infarction and Coronary Death among Women: Psychosocial Predictors from a 20-Year Follow-up of Women in the Framingham Study." *Am J Epidemiology* 135:854–864.

Friedman, H. S., and S. Booth-Kewley. 1987. "The 'Disease-Prone Personality': A Meta-Analytic View of the Construct." *Am Psychol* 42(6):539–555.

Hahn, R. A. 1995. *Sickness and Healing; An Anthropological Perspective*. New Haven, Conn.: Yale University Press.

Harris, H. W., and J. H. McClement. 1983. "Pulmonary Tuberculosis." In Hoeprich, P. D., ed., *Infectious Diseases*, pp. 378–404. New York: Harper and Row.

Jewett, D. L., G. Fein, and M. H. Greenberg. 1990. "A Double-blind Study of Symptom Provocation to Determine Food Sensitivity." *N Engl J Med* 323(7):429–433.

Kennedy, W. P. 1961. "The Nocebo Reaction." *Medical World* 91:203–205.

Kerckhoff, A. C., and K. W. Back. 1968. *The June Bug: A Study of Hysterical Contagion*. New York: Appleton-Century-Crofts.

Kissel, P., and D. Barrucand. 1964. *Placebos et Effet Placebo En Medecine*. Paris: Masson.

Lancman, M. E., J. J. Asconape, W. J. Craven, G. Howard, and J. K. Penry. 1994. "Predictive Value of Induction of Psychogenic Seizures by Suggestion." *Annals of Neurology* 35(3):359–361.

Luparello, T. J., N. Leist, C. H. Lourie, and P. Sweet. 1970. "The Interaction of Psychologic Stimuli and Pharmacologic Agents on Airway Reactivity in Asthmatic Subjects." *Psychosomatic Medicine* 32(5):509–513.

Luparello, T., H. A. Lyons, E. R. Bleecker, and E. R. McFadden. 1968. "Influences of Suggestion on Airway Reactivity in Asthmatic Subjects." *Psychosomatic Medicine* 30: 819–825.

Modan, B., M. Tirosh, E. Weissenberg, et al. 1983. "The Arjenyattah Epidemic: A Mass Phenomenon: Spread and Triggering Factors." *Lancet* 24/31:1472–1474.

Newman, S. C., and R. C. Bland. 1991. "Mortality in a Cohort of Patients with Schizophrenia: A Record Linkage Study." *Can J Psychiatry* 36:239–245.

Phillips, D. P. 1974. "The Influence of Suggestion on Suicide: Substantive and Theoretical Implications of the Werther Effect." *American Sociological Review* 39:340–354.

———. 1977. "Motor Vehicle Fatalities Increase Just after Publicized Suicide Stories." *Science* 196:1464–1465.

Phillips, D. P., and L. L. Carstensen. 1986. "Clustering of Teenage Suicides after Television News Stories about Suicide." *N Eng J Med* 315:685–689.

Reich, P. 1985. "Psychological Predisposition to Life-threatening Arrhythmias." *Ann Rev Med* 36:397–405.

Rosenzweig P., S. Brohier, and A. Zipfel. 1993. "The Placebo Effect in Healthy Volunteers: Influence of Experimental Conditions on the Adverse Events Profile During Phase I Studies." *Clinical Pharmacology and Therapeutics* 54(5):578–583.

Schachter S., and J. E. Singer. 1962. "Cognitive, Social, and Physiological Determinants of Emotional State." *Psychological Review* 69(5):379–399.

Schweiger, A., and A. Parducci. 1981. "Nocebo: The Psychologic Induction of Pain." *Pav J Biol Sci* 16:140–143.

Sirois, F. 1974. "Epidemic Hysteria." *Acta Psychiatrica Scandinavia* 51(252):7–44.

———. 1975. "À Propos de la Fréquence Des Épidémies D'hystérie." *Union Med Canada* 104:121–123.

Sternbach, R. A. 1964. "The Effects of Instructional Sets on Autonomic Responsivity." *Psychophysiology* 1(1):67–72.

Weisman, A. D., and T. P. Hackett. 1961. "Predilection to Death: Death and Dying as a Psychiatric Problem." *Psychosomatic Medicine* 23(3):232–256.

Weissman, M. M., J. S. Markowitz, R. Ouellette, S. Greenwald, and J. P. Kahn. 1990. "Panic Disorder and Cardiovascular/Cerebrovascular Problems: Results from a Community Survey." *Am J Psychiatry* 147:1504–1508.

Wells, K. B., A. Stewart, R. D. Hays, et al. 1989. "The Functioning and Well-Being of Depressed Patients." *JAMA* 262(7):914–919.

The Social Construction of Illness and the Social Production of Health

⚜ CONCEPTUAL TOOLS ⚜

■ *Taken-for-granted realities, like disease categories, are socially constructed within the context of each particular culture.* The social construction of reality, and therefore the social construction of illness, may be difficult for students to understand. In some ways, the argument is philosophical. It pertains to the difficult question of what knowledge is. Following the important sociological formulation of Peter Berger and Thomas Luckmann (1967), things and ideas are considered real in our everyday lives only when there is a social agreement that they are real. Things and concepts are labeled through language; they are the subject of discussion, and people act on the knowledge that they exist. Reality is a bit like the emperor's new clothes in that the reality derives from the social agreement that a thing exists, not from physical evidence per se. People gain cultural knowledge—including such categories and the cognitive models through which people learn to think—from the socialization process of childhood.

In this sense, illnesses exist because people put a label on them. In turn, when an illness category or label exists, then people pay attention to particular sets of symptoms and therefore decide that they have the illness. As we shall see in the section on culture and mental health, the social construction of mental illness categories can be mechanisms of social control. Only when illness categories are socially recognized can an individual make a legitimate claim to the "sick role," a special social identity that exempts one from some social obligations (like going to work or school) but that also entails other obligations (such as getting well as soon as possible and following the doctor's orders).

■ *Culture defines normality.* What is considered normal—in behavior, thinking, or even physical attributes—is cultural; that is, we learn it as children, and we share these assumptions with others in our social group. For example, to stare for hours at a blank wall is considered abnormal in our culture, but to stare at the TV for the same period is considered quite nor-

mal. What is the real difference between these behaviors? If, for example, a Tibetan monk stares at a wall in order to meditate, that might be considered normal. How we judge behaviors depends on cultural expectations.

Cultural behaviors and beliefs are often deeply held and seldom questioned by adults, who pass on their "obvious" knowledge and habits to their offspring. In this regard, cultural beliefs and values are largely unconscious factors in the motivation of individual behaviors. The fact that cultural beliefs define normality and what is socially acceptable can constrain an individual's behavioral choices. Members of all societies are *ethnocentric* in that they use their own arbitrary beliefs and values to judge people from another culture. What is considered normal and abnormal, acceptable and unacceptable, moral and immoral varies from culture to culture and even from subculture to subculture within a society.

■ *Illness categories may have important symbolic dimensions.* Medical anthropologists have shown that there is considerable cultural variation in the type and severity of symptoms regarded as important by different social groups. For example, in regions where amoebic infections are common, diarrhea can be considered a normal bowel function.

As biocultural creatures, people filter the biological feedback from their bodies through culturally constructed ethnomedical beliefs. Illness also has important symbolic dimensions. Susan Sontag (1978) describes illness as cultural metaphor and claims that particular illnesses (such as tuberculosis, cancer, AIDS) can have powerful social meanings in specific social contexts. The symbolic dimensions of illness most often have negative valuations and result in social stigma and ostracism (for example, leprosy). However, in some contexts, illness labels may be regarded positively and be attributes of personal identity.

The cultural meanings of an illness like leprosy can be maintained even when they are no longer scientifically justified. These cultural meanings vary from culture to culture.

■ *Medical systems reflect social realities.* Issues of socioeconomic class, gender hierarchies, and ethnic relations often play out in the context of a medical system. The epidemiological distribution of disease is not equitable from one social group to another. In general, the poor have higher rates of morbidity and mortality for all causes. Men and women generally have different rates of illness, although age-adjusted mortality rates are higher for men than for women. On the other hand, the risks associated with childbirth and motherhood are substantial in many parts of the world. In regard to illness behavior, women tend to seek health care more often than men. Social stratification, however, is clearly the single most important variable in determining both health status and access to medical care. Some societies draw from more than one medical tradition to produce and distribute services in a particular community or region.

Medical systems can be seen as sociocultural systems. There are particular social roles for practitioners and patients, and there is a hierarchy of power and prestige among practitioners. For the system to reproduce itself, medical practitioners must be trained. Practitioners must cooperate or compete with one another. Healing behaviors must be performed in particular fashions, and in some contexts these practices are regulated for the good of the profession. Most importantly, all healers must be compensated for their work. Finally, because politics and philosophy vary from society to society, this clearly influences the practice of medicine and access to medical care.

■ *Illness behavior can be considered a "hierarchy of resort."* When people perceive that they are ill, they act on this perception and seek medical care. Sociologists call these actions *illness behavior*. The primary components of illness behavior include acceptance of the sick role and seeking therapeutic interventions. Studies of illness behavior center on patterns of seeking health care; these patterns are called a *hierarchy of resort*. In general, people's hierarchies of resort begin with seeking solutions at home, usually from a female figure called "Mom" (or a linguistic variation thereof—actually, "Mama" is very common in the languages of the world). If household remedies do not work, the patient and his or her family move up the hierarchy of resort to a health care specialist. Depending on the society, the second step may be to go to a biomedical doctor or to a folk healer. If the patient is not cured on this level, and financial resources permit, the patient will seek care from a dif-

ferent, often more specialized, medical practitioner. Ethnographic descriptions of medical decision making and therapy-seeking behaviors comprise important aspects of the anthropological description of medical systems.

■ *The sick role is an important concept.* One area of sociological theory involves social statuses and roles—patterns of behavior that are expected by people fulfilling particular positions in a social system. The metaphor "all life is a stage" is intended here—we are actors playing roles. As individuals, we can simultaneously occupy different roles in relation to other people. For example, you may be somebody's son or daughter, somebody's student, somebody's lover, somebody's co-worker, and so on. How you act in a particular context depends in large part on what role you are playing at the time. Appropriate role behavior is learned as part of our culture. Society as a whole can function because people agree on what the roles are and what the expected behavior of a person is in each role. Cognitive psychologists and anthropologists have argued that we know the "play" (or the social scene), including the roles and scripts that they involve, because we share cultural models or schemata (general conceptions about how the world is supposed to function). This idea is closely linked to the social construction of reality that has been previously discussed.

In the inevitable event of sickness, our culture provides us with particular social roles: the sick patient, the healer, the supportive friend or family member. That way, everyone is expected to know what to do. When an individual adopts the sick role, a person's regular social responsibilities are temporarily suspended (for example, going to work or school). The sick role has its benefits, as we all know. At the same time, new social expectations and responsibilities are enforced (following the doctor's orders, gradually decreasing dependence on medical care, getting better). If people fail to meet these expectations—for example, if they get up and play instead of staying in bed and acting sick—then others think they are malingering, faking the sick role to reap its benefits. The same thing happens if patients fail to get well, as in the example of chronic fatigue syndrome.

■ *Because people live in households and as part of families, important characteristics of both health status and medical-care seeking are determined by these social groups.* All scientists have to decide the appropriate unit of analysis for understanding a particular phenomenon. In psychology and in biomedicine, that unit of analysis is usually the individual. The emphasis on the individual as an independent and autonomous unit is a feature of Western culture. Social scientists tend to look at things with the wider eye of larger units of analysis—families, social classes, tribes, ethnic groups, and so on. Medical anthropologists working in communities and public health settings have emphasized the importance of the household production of health. Because individuals' health status is affected by access to adequate nutrition, clean water, hygienic conditions, and medical care, people in a household have many of these elements in common. At the same time, familial roles might affect health differences within a household; for example, in many societies the male breadwinner eats first and children's nutritional needs are not given special attention. When sickness strikes a family, the entire group is often involved in health care decisions, particularly when there is a step to the next level of the hierarchy of resort. The family, sometimes extending beyond the household through other kinship links, has been called the *therapy management group,* a concept associated with the work of John Janzen (1978).

 **16**

Learning to Be a Leper: A Case Study in the Social Construction of Illness

Nancy E. Waxler

This selection returns us to the anthropological enterprise of cross-cultural comparison by examining the social meanings of a particular illness—leprosy—in the contexts of South Asia, North America, and Africa. The biomedical label for leprosy is Hansen's disease (HD); contrary to myth, this disease, characterized by a progressive degeneration of nerves in the limbs, is not highly infectious. The deformities associated with leprosy are the result of untreated secondary infections, partly because the victim has no sensation of pain in the extremities. With modern biomedical care, HD can be completely arrested. Although it may be possible to cure the disease, the illness and its social stigma are less easily treated.

An important research strategy in medical anthropology is cross-cultural comparison. Leprosy is a particularly interesting topic for such a comparison because the disease has undergone a striking social transformation. Even though biomedical science has disproved the idea of leprosy as being "unclean," these notions persist. Westerners fear and are disgusted by leprosy; it is, after all, a disease of Biblical proportions. But is this social stigma a cultural universal? Is the social reaction related to particular pathological features of the disease? What is it like to be a leper?

When people are diagnosed with a chronic disease, they must learn to adapt to it. The mechanisms for coping, however, are learned in a cultural context. People in the United States with leprosy react differently than people with HD in Ethiopia. In this selection, Nancy Waxler argues that the

Mycobacterium germ that causes leprosy the disease has only a small part in the large drama that is leprosy the illness. Also note her description of how charitable institutions, established to serve those suffering from leprosy, in the long term may function to perpetuate the problems of stigma.

Notice in this selection that the medical anthropologist is describing the experience of illness from the patient's perspective. This is an example of experience-near *ethnographies that are based on the qualitative research techniques of participant observation and interviewing. The phenomenon of the social construction of a stigmatized illness cannot be studied only by talking to people who have the disease. The social reaction to the disease—the social construction of a moral judgment about the condition—is equally important.*

As you read this selection, consider these questions:

- *How is the social stigma of leprosy different from the stigma of AIDS?*
- *If you were a physician and you were able to stop a case of Hansen's disease so that there were no deformities or long-term effects, what do you think could be done about the experience of the illness of leprosy?*
- *How is it that agencies designed to help people might in fact contribute to their stigmatization?*
- *What does the author mean when she says that people have "careers" with a chronic disease?*

People who feel ill often first discuss their symptoms with family members or friends and then later go to a physician who questions, evaluates, and perhaps prescribes treatment. In the course of this exploration the "trouble" itself is transformed from vague and disconnected symptoms to a labeled condition, that is, an illness that others in the society understand to have a particular explanation and social meaning. Thus, social negotiations turn symptoms into social facts that may have significant consequences for the sick person.

. . . [W]e shall look at several aspects of this "social labeling" process.[1] In particular, we shall stress that the definition of a specific disease and associated social expectations often depend as much on the society and culture as on the biological characteristics of the disease itself. People diagnosed as having a particular disease learn "how" to have it by negotiating with friends and relations as well as with people in the treatment system; this process is affected by society's beliefs and expectations for that disease. Finally,

symptoms → condition → societies meaning

society's definition of and expectations for a particular disease are sustained by social and organizational forces that may have little to do with the disease itself as a biological process.

Leprosy is a disease in which the process of social transformation is clear. Leprosy has a known cause, an effective treatment (but no cure), and thus a predictable outcome. From the perspective of the medical model, if the patient is treated quickly and regularly, the bacillus is controlled and the patient will recover; routine and scientifically neutral treatment is all that is required. But Westerners and many Asians—even those who have never seen a leprosy patient—may suspect that scientific treatment of the biological phenomenon misses the point. Often leprosy is feared; lepers are shunned; we say of a deviant community member, "He's like a leper." Doctors in Indian hospitals refuse to see cases; attendants in Ceylonese hospitals refuse to change dressings; wives begin divorce proceedings when husbands are diagnosed as lepers; patients leave their villages to become urban beggars. In some societies, then, routine treatment is neither given nor received. Responses to the disease by patient, family, and doctor are strongly influenced by social expectations and not simply by the biological characteristics of leprosy.

If the social transformation of the disease has such profound effects on those who experience it, then we must ask how a biological phenomenon has taken on such a definition. Is there some inherent quality of the disease—perhaps its communicability, threat to life, its disfiguring effects—that determines social expectations? Or are social definitions of particular diseases specific to certain societies and historical circumstances? Finally, why are certain social definitions perpetuated, for example, the terrible fear of leprosy, in the face of a known cause and effective treatment?

One way to consider these questions is to examine disease and illness cross-culturally. A cross-cultural analysis of leprosy controls for the nature of the disease but varies societal and historical factors, giving us an opportunity to ask whether the stigma of leprosy is universal (thus perhaps associated with biological phenomena) or whether social definitions differ from society to society. . . . [W]e shall document the truth of the second alternative, that there is considerable variation in the social and moral definition of leprosy across cultures, and speculate that this variation may be linked to specific historical events.

We shall also ask how patients respond when caught up in their own society's definition of the disease, and we shall show that the career of the diseased person reflects society's expectations. American lepers, though stigmatized, tend to respond aggressively, "taking on" the disease and the society; Ethiopian and Indian lepers stigmatize themselves and withdraw, complying with society's definition even before others recognize the disease.

Finally, we shall question how and why particular moral definitions of disease continue unchanged. Why are the stigma and fear of leprosy still prevalent in many countries when an effective treatment is readily available? In this regard we shall examine the organizational and social context in which care is offered and shall show that the medical organizations that treat leprosy may have had an important although inadvertent part in perpetuating the stigma of the disease.

Leprosy is an exotic disease, one that most of us have never seen. We examine it here for the same reasons that many anthropologists examine exotic cultures, to reflect on common phenomena. Studies of diseases such as leprosy that have clear and strong moral definitions in some societies provide insights into the moral component of all diseases. We can expect, then, that similar analytic principles might be useful in understanding our own society's definitions of tuberculosis, heart disease, schizophrenia, and cancer.

SOME MEDICAL FACTS ABOUT LEPROSY

Leprosy has been known for thousands of years as a chronic and communicable disease affecting the skin, eyes, internal organs, peripheral nerves, and mucous membranes. Not until 1873, however, did Hansen report the discovery of *Mycobacterium leprae*, now thought to be a causal factor in the disease, and only recently has an agent, the nine-banded armadillo, been discovered in which the bacteria can be cultivated experimentally. Pending effective cultivation and experimental tests, the exact relationship between the bacterium and the disease is not clear, although researchers assume that the bacterium plays a part in the disease.

Leprosy is assumed to be only mildly communicable, even though the mode of transmission is not entirely understood. It is usually suggested that long-term skin or respiratory contact of ten or fifteen years' duration is required for transmission. Alternatively, however, a long incubation period is also known. American soldiers, who presumably were infected abroad during World War II, became symptomatic 2.9 years later (for tuberculoid leprosy) and 9.3 years later (for lepromatous leprosy).[2] Further, some immunity factor also is hypothesized.

The common stereotype of the disease, in novels, films, even in fund-raising literature, is of a person whose fingers have fallen off, without a nose, with terrible ulcers on the skin. In fact, the most common symptoms of leprosy, especially in the early stages, are mild and unremarkable. Anesthetic skin (causing secondary problems such as accidental burns), raised patches resembling eczema, skin ulcers that do not heal, for example, are usual; the unremarkability of the symptoms often contribute to late treatment. Only after many years without treatment do leprosy patients experience severe malformation and dysfunction of the kind that might be readily recognized by the layperson.

Currently the most common treatment is sulfone drugs administered over a long period. In Sri Lanka, for example, leprosy patients are expected to continue treatment for a minimum of five years following diagnosis. No one terms these drugs a "cure," and presumably no cure will be known until the causal factors are understood more clearly. These drugs are known to arrest the growth of the bacteria, however, and to cause a drop in the bacteria count in most but not all patients; after three months the disease is usually no longer communicable. For patients whose disease has progressed to the stage of physical malformation, surgery is also used.

The World Health Organization[3] estimates the worldwide prevalence of leprosy to be about 10 million cases or 0.8 per thousand. Ninety-four percent of these cases are in tropical Africa and Asia. Of the total number of estimated cases, only one-third are registered with a health agency and only one-fifth are being treated. Although Westerners usually think of leprosy as a problem "over there," an average of 100 new cases of leprosy was reported each year in the United States during the twenty-year period following World War II; of these, approximately one-half were foreign-born residents.[4] In the Commonwealth of Massachusetts, an average of one case of leprosy per year has been reported since 1970.

If we construct a picture of the "typical" leprosy patient from the medical facts, then, we see a man or woman whose symptoms are mild enough to be unrecognizable to the layperson, who sometime in the past may have lived or worked closely with a leper. During the time the disease was harbored it is relatively unlikely that it was passed along to others. If the disease is diagnosed early and treated regularly with the appropriate drugs, the patient's symptoms will disappear and the disease will be arrested if not cured, leaving no visible signs.

This should be the "medical career" of the typical leprosy patient today. Even in many African and Asian countries, treatment is available and known to ordinary villagers, and thus it is quite possible for a leprosy patient to receive early outpatient treatment, exhibit few visible symptoms, and carry on ordinary social activities. Why is it possible, then, for lepers in Nigeria to follow this career and for Indian lepers, on the other hand, to experience profound changes in their whole life, to lose their occupations, their wives, their children, their very identities? That is, how and why does the moral definition of the disease vary across cultures?

IS LEPROSY UNIVERSALLY STIGMATIZED?

It is easy for Westerners to assume that leprosy is stigmatized in all societies. . . . This assumption has been made without question by a number of authors who have then offered a functional hypothesis about stigma. These authors suggest that because leprosy is universally stigmatized, stigma must function as a sort of social protection device. That is, the moral definition of leprosy was developed to explain and justify society's need to isolate lepers from the majority group that the communicable disease threatened. The assumption, then, is that the disease is indeed inherently life-threatening, that society must protect itself from such a disease by isolating those who are afflicted, and that the moral ideology regarding leprosy is society's justification for its own self-protection.

But does the moral definition of the disease come from the quality of the disease itself or from the social and historical conditions in which the disease exists? One way of answering this question is to investigate the extent to which the stigma of leprosy differs across societies. If we assume that the basic biological characteristics of leprosy are much the same everywhere in the world and we find that social and moral definitions are not, then we must conclude that these social definitions cannot be explained simply in terms of the biological nature of the disease itself. Reflecting on this hypothesis, we shall look at the social definitions of leprosy in India, Sri Lanka, and Nigeria.

The Indian definition of leprosy can be quickly understood by reference to one set of facts. Of 100 people with leprosy being treated in the city of Lucknow, 53 percent had been born and raised in rural villages; after their leprosy was discovered, all but 18 percent of this group had migrated to the city, away from home and family; 66 percent of these migrants never returned to visit their homes; many became beggars.[5] As Kapoor reports, "The attitude of the society towards these unfortunate people is so cruel and cynical that the victim of the disease feels isolated, despised and virtually excommunicated."[6] Such rejection of people with leprosy is also apparent in Indian leprosy hospitals themselves, where it has been reported that doctors in charge sometimes refuse to touch the patient's body when treatment or diagnosis is required.[7]

These informal norms were formalized in Indian law. Before the 1950s in India, all pauper lepers were segregated regardless of the level of infectiousness. Lepers were excluded from all inheritance in the joint family, were barred from traveling in trains with non-lepers, were not eligible for insurance, and were not allowed to serve in the military. In the 1950s the laws were changed to allow normal inheritance of property by leprosy patients but at the same time to provide for judicial separation and divorce when leprosy appeared in a married man or woman. A proposal has also been made for compulsory sterilization of all infectious male patients.[8]

From all reports, then, lepers are often physically and socially rejected in Indian society; some modern laws perpetuate these norms. There is great fear of contagion (an Indian friend advised, "If you talk to a leper, put your handkerchief in front of your nose and mouth"), and repulsion at the sight or even thought of a leper. Those who discover that they have the disease often leave or are pushed out of their homes, to migrate to the cities to the "normal" role of a beggar.

. . .

But if we look at Sri Lanka (formerly Ceylon), we see a different picture. Here, again, the general population fears leprosy, believes it to be extremely contagious, and to result in hideous deformities; few have seen a leper, however, even in a population where best estimates indicate that the prevalence is 0.37 per thousand.[9] One might expect that the Sri Lankan leper's life experience would be similar to the Indian's, including rejection and mobility. Our interviews of lepers receiving outpatient treatment indicate that this is not so.[10] Instead, we found that leprosy patients, after diagnosis, remain in their own homes and carry on the same occupation that they had before the disease appeared. The schoolteacher continues teaching; the housewife continues cooking and caring for children; only one man, a baker, left his job, he reported, because the physical symptoms prevented him from doing his work.

Families of patients remain intact as well. Those who were married before diagnosis remained married; several more were married after the disease appeared.

. . .

Thus, there is little of the overt rejection reported in India. Yet life is not entirely unchanged for Sri Lankan lepers. Most patients, in fact, withdraw from society to

some extent; they stigmatize themselves. When asked what advice they would give to other patients, our leprosy patients said, "Do not move around the village," "Do not visit others' homes unless it is absolutely necessary." They apply similar advice within their own families (and usually follow this advice), saying, "Use separate eating utensils and sleep separately." And there is general but not unanimous agreement that it is better *not* to tell nonfamily members about the illness; "Others will be afraid," "Others might stop visiting, even stop working with us." Leprosy patients, then, are fully aware of the stigma of the disease; their response is to avoid possible rejection by mild withdrawal and secrecy.

Yet often the secret of leprosy cannot be kept forever. When villagers discover that someone they know has leprosy, their first response is fear and rejection; but that often disappears over the years and relationships return to normal. One patient reported that when the villagers found out about his illness, "They went to the Montessori school my son was attending and asked the teachers to separate him from the others. Then the children began to harass my son. So I wrote a letter to the rural development society telling them they could call any doctor and give me an examination. They didn't do that but the harassment of my son stopped after that. I know the doctors would not say I had leprosy because the treatment is kept secret and they wouldn't tell what it was." For this man stigmatization early in the course of his illness also meant that villagers stopped using his well for bathing. "But now (seven years later) they use the well again and relations are back to normal."

Although the general population in Sri Lanka seems to favor rejection and isolation of lepers, the actual experience of many of these patients is quite different. Families accept the patient, marriages continue, and, over the years, neighbors who might have been afraid at first resume normal relations. Patients themselves sometimes withdraw into their families and avoid unnecessary nonfamily contact. This is not true, naturally, for all those with leprosy, but the general pattern, relative to the Indian one, is of acceptance or at least tolerance.

Nigeria provides an even more benign example.[11] Among the Hausa of Northern Nigeria, leprosy is highly prevalent, as it is in India. In this peasant agricultural, largely Muslim, society, indigenous beliefs about the cause of leprosy include gluttony, swearing falsely by the Koran, washing in the water a leprosy patient has used. Treatments may consist of burning and scraping the skin, purges, and potions. Although leprosy is common, modern methods and theories not understood, and traditional treatments probably ineffective, no one is afraid. "The Hausa, in contrast to the West, exhibit little fear or disgust concerning leprosy.

They do not seem to regard it with any special apprehension; it is not necessarily more unusual than any other of the great range of diseases that assail them."[12] Lepers continue to reside with their families, living a normal life until the very advanced stages of the disease. "At this point there seems to be a distinct change in vocation with many of the victims becoming beggars,"[13] but begging itself is an accepted, nonstigmatized role among Muslims.

. . .

Variation in the degree to which leprosy is stigmatized is apparent across Africa, with reports from Ethiopia[14] that resemble the experiences of Indian lepers (divorce, migration, begging), and mild rejection or none at all in Nigeria and Tanzania.[15]

How can we account for differences in the moral definition of leprosy that are apparent in different cultures? Perhaps the incidence of the disease, variations in subtypes, patterns of immunity, or effectiveness of treatment contribute to a society's perceptions. But these may play a minor role in comparison with the culture norms and historical circumstances in which the disease is found. Lepers in India may easily be rejected because a clear and elaborate hierarchical caste structure, justified by the ideology of impurity and sin, is available into which a threatening person may be placed. Caste beliefs and caste practices (not eating with, not touching, not sitting with) serve very well to handle society's fear of the leper. It is easy, then, for normal people in Indian society to equate leprosy with punishment of sins and to treat lepers as outcastes. The cultural background of Sri Lanka is quite similar to that of India, but with two crucial differences. The caste structure is less hierarchical (more than half of the population belongs to the high cultivators' caste), and the majority of the population is Buddhist, not Hindu. The Sinhalese experience with low-caste, and particularly outcaste groups, is relatively small; traditional caste obligations of family to family have generally disappeared, and the concern with who is who and how to behave in the company of other castes is narrowing. Further, Buddhism's stress on tolerance of differences and on compassion for others contrasts with Hindu values. These cultural and structural differences, then, may help explain why the general population in Sri Lanka fears and wants to reject lepers but the family and neighbors of leprosy patients actually accept them with little permanent stigma.

By examining leprosy in India, Sri Lanka, and Africa we have shown that lepers are not universally stigmatized. Thus it is unlikely that the social definition of leprosy arises entirely from biological qualities of the disease itself, that is from its degree of contagion or visible symptoms. Instead, stigma may be linked to particular historical and cultural conditions, specific to each society.

HOW DOES THE MORAL DEFINITION OF LEPROSY DEVELOP?

How does a disease come to be feared and stigmatized in some cultures, yet remain an unremarkable fact of life in others? This is obviously a complicated question to which there can be no single answer. We might, however, find some answers in historical conditions or in the cultural and social matrix in which the disease is embedded. Many explanations are buried in the past; in India the extreme stigma of leprosy is certainly not new. Nineteenth-century Hawaii, however, provides one well-documented case in which the moral definition of leprosy is related to specific historical, economic, and social circumstances.[16]

In the 1840s in Hawaii, and elsewhere in the West, leprosy had almost disappeared, and when it did occur was considered to be a hereditary household disease. It was of minor importance, not stigmatized, a disease that most people did not encounter. Soon after mid-century, however, Hawaii's economic and social situation began to change, reflecting the worldwide movement of people at the height of colonialism. Europeans moved out to the colonies; Americans traveled for purposes of trade. Chinese began to move the other way, to Hawaii to work on the plantations and to the American West during the gold rush. In 1851 the first group of 180 Chinese immigrants arrived in Hawaii, and by the 1860s the movement of Chinese to Hawaii had become a flood.

The Hawaiians believed that the Chinese had brought leprosy. In the 1850s Hawaiian authorities noted an increase in leprosy, but newspaper reference to leprosy "was purposely omitted . . . for fear of injuring . . . commercial development."[17] By 1862 it could not be ignored and was publicly described as a major outbreak of the disease. This raised several questions in the minds of Hawaiians, and in the minds of health officials around the world. If Hawaii had suddenly experienced a serious increase in leprosy, could one still cling to the idea that leprosy was hereditary? And if it were not hereditary, who carried the disease?

In 1865 Hawaii's official response to the outbreak of leprosy was quarantine of lepers, implying a belief in contagion. This was confirmed in 1874 by Hansen's discovery of the bacillus, *Mycobacterium leprae*. Within one or two decades, at a time of vastly increasing population movements, world opinion shifted from belief in inheritance to belief in contagion.

The Chinese who were believed to have brought leprosy to Hawaii and the western United States were "industrious, painstaking, persevering and frugal—qualities which in Caucasian Protestants undoubtedly would have been considered virtues."[18] Yet they were also viewed by white people, in that age of social Darwinism, as natural cultural inferiors. Further, they provided cheap labor, and their industriousness perhaps threatened poor Westerners who wanted work. Thus, "while there were many demographic–environmental factors at work other than the coincidence of Chinese immigration with the leprosy outbreak in Hawaii that might have triggered the epidemic, the Chinese, nevertheless, almost immediately came to bear the full brunt of responsibility, a stigmatization of them that soon reached monstrous proportions."[19]

. . .

The Chinese were blamed, stigmatized, and excluded. Yet if we look more carefully at Hawaiian Board of Health records, it is not at all clear that the Chinese actually brought leprosy. Writing in 1886, the then superintendent of the Molokai Leprosy Hospital inquired about early cases to discover that leprosy was recognized by missionaries in 1823 and by a physician familiar with the disease in 1840, a decade or more before the great influx of Chinese laborers.[20] Health data support the conclusion that the Chinese were not an important source of leprosy. In the period 1866–85, the Molokai Hospital admitted 3,076 patients, 2,997 of whom were native Hawaiians, 22 Chinese, and the remainder Europeans, Americans, and Africans.[21]. . .

In analyzing this phenomenon a hundred years later, we might conclude that the Chinese became convenient scapegoats for Western society. Whether they actually brought leprosy—and it is not clear that they did—the presence of the disease in Hawaii provided a rationale for rejection that in fact had other basic causes. First was the potential or real economic threat that native Western workers may have felt from Chinese laborers. If Chinese could be believed to have leprosy, that fact made a convenient excuse for excluding economic competitors. Second was the nineteenth-century belief in the inherent inferiority of nonwhite people. If the Chinese could be believed to have a threatening contagious disease, so much the better because that would confirm the Westerner's sense of superiority.

If the Chinese were stigmatized ostensibly because they brought leprosy, then the association could also work the other way; leprosy became stigmatized because it was common among the Chinese. This phenomenon may have occurred in the Western world, and particularly in Hawaii. The result, by the end of the nineteenth century, was the transformation of a relatively unknown disease into a socially and morally threatening phenomenon. In this case the moral defin-ition of the disease came from and was reinforced by the moral and social definition of those believed to carry it.

The association between particular historical events and the appearance of leprosy in Hawaii may explain why leprosy became a stigmatized disease there. In other cultures quite different circumstances may influence the moral definition of the disease. We can look again at Africa for evidence of another definitional process, the introduction of stigma by Western medicine.

In northern Tanzania, . . . there was traditionally little stigma attached to leprosy; patients lived with, ate with, slept with their families. Leprosy was an unremarkable disease. But in 1966 the Geita Leprosy Scheme was inaugurated, focusing not only on case finding and treatment but also on public education. Talks were given to school children in grades 5, 6, and 7 once every two years; key members of the community were also reached, although the general public was not directly educated about the disease. Information on cause, symptoms, mode of transmission, treatment, and social problems was included in each additional effort; thus Western medical notions about leprosy were introduced into the traditional system, largely through the children.

A survey conducted five years later showed how effective this educational effort had been. In response to almost all information questions about the disease, "The majority of the school children expressed the modern view of leprosy as being caused by certain bacteria and by physical contact with a patient, whereas the adult population and the leaders associated leprosy more frequently with such factors as heredity, witchcraft. . . ."[22] Whereas the educational program "stressed that there is no need to isolate the patient provided certain basic rules of hygiene are maintained, and that there is no reason to discontinue marriage to a leprosy patient,"[23] there was a surprising finding. School children, targets of this education, opposed the idea of leprosy patients sharing food and sleeping space with family members, and objected to leprosy patients marrying. "Another illustrative example of attitudes derived from health education is that of the sellers at the Sengerema market who, after a health education session by the Geita Leprosy Scheme some years ago, for the first time in Sengerema's history, urged their colleagues suffering from leprosy not to enter the market again."[24] Thus, together with scientific medicine's facts about causation and treatment, other attitudes had inadvertently been added to the society; the new idea of infection had presumably led Tanzanians to recommend avoidance and even rejection of people with leprosy.

In Tanzania, we see what could be the beginning of a new moral definition of leprosy, introduced without intent by public health educators. A somewhat similar phenomenon seems to have occurred in Nigeria[25] and elsewhere[26] when Western modes of treatment—isolation in leper colonies—were introduced by Christian missionaries. In neither instance is there evidence that the general public's attitude toward leprosy underwent a radical shift toward stigmatization. Yet what we see in this century in Tanzania and Nigeria may appear, in the next century, in a more institutionalized form.

The cases of Hawaii and Africa provided examples of two different processes through which an ordinary disease may take on a particular social and moral definition. In Hawaii it appears that the status of those believed to carry the disease—the inferior yet economically threatening Chinese coolies—may have been transferred to the disease itself. In Africa a new moral definition may have been inadvertently suggested by scientific medicine's public health educators. Thus, depending on specific historical/economic/cultural/medical "accidents," leprosy, and by implication perhaps all diseases, are transformed into illnesses having culture-specific social and moral definitions.

LEARNING TO BE A LEPER

A society's expectations for lepers, its beliefs about them, have a significant influence on their experiences as sick people. If we examine what a particular patient does when he discovers he has leprosy, we find that his response to leprosy is consistent with society's expectations for lepers. In fact, he learns to be a leper, the kind of leper his family and neighbors, even his doctors, expect him to be.

Ethiopia provides one example of the leprosy patient's confirmation of his society's beliefs about his disease. Leprosy there is feared and stigmatized. "People entering the bus which links the area around the leprosy hospital to the center of town will cover their nose and mouth. When there is an important visitor to the hospital . . . the patients may be confined to their wards."[27]

Those who discover that they have leprosy respond to this social definition in the way we might expect. Often they stigmatize themselves. In a sample of 100 leprosy patients interviewed in the leprosy outpatient clinic in Addis Ababa, Ethiopia, a fairly common patient career was apparent. One-fifth of the patients had been rejected by their families or had voluntarily left their homes. Half of the lepers continued to attend church, "although this does not mean that they actually entered the building. Seventeen refrained from going, mainly out of fear of being rejected."[28] Of those who remained married, one-third stopped having sexual relationships. But many marriages did not continue. One-half of all lepers who were married at the outbreak of the disease were later divorced; of these divorces, one-half were actually initiated by the patient. (This divorce rate is much higher than that of the general population.) Finally, one-fifth had migrated to the city to become beggars.

. . .

The response of Ethiopian lepers to their predicament is consistent with the fatalism of the Ethiopian peasant. Many American lepers, on the other hand, take a role that is almost a caricature of American values: They "fight back."

Leprosy patients treated at the U.S. Public Health Service hospital at Carville, Louisiana, begin with the assumption that the public fears and stigmatizes lepers. Some report experiences with families or communities that confirm the existence of fear and even rejection. And some leprosy patients accept the public definition of the disease by withdrawing to the haven of the Carville hospital, where they are allowed to live the remainder of their lives. Yet those who make this choice do not willingly accept the beliefs about leprosy that are associated with stigma, beliefs about extreme contagion, deformity, and incurability.

Instead, patients who voluntarily withdraw from society support another segment of the patient population, those whom Gussow and Tracy call "career patients."[29] It is these career patients who take on a peculiarly "American" role, one that is undoubtedly respected by the public. They become professional educators, acting as representatives of all lepers in an attempt to change the public's view of the disease. They give talks at Rotary clubs, organize seminars, speak about leprosy on the radio, conduct tours of the leprosy hospital, publish *The Star*. The content of their educational attempts is a new set of beliefs about leprosy, beliefs that are designed to replace the "old" ideas that justified stigma.

. . .

The assumption behind this new ideology, promoted by the career patients, is that American society's fear of leprosy will wither away as the public learns the "truth" about the disease. No longer will lepers feel wrongly labeled and no longer will they be stigmatized.

In a sense, these career patients are America's version of the Ethiopian beggar. Their response to leprosy is consistent with American values on activism, self-sufficiency, and change; when they see a problem, especially a problem for themselves, they try to solve it. They do not respond like the Ethiopian fatalists. At the same time, however, from the point of view of the public, they are not "normal." They are still lepers, whose role as educators depends on existence of the disease itself. "At the present time this status [as career patient] appears to be the only legitimate one the leprosy patient has available to him for life in open society."[30]

Lepers in the United States learn to be the kind of lepers Americans expect. To confirm the lay American's fears of leprosy, they withdraw, avoid, protect themselves, and protect others. But they do these things reluctantly and temporarily, until their active educational efforts succeed in changing public opinion. In the meantime, those who go openly into the outside world go labeled as "leper," fulfilling our expectations that lepers are indeed "different."

There is a world of difference between the Ethiopian leper begging in front of the train station and the American leper showing a film to the Lions' club. But underlying that difference is a more basic similarity: Lepers learn how to be lepers from the beliefs and expectations their society has for them. In every society the sick person is socialized to take a role the society expects.

HOW IS THE MORAL DEFINITION OF LEPROSY PERPETUATED?

Even though leprosy is sometimes feared and lepers stigmatized, and even though leprosy patients often willingly take on the deviant role that society expects, why do such moral definitions continue far beyond the time when effective treatment is readily available? Wouldn't one expect that as the disease becomes easily treatable the fear and threat would subside?

To examine this question we must return to the situation at the end of the nineteenth century, when although a pandemic of leprosy was feared by European and American observers, it did not occur. The public at the time believed leprosy to be highly contagious, but very few people actually contracted the disease. The panic died down. Leprosy was limited to tropical people, usually the poor, and did not become a threat to colonial settlers. Although an official statement was made in 1909 that leprosy was incurable,[31] by the 1920s a moderately successful treatment had been instituted, and by the 1940s a more effective one. We must ask why fear of leprosy and rejection of lepers continued in many societies when, in reality, most people in those societies had discovered that leprosy was relatively nonthreatening. Here, again, we shall look at social and organizational contexts in which the disease exists rather than at the biological qualities of the disease itself.

In the second half of the nineteenth century, when it was believed that leprosy was not only highly contagious but life-threatening, the churches acted. Father Damien established the leper hospital at Molokai, Hawaii, in 1860 and died there, from leprosy, in 1889. The Mission to Lepers was established in Great Britain in 1874. The Louisiana Home for the Lepers, now the U.S. Public Health Service Hospital at Carville, was founded by the Catholic church in 1894. During this time, of course, numerous missionaries were sent out, to Africa, India, Oceania, to treat lepers. Not until the 1920s did nonreligious organizations enter the field, and they still remain of minor importance compared with the worldwide involvement of missionaries. Even today the nursing staff at the U.S. Public Health Service Hospital at Carville is provided by the Sisters of Charity of St. Vincent de Paul.[32] Also today the American Leprosy Missions and the Leprosy Mission (of Great Britain), foundations that finance treatment centers all over the world, integrate Christian ideology with treatment goals. "The main object of the Mission is to minister in the name of Jesus Christ to the physical, mental and spiritual needs of sufferers from leprosy, to assist in their rehabilitation, and to work toward the eradication of leprosy."[33]

Thus certain groups, church groups in this case, came to "own" the disease. They set up hospitals, trained staff, searched for patients, collected and disseminated information, and spoke and acted "for" the lepers. Because leprosy was in many places greatly feared, those who did this work took on an aura of saintliness. . . .

We have introduced two important facts about leprosy since 1920. First, private church-related organizations became the main providers of treatment to leprosy patients, collecting funds mainly from the industrial West and funneling money to nonindustrial tropical countries. Second, in many (but not all) of these nonindustrial countries, leprosy was strongly stigmatized. One might expect that, once an effective treatment became known and once the missionary organizations began to provide this treatment, the stigmatization of leprosy would decline. Changes in definition of the disease might be slow, might take decades, but with effective and available treatment fear and thus stigma would disappear, even in India and Ethiopia.

Yet they have not disappeared. In fact we suspect that the organizations most committed to treating and curing may have, inadvertently, had a part in perpetuating the stigma of leprosy, through a complex and circular relation between the expectations that some societies have for people with leprosy and the organizational constraints and requirements for the leprosy organizations' own survival.

"Normals" in the community prefer to have deviant people of many sorts removed from view and cared for by others. . . .

Leprosy organizations have taken the responsibility for the care of lepers from "normals" and have in many societies done just what the community wants, removed the leper from view. Inpatient facilities are often completely contained villages providing not only treatment but also employment, education, and recreation. There is often no need for a leprosy patient to leave this "asylum" and, in fact, it is sometimes physically difficult to do so because leprosy hospitals are often found on islands (e.g., in Sri Lanka and the Philippines) or in the remote countryside. In fact, organizations justify the isolation of leprosy patients by reference to the community's stigmatization of lepers. "Some are rejected by their homes and families . . . for some there is, humanly speaking, no hope; their disabilities mean that they will be dependent for the rest of their lives. The Mission cares for such as these also."[34] Removal of lepers from the "normal" community serves to confirm the idea of stigma. People in Sri Lanka may say, "If lepers must be sent to a remote island for treatment then there must be something very terrible about them and their disease." Stigma is thus confirmed.

Leprosy organizations have not only removed threatening people from community view, they have also demanded little change on the part of "normals" by focusing their work largely on treatment and rehabilitation rather than on prevention or on public education to reduce stigma. . . .

Thus, leprosy organizations, by building permanent inpatient hospitals and stressing treatment of stigmatized patients rather than change in the public's view of the disease, have acted "for" the normal community. In many cases leprosy patients, even in the United States, remain permanently under organizational control and do not return to their communities.[35] We expect that so long as these organizations continue to remove leprosy patients, they will be supported by the community. . . .

Leprosy organizations, like many medical foundations, are dependent on public donation of funds. As Scott has suggested, funds may be contributed more generously if such organizations confirm popular beliefs by medical and social science. Spokespersons for these foundations have suggested as much, in discussions of the change from "leprosy" to "Hansen's disease," when they say: "There is a case for retaining the substance of current terminology related to *leprosy*

particularly because of its value to fund-raising." They explain that appeals for "overseas" charity, for Asian and African patients, must compete with 77,000 charities at home and "the evocation of a reaction to the word *leprosy* is an essential factor."[36] Thus, leprosy foundations may, to sustain themselves, find it necessary to allude to the idea of threat and to support the community in its willingness to stigmatize.

. . .

Westerners, vaguely threatened by a terrible disease, and certainly somewhat guilty about but very willing to turn the care of such patients over to others, can do only one thing, give donations. As the American Leprosy *Bulletin* suggests, the fact that immunity to standard drugs is occurring more frequently ". . . is nothing short of terrifying, simply because, to date, there is absolutely no other drug which is readily available, as free of negative side effects, as inexpensive and as effective as DDS has been up until now. . . . The quality of care must be raised until a high proportion of cases are found early and treated regularly. Five dollars per year is not enough. Thirty dollars is a more reasonable figure, but in many areas adequate care cannot be given for less than fifty to sixty dollars per patient per year."[37] All one needs to do, then, to be relieved of the burden of dealing with stigmatized people, is to give money, in this case, to keep the disease out of sight in the poor tropical countries.

Much of what is stated in these messages is, according to current scientific knowledge about leprosy, factually wrong. Leprosy is not a terrible or life-threatening disease, nor a real threat to Westerners. Service to lepers, like all service, requires devotion, but the degree of risk is not great. In fact, in a growing number of countries service to lepers is provided by government health service employees in the same way as it is for other diseases. It is apparently true that the immunity of some bacilli has become a problem that must be handled by greater expenditure and/or better planning based on epidemiological knowledge.[38]

Why do foundations dealing with leprosy arouse fears and suggest stigma—particularly in the face of scientific and experiential knowledge that leprosy is not highly contagious and can be treated effectively on an outpatient basis while the patient carries on normal activities? We have suggested that the economic and social commitments of the organizations, justified by an ideology about "important work that remains undone," requires continued financial and other support. To sustain financial support these organizations have learned that they survive only if they confirm society's preference for removal of deviant people from view. Thus, the organizations whose goals are "to assist in their [leprosy patients'] rehabilitation and to work toward the eradication of leprosy" at the same time perpetuate, through their actions (building inpatient hospitals and providing long-term care) and words (public education programs and fund-raising brochures) the community's ideas of stigma. It is not insignificant that the 1978 brochure of the Leprosy Mission is entitled *Set Apart*.

CONCLUSION

We began with a bacillus, mildly communicable, treatable, not life-threatening nor even deforming if treated early. Now we see that the bacillus itself is only a minor actor in the drama of leprosy. Instead, surrounding the disease in many societies is a set of social beliefs and expectations that profoundly affect the patient's experience and the doctor's work.

First we showed that the stigma of leprosy is not universal. In many societies, even where leprosy is common, leprosy is believed to be just another of the debilitating illnesses that many families must tolerate. Patients remain at home and marriages continue. In other societies, lepers are quickly divorced, pushed out of their homes, to end up as beggars. This cross-cultural variation in the stigma of leprosy led us to conclude that the source of a particular response is in the social and cultural matrix in which the disease exists.

In many societies beliefs about leprosy developed and stabilized long before written records were kept. In nineteenth-century Hawaii, however, we saw the economic and social threat of the Chinese immigrants become transformed into the social threat of the disease they were believed to carry. In Africa, we pointed to the very beginning of what could be a new, and stigmatized, notion of leprosy inadvertently introduced by public health educators. Thus, the moral definition of leprosy may arise from particular historical/social/medical circumstances, different in each society.

Second, we showed that the ideology surrounding leprosy provides a map for the leper. Moral definitions tell the leper how to "have" the illness. We contrasted Ethiopian and American experiences, profoundly different, but each exemplifying the effect of society's expectations on the leper's career.

Finally, once the moral definition becomes established, it is often perpetuated for reasons having very little to do with the disease itself. In the case of leprosy, even though effective treatment is available in the tropical countries where the disease is prevalent, and

even though the Christian missionary organizations that are often the main providers of treatment certainly do not intend to stigmatize, the stigma of leprosy continues. We have suggested that this moral definition of leprosy is often perpetuated by the very organizations that treat the disease through a complex and circular relationship between the community's preference for removing deviant people and the leprosy organizations' needs for society's support in order to survive. Both the organizations' actions (removing leprosy patients from society) and their ideologies (in the form of public educational materials) sustain the idea that leprosy is horrible and threatening, requires treatment by "special" people, and is an enormous, often hidden, and unending problem. These actions and beliefs, though not based on medical facts, are consistent with the normal community's definitions of the disease and thus receive most sympathy from prospective donors. To continue their work, then, the organizations that "own" leprosy must sustain the stigma of leprosy.

We have examined leprosy because it provides a clear example of the social transformation of disease. In some societies leprosy is transformed into an illness that has serious implications for the social career of the sick person. Similar transformations might occur with other diseases. The effects may be milder and the social transformations less obvious, but if we examine the beliefs, practices, and experiences of patients who suffer from other disease, we should see similar processes.

. . .

The social definition of illness [also] has an obvious effect on doctors. For example, not only must they treat the leprosy bacillus, they must also recognize and deal with the culture's beliefs about the disease. In India and Sri Lanka they must find the hidden patients and convince those in treatment to return for more. In Hawaii and Louisiana doctors must care for and also justify the continued hospitalization of large proportions of leprosy patients with inactive diseases who do not want to go home.[39] The social and cultural context in which the disease exists must be seen as part of the disease process itself.

Our understanding of leprosy can move beyond this "conservative" analysis of the relationship between social factors and disease. It is not simply that doctors are waiting outside the society with neutral values, waiting to step in to treat and to take into account society's peculiar transformations of disease. Instead the medical institution is part of society itself, and thus is implicated in the social and moral definition of disease. We have seen that missionary doctors who went to Africa and India took with them a particular conception of leprosy that required isolation hospitals, and this new treatment method implied that it was right and good that lepers be taken from their homes and isolated from their families. New threats and fears—even the idea of stigma—were thus introduced. These threats and fears, predominant in the West, have been strengthened over the years by medical and missionary organizations whose basic needs are to survive.

NOTES

1. Schur, E. M. *Labeling Deviant Behavior: Its Sociological Implications*. New York: Harper & Row, 1971.

2. Feldman, R. A. "Leprosy surveillance in the USA: 1949–1970," *International Journal of Leprosy*, 1968, 37: 458–60.

3. World Health Organization Expert Committee on Leprosy. *World Health Organization Technical Report Services*, No. 459. Geneva: World Health Organization, 1970.

4. Feldman. "Leprosy surveillance in the USA."

5. Kapoor, J. N. "Lepers in the city of Lucknow," *Indian Journal of Social Work*, 1961, 22:239–46.

6. Ibid., p. 239.

7. Ryrie, G. A. "The psychology of leprosy," *Leprosy Review*, 1951, 22:1, 13–24.

8. Kapoor, "Lepers in the city of Lucknow," p. 245.

9. Heffner, L. T. "A study of Hansen's disease in Ceylon," *Southern Medical Journal*, 1969, 62:977–85.

10. Waxler, N. E. "The social career of lepers in Sri Lanka." Unpublished study, 1977. The fact that our sample of leprosy patients was obtained from the outpatient leprosy clinic means that we have no information on half of the group estimated to remain untreated. Our conclusions may be biased but in ways that we cannot determine.

11. Shiloh, A. "A case study of disease and culture in action: leprosy among the Hausa of northern Nigeria," *Human Organization*, 1965, 24:140–7.

12. Ibid., p. 143.

13. Ibid.

14. Giel, R. and van Luijk, J. N. "Leprosy in Ethiopian society," *International Journal of Leprosy*, 1970, 38:187–98.

15. Hertroijs, A. R. "A study of some factors affecting the attendance of patients in a leprosy control scheme," *International Journal of Leprosy*, 1974, 42:419–27; van Etten and Anten, "Evaluation of health education."

16. For some of the analysis presented, the author is indebted to Gussow, Z., and Tracy, G., "Stigma and the leprosy phenomenon: the social history of a disease in the nineteenth and twentieth centuries," *Bulletin of the History of Medicine*, 1970, 44:424–49; Gussow, Z., and Tracy, G. "The use of archival materials in the analysis and interpretation of field data: a case study in the insti-

tutionalization of the myth of leprosy as 'leper,'" *American Anthropologist*, 1971, 73:695–709.

17. Gussow and Tracy, "Stigma and the leprosy phenomenon," p. 433.

18. Ibid., p. 441.

19. Gussow and Tracy, "The use of archival materials," p. 706.

20. Mouritz, A. "Report of the Superintendent of the Molokai Leprosy Hospital," in *Appendix to the Report on Leprosy of the President of the Board of Health to the Legislative Assembly*. Honolulu, Hawaii, 1886.

21. Ibid.

22. van Etten and Anten, "Evaluation of health education," p. 405.

23. Ibid., p. 417.

24. Ibid., p. 408.

25. Shiloh, "A case study of disease and culture in action."

26. "There was . . . no stigma attached to the disease amongst the Australian Aboriginals until segregation became law and sufferers were taken from their families and isolated. It seems that the Aboriginal people have known and coped with the disease at least since the influx of immigrants from leprosy endemic areas in the middle of the last century—and had no fear of it." Editorial, *The Medical Journal of Australia*, 1977, 2(11):345–7.

27. Giel and van Luijk. "Leprosy in Ethiopian society," p. 194.

28. Ibid., p. 190.

29. Gussow, Z., and Tracy, G. "Status, ideology, and adaptation to stigmatized illness: a study of leprosy," *Human Organization*, 1968, 27:316–25, p. 322. These authors assert that in the West the stigma of leprosy is a myth perpetuated by treatment agents. This "myth" is taken quite seriously by the patients themselves; whether it is actually true is not important for our analysis here.

30. Ibid., p. 324.

31. Gussow and Tracy, "The use of archival materials," p. 700.

32. Ibid., p. 703.

33. "Set apart." London: *The Leprosy Mission*, 1978.

34. "Set apart."

35. Bloombaun, M., and Gugelyk, T. "Voluntary confinement among lepers," *Journal of Health and Social Behavior*, 1970, 11:16–20.

36. *Hansen: Research Notes*, 1975, 6(1–2):202.

37. American Leprosy Missions, *Bulletin*, Fall 1978.

38. Some have suggested that drug-resistance requires development of a new treatment strategy that will interrupt transmission in large populations of leprosy patients. One part of this strategy, ironically, may be the need to provide "facilities for the hospitalization of a larger number of patients than at present during the first few months of treatment. This will require building or remodeling of facilities . . ." Lechat, M. "Sulfone resistance and leprosy control," *International Journal of Leprosy*, 1978, 46:64–7.

39. Bloombaum and Gugelyk, "Voluntary confinement among lepers."

17

Gender and Generation in Poor Women's Household Health Production Experiences

Lauren Clark

There are two rules students should keep in mind when considering the social organization of health and health-care seeking in almost any society: First, never underestimate the importance of social stratification; second, never underestimate the power and importance of gender. These rules are not obvious to many students in the United States because the principles of social stratification and gender are so pervasive and fundamental that they are taken for granted. They are so much a part of our cultural ideology that they are invisible—especially for those that benefit from them. Part of the U.S. cultural belief system is a secular ideology of individualism, capitalism, and opportunity. We grow up being taught that anyone can become president, even when on the slightest reflection we know that statement is not true. We grow up believing that each person is responsible for his or her success or failure. Our ideology tells us that all people are created equal, although we know that people grow up in families with remarkably different access to resources. In other words, our culture discourages us from thinking in terms of social classes that are, in large part, inherited from our parents. Some people think that it is "un-American" to think that way.

One of the most powerful observations of modern epidemiology is that there is a pervasive and powerful inverse correlation between health status and social class—health and wealth. The effect of social stratification in the United States is quite startling. For example, men over 30 living in Harlem in New York City have lower life expectancies than men living in Matlab, Bangladesh, a village in one of the poorest countries of the world. These men die at higher rates, not because of drugs or violence, but because of plain old garden-variety cardiovascular disease (McCord and Freeman 1990).

The importance of gender in health production is extremely important. In this selection, Lauren Clark examines the role of women and their access to social support in maintaining the health of their families. She uses ethnographic methods of multiple open-ended interviews with a sample of women from Mexican American and Anglo (white) households in southern Arizona; she also had the women keep health diaries of the illness episodes in their households over an extended time. There is a cross-cultural comparison built into this research design. By focusing on the roles and coping strategies of women in poor households, issues of cultural variation by ethnicity come into sharper focus. Social scientists call this research strategy controlling for variables. Notice how gender role expectations differ between these two groups and how this affects the social organization of health-seeking.

As you read this selection, consider these questions:

- *Why does the author call this the household "production" of health? What are the activities involved in the production of health?*

- *Do you think there are differences in the marriage characteristics between the poor Mexican American women and the poor Anglo women? Are there differences in the closeness of the extended (cross-generational) family structure? What are trade-offs in these social relations?*

- *How and why do poor women constitute "therapy management groups" for sickness in their households?*

Unfortunately, there is a universal dearth of information about the informal health care provided within the family, the preparation of women to provide such care effectively, how burdensome they find this aspect of their family responsibilities, and how much help they receive from their spouses.

—PIZURKI ET AL. (1987:11)

The informal health-producing work of women, like other kinds of women's domestic work, frequently eludes scientific scrutiny. The household production of health model emphasizes the consideration of factors other than advanced technology in producing health at the household level (Berman et al. 1988), thereby addressing previously overlooked proximate determinants of health outcomes. Gender comprises one of the nontechnologic factors profoundly influencing health production; culture is another. These two factors intersect when we realize women in both Mexican American and anglo culture assume responsibility for nursing their families through health and illness (Mirowsky and Ross 1987). Most sources estimate 70 percent to 95 percent of all health care is domestic—not professional—and women provide nearly 95 percent of all domestic care (Demers et al. 1980; Kleinman et al. 1978; Pizurki et al. 1987; Verbrugge and Ascione 1987).

This article examines the gendered and generational nature of women's domestic health work, or household health production, as it is sometimes called,[1] for mothers who lived in the southwestern United States during 1989–91. Mexican American and anglo households living in poverty were the units of analysis, approached through the lens of women's experiences. Circumstances of poverty and the cultural patterning of relations between genders and across generations shaped women's domestic health work and the social resources they assembled to help carry out that work. Women's accounts of the ways their femaleness and generational position predisposed them to accept disproportionate responsibility for household health adds complexity to feminist-oriented characterizations of women as the caretakers of humanity (Gilligan 1979, 1982; Graham 1982, 1983) and supplements the academic discourse about health promotion with private stories of conflict and negotiation in the household.

Research on household health production concludes that health-related labor is distributed on the basis of gender, and women's efforts shape health outcomes across generations (Berman et al. 1988; Browner 1989; Graham 1984a; Nichter and Kendall 1991). For their children, women provide primary contributions in several areas: scheduling physician's appointments; recording immunizations; transporting children to medical and dental appointments; waiting while services are provided; feeding and medicating ill children at home; and missing work to do all of these things (Antonucci and Davies 1980; Browner 1989; Carpenter 1980; Graham 1984b). For their husbands, women again provide significant labor in health care, particularly as their husbands age or if they become ill (Gannik 1990; Sommers and Shields 1987). As daughters and daughters-in-law, women predominate as unpaid care givers to the frail, noninstitutionalized elderly in the United States (Stone et al. 1987; Ward 1987).

Culture mediates the influence of gender and generational position as nontechnologic factors in household health production. Mexican and Mexican American cultural values emphasize extended family participation in illness decision making, maternal sacrifice for child welfare, and adult male privilege (Falicov 1982; Kay 1977; Krajewski-Jaime 1991; Martin 1990; Selby et al. 1990). Mexican American systems of support characteristically display strong nuclear family and kin network ties, in comparison to a heavier reliance by anglos on friends, neighbors, and co-workers (Falicov 1982; Heller et al. 1991; Keefe et al. 1979; Salgado de Snyder and Padilla 1987). Cultural elements may be part of the reason Hispanics, faced with the troubles of poverty and illness characteristic of most minority subgroups, share a mortality pattern more similar to anglos, even though their demographic profile is closer to that of African Americans (Gottlieb and Green 1987).

Less clear from past research is how the allocation of domestic health work is actually accomplished within households to arrive at a distribution of health work skewed by gender and generation. It is the dissension, conflict, negotiation, and cooperation in household health production that this article addresses through the experiences of poor Mexican American and anglo women. Using resources at hand, women weave together therapy management groups to accomplish health work in culturally informed ways. In addition to accomplishing health work, therapy management groups and gossip networks simultaneously reinforce and legitimate gender inequality in the household.

THE SAMPLE AND DATA COLLECTION

During 1989–91, I interviewed Mexican American and anglo women in southern Arizona about their household health production experiences. As the unit of analysis, the household was operationally defined as the group of kin and non-kin living in the same dwelling more than half the time and engaged in accomplishing shared task-oriented activities (Netting et al. 1984; Wilk 1989). Recruitment of women participants began at an eligibility center for low-income families seeking entry into or recertification for state or federally funded food aid programs. Informal recruitment at a low-income housing project and referral from participants in the study supplemented the pool of subjects recruited from the food and eligibility office. In the final sample, ten households were Mexican American and ten anglo. Criteria for household participation included: (1) household income below 150 percent of the federally defined, weighted poverty threshold (U.S. Bureau of the Census 1990); and (2) presence of one or more children under five years of age in the household. Poor households with young children were specifically recruited because children require significant amounts of care, typically provided by their mothers (Barnett and Baruch 1987; Coreil 1991; Cowan 1987), and poor, preschool-aged children carry a high morbidity burden (Black et al. 1982; Institute of Medicine 1993; Parker et al. 1982) that further heightens the care required on their behalf.

Twenty-six women representing the 20 households participated in interviews. Each woman was interviewed an average of three times in her home with an additional two informal visits or telephone contacts. Interviews were conducted in English because all of the Mexican American women were bilingual. As a second data source, the woman who reported primary responsibility for children's health in the household recorded daily symptoms, treatments, and medications for each household member for a three-week period in a health diary.[2] Third, a woman in each household showed to me and explained each of her medicines and remedies. These data comprised the household medication inventory. For completing each phase of the study, women were paid a nominal amount.

A total of 68 tape-recorded interviews (ranging from half an hour to two hours) was transcribed and analyzed. Health diary data for 2,268 person-days (a 75 percent completion rate) were examined for common symptoms of household members, treatments employed, social network contacts for health advice, and cost of chosen medications and treatments. From the medication inventory, 669 medications were catalogued.

Interviews were organized for analysis using Ethnograph software (Seidel et al. 1988). In analyzing the coded interviews, health diaries, and medication inventories, I looked for patterns in the women's management of both the routine and the extraordinary aspects of domestic health work and explored how managing household health involved or avoided other women and men in the household and beyond. The diary data were used to supplement and verify interview data; the medication inventories suggested relationships between stated illness behaviors and self-medication practices. The different data sources and collection methods provided credibility of the research findings through triangulation.[3]

DESCRIPTION OF PARTICIPATING HOUSEHOLDS

The Mexican American women in the study lived in households where the ratio of adults to children was 1:2. In contrast, the anglo women had a 1:1 adult to child ratio. The lower ratio of adults to children in the Mexican American households was primarily due to a higher average number of children (4.2 in the Mexican American households, as compared to 2.2 children on average in anglo households) rather than to a difference in spousal presence. In one-third of both anglo and Mexican American households, the women reported no male partner or husband. Of those women who reported a husband or partner involved in the operation of the household, half of the Mexican American women reported his presence was partial or sporadic. Therefore, the lower ratio of adults to children in the Mexican American households, conservatively estimated here, might have been even more exaggerated at times when male partners were absent.

All of the Mexican American women reported bilingualism. One-third were born in Mexico and half the women reported Spanish as their first language. The anglo women described themselves as Caucasians or simply Americans without any other primary ethnic identification.

For a family of four, the federally defined poverty threshold was $12,675 per year during the data collection phase of this study (U.S. Bureau of the Census 1990). Because the poverty threshold is based on family income per family size, higher thresholds of poverty apply to larger families. On average, Mexican American households in this study made 54 percent of the poverty threshold regardless of household size. As predicted by national data, the anglo households reported higher household incomes, averaging 102 percent of the poverty threshold.

RESULTS

Poor mothers of young children exhibited culturally linked patterns of household health production. Anglo women relied heavily on their husbands; Mexican American women more often incorporated female kin from the larger action set.[4] Mexican American women also reported deeper intrahousehold antagonisms with their husbands over household health production than did their anglo counterparts.

Gender Organizing Household Health Production

Statistics suggesting household health work is segregated by gender, with the majority of work falling to women (Demers et al. 1980; Kleinman et al. 1978;

Pizurki et al. 1987), were validated in women's personal narratives. Differentiating or illustrating men's and women's responsibilities for health in the household was the topic of 139 illness narratives, about half of those contributed by women in each ethnic group. Women's narratives constructing gendered responsibility for household health came in several varieties: some illuminated women's domestic health care talents and the corresponding ineptitudes of their husbands; some highlighted women's active part in illness management in contrast to men's more passive "helper" role; and others characterized women's daily worries and men's more technical or supervisory concerns. Commonalities between Mexican American and anglo women's narratives are described first, followed by a discussion of the differences between the two groups, particularly the factors exacerbating antagonisms between men and women in Mexican American households.

Recruiting men to help with routine, daily domestic health-related work in Mexican American and anglo households was hampered by a belief in the unique suitability of women (particularly mothers) for taking care of children, sick or well. Using her husband as a contrasting example, a Mexican American woman named Diana highlighted her own competence at knowing what needed to be done to care for an injured child and knowing how to do it. In this particular story, the couple's son fell on a stick that lodged in his eye. Diana reported:

> [My husband] can handle the minor stuff, but he panics when it's something big. [When the accident happened] you could see the stick was stuck. My husband was yelling at me like it was my fault. So needless to say, I went on the defensive, you know, I said, "Shut up. If you're not gonna help me, then just get the hell out of my way. I know what I'm doing." I went in [the house], I had the baby in my arms, and I called the emergency room. I [drove to the emergency room] and they got him immediately and they took it out.

Diana's responsibility narrative projected the image of a caring and competent mother in the interview situation, while replaying the superiority-of-motherly-knowledge theme. Diana's narrative shows how her husband also cast her as the household health authority by focusing on Diana's blameworthiness, the other side of responsibility.

Women in both ethnic groups took pride in their expertise in matters of household health. Like Diana, they believed they knew what they were doing. In constructing their narratives, they portrayed men in various unflattering ways. Some men were merely "out of touch" with children's normal health para-

meters; others were reluctant to take any responsibility for health or illness care; a few were hostile when drawn into the daily care and decisions surrounding household health maintenance. Whether these portrayals were merely convenient narrative foils to a woman's self-construction as health expert, or whether men were objectively less involved in household health production is a question partially addressed by the health diary and medication inventory. As triangulating data sources, both the health diary and the medication inventory affirm the more intensive and long-lasting involvement of women, particularly mothers, in shepherding children through the entire trajectory of an illness and reestablishing health maintenance thereafter.

In both Mexican American and anglo households, women described division of labor between men and women as following "traditional" gender-linked child care and health care roles. Some women reported their male partners would not participate in certain female-defined activities, such as "baby-sitting" their own children. Others said their husbands helped when it seemed convenient: "[my husband] is a real big help, but if he's already sitting down or in bed, you can just scratch him off the list. You are getting nothing from him," said Olive. Sarah differentiated between herself and her husband in terms of intensity of involvement with child health: "I think men have the stress of supporting the family, even though we're trying to be a more modern society. I'm more concerned with the actual welfare of Seth. Steve's concerned, but it's the constant thing going through my mind." Sarah attributed the contrasting concerns of herself and her husband to in essential difference, unmodified by modernity, between men and women.

In contrast to women, who were seen as familiar with and expert in matters of domestic health, men were portrayed as novices in household health production. "My husband will try and help [with the kids or the house], but it ends up in an argument because I go back after he's done and redo it my way, which hurts his feelings," said one anglo mother. "He doesn't help as much as I would like, but I think he helps as much as he can," said another, who said she wished he "changed diapers and gave baths." Several women wished their husbands would wake up with sick or fussy children at night or would consent to "baby-sit" them during the day occasionally. All the women characterized a man's role in the household as "helping" or "filling in."

Rhetoric dividing men from women, novices from experts, and slackers from workhorses echoed entrenched behavioral patterns of household health production as women saw it. In telling of her own recent illness, Diana, a Mexican American mother, illustrated the heterosexual antagonisms alienating her from her husband and isolating her as the indispensable provider of domestic services. Juxtaposed against her husband's aloof behavior was Diana's mother's helpfulness in maintaining the cohesiveness of the household. When Diana was ill with pneumonia, her husband passively refused to help with the house cleaning, meal preparation, or child care. When she asked him to fix simple lunches for the children, pick the eldest up from school, or supervise the elder's play, "he acted so resentful, like 'can't you do anything?'" So "my Mom ended up having to stay here and help me take care of the kids; I found my husband was very unsympathetic." But Diana assertively questioned his behavior, saying, "Don't you feel embarrassed? I'm a grown married woman and I had to ask my mom to come and take care of me." Although Diana used several different tactics and demonstrated tenacity in seeking a redistribution of labor within the household, her husband did not "help out." Instead of gaining his help, Diana eventually accepted her mother's aid instead. In households like Diana's, where an emphasis was placed on the essential differences between men's and women's capacities as nurturers or care givers, attempts to renegotiate responsibilities escalated whatever hostilities surrounded domestic health work. Women who characterized their husbands' responsibility for daily household health care as "filling in" when necessary, struck little agreement with their partners over what kinds of "filling in" were needed and when.

Moving from these general problems of gendered household health work into specific cultural situations, women in anglo households acted as though the resources and responsibilities for health production resided in the household itself. Only half the anglo women reported kin in the area to assist (or interfere) in household health matters. Aside from occasional telephone calls to distant relatives, advice from health care providers, or limited aid from friends or neighbors, anglo households managed child health matters in relative detachment from other social units.

With few kin available, anglo women typically facilitated husbands' involvement in domestic health work. For example, anglo women gave more instances than did Mexican American women of bartering with their spouses to realign domestic chores. But even with some negotiated spousal participation, mothers emphasized their ability to detect and diagnose children's symptoms and take care of "those little worries," as one woman called them. Interestingly, even when a temporary renegotiation of tasks proved workable, perceptions of gendered responsibilities remained constant. "As a mom I think those worries are

always in the back of your head. Is your child eating enough? Did he have a bowel movement today?" said one mother. "Is he eating dirt or sucking on a rock?" said another mother, "You get up five times in the night when it's cold to make sure they're covered up, and you can't have the heater too high or their skin gets all dried out." Women learned the care-giving role through years of socialization and honed their skills by participating in the day-to-day care of their children. "It seems to be common sense," said one mother. "I'm The Mom," said another, in reference to her ever-present household health responsibilities.

Mexican American women faced the same "little worries" as their anglo counterparts, but with more extra household help. Each of the Mexican American women reported extended family ties in the Arizona-Sonora border area and substantial amounts of intra-household friction between men and women over household health work allocation. If a mother is ill, her partner may be less willing to pitch in if he knows his mother-in-law or some other woman relative could be called upon, especially if the responsibilities he is asked to assume are ongoing and considered burdensome, and if he views household work as sex-typed. A heightened demand to redistribute household health work in Mexican American households arose from several factors. First, health status in Mexican American households was lower than in anglo households, as indicated by the number of underlying chronic health problems and women's perceived health status of self and other household members. Second, more Mexican American women (60 percent) were engaged in income generation (in both formal and informal sectors) than anglo women (40 percent). Third, Mexican American women reported higher rates of partially-absent male partners, and fourth, their larger households contained more children. These characteristics combined to increase the time constraints and sheer work load of women in Mexican American households, thereby exacerbating the discord between men and women over distribution of household health work. Given these conditions, the expression of Mexican American cultural values such as maternal sacrifice and extended family support are necessary compensatory strategies for dealing with a demanding domestic work load.

In both Mexican American and anglo households, conflict over a husband's nonparticipation in household health production could exceed a woman's limits of tolerance and resignation. Grace, an anglo woman, described her husband's failure to care for their children as a contributor to their divorce:

> I got two jobs. So here I am working 16 hours a day and then coming home and the girls are dirty and they're

not fed properly and they're not changed, and the baby's in dirty diapers, and he hasn't cleaned up or done the kitchen. And he's not working regular, you know. So finally I left.

Mexican American women also cited a man's non-participation in household health production activities as a nexus of conflict and a potential cause for divorce.

In summary, gender is constructed in women's household health production experiences as an explanatory factor in the organization of domestic health-related labor. Women reported that the everyday tasks of health production are taken as "natural" expressions of womanhood—by both men and women. Viewed as a gendered responsibility, household health production became an area of conflict between men and women when circumstances demanded flexibility and renegotiation of responsibilities. Mexican American women voiced more dissatisfaction with their husbands' participation in domestic health work than did anglo women. Related to Mexican American women's higher levels of gendered, intrahousehold conflict were heavier health-related household work loads and more employment in wage labor for Mexican American women, coupled with less spousal availability. Cultural resources mediated their response to these factors by encouraging maternal sacrifice and extrahousehold familial support. Geographic proximity of kin for Mexican American women made enactment of the cultural value of extrahousehold familial support possible.

Generation Connecting Households in Health Production

Women selectively recruited others from a cross-generational and gendered web of association outside the household to aid them in household health production. Often, cross-generational networks emphasized reciprocity. For the anglo women without kin in the area, reciprocity took the form of exchanging telephone calls, taking trips to visit, or sending holiday gifts and greetings. If relatives lived nearby, anglo women commonly exchanged goods and services between households. Annette, for example, organized informal cooperative activities with relatives. She saved money by purchasing bulk foods in conjunction with relatives; she helped butcher game killed by her brothers in exchange for a share of the meat; and she helped her recently widowed father adjust to his new life by telephoning and visiting often. In return, Annette's father pitched in when one of Annette's children was hospitalized and took over some child care

and transportation duties. Cross-generational networks of support and reciprocity like Annette's were typical in poor anglo women's experience.

Cross-generational ties between Mexican American women and their networks of extended kin also emphasized reciprocity in the exchange of goods and services, but in greater magnitude. The experiences of Lucia and Irma are illustrative. Lucia lived with her six children, apart from her ex-husband and her male partner. Her ex-husband refused to pay child support, and she had struck an agreement with her partner, Luke, not to "report him" to the welfare system. Consequently, food stamps, her monthly Aid to Families with Dependent Children check, and her telemarketing paycheck kept her barely solvent. Her ex-husband, her partner, and even her father had denied responsibility for her and the children in a number of confrontations over food, medical care, and housing. At one point, Lucia and the children were homeless. Without aid from family members, Lucia eventually secured shelter.

Luckily for Lucia, the relationships she cultivated with her partner's mother and his sisters did provide mutual support. Lucia grew increasingly closer to her partner's mother, Soledad. Soledad frequently asked Lucia to pick her up in Mexico and bring her across the border to visit her many grandchildren in southern Arizona. Lucia may have been counting on Soledad's friendship—and her dependence on the transportation Lucia provided—to stabilize Lucia's place in the family and solidify Luke's role as a father to their child. Lucia also befriended Luke's sister, who was mildly chronically ill herself. The sister earned a little extra money by watching Luke and Lucia's son during the day, and in return Lucia drove her to medical appointments and acted as her translator. Even a distant "cousin-in-law" in Luke's family benefited from Lucia's generosity because Lucia now and again spent her own food stamps to provide the cousin and her children with a meal. "I'll see she doesn't have anything, so I'll go ahead and buy food for all of us. But then I lose out on some of my food stamps, plus some of my gas. Why did I do it, [I'll ask myself]?"

Lucia recognized that she shared her resources because she benefited from her exchanges with Luke's mother, sister, and cousin. She particularly appreciated the traditional Mexican medical advice she began to absorb. Lucia, who had lived in the United States her whole life, reported learning about Mexican remedies from her "in-laws." "Soledad gives me a lot of advice. And different kinds of herbs, and medicine." When her baby had diarrhea, Luke's sister showed her how to prepare rice water, "mint tea, and another tea, I don't know what it was." On another occasion, the baby was constipated, and Luke's cousin-in-law shared some prescription medicine from Mexico that was added to the baby's bottle. Learning about herbal medicine felt like a return to her heritage, and Lucia described it as "things I'd forgotten, and I'm learning again." For her infant's coughs, colds, and earaches, Lucia reported several remedies gathered from her own experience with her five older children and augmented with cures recommended by her "mother-in-law." Lucia generally used

> lemon and honey for a cough, tea with *canela* (cinnamon) and a dash of lemon, along with two aspirins and to bed. And a rubdown with Vick's. And I learned about *ruda* (rue) from my mother-in-law. When children have earaches, just rub a little bit inside [the ear canal], as far as you can go with your finger tip. It stops the earache.

As Lucia's health production skills diversified and her network of support expanded, Luke remained as uninvolved as ever in the domestic life of Lucia and her children. But Lucia's cultivation of reciprocal relationships with his mother and other kin strengthened her social connection to Luke, gave her new treatment ideas for children's illnesses, and gave her a sense of homecoming to her Mexican heritage.

Irma is a second case study of intergenerational support counterbalancing a domestic life of intrahousehold heterosexual antagonism. At the time of our interviews, Irma was raising her own three children and had guardianship of her sister's three children as well. She was also working full-time and attending school part-time. Her aging and chronically ill parents helped Irma with the children and simultaneously required Irma's assistance in their health care. On weekdays while Irma worked, her mother cared for two of Irma's children and picked up the third after school. She bought the children gifts occasionally and loved them "more than her other grandchildren," Irma reported. For her part, Irma gave her mother daily insulin injections and frequently acted as a mediator between her parents and the professional health care system. During the study, Irma's father suffered a heart attack, and Irma supervised her father's hospitalization and took charge of her mother's welfare while he was hospitalized.

Because Irma lived with a man who spent about half of the year in Mexico working for relatives on a ranch, she relied heavily on her parents' assistance in child care. Even when Irma's partner was present during his sporadic stays in the home, he was sometimes remote and uninvolved. "At least he's a better father than he is a husband," Irma commented. The range of Irma's health work was evident during two months of the study when she responded to both chronic and

acute illnesses in her household, in her extended family, and in the neighborhood. In addition to caring for her parents during the heart attack episode, Irma took her niece to the emergency room with severe abdominal pain, gave a neighbor an injection he had purchased in Mexico, and counseled her recently released sister about her postprison options. Two of her children developed colds during the month, and according to her health diary, she rubbed Vick's Vaporub on their chests every night for a week. Her infant had a weeklong bout of diarrhea, and she took him to the doctor and modified his diet until he recovered. Irma's long list of illness-caring behaviors was not unique, but superimposed on her already hectic life, they would have been overwhelming without her parents' help.

In the face of intrahousehold conflict, cross-generational networks of women kin allayed the problems of health production in situations of poverty in many ways, such as sharing information, food, medicine, and child care. Neither intrahousehold conflict nor cross-generational support were tied exclusively to the Mexican American or anglo experience of domestic health work. In general, Mexican American women described heightened intrahousehold conflict and cultivated extrahousehold networks for assistance with therapy management, whereas the anglo women more typically worked to resolve or accommodate intrahousehold differences with their partners over domestic health matters and relied less on cross-generational networks of support. Still unknown is whether the inverse correlation of intrahousehold conflict to cross-generational support taps an underlying causal relationship.

DISCUSSION

Comparing Mexican American and anglo women in terms of a gendered construction of domestic health work shows similarities among women's experiences. Gender figured prominently as the criterion sifting out caregivers from noncaregivers, with women's "natural" suitability for care of children and the ill uncontested. Women's prominence in household health production has been cast as an "ideology of maternal competence" (Anderson and Elfert 1989), or what Sacks has called the "heart and soul" of women's work: the ability to "take responsibility and initiative for knowing what need[s] to be done, and knowing how to do it" (1989:89).

Interacting in informal "gossip networks" (Finerman 1989), women in this study told each other stories of their maternal competence and corresponding male hostility or naivete in household health matters, and their discourse can be understood as a framework reconstructing and legitimating existing gender roles. Creating a gendered self-identity of expertise in matters of household health through social interaction reaffirmed a woman's gendered relationship to work, to others in the household, and to the world (Berk 1985; West and Zimmerman 1987). Common among the women interviewed in this study (and the men whom they described) was the construction of essential differences between men and women—such as "maternal instincts"—that legitimated the gender-based inequality in their division of household labor (Coltrane 1989). Partitioning responsibility converged with partitioning blame when women's actions could not avert illness or accident, and blaming heightened intrahousehold conflict between women and men, or what Philipson (1982) has termed "heterosexual antagonisms."

Mexican American women experienced deeper heterosexual antagonisms. In comparison to their anglo counterparts, Mexican American women encountered a number of social and economic factors (such as frequent spousal absence, higher levels of waged labor, more children, more intense poverty, and greater involvement in their parents' illnesses) that increased their work load and constricted their time. Those factors, coupled with cultural notions of maternal sacrifice and reliance on extended kin, resulted in Mexican American women piecing together a household health production strategy characteristically reliant on women outside the household. In contrast, anglo women were more dependent on their own and their spouses' labor to produce health.

When health production was extended to include persons outside the household in larger therapy management groups (Janzen 1978, 1987) or illness-specific action sets (Chrisman and Kleinman 1983), who was selected to participate brought both immediate and long-term consequences. Women constituted therapy management groups to meet the immediate need for health production and simultaneously accomplish more far-reaching desires. In this study, women formulated therapy management groups along gender lines to accomplish therapy management but also reaffirm their cultural identity, reinforce their place in a social network, or reenact their gendered relationship to health work and others in the household. Similarly, Crandon-Malamud (1991) described how using culturally tied nomenclature in the identification of a symptom and then composing a therapy management group to deal with the problem is a metacommunicative act among the Kachitunos of Bolivia. Alignment of oneself with one or another medical system showed something of one's ethnic and religious self-identification. In a similar vein, Kay (1980)

found that certain Mexican American women went about the business of reclaiming their cultural identity by seeking older women kin to teach them birthing techniques and traditional cultural health practices.

CONCLUSION

Retelling women's private stories adds validity to a more public, academically oriented discourse about household health production (Linde 1986). Worthy of public description are the private aspects of poor and minority women's lives that have been previously dismissed—those considered too mundane, trivial, or ordinary—including their day-to-day household health-related work negotiated in gendered households and across generational networks.[5] Some of the nontechnologic variables constraining, inhibiting, or promoting household health production have received well-deserved attention in the public realm of academic discourse. Heavy maternal time demands, for example, reportedly impinge on the use of primary health care services. In the household, higher adult-to-child ratios and greater maternal time availability for infant care both increase the likelihood of professional health care use (Coreil 1991).

The private stories of illness and accident told by poor Mexican American and anglo women in this study reinforce with vivid detail the significance of assistance from adults in the household and in the larger therapy management group in health maintenance. But women's private stories add conditions to our public understanding. For example, simply estimating an adult-to-child ratio to predict the case of health production oversimplifies and overlooks variations in intrahousehold allocation of responsibility for health. Variability in men's reluctance to participate in domestic matters—whether illness care, income generation, or child care—is glossed over in adult-to-child ratios. Also the paradoxical ability of those in older generations to aid a young mother with advice or tangible aid in the household, yet simultaneously require assistance in their own health care, escapes measurement in adult-to-child ratios or social support indices.

The variables of intrahousehold heterosexual antagonism and extrahousehold female support so prominent in the private stories of poor Mexican American and anglo women lead us toward an examination of the many factors favoring women's care giving when households are entrenched in the lowest strata of a capitalistic welfare state and simultaneously submerged in culturally informed relationships between genders and across generations.

NOTES

1. Other labels describing the same idea include domestic medicine (Blake 1977), home health care or home medicine (Florance 1982; Risse 1977), self-care, self-health care, self-help, self-management, or medical self-care (Butler 1987; Goeppinger 1984; Morantz 1977; Orem 1985; Young 1977), extramarket health services (Carpenter et al. 1976), informal care (Anderson 1988), and lay care (Wood and Williams 1988). Most of these labels are obviously gender-neutral, although the work described is most often gender-specific. A preferable term, which I employ here, is women's domestic health work.

2. Several studies have relied on diaries to capture the daily health problems and domestic care usually forgotten because of their ordinariness (e.g., Duffy 1986; Freer 1980; Roghmann and Haggarty 1972a, 1972b, 1974; Verbrugge 1980). A health diary is "a prospective procedure to obtain reports of morbidity (illness and injury), disability and health actions" (Verbrugge 1980:73).

3. Extensive discussion of various means of assuring trustworthiness of qualitative research findings can be found in Guba (1981) and Lincoln and Guba (1985). Triangulation in qualitative nursing studies, in particular, is addressed in Duffy (1987), Knafl and Breitmayer (1989), and Mitchell (1986).

4. An action set (Chrisman and Kleinman 1983) is similar to a therapy management group (Janzen 1978, 1987). Both take health production out of the confined household and place it in the context of a wider, yet still limited, social network. Broader still is the gossip network that operates within and around the action set, discussing and evaluating maternal actions and medical treatment (Finerman 1989).

5. Examples of scholarship taking other aspects of ordinary women's daily life seriously include Ulrich (1990) and Buss (1985).

REFERENCES

Anderson, Robert. 1988. The Contribution of Informal Care to the Management of Stroke. International Disability Studies 10(3):107–112.

Anderson, Joan M., and Helen Elfert. 1989. Managing Chronic Illness in the Family: Women as Caretakers. Journal of Advanced Nursing 14:735–743.

Antonucci, Toni C., and S. Margaret Davies. 1980. The Role of Women in Family Health Care Planning. In Women's Lives: New Theory, Research and Policy. Dorothy G. McGuigan, ed. Pp. 325–336. Ann Arbor: University of Michigan Center for Continuing Education of Women.

Barnett, Rosalind C., and Grace K. Baruch. 1987. Mothers' Participation in Child Care: Patterns and Consequences. In Spouse, Parent, Worker: On Gender and Multiple Roles. Faye J. Crosby, ed. Pp. 91–108. New Haven, CT: Yale University Press.

Berk, Sarah Fenstermaker. 1985. The Gender Factory. New York: Plenum Books.

Berman, Peter, Carl Kendall, and Karabi Bhattacharyya. 1988. The Household Production of Health: Putting People at the Center of Health Improvement. In Toward More Efficacy in Child Survival Strategies. Ismail Sirogeldin and Henry Mosley, eds. Pp. 1–18. Baltimore, MD: Johns Hopkins.

Black, Robert E., Kenneth H. Brown, Stan Becker, and M. Yunus. 1982. Longitudinal Studies of Infectious Diseases and Physical Growth of Children in Rural Bangladesh. American Journal of Epidemiology 115(3):305–314.

Blake, John B. 1977. From Buchan to Fishbein: The Literature of Domestic Medicine. In Medicine Without Doctors: Home Health Care in American History. Guenter B. Risse, Ronald L. Numbers, and Judith Walzer Leavitt, eds. Pp. 11–30. New York: Science History Publications.

Browner, Carole H. 1989. Women, Household and Health in Latin America. Social Science & Medicine 28(5):461–473.

Buss, Fran Leeper. 1985. Dignity: Lower Income Women Tell of Their Lives and Struggles. Ann Arbor: University of Michigan Press.

Butler, Frieda R. 1987. Minority Wellness Promotion: A Behavioral Self-Management Approach. Journal of Gerontological Nursing 13(8):23–28.

Carpenter, Eugenia S. 1980. Children's Health Care and the Changing Role of Women. Medical Care 18(12):1208–1218.

Carpenter, Eugenia S., et al. 1976. Women's Roles in Extra-Market Health Services. Ann Arbor: University of Michigan School of Public Health.

Chrisman, Noel J., and Arthur Kleinman. 1983. Popular Health Care, Social Networks, and Cultural Meanings: The Orientation of Medical Anthropology. In Handbook of Health, Health Care, and Health Professions. David Mechanic, ed. Pp. 569–590. New York: Free Press.

Coltrane, Scott. 1989. Household Labor and the Routine Production of Gender. Social Problems 36(5):473–490.

Coreil, Jeannine. 1991. Maternal Time Allocation in Relation to Kind and Domain of Primary Health Care. Medical Anthropology Quarterly (n.s.) 5:221–235.

Cowan, Ruth S. 1987. Women's Work, Housework, and History: The Historical Roots of Inequality in Work-Force Participation. In Families and Work. Naomi Gerstel and H. E. Gross, eds. Pp. 164–177. Philadelphia, PA: Temple University Press.

Crandon-Malamud, Libbet. 1991. From the Fat of Our Souls. Berkeley: University of California Press.

Demers, Raymond Y., Rita Altamore, Henry Mustin, Arthur Kleinman, and Denise Leonardi. 1980. An Exploration of the Dimensions of Illness Behavior. Journal of Family Practice 11(7):1085–1092.

Duffy, Mary E. 1986. Primary Prevention Behaviors: The Female-Headed, One-Parent Family. Research in Nursing and Health 9:115–122.

———. 1987. Methodological Triangulation: A Vehicle for Merging Quantitative and Qualitative Research Methods. Image 20(1):22–24.

Falicov, Celia Jaes. 1982. Mexican Families. In Ethnicity in Family Therapy. Monica McGoldrick, John K. Pearce, and Joseph Giordano, eds. Pp. 134–163. New York: Guilford Press.

Finerman, Ruthbeth. 1989. Tracing Home-Based Health Care Change in an Andean Indian Community. Medical Anthropology Quarterly (n.s.) 3:162–174.

Florance, Valerie. 1982. Healing and the Home: Home Medicine in Pioneer Utah. In From Cottage to Market: The Professionalization of Women's Sphere. John R. Sillito, ed. Pp. 28–46. Salt Lake City, UT: Utah Women's History Association.

Freer, C. B. 1980. Self-Care: A Health Diary Study. Medical Care 18(8):853–861.

Gannik, Dorte. 1990. Women's Health Work in Everyday Life: A Case Study of How Men and Women Deal with Back Trouble. Paper presented at the Fourth International Congress on Women's Health Issues. Massey University, Palmerston North, New Zealand.

Gilligan, Carol. 1979. Woman's Place in Man's Lifecycle. Harvard Educational Review 49(4):431–446.

———. 1982. In a Different Voice: Psychological Theory and Women's Development. Cambridge, MA: Harvard University Press.

Goeppinger, Jean. 1984. Self-Health Care through Risk Appraisal and Reduction: Implications for Community Health Nursing. In Community Health Nursing. Marcia Stanhope and Jeanette Lancaster, eds. Pp. 316–329. St. Louis, MO: C. V. Mosby.

Gottlieb, Nell H., and Lawrence W. Green. 1987. Ethnicity and Lifestyle Health Risk: Some Possible Mechanisms. American Journal of Health Promotion (Summer):37–46.

Graham, Hilary. 1982. Coping or How Mothers Are Seen and Not Heard. In On the Problem of Men. S. Friedman and E. Sarah, eds. Pp. 101–116. London: Women's Press.

———. 1983. Caring: A Labour of Love. In A Labour of Love: Women, Work and Caring. Janet Finch and Dulcie Groves, eds. Pp. 13–30. London: Routledge and Kegan Paul.

———. 1984a. Providers, Negotiators, and Mediators: Women as the Hidden Carers. In Women, Health and Healing. Virginia Olesen and Ellen Lewin, eds. Pp. 25–52. New York: Tavistock.

———. 1984b. Women, Health and the Family. Sussex, Great Britain: Wheatsheaf Books.

Guba, Egon G. 1981. Criteria for Assessing the Trustworthiness of Naturalistic Inquiries. Educational Communication and Technology Journal 29:75–92.

Heller, Peter L., H. Paul Chalfant, Gustavo M. Quesada, and Maria del Carmen Rivera-Worley. 1981. Class, Familism and Utilization of Health Services in Durango, Mexico: A Replication. Social Science & Medicine 15A:539–541.

Institute of Medicine. 1993. Access to Health Care in America. Washington, DC: National Academy Press.

Janzen, John J. 1978. The Quest for Therapy in Lower Zaire. Berkeley: University of California Press.

———. 1987. Therapy Management: Concept, Reality, Process. Medical Anthropology Quarterly (n.s.) 1:68–84.

Kay, Margarita A. 1977. Health and Illness in a Mexican American Barrio. In Ethnic Medicine in the Southwest. Edward H. Spicer. ed. Pp. 99–166. Tucson: University of Arizona Press.

———. 1980. Mexican, Mexican American and Chicana Childbirth. In Twice a Minority: Mexican American

Women. Margarita Melville, ed. Pp. 52–65. St. Louis, MO: C.V. Mosby.

Keefe, Susan, Amado M. Padillo, and Manuel L. Carlos. 1979. The Mexican-American Extended Family as an Emotional Support System. Human Organization 38:144–152.

Kleinman, Arthur, Leon Eisenberg, and Byron Good. 1978. Culture, Illness and Care: Clinical Lessons from Anthropological and Cross-Cultural Research. Annals of Internal Medicine 88:251–258.

Knafl, Kathleen A., and Bonnie J. Breitmayer. 1989. Triangulation in Qualitative Research: Issues of Conceptual Clarity and Purpose. In Qualitative Nursing Research: A Contemporary Dialogue. Janice M. Morse, ed. Pp. 209–220. Rockville, MD: Aspen.

Krajewski-Jaime, Elvia R. 1991. Folk-Healing among Mexican-American Families as a Consideration in the Delivery of Child Welfare and Child Health Care Services. Child Welfare 70(2):157–167.

Lincoln, Yvonna S., and Egon G. Guba. 1985. Naturalistic Inquiry. Beverly Hills, CA: Sage.

Linde, Charlotte. 1986. Private Stories in Public Discourse. Poetics 15:183–202.

Martin. JoAnn. 1990. Motherhood and Power: The Production of a Women's Culture of Politics in a Mexican Community. American Ethnologist 17(3):470–490.

Mirowsky, J., and C. E. Ross. 1987. Support and Control in Mexican and Anglo Cultures. In Health and Behavior: Research Agenda for Hispanics. M. Gaviria and J. D. Arana, eds. Pp. 85–92. The Simon Bolivar Research Monograph Series, I. Chicago: University of Illinois.

Mitchell, Ellen S. 1986. Multiple Triangulation: A Methodology for Nursing Science. Advances in Nursing Science 8(3):18–26.

Morantz, Regina Markell. 1977. Nineteenth Century Health Reform and Women: A Program of Self-Help. In Medicine Without Doctors: Home Health Care in American History. Guenter B. Risse, Ronald L. Numbers, and Judith Walzer Leavitt, eds. Pp. 73–94. New York: Science History Publications.

Netting, Robert McC., Richard R. Wilk, and Eric J. Amould. 1984. Introduction. In Households. Robert McC. Netting, Richard R. Wilk, and Eric J. Amould, eds. Berkeley: University of California Press.

Nichter, Mark, and Carl Kendall. 1991. Beyond Child Survival: Anthropology and International Health in the 1990s. Medical Anthropology Quarterly (n.s.) 5:195–203.

Orem, Dorothea A. 1985. Nursing: Concepts of Practice. 3d ed. New York: McGraw-Hill.

Parker, Robert L., Gong You-Long, Shan Long-Gen, Huang De-Yu, and Alan R. Hinman. 1982. The Sample Household Health Interview Survey. American Journal of Public Health 72(supplement):65–70.

Philipson, Irene. 1982. Heterosexual Antagonisms and the Politics of Mothering. Socialist Review 12(6):55–77.

Pizurki, Helena, Alfonso Mejia, Irene Butter, and Leslie Ewart. 1987. Women as Providers of Health Care. Geneva: WHO.

Risse, Guenter B. 1977. Introduction. In Medicine Without Doctors: Home Health Care in American History. Guenter B. Risse, Ronald L. Numbers, and Judith Walzer Leavitt, eds. Pp. 1–10. New York: Science History Publications.

Roghmann, Klaus J., and Robert J. Haggerty. 1972a. The Diary as a Research Instrument in the Study of Health and Illness Behavior: Experiences with a Random Sample of Young Families. Medical Care 10(2):143–163.

———. 1972b. Family Stress and the Use of Health Services. International Journal of Epidemiology 1(3):279–286.

———. 1974. Measuring the Use of Health Services by Household Interviews: A Comparison of Procedures Used in Three Child Health Surveys. International Journal of Epidemiology 3(1):71–81.

Sacks, Karen B. 1989. What's a Life Story Got to Do With It? *In* Interpreting Women's Lives: Feminist Theory and Personal Narratives. The Personal Narratives Group, eds. Pp. 85–95. Bloomington: Indiana University Press.

Salgado de Snyder, V. N., and A. M. Padilla. 1987. Social Support Networks: Their Availability and Effectiveness. *In* Health and Behavior. Research Agenda for Hispanics. M. Gaviria and J. D. Arana, eds. Pp. 93–107. The Simon Bolivar Research Monograph Series, 1. Chicago: University of Illinois Press.

Seidel, John, Rolf Kjolseth, and Elaine Seymour. 1988. The Ethnograph (version 3.0). Corvallis, OR: Qualis Research Associates.

Selby, Henry A., Arthur D. Murphy, and Stephen A. Lorenzen. 1990. The Mexican Urban Household: Organizing for Self-Defense. Austin: University of Texas Press.

Sommers, Tish, and Laurie Shields. 1987. Women Take Care: The Consequences of Caregiving in Today's Society. Gainesville, FL: Triad Publishing.

Stone, Robyn, Gail Lee Cafferata, and Judith Sangl. 1987. Caregivers of the Frail Elderly: A National Profile. DHHS Publication #181–345:60026. Washington, DC: U.S. Government Printing Office.

Ulrich, Laurel T. 1990. A Midwife's Tale: The Life of Martha Ballard, Based on Her Diary, 1785–1812. New York: Alfred A. Knopf.

U.S. Bureau of the Census. 1980. Money Income and Poverty Status in the United States, 1989. Advance Data from the March 1990 Current Population Survey. Current Population Reports, Consumer Income. U.S. Department of Commerce Series p-60, No. 168. Washington, DC: U.S. Government Printing Office.

Verbrugge, Lois M. 1980. Health Diaries. Medical Care 18(1):73–95.

Verbrugge, Lois M., and Frank J. Ascione. 1987. Exploring the Iceberg: Common Symptoms and How People Care for Them. Medical Care 25(6):539–569.

Ward, Deborah H. 1987. The New Old Burden: Gender and Cost in Kin Care of Disabled Elderly. Ph.D. dissertation, Boston University, Boston.

West, Candice, and Don H. Zimmerman. 1987. Doing Gender. Gender and Society 1:125–151.

Wilk, Richard R. 1989. Decision Making and Resource Flows Within the Household: Beyond the Black Box. *In* The Household Economy. Richard R. Wilk, ed. Pp. 23–52. Boulder, CO: Westview.

Wood, Philip H. N., and Gareth H. Williams. 1988. Individual and Collective Initiates in Disablement. International Disability Studies 10(3):133–137.

Young, James Harvey. 1977. Patent Medicines and the Self-Help Syndrome. *In* Medicine Without Doctors: Home Health Care in American History. Guenter B. Risse, Ronald L. Numbers, and Judith Walzer Leavitt, eds. Pp. 95–118. New York: Science History Publication.

Healers in Cross-Cultural Perspective

✦ CONCEPTUAL TOOLS ✦

■ *Healers have special knowledge, and anthropologists may use the ethnographic strategy of becoming apprentices to study them.* Individual healers, their practices and performances, can be studied apart from a general ethnomedical system. As we have seen, the study of ethnomedicine may sometimes emphasize an idealized theory linking etiological categories, diagnostic techniques, and therapies. But many ethnomedical systems are not codified; there are no textbook ways to cure. The actual practice of an ethnomedical system can be highly idiosyncratic to a particular healer. As we saw in the story of Quesalid told by Lévi-Strauss, a shaman's knowledge is not generally shared with others. A shaman will have personal relationships with particular spirit helpers. The healer's medical knowledge is a product of his or her personal experience and biography, and the healer's theories and techniques may combine components from radically different belief systems. For example, in David Jones's ethnography *Sanapia: A Comanche Medicine Woman* (1972), that medical system combined traditional Comanche beliefs and herbal knowledge with fundamentalist Christian beliefs, as well as the peyote practices of the Native American church. These diverse elements are combined in Sanapia's unique "medicine way" that seems logically consistent to her.

One research methodology used by medical anthropologists is the intensive study of a single healer in his or her medical context. When anthropologists study a cultural system, they often depend on a small number of key informants who are intensively interviewed and followed over a period of time. The relationship between informants and anthropologists is like the relationship between teachers and students. But because the healer–informants' knowledge is very powerful—and takes years of devoted study to master—informants sometimes reveal the knowledge very gradually. In this regard, anthropologists become apprentices. This methodology has been used often.

Some cases, like the work of Carlos Casteneda (1973) who wrote about a probably fictitious Yaqui Indian shaman called Don Juan, are famous but not anthropologically reliable. Other anthropologists have studied Tibetan Buddhist priests (DesJarlais 1992), Malayan midwives, South American rain forest shaman (Harner 1968), as well as biomedical internist (Hahn and Gaines 1985) and surgeon (Katz 1990). These are cases of participant observation (although the anthropologist in the operating room is really observing rather than participating).

One anthropologist, Michael Harner, has become famous among New Age healers because he travels the country teaching the basic techniques of shamanism described in his book *The Way of the Shaman* (1990). There is a remarkable demand for this type of knowledge, possibly indicating people's distrust and discontent with biomedicine. Nevertheless, very few anthropologists condone the work of Harner, who has become a shaman and teaches others how to be spiritual healers.

■ *All acts of healing, however mundane, have an important element of ritual and drama.* To what extent are taking one's temperature with a thermometer and reading blood pressure with a cuff and stethoscope ritual acts? From the point of view of the patient, ritual may be the most important attribute. Because they have special knowledge, healers symbolically differentiate themselves with particular technologies, clothes, and vocabularies. The practice of an ethnomedical system must involve the correct use of these symbols in order to achieve the beliefs discussed previously. Therefore, a healing ritual can be described from a dramatic and theatrical point of view. A recent book edited by Carol Laderman and Marina Roseman (1996) provides multiple examples of this kind of analysis. Mystery is an important element in performing healing rituals throughout the world.

18

Dark Side of the Shaman

Michael F. Brown

The title of this selection reminds me of the Star Wars trilogy and the ways that participants in the struggle between the evil empire and the noble rebellion use the same amoral source of knowledge and power—"the force." In this regard, the healer or shaman has an equal and opposite counterpart in the sorcerer. The shaman heals, the sorcerer harms; you could say that one utilizes the placebo effect and the other the nocebo effect. But the struggle between healer and sorcerer is not simply fiction. For people living in societies with ethnomedical systems based on a personalistic logic (to use George Foster's typology, selection 12), this is a real struggle of life and death. In this selection, Michael Brown, who has done fieldwork with shaman of the Aguaruna of the Amazon, describes the dark and violent side of this struggle. Most North Americans know something about spiritual healing and the power of belief—books about this topic have been on the best-seller lists for years—but few seem to recognize the wider cultural context.

The people described in this selection are very much like the Yanomamo of northern Brazil and southern Venezuela who have become so widely known through the ethnographic films and writings of Napoleon Chagnon (1968) and similar to the Nambicuara described in one of the vignettes by Claude Lévi-Strauss.

When medical anthropologists study a particular healing system, they often use the methodological technique of becoming apprentices to a healer. This method has advantages and disadvantages. The primary benefit is the quality of detailed and contextual information researchers can gain. However, many shamanistic practices are idiosyncratic to a particular practitioner, and therefore anthropologists are unable to generalize their knowledge to the general ethnomedical practice of the society. With this kind of study, the anthropologist cannot discover intracultural variation.

Today in the United States alternative medicine is a large and popular movement involving millions of people and millions of dollars. The United States is a medically pluralistic society, and because of this, the National Institutes of Health has recently opened an office of Alternative and Complementary Medicine to encourage epidemiological and ethnographic research in this important area.

As you read this selection, consider these questions:

- *Why are the Aguaruna ambivalent about their local healer Yankush?*

- *What might be some benefits to Yankush for being a shaman? What are some costs or dangers associated with his profession?*

- *Why do you think alternative medicine and New Age healing are so popular in the United States and particularly in Santa Fe?*

- *Is it wrong or dangerous to borrow customs and ideas from other cultures without accepting the entire cultural package?*

Santa Fe, New Mexico, is a stronghold of that eclectic mix of mysticism and folk medicine called "New Age" thought. The community bulletin board of the public library, just around the corner from the plaza and the venerable Palace of the Governors, serves as a central bazaar for spiritual guides advertising instruction in alternative healing methods. Many of these workshops—for example, classes in holistic massage and rebirthing—have their philosophical roots in the experiments of the 1960s. Others resist easy classification: What, I've wondered, is Etheric Body Healing and Light Body Work, designed to "resonate the light forces within our being"? For thirty-five dollars an hour, another expert offers consultations in "defense and removal of psychic attack." Most of the classes, however, teach the healing arts of non-Western or tribal peoples. Of particular interest to the New Agers of Santa Fe is the tradition known as shamanism.

Shamans, who are found in societies all over the world, are believed to communicate directly with spirits to heal people struck down by illness. Anthropologists are fond of reminding their students that shamanism, not prostitution, is the world's oldest profession. When, in my role as curious ethnographer,

I've asked Santa Feans about their interest in this exotic form of healing, they have expressed their admiration for the beauty of the shamanistic tradition, the ability of shamans to "get in touch with their inner healing powers," and the superiority of spiritual treatments over the impersonal medical practice of our own society. Fifteen years ago, I would have sympathized with these romantic ideas. Two years of fieldwork in an Amazonian society, however, taught me that there is peril in the shaman's craft.

A man I shall call Yankush is a prominent shaman among the Aguaruna, a native people who make their home in the tropical forest of northeastern Peru. Once feared headhunters, the Aguaruna now direct their considerable energies to cultivating cash crops and protecting their lands from encroachment by settlers fleeing the poverty of Peru's highland and coastal regions.

Yankush is a vigorous, middle-aged man known for his nimble wit and ready laugh. Like every other able-bodied man in his village, Yankush works hard to feed his family by hunting, fishing, and helping his wife cultivate their fields. But when his kinfolk or friends fall ill, he takes on the role of *iwishín*—shaman—diagnosing the cause of the affliction and then, if possible, removing the source of the ailment from the patient's body.

In common with most peoples who preserve a lively shamanistic heritage, the Aguaruna believe that life-threatening illness is caused by sorcerers. Sorcerers are ordinary people who, driven by spite or envy, secretly introduce spirit darts into the bodies of their victims. If the dart isn't soon removed by a shaman, the victim dies. Often the shaman describes the dart as a piece of bone, a tiny thorn, a spider, or a blade of grass.

The Aguaruna do not regard sorcery as a quaint and colorful bit of traditional lore. It is attempted homicide, plain and simple. That the evidence of sorcery can only be seen by a shaman does not diminish the ordinary person's belief in the reality of the sorcerer's work, any more than our inability to see viruses with the naked eye leads us to question their existence. The Aguaruna insist that sorcerers, when discovered, must be executed for the good of society.

Shaman and sorcerer might seem locked in a simple struggle of good against evil, order against chaos, but things are not so straightforward. Shamans and sorcerers gain their power from the same source, both receiving spirit darts from a trusted instructor. Because the darts attempt to return to their original owner, apprentice shamans and sorcerers must induce them to remain in their bodies by purifying themselves. They spend months in jungle isolation, fasting and practicing sexual abstinence. By wrestling with the terrifying apparitions that come to plague their dreams, they steel themselves for a life of spiritual struggle.

There the paths of sorcerer and shaman divide. The sorcerer works in secret, using spirit darts to inflict suffering on his enemies. The shaman operates in the public eye and uses his own spirit darts to thwart the sorcerer's schemes of pain and untimely death. (I say "he," because to my knowledge all Aguaruna shamans are men. Occasionally, however, a woman is accused of sorcery.) Yet because shamans possess spirit darts, and with them the power to kill, the boundary between sorcerer and shaman is sometimes indistinct.

The ambiguities of the shaman's role were brought home to me during a healing session I attended in Yankush's house. The patients were two women: Yamanuanch, who complained of pains in her stomach and throat, and Chapaik, who suffered discomfort in her back and lower abdomen. Their illnesses did not seem life threatening, but they were persistent enough to raise fears that sorcery was at the root of the women's misery.

As darkness fell upon us, the patients and their kin waited for Yankush to enter into a trance induced by a bitter, hallucinogenic concoction he had taken just before sunset (it is made from a vine known as *ayahuasca*). While the visitors exchanged gossip and small talk, Yankush sat facing the wall of his house, whistling healing songs and waving a bundle of leaves that served as a fan and soft rattle. Abruptly, he told the two women to lie on banana leaves that had been spread on the floor, so that he could use his visionary powers to search their bodies for tiny points of light, the telltale signature of the sorcerer's darts. As Yankush's intoxication increased, his meditative singing gave way to violent retching. Gaining control of himself, he sucked noisily on the patients' bodies in an effort to remove the darts.

Family members of the patients shouted words of concern and support. "Others know you are curing. They can hurt you, be careful!" one of the spectators warned, referring to the sorcerers whose work the shaman hoped to undo. Torn by anxiety, Chapaik's husband addressed those present: "Who has done this bewitching? If my wife dies, I could kill any man out of anger!" In their cries of encouragement to Yankush, the participants expressed their high regard for the difficult work of the shaman, who at this point in the proceedings was frequently doubled over with nausea caused by the drug he had taken.

Suddenly there was a marked change of atmosphere. A woman named Chimi called out excitedly, "If there are any darts there when she gets back home, they may say that Yankush put them there. So take them all out!" Chimi's statement was an unusually blunt rendering of an ambivalence implicit in all relations between Aguaruna shamans and their clients. Because shamans control spirit darts, people fear that a shaman may be tempted to use the cover of healing as an opportunity to bewitch his own clients for personal reasons. The clients therefore remind the shaman that they expect results—and if such results are not forthcoming, the shaman himself may be suspected of, and punished for, sorcery.

Yankush is such a skilled healer that this threat scarcely caused him to miss a step. He sucked noisily on Yamanuanch's neck to cure her sore throat and, after singing about the sorcery darts lodged in her body, announced she would recover. For good measure, he recommended injections of a commercial antibiotic. Yankush also took pains to emphasize the intensity of his intoxication. Willingness to endure the rigors of a large dose of *ayahuasca* is a sign of his good faith as a healer. "Don't say I wasn't intoxicated enough," he reminded the participants.

As Yankush intensified his singing and rhythmic fanning of the leaf-bundle, he began to have visions of events taking place in distant villages. Suddenly he cried out, "In Achu they killed a person. A sorcerer was killed." "Who could it be?" the other participants asked one another, but before they could reflect on this too long, Yankush had moved on to other matters. "I'm concentrating to throw out sickness, like a tireless jaguar," he sang, referring to Chapaik, who complained of abdominal pains. "With my help she will become like the tapir, which doesn't know how to refuse any kind of food."

After two hours of arduous work, Yankush steered the healing session to its conclusion by reassuring the patients that they were well on their way to recovery. "In her body the sickness will end," he sang. "It's all right. She won't die. It's nothing," he added, returning to a normal speaking voice. Before departing, the patients and their kin discussed the particulars of Yankush's dietary recommendations and made plans for a final healing session to take place at a later date. As the sleepy participants left Yankush's house for their beds in other parts of the village, they expressed their contentment with the results of his efforts.

During the year I lived near Yankush, he conducted healing sessions like this one about twice a month. Eventually, I realized that his active practice was only partly a matter of choice. To allay suspicions and demonstrate his good faith as a healer, he felt compelled to take some cases he might otherwise have declined. Even so, when I traveled to other villages, people sometimes asked me how I could live in a community where a "sorcerer" practiced on a regular basis.

When a respected elder died suddenly of unknown causes in 1976, Yankush came under extraordinary pressure to identify the sorcerer responsible. From the images of his *ayahuasca* vision he drew the name of a young man from a distant region who happened to be visiting a nearby village. The man was put to death in a matter of days. Because Yankush was widely known to have fingered the sorcerer, he became the likely victim of a reprisal raid by members of the murdered man's family. Yankush's willingness to accept this risk in order to protect his community from future acts of sorcery was a source of his social prestige, but it was also a burden. I rarely saw him leave his house without a loaded shotgun.

In calling attention to the violent undercurrents of shamanism, my intention is not to disparage the healing traditions of the Aguaruna or of any other tribal people. I have no doubt that the cathartic drama I witnessed in Yankush's house made the two patients feel better. Medical anthropologists agree that rituals calling forth expressions of community support and concern for sick people often lead to a marked improvement in their sense of well-being. Shamans also serve their communities by administering herbal medications and other remedies and even, as in Yankush's case, helping to integrate traditional healing arts with the use of modern pharmaceuticals. At the same time, however, they help sustain a belief in sorcery that exacts a high price in anxiety and, from time to time, in human life.

In their attempts to understand this negative current, anthropologists have studied how shamanism and accusations of sorcery define local patterns of power and control. Belief in sorcery, for example, may provide a system of rules and punishments in societies that lack a police force, written laws, and a formal judicial system. It helps people assign a cause to their misfortunes. And it sustains religions that link human beings with the spirit world and with the tropical forest itself.

What I find unsettling, rather, is that New Age America seeks to embrace shamanism without any appreciation of its context. For my Santa Fe acquaintances, tribal lore is a supermarket from which they choose some tidbits while spurning others. They program computers or pursue other careers by day so that by night they can wrestle with spirit-jaguars and search for their power spots. Yankush's lifetime of discipline is reduced to a set of techniques for personal development, stripped of links to a specific landscape and cultural tradition.

New Age enthusiasts are right to admire the shamanistic tradition, but while advancing it as an alternative to our own healing practices, they brush aside its stark truths. For throughout the world, shamans see themselves as warriors in a struggle

against the shadows of the human heart. Shamanism affirms life but also spawns violence and death. The beauty of shamanism is matched by its power—and like all forms of power found in society, it inspires its share of discontent.

 19

Transcendental Medication

Melvin Konner

The author of this selection is a biological anthropologist, a skeptical scientist, and a physician (Konner 1982, 1987; see also selection 2). He is not one of the New Agers you read about in the last selection. Nevertheless, here Melvin Konner tells the story of becoming an apprentice healer when he and his wife Marjorie Shostak were doing anthropological field-work among the !Kung San hunter-gatherers of the Kalahari Desert of Botswana. Unlike the Amazonian peoples you have just read about, the !Kung do not take any drugs in order to induce the altered state of consciousness—the trance—necessary for healing. Rather, they use a technique that might be considered a form of both sensory deprivation and overload, by a long and repetitive dance and song called the N/um Tchai, or medicine dance. This is the most common and important ritual of the San peoples, and it has been studied in depth (Katz 1982; Shostak 1981). In this ritual, the n/um—medicine or sweat—that is stored in the stomachs of the "owners of medicine" is heated through dance and song until it causes the dancer to fall into a trance. In this state the healer can "lay on hands," transferring his protective sweat and energy to the assembled group or pull out the sicknesses from people. The N/um Tchai ritual is well depicted in an ethnographic film of the same name.

!Kung call the trance state kwi, or "half death." This interesting term reminds me of the ideas of Edward Tylor, one of the founders of the discipline of anthropology, who in his early book Primitive Religion *(1889) argued that the most fundamental religious belief, called* animism, *referred to a belief in souls. Tylor thought that the belief in souls meant a recognition that living things have a visible, corporeal element as well as an invisible, spiritual, life-giving ele-*

ment. He thought that the idea of souls was reinforced by and helped explain the everyday experiences of death, dreams, and trances—times when the body and soul become separated; the idea of animism also agrees with the relatively common experience of spirit possession in other cultures. Because a trance is temporary, it might be considered "half death," but it is clearly recognized as a dangerous and somewhat painful state. Among the !Kung, both men and women can become "owners of medicine," but women, because of the danger involved, usually curtail their healing careers when they first get pregnant.

In this selection, there is little doubt that trance involves an altered state of consciousness and that this ritual is quite dramatic. N/um Tchai ceremonies often continue all night. Like the band societies themselves, there is no clear leader and little job specialization. Some men, however, simply have a greater gift for going into trance, and they are afforded some prestige for this.

By trying his hand at the trance dance, Melvin Konner followed the long ethnographic tradition of participant observation. Although his research among the !Kung focused on patterns of infant rearing and the biology of breast-feeding, his research interests were much broader than that. The questions at the end of this selection about biology of belief and healing are currently being addressed in a new field called psychoneuroimmunology (Desowitz 1987).

As you read this selection, consider these questions:

■ *Why do you think that the touching of the patient by the healer seems so important in this healing ritual? Is the fact that* n/um *also means "sweat" relevant*

Dusk is closing. The horizon of the Kalahari Desert makes a distant, perfect circle, broken only by scrub bush and an occasional acacia. The human sounds of the evening meal are heard throughout the village camp, a rough ring of small grass shelters with a fire and a family in front of each. For some reason, on this night, there is an unusually high level of excitement among the people of the !Kung San band. Perhaps there is meat in the camp, or perhaps it is just the round moon rising. Perhaps someone has been ill. Or maybe no one has; what is about to happen will benefit the healthy almost as much as the sick.

The women have talked among themselves and decided to try. They may have been prodded by the men, or they may have tested the men's interest with questions—or they may have just decided, simply and unilaterally. They begin to clap in complex rhythms and to sing in a strange yodeling style that bridges octaves gracefully, creating a mesmerizing array of sounds. Gradually, they collect into a circle around a fire. Emotionally and musically they echo one another's enthusiasm. Someone stokes the fire as the dusk turns to dark.

Two of the men sitting cross-legged in front of a hut poke each other and stir. "These women are really singing," says one. "But we men are worthless." They chuckle and then become more serious, although the joking will begin again as the night wears on. They strap dance rattles onto their lower legs and get the feel of the sound that bounces back when their feet slap the ground. "Look," one of the women says, smiling. "These things might become men tonight." The dancing begins as other men join in, tracing a circle around the singing women. The men's feet slam to the ground repetitively and solidly. That sound becomes orchestrated with the clapping and singing of the women, and the network of echoing enthusiasm widens.

A newborn baby wakes and cries, and is adjusted in the sling at her mother's side. A toddler stumbles over to his mother, leans against her, and stares, wide-eyed, at the dancers. A pretty young woman whispers something into the ear of the woman next to her, both of them glance at one of the men dancing and burst out laughing. The fire is stoked again, and it burns more brightly.

Suddenly a man falls to the ground. Because he is in late middle age, the naïve observer wants to rush to his aid, but for the same reason his !Kung companions are unconcerned. (They have been expecting someone to fall, and the older and wiser among them, because of their experience, are most susceptible.) He lies there for a time, moaning softly and trembling. Other men drift over to him and kneel. They rub him gently, then vigorously, as one of them lifts the fallen man onto his lap. Finally, the man comes to a semblance of his senses and gets to his feet. Now he is in another state entirely, still trembling and moaning but walking, fully charged with energy. He bends over one of the women in the circle and places his hands on her shoulders. The trembling intensifies, taking on the rhythm of his breathing. With each breath, the amplitude of his voice and the tremor of his arms increase until the crescendo ends with a piercing shriek: "Kow-hee-dee-dee!" He seems to relax momentarily, then moves on and repeats the ritual with each woman in the circle.

Meanwhile, the circle of singers has swelled, more men have joined the dancing, and other villagers, mostly children and adolescents, have formed a spectators' circle outside the inner two. One of the onlookers is a pregnant woman with a fever. The man in the healing trance goes to her for the laying on of hands, exerting himself at exceptional length and with exceptional vigor. At one point he pauses and stares out into the blackness, shouting almost hysterically, "You all! You all get out of here! You all get out of here!" Then he stares for a time into the void beyond the circle of spectators, before returning to the task of healing.

How does the healing trance come about? Does it truly impart the power to heal? And if so, how?

If Lorna Marshall, Richard Lee, and Richard Katz —the three great students of this ritual—could be at your elbow while you watched the !Kung dance, they might provide the following information. The trance and its power to heal are due in large part to the energy of the community. If the women sing and clap well, the men will dance well; if the sound of the dance rattles is good and someone begins to fall into a trance, the clapping and singing will rise to a new plane of excitement; if that plane is high enough and the men are sufficiently trusting of the women and of one another, several may enter deep and prolonged trances, and their healing power may last until after dawn.

The power itself, called *n/um*, is said to reside in the flanks of the abdomen, the pit of the stomach, or the base of the spine, and to boil up in a very painful way during the trance. The power to heal is not exactly the same as susceptibility to trances, but both are said to grow steadily during early adulthood and then diminish after middle or late middle age. A young man may have all the courage and energy he needs but, lacking experience and control, may be quite useless as a healer; an elder may have all the experience required, but his energy will not be what it was. (The parallel to the life cycle of male sexuality is striking, and perhaps significant.) As many as half of all men in the tribe can attain the healing power, which is an act of great courage, since the !Kung San believe that in a deep enough trance the soul may leave the body forever. The trance itself is at once exotically self-involved and heroically selfless. The individual is elevated in a way that is almost unique in this egalitarian culture, and yet his identity is dissolved; the ritual is of, by, and for the whole community.

If the dancer is experienced, his soul can travel great distances, to the world of the spirits and gods, and communicate with them about the illnesses and problems of the people. This marginal condition, between life and death, can be controlled only by the healer's own skill and by the vigorous ministrations of other healers. Their taking him in their arms, embracing him, and rubbing him with their sweat are considered lifesaving. In the process, the healing power can be transferred from an older, "big" healer to a novice; the novice places himself and his life in the hands of the older man, who must convey the power while protecting the novice from the grave dangers—both spiritual and real—that lie in wait.

In 1970, when I lived with the !Kung San in northwestern Botswana, along the fringe of the Kalahari Desert, I became an apprentice healer myself. The music created by the combined instruments of voice, clapping, and dance rattles struck me as being what used to be called psychedelic. Its eerie beauty seemed to bore into my skull, loosening the moorings of my mind. The dancing delivered a shock wave to the base of the head each time my heels hit the ground. This happened perhaps a hundred times a minute and lasted between two and ten hours. The effects on the

brain and its blood vessels, and on the muscles of the head and neck, were direct and physical. Hyperventilation probably played a role, and perhaps smoke inhalation did as well. The sustained exertion may have depleted the blood of sugar, inducing light-headedness. And staring into the flames, while dancing those monotonous steps around and around the circle, seemed to have an effect all its own. ("Look not too long into the fire," warns Ishmael, the narrator of *Moby Dick*, for it may unhinge the mind.)

But more than any of these factors, what made it possible for me to enter into the trance (to the limited extent that I did) was trust. On the one night that was followed by a morning full of compliments, especially from the women, on how well I had done, I had it in the extreme—that "oceanic" feeling of oneness with the world, which Freud viewed as echoing our complete, blissful infant dependency. Whom did I trust? Everyone—the women; the other dancers, apprentices, and healers; the whole community—but especially my teacher, a man in his late forties (I was then twenty-six). He was not one of the most powerful healers, but he was strong enough to teach a novice like me. God had strengthened his healing power (and given him his own dancing song) in a dream, during the course of a long illness. He was a well-respected leader in the community, and most important, he was my friend.

Over the two years during which we worked closely together, my regard and affection for him matured into love. He was sensitive, wise, loyal, witty, bright, vigorous, generous—in a word, the perfect father. During that night I committed myself entirely into his hands, much as a suggestible person might do with a hypnotist. And as I drifted into a mental world not quite like any other I have experienced (although it shared some features with states induced by alcohol or marijuana), my mind focused on him and on my feeling for him. I felt sure that he would take care of me. He left me to my own devices for hours, and then at last, when I most needed some human contact, he took my arms and draped me over his shoulders. I suppose we looked rather comical—a six-foot-tall white man slumped over a five-foot-high African hunter-gatherer—but to me it seemed one of the most important events of my long and eventful stay in Africa.

All folk healing systems—and modern scientific medicine, too—are based on the relationship between the healer and the victim of illness. The behavioral and psychological features of this relationship—such elements as authority, trust, shared beliefs, teaching, nurturance, and kindness—significantly, and sometimes dramatically, affect the course of illness, promoting healing and preventing recurrence. Counseling and psychotherapy speed recovery from surgery and heart attack and mitigate the suffering of patients receiving radiotherapy for cancer. Even a room with a view reduces the amount of pain medication requested by patients recovering from surgery.

Call it placebo if you like, but the human touch has a real and measurable effect. Some aspects of it appear to act directly, through neuroendocrine mechanisms, which, though poorly understood, clearly serve as intermediaries between mind and body. Meditation, for example, decreases heart rate and blood pressure and thus helps relieve hypertension, and psychological stress has been shown in laboratory animals to decrease the number of "natural killer cells," which seek and destroy tumors and may provide resistance to cancer. On a more mundane level, the human touch can improve the patient's compliance with medical advice—an area in which modern physicians have not exactly excelled.

In my case, the deep and all-encompassing sense of trust did not last the whole night through. I drifted into a delusion that something terrible was happening to my wife, who was back resting in our grass hut, a mile or so away. This idea arose from an almost completely irrational fear of the Kalahari and all the creatures in it, animal and human. I darted from the circle, jumped into a Jeep truck, and began to drive. The trance was broken by the sound of the Jeep lodging itself on a tree stump.

What was happening in my mind and brain? No one can really say. We can guess that the neocortex, which is centrally involved in logical thought, was dulled, and probably have a piece of the truth; but it is possible as well that selected parts of my brain were heightened in their functioning. Because of the trance's superficial resemblance to a seizure and, more

important, because of the powerful shifts in emotion, we can presume the involvement of the limbic system, the structure, between the brain stem and the neocortex, that mediates the emotions and has been implicated in epilepsy. Finally, we can be pretty sure that the trance involves some alteration of the brain stem's reticular activating system, which is the regulator of consciousness, ushering us from sleep to waking, from concentration to reverie. But this is all what mathematicians call "hand waving"—lines of argument so vague and sweeping as to satisfy no one.

So, it is too soon to conclude that !Kung healing "works" (according to scientific standards), and too soon to give an adequate explanation of the trance itself. I suspect, though, that in the end we will have convincing evidence. In the meantime, we can give the !Kung credit for discovering a deeply insightful system of psychology, based on knowledge and methods comparable in interest to anything in the West—and with at least equal symbolic richness. Consider the case of a young mother who had a serious bout with malaria in the wake of her middle-aged father's death. The healer in charge of her care entered a deep trance, during which his soul left his body. Traveling the road to the spirit world, it caught up with her father, who held the daughters soul in his arms. After much discussion, the father was convinced that his daughter's need to remain on earth outweighed his own need for her and even his own considerable grief, so he returned her soul to the world of the living. A few days later, her fever and chills were gone.

Could the healer's report of his encounter with the father have influenced the course of the daughter's parasitic illness? Your guess is as good as mine. But mine is that the !Kung may have something to teach Western physicians about the psychological, and even spiritual, dimensions of illness.

20

"Psychic Surgery": Close Observation of a Popular Healing Practice

Philip Singer

This selection is a skeptical inquiry, examining the actual mechanisms of a Philippine "psychic surgeon," a healer who operates on patients and removes objects from their bodies without making an incision and without leaving a scar. Psychic surgeons are, as the author says, a minor industry in the Philippines, one that attracts a fair number of ill foreigners following their hierarchy of resort to more extreme and exotic locales.

The anthropologist does not deny the importance of belief in the healing process, but he does correctly point out that the claims of psychic surgeons about their physical activities can be examined by scientifically controlled close observation. In this case, the author hired three consultants—a magician, an audiovisual technician, and a forensic pathologist—to examine the physical artifacts of six operations held in a university laboratory. All the physical evidence suggests that the psychic surgeon and his wife were using a series of sleight-of-hand tricks in the healing sessions. The objects removed were human blood clots wrapped in tissue, but in some cases the blood type of the tissue removed did not match that of the patient.

The author reminds us of the famous case of the Kwakiutl shaman Quesalid, whom we read about in the selection by Claude Lévi-Strauss. Although the physical evidence shows that this particular psychic surgeon is a sleight-of-hand artist, patients still believe that real psychic surgeons exist. In other words, the belief could not be disputed by empirical observation; one of these believers is actually a physician.

What are we to take from this debunking? The psychic surgeons adapted their traditional practice to fit the changing world of biomedicine and "health tourists." People continue to come to them because they are powerful healers. What we miss in this analysis is the close observation of the patient—someone who has already committed an important act of faith by seeking out the psychic surgeon. The power of faith is to be found in the patient, and the sham of the ritual may be relatively unimportant.

As you read this selection, consider these questions:

- *Why do you think the psychic surgeon agreed to the conditions of this close observation? Why do you think Belk, the wealthy enthusiast, agreed to finance the trip to the United States? Why do you think the anthropologist was interested?*

- *Even if the specific techniques of psychic surgery are fraudulent, how might they still have healing power as a placebo? How does this phenomenon fit Lévi-Strauss's idea of the three beliefs in the "shamanistic complex"?*

- *What does the author mean by cognitive dissonance on the part of the believer-patients?*

- *Who do you think the patients are who travel to exotic locales like this in search of a cure?*

- *A very large percentage of biomedical surgical procedures in the United States have been described as unnecessary. In what way is this analogous to the psychic surgeries?*

Acceptable parapsychological research is commonly equated with carefully controlled experiments and statistical procedures for investigating such phenomena as the ability to control the fall of a coin or die (Roll, Beloff, and White 1983), "seeing," which Zener card has been turned up (Hansen 1990), or "controlling" the output of a random-number generator (Singer and Ankenbrandt 1982). Although such experiments rarely exhibit the degree of control or the mandatory replication that characterizes experiments in physics or chemistry, their form has helped create an intellectual climate of belief in "psi" phenomena. A striking example is Filipino "psychic surgery," the apparent entry into a patient's body with the bare hand and the extraction of a pathological agent in the form of objects like hair, seeds, dry palm leaves, or, more recently, blood and bodily tissue.

I suggest that anthropologists can study the phenomenon of psychic surgery from two different perspectives: (1) as cultural behavior and (2) as a biophysical phenomenon in and of itself. The former study can be accomplished by participant observation of the classical kind. The latter requires, in addition, specialist observers, such as magicians, audiovisual technicians, and pathologists. Furthermore, since the laws of physics and biology apply equally in Philippine barrios and air-conditioned laboratories and since "psychic surgery" purports to be a specific physical and biological phenomenon, it can be studied outside either its original or transplanted cultural context (i.e., in those places, from Singapore to Sedona, Arizona, where Philippine healers now travel to perform psychic surgery). Wherever the procedure is performed, the material behavior can be responsibly described by ascertaining the answers to the following questions. Is the body penetrated with bare hands? Are blood and tissue removed? Is the "opening" closed without a scar?

To answer these and other biophysical questions, I arranged a demonstration of "noninvasive psychic surgery" in cooperation with the Department of Physics at Oakland University in 1986. The question of healing was specifically not addressed, since almost every type of disease may respond to placebo treatment, including the common cold, hypertension, or multiple sclerosis (Netter 1977). Consequently the demonstration was planned to focus on the alleged phenomenon itself—the act of opening the body barehandedly and removing organic material, including blood and tissue, which can be analyzed for pathology. The demonstration involved observation and specific audiovisual research methods (Sorenson and Gajdusek 1963), but it was also conducted with an awareness of the historical, political, and cultural contexts of psychic surgery and its practitioners.

The psychic surgeon in this demonstration was the Reverend Philip S. Malicdan, founder of the "Cultural Minorities Spiritual Fraternization Church of the Philippines" (Government Permit No. 44125), Baguio City. Malicdan identifies himself as an Igorot or "Mountain people," educated at the Mission School (St. Mary's) in Sagada, Bontoc, the University of Philippines at Baguio, and the Lutheran Seminary at Baguio. He claims to have gained his power to open the body barehandedly while on a yearly fast in a cave, where he heard a voice say, "Go in peace with joy, and help the ill, and I will help you in all you do." He has established healing centers in Singapore, Australia, California, Korea, and the Netherlands, and he claims recently to have treated "Miss Austria and Miss Bolivia 1980 and her mother" (Malicdan 1986, personal communication).[1]

W. H. Belk, of the Belk Foundation and 350 Belk department stores, brought Malicdan and his wife Frances, who acts as his assistant, to his home in Charlotte, North Carolina, in August 1986 for a two-month visit. Belk's plan was to demonstrate the imminence of the Biblical "end time" through the "miracles" of psychic surgery. During their visit the Malicdans treated more than 400 patients in Charlotte. On the basis of a small anonymous grant, and with the cooperation of Belk and the Department of Physics, Oakland University, I was able to set up a demonstration by Malicdan on September 24, 1986, of allegedly noninvasive psychic surgery under relatively controlled conditions and with recording instrumentation.

The demonstration was held in the Kettering Magnetics Laboratory at Oakland University in Rochester, Michigan. Malicdan "operated" on eight subjects, men and women who were chosen both because they had an interest in the phenomenon of psychic surgery and because they had a medically diagnosed condition (e.g., varicose veins, hemorrhoids). Because Malicdan asked to have the procedure stopped at various points to allow him to rest, the entire demonstration took five hours, during which time he removed material from five of the eight subjects.

The research protocol was designed to produce one of two possible results: (1) discovery of sleight-of-hand or (2) production of anomalous phenomena which would then call for additional scientific research. While preparing the protocol, I consulted by telephone with the magician, James Randi, about using a magician in the demonstration. Randi advised a sequential approach, wherein the psychic surgeon would first be allowed to carry out his usual procedure with the magician closely observing; after the first demonstration the magician would set terms for any further enactments so as to catch the psychic surgeon "in the act." Randi concurred in my selection of Max Maven as the magician-observer. Maven was chosen on the recommendation of Charles Reynolds of Illusion Associates in New York City, a consultant to theatrical and television enterprises that use magical effects. In a letter accompanying his final report on the Malicdan demonstration, Maven wrote that he understood his role to be "that of [an] informed observer; we had specifically agreed that I would not 'grandstand'" (Maven 1987, personal communication).

As the technical consultant and audiovisual coordinator, I selected Tom Peterson of Cleveland, Ohio, who was technical advisor and consultant to the Kent State University parapsychology demonstrations and tests, held in 1975–76 under the sponsorship of Glenn Olds, then the university's president. Peterson also acts as consultant to police and fire departments in the use of high-speed photography and explosives and has served as an expert witness on the interpretation of surveillance film for the FBI, General Electric, and other clients.

The pathologist who collected all materials "removed" or "materialized" from subjects was Alexander S. Ullmann, M.D., Chief Pathologist, Crittenton Hospital, Rochester, Michigan. All specimens collected were preserved under sterile conditions, and Ullmann analyzed all such materials in his laboratory in comparison with samples of the subjects' blood. He also sent suitable samples to the Michigan State Police Crime Laboratory for testing that was beyond the capacity of the hospital laboratory.

THE OBSERVERS' REPORTS

After the demonstration all three specialist-observers (magician, audiovisual expert, and pathologist) concluded, without mutual consultation, that, as Max Maven put it, "Philip Malicdan is a willful fraud" (Maven 1987, personal communication). The three based their conclusions on different evidence and different forms of analysis.

In his report (1987) Maven points out that four different named "elements" of conjuring methodology were present in Malicdan's work.

1. "Natural law disguised" means that Malicdan seemed to have pushed his hands deeper into a patient's body than would seem possible.
2. "Secretly prepared materials" refers to the conjuror's "gimmick," "gaf," or "load," apparently produced from the patient's body. Malicdan's "load" consisted of tissue wrapped around blood-clots, a "very efficient [method] in that the *load-container* is the *load-item* itself." One unused specimen was found in the water-basin in which Malicdan washed his hands before an unexpected hand-search, and traces of another appeared on the bathroom floor after Mrs. Malicdan retreated there to avoid another search.
3. "Secret activities" involves the methods used by Mrs. Malicdan to transfer the "load" to her husband and by Philip Malicdan to conceal it until it could be used.
4. "Psychology" shows Malicdan at his most sophisticated. When he and Frances arrived in Michigan the day before the scheduled demonstration, they were shown the laboratory and approved the general arrangements, the lighting, etc. At that time Malicdan complained of high blood pressure symptoms and insisted on being examined by a physician, who prescribed medication. Maven pointed out that Malicdan used his disability in several ways. It allowed him to quit at any time; in fact, he threatened to do so more than once. It also allowed him to pause "to rest," while

he reassessed the situation and figured out how to get another "load." His condition also built sympathy for him and so allowed him to bend or dispense with previously agreed-on procedures. For instance, during one unannounced hand search, he actually held a "load" in his right hand and, in Maven's words, counted on Maven's not choosing "to be so 'cruel' to an overtly suffering man," whereas actually Maven refrained from the examination because insisting on it would, in his opinion, have led Malicdan to refuse to continue.

Maven's conclusion is that Frances Malicdan carried the loads, "which were passed to her husband by way of the water basin or probably at times by other methods." Tom Peterson, the audiovisual technical director, concurred in this conclusion.

Peterson used three videotape cameras to record "an unquestioned record of whatever took place, so that a valid conclusion would be drawn as to whether the alleged phenomenon was authentic or the result of illusion and trickery" and also "to serve as a base [for] scientists planning similar investigations" (Peterson 1986, personal communication). He provided an ideal protocol for the demonstration but noted afterwards that it had been "compromised and altered" by the Malicdans' actions. For example, after agreeing on the lighting arrangements on September 23, the next day Malicdan complained that the lights were too bright. ("The rays are being blocked.") In addition, Frances Malicdan introduced a satchel containing various oils and medications after the original search had been done and produced from it a dark-colored cloth which she and her husband insisted on using and which was, according to Peterson (1986, personal communication), a "perfect color and texture to disguise an object such as was found in the water bowl" (i.e., the "load"). Such tactics, as well as delays during which some cameras were turned off and observers became inattentive, were specifically mentioned by Peterson as opportunities for sleight-of-hand.

In these cases of delay, the overhead "clock reference" camera, which would record in any light and continued to operate during breaks when other cameras were turned off, proved invaluable. From it Peterson was able to note the tactics mentioned above and also "awkward or unnecessary movements," like Malicdan's attempt to readjust the drape on the operating table while holding a styrofoam cup almost empty of the coffee it had held (which he could more naturally have set down). Peterson also noted Malicdan's "sweep" of the surface of the water basin, after which on another camera "we see Frances Malicdan pick up something from the bowl and place it at the small of her back under the smock." (Both Malicdans were asked to dress in hospital scrub-suits before the demonstration but were not required to remove their underwear or submit to a strip-search.) When I mentioned a search at one point, Frances Malicdan expressed a need to go to the bathroom, where a blood smear was found on the floor. Peterson also cited the Malicdans' "singular ability to control the extent and duration of searches"—for example, by announcing that Malicdan "was ready to begin the healing" or by simply redirecting the search to a different location. Peterson's detailed analysis of the Malicdans' actions led him to conclude, like Maven, that "the tape record indicates beyond any doubt that sleight-of-hand was used to create the illusion of mysterious withdrawal of diseased tissue from within the patient" (1986, personal communication).

Ullmann provided evidence of a different kind. He was accompanied by his assistant, who acted as one of Malicdan's patients and also took blood samples to match with the blood and tissue allegedly removed by Malicdan. Ullmann's report pointed out that, without exception, the samples were in an "advanced state of degeneration," which "indicates to me that they were not removed at the time of their purported 'Psychic Surgery'" (Ullmann 1986, personal communication). He notes that in two cases where the samples were not too deteriorated to preclude analysis, Malicdan had apparently succeeded in taking Type B blood from patients whose blood type is O.

The tissue specimens, furthermore, showed no relationship to the parts of the various patients' bodies from which they had allegedly been removed. Ullmann concluded that probably the specimens "were removed—whether from humans or animals I do not know—possibly weeks or months before [the demonstration] and were kept under unsterile conditions to be produced at the appropriate time as fresh specimens" (1986, personal communication). This hypothesis is strengthened by the fact that Frances Malicdan is a medical technologist who would have had opportunities in the Philippines to obtain human blood and tissue. In addition, a friend of Henry Belk's who supervised the North Carolina treatment of patients told us that a "mysterious box," which she did not open, appeared in Belk's refrigerator at the beginning of the Malicdans' stay and disappeared when they left. But wherever the tissue specimens may have been between the Malicdan's arrival in the United States and the university demonstrations, Ullmann concurs with Maven and Peterson about the method of delivery: "I . . . assume that these blood clots were collected in the distant past and were kept in a dried state and were mixed with water (in the hand-washing basin) during Mr. Malicdan's hand-washing procedures immediately prior to the surgery" (Ullmann 1986, personal commu-

nication). He added that the seemingly human origin of the blood "found on the surface of the degenerated tissue specimens offers no proof for the human origin of the tissues, since the liquified blood becomes easily attached to the surface of any tissue and gives a positive result" (Ullmann 1986, personal communication).

DISCUSSION

The Reactions of Advocates of Psychic Surgery

The reactions of Henry Belk and some participants in the demonstration are interesting as examples of cognitive dissonance. After receiving Peterson's report, Belk wrote to him:

> I have read and carefully digested your report on Malicdan's alleged healings in Detroit. I have only these complaints. Conditions should have been even tighter. . . . The magician should have been eliminated. . . . Malicdan is a bastard and SOB (who is after money, greed, and Ego). . . . I never rule out FRAUD or its possibility. Yet equally I was healed by [other psychic surgeons], and it's a reputable, daily happening. *Truth will out. All is not fraud.* I am glad you were so thorough. But don't throw out the baby with the water! I admire you and a job well done. (Belk 1987, personal communication)

One of the four subjects from whom Malicdan allegedly extracted blood and tissue during the demonstration was Jewel Irwin Pookrum, M.D., in private practice at a holistic medical clinic in Detroit. Pookrum graduated from the Creighton School of Medicine and was Chief Resident in Gynecology at Henry Ford Hospital, Detroit. Malicdan "operated" on her for adhesions from two caesarean sections. She believes that since "psychic surgeons merge energy fields, theirs and the patient's," and since they "know the natural cleavage points in the cell," they can "enter the body without making an incision" (Pookrum 1986, personal communication). Even though the blood Malicdan allegedly removed or materialized from her was Type B rather than her own Type O, and even though the histologic report showed "completely degenerated and necrotic tissue with necrotic cellular debris in which no other tissue elements can be identified" (Ullmann 1986, personal communication), Pookrum insists today that what Malicdan removed was her adhesions. The fact that all tissues from the four subjects were not only necrotic but similar (though one allegedly came from a lump behind the left knee, another from the back of the neck, a third from an eye, a fourth from the heart region) did not shake her belief. She told me, "This has been just a monumental experience in my life and has truly awakened my horizon on many levels" (Pookrum 1986, personal communication).

The reactions of these believers in psychic surgery are reminiscent of Qaselid and his fellow Kwakiutl shamans, as recorded by Boas (1969[1930]). Though Qaselid provided a detailed description of his shamanic trickery, involving confederates and sleight-of-hand to produce "paranormal" materializations, he and his fellow shamans sustained their belief in the supernatural. After faking the materialization and removing the sickness, the conjuror sang his sacred song: "Do those supernatural ones really see it? Those supernatural ones see it plainly, those supernatural ones. No one can imitate our great friends, the supernatural ones" (Boas 1969[1930]:28). Qaselid learned all the sleight-of-hand tricks of various shamans but still continued to search for a true shaman endowed with true supernatural powers. After much time and searching and after learning many tricks, he believed that perhaps he had found a true shaman: "Only one shaman was seen by me, who sucked at a sick man and I never found out whether he was a real shaman or only made up. Only for this reason I believe that he is a shaman; he does not allow those who are made well to pay him. I truly never once saw him laugh" (Boas 1969[1930]:40–41). Like Qaselid, contemporary advocates of psychic surgery, such as Belk, rest their case on the likely existence of one "true" shaman.

Psychic Surgery: A Minor Philippine Industry

The evidence concerning the alleged phenomenon of psychic surgery points clearly to the conclusion that it is cultural behavior learned by its practitioners, just as it represents cultural behavior by those patients, Philippine and Western, who accept it as a gift of the spirit. From an anthropological point of view, the history of psychic surgery in the Philippines over the past 20 years presents a clear example of the process of acculturation which has been supported by the ruling oligarchy of the country. Far from being reluctant shamans "deculturated" by Western contact, psychic surgeons have made a vital transition from traditional shamanism ("extraction" from the body of leaves, seeds, worms, hair, etc.) to a simulacrum of Western scientific medicine ("extraction" of blood, tissue, tumors, organs) and from traditional shamanic concepts to Western religious concepts of the Holy Spirit and the saints, Far Eastern concepts of "karma," "prana," and "chakras"; parapsychological concepts of "etheric,"

"astral," and "bioplasmic" bodies; or quasi-scientific concepts like the bicameral mind or energy vibrations (Finkelstein 1985:131).

The dramatic transformations of psychic surgeons from barrio and village shamans to global healers is a matter of historical fact and can be dated. The turning point in this movement was the September 1965 article in *Psychic News* by Nelson Decker, a doctor of chiropractic in Los Angeles. Decker described "psychic surgery" and his month-long experience with Eleuterio Terte, the "father of psychic surgery," and Terte's leading disciple Tony Agpaoa. In his book on healers and healing, George W. Meek—engineering graduate of the University of Michigan, holder of patents relating to air and thermal control processes, and inventor of "Spiricom" (a device for speaking with the dead)—notes that "The native Filipino healers . . . were totally steeped in nature. . . . then things began to change! *Foreigners* started to show up in search of healing. These foreigners, upon returning home, showed films and extolled the 'miracles' of healing" (Meek 1977:100; emphasis in original). Meek acknowledges Henry Belk and Harold Sherman as pioneers in the study of Filipino healers, who laid the groundwork for the researchers who followed them.

By 1973 psychic surgery had achieved de facto acceptance by the Philippine Medical Association (PMA). The PMA concluded that an investigation they conducted had revealed nothing illegal, since psychic surgeons used no instruments and did not write prescriptions. An article in *Philippine Panarama* (August 25, 1973) adds, "Besides, . . . they bring in foreign tourists. These tourists go to these healing centers, and even Americans from Clark Air Base [go] in bus loads."

In 1983 the Philippine Healers' Circle, Inc., headed by the psychic surgeon Alex Orbito and with Malicdan as an officer, was inaugurated with a keynote speech by the Philippine government's Information Minister, who observed that the limits of modern medicine could be transcended by "psychic healing," which, he noted, includes removing tumors and other objects from patients' bodies by healers working bare-handed. In 1984 former President Ferdinand Marcos sent a personal message to the First Philippine Conference on Paranormal Healing, organized by the Philippine Healers' Circle. Marcos, a believer in psychic surgery (Singer and Ankenbrandt 1980:21), said in an address to the Conference (1984), "For over a decade now the Philippines have been the center of world attention for her incredible and admittedly controversial methods of spiritual healing." He added that "the Philippine government . . . is fully aware of the many benefits that have been reported to have resulted from them" (source not available). Indeed, by 1984 psychic surgeons were attending international anthropological meetings in Indonesia, South America, and Europe. Though Marcos is gone, political support for psychic surgeons appears to be constant. In 1985 and 1986 two more international conferences on "paranormal healing" were sponsored by psychic surgeons in the Philippines. In short, the existence today of hundreds of psychic surgeons in the Philippines does not indicate any new facts or scientific discoveries about biology or physics but rather clearly supports an anthropological principle that people learn cultural behavior from other people, generally when it is in their interest to do so. With psychic surgery we are dealing with syncretic cultural behavior, the meaning and import of which differs for practitioners and their Western clients and proponents.

NOTE

1. When I visited Malicdan at Baguio in the Philippines in February 1984, a group of 10 Canadians and two young German women were waiting for treatment. The Canadians' three-week package trip was arranged by a Canadian travel service at a cost of $4,000. This fee did not include treatments by Malicdan at $50 for the first and $25 for subsequent sessions. Just after treatment I spoke to a 75-year-old male patient who suffered from chronic bronchitis and sinus trouble and who said he felt much better after his psychic surgery than he did during the preceding six years after medication and surgery by physician specialists. One German woman said she had had diagnosed breast and uterine cancer which Malicdan cured in 1981. Her German physician allegedly told her afterward that she was "all clean." In 1984 she returned to Malicdan for "preventive" treatment.

REFERENCES

Boas, Franz. 1969[1930]. The Religion of the Kwakiutl Indians, Part 2. Translations. New York: AMS Press.

Finkelstein, Adrian. 1985. Your Past Lives and the Healing Process. Farmingdale, NY: Coleman Publishing.

Hansen, George P. 1990. Deception by Subjects in Psi Research. Journal of the American Society for Psychical Research 84:25–80.

Maven, Max. 1987. Report on Malicdan Demonstration. April 13. (Manuscript, files of the author.)

Meek, George, ed. 1977. Healers and the Healing Process: A Report on 10 Years of Research by 14 World Famous Investigators. Wheaton, IL: Theosophical Publishing House.

Netter, P. 1977. Placebo Effect. Münchener Medicinische Wochenschrift 119:203–206.

Roll, William G., J. Beloff, and R. White, eds. 1983. Research in Parapsychology 1982. Metuchen, NJ: Scarecrow Press.

Singer, Philip, and Kate Ware Ankenbrandt. 1980. The Ethnography of the Paranormal. New Directions in the Study of Man 4(1 and 2):19–34.

———. 1982. Comment on Magic: A Theoretical Reassessment, by Michael Winkelman. Current Anthropology 23:52–58.

Sorenson, E. R., and D. C. Gajdusek. 1963. Investigation of Non-Recurring Phenomena. Nature 200 (4902):112–115.

Culture, Illness, and Mental Health

✤ CONCEPTUAL TOOLS ✤

■ *Culture defines normality, and cultural rules determine who is crazy.* How do you know if you're normal? How do you know if your emotional feelings are appropriate or if your thought processes are disturbed? These are difficult questions because we have to compare ourselves with others, and yet there are no cross-culturally universal standards for normal behavior or thinking. Historical and cultural contexts vary. Saintly behavior in one context may be considered deranged in another. Over 120 years ago in the United States there was a mental illness affecting African American slaves called drapetomania. The symptoms of this illness included repeated attempts to run away from the owner's plantation, and slaves with this "illness" had less value. Twenty years ago, homosexuality was officially diagnosed as a mental illness, and then, in a revision of the *Diagnostic and Statistical Manual* (*DSM*) of the American Psychiatric Association, it was decided that homosexuality was no longer an illness. The powerful novels of Aleksandr Solzhenitsyn, like *The Gulag Archipelago* (1973), show how psychiatry can become a powerful tool of social control by the state—when any political dissidence becomes de facto evidence of insanity. The problem of the definition of normality is exactly the same as the problem of cultural relativity: Although we need to be tolerant of a range of variation of the definitions of normal thought and behavior, absolute relativism—an "anything goes" idea—is not acceptable. Boundaries of health and illness are difficult to set. Recognition of this cultural relativity and the function of mental illness categories as agents of social control have played a role in labeling theory and the antipsychiatry movement (Szasz 1974).

■ *Some mental conditions may be more pronounced or elaborated in particular cultural settings; these conditions have been labeled "culture-bound" or "culture-specific" syndromes* (Simons and Hughes 1985). This concept in medical anthropology and cross-cultural psychiatry has caused significant debate. Culture-bound syndromes (CBSs) seem exotic and usually have vernacular ethnomedical labels depending on the locality where they were first described. For

example, *latah* is an elaborated startle response that is founded in Malaysia (Simons 1985, 1996). People (usually older women) who have *latah* are often startled several times a day, because their response is so extreme and entertaining. Sometimes their attention can be captured and they mimic their tormentors; sometimes they say colorful obscenities. Another CBS is *koro,* an extreme anxiety reaction affecting males. A victim fears that his penis is shrinking up into his abdomen and that when it ascends all the way he will die. Epidemics of *koro* have been reported in China and Malaysia. Other CBSs include *pibloktoq* (arctic hysteria), *amok* (sudden mass assault), and the folk illness *susto* (soul loss or magical fright) that we will read about later (see selection 22). Some anthropologists have argued that the criteria for culture-bound syndromes fit particular conditions in the United States, including premenstrual syndrome (PMS) (Johnson 1987) and obesity (Ritenbaugh 1978). Most medical anthropologists do not believe that mental disorders can actually be limited to a particular society with a particular culture; rather, society *constructs* illness labels, and social customs may function to put people at elevated risk for certain kinds of stressors that may result in mental illness (Hahn 1995).

■ *Some cross-cultural psychiatrists believe that there are a very small number of universal mental illnesses, two of which correspond to biomedical labels of "schizophrenia" and "depression."* In contrast with labeling theorists who emphasize cultural relativity, some cross-cultural epidemiological studies of mental health have focused on commonalities of serious mental disorders. Schizophrenia-type illnesses—including cognitive impairment, auditory hallucinations, and inappropriate behaviors—appear to have some cross-cultural validity. There is also persuasive evidence that there is a genetic component to these illnesses. Depression-type illnesses are common throughout the world, although the local expression of the affective (emotional) disorder varies (Kleinman and Good 1985). Risk of depression-type illnesses also appears to have a genetic component. Evolutionary theorists have speculated as to why genes involved in the etiology of severe mental illnesses seem to persist in human populations (Allen and Sarich 1988). It is possible that mild expressions of these illnesses—for example, in creativity or social sensitivity—may be advantageous.

■ *Different cultures have their own ethnopsychiatric systems for diagnosing and curing mental illness. All ethnopsychiatric systems are based on cultural assumptions and social role expectations.* In ethnomedical studies, it is difficult to separate psychiatric practice from other kinds of medical interventions because other cultures may not rely on the same philosophical assumptions—for example, the separation of mind and body—as does Euroamerican medicine. The cross-cultural study of ethnopsychiatric systems is very interesting (Gaines 1992), and more epidemiological studies of the effectiveness of traditional therapies is warranted. For example, H. Kristian Heggenhougen (1984) has shown the effectiveness of religious healers in treating heroin addiction in Southeast Asia. Medical anthropologists have also examined the cultural assumptions embedded in a psychiatric category system like the *DSM*'s definitions of personality disorders. Charles Nuckolls has shown that U.S. pyschiatrists often arrive at diagnoses of personality disorders in the first few seconds of an interaction and that personality disorder categories hinge on definitions of appropriate gender attributes (Nuckolls 1996).

■ *Social stress is a serious cause of illness.* Generations of psychosomatic researchers have demonstrated that feelings of distress and hopelessness affect physical well-being. Although stress is difficult to define, its importance is obvious. Studies of stress show the interconnectedness of the physical, psychological, and social aspects of an individual. Recent studies by medical anthropologists have shown that the stresses of modernization and a growing discrepancy between rich and poor are serious world health problems (Des Jarlais, Kleinman, et al., 1995).

21

Do Psychiatric Disorders Differ in Different Cultures?

Arthur Kleinman

The author of this selection is a psychiatrist and a medical anthropologist, specializing in the study of China, who teaches at Harvard Medical School. The selection comes from a book, Rethinking Psychiatry *(Kleinman 1988), written for psychiatrists about cultural variation and mental health. The selection reviews a large and somewhat contradictory literature; as you will see when you critically review the literature, there is a lot that we do not know about the epidemiological distribution and symptomatological expression of mental illnesses across cultures.*

Here, Kleinman assumes that you understand what culture-bound syndromes are. (You may want to review Conceptual Tools *for this section.) The first part of the selection is about epidemiological studies of mental illness—the distribution across cultural groups and social categories—although it is difficult to evaluate this work because of the lack of international standardization of definitions. Despite these problems, it seems clear that rates of major mental illnesses vary from society to society. A famous study in this regard—Nancy Scheper-Hughes's* Saints, Scholars and Schizophrenics *(1979)—demonstrates that traditional patterns of social organization and family interaction, in combination with worsening economic conditions, result in elevated rates of schizophrenia (and institutionalization) in Ireland.*

The second and third parts of the selection concern the symptomatology of mental illness and illness behavior (how people react to their symptoms and seek help, or, in the case of depression, attempt suicide). This selection differs from many others in this book because it does not focus on a particular case; instead, it discusses a wide variety of cases. The answer to the question posed in the title is affirmative, but the ways in which psychiatric disorders vary remain complex.*

As you read this selection consider these questions:

- *If illnesses are socially constructed, how is it possible to compare mental illness rates and symptom-complexes across cultures? How can one compare psychiatric diagnoses across cultures when standards of normal behavior differ from culture to culture? Is this a silly task?*

- *Although it is clear that family patterning or genetic predispositions are involved in schizophrenia and depression, the author says that the actual causes of these illnesses are not known. Why do you think this may be the case?*

- *What is somatization in the expression of psychological discomfort? Why might it be important for a healer to be aware of the process of somatization?*

- *Why is suicide considered an illness behavior in the context of depression? Why is the study of suicide interesting?*

EPIDEMIOLOGY

The prevalence data (total cases at a particular time) for schizophrenia—a serious mental disorder of unknown cause characterized by delusions, hallucinations, associations of unrelated ideas, social withdrawal, and lack of emotional responsiveness and motivation—indicate a band of prevalence rates ranging from roughly two to ten cases per thousand population across a range of populations (Sartorius and Jablensky 1976). Lower rates have been reported in less developed societies and the highest rates in North America and certain European societies (Fortes and Mayer 1969;

Torrey 1980; Sikanerty and Eaton 1984). Although some incidence data (new cases in a defined period of time) are available for European societies, the data for non-Western societies are very limited and controversial. As we have seen in the World Health Organization studies, there is evidence for a wider range of incidence rates when the broader, heterogeneous sample of schizophrenic patients is used to calculate rates, and a narrower range when the more homogeneous sample is employed. Other studies report small-scale, preliterate societies with hardly any cases of schizophrenia and communities, often small, isolated Scandinavian ones,* with very high rates of schizophrenia (cf. Warner 1985 for the most comprehensive review).

It is hard to know what to make of these findings. They certainly represent a wider continuum than is suggested by the professional catechism that there is a relatively narrow band of prevalance of this psychiatric disorder cross-culturally. There are, furthermore, families that have much higher rates of this major mental illness than most others in the population. Twin studies, including those comparing twins of schizophrenic parents who are adopted out into nonschizophrenic families, indicate that there is a significant genetic basis to this disorder.[1] But the genetic contribution is controversial; most models of the disorder invoke an interaction between social environment, genetic endowment, and neurobiological processes, making for a complex causal nexus. It is clearer to say in 1987 that the cause is unknown, as Carpenter, McGlashan, and Strauss (1977), leading psychiatric researchers who have devoted their careers to the study of schizophrenia, concluded a decade ago. Perhaps the chief epidemiological conclusion is simply the finding of patients with the core symptoms of schizophrenia in a very wide variety of societies. This mental illness is no myth.

Schizophrenia in developing societies is much more likely to present with an acute than an indolent onset; chronic mode of onset is more common in Western societies. DSM-III's diagnostic criteria strictly limit cases of schizophrenia to those that have had a course of at least six months. Acute onset cases that are of less than six months' duration are not diagnosed as schizophrenia by the standards of DSM-III. The WHO's ICD-9 does not have this requirement. Thus, different categories and different phenomena interact to create incommensurate findings. Acute onset psychosis of short duration is probably not the same disease as chronic onset long-duration psychosis (Stevens 1987). Whether acute onset and chronic onset psychoses of the same duration are indeed the same disorder is unclear. Schizophrenia is probably a group of syndromes. From the cross-cultural perspective, schizophrenia is organized as much by taxonomies as it is by disease processes.

Warner (1985) advances a substantial body of evidence to suggest that the occurrence and course of schizophrenia are strongly conditioned by the political economy. Unemployment and economic depression in the West and the development of capitalist modes of wage labor in non-Western societies appear to lead to greater numbers of individuals manifesting schizophrenia and fewer of them improving. . . . Warner also

explains how analysts of the cross-cultural data base on the prevalence of schizophrenia could come to almost diametrically opposed views of the relative frequency of the disorder in non-Western and Western societies because of ideological commitments which lead psychiatrists to emphasize certain studies while discounting or even ignoring others.

The prevalence data for brief reactive psychosis—an acute psychosis closely associated with a serious stressful life event in a person without premorbid pathology and with recovery within days or weeks without any significant chronic symptoms or persistent disability—show that this disorder constitutes a much larger portion of acute psychoses in nonindustrialized, non-Western societies than in the industrialized West (Langness 1965; Manschreck 1978; Murphy 1982). Psychiatric researchers are concerned that such cases of brief reactive psychosis misdiagnosed as schizophrenia confound cross-cultural comparisons. But for the anthropologist, brief reactive psychoses are of particular interest because they are the one psychotic disorder that has enormously different prevalance rates cross-culturally. Moreover, they show great diversity in form—in an arc running from trance and possession states occurring outside culturally authorized settings to schizophreniform experiences—and such impressive cultural shaping that certain brief reactive psychoses are included in the culture-bound syndrome category. This group of psychiatric disorders is neither well-studied nor given a central place in psychiatry; yet for cultural analysis it is of very special significance. It is not surprising, then, that anthropological studies of individual brief reactive psychoses are more frequent than anthropological studies of schizophrenia. Studies disclose that of all forms of madness brief reactive psychoses bear the strongest causal relationship to immediate life event stressors, especially stressors that are of particular cultural salience, that they are the most culturally diverse of all psychoses, that they overlap with final common pathways of normal behavior (e.g., culturally approved trance states), and that they respond well to indigenous healing systems (Langness 1965; Kleinman 1980; Lewis 1971).

The epidemiology of nonpsychotic disorders around the globe is even more variable. Depression is the best case in point. The findings reveal a much greater range of variation than for schizophrenia. There simply are no studies in the non-Western world, however, comparable in rigor and standardization to the Epidemiological Catchment Area (ECA) studies sponsored by the NIMH in the United States. That set of studies, a particularly expensive undertaking involving investigators trained to use the same interview schedule (DIS), surveyed communities in five

---

*For example, Book et al. (1978) report a rate of 17 cases per 1000 for northern Sweden; and Torrey et al. (1984) report a rate of 12.6 per thousand for a high prevalence area in western Ireland.

sites. Six-month prevalance rates (i.e., total number of cases detected in a period of six months) for affective disorders (chiefly depression) ranged from 4.6 to 6.5 percent. Lifetime prevalence rates (i.e., total number of individuals in the study population who experienced an episode of depressive disease sometime during their life) ranged from 6.1 to 9.5 percent. Major depression, as in earlier research, was found to be more common in women and in urban areas (Blazer et al. 1985; Myers et al. 1984; Robins et al. 1984).

Reviewing the English-language literature for industrialized Western societies, Boyd and Weissman (1981) estimated the point prevalence (number of cases at a particular point in time) of clinical depression (not including manic-depressive disorder, a psychosis) in studies using newer, more reliable diagnostic techniques as 3.2 percent in males and 4.0 to 9.3 percent in females. The range of prevalence in reports from non-industrialized, non-Western societies is much greater.

Despite reports during the colonial period that depression was uncommon in India, Venkoba Rao (1984) states that recent studies indicate depression is a common disorder, though, because the variation of rates across different cultural areas in India is wide, he is uncertain just how common. Rao cites Indian rates of 1.5 to 32.9 per thousand in the general population. Among the highest rates currently reported are those for Africa: 14.3 percent for men and 22.6 percent for women in Uganda (Orley and Wing 1979). Ironically, an earlier generation of colonial psychiatrists, many of whom were paternalistic and racialist, claimed that depression was rare in Africa, India, and other non-Western culture areas owing to putative weaknesses in the cognitive and affective states of indigenous populations.[2]

Increased rates of depression in Africa and other non-Western cultures appear to be the result of the use of more culturally appropriate diagnostic criteria and standardized research methods in studies that sample the general population and therefore do not rely, as did an early generation of studies, on clinic-based figures that are biased by different patterns of help seeking. But Prince (1968) and H. B. M. Murphy (1982, p. 143) suggest, in addition to correction of methodological shortcomings, there has probably been a general increase in rates of depression in many non-Western societies due to the pressures and problems of modernization. Clearly, the findings of high rates of depression in Uganda must, at least in part, reflect the political chaos and murderous oppression that the members of that society have so tragically experienced.

Lin and Kleinman (1981) reviewed the epidemiological studies of mental illness in China since the early 1950s, which include some of the largest population surveys ever attempted, involving tens of thousands of respondents. They found that prior to 1981, with the exception of manic-depressive psychosis and involutional melancholia, a psychosis among the elderly, clinical depression was simply not reported. In the past few years the Chinese have begun to publish clinic-based studies that record higher rates of depression (an increase from 1 percent to 20 percent of outpatient samples), though rates still lower than in the West (see studies cited in Kleinman 1986). This increase is almost certainly the result of using newer Western-influenced diagnostic criteria and psychometric assessment tools. The WHO's comparative international study of *Depressive Disorders in Different Cultures* (Sartorius et al. 1983), a multicultural project involving centers in Japan, Iran, and other non-Western societies, does not cite prevalence rates among its findings. Tsung-yi Lin and his colleagues in Taiwan (1969) reported a great increase in the rates of neuroses including depression from the time of a first survey of three communities in the late 1940s to a second survey, conducted by the same research team with the same criteria and methods, 15 years later, during the period of Taiwan's rapid modernization. Clinicians in many non-Western societies have claimed similar increases, but pre- and post-epidemiological surveys, like Lin's, are few in number. There is a strong possibility that, at least in some societies, the norms and idioms for expressing distress have changed so substantially that the expression, not necessarily the occurrence, of depression is more common. We do know, however, that the rates of depression and other neurotic conditions are elevated in refugee, immigrant, and migrant populations owing to uprooting, loss, and the serious stress of the acculturation process (Beiser 1985, Beiser and Fleming 1986). Selective uprooting of those most vulnerable to mental illness does not play a significant role in forced migrations of the most recent Southeast Asian and South American refugees in North America, so that the data on refugees probably are an accurate reflection of psychiatric casualties of uprooting and acculturation.[3] Furthermore, at least in North America, leading psychiatric epidemiologists claim to have incidence data that the rate of depression among young adults is on the rise (*Psychiatric News* 15 May, 1988).

Some advance has also been made in understanding risk factors for depression. In a classic study, Brown and Harris (1978) convincingly demonstrated that among working-class women in England, relative powerlessness, absence of affective support, and the social pressures of child rearing and no job outside the home significantly increased their vulnerability to serious life event stressors, like loss; those with marginal self-esteem were pushed over the edge into generalized hopelessness and clinical depression. Kleinman

(1986) has found the same pattern of vulnerability and provoking agents among Chinese depressives, though the particular sources of their vulnerability differ. Good, Good and Moradi (1985) reported comparable findings among Iranian immigrants in the United States. Beiser (1987) has identified a mediating process in depressed and anxious Southeast Asian refugees to Canada: excessive nostalgia and preoccupation with self-perceptions of time past as ideally positive and future time as threatening and undesirable identify those at highest risk for developing distress at a later date. The causes of differential susceptibility remain a very important subject for cross-cultural comparisons.

For the other neurotic disorders, there is terribly little valid cross-cultural epidemiological data. In earlier epidemiological studies, either anxiety was mixed in with other neuroses or the criteria for distinguishing it from other disorders were not enumerated. In an earlier review of what cross-cultural literature does exist, my colleague Byron Good and I (1985) estimated that, with the exception of studies of Australian aborigines, anxiety disorders are diagnosed at a rate of 12 to 27 cases per thousand population. In the ECA studies, six-month prevalence rates of anxiety and somatoform (somatization disorder, hypochondriasis, psychogenic pain) disorders varied from 6.6 to 14.9 percent and lifetime rates from 10.4 to 25.1 percent (with differences largely due to different rates for phobias), making this combined category the commonest psychiatric condition in the United States. Iranian studies described prevalence rates of 27 and 8 per thousand in one project for anxiety disorders among villagers and city dwellers, respectively, and 48 and 38 per thousand for a mixed category of anxiety and somatoform disorders in another. Indian studies cite rates of 17.8, 20.5, and 12 per thousand population for the same category.

The studies of Australian aborigines are a marked contrast. Population surveys of 2,360 individuals turned up only one case of "overt anxiety" (Jones and Horne 1973). The Cornell-Aro Mental Health Project in Nigeria conducted by the psychiatrist-anthropologist Alexander Leighton and his colleagues (1963b) reported high levels of anxiety symptoms (this study did not make disease designations) in village and town residents, 36 and 27 percent, and found high levels of respondents who were significantly impaired, 19 and 16 percent. By contrast, the Sterling County study in Nova Scotia by the same team of investigators (Leighton et al. 1963a) found far fewer anxiety symptoms (13 and 10 percent) but twice the rate of impairment (38 and 32 percent). As with their findings for depression, Orley and Wing's (1979) comparison of Ugandan village women and London women found higher rates of anxiety disorders in the former. (Given the high rates of infectious diseases, many undiag-

nosed, among rural dwellers in the non-Western world, it is extremely difficult to know what to make of attempts to diagnose their anxiety and somatoform disorders.) Many researchers of the common culture-bound syndromes—especially fright and soul loss disorders, neurasthenia, and *taijinkyofusho*, a Japanese phobic reaction associated with fear of others—hypothesize that these conditions may represent culturally authorized final common behavioral pathways for anxiety disorders (Carr and Vitaliano 1985; Simons and Hughes, eds., 1985). Consequently, the cross-cultural epidemiological literature on depression and anxiety disorders indicates that these are common around the globe, particularly in patients in general medical clinics, though precise determination of comparative rates is not feasible at present and reasons for the wider cross-cultural disparities are uncertain.

Studies also generally show that these disorders are found at higher rates among women (though several studies show the reverse) and members of lower socioeconomic classes in a number of societies. The most recent studies of depression and gender have supported Brown's model of the effect of powerlessness and low self-esteem on the etiology of depression in women (Finkler 1985; Kleinman 1986; Good and Kleinman 1985; Lock 1986, 1987; Gaines and Farmer 1986). The definitive epidemiological data is not in, but women and certainly poor women appear to be at higher risk for mental illness in a number of societies.[4] For the major mental disorders, the social context . . . appears to be the chief source of cross-cultural diversity. But this is in part because genetic, temperament, and other biographical variables, which might explain why only some individuals exposed to the same pressures become ill, have not been systematically studied outside the Western world.

That research on American Indians and Hispanic Americans shows both very high and quite low rates in different studies warns us again of the importance of intracultural diversity. The association of depression with high rates of alcoholism in some (but not all) American Indian and Alaskan Native populations emphasizes as well the potentially important relationship between alcohol abuse and mental illness. For example, in the ECA studies, lifetime prevalence rates for substance abuse ranged from 15 to 18 percent with alcoholism 11.5 to 15.7 percent, and 15 percent of those with alcoholism had depression (Robins et al. 1984). Alcoholism rates are rising in a number of areas around the world, though, as Heath (1986) sagely cautions, the evidence for a worldwide epidemic, which some mental health professionals claim is happening, is simply not there. Nonetheless, alcohol rates in East Asian societies (Japan, Hong Kong, Taiwan, even China), which were traditionally very low by

Western standards, are now increasing, and this will complicate the cross-cultural epidemiology of mental disorders very considerably, because it will be necessary to determine if changes in rates of psychopathology are due to alcoholism (Lin and Lin 1984).

Our original question was, do psychiatric disorders differ cross-culturally? The epidemiological rates indicate significant differences. This is even true without taking into account culture-bound syndromes and trance and possession psychoses which occur outside of culturally authorized ritual settings. Those disorders by definition are found only or principally in non-Western societies. The epidemiological data, however, do not sustain the radical cultural relativist argument that mental disorders are incomparable in greatly different societies. The chief mental disorders are diagnosable worldwide; research is quite clear on this point. Thus, we are once again left with evidence of both cross-cultural universals and particularities, cross-cultural support for the dialectical view that "life requires both the determination of the environment and the physical body" (Kitaro 1970, p. 100).

SYMPTOMATOLOGY

A salient international finding, often replicated as I have noted, is the marked predominance of somatic symptoms among depressed and anxious patients in non-Western societies, albeit these symptoms are also common in the West (Kleinman and Good, eds., 1985; Good and Kleinman 1985; Kirmayer 1984; H. B. M. Murphy 1982; Weiss and Kleinman in press).[5] Particular symptoms and symptom patterns differ across patients in different cultures. Because the literature relevant to symptomatology comes from studies of depression and anxiety disorders, I will focus principally on these conditions.

I have shown (1986) that headaches, dizziness, and lack of energy form a symptom cluster in ancient Chinese society and in contemporary Taiwan and China which is the core of neurasthenic illness behavior associated with mixed depressive and anxiety disorders. These symptoms have been culturally salient for centuries in Chinese society and still today carry considerable cultural meaning. Indeed, Chinese patients appear to selectively perceive, label, and communicate these symptoms out of the diffuse complaints of psychophysiological arousal and the multiform somatic effects of stress. The association of a culturally salient somatic language of complaints with depression and/or anxiety disorders has also been recorded for clinical samples in Saudi Arabia (Racy 1980), Iraq (Baz-

zoui 1970), Benin (Binitie 1975), Peru (Mezzich and Rabb 1980), India (Teja et al. 1971; Sethi et al. 1973), and Hong Kong (Cheung et al. 1981), and among depressed patients in many non-Western cultures (Marsella 1979).

Data from the WHO's cross-cultural study of depression in clinical research centers in Montreal, Teheran, Basel, Nagasaki, and Tokyo disclose both similarities and differences in symptomatology (Sartorius et al. 1983). Sadness, joylessness, anxiety, tension, lack of energy, decreased interest and concentration, and feelings of inadequacy and worthlessness were found in three-fourths to all of the depressed patients at each center. One-third had hypochondriacal ideas, and 40 percent had some somatic complaints, obsessions, and phobias. More personality disorders were detected in Western centers, where concepts of such disorders may fit the Western diagnostic categories better, than in non-Western ones. Psychomotor agitation was more frequent in Teheran and symptoms of self-reproach higher in Europe. Marsella et al. (1985) reflect on their participation in this project and conclude the WHO comparison was not organized to pick up more center-specific symptoms, and it didn't.

Field (1958), working among the Ashanti in West Africa, in local healing shrines, found that anxiety was commonly expressed as self-accusation or fears of witchcraft. Studies in Nigerian society report that generalized anxiety disorders among Yoruba are associated with three clusters of primary symptoms—worries, dreams of witchcraft, and bodily complaints (Collis 1966; Anumonge 1970; Jegede 1978). Each of these takes a form appropriate in Yoruba culture. Predominant worries expressed by patients were those associated with procreation and maintenance of a large family. Lambo (1962), himself a Yoruba psychiatrist, long ago noted the close correlation between "morbid fear of bewitchment" and "acute anxiety states in Africa."

The combination of universal and culture-specific symptoms of depressive and anxiety disorders had been reported for Iranians (Good et al. 1985), Chinese (Kleinman and Kleinman 1985), and American Indians (Manson et al. 1985). Research on American Indians has shown that certain signs that might be taken as evidence of severe depression in other groups are normative for members of this ethnic group, including "prolonged" mourning, "flat affect," auditory hallucinations of spirit beings, and visual hallucinations of the recently dead (O'Nell in press).

The research literature also points out that feelings of guilt are much less commonly associated with depression in the non-Western world than in the West. H. B. M. Murphy (1982) attributed guilt to the influence of the Judeo-Christian heritage, including its effects on Islam. Melancholia, the traditional term for depressive disorder in the West, acquired this moral meaning from *acedia,* a religious expression of depression (Jackson 1985). But the literature purporting to demonstrate low frequency and severity of guilt in the Third World is flawed by the absence of consistent definitions, operationalized criteria, and methods of assessment. This is because many writers *assume* that guilt is a sign of higher levels of personality functioning—stronger egos, more intense superego development, higher differentiation—on the basis of outmoded and unsubstantiated psychoanalytic and evolutionary schemes. Weiss and Kleinman (in press) note that in spite of substantial findings of guilt in India (Venkoba Rao 1973; Teja et al. 1971; Ansari 1969), discussions in the Indian literature minimize its significance or interpret it as milder or of a different kind. For example, Venkoba Rao (1973) distinguished karmic guilt (concerned with deeds in a previous life) from present guilt. He felt that karmic guilt might actually protect against the other type.

Sartorius et al. (1983) did not find major differences in guilt between depressive patients in the West and Japan. Escobar and his co-workers (1983), in keeping with H. B. M. Murphy's (1982) hypothesis, found Christian patients in Colombia to have the same degree of guilt in the course of depression as found in depressed patients in North America. I (1986) discerned less guilt among depressives in China than is reported from the West, and noted that low self-esteem was also less common. I reviewed the work of Cheung and her colleagues (1981) in Hong Kong suggesting no major difference in guilt there and in the West, and wondered if her subjects are Christians or otherwise acculturated to Western values in that highly Westernized community. Since there are few studies that systematically look for other idioms of expressing guilt in the non-Western world, the finding of low preoccupation with guilt could be an artifact of reporting and of the research methodology.

For example, Field (1958) noted that the expression of guilt among her Ashanti informants occurred only in an idiom of witchcraft. Levy (1973), studying Tahitians, demonstrated in a subtle ethnographic and psychological study that shame and guilt were not discrete feelings, but intermixed. Lutz (1985), Rosaldo (1980), and other psychological anthropologists have studied individuals in small-scale preliterate societies whose concepts of self and emotions are radically different than in the West. These anthropologists repeatedly show that different meanings of guilt, sadness, and other emotions significantly influence the experience of those emotions (Lutz and White 1986). Guilt understood and experienced as existential suffering, or as loss of face, or as self-accusation of witchcraft is not the same emotional phenomenon. Thus, anthropologists hold that simple dichotomies between high and low levels of guilt or its presence and absence in very different societies distort a much more complex picture cross-culturally.

Suicide has also been said to be less common among depressed patients in the Third World (Headley, ed., 1983); it probably is, with some notable exceptions like Japan, less common in non-Western societies generally (La Fontaine 1975). But since most cases in developing societies probably go unrecorded, and since there is great variation across rural/urban, time, and ethnic boundaries, the cross-cultural epidemiology of suicide is anything but clear. Indeed, the low prevalence of suicide has been explained as the result of the alleged low level of guilt—a decidedly weak foundation.

I (1982) found less suicide among Chinese depressives in Hunan, but explained this finding by suggesting that somatization protects against this and other negative sequelae of a more intrapsychic, existential experience of depression. This explanation needs to be weighed against a history of salience of suicide in Chinese culture (Hsieh and Spence 1982). Mezzich and Raab (1980) report lower tendency toward suicide among depressed Peruvians than among matched North American depressives. They attribute this difference to strong teaching by the Catholic Church against suicide. Venkoba Rao points out several cultural factors in India that may protect against suicide. These include the emphasis on family obligations over individual rights, the legitimation of suicide, at least historically, under ritual conditions (*sati*), and the concept of *karma* (which would lead individuals to avoid suicide lest they be reborn in a less desirable state).

Attempted suicide in a number of Asian and Middle Eastern societies, as in North America, is higher among women than among men. But, unlike North America, completed suicides also appear to me more common among women in these societies (Headley, ed., 1983). Reasons for suicide and means of carrying it out vary greatly, but there is significant evidence that relative powerlessness, absence of alternative means of communicating despair, traditional use of suicide as a sanctioned idiom of distress, and its place in cultural mythology make particular categories of women (generally the young but in certain cultures the elderly too) more likely, perhaps driven, to take this last alternative.

There is also evidence that social change contributes to fluctuating suicide rates. For example, suicide rates in various of the Pacific Island cultures are increasing rapidly as those societies experience the problems of modernization. Also a recent report from Sri Lanka reports that the suicide rate tripled between 1955 and 1974, when it was highest among the Tamil ethnic minority in the northeast (Kearney and Miller 1985). The authors explain the increase as the result of rapid population growth, increased competition for education and employment, and the breakdown of a stable society, placing great pressure especially on Tamils. It is unclear from their report whether these rates are associated with increased depression, or what has happened during the current era of civil war. Poverty, economic failure, and exam failure are other important social factors contributing to suicide around the globe. Much of the anthropological work on suicide has indicated that it may (and often does) occur in individuals without mental illness who are under great social pressure or for whom it is one of a very few culturally authorized expressions of severe distress (La Fontaine 1975).

The review of the findings of the WHO's cross-cultural comparison of schizophrenia, as noted earlier, also discloses important differences in the mode of onset and symptoms of schizophrenia. Barrett (in press), furthermore, offers evidence that the sense of a split or divided self that is so strongly associated with both professional and lay discourses on schizophrenia in the West may emerge as salient because of the Western conception of the person as a bounded individual self. Patients in the West report feeling a split in personality. This aspect of schizophrenia appears to be less central to the experience of the disorder in China and other non-Western societies. In those societies, the expression of a feeling of split personality is as uncommon as is the mythology of a self divided against itself.[6]

Thus, we can conclude that the symptomatology of mental disorders differs very substantially cross-culturally. For schizophrenia, major depressive disorder, and anxiety disorders there are also significant uniformities. If we lump together with these mental illnesses culture-bound disorders and trance-possession and other dissociative psychoses (occurring outside ritually prescribed settings), then the variation in the symptoms of mental illness is much greater. Thus, the research literature on symptomatology points to the same pattern of cross-cultural findings as do the other aspects of mental illness we have reviewed: there are certain significant similarities and many very significant differences.[7]

ILLNESS BEHAVIOR

Few researchers have actually compared the illness behavior—i.e., meaningful experience of symptoms and patterns of coping and help seeking—of appropriately matched samples of depressed or anxious patients in different societies. Research does disclose, however, greatly different patterns of help seeking for mental illness in different societies and ethnic groups (Lin et al. 1978; Lin, Kleinman and Lin 1982). These studies find, for example, that North American Indian, Asian, and Caucasian ethnic patients follow distinctive pathways to the mental health center, arrive there at very different points in the course of illness, and experience greatly divergent types of involvement of their family members. Response to psychiatric treatment also differs. Lin et al. (1986) review the literature demonstrating distinctive pharmacokinetic and pharmacodynamic responses to tricyclic antidepressants among East Asian and Caucasian groups, disclosing different physiological responses to treatment in these ethnic groups. That is to say, biology-culture interactions are important in treatment, and are probably also significant in perception of symptoms (cf. Hoosain 1986).

Perhaps the best way to get at cultural influences on illness perception and experience in mental illnesses like depressive and anxiety disorders is to analyze those culture-bound syndromes that bear a family resemblance to these disorders, because certain of these syndromes have been described in considerable detail. Manson et al. (1985) disclose that among Hopi one culture-specific syndrome overlaps extensively with depressive symptomatology, whereas several others that appear to overlap actually are distinctive. Johnson and Johnson (1965) discovered among the Dakota Sioux a syndrome called *towatl ye sni* (or "totally discouraged"). This syndrome cut across various Western categories of psychopathology, but struck the authors as especially close to depression. Yet the beliefs and behaviors labeled *towatl ye sni* were also strongly culturally shaped and included feelings of deprivation, the experience of one's thoughts traveling to the dwelling place of dead relatives, an orientation to the past as the best time, willing death to become nearer to the dead, and preoccupations with ghosts and spirits.

Prince and Tcheng-Laroche (1987) show that *taijinkyofusho* among Japanese can be glossed as a phobia of interpersonal relations but is different from DSM-III social phobia inasmuch as patients feel guilty about embarrassing others with their behavior (e.g., blushing, unpleasant body odor, stuttering) rather than fearful of others' criticisms. In *taijinkyofusho* the emphasis is on the fear of discomfiting others through their sense of shame, a fear thoroughly in concert with Japanese cultural sensibilities but quite foreign to North American fears. This experience suggests that psychiatric classifications of phobias are unsufficient as presently cast to model a major illness experience in Japanese society. While similarities have been found between agoraphobia and one type of neurasthenia in Japan, *shinkeishitsu* associated with obsessions and phobias, there are also divergences. Agoraphobia in North America is found predominantly in women, *shinkeishitsu* in men. Western sufferers are afraid of being alone in public; Japanese patients avoid contact with others (least with intimates or strangers, most with acquaintances). The illness behavior of the Japanese is best described as "anthropophobic."

Littlewood and Lipsedge (1987) argue that anorexia nervosa might be regarded as a culture-specific illness behavior in the West, at times associated with personality disorder, at other times part of a constellation of psychiatric depression with somatic delusions. These British psychiatrists point out anorexia nervosa is not highly prevalent outside the West, with the exception of the educated class of industrialized societies like Japan who have been strongly influenced by Western aesthetic standards which value extreme slimness and which view strict dieting as an emblem of moral discipline. The historian Caroline Walker Bynum (in press), who traces the lineaments of anorexia to various Christian saints, concludes:

> The cultures within which female non-eating occurs and achieves significance as a form of sanctity or empowerment are all cultures which, on the one hand, associate the female with body and sexuality and, on the other, expect females to suffer and to serve (especially to offer food to) others.

Anorectic women in medieval Italy and modern Portugal participate, she avers, not in behavior whose cause is physiological, but in cultures which share similar perceptions of women's roles and symbolism of being female. Historical analysis does not lend support, furthermore, to psychodynamic interpretations of the nature of mother-daughter conflict or patriarchal control as the basis for anorectic behavior. The "starving disease" epidemic of our time, she shows, is also more than the fight among a male-dominated culture and a resisting female subculture for control of the bodies of adolescent girls that feminist psychologists have made it out to be. The symbolic meaning in modern Portuguese peasant society and medieval Italy of noneating as purity through suffering that brings women, who are otherwise symbolically polluting, closer to God, Bynum regards as the most availing explanation for anorexia in those societies. The noneating living, like the consecrated incorrupt dead, "symbolize restraint or purity that harnesses and channels, but does not destroy, fertility" (see also Bell 1985; Pina-Cabral 1986). Brian Turner (1985, pp. 180–201), a sociologist who has canvassed the social historical significance of bodily practices in the West, links the cultural analysis of anorexia with the political and economic forces in contemporary capitalism's consumer society to show that this is a disorder whose sign—slimness—is promoted by food and drug and other industries for which this bodily product of hedonism and narcissism holds powerful commercial significance.

What can be generalized from these and many, many other accounts is that illness behavior is always strongly shaped by culture even when the associated disease processes can be diagnosed with an international nosology. Whatever the causes of anorexia, which are likely to be multiple and interactive, the experience of anorexia and other chronic disorders is inseparable from their cultural context.

COURSE AND OUTCOME

A final aspect of illness behavior, but one deserving special attention, is course and outcome of disorder. Here the literature is particularly murky. The example of better outcome for schizophrenia in less developed societies is a beam of clear light. One of the more interesting (and better-supported) hypotheses to explain this finding is Waxler's (1977) theory that where schizophrenia is popularly viewed as an acute problem and patients suffering from it are accordingly expected to recover just like those who suffer from other acute disorders, there the cultural message is reinforced by familial and community responses to the patient that encourage normalization and discourage acceptance of a disabled role. In this view, chronicity is in large measure the result of social messages and interpersonal reactions to the patient that impede the patient's sense of self-control and undermine his optimism and its psychophysiological effects. Other factors such as the economics of disability, the investment of certain mental health programs in maintaining patients in long-term patient roles, and the very high demands that industrialized societies make on former patients in the absence of effective supports have also been implicated as obstacles to better outcome from schizophrenia (Lin and Kleinman in press; Warner 1985; Estroff 1981; Waxler 1977). The medical profession may inadvertently abet these forces, since in North American and Western European society its members have been trained to treat schizophrenic patients with the expectation that there is little that can be done to help them recover from a disorder that until recently was regarded as progressively disabling. In fact, more recent long-term research shows that even in the West, the course of many schizophrenic patients is much more hopeful than the professional stereotype (see Bleuler 1978; Harding et al. 1987; Alanen et al. 1986).

If we take suicide as an outcome, then somatized illness experience in major depressive disorder in the Third World would have a better outcome than psychologized depression in the West, inasmuch as there is less suicide among the former group. But given what has already been said about the relationship of guilt and low self-esteem to depression, and taking into account the tendency toward lower suicide rates generally in much of the nonindustrialized world, it is difficult to be certain if somatization per se protects against suicide. However, because of the findings for schizophrenia in developing societies, it is important that research be undertaken to compare the course of depressive and anxiety disorders in Western and non-Western societies. A leading hypothesis should be that somatized depression may have an easier course and better outcome than psychologized depression, owing to less morbid preoccupation with, and negative expectation in, the personal experience of the illness.

Overall, then, chronicity and disability may be at least partially separable from physiological disease processes and their causes. Just as there is no one-to-one correlation of symptom to pathology, there are a variety of courses for the same disorder. The meanings of the illness experience and the social context of the sick person together with his biography also shape these outcomes (Osterweis et al., eds., 1987). It is unlikely that all or even most non-Western settings encourage processes of adaptation and rehabilitation, but clearly contemporary industrialized societies place certain categories of the sick under constraints that foster chronicity and disability. This is a topic that is likely to receive much greater attention in future cross-cultural research.

NOTES

1. The genetic theory of schizophrenia, which up until several years ago seemed well established, is now in considerable disarray. Inheritance has not been proved (see Barnes 1987a). There is evidence of abnormalities in dopamine receptors in key regions of the brain. The response of patients to antipsychotic drugs also points to dopamine neurotransmission as disordered. But other biological findings are controversial (e.g., alleged altered brain blood flow and larger ventricles). There is still, after more than 30 years of intensive biological investigation, no clear-cut understanding of the biology of schizophrenia (Haracz 1982; Lewontin, Kamin and Rose 1984; Barrett in press). This does not deter psychiatrists and those who write the advertisements for drug companies from asserting without any hesitation that schizophrenia is a biologically based disorder. This belief is a central tenet of professional orthodoxy.

   The most convincing research on the genetics of a mental illness comes from Egeland et al. (1987), who studied bipolar (manic-depressive) disorder, which has a 0.5 to 1 percent prevalence rate in the West, among Old Order Amish in the U.S. They established that a gene or chromosome 11 is associated with dominant inheritance. But there is only partial "penetration," meaning that environ-

mental factors are still essential in the expression of the genetic vulnerability. Other research suggests different genetic factors in other populations in which bipolar disease has been studied.

2. The topic of colonial impediments to accurate psychiatric findings from India and Africa in the nineteenth and early twentieth centuries is reviewed in Weiss and Kleinman (in press).

3. The most recent Cuban migration to the U.S. did include patients with mental illness who were forced to depart for Florida. But this is not true of Vietnamese, Cambodian, Laotian, or South American refugee groups.

4. Showalter (1985) reviews evidence that the finding of greater rates of neurotic disorder among women seems to have been true as well of women in England during much of the nineteenth and twentieth centuries. Although her historical analysis indicates it affected women in all social classes, there is no epidemiological data to settle the issue.

5. This section of the chapter includes materials modified from a report of an NIHM contract for a Review of Cross-Cultural Studies of Depressive and Anxiety Disorders prepared by the author and his colleagues, Byron Good and Peter Guarnaccia, in May 1986.

6. One of the more impressive demonstrations of cultural differences in symptomatology of mental illness is the reports of Jilek-Aall et al. (1978) of the symptom patterns of Russian Doukhobor, Coast Salish Indian, and Mennonite patients, whom they treated in the Fraser Valley of British Columbia, Canada. These cross-cultural psychiatrists found "that while sexes could to some extent be differentiated on the basis of clinical symptoms, cultural factors came out as the more important differentiating criteria of symptom formation." For example, for the Doukhobor psychiatric patients, violent acts against property and relatively very paranoid delusions concerning legal authority and God or Devil were common. Prolonged mourning reactions, suicide attempts, identity confusion, marital maladjustment, and hallucinations of supernatural beings differentiated Canadian Indian patients from the other two ethnic groups; whereas gastrointestinal symptoms, hypochrondriasis, apathy, feelings of inadequacy and self-depreciation, guilt and fear of rejection or punishment by God, shame, sexual dysfunction, and general and phobic anxiety set Mennonite patients apart.

7. In a long-term study of manic-depressive disorder among Old Order Amish in Pennsylvania, Egeland (1986) describes how the biological bases of the disorder, group norms, and social conditions combine to form a pattern of expressing complaints that discloses just such uniformities and differences.

REFERENCES

Alanen, Y. O., et al. 1986. Toward Need-Specific Treatment of Schizophrenic Psychoses. New York: Springer Verlag.

Ansari, S. A. 1969. Symptomatology of Indian depressives. Transactions of the All India Institute of Mental Health 9:1–18.

Anumonge, A. 1979. Outpatient psychiatry in a Nigerian University general hospital. Social Psychiatry 5:96–99.

Barrett, R. in press. Schizophrenia and personhood. Medical Anthropology Quarterly.

Barzun, J. 1983. A Stroll with William James. Chicago: University of Chicago Press.

Bazzoui, W. 1970. Affective disorders in Iraq. British Journal of Psychiatry 117:195–203.

Beiser, M. 1958. A study of depression among traditional Africans, urban North Americans, and Southeast Asian Refugees. In Culture and Depression. A. Kleinman and B. Good, eds. Berkeley: University of California Press.

Beiser, M., and J. Fleming. 1986. Measuring psychiatric disorder among Southeast Asian refugees. Psychological Medicine 16:627–639.

Bell, R. 1985. Holy Anorexia. Chicago: University of Chicago Press.

Binitie, A. 1975. A factor-analytical study of depression across African and European cultures. British Journal of Psychiatry 127:559–563.

Blazer, D., et al. 1985. Psychiatric disorders: a rural/urban comparison. Archives of General Psychiatry 41:971–978.

Bleuler, M. 1978. The Schizophrenic Disorders: Long-Term Patient and Family Studies. New Haven, CT: Yale University Press.

Book, J. A., et al. 1978. Schizophrenia in a North Swedish geographical isolate 1900–1977. Clinical Genetics 14:373–394.

Boyd, J., and M. Weissman. 1981. Epidemiology of affective disorders. Archives of General Psychiatry 38:1039–1046.

Brown, G., and T. Harris. 1978. The Social Origins of Depression. New York: Free Press.

Bynum, C. W. in press. Holy anorexia in modern Portugal. Culture, Medicine, and Psychiatry.

Carpenter, W., T. McGlashen, and J. Strauss. 1977. The treatment of acute schizophrenia without drugs. American Journal of Psychiatry 134:14–20.

Carr, J., and P. Vitaliano. 1976. The Great Universe of Kota: Change and Mental Disorder in an Indian Village. Berkeley: University of California Press.

Cheung, F., et al. 1981. Somatization among Chinese depressives in general practices. International Journal of Psychiatry in Medicine 10:361–374.

Collis, R. J. M. 1966. Physical health and psychiatric disorders in Nigeria. Transactions of the American Philosophical Society New Series 56(4):1–45.

Escobar, J., et al. 1983. Depressive symptomatology in North and South American patients. American Journal of Psychiatry 140:47–51.

Estroff, S. 1981. Making It Crazy. Berkeley: University of California Press.

Field, M. D. 1958. Search for Security: An Ethno-Psychiatric Study in Rural Ghana. London: Faber & Faber.

Finkler, K. 1985. Symptomatic differences between the sexes in rural Mexico. Culture, Medicine, and Psychiatry 9:27–58.

Fortes, M., and D. Y. Mayer. 1969. Psychosis and social change among the Tallensi of Northern Ghana. In Psychiatry in a Changing Society. S. H. Foukes and G. S. Prince, eds. London: Tavistock.

Gaines, A., and P. Farmer. 1986. Visible saints: Social cynosures and dysphoria in the Mediterranean tradition. Culture, Medicine, and Psychiatry 10:295–330.

Good, B., et al. 1982. Toward a meaning-centered analysis of popular illness categories. In Cultural Conceptions of Mental Health and Therapy. A. Marsella and G. White, eds. Dordrecht, Holland: D. Reidel.

Good, B., and A. Kleinman. 1985. Culture and anxiety. In Anxiety and the Anxiety Disorders. J. P. Maser and A. H. Turns, eds. Hillsdale, NJ: Lawrence Erlbaum.

Good, M., J. D. Good, and R. Moradi. 1985. The interpretation of Iranian depressive illness. In Culture and Depression. B. Good and A. Kleinman, eds., Berkeley: University of California Press.

Gould, Stephen J. 1987. Animals and us. New York Review of Books 34(11):20–25.

Harding, C. M., et al. 1987. The Vermont longitudinal study of patients with severe mental illness. Parts 1 and 2. American Journal of Psychiatry 144:718–726, 727–735.

Headley, L. A., ed. 1983. Suicide in Asia and the Near East. Berkeley: University of California Press.

Heath, D. 1986. Drinking and drunkenness in transcultural perspective. Parts 1 and 2. Transcultural Psychiatry Research Review 23.

Hossain, R. 1986. Perception. In The Psychology of the Chinese People. M. Bond, ed. Hong Kong: Oxford University Press.

Hsieh, A., and J. Spence. 1982. Suicide and the family in premodern China. In Normal and Abnormal Behavior in Chinese Culture. T. Y. Lin and A. Kleinman, eds. Dordrecht, Holland: D. Reidel.

Jackson, S. 1985. Acedia: The sin and its relationship to sorrow and melancholia. In Culture and Depression. A Kleinman and B. Good, eds. Berkeley: University of California Press.

Jegede, R. O. 1978. Outpatient psychiatry in an urban clinic in a developing country. Social Psychiatry 13:93–98.

Johnson, D., and C. Johnson. 1965. Totally discouraged: A depressive syndrome of the Dakota Sioux. Transcultural Psychiatry Research Review 2:141–143.

Jones, I., and D. Horne. 1973. Diagnosis of psychiatric illness among tribal aborigines. Medical Journal of Australia 1:345–349.

Kearney, R., and B. Miller. 1985. The spiral of suicide and social change in Sri Lanka. Journal of Asian Studies 45:81–101.

Kirmayer, L. 1984. Culture, affect, and somatization. Parts 1 and 2. Transcultural Psychiatry Research Review 21(3): 159–188, 237–262.

Kitaro, N. 1970. Fundamental Problems of Philosophy: The World of Action and the Dialictical World. D. A. Dilworth, trans. Tokyo: Sophia University.

Kleinman, A. 1980. Patients and Healers in the Context of Culture. Berkeley: University of California Press.

Kleinman, A. 1982. Neurasthenia and depression. Culture, Medicine, and Psychiatry 6(2):117–190.

Kleinman, A. 1986. Social Origins of Distress and Disease: Depression, Neurasthenia and Pain in Modern China. New Haven, CT: Yale University Press.

Kleinman, A., and J. Kleinman. 1985. Somatization. *In* Culture and Depression. B. Good and A. Kleinman, eds. Berkeley: University of California Press.

LaFontaine, J. 1975. Anthropology. *In* A Handbook for the Study of Suicide. S. Perlin, ed. New York: Oxford University Press.

Lambo, T. 1962. Malignant anxiety. Journal of Mental Science 108:256–264.

Langness, L. L. 1965. Hysterical psychosis in the New Guinea highlands: A Bena Bena example. Psychiatry 28:259–277.

Leighton, A., et al. 1963. The Character of Danger: Psychiatric Symptoms in Selected Communities, Vol. II. New York: Basic Books.

Leighton, A., et al. 1963. Psychiatric Disorder Among the Yoruba. Ithaca, NY: Cornell University Press.

Levy, R. 1973. Tahitians: Mind and Experience in the Society Islands. Chicago: University of Chicago Press.

Lewis, I. S. 1971. Ecstatic Religion: An Anthropological Study of Spirit Possession and Shamanism. Harmoundsworth, England: Penguin.

Lin, K. M.., and A. Kleinman. 1981. Recent development of psychiatric epidemiology in China. Culture, Medicine, and Psychiatry 5:135–143.

Lin, K. M., and A. Kleinman. in press. Psychopathology and clinical course of schizophrenia: A cross-cultural perspective. Schizophrenia Bulletin.

Lin, K. M., A. Kleinman, and T. Y. Lin. 1982. Overview of mental disorders in Chinese culture. *In* Normal and Abnormal Behavior in Chinese Culture. A. Kleinman and T. Y. Lin, eds. Dordrecht, Holland: D. Reidel.

Lin, N., et al. 1985. Modeling the effects of social support. *In* Social Support, Life Events and Depression. N. Lin et al. eds. New York: Academic Press.

Lin, T. Y., et al. 1969. Mental disorders in Taiwan 15 years later. *In* Mental Health in Asia and the Pacific. W. Caudell and T. Y. Lin, eds. Honolulu: East West Center Press.

Lin, T. Y., et al. 1978. Ethnicity and patterns of help-seeking. Culture, Medicine, and Psychiatry 2:3–14.

Lin, T. Y., and D. Lin. 1982. Alcoholism among the Chinese. Culture, Medicine, Psychiatry 6:109–116.

Littlewood, R., and M. Lipsedge. 1987. The butterfly and the serpent: Culture, psychopathology and biomedicine. Culture, Medicine, and Psychiatry 11:289–336.

Lock, M. 1986. Ambiguities of aging: Japanese experience and perception of menopause. Culture, Medicine, and Psychiatry 10:23–46.

Lock, M. 1987. Protests of a good wife and wise mother: Somatization and medicalization in modern Japan. *In* Health and Medical Care in Japan. M. Lock and E. Norbeck, eds. Honolulu: University of Hawaii Press.

Lutz, C. 1985. Depression and the translation of emotional worlds. *In* Culture and Depression. A. Kleinman and B. Good, eds. Berkeley: University of California Press.

Lutz, C., and G. White. 1986. The anthropology of emotions. Annual Review of Anthropology 15:405–436.

Manschreck, T. 1978. Towards an explanation of recent trends in suicide in Western Samoa. Man 22(2):305–330.

Manson, S., et al. 1985. The depressive experience in American India communities. *In* Culture and Depression. B.

Good and A. Kleinman, eds. Berkeley: University of California Press.

Marsella, A. 1979. Depressive experience and disorder across cultures. *In* Handbook of Cross-Cultural Psychology Volume 6. H. Triandis and J. Draguns, eds. Boston: Allyn & Bacon.

Marsella, A., et al. 1985. Cross-cultural studies of depressive disorders. *In* Culture and Depression. A. Kleinman and B. Good, eds. Berkeley: University of California Press.

Mezzich, J., and E. Raab. 1980. Depressive symptomatology across the Americas. Archives of General Psychiatry 37:818–823.

Murphy, H. B. M. 1982. Comparative Psychiatry: The International and Intercultural Distribution of Mental Illness. New York: Springer-Verlag.

Murphy, J. 1982. Cultural shaping and mental disorders. *In* Deviance and Mental Illness. W. R. Gove, ed. Beverly Hills: Sage.

Myers, J. K., et al. 1984. Six-month prevalence of psychiatric disorders in three communities. Archives of General Psychiatry 41:959–967.

O'Nell, T. in press. Psychiatric investigations among American Indians and Alaska natives: a critical review. Culture, Medicine, and Psychiatry.

Orley, J., and J. Wing. 1979. Psychiatric disorders in two African villages. Archives of General Psychiatry 36: 513–520.

Osterweis, M., et al., eds. 1987. Pain and Disability. Washington, DC: National Academy Press.

Pina-Cabral, J. 1986. Sons of Adam, Daughters of Eve: The Peasant Worldview of the Alto Minho. London: Oxford University Press.

Prince, R. 1968. Changing picture of depressive syndromes in Africa. Canadian Journal of African Studies 1:177–192.

Prince, R., and F. Tcheng-Laroche. 1987. Culture-bound syndromes and international classifications of disease. Culture, Medicine, and Psychiatry 11(1):3–20.

Racy, J. 1980. Somatization in Saudi women. British Journal of Psychiatry 137:212–216.

Rao, A. V., 1973. Depressive illness and guilt in Indian culture. Indian Journal of Psychiatry 26:301–311.

Robins, L. N., et al. 1984. Lifetime prevalance of specific psychiatric disorders in three communities. Archives of General Psychiatry 41:949–958.

Rosaldo, M. 1980. Knowledge and Passion: Ilongot Notions of Self and Social Life. London: Cambridge University Press.

Sartorius, N., and A. Jablensky. 1976. Transcultural studies of schizophrenia. WHO Chronicle 30:481–485.

Sartorius, N., et al. 1983. Depressive Disorders in Different Cultures. Geneva: WHO.

Sethi, B. B., et al. 1973. Depression in India. Journal of Social and Biological Structures 9(4):345–352.

Sikanerty, R., and W. W. Eaton. 1984. Prevalence of schizophrenia in the Labali district of Ghana. Acta Psychiatrica Scandinavica 6:156–161.

Simons, R., and C. Hughes, eds. 1985. The Culture-Bound Syndromes. Dordrecht, Holland: D. Reidel.

Stevens, J. 1984. Brief psychosis: Do they contribute to the good prognosis and equal prevalence of schizophrenia in

developing societies? British Journal of Psychiatry 151:
393–396.

Teja, J. S., et al. 1971. Depression across cultures. British Journal of Psychiatry 119:253–260.

Torrey, E. F. 1980. Schizophrenia and Civilization. New York: Jason Aronson.

Torrey, E. F., et al. 1984. Endemic psychosis in western Ireland. American Journal of Psychiatry 141:966–969.

Turner, B. 1985. The Body and Society. Oxford: Basil Blackwell.

Warner, R. 1985. Recovery from Schizophrenia: Psychiatry and Social Economy. New York: Routledge and Kegan Paul.

Waxler, N. 1977. Is outcome for schizophrenia better in non-industrialized societies. Journal of Nervous and Mental Disease 167:144–158.

Weiss, M., and A. Kleinman. in press. Depression in cross-cultural perspective. In Contributions of Cross-Cultural Psychology to International Mental Health. P. Dasein et al., eds. New York: Plenum.

 22

The Epidemiology of a Folk Illness: Susto in Hispanic America

Arthur J. Rubel

This is a classic in the field of medical anthropology, and it represents the initial data collection of what became a larger and very significant study in the epidemiology of a folk illness called susto, *usually translated as "soul loss" or "magical fright." The important book from this study (the collaboration of a medical anthropologist, a psychological anthropologist, and a physician) is called* Susto: A Folk Illness *(Rubel, O'Neil, and Collado-Ardon 1984). This is a folk illness because it does not fit into the categorization system of biomedicine or psychiatry (the* DSM*). An epidemiological study of a folk illness involves the description of its distribution in regard to time, place, and person. Analysis of these data allows the researcher to make hypotheses about the causation of the illness. The symptom complex of* susto *reminds many students of "depression"—victims who have lost their souls feel tired, listless, have trouble sleeping, don't care about their appearance, have little appetite, and so forth. But the cultural meanings of* susto *are very different from what North Americans would call depression. The cultural interpretations of the cause of* susto, *in fact, differ for people of Indian descent and mainstream others of mixed descent (mestizos). You will notice that the Indian etiological theory is closely linked to the idea of* animism *(that all living things have souls). People get sick when their souls become separated from their bodies.*

In this selection, Arthur Rubel introduces us to the concept of stress, a concept that has much relevance to medical anthropology (Selye 1976). He also presents a fascinating model of the individual as a "linked open system" of physical, social, and psychological aspects that are clearly interconnected in the context of stress and support. The larger study is designed as a retrospective case-control study—a comparison of the life situations of people who have suffered from susto *and matched pairs who have not had the illness. Over the course of the longer study, it became possible to also do a prospective case-control study by following cases and controls over a ten-year period; one of the most surprising findings from this work was that people who had suffered from* susto *had a much greater likelihood of dying over this time period. This selection considers the issue of the sick role and its associated claims for a "time out" from regular responsibilities in the context of difficult-to-meet social demands (this is something students may know from personal experience).*

As you read this selection, consider these questions:

- *What are the rights and responsibilities of the sick role? Why might this be a good thing? How might the sick role be abused, and what happens to a person who is suspected of not really being sick?*

- *Why are there ethnic differences in the etiological explanations of* susto *between Indians and non-Indians?*
- *How is the treatment of* susto *different, for example, from the treatment of depression in U.S. society? How do the two conditions differ in regard to the blaming-the-victim question?*

- *What is the role of the family in the cure? How might this fit with Lévi-Strauss's analysis (selection 14) of the role of belief in healing?*
- *What is epidemiological about this research?*

This exploratory article seeks to assess the extent to which folk illness may be subjected to epidemiological studies, as are other illnesses. It is a working assumption of this paper that, in general, folk-illness phenomena are indeed amenable to such investigation if one is aware of special methodological problems which are concomitants of such research. A presentation of some of these general problems is followed by an examination of the Hispanic-American folk illness which I refer to as *susto.*

METHODOLOGICAL PROBLEMS

A work which has as its announced goal the description, distribution, and etiology of folk illness faces a number of methodological problems. Not the least of these is an acceptable definition of folk illness. In these pages "illness" refers to syndromes from which members of a particular group claim to suffer and for which their culture provides an etiology, diagnosis, preventive measures, and regimens of healing. I apply the prefix "folk" to those illnesses of which orthodox Western medicine professes neither understanding nor competence—a definition which, although somewhat cumbersome, has the value of subsuming a number of seemingly bizarre syndromes which are reported in anthropological, medical, and psychiatric literature from many areas of the world.

Another problem of basic importance is that, when modern epidemiologists or research-oriented physicians engage in systematic research on folk health phenomena, they find it difficult to agree with the population that a health problem indeed exists; furthermore, they tend to disagree with their patients on even the most fundamental premises about health and illness. The two groups perceive the same condition from premises which are fundamentally divergent. The problem is compounded by the fact that the health professional must elicit medical history and descriptions of the discomfort from people who hold an opposing point of view.

In recent years anthropologists have elucidated the underlying logic whereby a number of folk peoples understand illness, diagnosis, and healing, e.g., the work of Frake (1961) among the Subanun, of Metzger and Williams (1963) on the Tzeltal, and of Rubel (1960) among Mexican-Americans. These are steps along the way, but such studies do not inform us which components of the population do in fact become ill, nor under what circumstances illness occurs, nor what courses the illness follows when it does manifest itself. Investigations of folk illness are presently at a stage where we can assert with some degree of confidence only that certain syndromes appear to be confined to particular cultural or linguistic groups, e.g., Algonkians, Eskimos, or Mexican-Americans, and do not appear among others. That is to say, if one may divide the study of folk illness into two complementary areas of achievement—illness as a culture complex and the epidemiology of folk illness—then I submit that the first of these represents our present state of knowledge.

Monographs, articles, and more casual reports on exotic cultures abound with allusions to certain seemingly bizarre notions about illness. Sometimes these descriptive writings discuss the folk concept in some detail, but more often they do not. Often such reports titillate the reader by providing a few clinical case histories which reflect cultural beliefs about health and illness, but only in rare instances is one provided detailed descriptions about an individual patient's medical history, his or her response to the onset of the folk illness, or close observations of the course which the illness follows. Even more rarely does the reader encounter an extensive corpus of cases assembled either from published sources or from field observations.

The large collections of library data on the basis of which Parker (1960) and Teicher (1960) discuss the folk illness known as *wiitigo* are extremely valuable. The scrupulous attention paid by these scholars to the intricacies of a folk illness points up some of the more pressing problems faced by researchers who utilize library resources to derive epidemiological inferences as to causality. For example, the case materials on the *wiitigo* illness are reported by such diverse observers as anthropologists, explorers, missionaries, trappers, and Indians. Moreover, in these as in other instances, the descriptive reports often span years or even centuries of time and define the population involved in only the grossest terms. In the absence of precise chronological, social, or cultural parameters it is hazardous to attempt to infer rates of prevalence or incidence of a folk illness, much less the relationships which obtain between these rates and such demographic variables as age, sex, or marital status. Yet it is precisely from such inferences and associations that we may hope to gain an understanding of the nature of folk illness.

The methodical field worker who seeks cases of folk illness within a precisely delimited locale and time span is confronted by the problem of defining beforehand what it is that he seeks. Oftentimes, though the symptoms of presumed patients remain constant from place to place, the labels by which a disability is identified vary considerably. For heuristic and practical purposes I suggest that, in the present state of the study of folk illness, when several symptoms regularly cohere in any specified population, and members of that population respond to such manifestations in similarly patterned ways, the cluster of symptoms be defined as a disease entity. For, as Leighton (1961: 486) has commented, it will prove profitable to fasten our attention first on "the distribution of selected types of human patterns, and only later ask what the functional effect and consequences of these are. The determination of pathology is the last thing to be done rather than the first" (cf. also Blum 1962).

SUSTO IN HISPANIC AMERICA[1]

The general problems in the study of folk illness, to which we have alluded, apply equally to the investigation of a condition, here called *susto*, which is reported from many regions of the Spanish-speaking New World.[2] Though variously called *susto, pasmo, jani, espanto, pérdida de la sombra,* or other terms in different localities, the reference in this paper is always to a syndrome, rather than its variant labels, and for purposes of exposition this particular cluster of symptoms and its attendant beliefs and behaviors will be arbitrarily designated as *susto*.

Those who suffer from *susto* include Indian and non-Indian, male and female, rich and poor, rural dwellers and urbanites. In the United States it is endemic to the Spanish-speaking inhabitants of California, Colorado, New Mexico, and Texas (Clark 1959; Saunders 1954; Rubel 1960). In Hispanic America *susto* is often mentioned in the writings of anthropologists and others. In contrast to other well-known folk illnesses such as *wiitigo* and arctic hysteria, however, it is not confined uniquely either to the speakers of a single

group of related languages or to the members of one socio-cultural group. Peoples who speak unrelated aboriginal languages, e.g., Chinantec, Tzotzil, and Quechua, as well as Spanish-speaking non-Indians, appear to be equally susceptible to this syndrome.[3]

From the point of view of cultural analysis, the *susto* syndrome reflects the presence in Hispanic America of a trait complex which also occurs elsewhere in the world—a complex consisting of beliefs that an individual is composed of a corporeal being and one or more immaterial souls or spirits which may become detached from the body and wander freely. In Hispanic America, as elsewhere, these souls may leave the body during sleep, particularly when the individual is dreaming, but among peasant and urban groups they may also become detached as a consequence of an unsettling experience. The latter aspect of spirit separation from the corporeal being has attained such importance in Hispanic America as to justify being described as a cultural focus (Honigmann 1959: 128-129). I shall speak of it, together with its associated behavioral traits, as the *susto* focus. It is clearly distinct from the more widely diffused trait of soul separation. It is on the behavioral, rather than the cultural, nature of this focus that this paper concentrates.

Local embellishments on the basic cohering symptoms of *susto* make this entity appear far more inconstant than is really the case. When one concentrates on the constants which recur with great consistency among the various groups from which *susto* is reported, the basic syndrome appears as follows: (1) during sleep the patient evidences restlessness; (2) during waking hours patients are characterized by listlessness, loss of appetite, disinterest in dress and personal hygiene, loss of strength, depression, and introversion (Sal y Rosas 1958; Gillin 1945).[4]

A number of basic elements recur in the folk etiology of *susto*. Among Indians the soul is believed to be captured because the patient, wittingly or not, has disturbed the spirit guardians of the earth, rivers, ponds, forests, or animals, the soul being held captive until the affront has been expiated. By contrast, when a non-Indian is diagnosed as suffering from soul loss, the locale in which it occurred, e.g., a river or forest, is of no significance, nor are malevolent beings suspected.[5] In many though not all cases a fright occasioned by an unexpected accident or encounter is thought to have caused the illness.

The curing rites of the groups in which this syndrome manifests itself as a significant health phenomenon likewise share a number of basic features. There is an initial diagnostic session between healer and patient during which the cause of the particular episode is specified and agreed upon by the participants. The soul is then coaxed and entreated to rejoin the patient's body; in the case of Indians those spirits who hold the soul captive are begged and propitiated to release it, and in both Indian and non-Indian groups the officiant shows the soul the direction back to the host body. During healing rites a patient is massaged and often sweated, both apparently to relax him, and he is "swept" or rubbed with some object to remove the illness from his body. In the Peruvian highlands a guinea pig is utilized for the therapeutic rubbing, whereas some Guatemala Indians use hens' eggs, and in south Texas and parts of Mexico medicinal brushes are employed for the same purpose.

CASE HISTORIES

The fullest account of a case of *susto* (Gillin 1948) describes the condition of a Pokomam Indian woman from San Luis Jilotepecque in eastern Guatemala. The 63-year-old woman shared with neighbors a belief that her soul had been separated from the rest of her body and held captive by sentient beings. The capture of her soul was believed to have been precipitated when she discovered her husband philandering with a loose woman of the village. As a consequence of her discovery, the patient upbraided her husband, who retaliated by hitting his wife with a rock. When Gillin (1948: 348) encountered the woman,

> she was in a depressed state of mind, neglected her household duties and her pottery making, and reduced her contact with friends and relatives. Physical complaints included diarrhea, "pain in the stomach," loss of appetite, "pains in the back and legs," occasional fever. Verbalizations were wheedling and anxious; she alternated between moods of timorous anxiety and tension characterized by tremor of the hands and generally rapid and jerky movements, and moods of profound, though conscious, lethargy. Orientation was adequate for time and place and normal reflexes were present.

The next case (Rubel 1960) is from a small city in south Texas. The patient, Mrs. Benitez, was a non-Indian who had been born in Mexico but had resided in Texas for many years. She was in her middle thirties and was the mother of five children, all girls. Her husband had deserted his family more than five years before. During our acquaintance the patient was irregularly employed as an agricultural field laborer, but most of her family's income was in fact derived from welfare agencies. She was extraordinarily thin and wan and appeared much older than her years. She had had a long history of epileptoid attacks, involving the locking of her jaw and involuntary spasms of her legs, but she claimed not to be able to recall what had

occurred during such seizures. She expressed a feeling of constant tiredness and of complete social isolation, and she maintained that she had suffered recurrently from soul loss.

Another case concerns a middle-aged man, a baker by profession and a non-Indian, from Mexiquito in southern Texas. One day, according to his sister, when the baker was following his usual custom of delivering breads and cakes to workers at a vegetable-packing warehouse during the noon lunch hour, he stepped into an open ice chute as he moved across a wooden platform. His leg bent under the weight of his falling body, his shoulders hit the flooring, and the breads and cakes scattered in all directions. Noting his ludicrous predicament, the onlooking laborers commenced to laugh; then, perceiving him to be in great pain, they rushed to his assistance. He was immediately taken home to his mother, who initiated a treatment for the loss of his soul which had presumably been occasioned by the accident. She also massaged the injured leg and requested a neighbor to collect the inner bark of a tree known as *huisatche chino,* which she prepared by boiling and administered to the victim for the next eight days. The laughter of the onlookers and the consequent mortification and helpless anger of the victim apparently seemed so important to the informant that she mentioned them three times during the course of her short tale.

Another case from Mexiquito in Texas involved a family whom I shall call the Montalvos. Mr. Montalvo is a Spanish-speaking, native-born American citizen who neither speaks English nor reads or writes in any language. Since he has been old enough to work he has been an agricultural field laborer, except for a brief period when he was employed by a small construction company. His wife, who is likewise able to converse only in Spanish, came from a hamlet in arid northeastern Mexico where she grew up poor, illiterate, and anxious. The pathos of her life is compounded by an ever-present fear that her illegal presence in this country may be discovered, resulting in her arrest and deportation. During the course of our acquaintance the family spent a large proportion of its meager income and a substantial amount of time in efforts to secure the Mexican documents required to establish her legal residence in this country. The Montalvos had a seven-year-old daughter, a five-year-old son, and an infant boy who died shortly after I made the family's acquaintance.

On a Sunday outing Ricardo, the older boy, suffered an attack of *susto.* The rest of the family romped in and about the water of a local pond, but Ricardo demurred. Despite coaxing and taunts, especially from his sister, Ricardo would have nothing to do with the water but climbed into the automobile and went to sleep. He slept throughout the afternoon and did not even awake when he was taken home after dark and put to bed. That night he slept fitfully and several times talked aloud in his sleep. On the following morning the parents decided that Ricardo had suffered a *susto*. It was caused, they reasoned, not by fear of the water but by the family's insistence that he enter the pond—a demand to which he was unable to accede. They brought him to a local curer to have his soul coaxed back to his body and thus be healed of soul loss.

The next case involved Antonio, a young married man about 25 years of age, likewise a native-born American citizen who could neither read, write, nor communicate in English. He and his family before him were laborers employed in harvesting cotton and vegetables in south Texas and migrating every spring and summer to the north-central states for similar field labor. To all outward appearances Antonio seemed an outgoing fellow contented enough with his lot. He lived with his wife and children in a homemade shack with an earth-packed floor, walls of corrugated paper, and a roof of tin. There was, of course, no indoor plumbing, but Antonio and the owner of the lot on which his shack stood had fashioned a shower and water closet in an outhouse which both families used. Unlike her husband, Antonio's wife came from a hamlet in northeastern Mexico. She neither spoke nor understood English, but she was able to write Spanish by using self-taught block letters. Despite the family's impoverished condition she, too, seemed a cheerful and untroubled person.

On one occasion Antonio was sent to a hospital with a diagnosis of double pneumonia. His fever was successfully controlled, and he was placed in a ward for a recuperative period. One night he noticed a change in the condition of a wardmate, became alarmed, and tried to communicate his concern to the attendants, but for some reason he was unsuccessful. Some time later they discovered that the wardmate had died and removed the corpse from the room. Antonio was much upset by the incident. He became fitful, complained of restless nights, and exhibited little interest in his food or surroundings. Moreover, he found his body involuntarily "jumping" on the bed while he lay in a reclining position. After leaving the hospital he went home and asked that his mother, who lived in Mexico, be brought to his side. When she arrived she immediately began to coax his soul back to his body by means of a traditional cure (see below).

A woman from Laredo, Texas, suffered *susto* on at least two occasions, several years apart. Each instance occurred during the course of her family's seasonal migration for field labor in the north. Mr. Solís, the pa-

tient's husband, was a highly excitable and apparently alienated person who conceived of himself as earning a living "by the honest sweat of my brow" in face of the restricting regulations of the local and federal government and of the outright malice of his employers. His lack of other than agricultural skills and the absence of year-round employment in south Texas left the family no choice except migratory labor and precluded the children's regular attendance at school despite the family's strong motivation toward education and their manifest aspirations toward a better way of life. Mrs. Solís, though probably only in her middle forties, was constantly sickly, felt weak, and had no desire to eat anything, not even when she awoke in the morning. Moreover, she felt listless during the day and did not like to move about. She claimed she had suffered this condition for two years but had not brought it to a physician's attention.

The first episode of *susto* afflicted Mrs. Solís during her family's stay in an Indiana migrant labor camp. It occurred after she had unwillingly and helplessly witnessed an attack on a peaceable member of her husband's crew by drunken and bellicose members of another crew in which the victim was slashed in the abdominal region and removed to a hospital. Several years later, when she was pregnant, Mrs. Solís helplessly watched the family truck overturn, carrying with it the fruit of the crew's labor. As a consequence of this disturbing event she suffered a miscarriage and was again afflicted with *susto*.

In the seven cases of soul loss presented thus far—one from an Indian community in Guatemala and the remainder from non-Indian groups in south Texas—it has been possible to present relevant data on the patient's personality, on the family contexts, and on the causes presumed by the people involved to have precipitated the soul loss and illness. The following cases are less complete because all the relevant data are not available.

One case involved a young Chinantec Indian schoolboy from San Lucas Ojitlán in Oaxaca, Mexico. According to the boy's teacher, it was necessary one day to punish him for talking in class. The lad was instructed to stand by his desk with his hands outstretched and his palms up, and the teacher then slapped one upturned palm with a small wooden ruler. According to the instructor's account, the blows were not hard enough to have hurt the boy in a physical sense. Nevertheless, the illness which resulted from this chastisement was so serious as to keep the lad out of school for two weeks. During this period he was unable to eat and manifested considerable apathy. The child's mother recognized from these signs that her son's soul had left his body and had been captured by the spirit of the earth, and she took corrective steps which will be related later.

The following two cases are reported by Diaz de Solas (1957) from the Tzotzil-speaking Indians of San Bartolomé de Los Llanos in the Mexican state of Chiapas. In the first case an Indian mother seated her four-year-old son on a stone wall from which he could watch her while she gardened in the family corn field. After a while the child lost his balance and fell to the ground. Although he cried, he seemed to have been uninjured by the accident, nor was it thought that he had suffered *susto* as a result. The mother, however, lost her soul—a condition which the community considered to have been precipitated by her helplessness as she watched the child's fall.

The second case from San Bartolomé involved a man who suffered a *susto* as a result of an accident he was unable to prevent. This Indian was leading his heavily laden horse home from market, a trip which required the fording of a swiftly flowing stream. As they crossed the stream, the pack animal was swept downstream by the current. The owner saved himself, and was finally able to retrieve his horse, but the valuable load was lost. Subsequently the Indian sickened, and his condition was diagnosed as *susto;* his soul was presumed to have been taken captive by the spirit of the locale in which the accident occurred. In both the cases from San Bartolomé it was thought that the illness would continue until the annoyance suffered by the spirits, respectively of the earth and the river, had been expiated.

A very similar case occurred in another Tzotzil municipio, San Andrés Larrainzar, in the Chiapas highlands (cf. Guiteras-Holmes 1961: 269-275). An Indian was driving a horse laden with corn on a trip from one section (*paraje*) of San Andrés to another, and in the course of his journey they were forced to cross the Rio Tiwó. The man drove his animal into the river whilst he himself crossed over a small bridge. The horse was carried away by the current until it finally came to rest against a fallen tree trunk. Although the owner was able to rescue his horse, his load was lost. He felt very sad about his loss, and then he suffered an *espanto* (note the sequence!). At the end of a month the patient felt sad and sick, and had no desire to eat anything; as a consequence of these symptoms a curer was called into the case.

Foster (1951: 168-169) reports an incident in which a Popoluca Indian suffered the loss and capture of his soul. According to the patient's account,

> In August, 1939, I was in a boat near Cotzacoalcos [*sic*] which upset and threw me into the water. I struggled and tried to reach the shore, but couldn't make it. I was afraid of drowning. Finally I was rescued, but I became very ill. I couldn't eat; I couldn't even sit up. I was ill all through the fall and winter until March, getting worse and worse. I know what the matter was because I dreamed of Coatzacoalcos and knew my spirit was there.

The examples of *susto* reported in the preceding pages represent only a few of the references to the illness which were discovered in the literature. They have been selected for inclusion herein because they describe with some amplitude the circumstances surrounding the onset of a specific case of *susto* or because they provide some of the social or personality characteristics of the patients.

HEALING RITES

I now move to a discussion of the curing rites associated with the syndrome of *susto*. I shall first describe those utilized to heal some of the patients in the cases already presented and shall then refer to some generalized, but detailed, descriptions of healing procedures provided by the psychiatrist Sal y Rosas (1958) and the anthropologists Tschopik (1951), Weitlaner (1961), and Carrasco (1960).

In the case from San Luis Jilotepecque, Guatemala, described by Gillin (1948), the patient for whom the healing ceremonies were intended was the wife who had suffered from a philandering husband. The essentials of the treatment may be divided into several stages. During the first stage, that of diagnosis, the native curer pronounced to the patient a clear-cut and authoritative diagnosis of *espanto* or soul loss. Later the woman was required to consider and "confess" the actual events which had led up to the particular episode of soul loss (she had had a previous history of similar episodes). During the second stage, that of the actual healing rites, a group of persons who were socially significant to the patient was organized to attend a nocturnal ceremony. Some of them joined the patient and the healer in offering prayers to the Catholic saints of the village. Hens' eggs were then passed over the patient to absorb some of the illness. They were later deposited at the place where the soul loss had occurred, along with a collection of gifts to propitiate the spirits who held the patient's soul and who were now requested to release it. Following prayers and libations to the spirits, a procession was formed. It led from the place of the accident back to the woman's home, the healer making noises to indicate to the soul the appropriate direction. Finally, the patient was undressed, "shocked" by cold liquor sprayed from the mouth of the curer, then massaged, and finally "sweated" on a bed placed over a brazier filled with burning coals.

The essentials of the Pokomam ceremony, with the exception of certain details in the expiation rites, are found widely dispersed in Hispanic America among Indians and non-Indians alike. In the case involving the Chinantec schoolboy, for example, the healing rites were as follows.[6] The boy's mother proceeded to the schoolhouse, taking with her the shirt her son had worn on the day he had been punished. Inside the building she moved directly to the desk alongside of which her son had been chastised. She took his shirt, rolled it up, and proceeded to wipe the packed earth flooring, meanwhile murmuring:

> I come in the name of curer Garcia who at this time is unable to come. I come in order to reunite the spirit of my boy, José, who is sick. I come this time and this time only. It surely was not your intention to dispossess him of his spirit. Goodbye, I will return in four days to advise you as to his condition and to do whatever is necessary.

The mother then removed from her clothing a bottle of liquor mixed with the herb called *hoja de espanto* and sprayed some of this liquor from her mouth on the shirt, as well as on the earthen floor on which the desk rested, meanwhile crossing herself and making the sign of the cross over the wet shirt. She then picked up the shirt and excavated a little earth, which she carried home. Here her son donned his shirt, and the earth was placed in a receptacle containing liquor set beside the boy's cot. The mother next called on the services of a professional curer, who poured liquor from the receptacle into his own mouth and sprayed the patient on his face, chest, crown, and the back of his neck. The child was then placed on his cot, rolled in blankets, and a brazier of hot coals was placed under the cot to sweat him. Following the child's recovery, the curer went himself to the schoolhouse, where he offered thanks to the earth for releasing the child's soul and then ceremoniously bade it farewell.

Very similar ceremonies were employed to heal the Tzotzil Indian from San Andrés Larrainzar. In this instance a specialist was called into the case only after the illness had run its course unchecked for a month. His first act was to diagnose the entity as *susto* or soul loss. The healer then repaired to the ford where the mishap had occurred. Here he offered candles, incense, and a slaughtered cock to the local spirits. Returning to the home of his patient, he brought with him a quantity of water from the site where the incident had occurred; he required the patient to drink three glasses of this water and administered a small amount (mixed with salt) to the rescued horse. Following this he built a small altar in the patient's home on which incense and candles were offered.

In the non-Indian cases reported from Texas the cures, though similar in many respects, involved neither expiation nor propitiation. The major problem a Texas curer confronts is to induce the soul to return to the patient's body; it is not compounded by the conception of malevolent captors. In Antonio's case his mother placed him on the dirt floor of his shack, with his arms outstretched but his legs together so that he formed a human cross. She then dug a hole at the base of his feet, another above his head, and one at each of his extended hands, filling them with a liquid composed of water and medicinal herbs. Then she began to "sweep" the illness out of her son's body via the extremities, using a broom constructed of a desert bush with medicinal qualities. She and her son then prayed, entreating his lost and wandering soul to rejoin his body, after which she blew a spray of liquid from her mouth directly into her son's face, and Antonio sipped some of the medicinal liquid which his mother had scooped from the holes in the dirt floor.

Among the most meticulous descriptions of cures for *susto* are those provided by Sal y Rosas (1958: 177–184). In the main, his data pertain to the Quechua Indians of the Callejon de Huaylas region of Peru, but a number of his observations refer to other parts of that country as well. After diagnosis, according to Sal y Rosas, a patient reclines on a cot or on a blanket stretched on the floor, and alongside him is placed a mixture of various flower petals, leaves, and wheat or corn is placed beside him. The curer blesses the mixture and distributes it over the patient's body, commencing at his head and moving down to the legs and then the feet. Later the curer's helper carries the mixture, wrapped in the patient's clothing, to the locality where the illness was precipitated, scattering on his way a trail of petals, leaves, and flour to indicate to the soul the path by which it is to return to the body. He also leaves an offering of liquor, cigarettes, and coca leaves at the site as an inducement to the soul to return. He then holds up the patient's shirt and shakes it in the air to attract the soul's attention. Returning to the patient's house, the helper carefully follows the trail of petals, leaves, and flour and holds the shirt in plain sight so that the soul will encounter no trouble in finding its way. (In more serious cases of soul loss, the patient is rubbed with a live guinea pig, which is then taken and left as a gift to the spirits of the locality where the illness occurred, in exchange for the captive soul.)

Reports by Weitlaner (1961) and Carrasco (1960: 103–105, 110) of symptoms, etiology, and curing rites among Nahuatl-speaking and Chontal-speaking groups in western Mexico indicate that soul capture and its concomitant syndrome are remarkably similar to those reported among aboriginal groups with very different linguistic affiliations. Among these Chontal and Nahua groups the loss and capture of a soul is believed to be precipitated by a fall on a road or pathway, by slipping or falling near a body of water, or by a sudden encounter with animals, snakes, or even a corpse. Diagnosis and healing include the elicitation by a healer of the date, place, and other pertinent circumstances of the event the patient presumes to have brought on the illness. This is followed by expiation for the annoyance caused by the spirit guardians of the locale and by propitiation of these beings in exchange for the captive soul. The healer then attempts to coax and lead the absent soul back to its host body. Unlike other groups previously discussed, the Nahua and Chontal adorn their healing rites with elaborate symbolism in which ritual colors, numbers, and directions play important parts. Nevertheless, beneath these local embellishments, one quickly discerns the fundamentals of the widespread *susto* complex and the associated healing rites which these Indians share with the other groups mentioned.

SUMMARY OF DESCRIPTIVE DATA

One of the most noteworthy aspects of the *susto* phenomenon is the fact that a basic core of premises and assumptions—symptoms, etiology, and regimens of healing—recur with remarkable constancy among many Hispanic-American groups, Indian and non-Indian alike. In general, the following symptoms characterize victims of this illness: (1) while asleep a patient evidences restlessness, and (2) during waking hours he manifests listlessness, loss of appetite, disinterest in costume or personal hygiene, loss of strength and weight, depression, and introversion. In one unique instance, a Texas patient (Mrs. Benitez) subsumes under *susto* her epileptoid seizures in addition to the more usual loss of strength, depression, apathy, listlessness, and introversion. However, it should be noted that, when this victim of *susto* describes her own condition, she stresses the post-spasmodic depressive and introversive emotional states rather than the seizure itself.

Although Indian and non-Indian populations appear to be equally subject to *susto*, there are significant differences between them with respect to the nature of the causal agents. Unlike non-Indians, Indian groups conceive of the separation of the soul from the body as precipitated by an affront to the spirit guardians of a locality—guardians of the earth, water, or animals—

although the offense is usually caused unwittingly by the victim. Intentional or not, however, the mischief must be expiated and the spirits of the site propitiated before they will release the captured soul.

There are also other features of the precipitating events which recur with remarkable constancy. Thus one salient feature of all the cases cited is role helplessness. Significantly, however, a victim's helplessness appears in association with only some kinds of problems in role behavior, but not with others. In none of the instances cited, for example, do we discover a victim helpless in the face of role conflicts or expectations which are products of his or her cultural marginality or social mobility.[7] In other words, *susto* appears to communicate an individuals inability to fulfill adequately the expectations of the society in which he has been socialized; it does not seem to mark those role conflicts and uncertainties Indians confront as they pass into Ladino society or the problems posed to upwardly mobile Mexican-Americans in the process of being assimilated into the Anglo-American society of Texas.

In cases of soul capture, a healing specialist visits the site at which the mishap occurred, where he propitiates the spirits and then coaxes the released soul back to the body of the victim along a path clearly indicated by the healer. Sickness which has "entered" the victim's body is removed either by sweeping it out by means of medicinal branches or by passing hens' eggs, a fowl, or a guinea pig across the body of the victim in such a manner as to absorb the illness, removing it from the victim. Inasmuch as non-Indian groups neither attribute soul loss to malevolent sentient beings nor consider the site at which a mishap occurred to be important, it follows that neither expiation nor propitiation occur in their healing rites. Finally, the rites of both groups share such other elements as medicinal "sweeping" to remove internalized illness, recollection and verbalization by the patient of the event precipitating the separation of his soul from the body, simulation of the "shock" which was the immediate cause of that separation, and entreaties directed to a soul to return to the victim. The constancy with which similar precipitating events, symptoms, and healing methods recur among a variety of groups in Hispanic America makes the syndrome amenable to systematic epidemiological investigation.

AN EPIDEMIOLOGICAL MODEL

Epidemiology has been described by Wade Hampton Frost as "something more than the total of its established facts. It includes their orderly arrangement into chains of inference which extend more or less beyond the bound of direct observation" (Maxcy 1941: 1). In what follows I shall attempt to order the descriptive data into such "chains of inference." Let me first make clear that it is not my intent to investigate the truth of informants' statements as to whether or not those who complain of illness associated with a presumed loss of soul are really ill. It has been my experience (one which I share with others who write of this phenomenon) that individuals who claim to suffer an *asustado* condition are characterized by, if nothing else, a distinctive absence of well-being—the minimal criterion for defining illness.

It is hoped that my conceptual model and the hypotheses it generates will result in a later test of those hypotheses and their verification, modification, or rejection as may be required. Underlying this model is an assumption which holds that the *susto* syndrome is a product of the interaction between three open systems, each linked with the others (Caudill 1958: 4–7). The three systems in question are (1) an individual's state of health, (2) his personality system, and (3) the social system of which he is a member. The interaction between these three linked open systems is portrayed in the following simple diagram (see Cassell *et al.* 1960).[8]

Finally, I proffer the following tentative hypotheses:

I.   A *susto* syndrome will appear only in social situations which victims perceive as stressful. The syndrome is the vehicle by means of which people of Hispanic-American peasant and urban societies manifest their reactions to some forms of self-perceived stressful situations, but not others. People in these so-cieties not only choose to assume the sick role but also elect the kinds of symptoms by which to make manifest to others an absence of well-being (cf. Parsons and Fox 1952; Weinstein 1962).

II.   The social stresses which are reflected in the *susto* syndrome are intra-cultural and intra-societal in nature. Stresses occasioned by conflict between cultures or by an individual's cultural marginality or social mobility will be symbolized by symptoms of illness other than *susto*. In other words, the frustration or alienation which often result from efforts to identify with, and to be accepted by, members of a society or social stratum distinct from that into which one has been socialized will not be reflected by *susto*.

III. In Hispanic-American societies, the *susto* syndrome will appear as a consequence of an episode in which an individual is unable to meet the expectations of his own society for a social role in which he or she has been socialized.

Corollary 1: Because these societies differentially socialize males and females, and because society's expectations of male and female children differ from those held for mature men and women, it is expected that girls and women will be afflicted by *susto* and its concomitants as a consequence of experiences different from those which jeopardize the health of boys and men of the same society. For example, girls are socialized to be demure, dependent, and home-oriented, whereas boys are trained to show aggressiveness, independence, and orientations toward occupational and public responsibility roles. I should not expect many girls or women in these societies to manifest *susto*

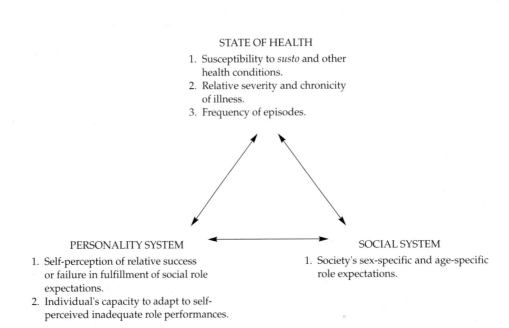

STATE OF HEALTH
1. Susceptibility to *susto* and other health conditions.
2. Relative severity and chronicity of illness.
3. Frequency of episodes.

PERSONALITY SYSTEM
1. Self-perception of relative success or failure in fulfillment of social role expectations.
2. Individual's capacity to adapt to self-perceived inadequate role performances.

SOCIAL SYSTEM
1. Society's sex-specific and age-specific role expectations.

under circumstances where the society has no reason to expect a female to fulfill a responsibility successfully. Neither should one expect a young man to suffer ill effects from his inability to carry out successfully a task usually assigned to females. If, for example, a girl of the same age as the Mexican-American boy, Ricardo, refused to enter the water because of timidity, it is my belief that the soul-loss syndrome would not have appeared. The girl's timidity would have been a demonstration of appropriate female behavior, whereas Ricardo's behavior was a far cry from the expectations which Mexican-Americans hold for boys and men.

Corollary 2: Since Hispanic-American societies attach greater importance to the successful accomplishment of some tasks than of others, the more importance which socializers attach to a particular task, the greater the likelihood will be that *susto* will occur in association with failure to perform that task adequately. It follows that, although females and males both risk illness as a consequence of failure adequately to perform sex-specific and age-specific tasks, not all such tasks are equally risky.

IV. Although all persons in a society may believe in the concept of soul loss and its attendant illness, not all members of that society will actually fall victim to this kind of illness. It is hypothesized that individual personalities act as contingency variables. That is, if two members of a society, matched for age and sex, fail to meet adequately the society's role expectations, one may respond to his self-perceived inadequacy by electing the sick role, i.e., *susto*, whereas the other may adapt in a different manner, e.g., by an expression of generalized anger or by displacement of hostility. Moreover, among those who do elect the *susto* syndrome, the severity, chronicity, and frequency of episodes will vary systematically with respect to personality and societal variables. The points which are of interest to us, of course, are (1) that some cultures provide *susto* as an adaptive mechanism to self-perceived social inadequacies, whereas others do not, and (2) that some but not all individuals with these cultural beliefs elect *susto* symptoms to indicate an absence of well-being.

Briefly, these hypotheses propose that *susto* illness in societies of Hispanic America may be understood as a product of a complex interaction between an individual's state of health and the role expectations which his society provides, mediated by aspects of that individual's personality.

SUMMARY

In this exploration of the health phenomenon which I call *susto*, I have sought to assess the extent to which this folk illness is amenable to epidemiological analysis. Despite localized embellishments on a general theme of soul-loss illness, there recurs in many societies a hard core of constant elements which lead one to conclude that this phenomenon is indeed subject to orderly description and analysis. Moreover, inferences of causality drawn from ethnographic data offer great potential for understanding the nature of folk illness and some facets of the relationships which obtain between health and social behavior. Finally, if one folk illness, *susto*, proves amenable to such investigation, other seemingly bizarre notions of illness demand the attention of epidemiologists and research physicians working in collaboration with anthropologists (see Fleck and Ianni 1958).

NOTES

1. Field work was carried out among the Chinantec of San Lucas Ojitlán in 1950 and in the Tzotzil municipios of San Bartolomé de Los Llanos, San Andrés Larrainzar, and Santa Catarina Pantelhó in 1957 and 1961. Between 1957 and 1959 I engaged in a study of health and social life of Mexican-Americans in south Texas. Work among the Tzotzil was supported by the University of Chicago Man-In-Nature Project, in Mexiquito by the Hogg Foundation for Mental Health, and in Laredo by the Migrant Health Branch of the United States Public Health Service. To all these organizations I wish to acknowledge my gratitude. A preliminary version of this paper was presented at the annual meeting of the Society for Applied Anthropology in Pittsburgh, 1960, and a short version appeared in *Research Reviews* 8: 13–19 (Chapel Hill, 1961). I wish to express my gratitude to R. N. Adams, Harriet Kupferer, Duane Metzger, Ralph Patrick, and Richard Simpson for their considered criticisms. Remaining defects are solely the author's responsibility. Assistance in the preparation of this manuscript was provided by the Research Fund of the University of North Carolina at Greensboro, to which I am very grateful.
2. Foster (1953) remarks on the absence of this or a similar syndrome in either historic or contemporary Spanish life.
3. In some countries, according to Adams (1957), this syndrome has a "spotty" distribution from town to town, a discovery which affords an exciting opportunity to pursue controlled comparative studies of the functional relationship between *susto* and other aspects of social life.
4. It is noteworthy that among one of Peru's highland groups, the Aymara of Chuquito, a disease entity identified as *kat'a*, which Tschopik equates with *susto*, manifests itself in quite a different set of symptoms, although

etiologically it is the equivalent of *susto* as described by Sal y Rosas, Gillin, and others (Tschopik 1951: 202, 211–212, 282–283). Furthermore, the Aymara rites for curing *kat'a* share all essential features with the Quechua rites described by Sal y Rosas (1958).

5. The importance of sentient beings in instances of Indian illness and their absence in cases of non-Indians are presumably a function of the utilization of sprites and other sentient beings in socialization procedures in Indian and non-Indian cultures. Fear of "bogy men" is, to be sure, used among both groups, but Indians to a far greater extent than Ladinos invoke the guardian spirits of woods, animals, caves, and streams (see Whiting and Child 1953).

6. For a curing rite remarkably similar in detail see Mak (1959: 128–129).

7. A notable exception is found in the Cakchiquel town of Magdalena Milpas Altas, where *susto* is interpreted as associated with acculturation stresses (see Adams 1951: 26–27). Furthermore, in Magdalena, as in many other localities in Middle America, the kidnapper of Indian souls is depicted as a Ladino (Adams and Rubel 1964). This does not, however, require an assumption that Indian-Ladino relations are the context in which soul loss actually occurs, for available case histories lead us away from such an assumption.

8. This represents an adaptation of a model prepared by the Department of Epidemiology, School of Public Health, University of North Carolina, to the members of which I owe my training in epidemiology.

REFERENCES

Adams, R. N. 1952. An Analysis of Medical Beliefs and Practices in a Guatemalan Indian Town. Guatemala.

———. 1957. Cultural Surveys of Panama-Nicaragua-Guatemala-El Salvador-Honduras. Washington.

Adams, R. N., and A. J. Rubel. Sickness and Social Relations. Handbook of Middle-American Indians (in press).

Blum, R. H. 1962. Case Identification in Psychiatric Epidemiology: Methods and Problems. Milbank Memorial Fund Quarterly 40: 253–289.

Carrasco, P. 1960. Pagan Rituals and Beliefs Among the Chontal Indians of Oaxaca. Anthropological Records 20: 87–117.

Cassel, J., R. Patrick, and D. Jenkins. 1960. Epidemiological Analysis of Health Implications of Culture Change: A Conceptual Model. Annals of the New York Academy of Sciences 84: 938–949.

Caudill, W. 1958. Effects of Social and Cultural Systems in Reactions to Stress. Memorandum to the Committee on Preventive Medicine and Social Science Research, Pamphlet, 14.

Clark, M. 1959. Health in the Mexican-American Culture. Berkeley.

Diaz de Solas, M. 1957. Personal Communication.

Fleck, A. C., and F. A. J. Ianni. 1958. Epidemiology and Anthropology: Some Suggested Affinities in Theory and Method. Human Organization 16: 38–41.

Foster, G. M. 1951. Some Wider Implications of Soul-Loss Illness Among the Sierra Popoluca Homenaje a Don Alfonso Caso, pp. 167–174.

———. 1953. Relationships Between Spanish and Spanish-American Folk Medicine. Journal of American Folklore 66: 201–247.

Frake, C. 1961. The Diagnosis of Disease Among the Subanun of Mindanao. American Anthropologist 63: 113–132.

Gillin, J. 1945. Moche: A Peruvian Coastal Community. Washington.

———. 1948. Magical Fright. Psychiatry 11: 387–400.

Guiteras-Holmes, C. 1961. Perils of the Soul. New York.

Honigmann, J. J. 1959. The World of Man. New York.

Leighton, A. 1961. Remarks. Milbank Memorial Fund Quarterly 39: 486.

Mak, C. 1959. Mixtec Medical Beliefs and Practices. America Indigena 19: 125–151.

Maxcy, K. A., ed. 1941. Papers of Wade Hampton Frost, M.D. New York.

Metzger, D., and G. Williams. 1963. Tenejapa Medicine I: The Curer. Southwestern Journal of Anthropology 19: 216–234.

Parker, S. 1960. The Wiitiko Psychosis in the Context of Ojibwa Personality and Culture. American Anthropologist 62: 603–623.

Parsons, T., and R. Fox. 1952. Illness, Therapy, and the Modern Urban American Family. Journal of Social Issues 8: 31–44.

Rubel, A. J. 1960. Concepts of Disease in Mexican-American Culture. American Anthropologist 62: 795–815.

Sal y Rosas, F. 1958. El mito del Jani o Susto de la medicina indigena del Peru. Revista de la Sanidad de Policia 18: 167–210. Lima.

Saunders, L. 1954. Cultural Differences and Medical Care. New York.

Teicher, M. I. 1960. Windigo Psychosis. Seattle.

Tschopik, H. 1951. The Aymara of Chucuito, Peru: Magic. Anthropological Papers of the American Museum of Natural History 44: 133–308.

Weinstein, E. A. 1962. Cultural Aspects of Delusion. New York.

Weitlaner, R. J. 1961. La ceremonia llamada "Levantar la sombra." Typescript.

Whiting, J. W. M., and I. L. Child. 1953. Child Training and Personality. New Haven.

Critical Medical Anthropology

❖ CONCEPTUAL TOOLS ❖

■ *What is "critical" about critical medical anthropology?* For the purposes of the following selections, it is important to clarify what is meant by a "critical" approach in critical medical anthropology (CMA). Although critical approaches may be skeptical or cynical, their primary aim is to examine the core assumptions of a given explanation for disease, to uncover the biases of a given epistemology. *Epistemology* can be broadly defined as a way of knowing something, and all epistemologies are conceptual frameworks that have particular biases. For example, one epistemological perspective on the AIDS epidemic is that the disease is caused by the moral qualities of particular groups of people, whereas another epistemology is that social and economic discrimination place particular groups of people at increased risk for disease. In each case, the explanation contains assumptions, and these assumptions affect how we define the AIDS problem and what we believe should be done about it. Because critical medical anthropologists attempt to be aware of the biases of epistemologies of health and illness, they emphasize that we always know things from a specific point of view. They also show how each point of view obscures some features and enlightens others.

■ *Why are critical approaches consciously political and reflexive?* The critical awareness that all explanations are merely points of view with their own built-in assumptions has been called reflexivity. Reflexivity refers to the commitment to be continually aware of the biases that inform any explanation, including one's own, and to critique explanations that ignore alternative interpretations. Critical medical anthropologists often advocate a more reflexive approach to explanations of health and disease, and frequently focus on the knowledge that has been systematically neglected by more traditional explanations within medical anthropology. In the AIDS example, a critical perspective would emphasize that particular individuals or groups (homosexuals, immigrants, and so on) are not inherently predisposed to the disease—an argument made frequently in popular discussions of the epidemic—but are often the victims of other social forces that are beyond their individual control. As one prominent medical anthropologist has noted, then, CMA tends to maintain a consciously political, activist perspective on disease, and these explanations often include passionate, emotional criticism.

23

The Mindful Body: A Prolegomenon to Future Work in Medical Anthropology

Nancy Scheper-Hughes
Margaret M. Lock

This is an important selection in critical medical anthropology (CMA) because, when it was first published, it announced an important new agenda for many culturally oriented anthropologists. It was also the first article in the new series of Medical Anthropology Quarterly, *so it had special symbolic importance. Like many important theoretical articles in anthropology this is not easy reading, but I think you'll find it well worth the effort. The analysis is critical in that it questions the underlying assumptions of epistemology of Western biomedicine (Gordon and Lock 1988). This has been an important area of recent research in medical anthropology (Lindenbaum and Lock 1993). This particular selection introduces medical anthropologists to a large literature on "the body," as a social construction more than a biological entity.*

Anthropologists argue that our everyday ways of thinking are learned from culture. The cognitive anthropologist Bradd Shore, in an important book Culture in Mind *(1995), calls these ways of thinking* cultural models. *The body–mind dualism described in this selection and so characteristic of biomedical thinking is a good example of such a cultural model. Like the medical student described in the*

beginning of the selection, most practitioners of biomedicine think of the "real cause of the headaches" as being biochemical. There is an unstated assumption that social and psychological stresses are not, in fact, real. This is not a small, picky difference; it is an important epistemological question. Part of the goal of CMA is to attempt to understand and describe the hidden cultural models of biomedical thinking.

As you read this selection, consider these questions:

- *What are the advantages and disadvantages of the cultural model of Cartesian dualism?*

- *Is it true that none of the "three bodies" described in this selection are the biological, corporeal body? Or is it the case that all of these levels refer to the biological, corporeal body?*

- *Why do you think the CMA approach would make some people within scientific biomedicine angry and defensive?*

- *What is the process of medicalization?*

> The body is the first and most natural tool of man.
> —Marcel Mauss (1979 [1950])

Despite its title this article does not pretend to offer a comprehensive review of the anthropology of the body, which has its antecedents in physical, psychological, and symbolic anthropology, as well as in ethnoscience, phenomenology, and semiotics.[1] Rather, it should be seen as an attempt to integrate aspects of anthropological discourse on the body into current work in medical anthropology. We refer to this as a prolegomenon because we believe that insofar as medical anthropology has failed to problematize the body, it is destined to fall prey to the biological fallacy and related assumptions that are paradigmatic to biomedicine. Foremost among these assumptions is the much-noted Cartesian dualism that separates

mind from body, spirit from matter, and real (i.e., visible, palpable) from unreal. Since this epistemological tradition is a cultural and historical construction and not one that is universally shared, it is essential that we begin our project in medical anthropology with a suspension of our usual belief and cultural commitment to the mind/body, seen/unseen, natural/supernatural, magical/rational, rational/irrational, and real/unreal oppositions and assumptions that have characterized much of ethnomedical anthropology to date. We will begin from an assumption of the body as simultaneously a physical and symbolic artifact, as both naturally and culturally produced, and as securely anchored in a particular historical moment.

In the following pages we will critically examine and call into question various concepts that have been privileged in Western thinking for centuries and which have determined the ways in which the body has been perceived in scientific biomedicine and in anthropology. This article is descriptive and diagnostic. Its goal is both the definition of an important domain for anthropological inquiry and an initial search for appropriate concepts and analytic tools.

We are writing for three audiences. First, we hope to introduce general anthropologists to the potential contributions of medical anthropology toward understanding an intellectual domain we all share—the body. Second, we want to draw the attention of medical anthropologists to writings on the body not usually recognized for their relevance to the field. And third, we wish to speak to clinicians and other health practitioners who daily minister to mindful bodies. The resulting effort is necessarily partial and fragmentary, representing a somewhat personal itinerary through paths of inquiry we believe to hold particular promise for theory building and further research in anthropology generally, and in medical anthropology particularly.

THE THREE BODIES

Essential to our task is a consideration of the relations among what we will refer to here as the "three bodies."[2] At the first and perhaps most self-evident level is the individual body, understood in the phenomenological sense of the lived experience of the body-self. We may reasonably assume that all people share at least some intuitive sense of the embodied self as existing apart from other individual bodies (Mauss 1985 [1938]). However, the constituent parts of the body—mind, matter, psyche, soul, self, etc.—and their relations to each other, and the ways in which the body is received and experienced in health and sickness are, of course, highly variable.

At the second level of analysis is the social body, referring to the representational uses of the body as a natural symbol with which to think about nature, society, and culture, as Mary Douglas (1970) suggested. Here our discussion follows the well-trodden path of social, symbolic, and structuralist anthropologists who have demonstrated the constant exchange of meanings between the "natural" and the social worlds. The body in health offers a model of organic wholeness; the body in sickness offers a model of social disharmony, conflict, and disintegration. Reciprocally, society in "sickness" and in "health" offers a model for understanding the body.

At the third level of analysis is the body politic, referring to the regulation, surveillance, and control of bodies (individual and collective) in reproduction and sexuality, in work and in leisure, in sickness and other forms of deviance and human difference. There are many types of polity, ranging from the acephalous anarchy of "simple" foraging societies, in which deviants may be punished by total social ostracism and consequently by death (see Briggs 1970; Turnbull 1962), through chieftainships, monarchies, oligarchies, democracies, and modern totalitarian states. In all of these polities the stability of the body politic rests on its ability to regulate populations (the social body) *and* to discipline individual bodies. A great deal has been written about the regulation and control of individual and social bodies in complex, industrialized societies. Foucault's work is exemplary in this regard (1973, 1975, 1979, 1980a). Less has been written about the ways in which preindustrial societies control their populations and institutionalize means for producing docile bodies and pliant minds in the service of some definition of collective stability, health, and social well-being.

The "three bodies" represent, then, not only three separate and overlapping units of analysis, but also three different theoretical approaches and epistemologies: phenomenology (individual body, the lived self), structuralism and symbolism (the social body), and poststructuralism (the body politic). Of these, the third body is the most dynamic in suggesting why and how certain kinds of bodies are socially produced. The following analysis will move back and forth between a discussion of "the bodies" as a useful heuristic concept for understanding cultures and societies, on the one hand, and for increasing our knowledge of the cultural sources and meanings of health and illness, on the other.

THE INDIVIDUAL BODY

How Real Is Real?
The Cartesian Legacy

A singular premise guiding Western science and clinical medicine (and one, we hasten to add, that is responsible for its awesome efficacy) is its commitment to a fundamental opposition between spirit and matter, mind and body, and (underlying this) real and unreal. We are reminded of a grand rounds presentation before a class of first-year medical students that concerned the case of a middle-aged woman suffering from chronic and debilitating headaches. In halting sentences the patient explained before the class of two hundred that her husband was an alcoholic who occasionally beat her, that she had been virtually housebound for the past five years looking after her senile and incontinent mother-in-law, and that she worries constantly about her teenage son who is flunking out of high school. Although the woman's story elicited considerable sympathy from the students, many grew restless with the line of clinical questioning, and one finally interrupted the professor to demand "But what is the *real* cause of the headaches?"

The medical student, like many of her classmates, interpreted the stream of social information as extraneous and irrelevant to the *real* biomedical diagnosis. She wanted information on the neurochemical changes which she understood as constituting the true causal explanation. This kind of radically materialist thinking, characteristic of clinical biomedicine, is the product of a Western epistemology extending as far back as Aristotle's starkly biological view of the human soul in *De Anima*. As a basis for clinical practice, it can be found in the Hippocratic corpus (ca. 400 B.C.). Hippocrates[3] and his students were determined to eradicate the vestiges of magico-religious thinking about the human body and to introduce a rational basis for clinical practice that would challenge the power of ancient folk healers or "charlatans" and "magi," as Hippocrates labeled his medical competitors. In a passage from his treatise on epilepsy, ironically entitled "On the Sacred Disease," Hippocrates (Adams 1939:355–356) cautioned the Greek *iatros* (physician) to treat only what was observable and palpable to the senses:

> I do not believe that the so-called Sacred Disease is any more divine or sacred than any other disease, but that on the contrary, just as other diseases have a nature and a definite cause, so does this one, too, have a nature and a cause. . . . It is my opinion that those who first called this disease sacred were the sort of people that we now call "magi." These magicians are vagabonds and charlatans, pretending to be holy and wise, and pretending to more knowledge than they have.

The natural/supernatural, real/unreal dichotomy has taken many forms over the course of Western history and civilization, but it was the philosopher-mathematician Rene Descartes (1596–1650) who most clearly formulated the ideas that are the immediate precursors of contemporary biomedical conceptions of the human organism. Descartes was determined to hold nothing as true until he had established the grounds of evidence for accepting it as such. The single category to be taken on faith, as it were, was the intuited perception of the body-self, expressed in Descartes' dictum: *Cogito, ergo sum*—I think, therefore I am. From this intuitive consciousness of his own

being, Descartes proceeded to argue the existence of two classes of substance that together constituted the human organism: palpable *body* and intangible *mind*. In his essay, "Passions of the Soul," Descartes sought to reconcile material body and divine soul by locating the soul in the pineal gland whence it directed the body's movements like an invisible rider on a horse. In this way Descartes, a devout Catholic, was able to preserve the soul as the domain of theology, and to legitimate the body as the domain of science. The rather artificial separation of mind and body, the so-called Cartesian dualism, freed biology to pursue the kind of radically materialist thinking expressed by the medical student above, much to the advantage of the natural and clinical sciences. However, it caused the mind (or soul) to recede to the background of clinical theory and practice for the next three hundred years.

The Cartesian legacy to clinical medicine and to the natural and social sciences is a rather mechanistic conception of the body and its functions, and a failure to conceptualize a "mindful" causation of somatic states. It would take a struggling psychoanalytic psychiatry and the gradual development of psychosomatic medicine in the early 20th century to begin the task of reuniting mind and body in clinical theory and practice. Yet, even in psychoanalytically informed psychiatry and in psychosomatic medicine there is a tendency to categorize and treat human afflictions as if they were either wholly organic or wholly psychological in origin: "it" is *in* the body, or "it" is *in* the mind. In her astute analysis of multidisciplinary case conferences on chronic pain patients, for example, Corbett (1986) discovered the intractability of Cartesian thinking among sophisticated clinicians. These physicians, psychiatrists, and clinical social workers "knew" that pain was "real" whether or not the source of it could be verified by diagnostic tests. Nonetheless, they could not help but express evident relief when a "true" (i.e., single, generally organic) cause could be discovered. Moreover, when diagnostic tests indicated some organic explanation, the psychological and social aspects of the pain tended to be all but forgotten, and when severe psychopathology could be diagnosed, the organic complications and indices tended to be ignored. Pain, it seems, was *either* physical *or* mental, biological *or* psycho-social—never both or something not-quite-either.

As both medical anthropologists and clinicians struggle to view humans and the experience of illness and suffering from an integrated perspective, they often find themselves trapped by the Cartesian legacy. We lack a precise vocabulary with which to deal with mind-body-society interactions and so are left suspended in hyphens, testifying to the disconnectedness of our thoughts. We are forced to resort to such fragmented concepts as the bio-social, the psycho-somatic, the somato-social as altogether feeble ways of expressing the myriad ways in which the mind speaks through the body, and the ways in which society is inscribed on the expectant canvas of human flesh. As Kundera (1984:15) recently observed: "The rise of science propelled man into tunnels of specialized knowledge. With every step forward in scientific knowledge, the less clearly he could see the world as a whole or his own self." Ironically, the conscious attempts to temper the materialism and the reductionism of biomedical science often end up inadvertently recreating the mind/body opposition in a new form. For example, Leon Eisenberg (1977) elaborated the distinction between disease and illness in an effort to distinguish the biomedical conception of "abnormalities in the structure and/or function or organs and organ systems" (*disease*) from the patient's subjective experience of malaise (*illness*). While Eisenberg and his associates' paradigm has certainly helped to create a single language and discourse for both clinicians and social scientists, one unanticipated effect has been that physicians are claiming *both* aspects of the sickness experience for the medical domain. As a result, the "illness" dimension of human distress (i.e., the social relations of sickness) are being medicalized and individualized, rather than politicized and collectivized (see Scheper-Hughes and Lock 1986). Medicalization inevitably entails a missed identification between the individual and the social bodies, and a tendency to transform the social into the biological.

Mind/body dualism is related to other conceptual oppositions in Western epistemology, such as those between nature and culture, passion and reason, individual and society—dichotomies that social thinkers as different as Durkheim, Mauss, Marx, and Freud understood as inevitable and often unresolvable contradictions and as natural and universal categories. Although Durkheim was primarily concerned with the relationship of the individual to society (an opposition we will discuss at greater length below), he devoted some attention to the mind/body, nature/society dichotomies. In *The Elementary Forms of the Religious Life* Durkheim wrote that "man is double" (1961[1915]:29), referring to the biological and the social. The physical body provided for the reproduction of society through sexuality and socialization. For Durkheim society represented the "highest reality in the intellectual and moral order." The body was the storehouse of emotions that were the raw materials, the "stuff," out of which mechanical solidarity was forged in the interests of the collectivity. Building on Durkheim, Mauss wrote of the "dominion of the conscious [will] over emotion and unconsciousness" (1979[1950]:122). The degree to which the random and chaotic impulses of the body

were disciplined and restrained by social institutions revealed the stamp of higher civilizations.

Freud introduced yet another interpretation of the mind/body, nature/culture, individual/society set of oppositions with his theory of dynamic psychology: the individual at war within himself. Freud proposed a human drama in which natural, biological drives locked horns with the domesticating requirements of the social and moral order. The resulting repressions of the libido through a largely painful process of socialization produced the many neuroses of modern life. Psychiatry was called on to diagnose and treat the dis-ease of wounded psyches whose egos were not in control of the rest of their minds. *Civilization and its Discontents* may be read as a psychoanalytic parable concerning the mind/body, nature/culture, and individual/society oppositions in Western epistemology.

For Marx and his associates the natural world existed as an external, objective reality that was transformed by human labor. Humans distinguish themselves from animals, Marx and Engels wrote, "as soon as they begin to produce their means of subsistence" (1970:42). In *Capital* Marx wrote that labor humanizes and domesticates nature. It gives life to inanimate objects, and it pushes back the natural frontier, leaving a human stamp on all that it touches.

Although the nature/culture opposition has been interpreted as the "very matrix of Western metaphysics" (Benoist 1978:59) and has "penetrated so deeply . . . that we have come to regard it as natural and inevitable" (Goody 1977:64), there have always been alternative ontologies. One of these is surely the view that culture is rooted *in* (rather than against) nature (i.e., biology), imitating it and emanating directly from it. Cultural materialists, for example, have tended to view social institutions as adaptive responses to certain fixed, biological foundations. M. Harris (1974, 1979) refers to culture as a "banal" or "vulgar" solution to the human condition insofar as it "rests on the ground and is built up out of guts, sex, energy" (1974:3). Mind collapses into body in these formulations.

Similarly, some human biologists and psychologists have suggested that the mind/body, nature/culture, individual/society oppositions are natural (and presumed universal) categories of thinking insofar as they are a cognitive and symbolic manifestation of human biology. Ornstein (1973), for example, understands mind/body dualism as an overly determined expression of human brain lateralization. According to this view, the uniquely human specialization of the brain's left hemisphere for cognitive, rational, and analytic functions and of the right hemisphere for intuitive, expressive, and artistic functions *within the context of left-hemisphere dominance* sets the stage for the symbolic and cultural dominance of reason over passion, mind over body, culture over nature, and male over female. This kind of biological reductionism is, however, rejected by most contemporary social anthropologists who stress, instead, the cultural sources of these oppositions in Western thought.

We should bear in mind that our epistemology is but one among many systems of knowledge regarding the relations held to obtain among mind, body, culture, nature, and society. We would point, for example, to those non-Western civilizations that have developed alternative epistemologies that tend to conceive of relations among similar entities in monistic rather than dualistic terms.

Representations of Holism in Non-Western Epistemologies

In defining relationships between any set of concepts, principles of exclusion and inclusion come into play. Representations of holism and monism tend toward inclusiveness. Two representations of holistic thought are particularly common. The first is a conception of harmonious wholes in which everything from the cosmos down to the individual organs of the human body are understood as a single unit. This is often expressed as the relationship of microcosm to macrocosm. A second representation of holistic thinking is that of *complementary* (not opposing) dualities, in which the relationship of parts to the whole is emphasized.

One of the better known representations of balanced complementarity is the ancient Chinese yin/yang cosmology, which first appears in the *I Ching* somewhat before the 3rd century B.C. In this view, the entire cosmos is understood as poised in a state of dynamic equilibrium, oscillating between the poles of yin and yang, masculine and feminine, light and dark, hot and cold. The human body is likewise understood as moving back and forth between the forces of yin and yang—sometimes dry, sometimes moist, sometimes flushed, and sometimes chilled. The evolving tradition of ancient Chinese medicine borrowed the yin/yang cosmology from the Taoists and from Confucianism a concern with social ethics, moral conduct, and the importance of maintaining harmonious relations among individual, family, community, and state. Conceptions of the healthy body were patterned after the healthy state: in both there is an emphasis on order, harmony, balance, and hierarchy within the context of mutual interdependencies. A rebellious spleen can be compared to an insubordinate servant, and a lazy intestine compared to an indolent son. In the *Nei Ching, The Yellow Emperor's Classic of Internal Medicine,* the Prime Minister counsels: "the

human body is an imitation of heaven and earth in all its details" (Veith 1966:115). The health of individuals depends on a balance in the natural world, while the health of each organ depends on its relationship to all other organs. Nothing can change without changing the whole. A conception of the human body as a mixture of yin and yang, forces of which the entire universe is composed, is altogether different from Western body conceptions based on absolute dichotomies and unresolvable differences. In ancient Chinese cosmology the emphasis is on balance and resonance; in Western cosmology, on tension and contradiction.

Islamic cosmology—a synthesis of early Greek philosophy, Judeo-Christian concepts, and prophetic revelations set down in the Qur'an—depicts humans as having dominance over nature, but this potential opposition is tempered by a sacred world view that stresses the complementarity of all phenomena (Jachimowicz 1975; Shariati 1979). At the core of Islamic belief lies the unifying concept of *Towhid,* which Shariati argues should be understood as going beyond the strictly religious meaning of "God is one, no more than one" to encompass a world view that represents all existence as essentially monistic. Guided by the principle of *Towhid* humans are responsible to one power, answerable to a single judge, and guided by one principle: the achievement of unity through the complementarities of spirit and body, this world and the hereafter, substance and meaning, natural and supernatural, etc.

The concept in Western philosophical traditions of an observing and reflexive "I," a mindful self that stands outside the body and apart from nature, is another heritage of Cartesian dualism that contrasts sharply with a Buddhist form of subjectivity and relation to the natural world. In writing about the Buddhist Sherpas of Nepal, Paul suggests that they do not perceive their interiority or their subjectivity as "hopelessly cut off and excluded from the rest of nature, but [rather as] . . . connected to, indeed identical with, the entire essential being of the cosmos" (1976:131).

In Buddhist traditions the natural world (the world of appearances) is a product of mind, in the sense that the entire cosmos is essentially "mind." Through meditation individual minds can merge with the universal mind. Understanding is reached not through analytic methods, but rather through an intuitive synthesis, achieved in moments of transcendence that are beyond speech, language, and the written word. For, the essence of world meaning is unspeakable and unthinkable. It is experientially received as a perception of the unity of mind and body, self and other, mind and nature, being and nothingness.

. . .

Person, Self, and Individual

The relation of individual to society, which has occupied so much of contemporary social theory, is based on a perceived "natural" opposition between the demands of the social and moral order and egocentric drives, impulses, wishes, and needs. The individual/society opposition, while fundamental to Western epistemology, is also rather unique to it. . . .

In all, Japan has been repeatedly described as a culture of "social relativism," in which the person is understood as acting within the context of a social relationship, never simply autonomously (Lebra 1976; Smith 1983). One's self-identity changes with the social context, particularly within the hierarchy of social relations at any given time. The child's identity is established through the responses of others; conformity and dependency, even in adulthood, are not understood as signs of weakness, but rather as the result of inner strength (Reischauer 1977:152). One fear, however, which haunts many contemporary Japanese is that of losing oneself completely, of becoming totally immersed in social obligations. One protective device is a distinction made between the external self (*tatemae*)—the persona, the mask, the social self that one presents to others—versus a more private self (*honne*), the less controlled, hidden self. Geertz has described a similar phenomenon among the Javanese and Balinese (1984:127–128).

. . .

Such sociocentric conceptions of the self have been widely documented for many parts of the world (see Shweder and Bourne 1982; Devisch 1985; Fortes 1959; Harris 1978) and have relevance to ethnomedical understanding. In cultures and societies lacking a highly individualized or articulated conception of the body-self it should not be surprising that sickness is often explained or attributed to malevolent social relations (i.e., sorcery), or to the breaking of social and moral codes, or to disharmony within the family or the village community. In such societies therapy, too, tends to be collectivized. Lévi-Strauss (1963) has noted that in transcendental and shamanic healing, the patient is almost incidental to the ritual, which is focused on the community at large. The !Kung of Botswana engage in weekly healing trance-dance rituals that are viewed as both curative and preventive (Katz 1982). Lorna Marshall has described the dance as "one concerted religious act of the !Kung [that] brings people into such union that they become like one organic being" (1965:270).

In contrast to societies in which the individual body-self tends to be fused with or absorbed by the social body, there are societies that view the individual as comprised of a multiplicity of selves. The Bororo (like the Gahuku-Gama) understand the individual only as reflected in relationship to other people. Hence, the person consists of many selves—the self as perceived by parents, by other kinsmen, by enemies, etc. The Cuna Indians of Panama say they have eight selves, each associated with a different part of the body. A Cuna individual's temperament is the result of domination by one of these aspects or parts of the body. An intellectual is one who is governed by the head, a thief governed by the hand, a romantic by the heart, and so forth.

. . .

Body Imagery

Closely related to conceptions of self (perhaps central to them) is what psychiatrists have labeled "body image" (Schilder 1970[1950]; Horowitz 1966). Body image refers to the collective and idiosyncratic representations an individual entertains about the body in its relationship to the environment, including internal and external perceptions, memories, affects, cognitions, and actions. The existing literature on body imagery (although largely psychiatric) has been virtually untapped by social and especially medical anthropologists, who could benefit a great deal from attention to body boundary conceptions, distortions in body perception, etc.

Some of the earliest and best work on body image was contained in clinical studies of individuals suffering from extremely distorted body perceptions that arose from neurological, organic, or psychiatric disorders (Head 1920; Schilder 1970[1950]; Luria 1972). The inability of some so-called schizophrenics to distinguish self from other, or self from inanimate objects has been analyzed from psychoanalytic and phenomenological perspectives (Minkowski 1958; Binswanger 1958; Laing 1965; Basaglia 1964). Sacks (1973[1970], 1985) has also written about rare neurological disorders that can play havoc with the individual's body image, producing deficits and excesses as well as metaphysical transports in mind-body experiences. Sack's message throughout his poignant medical case histories is that humanness is not dependent upon rationality or intelligence—i.e., an intact mind. There is, he suggests, something intangible, a soul-force or mind-self that produces humans even under the most devastating assaults on the brain, nervous system, and sense of bodily or mindful integrity.

While profound distortions in body imagery are rare, neurotic anxieties about the body, its orifices, boundaries, and fluids are quite common. Fisher and Cleveland (1958) demonstrated the relationship between patients' "choice" of symptoms and body image conceptions. The skin, for example, can be experienced as a protective hide and a defensive armour protecting the softer and more vulnerable internal organs. In the task of protecting the inside, however, the outside can take quite a beating, manifested in skin rashes and hives. Conversely, the skin can be imagined as a permeable screen, leaving the internal organs defenseless and prone to attacks of ulcers and colitis. Few medical anthropologists have examined social dimensions and collective representations of body imagery, although Kleinman's work on the somatization of depression in the aches and pains of Chinese and Chinese-American patients is one example (1980; Kleinman and Kleinman 1985). Another is Scheper-Hughes's description of impoverished Brazilian mothers' distorted perceptions of their breastmilk as sour, curdled, bitter, and diseased, a metaphorical projection of their inability to pass on anything untainted to their children (1984:541–544).

Particular organs, body fluids, and functions may also have special significance to a group of people. The liver, for example, absorbs a great deal of blame for many different ailments among the French, Spanish, Portuguese and Brazilians, but to our knowledge only the Pueblo Indians of the Southwest suffer from "flipped liver" (Leeman 1986). In their national fantasy about the medical significance of the liver the French have created a mystical "phantom organ," one altogether fierce in its tyranny over the rest of the body and its ability to inflict human suffering (Miller 1978:44). The English and the Germans are, by comparison, far more obsessed with the condition and health of their bowels. Dundes takes the Germanic fixation with the bowels, cleanliness, and anality as a fundamental constellation underlying German national character (1984), while Miller writes that "when an Englishman complains about constipation, you never know whether he is talking about his regularity, his lassitude, or his depression" (1978:45).

Once an organ captures the imagination of a people, there appears to be no end to the metaphorical uses to which it may be put. Among "old stock" American Midwestern farmers, for example, the backbone has great cultural and ethnomedical significance. When illness strikes at these industrious and "upright" people, being forced off their feet comes as a grave blow to the ego. Even among the elderly and infirm, well-being is defined as the ability to "get around," to be on one's feet. Obviously, the ability to stay "upright" is not confined to the mere technical problems of locomotion; it carries symbolic weight as well. As Erwin Strauss pointed out, the expression "to be upright" has two connotations to Americans: the first, to stand up, to be on one's feet; and the second, a moral implica-

tion "not to stoop to anything, to be honest and just, to be true to friends in danger, to stand by one's convictions" (1966b:137). Among rural Midwesterners laziness is a most serious moral failing, and "spinelessness" is as reviled as godlessness. It is little wonder that a therapy concerned with adjusting perceived malalignments of the spine—chiropractic medicine—would have its origins in middle America (Cobb 1958).

Blood, on the other hand, is a nearly universal symbol of human life, and some peoples, both ancient and contemporary, have taken the quality of the blood, pulse, and circulation as the primary diagnostic sign of health or illness. The traditional Chinese doctor, for example, made his diagnosis by feeling the pulse in both the patient's wrists and comparing them with his own, an elaborate ritual that could take several hours. The doctor was expected to take note of minute variations, and the *Nei Ching* states that the pulse can be "sharp as a hook, fine as a hair, taut as a musical string, dead as a rock, smooth as a flowing stream, or as continuous as a string of pearls" (Majno 1975:245). Snow (1974) has described the rich constellation of ethnomedical properties and significances attached to the quality of the blood by poor black Americans, who suffer from "high" or "low," fast and slow, thick and thin, bitter and sweet blood. Linke (1986) has analyzed the concept of blood as a predominant metaphor in European culture, especially its uses in political ideologies, such as during the Nazi era. Similarly, the multiple stigmas suffered by North American AIDS patients include a preoccupation with the "bad blood" of diseased homosexuals (Lancaster 1983).

Hispanic mothers from southern Mexico to northern New Mexico focus some of their body organ anxieties on the infant's fontanelle. Often, it exposes the newborn to the evil influences of night airs, as well as the envious looks and wishes of neighbors. Until it closes over, there is always the threat of *mollera caida*, "fallen fontanelle," a life-threatening pediatric disorder (Scheper-Hughes and Stewart 1983).

In short, ethnoanatomical perceptions, including body image, offer a rich source of data both on the social and cultural meanings of being human and on the various threats to health, well-being, and social integration that humans are believed to experience.

THE SOCIAL BODY

The Body as Symbol

Symbolic and structuralist anthropologists have demonstrated the extent to which humans find the body "good to think with." The human organism and its natural products of blood, milk, tears, semen, and excreta may be used as a cognitive map to represent other natural, supernatural, social, and even spatial relations. The body, as Mary Douglas observed, is a natural symbol supplying some of our richest sources of metaphor (1970:65). Cultural constructions of and about the body are useful in sustaining particular views of society and social relations.

Needham, for example, pointed out some of the frequently occurring associations to right- and left-handedness, especially the symbolic equations, on the one hand, between the left and that which is inferior, dark, dirty, and female, and, on the other hand, between the right and that which is superior, holy, light, dominant, and male. Needham called attention to such uses of the body as a convenient means of justifying particular social values and social arrangements, such as the "natural" dominance of males over females (1973:109). His point is that these common symbolic equations are not so much natural as they are useful, at least to those "on the top" and to the right.

. . .

Ethnobiological theories of reproduction usually reflect the particular character of their associated kinship system, as anthropologists have long observed. In societies with unilineal descent it is common to encounter folk theories that emphasize the reproductive contributions of females in matrilineal and of males in patrilineal societies. The matrilineal Ashanti make the distinction between flesh and blood that is inherited through women, and spirit that is inherited through males. The Brazilian Shavante, among whom patrilineages form the core of political factions, believe that the father fashions the infant through many acts of coitus, during which the mother is only passive and receptive. The fetus is "fully made," and conception is completed only in the fifth month of pregnancy. As one Shavante explained the process to Maybury-Lewis, while ticking the months off with his fingers: "Copulate. Copulate, copulate, copulate, copulate a lot. Pregnant. Copulate, copulate, copulate. Born" (1967:63).

Similarly, the Western theory of equal male and female contributions to conception that spans the reproductive biologies of Galen to Theodore Dobzhansky (1970) probably owes more to the theory's compatibility with the European extended and stem bilateral kinship system than to scientific evidence, which was lacking until relatively recently. The principle of one father, one mother, one act of copulation leading to each pregnancy was part of the Western tradition for more than a thousand years before the discovery of spermatozoa (in 1677), the female ova (in 1828), and

before the actual process of human fertilization was fully understood and described (in 1875) (Barnes 1973:66). For centuries the theory of equal male and female contributions to conception was supported by the erroneous belief that females had the same reproductive organs and functions as males, except that, as one 6th-century Bishop put it, "*theirs* are *inside* the body and not outside it" (Laquer 1986:3). To a great extent, talk about the body and about sexuality tends to be talk about the nature of society.

Of particular relevance to medical anthropologists are the frequently encountered symbolic equations between conceptions of the healthy body and the healthy society, as well as the diseased body and the malfunctioning society. Janzen (1981) has noted that every society possesses a utopian conception of health that can be applied metaphorically from society to body and vice versa. One of the most enduring ideologies of individual and social health is that of the vital balance, and of harmony, integration, and wholeness that are found in the ancient medical systems of China, Greece, India, and Persia, in contemporary Native American cultures of the Southwest (Shutler 1979), through the holistic health movement of the 20th century (Grossinger 1980). Conversely, illness and death can be attributed to social tensions, contradictions, and hostilities, as manifested in Mexican peasants' image of the limited good (Foster 1965), in the hot-cold syndrome and symbolic imbalance in Mexican folk medicine (Currier 1969), and in such folk idioms as witchcraft, evil eye, or "stress" (Scheper-Hughes and Lock 1986). Each of these beliefs exemplifies the link between the health or illness of the individual body and the social body.

The Embodied World

One of the most common and richly detailed symbolic uses of the human body in the non-Western world is to domesticate the spaces in which humans reside. Bastien has written extensively about the Qollahuaya-Andean Indians' individual and social body concepts (1978, 1985). The Qollahuayas live at the foot of Mt. Kaata in Bolivia and are known as powerful healers, the "lords of the medicine bag." Having practiced a sophisticated herbal medicine and surgery since A.D. 700, Qollahuayas "understand their own bodies in terms of the mountain, and they consider the mountain in terms of their own anatomy" (1985:598). The human body and the mountain consist of interrelated parts: head, chest and heart, stomach and viscera, breast and nipple. The mountain, like the body, must be fed blood and fat to keep it strong and healthy. Individual sickness is understood as a disintegration of the body, likened to a mountain landslide or an earthquake. Sickness is caused by disruptions between people and the land, specifically between residents of different sections of the mountain: the head (mountain top), heart (center village), or feet (the base of the mountain). Healers cure by gathering the various residents together to feed the mountain and to restore the wholeness and wellness that was compromised. "I am the same as the mountain," says Marcelino Yamahuaya the healer, "[the mountain] takes care of my body, and I must give food and drink to Pachemama" (Bastien 1985:597). Bastien concludes that Qollahuaya body concepts are fundamentally holistic rather than dualistic. He suggests that

> The whole is greater than the sum of the parts.
> . . .Wholeness (health) of the body is a process in which centripetal and centrifugal forces pull together and disperse fluids that provide emotions, thoughts, nutrients, and lubricants for members of the body. (1985:598)

. . .

We could multiply by the dozens ethnographic illustrations of the symbolic uses of the human body in classifying and "humanizing" natural phenomena, human artifacts, animals, and topography. Among some of the more well-known examples are the western Apache (Basso 1969), the Indonesian Atoni (Cunningham 1973); the Desana Indians of the Colombian-Brazilian border (Reichel-Dolmatoff 1971); the Pira-pirana of the Amazon (Hugh-Jones 1979); the Zinacantecos of Chiapas (Vogt 1970); and the Fali of northern Cameroon (Zahan 1979). In such essentially monistic and humanistic cosmologies as these, principles of separation and fusion, imminence and transcendence influence interpretations of illness and the practice of healing.

Manning and Fabrega (1973) have summarized the major differences between most of these non-Western ethnomedical systems and modern biomedicine. In the latter body and self are understood as distinct and separable entities; illness resides in either the body or the mind. Social relations are seen as partitioned, segmented, and situational—generally as discontinuous with health or sickness. By contrast, many ethnomedical systems do not logically distinguish body, mind, and self, and therefore illness cannot be situated in mind or body alone. Social relations are also understood as a key contributor to individual health and illness. In short, the body is seen as a unitary, integrated aspect of self and social relations. It is dependent on, and vulnerable to, the feelings, wishes, and actions of others, including spirits and dead ancestors. The body is not understood as a vast and complex machine, but rather as a microcosm of the universe.

. . .

However, the mind/body dichotomy and the body alienation characteristic of contemporary society may also be linked to capitalist modes of production in which manual and mental labors are divided and ordered into a hierarchy. Human labor, thus divided and fragmented, is by Marxist definition "alienated," and is reflected in the marked distortions of body movement, body imagery, and self-conception that E. P. Thompson (1967), among others, has described. Thompson discusses the subversion of natural, body time to the clock-work regimentation and work discipline required by industrialization. He juxtaposes the factory worker, whose labor is extracted in minute, recorded segments, with the Nuer pastoralist, for whom "the daily timepiece is the cattle clock" (Evans-Pritchard 1940:100), or the Aran Islander, whose work is managed by the amount of time left before twilight (Thompson 1967:59).

. . .

In contrast, the world in which most of us live is lacking a comfortable and familiar human shape. At least one source of body alienation in advanced industrial societies is the symbolic equation of humans and machines, originating in our industrial modes and relations of production and in the commodity fetishism of modern life, in which even the human body has been transformed into a commodity. Again, Manning and Fabrega capture this so well:

> In primitive society the body of man is the paradigm for the derivation of the parts and meanings of other significant objects; in modern society man has adopted the language of the machine to describe his body. This reversal, wherein man sees himself in terms of the external world, as a reflection of himself, is the representative formula for expressing the present situation of modern man. (1973:283)

We rely on the body-as-machine metaphor each time we describe our somatic or psychological states in mechanistic terms, saying that we are "worn out" or "wound up," or when we say that we are "run down" and that our "batteries need recharging." In recent years the metaphors have moved from a mechanical to an electrical mode (we are "turned off," "tuned in," we "get a charge" out of something), while the computer age has lent us a host of new expressions, including the all-too-familiar complaint: "my energy is down."

. . . The machines have changed since those early days of the assembly line. One thinks today not of the brutality of huge grinding gears and wheels, but rather of the sterile silence and sanitized pollution of the microelectronics industries to which the nimble fingers, strained eyes, and docile bodies of a new, largely female and Asian labor force are now melded. What has not changed to any appreciable degree is the relationship of human bodies to the machines under 20th-century forms of industrial capitalism.

. . .

THE BODY POLITIC

The relationships between individual and social bodies concern more, however, than metaphors and collective representations of the natural and the cultural. The relationships are also about power and control. Douglas (1966) contends, for example, that when a community experiences itself as threatened, it will respond by expanding the number of social controls regulating the group's boundaries. Points where outside threats may infiltrate and pollute the inside become the focus of particular regulation and surveillance. The three bodies—individual, social, and body politic—may be closed off, protected by a nervous vigilance about exits and entrances. Douglas had in mind witchcraft crazes and hysterias from the Salem trials through contemporary African societies and even political witch hunts in the United States. In each of these instances the body politic is likened to the human body in which what is "inside" is good and all that is "outside" is evil. The body politic under threat of attack is cast as vulnerable, leading to purges of traitors and social deviants, while individual hygiene may focus on the maintenance of ritual purity or on fears of losing blood, semen, tears, or milk.

Threats to the continued existence of the social group may be real or imaginary. Even when the threats are real, however, the true aggressors may not be known, and witchcraft can become the metaphor or the cultural idiom for distress. Lindenbaum (1979) has shown, for example, how an epidemic of Kuru among the South Fore of New Guinea led to sorcery accusations and counteraccusations and attempts to purify both the individual and collective bodies of their impurities and contaminants. Mullings suggests that witchcraft and sorcery were widely used in contemporary West Africa as "metaphors for social relations" (1984:164). In the context of a rapidly industrializing market town in Ghana, witchcraft accusations can express anxieties over social contradictions introduced by capitalism. Hence, accusations were directed at those individuals and families who, in the pursuit of economic success, appeared most competitive, greedy, and individualistic in their social relations. While Foster (1972) might label such witchcraft accusations a

symptom of envy among the less successful, Mullings argues that witchcraft accusations are an inchoate expression of resistance to the erosion of traditional social values based on reciprocity, sharing, and family and community loyalty. Mullings does not, of course, suggest that witchcraft and sorcery are unique to capitalist social and economic formations, but rather that in the context of increasing commoditization of human life, witchcraft accusations point to the social distortions and dis-ease in the body politic generated by capitalism.

When the sense of social order is threatened, as in the examples provided above, the symbols of self-control become intensified along with those of social control. Boundaries between the individual and political bodies become blurred, and there is strong concern with matters of ritual and sexual purity, often expressed in vigilance over social and bodily boundaries. Individuals may express high anxiety over what goes in and what comes out of the two bodies. In witchcraft-fearing societies, for example, there is often a concern with the disposal of one's excreta, hair cuttings, and nail parings. In small, threatened, and therefore often conservative peasant communities, a similar equation between social and bodily vigilance is likely to be found. For example, in Ballybran, rural Ireland, villagers were equally guarded about what they took into the body (as in sex and food) as they were about being "taken in" (as in "codding," flattery, and blarney) by outsiders, especially those with a social advantage over them. Concern with the penetration and violation of bodily exits, entrances, and boundaries extended to material symbols of the body—the home, with its doors, gates, fences, and stone boundaries, around which many protective rituals, prayers, and social customs served to create social distance and a sense of personal control and security (Scheper-Hughes 1979).

In addition to controlling bodies in a time of crisis, societies regularly reproduce and socialize the kind of bodies that they need. Aggressive (or threatened) societies, for example, often require fierce and foolhearty warriors. The Yanomamo, who, like all Amerindian peoples living in the Amazon, are constantly under siege from encroaching ranching and mining interests, place a great premium on aggressivity. The body of Yanomamo males is both medium and message: most adults' heads are criss-crossed by battle scars into which red dyes are rubbed. The men's mutilated crowns are kept clean and shaved for display; their scars are endowed with a religious as well as a political significance—they represent the rivers of blood on the moon where Pore, the Creator-Spirit of the Yanomamo, lives (Brain 1979:167–168). In creating a fine consonance among the physical, material, political, and spiritual planes of existence, many Yanomamo men are encouraged to put their bodies—especially their heads—in the service of the body politic. In many societies (including our own) the culturally and politically "correct" body is the beautiful, strong, and healthy body, although the meanings given to obesity and thinness, to the form and shape of body parts, to facial and dental structure, as well as the values placed on endurance, agility, fertility, and longevity (as indicators of strength and health), vary.

. . .

In our own increasingly "healthist" and body-conscious culture, the politically correct body for both sexes is the lean, strong, androgynous, and physically "fit" form through which the core cultural values of autonomy, toughness, competitiveness, youth, and self-control are readily manifest (Pollitt 1982). Health is increasingly viewed in the United States as an achieved rather than an ascribed status, and each individual is expected to "work hard" at being strong, fit, and healthy. Conversely, ill health is no longer viewed as accidental, a mere quirk of nature, but rather is attributed to the individual's failure to live right, to eat well, to exercise, etc. We might ask what our society "wants" from this kind of body. DeMause (1984) has speculated that the fitness/toughness craze is a reflection of an international preparation for war. A hardening and toughening of the national fiber corresponds to a toughening of individual bodies. In attitude and ideology the self-help and fitness movements articulate both a militarist and a Social Darwinist ethos: the fast and fit win; the fat and flabby lose and drop out of the human race (Scheper-Hughes and Stein 1987). Crawford (1980, 1985), however, has suggested that the fitness movement may reflect, instead, a pathetic and individualized (also wholly inadequate) defense against the threat of nuclear holocaust.

Rather than strong and fit, the politically (and economically) correct body can entail grotesque distortions of human anatomy, including in various times and places the bound feet of Chinese women (Daly 1978), the 16-inch waists of antebellum Southern socialites (Kunzle 1981), the tuberculin wanness of 19th-century Romantics (Sontag 1978), and the anorexics and bulimics of contemporary society. Crawford (1985) has interpreted the eating disorders and distortions in body image expressed in obsessional jogging, anorexia, and bulimia as a symbolic mediation of the contradictory demands of postindustrial American society. The double-binding injunction to be self-controlled, fit, and productive workers, and to be at the same time self-indulgent, pleasure-seeking consumers is especially destructive to the self-image of the "modern," "liberated" American woman. Expected to be fun-loving and sensual, she must also remain thin, lovely, and self-disciplined. Since one cannot be hedonistic and controlled simultaneously, one can alternate phases of binge eating, drinking, and drugging with phases of jogging, purging, and vomiting. Out of this cyclical resolution of the injunction to consume and to conserve is born, according to Crawford, the current epidemic of eating disorders (especially bulimia) among young women, some of whom literally eat and diet to death.

. . .

The body politic can, of course, exert its control over individual bodies in less dramatic and mundane, but no less brutal, ways. Foucault's (1973, 1975, 1979, 1980c) analyses of the role of medicine, criminal justice, psychiatry, and the various social sciences in producing new forms of power/knowledge over bodies are illustrative in this regard. The proliferation of disease categories and labels in medicine and psychiatry, resulting in ever more restricted definitions of the normal, has created a sick and deviant majority, a problem that medical and psychiatric anthropologists have been slow to explore. Radical changes in the organization of social and public life in advanced industrial societies, including the disappearance of traditional cultural idioms for the expression of individual and collective discontent (such as witchcraft, sorcery, rituals of reversal and travesty), have allowed medicine and psychiatry to assume a hegemonic role in shaping and responding to human distress. Apart from anarchic forms of random street violence and other forms of direct assault and confrontation, illness somatization has become a dominant metaphor for expressing individual and social complaint. Negative and hostile feelings can be shaped and transformed by doctors and psychiatrists into symptoms of new diseases such as PMS (premenstrual syndrome) or Attention Deficit Disorder (Martin 1987; Lock 1986a; Lock and Dunk 1987; Rubinstein and Brown 1984). In this way such negative social sentiments as female rage and schoolchildren's boredom or school phobias (Lock 1986b) can be recast as individual pathologies and "symptoms" rather than as socially significant "signs." This funneling of diffuse but real complaints into the idiom of sickness has led to the problem of "medicalization" and to the overproduction of illness in contemporary advanced industrial societies. In this process the role of doctors, social workers, psychiatrists, and criminologists as agents of social consensus is pivotal. As Hopper (1982) has suggested, the physician (and other social agents) is predisposed to "fail to see the secret indignation of the sick." The medical gaze is, then, a controlling gaze, through which active (although furtive) forms of protest are transformed into passive acts of "breakdown."

While the medicalization of life (and its political and social control functions) is understood by critical medical social scientists (Freidson 1972; Zola 1972; Roth 1972; Illich 1976; deVries 1982) as a fairly permanent feature of industrialized societies, few medical anthropologists have yet explored the immediate effects of "medicalization" in those areas of the world where the process is occurring for the first time. In the following passage, recorded by Bourdieu (1977:166), an old Kabyle woman explains what it meant to be sick before and after medicalization was a feature of Algerian peasant life:

> In the old days, folk didn't know what illness was. They went to bed and they died. It's only nowadays that we're learning words like liver, lung . . . intestines, stomach . . . , and I don't know what! People only used to know [pain in] the belly; that's what everyone who died died of, unless it was the fever. . . . Now everyone's sick, everyone's complaining of something. . . . Who's ill nowadays? Who's well? Everyone complains, but no one stays in bed; they all run to the doctor. Everyone knows what's wrong with him now.

Or *does* everyone? We would suggest the usefulness to the body politic of filtering more and more human unrest, dissatisfaction, longing, and protest into the idiom of sickness, which can then be safely managed by doctor-agents.

. . .

Biomedicine has often served the interests of the state with respect to the control of reproduction, sexuality, women, and sexual "deviants." A particularly poignant illustration of medical intervention in the definition of gender and sexual norms comes from Foucault's (1980b) introduction to the diary of Herculine Barbin, a 19th-century French hermaphrodite. At that time it was the opinion of medical science in Europe that nature produced in humans (unlike other animals) *only* two biological sexes. Once discovered to be sexually ambiguous, Herculine was forced in adulthood to conform to a medically and legally mandated sex and gender transformation, based on her "deviant" sexual preference for female partners. Although fully socialized to a healthy personal and social identity as an adult female, Herculine was forced to accept a medical diagnosis of her "true" sex as male, which resulted in her suicide a few years later.

EMOTION: MEDIATRIX OF THE THREE BODIES

An anthropology of the body necessarily entails a theory of emotions. Emotions affect the way in which the body, illness, and pain are experienced and are projected in images of the well or poorly functioning social body and body politic. To date, social anthropologists have tended to restrict their interest in emotions to occasions when they are formal, public, ritualized, and "distanced," such as the highly stylized mourning of the Basques (W. Douglas 1969) or the deep play of a Balinese cock fight (Geertz 1973). The more private and idiosyncratic emotions and passions of individuals have tended to be left to psychoanalytic and psychobiological anthropologists, who have reduced them to a discourse on innate drives, impulses, and instincts. This division of labor, based on a false dichotomy between cultural sentiments and natural passions, leads us right back to the mind/body, nature/culture, individual/society epistemological muddle with which we began this article. We would tend to join with Geertz (1980) in questioning whether any expression of human emotion and feeling—whether public or private, individual or collective, whether repressed or explosively expressed—is ever free of cultural shaping and cultural meaning. The most extreme statement of Geertz's position, shared by many of the newer psychological and medical anthropologists, would be that without culture we simply would not know how to feel.

Insofar as emotions entail both feelings and cognitive orientations, public morality, and cultural ideology, we suggest they provide an important "missing link" capable of bridging mind and body, individual, society, and body politic. As Blacking (1977:5) has stated, emotions are the catalyst that transforms knowledge into human understanding and that brings intensity and commitment to human action. Rosaldo (1984) has recently charged social and psychological anthropologists to pay more attention to the force and intensity of emotions in motivating human action.

Certainly, medical anthropologists have long been concerned with understanding the power of emotion and feelings in human life, and it is time that their specific contributions were recognized beyond the subdiscipline and the implications of their findings brought to bear on general theory in the parent discipline. We would refer in particular to those phenomenological, ethnopsychological, and medical anthropologists whose stock-in-trade is the exploration of sickness, madness, pain, depression, disability, and death—human events literally seething with emotion (e.g., Schieffelin 1976, 1979; M. Rosaldo 1980, 1984; Kleinman 1982, 1986; Lutz 1982, 1985; Levy and Rosaldo 1983; Kleinman and Good 1985).[4] It is sometimes during the experience of sickness, as in moments of deep trance or sexual transport, that mind and body, self and other, become one. Analyses of these events offer a key to understanding the mindful body, as well as the self, social body, and body politic.

Elaine Scarry claims to have discovered in the exploration of pain (especially pain intentionally inflicted through torture) a source of human creativity and destructiveness which she refers to as the "making and unmaking of the world" (1985). Pain destroys, disassembles, deconstructs the world of the victim. We would offer that illness, injury, disability, and death likewise deconstruct the world of the patient by virtue of their seeming randomness, arbitrariness, and hence their absurdity. Medical anthropologists are privileged, however, in that their domain includes not only the unmaking of the world in sickness and death, but also the remaking of the world in healing, especially during those intensely emotional and collective experiences of trance-dance, sings, and charismatic faith healing.

. . .

"Belief kills; belief heals," write Hahn and Kleinman (1983:16), although they might as accurately have stated it "feelings kill; feelings heal." Their essay is part of that tradition in psychiatry, psychosomatic medicine, and medical anthropology that seeks to understand human events in that murky realm (close to religion and parapsychology) where the causes of "sudden death" or of "miraculous cure" cannot be explained by conventional biomedical science.[5] At the one pole for Hahn and Kleinman is "culturogenic" death involving voodoo, bone pointing, evil eye, sorcery, fright, "stress," and other states involving strong and pathogenic emotions. These they label "nocebo" effects. At the other, and therapeutic, pole are unexplained cures attributed to faith, suggestion, catharsis, drama, and ritual. These they label placebo effects. Moerman (1983), reporting on remarkable improvements in coronary bypass surgery patients (in which the surgery was a technical failure), attributes cause to the powerfully metaphoric effects of the operation as a cosmic drama of death and rebirth. His analysis strikes many chords of resonance with previous interpretations of the "efficacy of symbols" in shamanic and other ethnomedical cures (e.g., Lévi-Strauss 1967; Edgerton 1971; Herrick 1983). What is apparent is that nocebo and placebo effects are integral to *all* sickness and healing, for they are concepts that refer in an incomplete and oblique way to the interactions between mind and body and among the three bodies: individual, social, and politic.

CONCLUDING OBSERVATIONS

We would like to think of medical anthropology as providing the key toward the development of a new epistemology and metaphysics of the mindful body

and of the emotional, social, and political sources of illness and healing. Clearly, biomedicine is still caught in the clutches of the Cartesian dichotomy and its related oppositions of nature and culture, natural and supernatural, real and unreal. If and when we tend to think reductionistically about the mind-body, it is because it is "good for us to think" in this way. To do otherwise, using a radically different metaphysics, would imply the "unmaking" of our own assumptive world and its culture-bound dimensions of reality. To admit the "as-ifness" of our ethnoepistemology is to court a Cartesian anxiety—the fear that in the absence of a sure, objective foundation for knowledge we would fall into the void, into the chaos of absolute relativism and subjectivity (see Geertz 1973:28–30).

We would conclude by suggesting that while the condition may be serious, it is far from hopeless. Despite the technologic and mechanistic turn that orthodox biomedicine has taken in the past few decades, the time is also one of great ferment and restlessness, with the appearance of alternative medical heterodoxies. And, as Cassell (1986:34) has recently pointed out, there is hardly a patient today who does not know that his mind has a powerful effect on his body both in sickness and in health. We might also add, with reference to our combined experience teaching in medical schools, that most clinical practitioners today know (although often in a nontheoretical and intuitive way) that mind and body are inseparable in the experiences of sickness, suffering, and healing, although they are without the vocabulary and concepts to address—let alone the tools to probe—this mindful body (Lock and Dunk 1987).

In our experience, most clinicians today know that back pain is real, even when no abnormalities appear under the penetrating gaze of the x-ray machine. And many are aware, further, of the social protest that is often expressed through this medium. Most surgeons know not to operate on a patient who is sure she will not survive what may be a rather minor surgical procedure. And, while most psychiatrists know that the effectiveness of tricyclic antidepressants has something to do with their effects on brain transmitters, few believe that chemical abnormalities are the sole causes of depression. Therefore, they invariably explore the painful life events and difficulties of their patients.

Consequently, physicians are increasingly looking to medical anthropology and to the other "softer" disciplines of cultural psychiatry, medical sociology, and psychiatric epidemiology for the answers to the ultimate and persistent existential questions that are not reducible to biological or to material "facts." Why *this* person, of all people? Why this particular disease? Why this particular organ or system? Why this "choice" of symptoms? Why now?

What we have tried to show in these pages is the interaction among the mind/body and the individual, social, and body politic in the production and expression of health and illness. Sickness is not just an isolated event, nor an unfortunate brush with nature. It is a form of communication—the language of the organs—through which nature, society, and culture speak simultaneously. The individual body should be seen as the most immediate, the proximate terrain where social truths and social contradictions are played out, as well as a locus of personal and social resistance, creativity, and struggle.

NOTES

1. See, for example, Bateson and Mead 1942; Hewes 1955; Belo 1960; Hertz 1960[1909]; Merleau-Ponty 1962; Darwin 1965[1872]; Strauss 1966a; Brown 1968; Schilder 1970 [1950]; Hinde 1974; Needham 1973; Davis 1975; Englehardt 1975; Blacking, ed. 1977; Daly 1978; Polhemus 1978; Betherat 1979; Bateson 1980; Rieber 1980; Kunzle 1981; Konner 1982; Johnson 1983.
2. Mary Douglas refers to "The Two Bodies," the physical and the social bodies in *Natural Symbols* (1970). More recently John O'Neill has written a book entitled *Five Bodies: The Human Shape of Modern Society* (1985), in which he discusses the physical body, the communicative body, the world's body, the social body, the body politic, consumer bodies, and medical bodies. We admit that this proliferation of bodies had our decidedly nonquantitative minds stumped for a bit, but the book is nonetheless a provocative and insightful work. We are indebted to both Douglas and O'Neill but also to Bryan Turner's *The Body and Society: Explorations in Social Theory* for helping us to define and delimit the tripartite domain we have mapped out here.
3. We do not wish to suggest that Hippocrates's understanding of the body was analogous to that of Descartes or of modern biomedical practitioners. Hippocrates's approach to medicine and healing can only be described as organic and holistic. Nonetheless, Hippocrates was, as the quote from his works demonstrates, especially concerned to introduce elements of rational science (observation, palpation, diagnosis, and prognosis) into clinical practice and to discredit all the "irrational" and magical practices of traditional folk healers.
4. This article is not intended to be a review of the field of medical anthropology. We would refer interested readers to a few excellent reviews of this type: Worsley 1982; Young 1982; Landy 1983. With particular regard to the ideas expressed in this article, however, see also Taussig 1980, 1984; Estroff 1981; Good and Good 1981; Nichter 1981; Obeyesekere 1981; Laderman 1983, 1984; Comaroff 1985; Devisch 1985; Hahn 1985; Helman 1985; Low 1985.
5. See also "The Surgeon As Priest" in Selzer (1974).

REFERENCES

Adams, F., transl. 1939. Hippocrates: The Genuine Works of Hippocrates. 2 vols. Baltimore: Williams & Wilkins.
Barnes, J. A. 1973. Genitrix:Genitor:: Nature: Culture? In The Character of Kinship. Jack Goody, ed. Cambridge: Cambridge University Press.
Basaglia, Franco. 1964. Silence in the Dialogue With the Psychotic. Journal of Existentialism 6(21):99–102.
Basso, Keith H. 1969. Western Apache Witchcraft. Tucson: University of Arizona Press.
Bastien, Joseph. 1978. Mountain of the Condor: Metaphor and Ritual in an Andean Ayllu. St. Paul, MN: West Publishing.
———. 1985. Qollahuaya-Andean Body Concepts: A Topographical-Hydraulic Model of Physiology. American Anthropologist 87:595–611.
Bateson, Gregory. 1980. Mind and Nature: A Necessary Unity. New York: Bantam Books.
Bateson, Gregory, and Margaret Mead. 1942. Balinese Character: A Photographic Essay. Special Publication of the New York Academy of Sciences, Vol. 11. New York: Ballantine Books.
Belo, Jane. 1960. Trance Dance in Bali. New York: Columbia University Press.
Benoist, Jean. 1978. The Structural Revolution. London: Weidenfeld and Nicolson.
Betherat, Therese. 1979. The Body Has Its Reasons. New York: Avon Books.
Binswanger, Ludwig. 1958. Insanity as Life-History Phenomenon. In Existence: A New Dimension in Psychiatry and Psychology. Rollo May, Ernest Angel, and Henri Ellenberger, eds. New York: Simon & Schuster.
Bourdieu, Pierre. 1977. Outline of a Theory of Practice. Cambridge Studies in Social Anthropology, Vol. 16. Cambridge: Cambridge University Press.
Brain, Robert. 1979. The Decorated Body. New York: Harper & Row.
Briggs, Jean. 1970. Never in Anger: Portrait of an Eskimo Family. Cambridge, MA: Harvard University Press.
Brown, Norman O. 1968. Life Against Death. New York: Vintage/Random House.
Cassell, Eric. 1986. Ideas in Conflict: The Rise and Fall and Rise and Fall of New Views of Disease. Daedalus 115:19–42.
Cobb, Beatrix. 1958. Why do People Return to Quacks? In Patients, Physicians, and Illness. E. Gartly Jaco, ed. Pp. 283–287. New York: Free Press.
Comaroff, Jean. 1985. Body of Power, Spirit of Resistance: The Culture and History of a South African People. Chicago: University of Chicago Press.
Corbett, Kitty King. 1986. Adding Insult to Injury: Cultural Dimensions of Frustration in Management of Chronic Back Pain. Ph.D. dissertation, Department of Anthropology, University of California, Berkeley.
Crawford, Robert. 1980. Healthism and the Medicalization of Everyday Life. International Journal of Health Services 10:365–388.
———. 1985. A Cultural Account of Health: Self Control, Release, and the Social Body. In Issues in the Political Economy of Health Care. J. McKinlay, ed. London: Tavistock.

Cunningham, Clark. 1973. Order in the Antoni House. *In* Right and Left: Essays on Dual Symbolic Classification. Rodney Needham, ed. Pp. 204–238. Chicago: University of Chicago Press.

Currier, Richard. 1969. The Hot-Cold Syndrome and Symbolic Balance in Mexican and Spanish-American Folk Medicine. *In* The Cross-Cultural Approach to Health Behavior. L. R. Lynch, ed. Pp. 255–273. Madison, NJ: Fairleigh Dickinson University Press.

Daly, Mary. 1978. Gyn/Ecology. Boston: Beacon Press.

Darwin, Charles. 1965[1872]. The Expression of Emotions in Man and Animals. Chicago: University of Chicago Press.

Davis, Martha. 1975. Towards Understanding Intrinsic Body Movements. New York: Arno.

deMause, Lloyd. 1984. Reagan's America. New York: Creative Books.

Devisch, Renaat. 1985. Symbol and Psychosomatic Symptom in Bodily Space-Time: The Case of the Yaka of Zaire. International Journal of Psychology 20:589–616.

deVries, Martin, ed. 1982. The Use and Abuse of Medicine. New York: Praeger.

Dobzhansky, Theodosius. 1970. Heredity. Encyclopedia Britannica 11:419–427.

Douglas, Mary. 1966. Purity and Danger. New York: Praeger.
———. 1970. Natural Symbols. New York: Vintage.

Douglas, William. 1969. Death in Murelaga: Funerary Ritual in a Spanish Basque Village. Seattle: University of Washington Press.

Dundes, Alan. 1984. Life Is Like a Chicken-Coop Ladder. New York: Columbia University Press.

Durkheim, Emile. 1961[1915]. The Elementary Forms of the Religious Life. Joseph Ward Swain, transl. New York: Collier.

Edgerton, Robert. 1971. A Traditional African Psychiatrist. Southwestern Journal of Anthropology 27:259–278.

Eisenberg, Leon. 1977. Disease and Illness: Distinctions Between Professional and Popular Ideas of Sickness. Culture, Medicine and Psychiatry 1:9–23.

Englehardt, H. T. 1975. Bioethics and the Process of Embodiment. Perspectives in Biology and Medicine 18(4):486–500.

Estroff, Sue E. 1981. Making It Crazy: An Ethnography of Psychiatric Clients in an American Community. Berkeley: University of California Press.

Evans-Pritchard, E. E. 1940. The Nuer. Oxford: Oxford University Press.

Fisher, S., and S. Cleveland. 1958. Body Image and Personality. Princeton, NJ: D. Van Nostrand.

Fortes, Meyer. 1959. Oedipus and Job in West African Religion. Cambridge: Cambridge University Press.

Foster, George. 1965. Peasant Society and the Image of the Limited Good. American Anthropologist 68:210–214.
———. 1972. The Anatomy of Envy: A Study in Symbolic Behavior. Current Anthropology 13(2):165–186.

Foucault, Michel. 1973. Madness and Civilization: A History of Insanity in the Age of Reason. New York: Vintage.
———. 1975. The Birth of the Clinic: An Archaeology of Medical Perception. New York: Vintage.
———. 1979. Discipline and Punish: The Birth of the Prison. New York: Vintage.
———. 1980a. The History of Sexuality, Vol. 1: An Introduction. New York: Vintage.
———. 1980b. Introduction. *In* Herculine Barbin: Being the Recently Discovered Memoirs of a Nineteenth-Century French Hermaphrodite. New York: Pantheon.
———. 1980c. Power/Knowledge: Selected Interviews and Other Writings. New York: Pantheon.

Freidson, Eliot. 1972. Client Control and Medical Practice. *In* Patients, Physicians, and Healers. E. Gartly Jaco, ed. Pp. 214–221. New York: Free Press.

Geertz, Clifford. 1973. The Interpretation of Cultures. New York: Basic Books.
———. 1980. Negara: The Theatre-State in Nineteenth-Century Bali. Princeton: Princeton University Press.
———. 1984. From the Native's Point of View: On the Nature of Anthropological Understanding. *In* Culture Theory. Richard Shweder and Robert LeVine, eds. Pp. 123–136. Cambridge: Cambridge University Press.

Good, Byron, and Mary Jo Good. 1981. The Meaning of Symptoms: A Cultural Hermeneutic Model for Clinical Practice. *In* The Relevance of Social Science for Medicine. Leon Eisenberg and Arthur Kleinman, eds. Dordrecht: Reidel.

Goody, Jack. 1977. The Domestication of the Savage Mind. Cambridge: Cambridge University Press.

Grossinger, Richard. 1980. Planet Medicine: From Stone Age Shamanism to Post-Industrial Healing. New York: Doubleday.

Hahn, Robert. 1985. Culture-Bound Syndromes Unbound. Social Science and Medicine 21:165–171.

Hahn, Robert and Arthur Kleinman. 1983. Belief as Pathogen, Belief as Medicine. Medical Anthropology Quarterly 14(4):3, 16–19.

Harris, Grace. 1978. Casting Out Anger: Religion among the Taita of Kenya. Cambridge: Cambridge University Press.

Harris, Marvin. 1974. Cows, Pigs, Wars and Witches. New York: Vintage.
———. 1979. Cultural Materialism: The Struggle for a Science of Culture. New York: Random House.

Head, Henry. 1920. Studies in Neurology. 2 vols. London: H. Frowde: Hodder Stoughton.

Helman, Cecil. 1985. Psyche, Soma and Society: The Social Construction of Psychosomatic Disorders. Culture, Medicine and Psychiatry 9:1–26.

Herrick, James. 1983. The Symbolic Roots of Three Potent Iroquois Medicinal Plants. *In* The Anthropology of Medicine. Lola Romanucci-Ross, Daniel Moerman, and L. Tancredi, eds. Pp. 134–155. New York: Bergin & Garvey.

Hertz, Robert. 1960[1909]. Death and the Right Hand. Aberdeen: Cohen and West.

Hewes, Gordon. 1955. World Distribution of Certain Postural Habits. American Anthropologist 57:123–132.

Hinde, Robert A. 1974. Biological Bases of Human Social Behaviour. New York: McGraw-Hill.

Hopper, Kim. 1982. Discussant comments following the organized session. "The Lure and Haven of Illness." 81st annual meeting of the American Anthropological Association, Washington, D.C.

Horowitz, M. J. 1966. Body Image. Archives of General Psychiatry 14:456–461.

Hugh-Jones, C. 1979. From the Milk of the River: Spatial and Temporal Process in Northwest Amazonia. Cambridge: Cambridge University Press.

Illich, Ivan. 1976. Medical Nemesis. New York: Pantheon.

Jachimowicz, Edith. 1975. Islamic Cosmology. In Ancient Cosmologies. Carmen Blacker and Michael Lowe, eds. London: George Allen and Unwin.

Janzen, John. 1981. The Need for a Taxonomy of Health in the Study of African Therapeutics. Social Science and Medicine 15B:185–194.

Johnson, Don. 1983. Body. Boston: Beacon Press.

Katz, Richard. 1982. Boiling Energy. Cambridge: Harvard University Press.

Kleinman, Arthur. 1980. Patients and Healers in the Context of Culture. Berkeley: University of California Press.

———. 1982. Neurasthenia and Depression: A Study of Somatization and Culture in China. Culture, Medicine and Psychiatry 6:117–190.

———. 1986. Social Origins of Distress and Disease: Depression and Neurasthenia in Modern China. New Haven, CT: Yale University Press.

Kleinman, Arthur, and Byron Good, eds. 1985. Culture and Depression: Studies in the Anthropology and Cross-Cultural Psychiatry of Affect and Disorder. Berkeley: University of California Press.

Kleinman, Arthur, and Joan Kleinman. 1985. Somatization: The Interconnections in Chinese Society Among Culture, Depressive Experiences, and Meanings of Pain. In Culture and Depression: Studies in the Anthropology and Cross-Cultural Psychiatry of Affect and Disorder. Arthur Kleinman and Byron Good, eds. Pp. 429–490. Berkeley: University of California Press.

Konner, Melvin. 1982. The Tangled Wing. New York: Holt, Rinehart & Winston.

Kundera, Milan. 1984. The Novel and Europe. New York Review of Books 31:15–19.

Kunzle, David. 1981. Fashion and Fetishism: A Social History of the Corset, Tight-Lacing, and Other Forms of Body Sculpture in the West. London: Rowan and Littlefield.

Laderman, Carol. 1983. Wives and Midwives: Childbirth and Nutrition in Rural Malaysia. Berkeley: University of California Press.

———. 1984. Food Ideology and Eating Behavior. Social Science and Medicine 19(5):547–560.

Lancaster, Roger Nelson. 1983. What AIDS Is Doing to Us. Christopher Street 7(3):48–52.

Landy, David. 1983. Medical Anthropology: A Critical Appraisal. In Advances in Medical Science, Vol. 1. Julio Ruffini, ed. Pp. 184–314. New York: Gordon and Breach.

Laquer, Thomas. 1986. Orgasm, Generation, and the Politics of Reproductive Biology. Representations 14:1–41.

Lebra, Takie Sugiyama. 1976. Japanese Patterns of Behavior. Honolulu: University Press of Hawaii.

Leeman, Larry. 1986. Pueblo Models of Communal Sickness and Wellbeing. Paper read at the Kroeber Anthropological Society Meetings. Berkeley, March 8.

Lévi-Strauss, Claude. 1963. The Sorcerer and His Magic. In Structural Anthropology. Pp. 167–185. New York: Basic Books.

———. 1967. The Efficacy of Symbols. In Structural Anthropology. Garden City, NY: Doubleday.

Levy, Robert, and Michelle Rosaldo, eds. 1983. Self and Emotion. Ethos 11(3).

Lindenbaum, Shirley. 1979. Kuru Sorcery: Disease and Danger in the New Guinea Highlands. Palo Alto, CA: Mayfield.

Linke, Uli. 1986. Where Blood Flows, a Tree Grows: A Study of Root Metaphors and German Culture. Ph.D. dissertation, Department of Anthropology, University of California, Berkeley.

Lock, Margaret. 1986a. Castigations of a Selfish Housewife: National Identity and Menopausal Rhetoric in Japan. Paper read at the American Ethnological Society Meetings, Wrightsville Beach, North Carolina.

———. 1986b. Plea for Acceptance: School Refusal Syndrome in Japan. Social Science and Medicine 23:99–112.

Lock, Margaret, and Pamela Dunk. 1987. My Nerves Are Broken: The Communication of Suffering in a Greek-Canadian Community. In Health in Canadian Society: Sociological Perspectives. D. Coburn, C. D'Arcy, P. New, and G. Torrence, eds. Toronto: Fitzhenry and Whiteside.

Low, Setha. 1985. Culturally Interpreted Symptoms or Culture-Bound Syndromes. Social Science and Medicine 21:187–197.

Luria, A. R. 1972. The Man With a Shattered Sword. New York: Basic Books.

Lutz, Catherine. 1982. The Domain of Emotion Words on Ifaluk. American Ethnologist 9:113–128.

———. 1985. Depression and the Translation of Emotional Worlds. In Culture and Depression. Arthur Kleinman and Byron Good, eds. Berkeley: University of California Press.

Majno, Guido. 1975. The Healing Hand: Man and Wound in the Ancient World. Cambridge, MA: Harvard University Press.

Manning, Peter, and Horacio Fabrega. 1973. The Experience of Self and Body: Health and Illness in the Chiapas Highlands. In Phenomenological Sociology. George Psathas, ed. Pp. 59–73. New York: Wiley.

Marshall, Lorna. 1965. The !Kung Bushmen of the Kalahari Desert. In Peoples of Africa. J. L. Gibbs, ed. New York: Holt, Rinehart & Winston.

Martin, Emily. 1987. The Woman in the Body. Boston: Beacon Press. (In press.)

Marx, Karl, and Frederick Engels. 1970. The German Ideology. New York: International Publishers.

Mauss, Marcel. 1979[1950]. Sociology and Psychology: Essays. London: Routledge & Kegan Paul.

———. 1985[1938]. A Category of the Human Mind: The Notion of the Person, the Notion of the Self. In The Category of the Person: Anthropology, Philosophy, History. M. Carrithers, S. Collins, and S. Lukes, eds. Pp. 1–25. Cambridge: Cambridge University Press.

Maybury-Lewis, David. 1967. Akwe-Shavante Society. Oxford: Clarendon Press.

Merleau-Ponty, Maurice. 1962. The Phenomenology of Perception. London: Routledge and Kegan Paul.

Miller, Jonathan. 1978. The Body in Question. New York: Vintage.

Minkowski, Eugene. 1958. Findings in a Case of Schizo-phrenic Depression. *In* Existence: A New Dimension in Psychiatry and Psychology. Rollo May, Ernest Angel, and Henri Ellenberger, eds. Pp. 127–138. New York: Simon & Schuster.

Moerman, Daniel. 1983. Physiology and Symbols: Anthro-pological Implications of the Placebo Effect. *In* The Anthropology of Medicine. Lola Romanucci-Ross, Daniel Moerman, and L. Tancredi, eds. Pp. 156–167. New York: Bergin & Garvey.

Mullings, Leith. 1984. Therapy, Ideology, and Social Change. Berkeley: University of California Press.

Needham, Rodney, ed. 1973. Right and Left: Essays on Dual Symbolic Classification. Chicago: University of Chicago Press.

Nichter, Mark. 1981. Idioms of Distress. Culture, Medicine and Psychiatry 5:379–408.

Obeyesekere, Gananath. 1981. Medusa's Hair: An Essay on Personal Symbols and Religious Experience. Chicago: University of Chicago Press.

Ornstein, R. E. 1973. Right and Left Thinking. Psychology Today May: 87–92.

Paul, Robert. 1976. The Sherpa Temple as a Model of the Psy-che. American Ethnologist 3:131–146.

Polhemus, Ted, ed. 1978. The Body Reader. New York: Pantheon.

Pollit, K. 1982. The Politically Correct Body. Mother Jones May:66–67.

Reichel-Dolmatoff, G. 1971. Amazonian Cosmos: The Sex-ual and Religious Symbolism of the Tukanao Indians. Chicago: University of Chicago Press.

Reischauer, Edwin O. 1977. The Japanese. Cambridge, MA: Harvard University Press.

Rieber, R. W. 1980. Body and Mind. New York: Academic Press.

Rosaldo, Michelle Z. 1980. Knowledge and Passion: Ilongot Notions of Self and Social Life. Cambridge: Cambridge University Press.

———. 1984. Toward an Anthropology of Self and Feeling. *In* Culture Theory. Richard Shweder and Robert LeVine, eds. Cambridge: Cambridge University Press.

Rosaldo, Renato. 1984. Grief and the Headhunter's Rage: On the Cultural Force of Emotions. *In* Text, Play, and Story. Edward Bruner, ed. Pp. 178–195. Washington, DC: American Ethnological Society.

Roth, Julius. 1972. Some Contingencies of the Moral Eval-uation and Control of Clientele: The Case of the Hos-pital Emergency Service. American Journal of Sociology 77:840–855.

Rubinstein, Robert A., and Ronald T. Brown. 1984. An Evaluation of the Validity of the Diagnostic Category of Attention Deficit Disorder. American Journal of Ortho-psychiatry 54(3):398–414.

Sacks, Oliver. 1973[1970]. Migraine: The Evolution of a Com-mon Disorder. Berkeley: University of California Press.

———. 1985. The Man Who Mistook His Wife For a Hat and Other Clinical Tales. New York: Summit Books.

Scarry, Elaine. 1985. The Body in Pain: The Making and Un-making of the World. Oxford: Oxford University Press.

Scheper-Hughes, Nancy. 1979. Saints, Scholars, and Schizo-phrenics: Mental Illness in Rural Ireland. Berkeley: Uni-versity of California Press.

———. 1984. Infant Mortality and Infant Care: Cultural and Economic Constraints on Nurturing in Northeast Brazil. Social Science and Medicine 19(5):533–546.

Scheper-Hughes, Nancy, and Margaret Lock. 1986. Speak-ing Truth to Illness: Metaphors, Reification, and a Peda-gogy for Patients. Medical Anthropology Quarterly 17(5): 137–140.

Scheper-Hughes, Nancy, and Howard Stein. 1987. Child-Abuse and the Unconscious. *In* Child Survival: Anthropo-logical Approaches to the Treatment and Maltreatment of Children. Nancy Scheper-Hughes, ed. Dordrecht: Reidel. (In press.)

Scheper-Hughes, Nancy, and D. Stewart. 1983. Curan-derismo in Taos County, New Mexico: A Possible Case of Anthropological Romanticism? Western Journal of Medi-cine 139(6):71–80.

Schieffelin, Edward L. 1976. The Sorrow of the Lonely and the Burning of the Dancers. New York: St. Martin's Press.

———. 1979. Mediators as Metaphors: Moving a Man to Tears on Papua New Guinea. *In* The Imagination of Real-ity: Essays in Southeast Asian Communication Systems. A. L. Becker and A. Yengoyan, eds. Norwood, NJ: Ablex Publishing.

Schilder, Paul. 1970[1950]. The Image and Appearance of the Human Body. New York: International Universities Press.

Selzer, Richard. 1974. Mortal Lessons: Notes on the Art of Surgery. New York: Simon & Schuster.

Shariati, Ali. 1979. On the Sociology of Islam. Hamid Algar, transl. Berkeley, CA: Mizan Press.

Shweder, Richard, and Edmund J. Bourne. 1982. Does the Concept of the Person Vary Cross-Culturally? *In* Cultural Conceptions of Mental Health and Therapy. Anthony J. Marsella and Geoffrey M. White, eds. Pp. 97–137. Dor-drecht: Reidel.

Shutler, Mary Elizabeth. 1979. Disease and Curing in a Yaqui Community. *In* Ethnic Medicine in the Southwest. E. Spicer, ed. Tucson: University of Arizona Press.

Smith, Robert V. 1983. Japanese Society: Tradition, Self, and the Social Order. Cambridge: Cambridge University Press.

Snow, Loudell. 1974. Folk Medical Beliefs and Their Implica-tions for Care of Patients: A Review Based on Studies Among Black Americans. Annals of Internal Medicine 81:82–96.

Sontag, Susan. 1978. Illness as Metaphor. New York: Farrar, Strauss, and Giroux.

Strauss, Erwin. 1966a. Phenomenological Psychology. New York: Basic Books.

———. 1966b. Upright Posture. *In* Phenomenological Psy-chology: The Selected Papers of Erwin W. Strauss. Pp. 137–165. New York: Basic Books.

Taussig, Michael. 1980. Reification and the Consciousness of the Patient. Social Science and Medicine. 14:3–13.

Thompson, E. P. 1967. Time, Work, Discipline, and Industrial Capitalism. Past and Present 38:56–97.

Turnbull, Colin. 1962. The Forest People. New York: Simon & Schuster.

Veith, Ilza. 1966. The Yellow Emperor's Classic of Internal Medicine. Berkeley: University of California Press.

Vogt, Evon. 1970. The Zinacantecos of Mexico: A Modern Mayan Way of Life. New York: Holt, Rinehart & Winston.

Worsely, Peter. 1982. Non-Western Medical Systems. Annual Review of Anthropology 11:315–348.

Young, Allan. 1982. Anthropologies of Illness and Sickness. Annual Review of Anthropology 11:257–285.

Zahan, Dominique. 1979. The Religion, Spirituality, and Thought of Traditional Africa. Chicago: University of Chicago Press.

Zola, I. K. 1972. Medicine as an Institution of Social Control. Sociological Review 20(4):487–504.

24

Beyond the Ivory Tower: Critical Praxis in Medical Anthropology

Merrill Singer

This selection provides an important view of the other side of critical medical anthropology (CMA) by focusing on the political economy of health. The author has played an important role in the development of CMA from a political-economic or Marxist point of view. In the past, there has been a tension between proponents of CMA, mostly working in academic settings, and many applied anthropologists working within the health care system. The critical stance of CMA, as Merrill Singer points out, is consciously political, which means that the criticism of CMA by other anthropologists is also a political criticism. Critics of CMA, including clinically applied medical anthropologists, argue that at least they are doing something about health problems. After all, applied anthropologists might say, the proponents of CMA are largely academicians in the ivory tower.

Here Singer addresses the question of whether CMA can be applied to real-world situations, and, if so, how? The word praxis in the title refers to practice or political action. The approach of this type of CMA has been greatly influenced by a 19th-century leader of social medicine in Germany, a physician named Virchow, whose view can be

summed up in his phrase, "Medicine is a social science and politics is nothing else than medicine on a grand scale" (in Rosen 1974:65). There are two extended case studies of critical praxis presented here: Singer's own work at the Hispanic Health Council in Hartford, Connecticut, and the U.S. farm labor movement. Typical of CMA, the author challenges the reader to reconsider the cognitive boundaries that separate health care and politics.

As you read this selection, consider these questions:

- *Is an anthropologist or health care practitioner working within the system of medicine and public health necessarily co-opted by that system? How critical can a clinical medical anthropologist be?*

- *Many medical anthropologists argue that the root cause of sickness and disease is poverty. If you believe that is true, how does that belief affect your life plans?*

- *Is there a role for academic anthropologists from the CMA point of view?*

Critical medical anthropology can be defined as a theoretical and practical effort to understand and respond to issues and problems of health, illness, and treatment in terms of the *interaction* between the macrolevel of political economy, the national level of political and class structure, the institutional level of the health care system, the community level of popular and folk beliefs and actions, the microlevel of illness experience, behavior, and meaning, human physiology, and environmental factors (Baer et al.

1986; Scheder 1988; Singer 1986, 1990a). This effort is peculiarly anthropological in the sense that it is holistic, historical, and immediately concerned with on-the-ground features of social life, social relationships, and social knowledge, as well as with culturally constituted systems of meaning. Additionally, critical medical anthropology is consciously political in that it

1.   Recognizes that health itself is a profoundly political issue (Navarro 1984)

2.   Is cognizant and critical of the colonial heritage of anthropology and the tendency of conventional medical anthropology to serve as a "handmaiden of biomedicine" (Greenwood et al. 1988)

3.   Balances concern for unbiased social science with an awareness of the sociohistoric origin and political nature of all scientific knowledge

4.   Acknowledges the fundamental importance of class, racial, and sexual inequity in determining the distribution of health, disease, living and working conditions, and health care

5.   Defines power as a fundamental variable in health-related research, policy, and programming

6.   Avoids the artificial separation of local settings and micropopulations from their wider political-economic contexts

7.   Asserts that its mission is emancipatory: it aims not simply to understand but to change culturally inappropriate, oppressive, and exploitive patterns in the health arena and beyond

8.   Sees commitment to change as fundamental to the discipline (Singer 1990c)

In what might be called the first phase of its development, critical medical anthropology struggled with issues of self-definition and acceptance within academic medical anthropology (Singer 1989a). The primary objectives of this phase were to develop a critique of and alternatives to the concepts, theories, scope, alignments, and self-image of conventional medical anthropology and to bring these alternative ideas into the usual forums of scholarly exchange. Although this first phase is far from over—there is much to be resolved among those who have found common cause behind the label critical medical anthropology (e.g., Morsy 1989), much to be clarified with colleagues who do not recognize or are undecided about the advantage of a critical approach (e.g., Csordas 1988; Estroff 1988), and much to be countered in the recent postmodernist suspension of interest in so-called totalizing paradigms (Singer 1990b)—it is not an exaggeration to say that critical medical anthro-

pology has had some impact on the field (e.g., B. Good 1994; M. Good 1990). We have moved, I believe, into a second phase in the evolution of the perspective.

One of the issues under examination in this new phase is the ability of critical medical anthropology to move beyond the academy, the scholarly conference, and the academic journal into the applied field of clinics, health education and development projects, federal health research institutes, international health bodies, private voluntary organizations, health movements, and community-based agencies. Simply put, the time has come to ask whether there is life beyond the ivory tower for critical medical anthropology, and, if so, what factors and forces will determine its entry, position, and program within the professional health world.

It is fairly evident why this question is being raised. As Pelto affirms, "medical anthropology is, on the whole, an applied field, in which the researchers ask the question, 'How can this situation be improved?'" (1988:436). But the answers medical anthropologists develop may not be those that are welcomed by power wielders. Too often, as Kendall found in his work in diarrheal disease control in Honduras, "when anthropological evidence clash[es] with the viewpoint of medical authorities and with the evidence collected from other sources, the former [is] not considered to be of sufficient weight to change the implementation strategy" (1989:289–290). Consequently, Wulff and Fiske observe: "Much of the literature in applied anthropology is neutral or negative reporting of the frustration of ignored or underutilized anthropological data—what 'might have been' if we could only get policymakers' attention" (1987:1). If conventional medical anthropology has had to struggle to get a shaky foothold in the health field, what does this portend for an approach that seeks not to serve neutrally but to challenge directly the underlying political structures and relations that it sees as responsible for much ill health and poor treatment? In this light, those who discount critical medical anthropology have questioned its relevance to the practical world of health care and its viability beyond the cloistered environs of the university campus. Writing of the clinic, Eisenberg and Kleinman assert:

> The patient who seeks help from the doctor is today's victim, not salvageable by tomorrow's hoped-for reform. His or her distress will not be put aright by injunctions for political action. (1981:18)

This and similar statements appear to assume that critical praxis begins and ends with the advocacy of global transformation; anything less would amount to little more than system-maintaining reformism, a notion shared by some critical thinkers. Following a review of the critical social science literature, for example, Morgan notes that "one begins to anticipate the concluding paragraphs of each article: socialist revolution is the only path to a more humane, equitable, and healthy society" (1987:138). By implication, there can be no applied critical medical anthropology because, as one critical colleague in an applied setting expressed it, "political economy leads you to put on macrostructural glasses but the applied setting forces you to be myopic" (Rick Jacobsen, personal communication, 1991).

Additional questions confront critical medical anthropologists who seek to work in applied settings. Pflanz asks what would happen to the applied medical social scientist "who even tried to show how far the values set up by medicine are deliberately fostered in order to strengthen an unholy alliance between physicians and an elite bourgeoisie" (1975:8). Others have wondered whether projects with a critical component can be approved by health professionals. Can applied research generated by critical theory gain funding? Indeed, are self-identified critical medical anthropologists even employable in applied work? In short, though it has been possible to develop a critical anthropology *of* health, there may well be insurmountable political barriers to the creation of a critical anthropology *in* health.

In this article I am concerned with developing a response to these questions that emerges from and is in harmony with critical theory and practice. I examine two apparent dilemmas confronting critical praxis: (1) If, as critical medical anthropologists, among others, have suggested, powerful social classes ultimately control the health care system, is the whole notion of critical praxis in health an exercise in futility? (2) If the health care system both reflects and reproduces the wider system of social inequality and social control, is critical praxis a contradiction in terms? The argument that there are openings for critical praxis in the health domain and that such work need not become easily co-opted liberal reform is illustrated here with two case examples.[1]

SOCIAL RELATIONS AND SOCIAL ACTION: THE STARTING POINTS OF SOCIAL SCIENCE

Questions about the relevance and viability of critical medical anthropology in the applied domain must be addressed, in part, in terms of an analysis of social relations and social action within the larger health field. These topics warrant renewed attention because a failure to squarely confront the issue of power continues to diminish the significance of work in medical anthropology. As Wolf (1990) indicates, the very term *power* leaves many anthropologists uncomfortable. Whereas Bloch (1983:121) sees "extraordinary theoretical cowardice" in this trait of the discipline, I am inclined to see one core element of anthropological culture: the potent desire to stay as close as possible to the ethnographic ground of experience, or, in Ortner's (1984:144) words, to describe "real people doing real things," things that matter. Though our inclination to create "an anthropology-with-one's-feet-on-the-ground" (Scheper-Hughes 1992:4) is a strength, as Wolf emphasizes, "we must take the further step of understanding the consequences of the exercise of power" (1990:594). Doing so in an age of "global dreams" and "global reach" requires lifting our feet and our gaze off the ground (Barnet and Cavanagh 1994; Barnet and Müller 1974).

Limitations in medical anthropology's effort to integrate a conception of power have been discussed at some length with reference especially to studies guided by the perspective of medical ecology (Singer 1989b, 1990a). . . .

. . . [There are, in fact, practical] "institutional and situational openings" for influence and activity at many points in health care systems. Community-based organizations, community health and mental health centers, women's clinics, union-run health programs, and similar entities—because they must address the concerns of poor, working class, and oppressed groups—are local-level examples of struggle-generated openings for critical intervention (Borrero et al. 1982; Chamberlin and Radebaugh 1976; Morgen 1986; Nash and Kirsch 1988; Rudd 1975; Schensul and Schensul 1982; Yee 1975). Progressive social movements concerned with improving the health and well-being of oppressed populations or with limiting the control over health wielded by physicians, the pharmaceutical and medical technology industries, or hospitals have also been instrumental in creating openings for critical involvement in the health field. The network of alternative health programs and practices created by the women's health movement, the gay and lesbian health crisis movement, self-care organizations, occupational health and safety efforts, environmental protection campaigns, and community-controlled hospitals are examples of health-care settings and activities in which critical medical anthropologists have found opportunities to make useful contributions (Baer 1990; Douglas and Scott 1978; Levin 1976; Marieskind and Ehrenreich 1975; McKnight 1986; Scheper-Hughes and Lovell

1986). Even state-run programs brought into existence because of popular pressure, such as those designed to address problems such as AIDS, homelessness, and hunger, can become important arenas of critical medical anthropological praxis (Guttmacher, personal communication, 1990; Hopper 1988; Susser and Conover 1987; Susser et al. 1989; Susser and Gonzalez 1991; Singer et al. 1991). At the international level, the health systems of a number of socialist countries have provided opportunities for critical medical anthropology practice in recent years (Donahue 1986, 1989; Guttmacher 1989).

In short, although structural barriers to critical application are both real and impinging, in a class-divided social formation riddled by contradiction and enlivened by diverse expressions of class and related struggle, various opportunities exist for critical medical anthropology to affect health. These diverse niches within the health system provide space for the formulation, testing, evaluation, and reformulation of critical praxis.

PRAXIS SHORT OF TRANSFORMATION

Beyond the issue of access lies the question of critical medical anthropology's ability to be something other than a system-maintaining approach to tinkering and patching in health. Unfortunately, like the good intentions paving the road to hell, the evolutionary pathway of capitalist society is lined with the remnants of progressive initiatives co-opted to serve oppressive ends (usually by providing cushioning for the roughest edges of inherently exploitative social relations, for example, many components of the welfare state). As Waitzkin notes:

> When oppressive social conditions exist, reforms to improve them seem reasonable. However, the history of reform in capitalist countries has shown that re-forms most often follow social protest, make incremental improvements that do not change overall patterns of oppression, and face cutbacks when protest recedes. (1981:359)

Thus, Piven and Cloward (1971) have effectively chronicled the history of public welfare in the United States in relation to public protest and the demand for relief from structurally imposed destitution. Health reforms share a common history. Hyman, for example, concluded from his evaluation of the long-term effects of nine reform projects designed to improve the health of poor and working people in New York that "regardless of the nature of the program, support or service,

they were underfinanced and thus hardly able to meet the overwhelming needs for health services in the . . . community" (1973:188). In addition to financial problems, most of the programs faced "organizational inhibiting constraints, or poor commitment as factors that prevented their achievement" (Hyman 1973:195). In a somewhat similar vein, Morgen (1986) documents the process of state co-optation of a feminist health clinic, a process involving an erosion of democratic decision making, a narrowing of the organizational mission to service delivery and away from social organizing and community education, and a loss of autonomy. Recently, Cain has argued that AIDS organizations tend to lose their critical edge as they move from being activist initiatives to established organizations.

> The literature shows how involvement with the state and the receipt of regular funding contribute to the formalization and bureaucratization of community organizations. The initial goals of many community groups are displaced by concerns with organizational maintenance and by the career interests of their workers. Once established, "inertial forces" within the groups can impede their ability to respond to changes in their environments, and they can be prone to internal fragmentation. The ability of indigenous workers to bring about social change can be limited by the organizations in which they work, and they can experience pressure to become more professional and earn academic credentials. (1993:666)

The conclusion sometimes drawn from such cases is that reform *by nature* is suspect because it only leads to further control. This is said to be especially true of medical reform because of the vital regulatory functions performed by biomedicine concomitant with the secularization of society. Echoing Foucault, Turner argues that "the rise of preventive medicine, social medicine and community medicine has extended . . . agencies of regulation deeper and deeper into social life" (1987:38). All of these socially oriented medical disciplines, it is asserted, are but newfangled "power techniques" deployed to more closely observe, know, regulate, and use individuals through the manipulation of their bodies (Foucault 1977). Using a dialectical approach, however, Navarro correctly identifies a weakness of this argument with reference to popular demand for a national health service.

> To see medicine only as control . . . is to fail to see the dialectical nature of medicine in which there is also a useful needed function. To believe otherwise is to think that when the majority of Americans demand a national health program, they are asking for more control. . . . The working class demands medical services because, in large degree, it gets benefits from the utiliza-

tion of these services. . . . But as long as these services exist under capitalism, they will be under the influence of the dominant class, which will try to use these medical services . . . to optimize its own interests. In the same degree that the capitalist and working classes are intrinsically in conflict . . . these two functions—the dominating and the useful in medicine—are also in contradiction. (1985:531)

Although the provision of medical care as a welfare function can serve to disarm social protest, it is nonetheless true that "by placing pressure on the 'system' real gains can be achieved—such as improved levels of access to care" (Jacobsen 1986:131). Following this line of reasoning, a distinction must be drawn between two fundamentally different categories of social and health reform. Gorz (1973) accomplished this task in his differentiation between "reformist and nonreformist reform." Gorz used the term *reformist reform,* or what, in the interest of clarity, I will here call *system-correcting praxis,* to designate the conscious implementation of minor material improvements that avoid any alteration of the basic structure of social relations in a social system. In his incisive critique of applied medical anthropology in Latin America, Bonfil Batalla aptly portrayed the underlying character of this type of reform.

> Sometimes it looks as if those who work along the road of slow evolution intend to achieve only minimal changes, so that the situation continues to be substantially the same; this is, in other words, to change what is necessary so that things remain the same. Those who act according to such a point of view may honestly believe that their work is useful and transforming; however, they have in fact aligned themselves with the conservative elements who oppose the structural transformations that cannot be postponed. (1966:92)

Characteristic of system-correcting praxis is its vulnerability to co-optation by dominant forces in a social system. The work of medical social scientists in the health field in Britain is exemplary here. As Susser (1974) showed, the history of British medical social science can be divided into three phases. In the first, medical social scientists "struggled for a place, any place" in the health system (Susser 1974:407). The second phase was marked by the acceptance of social scientists into the system because they were seen as serving a useful function by those with power over health policy. In the last phase, "social science can be said to have been co-opted by those at the administrative center of power" (Susser 1974:408).

Between the poles of reformist reform and complete structural transformation, Gorz identified a category of applied work that he labeled *non-reformist reform,* what I refer to here as *system-challenging praxis.*[2] Though system-correcting praxis tends to obscure the causes of suffering and sources of exploitation, system-challenging praxis is concerned with unmasking the origins of social inequity. Moreover, this type of praxis strives to heighten rather than dissipate social action and to make permanent changes in the social alignment of power. The deepest roots of system-challenging praxis in health lie in the work of the physician/activist Rudolph Virchow during the typhus epidemic of 1847 in Upper Silesia, an impoverished area of East Prussia. More recently, such praxis has found concrete expression in the village health worker model in international health development. As described by David Werner, who spent many years establishing a health care network of village health workers in an underdeveloped area in Mexico and worked with and studied them in a number of other countries as well, the village health worker is an internal agent-of-change, not only for health care, but for the awakening of his people to their human potential . . . and ultimately to their human rights" (1977:5). Indeed, in some settings there are real parallels between the work of village health workers and critical medical anthropology practitioners (e.g., see Scheper-Hughes 1992:17–18).

Sanders (1985) suggested two principles to guide system-challenging praxis: enhancing democratization and eliminating mystification. According to Sanders, critical health workers

> should show themselves to be in solidarity with the people by putting their skills at the disposal of those acting with the poorest and most powerless. Encouraging democratic control over the provision of health care and showing oneself to be willing to submit to the will of the majority, rather than asserting one's professional autonomy, is crucially important. And its accompaniment, constantly attempting to demystify medical knowledge and practice, is the second principle. (1985:219)

A third principle is suggested by the long struggle to improve living and working conditions expressed in Virchow's famous assertion that "medicine is a social science and politics is nothing else but medicine on a large scale" (in Rosen 1974:65). It has been well established that the major gains in health status and longevity that separate the United States and Europe from much of the rest of the world were in large part a product of improved social conditions (McKeown 1976; McKinlay and McKinlay 1977). In short, disease cannot simply be reduced to a pathological entity in nature but must be understood as the product of historically located sociopolitical processes. Consequently, medicine "ought to be . . . a form of applied sociology, since to understand the illness of a patient it is important (indeed necessary) to locate the patient in a social and personal environment" (Turner 1987:5). To cite one example:

> An insulin reaction in a diabetic postal worker might be ascribed (in a reductionist mode) to an excessive dose of insulin causing an outpouring of adrenaline, a failure of the pancreas to respond with appropriate glucagon secretion, etc. Alternatively, the cause might be sought in his having skipped breakfast because he was late for work; unaccustomed physical exertion demanded by a foreman; inability to break for a snack; or, at a deeper level, the constellation of class forces in U.S. society which assures capitalist domination of production and the moment to moment working lives of the proletariat. (Woolhandler and Himmelstein 1989:1208; also see de Beer 1986; Scheder 1988; Singer et al. 1992)

The larger lesson is that "disease . . . [all disease] must be put to the test of political practice" rather than be accepted routinely as natural, inevitable, or best responded to through clinical intervention" (Stark 1982:454). To evoke McKnight's axiom for critical health action: "To convert a medical problem into a political issue is central to health improvement" (1986:415).

Such conversion, which constitutes a reversal of the standard medical tendency to individualize and privatize sickness, is the first step in critical practice. Praxis, therefore, can never be reduced to an "anthropology for medicine" (cf. Petersdorf and Feinstein 1981) but must be guided by the recognition that the key determinants of health are social relations. Consequently, the system-challenging praxis that comprises the day-to-day work of critical practitioners must "be regarded as a means and not an end, as dynamic phases in a progressive struggle, not as stopping places" (Gorz 1973:84).

As this discussion implies, critical medical anthropology praxis must emerge from a recognition of a significant limitation in contemporary globalist approaches to social change (see Morgan 1987). In world system, dependency, and related globalist theories, there is "a tendency to assign all causality to the world capitalist system, and, in the process, to ignore the impact of local-level actors" (Schroder 1987:123–124). The corrective for this form of "global functionalism" (Smith 1985) is a restoration of a dialectical understanding of social process and organization. Such an approach directs attention toward opportunities for system-challenging critical action, such as the two examples that follow.

THE STRUGGLE FOR SYSTEM-CHALLENGING PRAXIS: TWO CASE EXAMPLES

Case 1: The Hispanic Health Council

In 1978, a community-based health institute called the Hispanic Health Council was formally organized in the Puerto Rican community of Hartford, Connecticut. The council began as a partnership between several university based applied medical anthropologists and a small group of health activists from the local Puerto Rican community. Although various factors contributed to the birth of this community-based organization, a tragic incident in the local community played a pivotal role in unleashing the energy needed to launch the organization. The incident began when the eight-month-old child of a young Puerto Rican mother who was monolingual in Spanish became ill. The baby developed a fever, became increasingly irritable, and started to vomit. Lacking a family physician or health insurance program, the mother hurried her child to the emergency room of one of the three hospitals in Hartford. The medical staff instructed the mother (in English) to give the baby liquids and aspirin. The mother found the treatment she received at the hands of the medical providers to be harsh and alienating. They, in turn, experienced the mother as "hysterical" and "overreactive." Nonetheless, when the child's condition continued to deteriorate, the mother responded by going the next day to a second emergency room. The experience was not very different from the first clinical encounter. Then, on the evening of the second day, the child's condition became critical and the police were called. The baby died of dehydration in the police car on the way to the last of the city's emergency rooms. This incident, which crystallized many of the problems Puerto Ricans faced in receiving adequate and appropriate treatment and care from dominant health care institutions, sparked a series of angry community demonstrations and produced a heightened awareness of health as a pressing political issue in the Puerto Rican community. Local activists came to the conclusion that an organized and sustained effort was needed to achieve meaningful change in this domain (Schensul and Borrero 1982).

Despite a sizeable increase in Hartford's Puerto Rican population since 1960, health care providers and institutions had made only a very limited effort to respond to the linguistic, cultural, social, and health needs of the Puerto Rican community. The initial goal of the council, as a result, was to ascertain the nature and contours of these needs. Specifically, in its first efforts the council attempted to determine the range of health and living conditions in the Puerto Rican community, assess popular health beliefs and illness behaviors, discern unmet needs for specific types of health care and services, and evaluate the organization, ethnic composition, attitudes, and behaviors of prominent health care institutions. This agenda contributed to the centrality of community research in the council's approach to health change, a development that has helped to sustain an opening for critical medical anthropology in the organization.

As data were collected, a primary organizational concern at the council became the translation of research findings into effective, empirically grounded, culturally appropriate interventions. Based on its various research projects, the council began to organize specific programs designed to impact the health scene in Hartford as it relates to Puerto Ricans and other groups suffering from poverty, discrimination, poor health, and linguistic and cultural differences with dominant institutions (Schensul et al. 1987).

For example, one of the interventions begun by the council was called Project Apoyo. The project trained and placed a bicultural, bilingual case coordinator in a local neonatal intensive care unit to assist Hispanic families during and after their infants' hospitalizations and to facilitate the transition from hospital to home and community.

> A key element in this case coordination approach was that of assuring adequate parent-professional communication, a function which goes well beyond the translation of information from one language to another. Rather, the goal was to help families understand, from their own perspective, the meaning and implications of professionals' communications about infants' medical problems, to help families deal with their own reactions to medically-related events, and to promote parent advocacy on behalf of their children. . . . The coordination function also included helping professionals to understand families' concerns and reactions and to appreciate cultural and social influences on parental perceptions and behaviors. (Allen et al. 1988:1)

This project was developed in response to a growing recognition of the lack of culturally sensitive services and training for service providers. Consequently, major discrepancies were found between the experience of Hispanic mothers and staff in the neonatal intensive care unit. Before placement of the project's case coordinator, nurses reported that most Hispanic mothers did not visit their hospitalized infants even once per day and that only about 7 percent called to check on the condition of their children. Moreover, nurses indicated that Hispanic mothers asked fewer

questions, were less realistic about the nature of their babies' problems, participated less in discharge planning, had poorer understanding of their children's conditions, and maintained poorer relations with unit staff than non-Hispanic mothers. Mothers, on the other hand, reported visiting the unit much more often than indicated in nurses' reports and generally saw themselves as being more involved in the care of their children than did the nurses. With the placement of the case coordinator, however, staff perceptions began to change.

> Nurses reported that the intervention caused noticeable behavioral changes in the Puerto Rican mothers. When a mother saw the coordinator in the unit, she was much more likely to feed, bathe, and interact with her baby. Nurses reported that prior to the intervention, mothers were intimidated by the unit (as most people are when they first see all the sick and small babies attached to machines), but throughout the intervention they came in and touched their babies, asked more questions, and generally appeared more involved. (Allen et al. 1988:53)

In short, Project Apoyo was able to demonstrate the importance of cultural differences in health care and the need for culturally appropriate treatment. Whatever the initial perceptions of nurses or mothers, both groups agreed that the intervention facilitated communication and participation in caregiving.

This knowledge, however, fell on deaf ears! At the project's conclusion, the council was unable to convince the local hospital to institutionalize the case coordinator role. Administrator perceptions of appropriate hospital investment, in high-technology equipment, buildings, and parking lots, have obstructed culturally sensitive treatment and communication.

Experiences such as the one described have shown the council that good research and innovative projects are not sufficient to make changes in the health care system. *Political action is also a necessary component of the council's repertoire.* Consequently, the council has been actively involved in various health and social struggles and has lent support and resources to most progressive initiatives launched by Puerto Rican and other activists concerned with changing oppressive social relations. For example, the council fought the effort to proclaim English the official language of Connecticut, organized local community response to a hit-and-run death of a Puerto Rican girl by a prominent attorney, and defended several Puerto Rican nationalists on trial in a local court. Research findings from council studies of the health and social status of Puerto Ricans in the city, the nature of the health care system, and illness beliefs and behaviors in the community provide vital information for exposing health problems, countering official stereotypes, questioning institutional and governmental policies, empowering local activists, and training community members in the sources of their pressing health problems. For example, a carefully structured community survey carried out by the council found that 41 percent of low-income families with school-aged children under 12 years old experience hunger each year (Damio and Cohen 1990). Rather than urging a stopgap response to this growing problem, the council launched a media and community drive to make fundamental, long-lasting changes in local, regional, and federal programs, policies, and institutional practices that contribute to hunger, as well as to seek ways of empowering the local community to respond directly to the threat of hunger.

Indeed, empowerment and community education have been central to the council's mission. For example, in response to the AIDS crisis, the council launched a variety of initiatives designed to counter both the homophobic portrayal of AIDS as a disease caused by gay people and the religious construction of the epidemic as divine retribution. Council research helped to determine the character of community beliefs and attitudes about AIDS (AIDS Community Research Group 1988, 1989), the nature and extent of AIDS-related risk behavior in the community, and the range of social, economic, and health problems faced by injection drug users attempting to avoid HIV infection (Singer et al. 1990). Based on this research, the council developed several AIDS initiatives. The Communidad y Responsibilidad Project, for example, was designed to serve as a community-centered, primary AIDS prevention, education, and support model for the Puerto Rican population. In particular, the aim of the project was to reach and mobilize Puerto Rican women, a group not only suffering increasingly from HIV infection but also having the capacity to offer education to all layers of the community—children, family, friends, neighborhood, and church. The project creatively drew on features of Puerto Rican culture to overcome existing linguistic, cultural, and socioeconomic barriers to develop in the inner-city Puerto Rican community the type of culturally congruent empowerment model that has appeared in recent years in the gay community in response to the AIDS crisis. In the project, a cadre of community members was trained as AIDS activists and provided with the resources and support to organize community discussions about the nature of the AIDS crisis in the Puerto Rican community, the need for collective community response to the epidemic, and the health and social support needs of Puerto Rican people with AIDS (Singer et al. 1994).[3] Despite opposition from various

corners, the council also played a leading role in advocating for the implementation of sterile needle exchange as an AIDS prevention strategy for injection drug users. Because of the broad support from community AIDS activists, Connecticut is the only state east of the Mississippi River that has an exchange program authorized by the state legislature (Singer, Irizarry, and Schensul 1991).

Activities such as these have provided an important critical edge to the Council's work, while opening opportunities for the efforts of several critical medical anthropologists and political activists on the council's staff. Like many community agencies, the council strives to please several audiences, including its board of directors, the professional Hispanic sector in Hartford, the poor and working-class Puerto Rican community, funders, and the health care institutions it is attempting to influence. As a result, there are contradictions in the council's work. Nonetheless, organizations such as the council, which must remain close to the struggles, overt and covert, of local communities, are important arenas for system-challenging praxis and for testing alternative approaches for applied work in critical medical anthropology.

Case 2: The U.S. Farm Labor Movement

As succinctly summarized by Friedland and Nelkin:

> For too many farmworkers life is poor, nasty, brutish, and short. Too many farmworkers are present-day slaves, subservient to and dependent upon the fluctuations of economies, the whims of growers, the vagaries of weather, the march of technology, and the decisions of government. This condition is the predictable consequence of economic and political powerlessness. (1971:ix)

The contribution of the oppressive life conditions experienced by farm laborers to adverse health outcomes through specific physiological mechanisms has been examined by Scheder (1988). Although numerous anthropologists over the years have provided support to farmworker efforts to improve their living and working conditions, Barger and Reza's (1985) contribution is notable because it has involved a sustained and systematic attempt to bring anthropological concepts and methods to this endeavor. Over the last decade, they have collaborated in a number of applied research and action projects in conjunction with farmworker organizations in the Midwest and in California. They describe the development of their collaboration as follows:

Ernesto Reza was a FLOC [Farm Labor Organizing Committee] staff member working with the boycott campaign and a doctoral student in organizational psychology at the University of Michigan. Ken Barger was an associate professor of anthropology at Indiana University at Indianapolis and coordinator of the Indianapolis Farm Worker Support Committee, a citizens' group involved in social action and advocacy on behalf of FLOC. We met in 1980 on a bus of FLOC farmworkers going to a UFW [United Farm Workers] convention in Texas, and on that trip we actively discussed ways in which FLOC and academics could cooperate. Contributing to our relationship were the personal values and views we shared that led us both to become involved in the farm labor cause. We also shared common academic interests in applied change. (Barger and Reza 1987:64)

Two of the projects they have worked on together, the Campbell's Labels Project and the California farmworker's survey, are discussed below.

Because of a radical imbalance of power at the site of production between farmworkers on the one hand and growers, law enforcement, and politicians on the other, since the 1960s the farmworkers movement in the United States has attempted to mobilize popular support for consumer boycotts of selected goods produced by agricultural corporations. As Barger and Reza indicate: "The rationale of [the] boycott . . . is that the combined social and economic power of millions of individual Americans who are concerned with justice can counterbalance the relative political powerlessness of farmworkers" (1989:271). In this regard, Barger and Reza helped to organize the Campbell's Labels Project in Indiana in 1981. The critical praxis of the project had two notable features. First, it was oriented toward changing the social context (the surrounding dominant society) of a targeted population (farmworkers) rather than the targeted population itself. Second, "the project included active involvement and commitment in advocating change, rather than a detached role of providing ideas and information but not assuming responsibility, which is more common to many applied academics" (Barger and Reza 1985: 269). The project was organized in response to the Campbell's Soup Company's "Labels for Education" program in which schools and churches were encouraged to collect labels from soup cans and to send these to the company in exchange for educational and athletic equipment. This promotional program—which was predicated on the inadequate funding of public schools—benefited the company by providing increased sales, tax deductions, advertisement, and improved public relations. The latter helped to counter some of the bad press Campbell's received in response

to its staunch refusal to negotiate with the Farm Labor Organizing Committee during a strike at the company's tomato field operation in 1978.

The action project was designed to encourage schools to review their involvement in the labels program with the intention of undercutting the company's promotional efforts. The project focused on providing education about the social issues involved directly to parents' organizations affiliated with local schools. The educational materials developed and widely distributed by the project did not specifically ask schools to drop involvement in the labels program but rather emphasized that school parents had an opportunity to "set a positive example of citizenship for their children by openly and responsibly examining the issues" (Barger and Reza 1985:271). The effort was supported by the involvement of teachers' organizations, church committees, and other community groups and through an active mass media campaign. In conjunction with the project, pre- and posttest telephone surveys of all local schools were conducted to test the impact of the campaign on involvement in the labels program. The posttest survey, implemented about six months after the project began, found that participation in the labels program had dropped by 43 percent whereas school awareness of the farmworkers' struggle had risen from 9 percent to 82 percent. Feedback from parents indicated that the education campaign was a major (although not the only) factor in school decisions to terminate involvement in the campaign. One additional indicator of the project's success was that Campbell's was forced to launch its own public relations effort to explain its refusal to negotiate with the farm worker union.

Based on the success of the labels project, Barger and Reza were contacted by United Farm Workers to conduct a scientific survey of farmworker attitudes in California. The purpose of the survey was to determine farmworkers' views of the farm labor movement as a vehicle for improving their living and working conditions. The study was a joint project with the National Farm Workers Ministry, an ecumenical group with a long history of involvement in farm labor issues. As described by Barger and Reza, the survey "was an example of a community action model of applied change, where our role as professionals was to support democratic self-determination of farmworkers" (1989:261).

The study targeted a random sample of 137 local farmworkers employed by Kern and Tulare county table grape growers (based on employment lists prepared for another purpose by employers) and a stratified random sample of 57 migrant farmworkers housed at local labor camps. The majority of the farmworkers (72%) were employed on farms not covered by United Farm Workers contracts. Interviews were conducted with a 200-item standardized, pretested questionnaire, which included both open and closed questions as well as validity checks. Completed interviews were coded and recoded for accuracy, entered into a computer file, and then rechecked against the original for accuracy. As Barger and Reza emphasize:

> We used the highest scientific standards possible in the research . . . because the study . . . focus[ed] on a major social issue. . . . [W]e wanted to be absolutely sure of the concepts and methods used in collecting and analyzing the data for two reasons. First, the results of applied work can impact directly on people's lives, and we therefore have a moral obligation to be sure that findings are both accurate and predictive. . . . And second, just because we are committed to our social convictions, we want to be sure our understandings are as accurate and predictive as possible, so that we can make effective changes. (1989:262)

Findings from the study show that farmworkers in California overwhelmingly supported the United Farm Workers as their collective bargaining agent (78%) and believed that it could offer the best alternative for improving their lives (83%). Endorsement of the union was as strong among those not already affiliated as among members. Moreover, farmworkers who were covered by union contracts reported significantly better living and working conditions, factors that, as Scheder's (1988) work shows, have direct and significant impact on farmworker health. Workers protected by the contracts expressed much higher job satisfaction, had greater employment benefits (including paid sick leave), had far greater access to health care, and reported significantly better social stability (e.g., residential and marital stability). As concisely summarized by one of the respondents: "Look at it. Things are much better off now than before the Union. We have better wages, more benefits, and bathrooms in the fields" (quoted in Barger and Reza 1989:266–267). In short, the study scientifically validated the United Farm Workers' claim to represent farmworkers, a claim that growers and politicians with vested political interests have attempted to discredit during the entire history of the farm workers movement. In addition to refuting allegations that the United Farm Workers lacks broad support among workers, the findings have been used by the union to expand services to members, lobby legislators on behalf of farmworkers' needs, improve contract clauses to better reflect farmworkers' concerns, and publicize the dismal state of farmworkers' living and working conditions.

In explaining their work, Barger and Reza specifically address a question raised by some critics of critical medical anthropology, namely: is there not a contradiction between social commitment and valid anthropological research (e.g., Estroff 1988; Wiley 1992)? According to Barger and Reza:

> We would like to make clear . . . that taking value positions does not mean that professional standards are compromised. . . . Since applied work inherently involves social changes and can therefore make direct impacts on people's lives, we need to be very sure of where we are valid in our understandings and also of where we are limited. . . . *Valid scientific research is . . . based on the control of biases and limitations (rather than their absence),* and such controls must be consciously included in the conceptualization of the issue, in the collection of data, in the analysis of data, and in making grounded interpretations of findings. We argue that it is because of the very value positions involved that the highest scientific standards are needed . . . because we have to have valid understandings if our contributions are to be effective and constructive. (1989:276–277, emphasis added)

Neither the commitment of Barger and Reza to democratic self-determination among farmworkers nor their conclusion that the poor health, noxious working conditions, poverty-level wages, and substandard housing and sanitation facilities experienced by this population are the product of economic exploitation by their employers precluded these researchers from conducting valid research. By extension, it is evident that all researchers (whatever their political orientation) are influenced in their choice of research areas, adoption of theoretical perspectives, and design of research methods by the values and commitments they hold near and dear. Questions of bias, however, tend to be raised only in certain cases. As Becker noted with reference to sociology:

> When do we accuse ourselves and our fellow sociologists of bias? I think inspection of representative instances would show that the accusation arises, in one important class of cases, when the research gives credence, in any serious way, to the perspectives of the subordinate group in some hierarchical relationship. (1967:240)

Additionally, the work of Barger and Reza illustrates that although the detached observer may gain certain social scientific insights, only the engaged observer is privy to others. Starn asserts, "Activism clearly can be a valuable angle of observation and interpretation in the flow of fieldwork" (1994:21). Moreover, engagement has long been recognized as an important arena for social science training. As Willhelm observed during the antiwar and related student demonstrations of the 1960s and 1970s "to partake of the student movements . . . sweeping the campuses of colleges and universities serves as a superior teacher to the introduction of society than a freshman sociology course" (1966:10).

CONCLUSION

Critical medical anthropology is predicated on the awareness that "no anthropologist can escape involvement" (Hastrup and Elsass 1990:302) and is characterized by its abiding concern with the question: involvement in whose interest? Ultimately, critical medical anthropology cannot achieve its goals without serious consideration of the appropriate application of critical knowledge to the practical domain of health because "the exercise of critical thought implies a discrimination between what is merely given and what ought to exist" (Lichtheim 1966:127). Unfortunately, an enduring effect of the 1960s antiwar movement—which grew out of and was sustained by campus activism—has been the tendency to assume that critical ideas have no natural home in the so-called real world outside the protective walls of the academy. There is a good deal of anti–working class sentiment embodied in such thinking, as well as a distorted sense of the origin of many counterhegemonic insights. Recognition that in complex stratified societies Gramscian counterhegemonic struggles ensue on various levels across multiple axes of oppression (e.g., struggles against racism, sexism, heterosexism, classism, ageism, discrimination against the physically challenged, environmental destruction) helps bring into focus the numerous opportunities for critical intervention. Having argued in this paper that there is life beyond the ivory tower for critical medical anthropology, I find it appropriate to ask what special attributes critical medical anthropology has to offer system-challenging movements in health care. Several are identifiable:

1.   The anthropological tradition of cultural relativism (whatever its limitations) and the discipline's enduring concern with insider understanding arm critical medical anthropology with an appreciation of and commitment to the principle of self-determination. Support of self-determination is further supported by the anthropological obligation to counter Western, colonial ethnocentrism and to create opportunities for the voices of so-called people without history (i.e., oppressed third world populations) to be heard on the contemporary world stage. Critical medical anthropology practice, as a consequence, brings recognition of the folly inherent in the act of imposing externally generated "solutions" to externally determined health problems and seeks in-

stead, as seen in the two cases presented above, to work in conjunction with struggling communities and groups in responding to their felt needs. To this collaboration, critical medical anthropology brings several attributes, including an understanding of research as a potentially potent weapon in social struggle.

2.   Critical medical anthropology is empowered by its understanding of local contexts in relationship to their location in the encompassing world or national systems (Wolf 1982). The earlier tendency in the discipline was to isolate social dynamics within artificially boundable cultures, but the holistic orientation of critical medical anthropology, as exemplified by the labels program boycott of struggling farm workers, guides attention to the optimum level for effective praxis.

3.   Recognition of the historic role of culture in the shaping of human behavior and social configuration, on the one hand, and of the contribution of social relations to the generation of culture, on the other, establishes the ground for an awareness of the social origin and ideological function of such concepts as disease, medicine, and social development. This awareness limits (but does not eliminate) the ever present threat of co-optation of community initiatives (Morgen 1986). In the case of the Hispanic Health Council, for example, anthropological reflexivity has helped to subject newfangled human service buzzwords such as "culture of poverty" or "strengthening family values" to political economic critique.

4.   Acknowledgement of the contested nature of culture and the inherent contradictions of social relations directs the gaze of critical medical anthropologists toward opportunities for expanding the focus of health-related struggles from immediate to ultimate causes of illness and disease. In other words, critical medical anthropology is oriented toward consciousness raising and empowerment through the unmasking of the structural roots of suffering and ill health. In working with chemically dependent pregnant women, for example, the Hispanic Health Council seeks to assist women both to stop using drugs and to understand addiction in light of oppressive social relations and, further, to view participation in social change on behalf of women's needs or the needs of oppressed communities as a therapeutic activity.

5.   Concern with social relations as a determinant force in social life directs critical attention to the alignment of forces in practical work. In an effort to offset the imbalance in social power across class, race, or other social divisions, critical praxis emphasizes collaboration and coalition building. Central to critical praxis is the forging of collaborative relations across social segments that heretofore have been subject to divide and conquer tactics. Historically, for example,

United Farm Workers was able to overcome a long history of failed efforts to organize farm workers when it united Chicano and Filipino farm workers in a common union struggle.

Providing a theoretical framework for the emergence of a critical anthropological praxis in health, based on a dialectical understanding of social relationship and social action, has been the major intent of this paper. Discussions of the "dynamic phases" in bringing to fruition what "ought to exist" as well as the obstacles to and strategies for its accomplishment remain important tasks in the second stage of critical medical anthropology's development.

NOTES

1. The selection of cases is based on the experience of the author, who has been an employee of the Hispanic Health Council for the past 12 years and previously spent several years as a full- or part-time boycott organizer for the United Farm Workers of America.
2. Elsewhere (Singer 1994), I have used the term *community-centered praxis* to label one type of system-challenging applied work; community-centered praxis refers to efforts that are carried out through community-based organizations or indigenous movements. The term is used to draw attention to the difference between initiatives that emerge from the community concerned and those, however well-intended, that are sponsored from the outside.
3. Funding for this project was provided by the Robert Wood Johnson Foundation.

REFERENCES

AIDS Community Research Group. 1988. AIDS: Knowledge, Attitudes and Behavior in an Ethnically Mixed Urban Neighborhood. Special Report to the Connecticut State Department of Health Services, Hartford.
———. 1989. AIDS: Knowledge, Attitudes and Behavior in Hartford's Neighborhoods. Special Report to the Connecticut State Department of Health Services, Hartford.
Allen, Lisa, Victor Herson, and Victoria Barrera. 1988. Coping with Neonatal Intensive Care: The Puerto Rican Experience. Hartford: Hispanic Health Council.
Baer, Hans. 1990. Kerr McKee and the NRC: From Indian Country to Silkwood to Gore. Social Science & Medicine 30(2):237–248.
Baer, Hans, Merrill Singer, and John Johnsen. 1986. Introduction: Toward a Critical Medical Anthropology. Social Science & Medicine 23(2):95–98.
Barbee, Evelyn. 1993. Racism in Nursing. Medical Anthropology Quarterly (n.s.) 7:346–362.
Barger, W. K., and Ernesto Reza. 1985. Processes in Applied Sociocultural Change and the Farmworker Movement in the Midwest. Human Organization 44(3):268–283.
———. 1987. Community Action and Social Adaptation: The Farmworker Movement in the Midwest. In Collaborative Research and Social Change. Donald Stull and Jean Schensul, eds. Pp. 55–76. Boulder, CO: Westview Press.
———. 1989. Policy and Community-Action Research: The Farm Labor Movement in California. In Making Our Research Useful. John van Willigen, Barbara Rylko-Bauer, and Ann McElroy, eds. Pp. 258–282. Boulder, CO: Westview Press.
Barnet, Richard, and John Cavanagh. 1974. Global Dreams: Imperial Corporations and the New World Order. New York: Simon and Schuster.
Barnet, Richard, and Ronald Müller. 1974. Global Reach: The Power of the Multinational Corporations. New York: Simon and Schuster.
Becker, Howard. 1967. Whose Side Are We On? Social Problems 4:239–247.
Bloch, Maurice. 1983. Marxism and Anthropology. Oxford: Oxford University Press.
Bonfil Batalla, Guillermo. 1966. Conservative Thought in Applied Anthropology: A Critique. Human Organization 25(2):89–92.
Borrero, Maria, Jean Schensul, and Robert Garcia. 1982. Research Based Training for Organizational Change. Urban Anthropology 11(1):129–153.
Cain, Roy. 1993. Community-Based AIDS Services: Formalization and Depoliticization. International Journal of Health Services 23(4):665–684.
Carey, James. 1990. Social System Effects on Local Level Morbidity and Adaptation in the Rural Peruvian Andes. Medical Anthropology Quarterly (n.s.) 4:266–295.
Chamberlin, R., and J. Radebaugh. 1976. Delivery of Primary Care—Union Style. New England Journal of Medicine 294:641–645.
Csordas, Thomas. 1988. The Conceptual Status of Hegemony and Critique in Medical Anthropology. Medical Anthropology Quarterly (n.s.) 2:416–421.
Damio, Grace, and Laura Cohen. 1990. Policy Report of the Hartford Community Childhood Hunger Identification Project. Hartford: Hispanic Health Council.
de Beer, Cedric. 1986. The South African Disease. Trenton: Africa World Press.
Donahue, John. 1986. The Nicaraguan Revolution. South Hadley, MA: Bergin and Garvey.
———. 1989. International Organizations, Health Services, and Nation Building in Nicaragua. Medical Anthropology Quarterly (n.s.) 3:258–269.
Doughterty, Molly, and Toni Tripp-Reimer. 1990. Nursing and Anthropology. In Medical Anthropology: Contemporary Theory and Method. Thomas Johnson and Carolyn Sargent, eds. Pp. 174–186. New York: Praeger.
Douglas, C., and J. Scott. 1978. Alternative Health Care in a Rural Community. Win Magazine 14:20–24.
Doyal, Lesley. 1979. The Political Economy of Health. Boston: Southend Press.

Eisenberg, Leon, and Arthur Kleinman, ed. 1981. Clinical Social Science. *In* The Relevance of Social Science for Medicine. Pp.1–23. Dordrecht: D. Reidel.

Estroff, Sue. 1988. Whose Hegemony? A Critical Commentary on Critical Medical Anthropology. Medical Anthropology Quarterly (n.s.) 2:421–426.

Forsyth, Gordon. 1966. Doctors and State Medicine: A Study of the British Health Service. London: Pitman Medical Publishers.

Foucault Michel. 1977. Discipline and Punish: The Birth of the Prison. New York: Pantheon Books.

Frankenberg, Ronald. 1988. Gramsci, Culture, and Medical Anthropology: Kundry and Parsifal? or Rat's Tail to Sea Serpent. Medical Anthropology Quarterly (n.s.) 2:324–337.

Friedland, William, and Dorothy Nelkin. 1971. Migrant Agricultural Workers in America's Northeast. New York: Holt, Rinehart and Winston.

Fresia, Jerry. 1988. Toward an American Revolution. Boston: South End Press.

Good, Byron. 1994. Medicine, Rationality, and Experience: An Anthropological Perspective. Cambridge: Cambridge University Press.

Good, Mary-Jo Delvecchio. 1990. The Practice of Biomedicine and the Discourse on Hope: A Preliminary Investigation into the Culture of American Oncology. *In* Anthropologies of Medicine: A colloquium on West European and North American Perspectives. Beatrix Pfeiderer and Gilles Bibeau, eds. Pp.121–135. Heidelberg: Vieweg.

Gorz, Andre. 1973. Socialism and Revolution. Garden City, NY: Basic Books.

Greenwood, Davydd, Shirley Lindenbaum, Margaret Lock, and Alan Young. 1988. Introduction. Theme Issue: Medical Anthropology. American Ethnologist 15(1):1–3.

Guttmacher, Sally. 1989. Minimizing Health Risks in Cuba. Medical Anthropology 11(2):167–180.

Habermas, Jürgen. 1984. The Theory of Communicative Action. Boston: Beacon Press.

Hastrup, Kirsten, and Peter Elsass. 1990. Anthropological Advocacy. Current Anthropology 31(3):301–311.

Hine, Darlene. 1989. Black Women in White: Racial Conflict and Cooperation in the Nursing Profession. 1890–1950. Bloomington: Indiana University Press.

Hopper, Kim. 1988. More Than Passing Strange: Homelessness and Mental Illness in New York City. American Ethnologist 15(1):155–167.

Hyman, Herbert Harvey. 1973. The Politics of Health Care: Nine Case Studies of Innovative Planning in New York. New York: Praeger.

Jackson, Eileen. 1993. Whiting-Out Difference: Why U.S. Nursing Research Fails Black Families. Medical Anthropology Quarterly (n.s.) 7:363–385.

Jackson, Jean. 1992. "After a While No One Believes You": Real and Unreal Pain. *In* Pain as Human Experience: An Anthropological Perspective. Mary-Jo Delvecchio Good, Paul Brodwin, Byron Good, and Arthur Kleinman, eds. Pp. 138–168. Berkeley: University of California Press.

Jacobsen, Rick. 1986. Using Organizations to Pursue Political Economic Analysis: The Case of Primary Health Care for the Poor. Medical Anthropology Quarterly 17(5):131–132.

Katon, Wayne, and Arthur Kleinman. 1981. Doctor-Patient Negotiation and Other Social Science Strategies in Patient Care. *In* The Relevance of Social Science for Medicine. Leon Eisenberg and Arthur Kleinman, eds. Pp. 253–279. Dordrecht: D. Reidel.

Kavanagh, Kathryn. 1993. Review of Anthropology and Nursing. Medical Anthropology Quarterly (n.s.) 7:405–407.

Kendall, Carl. 1989. The Use and Non-Use of Anthropology: The Diarrheal Disease Control Program in Honduras. *In* Making Our Research Useful. John van Willigen, Barbara Rylko-Bauer, and Ann McElroy, eds. Pp. 283–303. Boulder, CO: Westview Press.

Kleinman, Arthur. 1978. Concepts and a Model for the Comparison of Medical Systems as Cultural Systems. Social Science & Medicine 12:85–93.

———. 1980. Patients and Healers in the Context of Culture. Berkeley: University of California Press.

———. 1986. Social Origins of Distress and Disease. New Haven, CT: Yale University Press.

Lappé, Francis Moore, Joseph Collins, and David Kinley. 1981. AID as Obstacle. San Francisco: Institute for Food and Development Policy.

Lazarus, Ellen. 1988. Theoretical Considerations for the Study of the Doctor-Patient Relationship: Implications of a Perinatal Study. Medical Anthropology Quarterly (n.s.) 2:34–58.

Leininger, Madelyn. 1970. Nursing and Anthropology: Two Worlds to Blend. New York: Wiley.

Levin, Lowell. 1976. Self-Care: An International Perspective. Social Policy 7(2):70–75.

Lichtheim, George. 1966. Marxism in Modern France. New York: Columbia University Press.

Marieskind, Helen, and Barbara Ehrenreich. 1975. Toward Socialist Medicine: The Women's Health Movement. Social Policy 6(2):34–42.

McKeown, Thomas. 1976. The Role of Medicine. London: Nuffield Provincial Hospital Trust.

McKinlay, John, and Sonya McKinlay. 1977. The Questionable Contribution of Medical Measures to the Decline of Mortality in the United States in the 20th Century. Milbank Memorial Fund Quarterly 55:405–428.

McKnight, John. 1986. Politicizing Health Care. *In* The Sociology of Health and Illness. Peter Conrad and Rochelle Ker, eds. Pp. 10–23. New York: St. Martin's Press.

Morgan, Lynn. 1987. Dependency Theory in the Political Economy of Health: An Anthropological Critique. Medical Anthropology Quarterly (n.s.) 1:131–154.

Morgen, Sandra. 1986. The Dynamics of Cooptation in a Feminist Health Clinic. Social Science & Medicine 23(2):201–210.

Morsy, Soheir. 1989. Drop the Label: An "Emic" View of Critical Medical Anthropology. Anthropology Newsletter 30(2):13, 16.

Nash, June, and Max Kirsch. 1988. The Discourse of Medical Science in the Construction of Consensus Between Corporation and Community. Medical Anthropology Quarterly (n.s.) 2:158–171.

Navarro, Vincente. 1984. A Critique of the Ideological and Political Positions of the Willy Brandt Report and the

WHO Alma Ata Declaration. Social Science & Medicine 8:467–474.

———. 1985. U.S. Marxist Scholarship in the Analysis of Health and Medicine. International Journal of Health Services 15:525–545.

Ortner, Sherry. 1984. Theory in Anthropology since the Sixties. Comparative Studies in Society and History 26(1):126–166.

Pappas, Gregory. 1990. Some Implications for the Study of the Doctor-Patient Interaction: Power, Structure, and Agency in the Work of Howard Waitzkin and Arthur Kleinman. Social Science & Medicine 30(2):199–204.

Pelto, Pertti. 1988. A Note on Critical Medical Anthropology. Medical Anthropology Quarterly (n.s.) 2:435–437.

Petersdorf, Robert, and Alvan Feinstein. 1981. An Informal Appraisal of the Current Status of Medical Sociology. In The Relevance of Social Science for Medicine. Leon Eisenberg and Alan Kleinman, eds. Pp. 27–45. Dordrecht: D. Reidel.

Pflanz, Manfred. 1975. Relations between Social Scientists, Physicians and Medical Organizations in Health Research, Social Science & Medicine 9:7–13.

Piven, Francis Fox, and Richard Cloward. 1971. Regulating the Poor: The Functions of Public Welfare. New York: Vintage.

Rosen, George. 1974. From Medical Police to Social Medicine: Essays in the History of Health Care. New York: Neale Watson Publications.

Rudd, Paul. 1975. The United Farm Workers Clinic in Delano, California: A Study of the Rural Poor. Public Health Reports 90:331–339.

Sanders, David. 1985. The Struggle for Health. London: MacMillan.

Scheder, Jo. 1988. A Sickly-Sweet Harvest: Farmworker Diabetes and Social Equality. Medical Anthropology Quarterly (n.s.) 2:251–277.

Schensul, Jean, Donna Denelli-Hess, Maria Borrero, and Maprem Bhavati. 1987. Urban Comadronas: Maternal and Child Health Research and Policy Formulation in a Puerto Rican Community. In Collaborative Research and Social Change. Donald Stull and Jean Schensul, eds. Pp. 9–32. Boulder, CO: Westview Press.

Schensul, Stephen, and Maria Borrero. 1982. Introduction: The Hispanic Health Council. Urban Anthropology 11(1):1–8.

Schensul, Stephen, and Jean Schensul. 1982. Advocacy and Applied Anthropology. In Social Scientists as Advocates. G. Weber and G. McCall, eds. Pp. 121–165. Beverly Hills: Sage.

Scheper-Hughes, Nancy. 1990. Three Propositions for a Critically Applied Medical Anthropology. Social Science & Medicine 30(2):189–198.

———. 1992. Death Without Weeping: The Violence of Everyday Life in Brazil. Berkeley: University of California Press.

Scheper-Hughes, Nancy, and Anne Lovell. 1986. Breaking the Circuit of Social Control: Lessons in Public Psychiatry from Italy and Franco Basaglia. Social Science & Medicine 23(2):159–178.

Schoepf, Brooke. 1975. Human Relations versus Social Relations in Medical Care. In Topias and Utopias in Health. Stanley Ingman and Anthony Thomas, eds. Pp. 99–120. The Hague: Mouton.

Schroder, Barbara. 1987. Ethnic Identity and Non-Capitalist Relations of Production in Chimborazo, Ecuador. In Perspectives in U.S. Marxist Anthropology. David Hakken and Hanna Lessinger, eds. Pp. 123–139. Boulder, CO: Westview Press.

Sharma, Ursula. 1992. Complimentary Medicine Today: Practitioners and Patients. New York: Routledge.

Singer, Merrill. 1986. Developing a Critical Perspective in Medical Anthropology. Medical Anthropology Quarterly 17(5):128–129.

———. 1987. Cure, Care and Control: An Ectopic Encounter with Biomedical Obstetrics. In Encounter with Biomedicine: Case Studies in Medical Anthropology. Hans Baer, ed. Pp. 249–265. New York: Gordon and Breach.

———. 1989a. The Coming of Age of Critical Medical Anthropology. Social Science & Medicine 28:1193–1204.

———. 1989b. The Limitations of Medical Ecology: The Concept of Adaptation in the Context of Social Stratification and Social Transformation. Medical Anthropology 10:223–234.

———. 1990a. Reinventing Medical Anthropology: Toward a Critical Realignment. Social Science & Medicine 30(2): 179–188.

———. 1990b. Postmodernism and Medical Anthropology: Words of Caution. Medical Anthropology 12:289–304.

———. 1990c. On Anthropological Advocacy. Current Anthropology 31(5):548–549.

———. 1992. Matching Programs to Populations in Substance Abuse Treatment. Addictions Nursing Network 4(2):33–43.

———. 1994. Community Centered Praxis: Toward an Alternative Non-Dominative Applied Anthropology. Human Organization 53(4):336–344.

Singer, Merrill, Cándida Flores, Lani Davison, Georgine Burke, Zaida Castillo, Kelly Scalon, and Miydalia Rivera. 1990. SIDA: The Sociocultural and Socioeconomic Context of AIDS among Latinos. Medical Anthropology Quarterly (n.s.) 4:72–114.

———. 1991. Puerto Rican Community Organizing in Response to the AIDS Crisis. Human Organization 50(1):73–81.

———. 1992. Why Does Juan Garcia Have a Drinking Problem? The Perspective of Critical Medical Anthropology. Medical Anthropology 14(1):77–108.

———. 1994. Implementing a Community-Based AIDS Prevention Program for Ethnic Minorities: The Comunidad y Responsibilidad Project. In AIDS Prevention and Services. Johannes P. Van Vugt, ed. Pp. 59–92. Westport, CT: Bergin and Garvey.

Singer, Merrill, Lani Davison, and Gina Gerdes. 1988. Culture, Critical Theory, and Reproductive Illness Behavior in Haiti. Medical Anthropology Quarterly (n.s.) 2:370–385.

Singer, Merrill, Ray Irizarry, and Jean Schensul. 1991. Needle Access as an AIDS Prevention Strategy for IV Drug Users:

A Research Perspective. Human Organization 50(2): 142–153.

Smith, Carol. 1985. Local History in Global Context: Social and Economic Transitions in Western Guatemala. *In* Micro and Macro Levels of Analysis in Anthropology. Billie De Walt and Perrti Pelto, eds. Pp. 147–164. Boulder, CO: Westview Press.

Stark, Even. 1982. Doctors in Spite of Themselves: The Limits of Radical Health Criticism. International Journal of Health Services 12(3):419–455.

Starn, Orin. 1994. Rethinking the Politics of Anthropology: The Case of the Andes. Current Anthropology 35(1):13–38.

Susser, Ezra, and Sarah Conover. 1987. The Epidemiology of Homelessness and Mental Illness. *In* Psychiatric Epidemiology: Progress and Prospects. Brian Cooper, ed. Pp. 182–194. London: Croom Helm.

Susser, Ezra, Elmer Struening, and Sarah Connover. 1989. Psychiatric Problems in Homeless Men. Archives of General Psychiatry 46:845–850.

Susser, Ida, and M. Alfredo Gonzalez. 1991. Sex, Drugs and Videotape: The Prevention of AIDS in a New York City Shelter for Homeless Men. Medical Anthropology 14(2–4): 307–322.

Susser, Mervyn. 1974. Introduction to the Theme: A Critical Review of Sociology in Health. International Journal of Health Services 4:407–409.

Tripp-Reimer, Toni. 1984. Research in Cultural Diversity. Western Journal of Nursing 6(3):353–355.

Turner, Bryan. 1987. Medical Power and Social Knowledge. London: Sage.

Waitzkin, Howard. 1979. Medicine, Superstructure and Micropolitics. Social Science & Medicine 13A:601–609.

———. 1981. A Marxist Analysis of the Health Care Systems of Advanced Capitalist Societies. *In* The Relevance of Social Science for Medicine. Leon Eisenberg and Arthur Kleinman, eds. Pp. 333–339. Dordrecht: D. Reidel.

Wemer, David. 1977. The Village Health Worker—Lackey or Liberator? Palo Alto, CA: Hesperian Foundation.

Wiley, Andrea. 1992. Adaptation and the Biocultural Paradigm in Medical Anthropology: A Critical Review. Medical Anthropology Quarterly (n.s.) 6:216–236.

Willhelm, Sidney. 1966. Elites, Scholars, and Sociologists. Catalyst 2:1–10.

Wolf, Eric. 1982. Europe and the People without History. Berkeley: University of California Press.

———. 1990. Distinguished Lecture: Facing Power—Old Insights, New Questions. American Anthropologist 92(3): 586–596.

Woolhandler, Steffie, and David Himmelstein. 1989. Ideology in Medical Science: Class in the Clinic. Social Science & Medicine 28(11):1205–1209.

Wulff, Robert, and Shirley Fiske. 1987. Introduction. *In* Anthropological Praxis. Robert Wulff and Shirley Fiske, eds. Pp. 1–11. Boulder, CO: Westview Press.

Yee, Willie Kai. 1975. Dialectical Materialism and Community Mental Health Programs: An Analysis of the Lincoln Hospital Department of Psychiatry. *In* Topias and Utopias in Health. Stanley Ingman and Anthony Thomas, eds. Pp. 141–158. The Hague: Mouton.

Part II

APPLYING MEDICAL ANTHROPOLOGY

The selections in the second part of this book show you how medical anthropology can be used to analyze and improve real human health problems. Most of these selections are case studies of medical anthropology in action. In reality, however, this division between understanding and applying medical anthropology is arbitrary; it is impossible to separate theory and practice in the social sciences, especially in the field of health and healing. I believe that *all* the different approaches described in the first part of the book have relevance to the analysis and solution of health problems. All the approaches are anthropological because they are based on fundamental concepts, such as culture, and basic methods, such as participant observation and cross-cultural comparison. All the approaches can contribute to our society's struggle with health problems such as AIDS, malnutrition, and mental health. The underlying premise in the organization of this book is the dual goal of first understanding the diversity of theoretical perspectives in medical anthropology and then seeing how the discipline is applied to real human problems. Also, although it would have been easy to select all of the examples for this second half of the book solely from the United States, because there is so much medical anthropological work done here, it is very important to have a range of ethnographic examples.

There *is* a field called applied anthropology, and some of the selections in this half of the book probably do not fit within a strict definition of that field. Applied anthropology often refers to research and analysis done by anthropologists on a specific problem and for a specific client. For example, a coalition of health providers in an inner-city area may hire an anthropologist to help them understand why people with tuberculosis do not comply in taking the full course of their treatment medicine, or an international health project aimed at improving children's nutrition in certain demonstration projects in Africa may hire an anthropologist to do background studies of traditional infant feeding practices. In both cases, the applied anthropologist is hired to do specific work and to deliver a specific product—usually a report. In these examples, the anthropologist would be asked for advice in improving the program; sometimes the anthropologist

is regarded as a social and cultural troubleshooter, brought in to discover what went wrong. In a promising development, many of those in charge of health programs recognize the importance of social and cultural factors in the success of their projects, and therefore more applied medical anthropologists are now being asked to play a role in the design and management of those projects. Some anthropologists—such as those who work for the World Health Organization or the U.S. Centers for Disease Control and Prevention—claim that it is harder to design and implement successful health programs than to criticize such efforts from the sidelines. The greater recognition of applied medical anthropology is therefore a challenging opportunity for the field.

In applied medical anthropology, when a particular client defines a specific problem to be studied, it may seem to be an *atheoretical* enterprise, that it is simply a matter of applying the correct anthropological methods to the problem, like following a recipe in a cookbook. In reality, this is not the case because problems, theories, and methods are all linked. For example, there may be constraints on the medical anthropologist who is hired by a hospital. How critical can that person be and still keep the job? The client–employers want anthropologists to help them do their job better, so anthropologists may need to work within that system. In any case, there is not a single anthropological paradigm that can be applied to every problem. Research requires triangulation between a problem, an ethnographic context, and a theoretical orientation. For example, the problem might be the care of burn victims in a hospital setting, the setting might be the burn center itself and debridement (the removal of dead tissue), and the theoretical orientation might be the illness experience of patients, the psychology of pain, and the goals of the nursing staff. This example is from the work of a clinical anthropologist, Thomas Johnson, whose study of illness experience in a burn unit resulted in a small but significant change in debriding procedures (Johnson 1997). Patients said they could tolerate pain if they knew when it was going to end, but nurses doing the debridement had been working to get it done as quickly as possible. From listening to patients, the anthropologist realized that patients preferred to have predictable breaks during this painful process. By placing a large clock in the debridement room and agreeing upon a set schedule of debriding minutes followed by rest periods, the applied anthropologist was able to introduce an improvement for both patients and nurses. The problem, setting, and theory all worked together in focusing the research, implementation, and evaluation of a change. When looking at research proposals (or student's ideas for research papers), anthropologists look for the problem, the setting, and the theoretical orientation. Only after these three parameters are set can an appropriate methodology for research be selected.

The selections in Part II are divided into six areas: case studies in explanatory models; ethnicity and health care; stigma and coping with chronic illness; gender and women's health; culture and nutrition; and international health issues and programs. Within each topic area a wide variety of health problems are represented. But *how* are we to define health problems? Biomedicine defines health problems by categorizing human biological systems (neurology, orthopedics, internal medicine, ophthalmology, and so on) or points in the life cycle (pediatrics, obstetrics, geriatrics); it may also focus on specific diseases. Because anthropologists argue that health problems cannot be easily separated from aspects of sociopolitical organization, cultural beliefs, and ecology, it is impossible to define health problems as only *within* an individual human body. Clearly, this understanding of health problems requires a wider, socially oriented view, and medical anthropology offers a variety of angles (or lenses) for examining those problems. The same health issue—lower back pain, for example—might be seen through the lens of explanatory models if the goal is to improve the treatment or pain management of patients. On the other hand, this health issue might involve the political economy of health if the goal is to prevent back injuries that occur on the job. In fact, any single health problem may be explored from a diversity of medical anthropological perspectives; the "correct" perspective depends on what you want to know and what you want to do with that information. This diversity of perspectives is a strength of anthropology.

Students interested in further reading in applied anthropology may refer to the works listed in the references at the back of the book. There is also useful information on the Society for Applied Anthropology (SfAA) internet home page (http://www.telepath.com/sfaa) as well as the National Association of Practicing Anthropologists (NAPA) internet home page (http://www.oakland.edu/~dow/napa/napares/napa.htm). The film *Anthropologists at Work: Careers Making a Difference* (35 min., VHS) distributed by the American Anthropological Association is also a useful introduction.

Case Studies in Explanatory Models

✦ CONCEPTUAL TOOLS ✦

■ *The study of explanatory models has many practical uses.* Explanatory models (EMs) have been a major contribution of Arthur Kleinman and his colleagues, who introduced this concept to describe individuals' cognitive models of their own illnesses as these models relate to cultural issues in clinical settings. Kleinman has suggested that clinicians can elicit a patient's EM by asking questions like the following: What do you think caused your problem? Why do you think this illness happened at the particular time that it did? How bad do you think this illness is? What worries you most about this illness? What kind of treatment were you expecting to get? What are the most important results you expect to get from treatment? (see Brown, Gregg, and Ballard 1997; Kleinman 1988). These questions resemble those an anthropologist would ask to learn about a different ethnomedical system. In a clinical setting, asking these kinds of questions allows the health care provider to get the patient's cultural beliefs "out on the table" so that potential cultural problems might be avoided. If the patient thinks a condition is severe and will last a long time and the physician thinks the condition is mild and temporary, it is important to discuss this discrepancy in a way that does not condescend to the patient. Asking these questions also allows the health care provider to acknowledge legitimate differences in medical beliefs; it is a way to treat the patient with respect. In a public health or health education setting, eliciting EMs from community members (also called the folk model of illness) can help planners identify (or rule out) potential cultural conflicts. The case of *empacho* in selection 43 is an example of this. Ethnomedical beliefs about the etiology, diagnosis, and treatment of illnesses are important because when patients and healers rely on different ethnomedical systems there is increased risk of miscommunication. If peoples' behavior is logically linked to their modes of thinking, then it is essential to know what people think.

■ *The fallacy of empty vessels is that people in other societies lack health knowledge.* This idea is based on the important work of Steven Polgar, who developed this concept to describe cultural problems encountered in international health programs, but the idea is equally applicable in class-stratified, multicultural societies like the United States (Polgar 1962). The fallacy of empty vessels is that people in other societies (so-called target populations) do not have any health knowledge or beliefs. Rather they are "empty vessels," waiting to be filled with the knowledge of scientific medicine developed in modern, rich countries. The fallacy implies that as soon as people are educated about new scientific knowledge for prevention and treatment, they will certainly change their behaviors or accept the medical innovations. In reality, however, all peoples already have their own ethnomedical beliefs and practices, and these preexisting beliefs influence how new ideas are accepted. When one pours different liquid into already-filled vessels, a new mixture results, and when new biomedical ideas are introduced to people who already have an ethnomedical system, they are more likely to accept those ideas that fit with the preexisting system and reject those that do not. Such problems can be overcome, but only if one is aware of the fallacy of empty vessels. Understanding that people receive health messages within the context of their own beliefs is essential in order to achieve effective communication between physicians and patients, health promoters and the public.

■ *Questions of compliance or adherence are linked to issues of power.* Anthropologists hold that, in general, people's behavior is understandable and logical within their own social and cultural context. The challenge, therefore, is to understand the "other's" point of view. The idea of eliciting EMs from patients, or of studying the folk models of illness in a population, is based on the belief that compliance (adherence) can be improved through better communication. One important factor left out of this equation, however, is that people's behavior is sometimes constrained by their particular conditions of social class. Another factor is that there are power differentials between the givers and receivers of health messages. Health care providers are in a more powerful position, and they may expect their suggestions to be followed simply because of these power differences. In this regard, health care providers may perceive patient noncompliance as a problem of disobedience, expecting the receivers of health messages to comply like obedient and powerless children. This attitude does not fit well with a model of partnership between patient and provider.

■ *Medical pluralism exists in most social contexts.* In general, simple one-to-one relationships between a single society and a single ethnomedical system do not exist. As biomedicine has dispersed in nearly all areas of the world, traditional medical systems continue to thrive. Medical pluralism means that multiple medical systems coexist in a single social context, and therefore people choose from a variety of medical–therapy options to deal with their complaints. The pattern of health-seeking between different modalities of health systems available is called the *hierarchy of resort* (Romanucci-Ross 1969).

✤ 25

Ethnomedical Beliefs and Patient Adherence to a Treatment Regimen: A St. Lucian Example

William W. Dressler

This selection tests a relatively straightforward hypothesis: In the context of medical pluralism, are people who do not hold biomedical beliefs more or less likely to be noncompliant in taking medication for hypertension? In this research in St. Lucia, William Dressler uses the personalistic-naturalistic distinction in ethnomedical systems developed by George Foster (selection 12). When a theoretical ideal typology is tested in a research setting, it often becomes evident that the original categorizations were less clear-cut than expected. Three belief systems (personalistic, naturalistic, and biomedical) coexist in St. Lucia. Dressler interviewed people diagnosed with hypertension in the biomedical clinic to see whether they took their prescribed hypertension medicine. Essential hypertension, or high blood pressure, is a particularly interesting phenomenon to examine because it is a symptomless disease. It is diagnosed from readings with a blood pressure cuff and a stethoscope; this raised pressure in the cardiovascular system is clearly linked to high risk for stroke and premature death. The disease can be controlled through medication, but that medicine often has to be taken for a lifetime. Because of this set of features, the problem of compliance in taking the prescription is particularly difficult.

In this example, Dressler is not looking specifically at explanatory models about a specific illness (as we will see in the next selection, also dealing with hypertension) but rather people's overall ethnomedical cognitive model. Also notice how the anthropologist asks specific questions so that he may classify people by the quantitative analysis necessary to test the hypothesis. Although there is little mystery about the methodology of this research, it is not so obvious how to interpret the results.

As you read this selection, consider these questions:

■ *What do you think are the advantages and disadvantages of doing anthropological research using the quantitative, hypothesis-testing approach described in this selection?*

■ *How is it that a single society can have multiple and competing ethnomedical systems? Why don't some of these ethnomedical beliefs just die out?*

■ *Is it possible for a symptomless disease to be an illness?*

■ *How do you interpret the fact that language use becomes a powerful predictive marker of hypertension medication compliance?*

■ *Are applied medical anthropologists correct in their assumption that human behavior is generally predictable and almost always changeable?*

The study of "adherence to" or "compliance with" treatment regimens has become very important in recent years. These terms refer to the extent to which a patient persists in behaviors prescribed by a health professional (e.g., taking pills, changing diets), or restricts activities, such as smoking. These issues loom large in the treatment of chronic diseases such as high blood pressure (or essential hypertension). Hypertension is an asymptomatic disease which leads to heart disease, stroke, kidney disease and others if not treated, and treatment may last a lifetime. Yet an accepted estimate is that of all hypertensives, only one-fourth are under treatment, and only one-half of those adhere to their regimen (Kirscht and Rosenstock 1977).

This problem has stimulated the search for those factors, especially beliefs and attitudes, that are associated with adherence behavior (Blackwell 1973). These concerns converge with one of the more interesting theoretical issues in medical anthropology, namely, the relationship of ethnomedical beliefs to health-related behaviors.

A number of anthropologists have commented on the problem of adherence to treatment in relation to ethnomedical beliefs. Snow (1974) has reviewed much of the literature on folk medical beliefs among Black Americans, and she describes a wide range of beliefs dealing with both natural and supernatural causes and treatments of illness. She concludes that "the presence of an alternate medical system which at best is different from and at worst is in direct conflict with that of the health professional can only complicate matters. These beliefs . . . may greatly color the doctor/patient relationship and influence the decision to follow—or not—the doctor's orders" (1974:94). Similarly, Harwood (1971) and Logan (1973) have reviewed ethnomedical beliefs held by Hispanics in the New World. They have argued that an individual's commitment to (in the case of Hispanics) the humoral theory of medicine can seriously undermine the biomedical treatment of disease. Finally, Wiese (1976) suggests that food-related beliefs in Haiti might interfere with successful nutritional therapy.

Based on these studies, the hypothesis can be advanced that, within a mixed medical setting, the greater an individual's commitment to an ethnomedical belief system, the less likely it is that that individual will adhere to a treatment regimen prescribed within the Western medical setting.

I conducted research to evaluate this hypothesis in the West Indies, in a town in St. Lucia. The population of St. Lucia is predominantly Afro-American, and is descended from African slaves. Until recently, St. Lucia was a colonial dependency of Britain, although the original White settlers on the island were French. The French influence is most evident in language; virtually every St. Lucian speaks a French-English creole, locally termed Patois, as their first language (Lieberman and Dressler 1977).

The research reported here was conducted in a town of approximately five thousand inhabitants. The region is situated on the western coast of St. Lucia and is devoted to agriculture. The bulk of arable land is held by large estates planted in bananas, coconuts, citrus, and root crops. A large percentage of the population is employed as agricultural laborers. There is also a copra processing plant in the town, employing nearly three hundred persons. Other economic pursuits include fishing, small-scale retailing, and government service.

St. Lucia is especially appropriate for this study for two reasons. First, there is a very high prevalence of hypertension in St. Lucia. Despite the fact that hypertension is asymptomatic, the disease is of concern to the people of St. Lucia, and it occupies a prominent place in the ethnomedical belief system. Second, the medical system of St. Lucia is a mixed, traditional-Western system. Furthermore, the medical subsystems have coexisted for over a century, since the first Western-trained physicians visited St. Lucia in the 19th century.

THE MEDICAL SYSTEM

Foster (1976) has proposed two categories, the "naturalistic" and the "personalistic," to account for variation in ethnomedical belief systems. These categories will be used to describe the intracultural variation in ethnomedical beliefs in St. Lucia. There is, of course, a certain degree of overlap between these two categories. Nonetheless, they are useful in distinguishing two varieties of ethnomedical belief in St. Lucia, and they are emically valid. St. Lucians make a similar distinction themselves. Finally, the Western medical system is considered to be analytically and logically distinct.

The *personalistic system* refers to that subset of ethnomedical beliefs in which illness and other types of misfortune are explained by the active aggression of some agent which might be human, nonhuman, or supernatural (Foster 1976:775). In St. Lucia this set of beliefs is subsumed under the term *obeah*. Obeah is a West Indian form of sorcery. Obeah is not seen as a necessary or even sufficient cause of illness; however, these practices may be used to make any existing illness episode longer, more severe, and sometimes fatal.

Persons who practice obeah are referred to as *jagajey* and obtain their power directly from Satan. There are a number of malevolent agents that can be used by a jagajey, and these agents can be dangerous in their own right.

If obeah is suspected in an illness, a *gade* will be consulted. A gade is an ethnomedical specialist who has the power and knowledge to counteract obeah. The gade gains knowledge through dreams and uses divination to diagnose. Other kinds of illnesses can be treated by a gade, but only the gade can fight obeah.

The *naturalistic system* refers to that subset of ethnomedical beliefs in which forces of nature—such as cold and dampness—are thought to be major causes of illness (ibid.). In St. Lucia these beliefs are subsumed under the term "bush medicine." The most important factors in the environment which cause illness are imbalances in hot and cold (referring to actual temperature) and dietary factors. There is a degree of etiologic specificity in these beliefs; particular kinds of factors are associated with specific illnesses. For example, hypertension (referred to simply as "the pressure") is believed to be caused by chemical fertilizers that were introduced during the expansion of the banana industry and are now used in the growing of staple crops.

When an illness is believed to have been caused by a natural force, the treatment will be in the form of a "bush tea" made from local plants. Many people seek the advice of a bush medicine specialist. These individuals are known by no special cover term; they are simply recognized as being particularly knowledgeable in the domain of bush medicine. These specialists typically do not charge for their services.

The *Western system* refers to the government health-care delivery system. The most important segment of that system is the health center. The island is divided into seven medical districts, each staffed by a District Medical Officer (DMO). The DMO is an M.D., usually a White expatriate, whose function is to treat patients attending general medical clinics throughout the district. The health center that was located in the research community was staffed by two registered nurses, several student nurses and aides and a dispenser, in addition to the DMO.

With respect to hypertension, the treatment practices were as follows: if a patient presented an elevated blood pressure reading and no other evidence of hypertension, a tranquilizer was given. If some other sign of hypertension was present, reserpine, an antihypertensive drug, was prescribed. Hypertensives were given 30-day prescriptions that could be refilled six times, at which time they returned to the DMO for evaluation of control. In the interim, their blood pressure was monitored by a nurse at two-week intervals.

Those patients receiving tranquilizers were given a nonrefillable 30-day prescription.

METHODS

A sample of 40 hypertensives under treatment at the local health center was interviewed. This sample represents all those cases under treatment that could be contacted. The sample is thus not a probability sample, but neither is it merely accidental. The only systematic bias which might have occurred was an underrepresentation of males (as compared to a community-wide probability sample): there were 33 females and 7 males in the sample. Significance tests were used not for the purposes of generalizing to a universe, but to rule out the operation of random processes within the sample (Blalock 1972:239). Descriptive statistics for the sample are presented at the bottom of Table 1.

Adherence behavior was measured as a dichotomy on the basis of successful compliance with the medication regimen. During the course of an interview each respondent's most recent prescription for medication was examined. If the respondent had taken 70% or more of the tablets from the most recent prescription, and had properly refilled the prescription, then the respondent was considered to have successfully complied with the regimen. Using this criterion, 19, or 47.5%, of the respondents were compliant. This equals compliance rates found in most studies (Kirscht and Rosenstock 1977).

Ethnomedical beliefs were measured by presenting the respondents with statements and asking them first if they were aware of the statement, and second if they believed the statement to be true or false. The latter responses were used as evidence of commitment to beliefs. The following 16 items were used (the items were randomized on the interview schedule).

1. *Lespwi* are evil spirits who can hurt people.

2. *Bolom* are things that look like children but are really evil spirits.

3. *Lajablesse* are evil spirits who can hurt people.

4. A gade is a man who knows how to fight evil spirits and treat sicknesses.

5. If a person works obeah on you, it can make you sick or even kill you.

6. Jagajey are people who know how to work evil.

7. High blood pressure is caused by fertilizers (salt put on plants to make them grow).

TABLE 1   Descriptive Statistics and Correlation Matrix

	(1)	*(2)*	*(3)*	*(4)*	*(5)*	*(6)*	*(7)*	*(8)*	*(9)*
1. Language	—								
2. Travel	.533***	—							
3. Age	−.017	−.100	—						
4. Education	.731***	.406**	−.126	—					
5. Economic status	.060	.276*	.026	.241	—				
6. Personalistic beliefs	.285*	.288*	−.012	.366*	−.059	—			
7. Naturalistic beliefs	.364**	.198	.063	.308*	.076	.519***	—		
8. Western beliefs	.344**	.172	.107	.239	.007	.168	.425**	—	
9. Adherence	−.040	−.156	−.208	.026	.174	−.319*	−.172	−.060	—
Mean	.60	.45	63.8	3.7	3.2	2.5	2.5	.48	
Standard Deviation	.49	.50	10.3	2.4	2.1	1.4	.78	.50	

*p < .05
**p < .01
***p < .001

8. *Gwenabafay, twatas,* or *citronel* can be used to make a bush tea for *empwida.*

9. A tea made with Indian cucumber is good for high blood pressure.

10. Empwida is caused by being hot and eating or drinking something cold.

11. Eating green paw-paw is good for high blood pressure.

12. A person will get high blood pressure if his blood is too rich.

13. If a person has high blood pressure, he should not put salt on his food.

14. If high blood pressure is not treated, it can cause a stroke.

15. A person who has high blood pressure must always take pills.

16. High blood pressure can never be cured.

Three subscales were formed for purposes of analysis. Scale reliability was assessed using the coefficient of internal consistency, "alpha" (Kerlinger 1973:451–52). The *personalistic scale* is made up of items 1–6 (alpha = .80). The *naturalistic scale* is made up of items 7–12 (alpha = .65). The *Western scale* is made up of items 13–16 (alpha = .65). Each scale shows an acceptable degree of reliability.

The following variables were included as potential predictors of adherence because they have been shown to affect health behavior in other contexts (Woods and Graves 1973). *Economic status* was measured as a four-item index of the acquisition of material culture (electricity, plumbing, toilet, concrete house; alpha = .84). *Education* is a seven-point scale of years of education completed. *Age* is the respondent's age in years. *Travel*

was coded as a dichotomy, i.e., whether or not the respondent had ever traveled off the island. *Language* was coded as the language used during the interview (English = 1; Patois = 0).

A correlation matrix of all variables is presented in Table 1. The only variable significantly related to adherence to treatment is the personalistic belief scale; the higher an individual's acceptance of personalistic beliefs, the lower their compliance.

In order to control for the effects of the background variables, partial correlations were computed between the belief scales and adherence, controlling for economic status, education, age, travel, and language use. The partial correlation for adherence and personalistic beliefs was significant and negative (partial r = −.29, p < .05). The other partial correlations were not significant (r = −.17 for adherence and naturalistic beliefs; r = −.06 for adherence and Western beliefs).

DISCUSSION

It is of interest to examine the utility of Foster's (1976) scheme for classifying ethnomedical beliefs at the outset. There is, of course, a certain degree of ambiguity in applying the concepts of "personalistic" or "naturalistic." From one perspective, we could group these categories of belief under the rubric "ethnomedicine" and distinguish both from Western medicine. On the other hand, Western beliefs and bush medicine could be grouped as kinds of naturalistic beliefs and could be distinguished from personalistic beliefs. As it turns out, this seeming ambiguity reflects the empirical situation in St. Lucia accurately. When we examine the correlations among the three belief scales, personalistic and naturalistic beliefs are correlated, and naturalistic and Western beliefs are correlated, but personalistic and Western beliefs are uncorrelated. The personalistic and naturalistic systems share an emphasis on herbal and plant remedies, along with a lack of government recognition. The naturalistic and Western systems share an emphasis on natural forces or conditions as causes of disease. There is little or no similarity between personalistic and Western beliefs. Thus, this conceptual scheme proved useful in the analysis of the intracultural diversity of medical beliefs in St. Lucia.

Of additional interest are the patterns of relationships among the sociocultural variables and the three belief scales. In general, those individuals with greater English language facility, more exposure to the world through travel, and more education, tend to express more agreement with statements of medical beliefs of all kinds. These findings could be a methodological artifact. That is, individuals with greater English language facility and more education might answer more in the affirmative to please the investigator. It seems unlikely, however, that this would occur in the case of personalistic beliefs. On the other hand, it has been shown in a number of studies that "modernizing" individuals present more illness complaints. Perhaps modernizing individuals also express more concern with medical beliefs. Their concern with the cognitive domain of health might manifest itself both in more illness complaints *and* in an expression of more knowledge and affirmation of medical beliefs in an interview situation.

It is striking that these modernizing individuals express more agreement with statements of personalistic beliefs. These results run counter to the scholarly mainstream of research in modernization. The various conceptions of "modern" persons differ somewhat, but a recurring feature is that such persons believe in determinism and scientific knowledge and reject traditional beliefs.

These and other data clearly do not support this position. My findings corroborate those of Jahoda (1970), one of the few studies in this area. Jahoda examined the correlates of supernatural beliefs in a large sample of university students in Ghana. He found that "the modest trend was for subjects who had spent more years at the university and for those from a more literate home background to retain more supernatural beliefs" (ibid.: 126). If these results continue to be replicated in future research, the concept of "psychological modernization" will need revision. More research should be devoted to the modernization of traditional belief systems, the process that seems to be at work in St. Lucia, rather than the simple adoption of Western belief systems.

The only significant correlate of adherence to treatment for essential hypertension is the scale of personalistic beliefs. When sociocultural variables are controlled, the correlation is reduced somewhat, but the significant, inverse relationship remains.

It has been argued that the link between personalistic beliefs and adherence is motivational. It is hypothesized that those individuals believing in a personalistic system see themselves as under the control of external forces. Thus, there is little motivation for them to take their medication since control of their fate is out of their hands (Caplan et al. 1976:35). This hypothesis predicts that individuals should take *no* action to treat their illness. This is not consistent with the data in this study. Over half of the respondents (55%) report having used a bush tea for their high blood pressure, and this reported behavior is positively correlated with both personalistic beliefs ($r = .41, p < .01$) and naturalistic beliefs ($r = .36, p < .01$). Interestingly, the two behavioral responses (medication or bush tea) are independent of one another ($r = .05$, n.s.). Since these two behavioral responses are independent of one another, and related to personalistic beliefs in different directions, a motivational hypothesis fails to account for the observed correlations.

Some years ago, Buchler (1964) observed that people on Grand Caymans in the West Indies preferred to take medication in liquid form rather than as pills, which he related to their customary use of bush teas. Perhaps the same process is operating here. This would explain why individuals more committed to personalistic beliefs are more likely to use a bush tea, but less likely to take their pills as directed. This interpretation should be tested in future research.

In summary, partial support was found for the hypothesis I advanced. One dimension of ethnomedical beliefs does relate to adherence behavior, although the interpretation of that relationship is problematic. This is far from a definitive study. Rather, these data serve to illustrate some of the more general issues in the study of ethnomedical beliefs and health behavior.

REFERENCES

Blackwell, B. 1973. Patient Compliance. New England Journal of Medicine 289:249–52.

Blalock, H. M. 1972. Social Statistics. Second ed. New York: McGraw-Hill.

Buchler, I. R. 1964. Caymanian Folk Medicine: A Problem in Applied Anthropology. Human Organization 23:48–49.

Caplan, R. D., et al. 1976. Adhering to Medical Regimens. Ann Arbor: Institute for Social Research, The University of Michigan.

Foster, G. M. 1976. Disease Etiologies in Non-Western Medical Systems. American Anthropologist 78:773–82.

Harwood, A. 1971. The Hot-Cold Theory of Disease. Journal of the American Medical Association 216:1153–58.

Jahoda, G. 1970. Supernatural Beliefs and Changing Cognitive Structures Among Ghanian University Students. Journal of Cross-Cultural Psychology 1:115–30.

Kerlinger, F. 1973. Foundations of Behavioral Research. Second ed. New York: Holt, Rinehart and Winston.

Kirscht, J. P., and I. M. Rosenstock. 1977. Patient Adherence to Antihypertensive Medical Regimens. Journal of Community Health 3:115–24.

Lieberman, D., and W. W. Dressler. 1977. Bilingualism and Cognition of St. Lucian Disease Terms. Medical Anthropology 1:81–110.

Logan, M. H. 1973. Humoral Medicine in Guatemala and Peasant Acceptance of Modern Medicine. Human Organization 32:385–96.

Snow, L. 1974. Folk Medical Beliefs and Their Implications for Care of Patients. Annals of Internal Medicine 81:82–96.

Wiese, H. J. C. 1976. Maternal Nutrition and Traditional Food Behavior in Haiti. Human Organization 35:193–200.

Woods, C. M., and T. D. Graves. 1973. The Process of Medical Change in a Highland Guatemala Town. Los Angeles: Latin American Center, UCLA.

✤ 26

Health Beliefs and Compliance with Prescribed Medication for Hypertension Among Black Women—New Orleans 1985–86

Centers for Disease Control and Prevention
Based on Work by Suzanne Heurtin-Roberts and Efrain Reisin

This brief selection is from the no-nonsense publication of the Centers for Disease Control and Prevention, the Morbidity and Mortality Weekly Report (MMWR). *The selection summarizes some important ethnographic research by Suzanne Heurtin-Roberts and Efrain Reisin on the relationship between ethnomedical beliefs and compliance with taking prescribed antihypertension medicine. The research is important because it demonstrates that although there is variation in the African American community in regard to the belief in folk medical concepts, those who believe in the traditional ethnomedical categorizations are less likely to be compliant. The researchers also demonstrate that the medical staff at this inner-city hospital were generally unaware of the health beliefs of their patients, although medical anthropologists studying the ethnomedical beliefs within African American communities have known for a long time about the differences between "high blood" and "high pertension." These illness labels have been described in diverse regions of the United States: Washington State (Blumhagen 1980), western Michigan (Snow 1993), and eastern North Carolina (Mathews 1988).*

The folk model distinguishes between a chronic condition amenable to treatment and an episodic condition affected by emotional crises. "High blood" is considered to be a persistent condition of blood that is too thick, too rich, or too heavy. This blood is thought to rise up into the head and stay there, causing negative health consequences largely because the condition makes the heart work too hard. A variety of symptoms may indicate that "high blood" exists—red eyes, nosebleeds, headaches, tasting blood—due to blood rising to the head. "High blood" is caused in part by individual predisposition and is exacerbated by a diet rich in red, heavy, and sweet foods (including pork and red wine). People with "high blood" generally have that condition for life, and they need to avoid certain foods to prevent dangerous episodes. "High blood" can be treated by drinking blood-thinning agents like epsom salts or pickle juice (Heurtin-Roberts and Reisin 1990). On the other hand, "high pertension," or tension, is an episodic, emotional condition in which the blood suddenly rises and then falls, making the victim more likely to "fall out" or faint. "High pertension" is largely a matter of an individual's predisposition, as well as the result of par-

ticular emotional contexts. It cannot be treated or cured; the best that can be done is to avoid emotional trauma.

The findings of this study show that women who recognized the ethnomedical categories were more likely to be noncompliant than were women who only recognized the biomedical category of hypertension. Of the women who believed in the folk medical categories, those who believed their condition was the untreatable "high pertension" were the least likely to be compliant in taking the necessary medicine. The fact that health care workers were unaware of these folk categories and did not attempt to elicit the EMs of their patients clearly adds to the problem of compliance.

As you read this selection, consider these questions:

- *What kind of confusion might arise if a health care provider does not know that her patient believes in "high pertension" instead of the biomedical category "hypertension"?*

- *Why would the MMWR consider this study important enough to publish it as timely medical news?*

- *What kind of education project seems to be suggested by this research? Do you think it would be best to focus on health care providers or patients?*

- *Why does it seem very logical that a person who believed that she had "high pertension" would not think that taking medication regularly would be an important thing to do?*

- *Why might a person who thinks she has "high blood" think that taking hypertension medication regularly is a reasonable thing to do?*

In the United States, the prevalence of definite hypertension (i.e., having systolic blood pressure ≥160 mm Hg and/or diastolic blood pressure ≥ 95 mm Hg, and/or taking antihypertensive medication) is 1.5 times higher among blacks (25.7%) than among whites (16.8%).[1] Although hypertension-related mortality appears to be declining among blacks, this problem continues to be disproportionately higher among blacks than among whites, particularly in younger age groups.[2] Poor compliance with prescribed treatment is cited as the major reason for inadequate control of hypertension in blacks and whites.[3] Improved understanding of patients' beliefs about hypertension could aid the development of public health strategies to reduce or control the disease. This report summarizes a study of the relationship between beliefs about hypertension and compliance with antihypertensive treatment among black women who received health care at a public hospital clinic in New Orleans.

From May 1985 through July 1986, 54 (72%) of 75 black women aged 45–70 years receiving treatment for essential hypertension and possibly one other chronic disease unrelated to hypertension were included in the study. Each patient participated for 2 months. To elicit beliefs and attitudes about hypertension and general health, investigators interviewed each patient twice using a standardized questionnaire. Patients were visited in their homes at 2-week intervals to monitor blood pressure and compliance with prescribed medication. The 15 resident physicians who treated these patients at the clinic were interviewed about their awareness of patient health beliefs.

Based on medication diaries, field notes, and pill counts (at the initial visit and at 1 and 2 months after the initial visit), patient compliance was categorized as "poor" (pill use <60%) or "good" (use >80%). For women with pill use 60%–79% (n = 14) or for whom complete pill-use records were not available, diaries and field notes were used to determine whether compliance was "good" or "poor." The likelihood of poor compliance among women who professed folk beliefs was compared with the likelihood of poor compliance among women who believed in a biomedical model of hypertension.

The 54 patients conceptualized their disease as "pressure trouble" or simply "pressure." One group (n = 22) believed in the existence of the biomedical disease, hypertension; the other group (n = 32) believed instead in the existence of two diseases, "high blood" and "high-pertension," distinguished by folk etiology, symptomatology, and treatment.

Patients characterized "high blood" as a physical disease of the blood and heart in which the blood was too "hot," "rich," or "thick"; the level of the blood rose slowly in the body and remained high for extended periods. These participants considered "high blood" to be caused by heredity, poor diet, and "heat" (from either the body or the environment); to be predictable and controllable; and to be capable of resulting in illness or death. "High blood" was thought to be appropriately treated by dietary control (i.e., abstention from pork, hot or spicy foods, and "grease") and by various folk remedies such as ingestion of lemon juice, vinegar, or garlic water. Patients believed these treatments cooled and thinned the blood, causing its level in the body to drop.

Patients considered "high-pertension" to be a disease "of the nerves" caused by stress, worry, and an anxious personality. Unlike "high blood," "high-pertension" was believed to be volatile and episodic. These patients believed that at times of emotional excitement, the blood would "shoot up" rapidly toward the head, then "fall back" or "drop back" quickly. Rather than medication and dietary control, these patients considered the appropriate treatment for "high-pertension" to be mitigation of stress and emotional excitement through control of emotions and the social environment.

Of the 32 women who believed in either of the two folk illnesses, 20 (63%) complied poorly with antihypertensive treatment, compared with six (27%) of 22 who believed in biomedical hypertension (relative risk = 2.3; 95% confidence interval [CI] = 1.2–4.4). Differences in compliance were also related to self-diagnosis: women who believed they had "high-pertension" were 3.3 times as likely to comply poorly as women who believed they had biomedical hypertension (95% CI = 1.7–6.8). Those with "high blood" were 0.5 times as likely to be poor compilers (95% CI = 0.1–3.1). Patients who believed they had both folk illnesses were 2.4 times as likely to be poor compliers as those who believed they had biomedical hypertension (95% CI = 1.1–5.2).

The 15 resident physicians had limited knowledge of the existence among their patients of folk beliefs about hypertension. Only two physicians knew of their patients' beliefs about the role of blood and emotional states in hypertension. Although 12 of the 15 physicians were aware of folk terms for hypertension, eight believed such terms were simply folk expressions for the biomedical illness.

EDITORIAL NOTE

Compliance with drug therapy has been a major focus of research on the control of hypertension since 1979, when the Hypertension Detection and Follow-Up Program Cooperative Group[1] reported lower mortality in persons with moderate hypertension who received therapy. Although the benefits of drug therapy are well established, excess mortality associated with essential hypertension persists among black persons in the United States. The findings in this report suggest that physicians might decrease the excess mortality associated with hypertension through health education efforts and by taking into consideration their patients' beliefs.

This study (1) documented hypertension-related beliefs of a high-risk population under treatment, (2) demonstrated a measurable relationship between patients' perceptions of illness and compliance behavior, (3) determined that physicians treating these patients were unaware of their patients' perceptions of their illness, and (4) suggested the importance of training physicians to elicit patients' conceptions of the illness[4] before selecting a therapeutic regimen.

Limitations of the study sample are that it was small and facility-based and included only black women. Nonetheless, the findings about these patients' perceptions of hypertension are consistent with other studies that used larger, community-based samples of blacks[5,6] and facility-based samples of whites.[7] These studies advocate educating physicians about the importance of patient beliefs about hypertension.

REFERENCES

1. Drizd T, Dannenberg AL, Engel A, NCHS. Blood pressure levels in persons 18–74 years of age in 1976–80, and trends in blood pressure from 1960 to 1980 in the United States. Hyattsville, Maryland: US Department of Health and Human Services, Public Health Service, CDC, 1986; DHHS publication no. (PHS)86–1684. (Vital and health statistics; series 11, no. 234).

2. National Heart, Lung, and Blood Institute. The 1988 report of the Joint National Committee on Detection, Evaluation, and Treatment of High Blood Pressure. Arch Intern Med 1988; 148:1023–38.

3. National Heart, Lung, and Blood Institute. The 1984 report of the Joint National Committee on Detection, Evaluation, and Treatment of High Blood Pressure. Arch Intern Med 1984; 144:1045–57.

4. Kleinman A. Patients and healers in the context of culture: an exploration of the borderland between anthropology, medicine, and psychiatry. Berkeley, California: University of California Press, 1980:105–6.

5. Snow L. Traditional health beliefs and practices among lower class black Americans. Western J Med 1983; 139: 820–8.

6. Wilson RP. An ethnomedical analysis of health beliefs about hypertension among low income black Americans [Dissertation]. Stanford, California: Stanford University, 1985.

7. Blumhagen D. The meaning of hypertension. In: Chrisman NJ, Maretzki TW, eds. Clinically applied anthropology. Boston: Reidel Publishing, 1982.

27

The Hot-Cold Theory of Disease: Implications for the Treatment of Puerto Rican Patients

Alan Harwood

The hot-cold theory of disease is probably the most wide-spread humoral concept in the world. As we saw in Foster's typology (selection 12), the hot-cold theory is an example of a naturalistic approach—diseases are either hot or cold, and their remedies involve selecting the medicines or foods that counteract the natural character of the disease. The healthy human body is at equilibrium between the different humors. The hot-cold theory was brought to the New World by way of the Spanish conquest (Foster 1994), and the theory was simplified to drop the moist-dry distinction found in classical Hippocratic (or Gallenic) humoral theory. Of course, the hot-cold classifications do not refer to actual temperature but rather to the essential character of the thing (almost like nouns that have gender in Romance languages). There is no completely standardized system of hot-cold classification—for diseases or especially for foods or medicines. In parts of Latin America, a remedy may be categorized as hot in one valley and cold in an adjacent valley (Logan 1977). On the other hand, the classifications do not seem to be particularly arbitrary. Fevers are always hot, as are the symptoms that often accompany febrile illnesses (rashes, diarrhea). The symptom complex that North Americans call the common cold (nasal congestion, mucus, muscle aches) is always thought to be cold.

This famous selection was written for practicing physicians and published in a well-known medical journal. Alan Harwood, who studied the medical systems of Puerto Ricans in New York City (1977), had previously focused on espiritas *and mental health, but he realized the practical importance of understanding the hot-cold theory of illness. In this selection, he offers practical advice on how physicians can "work within" the people's ethnomedical system.*

Notice that there is a fundamental logic to the hot-cold theory, which probably accounts for its global popularity. If practicing physicians ignore this underlying cultural logic, their credibility may be suspect.

A French physician I know was once practicing medicine in a village in Bangladesh (where there is also the hot-cold distinction). He says that at the end of every doctor–patient interaction patients would ask him what to eat during therapy. At first, the physician said that it really didn't matter, that they should eat healthy food. People were not satisfied with such a silly answer. After learning about the basic categorization of hot and cold illnesses and foods, he was able to answer patients' questions in culturally acceptable ways. Consequently, his patients were much happier. When he left the village after a year, people told him that when he first came, they didn't think he knew anything, but then he became a good doctor.

The first two rules of Hippocrates are "First, do no harm" and second, "Know thy patient." Knowing the patient includes being aware of the patient's cultural beliefs.

As you read this selection, consider these questions:·

- *Why do Puerto Rican mothers think it sounds dangerous to give an antibiotic to a child who has a rash and fever illness?*

- *What methods does Harwood suggest to get around the cultural problem of the hot-cold theory?*

- *Do ethnomedical beliefs always present a problem to the practice of medicine?*

- *The problem of compliance (adherence) to a complete course of antibiotics is commonplace (even college-educated people fail to take the entire prescription). Why is this a problem? Does it seem wrong to blame cultural factors in this case, if hardly anyone is compliant?*

- *To what extent is the degree of acculturation important in answering these questions?*

To communicate effectively with a patient about his illness or treatment regimen, a physician must know something about how the patient conceives of disease, its etiology, and therapeutics in general. When the patient comes from a different sociocultural milieu than the physician, the likelihood is great that the two will face each other with quite different views on these matters. For this reason, the physician is unlikely to be able to anticipate or understand questions and problems the patient has that may ultimately prevent him from carrying through a prescribed regimen. In order to treat patients of a different sociocultural background effectively, the physician must therefore develop a special understanding of their medical beliefs and practices.

Although anthropologists have discussed the hot-cold theory of disease etiology in many Latin American cultures,[1,2] the direct implications of this theory for understanding and treating patients who subscribe to it have rarely been examined. (A number of works[3–8] discuss in a general fashion the medical implications of the hot-cold theory for treatment of Mexican-Americans, but no such attention has been accorded other Latin-American groups in the United States.) This communication describes the hot-cold etiological system as it is found among many Puerto Ricans in New York City and discusses specific ways in which patients' commitment to this belief system affects their medical treatment.

BACKGROUND: UNDERSTANDING THE HOT-COLD ETIOLOGICAL SYSTEM

The hot-cold system stems from Hippocratic humoral theories of disease which were carried to the western hemisphere by the Spanish and Portuguese in the 16th and 17th centuries. Medical schools, established in Mexico and Peru in this period, taught the system, and its tenets were also embodied in household medical references which were used throughout Spanish America by priests and others who provided European medical care to the indigenous and mestizo populations. Through these channels of influence the humoral theory became an integral part of Latin-American folk medical practice, where it persists today.

According to the Hippocratic theory, the bodily humors (blood, phlegm, black bile, and yellow bile) vary in both temperature and moistness. Health is conceived in this system as a state of balance among the four humors which manifests itself in a somewhat wet, warm body. Illness, on the other hand, is believed to result from a humoral imbalance which causes the body to become excessively dry, cold, hot, wet, or a combination of these states. Food, herbs, and other medications, which are also classified as wet or dry, hot or cold, are used therapeutically to restore the body to its supposed natural balance. Thus, according to the system, a "cold" disease, such as arthritis, is cured by administering "hot" foods or medications.

When the Hippocratic theory was incorporated into Latin American folk practice, the wet-dry dichotomy became insignificant as a basis for diagnostic and therapeutic decisions, and the hot-cold (caliente-frío) dimension came to dominate the system. In the Puerto Rican cultural variant of the system, diseases are grouped into hot and cold classes, while medications and foods are trichotomized as hot, cold, or an intermediate category, "cool" (fresco).[9,10] Cold-classified illnesses are treated with hot medication and foods, while hot illnesses are treated with cool substances.

Table 1 lists the major illnesses, foods, medicines, and herbs associated with the hot-cold system among Puerto Ricans in New York. The various herbs mentioned in the table are available in herb shops (botánicas), located in most sectors of the city with heavy concentrations of Latin American residents, or may be acquired from relatives who send them from the islands. The medicines, like magnesium carbonate and mannitol, are available at neighborhood pharmacies.

While there is general agreement about the assignment of foods and medicines to the categories listed in the table, the system allows for variation as well. In general, a person may categorize a food or medicine differently from the norm if it idiosyncratically produces physical symptoms which are typically classified as hot or cold. For example, a person may note that pineapple causes him to have diarrhea or some other hot reaction (eg, hives) and therefore considers it caliente, even though it is not generally so considered. Pork is a food which is particularly subject to variant categorization.

Although the terminology of the hot-cold system suggests that it is based on temperature, the thermal state in which foods and herbal remedies are taken is not relevant to the classification. For example, linden-flower tea may be served straight off the fire and is still considered cool, while cold beer, because of its alcoholic content, is considered hot. Temperature does play a role, however, in ideas about the etiology of disease in the system. Cold illnesses are believed to be caused by a chill, which may occur when a person moves from heated to unheated surroundings. For example, colds are commonly attributed to drafts, and arthritic pain in

Table I   The Hot-Cold Classification Among Puerto Ricans

	FRÍO (Cold)	*Fresco (Cool)*	*Caliente (Hot)*
Illnesses or bodily conditions	Arthritis Colds *Frialdad del estómago** Menstrual period Pain in the joints *Pasmo**		Constipation Diarrhea Rashes Tenesmus (*pujo*) Ulcers
Medicines and herbs		Bicarbonate of soda Linden flowers (*flor de tilo*) Mannitol (*maná de manito*) Mastic bark (*almácigo*) MgCO$_3$ (*magnesia boba*) Milk of magnesia Nightshade (*yerba mora*) Orange-flower water (*agua de azahar*) Sage	Anise Aspirin Castor oil Cinnamon Cod liver oil Fe tablets Penicillin Rue (*ruda*) Vitamins
Foods	Avocado Bananas Coconut Lima beans Sugar cane White beans	Barley water Bottled milk Chicken Fruits Honey Raisins Salt-cod (*bacalao*) Watercress	Alcoholic beverages Chili peppers Chocolate Coffee Corn meal Evaporated milk Garlic Kidney beans Onions Peas Tobacco

*For an explanation of these terms, see text.

the hands is often said to come from plunging the hands into cold water after they have been immersed in hot. Similarly an upset stomach may be attributed to eating too many cold-classed foods which are believed to chill the stomach, a condition known as *frialdad del estómago* (or *frío en el estómago*).

The term *pasmo* is used to describe two different conditions, both related to the hot-cold theory. In one of its uses, *pasmo* refers to tonic spasm of any voluntary muscle. This condition is usually attributed to a chill arising from exposure to cold air when the body is in an overheated state. In its other use, *pasmo* refers to a cough, stomach pain, or other cold-classified symptom which has become chronic. Many people attribute such lingering symptoms to a chill or the eating of cold-classified foods. (In describing this situation, patients most often use the verb *pasmarse* rather than the noun *pasmo*. For example, the statement, *Cuando tenía ronquera, tomé jugo de china y me pasmé*, best translates as "When I was hoarse with a cold, I drank orange juice and became chronically hoarse.")

New foods or medicines are incorporated into the hot-cold system according to the effect they have on

the body. Thus penicillin, because it can cause hot-classified symptoms (a rash or diarrhea), is categorized with hot substances, while a drug which might cause muscular spasms would be considered cold. The very fact that new items are still being incorporated into the hot-cold classification attests to its vitality in Puerto Rican culture.

The existence of a vital medical tradition such as this raises several important issues for those who practice medicine with a Puerto Rican clientele. The first of these issues is how the system specifically influences patients' behavior when they consult a physician, and the second is how the professional practitioner can work with patients who evaluate illness and therapeutics within the hot-cold framework. The following sections consider these two issues.

The data which will be discussed were derived from three sources: (1) from observations in 64 Puerto Rican households, made over a period of one year as part of an ethnographic study of medical beliefs and practices within the target area of the Dr. Martin Luther King, Jr., Neighborhood Health Center in the south Bronx; (2) responses to a questionnaire concerning postpartum practices and infant care, which was administered to all Latin American women living in the Martin Luther King Health Center area who had given birth in November and December, 1967 (questionnaire was administered as a focused interview three months after the women had given birth [number interviewed—27]); and (3) anecdotal reports from medical personnel at the Martin Luther King, Jr. Neighborhood Health Center.

THE HOT-COLD SYSTEM AND PATIENTS' BEHAVIOR

General Medical Care

Treatment of Colds   Common colds are seen as quite serious by many Puerto Ricans, since they are viewed as the start of a possible chain of illnesses, brought on by repeated chills and failure to effect a cure. Thus, an untreated or chronic cold is believed to lead to chronic shortness of breath or wheezing (*fatiga*), which in turn may develop into bronchitis or even tuberculosis.

All conditions in this prodromal sequence are considered cold in nature and treatable by hot remedies. Patients with any of these illnesses may thus face a dilemma when the physician outlines a treatment regimen which includes cold or cool substances, since these violate the patient's conception of proper treatment.

A common example of this situation is when a physician recommends fruit juices for a cold. Since most fruits are *fresco*, this regimen is unacceptable. The culturally preferred remedy for this condition is ginger tea, which is hot and usually taken instead of the recommended juice. As the patient nears recovery from a cold, a cathartic hot substance, usually anise or castor oil, is also routinely administered to clean the system of accumulated phlegm.

In the above example patients solve their dilemma concerning an unacceptable treatment regimen in a manner which does not impair therapy. This is not always true, however, and complications can arise. The regimen prescribed with diuretics provides a good example.

Use of Diuretics

When prescribing a diuretic, routine medical practice is to encourage the patient to eat bananas, oranges, raisins, or other dried fruit in order to maintain the potassium balance in the system. With patients who adhere to the hot-cold theory, however, this advice may have untoward consequences, since all these foods are considered either cold or cool. As a result, when the patient contracts a common cold or other cold-classified illness, he will stop eating these potassium sources because they are contraindicated for his immediate condition. Women particularly run into difficulty with this type of regimen, since many of them are careful to avoid both cold foods and acidic cool fruits during their menses. This practice therefore eliminates all potassium sources usually suggested to them. A way out of this dilemma might be for the physician to prescribe potassium in solution as a "vitamin" (and therefore hot) to be taken during menstruation or whenever the patient has a cold or to suggest hot foods rich in potassium (like coffee, cocoa, peas, etc), in addition to the usual cold foods, so that patients have enough options to make choices within the hot-cold system themselves.

Prophylactic Use of Penicillin

Another difficulty which arises in treating people who follow hot-cold medical practices results from the prophylactic use of penicillin for former rheumatic fever patients. Since rheumatic fever involves joint pains, it is considered a cold illness, and hot penicillin is therefore readily accepted as treatment. However, should a patient experience temporary diarrhea or constipation while participating in a maintenance program, he will usually stop taking his medication because in all likelihood he will attribute his symptoms to the hot penicillin. A way of dealing with this eventuality would be to encourage patients to take their penicillin with fruit juice or some other cool substance, since ingestion of something cool in conjunction with something hot is believed to neutralize any adverse effects of the hot substance. This important principle of "neutralization" is one which we shall return to a number of times in the ensuing discussion, since it is an effective method of working with patients within the hot-cold system, when this approach seems indicated. (The term neutralization is one which I have chosen to describe the activity involved and is not one which Spanish-speakers would use. They refer to the activity as "*refrescando el estómago*" "refreshing" or "cooling" the stomach.)

The Reinforcing Value of Hot-Cold Beliefs

The hot-cold classification should not be viewed as producing only problems for the medical professional.

In many instances it comports with and may therefore be used to reinforce standard treatment regimens. We have already noted that the use of penicillin for treatment of rheumatic fever fits the logic of the system. In addition, bland diets recommended for ulcer patients prohibit most of the foods which are considered hot and would therefore be avoided as a matter of course within the folk system. Similarly, the use of aspirin for relief of colds or arthritic pain accords with both therapeutic systems. Indeed, although the hot-cold and modern therapeutic systems differ in their basic premises, the behavior they imply is probably more similar than antipathetic. One may even conjecture that the viability of the hot-cold system is founded to some extent on this fundamental agreement in the health behavior implied by the two systems.

Pediatric Care

Infant Feeding   Perhaps the most important implication of the hot-cold classification for pediatric care concerns the feeding of infants. As noted in Table 1, evaporated milk, the formula base usually recommended to mothers on leaving the hospital, is considered hot, and whole milk is considered cool. Since infants tend to develop rashes, and rashes are believed to come from hot foods, mothers prefer to feed their infants cool foods instead of the hot evaporated milk formula.

In the sample of 27 Puerto Rican mothers described more fully above, 41% almost immediately on return home from the hospital curtailed their babies' intake of hot formula. Two strategies were used for doing this. Five mothers (19%) simply discontinued the evaporated milk formula after a few weeks and fed their babies only whole milk. Since it is believed dangerous to switch an infant too rapidly from hot to cool foods, mothers commonly feed their babies weak tea and mannitol (both cool substances) for 24 hours before starting the whole milk. (The fact that whole milk, besides being cool, is also considered more prestigious and easier to prepare by some mothers undoubtedly also contributes to its adoption.)

Rather than switching milks, six mothers who were interviewed in the same study (22%) used the neutralization principle in resolving the contradiction between their beliefs about infant feeding and the medically recommended procedure. These mothers either added a cool substance to the evaporated milk formula or fed something cool to the baby as a supplement. The cool substances used were barley water, magnesium carbonate, and mannitol. The latter two are a cathartic and diuretic, respectively, and were administered to the babies in sufficient quantity to cause diarrhea. This finding suggests a source of diarrhea in the Puerto Rican infant population which should be investigated in a more rigorous fashion. In the meantime, however, the pediatrician working with a mother who believes in the importance of the hot-cold classification might well reinforce the use of barley water as a neutralizer in preference to the two, possibly harmful substances.

Oral Medication for Children

The concept of neutralization is commonly employed by mothers when administering vitamins or other hot medications, such as aspirin or cod liver oil, to children. The cool substances most often used for this purpose are fruit juice, milk of magnesia, or mannitol. It is therefore advisable for the physician to find out which of these substances the mother is using, in order to avoid any which might have a detrimental effect on the child.

Childhood Diseases

As might be expected, measles, chickenpox, and other childhood diseases involving rashes are classified as hot in this nosology. Cool medications are therefore used in the home for these illnesses. For measles or chickenpox, raisins soaked in warm milk or water are commonly fed to children "to bring out the rash," ie, to "cool" the internal organs sufficiently so that the "heat" comes to the surface in the form of the rash. Cool herb teas are also used for this purpose.

Obstetric and Gynecologic Care—Antepartum Care

During pregnancy a woman is careful to avoid hot foods or medication to prevent her baby from being born with an "irritation" (a rash or red skin). To further guarantee this, many women "refresh" themselves repeatedly with either milk of magnesia (1 to 3 tablespoons a day) or commercial anti-acids (one to four doses a day), especially during the first and second trimesters. Since many abortifacients are considered hot, a woman who has used them unsuccessfully will be particularly diligent to prevent further irritation to the foetus by taking cool preparations.

An important consequence of the avoidance of hot substances during pregnancy is that many women will not take hot iron supplements or vitamins. These patients might be encouraged to take these prescriptions with fruit juice or an herb tea to "neutralize" them.

Postpartum Practices

After delivery women traditionally underwent a period of seclusion for 40 days (the *cuarentena*), during which time several practices associated with the hot-cold system were observed. Many of these are still followed, even though the full *cuarentena* rarely is. Many women avoid eating cool foods after delivery on the ground that they impede the flow of blood and therefore prevent complete emptying of the uterus and birth canal. Should the lochia flow toward the head, it is believed to cause nervousness or even insanity (*pulga del parto,* literally the "purge of parturition"). To help prevent this, certain tonics are drunk which contain mostly hot foods. One, for example, is made of chocolate, garlic, cinnamon, rue (*ruda,* an herb), mint, and pieces of cheese.

Similar beliefs attach to the menses. Cool foods are avoided at these times, since it is considered particularly important for the discharge from the womb to be complete. There is also an association, maintained mostly by older women, between strength and hot foods. Thus, a "weak" womb (*matriz débil*) is believed to "jump" about in the body cavity in search of something hot to fortify it. Rue, mixed with black coffee, rum, or cocoa, is taken as a remedy for this condition.

Table 2 summarizes the major points of the above discussion by indicating patients' reactions to particular symptoms and therapeutic regimens.

COMMUNICATION WITH PATIENTS INVOLVING HOT-COOL BELIEFS

In contemporary medical practice, communication with Spanish-speaking patients most frequently occurs in one of three contexts: (1) the physician speaking (usually in English) directly to his patient or, in a family practice, to various members of the family as well, (2) the physician speaking through a translator or health worker from the Hispanic community who filters the communication through his own set of medical standards or accommodations between the professional and folk therapeutic systems, and (3) health professionals informing the Spanish-speaking public through mass media or printed brochures. Each of these contexts obviously offers different opportunities for sharing information and for mutual accommodation between communicators. In the following discussion we shall be concerned only with the first two contexts, in which the physician or Hispanic health worker and patient have considerable latitude in accommodating to one another's definition of an illness or therapeutic course.

TABLE 2   Expectable Behavior of Patients Who Adhere to the Hot-Cold Theory*

Patient's Condition	*Expectable Behavior*
Common cold, arthritis, joint pains	Patient will not take cold-classified foods or medications, but will accept those classed as hot
Diarrhea, rash, ulcers	Patient will not take hot-classified medications and uses cool substances as therapy
Requires a diuretic as part of a treatment regimen and has been told to supplement his potassium intake by eating bananas, oranges, raisins, or dried fruit	Patient will not eat these cold-classified foods while he has a cold or other cold-classified condition (For female patients this includes the menses)
Requires penicillin or any other hot medication, particularly on an ongoing basis	Patient will stop taking hot medicine when he suffers any hot-classified symptom (eg, diarrhea, constipation, rash)
Infant requires formula, which contains hot-classified evaporated milk	Mother will put baby on cold-classified whole milk or will, after feeding formula, "refresh" the baby's stomach with various cool substances, some of which are diuretic
Pregnant	Avoids hot medicine and hot foods and takes cool medicine frequently
Postpartum and during menstruation	Avoids cool foods and medicines, particularly those which are acidic

*See text for discussion of ways of treating such patients appropriately.

For optimum therapeutic success, there are clearly two important pieces of information which must be interchanged between patient and physician in order to deal with any divergent views which may exist between them concerning the illness or treatment regimen: (1) the physician must determine if the patient's views undermine the treatment regimen, and (2) if so, a modus operandi must be reached whereby patient and physician agree on an appropriate treatment regimen.

Determining a Patient's Commitment to the Hot-Cold Theory

In identifying patients who are likely to adhere to the hot-cold system and the behavior it implies, degree of acculturation is, of course, a significant indicator. For, between different generations and among people of different educational backgrounds, the culture pattern takes different forms or may even be abandoned altogether. The elderly and recent adult migrants who never completed high school are most likely to espouse the hot-cold system openly and consciously to weigh therapeutic decisions within its framework. Among 64 Puerto Rican families in the ethnographic study, 23 (36%) had adults who fell into this category. People who have been born in the States, on the other hand, or who have received most of their primary and secondary education here are not likely to express agreement with the hot-cold system openly. They may, however, defend those parts of it which agree with standard medical practice (eg, the association between ulcers and hot foods) and almost certainly follow at least some of the practices entailed by the system at home. Even among the second generation American-born, the culture pattern may still survive in attenuated form. Remedies which stem from the hot-cold theory are remembered from childhood and may occasionally be used, even though an awareness of the underlying hot-cold system is completely lost.

In short, the process of acculturation through the generations creates subtle variations in the way hot-cold beliefs manifest themselves in the behavior of Puerto Rican patients. If the physician suspects that hot-cold theories have a bearing on the treatment regimen he is prescribing, it is therefore in the interests of good therapy to probe his patients' commitment to these beliefs. This is best done by indicating to the patient an awareness of the belief system but without implying judgment of it. An appropriate probe might be, "Some of my patients say that a particular medication or food pertinent to the proposed regimen is *caliente* or *fresco*. Do you think so?" Similar questions might also be posed to the person who prepares meals in the patient's family or who takes charge of his treatment.

In medical delivery systems where Spanish-speaking staff translate for physicians or work closely with families, their training should include an awareness of those illnesses in which the hot-cold classification might pose therapeutic problems so that they can discuss them at length with families.

Arriving at an Appropriate Regimen

Once the medical practitioner has determined that the hot-cold classification is relevant to his patient's treatment, the age and degree of acculturation of the patient should influence how he handles the situation. At this point, too, the physician's own attitude and temperament will play an important role in communication. Some physicians may by temperament wish to use their authority to establish a modus operandi with the patient over the regimen; some may take the view that if the patient is "educated" to understand the logic of the regimen, he will abandon old habits and follow it; others may opt to work within the hot-cold system to achieve the desired therapeutic goal.

From the standpoint of behavioral science, the most effective of these approaches—particularly with elderly or less acculturated patients—would be to work within the system, using notions like neutralization or other features of the classification discussed above to achieve the therapeutic goal. The probability of changing an individual patient's conception of disease etiology in a few encounters is small indeed—particularly with the hot-cold theory, which not only orders a great deal of health behavior but is also supported by prestige, developed through generations of use, as well as, in many instances, by empirical validation. Respect for the patient's tradition and an ability to work with the therapeutic choices inherent in it allows for development of a treatment regimen with the patient which does not contravene his deeply held ideas about illness and will therefore stand a much better chance of success.

REFERENCES

1. Foster GM: Relationships between Spanish and Spanish-American folk medicine. *J Amer Folklore* **66**:201–17, 1953.
2. Adams RN, Rubel AJ: Sickness and social relations: In Wauchope R (ed): *Handbook of Middle American Indians*. Austin, University of Texas Press, 1967.

3. Saunders L: *Cultural Differences and Medical Care*. New York, Russell Sage Foundation, 1954.
4. Saunders L, Samora J: A medical care program in a Colorado county, in Paul BD (ed): *Health, Culture and Community*. New York, Russell Sage Foundation, 1955.
5. Clark M: *Health in Mexican-American Culture*. Berkeley, University of California Press, 1959.
6. Samora J: Conceptions of health and disease among Spanish Americans. *Amer Catholic Sociol Rev* **22:**314–23, 1961.
7. Martinez C, Martin HW: Folk diseases among Mexican-Americans: etiology, symptoms, treatment. *JAMA* **196:** 161–4, 1966.
8. Weaver T: Use of hypothetical situations in a study of Spanish American illness referral systems. *Human Organization 29* **2:**140–154, 1970.
9. Steward JH (ed): *People of Puerto Rico: a Study in Social Anthropology*. Urbana, University of Illinois Press, 1956.
10. Padilla E: *Up from Puerto Rico*. New York, Columbia University Press, 1958.

Ethnicity and Health Care

✤ CONCEPTUAL TOOLS ✤

- *Race is not a useful biological category, but it is an important social category.* Most people believe the word *race* is a scientific term with a specific biological meaning. This is not the case when it comes to humans. Human biologists, including biological anthropologists, do not have a clear idea of how to define a race or what the significance of that category is if they have defined it. It is not possible to define a race in terms of either physical appearance (*phenotype*) or genetic makeup (*genotype*). This is partially because there is no way to determine the number of characteristics used to define the categories; the more characteristics used, the more categories there are. Moreover, genetic traits are independently assorted at conception. And, after all, all humans are biologically unique on an individual level while at the same time all are members of the single species, *Homo sapiens*.

  The term *race* is a historic artifact from an archaic biology. The idea that there are a few "races"—white, black, red, yellow—or their scientific-sounding equivalents—Caucasoid, Negroid, Mongoloid—simply doesn't make sense or serve a useful purpose in biological explanations (Goodman and Armelagos 1996). From an evolutionary perspective, it would make scientific sense to consider the concept of *populations* that might form breeding isolates, but for actual living humans such breeding isolates do not seem to exist. On the other hand, race as a social category is of incredible importance because it has been used as a biological rationalization for patterns of exploitation (slavery) or socioeconomic injustice (racism). Race is a social construction that has real biological consequences, for example, higher disease rates and lower life expectancies for members of minority groups.

- *The North American rule of racial hypodescent is one indication of the social construction of race.* In the United States, a child who has one African American parent and one white parent is automatically socially classified as an African American. This does not make biological sense, because the child inherits one-half of her genes from each parent. This traditional social rule is called *racial hypodescent*, meaning that the offspring is put into the lower-ranking category. The same rule functions for children of mixed-caste marriages in India. There are historical reasons for racial hypodescent in the United States because slave children became material property of the slave owner, even if he was the biological father. Other social rules of racial classification operate in different societies, like Brazil, with their own economic histories (Harris 1980).

- *Ethnicity is a useful and important social construct.* Often, when people in the United States use the term *race*, they are actually referring to social categories of identity and subcultural differences that should be called *ethnicity*. Ethnic categories are based on cultural distinctions of history, heredity, religion, language, and so forth. People identify with their own ethnic group, and they are identified by others as members of that group. At the same time, however, the boundaries between ethnic groups are permeable, bendable, and socially constructed, as shown in the important anthropological research of Fredrik Barth (1969). As is so evident in today's world, ethnic groups are often the focus of ethnocentrism, bigotry, and political violence.

- *Ethnicity interacts with social class.* People may use the term *race* when they are actually referring to differences in social class, that is, differences in access to material resources like money, property, or education. People in the United States may think that they live in a classless society, largely because just about everybody thinks they are members of the struggling middle class. In actuality, the United States is a highly stratified society in terms of wealth, meaning that we have a much more significant problem of poverty than most other industrialized nations. Members of ethnic minorities are more likely to be poorer and less powerful. Racist beliefs on the part of the dominant white ethnic groups exacerbate the problems of socioeconomic inequity.

■ *In a multicultural society, ethnocentrism is a constant problem.* The degree to which people identify with their ethnic group depends on various factors, including the degree of hostility of the dominant group, the length of time since immigration, the agglomeration of minorities in ethnic enclaves, and so forth. When individuals begin to identify more with the dominant culture—often as a result of education and upward social mobility—they become *acculturated* (an old anthropological term meaning that they have lost their traditional culture). Although the United States retains the myth of the melting pot, we are not a culturally homogenized society.

Ethnocentrism, the tendency to judge others using your own cultural criteria, is characteristic of all the world's societies, but it is an everyday problem in a multicultural, multiethnic society. Ethnocentrism can only be overcome through tolerance and vigilance.

■ *Knowledge about cultural variation in the folk models of illness is valuable and useful, but this is different from simple stereotyping.* Individuals hold explanatory models of their illnesses; when people in a group share some characteristics of an explanatory model it is called a *folk model of illness*. But not every member of an ethnic group will have identical beliefs about health and illness (Harwood 1981). The health care provider must learn to elicit this information from patients and to be sensitive to the possibility that cultural factors may interfere with effective communication.

Medical anthropologists do not advocate an ethnic "cookbook" approach to medical care and public health. What *is* most important is that health providers understand the range of health beliefs in a population and that they treat the people who hold these beliefs with respect and not ethnocentric derision (Clark 1983).

28

The State of Federal Health Statistics on Racial and Ethnic Groups

Robert A. Hahn

This selection is written by an anthropologist–epidemiologist working at the Centers for Disease Control (we encountered his work on nocebos in selection 15). The selection deals with a subject that may appear to be technical and trivial at first blush: how federal statistics in health studies are collected on the variables of ethnicity and racial groups. A closer examination of the problem, however, shows that the collection of this data is both messy and important. It is messy because the statistics are not collected in a coherent way. Studies show problems with both the validity *(Are they really measuring what they think they are measuring?) and the* reliability *(Can these results be repeated?) of these measures. Nevertheless, the measurement of these variables is important because they are used in identifying public (that is, political) priorities in health policies. They are also helpful in determining if we, as a society, are improving our health standards.*

When researching the field, anthropologists often ask obvious questions about things the local people take for granted. This is the case with questioning the meaning of measures of ethnicity and race in federal statistics. Robert Hahn's work on this topic—along with much political pressure for new ethnicity classifications on federal forms (such as, "multi-racial")—resulted in public congressional hearings throughout the country regarding the Office of Management and Budget's directive 15 defining ethnic and racial groups (Wright 1994) for the design of the federal census in 1997.

"Race" and "ethnicity" are not simple, commonsensical categories. They are complex, historically contextualized, social constructions. They reflect certain social realities that have biological consequences, as seen in disease prevalence and mortality rates.

As you read this selection, consider these questions:

- *Is the cultural rule of racial hypodescent (children automatically assigned to the lower social status of their parents) changing in the contemporary United States?*
- *How is it that children can be categorized in one race when they are born and another race when they die? What is the significance of these errors?*
- *Why do we collect data on race and ethnicity? Does this information serve a useful purpose?*
- *Why is "ethnicity" a preferable category to "race"?*
- *Why is it that almost all epidemiological and medical studies include the variable of race?*

Federal health statistics indicate that infant mortality in the United States in 1987 was 2.1 times higher among blacks and 1.2 times higher among American Indians than among whites,[1] that cumulative rates of the acquired immunodeficiency syndrome through May 1988 were 2.9 times higher among non-Hispanic blacks and 2.6 times higher among Hispanics than among non-Hispanic whites,[2] and that the proportion of persons not covered by any health insurance in 1986 was 1.6 times greater among blacks than among whites.[3]

The validity of such health statistics rests on logical assumptions that include the following:

1. The categories of "race" and "ethnicity" and specific racial and ethnic group designations are consistently defined and ascertained.

2. The categories and designations are understood by the populations questioned.

3. Survey enumeration, participation, and response rates are high and similar for all populations.

4. The responses of individuals are consistent in different data sources and at different times.

This report builds on previous research and examines these assumptions, focusing on birth, death, and population statistics in the United States.

Health statistics on racial and ethnic groups in the United States are calculated from data on the population provided by the Bureau of the Census (BC) and data on health events provided by the Centers for Disease Control's National Center for Health Statistics

(NCHS). The BC and NCHS have conducted many studies to assess and enhance the quality of their data. This report uses results of BC, NCHS, and other important studies conducted since the 1950s, recognizing that the system of data collection has evolved substantially over this period.

In the collection of information on race and ethnic groups, consistency of definition and procedure is not simply a matter of convenience for analysts. Sources of information on natality, mortality, and the population are highly interdependent. Birth and death rates are calculated on the basis of the census,[1,4] completeness of birth registration is assessed by census information,[5] intercensal estimates and estimates of completeness of coverage in the decennial census require information on births and deaths,[6] and infant mortality is computed as a ratio of infant deaths to infant births.[1]

Long-standing conceptual difficulties in the definition of "race" and "ethnicity" pose a challenge to the surveillance of health in US "racial" and "ethnic" groups. The validity of the concept of "race," for example, has been questioned,[7–9] and biological notions of "race" may be confused with cultural and behavioral notions of "ethnicity." Lack of scientific consensus has hindered the establishment of firm principles for surveillance of the health of racial and ethnic groups. Surveillance is also made difficult by multiple and changing perceptions of social identity in different segments of the population and by interests not consistent with scientific goals. While data-collection agencies have made notable improvements, this review suggests a need both to reconsider the scientific validity of the categories, "race" and "ethnicity," and to assess perceptions of social identity in the US population.

FOUR ASSUMPTIONS EXAMINED

Assumption 1: The Categories of "Race" and "Ethnicity" Are Consistently Defined and Ascertained by Federal Data-Collection Agencies

Background. Current regulations for the statistical classification of racial and ethnic groups by federal agencies were published in 1978 in Office of Management and Budget (OMB) directive 15, "Race and Ethnic Standards for Federal Statistics and Administrative Reporting."[10] Directive 15 was intended to set uniform standards for data collection and publication among federal agencies and to increase available information on persons of Hispanic origin, as required by Congress.[11,12] Directive 15 does not define the concepts of "race" or "ethnicity" and explicitly denies being "scientific or anthropological in nature." It presents brief rules for the classification of persons into four racial categories (American Indian or Alaskan Native, Asian or Pacific Islander, black, and white) and two ethnic categories (Hispanic origin and not of Hispanic origin); it requires categorization of whites and blacks as Hispanic or non-Hispanic.

Directive 15 employs four features to define categories of race and ethnicity: (1) descent from "the original peoples" of a specified region or nation, (2) a specific cultural origin, (3) cultural identification or affiliation, and (4) race itself. Defining characteristics are not further explained. Descent is used to define all six categories (of race and ethnicity together). Specific cultural origin is used to define Hispanics; however, American Indians and Alaskan Natives are similarly defined by "cultural identification through tribal affiliation or community recognition." "Black race" is tautologically defined by black race and African origin. The race and ethnicity categories of directive 15 are not mutually exclusive; for example, "Hispanic" is not exclusive of either "American Indian or Alaskan Native" or of "Asian or Pacific Islander." Supporting documents indicate that the categories of directive 15 were not intended to be exhaustive.[11]

Directive 15 does not clearly indicate whether race and ethnicity are to be ascertained on the basis of the respondent's or the interviewer/observer's perception. While the directive suggests that the respondent's self-perception or perhaps "recognition in his community" determines racial and ethnic identity, supporting documents imply that self-identification is not intended by the directive and is not the optimal method of ascertainment.[11] The difference between respondent and interviewer/observer ascertainment may be substantial, both conceptually and statistically. An NCHS study that compared respondent-reported race with interviewer-observed race in a nationally representative sample found that 5.8% of persons who reported themselves as "black" were classified as "white" by the interviewer and that 32.3% of self-reported Asians and 70% of self-reported American Indians were classified as "white" or "black."[13]

Definitions of "Race" and "Ethnicity" in NCHS and BC Statistics. As in directive 15, NCHS and BC documents do not define the concepts of "race" and "ethnicity" or consider the scientific principles on which classification schemes are based. ("The concept of race as used by the Census Bureau reflects self-identification; it does not denote any clear-cut scientific definition of biological stock."[14]) In addition, the terminology and categorization of racial and ethnic groups differ from source to source. For example, the category prescribed by directive 15, "American Indians," is labeled "Indian (Amer)" in the 1980 census and lists separately Eskimos and Aleuts; in natality documents, the category "American Indian" includes Aleuts and Eskimos; and in mortality documents, the category "Indian" includes American, Canadian, Eskimo, and Aleut.[1,4,14] Categorization of "American Indians" (and of other groups) is thus not strictly commensurate among sources and does not fully comply with directive 15.

Birth and Death Statistics. Procedures used to assign race and ethnicity also differ among sources of information. Until 1989, the race of a newborn was determined by a complex algorithm incorporating information on the race of the parents.[4] Races were treated unequally; for example, only infants with two white parents were white, while an infant with one white parent took the race of the parent whose race was other than white.[4] Beginning in 1989, while information on the race of the parents will still be available in computer files, published NCHS statistics uniformly assign the infant the race and ethnicity of its mother, diminishing the number of infants assigned to races other than white while increasing the number of infants assigned to the white race.[15] Statistics on Hispanic origins, published since 1984, have always assigned newborns the origin of their mothers.

On death certificates, parental race and ethnicity are not cited as definitional criteria, other than for fetal deaths. Race and ethnicity are determined by information about the decedent's identity given to funeral directors by next of kin[1]; however, with unknown frequency, funeral directors make independent assessments.

The Census. In the decennial census, respondents are asked to indicate their own racial and ethnic identity and that of household members.[14] Postcensal and intercensal population estimates incorporate information from several sources: previous and subsequent decennial censuses, subsequent registered births and deaths, and migration (ascertained from the Immigration and Naturalization Service by an algorithm including demographic information on the immigrants' nations of origin). Intercensal estimation procedures

tacitly (and erroneously) assume that race and ethnicity are commensurate in all sources.[6] Evidence presented below indicates that individuals may be assigned a different race at birth, during the course of life, and at death.

Assumption 2: Racial and Ethnic Categories Are Understood by the Populations Questioned

While popular understandings of race and ethnicity have not been comprehensively explored, there are indications that popular notions differ substantially from those of information-collection agencies. Interviewers in an NCHS survey, for example, report that "the phrase 'origin or descent' was poorly understood by many respondents,"[16] and the BC remarks that notions of "race," "ethnicity," and "ancestry" are not clearly distinguished from one another by census respondents.[17] The BC assumes it has asked meaningful questions when response rates are high[17]; however, survey respondents may answer questions they find unclear.[18] The BC also assumes its results are valid when overall counts are similar in reinterview surveys,[19] but overall counts may be similar even when large proportions of respondents have changed their responses.

Terminology for race and ethnic groups also differs among segments of the population. The category "white" is understood by some Hispanics to be synonymous with "Anglos," ie, non-Hispanics. Perhaps for this reason, in the 1980 census, almost 40% of persons who classified themselves as Hispanic answered "other" to the question intended to elicit racial identity.[20] (The 1980 census question intended to elicit "race" did not use the word *race*, causing confusion for both respondents and analysts.) While 1980 census documents report these persons as "other," intercensal estimates have reassigned them a race in proportion to Hispanics who specified "black" or "white" race, to comply with requirements of OMB directive 15.[20] However, the BC also estimates that, among persons (in 27 states) who specified a race, 32.7% of whites and 92.9% of blacks who reported being Mexican-American did so erroneously; thus, approximately 33.4% of the estimated Mexican-American population in the states examined was misclassified.[21] Thus, persons who apparently did not find an appropriate option on the "race" question have been assigned a race on the basis of persons who answered the question, but commonly in error.

Other questionnaire terms are also misinterpreted. The category "South and Central American" (in the

1970 census) was thought by some respondents to refer to natives of southern and central regions of the United States, and "Alaska Native" was thought to refer to persons born in Alaska.[17] Finally, categories such as "Other" and "Mexican-(Amer)" that appeared in the 1980 census are also reported to be misunderstood, particularly by recent immigrants and minority respondents.[17]

Assumption 3: Survey Enumeration, Participation, and Response Rates Are High and Similar for All Racial and Ethnic Populations

Underregistration of Births. Underregistration of births overall appears to be negligible but varies by race. The most recent survey estimated that birth underregistration between 1964 and 1968 was 0.6% for whites and 2.0% for "Negro and other races."[5] However, the inclusion of blacks and other groups in a single category may mask diversity. The earlier survey of births in 1950 found an underregistration of 1.4% for whites, 6.3% for blacks, and 14.9% for American Indians, indicating a marked improvement from 1950 to 1964–1968 but also indicating a marked racial disparity.[22]

Misclassification of Race at Death. In the registration of deaths, the problem is less one of underregistration than of misclassification—incorrectly assigning race to decedents. The net result is similar to underregistration and undercounting—deaths are undercounted in one race and overcounted in another. Study of a sample of 1986 US death certificates indicated that, while white race was misclassified on only 0.5% and black race on only 1.0% of certificates, Asians were misclassified on 21.1% of certificates and American Indians on 23.7%.[23] Most misclassified decedents were falsely reported to be white, exaggerating white mortality and minimizing mortality among races other than white. Misclassification appears not to have decreased in the last 25 years; similar results have been found in studies of US deaths in 1960[24] and infant deaths in Washington State between 1968 and 1977.[25]

Census Enumeration Miscounts. Differential miscounting by race and ethnicity has also occurred in the census. It is estimated that the 1980 census undercounted blacks by 5.9% and whites and others by 0.7%; Hispanics were undercounted by as much as 7.8%.[6] The 1980 census has been shown to have "over-

counted" American Indians by approximately 358,000, 33.7% above the population estimated from previous censuses and intervening births and deaths; the overcount is probably a result of increasing "Indian" self-identification.[26]

Nonresponse. A small proportion of nonresponses to racial identity questions on birth and death certificates is imputed by an algorithm that assigns the decedent the race of the preceding computer record, while nonresponse on Hispanic origins on infant death certificates is reported to be as high as 8%.[1] In 1988, the most recent year of published mortality statistics, only 18 states (with an estimated 80% of the Hispanic population) met NCHS standards for the reporting of infant mortality by Hispanic origin.[1,4]

Nonresponse to the "race" question on the 1980 census was only 1.5%; however, as noted, 40% of persons identifying themselves as Hispanic (almost 6 million persons) chose the "other" category on this question. The Hispanic-origin question on the 1980 census was unanswered by 2.3% of respondents, the ancestry question by 12%.[17,27]

The effects of miscounts and misclassification may be substantial.[6] For example, computer-linked statistics on US infants dying in 1983 and 1984 indicate that infant mortality was 1.57 times higher among American Indians than among whites (using the uniform rule assigning a newborn and decedent infant the race of its mother).[28] This is almost 50% higher than the 1.06 ratio based on published information in which infants may be assigned a different race at birth and at death.[29,30]

Assumption 4: Individual Responses to Questions of Racial and Ethnic Identity Are Consistent in Different Surveys and Different Times

Given that persons of different racial and ethnic groups are covered by surveys and have responded to questions about "race" and "ethnicity," available evidence indicates substantial inconsistency in responses. The BC researchers Siegel and Passel[31] suggest that inconsistency may be explained by two phenomena: "fuzzy group boundaries," ambiguity about the criteria of group membership, and "shifting identity," changes of individuals' group identity over time.

Siegel and Passel's study of coverage in the 1970 census compared five indicators of self-reported Hispanic identity: Hispanic origins, use of the Spanish language, Hispanic heritage, surname, and birthplace or parentage.[31] With different indicators, estimates of the Hispanic population ranged from 5.2 million (persons of Hispanic heritage) to 1.8 times as many, 9.6 million (persons using the Spanish language). The BC researchers conclude, "A central problem is the inability of the census data to reflect a clear, unambiguous, and objective definition of exactly who is a member of the Hispanic population."

The category "American Indian" is also characterized by boundary fuzziness and shifting identification, as indicated above by apparent population "overcounts." In a 1980 reinterview study, 41% of persons who identified themselves as American Indian had reported themselves as white in the 1980 census.[19] Also in the 1980 census, while an estimated 6.8 million persons reported American Indian ancestry, only 1.2 million reported American Indian race. Ancestry was not simply a broader category; only 73% of those reporting American Indian race claimed American Indian ancestry, the remainder claiming European, other, or unknown ancestries.[32] In questioning about perceived identity, the circumstances and terminology used appear to have important effects on responses.

Shifting perception of identity has also been found in other race and ethnic groups. In answer to the 1980 census "race" question, 26.5 million people identified themselves as "black or Negro," while only an estimated 21 million claimed Afro-American ancestry.[33] In March 1971 and again in March 1972, the BC's Current Population Survey interviewed a large sample of persons in US households, eliciting the ethnic identity of all household members; from one year to the next, 34.3% of household members were reported to have different ethnic identities.[34]

COMMENT

Because of their frequent association with health status, "race" and "ethnicity," along with age and sex, are categories by which populations are commonly divided in health research and planning. Such categorization assumes that "race" and "ethnicity" are valid concepts that can be correctly identified and classified. The validity of the concept of "race" has been questioned in recent decades.[7-9] Even if conceptually valid, it may be that race cannot be readily assessed by survey procedures.

Particularly for nonwhite populations and for Hispanics, the quality of statistical information on the health of racial and ethnic populations in the United States is problematic. Better-quality information would

enable more effective health research and program planning. While the system of health statistics on racial and ethnic groups has not been comprehensively evaluated, available evidence suggests that certain underlying assumptions do not always hold. Conceptual definitions are lacking and the potential scientific bases for definition are largely ignored; procedures for data ascertainment vary from source to source; undercounting and misclassification can differ by orders of magnitude between whites and races other than white or black; and the responses of individuals may be inconsistent for different indicators, in different surveys, and at different times. In information systems that rely on separate sources, inconsistent definitions and procedures for assigning race and ethnicity may produce computed results of questionable validity. Counts, rates, and rate ratios may be inaccurate.

Further improvement of the system of health statistics may require several steps:

1. Clear goals (and possibly diverse ones) for the definition of categories of "race" and "ethnicity" need to be established for planning, public health surveillance, administration, and research.

2. Extensive efforts should be made to scientifically validate the categories "race" and "ethnicity" and to establish basic scientific and anthropological principles for the public health surveillance of racial and ethnic populations. In the validation of "race," genetic, physical anthropological, archaeological, linguistic, and migration evidence should be weighed. In the validation of "ethnicity," concepts of social identity and changes in social identity in various populations should be assessed and compared. If valid, categories must be clearly defined, standardized, and operationalized so that researchers and respondents know what the categories mean and so that information is compatible from source to source. The design, development, and management of programs and administrative activities should also be based on scientific principles.

3. To ensure that respondents to public health surveillance understand survey instruments, the way in which different segments of the population identify themselves by "race," "ethnicity," or other characteristics should be comprehensively assessed and incorporated into surveillance design.

4. To ensure the quality of health statistics of racial and ethnic populations, the surveillance system should be periodically and systematically evaluated.[35]

The assessment of demographic identity in a society of culturally diverse and rapidly changing populations with different needs and interests is extremely difficult. In meeting this challenge, federal agencies have made notable improvements, for example, the new NCHS rule assigning infants the race of their mother in published statistics and the NCHS linked birth/infant-death computer tape. A Public Health Service Task Force on Minority Health Data has recently been constituted to further address data problems and needs. With additional collaborative work by federal, state, and local organizations in the collection, analysis, and reporting of population and health statistics, substantial progress toward resolution of the problems outlined in this report is possible.

REFERENCES

1. *Vital Statistics of the United States 1987: Mortality*. Washington, DC: US Dept of Health and Human Services; 1990:IIA. Publication PHS 90–1101.

2. Selik RM, Castro KG, Pappaiouanou M. Racial/ethnic differences in the risk of AIDS in the United States. *Am J Public Health*. 1988;78:1539–1545.

3. *Health, United States, 1989*. Hyattsville, Md: National Center for Health Statistics; 1990.

4. *Vital Statistics of the United States 1987: Nationality*. Washington, DC: US Dept of Health and Human Services; 1989:I. Publication PHS 89–1100.

5. *1970 Census of Population and Housing: Evaluation and Research Program: Test of Birth Registration Completeness 1964 to 1968*. Washington, DC: Bureau of the Census; 1973. US Dept of Commerce publication PHC-E-2.

6. Fay RE, Passel JS, Robinson GJ, Cowan CD. *The Coverage of the Population in the 1980 Census*. Washington, DC: Bureau of the Census; 1988. US Dept of Commerce publication PHC80-E4.

7. Montagu A. *The Idea of Race*. Lincoln, Neb: University of Nebraska Press; 1965.

8. Lewontin RC. The apportionment of human diversity. *Evol Biol*. 1972;6:381–398.

9. Gould SJ. Why we should not name human races: a biological view. In: Gould SJ. ed. *Ever Since Darwin*. New York, NY: WW Norton & Co Inc; 1977:231–236.

10. Office of Management and Budget. Directive No. 15: race and ethnic standards for federal statistics and administrative reporting. In *Statistical Policy Handbook*. Washington, DC: Office of Federal Statistical Policy and Standards, US Dept of Commerce; 1978:37–38.

11. Wallman KK, Hodgdon J. Race and ethnic standards for federal statistics and administrative reporting. *Stat Rep*. 1977;77:450–454.

12. Wallman KK. Statistics for Americans of Spanish origin or descent. *Stat Rep*. 1978;78:148–152.

13. Massey J. Using interviewer observed race and respondent reported race in the Health Interview survey. In: *Proceedings of American Statistical Association Meetings: Social Statistics Section*. Alexandria, Va: American Statistical Association; 1980:425–428.

14. *1980 Census of Population: General Social and Economic Characteristics: United States Summary*. Washington, DC: Bureau of the census; 1983. US Dept of Commerce publication PC80-1-C.

15. Heuser RL. Race and ethnicity in U.S. natality tabulations. Presented at the 117th Annual Meeting of the American Public Health Association; October 24, 1989; Chicago, Ill.

16. Drury TF, May CS, Poe GS. Going beyond interviewer observations of race in the National Health Interview Survey. In: *Classification Issues in Measuring the Health Status of Minorities*. Hyattsville, Md: National Center for Health Statistics; 1980:5–17.

17. McKenney NR, Cresce AR, Johnson PA. U.S. development of the race and ethnic items for the 1990 census. Presented at the Annual Meeting of the Population Association of America; April 21–23, 1988; New Orleans, La.

18. Suchman L, Jordan B. Interactional troubles in face-to-face survey interviews. *J Am Stat Assoc*. 1990;85:232–244.

19. *Content Reinterview Study: Accuracy of Data for Selected Population and Housing Characteristics as Measured by Reinterview*. Washington, DC: Bureau of the Census; 1986. US Dept of Commerce publication PHC80-E2.

20. Hollmann FW. *United States Population Estimates, by Age, Sex, Race, and Hispanic Origin: 1986 to 1988*. Washington. DC: Bureau of the Census; 1990. US Dept of Commerce, ser P-25, No. 1045.

21. *Persons of Spanish Origin by State: 1980*. Washington, DC: Bureau of the Census; 1982. US Dept of Commerce publication PC80-SI-7.

22. *Vital Statistics of the United States 1950*. Washington, DC: US Dept of Health, Education, and Welfare; 1954;I.

23. Poe GS, Powell-Griner E, McLaughlin JK, Robinson K, Placek J. A comparability study of the responses to the 1986 National Mortality Follow-back Survey to similar demographic items from the death certificate. Unpublished results.

24. Hambright TZ. Comparability of marital status, race, nativity, and country of origin on the death certificate and matching census record: United States—May-August 1960. *Vital Health Stat [2]*. 1969:1–47. Ser 2, No. 34.

25. Frost F, Shy KK. Racial differences between linked birth and infant death records in Washington State. *Am J Public Health*. 1980;70:974–976.

26. Passel JS, Berman PA. Quality of the 1980 census data for American Indians. *Soc Biol*. 1986;33:163–182.

27. Farley R. *Race and Ethnicity in the U.S. Census: An Evaluation of the 1980 Ancestry Question*. Washington, DC: Bureau of the Census; 1990.

28. Kleinman, JC. Infant mortality among racial/ethnic minority groups, 1983–1984. *MMWR*. 1990;39(SS–2):31–39.

29. *Vital Statistics of the United States 1983: Mortality*. Washington, DC: US Dept of Health and Human Services; 1987;IIA. Publication PHS 87-1101.

30. *Vital Statistics of the United States 1984: Mortality*. Washington, DC: US Dept of Health and Human Services; 1987;IIA. Publication PHS 87-1122.

31. Siegel JS, Passel JS. Coverage of the Hispanic population of the United States in the 1970 census. Washington, DC: Bureau of the Census; 1979. Current Population Reports. US Dept of Commerce publication P23, No. 82.

32. Snipp CM. Who are American Indians? some observations about the perils and pitfalls of data for race and ethnicity. *Popul Res Policy Rev.* 1986;5:237–252.

33. *1980 Census of Population: Ancestry of the Population by State: 1980.* Washington, DC: Bureau of the Census; 1983.

Current Population Reports. US Dept of Commerce publication PC80-S1-10.

34. Johnson CE Jr. *Consistency of Reporting of Ethnic Origin in the Current Population Survey.* Washington, DC: Bureau of the Census; 1974. US Dept of Commerce Technical Paper No. 31.

35. Centers for Disease Control. Guidelines for evaluating surveillance systems. *MMWR.* 1988:37(S-5):1–18.

✤ 29

Ethnic Variations in the Chronic Pain Experience

Maryann S. Bates

W. Thomas Edwards

In this selection an anthropologist–physician team explores a question with a long and controversial history in medical anthropology. Mark Zborowski's famous old study in medical anthropology from the late 1940s "Cultural Components in Response to Pain" (1952), compared the cultural rules about reporting pain among ethnic groups in a northeastern U.S. hospital. The study compared white ethnics—including Jewish Americans, Italian Americans, Irish Americans, and "Old Americans" or "Yankees." The basic finding was that pain meant different things to people from different ethnic subcultural backgrounds (Zborowski 1969). In some groups it was permissible to complain about pain whereas in others group members were expected to dispassionately "report" about pain, if they mentioned it at all. Pain brought different worries to people. Members from some groups were worried about the long-term implications of pain (What is causing this?) and were less likely to want analgesics because they might mask a more serious problem. Others worried about the immediate pain and wanted painkillers. The study showed that the health care providers were more comfortable with patients who were culturally more like themselves; they did not like patients whose cultural style allowed or even encouraged "complaining." The anthropologist observed that, as a result, health care givers did not meet the emotional needs of some patients.

It is obvious that people differ in their reactions to pain. The question is whether this variation is idiosyncratic to in-dividuals or if there are social groups who share particular attitudinal and behavioral patterns. Our society tends to emphasize individual variation, but many societies expect, for example, that boys will tolerate more pain than girls or that crying and complaining are less acceptable for boys. A similar cultural rule might separate children and adults. However, these gender or age differences are clearly not cultural universals.

Pain cannot be measured directly; there is no objective machine that might be called a "dolorimeter." Rather, pain has to be interpreted through each particular patient. Variation in the experience of pain might be related to the particular sociocultural context (DelVecchio Good et al. 1992) or even to the expectations of pain (such as nocebo phenomenon in selection 15).

In this selection, the medical anthropologists go beyond these past descriptive studies of the cultural components of pain response. Notice the quantitative orientation of the research design and the way that psychological variables (like locus of control) can be incorporated into cross-cultural comparison. Notice that intragroup variation is also an important question facing the researchers.

As you read this selection, consider these questions:

- *Why has chronic pain been described as one of modern medicine's greatest failures?*

- *How can the authors assert that reaction to pain is a learned response? Isn't pain a question of the neurophysiology of the nervous system? Why are health care providers concerned with pain? What can pain tell clinicians?*

- *What might be the evolutionary function of pain? (Remember from selection 16 that leprosy involves the absence of pain.)*

- *In this kind of research, is there a problem with comparing ethnic groups? What about the issue of stereotyping?*

- *What can clinicians do with this knowledge?*

Chronic pain has been called one of modern medicine's greatest failures and is currently one of its greatest challenges[1,2] (see . . . [note 1] for a comparison of chronic and acute pain). In spite of increased research and the emergence of over 1200 chronic pain treatment centers in the United States over the past two decades,[3] most chronic pain sufferers have not found substantial or lasting relief. It is estimated that 50 to 80 million Americans suffer from chronic pain.[3,4] In the United States alone, the annual cost of chronic pain, in health care, drugs, disability compensation, lost wages, etc, exceeds $50 billion.[5] Despite the high incidence and costs, effective treatments or cures for chronic pain remain elusive.

There has been considerable research on the psychosocial and behavioral aspects of chronic pain.[3,6–9] However, despite findings of ethnic variations in acute and experimental pain,[10–14] most studies of and treatment programs for *chronic* pain have ignored the possible influence of ethnic or cultural background on the pain experience.

In a study of a multiethnic group of chronic pain sufferers, we found a significant relationship between ethnic background and variation in the perception of chronic pain intensity and in behavioral, psychological, and attitudinal responses to the pain.

Textbooks generally define pain as an uncomfortable, unpleasant sensation, related to current or impending tissue damage, that motivates the sufferer to avoid the perceived pain stimulus.[15] However, there is no known physiological measure that can be relied on to vary in accordance with degree of clinical pain intensity.[16,17] Thus, human perception of pain intensity is a subjective experience communicated to others through written, oral, or behavioral means. Clinicians depend on this communication when making diagnostic and treatment decisions. There is also a psychological response to pain, such as fear or anger, and humans often attempt to attach meaning to their pain. Thus, the human pain experience is a complex phenomenon involving sensory, motivational, psychological, emotional, and cognitive components.

Social scientists have various views on the precise definition of the term *culture;* for our purposes, culture is defined as the patterned ways in which humans have learned to think about and act in their world. These learned, shared, patterned ways of thinking and acting replicate human social structures.[18] As Kleinman notes, one's cultural orientation guides one's "conventional common sense about how to understand and treat illness; thus we can say of illness experience that it is always culturally shaped."[18(p5)] However, each individual's expectations regarding illness are also shaped by a specific social situation and life history. Therefore, despite the cultural patterning of the illness experience, each person nonetheless has a somewhat distinct illness experience.[18]

While cultural orientation is a component of one's ethnic heritage, ethnicity refers specifically to the condition of belonging to a particular ethnic group. An ethnic group is a social group, within a larger cultural system, that is accorded its own identity (by members and nonmembers) on the basis of variable traits that may include, but are not limited to, religion, language, ancestry, or other historical factors. In a broad sense, ethnic identity refers to the individual's sense of belonging in an ethnic group and to the parts of that individual's thinking, perceptions, feelings, and behaviors that are due to group membership.[19] Ethnic identity has many components, including ethnic awareness, which involves an understanding of one's own and other groups; ethnic self-identification; and attitudes and behavioral patterns specific to one's group.[19(p13)] While an ethnic group may share some characteristics of the dominant culture, such a group is unique in its world view and its system of values; its interactive roles, its behavioral styles, and often its language are distinctive to and shared by members.[20(p39)]

There is evidence that ethnic or cultural background influences the meaning people give to symptoms, including pain, and influences the ways in which illnesses and pain are defined and treated.[11–14,21] Zborowski's pioneering research[13] on ethnic group influences on pain suggests that a person's cultural or ethnic group becomes a conditioning influence in the formation of the person's attitudes toward and responses to pain. Culture thus represents the symbolic and linguistic system within which one's pain experiences are labeled and acted on.[22]

Therefore, knowledge of cultural or ethnic group beliefs, attitudes, norms for behavior, and meanings regarding pain may provide one major clue in understanding an individual's response to pain. However, despite evidence that ethnic identity is associated with variation in acute and experimental pain response,[13,14,23,24] with one exception,[25] studies of *chronic* pain have given insufficient attention to cultural factors. Lipton and Marbach studied chronic and acute facial pain, but they did not differentiate between the two types in their research report.[11] As chronic pain is now recognized as different from acute pain,[26–29] studies must differentiate between the two.

Kotarba's study of the social dimensions of chronic pain did not focus on the influence of ethnic or sociocultural variables on chronic pain perception.[28] He focused on how chronic pain affects a person's behavior and relationships in social situations. However, in suggesting that "chronic pain experiences" are strikingly similar across various socioeconomic and cultural groups, he appears to imply that a single model of the chronic pain "career" is sufficient for describing the experiences of all chronic pain sufferers.[28] Because culture is a major means by which humans interpret all shared experiences, and pain is a human experience familiar to all cultures, it would be most remarkable if culture did not influence the interpretation of *all* types of pain.[30]

Although some have suggested the possibility of biological or genetic reasons for differences in pain intensity between ethnic groups,[31] there is currently no firm evidence that proves ethnic or racial differences in the neurophysiological systems responsible for human pain perception.[32] Therefore, at this time, we assume that all (physically normal) humans have essentially similar neurophysiological systems of pain perception. Human pain perception and response are, at least in part, learned. People learn in social communities; this is where conventional ways of interpreting and responding to pain are acquired.

We hypothesize that people from similar cultural or ethnic backgrounds are likely to show similar pain perception and response patterns, and we term such patterning as cultural.[33] To test this hypothesis, we conducted research to answer the following questions:

1. Are there statistically significant differences in (a) perception of chronic pain intensity and (b) behavioral, psychological, and attitudinal responses to pain among ethnic groups? How strongly, if at all, does this variability correlate with ethnic variability when controlling for the influence of other sociodemographic, medical, and psychological variables?

2. Are there specific cultural, sociodemographic, psychological, and/or medical variables that serve as predictors of *intragroup* variation in pain perception and/or response within ethnic groups?

RESEARCH DESIGN AND METHODOLOGY

Our project was conducted at the Pain Control Center (PCC) at the University of Massachusetts Medical Center in Worcester from May 1987 to February 1988. The PCC is an outpatient multidisciplinary chronic pain treatment facility. The project was approved by the Committee for the Protection of Human Subjects in Research at the Medical Center. Informed consent was obtained from each participant.

Ethnic identity was determined with an Ethnicity and Pain Survey (see . . . [note 2] for information on obtaining copies of this survey and of the questionnaires used in this study), which assessed: (1) language spoken in the childhood home, (2) birthplace of patient, parents, and grandparents (if the patient was greater than third-generation US-born and self-identified with an ethnic group, we also assessed birthplace of great-grandparents), and (3) primary ethnic group self-identification. All patients who reported more than one primary ethnic affiliation were eliminated from further consideration, because we wanted to study distinct ethnic groups. The center's patient population (approximately 6000 visits per year) represented 28 different ethnic groups.

The six largest ethnic/cultural groups at the PCC were used in the full study. The first group is "Old Americans" (n = 100). This category was originally defined by Zborowski in his pioneering work[13] and involves US-born Anglo patients, mainly of third or greater generation, who identify with no ethnic group but define themselves as Americans; the majority are Protestants. The other groups are Hispanics (n = 44), Irish (n = 60), Italians (n = 50), French Canadians (n = 90), and Polish (n = 28). All patients treated at the PCC during the study period who identified one of the six groups as their sole primary affiliation and whose ancestry matched the self-identification were asked to participate. Of the 438 patients asked, 372 (85%) agreed.

According to the 1980 census,[34] the major ancestry groups in Worcester and the surrounding congressional district, which has a total of population of

521 959, are French (65 934), Polish (35 245), Irish (34 148), English (33 457), black American (27 594), Italian (25 918), and Hispanic or "of Spanish origin" (19 086).[34] Thus, the six largest groups in our study are a reflection of the predominant ancestral groups, with the exception of black Americans, that make up the population of Worcester and the surrounding region. We encountered only seven black Americans in the patient population during the study—obviously too small a group to include in the analysis.

Dependent and Independent Variables and Their Measures

The *dependent variable* in our study is the reported *chronic pain experience*. Based on the findings of Zborowski,[13] Zola,[14] and Lipton and Marbach,[11] we determined that the aspects of the pain experience that may vary can be categorized into three major areas:

1. *Pain perception,* or perceived pain intensity, was determined from the McGill Pain Questionnaire (MPQ), a standardized instrument for assessing pain severity. The Pain Control Center Questionnaire (PCCQ) assessed pain location and duration.

2. *Behavioral response,* including the effects of the chronic pain on social, occupational, and daily activities, was determined from the Ethnicity and Pain Questionnaire (EPQ), devised for this study. . . .

The EPQ questions are worded in the form of statements with response selections based on a Likert-type scale: (0) not applicable, (1) disagree somewhat, (2) disagree strongly, (3) agree somewhat, and (4) agree strongly. This scale is often used as an interval measure in social science studies of medical or psychological populations.[11,35]

Behavioral response was also assessed by the PCCQ, which uses a Likert-scale chart to indicate to what degree the pain causes interference with daily activities such as working, walking, household chores, driving, eating, and recreation. In addition, behavioral response was assessed through interviews with and observations of the patients and through reports on their behavior by the medical providers.

3. *Attitudinal and emotional/psychological response* includes the degree of worries, anger, fear, depression, and tension; degree of stoicism or expressiveness associated with the pain; and the patients' attitudes toward the chronic pain experience. These were determined from the EPQ, the PCCQ, and interviews and observations.

The *independent variables* are those that other studies indicate may be related to pain intensity or response variation,[11,13–14,24,36–39] and they include:

1. *Ethnic group identification and degree of heritage consistency.* Ethnic identity was determined by assessing each subject's enculturative environment using the Ethnicity and Pain Survey as described above. Estes and Zitzow define heritage consistency as the degree to which one's life-style reflects one's traditional culture.[40,41] The EPQ covers heritage consistency with questions such as: Was the patient born and/or raised in the ethnic group's country of origin or in an ethnic neighborhood? Does the patient live in an ethnic neighborhood as an adult, maintain regular contact with the extended family, engage primarily in social activities with members of the ethnic group, and have knowledge of and pride in the ancestral culture and language? Does that heritage still play an important role in the patient's present life-style? A high aggregated score on these questions indicates strong ties to one's group or a high degree of heritage consistency.[41]

2. *Sociodemographic background,* including age, gender, socioeconomic status (SES; assessed by occupation, education, and household income), worker's compensation status, and religion, came from the PCCQ.

3. *Pain treatment history,* including number of types of past treatments and surgeries for pain, was determined from the patients' medical records, the PCCQ, and interviews with patients.

4. *Current number and types of medications for pain* were determined from the patients' medical records and interviews.

5. *Clinical diagnosis of pathology* associated with the pain was abstracted from medical files based on the PCC physician's notes.

6. *Locus of control (LOC) style.* An internal LOC style of psychological coping involves a perception that life events and circumstances are the result of one's own actions, whereas an external LOC style involves a view that life events and circumstances are beyond one's own control and in the hands of fate, chance, or other people.[42] Numerous studies have found a relationship between LOC style and variation in ways of coping with or responding to stressful life events, including illness.[42–45] Internal or external LOC style was determined by 10 questions on the EPQ that were taken from Rotter's original LOC scale.[45]

. . .

In addition, the total pain rating index (PRIT) of the MPQ was selected to measure each patient's perception of overall pain intensity. The MPQ is currently considered to be one of the best measures of overall pain severity and is widely used in the assessment of both acute and chronic pain.[46–49] Numerous studies have confirmed the validity of this instrument,[16,17,46–49] and it has been extensively used internationally (languages include English, French, Swedish, and Spanish).[27,50–54]

The questionnaires were generally administered during interviews. The 33 Hispanic patients not fluent in English were interviewed using the Spanish versions of the questionnaires. Qualitative data were also collected through informal discussions with and observations of patients, during both interviews and repeat informal visits, either in the waiting room or in procedure rooms after treatments.

Data that could be analyzed statistically were coded and entered on the "dBase III Plus" data management system, and the analysis was performed using SPSSx analysis software. This analysis included appropriate statistical tests, such as F tests, Duncan's Multiple Range tests, Student's t tests, χ^2 tests, Pearson Correlation Coefficients, and multiple regression analysis. We set α at 0.05.

RESULTS

We compared the characteristics of the groups by performing one-way analyses of variance (ANOVA) and, where appropriate, Duncan's Multiple Range tests for each of the independent variables across the six groups to determine the specific groups that differed for each variable.

Ethnic Characteristics

The "Old American" group, those US-born Anglo patients who identify with no ethnic group, was used because, as Zborowski noted in 1952 (and we still find accurate today), "the values and attitudes of this group dominate in the country and are held by [many] members of the medical profession."[33(p19)] In our study, Old Americans often cited a secondary self-identification as a "Yankee" or "New Englander." Our qualitative data suggest that common cultural elements within this group include those previously identified for Anglo-Saxon Protestants.[55,56] Our research and Zborowski's earlier research[13] indicate that Old Americans value stoicism in the face of pain and tend to describe their pain symptoms to providers in a matter-of-fact, unemotional manner with the expectation that this will lead to correct diagnosis and treatment.[13(pp24–25)]

The Hispanic group is the most recent to come to the US mainland; 35 of 44 members were born outside the US mainland—34 in Puerto Rico (see . . . [note 3]) and 1 in Costa Rica—and most arrived within the last 5 years. The majority of the Hispanics (33 of 44) do not speak English fluently. The majority in the Polish and Italian groups are members of the first or second US-born generation . . . ; all speak English, and many adults also speak Polish or Italian. The majority of Irish and French Canadians are members of the second or third generation, or beyond . . . ; the vast majority of adults in both groups speak only English.

The Hispanic, Italian, and Polish groups have the highest heritage-consistency means (F = 4.94; $P < .01$), that is, the strongest ties to their ethnic groups and life-styles that most strongly reflect their ethnic cultures. . . . A Duncan's Multiple Range test shows that the significant differences in these means are between the Old American group and each of the other five groups and between the Hispanic group and the French Canadians and Irish.

Sociodemographic Characteristics

There are few significant sociodemographic differences among the six groups (no significant differences in mean age, household income, or gender distributions), except that the Hispanic group has a significantly lower mean for years of education. . . . There is a significant difference in religious affiliation between the Old Americans and the other groups, the Old Americans being the only group with more Protestants than Catholics. . . .

Medical Characteristics

The population mean for duration of pain is 50.3 months. There is no significant difference in duration means among the ethnic groups. . . . Diagnosis was determined by each patient's PCC physician. However, as is often the case with chronic pain, even after exhaustive diagnostic tests, the exact cause of the pain could not be identified for many patients. Thus, the diagnosis was often of a general nature, such as radicular or mechanical low back pain. The majority of patients in all six groups fall into one of three major diagnostic categories: (1) low back pain, including degenerative and herniated discs and mechanical, radicular, and postsurgical lower back pain; (2) arthritis, including rheumatoid and osteoarthritis; and (3) neuropathy, including neuritis, neuralgia and other neuropathies. There are no significant differences in the distributions of these diagnoses or in the mean number of pain medications being taken among the six groups. . . . There are also no significant differences in the distributions of the most common current pain medication classes among the six groups (F = 10.7; P = .95). The most common pain medication classes being taken by patients are nonopiate analgesics, opiate analgesics, antidepressants, anti-inflammatories, and muscle relaxants.

Psychological Characteristics, LOC Style

There is a significant relationship between LOC style and ethnic identity, as there is a significant difference in the distribution of the two styles across the ethnic groups (χ^2 = 22.52; P < .01). In the Old American group, 50% of members are in the external LOC group and 50% are in the internal LOC group. Among Hispanics, over 80% are in the external group. In contrast, 90% of the Polish are in the internal group, as are approximately 60% of the French Canadians, 65% of the Italians, and 65% of the Irish. . . . Thus, except for the Old American group, ethnic identity is a predictor of LOC style. As it is impossible for LOC style to influence ethnic identity, that identity (one's socialization within the ethnic group) probably has an effect on the LOC style one is most likely to develop. There are no significant relationships between the distribution of the two LOC styles and the other sociodemographic variables in this study, including age, gender, SES, and religion.

Interethnic Group Variation in Perception of Pain Intensity

The one-way ANOVA demonstrates that ethnic identity is associated with statistically significant differences in perceptions of pain intensity as measured by the MPQ-PRIT (F = 4.08; P < .01). The MPQ-PRIT's highest possible score, representing excruciating, unbearably intense pain, is 78. The Hispanic mean of 40.6 was the highest, with the Italian mean of 32.3 second highest. The Polish group had the lowest mean, 29.2, and the French-Canadian group had a mean of 29.3. The Old Americans and the Irish had intermediate means of 30.3 and 31.5, respectively. . . . A Duncan's Multiple Range test determined that the significant differences in intensity were between the Hispanics and each of the other groups. Regression analyses, discussed below, also revealed a significant difference in intensity between the Polish and the Old American groups when controlling for other significant variables.

The ANOVA shows that the only other independent variables in the PCC study that were significantly associated with intensity variation were age cohort (F = 3.05; P < .05) and LOC style (F = 6.86; P < .01). . . . There was also a significant interaction between ethnic identity and LOC style: among Old American and Polish patients, the internal LOC group had a higher pain intensity mean than the external LOC group, yet conversely, among patients in each of the other ethnic categories, the internal LOC group had a lower intensity mean than the external group. . . . The relationship between ethnicity and LOC style is clearly complex.

The ANOVAs show no significant relationships between variation in pain intensity, measured by the MPQ-PRIT, and gender (F = .28; P = .60; see . . . [note] 4), worker's compensation status (F = .10; P = .76), religion (F = 1.21; P = .31), SES (for example, education: F = .67; P = .57), diagnosis (F = .77; P = .47), and medication type (F = 2.20; P = .07).[30(pp95–101)]

Since age, LOC style, and ethnic identity are the only independent variables significantly associated with intensity variation in the ANOVA, we used multiple regression analysis to examine their relationships. As ethnic identity and LOC style are qualitative, they were treated as dummy variables. Because of the interaction of LOC style and ethnic identity, an interaction term for the Old American and the Polish groups was included in the regression equation to control for the differing effect of LOC style in those two groups. Because the Hispanic group had the highest intensity mean, it was used as the ethnic group constant in the initial regression analysis. In this analysis, ethnic identity and LOC style remain significantly associated with pain intensity variation after controlling for the influence of age and of each other; however, age does not remain significant. . . . The regression analysis shows that 22% (R^2 = .2183) of the variation in intensity is explained by the variation in age, ethnic identity, and LOC style. In this analysis, the significant ethnic differences are between the Hispanic group and the Old American, French-Canadian, and Irish groups. A similar regression analysis was performed using the group with the lowest intensity mean (Polish) as the constant. It shows that the differences between intensity means for the Polish and the Old American groups are significant when controlling for age and LOC style. . . .

Intraethnic Group Variation in Perception of Pain Intensity

A similar pattern of ethnic and psychological influences is evident in intragroup pain intensity variation, as such variation is most often associated with differences in degree of heritage consistency and LOC style. In the Hispanic, French-Canadian, Polish, and Irish groups, high heritage consistency is correlated with lower pain intensities; however, this difference attains statistical significance only among the French Canadians and Irish. . . . Within the Hispanic, Italian, French-Canadian, and Irish groups, the subgroup with an internal LOC style has a lower intensity mean than the subgroup with an external style; but this difference attains statistical significance only in the French-Canadian and Hispanic groups (Old American group: $F = 5.01$, $P = 0.06$; Hispanic group: $F = 5.01$, $P < .05$; Italian group: $F = 3.89$, $P = 0.06$; French-Canadian group: $F = 3.93$, $P < .05$; Irish group: $F = 2.99$, $P = 0.21$; Polish group: $F = 2.80$, $P = 0.14$). . . .

With only one exception, there are no significant intragroup variations in intensity related to diagnosis, pain medications, age, gender, worker's compensation status, or SES. The exception is in the Irish group, which shows a significant difference in intensity related to occupation. . . . The occupations were categorized as follows: (1) no salaried occupation, (2) unskilled, (3) semiskilled, (4) skilled, and (5) professional. Among the Irish, the unskilled group has the highest intensity mean of 44.2, while the skilled group's mean of 26.0 is significantly lower. . . .

Interethnic Group Variation in Pain Response

There are significant variations in behavioral, attitudinal, psychological, and emotional responses to chronic pain in the total study population in numerous areas. . . .

Behavioral Response There are significant differences among several groups in pain-related work stoppage, inside and outside the home. . . . A Duncan's Multiple Range test determined that the significant differences in work stoppage means are between the Italians and Old Americans and between the Hispanic group and the Old American, Polish, Irish, and French-Canadian groups. The ethnic differences remain in regression analyses when other variables are controlled. . . .

Self-reported expression of pain is highest among the Hispanic group (a mean of 15.3 out of a possible aggregated score of 20). The Italian group has the second highest mean (12.7), while the Old Americans have the lowest (10.3). . . . A Duncan's Multiple Range test shows that the significant differences in expressiveness means are between the Old American group and the

Italian, Hispanic, and French-Canadian groups and between the Hispanics and each of the other groups. These ethnic differences remain in regression analysis when controlling for other independent variables that were significant in the ANOVA. . . .

Some significant differences appear in the degree to which patients asked family and friends for advice regarding pain treatments. The Hispanic group reported seeking advice most often, the Old American group least often. . . . A Duncan's Multiple Range test shows the significant difference in seeking advice is between the Hispanics and each of the other groups except the Polish. These differences remain significant in regression analysis. . . .

There are no ethnic group differences, however, in the behavioral category labeled "total interference in all daily activities," which was determined by adding each patient's scores on all of the items on the activity interface chart ($F = .60$; $P = .63$). Nor are there any significant ethnic differences in patients' reported compliance with physicians' directions on medications or treatments ($F = 2.11$; $P = .07$).

Attitudinal Response Several attitudinal response areas show significant differences among the ethnic groups. For example, patients were asked if and how strongly they agreed with the statement "As long as I am in pain, I will never have a fulfilling and happy life." The Hispanics had the highest mean, the Italians the second highest and the Polish the lowest. . . . The Duncan's Multiple Range test shows that the significant differences are between the Italian and the Old American groups, between the Polish and both the Irish and French-Canadian groups, and between the Hispanic and each of the other five groups. These ethnic differences remain in regression analysis when controlling for LOC style and other independent variables. . . .

Patients were asked about their attitudes regarding their current health using the categories of "healthy" or "unhealthy/disabled." Using a χ^2 crosstabulation, we discovered significant differences in the distributions of the two health-status attitudes across the six ethnic groups . . . , although there is no significant difference in the distributions of the three main *diagnostic* categories across the six groups. . . . Sixtyone percent of the Old Americans and 58% of the French Canadians defined themselves as healthy, while only 16% of the Hispanics, 44% of the Polish, 45% of the Irish, and 47% of the Italians defined themselves as healthy.

Two other attitudinal response areas show no significant ethnic differences. These are patients' reported beliefs concerning support from family and friends during the pain experience (F = 1.07; P = .38) and patients' attitudes regarding their ability eventually to overcome the pain (F = .95; P = .45).

Psychological/Emotional Response Finally, several psychological/emotional response areas show significant intergroup differences, including differences in degree of worries, tension, and anger associated with the pain. . . . The Hispanic group had the highest mean in each of these response areas, the Italian group had the second highest, and the Polish group had the lowest. These differences remain in regression analysis when other significant variables are controlled. . . . In one area, degree of depression, the F ratio is not statistically significant for differences among all six groups (F = 2.04; P = .08); however, a Duncan's Multiple Range test does show a significant difference in depression means between the Hispanic and the Polish and Irish groups.

Intraethnic Group Variation in Pain Response

Significant variations in pain response also appear *within* several of the PCC groups. (It should be noted that the sample size of the Polish group, n = 28, made statistically valid intragroup comparisons difficult; for those categories where valid comparisons could be made, little variation was found, due perhaps to actual group homogeneity or, obviously, to small sample size.) Surprisingly, there are very few intragroup variations in pain response related to SES. Most frequently, intragroup response variations are related to degree of heritage consistency, patient's generation, and LOC style.

Heritage consistency is related to response variation within the Hispanic, Italian, French-Canadian, and Irish groups. For each group, we ran a Pearson's Correlation Coefficient to test for a correlation between heritage consistency and variation in total interference in daily activities. We found that for the Italian and Irish groups, high heritage consistency is correlated with significantly lower levels of total interference with daily activities. . . .

In the French-Canadian and Irish groups, high heritage consistency is significantly related to lower degrees of depression and is correlated with higher degrees of reported social support from family and friends during the pain experience. . . . Such high degrees of social support may well help to lessen the depression associated with the pain.

There is also a correlation between heritage consistency and support of family and friends within the Hispanic group. Again, high heritage consistency correlates with reports of high degrees of support from family and friends during the pain experience. . . . Hispanics with high heritage consistency also report a significantly higher degree of expressiveness of their pain. . . .

Generation is also related to intragroup variations. Using a Pearson Correlation, we determined that, in the Hispanic group, as generation goes up, fear level goes up as well (thus, being first- or second-generation US mainland–born correlates with higher levels of fear associated with the pain experience). . . . Given that US mainland–born Hispanics report less strong ties to the local Hispanic community than do the immigrants and that, as mentioned above, heritage consistency correlates with support from family and friends, it appears that strong social support may help reduce the fears of the immigrant group. Generation in the Hispanic group also correlates with degree of expressiveness: as generation goes up, degree of expressiveness goes down. . . . It is likely that the lower expressiveness of the US mainland–born Hispanics is due to their increased assimilation to the Old American standard of nonexpressiveness of pain.

In the French-Canadian group, generation is related to differences in degree of tension associated with the pain. As generation goes up among French Canadians, degree of tension goes up as well. . . . Again, the likely explanation is that the greater the generation, the less strong are the ties to the local ethnic community; this may result in less social support, which could conceivably increase the patient's tension level. In fact, French Canadians do show correlations between both generation and degree of heritage consistency and degree of support from family and friends. As generation goes up, reported social support goes down; as heritage consistency goes up, social support goes up as well. . . .

LOC style is related to significant variations in emotional response to pain (tension, anger, and/or fear) within the Old American, Italian, and French-Canadian groups. In each case, the external LOC subgroup has a significantly higher response mean than the internal subgroup. . . .

DISCUSSION

Analyses show that *the most frequent and consistent differences in pain intensity and response in the total study population are related to variation in ethnic identity and LOC style.* The ethnic pattern is consistent: the

Hispanic group has the highest intensity mean, the greatest interference with work and social activities, the highest degree of emotional and psychological stress, and the highest pain expressiveness; the Italian group is second highest in each of these categories; and either the Polish or the Old American group is lowest in each category.

The Irish and French-Canadian groups do not differ significantly from each other in pain intensity means, rarely differ significantly from each other in pain response, and often do not differ significantly from the Old American group. However, the French Canadians and Irish do generally differ significantly from the Hispanics and often from the Italians and Polish. Thus, our analyses show that the most pronounced interethnic differences in pain intensity and response (ie, the highest and lowest means) usually are associated with the Hispanic, Italian, and Polish groups. These three ethnic groups have the highest means for heritage consistency, indicating close ethnic ties and life-styles reflective of their ethnic heritages. These three are the only groups that have majorities in the immigrant or first- or second-generation US-born categories. Thus, in the PCC study population, the groups that appear least assimilated to Old American culture show the greatest variation in pain intensity and response.

Furthermore, the intragroup analyses demonstrate that, *within* several ethnic groups, those who are immigrants or first-generation US-born, who have high degrees of heritage consistency, and who believe they have the strong support of family and friends report less severe (although not necessarily less expensive) responses to the pain in several areas. Therefore, in this study population, *both generation and degree of heritage consistency appear to modify the effect of ethnic affiliation on the pain experience.*

Our findings of significant interethnic and intraethnic group differences in the pain experience have implications for future treatment programs. The medical, psychological, and social science literature often represents chronic pain patients as a homogeneous group[7,26,28] with the following characteristics: "preoccupation with pain, strong and ambivalent dependency needs, feelings of isolation and loneliness, . . . inability to take care of self-needs, passivity, lack of insight into patterns of self-defeating behavior, [and] inability to deal appropriately with anger and hostility."[26(p472)] Given the variation found in the PCC population, we suggest that the widespread perception of a single, homogeneous type of chronic pain patient leads to homogeneous care and treatment programs that may be ineffective for many patients. The assumption of homogeneity may cause providers to miss important clues that could help them to better

understand the individual patient's chronic pain experience. In the PCC study population, ethnicity is an important factor in the individual's pain experience, affecting it directly and, through LOC style, indirectly, because ethnicity, unlike the other sociodemographic variables, is a predictor of LOC style.

The relationship among LOC style, ethnic background, and pain intensity is complex. Indeed, within two of our groups (Old Americans and Polish), an internal LOC style is associated with higher pain intensities, while within each of our other four groups, an internal LOC style is associated with lower pain intensities. We will therefore pursue further research to clarify the relationships among ethnic background, LOC style, and pain intensity and response variation. This is an especially important area for future research, as it would seem possible to determine the effect of LOC style on an individual's pain experience. Once this relationship is determined, if an external style is associated with severe pain and life disruption, providers can assist in the establishment of a program in which the patient sets and attains self-defined, culturally relevant, realistic goals. Such programs should help patients attain a sense of control over their life circumstances and their pain.

We stress that ethnic stereotyping is as dangerous as inattention to cultural variables. (See Stein[57] for an illustration of this danger.) There is significant intragroup variation in our study, and others have found significant intragroup variation in other populations of pain sufferers.[11] Clinicians must acknowledge that not all patients are alike, that pain does not have the same meaning and significance for different patients, and that patients may exhibit different coping strategies and different responses to the pain and to treatments provided. If clinicians are to treat multiethnic chronic pain sufferers successfully, they must be able to unlock the "illness reality" of each particular patient and thereby provide more humane and personal care and treatment.[11]

Chronic pain is a complex, poorly understood, and very expensive condition that often frustrates both providers and patients. Because they recognize there are currently no treatments that are highly effective for all sufferers, many providers are open to new approaches. We suggest that a major component of patient assessment be a detailed psychosocial and cultural history, taken by providers who are aware of both the complexity of cultural and psychosocial variables in the chronic pain experience and of their own cultural backgrounds and biases.

The work of Kleinman[18,58,59] and Kleinman et al,[60] regarding explanatory models and how to use a structured but open-ended interview to determine the meanings and explanations the patient attaches to the situation, would be helpful in effective history-taking and interpretation. Medical anthropologists, medical sociologists, or other "culture brokers" could be useful as consultants during history-taking and in developing more effective chronic pain programs for multiethnic populations. Such programs must treat patients as individuals with specific physical, cultural, and psychosocial characteristics and cognitive interpretations that are likely to influence the chronic pain experience.

Suggestions for Future Research

We acknowledge that our findings are certainly of a preliminary nature and that further research is needed to explore more fully how ethnicity relates to variation in the chronic pain experience. We believe that, in addition to the need to study the relationships among LOC style, ethnic background, and variation in the pain experience discussed above, other very important areas in need of further study are: (1) how ethnicity influences the meaning the sufferer attaches to pain and how those meanings influence perception of pain and (2) how ethnicity influences the communication of the pain experience. These areas of study are critical because the clinician depends on the patient's subjective perception and report of pain for diagnosis and treatment.

It should be stressed that culture does not affect patients alone. It is likely that medical providers' and specialists' own cultural backgrounds affect not only the communications and interactions between pain sufferer and provider, but also the care and treatment provided. At the PCC, we noted instances in which several nurses (many of whom are of New England ancestry) were somewhat judgmental toward the expressive Hispanics; the nurses did not believe the expressiveness was appropriate. This judgment was clearly related to these nurses' own cultural backgrounds.

A study by Westbrook et al[61] compared evaluations of a single set of clinical patients' case histories (not chronic pain patients) by Swedish and Australian health care providers. The study found significant differences between the Swedish and Australian providers' evaluations and proposed treatment regimes. The authors attributed the differences to the different cultural backgrounds of the two sets of providers and to the different health care models of the medical education systems in Sweden and Australia.[62] The study raises interesting questions about how providers' cultural and educational backgrounds influence their evaluation of patients and the care and treatment provided.

Like Westbrook et al, our study suggests a need to investigate how providers' cultural and educational backgrounds affect the way they perceive, communicate with, care for, and treat chronic pain patients. Given the obvious stereotyping of such patients in much of the current literature, one can readily imagine how training that defines chronic pain patients as a homogeneous group with significant "psycho-socio-economic disorders"[26(p472)] would influence providers' perceptions and treatment of pain sufferers.

Finally, one admitted limitation of our research design is that the PCC population does not represent the full range of chronic pain sufferers. Those who exclusively use other forms of treatment, such as general practitioners or religious, folk, or traditional healers, are not represented in this study. Our study findings cannot be generalized to include all pain sufferers; they should be applied only to similar diagnostic and clinical populations. Populations of chronic pain sufferers in other settings should be investigated in future studies.

NOTES

1. Acute pain serves the biological function of warning the individual that something is wrong and provides a diagnostic aid for the clinician.[29(pxi)] In contrast, chronic pain, defined as pain that continues beyond the period when it may help in detecting or healing an injury or disease, fails to respond to normal forms of biomedical intervention, and persists for at least 6 months, is now seen as a disabling disease in itself.[2,26,29] Chronic pain also imposes severe physical and psychological stress (such as depression and insomnia), as well as socioeconomic stress (severe disruption of social and work life), on the patient and family.[4,26,29,62]

2. Copies of the Ethnicity and Pain Survey, Ethnicity and Pain Questionnaire, Pain Control Center Questionnaire, and McGill Pain Questionnaire used in this study, in both English and Spanish, can be obtained by contacting Maryann S. Bates, PhD, Division of Human Development, School of Education and Human Development, State University of New York, PO Box 6000, Binghamton, NY 13902-6000, USA.

3. As Puerto Rico is a US commonwealth, all island-born Puerto Ricans are US citizens; technically, all Puerto Ricans are US-born. Thus, we refer to island-born Puerto Ricans as immigrants to the mainland United States and to those born in the continental United States as US mainland–born.

4. In the total PCC population, gender is related to statistically significant differences in degree of interference with daily household chores and in degree of having to stop work, inside and outside the home, because of the pain. Women reported a significantly greater degree of interference in household chores and of having to stop work, probably because they have more daily household chores and work inside the home than do men. On a qualitative

level, we were surprised to note few differences between men and women, even in regard to crying and emotionality, when describing the pain experience. The one noticeable exception was in the Hispanic group. Among Hispanic men, there was an openly expressed sense of having lost their manhood because they could no longer work and improve their families' standard of living. We did not find a corresponding sense among Hispanic women of loss of womanhood due to the pain experience. While numerous PCC patients of both genders expressed distress at having to cease because of pain, the effect of ceasing employment clearly had a more dramatic and severe effect on the Hispanic men and their sense of self-worth. This reaction was very likely related to the *machismo* values of the Hispanic community.

REFERENCES

1. Melzack R, Wall DP. *The Challenge of Pain.* New York, NY: Basic Books, 1983.
2. Melzack R, Wall DP. *The Textbook of Pain.* New York, NY: Churchill Livingstone; 1989.
3. Holzman AD, Turk DC, eds. *Pain Management.* Oxford, England: Pergamon Press; 1986.
4. Bonica J. Introduction. In: Aronoff G, ed. *Evaluation and Treatment of Chronic Pain.* Baltimore, Md: Urban and Schwarzenberg; 1985:xxxi–xliv.
5. Lipton S. Introduction. In: Lipton S, et al, eds. *Advances in Pain Research and Therapy.* New York, NY: Raven Press; 1990:xxvii–xxxiii.
6. Brennan S, et al. The prediction of chronic pain outcome by psychological variables. *Int J Psychiatry Med.* 1987;16:373–387.
7. Dorsel T. Chronic pain behavior patterns: a simple theoretical framework for health care providers. *Psychol Rep.* 1989;65:783–786.
8. Fordyce W. *Behavioral Methods for Chronic Pain and Illness.* St. Louis, Mo: Mosby; 1976.
9. Osterweis M, Kleinman A, Mechanic D, eds. *Pain and Disability.* Washington, DC: National Academy Press; 1987.
10. Buss AH, Portnoy NW. Pain tolerance and group identification. *J Personality Soc Psychol.* 1967;6:106–108.
11. Lipton JA, Marbach JJ. Ethnicity and the pain experience. *Soc Sci Med.* 1984;19:1279–1298.
12. Weisenberg M. et al. Pain: anxiety and attitudes in black, white and Puerto Rican patients. *Psychosom Med.* 1975;37:123–135.
13. Zborowski M. Cultural components in responses to pain. *J Soc Issues.* 1952;8:16–30.
14. Zola IK. Culture and symptoms—an analysis of patients presenting complaints. *Am Sociol Rev.* 1966;31:615–630.
15. Mountcastle VB. *Medical Physiology.* St. Louis, Mo: C. V. Mosby; 1974.
16. Elton D, Burrows GD, Stanley GV. Clinical measurement of pain. *Med J Australia.* 1979;24:109–111.
17. Gracely RH. Subjective quantification of pain perception. In: Bromm B, ed. *Pain Measurement in Man.* Amsterdam, Holland: Elsevier Publishers; 1984:371–387.
18. Kleinman A. *The Illness Narratives.* New York, NY: Basic Books, Inc; 1988.
19. Rotheram MJ, Phinney J. Definitions and perspectives in the study of children's ethnic socialization. In: Phinney J, Rotheram MJ, eds. *Children's Ethnic Socialization.* Newbury Park, Calif: Sage Publications; 1987:10–28.
20. Gilbert MJ. Cultural relevance in the delivery of human services. In: Keefe SE, ed. *Negotiating Ethnicity: The Impact of Anthropological Theory and Practice.* Washington, DC: National Association for the Practice of Anthropology; 1989;8:39–48.
21. Harwood A. *Rx: Spiritist as Needed. A Study of a Puerto Rican Community Mental Health Resource.* New York, NY: John Wiley and Sons; 1977.
22. Angel R, Guarnaccia P. Mind, body, and culture: somatization among Hispanics. *Soc Sci Med.* 1989;28:1229–1238.
23. Knox VJ, Shum K, McLaughlin D. Response to cold pressor pain and to acupuncture analgesia in Oriental and Occidental subjects. *Pain.* 1977;4:49–57.
24. Weisenberg M. *Pain: Clinical and Experimental Perspectives.* St. Louis, Mo: Mosby; 1975.
25. Lawlis G, Achterberg J, Kenner L, Kopetz K. Ethnic and sex differences in response to clinical and induced pain in chronic spinal pain patients. *Spine.* 1984;9:751–754.
26. Aronoff GM. *Evaluation and Treatment of Chronic Pain.* Baltimore, Md: Urban and Schwarzenberg; 1985.
27. Fox E, Melzack R. Comparison of transcutaneous electrical stimulation and acupuncture in the treatment of chronic pain. In: Bonica J, Albe-Fessard D, eds. *Advances in Pain Research and Therapy.* New York, NY: Raven Press; 1976:797–801.
28. Kotarba JA. *Chronic Pain: Its Social Dimensions.* Beverly Hills, Calif: Sage Publications; 1983.
29. Leroy PL. *Current Concepts in the Management of Chronic Pain.* Miami, Fla: Symposia Specialists; 1977.
30. Bates MS. *Biocultural Dimensions of Chronic Pain.* Ann Arbor, Mich: University Microfilms; 1988. Dissertation (University of Massachusetts).
31. Woodrow K, Friedman G, Siegelaub M, Collen M. Pain tolerance: differences according to age, sex, and race. *Psychosom Med.* 1972;34:548–555.
32. Reid V, Bush J. Ethnic Factors influencing pain expression: implications for clinical assessment. In: Miller TW, ed. *Chronic Pain.* Madison, Conn: Internal Universities Press, Inc; 1990:117–146.
33. Bates MS. Ethnicity and pain: a biocultural model. *Soc Sci Med.* 1987;24:47–50.
34. Bureau of the Census. *1980 Census of the Population.* Vol 1, chapter C, part 23: Massachusetts. Washington, DC: US Dept of Commerce; 1983.
35. Guagnano G, et al. Locus of control; demographic factors and their interactions. *J Soc Behav Personality.* 1986;1:365–380.
36. Sargent C. Between death and shame: dimensions of pain in Bariba culture. *Soc Sci Med.* 1986;19:1299–1304.

37. Sternbach RA, *Pain Patients' Traits and Treatments.* New York, NY: Academic Press; 1974.

38. Sternbach RA. Behavior therapy. In: Melzack R, Wall D. eds. *The Textbook of Pain.* New York, NY: Churchill Livingstone; 1984:800–805.

39. Zborowski M. *People in Pain.* San Francisco, Calif: Jossey-Bass; 1969.

40. Estes G, Zitzow D. Heritage consistency as a consideration in counseling Native Americans. Presented at the National Indian Educational Association Convention; November 1980; Dallas, Tex.

41. Spector RE. *Cultural Diversity in Health and Illness.* Norwalk, Conn: Appleton-Century-Crofts; 1985.

42. Coreil J, Marshall PA. Locus of illness control: a cross-cultural study. *Human Organization.* 1982;41:131–138.

43. Afflek G, et al. Appraisals of control and predictability in adapting to chronic diseases. *J Personality Soc Psychol.* 1987;54:273–279.

44. Lefcourt H. Locus of control and coping with life's events. In: Staub E, ed. *Personality.* Englewood Cliffs, NJ: Prentice Hall; 1980.

45. Rotter JB. *Generalized Expectancies for Internal Versus External Control of Reinforcement.* New York, NY: American Psychological Association Monographs; 1966.

46. Melzack R. The McGill Pain Questionnaire: major properties and scoring methods. *Pain.* 1975;1:277–299.

47. Melzack R. Measurement of the dimensions of pain experience. In: Bromm B, ed. *Pain Measurement in Man.* Amsterdam, The Netherlands: Elsevier Science Publishers; 1984:327–347.

48. Melzack R, Torgenson W. On the language of pain. *Anesthesiology.* 1971;34:50–59.

49. Turk DC, Rudy TE, Salovey P. The McGill Pain Questionnaire reconsidered: confirming the factor structure and examining appropriate uses. *Pain.* 1985;21:385–397.

50. Fotopoulos S, et al. Psychophysiological control of cancer pain. In: Bonica J, ed. *Advances in Pain Research and Therapy.* New York, NY: Raven Press; 1979:231–243.

51. Lahuerta J, Smith BA, Martinez-Lage JM. An adaptation of the McGill Pain Questionnaire to the Spanish language. *Schmerz.* 1982;3:132–134.

52. Kremer E, Atkinson S. Pain measurement construct validity of the affective dimensions of the McGill Pain Questionnaire with chronic benign pain patients. *Pain.* 1981;11:93–100.

53. Molina JC, Coppo C, del Docente P. The Argentine Pain Questionnaire. *Pain.* 1984;20(suppl):S42.

54. Prieto E, et al. The language of low back pain: factor structure of the McGill Pain Questionnaire. *Pain.* 1980;8:11–20.

55. Hsu F. *Psychological Anthropology.* Cambridge, Mass: Schenkman; 1972.

56. Mithun J. The role of the family in acculturation and assimilation in America: a psychocultural dimension. In: McCready W, ed. *Culture, Ethnicity, and Identity: Current Issues in Research.* New York, NY: Academic Press; 1983: 209–221.

57. Stein H. The culture of the patient as a red herring in clinical decision making: a case study. *Med Anthropol Q.* 1985;17:2–5.

58. Kleinman A. *Patients and Healers in the Context of Culture.* Berkeley, Calif: University of California Press; 1980.

59. Kleinman A. *Social Origins of Distress and Disease: Depression, Neurasthenia, and Pain in Modern China.* New Haven, Conn: Yale University Press; 1986.

60. Kleinman A, Eisenberg L, Good B. Clinical lessons from anthropologic and cross-cultural research. *Ann Intern Med.* 1978;88:251–258.

61. Westbrook MT, Nordholm LA, McGee JE. Cultural differences in reactions to patient behavior: a comparison of Swedish and Australian health professionals. *Soc Sci Med.* 1984;19:939–947.

62. Kores RC, Murphy WD, Rosenthal TL, Elias DB, North WC. Predicting outcome of chronic pain treatment via a modified self-efficacy scale. *Behav Res Therapy.* 1990; 28:165–169.

 **30**

A Case of Lead Poisoning from Folk Remedies in Mexican American Communities

Robert T. Trotter II

It is important to realize that not all medical remedies are helpful or even harmless. This is the case for both biomedicine and folk medicine. Physician-caused illness, called iatrogenic illness (Illich 1976), is a serious problem in the United States. Mistakes in hospital treatment—most often avoidable drug interactions—are a major cause of morbidity today. (The American Iatrogenic Association estimates that 80,000 deaths per year in the United States are in some way related to physician errors.) Illnesses caused by folk medical treatments are less well documented, but they certainly exist. For example, Marcia Inhorn (1994) has shown how both biomedical and ethnomedical treatments of infertility may actually add to the problem of tubal-factor infertility.

In general, medical anthropologists would expect that people would drop harmful treatments after they have had experience with them. But when the link between cause and effect is clouded—often because of a time delay in the effects—a faulty ethnomedical treatment might be continued. Also, because medical systems evolve, people often value novelty, and treatments are used (both in biomedicine and ethnomedicine) before they are completely tested.

This selection comes from a book of applied anthropology called Anthropological Praxis: Translating Knowledge into Action *(Wulff and Fiske 1987) that consists of first-person reports of how medical anthropologists' work made a difference in the world. To some students, the examples in* Anthropological Praxis *are self-congratulatory, but please do not let that stand in your way. This selection*

presents the case of a medical anthropologist who discovers a real public health threat in the course of a study and then takes action to remove that threat in his local area.

The folk medical problem of empacho, *dealt with here, is something that we will encounter again in selection 44. Because this illness is not recognized by standard biomedicine, people turn to folk medicine for cures. The problem of lead-based treatment in Latino folk medicine has persisted and is reported in the epidemiological literature (Weller et al. 1992). If you live in a multicultural urban area, it is easy to find folk medicine pharmacies—New Age shops,* botanicas, *Chinese pharmacies, or homeopathic drug stores—and as a student of medical anthropology, you should see what is inside.*

As you read this selection, consider these questions:

- *What are* greta *and* azarcon *used for? Do the people buying these medicines know what they are made of? Do you know what your over-the-counter medicines are made of?*

- *How did Robert Trotter combine his interests in a research study and social action in this case?*

- *Why was there a need for a "communication bridge" in this case? Was the gap more than between the Hispanic community and the Anglo community?*

- *Are medical anthropologists being ethnocentric when they identify negative aspects of folk medical practices?*

PROBLEM AND CLIENT

Three sources of lead poisoning most commonly affect children in the United States: eating lead-based paint chips, living and playing near a smelter where even the dust has a high lead content, and eating off pottery with an improperly treated lead glaze. This chapter describes the discovery of a fourth source of lead poisoning, one resulting from folk medicine practices in Mexican American communities.

In summer 1981, a team of emergency room health professionals in Los Angeles discovered an unusual case of lead poisoning. They treated a child with classic symptoms of heavy metal poisoning. When they pumped the child's stomach, they found a bright orange powder. Laboratory analysis of the powder determined that it was lead tetroxide (PbO_4) with an elemental lead content of more than 90 percent. After being strenuously questioned, the child's mother admitted giving the child a powdered remedy called *azarcon*. She also said that the powder was used to treat a folk illness called *empacho,* which translates roughly as a combination of indigestion and constipation. Empacho is believed by people who treat it to be caused by a bolus of food sticking to the intestinal wall. Unfortunately, this case was not handled in a culturally sensitive way, and the child was not brought back for follow-up. However, a general public health alert was sent out (see MMWR 1981, 1982; Trotter et al 1984).

As a result of the public health alert, a second case of lead poisoning from azarcon was discovered in Greeley, Colorado, by a nurse from the Sunrise Health Clinic who was culturally sensitive to the parents' claim that the child was not eating paint (the most commonly suspected cause). Having read about the azarcon case in Los Angeles, the nurse asked the mother if she was treating the child for empacho, and, when she answered yes, asked it the mother was using azarcon as a remedy. Analysis of the powder that the mother was keeping with the family's medicines confirmed that it was lead tetroxide.

Until this time, the use of lead as a home remedy had been assumed to occur only in isolated cases, and no anthropological input had been sought. However, additional questioning by the Los Angeles County Health Department and by individuals at the Sunrise Community Health Center turned up apparent widespread knowledge of azarcon in both Mexican American communities. The U.S. Public Health Service decided at this point that an anthropologist's study of this potential problem would be useful.

About six months after the azarcon problem was discovered, I was called by a friend who worked in the Region VI office for the Public Health Service (PHS) in Dallas. He asked me if I had ever heard of a remedy called azarcon while I was doing my research on Mexican American folk medicine. I had not. He then told me about the cases found in Los Angeles and Greeley and asked me to look for azarcon in south Texas.

I searched all the herb shops in four towns, including the one in the market in Reynosa, Mexico, and talked with *curanderos* (folk healers) living on the U.S.-Mexican border. I did not find azarcon nor did I find anyone who knew what it was. I reported this fact to my friend, and we both were relieved that the problem seemed to be confined to the western United States. Not long after I received a packet of information from the Los Angeles County Health Department, which had conducted a small survey on azarcon. Among other findings they had discovered some alternate names for the preparation. I went back to the herb shops to look for azarcon under its alternate names because the common names of remedies often change drastically from region to region.

The most important alternate name turned out to be *greta.* When I asked for greta in Texas I was sold a heavy yellow powder that, when analyzed, was found to be lead oxide (PbO) with an elemental lead content of approximately 90 percent. The shop owners told me that greta was used to treat empacho. So we now had confirmation that two related lead-based remedies were being used to treat empacho in Mexican American communities. In fact, a wholesale distributor in Texas, which was also selling over 200 other remedies to retail outlets, was supplying greta to more than 120 herb shops (*yerberias*). This finding drastically shaped both the scope and the content of the health education project that we started soon after this discovery. Because of the geographical scope of the problem and the multiple compounds involved, in the end six interacting clients utilized applied anthropology services to deal with the threat of greta and azarcon.

My first client was the Region VI Office of PHS. As previously described, it sponsored my initial narrowly focused ethnographic study to find azarcon—before our knowledge of greta. The second client group that requested my help was the task force formed to create and implement a health education project directed at eliminating the use of azarcon in Mexican American communities in Colorado and California. The project was sponsored through a federally funded migrant and community health center, the Sunrise Health Center, but was funded by the foundation of a private corporation. Our objective was to develop culturally sensitive health awareness materials that would reduce the risk of people using azarcon without attacking or denigrating the folk medical system. We knew that attacks on folk beliefs would produce strong resistance to the whole campaign and make people ignore our message. I was asked to participate because of my research on Mexican American folk medicine, in the hopes that my ethnographic data could be used to help design a health awareness campaign that would encourage a switch to nonpoisonous remedies.

The technique behind this approach has been successfully used by all major advertising agencies for decades: It is relatively easy to get people to switch from one product to another when both products perform the same function. It is difficult or impossible to get people to stop using a product for which there is a felt need, regardless of the known potential for harm for that product, unless one provides an acceptable alternative. Thus, it is easy to get a smoker to switch from Camel filters to Winstons but very hard to get that person to stop smoking altogether. So we decided that we would attempt to give people the alternative of switching from greta or azarcon to another remedy for empacho, such as *te de manzanilla* (chamomile), known to be harmless, rather than trying to get people to stop treating empacho altogether.

The discovery of greta use in Texas and Mexico produced a third client. The Food and Drug Administration (FDA) decided it needed basic ethnographic information on the use of greta. It wanted to know who used greta, what it was used for, how it was used, and where it could be purchased. Lead oxide is most commonly used as an industrial compound (as an adherent in marine paints) and as a color component in the paint used to make the "no passing" stripes on U.S. highways. It has never been considered either a food additive or a potential drug. Therefore, the FDA needed verifiable data that the compound was being used as a "drug." The FDA asked me to conduct a short, thorough ethnography in the herb shops where I had found the greta. This study included collecting samples and interviewing the owners (and a number of clients who wandered in to buy other remedies) about the ways that greta was used, what it was used to treat, how it was prepared, and the size of dose given for children and adults. These data allowed the FDA to determine that greta was a food additive and enabled it to exercise its authority to issue a Class I recall to ban the sale of these lead compounds as remedies. The information I gathered was important because herbal remedies do not normally fall under the jurisdiction of the FDA,[1] except in terms of the cleanliness requirements surrounding their packaging.

The discovery of greta in Texas caused the regional office of Health and Human Services (HHS) to request my assistance in creating and executing a survey along the U.S./Mexican border to discover how much knowledge people had about greta and azarcon and how many people used them. HHS felt that the use might be much more extensive than was suggested by the relatively small number of poisonings discovered in clinics. The survey indicated that as many as 10 percent of the Mexican American households along the border had at one time used greta or azarcon. The survey also turned up several other potentially toxic compounds that included mercury and laundry bluing (Trotter 1985).

The fifth group to request data was the Hidalgo County Health Care Corporation, a local migrant clinic. It asked for a survey to determine the level of greta and azarcon use in the local population compared with their clinic population. The HHS regional survey had only sampled clinic populations. The Hidalgo County research project involved simultaneously sampling at the clinics and in the communities from which the clinic population is derived. Over a two-

week period, a stratified random sample of informants at the clinic sites were given a questionnaire designed for the HHS regional survey. At the same time, a random stratified block cluster sample of households in the catchment communities were administered the same questionnaire. The results indicated that no significant difference existed between the two populations in terms of their knowledge about and use of greta and azarcon. The data showed trends that suggested that the clinic populations were more likely to treat folk illnesses than was the population at large.

My final client was the Migrant Health Service, a division of the PHS. The Migrant Health Service requested consultation on the necessity of a lead initiative for the entire United States, based on the results of the ethnographic and survey research conducted for other groups involved in the overall project. In the end, it was decided that a nationwide lead initiative was not necessary. Instead, the areas of high greta and azarcon use were targeted for a special initiative and received special notification of the problem.

PROCESS AND PLAYERS

The wide geographical distribution of greta and azarcon use, their employment as traditional remedies, and their inclusion in the treatment of a folk illness made this problem ideal for intervention by an anthropologist. Among other qualities, we tend to have a high ambiguity quotient: We tolerate poorly defined research objectives and virtually boundary-free problems that must be analyzed and solved simultaneously. The fact that the project rapidly developed a multiple-client base also made it very suitable for applied anthropology rather than for another social science. Anthropologists are often called upon to serve diverse, even conflicting, roles as culturebrokers. Multiple clients are no different from multiple community interest groups. Serving as a go-between in one setting develops the skills for doing so in any other setting.

From this perspective, my participation was requested by various clients because medical anthropologists have become known for being comfortable and competent in dealing with the types of issues presented by the greta and azarcon problem (problems that do not fit existing, well-defined categories or public health procedures). I did not become involved through a disguised or accidental process; my expertise was specifically sought because of the clients' recognition that they wanted a particular set of skills. This was particularly clear for the group creating the health education program. It deliberately sought an anthropologist with current knowledge about the Mexican American folk medical system. I was chosen because several people in the group had either read articles I had written or had heard me speak publicly about folk medicine. Likewise the migrant health program of PHS wanted someone with the same knowledge base, and I had previously worked with several of the individuals there.

My role evolved into a combination of researcher, consultant, communication bridge, and developer of program elements. My goal was to help create a culturally sensitive and effective method for reducing the use of these two folk remedies without interfering with the overall use of folk medicine. Another of my critical roles was that of information broker between the various client groups, some of which had not previously been in communication. Some of these groups had severe organizational barriers to communication with one another. One such barrier was simply organizational distance; the Washington-based migrant health officials only dealt with the local programs within certain contexts, such as regional and national meetings, or when a problem occurred in the operation of a clinic. I provided a good temporary (higher intensity) communication bridge to facilitate the exchange of information for this project. In the same way, the PHS and FDA had little need for contact, except for the temporary mutual need to solve different aspects of the greta/azarcon problem. But each of these groups found it useful to have the information available to, or available from, the others.

My final role was that of a scholar to publish the results of the study. The group developing the health education project wanted my findings published in order to disseminate the information about greta and azarcon as widely as possible. PHS wanted my results because it was finding it more and more difficult to put money into projects on the sole basis of an emotional appeal. The federal government (and increasing numbers of state and local governments) are reluctant to recognize "problems" that are not sufficiently documented and shown to be "real." One of the favored forms of documentation is publication in scientific journals. So following the normal process of publishing the results of an investigation allows an agency or organization to demonstrate a need for a specific program. The agency can support a request for a short-term (emergency) effort or can request a future increase in funds (or at least the maintenance of their prior funding levels). Scholarly documentation of problems and program effectiveness is particularly useful for programs that receive federal funds on an annual basis. When the preliminary results of my ethnographic research were published in *Medical Anthropology Quarterly* (Trotter et al. 1984), the officials

in the migrant health program felt they could reasonably justify the expenditure of funds to deal with the part of the greta and azarcon problem that affected their clients.

Publication can provide other long-term benefits. Naming members of the nonscholar staff as co-authors of publications not only gives them appropriate recognition for their contributions but also can increase the opportunities for future funding. Sharing a publication and its visibility tends to be excellent public relations. Clients can use the prestige of being an author in the development of their own careers. This tends to improve the chances of the anthropologist securing additional consultant work from that source. It produces a win/win situation.

RESULTS AND EVALUATION

Because this project involved several clients, it also had multiple results and multiple levels of outcomes. The Sunrise Clinic health education project resulted in considerable media exposure on the existence and dangers of greta and azarcon. This exposure included radio public service announcements broadcast on Spanish radio stations, a special television program aired in Los Angeles county, and an information packet sent to migrant clinics. These informational campaigns contained the suggestion that people switch to other remedies because greta and azarcon were hazardous.

The other major accomplishment of the Sunrise project was the production and distribution of a poster designed by Mexican American commercial design students at Pan American University. The students were provided an in-depth briefing on the problem and our investigation; then were turned loose to create a culturally appropriate poster. A small cash prize was given to the student with the best design. Twenty posters were completed and turned over to a group of Mexican American clients and staff at the clinic to judge for most effective design. The final poster, which combines the elements in two of the submissions, uses the culturally emotive symbol of La Meurte (a skeleton) to warn of the dangers of the use of greta and azarcon. The dominant impact of the poster is visual/emotional—to trigger the client into asking the clinic staff about greta and azarcon. The group felt that too many words would dilute the impact of the poster, so we did not attempt to incorporate the theme of product switch into the design. Posters with this design have been placed in over 5,000 clinics and other public access sites in each state with a concentration of Mexican Americans.[2]

The success of the overall campaign is demonstrated by the fact that some two years after the project was completed, interest had died down, and both greta and azarcon were hard to find in the United States. Another measure of the campaign's lasting success is illustrated by the doctor in El Paso who treated a child with classic lead poisoning symptoms. Not only did he recognize the probable cause of the symptoms (lead poisoning has such common symptoms that it is rarely suspected), he immediately asked the mother if the child was being treated with greta or azarcon. It turned out to be greta, and the child was immediately treated, with no serious long-term problems. The doctor was very happy that he had caught a problem that others might have missed, and we were pleased to discover that the project had at least a qualitative measure of success. Based on anecdotal information, the project appears to have had an important effect on public knowledge about these remedies and has reduced their use by some degree. However, no scientific effort was made to determine exactly how much change has occurred. Even with the increased information, these compounds will continue to be used regardless of the effectiveness of the campaign. Knowledge does not always drive behavior, as is evident in all the results of nonsmoking campaigns.

The work completed for the FDA was successful within the parameters set by the client. The data were sufficient to allow the agency to determine that the consumption of greta and azarcon fell within their jurisdiction, and it was able to successfully conduct a recall. Additionally, the data and the agency's recognition of its validity allow it to deal with future incidences of the sale of these two compounds as home remedies. This is a positive benefit because reuse of the compound is virtually assured by the fact that Mexico is the primary source of folk knowledge about the use of greta and azarcon and the source of the compounds themselves. Unfortunately, the public health sector in Mexico has not been able to devote many resources to this particular problem.

My work for the regional office of HHS resulted in data that allowed policy to be set and lead screening procedures to be amended at both national and regional levels to deal with this new source of lead poisoning. The basic policies dictated the creation of the new lead protocols. The agency pinpointed potential areas of high usage of the compounds and recommended cost-effective lead screening programs to be undertaken at selected sites. The screening is accomplished by drawing small samples of blood and testing it chemically for the effects or presence of lead. Because of the survey and accompanying ethnographic data the lead screening protocols for migrant and public health services were modified to include

ethnomedical sources of poisoning, such as greta and azarcon. Clinics were alerted to this source, and a growing number of cases have subsequently been discovered that would have otherwise been overlooked.

The data provided to HHS also permitted cost avoidances. Just after the discovery of greta and azarcon there was a rush to do something, which included a preliminary decision to buy some very expensive equipment for a large number of clinics. However, the data allowed a more cost effective decision to be made: to only do lead screening in those areas where there was a demonstrated risk. This approach avoided the purchase of equipment that would have been misused or not used at all because no funds were available to train clinic staffs to use these complex instruments after they were purchased.

The survey of greta and azarcon use (Trotter 1985) turned out to be an excellent educational and informational device. It was conducted at thirty migrant and public health clinics in Texas, New Mexico, and Arizona. As a result of the open-ended ethnographic structuring of the survey instrument, several other potentially toxic compounds, with regional but not universal usage, were also discovered. This finding alerted the local clinics both to the current use of home treatments of illnesses in their area and to some of the specific health education needs of their clients. In my opinion, the education benefits of conducting this type of survey have an untapped potential as an educational device for health care providers.

A project is only half successful, regardless of its results, if it does not produce additional opportunities for anthropologists to practice anthropology. These serendipitous results can be as simple as further work for the same client or as important as the development of new theories for the discipline. Yet rarely are these spin-offs mentioned or considered an important aspect of anthropological praxis. Even when a project has clear closure (rare for many of the types of applied problems tackled by anthropologists), the process of solving the problem should set up personal and professional relationships that carry beyond that temporary closure. Regardless of the products they produce, successful applied scientists are process oriented; they are constantly moving from one point on a continuum to the next.

The additional opportunities created by the greta and azarcon problem may have more long-lasting effects on the cross-cultural delivery of health care in the United States than the original projects had. The first spin-off was an invitation to participate in a program review for the Migrant Health Services division of PHS in Washington, D.C. The program review brought together a group of experts from around the United States to review, revise, and set new policies for the delivery of health care services in all migrant health clinics in the United States. The policies that were adopted are strongly cross cultural. They include the development of a Public Health Service Corps provider orientation package that specifically addresses cultural sensitivity, basic anthropological concepts of culture, and awareness of the qualitative aspects of migrant lifestyles, health beliefs, and medical needs. I am in the process of developing this package. Other policies and goals include statements on program coordination, continuity of care, information needs (e.g., research), and services. All have been shaped by the participation of anthropologists in the policy-making body.

Additionally, Indiana Health Centers, Inc., a private, nonprofit corporation that runs the migrant health clinics in Indiana, asked me to spend a week as a consultant for its program. The primary purpose of the consultation was to conduct public and clinic seminars on ethnomedicine and its importance to the delivery of health care to Mexican Americans. A latent purpose was to legitimize the use of culturally appropriate health services and to integrate them into the scientific medical system. One indication that the process worked is the clinic's decision to incorporate four of the most common Mexican American folk illnesses into their diagnostic system, which includes a computer coding and retrieval system. At the end of the year, the clinics will use these to set goals, determine funding and educational needs, and determine policy for the program, along with all other diagnostic data derived from their computer system.

To disperse the data as widely and rapidly as possible, four different articles on greta and azarcon were submitted to a variety of journals. Each article was targeted for a particular audience. The most important audiences were thought to be health professionals, medical anthropologists, public health personnel, and an international pharmacological audience. Each audience needed to know about the data and had an opportunity to help solve the problem of lead poisoning caused by folk remedies. However, this process of multiple submissions conflicts directly with the practice of avoiding prior publication.

The Hidalgo County Health Care Corporation was provided with reports showing that greta and azarcon use was comparable between their clinic and catchment populations. These data were also passed along to the regional and national offices of PHS. In this case the client used the data to create priorities for the next funding cycle. Each funding request requires goals and priorities, and better funding opportunities exist if the clinic demonstrates changing as well as expanding needs and services, especially in the area of patient education. The data allowed it to successfully compete for funding for its patient education goals by demonstrating a need for further health education on home remedies.

Perhaps the most important overall result of this project was the increased awareness of the utility of anthropology in solving culturally related health care problems in at least one segment of the medical care delivery system. For many years anthropologists have been saying that knowledge of folk medicine was important to the delivery of health care. But the only examples of how such knowledge was useful were couched in terms of "better rapport" with patients, "potentially reducing recidivism," or were tied to the "interface between culture and psychological processes." Patient rapport is an abominably low priority for practicing physicians and for most health clinics that are experiencing a patient overload. Likewise the cultural/psychological aspect has low prestige and is of interest to a small group of practitioners but not to the larger group dealing with physical medicine.

Now anthropologists are becoming visible to the greater part of medicine. Our discovery of the use of greta and azarcon and the subsequent discoveries that similar remedies are causing lead poisoning in Hmong, Saudi Arabian, and Chinese communities have finally demonstrated a clear link between anthropological research and the dominant biophysical side of modern medicine. Anthropological knowledge, research methods, and theoretical orientations are finally being used to solve epidemiological problems overlooked by the established disciplines. For some of our potential clients, this approach, for the first time, makes anthropology a potentially valuable source for consultation and for funding.

I was also invited by the Pennsylvania Department of Education, Migrant Education Division, to participate in its Project HAPPIER (Health Awareness Patterns Preventing Illness and Encouraging Responsibility). Project HAPPIER, which has a national scope, is funded through discretionary (143c) funds from the Office of the Secretary of Education. The objective of the project was to provide a major health resource guide and the data necessary to target health education in migrant clinics and for migrant educators, nationwide. My initial role was to conduct an analysis of national migrant health education needs, including an eight-state survey of migrant health beliefs and health education needs, as seen from the perspective of the migrants themselves. Although the survey provided excellent information, several important cultural groups were not well represented. Therefore, the following year I helped conduct a separate needs assessment in Puerto Rico to gather data on one of the underrepresented groups. The goals of the surveys were to improve our knowledge about migrant health status in all three migrant streams and to provide information that would allow the states and Puerto Rico to offer migrant children sufficient health education to improve the health status of the current and the next migrant generation. The preliminary results of the study indicate that migrants both want and need health education. This finding points up the possibility of exploring a number of areas for research and program development (spin-offs from spin-offs).

Other opportunities that resulted from the original project included the more traditional requests for speaking engagements, lectures, and so on. These occasions afforded visibility that created new project opportunities and acted as a source of income. In most academic settings these activities also count toward merit and promotion points.

Although it is very important to direct one's best effort toward each project, I feel that the best applied anthropologists also follow what I call the "basic fission theory of anthropological praxis." Each project undertaken by an applied anthropologist should produce at least four others (up to the capacity, skill, and time commitment available to the individual anthropologist). One indicator of success in anthropological praxis is a continued demand for the services offered; it is easiest to generate this demand by current success. An anthropologist should look for spin-offs during a project, not just after it is completed.

THE ANTHROPOLOGICAL DIFFERENCE

I believe that the anthropological difference I added to the greta/azarcon project comes from the training that all anthropologists receive. It includes our strong focus on culture combined with our willingness to innovate, to look for explanations in areas that have been neglected by other investigators. The difference is not so much a part of anthropological theory and methods as it is a part of the personal orientation many of us have and that we try to pass along to others. For example, the health officials who originally investigated the case of lead poisoning in Greeley assumed that the little girl could only have contracted lead poisoning in the same way all other children get lead poisoning—from the environment.[3] In her case, the only accessible source of lead was a fence some 200 yards from her house. Although her parents insisted that she never played near that fence, they were ignored until the child had gone through chelation therapy and, in a follow-up screening, was determined to have re-elevated blood lead levels without access to the fence. Then the publicity on the California case caused a culturally sensitive

worker (who had been exposed to transcultural nursing concepts) to ask about azarcon, and the case was solved.

Another anthropological contribution to this project was in the design and administration of the research requested by the clients. The methodological contributions an anthropologist can make to a project may be as important or even more important to the client than his or her contributions of theory. It is relatively easy to find someone who has a theoretical explanation for known behavior; it is also easy to find someone who can administer surveys. It is much harder to find someone who can combine ethnographic data collection and theory grounded in real behavior with survey methodology that can determine the scope of a behavior. These projects demanded both types of expertise. I had to discover both the basic patterns of and reasons for the continued use of home remedies in an urban-industrial society and a cultural context within which the educational and intervention process could take place. At the same time, I had the vitally important task of discovering how widespread the use of these remedies had become and if other hazardous remedies were being used to treat the same folk illness. A combination of ethnography and survey accomplished these goals.

The final area of anthropological contribution was in the design of the educational material and the programmatic responses to the problem of greta and azarcon. The major contribution there was to ensure that the materials used or developed were culturally appropriate rather than trying to force inappropriate change on people who would resent it, making the effort useless in the long run.

In some ways this cluster of projects indicates a potential new era for anthropology in health-related fields. In these instances the services of an anthropologist were deliberately sought because of the clients' sophisticated knowledge of the type of services they needed and the exact type of expertise they wanted. They needed descriptive ethnographic data to determine a method in which to produce a product switch from one remedy to other, nontoxic ones. In addition they needed a survey built on a solid ethnographic base that did not presume a closed field of knowledge about the subject. More and more of today's anthropologists are equally comfortable with quantitative and qualitative methods of data collection. This combination of research methods is actually stronger than either pure ethnography or pure statistical analysis, but it requires a much more methodologically sophisticated researcher. In some ways, the flexibility of approach—an eclectic orientation to methodology and analysis—has always marked the anthropological difference and may herald a subtle but real advantage not only for anthropological praxis but also for the future employment of anthropologists in many industries. If, as many claim, we are now in an information-driven age, anthropologists should have an advantage in the information service market, given the importance or centrality of communications research and information handling in the history of anthropology.

NOTES

1. Most of the people buying and selling greta and azarcon believe they are herbal compounds, probably because the overwhelming majority of Mexican American home remedies are botanicals.
2. Other Hispanic groups were not targeted for this campaign. A broad search among anthropologists working with other Hispanic populations in the United States indicated that the two compounds were not present in their ethnomedical pharmacopoeias.
3. Two traditional sources of lead poisoning are the consumption of lead paint chips, primarily by children living in dilapidated urban areas, and occupational exposure to high concentrations of lead by workers and children of workers in high lead use industries, such as battery manufacturing. The third source is environmental pollution.

The most common victims of this type of poisoning are children whose normal hand-to-mouth activities give them an overdose of lead from playing on soil with a high lead content (such as that near heavily traveled roads or industries such as smelters that have high lead emission levels). Epidemiological investigations are conducted when a child or adult is detected as having high blood lead levels. These investigations invariably concentrate on discovering which of these sources caused the problem.

REFERENCES

Ackerman et al. 1982. Lead Poisoning from Lead Tetroxide Used as a Folk Remedy—Colorado. *MMWR* (Center for Disease Control, Morbidity and Mortality Weekly Report) 30(52):647–648.

Trotter, Robert T., II. 1985. Greta and Azarcon: A Survey of Episodic Lead Poisoning from a Folk Remedy. *Human Organization* 44(1):64–72.

Trotter, Robert T., II, Alan Ackerman, Dorothy Rodman, Abel Martinez, and Frank Sorvillo. 1984. Azarcon and Greta: Ethnomedical Solution to an Epidemiological Mystery. *Medical Anthropology Quarterly* 14(3):3,18.

Vashistha, et al. 1981. Use of Lead Tetroxide as a Folk Remedy for Gastrointestinal Illness. *MMWR* 30(43):546–547.

 31

Why Does Juan García Have a Drinking Problem?
The Perspective of Critical Medical Anthropology

Merrill Singer
Freddie Valentín
Hans Baer
Zhongke Jia

. . . anthropology, in spite of its limitations, may play a part in documenting what the West has done to other societies.
—SIDNEY MINTZ (1989:794)

We will try to be objective but in no way will we be impartial.
—MANUEL MALDONADO-DENIS (1980:26)

Medical anthropological studies of health and ethnicity can be accomplished using a wide array of theoretical perspec-

tives. This selection uses the political-economic perspective of critical medical anthropology (CMA) to examine the question of alcohol abuse in a Puerto Rican community in Hartford, Connecticut. Three of the authors are employees of the Hispanic Health Council, whose work we encountered in selection 24. The council's research and projects focus on ethnic communities that themselves reflect cultural varia-tion (Cubans, Mexicans, Puerto Ricans, Dominicans, and so on). From the perspective of CMA, ethnicity is a variable that must be understood in the context of class stratification and international political-economic relations. To understand why a particular Puerto Rican man has a drinking problem, the authors argue, it is first necessary to recognize the wider, macro context.

The disease concept of alcoholism is discussed in the first part of this selection. This is a modern idea that medicalizes an individual's "out of control" behavior. As a disease, alcoholism does not provoke the same moral judgment as it did earlier this century in the United States. Recently, alcoholism has been discussed using the model of an addiction to a toxic substance, again emphasizing the individual level. These medical models clearly have explanatory power, but the social epidemiological distribution of heavy drinking or problem drinking is not random. There are larger reasons—political, economic, historical, and social—why some people are more at risk for this problem. The CMA approach examines these other factors.

Notice that the research methodologies used by these CMA researchers are not very different from standard med-

ical social science; in this example, the data set is based on interviews with a random sample of men from an ethnic enclave. But the interpretation of the data emphasizes the macro factors.

As you read this selection, consider these questions:

- *Given the political-economic argument the authors make, how can the variation in problem drinking rates between ethnic groups be explained?*

- *How did Juan García's life compare with the American dream? How do you think García would have explained his own drinking problem?*

- *How does this analysis show the relatedness of ethnicity and social class?*

- *Given the explanation of the health problem here by the CMA perspective, what kinds of solutions are possible?*

- *Why does the Alcoholics Anonymous program work? Do you think it is cross-culturally valid?*

Critical medical anthropology as a named theoretical perspective is about a decade old (Baer and Singer 1982), although its main roots within the subdiscipline, as expressed in the work of researchers like Soheir Morsy, Alan Young, Anthony Thomas, and Ronald Frankenberg, are somewhat older. Because of its links to the social analysis of Marx and Engels, and because it began as a challenge to medical anthropology, critical medical anthropology has been a somewhat controversial approach. Those who do not embrace it have issued a number of potentially damaging critiques, including the argument that critical medical anthropology: (1) is not suited to the applied and practical agenda of medical anthropology; (2) does not foster scientific research; (3) tends to be concentrated on macro-level systems and hence overlooks the lived experience of illness sufferers; (4) does not effectively demonstrate the links between microprocesses and macro-forces; and (5) is a passing trend whose popularity rests primarily on anthropology's fickle tendency to follow fashion. . . .

. . . Consequently, this paper, which is concerned with articulating the perspective of critical medical anthropology: targets an applied issue; is based on empirical research; incorporates the individual level; is concerned with showing the direct casual links between on-the-ground sociocultural/behavioral patterns and the macro-level; and situates its approach within the broader perspective of the political economy of health, which is at least as old as anthropology itself.[1]

In this paper we examine the health issue of problem drinking among Puerto Rican men. Over the years, medical anthropologists have exhibited an enduring interest in substance use and abuse, although attention has been especially concentrated since the early 1970s (Agar 1973; Bennett 1988; Douglas 1987; Heath 1976, 1978, 1980, 1987a, 1987b; Partridge 1978), producing both the Alcohol and Drug Study Group of the Society for Medical Anthropology in 1979, and a rapid expansion of the anthropological substance literature in recent years. Anthropologists bring a range of perspectives to the study of drinking in particular, and they have made a number of significant contributions to this field. However, from the viewpoint of critical medical anthropology, we have argued that

the anthropological examination of drinking has failed to systematically consider the world-transforming effects of a global market and the global labor processes associated with the evolution of the capitalist mode of production. Anthropological concentration on the intricacies of individual cases, while a necessary and useful method for appreciating the rich detail of cultural variation and insider understandings, has somewhat blinded researchers to the uniform processes underlying global social change, including changes in drinking patterns. While the literature notes some of the effects of incorporation into the capitalist world-system, rarely does it attempt to comprehend alcoholism in terms of the specific dynamics of this system. Rather, the central thrust has been to locate problem drinking within the context of normative drinking and normative drinking within the context of prevailing local cultural patterns. (Singer 1986a:115)

Although anthropological contribution to the U.S. Latino drinking literature has been somewhat limited, a number of studies are available (Ames and Mora 1988; Gordon 1978, 1981, 1985a; Gilbert 1985, 1987, 1988; Gilbert and Cervantes 1987; Page et al. 1985; Singer and Borrero 1984; Singer, Davison and Yalin 1987; Trotter 1982, 1985; Trotter and Chavira 1978). To date, most studies have been concerned with Mexican Americans. Drinking among Puerto Rican men has been a relatively neglected topic, although it has been suggested that this population is particularly at risk for alcohol-related problems (Abad and Suares 1974).

The goal of this paper is to deepen our understanding of problem drinking among Puerto Rican men by bringing to bear the perspective of critical medical anthropology. We begin with a review of the origin and perspective of critical medical anthropology after which we present the case of Juan García (pseudonym), a Puerto Rican man who in 1971 died with a bottle in his hand and booze in his belly. Following a location of this case in its historic and political-economic contexts, we present findings from two community studies[2] of drinking behavior and drinking-related health and social consequences among Puerto Rican men and adolescents to demonstrate the representativeness of the case material. In this paper, it is argued that the holistic model of critical medical anthropology advances our understanding beyond narrow psychologistic or other approaches commonly employed in social scientific alcohol research. More broadly, we assert this perspective is useful in examining a wide range of topics of concern to the subdiscipline.

. . .

Specific concern within the political-economic perspective with issues of health—including, it bears noting, the special topic of problem drinking—can be traced on the one hand to Frederick Engels' study of the working class of Manchester and on the other to Rudolf Virchow's examination of a typhus epidemic in East Prussia. Both of these seminal studies, which possibly constitute the earliest examples of medical anthropology field work, occurred in the 1840s. Each of these researchers undertook an intensive examination of local conditions, using ethnographic observation and informal interviewing, and attempted to describe and interpret research findings in light of broader political and economic forces. The current study, in fact, can be read as an extension and elaboration of the approach developed by Engels and Virchow in their respective work. Specifically, our analysis of problem drinking among Puerto Rican men, as well as studies

of mood-altering substance use by other critical medical anthropologists (e.g., Stebbins 1987, 1990), is directly influenced by Engels' examination of drinking and opiate use in his Manchester study.

Beyond theory, critical medical anthropology is committed inherently to the development of appropriate practical expression. Indeed, the data for this essay were drawn from research that Singer and Valentín have conducted over the last seven years through the Hispanic Health Council, a community action agency dedicated to creating short- and long-term health improvements in the Latino community of Hartford, CT and beyond (e.g., Singer, Irazzary, and Schensul 1990; Singer et al. 1991). Critical medical anthropology rejects a simple dichotomy between "anthropology of medicine" and "anthropology in medicine" that separates theoretical from applied objectives. Rather, critical medical anthropologists seek to place their expertise at the disposal of labor unions, peace organizations, environmental groups, ethnic community agencies, women's health collectives, health consumer associations, self-help and self-care movements, alternative health efforts, national liberation struggles, and other bodies or initiatives that aim to liberate people from oppressive health and social conditions. In sum, through their theoretical and applied work, critical medical anthropologists strive to contribute to the larger effort to create a new health system that will "serve the people," including the area of alcoholism, which has proven to be an especially intractable problem under particular social conditions.[3] . . .

. . . The medicalization of problem drinking, however thoroughly institutionalized at this point, involved a process that began in 1785 with Benjamin Rush (Rush 1785/1943) but was only completed relatively recently. As the National Council on Alcoholism stated in an educational pamphlet a number of years ago: "The main task of those working to combat alcoholism . . . is to remove the stigma from this disease and make it as 'respectable' as other major diseases such as cancer and tuberculosis" (quoted in Davies 1979:449). A significant step in this process was a 1944 statement of the American Hospital Association proposing that "the primary attack on alcoholism should be through the general hospital" (quoted in Chafetz and Yoerg 1977:599). Four years later, the World Health Organization included alcoholism in its International Classification of Diseases. But it was not until 1956 that the American Medical Association declared alcoholism to be an officially recognized disease in U.S. biomedicine. Four years later, E. M. Jellinek published his seminal book, *The Disease Concept of Alcoholism*. Finally, in 1971 the National Institute on Alcohol Abuse and Alcoholism was established "premised on the belief that alcoholism is a disease and an important health problem" (Conrad and Schneider 1980:108).

Since then, the disease concept has become "everyone's official dogma, with medical organizations, alcoholics themselves, and well-meaning people speaking on their behalf urging governments and employers to accept and act on its implications" (Kendell 1979:367). And with notable success! As Schaefer (1982:302) points out, "Alcoholism is a growth industry. Empty hospital beds are turned into alcoholism 'slots'. The disease concept has become . . . integrated into the political and economic consciousness." While ambiguity remains about how much blame to lay at the feet of the drinker for causing his/her own problems, research indicates that the majority of people in the U.S. accept alcoholism as a bonafide if confusing disease (Mulford and Miller 1964; Chrisman 1985).

. . .

From the perspective of critical medical anthropology, the conventional disease model of alcoholism must be understood as an ideological construct comprehensible only in terms of the historic and political-economic contexts of its origin (see Conrad and Schneider 1980; Mishler 1981). The disease concept achieved several things, including: (1) offering "a plausible solution to the apparent irrationality of . . . [problem drinking] behavior" (Conrad and Schneider 1980:87); (2) guaranteeing social status as well as a livelihood to a wide array of individuals, institutions, and organizations, within and outside of biomedicine (Trice and Roman 1972); and (3) limiting the growing burden on the criminal justice system produced by public drunkenness, the most common arrest made by police nationally (Park 1983). In the perspective of critical medical anthropology, however, it hinders *exploration of alternative, politically more challenging understandings of destructive drinking* (Singer 1986a). This point is argued below by presenting the case of Juan García in terms of contrasting conventional psychologistic and critical medical anthropological interpretations.

THE CASE OF JUAN GARCÍA

Juan was born in Puerto Rico in 1909. The offspring of an adulterous relationship, he deeply resented his father. At age eight, Juan's mother died and he went to live with an aunt, and later, after his father died, was raised by his father's wife. As expression of his undying hatred of his father, Juan took his mother's surname, García.

As a young man, he became romantically involved with a cousin named Zoraida, who had been deserted with a small daughter by her husband. They lived together for a number of years in a tiny wooden shack, eking out a meager living farming a small plot of land. Then one day, Zoraida's ex-husband came and took his daughter away. Because of his wealth and social standing, there was little Juan and Zoraida could do. In resigning themselves to the loss, they began a new family of their own.

Over the years, Zoraida bore 19 children with Juan, although most did not survive infancy. According to Juan's daughter, who was the source of our information about Juan:

> My mother went to a spiritual healer in Puerto Rico and they told her witchcraft had been done on her, and that all her children born in Puerto Rico would die; her children would only survive if she crossed water.

Given their intensely spiritual perspective, the couple decided to leave Puerto Rico and migrate "across water" to the US. It was to New York, to the burgeoning Puerto Rican community in Brooklyn, that Juan and Zoraida moved in 1946.

New to U.S. society and to urban life, Juan had great difficulty finding employment. Unskilled and uneducated, and monolingual in Spanish, he was only able to find manual labor at low wages. Eventually, he began working as a janitor in an appliance factory. Here, a fellow worker taught him to draft blueprints, enabling him to move up to the position of draftsman.

Juan's daughter remembers her parents as strict disciplinarians with a strong bent for privacy. Still, family life was stable and reasonably comfortable until Juan lost his job when the appliance factory where he worked moved out of state. At the time, he was in his mid-fifties and despite his efforts was never again able to locate steady employment. At first he received unemployment benefits, but when these ran out, the García family was forced to go on welfare. This greatly embarrassed Juan. Always a heavy drinker, he now began to drink and act abusively. According to his daughter:

> A big cloud came over us and everything kept getting worse and worse in the house. This was 1964, 1965, 1966. . . . The pressure would work on him and he used to drink and then beat my mother. But my mother wouldn't hit him back. . . . I went a year and a half without speaking to my father. He would say that I wasn't his daughter. We respected our father, but he lost our respect cause of the way he used to treat us. He would beat me and I would curse at him. . . . When my mother couldn't take the pressure any more, she would drink too. . . . My parents would get into fights and we had to get in between. Once they had a fight and my father moved out.

By the time Juan died of alcohol-related causes in 1971, he was a broken man, impoverished, friendless, and isolated from his family.

If we think of problem drinking as an individual problem, then it makes sense to say that Juan suffered from a behavioral disorder characterized by a preoccupation with alcohol to the detriment of physical and mental health, by a loss of control over drinking, and by a self-destructive attitude in dealing with personal relationships and life situations. Moreover, there is evidence that he was an insecure, emotionally immature individual who used alcohol as a crutch to support himself in the face of adversity. Finally, without probing too deeply, we even can find, in Juan's troubled relationship with his father, a basis in infantile experience for the development of these destructive patterns. In short, in professional alcohol treatment circles, among many recovered alcoholics, and in society generally, Juan could be diagnosed as having suffered from the disease of alcoholism.

In so labeling him, however, do we hide more than we reveal? By remaining at the level of the individual actor, that is, by locating Juan's problem *within* Juan, do we not pretend that the events of his life and the nature of his drinking make sense separate from their wider historic and political-economic contexts? As Wolf (1982) reminds us, approaches that disassemble interconnected social processes and fail to reassemble them falsify reality. Only by placing the subjects of our investigation "back into the field from which they were abstracted," he argues, "can we hope to avoid misleading inferences and increase our share of understanding" (Wolf 1982:3). To really make sense of Juan's drinking, to move beyond individualized and privatized formulations, to avoid artificial and unsatisfying psychologistic labeling, the critical perspective moves to the wider field, to an historic and political-economic appraisal of Puerto Ricans and alcohol.

HISTORIC AND POLITICAL ECONOMIC CONTEXT

When Columbus first set foot on Puerto Rico on November 19, 1493, he found a horticultural tribal society possessed of alcohol but devoid of alcoholism. While there is limited information on this period, based on the wider ethnographic record it is almost certain that the consumption of fermented beverages by the indigenous Taíno (Arawak) and Carib peoples of Puerto Rico was socially sanctioned and controlled, and produced little in the way of health or social problems. As Davila (1987:10) writes, the available literature suggests that "the Taíno made beer from a

fermentable root crop called manioc, and . . . they might also have fermented some of the fruits they grew. However, the existing evidence suggests that alcohol was used more in a ritual context than in a social one." Heath notes that among many indigenous peoples of what was to become Latin America, periodic fiestas in which most of the adults drank until intoxicated was a common pattern. However, "both drinking and drunkenness were socially approved in the context of veneration of major deities, as an integral part of significant agricultural ceremonies, or in celebration of important events in the lives of local leaders" (Heath 1984:9). At times other than these special occasions, alcohol consumption was limited and nondisruptive, controlled by rather than a threat to the social group.

These and other features of Arawak life greatly impressed Columbus. He also was quick to notice the limited military capacity of the Indians, given their lack of metal weapons. Setting the tone for what was to follow, in one of his first log entries describing the Arawak, Columbus noted: "With fifty men we could subjugate them all and make them do whatever we want" (recorded in Zinn 1980:1). In effect, this was soon to happen, prompted by the discovery of gold on the Island. Under the Spanish *encomienda* system, ostensibly set up to "protect" the Indians and assimilate them to Spanish culture, indigenous men, women and children were forced to work long hours in Spanish mines. Within 100 years of the arrival of the Columbus, most of the indigenous people were gone, victims of the first phase of "primitive accumulation" by the emergent capitalist economy of Europe.

Once the gold mines were exhausted, the island of Puerto Rico, like its neighbors, became a center of sugar production for export to the European market (History Task Force 1979). Almost unknown in Europe before the thirteenth century, 300 years later sugar was a staple of the European diet. Along with its derivatives, molasses and rum, it became one of the substances Mintz (1971) has termed the "proletarian hunger-killers" during the take-off phase of the Industrial Revolution. In time, rum became an essential part of the diet for the rural laboring classes of Puerto Rico.

This process was facilitated by two factors. First, alcohol consumption among Spanish settlers was a normal part of everyday activity. Prior to colonial contact, in fact, the Spanish had little access to mood-altering substances other than alcohol. As Heath (1984:14) indicates, among the Spanish, alcoholic beverages were consumed "to relieve thirst, with meals, and as a regular refreshment, in all of the ways that coffee, tea, water, or soft drinks are now used. . . ." Alcohol "thus permeated every aspect of . . . life" among the settlers (Davila 1987:11). Second, there was a daily distribution of rum to day workers and slaves on the sugar plantations (Mintz 1971). Not until 1609 did King Felipe III of Spain forbid the use of alcohol as a medium for the payment of Indian laborers (Heath 1984). Rum distilleries, in fact, were one of the few industrial enterprises launched by the Spanish during their several hundred year reign in Puerto Rico. Commercial production was supplemented by a home brew called *ron cañita* (little cane rum) made with a locally crafted still called an *alambique* and widely consumed among poor and working people (Carrion 1983). . . .

The U.S. acquisition of Puerto Rico in 1898 as war booty from the Spanish-American War—an event marking the beginning of "a major political realignment of world capitalism" (Bonilla 1985:152)—ushered in a new phase in Puerto Rican history and Puerto Rican drinking. At the moment of the U.S. invasion of Puerto Rico, 91% of the land under cultivation was owned by its occupants and an equal percentage of the existing farms were possessed by locally resident farmers (Diffie and Diffie 1931). Intervention, as Mintz (1974) has shown, produced a radical increase in the concentration of agricultural lands, the extension of areas devoted to commercial cultivation for export, and the mechanization of agricultural production processes. Indeed, it was through gaining control over sugar and the related production "that the United States consolidated its economic hegemony over the Island" (History Task Force 1979:95). Shortly after assuming office, Guy V. Henry, the U.S. appointed Military Governor of Puerto Rico, issued three rulings that facilitated this process: a freeze on credit, a devaluation of the peso, and a fix on land prices. Devaluation and the credit freeze made it impossible for farmers to meet their business expenses. As a result, they were forced to sell their property to pay their debts and thousands of small proprietors went out of business. The fix on land prices ensured that farm lands would be available at artificially low prices for interested buyers. At the time, the principal buyers in the market were either North American corporations or Puerto Rican companies directly linked to U.S. commerce. As a result, within "the short span of four years, four North American corporations . . . dedicated to sugar production came to control directly [275,030 square meters] of agricultural land" (Herrero, Sánchez, and Gutierrez 1975:56). As contrasted with the rural situation prior to U.S. intervention, by 1926 four out of five Puerto Ricans were landless (Clark 1930). The inevitable sequel to the consolidation of coastal flat lands for sugar cane plantations was a large migration out of the mountains to the coast, and the formation of "a vast rural proletariat, whose existence was determined by seasonal employment" (Maldonado-Denis 1976:44).

In the newly expanded labor force of sugar cane workers, a group that formed a large percentage of the Puerto Rican population until well into the twentieth century, drinking was a regular social activity. Mintz, who spent several years studying this population, notes the importance of drinking in men's social interaction. During the harvest season, the day followed a regular cycle. Work began early, with the men getting to the fields at sunrise and working until three or four in the afternoon, while women stayed at home caring for children, cleaning, doing the laundry, and preparing the hot lunches they would bring to their husbands in the fields.

> It is in the late afternoon that the social life of the day begins. . . . After dinner the street becomes the setting for conversation and flirting. Loafing groups gather in front of the small stores or in the yards of older men, where they squat and gossip; marriageable boys and girls promenade along the highway. Small groups form and dissolve into the bars. The women remain home. . . . The bachelors stand at the bar drinking their rum neat—each drink downed in a swallow from a tiny paper cup. The more affluent buy half pints of rum . . . and finish them sitting at the tables. (Mintz 1960:16–17)

During this period, a deeply rooted belief, reflecting the alienated character of work under capitalism, began to be established. This is the culturally constituted idea that *alcohol is a man's reward for labor*: "I worked hard, so I deserve a drink" (Davila 1987:11). Gilbert (1985:265–266), who notes a similar belief based on her research among Mexican American men, describes the widespread practice of "respite drinking," "that is to say, drinking as a respite from labor or after a hard day's work." As Marx asserts, under capitalism

> labor is external to the worker, i.e., it does not belong to his essential being; . . . in his work, therefore, he does not affirm himself but denies himself. . . . The worker therefore only feels himself outside his work, and in his work feels outside himself. He is at home when he is not working, and when he is working he is not at home. His labor is not voluntary, but coerced; it is forced labor. It is therefore not satisfying a need; it is merely a means to satisfy needs external to it. Its alien character emerges clearly in the fact that as soon as no physical or other compulsion exists, labor is shunned like the plague. (Marx 1964:110–111)

Because labor for cane workers was not intrinsically rewarding, its performance required external motivation, a role which alcohol in part—probably because of its ability in many contexts to produce euphoria, reduce anxiety and tension, and enhance self-confidence, as well has having a low cost and ready availability—filled. Serving as a valued recompense for the difficult and self-mortifying work undertaken by men, alcohol consumption became culturally entrenched as an emotionally charged symbol of manhood itself. Vital to the power of this symbolism was the emergent reconceptualization of what it meant to be a man in terms of sole responsibility for the economic well being of one's family. Although there existed a sexual division of labor prior to the U.S. domination of Puerto Rico, in rural agricultural life work was a domestic affair that required family interdependence and close proximity. Proletarianization produced a devaluation of female labor as homemaking, while relegating it to an unpaid status. Additionally, it "led to Puerto Rican masculinity being defined in terms of being paid laborers and *buenos proveedores* (good providers)" (De La Cancela 1988: 42–43). In this context, drinking came to be seen as a privilege "earned by masculine self-sufficiency and assumption of the provider role" (Gilbert 1985:266; also see Rodriguez-Andrew et al. 1988). In the words of one of Gilbert's informants: " 'Yo soy el hombre de la casa, si quiero tomar, tomo cuando me de la gana' (I am the man of the house, and if I want to drink, I drink when I feel like it)."

The 1930s marked a significant turning point in the lives of the sugar cane workers as well as most other Puerto Ricans. Prior to the Depression, sugar cane provided one-sixth of Puerto Rico's total income, one-fourth of its jobs, and two-thirds of the dollars it earned from the export of goods. One out of every three factories on the Island was a sugar mill, a sugar refinery, a rum distillery, or molasses plant. The Depression nearly destroyed this economic base. Sugar prices fell drastically, while two hurricanes (1928 and 1932) all but demolished what remained of the damaged economy.

In response, control of Puerto Rico was transferred from the U.S. War Department to the Department of the Interior, and federal taxes on Puerto Rican rum sold in the U.S. were remitted to the Puerto Rican treasury, thus providing the island's Commonwealth government with $160 million in working capital. This money was used to build a number of government-owned manufacturing plants. However, concern in the U.S. Congress with "the crazy socialistic experiment going on down in Puerto Rico" (quoted in Wagenheim 1975:108) led to the sale of these factories to local capitalists. The Commonwealth government also launched Operation Bootstrap at this time "to promote industry, tourism and rum" (Wagenheim 1975:108). Operation Bootstrap was an ambitious initiative designed to reduce the high unemployment rate caused by the stagnation of a rural economy that had been heavily

dependent on the production of a small number of cash crops for export. The program offered foreign investors, 90 percent of whom came from the United States, tax holidays of over ten years, the installation of infrastructural features such as plants, roads, running water and electricity, and most importantly, an abundant supply of cheap labor.

Significantly, however, as Maldonado-Denis (1980: 31–32) points out, "What is altered in the change from the sugar economy based on the plantation to the new industrialization is merely the form of dependency, not its substance." In line with the unplanned nature of capitalist economy—at the world level, displaced agricultural workers quickly came to be defined as both an undesired "surplus population" and a *cause* of Puerto Rico's economic underdevelopment. As Day (1967:441) indicates, in a capitalist economy "if there is some cost to maintain [a] . . . surplus, it is likely to be 'pushed out'." This is precisely what occurred. Between 1952 and 1971, the total number of agricultural workers in Puerto Rico declined from 120,000 to 75,000 (Dugal 1973). So extensive was the exodus from rural areas that it threatened "to convert many towns in the interior of the Island to ghost-towns" (Maldonado-Denis 1980:33). Male workers, in particular, were affected by industrialization, because over half of the new jobs created by Operation Bootstrap went to women (Safa 1986).

Although Juan and Zoraida understood their decision to leave Puerto Rico as part of an effort to protect their children from witchcraft, the folk healer's message and its interpretation by Juan and Zoraida must be located in this broader political-economic context. As Maldonado-Denis (1980:33) cogently observes, the "dislocation of Puerto Rican agriculture—and the ensuing uprooting of its rural population—is the result of profound changes in the structure of the Puerto Rican economy and not the result of mere individual decisions arrived at because of fortuitous events." However, "migrants do no usually see the larger structural forces that create [their] personal situation" and channel their personal decisions (Rodriguez 1989:13).

The first significant labor migration of Puerto Ricans to the U.S. began in the 1920s, with the biggest push coming after World War II. The focus for most migrants until the 1970s was New York City. As noted, it was to New York that Juan and Zoraida, along with 70,000 other Puerto Ricans, migrated in 1946. As many as 60% of these migrants came from the rural zones of the Island. They arrived during a post-war boom in the New York economy that created an urgent demand for new labor (Maldonado-Denis 1972). Employment was the primary motivation for migration and many found blue collar jobs, although often at wages lower than those of Euro-American and even African American workers performing similar toil (Maldonado 1976; Rodriguez 1980).

By the time of the post-war migrations, heavy alcohol consumption among men was woven deeply into the cultural fabric of Puerto Rico. However, as Coombs and Globetti (1986:77) conclude in their review of the literature on drinking in Latin America generally, "Until recently, most studies, conducted mainly in small communities or rural areas, found relatively few visible ill effects. Little guilt or moral significance was attached to alcohol use or even drunkenness." This description appears to hold true for Puerto Ricans as well. According to Marilyn Aquírre-Molina

> If we look at the Puerto Rican experience, we can clearly see how alcohol use and the alcohol industry are entrenched within the population . . . [D]istilled spirit is very available (at low cost), and part of the national pride for production of the world's finest rum. . . . Alcohol consumption has an important role in social settings—consumption is an integral part of many or most Hispanic functions. . . . At parties, or similar gatherings, a child observes that there's a great deal of tolerance for drinking, and it is encouraged by and for the men. A non-drinking male is considered antisocial. . . . Tolerance for drinking is further evidenced in the attitude that there is no disgrace or dishonor for a man to be drunk. . . . [I]t becomes evident that alcohol use is part of the socio-cultural system of the Hispanic, used within the contexts of recreation, hospitality [and] festivity. (Aguírre-Molina 1979:3–6)

Adds Davlia (1987:17), "In our culture, weakness in drinking ability is always humiliating to a man because a true man drinks frequently and in quantity. Therefore, for a Puerto Rican man not to maintain dignity when drinking would be an absolute proof of his weakness, as would be his refusal to accept a drink." Refusal to drink among Puerto Rican men, in fact, can be interpreted as an expression of homosexuality because drinking is defined as a diacritical male activity (Singer, Davison, and Yalin 1987). In Puerto Rico, these attitudes are supported by an extensive advertising effort by the rum industry, few restrictions on sales, ready availability of distilled spirits at food stores, and low cost for alcoholic beverages (Canino et al. 1987).

Most aspects of Puerto Rican life were transformed by the migration, drinking patterns included. According to Gordon

> Puerto Ricans have . . . adopted U.S. drinking customs and *added* them to their traditional drinking customs. . . . They follow the pattern of weekday drinking typical of the American workingman. . . . Weekday drinking among Puerto Ricans does not affect the importance of their traditional weekend fiesta drinking more com-

monly seen in a rural society (emphasis added). (Gordon 1985a:308)

. . .

While it is evident from Mintz's (1960) account of sugar cane workers that many Puerto Rican men had adopted working class drinking patterns even prior to migration, these behaviors were generalized and amplified following movement to the U.S. As a consequence of cultural pressure to maintain traditional drinking patterns as well as adopt U.S. working class norms, many Puerto Rican men have adopted a heavy drinking pattern. The development of this pattern was facilitated by the high density of businesses in poor, inner city neighborhoods that dispense alcohol, especially beer, for on- and off-premise consumption; multiple encouragements to drink in the media, including advertisements, films, and television programs (Maxwell and Jacobson 1989); and structural factors that have contributed first to a redefinition and ultimately to the marginalization of the Puerto Rican man. This last factor was especially important in transforming heavy drinking into problem drinking in this population.

As suggested above, the transition from yeoman farmer to rural proletariat began a process of reconceptualizing the meaning of masculinity among Puerto Ricans. This transition was completed with the migration. Work-related definitions of manliness and provider-based evaluations of self-worth became dominant. To be *un hombre hecho y derecho* (a complete man) now meant demonstrating an ability to be successful as an income earner in the public sphere. This is "the great American dream of dignity through upward mobility" analyzed so effectively by Sennett and Cobb (1973:169), a dream that threatens always to turn into a nightmare for the working man. And the name of this nightmare, as every worker knows so well, is unemployment. The fear of unemployment is not solely an economic worry, it is equally a dread of being blamed and of blaming oneself for inadequacy, for letting down one's family, for failing while others succeed. The "plea . . . to be relieved of having to prove oneself this way, to gain a hold instead on the innate meaningfulness of actions" is a central theme in the lives of working people (Sennett and Cobb 1973:246).

Juan's hard work, enabling his movement from janitor to draftsman, achieved without formal education or training, is the embodiment of the dream and the fear of the working man. During the period that Juan was successful at realizing the dream, his daughter remembers her family life as stable and happy. These golden years provided a stark contrast with what was to follow. Throughout this period Juan drank heavily, and yet he had no drinking problem.

Alcohol was his culturally validated reward for living up to the stringent requirements of the male role in capitalist society. The swift turn around in Juan's life following the loss of his job suggests that Puerto Rican male drinking problems should be considered in relationship to the problem of unemployment.

Several studies, in fact, indicate a direct association between unemployment and problem drinking. In his study of alcohol-related problems in Toronto, for example, Smart (1979) reports that 21% of unemployed respondents suffer from three or more alcohol-related problems compared to only 6% of employed workers. While an increase in consumption levels following unemployment has not been found in all studies of small groups of workers in particular settings (e.g., Iversen and Klausen 1986), a national study by McCornac and Filante (1984) of distilled spirit consumption and employment in the U.S. at the time of Juan's death supports this linkage. Their study concludes,

> The unemployment rate had a positive and significant impact on the consumption of distilled spirits in both the cross-sectional and pooled analyses. During a recessionary period, rising unemployment stimulates consumption while decreasing real per capita income decreases consumption. However, the two effects are not equal. From 1972–1973 to 1974–1975, the rate of unemployment rose by 37% . . . while real per capita income declined by less than 1%. Thus, the net effect of simultaneous changes in these two variables was to increase consumptions by approximately 8%. The important implication of this finding is that the negative consequences of higher rates of unemployment can be extended to include the increased social and economic costs of an increase in the use of distilled spirits. (McCornac and Filante 1984:177–178)

Similarly, analysis of national data on long and short term trends in alcohol consumption and mortality by Brenner (1975) shows an increase in alcohol consumption and alcohol-related health and social problems during periods of economic recession and rising unemployment. His study, covering the years during Juan's period of heaviest drinking and subsequent death, finds that "National recessions in personal income and employment are consistently followed, within 2 to 3 years, by increases in cirrhosis mortality rates" (Brenner 1975:1282). Economic disruptions, he argues, create conditions of social stress, which in turn stimulate increased anxiety-avoidance drinking and consequent health problems. Research by Pearlin and Radabaugh (1976:661) indicates that anxiety is "especially likely to result in the use of alcohol as a tranquilizer if a sense of control is lacking and self-esteem is low." The key variable in this equation, as Seeman and Anderson (1983) stress, is powerlessness. Based on

their study of drinking among men in Los Angeles, they argue, "The conclusion is inescapable that the sense of powerlessness is related to the experience of drinking problems quite apart from the sheer quantity of alcohol consumed" (Seeman and Anderson 1983:71). Increased alcohol consumption and alcohol-related problems and mortality have been found to be associated in several studies (Makela et al. 1981; Wilson 1984).

The major economic factor of concern here, of course, was the flight of the appliance factory where Juan was employed to a cheap labor market outside of the industrial Northeast. Juan was not alone in losing his job to the corporate transfer of production. About the same time, thousands of U.S. workers were being laid off by the "runaway shop"; 900,000 U.S. production jobs were lost, for example, between 1967 and 1971 alone (Barnet and Muller 1974). In New York City, during this period, 25% of the largest companies relocated, reflecting a shift away from a production-centered economy. This transition has intensified the problem of Puerto Rican unemployment (Maldonado-Denis 1980; Rodriguez 1980). Mills and his co-workers, in their study of Puerto Rican migrants in New York, found that lacking specialized job skills Puerto Rican workers are at the mercy of economic forces. During periods of economic upturn they are welcomed, but when the business cycle "is on the way down, or in the middle of one of its periodic breakdowns, there is a savage struggle for even the low wage jobs . . ." (Mills et al. 1967:82).

Consequently, at the time that Juan died in 1971, Puerto Ricans had one of the highest unemployment rates of all ethnic groups in the country. While 6% of all men in the U.S. were jobless, for Puerto Rican men the rate of unemployment was 8.8%. Significantly, the actual rate of unemployment for Puerto Rican men was even higher than these figures suggest because, as measured by the Department of Labor, the unemployment rate does not include numerous individuals who have given up on the possibility of ever locating employment. If discouraged workers were included, the "unemployment among Puerto Rican men would be more accurately depicted—not at the 'official' rate of 8.8 percent—but at the 'adjusted' (and more realistic) level of 18.7 percent" (Maldonado-Denis 1980:79–80).

For many older workers like Juan, whose age made them dispensable, and many younger Puerto Rican workers as well, whose ethnicity and lack of recognized skills made them equally discardable, the changing economic scene in New York meant permanent unemployment. Increased drinking and rising rates of problem drinking were products of the consequent sense of worthlessness and failure in men geared to defining masculinity in terms of being *un buen proveedor* (Canino and Canino 1980:537–538). As De La Cancela (1989:146) asserts, "living with limited options, uncertainty, and violence breeds fertile ground for ego-exalting substance use among Latinos." Pappas identifies the general reasons in this ethnography of the effects of factory closing on rubber workers in Barberton, Ohio. Beyond a salary, a job provides workers with a feeling of purpose and means of participation in the surrounding social world. In addition to contributing to the experience of uselessness, loss of work fragments social networks and produces increased isolation, placing increased strain on domestic relations. Restriction of the quantity of outside social interaction "narrows the psychic space in which the unemployed maneuver" (Pappas 1989:86).

. . .

Within the context of Puerto Rican culture, these general processes take on a particular slant. Drinking among Latino males is commonly linked both in the alcohol literature and in popular thinking with the concept of *machismo,* or the notable Latino emphasis on appearing manly at all times, particularly in public. Some have gone so far as to lay blame for the high rates of drinking found among Latino males on *machismo.* It is certainly the case that drinking is culturally defined as a male thing to do, as a culturally approved means of expressing prowess as a male. But this does not lead directly to alcoholism. Rather, it is the combination of a cultural emphasis on drinking as proper, appropriate, and manly, with political and economic subordination in a system in which most alternative expressions of manliness are barred to Puerto Rican access that is of real significance (Singer 1987b). This interpretation underscores De La Cancela's (1986: 292) argument that "just as capitalism obscures the necessity of institutionalized unemployment by defining the unemployed as somehow lacking in the required skills to succeed, *machismo* obscures the alienation effects of capitalism on individuals by embodying the alienation in male-female sex-role terms. . . ."

Unemployment blocked Juan, as it has so many other Puerto Rican men, from the major socially sanctioned route to success as a man. It did not, however, exterminate the ever present and powerful need to achieve the cultural values of *machismo* (mastery), *dignidad* (honor and dignity of the family), and *respecto* (respect of one's peers). In a sense, however counterproductive, drinking was all that was left for Juan that was manly in his understanding. Hard drinking replaced hard work, and alcohol, as a medium of cultural expression, was transformed from compensation for the sacrifices of achieving success into salve for the tortures of failure.

JUAN IS NOT ALONE

The "personal problems" of the unemployed workers of Barberton, like the problems experienced by Juan García, constitute part of the human fallout of so-called economic development. Although often portrayed as natural and inevitable, changes in the nature and location of production exact enormous human costs, costs that tend to be born disporportionately by the poor and working classes. The extent of the agony for Puerto Rican men is captured by Davila

> I have a father who is an alcoholic and a brother who died of cirrhosis of the liver a year ago at the age of 42. I have a young son who is having alcohol problems of his own. I have cousins and uncles who have died of alcoholism. I have friends who likewise have died of alcoholism or are currently alcoholic. And I am a recovering alcoholic. . . . All the persons I have listed are Puerto Rican . . . they are all men. (Davila 1987:17–18)

A study comparing mortality differentials among various Latino subgroups residing in the U.S. during the years 1979–1981 found that Puerto Rican population had a distinct pattern of mortality from chronic liver disease and cirrhosis. The age-adjusted death rate among Puerto Ricans from liver-related problems, which are common among heavy drinkers, is about twice that among Mexicans and almost three times the rate among Cubans. Further, the rate among Puerto Ricans is over two times the African American rate and triple the Euro-American rate (Rosenwaike 1987). In fact, New York Board of Health data for 1979–81 indicate that cirrhosis was the second leading cause of death among Island-born Puerto Ricans age 15–45 (cited in Gordon 1985b).

These data suggest that Juan's case, while having special features peculiar to his individual life course, is not, on the whole, unique. His life and his death, in fact, are emblematic of the broad experience of working class Puerto Rican men in the U.S., a conclusion supported by findings from our studies of drinking patterns and experiences among Puerto Rican men and adolescents in Hartford, CT. For both studies, the sampling frame consisted of all Puerto Rican households in high-density Puerto Rican neighborhoods as defined by census reports (25% Latino surnames). In the first of these studies, interviews were conducted with a randomly selected sample of Puerto Rican adolescents age 14–17 years. The sampling unit consisted of 210 adolescents (one adolescent subject per participating household), of which 88 were boys.

A series of national household surveys (Abelson and Atkinson 1975; Abelson and Fishburne 1976; Abelson et al. 1977) of drinking among adolescents indicates that over half of the adolescents in the U.S. report using alcohol during the past year, compared to 31% of the Puerto Rican adolescents in our sample. In the national samples, about one-third of participants report drinking within the month prior to the survey, compared to 14% in our sample. Similarly, Rachal et al. (1976), in a national sample of over 13,000 adolescents in grades 7–12, found that 55% reported usually drink at least once a month, compared to 10% in our sample. Regarding the quantity of alcohol consumed per drinking episode, these researchers found that 55% of their sample reported more than one drink per drinking occasion, compared to only 19% in our sample. In short, as have other researchers (Welte and Barnes 1987), we found a lower drinking prevalence among Puerto Rican adolescents than tends to be found for the general U.S. adolescent population.

. . .

The existing literature suggests that *family controls* are a major factor limiting alcohol consumption among Latino youth to levels below those of their white counterparts. This was found to be a primary reason given for not drinking by the adolescents in our study. Based on his research among Mexican-Americans in Texas, Trotter (1985:286) states: "Unmarried children who smoke or drink in front of parents are often thought to be extremely disrespectful, and to shame their family." This explanation fits with the cultural understanding that drinking is an earned reward for assuming the responsibilities of employment and family support, roles not open to dependent children.

Our second study examined drinking patterns in 398 Puerto Rican men, 18–48 years of age, recruited to a research sample structured by type of residence (private home, rented apartment, housing project). These primary sampling units were chosen because of expected differences in socio-economic status and the sense from prior research that residents in rented apartments in low income neighborhoods often are under greater economic pressure than households in rent controlled housing projects or owners of private homes or condominiums. The housing project included in this study is located at some distance from the central city area and tends to be in better repair than other Hartford housing projects. Respondents living in targeted neighborhoods (selected because of census data indicating a high density Spanish surname population) were randomly recruited and interviewed in their place of residence.

Among the men in the sample, 84% were born in Puerto Rico and half had been living in the U.S. for under ten years. Most of the other men were born in the U.S., 37% in Hartford. Fifty-four percent were married or living with a partner, and 83% had a high school education or less. Data on these respondents in-

dicate the economic difficulties faced by Puerto Rican men generally. Thirty-three percent reported that they were unemployed and looking for work and another 17% worked only part-time at the time of the interview. More than half of the men (55%) reported annual household incomes of under $8,000; 85% reported incomes under $15,000. Rates of unemployment for men across the three residential subgroups was as follows: private home: 3%; rented apartment: 44.3%; housing project: 68.5%. Additionally, rates of part-time employment across these three residence types were 12%, 19.8%, and 10.8% respectively. These data are consistent with other research in Hartford indicating "that whites . . . on average have a higher socio-economic level than the Black and Hispanic samples, and *the Hispanic group is consistently ranked lowest . . .* in socio-economic indicators in Hartford" (AIDS Community Research Group 1988:9; emphasis in original).

About 80% of the men in our study reported that they have consumed alcohol. Of these, 31% indicated that they drink at least once a week. Regarding quantities normally consumed when drinking, we found that 53% of the drinkers reported having at least 3 drinks per drinking occasion. Ten percent indicated that they normally drink until "high" or drunk, although drinking for these effects was reported as a motivation for consumption by 41% . . . . Almost 20% of the men reported having eight drinks per drinking occasion at least 1–3 times per month during the last year. Another 7.5% reported this level of drinking 3–11 times during the last year. The majority of the men, however, reported lower levels of drinking.

. . . Approximately 10% of the men in the study reported they felt that their drinking was not completely under control during the last year. If a longer time period is included (since a man's first drink), approximately 20% reported having felt out of control.

Additionally, 34% of the men stated that drinking as a means of forgetting about problems was a very to somewhat important motivation for them to drink, while almost a quarter reported they drink because they have nothing else to do.

Data show that between 7–28% of the men reported at least one drinking-related problem. Notably, 28.4% of the men indicated that drinking has had a harmful effect on their home life or marriage.

Table I compares negative drinking consequences among Puerto Rican men (21 years-of-age and older) with findings among men from a national probability sample of the general population aged 21 or older (Cahalan 1982). The problem drinking scales displayed on this table were constructed by combining responses from several related questions following Cahalan (1982). In most cases, quite similar questions

TABLE I   Prevalence of Drinking-Related Problems Among Men (21 years and older) over Last 12 Months

Drinking Related Problems	Total National Probability Sample N = 751	Total Hartford Puerto Rican Sample N = 352*	Hartford Puerto Rican Drinkers N = 180*
Health problems associated with drinking	4.0	9.4	31.7
Acting belligerently under the influence	8.0	9.1	48.5
Friends complain about drinking	3.0	30.7	35.9
Symptomatic drinking	20.0	19.9	36.5
Job-related drinking problems	7.0	6.8	19.7
Problems with law, police, accidents	2.0	4.8	38.6
Engaging in binge drinking	1.0	4.5	50.0
Spouse complains about drinking	2.0	7.7	13.0

*Excludes participants under 21 years of age

(pertinent to these scales) appear on both the national and Hartford instruments. Symptomatic drinking refers to signs of physical dependence and loss of control suggestive of Jellinek's gamma alcoholism (e.g., drinking to relieve a hangover, blackouts, having difficulty stopping drinking). Three variables used to construct this scale (tossing down drinks quickly, sneaking drinks, drinking before a party to ensure having enough alcohol) were not included in our survey, possibly resulting in a lower score for Puerto Rican men. Half of the variables used to construct an additional scale on psychological dependence for the national study were not included in our instrument and consequently this item is not included in the table.

In the national sample, 25% of the respondents were abstainers compared to 20% in our study. Additionally, it is evident from Table I that the prevalence of drinking-related problems is higher for the Hartford sample on most of the scales, supporting the epidemiological data suggesting higher problem drinking rates among Puerto Rican men. These differences are especially notable on the two scales (complaints about drinking by friends or spouses) that involve the impact of drinking on personal relationships. The final column on this table reports problem frequencies just for drinkers in the Hartford study (i.e., abstainers are not included). Positive responses on two of the scales, belligerence (getting into heated arguments while drinking) and binge drinking (being intoxicated for several days at a time), were reported by approximately half of the Puerto Rican drinkers.

Overall, we found high rates of heavy and problem drinking in our study of Puerto Rican men, with the heaviest and most problematic drinking occurring among men who lived in rented apartments in high density, low income, inner city neighborhoods. The correlation coefficients between employment and the

problem drinking scales reported in Table I are displayed in Table II. As this table indicates, there is a negative correlation between being employed and all eight problem drinking scales. Unemployment, in sum, is a clear correlate of problem drinking in Puerto Rican men.

Our research suggests that the onset of drinking problems among Puerto Rican males is associated with a *post-adolescent transition* into the world of adult responsibilities and sociocultural expectations. Specifically, findings from our second study indicate this transition occurs in the mid-20s. After that point, rates of problem drinking continue to rise until Puerto Rican men are well into their forties (cf. Caetano 1983). Confronted repeatedly with setbacks in attaining regular and rewarding employment, and unable to support their families, many Puerto Rican men in Hartford drink to forget their problems and their boredom, while seeking through heavy and often problem drinking what they cannot achieve otherwise in society: respect, dignity, and validation of their

Table II   Zero-Order Correlation Coefficients Between Employment and Drinking-Related Problems Among Puerto Rican Men

Drinking Related Problems	Correlation Coefficient (r)
Health problems associated with drinking	−.1805
Acting belligerently under the influence	−.0634
Friends complain about drinking	−.0069
Symptomatic drinking	−.1165
Job-related drinking problems	−.0573
Problems with law, police, accidents	−.2171
Engaging in binge drinking	−.3371
Spouse complains about drinking	−.1530

masculine identity. While 38.5% of the men in our sample who reported two or more drinking related health or social problems indicated that they drink to forget about their personal worries, the figure was 7.1% for problem-free drinkers. Similarly, 30.8% of problem drinkers reported drinking to release tension compared to 6.5% of problem-free drinkers. As our data show, not all Puerto Rican men become involved in problem drinking (or the use of other mind-altering drugs). Indeed, the majority do not. That so many do however reveals the folly of remaining at the micro-level in developing an explanation of this phenomenon.

CONCLUSION

In this examination of the broader context of Juan's drinking, we see the intersection of biography and history, that critical link uniting "the innermost acts of the individual with the widest kinds of social-historical phenomena" (Gerth and Mills 1964:xvi). In reviewing the social environment of "Juan's disease," we have not, we believe, "depersonalize[d] the subject matter and the content of medical anthropology" (Scheper-Hughes and Lock 1986:137). The goal of critical medical anthropology is not to obliterate the individual nor the poignant and personal expressions produced by the loss and struggle to regain well-being. Nor does this perspective seek to eliminate psychology, culture, the environment, or biology from a holistic medical anthropology. Instead, by taking "cognizance of processes that transcend separable cases" (Wolf 1982:17), we attempt to unmask the ways in which suffering, as well as curing, illness behavior, provider-patient interactions, etc., have levels of meaning and cause beyond the narrow confines of immediate experience. As Mintz (1989:791) suggests, "When we can accurately specify the effects of policies readily imposed by external authority, the relationships between outside and inside, and between the living of life events and the weight of the world system, are clear." Situated in relationship to relevant history and political economy, Juan's drinking loses the bewildering quality commonly attached to destructive behavior. This is achieved by an exploration of the macro-micro nexus which includes and requires an examination of symbolic, environmental, and psychological factors, but does not reduce analysis to any of these factors.

. . .

As Juan's case reveals, however misdirected and self-destructive, problem drinking is a dramatic and nagging reminder that medical anthropology must be more than the study of health systems and political-economic structures, it must be sensitive also to the symbolically expressed experiential and meaning frames of struggling human beings reacting to and attempting to shape their world, although never "under circumstances chosen by themselves" (Marx 1963:15). In its disruptiveness, problem drinking, in any type of society or social system (Singer 1986a), brings to light the dynamic tensions between structure and agency, society and the individual, general processes and particular human responses. Addressing these issues is the special contribution of critical medical anthropology to the wider arena of the political economy of health.

Thus, we argue for the adoption of a broad theoretical framework designed to explore and explain macro-micro linkages and to channel praxis accordingly. The success of critical medical anthropology in providing such a framework will determine its utility and endurance.

NOTES

1. Other critiques of critical medical anthropology have been addressed in Singer, Baer, and Lazarus (1989) and Singer (1989c). A recent critique, noteworthy for its distortions of the perspective, was penned by McElroy (1990). She alleges that critical medical anthropology is antiscience because it does not take Western biological categories at face value, asserting instead that political-economic factors shape even scientific thinking. The failures of medical ecology notwithstanding (Singer 1989a; Baer 1990b; Trostle 1990), at issue is not the reality of biology or a questioning of biological factors in disease etiology. As a materialist approach, critical medical anthropology hardly rejects the natural science paradigm. Instead, we call for a better science of humanity, one that recognizes the social origins and functions of science. Moreover, as demonstrated by Scheder (1988), critical medical anthropology is as much concerned with the political economy of disease as it is with the political economy of illness, treatment or related domains. The point is that critical medical anthropology views disease as both naturally and socially produced, but views "nature" as both naturally and socially produced as well.
2. These studies were supported by National Institute on Alcohol Abuse and Alcoholism grants R23 AA06057 and R01 AA07161. Preparation of this paper was supported by the latter grant. Merrill Singer served as Principal Investigator for both grants, while Freddie Valentín was Project Director and Zhongke Jia was Data Manager on the second study.
3. Despite the focus of this paper, it should be emphasized that these conditions are not found only in capitalist soci-

ety, nor are alcohol-related problems found exclusively in oppressed social classes and ethnic minority communities. These points are elaborated in Singer (1986a).

4. Most recently, a growing number of alcohol researchers have abandoned the notion of alcoholism in favor of alcohol dependency, because, it is believed, this labels an demonstrably organic condition. However, the barometers (e.g., DSM-III R and ICD 10) used to measure this organic condition still include behavioral and experiential factors which anthropological researchers have long argued are open to sociocultural influence (e.g., "a narrowing of the personal repertoire of patterns of alcohol use," "a great deal of time spent drinking or recovering from the effects of drinking"). In this paper, we employ the term *problem drinking* to refer to drinking patterns associated with negative health and social consequences for the drinker and his social network.

REFERENCES

Abad, V., and J. Suares. 1974. Cross Cultural Aspects of Alcoholism among Puerto Ricans. Proceedings of the Fourth Annual Alcoholism Conference of the National Institute on Alcohol Abuse and Alcoholism. Washington, D.C.

Abelson, H., and R. Atkinson. 1975. Public Experience with Psychoactive Substances. Princeton, NJ: Response Analysis Corporation.

Abelson, H., and P. Fishburne. 1976. Nonmedical Use of Psychoactive Substances. Princeton, NJ: Response Analysis Corporation.

Abelson, H. et al. 1977. National Survey of Drug Abuse, 1977. Rockville, MD: NIAAA AIDS Community Research Group.

———. 1988. AIDS: Knowledge, Attitudes and Behavior in an Ethically Mixed Urban Neighborhood. Special Report to the Connecticut State Department of Health Services, Hartford, CT.

Agar, M. 1973. Ripping and Running. New York: Academy Press.

Aguírre-Molina, M. 1979. Alcohol and the Hispanic Woman. Paper presented at the Conference on Women in Crisis, New York, NY.

Ames, G., and J. Mora. 1988. Alcohol Problem Prevention in Mexican American Populations. *In* Alcohol Consumption among Mexicans and Mexican Americans. M. J. Gilbert, ed. Pp. 253–280. New York: Plenum.

Baer, H. 1989. The American Dominative Medical System as a Reflection of Social Relations in the Larger Society. Social Science and Medicine 28(11):1103–1112.

———. 1990a. Kerr-McGee and the NRC. From Indian Country to Silkwood to Gore. Social Science and Medicine 30(2):237–248.

———. 1990b. Biocultural Approaches in Medical Anthropology: A Critical Medical Anthropology Commentary. Medical Anthropology Quarterly 4:344–348.

Baer, H., and M. Singer. 1982. Why Not Have a Critical Medical Anthropology? Paper presented at the Annual Meeting of the American Anthropological Association, Washington, D.C.

Baer, H., M. Singer, and J. Johnsen. 1986. Introduction: Toward a Critical Medical Anthropology. Social Science and Medicine 23(2):95–98.

Barnet, R., and R. Muller. 1974. Global Reach. New York: Simon and Schuster.

Bennett, L. 1988. Alcohol in Context: Anthropological Perspective. Drugs and Society 2(3/4):89–131.

Bonilla, F. 1985. Ethnic Orbits: The Circulation of Capitals and Peoples. Contemporary Marxism 10:148–167.

Brenner, H. 1975. Trends in Alcohol Consumption and Associated Illnesses. American Journal of Public Health 65:1279–1292.

Brown, R. 1979. Rockefeller Medicine Men. Berkeley, CA: University of California Press.

Caetano, R. 1983. Drinking Patterns and Alcohol Problems among Hispanics in the U.S.: A Review. Drug and Alcohol Dependence 12:37–59.

Cahalan, D. 1982. Epidemiology: Alcohol Use in American Society. *In* Alcohol, Science and Society Revisited. E. Gomberg, H. White, and J. Carpenter, eds. Pp. 96–118. Ann Arbor, MI: University of Michigan Press.

Canino, G., et al. 1987. The Prevalence of Alcohol Use and/or Dependence in Puerto Rico. *In* Health and Behavior: Research Agenda for Hispanics. The Research Monograph Series, vol. 1. M. Garria and M. Arana, eds. Pp. 127–144. Bloomington, IN: The University of Indiana Press.

Canino, I., and G. Canino. 1980. Impact of Stress on the Puerto Rican Family: Treatment Considerations. American Journal of Orthopsychiatry 50:535–541.

Carrión, A. 1983. Puerto Rico: A Political and Cultural History. Chicago, IL: Aldine.

Chafetz, M., and H. Demone. 1962. Alcoholism and Society. New York: Oxford University Press.

Chafetz, M., and R. Yoerg. 1977. Public Health Treatment Programs in Alcoholism. *In* Treatment and Rehabilitation of the Chronic Alcoholic. B. Kissin and H. Begleiter, eds. Pp. 593–614. New York: Plenum.

Chrisman, N. 1985. Alcoholism: Illness or Disease? *In* The American Experience with Alcohol. L. Bennett and G. Ames, eds. Pp. 7–22. New York: Plenum.

Clark, V. 1930. Puerto Rico and Its Problems. Washington, D.C.: The Brookings Institution.

Coll y Toste, C. 1969. Historia de la esclavitud en Puerto Rico. San Juan, PR: Sociedad de Autores Puerutorriqueños.

Conrad, P., and J. Schneider. 1980. Deviance and Medicalization: From Badness to Sickness. St. Louis, MO: C. V. Mosby.

Coombs, D., and G. Globetti. 1986. Alcohol Use and Alcoholism in Latin America: Changing Patterns and Sociocultural Explanations. The International Journal of the Addictions 21:59–81.

Davies, P. 1979. Motivation, Responsibility and Sickness in the Psychiatric Treatment of Alcoholism. British Journal of Psychiatry 134:449–458.

Davila, R. 1987. The History of Puerto Rican Drinking Patterns. *In* Alcohol Use and Abuse among Hispanic

Adolescents. M. Singer, L. Davison, and F. Yalin. Pp. 7–18. Hartford, CT: Hispanic Health Council.

Day, R. 1967. The Economics of Technological Change and the Demise of the Share Cropper. American Economic Review 47:427–449.

De La Cancela, V. 1986. A Critical Analysis of Puerto Rican Machismo: Implications for Clinical Practice. Psychotherapy 23(2):291–296.

———. 1988. Labor Pains: Puerto Rican Males in Transition. Centro Bulletin 2:41–55.

———. 1989. Minority AIDS Prevention: Moving Beyond Cultural Perspectives Toward Sociopolitical Empowerment. AIDS Education and Prevention 1:141–153.

De Ropp, R. 1976. Drugs and the Mind. New York: Delta.

Diffie, B., and J. Diffie. 1931. Puerto Rico: A Broken Pledge. New York: Vanguard Press.

Douglas, M., ed. 1987. Constructive Drinking: Perspectives on Drinking from Anthropology. New York: Cambridge University Press.

Dugal, V. 1973. Two Papers on the Economy of Puerto Rico. San German, Puerto Rico: The Caribbean Institute and Study Center for Latin America.

Elling, R. 1981. The Capitalist World-System and International Health. International Journal of Health Services 11:21–51.

Gerth, H., and C. W. Mills. 1964. Character and Social Structure. New York: Harbinger Books.

Gilbert, M. J. 1985. Mexican-Americans in California: Intracultural Variation in Attitudes and Behavior Related to Alcohol. In The American Experience with Alcohol. L. Bennett and G. Ames, eds. Pp. 255–278. New York: Plenum.

———. 1987. Alcohol Consumption Patterns in Immigrant and Later Generation Mexican American Women. Hispanic Journal of the Behavioral Sciences 9:299–314.

———. 1988. Alcohol Consumption among Mexicans and Mexican Americans: A Binational Perspective, Spanish Speaking Mental Health Research Center. Los Angeles, CA: University of California.

Gilbert, M. J., and R. Cervantes. 1987. Mexican Americans and Alcohol. Monograph No. 11, Spanish Speaking Mental Health Research Center. Los Angeles, CA: University of California.

Gordon, A. 1978. Hispanic Drinking after Migration: The Case of Dominicans. Medical Anthropology 10: 154–171.

———. 1981. The Cultural Context of Drinking and Indigenous Therapy for Alcohol Problems in Three Migrant Hispanic Cultures; An Ethnographic Report. In Cultural Factors in Alcohol Research and Treatment of Drinking Problems. Journal of Studies on Alcohol (Special Supplement No. 9. D. Health, J. Waddell, and J. Topper, eds. Pp. 217–240.

———. 1985a. Alcohol and Hispanics in the Northeast. In The American Experience with Alcohol. L. Bennett and G. Ames, eds. Pp. 297–314. New York: Plenum.

———. 1985b. State of the Art Review: Caribbean Hispanics and their Alcohol Use. Paper presented at the National Institute on Alcohol Abuse and Alcoholism Conference on the Epidemiology of Alcohol Use and Abuse Among U.S. Minorities, Bethesda, MD.

Heath, D. 1976. Anthropological Perspectives on Alcohol: An Historical Review. In Cross-cultural Approaches to the Study of Alcohol: An Interdisciplinary Perspective. M. Everett, J. Waddell, and D. Heath, eds. Pp. 42–101. The Hague: Mouton.

———. 1978. The Sociocultural Model of Alcohol Use: Problems and Prospects. Journal of Operational Psychiatry 9:56–66.

———. 1980. A Critical Review of the Sociocultural Model of Alcohol Use. In Normative Approaches to the Prevention of Alcohol Abuse and Alcoholism. T. Hartford, D. Parker and L. Light, eds. Pp. 1–18. NIAAA Research Monographs No. 3, DHEW Pub. No. ADM-79-847. Washington, D.C.: U.S. Government Printing Office.

———. 1984. Historical and Cultural Factors Affecting Alcohol Availability and Consumption in Latin America. Research Papers in Anthropology, No. 2, Department of Anthropology, Brown University, Providence, RI.

———. 1987a. A Decade of Development in the Anthropology Study of Alcohol Use: 1970–1989. In Constructive Drinking. M. Douglas, ed. Pp. 16–70. New York: Cambridge University Press.

———. 1987b. Anthropology and Alcohol Studies: Current Issues. Annual Review of Anthropology 16: 99–120.

Herrero, J., V. Sánchez Cardona, and E. Gutierrez. 1975. La Politicia monetaria del '98. El Nuevo Día, 30 July 1975.

History Task Force. 1979. Labor Migration Under Capitalism: The Puerto Rican Experience. New York: Monthly Review Press.

Iversen, L., and H. Klausen. 1986. Alcohol Consumption among Laid-Off Workers Before and After Closure of a Danish Ship-Yard: A 2-Year Follow-up Study. Social Science and Medicine 22:107–109.

Jessor, R. 1984. Adolescent Problem Drinking: Psychosocial Aspects and Developmental Outcomes. In Proceedings: NIAAA-WHO Collaborating Center Designation Meeting & Alcohol Research Seminar. Pp. 104–143. Rockville, MD: U.S. Department of Health and Human Services.

Keesing, R. 1987. Anthropology as Interpretive Quest. Current Anthropology 28:161–176.

Kendell, R. E. 1979. Alcoholism: A Medical or Political Problem? British Medical Journal 1:367–371.

Makela, K., et al. 1981. Alcohol, Society and the State. Toronto: Addiction Research Foundation.

Maldonado-Denis, M. 1972. Puerto Rico: A Socio-Historic Interpretation. New York: Vintage Books.

———. 1980. The Emigration Dialectic: Puerto Rico and the USA. New York: International Publishers.

Maldonado, R. 1976. Why Puerto Ricans Migrated to the United States in 1947–73. Monthly Labor Review (September):7–18.

Marx, K. 1963. The 18th Brumaire of Louis Bonaparte. New York: International Publishers.

———. 1964. The Economic and Philosophic Manuscripts of 1844. New York: International Publishers.

Marx, K., and F. Engels. 1967. On Religion. New York: Schocken Books.

Maxwell, B., and Jacobson, M. 1989. Marketing Disease to Hispanics. Washington, D.C.: Center for Science in the Public Interest.

McCornac, D., and R. Filante. 1984. The Demand for Distilled Spirits: An Empirical Investigation. Journal of Studies on Alcohol 45:176–178.

McElroy, A. 1990. Biocultural Models in Studies of Human Health and Adaptation. Medical Anthropology Quarterly 4:243–265.

McKinlay, J. 1986. A Case for Refocusing Upstream: The Political Economy of Illness. In The Sociology of Health and Illness: Critical Perspectives. P. Conrad and R. Kern, eds. Pp. 484–498. New York: St. Martin's Press.

Mills, C. W., et al. 1967. The Puerto Rican Journey. New York: Russell and Russell.

Mintz, S. 1960. Worker in the Cane. New Haven, CT: Yale University Press.

———. 1971. The Caribbean as a Socio-cultural Area. In Peoples and Cultures of the Caribbean. M. Horowitz, ed. Pp. 17–46. Garden City, NY: Natural History Press.

———. 1974. Caribbean Transformation. Chicago, IL: Aldine.

———. 1989. The Sensation of Moving, While Standing Still. American Ethnologist 169(4):786–796.

Mishler, E. 1981. The Social Construction of Illness. In Social Contexts of Health, Illness, and Patient Care. E. Mishler, et al., eds. Pp. 141–168. Cambridge: Cambridge University Press.

Morgan, Lynn. 1987. Dependency Theory in the Political Economy of Health: An Anthropological Critique. Medical Anthropology Quarterly 1:131–154.

Morsy, S. 1990. Political Economy in Medical Anthropology. In Medical Anthropology: Contemporary Theory and Method. T. Johnson and C. Sargent, eds. Westport, CT: Praeger.

Mulford, H., and D. Miller. 1964. Measuring Public Acceptance of the Alcoholic as a Sick Person. Quarterly Journal of Studies on Alcohol 25:314–323.

Navarro, V. 1977. Social Security and Medicine in the U.S.S.R. Lexington, MA: Lexington Books.

Noble, D. 1979. America by Design: Science, Technology, and the Rise of Corporate Capitalism. New York: Alfred A. Knopf.

Osherson, S., and L. AmaraSingham. 1981. The Machine Metaphor in Medicine. In Social Contexts of Health, Illness, and Patient Care. E. Mishler, et al., eds. Pp. 218–249. Cambridge: Cambridge University Press.

Page, B., L. Rio, J. Sweeney, and C. McKay. 1985. Alcohol and Adaptation to Exile in Miami's Cuban Population. In The American Experience with Alcohol. L. Bennett and G. Ames, eds. Pp. 315–332. New York: Plenum.

Pappas, G. 1989. The Magic City: Unemployment in a Working Class Community. Ithaca, NY: Cornell University Press.

Park, P. 1983. Social-Class Factors in Alcoholism. In The Pathogenesis of Alcoholism, vol 6, Psychosocial Factors. B. Kissin and H. Begleiter, eds. Pp. 365–404. New York: Plenum.

Partridge, W. 1978. Uses and Nonuses of Anthropological Data on Drug Abuse. In Applied Anthropology in America. E. Eddy and W. Partridge, eds. Pp. 350–372. New York: Columbia University Press.

Pearlin, L., and C. Radabaugh. 1976. Economic Strains and the Coping Functions of Alcohol. American Journal of Sociology 82:652–663.

———. 1982. Ethnic and Racial Variation in Alcohol Use and Abuse. In Special Populations Issues. Pp. 239–311. Washington, D.C.: U.S. Department of Health and Human Services.

Rachal, J., J. Williams, M. Brehm, B. Cavanaugh, R. Moore, and W. Eckerman. 1975. Final Report: A National Study of Adolescent Drinking Behavior, Attitudes, and Correlates. Research Triangle Park, NC: Research Triangle Institute.

Rodriguez, C. 1980. Economic Survival in New York. In The Puerto Rican Struggle. C. Rodriguez, V. Sanchez Korrol, and J. Alers, eds. Pp. 31–46. Maplewood, NJ: Waterfront Press.

———. 1989. Puerto Ricans: Born in the U.S.A. Boston, MA: Unwin Hyman.

Rodriguez-Andrew, S., M. J. Gilbert, and R. Trotter. 1988. Mexican American Cultural Norms Related to Alcohol Use as Reflected in Drinking Settings and Language Use. In Alcohol Consumption among Mexicans and Mexican-Americans: A Binational Perspective. M. J. Gilbert, ed. Pp. 103–126. Los Angeles, CA: Spanish Speaking Mental Health Research Center, University of California.

Rosenwaike, I. 1987. Mortality Differentials among Persons Born in Cuba, Mexico, and Puerto Rico Residing in the United States, 1979–1981. American Journal of Public Health 77:603–606.

Rush, B. 1943. An Inquiry into the Effects of Ardent Spirits upon the Human Body and Mind. Quarterly Journal of Studies on Alcohol 4:321–341.

Safa, H. 1986. Female Employment in the Puerto Rican Working Class. In Women and Change in Latin America. J. Nash and H. Safa, eds. Pp. 84–105. South Hadley, MA: Bergin & Garvey.

Schaefer, J. M. 1982. Ethnic and Racial Variation in Alcohol Use and Abuse. In Special Population Issues. Pp. 239–311. Washington, D.C.: U.S. Department of Health and Human Services.

Scheder, J. 1988. A Sickly-Sweet Harvest: Farmworkers Diabetes and Social Equality. Medical Anthropology Quarterly 2:251–277.

Scheper-Hughes, N. 1990. Three Propositions for a Critically Applied Medical Anthropology. Social Science and Medicine 30(2):179–188.

Scheper-Hughes, N., and M. Lock. 1986. "Speaking Truth" to Illness: Metaphors, Reification, and a Pedagogy for Patients. Medical Anthropology Quarterly 17:137–140.

Seeman, M., and C. Anderson. 1983. Alienation and Alcohol: The Role of Work, Mastery, and Community in Drinking Behavior. American Sociological Review 48:60–77.

Sennett, R., and J. Cobb. 1973. The Hidden Injuries of Class. New York: Vintage Books.

Singer, M. 1986a. Toward a Political-Economy of Alcoholism: The Missing Link in the Anthropology of Drinking. Social Science and Medicine 23:113–130.

———. 1986b. Developing a Critical Perspective in Medical Anthropology. Medical Anthropology Quarterly 17(5): 128–129.

———. 1987a. Cure, Care and Control: An Ectopic Encounter with Biomedical Obstretics. *In* Encounters with Biomedicine: Case Studies in Medical Anthropology. H. Baer, ed. Pp. 249–265. New York: Gordon and Breach.

———. 1987b. Similarities and Differences in Alcohol Use and Abuse among Hispanic and Non-Hispanic Drinkers. *In* Alcohol Use and Abuse among Hispanic Adolescents. M. Singer, L. Davison, and F. Yalin, eds. Pp. 44–49. Hartford, CT: Hispanic Health Council.

———. 1989a. The Limitations of Medical Ecology: The Concept of Adaptation in the Context of Social Stratification and Social Transformation. Medical Anthropology 10(4):223–234.

———. 1989b. The Coming of Age of Critical Medical Anthropology. Social Science and Medicine 28(11):1193–1204.

———. 1989c. Keep the Label and the Perspective: A Response to "Emic" Critiques of Critical Medical Anthropology. Anthropology Newsletter 30(3):15, 19.

———. 1990a. Postmodernism and Medical Anthropology: Words of Caution. Medical Anthropology 12:289–304.

———. 1990b. Reinventing Medical Anthropology: Toward a Critical Re-Alignment. Social Science and Medicine 30(2):179–188.

Singer, M., H. Baer, and E. Lazarus. 1989. Critical Medical Anthropology in Question. Social Science and Medicine 30(2):5–8.

Singer, M., and M. Borrero. 1984. Indigenous Treatment for Alcoholism: The Case of Puerto Rican Spiritualism. Medical Anthropology 8:246–273.

Singer, M., L. Davison, and F. Yalin, eds. 1987. Alcohol Use and Abuse among Hispanic Adolescents. Hartford, CT: Hispanic Health Council.

Singer, M., C. Flores, L. Davison, G. Burke, and Z. Castillo. 1991. Puerto Rican Community Mobilizing in Response to the AIDS Crisis. Human Organization 50(1):73–81.

Singer, M., R. Irizarry, and J. Schensul. 1990. Needle Access as an AIDS Prevention Strategy for IV Drug Users: A Research Perspective. Human Organization 50(2):142–153.

Smart, R. 1979. Drinking Problems among Employed, Unemployed and Shiftworkers. Journal of Occupational Medicine 21:731–735.

Stebbins, K. 1987. Tobacco or Health in the Third World? A Political-Economic Analysis with Special Reference to Mexico. International Journal of Health Services 17:523–538.

———. 1990. Transnational Tobacco Companies and Health in Underdeveloped Countries: Recommendations for Avoiding a Smoking Epidemic. Social Science and Medicine 30(2):227–236.

Trice, H., and P. Roman. 1972. Spirits and Demons at Work: Alcohol and Other Drugs on the Job. Ithaca, NY: New York State School of Industrial and Labor Relations, Cornell University.

Trostle, J. 1990. Comments on Defining the Shape of Biocultural Studies. Medical Anthropology Quarterly 4:371–373.

Trotter, R. 1982. Ethnic and Sexual Patterns of Alcohol Use: Anglo and Mexican American College Students. Adolescence 17:305–325.

———. 1985. Mexican-American Experience with Alcohol: South Texas Examples. *In* The American Experience with Alcohol. L. Bennett and G. Ames, eds. Pp. 279–296. New York: Plenum.

Trotter, R., and J. Chavira. 1978. Discovering New Models for Alcohol Counseling in Minority Groups. *In* Modern Medicine and Medical Anthropology in the United States-Mexico Border Population. B. Velimirov, ed. Pp. 164–171. Washington, D.C.: Pan American Health Organization.

Wagenheim, K. 1973. The Puerto Ricans. New York: Anchor Books.

———. 1975. Puerto Rico: A Profile. New York: Praeger.

Wallerstein, E. 1979. The Capitalist World-Economy. Cambridge: Cambridge University Press.

Welte, J., and G. Barnes. 1987. Alcohol Use among Adolescent Minority Groups. Journal of Studies on Alcohol 48(4):329–346.

Wilson, R. 1984. Changing Validity of the Cirrhosis Mortality-Alcoholic Beverage Sales Construct: U.S. Trends, 1970–1977. Journal of Studies on Alcohol 45:53–58.

Wolf, E. 1982. Europe and the People without History. Berkeley, CA: University of California Press.

Zinn, H. 1980. A People's History of the United States. New York: Harper & Row.

32

A Teaching Framework for Cross-Cultural Health Care

Elois Ann Berlin
William C. Fowkes, Jr.

This is an excellent selection for completing and summarizing the section on ethnicity and health care. It is essentially a lecture to clinicians and medical students about the fundamental characteristics of successful cross-cultural medical practice. The key is effective communication between patient and health care giver. Effective communication is a fundamental aspect of all human relationships, yet it is surprisingly difficult to achieve. In this selection, the authors use the acronym LEARN as a mnemonic device (listen, explain, acknowledge, recommend, negotiate). It represents the key attributes of an effective cross-cultural communication process. The authors describe each stage in this communication process with a short case study from a multicultural hospital setting.

Language can be a barrier to effective communication because, in addition to different words and grammar, cultural beliefs and values underlie the communication process. Different cultural backgrounds, like different languages, represent communication obstacles that can be overcome. The challenge of communication and cooperation among people of different ethnic groups can be found in the LEARN acronym. Many times, health care providers fail to listen and to identify a patient's concerns. Often, people in power think of themselves as giving orders to subordinates, rather than teaching, explaining, and recommending. Along with this old-fashioned idea that the doctor's orders are the law to be obeyed, noncompliance is nothing more than disobedience.

But this model no longer works. Today, a buzz word in clinical practice is the "therapeutic alliance" of physician and patient, meaning that healing requires a partnership based on mutual understanding, respect, and cooperation. Such a partnership is more difficult to achieve across the cultural divide of an ethnic boundary. The key to such a partnership is effective communication.

Other guides for cross-cultural clinical practice can be found in the collection Ethnicity and Health Care *(Harwood 1981), special issues of the* Western Journal of Medicine *(Barker and Clark 1992; Clark 1983), and chapters in behavioral science textbooks for medical students (Brown, Gregg, and Ballard 1997).*

As you read this selection, consider these questions:

- *Why is it important for doctors to know about cross-cultural medicine? After all, isn't medicine a universal science?*

- *Do you think that following the advice in the LEARN acronym would take more of a physician's time? Would it be worth the trouble?*

- *To what extent do social class differences and educational differences complicate effective communication between health care givers and patients?*

- *Do you think that medical school students would listen to this lecture? Could they learn from it?*

Health care providers are finding themselves dealing with increasingly diverse patient populations. Fueled by armed conflict, political unrest and economic instability, the influx of immigrants into the United States is prompting a structural shift in the demographic representation of minorities. The impact is especially acute in states like California, which are subject to secondary migration or relocation after preliminary resettlement. These migration patterns, in combination with reproductive patterns, set a trend that is predictive of what has been termed *minoritization*.

In addition to language and socioeconomic barriers recognized to stand between minority populations and the health care system,[1-3] there is an increasing awareness of the impact of diverse health and disease belief systems on the interaction of health care providers and patients of a different cultural heritage.[4-10]

Overcoming these obstacles is aided by the incorporation of new tolls for cross-cultural communication. At the Family Practice Residency at San Jose Health Center, we have begun to develop a set of guidelines for health care providers in a practice that serves a

303

multicultural patient population. We have structured these guidelines around the following mnemonic:

Guidelines for Health Practitioners: LEARN

L   *Listen* with sympathy and understanding to the patient's perception of the problem

E   *Explain* your perceptions of the problem

A   *Acknowledge* and discuss the differences and similarities

R   *Recommend* treatment

N   *Negotiate* agreement

It should be emphasized that the LEARN model is not intended to replace completely the normal structure of the medical interview. Rather, it is intended as a supplement to history taking. The difference in focus is between a patient's factual subjective report of onset and duration and characteristics of symptoms and a patient's theoretical explanation of the reasons for the problem.

DISCUSSION OF GUIDELINES

Listen

Interview techniques have been proposed that aid in elicitation of a patient's conception of the cause, process, duration and outcome of an illness as well as healing strategies and resources that the patient considers to be appropriate.[4,6] Understanding a patient's conceptualizations and preferences constitutes the first step. Questions such as, What do you feel may be causing your problem? How do you feel the illness is affecting you? and What do you feel might be of benefit? are examples of the shift in focus.

Explain

Explanation or communication of a "Western medicine" model is the next step. This may be a biomedical model but often the provider is making an educated guess, for example, that a patient's diarrhea is indeed due to an intestinal virus as opposed to toxins from contaminated food or psychosocial stress. In the primary care setting, treatment is frequently initiated without a definite diagnosis or biomedical model. However, it is critical to the success of the interaction that the care-giver have a strategy and that the strategy be conveyed to the patient.

Acknowledge

Acknowledgment of a patient's explanatory model occurs next or is integrated into the previous explanatory step. Based on an understanding of the explanatory models of both patient and provider, areas of agreement can be pointed out and potential conceptual conflicts understood and resolved. Resolution may involve bridging the conceptual gap between disparate belief systems. In many instances there is no therapeutic dilemma involved and a patient's own model can be incorporated into the system of care. If the provider feels that a patient's explanatory model and its consequences may have possible deleterious effects, such as a toxic medicinal substance, then an attempt must be made to market a more appropriate model leading to the next step. An example of a counterproductive explanatory model and resultant intervention is the consumption of pickle brine for hypertension—called "high blood" by some southern blacks. "High blood" is characterized by too much blood and treated by avoiding rich foods and consuming pickle brine, an "astringent" substance. The high sodium content of pickle brine would likely be deleterious in the face of blood pressure elevation.[10]

Recommend

Within the constraints imposed by a patient's and provider's explanatory models, a treatment plan can be developed. Patient involvement in the treatment plan is important. This step constitutes an extension of such an effort to include cultural parameters when appropriate culturally relevant approaches can be incorporated into the recommendation to enhance the acceptability of the treatment plan.

Negotiate

Negotiation is perhaps the key concept of the proposed LEARN model. It is necessary to understand a patient's perceptions and to communicate the provider's perspective so that a treatment plan can be developed and negotiated. There may be a variety of options from the biomedical, psychosocial or cultural approaches that could be appropriately applied. The final treatment plan should be an amalgamation resulting from a unique partnership in decision making between provider and patient. A patient can truly be involved in the instrumentation of recovery if the therapeutic process fits within the cultural framework of healing and health.

APPLICATION OF GUIDELINES

To illustrate the application of the LEARN model, we have selected examples from the experiences of our staff and students. We have chosen a separate case to exemplify each concept of LEARN. Although all or most steps in the model are involved in every clinical encounter, the cases were chosen to best illustrate each concept specifically.

■ *Listen*

A 28-year-old Vietnamese woman, a social work student, was first seen in the Family Practice Center in autumn of 1982 because of weight loss, mood swings, nervousness, sweaty palms and an increased number of bowel movements. She had lived in the United States for five years. Initially she volunteered that she had been extremely depressed ten years earlier and had once attempted suicide. She had an established diagnosis of retinitis pigmentosa and was legally blind. She was living with her mother and two siblings and was entering college to study social work. On initial examination there were findings consistent with retinitis pigmentosa. Lid lag was also noted. Initial laboratory studies elicited values consistent with mild hyperthyroidism and she was started on a regimen of propranolol hydrochloride taken orally.

She was seen regularly and had a constellation of symptoms including abdominal pain, mute attacks during which she could not open her mouth, twitching and palpitations. After taking propranolol she felt very fatigued and weak and had an episode of syncope after which she refused to take further medication. Additional symptoms developed including squeezing substernal chest pain. Repeat thyroid function testing was normal.

There was no apparent physical explanation for the symptoms and it was felt that she was suffering from anxiety and depression related to her disability and life stress. Supportive approaches were instituted with regular counseling visits. Relaxation training and a life journal were begun. The technique used for relaxation included both breathing exercises and visualization.

Shortly after these measures were instituted the patient presented in a very agitated state and said that the pleasant visual images she attempted to conjure turned "dark and scary." She also related that a childhood diary had been taken from her by one of her sisters and that the contents had been ridiculed. This made it very difficult for her to keep the recommended life journal. At this time, with encouragement, she related some very important events in her childhood. When she was 8 to 10 years of age her affliction was felt by her family to be due to her posses-

sion by an evil spirit, and a healer was summoned. The attempt at exorcism failed and this was interpreted as a sign that her illness was a form of punishment for her transgressions in a past life. She was virtually locked away in a back room for several years before the events that led to her immigration.

She stated she no longer held this set of beliefs, but she continued to worry about whether she was a good person. Her physician agreed with her rejection of the ideas held by her family and suggested that her studies in social work and her commitment to help people were indeed evidence of her goodness and worth.

She moved out of her home to campus housing and has improved somewhat. She continues to visit the Family Practice Center for supportive care.

Cultural Context

The medicoreligious beliefs of Vietnam derive from such a variety of sources that specification of exact religious context of the healing rituals of this patient's early life is difficult.

There have been historical interchanges of Ayurvedic medicine, with its roots in Galenic humoral pathology, influenced by Hinduism and Buddhism, especially in Southeast Asia.[11–16] Chinese medicine, which is more closely related to Confucian and Taoist religious philosophies, has made an additional contribution. More recent influences come from Catholicism and Western medicine. Local indigenous beliefs and practices also no doubt exert some influence.[17 (pp xviii–xxix)]

Attribution of illness to possession by spirits or demons is consistent with all of these religious traditions (including Catholicism, at least historically). Whichever temple and priest or shaman the patient's family applied to for help, her status as a victim of a malevolent source would have been validated by successful exorcism. This would have been confirmed by the return of her eyes to normal appearance. Failure of repeated exorcistic rites to alleviate the symptoms led to the conclusion that her deviant appearance was a mystical mark, a sign of evil committed in a former life. This conclusion transformed her from victim to perpetrator. In a family whose members include all of the living, dead and as yet unborn, the final diagnosis shamed the family in perpetuity. This was the justification for confining the child in the house and restricting her social interactions. The family was, literally, attempting to hide their shame. The psychologic burden that this explanation placed on the patient resulted in somatization of complaints. Mental illness, which bears strong negative sanctions for similar reasons, would have constituted yet another mark against the family.

The patient migrated with her family to the United States when she was an adolescent. The process of acculturation and an alternative biomedical diagnosis provided a context for a change of attitudes and perception of self-worth. Although several people whom the patient had consulted over time (social workers and health care providers) had felt that there was a troubling "cultural component" in her medical history, the patient had never been able to discuss it fully. Careful probing and an open, nonjudgmental attitude on the part of the resident physician allowed the patient to divulge the complete background information and to acknowledge the lingering self-doubt these experiences had produced. She was then able to initiate steps for improvement such as removing herself from the family context, which produced continuing stress and reinforced a negative self-image, and continuing her studies in a helping profession, which confirmed her goodness.

■ *Explain*

A 21-month-old Mexican-American male infant with recurrent onset of fever, runny nose and noisy breathing was brought to the clinic by his mother. The mother noted that the child had been sleeping restlessly and making sighing noises while asleep.

On physical examination, he was found to have edematous mucous membranes and mucoid nasal discharge consistent with an upper respiratory tract infection (URI).

The mother stated that she was very concerned because two months earlier the child had had a major motor seizure that she associated with a high fever. She felt that the seizure had precipitated *susto* (fright disease), as evidenced by the sighing and restlessness during sleep, and wanted a regimen to control fever and prevent a worsening of the child's *susto*.

The resident physician discussed upper respiratory tract infections and their effects on breathing. He suggested a decongestant for relief of symptoms. He also confirmed the relationship of fever to seizures and advised continued use of antipyretics. He demonstrated the use of sponge baths to reduce fever and emphasized the importance of fever control in preventing seizures. In addition, he suggested that the mother consult a *curandera* (folk healer) concerning her questions about *susto*. The patient has subsequently been seen for routine visits and has had no further seizures or other significant problems.

Cultural Context

Susto is a Latin-American folk illness that is caused by fright.[18–22] The source or cause of fright might be any-thing from a simple startle response to an encounter with spirits. Children are particularly susceptible to *susto*. Symptoms vary widely, but the sighing and restlessness or poor sleep pattern exhibited by the patient are common manifestations. The mother's explanatory model for this case of *susto* was as follows:

URI → fever → seizures → *susto* → sleep disturbance

The provider was able to give a detailed biomedical explanation of that portion of the patient's explanatory model to which it was applicable and to recommend consultation with a folk specialist for that portion that lay outside the purview of modern medicine.

■ *Acknowledge*

A 25-year-old Vietnamese woman was seen for a routine prenatal examination. As part of her evaluation she had blood drawn for laboratory testing. Within the next few days she returned with a variety of symptoms including weakness, fatigue and coryza. She attributed this to having blood removed, feeling that removal of blood weakens the system and causes illness.

Her provider, a Vietnamese physician, was aware of the belief and acknowledged it, but also explained how much blood volume she actually had and gave the example of persons donating blood, a much larger volume, without symptoms.

She was pleased with the explanation, seemed to feel less fearful and her symptoms abated.

Cultural Context

The probable influence of Chinese medicine or Ayurvedic medicine (or both) in Southeast Asia is seen in this patient's response to blood tests. Edwards[23] describes the following physiological process from Chinese medical theory: "The connection between food, [blood], sex and health is found in the transformational formula in which seven units of the precursor yields one unit of the subsequent product:

Food → blood → *jing* → *qi* → *shen*"

Edwards defines the terms as follows: *jing* = "sexual fluid," which is a vital substance; *qi* = "breath" or "life energy" (also written *chi*); *shen* = "ethereal energy." A similar process has been described from Ayurvedic medical theory, which could be outlined as follows:

Food → chyle → blood → flesh → fat
bones → marrow → semen[24]

Because several physiological systems are involved in the production, transportation and storage process—that is, digestive, genitourinary, circulatory and respiratory—symptoms can be diffuse and varied. Since all descriptions indicate a geometric reduction between precursor and product, the consequences of interruption of the cycle would increase geometrically in seriousness at each earlier step in the process.

The patient's and the provider's explanatory models were similar in that they both believed blood loss to constitute a potential threat to health. Their explanations differed in the amount of blood that must be lost to pose a problem. By relating the amount of blood removed to the total blood volume and comparing this with the much larger quantities safely removed from blood donors, the physician was able to reassure the patient and to effect alleviation of symptoms.

■ *Recommend*

A 38-year-old Mexican-American man was seen in the Family Practice Center for chronic genitourinary problems. He had experienced hematuria and right flank pain two years before. In addition there had been recurrent episodes over 18 years of right flank pain and dysuria, diagnosed as urinary tract infections. He did not use analgesics. Examination of the external genitalia and prostate was unremarkable. He had no abdominal or flank tenderness. Analysis of urine showed 50 to 100 leukocytes per high dry field. An intravenous pyelogram showed a localized hydronephrotic area in the upper pole of the right kidney.

He was seen by a urologist who carried out retrograde pyelograms. These showed a large calyceal diverticulum connected with the right collecting system, with hydronephrosis of the upper pole of the kidney.

Surgical treatment was recommended. The patient expressed considerable reluctance to have an operation. When questioned by his family physician he expressed concern that his "blood was low" and that he would have trouble going through an operation under the circumstances. His physician discussed the amount of blood that could be expected to be lost with a partial nephrectomy and also the total available blood supply in the body. He suggested that a surgical procedure be delayed for a period to allow the patient to "build up his blood" with appropriate medication. This was quite acceptable to the patient and the consultant urologist.

He subsequently underwent uneventful partial right nephrectomy.

Cultural Context

Blood is "hot" according to the hot-cold system of humoral pathology as practiced in Latin America. Blood is also associated with strength, both in the health and the sexual sense. Having a large supply of blood makes one strong and healthy, but is also associated with virility and hence with machismo. Menstrual blood, semen and sexual activity are very hot.[25] Men's blood is hotter than women's blood.

The patient felt a need to build up his blood supply in order to have reserve strength for an operation because he expected a significant amount of blood to be lost during it. He was willing to accept the recommendation that he take iron to help build blood. However, an equally acceptable way to build blood would have been to eat blood products such as fried blood or blood sausage. Organ meats are good for building up strength and blood supply. In the Mexican-American folk system, an abundant and varied diet builds physical reserves, including a healthy supply of blood.

By describing the surgical procedure, including control of bleeding, the resident physician was able to alleviate some of the patient's concerns about blood loss. The provider was then able to recommend a treatment plan acceptable to the patient by prescribing "blood building" medicines and by scheduling the operation following a delay of fixed duration that the patient concurred would be adequate to prepare himself.

■ *Negotiate*

A 48-year-old black man was seen because of severe hypertension and congestive heart failure associated with far-advanced renal insufficiency. Initially he was managed conservatively. It became obvious, however, that he had reached a stage at which renal dialysis was his only hope for survival.

When he was approached about the possibility of hemodialysis he declined, stating that he was a devout Christian and felt that the will of God was of prime importance and that he would wait for God's intervention rather than accept dialysis.

His physician acknowledged the importance of God's influence, but suggested that the opportunity for dialysis as a means to control his condition might be the way God had intended for him to survive. Indeed, there was nothing in the Bible that prohibited dialysis and God helps those who help themselves.

The following day the patient consented to hemodialysis and now has a functioning bovine shunt and is doing well.

Cultural Context

The socioreligious context of this patient's explanatory model was fundamentalist Protestantism. The direct intervention and control of health by God is supported in the Old Testament (Exodus 4: 11): ". . . who maketh the dumb or deaf, or the seeing or the blind? Have not I the Lord?" The New Testament contains dozens of examples of the healing powers of Christ.[26] While one common alternative to treatment is faith healing,[27] this patient seemed to be relying on the Old Testament with healing based on direct intervention by God. He suggested that he felt that God did not intend him to die yet and would intervene on his behalf. The provider was able to call on other aspects of Christian beliefs such as "the Lord helps those who help themselves" and that God sometimes works through human agents: "For to one is given by the Spirit the word of wisdom; . . . to another the gift of healing by the same Spirit" (I Corinthians 12:8–9).

The implication was drawn that the physicians and dialysis might be the instruments through which God intended to intervene. Medical intervention was thus translated into a construct that did not violate the tenets of the patient's faith. By using beliefs from the patient's own religious background, the provider was able to negotiate acceptance of recommended biomedical treatment.

SUMMARY AND CONCLUSIONS

Given current demographic trends it is probably unrealistic to assume that health care providers can gain in-depth knowledge about the health-affecting beliefs and practices of every ethnic or cultural group they are likely to encounter in practice. The processes of acculturation, interethnic variation and social change also serve as confounding agents in predicting knowledge, behavior and attitudes. Social class differences, too, provide striking variability. We have, therefore, chosen a process-oriented model by which the cultural, social and personal information relevant to a given illness episode can be elicited, discussed and negotiated or incorporated.

However, it is common in our experience for patients of different beliefs to be reluctant to discuss this problem for fear of criticism or ridicule. It is certainly of value for providers who deal with culturally diverse patients to have some understanding of common basic conceptions of health, illness and anatomy held by these persons. Much work needs to be done in codifying these conceptions and making them available to professionals in medicine.

The foregoing examples serve to illustrate some of the means the members of a family practice residency program have used for enhancing communication and promoting the integration of patients' and providers' perceptions of needs and solutions into the therapeutic process.

REFERENCES

1. Bullough B, Bullough V: Poverty, Ethnic Identity and Health Care. New York: Appleton-Century-Crofts, 1972
2. Quesada GM: Language and communication barriers for health delivery to a minority group. Soc Sci Med 1976 June; 10:323–327
3. Language Access Task Force, Velez M (Chief Author): Health Care for Non-English Speaking Populations: Access and Quality. West Bay Health Systems Agency. San Francisco, Western Center for Health Planning, 1982
4. Harwood A (Ed): Ethnicity and Medical Care. Cambridge, Mass, Harvard University Press, 1981
5. Hill CE: A folk medical belief system in the American South: Some practical considerations. South Med 1976 Dec. pp 11–17
6. Kleinman A, Eisenberg L, Good B: Culture, illness and care: Clinical lessons from anthropological and cross cultural research. Ann Intern Med 1978; 89:251–258
7. Martinez RA (Ed): Hispanic Culture and Health Care: Fact, Fiction and Folklore. St Louis, CV Mosby, 1978
8. Mason JC: Ethnicity and clinical care. Indiana Phys Assist Health Practitioner 1980 Nov; 30:30–39
9. Muecke MA: Caring for Southeast Asian refugee patients in the USA. Am J Public Health 1983; 73:431–438
10. Snow LF: Folk medical beliefs and their implications for care of patients: A review based on studies among Black Americans. Ann Intern Med 1974; 81:82–96
11. Basham AL: The practice of medicine in ancient and medieval India. In Leslie C (Ed): Asian Medical Systems. Berkeley and Los Angeles, University of California Press, 1976, pp 18–43
12. Burgel JC: Secular and religious features of medieval Arabic medicine, In Leslie C (Ed): Asian Medical Systems, Berkeley and Los Angeles, University of California Press, 1976, pp 44–62
13. Gard RA: Buddhism. New York, George Braziller, 1962
14. Obeyesekere G: The impact of Ayurvedic ideas on the culture and the individual in Sri-Lanka. In Leslie C (Ed): Asian Medical Systems. Berkeley and Los Angeles, University of California Press, 1976, pp 201–226
15. Olness K: Indochinese refugees—Cultural aspects of working with Lao refugees. Minn Med 1979 Dec; 62:871–874
16. Renou L: Hinduism. New York, George Braziller, 1961
17. Whitmore JK (Ed): An Introduction to Indochinese History, Culture, Language and Life—For Persons Involved With the Indochinese Refugee Education and Resettlement Project in the State of Michigan, Ann Arbor, Center for South and Southeast Asian Studies, University of Michigan, 1979
18. Klein J: Susto: The anthropological study of diseases of adaptation. Soc Sci Med 1978 Jan; 12:23–28
19. O'Nell CW, Selby HA: Sex differences in the incidence of susto in the Zapotec Pueblos: An analysis of the relationships between sex role expectations and a folk illness. Ethnology 1968; 7:95–105
20. O'Nell CW: An investigation of reported "fright" as a factor in the etiology of susto. "Magical Fright." Ethos 1975; 3:41–63

21. Rubel AJ: The epidemiology of folk illness: Susto in Hispanic America. Ethnology 1964; 3:268–283

22. Uzzell D: Susto revisited: Illness as a strategic role. Am Ethnol 1974; 1:369–378

23. Edwards JW: Semen anxiety in South Asian cultures: Cultural and transcultural significance. Med Anthropol, in press

24. Zimmer HR: Hindu Medicine. Baltimore, Johns Hopkins Press, 1948

25. Ingham JM: On Mexican folk medicine. Am Anthropol 1970; 72: 76–87

26. Henderson G, Primeaux M: Religious beliefs and healing. *In* Henderson G, Primeaux M (Eds): Transcultural Health Care. Menlo Park, Calif., Addison-Wesley, 1981, pp 185–195

27. Baer HA: Prophets and advisers in black spiritual churches: Therapy, palliative, or opiate? Cult Med Psychiatry 1981 Jun; 5:145–170

Stigma and Coping with Chronic Illness

✤ CONCEPTUAL TOOLS ✤

■ *The illness experience may include social and psychological dimensions that cannot be cured with medicine.* Medical anthropologists use the term *illness experience* to refer to a patient-centered view of sickness, especially the social and psychological aspects (Kleinman 1988). Attention to the overall illness experience—the human aspects of the illness experience—is not a strength of biomedicine. In fact, many see that this major failing of biomedicine is the reason more and more people in the United States use alternative health care systems (Eisenberg et al. 1993). The human suffering of some illnesses may be in the form of discrimination, stigma, damaged self-concept, and social ostracism. Suffering related to the social and psychological dimensions of illness may be worse and last longer than the disease itself; this is especially the case with chronic illnesses. The social meanings of illnesses can also vary from culture to culture.

■ *Stigma is the negative social attribution placed on people because of their disability or illness.* Based on the famous work of Erving Goffman (1963), *stigma* is defined as a sociological phenomenon in which an individual is devalued and shunned because the illness or disability makes her or him different or "not normal." The stigmatized condition becomes the "master status" that overpowers all other social attributes. This is especially prevalent when a chronic condition is obvious and public. Stigma creates long-lasting suffering.

■ *Chronic illnesses have different and more complex social dimensions than acute illnesses.* The rights and responsibilities of the sick role usually refer to the time-limited illness experience when an individual is sick and then cured. Chronic illnesses or disabilities do not follow the conventions of the sick role. Instead, chronic illnesses become part of people's core social identities. The illness experience is a continuing one, to which an individual must adapt. These adjustments may be difficult, especially because of sociocultural expectations about being normal.

■ *The illness experience may be powerful.* Practitioners of biomedicine are so unfamiliar with the illness experience that a significant number of physicians have written books about their personal stories of being sick (Hahn 1995). The movie *The Doctor* is an example of this genre, wherein the personal illness experience functions as a revelation and results in a conversion to a new way of practicing medicine. However, medical anthropologists have traditionally taken the patient's point of view in understanding the illness experience, and the ethnographic method emphasizes the native's *emic* analysis (that is, explaining things from the insider's point of view). More recently, some anthropologists have become autobiographical and reflexive in their ethnographic descriptions. This means that the position of the anthropologist and his or her relationship with the subject of study is included in the ethnography, in part because the author recognizes that it is impossible to be completely objective. A good example of this approach is found in selection 35 by Robert Murphy on the subject of his own paralysis.

■ *The anthropological study of aging has much in common with medical anthropology.* Aging is a normal part of the human life cycle. In U.S. society, however, the process of aging has been medicalized. A significant number of anthropological studies of communities of the elderly, including the particular contexts of nursing homes (Savishinsky 1991; Sokolovsky 1983), have shown how the lives of the elderly are shaped by their interactions with the medical system. In addition, the elderly often live in circumstances of age segregation, separated from their families, almost as if old age itself was a stigmatized condition.

33

Coping with Stigma: Lifelong Adaptation of Deaf People

Gaylene Becker

Usually when people think of an illness that carries stigma, they think of the classic case of leprosy, as we saw in selection 16. What comes to mind are images of dirty bandages, lost fingers or toes, open sores, or the social ostracism of being unclean. Stigma means that people fear the individual who is sick. The suffering from stigma can be worse than the physical pain. In fact, the irony that Hansen's disease (leprosy) is not very contagious must add to the suffering of stigma. Disfigurement from an illness—as in the case of neurofibromatosis, the condition of the so-called Elephant Man—is worse because people assume that the individual inside is also disfigured. Stigma is the grotesque side of the beauty myth (Wolf 1992).

Medical anthropologists have studied the illness experience of people with chronic health problems, including congenital conditions like the extremely short stature of little people or dwarfs (Ablon 1988). People with such conditions have to learn to adapt to their life situation physically, socially, and psychologically.

This selection concerns stigma and lifelong adaptations of deaf people, a group with no obvious physical disability. However, their disability affects their social interactions. In this selection, Gaylene Becker refers to deafness as an "invisible disability." Deaf people have to interact with the hearing world, but that interaction is sometimes difficult or emotion-

ally painful. Often, hearing people condescend to deaf people, which is one theme of the award-winning film Children of a Lesser God. *Although deafness is not a disease, the deaf form a community with special needs. Several years ago, college students at Gallaudete University (a university for the deaf) engaged in a nationally recognized protest when a hearing president was appointed by the university's board of trustees. The Americans with Disabilities Act has guaranteed hearing-impaired people access to public facilities and events, but the issues of stigma still remain.*

As you read this selection, consider these questions:

- *Why might an "invisible disability" involve a different set of problems?*

- *Is the creation of social stigma simply part of human nature? Or does our culture define what is normal?*

- *To what extent does the term* adapt *used in this selection have the same meaning as the concept of adaptation used in the first part of this book?*

- *What are the advantages and disadvantages of hearing-impaired people attending separate schools or being mainstreamed? Is participation in a separate community a normal human need or an adaptation to ostracism?*

INTRODUCTION

Mrs. Simpson[1] was sitting in her small, cluttered apartment in senior citizen housing, relating the story of her life. Suddenly, she became agitated, jumped up, and enacted a drama from her childhood.

> I was playing in the school yard with some other girls and a boy came along. He pointed at me. "Deafy," he screamed. "Deaf and dumb," and he threw something like acid in my face. It was a terrible day in my life. Why should he hate me just because I am deaf?

Stigma is a universal phenomenon. In every society certain conditions are stigmatized, whether they are based on physical "blemishes," or on behaviour that deviates from the norm.[2] Societies develop negative attitudes in response to the stigmatizing condition. Individuals with such a blemish or behaviour quickly become aware of the way others view them. The stigmatized individual must struggle with these negative attitudes and with the devalued status that accompanies them and develop strategies for handling the stigma. The individual who fails to do this cannot function adequately. In American society, failure to learn coping skills often results in institutionalization, or at best, existence on the fringes of society. When sufficient numbers of stigmatized people form a subsociety, they build coping strategies for dealing with stigma into their subculture.

This paper describes the ways in which older deaf people perceive and deal with stigma. The author studied 200 people in the San Francisco Bay Area who were born deaf or became deaf in the first few years of life. They were all over the age of 60 at the time of the study and communicated in American Sign Language. Fieldwork was conducted in sign language, utilizing traditional anthropological field techniques of participant observation and in-depth interviewing. The 200 people formed a natural group, and from this group 60 were selected for in-depth interviewing. Participant-observation activities took place wherever aged deaf people congregated—in senior citizen centers, at deaf clubs, at funerals, and in people's homes. The author did participant-observation almost daily during the one-year period of the research.

Deafness is called an invisible disability because it is only noticeable when a person attempts to communicate.[3] No visible indicators, such as the white cane of the blind person, give other people cues about what to expect in communication with a deaf person. Once the disability is known, the impact of it may be heightened.[4] Hearing people often "freeze" and withdraw from the situation or behave inappropriately. This type of behaviour is so common that Schlesinger and Meadow[5] have labeled it "shock withdrawal paralysis." Such a response to the deaf individual is in part due to the stigma attached to sign language, and is a continuous reminder to deaf people that they vary from the norm.

THE ROOTS OF STIGMA

The experience of stigma is inextricably intertwined with the condition of deafness for most deaf people and arises in the first few years of life. The great majority of aged deaf people had hearing parents with whom they were never able to satisfactorily communicate. These individuals did not begin to acquire language until they went to school at the age of five or six. The inability of parents to teach their children language and to socialize them created an emotional crisis that was exacerbated by the controversy over educational methods for deaf children. Parents faced a dilemma. They had to make a choice: whether to have their children learn the "oral" method that taught speech and lipreading, or whether to send children away to a school where they would learn sign language. One hearing parent said of this decision, "It was agonizing. My in-laws were against me. They said I just wanted to get rid of the deaf one—by sending him off to a state school. I decided it was in his best interest, but it wasn't easy to let him go."

American Sign Language was, and is, forbidden in oral schools, and its use brought punishment to the individual. In those state schools where it was used, the stigma surrounding it created a common bond among deaf children. In old age people still discuss their first awareness of being stigmatized. One woman said, "My father didn't want to send his child to an 'asylum'—it would bring shame on the family," while another respondent said, "My mother dragged me out of that school—she said it was not nice to sign."

In contrast, deaf individuals in the study group who had deaf parents did not experience these conflicts. Eight percent of the deaf population have deaf parents,[6] from whom they learn sign language and with whom they develop adequate communication. Meadow[7] found that such individuals have higher self-esteem than deaf people with hearing parents. Deaf people from deaf families see themselves as carrying on a cultural tradition to which little or no stigma is attached. Instead, they have a strong and positive identification that carries them through life.

American Sign Language, made up of signs, gestures, finger-spelling, facial expressions, and body language, is often embarrassing or frightening to the uninitiated. In any case, it is negatively perceived. It is distinct from English and follows different grammatical and syntactical construction.[8] Until the past few years, when sign language systems based on English were introduced, American Sign Language was the only system of manual signs in common use in the United States. Regardless of the type of education they received as children, in adulthood American Sign Language is the main means of communication for most deaf Americans.

The negative attitudes of hearing parents and the general public toward sign language creates conflict about the language for its users. One informant reported that whenever she started to leave the house to visit deaf friends, her mother said, "Oh, you're not going out with those deaf, are you?" (referring to her signing friends). The stigma attached to sign language further influenced deaf people's perspective of the world, so that they saw the world as being divided into two kinds of people: those who could hear and those who were deaf.

In adulthood deaf people demonstrate considerable ambivalence about their own language. Various informants talked to me about how sign language is "negative," making the sign with particular force. Many individuals talked about how they are "for" total communication, a recent innovative method in deaf education, because it combines sign language with speech and lipreading and is thus more acceptable. Most noticeable, however, is the way signs change in the privacy of the group. In groups of deaf people sign language becomes bigger and bolder than in public. Facial expression and body language take on new dimensions, and the richness of the language is exploited to its fullest.

IDENTITY

American Sign Language is a symbolic badge of identity in the deaf community. Identity provides the individual with a sense of self and enables him or her to relate that sense of self to the surrounding world. Clark and Kiefer[9] define identity as "that cognitive structure which gives a sense of coherence, continuity, and social relatedness to one's image of oneself." Deaf identity is crystalized early in life and is maintained throughout the life course. As individuals age, deafness defines their relationship to society.

Deaf-hearing interactions are characterized by ambiguity. Ambiguity regarding the degree of impairment in disability has the most negative impact on interpersonal relationships.[10] An informant commented, "People often talk to me and I can't answer. I shake my head and point to my ear. But they don't understand—they think I'm stuck up."

Regardless of the actual quantity of interaction with either hearing or deaf people, conflict is kept alive in the person's mind by the inconsistencies between self-perception with reference to the in-group and to the outside world. A deaf man said, "It's not very nice, but have you heard the expression, 'deafy'?" As the author nodded yes, he continued, "It's sad to say, but I know people I would have to call deafies. The major characteristic of the deafy is fear of association with hearing people."

The sign, deafy (the thumb is put against the ear and the fingers wave back and forth), is probably the most stigmatized expression in sign language. It symbolizes negative experience in deaf-hearing interaction, and stands for deaf and dumb, in the literal sense. In talking about oneself in front of hearing people, the expression is used in several ways: (1) by highly educated people as a form of irony or sarcasm, (2) by people with minimal English language skills who are forced to convey their lack of understanding of the situation to a hearing person, and (3) to express anger and frustration at the hearing world for its construed wrongs against the deaf. For example, in a bitter denouncement of the oral method, one informant finished up with "I didn't learn anything—that's why I'm a deafy."

Early fears about the hearing world have been maintained, characterized by the fear of being seen as a deafy by the hearing world. This often leads to negative predictions about the fate of any deaf-hearing interaction. For example, a number of deaf people predicted that a program that planned to integrate deaf and hearing aged would fail. In explanation, one informant said, "Deaf don't like to be around hearing." Another informant acknowledged this attitude, and said, "Some deaf people get mad dealing with hearing people, but my attitude is just to be calm—they (hearing people) will gradually get used to it (the deafness)."

Many deaf people indeed have feelings of inferiority which they express by the elaboration of signs that connote stupidity. Sign language has a large number of signs for inferior mental ability, e.g. stupid, ignorant, pea-brain, know-nothing, and dummy. One informant demonstrated how he felt about himself when he said to the researcher, "I'm dumb . . . You're hearing—smart," while another informant said of herself, "Me—no voice—dumb." This perception, which correlates hearing with intelligence and deafness with dumbness, was almost universal in individuals' comments and underlines the stigmatized way individuals see themselves.

THE INFLUENCE OF COPING MECHANISMS ON SELF-ESTEEM

Deaf identity is also shaped by social factors that engender a positive sense of self. The commonality of experiences, the frequent interaction with other deaf people, and successful communication about intimate aspects of everyday life help develop a sense of self-esteem that grows with time.[11]

In the process of personal development, deaf people have evolved a range of coping mechanisms to deal with stigma. The primary way they do this is a normalization process. The term "normalizing" has been used to describe the response of chronically ill and disabled people in different situations. In this context, normalizing refers to a strategy of social interaction. For example, Davis[12] uses the term to analyze the social behaviour of children with polio, while Strauss[13] discusses normalizing in terms of disease management. Normalizing is situational, and everyone experiences the need to normalize at one time or another. The concept covers a broad area of behavior. Normalization can occur within any group that is set apart by deviance or social marginality. Within the tightly knit reference group of elderly deaf that I studied the normalization process took place primarily within the group. The introduction of outsiders invites cognitive dissonance. During the initial field experience, people were reticent to talk to me. As a hearing person I was a threat to their feelings of normality. Outsiders serve as reminders (both in fact and fantasy) that the world is not necessarily the way it is perceived by the in-group. For this reason, the in-group seldom accepts outsiders who are not deaf. Even adult children of deaf parents who are native signers are on the margin of the group if they can hear.

In contrast, interaction within the in-group enhances feelings of normality, reinforces positive feelings about one's abilities and validates one's worth. An informant said, "At the suggestion of the minister, my parents finally sent me to the state school when I was 18 to learn sign language. I made a lot of friends there and it made me realize how lonely and friendless my childhood had been." He began to socialize with deaf people, going to the Deaf Club and to social events at the state school. After dating a number of deaf women, he met his wife-to-be. She had grown up in state schools and had an extensive network of friends from childhood. When they married, he was included in this social network and developed his own friendships within the group. As the years passed, he took on leadership responsibilities in the church and deaf social organizations in which he and his wife were members. His interactions with hearing people were gradually reduced and when he retired, his social life with hearing people ended.

This story records a typical reaction to the difficulties inherent in deaf-hearing relationships. Once the individual has begun to reconcile the dilemma of trying to function as a hearing person and to begin to accept his or her deafness as a reality of life, he or she can devote energy formerly used in frustrating interactions to develop more fully as a person and to establish meaningful relationships with peers.

Membership in a deaf community that integrates the use of sign language and shared experience fosters self-esteem. During the course of fieldwork with the aged deaf, a pattern in the interaction of deaf people could be observed to recur. When individuals were in a group of deaf people they were talkative, confident, outgoing, and relaxed. When they were interacting with people with normal hearing, whether alone or with only a few deaf people present, they became quiet and hesitant. Thus, their self-perceptions shaped two different kinds of behaviour, one convivial, so-

ciable, and gregarious, the other wary, timorous, and withdrawn. This dichotomy in their behaviour reflects the ultimate ways in which they have adapted to their disability, and softened the effects of stigmatizing situations.

VALUES AND SOCIAL BEHAVIOR

Among the aged deaf I studied, being deaf is the single most important factor in their lives. One owes allegiance to deafness because of early communication problems where individuals could communicate only with peers. One must further the good of the community, putting it before oneself, if necessary. Conformity to a group norm serves important functions, especially for those who must continuously deal with their own nonconformity. Conformity decreases feelings of deviance and, at the same time, heightens feelings of belongingness, a process that occurs both consciously and unconsciously. This process is related to deviance disavowal. Davis[14] used this term in discussing the response of nonstigmatized individuals' behaviour toward the stigmatized. As part of the normalization process, however, the aged deaf dissociate themselves from others who suffer from a different social stigma: ethnic and racial minorities, the socially deviant, and those with other disabilities. For example, after stating that her hearing niece had been hospitalized in a mental institution, one woman added quickly, "But I never see her. I don't have anything to do with her."

In the process of normalization, symbols of stigma undergo a transformation in which the negative aspects of the symbol become a means of self-affirmation. One example is the single sign for "I love you." This has become a much-used symbol in the 1970's—in greeting one another, in speeches, on bumper stickers, and in graphics intended to educate the hearing world about deafness. The sign originated in the California School for the Deaf some 40 years ago when the school used the oral method and signing was prohibited. Students would arrange their fingers in the sign configuration and walk down the hall, dangling a hand casually at their side or holding it against their books.[15] Through this maneuver the students demonstrated deaf solidarity against a hearing world. The sign has thus undergone a profound transformation. The stigmatized origin of the sign has been forgotten, and it has become a powerful symbol of unity and affection that is now used by deaf people all over the United States.

CONCLUSION

In efforts to counteract what Goffman[16] refers to as spoiled identity, and to develop as individuals, aged deaf people have lived their lives on two levels: (1) the superficial interactions with hearing "strangers," and (2) the intimate interactions with deaf peers. As time passes, intimate interactions become increasingly important to the self-concept. The awkward, tension-laden interaction with strangers, although they are reminders of one's deafness, become easier to avoid as people age. By limiting the intensity and frequency of their contacts with the hearing world, elderly deaf people reduce the level of frustration with which they must live. The combination of deaf identity and a strong system of social support sustain elderly deaf people against isolation and loss of self-worth. Thus, they have created a climate that enables them to adapt to their disability.

REFERENCES

1. A pseudonym is used to protect confidentiality.
2. Goffman E. *Stigma: Notes on the Management of Spoiled Identity.* Prentice Hall, Englewood Cliffs, NJ, 1963.
3. Meadow K. P. Personal and social development of deaf persons. In *Psychology of Deafness for Rehabilitation Counselors* (Edited by Bolton B.). University Park Press, Baltimore, 1976.
4. Davis F. Deviance disavowal: the management of strained interaction by the visibly handicapped. *Soc. Probl.* **9**, 120, 1961.
5. Schlesinger H. S. and Meadow K. P. *Sound and Sign,* Univ. of California Press, Berkeley, 1972.
6. Schein J. and Delk M. T. *The Deaf Population of the United States.* National Association of the Deaf, Silver Springs, MD, 1974.
7. Meadow K. P. Parental response to the medical ambiguities of deafness. *J. Hlth Soc. Behav.* **9**, 299, 1968.
8. Stokoe W. C. Sign language structure: an outline of the visual communication systems of the American deaf. Occasional Papers No. 8, University of Buffalo, Buffalo, NY, 1960.
9. Clark M. M. and Kiefer C. Working paper on ethnic identity. Mimeo, Human Development Program, University of California, San Francisco, 1971.
10. Zahn M. A. Incapacity, impotence, and invisible impairments: their effects upon interpersonal relations. *J. Health and Hum. Behav.* **14**, 115, 1973.
11. Mead G. H. *Mind, Self, and Society,* Univ. of Chicago Press, Chicago, 1934.
12. Davis F. *Passage through Crisis.* Bobbs Merrill, Indianapolis, 1963.
13. Strauss A. L. *Chronic Illness and the Quality of Life.* Mosby, St. Louis, MO, 1975.
14. Davis F. Deviance disavowal: the management of strained interaction by the visibly handicapped. *Soc. Prob.* **9**, 120, 1961.
15. I am indebted to George Attletweed for calling the history of this sign to my attention.
16. Goffman E. *Stigma: Notes on the Management of Spoiled Identity.* Prentice Hall, Englewood Cliffs, NJ, 1963.

 34

Genital Herpes: An Ethnographic Inquiry into Being Discreditable in American Society

Marcia C. Inhorn

For many students, this selection will hit close to home. Sexually transmitted diseases (STDs) are a risk, a worry, and a problem to many sexually active college-age people. Some STDs are caused by viruses and cannot be cured with antibiotics, and there are now some antibiotic-resistant strains of bacterial STDs. The most famous STD today is HIV/AIDS, and it is causing massive mortality and untold suffering. On a global level, roughly one-half of the victims of HIV/AIDS are women—and most have "done" nothing more than have sex with their husbands. Nonetheless, they are often blamed for their condition (Farmer, Connor, and Simmons 1996).

Throughout the world, STDs are frequently stigmatized conditions that reflect on the morality of the patient (Gregg 1983). Often there is also a double standard in terms of stigma. In this selection, Marcia Inhorn analyzes the problem of information management—that is, the decision of whom to tell about one's condition. The problem of living with herpes is less a medical problem than a social and psychological problem. The fact of having a secret, and the shame associated with having the truth come out, is part of the illness experience of people with genital herpes.

This selection may seem dated, in large part because the HIV/AIDS epidemic changed the situation enormously. At the time it was written, the emerging genital herpes epidemic seemed terrible and noteworthy. Many people had recognized that a marked increase in STD prevalence accompanied the sexual revolution in the late 1960s and 1970s (the era before AIDS). Some people did not consider these infections to be serious problems until the herpes epidemic and other "new," untreatable, and potentially lethal STDs like AIDS. This attitude, however, ignored the fact that STDs, particularly in women, could result in long-term infertility. The big change in attitude came with AIDS; public health workers believe that the risk of AIDS has made the general population more careful about STDs.

This selection suggests that the media play an important role in the social construction of new epidemics—after all, new diseases are news. However, given the changing nature of epidemiological information and the suffering caused by stigma, the role of the media can be a two-edged sword. There is value in informing the public, but there is also the danger associated with irrational social reaction to epidemics.

As you read this selection, consider these questions:

- *Does the stigmatization of genital herpes mean that the normal rules of the sick role are not applicable?*

- *Why is information management a problem associated with this illness?*

- *What does the author mean by "discreditable"? Why would an infection make someone less creditable?*

- *What are the functions of self-help groups, like the voluntary association called HELP?*

- *Can the stigmatization of an illness change over time? Why?*

INTRODUCTION

In her widely acclaimed book *Illness As Metaphor*, Susan Sontag (1979) ruminates over Western society's use of illness as a symbol of corruption and decay and the subsequent social stigma attached to sufferers of those metaphorically manipulated afflictions. She states:

> Leprosy, in its heyday aroused a . . . disproportionate sense of horror. In the Middle Ages, the leper was a social text in which corruption was made visible; an exemplum, an emblem of decay. Nothing is more punitive than to give a disease a meaning—that meaning being invariably a moralistic one. Any important disease whose causality is murky, and for which treatment is ineffectual, tends to be awash in significance. (1979:57)

Writing in the late 1970s, she adds:

> In the last two centuries, the diseases most often used as metaphors for evil were syphilis, tuberculosis, and cancer—all diseases imagined to be, preeminently, the diseases of individuals. (1979:58)

Without question, if Sontag were to rewrite her thought-provoking treatise for the 1980s, two "diseases of individuals" would have to be added to the list of metaphorical maledictions in the United States. The diseases, of course, are genital herpes and, most recently, acquired immunodeficiency syndrome (AIDS).

This paper will deal with only the first of these two recent additions—the condition that has been dubbed by the popular media as "the new scarlet letter." Genital herpes is a sexually transmitted disease (STD) that tends to affect otherwise healthy, predominantly Caucasian, educated, well-employed, middle- to upper-middle-class men and women and, in so doing, may exert upon these never before-traumatized individuals a profound psychosocial impact out of proportion to the otherwise benign, non-life-threatening physical condition itself. The reason for the psychosocial ramifications, according to genital herpes patients,[1] is quite clear: namely, that the popular media have transformed genital herpes into a socially stigmatized condition of major proportions. This transformation, furthermore, has taken place only within the past five years, and its effects have diminished only slightly with the media's more current fascination over AIDS. Thus, to use Goffman's definition, the individual with genital herpes can now be seen as possessing an attribute that makes him different from others in the category of persons available for him to be, and of a less desirable kind—in the extreme, a person who is quite thoroughly bad, or dangerous, or weak. He is thus reduced in our minds from a whole and usual person to a tainted, discounted one. Such an attribute is a stigma, especially, when its discrediting effect is very extensive. (1963:3)

QUESTIONS AND METHODS

With this in mind, the question remains: What is it like to be an individual with genital herpes in the mid-1980s? This is the question to be addressed in this paper and is not unlike the one that other anthropologists, who have chosen to study so-called "marginal" members of their own societies, have asked in recent years.

This article represents the results of two months of field work among a group of American adults of heterogeneous backgrounds and origins who have been brought together because of their "marginalized" status as genital herpes patients. All of the individuals who participated in this study are members (or, in some cases, are temporarily attending meetings) of HELP, a nationwide, volunteer-run, self-help organization for individuals with genital herpes. Through observation of three meetings (two for both men and women and one for women only) of a large metropolitan chapter of HELP, many of the concerns of individuals with newly diagnosed or recurrent genital herpes were recorded, and volunteers were recruited for follow-up, confidential telephone interviews. Eight individuals (four men and four women), ranging in age from the mid-20s to late-30s, agreed to be interviewed, each interview lasting from one to two hours. In addition, three sexually active individuals (two women and one man) of the same age group who do not have genital herpes were interviewed to elicit representative attitudes toward this disease from the so-called "normal" sector of the sexually active heterosexual population.

These data were supplemented by a thorough search of the recent medical (including nursing) literature on genital herpes; the "popular" literature (including recent articles in the press); and six years' worth of *The Helper*, the quarterly publication for HELP members, published by the sponsoring American Social Health Association (ASHA) in Palo Alto, California (ASHA 1979–84).

This paper integrates information from these varied sources as the key issues in the life experiences of individuals with genital herpes are discussed. These issues fall into two broad categories: (1) clinical concerns, revolving primarily around prevention of recurrence or of transmission of the disease to sexual partners; and (2) problems of "information manage-

ment," as first defined by Goffman (1963). This paper will address only the second category: issues of information disclosure—to lovers, friends, and family—and the importance of "disclosure selectivity" in the lives of individuals with genital herpes.[2] This will be followed by a discussion of the role of self-help groups in information management counseling, and, finally, of the role of the media in the recent stigmatization of this condition and the impact of this stigmatization on the lives of genital herpes patients.

TO TELL OR NOT TO TELL

For individuals with genital herpes, the greatest degree of discomfort often has very little to do with physical pain per se, but, rather, with the psychological suffering encumbered in the issue of "information management." In his now-classic book on stigma, Goffman (1963) explains the special problems of disclosure faced by those with a "discreditable" stigma, such as genital herpes. He states:

when his differentness is not immediately apparent, and is not known beforehand (or at least known by him to be known to the others), when in fact his is a discreditable, not a discredited person, then the second main possibility in his life is to be found. The issue is not that of managing tension generated during social contacts, but rather that of managing information about his failing. To display or not to display; to tell or not to tell; to let on or not to let on; to lie or not to lie; and in each case, to whom, how, when, and where. (1963:42)

Indeed, Goffman's explication of the problems of the "discreditable" persona are quite germane to the discussion of genital herpes. Genital herpes is truly a discreditable condition—one that is essentially "invisible" (except, of course, when the individual is experiencing an outbreak and is having difficulty functioning), but, in certain instances, must be exposed with unpredictable outcomes to significant others. Indeed, this issue—more than anything else—seems to be *the* crucial variable in the lives of those with genital herpes; its importance cannot be underestimated.

Sexual Partners

Many individuals who volunteered information at HELP meetings, and other respondents, did not know precisely from whom or how they had contracted genital herpes. In most cases, however, this was not attributable to sheer number of sexual partners (i.e., so-called "promiscuity"), but, rather, to the insidious nature of the disease; namely, it may have appeared for the first time during periods of sexual inactivity or during periods of monogamy with a supposedly uninfected sexual partner.

For others, the disease was clearly contracted from a known sexual partner, who either did not tell of his or her problem or, in some cases, miscalculated the length of an outbreak and, hence, the period of contagion. For those who were "lied to" by their partners, a degree of anger or outright rage was felt by all.

Indeed, the issue of "honesty" was raised by all individuals interviewed and appears to be *the* major information management dilemma faced by genital herpes patients—or, as Goffman would put it, "to tell or not to tell; to let on or not to let on; to lie or not to lie" (1963:42). Although the decision to disclose information about one's genital herpes is optional in most cases, it seems that, for most individuals, this matter of choice disappears—either morally or practically—when it comes to telling a potential sexual partner. Yet, the individual with genital herpes is caught in a "double bind" when it comes to forming intimate, "post-stigma" relationships, for, if this "failing" is revealed too soon, the other party may flee, while, if disclosed too late, guilt, accusations or dishonesty, and actual transmission of the stigmatized viral condition may ensue.

For example, one married man said he considers himself fortunate to be in a permanent relationship because of the disclosure implications faced by single men and women. He explained:

> If I weren't in a relationship, I know I'd have a lot more to deal with. Having to tell someone after two or three dates, "I have herpes. Will you go to bed with me?" is not a pleasant thought. I would say "No" myself if I didn't have it! So I see all these single people in the group [HELP] having to come up with little schemes to delay sex and build up other aspects of the relationship first.

Such "sex-delaying" schemes and ways to "break the news" are the topics of much conversation, both at the HELP meetings and in *The Helper*. At one meeting, the group leader suggested some "do's and don'ts" for telling a partner, including: (1) don't make it into a dramatic production; (2) don't use words like "incurable," "highly contagious," and "venereal"; (3) don't give more information than the person can handle (e.g., an hour on the statistics alone); (4) do present it in a matter-of-fact tone of voice; (5) do pick a quiet, relaxed moment to tell; (6) don't wait until you're in bed with your clothes off; and (7) don't wait until you've had sex with the person 16 times.[3] However, according to most informants, this suggested approach is easier said than done, and actual disclosure experiences ranged from "histrionics" on the part of several informants to avoidance of sexuality altogether in the case of others.

According to informants, the reason disclosure to intimates is so difficult is because of an overwhelming fear of rejection—a fear that appears to loom large in the minds of those with genital herpes. Several informants admitted that they now avoid, to a great degree, intimate relationships because of their fear of potential rejection. Others, primarily women, said that they had stayed in problematical relationships much longer than they would have had they not had genital herpes, because of their timidity in striking up new sexual partnerships. Virtually all informants stated that their sex lives had changed significantly as a result of genital herpes and that they were now much more circumspect about entering into new situations of intimacy.

Nevertheless, despite this overriding pessimism, actual experiences with new sexual partners suggest that the worst fears of rejection are rarely realized. Of the six individuals with genital herpes who had attempted to have post-herpes sexual relationships, only two could cite definite cases of rejection because of the disease; most informants had at least two, and often many more, instances of acceptance. Furthermore, of the three individuals interviewed who did not have genital herpes, two of them had already engaged in sexual relationships with partners whom they knew had herpes—and said that they would do it again if the situation ever arose. The third individual, furthermore, concurred that genital herpes would be a "superfluous" factor in deciding whether or not to have a relationship. All three individuals added, however, that their attitudes toward genital herpes had changed drastically—toward a more positive, enlightened view—over time.

Friends

Likewise, many of the individuals with genital herpes were extremely reluctant to tell their friends—or their "pre-stigma" acquaintances (Goffman 1963:35)—about their newly acquired problem. Although some individuals attending the HELP meetings said they had told most of their friends and acquaintances about their condition, two of those interviewed, both male, had not divulged this information to any pre-stigma acquaintances, and the other six said they had told only a few of their closest friends, most of whom had reacted supportively.

At least part of the reason why most individuals chose not to tell more than a few close friends was their paranoia over widespread exposure of their "failing" and a desire to uphold their pre-stigma reputation.

This, in turn, was related to the aforementioned fear of rejection: of being made a pariah by one's larger circle of friends and acquaintances. This paranoia over exposure was understandable when one considers that most of the individuals attending the meetings—and certainly those interviewed—appeared to be bright, attractive, articulate, highly successful individuals, with positions of responsibility in the community. Widespread knowledge of the stigmatized condition would not only spoil the well-developed image, but might cast doubt on the so-called "moral character" of the individuals involved—especially considering the route of transmission of the disease. Thus, most of the individuals interviewed were extremely protective of their "secret," and the fear of exposure was a possibility that haunted many of their lives. As one woman stated:

> Some of my very closest friends don't even know. You have to *really* know who you trust, because if you tell one wrong person, and that person tells one person, then 101 people already know. If I have even a one-percent doubt in my mind, I don't tell.

Families

The fear of telling "Mom and Dad" was often even more pronounced in interviews with genital herpes patients. By telling parents or brothers and sisters about the condition, the genital herpes patient not only admits to his or her own sexuality, but that the sexual activity may have been of a questionable nature. Thus, unlike many other stigmatized conditions, in which family members are intimately involved in the individual's welfare (see, for example, Ablon 1984 or Ablon, Ames, and Cunningham 1984), genital herpes seems to be a condition with little involvement of the family group itself, since families, particularly parents, are rarely informed directly about their now "discreditable" member. Instead, informants, if they divulged this information at all, tended to choose only one member of the family, usually the "closest" sibling. In most cases, too, the disclosure was accompanied by promises of secrecy, especially regarding exposure to parents.

One informant, who told her brother about her condition, added:

> As for my parents, I *can't* tell them. The sad part is that if you had the flu or pneumonia, your family would stand by you. But you're a pariah if it's something like this.

Another informant, who also told a brother about herpes, explained:

> It's helped psychologically to have someone to talk to about it. Herpes is not one of your major two or three diseases, but it can get depressing. Most people are not in stable relationships when they get it, and they're lonely. Loneliness is the main aspect of the disease.

HELP: EDUCATIONAL AND SOCIAL FUNCTIONS

This last statement—that "loneliness is the main aspect of the disease"—explains why many individuals with genital herpes seek out HELP, if only temporarily. HELP, a program of the ASHA's Herpes Resource Center,[4] is the country's only, self-help organization for individuals with genital herpes. Of the more than 80 local chapters nationwide, most are located in major metropolitan areas.

For many individuals, this volunteer-run, self-help organization is a source of clinical information,[5] but its major function is as a support system of "sympathetic others," who can serve as role models, confidantes, and advisors during both clinical and emotional crises. Many individuals use the group intensively during the primary stages of their illness and then later settle into less frequent attendance patterns or, in some cases, stop going. Others use the group less as a resource and more as a social club. As one informant stated: "The honest truth is that I go to HELP to meet a woman. Sometimes I just think it would be easier having a relationship with someone who already understands."

Meeting others with similar "moral careers" (Goffman 1963) for the purpose of trouble-free dating and sex may be a covert function of the group; in fact, several individuals at the meetings mentioned their desires to date someone who also had genital herpes, for this, they believed, would solve some of their anxieties over information disclosure and transmission. Herpes "dating services" were also discussed at meetings; however, several members shared their negative experiences with these services, which are expensive and seemingly ineffectual, according to informants.

However, when the issue of "endogamous" dating was raised at meetings, the group leader provided convincing clinical evidence to discourage this practice: namely, the possibility of contracting two different strains of herpes virus, thereby exacerbating the recurrence problem. As a result of these clinical discussions, most of the individuals interviewed said they preferred to have sexual relations with individuals who did not have genital herpes, despite the difficulties encumbered in having to divulge their "secret stigma."

THE MEDIA AND THE PROCESS OF STIGMATIZATION

Without question, if genital herpes were to be ranked today by degree of social stigma in the long list of STDs, it would take second place, with AIDs assuming the top position. If, however, one were to rank genital herpes by degree of social stigma in a list of STDs normally found among heterosexuals alone (thereby eliminating AIDS), it would surely attain top billing—outranking the now curable syphilis and gonorrhea. Indeed, if one were to rank genital herpes in terms of stigma among all the diseases known to American society, it would certainly fall among the top dozen diseases, and possibly even among the top four or five. The reason for this notoriety is believed to be due to the media—and a process of stigmatization that took place almost overnight. As one informant stated, "We are victims of the media."

According to everyone interviewed, including those without genital herpes, the media have caused most of the problems for individuals with genital herpes. Those who could remember—particularly those who had already contracted the disease by the end of the 1970s—say that the media seemed to pick up on genital herpes in the very early 1980s, with a strong emphasis on the "incurable," "recurrent" nature of the disease. This culminated in August 1982, when *Time* magazine printed a cover story in which genital herpes was called "the new scarlet letter" (Leo 1982). At HELP meetings and in interviews, several persons pointed directly to this article as the lynchpin in the subsequent "epidemic" of paranoia and fear of herpes in the United States.

Although the media's sensationalist enthusiasm for genital herpes diminished substantially with the onset of AIDS, resurgences of interest have continued to occur, as seen most recently in the "little Johnny Bigley" case, in which a three-year-old child, affected at birth by neonatal Herpes simplex Type 1, caused fearful parents to remove their children from his classroom, thereby creating nationwide panic. The fact that such a "herpes scare" could take place in 1985 indicates that fear of genital herpes is still very strong in the United States, that misinformation and misconceptions about the disease abound, and that a corrective educational effort by the media has yet to take place.

As a result, a great deal of anger is directed at the press; this was evident at HELP meetings, in interviews with informants, and even in *The Helper* publication, which had initially condoned the media's attention. One informant explained his frustration in this way: "Before the scarlet letter cover, you could screw around as much as you wanted—as long as you didn't have a conscience. But now, everything's changed." Or, as another informant concluded, "The best thing that ever happened to herpes was AIDS."

Even those individuals without genital herpes who were interviewed said they thought the media were responsible for the public's fear of the condition. One person noted that the media have done a further disservice ("adding insult to injury") by lumping herpes with AIDS in terms of health risk, even though they are "orders of magnitude different in their severity."

But how does this media-generated social stigma translate into everyday life for those with genital herpes? According to all informants, the innocent jokes and cruel remarks made about herpes hurt the most—turning otherwise average days into bad ones and even souring friendships. As one woman explained:

> It's still an "hysterical" issue for people—in both senses of the word. For instance, I'll be talking with a group of friends about our love lives, and someone will say, "Boy, you're lucky you didn't catch herpes from him!" Then everyone laughs. They would never in a million years imagine that I have it, and, if they knew, some of them probably wouldn't sit in the same room with me for fear of catching it. I never say anything, but I really think those kinds of remarks are insensitive. Nowadays, you never know who might have it—maybe even your best friend. So it's better to just keep your mouth shut.

Another said that herpes has become "funny" because (1) it is sexually transmitted, and (2) it is incurable. Underlying this humor, however, is a great deal of fear. He asserted:

> People always joke about that which they're most afraid of. There is a lot of ignorance out there, and where there's ignorance, there's fear, and where there's fear, there's humor. That's the syllogism.

Thus, although most informants could accept the jokes on an intellectual level, humor about herpes also presented something of a Catch 22; namely, most informants said their natural desire to lash out at these offensive remarks was curbed by their fear of exposure and subsequent rejection. Hence, most informants simply "kept their mouths shut" to prevent being "treated like a leper" in social settings. Indeed, the terms "leper" or "leprosy" were used at least once by five informants and by two of the individuals without herpes also interviewed. Although most informants said they did not regard themselves as "lepers," they acknowledged that the public may regard herpes as being like leprosy—contagious and to be avoided at all costs. This attitude, although understandable, is unfair considering the relatively benign nature of the disease, and has made living with herpes much more difficult, according to all those questioned.

CONCLUSION

The "invisible" nature of genital herpes is, in some senses, its most perplexing attribute—creating emotional, practical, and ethical dilemmas in the private, "discreditable" domain of information management (Goffman 1963). This article has attempted to explicate that domain, through an ethnographic inquiry into the lives of some marginalized members of our own society. Interviews with eight young adults, all affected by genital herpes, reveal how fear of disclosure—and subsequent rejection—plays a powerful role in the daily lives of these individuals. Deciding whether or not and how to tell friends, families, acquaintances, strangers, and worst of all, potential lovers about one's "secret stigma" proves to be a continuous conundrum for most. To tell or not to tell, to lie or not to lie, to let or not to let on—these are the questions that individuals with genital herpes must face with each relationship, new or old, and the answers are not easily forthcoming.

Most individuals opt to solve these problems in the following ways: (1) by dividing the world into two groups, a select group of trusted "insiders," and the "outsiders," who would be too distraught (e.g., parents), too rejecting, or too garrulous to be trusted with the secret; (2) by limiting sexual partners, so as to avoid transmission of the virus and, more important, to avoid the issue of disclosure to intimates; and (3) by joining HELP, a self-help group for genital herpes patients, which offers both emotional and clinical support.

These steps are necessary, informants insist, because of the recent stigmatization of the disease. Namely, in the early 1980s, the media transformed genital herpes from an unknown, relatively benign, nonstigmatized condition into an "incurable, highly contagious, recurrent venereal disease, threatening the life, liberty, and happiness of every American who uses public toilets." This loathsome and leprous image, informants say, is entirely undeserved, for genital herpes is non-life-threatening, nonapparent, and easily preventable when proper precautions are taken. But because genial herpes has now been lumped with such stigmatized conditions as leprosy, AIDS, tuberculosis, and cancer, life has become difficult for those with the disease, who fear social outcasting, cruel humor, and other forms of outright stigmatization.

Whether genital herpes will continue to be stigmatized in American society remains to be seen. In all probability, the degree of stigma will diminish substantially if a vaccine to prevent transmission or, better yet, a true antiviral agent becomes available. But until that time, we, as medical anthropologists, have a rare opportunity to study the processes of stigmatization and marginalization at home. Once we understand how discreditable stigmas—the "new scarlet letters"—of our own complex society are created, maintained, and managed by individual members, we may be able to shed light on the phenomenon of acquired deviancy—on becoming society's discreditable members—the world over.

NOTES

1. I prefer to use the term "patient" rather than "victim" or "sufferer."
2. Information on clinical concerns of genital herpes patients may be obtained from the author.
3. Likewise, in an article on "Talking About Herpes" in *The Helper* (Summer 1984), some additional advice was preferred, including (1) don't tell a lie about herpes; (2) do assume that the person you are about to tell has little, if any, accurate information about herpes; (3) do be prepared to dispel fears and misconceptions; (4) don't worry in advance about telling (because it doesn't help); (5) don't feel as though you have to be a walking encyclopedia about every herpes-related nuance; (6) do use appropriate analogies wherever possible; (7) don't forget to emphasize how preventable herpes is; and (8) don't be surprised to learn that the person you are anxious to tell has wanted to tell you, too.
4. In 1982, the ASHA changed the name of its genital herpes self-help organization from Herpetics Engaged in Living Productively (HELP) to the Herpes Resource Center (HRC), because the term "herpetics" was viewed negatively by its membership. However, the acronym HELP is still used by the 80-odd local chapters, and the ASHA's publication is still called *The Helper*. Thus, the acronym HELP has been used throughout this paper to conform to current usage.
5. HELP also serves a number of other less widely discussed but important functions. These include (1) research fund drives; (2) lobbying; (3) provision of a telephone "hotline"; (4) symposia coordination; (5) epidemiological, demographic, and psychosocial surveys of the membership; (6) formulation of medical advisory boards; (7) public relations and media interviews; (8) legal advice; (9) announcements of clinical trials; (10) announcements of new clinics and chapters; and (11) review and evaluation of the medical and popular literature on genital herpes. To see how HELP compares with other national self-help organizations, refer to Borman et al. 1982; Borman and Lieberman 1976; Killilea 1976; and Silverman 1978.

REFERENCES

Ablon, J. 1984. Little People in America. New York: Praeger.

Ablon, J., G. Ames, and W. Cunningham. 1984. To All Appearances: The Ideal American Family. *In* Power to

Change. E. Kauffman. ed. Pp. 199–235. New York: Gardner Press.

American Social Health Association. 1979–84. The Helper. J. A. Graves. ed. Palo Alto, CA: American Social Health Association.

Borman, L. D., L. E. Borck, R. Hess, and F. L. Pasquale. 1982. Helping People to Help Themselves: Self-Help and Prevention. *In* Prevention in Human Services. R. Hess. ed. Pp. 1–129. New York: The Haworth Press.

Borman, L. D., and M. A. Lieberman. 1976. Self-Help Groups. The Journal of Applied Behavioral Science (Special Issue) 12(3):261–463.

Goffman, E. 1963. Stigma: Notes on the Management of Spoiled Identity. Englewood Cliffs, NJ: Prentice-Hall.

Killilea, M. 1976. Mutual Help Organizations: Interpretations in the Literature. *In* Support Systems and Mutual Help. G. Caplan and M. Killilea. eds. Pp. 37–93. New York: Grune & Stratton.

Leo, J. 1982. The New Scarlet Letter. Time 120(5):62–66.

Silverman, P. R. 1978. Mutual Help Groups: A Guide for Mental Health Workers. Rockville, MD: National Institute of Mental Health.

Sontag, S. 1979. Illness As Metaphor. New York: Vintage Books.

✤ 35

The Damaged Self

Robert F. Murphy

As Gregor Samsa awoke one morning from uneasy dreams he found himself transformed in his bed into a gigantic insect. He was lying on his hard, as if it were armor-plated, back and when he lifted his head a little he could see his domelike brown belly divided into stiff arched segments. . . . What has happened to me? he thought. It was no dream.

—FRANZ KAFKA, *The Metamorphosis*

This selection is autobiographical, written by an anthropology professor at Columbia University. Robert Murphy has done anthropological fieldwork in the Amazon and other parts of the world (Murphy and Murphy 1985; Murphy and Quain 1955). His research into the world of the disabled and wheelchair-bound began after a slow-growing cancer began pinching his spinal cord, ultimately leaving his legs paralyzed. This selection is a chapter from his book, The Body Silent *(1987) that both tells a poignant personal story and provides keen anthropological observations on the illness experiences of disabled people.*

The focus of this selection is on the self: the cultural construction of the individual as a social, corporeal, and psychological entity. Murphy uses Freudian theory to explore the notion of self and how the illness experience changes that notion. The relationship between the self and the body is particularly important. In recent years, the anthropology of the body—the study of the symbolic meanings of the body and the embodiment of meaning through lived experience—has become an increasingly important theme. Murphy's experience with a damaged body and an incurable disease resulted in many powerful insights about the world. (A similarly powerful book from this perspective is Reynolds Price's A Whole New Life *[1994].) Some insights come from the daily struggle to do simple things and the loss of taken-for-granted abilities. Murphy talks about the sex life of paraplegics in this vein. Further insights come from interactions with others who are affected not only by the physical reality of the wheelchair but also by cultural notions of stigma and the social creation of the "other." The necessity of adapting to new life circumstances—and the emotional impact of those adaptions—is a theme we saw in the selection by Gaylene Becker on the lives of deaf people. The disabled must adapt to limitations in mobility and to living daily with pain, but the nonphysical aspects of the illness experience remain very important. In this selection, Robert Murphy frankly discusses the suffering caused by depression and decreased self-esteem as well as criticizing biomedicine for its inability to deal with the entire self.*

As you read this selection, consider these questions:

■ *Why are children often afraid when they see a disabled person? How are definitions of "normal" learned?*

■ *Murphy's paralysis developed relatively slowly, whereas most spinal-cord injuries occur suddenly as a result of car crashes and other accidents. Would the cause of the injury have any relation to the illness experience? To the way that others treat the disabled?*

■ *What does Murphy mean by "unmarked categories" and the creation of the "other"? Is his analogy to the importance of race and the experience of racism relevant here?*

■ *Think for a moment about what your life would be like if you were suddenly confined to a wheelchair. How would your life be different? How would your relationship with your body be different? How would people treat you differently?*

From the time my tumor was first diagnosed through my entry into wheelchair life, I had an increasing apprehension that I had lost much more than the full use of my legs. I had also lost a part of my self. It was not just that people acted differently toward me, which they did, but rather that I felt differently toward myself. I had changed in my own mind, in my self-image, and in the basic conditions of my existence. It left me feeling alone and isolated, despite strong support from family and friends; moreover, it was a change for the worse, a diminution of everything I used to be. This was particularly frightening for somebody who had clawed his way up from poverty to a position of respect. I had become a person of substance, and that substance was oozing away. It threatened everything that Yolanda and I had put together over the years. In middle age, the ground beneath me had convulsed. And I had no idea why and how this had happened.

I cannot remember ever before thinking about physical disability, except as something that happened to other, less fortunate, people. It certainly had no relevance to me. A disabled person could enter my field of vision, but my mind would fail to register him—a kind of selective blindness quite common among people of our culture. During a year that I spent in the Sahel and Sudan zones of Nigeria and Niger, a region of endemic leprosy and missing hands, feet, and noses, the plight of those people was as alien to me as were their language, culture, and circumstances. Because of this gulf, I had no empathy for them and just enough sympathy to drop coins into cups extended from the ends of stumps. A few pennies were all that it took to buy the dubious grace of almsgiving. It was a bargain, a gesture that did not assert my oneness with them, but rather my separation from them.

With the onset of my own impairment, I became almost morbidly sensitive to the social position and treatment of the disabled, and I began to notice nuances of behavior that would have gone over my head in times past. One of my earliest observations was that social relations between the disabled and the able-bodied are tense, awkward, and problematic. This is something that every handicapped person knows, but it surprised me at the time. For example, when I was in the hospital, a young woman visitor entered my room with a look of total consternation on her face.

She exclaimed that she had just seen an awful sight, a girl who was missing half of her skull. I knew the girl as a very sweet, but quite retarded, teenaged patient who used to drop in on me a few times a day; we always had the same conversation. I asked my guest why the sight bothered her so much, but she couldn't tell me. She in turn asked why it didn't trouble me. After a moment's thought, I replied that I was one of "them," a notion that she rejected vehemently. But why did my visitor, a poised and intelligent person, react in this way? It aroused my curiosity.

There is something quite significant in this small encounter, for it had elements of what Erving Goffman called "one of the primal scenes of sociology."[1] Borrowing the Freudian metaphor of the primal scene (the child's traumatic witnessing of the mother and father in sexual intercourse), Goffman used the phrase to mean any social confrontation of people in which there is some great flaw, such as when one of the parties has no nose. This robs the encounter of firm cultural guidelines, traumatizing it and leaving the people involved wholly uncertain about what to expect from each other. It has the potential for social calamity.

The intensely problematic character of relations between those with damaged bodies and the more-or-less unmarked cannot be shrugged off simply as a result of the latter's ineptitude, bias, stupidity, and so forth, although they do play a part. Even the best-intentioned able-bodied people have difficulty anticipating the reactions of the disabled, for interpretations are warped by the impairment. To complicate matters, the disabled also enter the social arena with a skewed perspective. Not only are the bodies altered, but their ways of thinking about themselves and about the person and objects of the external world have become profoundly transformed. They have experienced a revolution of consciousness. They have undergone a metamorphosis.

Nobody has ever asked me what it is like to be a paraplegic—and now a quadriplegic—for this would violate all the rules of middle-class etiquette. A few have asked me what caused my condition, and, after hearing the answer, have looked as though they wished they hadn't. After all, tumors can happen to anybody—even to them. Polite manners may protect us from most such intrusions, but it is remarkable that physicians seldom ask either. They like "hard facts" obtainable through modern technology or old-fashioned jabbing with a pin and asking whether you feel it. These tests supposedly provide good, "objective" measures of neurological damage, but, like sociological questionnaires, they reduce experience to neat distinctions of black or white and ignore the broad range of ideation and emotion that always accompanies disability. The full subjective states of the patient are of little concern in the medical model of disability, which holds that the problem arises wholly from some anatomic or physiological disorder and is correctable by standard modes of therapy—drugs, surgery, radiation, or whatever. What goes on inside the patient's head is another department, and if there are signs of serious pyschological malaise, he is packed off to the proper specialist.

The medical people have had little curiosity about what I think about my condition, although they do know its sensory symptoms: a constant tingling in my hands, forearms, and feet and a steady, low threshold of pain in my legs. The discomfort is similar to the soreness and burning sensation experienced with torn or severely strained muscles and has much to do with the fact that the musculature of my trunk and legs is always in spasm, despite a generous daily dosage of muscle relaxants. The curious thing about this condition is that a knife could be run through my leg now and I wouldn't feel it. Aside from the tingle and the ache, my legs are otherwise numb and bereft of sensation. For the past four years, I have not tried to move them, for the tumor has long since passed the point at which therapy could maintain function; they don't even twitch anymore.

For a while, I occasionally tried to will the legs to move, but each futile attempt was psychologically devastating, leaving me feeling broken and helpless. I soon stopped trying. The average nondisabled person could be driven to the edge of breakdown if his legs were pinioned and rendered totally immobile for long periods, and an accident victim in a body cast finds his only comfort in the fact that his situation is temporary. I was saved from this, however, because the slow process of paralysis of my limbs was paralleled by a progressive atrophy of the need and impulse for physical activity. I was losing the will to move.

My upper body functions have suffered some impairment ever since the tumor became symptomatic, although the lower body has deteriorated at a much faster rate. In addition to the diminished lung capacity and, consequently, more rapid and shallow breathing, the musculature of the arms and hands has progressively weakened, their range of movement has be-

come steadily more narrow, my fingers have stiffened, and my hands have become increasingly numb and insensitive to touch and temperature. In common with other paralytics, I have to be careful with hot water or hot dishes and pots, for I can burn myself without knowing it. To complicate the hand problems, the fingers of quadriplegics curl inward toward the palms, a process that by the spring of 1986 has made my left hand almost useless.

Beyond these physical symptoms, I have been overtaken by a profound and deepening sense of tiredness—a total, draining weariness that I must resist every waking minute. It starts in the morning when I struggle to awaken, fighting my way out of the comfort and forgetfulness of sleep into self-awareness and renewed disability. Facing the world every day is an ordeal for everybody, and it is no accident that strokes and heart attacks peak at 8 to 9 A.M. It is much worse to confront the day with a serious deficit. The wish to turn my back to the world continues through the daily ablutions, which grow longer and more tedious every year; it now takes me a quarter hour to shave. I am fully able to face life by 10 A.M., but by 4 or 5 P.M., I start to flag. Between these hours, I teach, talk to students, and attend meetings, after which I go home and lie down for a couple of hours. I also conserve strength by spending two, or at most three, days a week at the university. Like most professors, I don't pass the other days in idleness. I read student exams, reports, and doctoral dissertations; I keep up on books and journals in my field; and I do research and writing. But the professorial life allows me to work at home at my own tempo, sometimes while lying in bed. In no other line of work, I tell my graduate students, could such a wreck be 100 percent employed—it has to be an easy job!

But there is another aspect of my fatigue that cannot be eased by rest. This is a sense of tiredness and ennui with practically everything and everybody, a desire to withdraw from the world, to crawl into a hole and pull the lid over my head. The average person will recognize this wish, for everybody at some time or other feels that things have become too much to handle and he or she wishes for surcease, for even temporary remission. How tempting to tell all and sundry—family, work, and society—to go to hell and leave him alone. Who hasn't said this, even if only under his breath? When an ordinary citizen is overcome by these feelings every day and all day, however, his family and friends will urge him to seek professional help, for these are the sure symptoms of depression. In contrast, the deeply impaired harbor these urges chronically, sometimes because they are depressed but more often because they must each day face an inimical world, using the limited resources of a damaged body.

Many give in to the impulse to withdraw, retreating into a little universe sustained by monthly Social Security disability checks, a life circumscribed by the four walls of an apartment and linked to outside society by a television set. Constantina Safilios-Rothschild, a sociologist, has noted that disability may provide a pretext for withdrawal from work for some older workers dissatisfied and weary with their jobs, a kind of "secondary gain" bought at great price.[2] But this is not the source of the isolation; it's just making the best of a bad thing. Many other disabled people go forth to battle the world every day, but even they must wage a constant rear-guard action against the backward pull. This is a powerful centripetal force, for it is commonly exacerbated by an altered sense of selfhood, one that has been savaged by the partial destruction of the body. Disability is not simply a physical affair for us; it is our ontology, a condition of our being in the world.

Of all the psychological syndromes associated with disability, the most pervasive, and the most destructive, is a radical loss of self-esteem. This sense of damage to the self, the acquisition of what Erving Goffman called a "stigma," or a "spoiled identity,"[3] grew upon me during my first months in a wheelchair, and it hit me hardest when I returned to the university in the fall of 1977. By then, I could no longer hold on to the myth that I was using a wheelchair during convalescence. I had to face the unpalatable fact that I was wedded permanently to it; it had become an indispensable extension of my body. Strangely, I also felt this as a major blow to my pride.

The damage to my ego showed most painfully in an odd and wholly irrational sense of embarrassment and lowered self-worth when I was with people on my social periphery. Most of my colleagues in the anthropology department were old friends, some even from our undergraduate years, and they generally were warm and supportive. But people from other departments and the administration were another matter. During my first semester back at the university, I attended a few lunch meetings at the Faculty Club, but I began to notice that these were strained occasions. People whom I knew did not look my way. And persons with whom I had a nodding acquaintance did not nod; they, too, were busily looking off in another direction. Others gave my wheelchair a wide berth, as if it were surrounded by a penumbra of contamination. These were not happy encounters.

My social isolation became acute during stand-up gatherings, such as receptions and cocktail parties. I discovered that I was now three-and-a-half feet tall, and most social interaction was taking place two feet above me. When speaking to a standing person, I have to crane my neck back and look upward, a position that stretches my larynx and further weakens my diminished vocal strength. Conversation in such settings has become an effort. Moreover, it was commonplace that I would be virtually ignored in a crowd for long periods, broken by short bursts of patronization. There was no escape from these intermittent attentions, for it is very difficult to maneuver a wheelchair through a crowd. My low stature and relative immobility thus made me the defenseless recipient of overtures, rather than their instigator. This is a common plaint of the motor-disabled: They have limited choice in socializing and often must wait for the others to come to them. As a consequence, I now attend only small, sit-down gatherings.

Not having yet read the literature on the sociology of disability, I did not immediately recognize the pattern of avoidance. Perhaps this was for the best, as my initial hurt and puzzlement ultimately led me to research the subject. In the meantime, I stopped going to the Faculty Club and curtailed my contacts with the university-at-large. This is not hard to do at Columbia, as each department lies within a Maginot Line, everybody is very busy, and the general social atmosphere runs from tepid to cool. None of this is surprising, for it is also the dominant ethos of New York City. On the positive side, this same general mood allows one to work in peace. They leave you alone at Columbia, and I wanted more than ever to be left alone.

Withdrawal only compounds the disabled person's subjective feelings of damage and lowered worth, sentiments that become manifest as shame and guilt. I once suggested to a housebound elderly woman that she should use a walker for going outside. "I would never do that," she replied. "I'd be ashamed to be seen." "It's not your fault that you have arthritis," I argued. I added that I used a walker, and I wasn't ashamed—this was untrue, of course, and I knew it. But why should anyone feel shame about his disability? Even more mysterious, why should anyone feel a sense of guilt? In what way could I be responsible for my physical state? It could not be attributed to smoking or drinking, the favorite whipping boys of amateur diagnosticians, and it wasn't the result of an accident, with its possibilities for lifestyle culpability, the accusation that one bought it by living dangerously. No, I didn't do a damned thing to earn my tumor, nor was there any way that I could have prevented it. But such feelings are endemic among the disabled. One young woman, who had been born without lower limbs, told me that she had felt guilt for this since childhood, as had her parents (from whom she probably acquired the guilt). Indeed, a mutuality of guilt is the very life-stuff of the paralytic's family, just as it is, on a smaller scale, central to the cohesion—and turmoil—of all modern families.

Guilt and shame are not in fact as separate as they are often represented to be. In simple form, both are said to involve an assault on the ego: Guilt is the attack of the superego, or conscience, and shame arises from the opprobrium of others. Of the two, I believe that shame is the more potent. The sociologist George Herbert Mead wrote that an individual's concept of his or her self is a reflection, or, more accurately, a refraction, as in a fun-house mirror, of the way he or she is treated by others.[4] And if a person is treated with ridicule, contempt, or aversion, then his own ego is diminished, his dignity and humanity are called into question. Shaming is an especially potent means of social control in small-scale societies, where everybody is known and behavior is highly visible, but it is less effective in complex societies like our own, where we can compartmentalize our lives and exist in relative anonymity. But a wheelchair cannot be hidden; it is brutally visible. And to the extent that the wheelchair's occupant is treated with aversion, even disdain, his sense of worth suffers. Damage to the body, then, causes diminution of the self, which is further magnified by debasement by others.

Shame and guilt are one in that both lower self-esteem and undercut the facade of dignity we present to the world. Moreover, in our culture they tend to stimulate each other. The usual formula is that a wrongful act leads to a guilty conscience; if the guilt becomes publicly known, then shame must be added to the sequence, followed by punishment. There is then a causal chain that goes from wrongful act to guilt to shame to punishment. A fascinating aspect of disability is that it diametrically and completely reverses this progression, while preserving every step. The sequence of the person damaged in body goes from punishment (the impairment) to shame to guilt and, finally, to the crime. This is not a real crime but a self-delusion that lurks in our fears and fantasies, in the haunting, never-articulated question: What did I do to deserve this?

In this topsy-turvy world of reversed causality, the punishment—for this is how crippling is unconsciously apprehended—begets the crime. All of this happens despite the fact that the individual may be in no way to blame for his condition; real responsibility is irrelevant. This transmutation of body impairment into guilt is a neat inversion of the Freudian Oedipal drama. According to the psychoanalytic interpretation of the myth, Oedipus unknowingly kills his father and marries his own mother, for which crime the Fates pursue him to Colonnus, where he blinds himself. Blinding is seen as a symbolic form of castration, which is, in turn, the fitting punishment for incest. According to Freud, in male socialization it is the threat of castration by the father—even if only a fantasized threat—that forces the child to relinquish and repress the guilt-ridden wish to possess the mother. It

should be noted, however, that in the myth the father did not blind Oedipus; Oedipus did it to himself. What is usually forgotten in discussions of the Greek tragedy is that the father, after hearing from a soothsayer that his son would one day slay him, crippled young Oedipus. In fact, the name Oedipus can be translated as "Swollen Foot" or, loosely, "Gimpy."

That crippling can be just as proper a punishment for incest as blinding finds ethnographic support. In my own fieldwork, I recorded a Mundurucu myth in which a man who committed incest with his surrogate mother was physically deformed by her husband, a god, and later blinded. And among West African Moslems there is a widespread religious cult centered on a female succubus named Dogwa. (In Morocco, this cult figure is called Aisha Kandisha.) Dogwa is both nuturant and sexually seductive to her devotees; she is both mother and lover. In the former role, she can bring wealth to her followers, but in the latter, she jealously takes swift retaliation against infidelity. Appropriately, the punishment is crippling or blinding. It is worth noting that no father figure is involved here. Instead there is the ambivalent mother, the giver and nurturer of life and its potential destroyer. Incest, or even the unconscious wish for it, is a dangerous game, and I would hazard the guess that the unconscious, diffuse sense of guilt that so often bedevils the disabled arises in the first place from the chimerical notion that the crippling is a punishment for this repressed, elusive, and forbidden desire. There may be no such thing as Original Sin, but original guilt lurks in the dark recesses of the minds of all humans. These ashes of our first love are the basic stuff of the indefinable, unarticulated, and haunting sense that the visitation of paralysis is a form of atonement—a Draconian penance.

Paralytic disability constitutes emasculation of a more direct and total nature. For the male, the weakening and atrophy of the body threaten all the cultural values of masculinity: strength, activeness, speed, virility, stamina, and fortitude. Many disabled men, and women, try to compensate for their deficiencies by becoming involved in athletics. Paraplegics play wheelchair basketball, engage in racing, enter marathons, and do weight-lifting and many other active things. Those too old or too impaired for physical displays may instead show their competence by becoming "super-crips." Just as "super-moms" supposedly go off to work every morning, cook Cordon Bleu dinners at night, play with the kids, and then become red-hot lovers after the children are put to bed, the super-crip works harder than other people, travels extensively, goes to everything, and takes part in anything that comes along. This is how he shows the world that he is like everybody else, only better.

Becoming a super-crip, or super-mom, often depends less on the personal qualities of the individual than on very fortunate circumstances. In my own case, I was well established in my profession at the time of my disability, so my activity was just a matter of persistence. The real super-crips are those who do it all after they become impaired, like one woman who, after partial remission from totally paralytic multiple sclerosis, went on to finish college and then obtain a Ph.D. She refused to let the disease rob her of a future. There are many such people, but, like super-moms, they are still a minority. The vast majority, as we will see, are unable to conquer the formidable physical and social obstacles that confront them, and they live in the penumbra of society, condemned to lives as outsiders.

Afflictions of the spinal cord have a further devastating effect upon masculinity, aside from paralysis, for they commonly produce some degree of impotence or sexual malfunction. Depending on the extent of damage to the cord, the numbed genital area sends no signals to the brain, nor do the libidinal centers of the brain get messages through to the genitalia and the physiological processes that produce erections. This can result in total and permanent impotence, sporadic impotence, or difficulty in sustaining an erection until orgasm. There are some paraplegic men, on the other hand, who can maintain an erection but are unable to achieve orgasm, even after steady intercourse of a half hour to an hour. The effects of this on the male psyche are profound. We usually think of "castration anxiety" as an Oedipal thing, but there is a sort of symbolic castration in impotence that creates a kind of existential anxiety among all men. It is no accident that impotence is a major problem in those lands where masculine values are strongest, nor was it fortuitous that the new sexual freedom in America, with its emphasis on female gratification and male performance, has yielded a bumper crop of impotent men. After all, being a man does not mean just having a penis—it means having a sexually useful one. Anything less than that is indeed a kind of castration, although I am using this lurid Freudian term primarily as a metaphor for loss of both sexual and social power.

Most forms of paraplegia and quadriplegia cause male impotence and female inability to orgasm. But paralytic women need not be aroused or experience orgasmic pleasure to engage in genital sex, and many indulge regularly in intercourse and even bear children, although by Caesarean section. Human sexuality, Freud tells us, is polymorphously perverse, meaning that the entire body is erogenous, and the joys of sex varied. Paraplegic women claim to derive psychological gratification from the sex act itself, as well as from the stimulation of other parts of their bodies and the knowledge that they are still able to give pleasure to others. They may derive less physical gratification from sex than before becoming disabled, but they are still active participants. Males have far more circumscribed anatomical limits. Other than having a surgical implant that produces a simulated erection, the man can no longer engage in genital sex. He either becomes celibate or practices oral sex—or any of the many other variations in sexual expression devised by our innovative species. Whatever the alternative, his standing as a man has been compromised far more than has been the woman's status. He has been effectively emasculated.

Even in those cases in which the paraplegic male retains potency, his stance during the sex act changes. Most must lie still on their backs during intercourse, and it is the woman who must do the mounting and thrusting. In modern America, this is an acceptable alternative position, but in some cultures it would be considered a violation of male dominance: Men are on top in society and they should be on top in sex, and that's the end of the matter. And even in the relatively liberated United States of the 1980s, the male usually takes the more active role and the position on top. But the paraplegic male, whether engaging in genital or oral sex, always takes a passive role. Most paralytic men accept this limitation, for they discover that the wells of passion are in the brain, not between the legs, and that pleasure is possible even without orgasm. One man, who had enjoyed an intensely erotic relationship with his wife before an auto accident made him paraplegic and impotent, reported that they simply continued oral sex. The wife derives complete orgasmic satisfaction and the husband achieves deep psychological pleasure, which he describes as a "mental orgasm." The sex lives of most paralyzed men, however, remain symbolic of a more general passivity and dependency that touches every aspect of their existence and is the antithesis of the male values of direction, activity, initiative, and control.

The sexual problems of the disabled are aggravated by a widespread view that they are either malignantly sexual, like libidinous dwarfs, or, more commonly, completely asexual, an attribute frequently ascribed to the elderly as well. These erroneous notions, which I suspect arise from the sexual anxieties of their holders, fail to recognize that a large majority of disabled people have the same urges as the able-bodied, and are just as competent in expressing them. Spinal cord injuries raise special problems, but motor-disabled people with cerebral palsy, the aftereffects of polio, and many other conditions often can lead almost normal sex lives. That asexuality is also attributed sometimes to the blind underlines the utter irrationality of the belief.

Given the prevalence of such ignorance, I was pleased to read in 1985 that educational television was airing a film on sex among the disabled, and I made it a point to watch it. At the beginning of the film, there appeared on the screen a warning that there would be nude scenes, leading me to the happy expectation that a para- or quadriplegic would be shown making love. Not so, for the only nudes were a couple of very healthy-looking young women. And, in deliberate counterpoint, most of the disabled people shown were grossly disfigured. It was a modern-day version of *Beauty and the Beast,* a film that served to perpetuate, not combat, a prejudice. The producers meant well, but they merely illustrated the depth of the problem. This episode reminded me that when one young woman began research among paraplegics, a female friend asked her, "But you wouldn't go to bed with one of them, would you?" These are indeed primal scenes.

One of Sigmund Freud's enduring contributions to our age was his rejection of classical philosophy's disembodiment of the mind. Instead, Freud started with a theory of instincts that located much of human motivation and thought in the needs of the body, especially the sexual drive. This was not a simple single-direction mechanical determinism, however, for Freud's theories held that causality is a two-way street. The human mind also uses its symbolic capacity to reach out and encompass the body, making it just as much a part of the mind as the mind is of the body. The body, particularly the more explicitly erogenous zones, becomes incorporated into human thought, into the very structure of the personality, and the sexual symbolism of pleasure and desire is used by the mind in molding one's orientation to the world. Sex thus invades thought, but is also intensified and transformed by thought. And so it is that the loss of the use of one's legs, or any other vital function, is an infringement also on the integrity of the mind, an assault on character, a vitiation of power.

The unity of mind and body is also an important element in phenomenological philosophy. This school, which arose in the early twentieth century from the writings of Edmund Husserl, sidesteps the old philosophical question of "how do we know the world [or reality, or truth]" and says that the world is whatever we make it out to be; it is created within the stream of conscious experience. And the way we experience and understand reality is in good part shaped by the language categories through which we sort out what we take to be real, and by the cultural symbolism through which we find significance and meaning in the mess of sense impressions continually bombarding us. Reality, then, isn't a hard-and-fast thing, the same for everybody, but a consensual matter, a social construct, that must be reaffirmed and re-created in all our interactions with other people. It would follow from this relativistic view of the human grasp of the world that people of different cultures inhabit somewhat different realities, as do people of the same culture but of radically different circumstances—people, for example, who can't walk.

In his 1962 book *The Phenomenology of Perception,* the French philosopher Maurice Merleau-Ponty states that the starting point for our apprehension and construction of the world is the body.[5] This goes beyond the obvious fact that our sense organs are parts of the body, for he stresses that the landscape of the body is, explicitly or implicitly, the means and the perspective by which we place ourselves in environments and experience their dimensions. As Simone de Beauvoir says, the body is not a thing, an entity separate from the mind and from the rest of the world in which it is situated. The body is also a set of relationships that link the outer world and the mind into a system. Merleau-Ponty illustrates this by reference to the phenomenon of the "phantom limb," the amputee's illusion that he still possesses the missing arm or leg. He writes, "What it is in us which refuses mutilation and disablement is an *I* [Merleau-Ponty's emphasis] committed to a certain physical and interhuman world, who continues to tend towards his world despite handicaps and amputations and who, to this extent, does not recognize them *de jure* [openly and avowedly]."[6] The amputee is missing more than a limb: He is also missing one of his conceptual links to the world, an anchor of his very existence.

Gelya Frank, an anthropologist, has written a life history of a woman born without her four limbs, documenting the laborious process by which she became "embodied" and grew to accept her condition and develop self-love.[7] Frank sees her as a kind of Venus de Milo whose beauty is curiously enhanced, like the statue's, by her lack of limbs. Embodiment is a problem for those born with deficiencies, but at least they can be socialized to their limitations from infancy. On the other hand, most paraplegics and quadriplegics come to their lot through "the slings and arrows of outrageous fortune" and have a different problem—they have to become reembodied to their impairments. And if the loss of function is grave enough, they may even have to become disembodied.

My own sense of disembodiment is somewhat akin to that of Christina, the "disembodied lady" discussed by Oliver Sacks in his book *The Man Who Mistook His Wife for a Hat.*[8] Because of an allergic reaction to an antibiotic drug, Christina lost all sense of her body—a failure of her faculty of proprioception, the delicate, subliminal feedback mechanism that tells the brain about the position, tension, and general feeling of the body and its parts. It is this "sixth sense" that allows for coordination of movement; without it, talking, walking, even standing, are virtually impossible. In similar fashion, I no longer know where my feet are, and without the low-level pain I still feel, I would hardly know I had legs. Indeed, one of the early symptoms of my malady was a tendency to lose my balance when I would take off my pants in the dark, something that happened to me often in my drinking days. Christina's troubles differ from those of the paralytic, however, for her loss has been more complete. Besides, she became disembodied while still capable of movement, and she compensated by using her eyes to coordinate her physical actions. Quadriplegics, too, must watch what they are doing, and I have spilled drinks held in my hand because my wrist had turned and my brain didn't register it. But by the time the paralytic's failure of proprioception is as complete as Christina's, the limb is no longer movable, and the condition is moot.

I have also become rather emotionally detached from my body, often referring to one of my limbs as *the* leg or *the* arm. People who help me on a regular basis have also fallen into this pattern ("I'll hold the arms and you grab the legs"), as if this depersonalization would compensate for what otherwise would be an intolerable violation of my personal space. The paralytic becomes accustomed to being lifted, rolled, pushed, pulled, and twisted, and he survives this treatment by putting emotional distance between himself and his body. Others join in this effort, and I well remember that after I came to from neurosurgery in 1976, there was a sign pinned to my sheet that read, Do Not Lift By Arms. I weakly suggested to the nurse that they print another sign saying This Side Up.

As my condition has deteriorated, I have come increasingly to look upon my body as a faulty life-support system, the only function of which is to sustain my head. It is all a bit like *Donovan's Brain,* an old science-fiction movie in which a quite nefarious brain is kept alive in a jar with mysterious wires and tubes attached to it. Murphy's brain is similarly sitting on a body that has no movement or tactile sense below the arms and shoulders, and that functions mainly to oxygenate the blood, receive nourishment, and eliminate wastes. In none of these capacities does it do a very good job. My solution to this dilemma is radical dissociation from the body, a kind of etherealization of identity. Perhaps one reason for my success in this adaptation is that I never did take much pride in my body. I am of medium height, rather scrawny, and militantly nonathletic. I was never much to look at, but that didn't bother me greatly. From boyhood onward, I cultivated my wits instead. It is a very different matter for an athletically inclined boy or a girl on the threshold of dating and courtship.

Those who have lost use of some parts of their bodies learn to cultivate the others. The blind develop acute sensitivity to sounds, and quadriplegics, who cannot handle heavy telephone directories, have a remarkable knack for remembering phone numbers. But of a more fundamental order, the quadriplegic's body can no longer speak a "silent language" in the expression of emotions or concepts too elusive for ordinary speech, for the delicate feedback loops between thought and movement have been broken. Proximity, gesture, and body-set have been muted, and the body's ability to articulate thought has been stilled. It is perhaps for this reason that writing has become almost an addiction for me, for in it thought and mind become a system, united in conjunction with the movements of my hands and the responses of the machine. Of even more profound impact on existential states, the thinking activity of the brain cannot be dissolved into motion, and the mind can no longer be lost in an internal dialogue with physical movement. This leaves one adrift in a lonely monologue, an inner soliloquy without rest or surcease, and often without subject matter. Consciousness is overtaken and devoured in contemplation, meditation, ratiocination, and reflection without end, relieved only by one's remaining movements, and sleep.

My thoughts and sense of being alive have been driven back into my brain, where I now reside. More than ever before, it is the base from which I reach out and grasp the world. Many paralytics say that they no longer feel attached to their bodies, which is another way of expressing the shattering of Merleau-Ponty's mind-body system. But it also has a few positive aspects. Just as an anthropologist gets a better perspective on his own culture through long and deep study of a radically different one, my extended sojourn in disability has given me, like it or not, a measure of estrangement far beyond the yield of any trip. I now stand somewhat apart from American culture, making me in many ways a stranger. And with this estrangement has come a greater urge to penetrate the veneer of cultural differences and reach an understanding of the underlying unity of all human experience.

My own disembodied thoughts are crude when compared with those of many people. A blind Milton painted sweeping landscapes of the heavens in *Paradise Lost,* and Beethoven crafted the Ninth Symphony despite—or perhaps because of—being deaf. And today one of the world's leading cosmologists, a Cambridge physicist named Stephen Hawking, travels through quarks and black holes in a journey across space and time to the birth of the universe. These are voyages of the mind, for Hawking has an advanced case of amyotrophic lateral sclerosis (familiarly known as Lou Gehrig's disease), which has left him with only slight movement in one hand and an inability to speak above a whisper. There are not many Miltons, Beethovens, and Hawkings, however, and their example may be small comfort to a twenty-year-old quadriplegic who has made the mistake of diving into shallow water. For most disabled people, the loss of synchrony between mind and body has few compensations.

Many years ago, long before I became disabled, I was talking to a black anthropologist, a friend from our days as fellow graduate students, and the subject turned to race. In the course of our conversation, my friend said, "I always think of myself as being black, just as you always think of yourself as white." I protested this, saying that even though I did think of myself as white when talking to a black person, my skin color was not in the forefront of my conscious mind at other times. My friend didn't believe me. But I was neither mistaken nor misleading in my observation, for I grew up in and still lived in a white world. Whiteness was taken for granted; it was standard and part of the usual order of things. I lived in white neighborhoods; I sailed on a white warship (except for the officers' stewards, who were black); I went to white schools (P.S. 114 in Rockaway Beach never had a black student during my eight years there); and I work in a profession that is still ninety-five percent white. Why think of my whiteness when most of my contacts are with white people? The comedian Martin Mull once did a television program entitled "The History of White People in America," a howlingly funny title because its redundancy fractures logic. White is normal; it's what ethnolinguists call an "unmarked category," a word that is dominant within its class and against which other words of that class are contrasted. Why, I would no more have thought of myself as white than I would have thought of myself as walking on two legs.

Before my disability, I was standard White, Anglo-Saxon, Agnostic Male (WASAM?), a member of the dominant part of the society. My roots in tattered-lace-curtain Irish Catholicism made me uneasy in academia, but I never gave much thought to the other components of my identity. My black friend was forced by the reality of white society always to think of himself as black. It was his first line of defense against a hostile environment. His was an embattled identity. And in exactly the same way, from the time I first took to the wheelchair up to the present, the fact that I am physically handicapped has been in the background of my conscious thoughts. Busy though I might be with other matters and problems, it lingers as a shadow in the corner of my mind, waiting, ready to come out at any moment to fill my meditations. It is a Presence. I, too, had acquired an embattled identity, a sense of

who and what I was that was no longer dominated by my past social attributes, but rather by my physical defects.

One of the more interesting parallels between the stigma of handicap and other forms of embattlement is a sensitivity to nomenclature. One must refer to Negroes as *blacks* today, a term that would have been insulting forty years ago, when the polite word was *colored*. Likewise, the term *lady* is now considered patronizing, and *girl* seems reserved for the prepubescent. It is not surprising, then, that many people in wheelchairs take offense at the brutally direct word *paralysis*, and I have heard spirited arguments over the relative meanings and virtues of *handicapped* and *disabled*. Words such as *crip* and *gimp* are forbidden to the able-bodied, although they are used by the disabled among themselves; ethnic pejorative words are bandied about in the same way. I have treated *handicapped* and *disabled* as synonyms, for what I find most interesting about the debate over the words is the debate itself. It reveals a stance of defensiveness against belittlement that is seldom relaxed; it bespeaks a constant awareness of one's deficiencies. And in the process, even the vocabulary of disability has become emotionally charged. People have a hard time deciding what to say to the disabled, and their troubles are compounded by the fact that they are uncertain about what words to use.

In all the years since the onset of my illness, I have never consciously asked, "Why me?" I feel that this is a foolish question that assumes some cosmic sense of purpose and direction in the universe that simply does not exist. My outlook is quite fatalistic, an attitude that actually predisposes me to get all the pleasure out of life that I can, while I can. Nonetheless, though I may not brood over my impairment, it is always on my mind in spoken or unspoken form, and I believe this is true of all disabled people. It is a precondition of my plans and projects, a first premise of all my thoughts. Just as my former sense of embodiment remained taken for granted, positive, and unconscious, my sense of disembodiment is problematic, negative, and conscious. My identity has lost its stable moorings and has become contingent on a physical flaw.

This consuming consciousness of handicap even invades one's dreams. When I first became disabled, I was still walking, after a fashion, and I remained perfectly normal in my dreams. But as the years passed and I lost the ability to stand or walk, a curious change occurred. In every dream I start out walking and moving freely, often in perilous places; significantly, I am never in a wheelchair. I am climbing high on the mast of a ship in rough seas—something I did occasionally in an earlier incarnation—or I am on a ladder, painting a house. But in the middle of the dream, I remember that I can't walk, at which point I falter and fall. The dream is a perfect enactment of failure of power, the realization that what most men unconsciously fear had in fact happened to me. In other dreams, I am just walking about aimlessly when suddenly I remember my disability. Sometimes I sit down, but often I just stand puzzled until I awaken, the dream dissolves, the room comes into view, and I return to the reality that my paralysis is not a transient thing—it is an awakening much like that of Gregor Samsa in Kafka's *The Metamorphosis*. But perhaps more significant than the content of my dreams is the fact that since 1978 I have never once dreamed of anything else. Even in sleep, disability keeps its tyrannical hold over the mind.

The totality of the impact of serious physical impairment on conscious thought, as well as its firm implantation in the unconscious mind, gives disability a far stronger purchase on one's sense of who and what he is than do any social roles—even key ones such as age, occupation, and ethnicity. These can be manipulated, neutralized, and suspended, and in this way can become adjusted somewhat to each other. Moreover, each role can be played before a separate audience, allowing us to lead multiple lives. One cannot, however, shelve a disability or hide it from the world. A serious disability inundates all other claims to social standing, relegating to secondary status all the attainments of life, all other social roles, even sexuality. It is not a role; it is an identity, a dominant characteristic to which all social roles must be adjusted. And just as the paralytic cannot clear his mind of his impairment, society will not let him forget it.

Given the magnitude of this assault on the self, it is understandable that another major component of the subjective life of the handicapped is anger,[9] a disposition so diffuse and subtle, so carefully managed, that I became aware of it in myself only through writing this book. The anger of the disabled takes two forms. The first is an existential anger, a pervasive bitterness at one's fate, a hoarse and futile cry of rage against fortune. It is a sentiment fueled by the self-hate generated by unconscious shame and guilt, and it bears more than casual resemblance to the anger of America's black people. And, just as among blacks, it becomes expressed in hostility toward the dominant society, then toward people of one's own kind, and finally it is turned inward into an attack on the self. It is a very destructive emotion. In my own case, I have escaped its worst ravages only because my impairment has been so slow that I have been able to adjust to it mentally, and I am old enough to know that I am just a statistic, not the victim of a divine conspiracy. I suspect, although I lack conclusive data on this, that

anger is much greater among those suddenly disabled and the young, for their impairment happens too quickly to permit assimilation, and it clouds an entire lifetime.

The other kind of anger is a situational one, a reaction to frustration or to perceived poor treatment. I have a good supply of this type. A paralytic may struggle to walk and become enraged when he cannot move his leg. Or a quadriplegic may pick up a cup of coffee with stiffened hands and drop it on his lap, precipitating an angry outburst. I had to give up spaghetti because I could no longer twirl it on my fork, and dinner would end for me in a sloppy mess. This would so upset me that I would lose my appetite. Or I may try unsuccessfully for a minute or so to pick up a paper from my desk or turn a page, casual maneuvers for most but a major challenge to me, because my fingers have lost both strength and dexterity. Such frustrations happen to me, and to other paralytics, several times a day. They are minor but cumulative, and they acquire special intensity from the more generalized existential anger often lurking below the surface.

The kind and virulence of the anger of the disabled vary greatly, for each person has a different history, but I have the impression that the depth and type of disability are critical. The extent of disablement obviously influences both existential and situational rage, but anger also seems to be most intense among people with communication disorders—primarily deaf-mutes and people with cerebral palsy and certain kinds of stroke. Most of us have watched the transparent suffering of the speech-impaired as they struggle to convey meaning to their agonized listeners. It is small wonder that the deaf form tightly circumscribed little communities, or that they occasionally explode into overt hostility at those who can hear and speak.

The anger of the disabled arises in the first place from their own lack of physical functions, but, as we will see, it is aggravated by their interaction with the able-bodied world. They daily suffer snub, avoidance, patronization, and occasional outright cruelty, and even when none of these occur, they sometimes imagine the affronts. But whatever the source of the grievance, the disabled have limited ways of showing it. Quadriplegics cannot stalk off in high (or low) dudgeon, nor can they even use body language. To make matters worse, as the price for normal relations, they must comfort others about their condition. They cannot show fear, sorrow, depression, sexuality, or anger, for this disturbs the able-bodied. The unsound of limb are permitted only to laugh. The rest of the emotions, including anger and the expression of hostility, must be bottled up, repressed, and allowed to simmer or be released in the backstage area of the home. This is where

I let loose most of the day's frustrations and irritations, much to Yolanda's chagrin. But I never vent to her the full despair and foreboding I sometimes feel, and rarely even express it to myself. As for the rest of the world, I must sustain their faith in their own immunity by looking resolutely cheery. Have a nice day!

In summary, from my own experience and research and the work of others I have found that the four most far-reaching changes in the consciousness of the disabled are: lowered self-esteem; the invasion and occupation of thought by physical deficits; a strong undercurrent of anger; and the acquisition of a new, total, and undesirable identity. I can only liken the situation to a curious kind of "invasion of the body snatchers," in which the alien intruder and the old occupant coexist in mutual hostility in the same body. It is also a metamorphosis in the exact sense. One morning in the hospital, a nurse was washing me when she was called away by another nurse, who needed help in moving a patient. "I'll be right back," she said as she left, which all hospital denizens know is but a fond hope. She left me lying on my back without the call bell or the TV remote, the door was closed, and she was gone for a half hour. Wondering whether she had forgotten me, I tried to roll onto my side to reach the bell. But I was already quadriplegic, and, try as I might, I couldn't make it. I finally gave up and was almost immediately overcome by a claustrophobic panic, feeling trapped and immobile in my own body. I thought then of Kafka's giant bug, as it rocked from side to side, wiggling its useless legs, trying to get off its back—and I understood the story for the first time.

At the beginning of this chapter, I spoke of the feeling of aloneness, the desire to shrink from society into the inner recesses of the self, that invades the thoughts of the disabled—a feeling that I attributed in part to the deep physical tiredness that accompanies most debility and the formidable physical obstacles posed by the outside world. But we have added other elements to this urge to withdraw. The individual has also been alienated from his old, carefully nurtured, and closely guarded sense of self by a new, foreign, and unwelcome identity. And he becomes alienated from others by a double-barreled mechanism: Due to his depreciated self-image, he has a tendency to withdraw from his old associations into social isolation. And, as if in covert cooperation with this retreat, society—or at least American society—helps to wall him off.

The physical and emotional sequestering of the disabled is often dramatic. One quadriplegic man, married and the father of two children, told us that he never leaves the house and nobody visits their home, not even the friends of his children. He confessed to feelings of shame about his condition. I was struck by the similarity between that family and the one begotten by my father. Another quadriplegic we met attends college through a program that allows home study. Even though he is capable of leaving his house with help, he never does so, and instructors from the college have to meet him at his home. He is trying to break out of his shell, but he is not quite ready. Many disabled people blame their isolation on a hostile society, and often they are right. But there is also that powerful pull backward into the self. It is an urge that I have felt all my life, a centripetal force that is a universal feature of the emotional makeup of our species. Our lives are built upon a constant struggle between the need to reach out to others and a contrary urge to fall back into ourselves. Among the disabled, the inward pull becomes compelling, often irresistible, outlining in stark relief a human propensity that is often perceived only dimly.

The generality of my inquiry was brought home to me vividly one day while listening to a paper delivered by my colleague Katherine Newman. Newman has been doing important research on four groups of people who have experienced severe economic loss: divorced women, air-traffic controllers fired after going out on strike in 1981, laid-off blue-collar workers, and long-time-unemployed middle-management people. Newman described a pattern of consistent responses from all four groups. All experienced a deep sense of loss and went through a period of "mourning" quite similar to that reported among the traumatically disabled. Their feelings of depression were aggravated by a process of self-abasement, accentuated in the case of the divorcées by a sense of sexual inadequacy. Common to most members of the four groups was the idea that they somehow were responsible for the loss, that they had failed as providers. They felt culpable, even in cases where they clearly were innocent victims of impersonal economic circumstance. Here, too, the American ideology of success, combined with vestiges of Calvinism, takes the anger that should be aimed at the system and turns it inward upon the self. With their guilt came shame, and Newman's informants frequently surrendered to that sentiment by sharp curtailment of their social contacts. These tendencies often were reinforced by society's penchant for blaming the victim; their self-condemnation was joined by the censure of others. The stricken individual, and his or her family, withdraws into humiliation, and all tend to be avoided just as if a pox had visited them.

The psychological devastation wrought by unemployment has been studied for more than half a century, but Newman's brilliant exposition makes vividly clear the striking parallels between economic and physical disability, the despoilment of identity that is the common fallout of the damaged self. It is a commentary on the importance of economic status in America that downward mobility fosters the same social and psychological results as crippling. And it is worth noting at this point that the social and emotional ravages of physical disability often are magnified by the individual's loss of livelihood. My own case is a rare exception.

Most of Newman's subjects will eventually make their way back to some kind of economic viability, and here they part company with the handicapped, to whom something more devastating has happened. The disabled have become changed in the minds of the rest of society into a kind of quasi-human. In only a few months, I had moved subtly from the center of my society to its perimeter. I had acquired a new identity that was contingent on my defects and that either compromised or radically altered my prior claims to personhood. In my middle age, I had become a changeling, the lot of all disabled people. They are afflicted with a malady of the body that is translated into a cancer within the self and a disease of social relationships. They have experienced a transformation of the essen-

tial condition of their being in the world. They have become aliens, even exiles, in their own lands.

REFERENCES

1. Erving Goffman, *Stigma: Notes on the Management of Spoiled Identity* (Englewood Cliffs, N.J.: Prentice-Hall, 1963).
2. Constantina Safilios-Rothschild, *The Sociology and Social Psychology of Disability and Rehabilitation* (New York: Random House, 1970).
3. Goffman, *Stigma*.
4. George Herbert Mead, *Mind, Self and Society* (Chicago: University of Chicago Press, 1934).
5. Maurice Merleau-Ponty, *The Phenomenology of Perception* (New York: Humanities Press, 1962).
6. Ibid., p. 81.
7. Gelya Frank, "Venus on Wheels: The Life History of a Congenital Amputee," Ph.D. dissertation, Department of Anthropology, University of California, Los Angeles, 1981.
8. Oliver Sacks, *The Man Who Mistook His Wife for a Hat*, pp. 42–52.
9. See Siller, "Psychological Situation of the Disabled."

✤ **36**

AIDS as Human Suffering

Paul Farmer
Arthur Kleinman

This is a powerful selection. It compares the illness experience, and death, of two people with AIDS. One is a gay man in a New York City hospital and the other is a poor woman in rural Haiti. The selection's cross-cultural comparison emphasizes the social and cultural dimensions of AIDS and the fact that stigma and cultural values can greatly increase the human suffering from the disease.

The AIDS pandemic is a terrible thing. A pandemic is a global epidemic; many people in the United States, who immediately think of homosexual men when one mentions AIDS, forget that the majority of people with AIDS are found in Third World countries. Many people in biomedi-

cine think of AIDS as a disease and as a scientific challenge and forget the human suffering of the illness experience.

From the view of epidemiology, an epidemic is a disease with greater than expected frequency (incidence). By definition, therefore, a newly discovered or identified disease is an epidemic. Epidemics are media events, in part because the discovery of a disease's biological cause makes an exciting story. Throughout history, there has been a pattern of infectious diseases changing from epidemic to endemic (meaning the diseases are permanently transmitted within a population). In other words, new diseases in a population often begin with high mortality rates and then, through processes of mutual adaptation of host and pathogen over time, diseases may become both more common and less virulent. Whether AIDS will follow this pattern is a matter of conjecture. Recently, because of stunning advances in clinical treatments for people who are HIV positive, AIDS has become more like a long-term chronic disease. But this medical progress appears to be primarily among white males with medical insurance; there is less improvement among ethnic minorities. For people in Third World countries, where economic resources do not permit even HIV testing, the scientific breakthroughs in clinical treatment of AIDS seem unlikely in the foreseeable future.

Medical anthropologists have contributed a great deal to the study of HIV transmission and prevention since the very beginning of the epidemic. The literature is large, and interested students might begin with an anthropology and AIDS bibliography (Bolton and Orozco, 1994). The design of culturally appropriate prevention strategies has been another area of interest to many applied medical anthropologists.

Paul Farmer, one of the authors of this selection, has done anthropological fieldwork on the impact of the AIDS epidemic on a small Haitian community where, in one sense, AIDS was thought of as a disease that could be "sent" through sorcery (Farmer 1988). Toward the beginning of the

AIDS epidemic, Haitians were singled out by the Centers for Disease Control as an ethnic "risk group" for the disease, and this erroneous epidemiological fact had some serious repercussions in terms of stigma and discrimination. Farmer is also a physician; he has worked in a rural health center in Haiti that has had marked success. The lessons learned from that project have been expanded to a nongovernmental agency called Partners in Health that has projects all over the world (Farmer, Connors, and Simmons 1996).

As you read this selection, consider these questions:

- *In what ways were Robert's and Anita's deaths different? How do those differences reflect cultural values? Which kind of death would you prefer?*

- *How is the stigma from HIV/AIDS different from something like a spinal-cord injury, as we saw in the last selection?*

- *Examine the nonmedical sources of human suffering caused by AIDS listed at the end of this selection. What kind of solutions would you suggest?*

- *How might culture be a factor in the distribution of disease? Could Robert or Anita have avoided their disease? How?*

That the dominant discourse on AIDS at the close of the twentieth century is in the rational-technical language of disease control was certainly to be expected and even necessary. We anticipate hearing a great deal about the molecular biology of the virus, the clinical epidemiology of the disease's course, and the pharmacological engineering of effective treatments. Other of contemporary society's key idioms for describing life's troubles also express our reaction to AIDS: the political-economic talk of public-policy experts, the social-welfare jargon of the politicians and bureaucrats, and the latest psychological terminology of mental-health professionals. Beneath the action-oriented verbs and reassuringly new nouns of these experts' distancing terminology, the more earthy, emotional rumblings of the frightened, the accusatory, the hate-filled, and the confused members of the public are reminders that our response to AIDS emerges from deep and dividing forces in our experience and our culture.

AIDS AND HUMAN MEANINGS

Listen to the words of persons with AIDS and others affected by our society's reaction to the new syndrome:

- "I'm 42 years old. I have AIDS. I have no job. I do get $300 a month from social security and the state. I will soon receive $64 a month in food stamps. I am severely depressed. I cannot live on $300 a month. After $120 a month for rent and $120 a month for therapy, I am left with $60 for food and vitamins and other doctors and maybe acupuncture treatments and my share of utilities and oil and wood for heat. I'm sure I've forgotten several expenses like a movie once in a while and a newspaper and a book."[1]

- "I don't know what my life expectancy is going to be, but I certainly know the quality has improved. I know that not accepting the shame or the guilt or the stigma that people would throw on me has certainly extended my life expectancy. I know that being very up-front with my friends, and my family and coworkers, reduced a tremendous amount of stress, and I would encourage people to be very open with friends, and if they can't handle it, then that's their problem and they're going to have to cope with it."

- "Here we are at an international AIDS conference. Yesterday a woman came up to me and said, 'May I have two minutes of your time?' She said, 'I'm asking doctors how they feel about treating AIDS patients.' And I said, 'Well, actually I'm not a doctor. I'm an AIDS patient,' and as she was shaking hands, her hand whipped away, she took two steps backward, and the look of horror on her face was absolutely diabolical."

■ "My wife and I have lived here [in the United States] for fifteen years, and we speak English well, and I do O.K. driving. But the hardest time I've had in all my life, harder than Haiti, was when people would refuse to get in my cab when they discovered I was from Haiti [and therefore in their minds, a potential carrier of HIV]. It got so we would pretend to be from somewhere else, which is the worst thing you can do, I think."

All illnesses are metaphors. They absorb and radiate the personalities and social conditions of those who experience symptoms and treatments. Only a few illnesses, however, carry such cultural salience that they become icons of the times. Like tuberculosis in *fin de siècle* Europe, like cancer in the first half of the American century, and like leprosy from Leviticus to the present, AIDS speaks of the menace and losses of the times. It marks the sick person, encasing the afflicted in an exoskeleton of peculiarly powerful meanings: the terror of a lingering and untimely death, the panic of contagion, the guilt of "self-earned" illness.

AIDS has offered a new idiom for old gripes. We have used it to blame others: gay men, drug addicts, inner-city ethnics, Haitians, Africans. And we in the United States have, in turn, been accused of spreading and even creating the virus that causes AIDS. The steady progression of persons with AIDS toward the grave, so often via the poor house, has assaulted the comforting idea that risk can be managed. The world turns out to be less controllable and more dangerous, life more fragile than our insurance and welfare models pretend. We have relegated the threat of having to endure irremediable pain and early death—indeed, the very image of suffering as the paramount reality of daily existence—to past periods in history and to other, poorer societies. Optimism has its place in the scale of American virtues; stoicism and resignation in the face of unremitting hardship—unnecessary character traits in a land of plenty—do not. Suffering had almost vanished from public and private images of our society.

Throughout history and across cultures, life-threatening disorders have provoked questions of control (What do we do?) and bafflement (Why me?). When bubonic plague depopulated fourteenth-century Europe by perhaps as many as half to three-fourths of the population, the black death was construed as a religious problem and a challenge to the moral authority as much or even more than as a

public-health problem. In the late twentieth century, it is not surprising that great advances in scientific knowledge and technological intervention have created our chief responses to questions of control and bafflement. Yet bafflement is not driven away by the advance of scientific knowledge, for it points to another aspect of the experience of persons with AIDS that has not received the attention it warrants. It points to a concern that in other periods and in other cultures is at the very center of the societal reaction to dread disease, a concern that resonates with that which is most at stake in the human experience of AIDS even if it receives little attention in academic journals—namely, suffering.

A mortal disease forces questions of dread, of death, and of ultimate meaning to arise. Suffering is a culturally and personally distinctive form of affliction of the human spirit. If pain is distress of the body, suffering is distress of the person and of his or her family and friends. The affliction and death of persons with AIDS create master symbols of suffering; the ethical and emotional responses to AIDS are collective representations of how societies deal with suffering. The stories of sickness of people with AIDS are texts of suffering that we can scan for evidence of how cultures and communities and individuals elaborate the unique textures of personal experience out of the impersonal cellular invasion of viral RNA. Furthermore, these illness narratives point toward issues in the AIDS epidemic every bit as salient as control of the spread of infection and treatment of its biological effects.

Viewed from the perspective of suffering, AIDS must rank with smallpox, plague, and leprosy in its capacity to menace and hurt, to burden and spoil human experience, and to elicit questions about the nature of life and its significance. Suffering extends from those afflicted with AIDS to their families and intimates, to the practitioners and institutions who care for them, and to their neighborhoods and the rest of society, who feel threatened by perceived sources of the epidemic and who are thus affected profoundly yet differently by its consequences. If we minimize the significance of AIDS as human tragedy, we dehumanize people with AIDS as well as those engaged in the public-health and clinical response to the epidemic. Ultimately, we dehumanize us all.

ROBERT AND THE DIAGNOSTIC DILEMMA

It was in a large teaching hospital in Boston that we first met Robert, a forty-four-year-old man with AIDS.[2]

Robert was not from Boston, but from Chicago, where he had already weathered several of the infections known to strike people with compromised immune function. His most recent battle had been with an organism similar to that which causes tuberculosis but is usually harmless to those with intact immune systems. The infection and the many drugs used to treat it had left him debilitated and depressed, and he had come east to visit his sister and regain his strength. On his way home, he was prevented from boarding his plane "for medical reasons." Beset with fever, cough, and severe shortness of breath, Robert went that night to the teaching hospital's emergency ward. Aware of his condition and its prognosis, Robert hoped that the staff there would help him to "get into shape" for the flight back to Chicago.

The physicians in the emergency ward saw their task as straightforward: to identify the cause of Robert's symptoms and, if possible, to treat it. In contemporary medical practice, identifying the cause of respiratory distress in a patient with AIDS entails following what is often called an algorithm. An algorithm, in the culture of biomedicine, is a series of sequential choices, often represented diagrammatically, which helps physicians to make diagnoses and select treatments. In Robert's case, step one, a chest X-ray, suggested the opportunistic lung parasite *Pneumocystis* as a cause for his respiratory distress; step two, examination of his sputum, confirmed it. He was then transferred to a ward in order to begin treatment of his lung infection. Robert was given the drug of choice, but did not improve. His fever, in fact, rose and he seemed more ill than ever.

After a few days of decline, Robert was found to have trismus: his jaw was locked shut. Because he had previously had oral candidiasis ("thrush"), his trismus and neck pain were thought to suggest the spread of the fungal infection back down the throat and pharynx and into the esophagus—a far more serious process than thrush, which is usually controlled by antifungal agents. Because Robert was unable to open his mouth, the algorithm for documenting esophagitis could not be followed. And so a "GI consult"—Robert has already had several—was called. It was hoped that the gastroenterologists, specialists at passing tubes into both ends of the gastrointestinal tract, would be better able to evaluate the nature of Robert's trismus. Robert had jumped ahead to the point in the algorithm that called for "invasive studies." The trouble is that on the night of his admission he had already declined a similar procedure.

Robert's jaw remained shut. Although he was already emaciated from two years of battle, he refused a feeding tube. Patient refusal is never part of an algorithm, and so the team turned to a new kind of logic: Is Robert mentally competent to make such a decision? Is he suffering from AIDS dementia? He was, in the words of one of those treating him, "not with the program." Another member of the team suggested that Robert had "reached the end of the algorithm" but the others disagreed. More diagnostic studies were suggested: in addition to esophagoscopy with biopsy and culture, a CT scan of the neck and head, repeated blood cultures, even a neurological consult. When these studies were mentioned to the patient, his silent stare seemed to fill with anger and despair. Doctors glanced uncomfortably at each other over their pale blue masks. Their suspicions were soon confirmed. In a shaky but decipherable hand, Robert wrote a note: "I just want to be kept clean."

Robert got a good deal more than he asked for, including the feeding tube, the endoscopy, and the CT scan of the neck. He died within hours of the last of these procedures. His physicians felt that they could not have withheld care without having some idea of what was going on.

In the discourse of contemporary biomedicine, Robert's doctors had been confronted with "a diagnostic dilemma." They had not cast the scenario described above as a moral dilemma but had discussed it in rounds as "a compliance problem." This way of talking about the case brings into relief a number of issues in the contemporary United States—not just in the culture of biomedicine but in the larger culture as well. In anthropology, one of the preferred means of examining culturally salient issues is through ethnology: in this case, we shall compare Robert's death in Boston to death from AIDS in a radically different place.

ANITA AND A DECENT DEATH

The setting is now a small Haitian village. Consisting of fewer than a thousand persons, Do Kay is composed substantially of peasant farmers who were displaced some thirty years ago by Haiti's largest dam. By all the standard measures, Kay is now very poor; its older inhabitants often blame their poverty on the massive buttress dam a few miles away and note bitterly that it has brought them neither electricity nor water.

When the first author of this paper began working in Kay, in May of 1983, the word *SIDA*, meaning AIDS, was just beginning to make its way into the rural Haitian lexicon. Interest in the illness was almost universal less than three years later. It was about then that Anita's intractable cough was attributed to tuberculosis.

Questions about her illness often evoked long responses. She resisted our attempts to focus discussions. "Let me tell you the story from the beginning," she once said; "otherwise you will understand nothing at all."

As a little girl, Anita recalls, she was frightened by the arguments her parents would have in the dry seasons. When her mother began coughing, the family sold their livestock in order to buy "a consultation" with a distinguished doctor in the capital. Tuberculosis, he told them, and the family felt there was little they could do other than take irregular trips to Port-au-Prince and make equally irregular attempts to placate the gods who might protect the woman. Anita dropped out of school to help take care of her mother, who died shortly after the girl's thirteenth birthday.

It was very nearly the *coup de grâce* for her father, who became depressed and abusive. Anita, the oldest of five children, bore the brunt of his spleen. "One day, I'd just had it with his yelling. I took what money I could find, about $2, and left for the city. I didn't know where to go." Anita had the good fortune to find a family in need of a maid. The two women in the household had jobs in a U.S.-owned assembly plant; the husband of one ran a snack concession out of the house. Anita received a meal a day, a bit of dry floor to sleep on, and $10 per month for what sounded like incessant labor. She was not unhappy with the arrangement, which lasted until both women were fired for participating in "political meetings."

Anita wandered about for two days until she happened upon a kinswoman selling gum and candies near a downtown theater. She was, Anita related, "a sort of aunt." Anita could come and stay with her, the aunt said, as long as she could help pay the rent. And so Anita moved into Cité Simone, the sprawling slum on the northern fringes of the capital.

It was through the offices of her aunt that she met Vincent, one of the few men in the neighborhood with anything resembling a job: "He unloaded the whites' luggage at the airport." Vincent made a living from tourists' tips. In 1982, the year before Haiti became associated, in the North American press, with AIDS, the city of Port-au-Prince counted tourism as its chief industry. In the setting of an unemployment rate of greater than 60 percent, Vincent could command considerable respect. He turned his attention to Anita. "What could I do, really? He had a good job. My aunt thought I should go with him." Anita was not yet fifteen when she entered her first and only sexual union. Her lover set her up in a shack in the same neighborhood. Anita cooked and washed and waited for him.

When Vincent fell ill, Anita again became a nurse. It began insidiously, she recalls: night sweats, loss of appetite, swollen lymph nodes. Then came months of unpredictable and debilitating diarrhea. "We tried everything—doctors, charlatans, herbal remedies, injections, prayers." After a year of decline, she took Vincent to his hometown in the south of Haiti. There it was revealed that Vincent's illness was the result of malign magic: "It was one of the men at the airport who did this to him. The man wanted Vincent's job. He sent an AIDS death to him."

The voodoo priest who heard their story and deciphered the signs was straightforward. He told Anita and Vincent's family that the sick man's chances were slim, even with the appropriate interventions. There were, however, steps to be taken. He outlined them, and the family followed them, but still Vincent succumbed. "When he died, I felt spent. I couldn't get out of bed. I thought that his family would try to help me to get better, but they didn't. I knew I needed to go home."

She made it as far as Croix-des-Bouquets, a large market town at least two hours from Kay. There she collapsed, feverish and coughing, and was taken in by a woman who lived near the market. She stayed for a month, unable to walk, until her father came to take her back home. Five years had elapsed since she'd last seen him. Anita's father was by then a friendly but broken-down man with a leaking roof over his one-room, dirt-floor hut. It was no place for a sick woman, the villagers said, and Anita's godmother, honoring twenty-year-old vows, made room in her overcrowded but dry house.

Anita was diagnosed as having tuberculosis, and she responded to antituberculosis therapy. But six months after the initiation of treatment, she declined rapidly. Convinced that she was indeed taking her medications, we were concerned about AIDS, especially on hearing of the death of her lover. Anita's father was poised to sell his last bit of land in order to "buy more nourishing food for the child." It was imperative that the underlying cause of Anita's poor response to treatment be found. A laboratory test confirmed our suspicions.

Anita's father and godmother alone were apprised of the test results. When asked what she knew about AIDS, the godmother responded, "AIDS is an infectious disease that has no cure. You can get it from the blood of an infected person." For this reason, she said, she had nothing to fear in caring for Anita. Further, she was adamant that Anita not be told of her diagnosis—"That will only make her suffer more"—and skeptical about the value of the AIDS clinic in Port-au-Prince. "Why should we take her there?" asked Anita's godmother wearily. "She will not recover from this disease. She will have to endure the heat and humiliation of the clinic. She will not find a cool place to lie down. What she might find is a pill or an injection to make her feel more comfortable for a short time. I can do better than that."

And that is what Anita's godmother proceeded to do. She attempted to sit Anita up every day and encouraged her to drink a broth promised to "make her better." The godmother kept her as clean as possible, consecrating the family's two sheets to her goddaughter. She gave Anita her pillow and stuffed a sack with rags for herself. The only thing she requested from us at the clinic was "a beautiful soft wool blanket that will not irritate the child's skin."

In one of several thoughtful interviews accorded us, Anita's godmother insisted that "for some people, a decent death is as important as a decent life. . . . The child has had a hard life; her life has always been difficult. It's important that she be washed of bitterness and regret before she dies." Anita was herself very philosophic in her last months. She seemed to know of her diagnosis. Although she never mentioned the word *SIDA*, she did speak of the resignation appropriate to "diseases from which you cannot escape." She stated, too, that she was "dying from the sickness that took Vincent," although she denied that she had been the victim of witchcraft—"I simply caught it from him."

Anita did not ask to be taken to a hospital, nor did her slow decline occasion any request for further diagnostic tests. What she most wanted was a radio—"for the news and the music"—and a lambswool blanket. She especially enjoyed the opportunity to "recount my life," and we were able to listen to her narrative until hours before her death.

AIDS IN CULTURAL CONTEXT

The way in which a person, a family, or a community responds to AIDS may reveal a great deal about core cultural values. Robert's story underlines our reliance on technological answers to moral and medical questions. "Americans love machines more than life itself," asserts author Philip Slater in a compelling analysis of middle-class North American culture. "Any challenge to the technological-over-social priority threatens to expose the fact that Americans have lost their manhood and their capacity to control their environment."[3] One of the less noticed but perhaps one of the farthest-reaching consequences of the AIDS epidemic has been the weakening of North America's traditional confidence in the ability of its experts to solve every kind of problem. In the words of one person with the disorder, "The terror of AIDS lies in the collapse of our faith in technology."[4]

This core cultural value is nowhere more evident than in contemporary tertiary medicine, which re-

mains the locus of care for the vast majority of AIDS patients. Despite the uniformity of treatment outcome, despite the lack of proven efficacy of many diagnostic and therapeutic procedures, despite their high costs, it has been difficult for practitioners to limit their recourse to these interventions. "When you're at Disney World," remarked one of Robert's physicians ironically, "you take all the rides."

Robert's illness raises issues that turn about questions of autonomy and accountability. The concept of autonomous individuals who are solely responsible for their fate, including their illness, is a powerful cultural premise in North American society. On the positive side, this concept supports concern for individual rights and respect for individual differences and achievement. A more ominous aspect of this core cultural orientation is that it often justifies blaming the victims. Illness is said to be the outcome of the free choice of high-risk behavior.

This has been especially true in the AIDS epidemic, which has reified an invidious distinction between "innocent victims"—infants and hemophiliacs—and, by implication, "the guilty"—persons with AIDS who are homosexuals or intravenous drug users. Robert's lonely and medicalized death is what so many North Americans fear: "He was terrified. He knew what AIDS meant. He knew what happens. Your friends desert you, your lover kicks you out into the street. You get fired, you get evicted from your apartment. You're a leper. You die alone."[5] The conflation of correlation and responsibility has the effect of making sufferers feel guilt and shame. The validity of their experience is contested. Suffering, once delegitimated, is complicated and even distorted; our response to the sufferer, blocked.

In contrast, in Haiti and in many African and Asian societies, where individual rights are often underemphasized and also frequently unprotected, and where the idea of personal accountability is less powerful than is the idea of the primacy of social relationships, blaming the victim is also a less frequent response to AIDS. Noticeably absent is the revulsion with which AIDS patients have been faced in the United States, in both clinical settings and in their communities. This striking difference cannot be ascribed to Haitian ignorance of modes of transmission. On the contrary, the Haitians we have interviewed have ideas of etiology and epidemiology that reflect the incursion of the "North American ideology" of AIDS—that the disease is caused by a virus and is somehow related to homosexuality and contaminated blood. These are subsumed, however, in properly Haitian beliefs about illness causation. Long before the advent of AIDS to Do Kay, we might have asked the following question: some fatal diseases are known to be caused by "microbes" but may also be "sent" by someone; is *SIDA* such a disease?

Differences in the responses of caregivers to Robert and Anita—such as whether to inform them of their diagnosis or undertake terminal care as a family or a community responsibility—also reflect the ego-centered orientation in North American cities and the more sociocentric orientation in the Haitian village. An ironic twist is that it is in the impersonal therapeutic setting of North American healthcare institutions that concern for the patient's personhood is articulated. It is, however, a cool bioethical attention to abstract individual rights rather than a validation of humane responses to concrete existential needs. Perhaps this cultural logic—of medicine as technology, of individual autonomy as the most inviolable of rights, and so of individuals as responsible for most of the ills that befall them—helps us to understand how Robert's lonely death, so rich in all the technology applied to his last hours, could be so poor in all those supportive human virtues that resonate from the poverty-stricken village where Anita died among friends.

A core clinical task would seem to be helping patients to die a decent death. For all the millions of words spilled on the denial of death in our society and the various psychotechniques advertised to aid us to overcome this societal silence, AIDS testifies vividly that our secular public culture is simply unable to come to terms with mortality.

A final question might be asked in examining the stories of Robert and Anita: just how representative are they of the millions already exposed to HIV? As a middle-class, white gay male, Robert is thought by many to be a "typical victim of AIDS." But he is becoming increasingly less typical in the United States, where the epidemic is claiming more and more blacks and Hispanics, and Robert would not be sociologically representative of the typical AIDS patient in much of the rest of the world. In many Third World settings, sex differences in the epidemiology of HIV infection are unremarkable: in Haiti, for example, there is almost parity between the sexes. Most importantly, most people with AIDS are not middle-class and insured. All this points to the fact that the virus that causes AIDS might exact its greatest toll in the Third World.

AIDS IN GLOBAL CONTEXT

Although the pandemic appears to be most serious in North America and Europe, per capita rates reveal that fully seventeen of the twenty countries most affected by AIDS are in Africa or the Caribbean. Further, although there is heartening evidence that the epi-demic is being more effectively addressed in the North American gay community, there is no indication that the spread of HIV has been curbed in the communities in which women like Anita struggle. Although early reports of high HIV seroprevalence were clearly based on faulty research, even recent and revised estimates remain grim: "In urban areas in some sub-Saharan countries, up to 25% of young adults are *already* HIV carriers, with rates among those reporting to clinics for sexually transmitted diseases passing 30%, and among female prostitutes up to 90%."[6] In other words, the countries most affected are precisely those that can least afford it.

These figures also remind us that AIDS has felled many like Anita—the poor, women of color, victims of many sorts of oppression and misfortune. Although heterosexual contact seems to be the means of spreading in many instances, not all who contract the disease are "promiscuous," a label that has often offended people in Africa, Haiti, and elsewhere. *Promiscuous* fails utterly to capture the dilemmas of millions like Anita. In an essay entitled "The Myth of African Promiscuity," one Kenyan scholar refers to the "'new poor': the massive pool of young women living in the most deprived conditions in shanty towns and slums across Africa, who are available for the promise of a meal, new clothes, or a few pounds."[7]

Equally problematic, and of course related, is the term *prostitute*. It is often used indiscriminately to refer to a broad spectrum of sexual activity. In North America, the label has been misused in investigations of HIV seroprevalence: "the category *prostitute* is taken as an undifferentiated 'risk group' rather than as an occupational category whose members should, for epidemiological purposes, be divided into IV drug users and nonusers—with significantly different rates of HIV infection—as other groups are."[8] A more historical view reminds us that prostitutes have often been victims of scapegoating and that there has long been more energy for investigation of the alleged moral shortcomings of sex workers than for the economic underpinnings of their work.

The implications of this sort of comparative exercise, which remains a cornerstone of social anthropology, are manifold. The differences speak directly to those who would apply imported models of prevention to rural Haiti or Africa or any other Third World setting. A substantial public-health literature, reflecting the fundamentally interventionist perspective of that discipline, is inarguably necessary in the midst of an epidemic without cure or promising treatment. The same must be true for the burgeoning biomedical literature on AIDS. But with what consequences have these disciplines ignored the issue of AIDS as suffering? Whether reduced to parasite-host interactions or to questions of shifting incidence and prevalence among risk groups, AIDS has meant suffering on a large scale, and this suffering is not captured in these expert discourses on the epidemic.

The meaning of suffering in this context is distinctive not only on account of different beliefs about illness and treatment responses but because of the brute reality of grinding poverty, high child and maternal mortality, routinized demoralization and oppression, and suffering as a central part of existence. The response to AIDS in such settings must deal with this wider context of human misery and its social sources. Surely it is unethical—in the broadest sense, if not in the narrow technical biomedical limits to the term—for international health experts to turn their backs on the suffering of people with AIDS in the Third World and to concentrate solely on the prevention of new cases.

DEALING WITH AIDS AS SUFFERING

To what practical suggestions does a view of AIDS as human suffering lead?

Suffering Compounded by Inappropriate Use of Resources

The majority of all medical-care costs for AIDS patients is generated by acute inpatient care. In many ways, however, infection with HIV is more like a chronic disease. Based on cases of transfusion-associated HIV transmission in the United States, the mean time between exposure to the virus and the development of AIDS is over eight years. This period may well be lengthened by drugs already available. And as the medical profession becomes more skilled at managing the AIDS condition, the average time of survival of patients with the full-blown syndrome will also be extended. For many with AIDS, outpatient treatment will be both more cost-effective and more humane. For the terminally ill, home or hospice care may be preferred to acute-care settings, especially for people who "just want to be kept clean." Helping patients to die a decent death was once an accepted aspect of the work of health professionals. It must be recognized and appropriately supported as a core clinical task in the care of persons with AIDS.

Not a small component of humane care for people with AIDS is soliciting their stories of sickness, listening to their narratives of the illness, so as to help them give meaning to their suffering. Restoring this seem-

ingly forgotten healing skill will require a transformation in the work and training of practitioners and a reorganization of time and objectives in health-care delivery systems.

The practitioner should initiate informed negotiation with alternative lay perspectives on care and provide what amounts to brief medical psychotherapy for the threats and losses that make chronic illness so difficult to bear. But such a transformation in the provision of care will require a significant shift in the allocation of resources, including a commitment to funding psychosocial services as well as appropriate providers—visiting nurses, home health aides, physical and occupational therapists, general practitioners, and other members of teams specializing in long-term, outpatient care.

Suffering Magnified by Discrimination

In a recent study of the U.S. response to AIDS, the spread of HIV was compared to that of polio, another virus that struck young people, triggered public panic, and received regular attention in the popular media. "Although these parallels are strong," notes the author, "one difference is crucial: there was little early sympathy for victims of AIDS because those initially at risk—homosexual men, Haitian immigrants, and drug addicts—were not in the mainstream of society. In contrast, sympathy for polio patients was extensive."[9] This lack of sympathy is part of a spectrum that extends to hostility and even violence, and that has led to discrimination in housing, employment, insurance, and the granting of visas.[10] The victims of such discrimination have been not only people with AIDS or other manifestations of HIV infection but those thought to be in "risk groups."

In some cases, these prejudices are only slightly muted in clinical settings. In our own experience in U.S. hospitals, there is markedly more sympathy for those referred to as "the innocent victims"—patients with transfusion-associated AIDS and HIV-infected babies. At other times, irrational infection-control precautions do little more than heighten patients' feelings of rejection. Blame and recrimination are reactions to the diseases in rural Haiti as well—but there the finger is not often pointed at those with the disease.

Although the President's Commission on AIDS called for major coordinated efforts to address discrimination, what has been done has been desultory, unsystematic, and limited in reach. While legislation is crucial, so too is the development of public-education programs that address discrimination and suffering.

Suffering Augmented by Fear

Underlying at least some of the discrimination, spite, and other inappropriate responses to AIDS is fear. We refer not to the behavior-modifying fear of "the worried well" but to the more visceral fear that has played so prominent a role in the epidemic. It is fear that prompts someone to refuse to get into a taxi driven by a Haitian man; it is fear that leads a reporter to wrench her hand from that of a person with AIDS; it is fear that underpins some calls for widespread HIV-antibody testing, and fear that has led some health professionals to react to patients in degrading fashion. The fact that so much of this fear is "irrational" has thus far had little bearing on its persistence.

Dissemination of even a few key facts—by people with AIDS, leaders of local communities, elected officials and other policy-makers, teachers, and health professionals—should help to assuage fear. HIV is transmitted through parenteral, mucous-membrane, or open-wound contact with contaminated blood or body fluids and not through casual contact. Although the risk of transmission of HIV to health-care professionals is not zero, it is extremely low, even after percutaneous exposure (studies show that, of more than 1,300 exposed health-care workers, only four seroconverted[11]).

Suffering Amplified by Social Death

In several memoirs published in North America, persons with AIDS have complained of the immediate social death their diagnosis has engendered. "For some of my friends and family, I was dead as soon as they heard I had AIDS," a community activist informed us. "That was over two years ago." Even asymptomatic but seropositive individuals, whose life expectancy is often better than that of persons with most cancers and many common cardiovascular disorders, have experienced this reaction. Many North Americans with AIDS have made it clear that they do not wish to be referred to as victims: "As a person with AIDS," writes Navarre, "I can attest to the sense of diminishment at seeing and hearing myself referred to as an AIDS victim, an AIDS sufferer, an AIDS case—as anything but what I am, a person with AIDS. I am a person with a condition. I am not that condition."[12]

It is nonetheless necessary to plan humane care for persons with a chronic and deadly disease—"without needlessly assaulting my denial," as a young man recently put it. The very notion of hospice care will need rethinking if its intended clients are a group of young and previously vigorous persons. Similarly, our cross-cultural research has shown us that preferred means of coping with a fatal disease are shaped by biography and culture. There are no set "stages" that someone with AIDS will go through, and there can be no standard professional response.

Suffering Generated by Inequities

AIDS is caused, we know, by a retrovirus. But we need not look to Haiti to see that inequities have sculpted the AIDS epidemic. The disease, it has been aptly noted, "moves along the fault lines of our society."[13] Of all infants born with AIDS in the United States, approximately 80 percent are black or Hispanic.[14] Most of these are the children of IV drug users, and attempts to stem the virus may force us to confront substance abuse in the context of our own society. For as Robert Gallo and Luc Montagnier assert, "efforts to control AIDS must be aimed in part at eradicating the conditions that give rise to drug addiction."[15]

There are inequities in the way we care for AIDS patients. In the hospital where Robert died, AZT—the sole agent with proven efficacy in treating HIV infection—is not on formulary. Patients needing the drug who are not in a research protocol have to send someone to the drugstore to buy it—if they happen to have the $10,000 per year AZT can cost or an insurance policy that covers these costs. Such factors may prove important in explaining the striking ethnic differences in average time of survival following diagnosis of AIDS. In one report it was noted that, "while the average lifespan of a white person after diagnosis is two years, the average minority person survives only 19 weeks."[16]

From rural Haiti, it is not the local disparities but rather the international inequities that are glaring. In poor countries, drugs like AZT are simply not available. As noted above, the AIDS pandemic is most severe in the countries that can least afford a disaster of these dimensions. A view of AIDS as human suffering forces us to lift our eyes from local settings to the true dimensions of this worldwide tragedy.

Compassionate involvement with persons who have AIDS may require listening carefully to their stories, whether narratives of suffering or simply attempts to recount their lives. Otherwise, as Anita pointed out, we may understand nothing at all.

NOTES

1. The first three of the four quotations cited here are the voices of persons with AIDS who attended the Third International Conference on AIDS, held in Washington,

D.C. in June 1987. Their comments are published passim in 4 (1) (Winter/ Spring 1988) of *New England Journal of Public Policy*. All subsequent unreferenced quotations are from tape-recorded interviews accorded the first author.

2. All informants' names are pseudonyms, as are "Do Kay" and "Ba Kay." Other geographical designations are as cited.

3. Philip Slater, *The Pursuit of Loneliness: American Culture at the Breaking Point* (Boston: Beacon Press, 1970), 49, 51.

4. Emmanuel Dreuilhe, *Mortal Embrace: Living with AIDS* (New York: Hill and Wang, 1988), 20.

5. George Whitmore, *Someone Was Here: Profiles in the AIDS Epidemic* (New York: New American Library, 1988), 26.

6. Renée Sabatier, *Blaming Others: Prejudice, Race, and Worldwide AIDS* (Philadelphia: New Society Publishers, 1988), 15.

7. Professor Aina, ibid., 80.

8. Jan Zita Grover, "AIDS: Keywords," in *AIDS: Cultural Analysis/Cultural Activism* (Cambridge: MIT Press, 1988), 25–26.

9. Sandra Panem, *The AIDS Bureaucracy* (Cambridge: Harvard University Press, 1988), 15.

10. See Sabatier for an overview of AIDS-related discrimination. As regards Haiti and Haitians, see Paul Farmer, "AIDS and Accusation: Haiti, Haitians, and the Geography of Blame," in *Cultural Aspects of AIDS: Anthropology and the Global Pandemic* (New York: Praeger, in press). The degree of antipathy is suggested by a recent *New York Times*–CBS News poll of 1,606 persons: "Only 36 percent of those interviewed said they had a lot or some sympathy 'for people who get AIDS from homosexual activity,' and 26 percent said they had a lot or some sympathy 'for people who get AIDS from sharing needles while using illegal drugs'" (*New York Times,* 14 October 1988, Al2).

11. Infectious Diseases Society of America, 276.

12. Max Navarre, "Fighting the Victim Label," in *AIDS: Cultural Analysis/Cultural Activism* (Cambridge: MIT Press, 1988), 143.

13. Mary Catherine Bateson and Richard Goldsby, *Thinking AIDS: The Social Response to the Biological Threat* (Reading, Mass.: Addison-Wesley, 1988), 2.

14. Samuel Friedman, Jo Sotheran, Abu Abdul-Quadar, Beny Primm, Don Des Jarlais, Paula Kleinman, Conrad Mauge, Douglas Goldsmith, Wafaa El-Sadr, and Robert Maslansky, "The AIDS Epidemic among Blacks and Hispanics," *The Milbank Quarterly 65,* suppl. 2 (1987): 455–99.

15. Robert Gallo and Luc Montagnier, "AIDS in 1988," *Scientific American* 259 (4) (October 1988):48.

16. Sabatier, 19.

Gender and Women's Health

✤ CONCEPTUAL TOOLS ✤

■ *Gender and sex are different categories.* In general, anthropologists use the term *sex* to refer to biologically based differences between men and women and *gender* to refer to the more important and more pervasive social, cultural, economic, and political differences between men and women. Gender is a cultural construct, and cultural ideas about women's health and women's bodies differ from social group to social group and across historical periods. There are biomedical consequences to the cultural constructions of gender differences. Prevalence of disease is often different for women and men, not because of biology but because of differential access to resources or exposure to both social and epidemiological stressors. There are also problems of underreporting and underrecognition of some diseases, like heart disease, in women. Gender issues do not only pertain to women; male gender rules and expectations are also culturally constructed. This may be why men have lower life expectancies than women at every age and in every country reporting vital statistics to the World Health Organization (WHO). There is little doubt that gender roles affect health.

■ *Women's reproductive health represents an important and widely studied area of medical anthropology.* Historically, the study of women had been neglected in the field of anthropology, but this situation has changed in the past twenty years (Morgen 1989). Feminist perspectives (a type of critical theory) have made major contributions to our understanding of health and medical systems. Women's reproductive health issues include a wide variety of concerns, including obstetric practice in childbirth and the risk of maternal mortality; cultural beliefs about menstruation and health, diet, infertility, abortion, contraception, and menopause (Sargent and Brettell 1996). An important critique of the literature on women's health is that women have been "essentialized" as reproducers—their most essential characteristic has been their ability to reproduce. Consequently, women's health is equated with reproductive health, and other aspects of health are underemphasized.

■ *There is little research on what women themselves deem to be their health concerns.* There is little research based on what *women* have identified as their health problems. In general, the identification of women's health problems has not come from women themselves. We know even less about the health issues, concerns, and experiences of women who are not white, and not middle class. There has been very little research examining the intersection of gender, race, class, age, sexual orientation, religion, and women's health. This absence of women's perspective is particularly ironic in that women are very often the "producers of health"—in other words, women are in charge of health issues on the household level.

■ *New reproductive technologies, such as in vitro fertilization, represent interesting case studies of the process of medicalization.* Medical anthropologists have documented enduring sexism in biomedicine, most often in the field of obstetrics (Hahn 1987). Historically, biomedicine has medicalized and often pathologized normal physiological processes, like pregnancy, childbirth, and breast-feeding. Normal stages in women's reproductive life cycle are turned into diseases. For example, "moodiness" around the time of the period becomes "PMS," which in turn becomes a psychiatric condition. Male medical authority has been allowed to define women's bodies and their health, and women's lives—especially their reproductive lives—have increasingly come under medical control.

■ *The language of biomedicine and the speech of biomedical practitioners can demonstrate power relations.* Medical anthropologists studying biomedicine are interested in issues of power relations, and power differentials are often involved in interactions between men and women. We can see this, for example, in the case of doctor–patient interactions in which male physicians may intimidate female patients in the course of giving instructions on care. Medical arguments on women's health are often political or moral discussions (discourses) in the guise of health issues.

For example, a recent study of beliefs about cervical cancer showed a marked difference between the Latina immigrants' beliefs and those of their physicians, who viewed cervical cancer as a consequence of immorality and "promiscuity" (Martinez, Chavez, and Hubbell 1997).

■ *Women's health is politicized.* Women's health is often the site of political struggle. The most notable example, of course, is the continuing debate over abortion (Ginsburg 1989). Among the many other issues is the targeting of poor women in international birth control and population control efforts.

37

Medical Metaphors of Women's Bodies: Menstruation and Menopause

Emily Martin

This selection explores the cultural and historical underpinnings of medical knowledge about women's bodies and medical authority over women. Emily Martin's approach fits within epistemologically oriented critical medical anthropology (as in selection 23). Her approach critically examines the cultural assumptions as they developed and as they are used in a field of expertise—biomedicine. This type of analysis is more typical of the work by humanities scholars (more specifically, cultural studies) largely because it focuses on the underlying conditions of the discourse, particularly the written communication of experts. This selection is part of Martin's book, The Woman in the Body: A Cultural Analysis of Reproduction *(1987). Because it is historical in its orientation, the primary sources of evidence in this analysis are texts (and textbooks) of medical knowledge.*

Feminist critiques like this one powerfully remind us of the processes through which objective facts are, in actuality, culturally constructed. Ethnographic studies of scientists in their laboratories and "doing science" have demonstrated that this production of knowledge is not value-neutral or culturally neutral; the studies of laboratory scientists (Latour 1986) are very much like the ethnographic studies of medical doctors working in clinics (Hahn and Gaines 1985) in that metaphors and stories are often used for communicating local cultural knowledge. The feminist analysis here demonstrates how the use of language and particular metaphors can influence how women are treated. Metaphors are shorthand for ways of thinking; they reflect implicit understandings among members of a social group. Metaphors, therefore, have real and practical implications for social relations, and these are important considering our previous readings on suffering and stigma.

Why are both menopause and menstruation considered pathological, or at least described with negative metaphors? Emily Martin traces these ideas to a more general medical metaphor of the body as a machine or a factory. The "product" of a female factory is a baby. As a factory, the body is organized with a centralized information system, and failure to follow the master plan must be seen as disorganization.

In a very readable book comparing the medical beliefs of Germany, France, Britain, and the United States, Lynn Payer (1988) describes the U.S. ethnomedical system as being based on the metaphor of the body as a machine. It was for this reason, she argues, that U.S. biomedical researchers thought it feasible to build a mechanical heart, whereas European biomedical researchers saw this effort as folly. The idea is that the cultural metaphor of the machine with replaceable parts allowed and encouraged a type of habitual thinking. In the same way, gender-related metaphors in biomedical discourse encourage specific treatment of women.

As you read this selection, consider these questions:

- *In what types of metaphors are women "essentialized" as reproducers from the biomedical viewpoint?*
- *Is it possible for this type of analysis to fit with the evolutionary medical analyses introduced in the first part of this book (selection 3)?*
- *Is the use of negative metaphors in texts a male plot? Or do women themselves incorporate these cultural models in their discourse and thinking?*
- *How might this analysis fit with the creation of premenstrual syndrome as a pathology?*

It is difficult to see how our current scientific ideas are infused by cultural assumptions; it is easier to see how scientific ideas from the past, ideas that now seem wrong or too simple, might have been affected by cultural ideas of an earlier time. To lay the groundwork for a look at contemporary scientific views of menstruation and menopause, I begin with the past.

It was an accepted notion in medical literature from the ancient Greeks until the late 18th century that male and female bodies were structurally similar. As

345

Nemesius, Bishop of Emesa, Syria, in the fourth century, put it, "women have the same genitals as men, except that theirs are inside the body and not outside it." Although increasingly detailed anatomical understanding (such as the discovery of the nature of the ovaries in the last half of the 17th century) changed the details, medical scholars from Galen in second-century Greece to Harvey in 17th-century Britain all assumed that women's internal organs were structurally analogous to men's external ones.[1]

Although the genders were structurally similar, they were not equal. For one thing, what could be seen of men's bodies was assumed as the pattern for what could not be seen of women's. For another, just as humans as a species possessed more "heat" than other animals and hence were considered more perfect, so men possessed more "heat" than women and hence were considered more perfect. The relative coolness of the female prevented her reproductive organs from extruding outside the body but, happily for the species, kept them inside where they provided a protected place for conception and gestation.[1, p.10]

During the centuries when male and female bodies were seen as composed of analogous structures, a connected set of metaphors was used to convey how the parts of male and female bodies functioned. These metaphors were dominant in classical medicine and continued to operate through the 19th century:[2, p. 5]

> The body was seen, metaphorically, as a system of dynamic interactions with its environment. Health or disease resulted from a cumulative interaction between constitutional endowment and environmental circumstance. One could not well live without food and air and water; one had to live in a particular climate, subject one's body to a particular style of life and work. Each of these factors implied a necessary and continuing physiological adjustment. The body was always in a state of becoming—and thus always in jeopardy.

Two subsidiary assumptions governed this interaction: first, that "every part of the body was related inevitably and inextricably with every other," and second, that "the body was seen as a system of intake and outgo—a system which had, necessarily, to remain in balance if the individual were to remain healthy."[2, pp. 5–6]

Given these assumptions, changes in the relationship of body functions occurred constantly throughout life, though more acutely at some times than at others. In Edward Tilt's influential mid-19th century account, for example, after the menopause, blood that once flowed out of the body as menstruation was then turned into fat:[3, p. 54]

> Fat accumulates in women after the change of life, as it accumulates in animals from whom the ovaries have been removed. The withdrawal of the sexual stimulus from the ganglionic nervous system, enables it to turn into fat and self-aggrandisement that blood which might otherwise have perpetuated the race.

During the transition to menopause, or the "dodging time," the blood cannot be turned into fat, so it was either discharged as hemorrhage or through other compensating mechanisms, the most important of which was "the flush":[3, pp. 54, 57]

> As for thirty-two years it had been habitual for women to lose about 3 oz. of blood every month, so it would have been indeed singular, if there did not exist some well-continued compensating discharges acting as wastegates to protect the system, until health could be permanently re-established by striking new balances in the allotment of blood to the various parts. . . . The flushes determine the perspirations. Both evidence a strong effect of conservative power, and as they constitute the most important and habitual safety-valve of the system at the change of life, it is worth while studying them.

In this account, compensating mechanisms such as the "flush" are seen as having the positive function of keeping intake and outgo in balance.

These balancing acts had exact analogues in men. In Hippocrates' view of purification, one that was still current in the 17th century,[4, p. 50]

> women were of a colder and less active disposition than men, so that while men could sweat in order to remove the impurities from their blood, the colder dispositions of women did not allow them to be purified in that way. Females menstruated to rid their bodies of impurities.

Or in another view, expounded by Galen in the second century and still accepted in the 18th century, menstruation was the shedding of an excess of blood, a plethora.[4, p. 50] But what women did through menstruation men could do in other ways such as by having blood let.[5] In either view of the mechanism of menstruation process itself not only had analogues in men, it was seen as inherently health maintaining. Menstrual blood, to be sure, was often seen as foul and unclean[4, p. 50] but the process of excreting it was not intrinsically pathological. In fact, failure to excrete was taken as a sign of disease, and a great variety of remedies existed even into the 19th century specifically to reestablish menstrual flow if it stopped.[6]

By 1800, according to Laqueur's important recent study, this long-established tradition that saw male and female bodies as similar both in structure and in function began to come "under devastating attack. Writers of all sorts were determined to base what they insisted were fundamental differences between male and female sexuality and thus between man and woman, on discoverable biological distinctions."[1] Laqueur argues that this attempt to ground differences between the genders in biology grew out of the crumbling of old ideas about the existing order of politics and society as laid down by the order of nature. In the old ideas, men dominated the public world and the world of morality and order by virtue of their greater perfection, a result of their excess heat. Men and women were arranged in a hierarchy in which they differed by degree of heat. They were not different in kind.[1, p. 8]

The new liberal claims of Hobbes and Locke in the 17th century and the French revolution were factors that led to a loss of certainty that the social order could be grounded in the natural order. If the social order were merely convention, it could not provide a secure enough basis to hold women and men in their places. But after 1800 the social and biological sciences were brought to the rescue of male superiority. "Scientists in areas as diverse as zoology, embryology, physiology, heredity, anthropology, and psychology had little difficulty in proving that the pattern of male-female relations that characterized the English middle classes was natural, inevitable, progressive."[7, p. 180]

The assertion was that men's and women's social roles themselves were grounded in nature, by virtue of the dictates of their bodies. In the words of one 19th century theorist:[7, p. 190]

> the attempt to alter the present relations of the sexes is not a rebellion against some arbitrary law instituted by a despot or a majority—not an attempt to break the yoke of a mere convention; it is a struggle against Nature; a war undertaken to reverse the very conditions under which not man alone, but all mammalian species have reached their present development.

The doctrine of the two spheres—men as workers in the public, wage-earning sphere outside the home and women (except for the lower classes) as wives and mothers in the private, domestic sphere of kinship and morality inside the home—replaced the old hierarchy based on body heat.

During the latter part of the 19th century, new metaphors that posited fundamental differences between the sexes began to appear. One 19th century biologist, Patrick Geddes, perceived two opposite kinds of processes at the level of the cell "upbuilding, constructive, synthetic processes" summed up as an-

abolism, "disruptive, descending series of chemical changes" summed up as katabolism.[8] The relationship between the two terms was described in frankly economic terms:[8, p. 133]

> The processes of income and expenditure must balance, but only to the usual extent, that expenditure must not altogether outrun income, else the cell's capital of living matter will be lost—a fate which is often not successfully avoided. . . . Just as our expenditure and income should balance at the year's end, but may vastly outstrip each other at particular times, so it is with the cell of the body. Income too may continuously preponderate, and we increase in wealth, or similarly, in weight, or in anabolism. Conversely, expenditure may predominate, but business may be prosecuted at a loss; and similarly, we may live on for a while with loss of weight, or in katabolism. This losing game of life is what we call a katabolic habit.

Geddes saw these processes not only at the level of the cell, but also at the level of entire organisms. In the human species, as well as almost all higher animals, females were predominantly anabolic, males katabolic. Although in the terms of his saving-spending metaphor it is not at all clear whether katabolism would be an asset, when Geddes presents male-female differences, there is no doubt which he thought preferable:[8, pp. 270–271]

> It is generally true that the males are more active, energetic, eager, passionate, and variable; the females more passive, conservative, sluggish, and stable. . . . The more active males, with a consequently wider range of experience, may have bigger brains and more intelligence; but the females, especially as mothers, have indubitably a larger and more habitual share of the altruistic emotions. The males being usually stronger, have greater independence and courage; the females excel in constancy of affection and in sympathy.

In Geddes, the doctrine of separate spheres was laid on a foundation of separate and fundamentally different biology in men and women, at the level of the cell. One of the striking contradictions in his account is that he did not carry over the implications of his economic metaphors to his discussion of male-female differences. If he had, females might have come off as wisely conserving their energy and never spending beyond their means, males as in the "losing game of life," letting expenditures outrun income.

Geddes may have failed to draw the logical conclusions from his metaphor, but we have to acknowledge that metaphors were never meant to be logical. Other 19th century writers developed metaphors in exactly opposite directions: women spent and men saved. The Reverend John Todd saw women as voracious spenders in the marketplace, and so consumers of all that a man could earn. If unchecked, a woman would ruin a man, by her own extravagant spending, by her demands on him to spend, or in another realm, by her excessive demands on him for sex. Losing too much sperm meant losing that which sperm was believed to manufacture: a man's lifeblood.[9]

Todd and Geddes were not alone in the 19th century in using images of business loss and gain to describe physiological processes. Susan Sontag has suggested that 19th century fantasies about disease, especially tuberculosis, "echo the attitudes of early capitalist accumulation. One has a limited amount of energy, which must be properly spent. . . . Energy, like savings, can be depleted, can run out or be used up, through reckless expenditure. The body will start 'consuming' itself, the patient will 'waste away.'"[10, pp. 61–62]

Despite the variety of ways that spending-saving metaphors could be related to gender, the radical difference between these metaphors and the earlier intake-outgo metaphor is key. Whereas in the earlier model, male and female ways of secreting were not only analogous but desirable, now the way became open to denigrate, as Geddes overtly did, functions that for the first time were seen as uniquely female, without analogue in males. For our purposes, what happened to accounts of menstruation is most interesting: by the 19th century, the process itself is seen as soundly pathological. In Geddes' terms,[8, p. 244]

> it yet evidently lies on the borders of pathological change, as is evidenced not only by the pain which so frequently accompanies it, and the local and constitutional disorders which so frequently arise in this connection, but by the general systemic disturbance and local histological changes of which the discharge is merely the outward expression and result.

Whereas in earlier accounts the blood itself may have been considered impure, now the process itself is seen as a disorder.

Nineteenth century writers were extremely prone to stress the debilitating nature of menstruation and its adverse impact on the lives and activities of women.[11] Medical images of menstruation as pathological were remarkably vivid by the end of the century. For Walter Heape, the militant anti-suffragist and Cambridge zoologist, in menstruation the entire epithelium was torn away, "leaving behind a ragged wreck of tissue, torn glands, ruptured vessels, jagged edges of stroma, and masses of blood corpuscles, which it would seem hardly possible to heal satisfactorily without the aid of surgical treatment.[1, p. 32] A few years later, Havelock Ellis could see women as being "periodically

wounded" in their most sensitive spot and "emphasize the fact that even in the healthiest woman, a worm however harmless and unperceived, gnaws periodically at the roots of life."[12, p. 284]

If menstruation was consistently seen as pathological, menopause, another function which by this time was regarded as without analogue in men, often was too: many 19th century medical accounts of menopause saw it as a crisis likely to bring on an increase of disease.[11, pp. 30–31] Sometimes the metaphor of the body as a small business that is either winning or losing was applied to menopause too. A late 19th century account specifically argued against Tilt's earlier adjustment model: "When the period of fruitfulness is ended the activity of the tissues has reached its culmination, the secreting power of the glandular organs begins to diminish, the epithelium becomes less sensitive and less susceptible to infectious influences, and atrophy and degeneration take the place of the active up-building processes."[13, pp. 25–26] But there were other sides to the picture. Most practitioners felt the "climacteric disease," a more general disease of old age, was far worse for men than for women. And some regarded the period after menopause far more positively than it is being seen medically in our century, as the "'Indian summer' of a woman's life—a period of increased vigor, optimism, and even of physical beauty."[11, p. 30]

Perhaps the 19th century's concern with conserving energy and limiting expenditure can help account for the seeming anomaly of at least some positive medical views of menopause and the climacteric. As an early 20th century popular health account put it:[14, p. 413]

> [Menopause] is merely a conservative process of nature to provide for a higher and more stable phase of existence, an economic lopping off of a function no longer needed, preparing the individual for different forms of activity, but is in no sense pathologic. It is not sexual or physical decrepitude, but belongs to the age of invigoration, marking the fullness of the bodily and mental powers.

Those few writers who saw menopause as an "economic" physiological function might have drawn very positive conclusions from Geddes' description of females as anabolic, stressing their "thriftiness" instead of their passivity, their "growing bank accounts" instead of their sluggishness.

If the shift from the body as an intake-outgo system to the body as a small business trying to spend, save, or balance its accounts is a radical one, with deep importance for medical models of female bodies, so too is another shift that began in the 20th century with the development of scientific medicine. One of the early 20th century engineers of our system of scientific medicine, Frederick T. Gates, who advised John D. Rockefeller on how to use his philanthropies to aid scientific medicine, developed a series of interrelated metaphors to explain the scientific view of how the body works:[15, pp. 170–171]

> It is interesting to note the striking comparisons between the human body and the safety and hygienic appliances of a great city. Just as in the streets of a great city we have "white angels" posted everywhere to gather up poisonous materials from the streets, so in the great streets and avenues of the body, namely the arteries and the blood vessels, there are brigades of corpuscles, white in color like the "white angels," whose function it is to gather up into sacks, formed by their own bodies, and disinfect or eliminate all poisonous substances found in the blood. The body has a network of insulated nerves, like telephone wires, which transmit instantaneous alarms at every point of danger. The body is furnished with the most elaborate police system, with hundreds of police stations to which the criminal elements are carried by the police and jailed. I refer to the great numbers of sanitary glands, skillfully placed at points where vicious germs find entrance, especially about the mouth and throat. The body has a most complete and elaborate sewer system. There are wonderful laboratories placed at convenient points for a subtle brewing of skillful medicines. . . . The fact is that the human body is made up of an infinite number of microscopic cells. Each one of these cells is a small chemical laboratory, into which its own appropriate raw material is constantly being introduced, the processes of chemical separation and combination are constantly taking place automatically, and its own appropriate finished product being necessary for the life and health of the body. Not only is this so, but the great organs of the body like the liver, stomach, pancreas, kidneys, gall bladder are great local manufacturing centers, formed of groups of cells in infinite numbers, manufacturing the same sorts of products, just as industries of the same kind are often grouped in specific districts.

Although such a full-blown description of the body as a model of an industrial society is not often found in contemporary accounts of physiology, elements of the images that occurred to Gates are commonplace. In recent years, the "imagery of the biochemistry of the cell [has] been that of the factory, where functions [are] specialized for the conversion of energy into particular products and which [has] its own part to play in the economy of the organism as a whole."[16, p. 58]

Still more recently, economic functions of greater complexity have been added: adenosine triphosphate (ATP) is seen as the body's "energy currency": "Produced in particular cellular regions, it [is] placed in an 'energy bank' in which it [is] maintained in two forms, those of 'current account' and 'deposit account.' Ultimately, the cell's and the body's energy books must balance by an appropriate mix of monetary and fiscal policies."[16, p. 59] Here we have not just the simpler 19th century saving and spending, but two distinct forms of money in the bank, presumably invested at different levels of profit.

Development of the new molecular biology brought additional metaphors based on information science, management and control. In this model, flow of information between deoxyribonucleic acid (DNA) and ribonucleic acid (RNA) leads to the production of protein. Molecular biologists conceive of the cell as "an assembly line factory in which the DNA blueprints are interpreted and raw materials fabricated to produce the protein end products in response to a series of regulated requirements."[16, p. 59] The cell is still seen as a factory, but, compared to Gates' description, there is enormous elaboration of the flow of information from one "department" of the body to another and exaggeration of the amount of control exerted by the center. For example, from a college physiology text:[17, pp. 7–8]

> All the systems of the body, if they are to function effectively, must be subjected to some form of control. . . . The precise control of body function is brought about by means of the operation of the nervous system and of the hormonal or endocrine system. . . . The most important thing to note about any control system is that before it can control anything it must be supplied with information. . . . Therefore the first essential in any control system is an adequate system of collecting information about the state of the body. . . . Once the CNS [central nervous system] knows what is happening, it must then have a means for rectifying the situation if something is going wrong. There are two available methods for doing this, by using nerve fibres and by using hormones. The motor nerve fibers . . . carry instructions from the CNS to the muscles and glands throughout the body. . . . As far as hormones are concerned the brain acts via the pituitary gland . . . the pituitary secretes a large number of hormones . . . the rate of secretion of each one of these is under the direct control of the brain.

Although there is increasing attention to describing physiological processes as positive and negative feedback loops, so that like a thermostat system, no single element has preeminent control over any other, most descriptions of specific processes give preeminent control to the brain, as we will see below.

In over-all descriptions of female reproduction, the dominant image is that of a signaling system. Lein, in a textbook designed for junior colleges, spells it out in detail,[18, p. 14]

Hormones are chemical signals to which distant tissues or organs are able to respond. Whereas the nervous system has characteristics in common with a telephone network, the endocrine glands perform in a manner somewhat analogous to radio transmission. A radio transmitter may blanket an entire region with its signal, but a response occurs only if a radio receiver is turned on and tuned to the proper frequency . . . the radio receiver in biological systems is a tissue whose cells possess active receptor sites for a particular hormone or hormones.

The signal-response metaphor is found almost universally in current texts for premedical and medical students:[19, p. 885; 20, p. 129; 21, p. 115; emphasis added]

The hypothalamus *receives signals* from almost all possible sources in the nervous system.

The endometrium *responds directly* to stimulation or withdrawal of estrogen and progesterone. In turn, regulation of the secretion of these steroids involves a well-integrated, highly structured series of activities by the hypothalamus and the anterior lobe of the pituitary. Although the ovaries do not function autonomously, they *influence*, through *feedback* mechanisms, the level of performance *programmed* by the hypothalamic-pituitary axis.

As a result of strong stimulation of FSH [follicle-stimulating hormone], a number of follicles *respond* with growth.

And the same idea is found, more obviously, in popular health books:[22, p. 6; 23, p. 6; emphasis added]

Each month from menarch on, [the hypothalamus] acts as elegant interpreter of the body's rhythms, *transmitting messages* to the pituitary gland that set the menstrual cycle in motion.

Each month, *in response to a message* from the pituitary gland, one of the unripe egg cells develops inside a tiny microscopic ring of cells, which gradually increases to form a little balloon or cyst called the Graafian follicle.

Although most accounts stress signals or stimuli traveling in a "loop" from hypothalamus to pituitary to ovary and back again, carrying positive or negative feedback, one element in the loop, the hypothalamus, part of the brain, is often seen as predominant. Just as in the general model of the central nervous system, the female brain-hormone-ovary system is usually described not as a feedback loop like a thermostat system, but as a hierarchy, in which the "directions" or "orders" of one element dominate:[24, p. 1615; 19, p. 885; emphasis added]

Both positive and negative feedback control must be invoked, together with *superimposition* of control by the

CNS through neurotransmitters released into the hypophyseal portal circulation.

Almost all secretion by the pituitary is *controlled* by either hormonal or nervous signals from the hypothalamus. . . . The hypothalamus is a collecting center for information concerned with the internal well-being of the body, and in turn much of this information is used *to control* secretions of the many globally important pituitary hormones.

As Lein puts it into ordinary language:[18, p. 84]

The cerebrum, that part of the brain that provides awareness and mood, can play a significant role in the control of the menstrual cycle. As explained before, it seems evident that these higher regions of the brain exert their influence by modifying the actions of the hypothalamus. So even though the hypothalamus is a kind of master gland dominating the anterior pituitary, and through it the ovaries also, it does not act with complete independence or without influence from outside itself . . . there are also pathways of control from the higher centers of the brain.

So this is a communication system organized hierarchically, not a committee reaching decisions by mutual influence. The hierarchical nature of the organization is reflected in some popular literature meant to explain the nature of menstruation simply: "From first menstrual cycle to menopause, the hypothalamus acts as the conductor of a highly trained orchestra. Once its baton signals the downbeat to the pituitary, the hypothalamus-pituitary-ovarian axis is united in purpose and begins to play its symphonic message, preparing a woman's body for conception and childbearing."[22, p. 6] Carrying the metaphor further, the follicles vie with each other for the role of producing the egg like violinists trying for the position of concertmaster; a burst of estrogen is emitted from the follicle like a "clap of tympani."[21, p. 6]

The basic images chosen here—an information-transmitting system with a hierarchical structure—have an obvious relation to the dominant form of organization in our society.[25] What I want to show is how this set of metaphors, once chosen as the basis for the description of physiological events, has profound implications for the way in which a change in the basic organization of the system will be perceived. In terms of female reproduction, this basic change is of course menopause. Many criticisms have been made of the medical propensity to see menopause as a pathological state.[26] I would like to suggest that the tenacity of this view comes not only from the negative stereotypes associated with aging women in our society, but as a logical outgrowth of seeing the body as a hierarchical information-processing system in the first place.

(Another part of the reason menopause is seen so negatively is related to metaphors of production, which I discuss later.)

What is the language in which menopause is described? In menopause, according to a college text, the ovaries become "unresponsive" to stimulation from the gonadotropins, to which they used to respond. As a result the ovaries "regress." On the other end of the cycle, the hypothalamus has gotten estrogen "addiction" from all those years of menstruating. As a result of the "withdrawal" of estrogen at menopause, the hypothalamus begins to give "inappropriate orders."[18, pp. 79, 97] In a more popular account, "the pituitary gland during the change of life becomes disturbed when the ovaries fail to respond to its secretions, which tends to affect its control over other glands. This results in a temporary imbalance existing among all the endocrine glands of the body, which could very well lead to disturbances that may involve a person's nervous system."[27, p. 11]

In both medical texts and popular books, what is being described is the breakdown of a system of authority. The cause of ovarian "decline" is the "decreasing ability of the aging ovaries to respond to pituitary gonadotropins."[28] At every point in this system, functions "fail," and falter. Follicles "fail to muster the strength" to reach ovulation.[22, p. 18] As functions fail, so do the members of the system decline: "breasts and genital organs gradually atrophy,"[28, p. 598] "wither,"[22, p. 181] and become "senile."[21, p. 121] Diminished, atrophied relics of their former vigorous, functioning selves, the "senile ovaries" are an example of the vivid imagery brought to this process. A text whose detailed illustrations make it a primary resource for medical students despite its early date describes the ovaries this way:[21, p. 116]

> [T]he *senile ovary* is a shrunken and puckered organ, containing few if any follicles, and made up for the most part of old corpora albincantia and corpora atretica, the bleached and functionless remainders of corpora lutia and follicles embedded in a dense connective tissue stroma.

In more recent accounts, it is commonly said that ovaries cease to respond and fail to produce. Everywhere else there is regression, decline, atrophy, shrinkage, and disturbance.

The key to the problem connoted by these descriptions is functionlessness. Susan Sontag has written of our obsessive fear of cancer, a disease that we see as entailing a nightmare of excessive growth and rampant production. These images frighten us in part because in our stage of advanced capitalism, they are close to a reality we find difficult to see clearly: broken-down hi-

erarchy and organization members who no longer play their designated parts represent nightmare images for us. One woman I talked to said her doctor gave her two choices for treatment of her menopause: she could take estrogen and get cancer or she could not take it and have her bones dissolve. Like this woman, our imagery of the body as a hierarchical organization gives us no good choice when the basis of the organization seems to us to have changed drastically. We are left with breakdown, decay, and atrophy. Bad as they are, these might be preferable to continued activity, which because it is not properly hierarchically controlled, leads to chaos, unmanaged growth, and disaster.

But let us return to the metaphor of the factory producing substances, which dominates the imagery used to describe cells. At the cellular level DNA communicates with RNA, all for the purpose of the cell's production of proteins. In a similar way, the system of communication involving female reproduction is thought to be geared toward production of various things: the ovaries produce estrogen, the pituitary produces follicle-stimulating hormone and luteinizing hormone, and so on. Follicles also produce eggs in a sense, although this is usually described as "maturing" them since the entire set of eggs a woman has for her lifetime is known to be present at birth. Beyond all this the system is seen as organized for a single preeminent purpose: "transport" of the egg along its journey from the ovary to the uterus[28, p. 580] and preparation of an appropriate place for the egg to grow if it is fertilized. In a chapter titled "Prepregnancy Reproductive Functions of the Female, and the Female Hormones," Guyton puts it all together: "Female reproductive functions can be divided into two major phases: first, preparation of the female body for conception and gestation, and second, the period of gestation itself."[19, p. 968] This view may seem commonsensical, and entirely justified by the evolutionary development of the species with its need for reproduction to ensure survival.

Yet I suggest that assuming this view of the purpose for the process slants description and understanding of the female cycle unnecessarily. Let us look at how medical textbooks describe menstruation. They see the action of progesterone and estrogen on the lining of the uterus as "ideally suited to provide a hospitable environment for implantation and survival of the embryo"[28, p. 576] or as intended to lead to "the monthly renewal of the tissue that will cradle [the ovum]."[18, p. 43] As Guyton summarizes, "The whole purpose of all these endometrial changes is to produce a highly secretory endometrium containing large amounts of stored nutrients that can provide appropriate conditions for implantation of a fertilized ovum during the latter half of the monthly cycle."[19, p. 976] Given this teleological interpretation of the purpose of the increased amount of endometrial tissue, it should be no surprise that when a fertilized egg does not implant, these texts describe the next event in very negative terms. The fall in blood progesterone and estrogen "deprives" the "highly developed endometrial lining of its hormonal support," "constriction" of blood vessels leads to a "diminished" supply of oxygen and nutrients, and finally "disintegration starts, the entire lining begins to slough, and the menstrual flow begins." Blood vessels in the endometrium "hemorrhage" and the menstrual flow "consists of this blood mixed with endometrial debris."[28, p. 577] The "loss" of hormonal stimulation causes "necrosis" (death of tissue).[19, p. 976]

The construction of these events in terms of a purpose that has failed is beautifully captured in a standard text for medical students (a text otherwise noteworthy for its extremely objective, factual descriptions) in which a discussion of the events covered in the last paragraph (sloughing, hemorrhaging) ends with the statement, "When fertilization fails to occur, the endometrium is shed, and a new cycle starts. This is why it used to be taught that 'menstruation is the uterus crying for lack of a baby.'"[29, p. 63]

I am arguing that just as seeing menopause as a kind of failure of the authority structure in the body contributes to our negative view of it, so does seeing menstruation as failed production contribute to our negative view of it. We have seen how Sontag describes our horror of production out of control. But another kind of horror for us is *lack* of production: the disused factory, the failed business, the idle machine. Winner terms the stopping and breakdown of technological systems in modern society "apraxia" and describes it as "the ultimate horror, a condition to be avoided at all costs."[30] This horror of idle workers or machines seems to have been present even at earlier stages of industrialization. A 19th century inventor, Thomas Ewbank, elaborated his view that the whole world "was designed for a Factory."[31] "It is only as a Factory, a *General Factory*, that the whole materials and influences of the earth are to be brought into play."[31, p. 23] In this great workshop, humans' role is to produce: "God employs no idlers—creates none."[31, p. 27] Ewbank continues:[31, p. 141]

> Like artificial motors, we are created for the work we can do—for the useful and productive ideas we can stamp upon matter. Engines running daily without doing any work resemble men who live without labor; both are spendthrifts dissipating means that would be productive if given to others.

Menstruation not only carries with it the connotation of a productive system that has failed to produce,

it also carries the idea of production gone awry, making products of no use, not to specification, unsalable, wasted, scrap. However disgusting it may be, menstrual blood will come out. Production gone awry is also an image that fills us with dismay and horror. Amid the glorification of machinery common in the 19th century were also fears of what machines could do if they went out of control. Capturing this fear, one satirist wrote of a steam-operated shaving machine that "sliced the noses off too many customers."[32] This image is close to the one Melville created in *The Bell-Tower*, in which an inventor, who can be seen as an allegory of America, is killed by his mechanical slave,[32, p.153] as well as to Mumford's[33] sorcerer's apprentice applied to modern machinery:[34, p. 180]

> Our civilization has cleverly found a magic formula for setting both industrial and academic brooms and pails of water to work by themselves, in ever-increasing quantities at an ever-increasing speed. But we have lost the Master Magician's spell for altering the tempo of this process, or halting it when it ceases to serve human functions and purposes.

Of course, how much one is gripped by the need to produce goods efficiently and properly depends on one's relationship to those goods. While packing pickles on an assembly line, I remember the foreman often holding up improperly packed bottles to show to us workers and trying to elicit shame at the bad job we were doing. But his job depended on efficient production, which meant many bottles filled right the first time. This factory did not yet have any effective method of quality control, and as soon as our supervisor was out of sight, our efforts went toward filling as few bottles as we could while still concealing who had filled which bottle. In other factories, workers seem to express a certain grim pleasure when they can register objections to company policy by enacting imagery of machinery out of control. Noble reports an incident in which workers resented a supervisor's order to "shut down their machines, pick up brooms, and get to work cleaning the area. But he forgot to tell them to stop. So, like the sorcerer's apprentice, diligently and obediently working to rule, they continued sweeping up all day long."[35, p. 312]

Perhaps one reason the negative image of failed production is attached to menstruation is precisely that women are in some sinister sense out of control when they menstruate. They are not reproducing, not continuing the species, not preparing to stay at home with the baby, not providing a safe, warm womb to nurture a man's sperm. I think it is plain that the negative power behind the image of failure to produce can be considerable when applied metaphorically to women's bodies. Vern Bullough comments optimistically that "no reputable scientist today would regard menstruation as pathological,"[36] but this paragraph from a recent college text belies his hope:[37, p. 525]

> If fertilization and pregnancy do not occur, the corpus luteum degenerates and the levels of estrogens and progesterone decline. As the levels of these hormones decrease and their stimulatory effects are withdrawn, blood vessels of the endometrium undergo prolonged spasms (contractions) that reduce the blood flow to the area of the endometrium supplied by the vessels. The resulting lack of blood causes the tissues of the affected region to degenerate. After some time, the vessels relax, which allows blood to flow through them again. However, capillaries in the area have become so weakened that blood leaks through them. This blood and the deteriorating endometrial tissue are discharged from the uterus as the menstrual flow. As a new ovarian cycle begins and the level of estrogens rises, the functional layer of the endometrium undergoes repair and once again begins to proliferate.

In rapid succession the reader is confronted with "degenerate," "decline," "withdrawn," "spasms," "lack," "degenerate," "weakened," "leak," "deteriorate," "discharge," and, after all that, "repair."

In another standard text, we read:[38, p. 624]

> The sudden lack of these two hormones [estrogen and progesterone] causes the blood vessels of the endometrium to become spastic so that blood flow to the surface layers of the endometrium almost ceases. As a result, much of the endometrial tissue dies and sloughs into the uterine cavity. Then, small amounts of blood ooze from the denuded endometrial wall, causing a blood loss of about 50 ml during the next few days. The sloughed endometrial tissue plus the blood and much serous exudate from the denuded uterine surface, all together called the *menstrum*, is gradually expelled by intermittent contractions of the uterine muscle for about 3 to 5 days. This process is called *menstruation*.

The illustration that accompanies this text captures very well the imagery of catastrophic disintegration: "ceasing," "dying," "losing," "denuding," and "expelling."

These are not neutral terms; rather, they convey failure and dissolution. Of course, not all texts contain such a plethora of negative terms in their descriptions of menstruation, but unacknowledged cultural attitudes can seep into scientific writing through evaluative words. Coming at this point from a slightly different angle, consider this extract from a text that describes male reproductive physiology, "The mechanisms which guide the *remarkable* cellular transformation from spermatid to mature sperm remain

uncertain. . . . Perhaps the most *amazing* characteristic of spermatogenesis is its *sheer magnitude:* the normal human male may manufacture several hundred million sperm per day."[28, pp. 483–484; emphasis added] As we will see, this text has no parallel appreciation of the female processes such as menstruation or ovulation, and it is surely no accident that this "remarkable" process involves precisely what menstruation does not in the medical view: production of something deemed valuable. Although this text sees such massive sperm production as unabashedly positive, in fact, only about one out of every 100 billion sperm ever makes it to fertilize an egg: from the very same point of view that sees menstruation as a waste product, surely here is something really worth crying about!

When this text turns to female reproduction, it describes menstruation in the same terms of failed production we saw earlier:[28, p. 577; emphasis added]

> The fall in blood progesterone and estrogen, which results from *regression* of the corpus luteum, *deprives* the highly developed endometrial lining of its hormonal support; the immediate result is *profound constriction* of the uterine blood vessels due to production of vasoconstrictor prostaglandins, which leads to *diminished* supply of oxygen and nutrients. *Disintegration* starts, and the entire lining (except for a thin, deep layer which will regenerate the endometrium in the next cycle) begins to slough. . . . The endometrial arterioles dilate, resulting in *hemorrhage* through the weakened capillary walls; the menstrual flow consists of this blood mixed with endometrial debris. . . . The menstrual flow ceases as the endometrium *repairs* itself and then grows under the influence of rising blood estrogen concentration.

And ovulation fares no better. In fact part of the reason ovulation does not merit the enthusiasm that spermatogenesis does may be that all the ovarian follicles containing ova are already present at birth. Far from being *produced* as sperm is, they seem to merely sit on the shelf, as it were, slowly degenerating and aging like overstocked inventory:[28, pp. 567–568]

> At birth, normal human ovaries contain an estimated one million follicles, and no new ones appear after birth. Thus, in marked contrast to the male, the newborn female already has all the germ cells she will ever have. Only a few, perhaps 400, are destined to reach full maturity during her active productive life. All the others degenerate at some point in their development so that few, if any, remain by the time she reaches menopause at approximately 50 years of age. One result of this is that the ova which are released (ovulated) near menopause are 30 to 35 years older than those ovulated just after puberty; it has been suggested that certain congenital defects, much commoner among children of

older women, are the result of aging changes in the ovum.

How different it would sound if texts like this one stressed the vast excess of follicles produced in a female fetus, compared to the number she will actually need. In addition, males are also born with a complement of germ cells (spermatogonia) that divide from time to time, and most of which will eventually differentiate into sperm. This text could easily discuss the fact that these male germ cells and their progeny are also subject to aging, much as female germ cells are. Although we would still be operating within the terms of the production metaphor, at least it would be applied in an evenhanded way to both males and females.

One response to my argument would be that menstruation just *is* in some objective sense a process of breakdown and deterioration. The particular words are chosen to describe it because they best fit the reality of what is happening. My counterargument is to look at other processes in the body, that are fundamentally analogous to menstruation in that they involve the shedding of a lining to see whether they also are described as breakdown and deterioration. The lining of the stomach, for example, is shed and replaced regularly, and seminal fluid picks up shedded cellular material as it goes through the various male ducts.

The lining of the stomach must protect itself against being digested by the hydrochloric acid produced in digestion. In the several texts quoted above, emphasis is on the *secretion* of mucus,[37, p. 419] the *barrier* that mucus cells present to stomach acid,[29, p. 776] and—in a phrase that gives the story away—the periodic *renewal* of the lining of the stomach.[37, p. 423] There is no reference to degenerating, weakening, deterioration, or repair, or even the more neutral shedding, sloughing, or replacement. As described in an introductory physiology text:[38, pp. 498–499]

> The primary function of the gastric secretions is to begin the digestion of proteins. Unfortunately, though, the wall of the stomach is itself constructed mainly of smooth muscle which itself is mainly protein. Therefore, the surface of the stomach must be exceptionally well protected at all times against its own digestion. This function is performed mainly by mucus that is secreted in great abundance in all parts of the stomach. The entire surface of the stomach is covered by a layer of very small *mucous cells*, which themselves are composed almost entirely of mucus; this mucus prevents gastric secretions from ever touching the deeper layers of the stomach wall.

The emphasis here is on production of mucus and protection of the stomach wall. It is not even mentioned,

although it is analogous to menstruation, that the mucus cell layers must be continually sloughed off (and digested). Although all the general physiology texts I consulted describe menstruation as a process of disintegration needing repair, only specialized texts for medical students describe the stomach lining even in the more neutral terms of "sloughing" and "renewal."[39] One can choose to look at what happens to the lining of stomachs and uteruses negatively as breakdown and decay needing repair, or positively as continual production and replenishment. Of these two sides of the same coin, stomachs, which women *and* men have, fall on the positive side; uteruses, which only women have, fall on the negative.

One other analogous process is not handled negatively in the general physiology texts. Although it is well known to those researchers who work with male ejaculates that a very large proportion of the ejaculate is composed of shedded cellular material, the texts make no mention of a shedding process let alone processes of deterioration and repair in the male reproductive tract.[28, pp. 557–558]

What applies to menstruation once a month applies to menopause once in every lifetime. As we have seen, part of the current imagery attached to menopause is that of a breakdown of central control. Inextricably connected to this imagery is another aspect of the metaphor of failed production. Recall the metaphors of balanced intake and outgo that were applied to menopause up to the mid-19th century, later to be replaced by metaphors of degeneration. In the early 1960s, new research on the role of estrogens in heart disease led to arguments that failure of female reproductive organs to produce much estrogen after menopause was debilitating to health.

This change is marked unmistakably in the successive editions of a major gynecology text. In the 1940s and 1950s, menopause was described as usually not entailing "any very profound alteration in the woman's life current."[40] By the 1965 edition, dramatic changes had occurred: "In the past few years there has been a radical change in viewpoint and some would regard the menopause as a possible pathological state rather than a physiological one and discuss therapeutic prevention rather than the amelioration of symptoms."[41]

In many current accounts, menopause is described as a state in which ovaries fail to produce estrogen. The 1981 World Health Organization report defines menopause as an estrogen deficiency disease.[42] Failure to produce estrogen is the leitmotif of another current text:[19, p. 979]

> This period during which the cycles cease and the female sex hormones diminish rapidly to almost none at all is called the *menopause*. The cause of the menopause

is the "burning out" of the ovaries. . . . Estrogens are produced in subcritical quantities for a short time after the menopause, but over a few years, as the final remaining primordial follicles become atretic, the production of estrogens by the ovaries falls almost to zero.

Loss of ability to produce estrogen is seen as central to a woman's life: "At the time of the menopause a woman must readjust her life from one that has been physiologically stimulated by estrogen and progesterone production to one devoid of those hormones."[19, p. 979]

Of course, I am not implying that the ovaries do not indeed produce much less estrogen than before. I am pointing to the choice of these textbook authors to emphasize above all else the negative aspects of ovaries failing to produce female hormones. By contrast, one current text shows us a positive view of the decline in estrogen production:[43, p. 799]

It would seem that although menopausal women do have an estrogen milieu which is lower than necessary for *reproductive* function, it is not negligible or absent but is perhaps satisfactory for *maintenance* of *support tissues*. The menopause could then be regarded as a physiologic phenomenon which is protective in nature—protective from undesirable reproduction and the associated growth stimuli.

I have presented the underlying metaphors contained in medical descriptions of menopause and menstruation to show that these ways of describing events are but one way of fitting an interpretation to the facts. Yet seeing that female organs are imagined to function within a hierarchical order whose members signal each other to produce various substances, all for the purpose of transporting eggs to a place where they can be fertilized and then grown, may not provide us with enough of a jolt to begin to see the contingent nature of these descriptions. Even seeing that the metaphors we choose fit very well with traditional roles assigned to women may still not be enough to make us question whether there might be another way. Here I suggest some other ways that menstruation and menopause could be described.

First, consider the teleological nature of the system, its assumed goal of implanting a fertilized egg. What if a woman has done everything in her power to avoid having an egg implant in her uterus, such as birth control or abstinence from heterosexual sex? Is it still appropriate to speak of the single purpose of her menstrual cycle as dedicated to implantation? From the woman's vantage point, it might capture the sense of events better to say the purpose of the cycle is the production of menstrual flow. Think for a moment how that might change the description in medical

texts: "A drop in the formerly high levels of progesterone and estrogen creates the perfect environment for reducing the excess layers of endometrial tissue. Constriction of capillary blood vessels causes a lower level of oxygen and nutrients and paves the way for a vigorous production of menstrual fluids. As a part of the renewal of the remaining endometrium, the capillaries begin to reopen, contributing some blood and serous fluid to the volume of endometrial material already beginning to flow." I can see no reason why the menstrual blood itself could not be seen as the desired "product" of the female cycle, except when the woman intends to become pregnant.

Would it be similarly possible to change the nature of the relationships assumed among the members of the organization—the hypothalamus, pituitary, ovaries, and so on? Why not, instead of an organization with a controller, a team playing a game? When a woman wants to get pregnant, it would be appropriate to describe her pituitary, ovaries, and so on as combining together, communicating with each other, to get the ball, so to speak, into the basket. The image of hierarchical control could give way to specialized function, the way a basketball team needs a center as well as a defense. When she did not want to become pregnant, the purpose of this activity could be considered the production of menstrual flow.

Eliminating the hierarchical organization and the idea of a single purpose to the menstrual cycle also greatly enlarges the ways we could think of menopause. A team which in its youth played vigorous soccer might, in advancing years, decide to enjoy a quieter "new game" where players still interact with each other in satisfying ways but where gentle interaction *itself* is the point of the game, not getting the ball into the basket or the flow into the vagina.

REFERENCES

1. Laqueur, T. Female orgasm, generation, and the politics of reproductive biology. *Representations* 14:1–82, 1986.
2. Rosenberg, C. E. The therapeutic revolution: Medicine, meaning, and social change in nineteenth-century America. In *The Therapeutic Revolution: Essays in the Social History of American Medicine*, edited by M. J. Vogel and C. E. Rosenberg, pp. 3–25. University of Pennsylvania Press, Philadelphia, 1979.
3. Tilt, E. J. *The Change of Life in Health and Disease.* John Churchill, London, 1857.
4. Crawford, P. Attitudes to menstruation in seventeenth-century England. *Past and Present* 91: 47–73, 1981.
5. Rothstein, W. G *American Physicians in the Nineteenth Century, From Sects to Science.* Johns Hopkins University Press, Baltimore, 1972.

6. Luker, K. *Abortion and the Politics of Motherhood*. University of California Press, Berkeley, 1984.

7. Fee, E. Science and the woman problem: Historical perspectives. In *Sex Difference: Social and Biological Perspectives*, edited by M. S. Teitelbaum, pp. 175–223. Doubleday, New York, 1976.

8. Geddes, P., and Thompson, J. A. *The Evolution of Sex*. Scribner and Welford, New York, 1890.

9. Barker-Benfield, G. J. *The Horrors of the Half-known Life: Male Attitudes Toward Women and Sexuality in Nineteenth-Century America*. Harper & Row, New York, 1976.

10. Sontag, S. *Illness as Metaphor*. Vintage, New York, 1979.

11. Smith-Rosenberg, C. Puberty to menopause: The cycle of femininity in nineteenth-century America. In *Clio's Consciousness Raised*, edited by M. Hartman and L. W. Banner, pp. 23–37. Harper, New York, 1974.

12. Ellis, H. *Man and Woman*. Walter Scott, London, 1904.

13. Currier, A. F. *The Menopause*. Appleton, New York, 1897.

14. Taylor, J. M. The conservation of energy in those of advancing years. *Popular Science Monthly* 64: 343–414, 541–549, 1904.

15. Berliner, H. Medical modes of production. In *The Problem of Medical Knowledge: Examining the Social Construction of Medicine*, edited by P. Wright and A. Treacher, pp. 162–217. Edinburgh University Press, Edinburgh, 1982.

16. Lewontin, R. C. et al. *Not in Our Genes. Biology, Ideology, and Human Nature,* Pantheon, New York, 1984.

17. Horrobin, D. F *Introduction to Human Physiology*. F. A. Davis, Philadelphia, 1973.

18. Lein, A. *The Cycling Female: Her Menstrual Rhythm*. W. H. Freeman, San Francisco, 1979.

19. Guyton, A. C. *Textbook of Medical Physiology*. W. B. Saunders, Philadelphia, 1986.

20. Benson, R. C. *Current Obstetric and Gynecologic Diagnosis and Treatment*. Lange Medical Publishers, Los Altos, Cal., 1982.

21. Netter, F. H. *A Compilation of Paintings on the Normal and Pathological Anatomy of the Reproductive System*. The CIBA Collection of Medical Illustrations, Vol. 2. CIBA, Summit, NJ, 1965.

22. Norris, R. V. *PMS: Premenstrual Syndrome*. Berkeley Books, New York, 1984.

23. Dalton, K., and Greene, R. The premenstrual syndrome. *Br. Med. J.* May 1953, pp. 1016–1017.

24. Mountcastle, V. B. *Medical Physiology*, Ed. 14, Vol. II. C. V. Mosby Co., St. Louis, 1980.

25. Giddens, A. *The Class Structure of Advanced Societies*. Harper & Row, New York, 1973.

26. McCrea, F. B. The politics of menopause: The "discovery" of a deficiency disease. *Social Problems* 31(1): 111–123, 1983.

27. O'Neill, D. J. *Menopause and Its Effect on the Family*. University Press of America, Washington, D.C., 1982.

28. Vander, A. J. et al. *Human Physiology: The Mechanisms of Body Function,* Ed. 4. McGraw-Hill, New York, 1985.

29. Ganong, W. F. *Review of Medical Physiology,* Ed. 11. Lange Medical Publishers, Los Altos, Cal., 1983.

30. Winner, L. *Autonomous Technology: Technics-out-of-Control as a Theme in Political Thought*. The MIT Press, Cambridge, Mass., 1977.

31. Ewbank, T. *The World a Workshop: Or the Physical Relationship of Man to the Earth*. D. Appleton, New York, 1855.

32. Fisher, M. *Workshops in the Wilderness: The European Response to American Industrialization, 1830–1860*. Oxford University Press, New York, 1967.

33. Mumford, L. *The Myth of the Machine: Technics and Human Development,* Vol. 1. Harcourt, Brace and World, New York, 1967.

34. Mumford, L. *The Myth of the Machine: The Pentagon of Power,* Vol. 2. Harcourt, Brace and World, New York, 1970.

35. Noble, D. *The Forces of Production*. Knopf, New York, 1984.

36. Bullough, V. L. Sex and the medical model. *J. Sex Res.* 11(4): 291–303, 1975.

37. Mason, E. B. *Human Physiology*. Benjamin/Cummings Publishing Co., Menlo Park, Cal., 1983.

38. Guyton, A. C. *Physiology of the Human Body,* Ed. 6. Saunders College Publishing, Philadelphia, 1984.

39. Sernka, T., and Jacobson, E. *Gastrointestinal Physiology: The Essentials*. Williams & Wilkins, Baltimore, 1983.

40. Novak, E. *Textbook of Gynecology,* Ed. 2. Williams & Wilkins, Baltimore, 1944.

41. Novak, E., et al. *Novak's Textbook of Gynecology,* Ed. 7. Williams & Wilkins, Baltimore, 1965.

42. Kaufert, P. A., and Gilbert, P. Women, menopause, and medicalization. *Cult. Med. Psychiatry* 10(1):7–21, 1986.

43. Jones, H. W., and Jones, G. S. *Novak's Textbook of Gynecology,* Ed. 10. Williams & Wilkins, Baltimore, 1981.

38

Turn-Taking in Doctor–Patient Dialogues

Candace West

This selection is an example of a sociolinguistic *analysis. The researcher examines speech events (things people actually say instead of a language's grammatical rules) in order to examine aspects of social reality. The speech events in this case are dialogues between patients and doctors. Among the topics sociolinguistics examines are pronunciation differences between social classes, dialect differences, and social context (Coulmas 1997). In this study, Candace West begins with the postulation that the social relationship between doctor and patient is asymmetrical. These social differences are apparent not only in patterns of speech, but also in modes of dress—for example, the contrast between the doctor's white coat and the patient's open-backed examination gown. Social asymmetry is a key to the establishment of medical authority.*

One sociolinguistic variable is turn-taking, including interruptions and overlapping conversations. The social implications of two people talking at the same time vary in different cultural contexts. To a person from the northeastern United States, for example, overlapping conversations might be considered a sign of enthusiasm and friendliness; to someone from the southern United States, the same sociolinguistic behavior might be regarded as rude and obnoxious. Differences in speech patterns between men and women are

the topic of a best-selling book by Deborah Tannen, You Just Don't Understand *(1990). Although people are often unaware of their speech behavior, this is at the root of many miscommunications.*

This study shows that doctors interrupt patients more often than vice versa, but it also suggests that male patients interrupt female doctors more often. The study raises issues of communication, authority, and trust in the healer (as discussed in selection 14), as well as the attributes of effective communication (the LEARN model discussed in selection 32).

As you read this selection, consider these questions:

- *What do dialogue interruptions signify in terms of either the patient or the doctor listening to the other?*

- *What does the author mean by "master–status"? How is this signified in the term* lady doctor*?*

- *Why do sociolinguists transcribe conversations with those diacritical marks and strange spellings? What information do these convey?*

- *From their own perspective, why do doctors interrupt patients?*

Whatever else transpires in physicians' interactions with patients must somehow be reconciled with the organization of their turns at talk. To date, such activities as history taking, examination, diagnosis and treatment have not yet been consigned to computers. Hence, performance of these tasks relies largely on the face-to-face exchange of speech between doctors and their patients.

In everyday life, we appear to recognize the significance of orderly speech exchange for attainment of conversational goals. Getting across the content of a message often seems contingent on such matters as being able to get a word in edgewise, sustaining a train of thought without interruption, and receiving some indication that one's conversational partners are in fact listening.

But little attention has been paid to the implications of talk's turn-taking organization for participants

in medical encounters. Part of the neglect may stem from an overemphasis on the importance of physicians' contributions to these exchanges. Physicians are, after all, the ones to perform examinations, issue diagnoses, and formulate "orders" for treatment. However, insofar as such tasks are dependent on patients' contributions to talk (e.g., expressing concerns, reporting symptoms, or indicating "where it hurts"), physicians' performance of their clinical work is ultimately contingent on the ordering of their talk with patients.

Elsewhere, the substance of spoken interaction is found to be a fundamental means of ordering social activities and organizing social relationships. For example, there is now an extensive body of research suggesting that males interrupt females far more often than the reverse, across a variety of situations (Argyle et al., 1968; Eakins and Eakins, 1976; McMillan et al., 1977; Natale et al., 1979; Octigan and Niederman, 1979;

Willis and Williams, 1976). Findings of my own earlier work indicate that males' interruptions of females in cross-sex conversations constitute an exercise of power and control over their conversational partners (Zimmerman and West, 1975; West and Zimmerman, 1977; West, 1979; 1982; West and Zimmerman, 1983).

Of course, power is an important facet of many other social relationships, such as those between whites and Blacks, bosses and employees, and—of particular interest here—doctors and patients. Recall Parsons's perspective on the matter, summarized by Wolinsky (1980): "The practitioner must have control over the interaction with the patient, ensuring that the patient will comply with the prescribed regimen" (p. 163). Insofar as the physician-patient relationship is, as some have contended, *essentially* asymmetrical by our cultural standards, it is here that we would expect to find highlighted the dynamics of micropolitical exchange, through, among other things, a greater proportion of interruptions initiated by superordinate parties to talk:

> In front of, and defending the political-economic structure that determines our lives and defines the context of human relationships, there is the micropolitical structure that helps maintain it. This micropolitical structure is the substance of our everyday experience. The humiliation of being a subordinate is often felt most sharply and painfully when one is ignored or interrupted while speaking, towered over or forced to move by another's bodily presence, or cowed unknowingly into dropping the eyes, the head, the shoulders. (Henley, 1977:3)

. . . I report results of my analysis of the organization of turn-taking between patients and family physicians. My preliminary findings offer some empirical support for the archetypal relationship thought to exist between doctors and patients: Physicians interrupt patients far more often than the reverse, *except* when the doctor is a "lady." Then, I find that gender seems to have a greater impact than professional status where women physicians are concerned. Consideration of these results leads me to address such issues as the respective parts played by power, status, and gender in social interaction.

. . .

THE MODEL

Sacks et al. (1974) observe that speech exchange systems in general are arranged to ensure that (1) one party talks at a time and (2) speaker change recurs. These features are seen to normatively organize a variety of forms of talk, including casual conversation, formal debate, and high ceremony. Conversation is distinguished from other forms of exchange by its variable distributions of turn size, turn order and turn content. . . .

Within this framework, a turn at talk consists not merely of the temporal duration of an utterance but of the right and obligation to speak which is allocated to a particular speaker. Turns are built out of what Sacks et al. term "unit-types," consisting of possibly complete words, phrases, clauses or sentences, depending on their context. Further, unit-types are described as "projective" devices, in that they allow enough information prior to their completion to allow the hearer to anticipate an upcoming transition place. In other words, the end of a possibly complete unit-type is the proper place for transition to occur between speaker turns.

My prior research has led me to distinguish between two general categories of simultaneous speech: *overlaps* (briefly, errors in transition timing) and *interruptions* (violations of speaker turns). Overlaps are defined as stretches of simultaneous speech initiated by a "next" speaker just as the current speaker arrives at a possible transition place (Zimmerman and West, 1975: 113–115). Jefferson and Schegloff (1975) note that such instances of simultaneity are common where the current speaker stretches or drawls the final syllable of an utterance, or adds a tag-question to an otherwise complete statement:

(Dyad 19:305–307)

Patient:	I li:ve better and so I- they don' bo:ther me too mu:ch, ⎡ y'know? ⎤
Physician:	⎣ O::kay. ⎦

Here (as indicated by the brackets), the physician starts her "Okay" just at what would ordinarily be the proper completion point for the patient's utterance ("They don't bother me too much"). However, the patient's addition of a tag-question ("Y'know?") results in their collision. I regard such an instance of simultaneous speech as a possible error in transition timing rather than as an indication that the physician is not listening. Indeed, one must listen very carefully in order to anticipate the upcoming completion of a current speaker's utterance and begin speaking precisely on cue, with no silence intervening between turns.

A related form of simultaneity "provoked" by careful listening is what Jefferson (1973) terms a "display of independent knowledge." For example, "saying the same thing at the same time" as someone else indicates not only that one is attending to them, but also that one is listening carefully enough to predict what they are going to say:

(Dyad 1:325–331)

Physician:	An::d Ornade ha:s one called isopropamide iodide, <u>an:d</u> it ha:s uh, phenylpropanolamine an'::Neosynephrine [Ye:ah it's a small amount- it's not that-
Patient:	So it- a small amount's but not that-] =
Patient:	= Right =
Physician:	= It's six of one und half a doz [en a the] other
Patient:	[Uh-huh]

In this excerpt, for example, just as the physician says "It's a small amount, it's not that" the patient independently produces the same thing—thus displaying her careful attention to both the form and content of the physician's emerging utterance.

In contrast, the fragment below illustrates an instance of interruption. An interruption is an initiation of simultaneous speech which intrudes deeply into the internal structure of a current speaker's utterance; operationally, it is found more than a syllable away from a possibly complete unit-type's boundaries (Zimmerman and West, 1975:113–115). Unlike overlaps or displays of independent knowledge, interruptions have no rationale for their occurrence in considerations of active listening (e.g., concerns for minimizing silence between speaker turns or displaying independent understanding). In fact, inasmuch as the rules for turn-taking assign the turnspace to the current speaker until a possible turn-transition point is reached (Sacks et al., 1974:706), an interrupting speaker is engaged in *violation of the current speaker's right* to be engaged in speaking. The following excerpt offers an illustration of the potential effects of such intrusion:

(Dyad 1:945–954)

((Here, the physician and patient have been discussing the effectiveness of sleeping pills when used over an extended time period. The physician argues that the patient will be better off doing without such medication; the patient argues that her anxieties over a forthcoming trip will interfere with her effectiveness on the job for which the trip is to be taken.))

Physician:	. . . prob'ly settle dow:n gradjully, a little bit, once yuh get used to it.=
Patient:	= The- press:: [ure's gonna-
Physician:	[Well if it doe::sn',]
Physician:	Seco<u>bar</u>:bital's not gonna help.
	(.2)
Patient:	We:ll,
	(.2)
Physician:	It's gonna make things worse.

The physician's intrusion ("Well if it doesn', Secobarbital's not gonna help") occurs where the patient is nowhere near completion of her utterance, and the patient drops out almost instantly, leaving her utterance hanging incomplete. As I note in the preface to this fragment, this physician and patient had been arguing about whether or not he ought to issue her a prescription for sleeping pills. One might imagine that his exasperation with the argument might have prompted him to cut off the patient's protests, especially since this patient was requesting refills for sixteen other medications (including Valium and Serax) prior to departing on her trip. However, the *method* used by the doctor to superimpose his opinion over that of the patient is interruption of her turn at talk, that is, violation of her speaking right. Later in this chapter, I will focus on the content of such interruptions between speakers in the physician-patient exchanges in my collection.

INTERRUPTIONS IN MEDICAL DIALOGUES

Instances of simultaneous speech were first located in the 532 pages of transcribed exchanges. Using the criteria specified in the preceding discussion, I separated instances of interruption (i.e., deep intrusions into the internal structure of speakers' utterances) from other types of simultaneity. Then I compared the initiations of interruptions by physician and patient in each dyad in the collection.

Recall Parsons's suggestion that the physician-patient relationship is *essentially* an asymmetrical one. Distributions of physician-initiated and patient-initiated interruptions would lend support to such a claim.

Inspecting Table 1, we see that a total of 188 instances of interruption occurred. Of these, physicians initiated 67 percent (126) and patients initiated 33 percent (62). Thus, doctors interrupted patients far more often than vice versa. Interruptions display further patterned asymmetries according to patients' race and gender. For example, the ratios of physicians' interruptions to patients' interruptions are: 1.1 (or nearly equal) for white male patients; 1.8 for white female patients; 2.6 for Black male patients; and 4.4 for Black female patients. Moreover, in the two dyads characterized by

TABLE 1   Interruptions in Encounters Between Patients and Male Physicians

	Percentage of Physician Interruptions		Percentage of Patient Interruptions	
Black female patient, 16 years	91	(10)	9	(1)
Black female patient, 20 years	100	(1)	—	(0)
Black female patient, 31 years	77	(20)	23	(6)
White female patient, 17 years	100	(1)	—	(0)
White female patient, 32 years	67	(10)	33	(5)
White female patient, 36 years	69	(11)	31	(5)
White female patient, 53 years	73	(29)	27	(11)
White female patient, 58 years	80	(4)	20	(1)
White female patient, 82 years[1]	37	(7)	63	(12)
Black male patient, 17 years	56	(5)	44	(4)
Black male patient, 26 years	100	(7)	—	(0)
Black male patient, 36 years	67	(4)	33	(2)
White male patient, 16 years	100	(1)	—	(0)
White male patient, 16 years	67	(2)	33	(1)
White male patient, 31 years	60	(3)	40	(2)
White male patient, 36 years	58	(7)	42	(5)
White male patient, 56 years[2]	36	(4)	64	(7)
TOTAL	67	(126)	33	(62)

1. This patient is hard of hearing.

2. This patient is mentally retarded.

more patient-initiated than physician-initiated interruption (those to which footnotes 1 and 2 are appended), the patient is hard of hearing on the one hand, and mentally retarded on the other. With the exception of these exchanges, doctors interrupted patients more in every dialogue in this group. However, this group is comprised only of interchanges between patients and *male* physicians.

Table 2 presents the distribution of interruptions between patients and *female* physicians. And in this case we can see that the statistical asymmetries depicted in Table 1 are exactly reversed. Whereas male physicians (in the aggregate) contribute 67 percent of

TABLE 2   Interruptions in Encounters Between Patients and Female Physicians

	Percentage of Physician Interruptions		Percentage of Patient Interruptions	
Black female patient, 52 years	50	(7)	50	(7)
Black female patient, 67 years	40	(6)	60	(9)
Black male patient, 58 years	28	(5)	72	(13)
White male patient, 38 years	8	(1)	92	(11)
TOTAL	32	(19)	68	(40)

all interruptions relative to their patients' 33 percent, female physicians (in the aggregate) initiate only 32 percent of interruptions relative to their patients' 68 percent. Moreover, patients in exchanges with female physicians interrupt as much or more than their physicians in each dyad in this collection.

Although the group of exchanges involving women doctors contains only four dyads, it is at least worth noting that the two interactions that approximate symmetrical relationships between the parties involved (the first two listed in Table 2) are same-sex exchanges between women doctors and women patients. These symmetries are more striking when one considers the differences in race and age between them (the patients in both dyads are Black and the physicians are white; the patients are both considerably older than their physicians). My earlier research on same-sex exchanges between white females conversing in public places also suggested that casual conversation between females tends to display symmetrical distributions of interruptions.

Obviously, the variety of race, age, and gender combinations in a sample of this size precludes extensive extrapolation regarding the composite effects of these factors. There is, for example, only one white male patient engaged in an exchange with a white female physician; similarly, there is only one sixty-seven-year-old patient involved in talk with a physician of half her years. Still, the consistency of patterns of physician and patient-initiated interruption displayed in Tables 1 and 2 offers some empirical evidence for the asymmetrical relationship posited between physicians and patients—*except* when the doctor is a "lady."

. . . Insofar as interruptions constitute violations of persons' rights to be engaged in speaking, there is ample evidence in the transcripts that patients' rights to speak are systematically and disproportionately violated by their male doctors. However, when physicians are women, the asymmetrical relationship between doctor and patient is exactly reversed: the posited asymmetry is stood on its head when women doctors are involved. In order to discuss the implications of these results, I move now to consider the relationship between asymmetrical patterns of interruption and interactional control.

Conversational Dominance

In previously comparing conversations between men and women and exchanges between parents and children, I suggested that males' use of interruptions might display dominance or control to females (and to any witnesses), just as parents' interruptions communicated aspects of parental control to children and to others present (West and Zimmerman, 1977:527). If patients can be likened to children (as claimed by Parsons and Fox, 1952), then we might regard the violations of their speaking rights by male physicians as displays of the physicians' interactional control. Parsons's contention was that patients' situational dependency on physicians, physicians' professional prestige, and their authority over patients all ensure physicians the necessary leverage for controlling interpersonal encounters. But, if physicians' control is to be exerted in actual dialogues with patients, one would expect some ready vehicle might be available in any medical exchange for demonstrating the physician's power.

While medical sociologists place heavy emphasis on social roles as determinants of behavior, the actual behaviors of persons in social roles remain to be enacted in everyday life. In short, such scripts as may exist for the physician-patient encounter must always be negotiated on the basis of situational exigencies, However, as Zimmerman notes:

> It would surely be odd if a society were designed so that its institutions were partly constructed of role-relationships, but lacked any systematic mechanism for articulating societal roles within the features of various interactional settings. . . . [And] stranger still if this articulation were itself not socially organized. Strangest of all would be a state of affairs in which the instantiation of a role in an actual situation had no bearing on the understanding of roles in general, or the sense of "objectivity" and transcendence of the role. (Zimmerman, 1978:12)

His observations invite us to look more closely at the ways in which the respective roles of patient and doctor might be played out in the organization of actual interactions between the two.

Hence, rather than regarding the physician's authority as superimposed onto encounters with patients in "well-rehearsed," script-like fashion (cf. Wilson, 1970), we must examine the dynamics of actual medical exchanges to see how power and control are constituted between participants in those exchanges. A telling example is offered by the fragment used earlier to demonstrate the potential effects of interruption itself. There, a disagreement between a (white male) physician and (white female) patient was ultimately resolved by the doctor's interruption of the patient's opinion (regarding sleeping pills) with his own contrary opinion ("They won't help"). In that excerpt we saw interruption used to advance the physician's (expert) perspective while simultaneously cutting off the patient's (lay) point of view.

Another example of the relationship between interruptions and interactional dominance was fur-

nished by a friend—in this case, a male physician. Prior to writing up the results of this analysis, I discussed with him the tendency of male physicians to interrupt patients in these encounters. My friend did not find this trend a surprising one, and explained, "That's because so many patients are still answering your last question when you're trying to ask them the *next* one!" His "explanation" was of interest for two reasons. First, it fails as an explanation on the grounds that answers follow questions, not the other way around. Hence, a speaker interrupting an answer with a "next question" is disavowing the obligation to listen to the answer to a prior question. . . . But second, my doctor-friend's explanation was of empirical interest, since I had already begun to notice that a great many physician-initiated interruptions in these data were composed of doctors' questions to their patients.

Consider the following fragment, which shows the staccato pace at which physicians' "next" questions can follow their "last" ones:

(Dyad 20:053–074)

Patient: It us:ually be (1.0) ((she reaches down to touch her calf with her left hand)) i:n he:ah.

You: know, it jus' [be a li:l-
Physician: [Can y' pull up]
yer cuff there for me? (.6) Duh yuh have the <u>pain</u> right <u>no::w</u>?
(.2)

Patient: <u>Um</u>-um. No, it [ha::ppens
Physician: [It's not happ'ning
right now::?]

Patient: ss-°some- Only one: time when ah w
[as heah.]
Physician: [Can y] uh take yer shoe: off for me please?
(.8)
((Patient removes her shoe))

Patient: [But I-]
Physician: [WHU:] :T'RE YUH DO::ING, when yuh <u>no:dice</u> the <u>pai:n</u>
(.4)
((Physician bends over to touch the muscles in the patient's legs))

Patient: We:ll, I thi:nk that- Well, <u>so:me</u>time I jus' be si:ttin' theah. (1.0) An' yih: know: ih ji:st- (1.2) ((she shrugs, holding up both palms)) Then I fee:l a liddul pai:n in theah. (.2) Yih know, ji:st- gra:dually (.4) It gradually
c [ome o:n.]
Physician: [Take thi:s] shoe: off?

We can note here that each of the physician's intrusions into his (Black female) patient's turn at talk is patently reasonable and warranted by the external constraints of medical examination and treatment. To ask where a patient is feeling pain, how often, when, or under what conditions is all justified by, even required for, precise diagnosis of a problem (cf. Cicourel, 1975; 1978). However, when these inquiries cut off what the patient is in the process of saying, particularly when what she is saying is presumably the necessary response to a "prior" needed question, then the physician is not only violating the patient's rights to speak, but he is also systematically cutting off potentially valuable information *on which he must himself rely* to achieve a diagnosis (see also Frankel, 1984).

Just below, a similar pattern is evident:

(Dyad 2:085–099)

((Here, the doctor is inquiring about a recent injury to the patient's back caused by an auto accident.))

Patient:	When I'm sitting u̲pright. Y'know =
Physician:	= More so than it was even before?
Patient:	Yay::es =
Physician:	= Swelling 'r anything like that thet chew've no:ticed?
	(.)
Patient:	Nuh:o, not the ⎡ t I've nodi-
Physician:	⎢ TEN:::DER
	⎣ duh the tou ⎤ ch?
	press:ing any?
Patient:	No::, jus'when it's- si::tting.
Physician:	Okay: =
Patient:	= Er lying on it.
Physician:	Even ly:ing. Stan:ding up? walking aroun:d?
	((singsong))
Patient:	No: ⎡ jis-
Physician:	⎣ Not ⎤ so mu:ch. Jis'- ly:ing on it. Si:tting on it. Jis' then.

In this excerpt, the longest pause to ensue between the Black female patient's response and the white male physician's next query is one tenth of one second (marked by the period in parentheses). And, on two occasions, the physician's "next" utterance cuts off the patient's completion of her answer to his "last" one. The staccato pacing and intrusions into the patient's turnspaces demonstrate that—in essence and in fact— a simple "yes" or "no" is all this doctor will listen to. Such practices also serve to demonstrate who is in control in this exchange.

In the case of both excerpts, it appears that the use of interruptions by male doctors is a *display* of dominance or control to the patient, just as males' and parents' interruptions (in my previous research) were employed to communicate control in cross-sex and parent-child exchanges. But also in these exchanges (as in the cross-sex and parent-child data), I find that the use of interruptions is *in fact* a control device, as the intrusions (especially when repeated) disorganize the local construction of conversational activities. Insofar as the over-arching conversational activity is, in the medical exchange, attending to the patient's health, we can only speculate on the potential benefits being lost when doctors interrupt their patients.

Although Parsons tends to equate physicians' interactional control over patients with the ability to treat them, I contend that this sort of control is more likely to hinder than to help physicians' efforts at healing. While it may be true, as he claimed, that patients consult physicians because they do not know what is wrong with them nor what to do about it (Parsons, 1951:439), it is equally true that physicians must listen to patients in order to know what brings them there for treatment. Thus, the doctor—as well as the patient—has much to lose when one or the other of them is unable to "get a word in edgewise."

The Case of Female Physicians

The above analysis notwithstanding, the fact remains that results for four of the 21 exchanges in this collection do not display the asymmetrical pattern implied by Parsons's description. Exchanges between two women doctors and two women patients evidence distributions of interruptions that approach symmetry. Moreover, exchanges between female physicians and male patients show the male patients (not the female physicians) interrupting most (92 percent of interruptions in one exchange and 72 percent in another). It must be noted that there are only two female physicians interacting with two male patients in the collection of materials I analyze. Thus, attention to these dyads approximates a variant of case study rather than a survey of such participants generally. However, since these proportions parallel—rather than contradict—the actual distributions of females and males in medicine (where women, notes Judith Lorber, are "invisible professionals and ubiquitous patients," 1975), they would seem to warrant at least preliminary consideration here.

Permit me a brief digression to recall a somewhat dated riddle concerning a father and son who go for a ride in the country in the father's new sports car. Speeding too quickly around a corner, the father loses control of the wheel, and the car crashes into an embankment. The father is killed instantly, but the son is rushed to the local emergency room, where he is met by the hospital staff on call for emergency treatment. A surgeon rushes over to the stretcher, pulls back the blanket, and exclaims: "My God! I can't operate—that's my son!" The punchline of the riddle is: How can this be? If the boy's father was killed in the accident, then who is the surgeon?

The answer to the riddle—more obvious now, perhaps, than when it first came into vogue—is that the surgeon is the boy's *mother.* The usefulness of the riddle, as a heuristic device, rests in its illumination of the sorts of auxiliary traits that have come to accompany the status of "surgeon" in our culture. As Everett Hughes observes:

> There tends to grow up about a status, in addition to its specifically determining traits [e.g., formal and technical competence], a complex of auxiliary characteristics which come to be expected of its incumbents. It seems entirely natural to Roman Catholics that all priests should be men, although piety seems more common among women. . . . Most doctors, engineers, lawyers, professors, managers, and supervisors in industrial plants are men, although no law requires that they be so. (1945: 353–354)

In our society, notes Hughes, the auxiliary characteristics that have grown up around the status "physician" include "white," "Protestant," and "male." Therefore, when persons assume the powerful status of physician and are not possessed of whiteness, Protestantism, or maleness, there tends to be what Hughes terms a "status contradiction," or even a "status dilemma"—"for the individual concerned and for other people who have to deal with him" (1945:357).

The case of the "lady doctor" provides an illuminating example, the adjective "lady" (or "woman" or "female") only underscoring the presumed maleness of the status "physician." Hughes argues that particular statuses (e.g., "Black") serve as "master-status determining traits," that is, traits which tend to have more salience than any others with which they may be combined. Thus, for persons (e.g., women) whose master-status conflicts with other very powerful statuses (e.g., physician), there is likely to be a dilemma over whether they are to be treated as members of the social category "women" *or* as practitioners of the profession "physician." Most important, as noted above, dilemmas of status extend not only to the individuals possessed of conflicting status-determining characteristics, but to those who must "deal with" them as well.

In the context of this analysis, we are well-advised to remember Zimmerman's (1978) observation that the appropriate behaviors of persons occupying social roles remain to be acted out in everyday life. Hughes's (1945) description might lead us to an overly deterministic perspective that portrays "choices" between two conflicting status-determining characteristics (e.g., "woman" and "physician"), as if the resolution of status dilemmas were an individual matter. However, the issue is more complicated than can be described by the "choice" or "nonchoice" of individuals who are caught in status dilemmas, since they must interact with others in their social worlds. For example, the Black man who would "pass" as a white one must rely on others' willingness to read various physical characteristics and elements of demeanor as constitutive of his "whiteness." Similarly, the woman who would become a physician must rely on others' willingness to honor her displays of professionalism over those of her gender.

While the evidence is tentative, there is reason to believe that Hughes's (1945) and Zimmerman's (1978) analyses might be pertinent to findings here presented. Recall, for example, that the four female physicians included in these exchanges were among the first cohort of women ever to enter the residency program at the Center. Moreover, at the time they began their training, there was only one woman physician on the staff of the faculty at the Center. (At the time of this writing, there is still only one faculty member who might ease the special adjustments of this "new and peculiar" cohort, through what might be termed role modeling, mentoring, or special advising, Shapiro et al., 1978.) Even the faculty supervising residents displayed a heightened awareness of the "special" status of the first cohort of women. For example, those who assisted me in my data collection took great pains to include "our new women residents" in the final corpus of exchanges. Through such descriptions they helped make gender a salient characteristic for women residents (e.g., not once did I hear a doctor who was male described as a "man resident").

More pertinent still, for purposes of this data analysis, are the words of patients themselves. Consider the fragment below, excerpted from the final moments of one (white) female physician's first meeting with a new (Black female) patient:

(Dyad 11:740–747)

Physician: OKa:y!
                     (.6)
   Patient: °O:kay.
                     (.6)
Physician: We:ll, I've enjo:yed <u>mee</u>:ting you! hh
                     (.2)
   Patient: I ha:ve <u>too</u>::. Enjoy:ed meeting you:,
                cuz I've nev-.hh (.6) Nev:uh <u>ha:d</u>

a fe:male docktuh befoah!-hunh-hungh-hungh-hungh-hungh!

"Enjoyable" or otherwise, meetings with female physicians are apparently rare in this patient's experience.

Another (Black male) patient, asked by his (white) female physician if he was having any problems passing urine, responded "You know, the <u>doctor</u> asked me that" (transcribing conventions simplified here). In this instance, it was difficult to tell who "the doctor" *was;* "the doctor" was *not,* evidently, the female physician who was treating him.

Finally, consider the excerpt below, in which a (white) female physician attempts to provide her professional opinion on a (Black male) patient's problem:

(Dyad 4:213–231)

((To this point, the patient has complained about his weight, and the doctor and patient have been discussing possible strategies for reducing. One suggestion offered by the physician was to slow down while eating; but the patient has *just countered* that suggestion with a complaint—he does not like cold food.))

Patient:　. . . An' they take twe:nny 'r thirdy minutes

.

.　((five lines deleted))

.

Tuh eat.

Physician:　Wull what chew ⌈ could DO:

Patient:　　　　　　　　　⌊ An' then by the

time they get through: their foo:d is col::d an' uh- 'ey li:kes it y'know

Physician:　⌈ engh-hengh-hengh-hengh-hengh ⌉ .hh

Patient:　⌊ An' th' they enjoy that ⌋ but I- I 'on't <u>like</u> cole foo:d.

(.2)

Physician:　One thing yuh could <u>d</u> ⌈ o::

Patient:　　　　　　　　　　　　⌊ Spesh'ly

food thet's not suhpoze: be <u>col'</u> =

Physician:　= O: kay.h = is tuh ea:t, say, the <u>meat</u> firs'. Yuh know:, but if yuh have a <u>sal</u>:ad tuh eat, t'sa:ve that till <u>after</u> yuh eat the meat. (.) Cuz the sal:ad's suhpose tuh be co:ld.

Note that the physician's attempts to advance her solution are interrupted repeatedly by the patient's ongoing elaboration of his (already evident) problem.

In this same exchange, the patient earlier questioned his physician about a medication he is taking for high blood pressure. He said that he had heard a radio report indicating that this medicine "might" cause cancer. It was a controversial report since a great many people take that particular drug to help control their blood pressure elevations. The patient's concern is certainly one with which many of us can identify and it is especially poignant in these times (in which everything from saccharin to fluorescent lighting has been linked to some potentially serious health hazard). In the case of the patient's medication, the radio report was followed by a subsequent announcement advising people to continue taking their medicine since the research had confirmed no cause-and-effect relationship between the medication and cancer. The patient said that he never heard anything further (following the subsequent announcement).

Following this initial expression of concern, the doctor checked the patient's blood pressure and explained to him that she has looked into this problem. There is, she said, no alternative medication available, and there is, in her opinion, no better present alternative than to continue with his medication. At this juncture, the patient shifts to a slightly different complaint:

(Dyad 4:430–454)

Patient:　. . . If there wuz any way <u>poss</u>ible duh git me some diffrun' type a pill thet li:ke yuh take twi:ce a da::y instead of three:, .hh an' have th' same effeck with this (allernate) 'n u:h <u>wah</u>dur pi:ll,

Physician:　OhKa:y, that's egzackly what we: were try:ing tuh do:: .hh =

Patient:　= Ah kno:w, but tho:se- I- (.) heard ⌈ what ⌉ th'man sai:d.

Physician:　　　　　　　⌊ We .ll., ⌋

(.)

Physician:　Ay:::e- checked <u>in</u>:ta tha:t, oka::y? an:::d (1.0) No:t No:t- ex<u>ten</u>sively, I didn' search all the lidda'chure =

Patient:　= ((clears his throat))

(.4)

Physician:　.h Bu::t uh:m (.6) ((sniff)) Ah feel <u>comf</u>'trable us:in' thuh dru:::g? An' would take it muhself::: °If I needed tuh. ((Looking directly at the patient))

(6.0)

Physician:　So it ⌈ 's u:p- .hh It's u:p ⌉ :: =

　　　　　　│ tuh you::

Patient:　　│ But if all they sa:y-   │ = Ah

　　　　　　⌊ if there's <u>any</u>- ⌋

know::w, it's u:h-uh ⌈ bud it's u:h ⌉ Ah'm try:in'

Physician:　　　　　　　⌊ It's up tuh you: ⌋

Patient: to: uh- .h ((clears throat)) i:s there:
            <u>any</u> <u>oth</u>er <u>ty::pe</u> that chew could u:h
            fi:gger . . .

To spare us, I have omitted the next several lines, in which the physician again asserts that there is nothing else the patient can take and in which the patient again asserts his desire to get around taking this medication. Below, however, is the resolution of their argument:

(Dyad 4:471–479)

Physician: <u>If</u> <u>I</u> brought cha some <u>arduhcul</u>(s)
            saying thet this wuz Ok<u>ay:::</u>, would
            juh bih<u>lie:::ve</u> me? .h
Patient: Ye:ah, su:re, defin ⌈at'ly.   ⌉
Physician: ⌊Oka:y.   ⌋
                            (.)
Physician: O ⌈Kay:, ⌉ o::kay=
Patient: ⌊But u:h-⌋ =((clears throat)) .h
            Whether I would cha:nge to it'r no:t,
            it would be a diff- y'know, a nuther
            thi::ng,

The patient might "believe" this woman physician if she brought him some articles supporting her opinions, but whether or not he would follow her advice "would be a nuther thi::ng."

My concern here is not the possible carcinogenic effects of the drug (though important)—nor the alternatives to it. Rather, I am interested in the way in which this woman physician is "heard" by her (male) patient. . . . As noted earlier, Parsons claimed that the therapeutic practice of medicine is predicated on institutionalized asymmetry between physician and patient. In his view, physicians are in a position of situational authority vis-à-vis their patients, since only physicians are possessed of the technical qualifications (and institutional certification) to provide medical care.

Yet, in these excerpts we see that neither technical qualifications (conferred by the training and medical degree) nor personal assurances ("I would take this myself," "I checked into it") are sufficient for the woman physician to have her authority (*as a physician*) respected by the patient. Elsewhere, Hughes (1958) suggests that clients of professionals do not simply grant them authority and autonomy as faits accompli. Given a recent history of increasing challenges to medical authority in the United States (cf. Reeder, 1972), it is entirely possible that patients in general are taking increased initiative in their own health care and questioning physicians' opinions more frequently. But nowhere in these data did I find a patient who questioned the opinion of a male physician as forcefully or as repeatedly as the case noted here.

SUMMARY AND CONCLUSIONS

Employing the model of turn-taking in conversation of Sacks et al. (1974), I established a theoretical basis for distinguishing interruptions from other types of simultaneous speech events in an attempt to examine the empirical bases for such claims as Parsons's (1951; 1975) regarding the essential asymmetry of the physician-patient relationship.

Exchanges between patients and male physicians in this collection lend support to the asymmetrical archetype: Male doctors interrupt their patients far more often than the reverse, and they appear to use interruptions as devices for exercising control in their interactions with patients. However, there is no evidence to suggest that this pattern of physician-initiated interruption is conducive to patients' good health. If anything, it appears that this sort of control is likely to hinder physicians' efforts at healing. Moreover, where female physicians are involved the asymmetrical relationship is exactly reversed: Patients interrupt their female doctors as much or more in each exchange in this collection. Thus, my results for women physicians conflict with Parsons's description of the general pattern.

At present, any discussion of the implications of this gender-associated difference must be speculative. The corpus of materials does not constitute a random sample, and simple projections from these results to physicians and patients in general cannot be justified by the usual logic of statistical inference. But, in engaging in such discussion, I would hope to eliminate possible misinterpretations of its significance. I am not claiming that female physicians are "better listeners" than their male colleagues (although they may be). These analyses have focused on the distribution of interruptions *between* physicians and patients. Whereas female physicians in this collection were interrupted by patients far more often than vice versa, it makes as much sense to attribute this finding to their patients' gender-associated "disrespect" (particularly in light of Hughes's and Zimmerman's suggestions) as it does to attribute it to the physicians' own communication skills. Neither inference is entirely warranted at this point.

What *is* tenable, for the findings reported here, is the suggestion that gender may have primacy over professional status where women physicians are concerned, that gender may amount to a "master–status" (Hughes, 1945), even where other power relations are involved.

39

Accounting for Amniocentesis

Rayna Rapp

The term accounting *in the title of this selection has two meanings. First, an account is an individual's story, like the three stories about amniocentesis at the beginning of the selection. An account represents an individual's creation of meaning out of life experiences. Medical anthropologists, as ethnographers, regularly collect people's stories—about their lives, their illness experiences, their decisions, and so forth. An account is one part of the discourse, or talk, that an ethnographer can directly observe. The second meaning of* accounting *in the title is a kind of analysis—the breaking down of a phenomenon into its essential components. To do an accounting of the complex procedure of amniocentesis, it is necessary to take on the viewpoints of different actors—in this case, the mothers, genetic counselors, and laboratory workers. The single term* accounting *has multiple layers of meaning that cannot be reconciled because they often involve contradictions or binary opposites (*antinomies, *in the author's terms).*

New reproductive technologies—in vitro fertilization (so-called test-tube babies), sonograms (ultrasound pictures), genetic screening through amniocentesis, and other testing procedures—have been both wondrous and troubling biomedical developments with regard to women's health. On the one hand, these technologies might prevent untold suffering due to infertility or prevent the birth of children with terrible medical problems. Also, biomedical technology gives people more control over their reproductive lives. On the other hand, they can be seen as symbols of biomedical dominance (hegemony) over women's lives and as technological intrusions into normal physiological processes. Some people wonder if this is a good thing—for example, consider the use of amniocentesis for preferential abortions of females in some cultures (Miller 1987).

Genetic screening through amniocentesis is closely bound up with the ongoing U.S. cultural debate over abortion, a debate that is poised at the intersection of politics, religion, women's rights, biomedicine, and social class. Faye Ginsburg's book Contested Lives *is an ethnographic case study of the debate in a single U.S. community (1989). In that book, Ginsburg centers her research on women's stories from both sides of the abortion debate; as an ethnographer, she uses women's accounts grounded in the context of their own lives to provide honest and insightful analyses of the plurality of U.S. culture. In this selection, Rayna Rapp uses the same ethnographic attention to women's stories analyzed from multiple viewpoints to demonstrate the cultural complexities of gender and women's health.*

As you read this selection, consider these questions:

- *Why did Rayna Rapp include working in a laboratory setting as part of her field research on amniocentesis? What does the author mean by a "gendered workplace"?*

- *What does Rapp mean by the idea of the anthropologist "situating herself within the context of the research"? Why is this relevant?*

- *Why is the amniocentesis test stressful for mothers? Why would some women not need the test and others refuse the test?*

- *How is ethnicity a factor in amniocentesis and reproductive decision making?*

- *What does Rayna Rapp mean by her sixth point, that "disabilities, like pregnancies, are socially constructed"?*

MULTIPLE BEGINNINGS

Here are three amniocentesis stories, drawn from my New York–based fieldwork, any one of which raises the problem of how to understand the development and routinization of prenatal diagnosis:

On Tuesdays, Alfredo returns to the lab around three o'clock in the afternoon. On this particular Tues-

day, there are four fluids in the specimen case he carries, two from Woodhull Hospital in Bushwick, Brooklyn, and two from St. Luke's on Manhattan's Upper West Side. Susan, the head of the lab, assigns one fluid each to Shedeh, Tom, Doris, and Moira. Shedeh will team up with Doris, who is still in training, to make sure all steps of the lab protocol are followed as the samples are logged and numbered, spun down, siphoned, divided, fed, and incubated. The fluids (or soup, as the lab techs call it) will be fed at six days and again at eleven. At fourteen days, there should be enough fetal cells in metaphase ready to read. By that time, the techs will have completed staining, scoping, photographing, and karyotyping cells from the earlier cases on which each was working. Turnaround time at the lab is twenty-one days, and it would be shorter if there were more technicians. The techs cooperate on cutting and scoping under time pressure, completing one another's karyotypes, rushing results, and feeding one another's soup. Seated on swivel chairs at the microscope, or around the cutting table, they talk about baby showers and lunch menus, rock concerts and New York rents as they work. Moira declares that "her" fetus is a wimp: "It's got a wimpy Y and the bikini on the X is pretty gross." Wimpy or not, this fetus is 46XY, which will be reported as a normal diagnosis. I am at the cutting table, struggling to tell number 13 chromosomes from number 14s, listening attentively to lab banter, and wondering what is happening to the woman from whose pregnant belly these "wimpy" fetal cells have been drawn.

Upstairs, Elena is answering telephones, directing patients calling for results to various genetic counselors; Henrietta is the most reassuring, the least likely to tell a twenty-one-week pregnant woman to call back in another week. She'll walk downstairs, trace a sample from the day it was logged to the scope on which it is being read, and try hard to get information she can share on the phone: "The chromosome studies aren't completed yet, but the biochemical results are just fine, and we should have the chromosomes by Friday. Call back, its okay to call back." But in this case, Mrs. Ramirez speaks only Spanish, and Henrietta doesn't. Iris Mendez, the Sarah Lawrence student on an internship, may do the phone work, or Elena will take matters into her own hands—pestering, then translating for one of the counselors who says she is too busy to take on the case.

Mrs. Ramirez is a Honduran immigrant domestic worker who settled in East Harlem three years ago. Before coming to New York, she had three children, the last in a hospital. Before she registered at St. Luke's prenatal clinic in her fifteenth week of this pregnancy, she had never heard of "the needle test." Now she is having amniocentesis. Why and how has this "choice" to use a new and very expensive reproductive technology been made? What must I learn about migration, medicine, and motherhood to understand how amniocentesis becomes routinized for both the lab techs and women like Mrs. Ramirez?

In February, Tom found something ambiguous on the number 9 chromosomes of the sample he was

scoping. Susan told him to check forty cells from all three flasks, rather than twenty from two. But the ambiguity persisted; it wasn't an in vitro artifact, or a random find. He, Susan, and the techs discussed it, and then called Dr. Judith Schwartz, the geneticist in charge of the lab. Judith agreed: there was additional chromosomal material on the top, short arm of the number 9 chromosomes. She called it "9P+": 9 for the pair of chromosomes on which it was located, P to designate the short arm, and plus to indicate additional chromosomal material. First she scanned the literature for an interpretation. Then she phoned the head obstetrician at Woodhull's prenatal clinic in charge of the case and made an appointment for the woman to be called in.

A week's research revealed nothing on "9P+," but twelve clinical reports on "trisomy 9," the closest diagnosis to which Judith could assimilate her case. The move to stabilize a label and an interpretation was not frivolous: the added material (the "plus" on the p arm) had banding patterns that suggested it was a partial replication of the #9, a trisomymanqué. After careful reading, many phone consultations with colleagues, and a meeting with Malve, the genetic counselor who had done the intake interview with the patient at Woodhull, Judith sent Malve off to explain the problem. The patient listened, and decided to keep the pregnancy. Malve was upset by her decision, and thought she hadn't understood what Judith's research revealed: in all twelve cases she could find of trisomy 9, the babies were born with visible and structurally significant physical anomalies and some degree of mental retardation. She asked Judith to counsel the patient directly. Judith did. The patient kept the pregnancy.

The baby was born in early June, and in late July, Judith Schwartz contacted the new mother through her obstetrician, asking if she would be willing to bring her child to the genetics laboratory for a consultation. The mother agreed. On a Wednesday afternoon, the "trisomy 9" came visiting: he was a six-week-old Haitian boy named Étienne St.-Croix. His mother, Veronique, spoke reasonable English and good French. His grandmother, Marie-Lucie, who carried the child, spoke Creole and some French. The two geneticists spoke English, Polish, Hebrew, and Korean between them. I translated in French, ostensibly for the grandmother and mother. Here is what happened:

Judith was gracious with Veronique but after a moment's chit-chat asked to examine the baby. She never spoke directly to the mother again during the examination. Instead, she and Maxine, the other geneticist, both trained in pediatrics, handled the newborn with confidence and interest. Malve took notes as

Judith measured and consulted with Maxine. "Note the oblique palpebral fissure and micrognathia," Judith called out. "Yes," answered Veronique in perfect time to the conversation, "he has the nose of my Uncle Hervé and the ears of Aunt Mathilde." As the geneticists pathologized the mother "genealogized," the genetic counselor remained silent, furiously taking notes, and the anthropologist tried to keep score. When the examination was over, the geneticists apologized to the baby for any discomfort they had caused him, and Judith, herself a practicing Jew, asked the mother one direct question. "I notice you haven't circumcised your baby. Are you planning to?" "Yes," Veronique replied, "we'll do it in about another week." "May we have the foreskin?" Judith queried. "With the foreskin, we can keep growing trisomy 9 cells for research, and study the tissue as your baby develops." Veronique gave her a firm and determined "yes," and the consultation was over.

Walking Veronique and Marie-Lucie to the subway to direct them home to Brooklyn, I asked what Veronique had thought about the experience: from the amniocentesis to the diagnosis to the genetic consultation.

At first, I was very frightened. I am thirty seven, I wanted a baby, it is my husband's second marriage, my mother-in-law is for me, not the first wife, my mother-in-law wanted me to have a baby, too. If it had been Down's, maybe, just maybe I would have had an abortion. Once I had an abortion, but now I am a Seventh Day Adventist, and I don't believe in abortion anymore. Maybe for Down's, just maybe. But when they told me this, who knows? I was so scared, but the more they talked, the less they said. They do not know what this is. And I do not know, either. So now, it's my baby. We'll just have to wait and see what happens. And so will they.

How do geneticists, genetic counselors, pregnant Haitians and anthropologists come to their interpretations of inherently ambiguous situations? How are the intersecting discourses of "genetics," "marriage and family life," and "medical anthropology" constructed, and how do they express contradictory processes?

. . .

Pat was thirty-seven when she accidentally got pregnant, and decided to keep the baby. "It was my best shot at ever having a second child. My first one was already eighteen, she didn't want this, but ever since I divorced her father, I knew I wanted another marriage, another baby. I couldn't get the marriage, but I got the kid." Pat's obstetrician recommended amniocentesis because she was over thirty-five and without much reflection she undertook the test. When the results came back positive, no one was more

shocked than she. Her OB wanted to perform an abortion right away, but she stalled for time. The more she thought, the more ambivalent she became.

I did some research, I visited this group home for adult retardeds in my neighborhood. You know, it was kind of nice. They looked pretty happy, they had jobs, they went bowling. I thought about it. Maybe if I was married, maybe if I had another shot at it. But this was it: take it or leave it. So I took it. I called the Mormons back. Oh, I hadn't been to temple for years. But I knew, in my heart of hearts, they'd convince me not to have an abortion. And they did. One man, he just came and prayed with me, he still comes. Stevie gets a lot of colds, I can't always make it to temple. But when we don't make it, he comes over and prays with us. And the Down's support group, that's helpful too. They told me about schools, and special programs. Stevie's doing really well, he'll learn to read this year, I know he will. And if he doesn't, that's okay, too. This kid has been a blessing, he makes me ask myself, "why are we put here on earth?" There must be a reason, and Stevie's reason was to teach love, to stop haters dead in their tracks. Everyone who meets him loves him. They may start out talking behind his back, but pretty soon, they're rooting for him, 'cause he's such a neat kid. He's taught me a lot about love, and acceptance. So when I see a girl who's pregnant, I always tell her about Stevie, I always say, "don't have that test, you don't need that test to love your baby the way it is." Oh, for some of them, maybe abortion is a good thing, I don't know. But for me, Stevie was just what I needed.

How can I account for Pat's "choice" in a way that preserves her agency while noting the power of religion, class, gender ideology, and personal reproductive history in it? How can I describe the shifting powers of sexual mores and medicalization in American culture as they both construct and constrain the range of what she might "choose"?

THE PROBLEM OF THE EXCLUDED MIDDLE

If anthropology can be said to have one foot in the sciences and one in the humanities, medical anthropology is thus doubly marked. . . . [It] must find a workable bridge linking biology and culture, matter and symbol, body and mind, action and thought. Medical anthropologists are challenged . . . to resolve the central issues in anthropological theory . . . and to contribute to contemporary discussions concerning the status of science as a component of culture.

—LINDENBAUM AND LOCK (1993)

Like all fields of critical inquiry, medical anthropology must simultaneously construct and deconstruct itself. The field seems balanced on a fulcrum, seesawing between biology and history, medicine and meaning systems, epidemiology and emic explanations. This construction tempts us to investigate an amalgam of the body biological and the body politic. When we begin with this orientation, the terrain on which our investigation rests appears stable: we can describe or measure how biology and culture intersect, assuming that each "factor" is distinct, if interactive.

Yet we also know that such bounded representations of biological and social bodies are deeply linked to nature/culture oppositions in the history of Western thought. Deconstructing such antimonies is a prerequisite for providing more powerful accounts of how illness and health operate in the lives of our informants, as well as in the disciplines of medicine and medical anthropology. Antimonies of nature and culture exclude precisely that "middle ground" on which the contest for the meaning and management of illness and health is constructed. It is not a coincidence that such antimonies also position "science" or "medicine" on the high ground of the theoretical seesaw, thus silencing competing interpretations or reducing them to ethnosciences. Binary formulations leave medical anthropologists remarkably free to construct an external role for themselves: we view ourselves as participant-*observers* with license to describe the relation between the parts, rather than observing *participants* in the social phenomena our narratives help to construct.

This triple exclusion—of the middle ground on which contests for meaning occur, of all other interpretations as less-than-scientific, and of medical anthropologists as "outside" their objects of study—became especially clear to me as I began to study the routinization of amniocentesis beginning in 1983. Combing the literature on "patient reactions to prenatal diagnosis," I found four overlapping medical discourses: geneticists spoke of the benefits and burdens their evolving technical knowledge conferred on patients (a discourse that has rapidly intensified as the Human Genome Initiative gets under way); health economists deployed their famous cost/benefit analysis to suggest which diseases and patient populations should be most effectively screened; social workers and sociologists interrogated the psychological stability and decision-making strategies of "couples" faced with "reproductive choices"; and bioethicists commented on the legal, ethical, and social implications of practices in the field of human genetics. Later, a fifth discourse, penned by feminists who are on the whole opposed to the new reproductive technologies as a "male takeover" of motherhood, was added to the literature (Arditti, Duelli-Klein, and Minden 1984;

Baruch, d'Amato, and Seager 1988; Corea 1985; Rothman 1986; Spallone & Steinberg 1987; Stanworth 1987). Absent from the published texts were descriptions of the multilayered and contradictory processes by which a new reproductive technology was being produced, a new work force and patient populations created, or a language articulated to describe the impact of these processes on representations of pregnancy, maternity, children, and family life.

Yet if we return to the stories that open this chapter, we can identify many multilayered forces at work. They include (at least) the following seven processes, in narrative order:

First, it is important to analyze "laboratory life." The laboratory labors through which prenatal diagnoses are constructed are carried out by a class-stratified, multiethnic new work force, most of whose members are women. From the Puerto Rican driver to the Iranian, Polish Catholic, Southern African-American, and suburban Jewish lab techs, to the Polish-Israeli-American and Korean-American geneticists, this is a work force that resembles the multinational make-up of New York's population. Brain drains, civil wars, labor migrations, upward and downward mobility: these world-scale political economic forces structure the possibilities of who becomes a worker in the scientific labor force. During the two months that I "interned" at the lab, three of the twelve technicians left and were replaced. One Lebanese, one Chinese, and one U.S.-born white Anglo-Saxon were succeeded by an Armenian-Iranian, a Southern African-American, and a New York–born Puerto Rican.

This rapid turnover in the labor force of medical technology is business-as-usual, according to the two geneticists who run the lab. And genetic counseling, too, is a field where job mobility is fast and continuous. During the three years that I have been observing their rounds, five lab counselors have filled two and a half permanent slots, and three to five student interns pass through the lab each year. Work culture is thus based on medical language, and there is little continuity for long-term connections through which counter-discourses might develop.

The world of prenatal diagnosis is distinctly female. Not only are pregnant women the clients for this new reproductive service, but virtually all the workers in this "industry" are female as well. Most lab technicians are women. Geneticists working in this field are disproportionately women, and more than 98 percent of all genetic counselors are female. This new "allied health professional" has been created in the last fifteen years explicitly to serve as "interface" between the DNA revolution and the public who will reap its consequences. Janus-faced experts in a technical and rapidly changing science, genetic counselors balance between science and social work, speaking both epidemiology and empathy to their clients. Trained in aspects of molecular genetics which many physicians do not understand, they are situated in the medical hierarchy like social workers. The cytogenetics, human genetics, molecular genetics, and counseling labors that construct prenatal diagnoses are often described as appropriately "feminine" because they focus on pregnancy, and the nine-to-five working hours do not disrupt family responsibilities. A new field of employment on the frontier of genetics thus emerges with job descriptions, prestige, and pay scales that reproduce familiar gender hierarchies.

Second, we need to consider the recruitment of highly diverse female patient populations. While nationally amniocentesis is becoming something of a ritual for white, middle-class families in which women have delayed childbearing to further education and careers, in New York City the situation is somewhat different. The Prenatal Diagnosis Laboratory of the Health Department was set up in 1978 explicitly to offer amniocentesis to low-income, hence disproportionately non-white, women. The lab is subsidized by both the state and city of New York. It accepts Medicaid and all third-party insurance, and has a sliding-scale fee that begins at zero. The amniotic fluid samples it analyzes reflect this economic outreach to the urban poor: the lab population is approximately one-third Hispanic, one-third African-American, and one-third white; half are private patients, and half are seen at public clinics, according to the racial/ethnic categories provided by both the city and state health departments.

· · ·

New York City's Health Department has historically been a leader in providing maternal and child health services, at least since the Progressive Era, providing the most liberal, expansive, and often the earliest nutritional, well-baby, and family planning services (Duffy 1968; Rosenberg 1976, 1987; Rosenkrantz et al., 1978; Rosner 1982). But this cutting edge, then and now, is also a double-edged sword. Services and surveillance, routine care and social control are inextricably linked in extending public health measures to the poor. It is not only "their" well-being, but "our" cost-effectiveness which is continually at issue. There is thus no way to separate eugenic and choice-enhancing aspects of prenatal diagnosis when provided by public health planning and moneys.

Third, science itself can be viewed as constructed by social and cultural processes (e.g., Latour 1987;

Traweek 1988; Woolgar 1988). There is an immense lumpiness to science once one steps through the looking-glass into the laboratory. The neutral and distanced discourse of medical journals, the triumphalism of the Tuesday *New York Times* "Science" section, the reassuring "commonsense solutions" of the Phil Donahue show all occasionally claim to evaluate progress in human genetics. But none can contain the ambiguities of the DNA research frontier. There is an anxiety-provoking plethora of "information" disembedded from any cultural context for its interpretation that genetics currently represents. Prenatal diagnosis provides a proliferation of information for consumers without guideposts, for doctors to deploy as stage directions in a play whose acts are as yet unwritten, for technicians in search of metaphors. All participants are constantly negotiating a system of interpretation for both producers and consumers of "scientific knowledge." The laboratory is at once the factory of prenatal diagnoses and an empire of signs. While medical genetic discourse claims universal authority, it continuously confronts the contested nature of much of its findings, and the diversity of interpretations to which even "universal biological facts" lend themselves. The path connecting "scientific information" to "medical policy," "counseling protocols," and "popular culture" is rocky at best.

Fourth, we should note that the relationship between science and religion is unstable in many ways. Not only do different religions hold diverse stances toward reproductive technologies (Office of Technology Assessment 1988) but practitioners within religions may vary widely in their interpretations of official doctrine and personal adherence. Mrs. Ramirez, whose story opened this essay, is a practicing Catholic, but she would consider abortion of a fetus with a serious disability despite church teachings. One of her co-religionists from Ecuador expressed it succinctly:

> Could I abort if the baby was going to have that problem? God would forgive me, surely, yes, I could abort. Latin Catholics, we are raised to fear God, and to believe in His love and mercy. Now, if I were Evangelical, that's another story. It's too much work, being Evangelical. My sisters are both Evangelicals, they go to church all the time. There's no time for abortion for them. (Maria Acosta, 41)

Many Hispanic Catholic women reported multiple early abortions. To them, late abortion was a mortal sin. Finely honed, female-centered theological distinctions and practices are carved out of a monolithic theology. Likewise, "Protestants" display a wide array of beliefs and practices. Some of these differences can be linked to specific churches. Fundamentalists are most likely to preach against the test and Pat Carlson beat a beeline to her Mormon roots when she wanted to be talked out of an abortion following a positive prenatal diagnosis. Mainline groups like Episcopalians, Dutch Reformists, and Methodists are either silent or supportive on the topic of amniocentesis.

. . .

These many stories should alert us to the fact that religions continue to proliferate and make claims on personal, ethnic, and communal identity throughout American cultural life. Far from representing a "culture lag" that science will soon overtake, religious adherence might better be viewed as a continuous aspect of contemporary social life (Harding 1987). Religious identity provides one resource in the complex and often contradictory repertoire of possible identities a pregnant woman brings to her decision to use or reject amniocentesis. There is no definitive "Catholic" or "Jewish" or "Protestant" position on reproductive technology, when viewed from the pregnant woman's point of view. Rather, each pregnancy is assessed in light of the competing claims on maternity the individual acknowledges and to which she responds.

Fifth, both maternalist and medical discourses require careful deconstruction. The debates (between "pharmocrats and feminists," in Gena Corea's felicitous phrase) over whether the new reproductive technologies, including amniocentesis, offer progress or degradation to family life are phrased "as if" motherhood were being revolutionized. The discourse of maternalism—technocratic or resistant romantic, the one aligned with science, the other with nurture—obviously holds ideological weight in the words of a Pat Carlson or a Veronique St.-Croix. But it is not the only or overriding basis on which a decision to use or reject amniocentesis, or pursue its consequences, is made. The dramatic discourses of modern pregnancy as allied with either nature or culture too often echo each other. Each sounds like a unified voice, but the women with whom I have spoken are always polyphonic.

Every pregnancy is embedded in its own specific context: the proximity and judgment of male partners, mothers, sisters, and friends all weigh heavily on an amniocentesis decision. Many women told me they brought their partners to see the sonogram: "Frank just isn't as committed to this pregnancy as he should be," commented white middle-class psychologist Marcia Lang, "but once he sees the baby moving, I know he'll get excited." Juana Martes, a Dominican home care attendant, also thought men should see the sonogram that accompanies the test: "When the little

creature moves, they begin to know what women feel, how they suffer for it to be born, and then they respect their wives." Ecuadorian-born Coralina Bollo felt pressured into having the test by her U.S.-born husband; Flora Blanca had to keep her decision to have it secret from her disapproving *companero*. Laura Escobar's Egyptian-born Muslim husband Ibrim reluctantly agreed to the test, stressing that he didn't believe in abortion. He *knew* God would protect his unborn child. Laura turned to me, and in Spanish (which her husband does not speak) said, "When God provides a problem, he also provides a cure."

The fact of decision making involved in amniocentesis reveals the existing gender negotiations within which a specific pregnancy is undertaken. There is a complex choreography of domination, manipulation, negotiation, and, sometimes, resistance in the gender tales women tell about their decisions to use or reject this piece of reproductive technology.

Sixth, disabilities, like pregnancies, are socially constructed. Pat Carlson's decision to continue her pregnancy after a prenatal diagnosis of Down's syndrome is quite a rare event: 90 to 95 percent of women receiving this diagnosis go on to terminate their pregnancies. Likewise, a diagnosis like Tay-Sachs disease carries an abortion rate that is almost 100 percent, although prenatal diagnosis of a similarly recessively transmitted disease, sickle cell anemia, probably leads to abortion only 40 percent of the time.[1] Different rates of abortion seem linked to at least two factors: the knowledge pregnant women and their supporters have about the condition's consequences (which vary, of course, by disease), and the local values (suggested by religious, familial, and ethnic experiences) they hold about it. One genetic counselor encountered two patients, each of whom chose to abort a fetus after learning that its status included XXY sex chromosomes (Klinefelter's syndrome, which affects growth, fertility, and possibly intelligence and learning abilities). One professional couple told her, "If he can't grow up to have a shot at becoming the President, we don't want him." A low-income family said of the same condition, "A baby will have to face so many problems in this world, it isn't fair to add this one to the burdens he'll have."

From a patient's point of view, most diagnoses are inherently ambiguous (Rothman 1986). An extra chromosome spells out the diagnosis of Down's syndrome, but it does not distinguish mildly from severely retarded children, or indicate whether this particular fetus will need open heart surgery. A missing X chromosome indicates a Turner's syndrome female (who will be short-statured and infertile), but cannot speak to the meaning of fertility in the particular family into which she may be born. Homozygous status for the sickle cell gene cannot predict the severity of anemia a particular child will develop. All such diagnoses are interpreted in light of prior reproductive histories and experiences, community values, and aspirations that particular women and their families hold for the pregnancy being examined.

And some constituencies contest the powerful medical definitions of disabilities that predominate in contemporary American society. The disability rights movement points out that socially constructed attitudes of stigma and prejudice, not absolute biological capacities, lie behind the segregation of disabled children and adults.[2] Many disability rights groups focus on legal and policy solutions to their members' problems, often using a civil rights perspective. The discourse of civil rights influenced a series of federal laws in the mid-1970s and the recent "Americans With Disabilities Act," which explicitly deployed models developed in the battles against racial discrimination to mandate access to education, housing, employment, and public facilities for disabled citizens. The movement contains many divided allies and is continuously debating such questions as the relation of mental to physical disabilities and the ethics of prenatal diagnosis for any or all disability. But virtually all members of and advocates for disabled groups insist on the social, rather than the medical, definition of the problems they must confront.

The discursive and material resources available for families of disabled children vary greatly along the fault lines set up by race, class, religious, and ethnic differences in contemporary America. Disability is socially constructed, reflecting not only the hegemonic claims of medicine and counterclaims of families and activists, but cross-cutting differences within the very category of "disability" as well.

Seventh, medical anthropologists must account for their own presence in the problems they study. Why should an anthropologist learn to cut karyotypes in a basement laboratory on First Avenue, follow genetic counselors through their rounds at Harlem hospital, and take the E train to Queens for home visits? Without indulging in a narcissistic exercise, it seems evident that this investigation into the social impact and cultural meaning of prenatal diagnosis is supported by almost twenty years of feminist mobilization in the discipline of anthropology. "People like me" teach women's studies courses, as well as anthropology courses, where the contradictions generated around the concepts of "reproduction" or "motherhood" glide across disciplinary boundaries. They also surface in our personal lives. Members of the same generation who produced the field of "feminist an-

thropology" often delayed childbearing for the establishment of education and careers, and now we study comparative reproduction. That a cultural anthropologist who has sustained two amniocenteses should query the power of medical discourse and the meaning of cultural differences in this experience seems like an obvious next move.

These seven proliferating processes make it difficult ever to completely frame our "unit" of analysis. Some of the layers described here are clearly local and particular—for example, the funding priorities of New York City's health department or the existence of a permanently and luxuriantly polyglot class of working poor women in the city. Other forces pertain more generally to the political economy of advanced capitalism, where scientific discourse and practices deeply influence contemporary cultural representations of health and illness, pregnancy, disability, and gender. And all layers are, of course, historically contingent.

ENDINGS ARE REALLY BEGINNINGS

In the "middle ground" partially described above, science (in medicine and medical anthropology) cannot provide stable, authoritative discourses against which to measure all other cultural practices. For scientific knowledge, like the other cultural discourses and social practices described above, is also historically contingent. To say that accounts of science (or pregnancy, or ethnic diversity, or anything else) are historically contingent is not to deny their power to intervene in what used to be called "the real world," nor to collapse this discussion into rampant relativism. The temptations of pure relativism can be avoided if the study of power relations, rather than pluralism, lies at the heart of the investigation.

This focus on power is one that was given to me by the people who consented to be interviewed for this study, for they frequently provided insightful comments on the force fields within which their own options and possibilities were inscribed. In the narratives of pregnant women and mothers of disabled children, for example, television looms large. Sonograms provide images of the fetus in utero on a television screen. These images of floating fetuses, beating hearts, and imagined sex organs all have multiple medical, religious, and political interpretations for parents-to-be and the health professionals who orchestrate the viewing (Rapp 1991). Televisions provide multiple viewing points for the cultural problem of prenatal diagnosis. When I asked where women had first learned about amniocentesis, many respondents without formal education answered, "Dallas." In 1986, it took three episodes for the drama of a prenatal diagnosis of Down's syndrome to unfold on the show, with a predictably genderized outcome: "the mother" wanted to keep the pregnancy, "the father" pressured for an abortion, "the resolution" was a miscarriage, rather than a decision. My seven-year-old daughter has accompanied me part of the way on this intellectual journey, learning to identify children and adults with Down's syndrome from her avid addiction to watching "Life Goes On" on Sunday nights. And when I asked Pat Carlson, whose story opens this essay, what would make her son Stevie's life more integrated, I expected an answer about "education" but I got one about television. "Pampers commercials," she replied. "Why Pampers?" I asked. "If they can show all those black and brown kids on TV ads these days, why can't they just show kids like Stevie?" Pat asked. Television is not a neutral presence in the life ways of health care workers, pregnant women, or families with Down's syndrome members. It may well be the most powerful panopticon through which the "information revolution" is constructed, represented, and enforced. The power of television vibrates through any "history of the present" in contemporary American culture.

Power relations are, of course, historically contingent. If, for example, the Chinese invent an earlier fetal sex chromosomal detection technology via maternal-fetal blood centrifuge to mediate the contradiction between their one-child family policy and a patriarchal kinship system, it will surely echo through protocol studies funded in Washington, D.C. down to the basement of the Prenatal Diagnosis Laboratory in New York City. There, visiting Chinese geneticists will undoubtedly enhance international scientific cooperation by teaching it to American colleagues. If the Reagan and Bush appointments to the Supreme Court do, indeed, augur the piecemeal reversal of legal abortion in the United States, prenatal diagnosis might fall victim to our particular, contemporary politicization of the court system. However, a more likely scenario would have to take into account powerful national polls indicating that over 80 percent of Americans support legal abortion when the fetus is defective, a consensus that makes disability rights activists desperate. This hypermedicalization of abortion rights, which posits a "grave fetal defect" as the only basis for a legal abortion, lies at the heart of *Doe v. Bamgaertner*, a legal case generated in Utah explicitly to test *Roe v. Wade*. Geneticists and genetic counselors were brought into the construction of the oppositional brief to describe the arcane range of possible, diagnosable fetal conditions on the one hand, and the subjective meaning of "grave" on the other. The cultural contest over abortion rights thus includes medical experts as liberals; a century ago, physicians served as strategists for campaigns to illegalize the procedure. As this moment in struggles over reproductive rights plays itself out, we can imagine that abortion services could become severely restricted and entirely remedicalized, and prenatal diagnosis would become one obvious and popular route to ending an undesired pregnancy.

Finally, power must remain central to any analysis of the permanent condition of heterogeneity that characterizes the culture of advanced capitalism. The relation of world-structured power domains and local cultures is intimately tied to this question of heterogeneity. If advanced capitalism has enormously homogenizing tendencies that threaten to engulf and flatten cultural particularities, it also sets up uneven conditions for the continuous production of cultural heterogeneity. I want to claim this as a historical as well as contemporary truth. Had I been studying childbirth in New York City at the turn of the century, it would have been Lithuanian holdouts against hospitals, rather than Haitian incomprehension of genetic testing that I would have been querying. There is no way out of this problem. And it has for me a politics that needs underlining. At least two concrete goals flow from this understanding. The first, a familiar theme in medical anthropology, is that health care professionals who often come from the dominant culture can never escape confrontation with multicultural rationalities. They may, however, be able to learn about cultural differences. Genetic counselors, unlike doctors, are new health professionals in a small and still-developing "woman's" field. Helping them to pluralize would be a service to wo*men*, rather than wo*man*, I imagine. Their commitment to medical discourse and dominant representations of pregnancy and motherhood makes this task a difficult one, but many conscientious counselors are committed to exploring how best to serve underserved, often minority, patient populations (Marfatia, Punales, and Rapp 1990; cf. Rapp 1988).

Second, we need a discussion of what popular scientific literacy might mean, especially but not exclusively for diverse American women, given the gender biases, racial prejudices, class structures, and attitudes toward disability which serve as effective barriers to restructuring the power dynamics of scientific discourse as it shapes American cultural life. While one subtext of the present account is to demedicalize prenatal diagnosis and disability, another, paradoxically, is to suggest that many, perhaps the majority, of women whose lives it affects *still lack access* to the discursive tools and social services on which both scientific literacy and a truly "informed consent" might rest. Historically contingent accounts lead us back to the problem of coping with diversity in a complex society that simultaneously and continuously produces, reproduces, and then denies its own heterogeneous nature. Beyond its theoretical recognition, what are we to do with the abundant inequalities and differences a critical, feminist, medical anthropology must represent amongst American women?

NOTES

1. These statistics were compiled from the Laboratory's "positive diagnosis" files covering the last five years. There is no national monitoring of either amniocentesis or abortion following positive prenatal diagnosis, although the Council of Regional Networks of Genetic Services is currently developing a national data base. The best comparative figures, which approximate those of the Lab, are provided by Hook 1981.
2. For a popular, inspiring, and highly controversial digest of disability rights activism, see *The Disability Rag*. Other resources by and for disabled people and their supporters include *The Exceptional Parent* and the *Siblings Network Newsletter*, and newsletters published by many of the groups organized around specific disabilities (e.g., *National Down's Syndrome Society Newsletter; Neurofibromatosis Newsletter*). Social scientific analyses of the impact of disabilities on family life are provided by Gliedman 1980; Featherstone 1981; Goffman 1963. Personal narratives concerning the lives of families with disabled children appear in Featherstone 1981 and Jablow 1982. Stray-Gundersen 1986 combines perspectives by parents and health professionals.

REFERENCES

Arditti, Rita, Renate Duelli-Klein, and Shelley Minden, eds. 1984. *Test-Tube Woman: What Future for Motherhood?* Boston: Routledge & Kegan Paul.

Baruch, Elaine H., Amadeo F. D'Amado, and Joni Seager, eds. 1988. *Embryos, Ethics and Women's Rights.* New York: Harrington Press.

Corea, Gena. 1984. *The Mother Machine.* New York: Harper & Row.

Duffy, John. 1968. *A History of Public Health in New York City.* New York: Russell Sage Foundation.

Featherstone, Helen. 1981. *A Difference in the Family: Living With a Disabled Child.* New York: Penguin.

Goffman, Erving. 1963. *Stigma: Notes Toward the Management of a Spoiled Identity.* Englewood Cliffs, NJ: Prentice-Hall.

Gliedman, John, and William Roth. 1980. *The Unexpected Minority: Handicapped Children in America.* New York: Harcourt, Brace, Jovanovich.

Harding, Susan. 1987. Convicted by the Holy Spirit. *American Ethnologist* 14:167–181.

Hook, Ernest B. 1981. Rates of Chromosomal Abnormalities at Different Maternal Ages. *Obstetrics and Gynecology* 58:282–285.

Jablow, Martha. 1982. *Cara: Growing with a Retarded Child.* Philadelphia: Temple University Press.

Latour, Bruno. 1987. *Science in Action.* Cambridge, Mass.: Harvard University Press.

Lindenbaum, Shirley and Margaret Lock, eds. 1993. Preface. In *Knowledge, Power, and Practice: The Anthropology of Medicine and Everyday Life.* Berkeley, Los Angeles, Oxford: University of California Press.

Marfatia, Lavanya, Diana Punales, and Rayna Rapp. 1990. When an Old Reproductive Technology Becomes a New Reproductive Technology: Amniocentesis and Underserved Populations. *Birth Defects* 26:109–126.

Office of Technology Assessment, Congress of the United States. 1988. *Appendix F: Religious Perspectives in Infertility: Medical and Social Choices.* Washington, D.C.: Government Printing Office.

Rapp, Rayna. 1988. Chromosomes and Communication: The Discourse of Genetic Counseling. *Medical Anthropology Quarterly.* 2:143–157.

———. 1991. Constructing Amniocentesis: Medical and Maternal Voices. In *Uncertain Terms: Negotiating Gender in American Culture*, 28–42 Faye Ginsburg and Anna Tsing, eds. Boston: Beacon.

Rosenberg, Charles. 1976. *No Other Gods: On Science in American Social Thought.* Baltimore: Johns Hopkins University Press.

———. 1987. *The Care of Strangers: The Rise of America's Hospital System.* New York: Basic Books.

Rosenkrantz, Barbara Gutmann, and Elizabeth Lomax. 1978. *Science and Patterns of Child Care.* San Francisco: W. H. Freeman.

Rosner, David. 1982. *A Once Charitable Enterprise: Hospitals and Health Care in Brooklyn and Cambridge.* New York: Cambridge University Press.

Rothman, Barbara Katz. 1986. *The Tentative Pregnancy.* New York: Norton.

Stanworth, Michelle, ed. 1987. *Reproductive Technologies.* Minneapolis: University of Minnesota Press.

Spallone, Patricia, and Deborah Steinberg, eds. 1987. *The Myth of Genetic Engineering and Reproductive Progress.* Elmsford, N.Y.: Pergamon.

Stray-Gundersen, Karen, ed. 1986. *Babies with Down Syndrome.* Kensington, Maryland: Woodbine House.

Traweek, Sharon. 1988. *Beamtimes and Lifetimes.* Cambridge, Mass.: Harvard University Press.

Woolgar, Steven. 1988. *Science: The Very Idea.* London: Tavistock.

40

Culture, Scarcity, and Maternal Thinking: Maternal Detachment and Infant Survival in a Brazilian Shantytown

Nancy Scheper-Hughes

This selection is an early report from the important and disturbing medical anthropological research by Nancy Scheper-Hughes, culminating in her book, Death Without Weeping *(1992). Based on research in an extremely poor shantytown neighborhood in northeastern Brazil where she had been a Peace Corps volunteer eighteen years earlier, this selection emphasizes questions drawn from medical anthropology, psychological anthropology, international health, and feminist studies. The research findings run counter to biosocial evolutionary analyses of the universality of "mother love." As such, they also challenge universal, biologically based gender roles, instead emphasizing the importance of culture and political-economic context in explaining human behavior. In many ways, the extreme poverty and hopelessness of the mothers of Alto do Cruzeiro are reminiscent of Colin Turnbull's dramatic, depressing ethnography of the Ik—a resettled African population whose circumstances resulted in loss of social cooperation and support and high death rates (Turnbull 1972). In this selection, Scheper-Hughes argues that high child mortality is the result of political economy, not medical technology. An important intervening variable appears to be maternal detachment from infants who are failing to thrive.*

From an ethnomedical perspective, the author discusses a folk category of doença de crianca *that is used by mothers to explain why certain children will not thrive and are destined for early death. There are other cultural attributes associated with these tragic circumstances: beliefs about sour or insufficient breast milk, sanctions against strong maternal sentiments toward children, and patterns of enculturation that routinize infant death.*

At the end of this ethnographic case study, Scheper-Hughes questions some generalized theories about motherhood and mother–infant relationships, including maternal bonding and maternal thinking. Mundane and avoidable circumstances of poverty—especially endemic hunger, lack of clean water, unsanitary conditions, inadequate housing, unemployment, and low wages—are often-repeated themes in medical anthropology. The human face of such situations—including physical and mental suffering—is illustrated more clearly by ethnographic accounts of scarcity and maternal behavior than by cold statistics.

As you read this selection, consider these questions:

- *What did the researcher gain by collecting reproductive histories of the women from Alto? Were you surprised by the statistics from that survey?*
- *Why don't women believe in the sufficiency of breast milk for infant feeding for the first six months (as recommended by the World Health Organization)?*
- *Why is infant mortality a women's health issue?*
- *Is there an advantage for mothers in limiting their attachment to infants? Or do you think that this is a question of cultural rules about the expression of feelings (as in the case of pain, selection 29)?*
- *Some people are offended by this selection. Why do you think that is the case?*
- *Is malnutrition a medical problem or a political problem?*

Maternal practices begin in love, a love which for most mothers is as intense, confusing, ambivalent, poignantly sweet as any they will experience.

—SARA RUDDICK (1980:344)

This paper is about culture, scarcity, and maternal thinking. It explores maternal beliefs, sentiments, and practices bearing on child treatment and child survival among women of Alto do Cruzeiro, a hillside shantytown of recent rural migrants. It is set in Northeast Brazil, a region dominated by the vestiges of a semifeudal plantation economy which, in its death throes, has spawned a new class: a rural proletariat of unattached and often desperate rural laborers living on the margins of the economy in shantytowns and invasion barrios grafted onto interior market towns. *O Nordeste* is a land of contrasts: cloying fields of sugar cane amidst hunger and disease; a land of authoritarian landlords and libertarian social bandits; of conservative Afro-Brazilian possession cults, and a radical, politicized Catholicism. In short, the Northeast is the heart of the Third World in Brazil—its mothers and babies heirs to the so-called Brazilian Economic Miracle, a policy of capital accumulation that has increased both the Gross National Product and the Gross National Indifference to a childhood mortality rate that has been steadily rising throughout the nation since the late 1960s.[1]

Approximately 1 million children under the age of 5 die each year in Brazil, largely the result of parasitic infections interacting with infectious disease and chronic undernutrition. Of these, few could be saved (for long) by the miracles of modern medicine. Infant and childhood mortality in the Third World is a problem of *political economy*, not of *medical technology*. Here, however, I will discuss another pair of childhood pathogens—maternal detachment and indifference toward infants and babies judged too weak or too vulnerable to survive the pernicious conditions of shantytown life. The following analysis of the reproductive histories of 72 women of Alto do Cruzeiro explores the links between *economic* and *maternal* deprivation, between material and emotional scarcity. It discusses the social and economic context that shapes the expression of maternal sentiments and the cultural meanings of mother love and child death, and determines the experiences of attachment, separation, and loss. It identifies a unifying metaphor of life as a *luta*, a struggle, between strong and weak, or between weak and weaker still, that is invoked by Alto women to explain the necessity of allowing some—especially their very sick—babies to die *"a mingua,"* that is, without attention, care, or protection. This same metaphor is projected on to body imagery in mothers' perception of their bodies as "wasted" and their breasts as "sucked dry" by the mouths of their infants, producing the disquieting image of hungry women hungrily consumed by their own children.

Finally, it is argued that maternal thinking and practices are *socially produced* rather than determined by a psychobiological script of innate or universal emotions such as has been suggested in the biomedical literature on "maternal bonding" and, more recently, in the new feminist scholarship on maternal sentiments.

BACKGROUND/CASE STUDIES

Two events, occurring more or less simultaneously, first captured my attention and started me thinking about maternal behavior under particularly adverse conditions. One event was public and idiosyncratic, the other was private and altogether commonplace. One aroused community sentiments of anger and hostility; the other aroused no public sentiments at all. Both concerned the survival of children in similarly unfortunate circumstances.

Rosa

During a drought in the summer of 1967 while I was then a Peace Corps health and community development worker living in Alto do Cruzeiro in the interior market town of Ladeiras (a pseudonym), I was drawn one day by curiosity to the jail cell of a young woman from an outlying rural district who had just been apprehended for the murder of her infant son and 1-year-old daughter. The infant had been smothered, while the little girl had been hacked with a machete and dashed against a tree trunk. Rosa, the mother, became, for a brief period, a central attraction in Ladeiras as both rich and poor passed her barred window in order to rain down slurs on her head: "beast"; "disgraceful wretch"; "women without shame"; "unnatural creature." Face-to-face with the withdrawn and timid girl, I asked her the obvious, "Why did you do it?" And she replied, as she must have for the hundredth time: "to stop them from crying for milk." After a pause she added (perhaps to her own defense): *"bichinos não sente nada"*—little things have no feelings. Embarrassed, I withdrew quickly, and left the girl (for she was little more than that) alone to ponder her "crime."

Lourdes and Ze

I lived at that time on the *Alto*, not far from the makeshift lean-to of Lourdes, a young girl of 17, single and pregnant for the second time. Conditions on the Alto do Cruzeiro were then, as now, appalling: contaminated drinking water, food shortages, unchecked infectious disease, lack of sanitation, and crowded living conditions decimated especially the oldest and youngest residents of the hill. Lourdes's first born, Ze-Ze, was about a year old and severely marasmic (i.e., malnourished)—toothless, hairless, and unable even to sit up, he spent his days curled up in a hammock or lying on a piece of cardboard on the mud floor where he was harassed by stray dogs and goats. I became involved with Zezino after I was called on to help Lourdes with the birth of her second child, a son about whom a great fuss was made because he was both fair (*loiro*) and robust (*forte*). With Lourdes's limited energy

376 Gender and Women's Health

and attention now given over to the newborn, Zezino's condition worsened and I decided to intervene. I carried him off to the cooperative day care nursery (*creche*) I had organized with the more activist women of the hill. My efforts to rescue Ze were laughed at by the other women, and Zezino himself resisted my efforts to save him with a perversity perhaps only equal to my own. He refused to eat and wailed pitifully whenever I approached him. The *creche* mothers advised me to leave Zezino alone. They said they had seen many babies like this one and that "if a baby *wants* to die, it *will* die" and that this one was completely *disanimado*, lifeless, without fight. It was wrong, they cautioned, to fight death. But this was a philosophy alien to me and I continued to do battle with the little boy until finally he succumbed: he ate, gained weight, his hair grew in, and his face filled out. Gradually, too, he developed a strong attachment to me. Long before he could walk he would spring to my back where he would wrap his spindly arms and legs around me. His anger at being loosed from that position could be formidable. He even learned to smile. But along with the other women of the *creche* I wondered whether Ze would ever be "right" again, whether he could develop normally after the traumas he had been through. Worse, there were the traumas yet to come since I had to return him to Lourdes in her miserable conditions. And what of Lourdes—was this fair to her? Lourdes did agree to take Zezino back and she seemed more interested in him now that he looked more human than monkey, while my own investment in the child began to wane. By this time I was well socialized into shantytown culture and I never again put so much effort where the odds were so poor.

I returned to the Alto in the summer of 1982, 18 years later. Among the women of the Alto who formed my research sample was Lourdes, still in desperate straits and still fighting to put together the semblance of a life for her five living children, the oldest of whom was Ze, now a young man of 20, and filling in as "head" of the household—a slight, quiet, reserved young man with a droll sense of humor. Much was made of the reunion between Zezino and me, and the story was told several times of how I had wisked Zezino off when he was all but given up for dead and had force fed him like a fiesta turkey. Ze laughed the hardest of all, his arm protectively around his mother's shoulders. When I asked Ze later in private the question I asked all my informants—Who has been your greatest friend and ally in life, the one person on whom you could always depend—he took a long drag on his cigarette and replied, "My mother, of course."

I introduce these vignettes as caveats to the following analysis. With respect to the first story, it was to point out that severe child battering leading to death is universally recognized as *criminally deviant* in *Nordestino* society and culture. It is, to this day, so rare as to be almost unthinkable, so abhorrent that the perpetrator is scarcely thought of as human. "Mother love" is a commonsense and richly elaborated motif in Brazilian culture, celebrated in literature, art, and verse, in public ceremonies, in music and folklore, and in the continuing folk Catholic devotion to the Virgin Mother. Nonetheless, selective neglect accompanied by maternal detachment is both widespread among the poorer populations of Ladeiras but "invisible"—generally unrecognized by those outside shantytown culture, even by professionals such as clinic doctors and teachers who come into frequent contact with severely neglected babies and young children. *Within* the shantytown, child death *a mingua* (accompanied by maternal indifference and neglect) is understood as an appropriate maternal response to a deficiency *in* the child. Part of learning how to mother on the Alto includes learning when to "let go."

I also want to point out, with reference to the second vignette, that although the data indicate that Alto mothers do sometimes withdraw care and affection from some of their babies, such behaviors do not invariably lead to death, nor are the distanced maternal emotions irreversible. One of the benefits of returning to the same community where I had previously worked was the chance to observe the positive outcomes of several memorable cases of selective neglect—children who, like Ze, survived and were later able to win their way inside the domestic circle of protective custody and love. It is also essential to note that selective neglect is not analogous to what we mean in the United States by "child abuse"; it is not motivated by anger, hate, or aggression toward the child. Such sentiments—part of the "classic" child abuse syndrome identified in the United States (Steele and Pollock 1968; Gill 1970; Bourne and Newberger 1979; Gelles 1973; Kempe and Helfer 1980)—appear altogether lacking among women of the Alto who are far more likely to express *pity for*, than anger against, a dependent child, who are disinclined to strike what is seen as an innocent and irrational creature, and who, to the best of my knowledge, never project images of evil or badness onto a small child.

THE SAMPLE: THE WOMEN OF O CRUZEIRO

My first sample of 72 Alto women was an opportunistic one, comprised of the first women to volunteer for the study following an open meeting I called at the *creche* and social center at the top of the hill. Many more women volunteered over the next several weeks than I could possibly have interviewed during the brief period of my stay (8 weeks). The only criterion for inclusion in the sample was that the woman had been pregnant at least once. All understood that I was studying reproduction and mothering within the context of women's lives on the Alto.

The interviews elicited demographic information, work history, patterns of migration, marital history. This was followed by a discussion of each pregnancy and its outcome. For each live birth the following information was recorded: location of, and assistance with, the delivery; mother's perceptions of the infant's weight, health status, temperament; infant feeding practices; history of early childhood illnesses, how treated, and outcomes, including mortality. Following the reproductive history I asked each mother a series of open-ended, provocative, and evaluative questions, including: Why do so many infants die here? What do infants need most in order to survive the first year of life? What could most improve the situation of mothers and infants here? Who has been your greatest source of comfort and support throughout your adult life? How many children are enough to raise? Do you prefer to raise sons or daughters and why?

As both psychological anthropologist and feminist I was concerned not only with raising questions about *behavior* and *practice* (i.e., *did* some of these women selectively neglect some of their infants and place them at risk) but also with questions of *meaning* and *motivation*, how and why they might do this. I wanted to know what infant death and loss meant to them, and how they explained and interpreted their actions as women and mothers. I wanted to know what were the effects of chronic scarcity and deprivation on women's abilities to nurture, to attend, indeed even to love. And, finally, I wanted to know what were the consequences of continual loss of infants and babies for the world views of Alto mothers, as, at a later stage, I hope to explore the consequences of selective neglect on the personalities, beliefs, and sentiments of those children—like Ze-Ze—who *do* survive in spite of their inauspicious and inhospitable early experiences. What follows here is a discussion of the initial findings from the first and exploratory stage of the research.

I was able to work efficiently during this initial period because I was both known and trusted on the Alto as the *Americana* who had once lived and worked with them. In fact, several of the older women and their adult daughters (now grandmothers and mothers) in my sample were the very same young mothers and toddlers with whom I had worked 20 years ago (1964–1966) in the construction and operation of a cooperative day care center for working mothers. My previous work and association with the midwives of the Alto and my attendance at numerous home births years ago now gave me access to the homes of young women who gave birth during the research period.

The women interviewed ranged in age from 17 to 71; the median age of 39 meant that most were still potentially fertile. A profile of the average woman in my sample could read as follows. She was born on an *engenho* (sugar plantation) where she grew up working "at the foot of the cane." She attended school briefly and while she can do sums with great facility, she cannot read. After marriage she moved several times always in search of better work conditions for her husband or a better life for the children, preferably a *vida na rua* (a life on urban streets) rather than in the *mata,* the rural backwaters. Her husband or present companion is a "good" man, but described as *meio-fraco,* weak-poor, unskilled, unemployed, or worse, sickly and dependent, or perhaps, a *cachazeiro,* a drunkard. They have been separated from time to time. She works at least part time in the marketplace, hiring herself out in the fields. The combined weekly household income in 1982, Cr$5000 ($25.00), put the family on the borders between *pobreza* and *pobretão*—poverty and absolute misery. The nuclear family is counted from above and below—including the little angels in heaven, and *os desgraçados,* the living but sinful children on earth.

REPRODUCTIVE HISTORIES

The 72 women reported a staggering *686* pregnancies and 251 childhood deaths (birth to 5 years). The average woman (speaking statistically) experienced 9.5 pregnancies, 1.4 miscarriages, abortions, or stillbirths, and 3.5 deaths of children. She has 4.5 living children. Many infants and toddlers were, however, reported by their mothers to be sick or frail at the time of the interview, and at least some of these could be anticipated to join the mortality statistics in the months and years ahead (see Table 1).

Alto babies are at greatest risk during the first year of life: 70% of the deaths had occurred between birth and 6 months, and 82% by the end of the first year. No doubt contributing to the high mortality in the first year is the erosion of breastfeeding which, the interviews with my older informants reveal, had begun on the plantation long before commercial powdered milk was available. All Alto infants are reared from birth on *mingaus* and *papas,* cereals of rice or manioc flour mixed with milk and sugar. The breast, when offered at all, is only a supplement to the staple baby food, *mingau.* Central to the precipitous decline in breastfeeding among Alto mothers[2] is not so much a positive valuation of commercial powdered milk as a pervasive devaluation of breastmilk related to women's often distorted perceptions of their bodies, and breasts in particular, to be discussed below.

Sex, Birth Order, and Temperament

I probed the circumstances surrounding each pregnancy, birth, and death, and I elicited infant care practices and mothers' theories of infant development and infant needs. In addition, I probed for patterns of preferential treatment or neglect, and I asked the women to share with me their thoughts and feelings about motherhood, family life, about joy and affliction, about loss and grief. Neither the reproductive histories nor the interviews revealed a strong sex or birth order bias.

The 72 mothers reported a total of 251 deaths of offspring from birth to 5 years; 129 males and 122 females (Table 2). Despite a fairly pervasive ideology of male dominance in Brazilian culture, the women of the Alto expressed no consistent pattern of sex preference, and virtually all agreed that a mother would want to have a balance between sons and daughters. Both sexes were valued in children, although for different reasons. Boys were said by mothers to be "easy" to care for and were independent from an early age. Sons could be sent out to "forage" in the market and were unashamed to beg or steal, if necessity came to that. Sons were also enjoyed for their skill in street games and sports, an important aspect of community life on the Alto. But daughters were highly valued as well: they were not only useful at home, but were a mother's lifelong friend and intimate. Alto mothers and daughters strive to stay in proximity to each other throughout the life cycle; distance, dissension, and alienation between mothers and daughters occurs, but is considered both tragic and deviant. "Obviously," Alto mothers would conclude, a woman would want to have at least one casal (a boy-girl pair) and preferably two pairs, spaced closely together.

With respect to birth order among the subset of completed families, the most "protected" cohorts were those children occupying a middle rank, neither among the first or last born. Although childhood deaths often occurred in runs, this usually reflected external life circumstances of the mother during that period of her reproductive career, and there were no strong correlations between birth order and survivability. However, the casula, the last born child to survive infancy, was particularly loved and indulged.

Far more significant with respect to maternal investment was the mother's perception of the baby's

TABLE 1   Reproductive Histories Summary

Total pregnancies	686 (9.5/woman)
Total living children	329 (4.5/woman)
Miscarriages/abortions	85
Stillbirths	16
Childhood deaths (birth–5 yrs.)	251 (3.5/woman)
Childhood deaths (6–12 yrs.)	5

85 and 16 → 101 (1.4/woman)

N = 72 women; ages 19–71; median age 39.

constitution and temperament—the infant's qualities of readiness for the uphill struggle that is life. The mothers readily expressed a preference for babies who evidenced early on the physical and psychological characteristics of "fighters" and "survivors." Active, quick, sharp, playful, and developmentally precocious babies were much preferred to quiet, docile, passive, inactive, or developmentally delayed babies. Mothers spoke fondly of those babies who were a little brabo (wild), who were sabido (wise before their years), and who were jeitoso (skillful with objects, words, tasks, people). One young mother explained:

> I prefer a more active baby, because when they are quick and lively they will never be at a loss in life. The worst temperament in a baby is one that is dull and morto de espirito [lifeless], a baby so calm it just sits there without any energy. When they grow up they're good for nothing.

The vividly expressed disaffection of Alto mothers for their quieter and slower babies was particularly unfortunate in an area where malnutrition, parasitic infections, and dehydrations artificially produce these symptoms in a great many babies. A particularly lethal form of negative feedback results when some Alto mothers reject and withdraw their affections from their passive and less demanding babies whose disvalued "character traits" are primarily the symptoms of chronic hunger. This pattern is revealed in the

TABLE 2   Sex and Age at Death (Birth–5 Years)

	Male	Female	Total		
Postpartum (1–14 days)	21	12	33		
15 days–7 weeks	18	8	26	175 (70%)	205 (82%)
2 mos.–6 mos.	57	59	116		
7 mos.–1 year	13	17	30		
13 mos.–2 years	12	15	27		
2 1/2 yrs.–5 yrs.	8	11	19		
Totals:	129	122	251		

N = 251.

TABLE 3   Causes of Infant/Childhood Deaths (Mothers' Explanations)

I. *The Natural Realm* (locus of responsibility: natural pathogens)
    A. Gastroenteric (various types of diarrhea) — 71
    B. Other Infectious, Communicable Diseases — 41
    C. Teething (*denticão*) — 13
    D. Skin, Liver, Blood Diseases — 13
    Total: 138

II. *Supernatural Realm* (locus of responsibility: God, the saints)
    A. *De Repente* (taken suddenly by God, saints) — 9
    B. *Castigo* (punishment for sin of the parent) — 3
    Total: 12

III. *The Social Realm* (locus of responsibility: human agency is directly or indirectly implied)
    A. Malignant Emotions (envy, shock, fear) — 14
    B. *Resguardo Quebrado* (postpartum or illness precautions broken) — 5
    C. *Mal Trato* (poor care, including poor medical care) — 6
    D. *Doença de Crianca* ("ugly diseases" involving benign neglect) — 39
    E. *Fraqueza* (perceived constitutional weakness that involves maternal under-investment) — 37
    Total: 101

mother's explanations of their children's causes of death.

PERCEIVED CAUSES OF CHILDHOOD MORTALITY

Although uneducated and, for the most part, illiterate, the shantytown mothers interviewed were all too keenly aware that the primary cause of infant mortality was gastroenteric and other infectious diseases resulting from living in, as they so graphically phrased it, a *porcaria*, a pig sty. When asked why, *in general,* so many babies and young children of O Cruzeiro die, the women were quick to reply: "they die because we are poor, because we are hungry"; "they die because the water we drink is filthy with germs"; "they die because we can't keep them in shoes or away from this human garbage dump we live in"; "they die because we get worthless medical care: 'street medicine,' 'medicine on the run'"; "they die because we have no safe place to leave them when we go off to work."

When asked what it is that infants need most to survive the first year of life, the Alto mothers in my sample invariably answered "good food, proper nutrition, milk, vitamins." I soon became bored with its concreteness. The irony, however, was that not a single mother had stated either a lack of food or insufficient

milk was a primary or even a contributing cause of death for any of her *own* children. Perhaps they must exercise this denial because the alternative—the recognition that a child is slowly starving to death—is too painful.

Table 3 offers a condensed rendering of these women's perceptions of the major pathogens affecting the lives of their children. Certainly naturalistic explanations predominated in which biomedical conceptions of contagion and infection blend with aspects of humoral pathology and belief in the etiological significance of teething. While *a vontage de Deus,* God's will, was understood as the ultimate cause of all human events (including the death of one's children), in very few instances did mothers attribute particular deaths to the immediate action or will of God or the saints. Human agency (although not necessarily guilt and responsibility) was imputed to the deaths of 101 of the children. This includes deaths attributed to poor care (*mal trato*), to uncontrolled pathogenic emotions (such as anger or envy resulting in evil eye, or fear resulting in the folk syndrome *susto* [magical fright]), and to breaking of customary precautions (*resguardas*) surrounding childbirth and the 40 days following, and attached to common childhood ailments. Finally, the interviews revealed a pattern of passive selective neglect expressed in the medium of folk diagnoses of *doença de crianca* (sickness of the child) and of *fraqueza* (weakness) implying in both cases a will toward death in the child.

Underlying and uniting these etiological notions is a world view in which all of life is conceptualized as *luta*, a power struggle between strong and weak. Death can be stronger than young life, and so mothers can speak of a baby whose drive toward life was not sufficiently strong or well developed, or who had an aversion (*disgosto*) to life. A pregnant woman who is "used up" (*acabado*) from too many previous pregnancies is said to transfer this weakness to the fetus who is then born frail and skinny, unfit for the *luta* ahead. Conversely, when a mother says that her infant suffered many crises during its first year but *vingou* (triumphed) in any case, she is giving proud testimony to the child's inner vitality, his or her will to live, to *lutar* (fight). If an infant succumbs to *denticão* (teething) it is understood that she died because the "force of the teeth" overwhelmed the delicate little system. The folk pediatric illness *gasto* is almost always fatal because the infant's alimentary canal is reduced to a sieve: whatever goes into the mouth comes out directly in violent bouts of vomiting and bloody diarrhea. The baby becomes *gasto* (spent, wasted), his [her?] vital fluids and energy gone. Most disquieting, however, is the image mothers convey of those of their babies who were said to have died of thirst, their tongues blackened and hanging out of their mouths because their mothers were too weak, ruined, or diseased to breast-feed them. One young mother said:

> They are born already starving in the womb. They are born bruised and discolored, their tongues swollen in their mouths. If we were to nurse them constantly we would all die of tuberculosis. Weak people can't give much milk.

When I challenged a young and vigorous Alto woman about her inability to breastfeed, she responded angrily, pointing to her breast, "Look. They can suck and suck all they want, but all they will get from me is blood." Once again we have the metaphor of *a luta*—the struggle between weak and weaker over scarce resources. Another reason given by Alto mothers for their failure to breastfeed their babies for more than the first few weeks of life was that their infant had rejected the breast. And why not? For I was told repeatedly by mothers of newborns that their breastmilk was "foul" or "worthless" and for many different reasons. The milk was said to be either "salty" or "bitter" or "watery" or "sour" or "infected" or "dirty" or "diseased." In all, their own milk was rejected as unfit for infants and little more than a vehicle for contamination.

I do not know to what extent mothers' perceptions of breastmilk insufficiency is a function of their nutritional status or of their reliance on supplementary infant feedings of *mingau*, which surely interferes with the mother's own milk production. But I do know that once the breastmilk falters Alto mothers are quick to interpret this as a symptom of their own *fraqueza*, their physical and moral weakness. Similarly, when these young women refer to their breastmilk as scanty, curdled, bitter, or sour, they are also speaking metaphorically to the scarcity and bitterness of their lives as women of the Alto. What has been taken from these women is their faith in their ability to give. As the mothers stated earlier "We have *nothing* to give our children" and "Weak people can't give much milk."

In all, the etiological system and body imagery can be understood as a projection, a microcosm of the hierarchical social order in which strength, force, and power win out. It is a response to, a defense against, and a reflection of the miserable conditions of Alto life. It is these survivor values and perceptions that make Alto mothers reluctant to care for those infants and babies seen as deficient in vital energy, in *animacão*. Multiple births fare poorly on the Alto: few twins and triplets survive infancy. An obstetrical nurse in Ladeiras reported that poor mothers will take the stronger of a set of twins and leave the smaller or frailer for the hospital staff to dispose of as they see fit.

All the mothers agreed that it is best if the weak and disabled die as infants and that they die without a prolonged and wasted struggle. Celia, for example, could speak of her two infants having given her "no trouble" in dying. They just "rolled their eyes to the back of their heads and were still." It is the more gradual, protracted deaths—the deaths of *doença de crianca*—that Alto mothers particularly fear.

DOENÇA DE CRIANCA: ETHNOMEDICAL SELECTIVE NEGLECT

The Alto mothers spoke frequently and covertly of a cluster of childhood illnesses that are both greatly feared and from which they withdraw treatment and care. They used a euphemism, "sickness of the child," in order to avoid discussing the many anxiety-provoking symptoms and conditions subsumed under the term. The women volunteered that a child with a *doença de crianca* was best left to die a *mingua*, meaning a child allowed to slowly wither away without sufficient care, food, love, or attention. It meant, quite simply, a death by neglect. The women did not like talking about this subject, but neither did they deny or conceal their own behavior or their feelings.

Doença de crianca was used to refer to any serious childhood condition which, while not necessarily life-threatening, was believed likely to leave the mother with a permanently disabled, frail, or dependent child. Various paralyses, epilepsy, childhood autism, and developmental disabilities were discussed in this context. The symptoms that mothers particularly feared and which they were likely to label as symptoms of a "sickness of the child" included deliriums from high fevers, fit-like convulsions, extreme passivity and immobility, retarded verbal or motor skills, disinterest in food, play, social interaction, changes in skin color, loss of body liquids and body fat, sunken eyes. The etiology was multicausal; many things caused *doença de crianca* including frights (*pasmo, susto*), germs and other microbes, evil eye, and complications resulting from otherwise normal childhood illnesses. Measles, diarrhea, even a common cold could, without taking proper precautions, "turn into" (*virar*) a dreaded sickness of the child, thereby marking the child as beyond hope of a normal recovery.

The expansiveness and flexibility of the folk diagnosis allows Alto mothers a great deal of latitude in deciding which of their children are not favored for normal development and from which she may withdraw her attentions. The woman does not hold herself responsible for the death and nor is she blamed by the immediate female community (men seem to have little knowledge of the matter); the cause of death is a perceived deficiency in the child, not a deficiency in the mother. Thirty-nine babies were said to have died of a sickness of the child, but the same behaviors are implied in an additional 37 deaths attributed to *fraqueza* (innate weakness of the child). The following statements of mothers are indicative:

> There are various "qualities" of *doença de crianca*. Some die with rose colored marks all over their body; others die black colored. It's very ugly—with this disease it takes a very long time for them to die. It takes a lot out of the mother. It makes you sad. This sickness we don't treat. If you treat it the child will never be right. Some become crazy. Others are just weak and sickly their whole life.

> They die because they have to die. If they were meant to live, it would happen that way as well. I think that if they were always weak, they wouldn't be able to defend themselves in life. So, it is really better to let the weak ones die.

> There are two diseases we don't like to talk about because they are the ugliest things in the world. So we just say *doença de crianca* and leave it at that. One of these is what some people call *gotas de serena* [literally "evening mist"] which is a kind of madness, like rabies in a dog. The other is *pasmo*, a terrible paralysis that the child gets from a bad shock. His skin turns black and he just sits there still and dumb in the hammock, really lifeless. We are afraid of these sicknesses of the child. It is best to leave them die.

> (*Doença de crianca*) can come from many different things. It can come from a fright the child has, but also from dirty laundry, or from strong germs that enter through the fingernails. Look, we don't like talking about this. We don't mention its name. We are afraid of calling it up.

It became painfully apparent that Alto mothers were often describing the symptoms of severe malnutrition and gastroenteric illness further complicated by their own selective inattention. Untreated diarrheas and dehydration contributed to the baby's passivity, his or her disinterest in food, and developmental delays. High fevers often produced the fit-like convulsions that mothers feared as harbingers of permanent madness or epilepsy. Because these hungry and dehydrated babies are so passive and uncomplaining, their mothers can easily forget to attend to their needs, and can distance themselves emotionally from what comes to appear as an *unnatural* child, an angel of death that was never meant to live. Many such babies are left alone in their hammocks while their mothers are out working, and not even a sibling or a neighbor woman is within earshot when their feeble cries signal a final

crisis, and so they die alone and unattended—*a mingua* as people say. A mother speaks of having "pity" for such a child, but her grief is as attenuated as her attachment to a baby who never demonstrated more than a fragile hold on life. The dead baby is washed and dressed in white satin and covered with sweet-smelling flowers. The coffin is simple: a cardboard or inexpensive wooden box decorated with a lining of purple tissue paper and a silver paper cross. Alto children form the funeral procession. In this way they are socialized to accept as natural and commonplace the burial of siblings and playmates; as later, perhaps they will have to bury their own children and grandchildren.

BONDING THEORY AND THE BIOLOGICAL BASIS OF MOTHER LOVE

In recent years there has been considerable interest in exploring the biological components of mother-infant attachment. The observations of species specific maternal behavior patterns such as nesting, grooming, and retrieving which have been studied in animal mothers immediately after birth led a number of ethnologists, human biologists, anthropologists, pediatricians, and developmental psychologists to posit the parallel existence of a sequence of largely *innate* behaviors in human mothers' responses to their newborn. Such maternal behaviors as smiling, gazing, cooing, nuzzling, sniffing, fondling, and enfolding the newborn immediately postpartum has been observed, recorded, and quantified in order to demonstrate the existence of a universal psychobiological script referred to as "mother-infant bonding" (Klaus and Kennell 1976).

Maternal bonding (or loving and attentive, if somewhat mindless, attachment to the newborn) is said to be "triggered" in mothers in response to instinctual infant behaviors, especially crying, sucking, clinging and smiling. The automatic "milk let-down" reflex in lactating mothers' responses to hungry infant cries is often cited as evidence of the unlearned and innate components of mothering. Klaus and Kennell and their associates have identified a "critical" or "sensitive" period for maternal bonding that is said to occur immediately postpartum:

> There is a sensitive period in the first *minutes* and hours of life during which it is *necessary* that the mother and father have close contact with the neonate for later development to be optimal. (Klaus and Kennell 1976:14)

If the mother and the infant are separated during this time (as is customary in hospital delivery), maternal bonding may be inhibited, suggest Klaus and Kennell, with consequences as serious as maternal indifference toward, or even rejection of, the infant when the two are reunited. Unlike other mammals, however, rarely are these consequences irreversible in *human* mothers:

> The process that takes place during the maternal sensitive period differs from imprinting in that there is not a point beyond which the formation of an attachment is precluded. This is the *optimal* but not the sole period for an attachment to develop. Although the process can occur at a later time, it will be more difficult and take longer to achieve. (Kennell, Trause, and Klaus 1975:88)

Support for the evolutionary genetic basis of human bonding has come from recent studies of hunter-gatherer populations. Research by Draper, Howell, and Konner (see Lee and DeVore 1976) indicates that the relationship between mother and infant in such small, mobile social groups is characterized by: a high degree of physical skin-on-skin contact (for over 70% of the day and night in the early months of life); continuous and prolonged nursing (up to 4 or 5 years); close, attentive, and seemingly "indulgent" maternal behavior. These behaviors "typical of most primate species living in large groups [and of most] hunter-gatherers known today . . . probably represents the usual social environment for development in our species going back millions of years" (SSRC Committee on Biosocial Science n.d.:2). Maternal bonding, therefore, is thought to be part of our evolutionary inheritance.

Alice Rossi suggests that while "biologically males have only one innate orientation, a sexual one that draws them to women, women have two such orientations, a sexual one toward men, and a reproductive one toward the young" (1977:5). Human mothering has a strong unlearned component, argues Rossi, because of the precarious timing of human birth. The extremely immature and dependent human neonate requires particularly close attention and care in order to assure its survival. Therefore, it was particularly advantageous for a "maternal instinct" to become genetically encoded in women's evolutionary psychology.

The by now extensive maternal-infant bonding literature[3] has had, among other effects, a profound influence upon changes in the obstetrical management of pregnancy, labor, and delivery in this country and elsewhere. Many hospitals now have "birthing rooms" and rooming-in wards in order to enhance early mother-infant interaction and maternal bonding.

Unfortunately, however, some of the "disciples" of Klaus and Kennell enlarged the claims made for the significance of early bonding. This lead to the naïve belief among some health professionals that if early contact was *necessary* to ensure *optimal* parenting, perhaps this was *all* that was needed to ensure *competent* parenting. A number of hospital-based intervention programs, based on this shaky assumption, were launched in the 1970s when belief in the critical importance of early bonding was at its height (see Lamb 1982b). Some programs identified high-risk populations for "inadequate" parenting (usually this meant the poor, nonwhite teenage or single mothers, mothers of low birth-weight infants, previous child abusers) and manipulated the hospital environment in order to "promote" bonding in the high-risk mothers who were sometimes observed against a matched control group. Rarely was there any attention paid to providing a supportive environment for the mother and child once they left the hospital. Similarly, the child abuse literature is replete with references to abuse and neglect as the consequence of failures in early maternal bonding.[4]

Recently, the scientific basis of bonding theory has been called into question,[5] and several longitudinal studies have not supported claims for any *long-term* effects of early mother-infant interaction (Ali and Lowry 1981; Rutter 1972; Chess and Thomas 1982; Curry 1979; deChateau 1980; deChateau and Wiberg 1977). As the scientific status of maternal bonding has receded, however, a view of womanhood positing the powerful effects of reproduction and mothering on females has arisen among some feminists (Rosaldo and Lamphere 1974; Ortner 1974; Chodorow 1978; Marks and de Courtivron, eds. 1980; Ruddick 1980; Gilligan 1982; Greer 1984). Sara Ruddick, for example, in a widely cited article published in *Feminist Studies* (1980:346–347) posits certain

> features of the mothering experience which are *invariant* and nearly *unchangeable,* and others, which, though changeable, are nearly universal. It is therefore possible to identify interests that appear to govern maternal practice throughout the species.

These *interests* concern demands for the *preservation, growth,* and *acceptability* of offspring. Ruddick refers to women's experience of a "social-biological pride in the function of their reproductive processes" (1980:344) and of a "sense of well-being" when their children flourish. Although she acknowledges that some economic and social conditions, such as poverty and isolation "may make [maternal] love frantic" (p. 344), she nonetheless maintains that these "do not kill the love." And she adds, "For whatever reasons, mothers typically find it not only *natural* but compelling to protect and foster the growth of their children" (1980:344). In stating her strong case for a *generalized* mode of "maternal thinking" Ruddick does specify that her model is based on her "knowledge of the institutions of motherhood in middle-class, white, Protestant, capitalist, patriarchal America" (p. 347) and she does call upon others "to correct her interpretations and to translate across cultures."

This is precisely what I shall do for the remainder of this paper in response to both the "bonding" and the "maternal sentiments" literature.

CULTURE, SCARCITY, AND HUMAN NEEDS

> I have seen death without weeping
> The destiny of the Northeast is death
> Cattle they kill
> To the people they do something worse
> —Traveling *repentista* singer, Brazil

Whenever we social and behavioral scientists involve ourselves in the study of women's lives—most especially thinking and behavior surrounding reproduction and maternity—we frequently come up against psychobiological theories of *human* nature that have been uncritically derived from assumptions and values implicit in the structure of the modern, Western, bourgeois family. Theories of innate maternal scripts such as "bonding," "maternal thinking," or "maternal instincts" are both culture and history bound, the reflection of a very specific and very recent reproductive strategy: to give birth to few babies and invest heavily in each one. This is a reproductive strategy that was a stranger to most of European history through the early modern period,[6] and it does not reflect the "maternal thinking" of a great many women living in the Third World today where an alternative strategy holds: to give birth to many children, invest selectively based on culturally derived favored characteristics, and hope that a few survive infancy and the early years of life. This reproductive strategy requires a very different conception of maternal thinking, and just as surely elicits different kinds of maternal attachments, feelings, and sentiments—such as, for example, those implicated in the selective neglect of "high risk" babies on the Alto do Cruzeiro. Since this reproductive strategy is characteristic of much of the world's poorer population today, it would seem that some revision of the maternal bonding/maternal thinking as a universal human script is in order.

As might be expected, women whose cumulative experiences lead them to resignation with respect to

high fertility *and* to an expectation of frequent failure to rear healthy, living children will respond differently to their newborn than middle-class mothers with both greater control over their fertility *and* a high expectation for the health and viability of their children. Infant life *and* infant death carry different meanings, weight, and significance to Alto women than to the mothers generally studied in "bonding" research. Despite the fact that the birth and neonatal environment on Alto do Cruzeiro should be optimal for intense, early bonding to occur, mother-infant attachment is often muted and *protectively distanced*.

The traditional birth environment among Alto women is a home birth attended by a lay midwife and by several supportive female friends and relatives, especially the woman's mother. Virtually all the mothers in my sample over 40 gave birth at home with a traditional *parteira*; half the younger women still prefer home to hospital delivery, although "charity cases" are accepted in the maternity wing of the town hospital. Even those who do give birth in the town *maternidade* stay for less than 2 days and keep their newborns in a small crib next to the hospital bed.

Alto mothers and infants sleep together until the baby is considered old enough to sleep in its own small hammock or cot next to the mother's bed. Co-sleeping lasts from 1 month to 6 months. Breastfeeding, although greatly attenuated, is the norm for the first few weeks (generally 1 month to 6 weeks in this sample). Although Alto infants are not tied to the mother's person in shawl or sling, the infant spends a good many hours of the day in the arms or, when slightly older, balancing on the hip of the mother or any one of a number of convenient mother surrogates: siblings of both sexes, neighbors, visiting anthropologists. There is a great deal of physical affection expressed toward infants who are frequently stroked, tickled, teased, sniffed (kissing is thought inappropriate), and babbled to by all in the household. In short, all the conditions conducive to "bonding," as described in the medical and psychological literature, can be said to obtain in O Cruzeiro.

Nonetheless, Alto mothers protect themselves from strong, emotional attachment to their infants through a form of nurturance that is, from the start, somewhat "impersonal," for lack of a better word. Many Alto babies remain not only unchristened but *unnamed* until they begin to walk or talk *or* until a medical crisis (and the possibility of death) prompts a hurried, emergency baptism. In such cases (and I have been present at several of these) the name given the child is incidental. In some cases I or another casual onlooker was asked to pick a name spontaneously. Often the infant simply inherits the name of the last infant to have died in the family. Unnamed babies are simply called *ne-ne* (baby) or given a Brazilian generic name, Ze (Joe) or Maria. Adult affection for the *ne-ne* is diffuse and not focused on any particular characteristics of the infant as a little persona.

The circulation of babies through informal adoption or abandonment is commonplace on the Alto. Mothers in dire straits will sometimes ask a current or former employer to take their baby as a foster child or even as a future household servant. Young and unmarried women will sometimes leave a 5- or 6-month-old baby on the doorstep of an Alto woman known to be particularly tender-hearted. This happened to a dear friend and key informant during the summer of my stay in 1982, and brought back poignant memories to us both of the occasions during 1965–1966 when we had to cope with several babies abandoned at the cooperative day care center we had organized on the hill.

Given the extraordinary incidence of infant mortality on the Alto, child funerals are an almost daily occurrence and are dispatched with a quality of *la belle indifferance* that outsiders sometimes find quite shocking (see, for example, Scrimshaw 1978). The infant coffin-maker is a village-level specialist found in every community of Northeastern Brazil. He sometimes works in the medium of cardboard, paper maché and scrap material. A brief wake is held in the home when an infant over 6 months dies. Household visitors are expected to admire the sweet angel, but not to grieve. Mothers are scolded by other women if they shed tears for an infant, and few do. There do exist cases of Alto women who refuse to forget the death of a particularly favored baby, but their emotions tend to be dismissed as inappropriate or even as symptomatic of a kind of insanity.

The mundaneness and the high expectancy of infant death is shared by physicians and politicians of the town. In pointing out to the mayor of Ladeiras the rather extraordinary rate of child mortality for the community, he replied that he was aware of the problem and that he had, in fact, fulfilled a campaign promise in that regard: a free baby coffin to all registered voters according to their family's needs.

In all, what is constructed as an environment in which loss is anticipated and bets are hedged. "Mother love" with its attendant emotions of *holding*, *keeping*, and *preserving* is replaced by an estranged and guarded "watchful waiting." What makes this possible is a cultural conception of the child as human, but significantly less human than the grown child or adult. There is socialized in the Alto mother an emotion of estrangement toward the infant that is protective to her, but potentially lethal to the child. Maria

Piers (1978:37) refers to this state of primitive unconnectedness as "basic strangeness":

> Basic strangeness precedes basic trust. It marks the beginning of life and its end. In the intervening years, however, many situations occur that drive us back partially or wholly into that state. Basic strangeness denotes the opposite of empathy. It is a state in which we "turn off" toward others and are unable to experience them as fellow human beings. Instead, we may value them as inanimate objects.

Piers suggests that the single most frequent cause of such total estrangement is "abject poverty" leading to physical weakness and hopelessness. In such a condition, "even one's own child may appear as a competitor" (1978:39). In human parenting nothing can be taken for granted, least of all that the parent would sacrifice her life and resources for her child. Human mothers who reach the limit of their endurance can and often do become both estranged from and indifferent toward their children. Certainly Piers's concept is worthy of further refinement and investigation.

However, I do not wish to suggest by the foregoing that Alto mothers never suffer the loss of their infants. Indeed, amidst the generally passive and emotionally flat narrations of their lives as women, workers, and mothers, the pain of a particularly unresolved or poignant loss would break through and shatter the equanimity and resignation that is the norm. There would be memories of *particular* babies in whom a mother's hopes for the future *had* been invested, and she would weep in the telling of *that* death of all the deaths and losses she had endured. In the presence of so "deviant" a response I would be at a loss for how to proceed, or indeed, whether to proceed at all. But invariably my Alto assistant, Irene, or another woman would come to the rescue. "No, Dona Maria," she would scold the grieving woman, "of course you will not go mad with grief. You *will* conform. You will go on. You have *your own life* ahead."

The reproductive and life histories of these shantytown women lead me to question the validity of such ill-defined terms as maternal bonding, attachment, maternal thinking, critical period, and separation anxiety that fill the literature on mother-infant interaction. The terms and concepts seem wholly inadequate to convey the experience of mothering under the less than optimum conditions that prevail throughout much of the world today. The classical maternal bonding model focuses altogether too much attention on too few critical variables and on too brief a period in the mother-child life cycle. The model grossly underestimates the power and significance of social and cultural factors that influence and shape maternal thinking over time: the cultural meanings of sexuality, fertility, death, and survival; mother's assessment of her economic, social support, and psychological resources; family size and composition; characteristics and evaluation of the infant—its strength, beauty, viability, temperament, and "winsomeness."

The bonding model has neither relevance to, nor resonance with, the experiences of the women of O Cruzeiro for whom the life history of attachments follows a torturous path marked by many interruptions, separations, rejections, and losses reflecting the precariousness of their own existence and survival. But it is also important to note that an early lack of attachment, an indifferent commitment, or even a hostile rejection of an infant does not preclude the possibility of an enfolding drama of mother-child attachments later on, as some of the memorable survivors of early and severe selective neglect, like Ze-Ze, would indicate. That there must be a biological basis to human emotions is not disputed. It is argued, however, that the nature of human love and attachments is a complex phenomenon, socially constructed and made meaningful through culture. A more contextualized model of maternal thinking and sentiments is needed.

Finally, in concluding this paper, I wish to make it abundantly clear that there are many conditions on the Alto do Cruzeiro that are hostile to child survival. Most serious are the ones I scarcely mentioned: contaminated water, unchecked infectious disease, food shortages, the absence of day care facilities, and grossly inadequate medical care. I have focused instead on maternal thinking and behaviors that may also contribute to childhood mortality in order to address the indignities and inhumanities forced on poor women who must make choices and decisions that no woman should have to make. In the final analysis, the selective neglect of children must be understood as a direct consequence of the "selective neglect" of their mothers who have been excluded from participating in what was once called the Economic Miracle of modern Brazil.

NOTES

1. See Paim, Netto-Dias, and De Araujo 1980. Also, see Wood 1977. A recent PAHO investigation of childhood mortality in a dozen urban and rural sites in eight Latin American countries found the city of Recife in Pernambuco, Northeast Brazil, to have the highest infant mortality of all urban centers sampled.
2. See Goldberg, Rodrigues, Thome, and Morris 1982; Grant 1983; Berquo, Cukier, and Spindel 1984. A recent UNICEF report noted that in Brazil the percentage of babies breastfed *for any length of time* has fallen from 96% in 1940

to under 40% in 1974. This same report cites another study which found that among a large sample of children of poor parents in the South of Brazil, bottle-fed babies were between three and four times more likely to be seriously malnourished than breastfed babies.
3. See, for example, Klaus and Kennell 1976, 1982; Kennel, Voos, and Klaus 1979; Klaus, Jerauld, and Kreger 1972; Lozoff, Brittenham, and Trause 1977.
4. See, for example, Hurd 1975 and Schwarzbeck 1977.
5. See, for example, Sveja, Campos, and Emede 1980; Lamb 1982a, 1982b, and 1982c; Korsch 1983.
6. Contemporary historians of European and American family life in the early modern period have described child-rearing practices that were at best harshly pragmatic, and at worst sadistic and passively infanticidal. (See, for example, Aries 1962; de Mause 1974; Fox and Quitt 1980; Laslett 1965; Shorter 1975; Stone 1977).

REFERENCES

Ali, Z., and M. Lowry. 1981. Early Maternal-Child Contact: Effect on Later Behavior. *Developmental Medicine and Child Neurology* 23:337–345.

Aries, Philipe. 1962. *Centuries of Childhood: A Social History of Family Life.* New York: Vantage.

Berquo, Elza, Rosa Cukier, and Cheywa Spindel. 1984. *Caracterizaçao e Determinantes Do Aleitamento Materno na Grande São Paulo e na Grande Recife.* CEBRAP—Centro Brasileiro de Analise e Planejamento, Nova Serie Numero 2.

Bourne, Richard, and Eli Newberger, eds. 1979. *Critical Perspectives on Child Abuse and Neglect.* Lexington, MA: Lexington Books.

Chess, Stella, and Alexander Thomas. 1982. Infant Bonding: Mystique and Reality. *American Journal of Orthopsychiatry* 52(2):213–222.

Chodorow, Nancy. 1978. *The Reproduction of Mothering: Psychoanalysis and the Sociology of Gender.* Berkeley: University of California Press.

Curry, M.A.H. 1979. Contact During the First Hour with the Wrapped or Naked Newborn: Effects of Maternal Attachment Behaviors at 36 Hours and Three Months. *Birth and Family Journal* 6:227–235.

DeChateau, P. 1980. *Parent-Neonate Interaction and Its Long-Term Effects: Early Experiences and Early Behavior* (E. G. Simmel, ed.) New York: Academic Press.

DeChateau, P., and B. Wiberg. 1977. Long-Term Effects on Mother-Infant Behavior of Extra Contact During the First Hour Post Partum. *Acta Paedietrica Scandinavica* 66: 145–151.

De Mause, Lloyd. 1974. *The History of Childhood.* New York: The Psychohistory Press.

Fox, Vivian, and Martin H. Quitt. 1980. *Loving, Parenting and Dying: The Family Cycle in England and America.* New York: The Psychohistory Press.

Gelles, Richard. 1973. Child Abuse as Psychopathology. *American Journal of Orthopsychiatry* 43(4):611–621.

Gilligan, Carol. 1982. *In a Different Voice: Psychological Theory and Women's Development.* Cambridge: Harvard University Press.

Gills, David. 1970. *Violence Against Children.* Cambridge: Harvard University Press.

Goldberg, H., W. Rodrigues, M. Thome, and Morris. 1982. Infant Mortality and Breastfeeding in Northeastern Brazil. Paper presented at the Population Association of America Annual Meeting, San Diego, California.

Grant, J. 1983. The State of the World's Children, 1982–1983. UNICEF, Information Division, Geneva, Switzerland.

Greer, Germaine. 1984. *Sex and Destiny: Politics and Human Fertility.* New York: Harper & Row.

Hurd, J. L. M. 1975. Assessing Maternal Attachment: First Step Toward the Prevention of Child Abuse. *Journal of Obstetric, Gynecologic and Neonatal Nursing* 4(4):25–30.

Kempe, H., and R. Helfer. 1980. *The Battered Child.* Chicago: The University of Chicago Press.

Kennel, J. H., M. A. Trause, and M. H. Klaus. 1975. *Parent-Infant Interaction.* CIBA Foundation Symposium, No. 33. Amsterdam: Elsevier.

Kennel, J. H., V. K. Voos, and M. H. Klaus. 1979. Parent-Infant Bonding. *Handbook of Infant Development* (J. D. Osfsky, ed.). New York: Wiley.

Klaus, M. H., R. Jerauld, and N. C. Kreger. 1972. Maternal Attachment: Importance of the First Post-Partum Days. *New England Journal of Medicine* 286:460–463.

Klaus, M., and J. K. Kennell, eds. 1976. *Maternal-Infant Bonding.* St. Louis: C. V. Mosby (revised edition entitled *Parent-Infant Bonding,* 1982).

Korsch, Barbara. 1983. More on Parent-Infant Bonding. *Journal of Pediatrics* (February):249–250.

Lamb, Michael. 1982a. Maternal Attachment and Mother-Neonate Bonding: A Critical Review. *Advances in Developmental Psychology.* Vol. 2, pp. 1–39. Hillsdale, NJ: Lawrence Erlbaum Associates.

———. 1982b. Early Contacts and Maternal-Infant Bonding: One Decade Later. *Pediatrics* 70(5):763–768.

———. 1982c. The Bonding Phenomenon: Misinterpretations and Their Implications. *Journal of Pediatrics* 10(4):555–557.

Laslett, Peter. 1965. *The World We Have Lost.* London: Methuen.

Lee, R. B., and I. De Vore. 1976. *Kalahari Hunter-Gatherers.* Cambridge: Harvard University Press.

Lozoff, B., G. M. Brittenham, and M. A. Trause. 1977. The Mother-Newborn Relationship: Limits of Adaptability. *Journal of Pediatrics* 91:1–12.

Marks, Elaine, and Isabelle De Courtivron, eds. 1980. *New French Feminisms.* New York: Schocken.

Ortner, Sherry. 1974. Is Female to Male as Nature is to Culture? *Women, Culture, and Society* (M. Rosaldo and L. Lamphere, eds.), pp. 67–88. Stanford: Stanford University Press.

Paim, S., C. Netto-Dias, and J. DeAraujo. 1980. Influencia de Fatores Sociais e Ambientais na Mortalidade Infantil. *Boln. Of. Sanit. Pan-Am* LXXXVIII:327–340.

Piers, Marta. 1978. *Infanticide.* New York: W. W. Norton.

Rosaldo, Michelle, and Louise Lamphere. 1974. Introduction. *Women, Culture, and Society* (M. Rosaldo and L. Lamphere, eds.), pp. 1–16. Stanford: Stanford University Press.

Rossi, Alice. 1977. A Biosocial Perspective on Parenting. *Daedalus* 106(2):1–32.

Ruddick, Sara. 1980. Maternal Thinking. *Feminist Studies* 6:342–364.

Rutter, Michael. 1972. *Maternal Deprivation Reassessed.* New York: Penguin.

Schwarzbeck, C. 1977. Identification of Infants at Risk for Child Abuse: Observations and Inferences in the Examination of the Mother-Infant Dyad. *Child Abuse: Where Do We Go From Here?* Conference Proceedings, Feb. 18–20, 1977. Washington, D.C.: Children's Hospital National Medical Center, Child Protection Center, pp. 67–69.

Scrimshaw, Susan. 1978. Infant Mortality and Maternal Behavior in the Regulation of Family Size. *Population and Development Review* 4:383–403.

Shorter, Edward. 1975. *The Making of the Modern Family.* New York: Basic Books.

SSRC Committee on Biosocial Science. n.d. Biosocial Foundations of Parenting and Offspring Development. New York: SSRC, unpublished report.

Steele, Brandt, and Carl Pollock. 1968. A Psychiatric Study of Parents Who Abuse Their Children. *The Battered Child* (R. E. Helfer and C. H. Kempe, eds.), pp. 103–147. Chicago: University of Chicago Press.

Stone, Lawrence. 1977. *The Family, Sex, and Marriage in England, 1500–1800.* New York: Harper & Row.

Svejda, M. J., J. J. Campos, and R. N. Emede. 1980. Mother-Infant "Bonding": Failure to Generalize. *Child Development* 51:775–779.

Wood, Charles. 1977. Infant Mortality Trends and Capitalist Development in Brazil. *Latin American Perspectives* 4(4): 56–65.

Culture and Nutrition: Fat and Thin

✤ CONCEPTUAL TOOLS ✤

■ *Nutrition is a key aspect of health, and eating habits are largely shaped by culture and political economy.* Nutritional anthropologists study how and what people in different cultures eat. This includes measures of actual food preparation and intake as well as the symbolic meanings of food. Children's growth and development require the regular consumption of calories, protein, and essential micronutrients. Malnourished children are less able to survive inevitable bouts of infectious disease. There have always been food shortages, and still today many people of the world are malnourished. The social epidemiological distribution of malnutrition is never random.

■ *Malnutrition can be in the form of protein-calorie malnutrition (PCM), micronutrient malnutrition, and overnutrition.* Nutritional needs change over the life cycle, and lack of adequate food during gestation and childhood may have lifelong effects on physical and mental health. Food shortages have immediate impacts on children. PCM refers to overall nutritional intake and the bioavailability of energy from calories as well as protein; PCM may even be considered a biomedical label for hunger (Cassidy 1982). In some parts of the world, the traditional diet may be deficient in particular vitamins and minerals. Micronutrient malnutrition diseases include goiter and cretinism from iodine deficiency, night blindness from vitamin A deficiency, scurvy from vitamin C deficiency, and a host of others. In the developed world, overnutrition is a widespread and intractable problem.

■ *Within the same household, everyone may not have the same access to food.* Although children and pregnant women have the greatest nutritional needs, they do not always receive adequate or appropriate foods. The "breadwinner effect" is a common scenario in many cultures, in which people doing physical labor receive the largest portion of food. Sometimes a significant portion of the household budget may be used for nonnutritive consumables like cigarettes and alcohol. Within households, those most vulnerable are probably "weanlings"—toddlers who no longer get breast milk and who have to adapt to adult foods. Some nutritional interventions in Third World countries have emphasized the development of appropriate weaning foods (Dettwyler and Fishman 1992).

■ *"Positive deviance" refers to exceptional cases that have good health outcomes.* There is considerable variation among individuals within any society and culture. As medical anthropologists study how cultural patterns might play a role in causing health problems, they must also be on the lookout for individuals who have chosen different successful strategies. Solutions to health problems may be found among such cultural innovators or "positive deviants." International health programs can develop and promote these local solutions.

■ *Some nutritional problems require study on multiple levels of analysis.* To understand nutritional problems, medical anthropologists often think it is useful to examine different levels—the individual, the household, the society, and the regional economy. For nutritional problems like anorexia nervosa, there are clearly several levels of interaction: individual beliefs, family dynamics, social pressures, cultural beliefs, and a larger sociocultural context. Anthropologists study these problems at all of these levels.

41

The Biocultural Approach in Nutritional Anthropology: Case Studies of Malnutrition in Mali

Katherine A. Dettwyler

Medical anthropological research dealing with nutritional issues is, almost by definition, biocultural in its approach. What foods people eat and how much they eat are determined not simply by hunger, a biological drive, but more importantly by political-ecological factors that determine the availability of food and cultural factors that shape the acceptability and preparation of food. As we saw in selection 4 by Reynaldo Martorell, which questioned the "small but healthy" hypothesis, nutritional anthropologists must be concerned about measures of childhood growth and development. Such measures reflect the biological consequences of nutritional intake. Researchers can assess the nutritional status of children by using standards, like the National Center for Health Statistics (NCHS) standards used in this selection.

Undernutrition takes two forms. First is overall protein and calorie deficit, as described here in case studies from the African country of Mali. Marasmus, a type of overall wasting, and kwashiorkor, an illness of protein deficiency often related to weaning, are particular types of malnutrition. In the poor countries of the world, there is a well-documented relation between undernutrition and infectious disease. Poorly nourished children have a harder time recovering from bouts of infectious disease, while at the same time illness episodes slow growth rates. This situation is often found in relation to inappropriate infant formula feeding wherein babies may be given an extremely diluted solution of "milk" made with water that is full of pathogens. The interaction of disease and malnutrition means that underweight children are more likely to die, as was sadly noted by the Brazilian shantytown mothers studied by Nancy Scheper-Hughes in selection 40.

Malnutrition can also be the result of the lack of a specific micronutrient such as iodine or vitamin A; a severe deficiency of iodine, for example, can result in goiter and mental retardation (Fernandez 1990; Greene 1977). Such consequences can be avoided by relatively simple programs of adding iodine to salt. Whether such well-aimed "magic bullets" will do much to solve problems of world hunger, however, is another question.

In this selection, Katherine Dettwyler provides individual case studies of child malnutrition in Mali. These are like the cases she describes in her book of anthropological fieldwork, Dancing Skeletons (1994). Mali is one of the poorest countries of the world, and as a consequence both child malnutrition and death rates are very high. This selection demonstrates that the relationship between socioeconomic status and malnutrition is not simple, for some of the cases here are the children of low-status mothers within a relatively prosperous extended family household. The vast majority of malnutrition in Third World countries does not have a single identifiable cause. Local agricultural production and the marketing of food are central factors, but issues regarding the status of women or cultural rules about child feeding also must be considered.

As you read this selection, consider these questions:

- What are the particular situations of these Malian mothers and children that result in child malnutrition and early death? In any one of these cases, how might these tragic outcomes have been avoided?

- Why is this study of malnutrition considered biocultural? Are there cultural factors that might not get included in regular nutrition surveys?

- What does the author mean when she says that in many instances children are severely malnourished because they "have fallen through the safety net of overlapping support systems that normally ensure a minimum level of nutrition and health for children in the community"? Why is she impressed that the traditional system is actually working?

- Do you think it is relevant that two of the case studies are of twins?

Socioeconomic status is often cited as the most important factor influencing nutritional status in children, and, in general, national rates of malnutrition are negatively correlated with per capita income. As Pryer and Crook (1988:5) have stated, "Appalling environmental conditions and intense poverty are likely to be the two most important determinants of health and nutritional status of the slum and shanty town dwellers in many of the cities of the developing countries." Although not disputing this conclusion, a number of ethnographic studies have highlighted the role that cultural beliefs and practices regarding infant feeding and care also play in determining health and nutritional status in young children (Daniggelis 1987a, 1987b; Guldan 1988; Hull and Simpson 1985; Marshall 1985; Zeitlin and Guldan 1988).

The work of Zeitlin and her colleagues has focused on the role of psychosocial and behavioral aspects of child care and feeding in determining "positive deviance" in child health—those children who manage to thrive under conditions of environmental adversity (see Zeitlin, Ghassemi, and Mansour 1990 for a review of the literature on positive deviance). Others have focused on attributes of those children who fare particularly poorly under such conditions, including how they are perceived by their caretakers. For example, in a study of childhood deaths in northeastern Brazil, Scheper-Hughes found that mothers "gave up" on severely malnourished children and neglected them until they died (Scheper-Hughes 1987). Likewise, Mull and Mull report that among the Tarahumara of Mexico, children who are perceived as being "handicapped" may be allowed to starve to death, or are killed outright (Mull and Mull 1987). In Kenya, de Vries (1987) found that Masai infants who cry a lot are perceived as being fighters, with the personality and will necessary to survive the harsh conditions of life. These children are given more attention and nursed more often than quiet, placid babies. The quieter babies thus suffer and die more often from malnutrition.

The work of Bledsoe, Ewbank, and Isiugo-Abanihe (1988) and Bledsoe (1991) has focused on intrahousehold food distribution patterns and the effect of being a foster child on access to food and health care resources, growth, and health among the Mende of Sierra Leone. Bledsoe finds that, compared to "born" children of the household, young "fosters" have less access to food resources but are expected to perform more labor (Bledsoe 1991). Fosters also suffer more from malnutrition, but are taken to the hospital less often than "born" children (Bledsoe, Ewbank, and Isiugo-Abanihe 1988).

These examples could all be described as instances of "socio-cultural malnutrition," a term coined by Gokulanathan and Verghese to refer to growth failure in children that is "due to factors other than poverty and the lack of availability of food materials" (1969:118). Research in Mali (West Africa) suggests that sociocultural malnutrition contributes to the overall malnutrition picture. A number of studies in Mali have compared expenditures for food and dietary intakes of groups at different levels of socioeconomic status and from different parts of the country. All of these studies have concluded that relative income is not closely related to diet in Mali (Diakite 1968; Clairin et al. 1967; May 1968; Mondot-Bernard and Labonne 1982). Members of all social classes consume the same foods in the same quantities, and rising income is not correlated with an increase in quantity or an improvement in the nutritional quality of the diet.

In 1982 and 1983, and again in 1989, the author conducted research in a periurban community in Mali, focusing on the relationship between infant/child feeding beliefs and practices and the growth and development of children. The 1982–83 research was based on a mixed-longitudinal study of 136 children under four years of age. The 1989 research included a follow-up study of the children in the earlier sample. Previous publications based on this research have described the systems of beliefs concerning infant and child feeding practices (Dettwyler 1985, 1986), breastfeeding and weaning (Dettwyler 1985, 1987), the role of anorexia in malnutrition (Dettwyler 1989a), infant feeding styles (Dettwyler 1989b), and the relationship between relative poverty and nutritional status and growth in the entire sample (Dettwyler 1985, 1986).

Treating the growth data in cross section, average growth for all children in the 1982–83 sample during the first three years of life corresponds closely to the fifth percentile of NCHS standards (Hamill et al. 1979; . . .). A few children were growing at or above the NCHS fiftieth percentile, even though they came from relatively poor families (cf. "positive deviants," Zeitlin, Ghassemi, and Mansour 1990), while others were well below the fifth percentile, including some from relatively well-off families. The children in the latter group can be described as having fallen through the safety net of overlapping support systems that normally ensure a minimal level of nutrition and health for children in the community.

The data clearly indicate that relative poverty is not an accurate predictor of the observed variation in nutritional status and growth in this community, and that differences in maternal attitudes, experience, and other factors are responsible (Dettwyler 1986). In Mali, these factors include maternal age, marital problems, untreated illness, allocation of household resources, maternal attitudes, maternal competence and experience, support networks, and the position of the mother within the social structure of a polygynous, patrilineal society. In this paper, case studies of three families from the research community illustrate how sociocultural malnutrition in young children in Mali can be viewed as a consequence of the interactions among many factors. It is hoped that the case studies will demonstrate the value of a biocultural approach in which detailed ethnographic data, gathered in conjunction with traditional anthropometric measurements, can illuminate the intricate interactions between culture and biology.

DEMOGRAPHIC AND ETHNOGRAPHIC BACKGROUND OF THE SAMPLE

The study community of Farimabougou (a pseudonym) is one of approximately ten periurban communities located across the Niger River from the capital city of Bamako. During 1982 and 1983, a sample of 136 children were visited every four to eight weeks. The sample was constructed in a flexible, random manner, by walking the streets of the community, looking for families with young infants (not yet eating solid foods), explaining the project, and recruiting families willing to cooperate over an extended period of time. The study compounds were widely distributed and included all sectors of the community. A few infants, usually from neighboring compounds, were added to the study at the request of their mothers. Only three families dropped out of the study due to lack of interest. Several families were dropped because the index infant died during the measles epidemic that occurred during the initial month of the study. The final sample of 136 children came from 117 compounds and included 20 sibling pairs.

Growth data were collected at each visit, and multiple, semistructured interviews of mothers and other caretakers, as well as participant-observation of child feeding activities, were used to collect data on infant feeding beliefs and practices and infant health. Growth data included anthropometric measures of weight, and of arm, head, and chest circumference, as well as number of teeth erupted and general stage of motor and language development. Exact ages were determined from birth certificates, and the records of the local maternity clinic provided birth weights for some of the children.[1] All interviews were conducted by the author in Bambara, the native language of most of the informants, with the assistance of a Malian interpreter. A follow-up study of the same children was conducted in 1989. Approximately half of the children were relocated, measured again when possible, and their mothers interviewed again.

A brief description of the community will provide a wider context for the case studies that follow. Traditionally, the Malian economy has been based on subsistence agriculture. Bamako and Farimabougou, however, operate primarily on a cash economy. Most food is purchased in the daily market using cash obtained from the wage labor of fathers and, occasionally, mothers. Farimabougou is a poor community. In 1979, the World Bank defined the "urban poverty threshold" for Bamako as approximately $60.00 per month per household, and reported that the average income in Farimabougou is 40 percent lower than that of Bamako, with almost half of the households in Farimabougou below the urban poverty threshold (World Bank 1979).

In terms of ethnic identity, the parents of children in the study identify themselves primarily as Bambara or Mandinka (67%); the rest are divided among Fulani, Senoufo, Songhrai, Bobo, and Dogon. According to information provided by the Institut du Sahel (T. T. Kane, pers. comm. 1989), in 1989 Mali had a crude birth rate of 47/1,000 and a crude death rate of 20/1,000, resulting in a natural growth rate of 2.7 percent. The infant mortality rate was 130/1,000, and the juvenile mortality rate was 159/1,000. Life expectancy at birth was 47 years. The average number of births was 6.7 per woman. Data for these variables specific to Farimabougou do not exist.

During the 1982–83 study in Farimabougou, the average age for the introduction of solid foods was 7.9 months, with 14.4 months as the average age when children began eating the adult staples (millet and rice). The average age of weaning was 20.8 months, and women experienced an average duration of lactational amenorrhea of 10.1 months. The average pregnancy interval was 19.4 months, and the average interbirth interval was 26.5 months.

Two of the case studies reported here involved twins. According to local maternity clinic records, the rate of twinning in Farimabougou was 17.8/1,000 births in 1981 and 1982; this is almost identical to the rate reported by Imperato for the Bambara and Mandinka (17.9/1,000). According to Imperato:

> Twin births are extremely common among the Bambara and Malinke . . . Because twins are regarded among the Bambara and the Malinke as a blessing bestowed by the supreme being, their birth is received with great rejoicing. (Imperato 1977:119)

In terms of child care in general, and infant feeding practices in particular, twins are not treated differently from single births. Twins often start life smaller than singleton births, and must share one mother's milk. In two of the case studies below, being a twin undoubtedly adds yet another risk factor for malnutrition. At the same time, other sets of twins in the sample survived and flourished.

In 1982–83, the houses in Farimabougou were mostly of mud-brick construction with corrugated iron roofs and were located inside mud-walled compounds that were closely packed along narrow dirt streets. Compounds had neither running water nor electricity. Each compound had a pit latrine. Household garbage was thrown into a pit inside the compound, or out into the street.

The Malian diet is based on millet and rice, accompanied by various sauces. Animal protein in the diet comes from beef, mutton, or fish, which are often pounded before being added to the sauce. According to several food consumption surveys, with the exception of years of severe drought and of certain areas of far northern Mali, adult Malians have an adequate diet (Clarin et al. 1967; Diakite 1968; May 1968; Mondot-Bernard and Labonne 1982).

The traditional social organization of the Bambara consists of extended families living in large compounds, polygynous marriages, patrilineal descent, and patrilocal residence (N'Diaye 1970). This type of compound social organization is seldom realized in Farimabougou. Usually only one adult male from a rural family migrates to the city, and he usually has only one wife due to economic constraints. Thus, most of the children in the larger sample came from parents in monogamous marriages and lived in compounds containing only nuclear family members.

Except for a few Christian families, the people of Farimabougou are Moslem. For the most part, however, women do not strictly follow Muslim teachings. They are not secluded, they seldom go to the mosque or pray at home, they rarely fast during Ramadan, and they are not familiar with Koranic guidelines concerning infant feeding. Islamic beliefs coexist with traditional religious beliefs and practices. Sickness and death are usually attributed to Allah rather than to organic causes, witchcraft, or sorcery.

The majority of women who participated in the study were born in rural villages and had lived in the urban environment for less than 20 years at the time of the initial study. They have had little or no formal education, speak Bambara but not French, and can neither read nor write.

Health services for the residents of Farimabougou are provided primarily by traditional herbalists who sell leaves in the market, and by a government-run PMI (maternal/child health center) located approximately three kilometers away. Although the PMI visits

are free, the numerous medicines that are usually prescribed are very expensive. Most children are born at the PMI, but mothers do not often take sick children to the PMI for treatment, preferring to try traditional cures first. The nearest hospital is located in downtown Bamako, at least 20 minutes away by public transportation. In 1982–83, few children had been vaccinated against any of the major childhood diseases, and oral rehydration solution as a treatment for diarrhea was virtually unknown. Measles, malaria, upper respiratory infections, and diarrhea were the major illnesses of young children. According to Imperato, who has written in detail about traditional Bambara beliefs concerning measles:

> Measles is the most important disease of childhood in Africa. It occurs throughout the continent, the incidence being highest in most areas every third year. Measles epidemics occur at the peak of the dry season in West Africa, from March through May, when stores of food and human nutritional levels are at their lowest . . . From 1958 through 1975, the annual number of measles cases reported in Mali has ranged from 10,000 to 40,000, with case mortalities of 15–20 percent. (Imperato 1977:138)

A serious outbreak of measles occurred during the initial study in May of 1982. There were only a few cases of measles in 1983.

Malaria affects children primarily during the rainy season (July–September). Only one child death was attributed to malaria during the initial study. Of the seven child deaths that occurred between the two studies, four were reported to be due to malaria, and three to measles.

In general, women welcome new pregnancies. Children are viewed as a source of wealth and prestige; the more children you have, the higher the family income will be, the more people there will be to support you when you are old, and the higher your status as a wife. Infertility is considered a tragedy. The Bambara believe that it is good luck to have a female child first, but both male and female children are valued. The growth data as well as interview data reveal no significant sex bias in terms of nutrition or health care. Thus, being a female is not a risk factor for malnutrition in this community. Although children are highly valued, there is little understanding of the importance of proper nutrition and health care during the first few years of life. Infant mortality rates are very high, and mothers seem resigned to the fact that many children die, even if you "search for medicine" for them. It is considered to be a much greater loss if an older child or an adult dies than if a young infant dies.

Compared to conditions in 1983, Farimabougou had changed little by 1989. Treated water was available from common stand-pipes located on the main roads, but most people continued to obtain water from the wells in their compounds. The community still lacked electricity, sewage treatment, and garbage disposal service. The major noticeable physical change was a building boom on the periphery of the community. Although construction of many houses has begun, few are completed. Block after block of half-finished cement houses, destined to be middle-class neighborhoods, surround the original mud-brick community.

In terms of health care, several changes were apparent. One is that many of the children under 3 years of age had been vaccinated against measles, tetanus, polio, and tuberculosis, primarily by a traveling van of health workers who visit the market periodically. Women said that measles no longer kills many children, and that only a few children in Farimabougou died of measles during the hot season of 1989. Women were still reluctant to take children to PMI for immunizations, however. The local PMI had acquired a bad reputation among mothers because of long waits and "rude treatment" by the health workers, and was used even less than it was in 1983. By 1989, many mothers had heard of oral rehydration solution, and approximately 10 percent reported that they use it for the treatment of diarrhea in young children. Other women still used traditional herbal cures for diarrhea or did not treat diarrhea at all.

The three case studies given here, involving seven children, represent children with some of the poorest growth in the sample. Their growth data are not as complete as those of some of the other children for several reasons. Often the children were too sick or miserable to measure, and one child died early in the study. However, their family situations, though unique in their specific combinations of factors, are not atypical. These case studies clearly illustrate that malnutrition is often the result of a complex set of factors acting in combination.

CASE STUDIES

Case Study 1: Children #5 and #6

Children #5 and #6 were fraternal twins, a boy named Al-Hassane and a girl named Assanatu (all the names have been changed). Birth records in the local PMI record their birth weights as 2.2 and 1.5 kilos, respectively; the records do not indicate if the twins were premature. Jeneba, the twins' mother, had been married before and given birth to four children. Two were still alive and lived with their father's brothers. The other

two, a set of twin boys, had died at 6 months of age from diarrhea, according to Jeneba. After her first husband died in 1980, Jeneba remarried; she gave birth to Al-Hassane and Assanatu in 1981. Her second husband was a widower with teenaged children from his first marriage. He was employed at the national airport in a salaried position, but his wife did not know how much money he made.

Al-Hassane and Assanatu entered the study at the age of 8 months. . . . At 8 months of age, both children fell below the fifth percentile of NCHS standards for weight-for-age. The boy's weight, 6.3 kilos, falls in the "moderately malnourished" category according to the World Health Organization's system of classification by standard deviations below the median (between 2 and 3 SD below the median). The girl's weight, 5.0 kilos, places her in the "severely malnourished" category, more than three standard deviations below the median for her age. The children were receiving only breast milk at this time, although the girl sometimes ate a little millet porridge. The mother reported that because she had insufficient breast milk for twins, she had occasionally given them formula as a supplement when they were younger. However, their father had stopped providing money for this purpose.

At the next visit, when the children were 9 months of age, their mother was sick with malaria. The children were still nursing, and both had begun to eat solid food on a regular basis during the previous month. They had eaten no solid food for two days, however, because the mother was too ill to cook and had no one to help her. Pryer and Crook have noted that in urban regions of Third World Countries, "adults who are ill or malnourished are very likely to be unable to cope with the time-intensive demands of child care" (Pryer and Crook 1988). Jeneba's husband's older children, from his first marriage, were cooking for him and for themselves, but would not help their stepmother care for her children. At this visit, Al-Hassane's weight had dropped to 5.5 kilos, while Assanatu's had remained at 5.0 kilos. Both children now fell into the "severely malnourished" category.

At 10 months, the boy's weight had returned to 6.0 kilos, but the girl's remained at 5.0 kilos. A 24-hour dietary recall revealed that for breakfast they had eaten millet porridge flavored with sweetened condensed milk. For lunch, they had rice flavored with beef bouillon cubes; in the late afternoon, they had eaten some boiled sweet potatoes. According to their mother, they had not eaten any dinner the night before, because they were already asleep when the meal was served. She said that they were usually asleep when the evening meal was prepared.

At 11 months, Al-Hassane had regained his 8-month weight of 6.3 kilos, but Assanatu still had not gained any weight. At 12 months, the children were sick with fever and diarrhea, but both had gained a little weight since the previous month. At 15 months, Al-Hassane had lost 1.0 kilo of weight since the previous visit. His mother said he had been chronically ill with fever and diarrhea caused by teething and had refused to eat any food for the previous month. Assanatu had not been sick and had gained 0.5 kilo during the preceding three months. At this visit, the mother confided that she was thinking of leaving her husband because they were not getting along. She was especially upset over her stepchildren's refusal to accept her or her children as part of the family, and their refusal to help with the domestic labor.

The next month when I went to visit the compound, I was told that Jeneba had indeed taken the twins and left. After four months, I relocated them at her first husband's compound. At 19 months, Al-Hassane weighed 8.6 kilos (moderately malnourished), a gain of more than 3.0 kilos in four months. This weight gain represents marked catch-up growth in response to the changed environment, especially an improvement in diet; normal weight gain for males between 15 and 19 months is 0.80 kilos. Assanatu had gained 1.1 kilos in the same time period, which also represents some catch-up growth; normal weight gain for females is 0.75 kilos. However, at 7.1 kilos, she was still classified as "severely malnourished."

Jeneba said they had been completely healthy ever since she had moved. She now had access to money to provide them with proper food, as well as help with the domestic labor, and emotional support from her relatives. Her first husband's family was providing money for food and medical care. A 24-hour dietary recall at this time revealed that they had eaten rice porridge with sugar for breakfast. At the morning market, they had eaten meat brochettes (small pieces of beef cooked on a skewer). For lunch, they had rice with fish and onion sauce, with leftovers in the late afternoon. At night, they had eaten millet porridge.

. . .

Assanatu was always significantly smaller than her brother, especially for head circumference. Her weight gains and losses were never as dramatic as Al-Hassane's either. However, she was slightly advanced in motor development, suffered less from teething, and generally seemed more alert and happy. These differences may reflect the tendency of females to be less affected by stressful environmental conditions than males (Stini 1985; Stinson 1985). Assanatu seemed to respond by not growing in size, but continuing to advance developmentally. Al-Hassane was bigger, but developmentally delayed. Both children seemed to be treated the same by their mother, in terms of access to food and medical resources.

Follow-Up In 1989, contact was re-established with the family. According to Jeneba, Al-Hassane died at 3 years of age, when he had the measles. Assanatu had the measles at the same time, but recovered. Today, at almost 8 years of age, Assanatu's weight of 18.6 kilos is below the fifth percentile of NCHS standards. She would be considered "mildly malnourished" by the WHO classification. Her height, 121.0 centimeters, is just below the twenty-fifth percentile of NCHS standards, well within "normal" limits. The main legacy of her early childhood malnutrition is a small head circumference. Most brain growth occurs during the first 3 years of life, and inadequate nutrition during this time cannot be overcome by improved conditions in later childhood. Assanatu's head circumference, 47.3 centimeters, is the median for a child of only 18 months by NCHS standards, and falls well below those of the other girls her age in the follow-up study, whose head circumferences range from 49 to 53 centimeters. Her mother reports that she is "not very smart," and although she went to Koranic school for a while, she no longer attends "because she couldn't keep up." She also reports that Assanatu suffers often from malaria, and "doesn't like to eat very much." Jeneba never returned to her second husband, and he provides no support for Assanatu. They still live with her first husband's family, along with a man to whom Jeneba is not legally married. She has had one child with this man, and is now pregnant with her eighth child.

In this case, a variety of factors combined to provide a less than satisfactory environment for proper growth for the twins. In addition to beginning life with low birth weights and having to share their mother's breast milk, the twins did not receive supplementary solid foods on a regular basis until 9 months of age, by which time both were already severely malnourished. The late addition of solids to the diet is typical of this community. Although their father had a steady, salaried job, their mother had little direct access to this income; she was dependent on her husband's good will and could not always count on money for formula to supplement her breast milk. Marital discord led her to return to her first husband's family. Even though the twins belonged to a different patrilineage, her first husband's family welcomed them and provided help with child care, as well as financial and emotional support. The twins responded with substantial catch-up growth and improved health. Al-Hassane's poor nutritional status during the first 2 years of life undoubtedly played a role in his death from measles at the age of 3 years, and Assanatu's early deprivation has led apparently to some mild, but probably permanent, mental deficiencies.

It is interesting to speculate on the different paths taken by these two children. Assanatu seemed to conserve her resources through poorer physical growth. Did this allow her to survive by reserving scarce resources for fighting disease? Did Al-Hassane's strategy of spending resources on growth mean that there were insufficient resources for fighting disease? If so, how do we account for individual or population differences in resource allocation?

Assanatu's functional impairments affect her directly, but they also affect her family and the society at large. She will never be able to make as much of a contribution as she might have if she had been adequately nourished, and this observation holds for many children who survive severe cases of early childhood malnutrition.

Case Study II: Children #76 and #77

Children #76 and #77 were a set of identical twin girls, named Fatoumata and Oumou. They were their mother's first and second children. Their mother, Aminata, was approximately 16 years old, and unmarried. The twins' father, who had not been allowed to marry her, did not contribute anything to their support. Aminata lived in a large compound containing one elderly woman, this woman's four adult sons, and their wives and children. Aminata was the foster child of a wife of one of the adult men in the compound.

I first encountered the twins when they were 14 months of age. They were never officially part of the growth study, but lived in the compound next to a family that was, so I saw them on a regular basis. They were not included in the official growth study for several reasons. First, the original sample was constructed to maximize the spread of families throughout the town, and I tried not to include immediate neighbors. Second, the twins were often so sick and miserable that it seemed unkind to bother them by taking measurements. Third, and most important, I was conducting a naturalistic study of traditional Malian patterns of infant feeding and their effects on growth and development. In this case, I often gave Aminata advice, and occasionally money to buy fish, and for several months I brought her home-made formula (powdered milk, sugar, oil, water). In addition, when the twins had the measles, I bought the ingredients for oral rehydration solution and showed Aminata how to mix and administer it. Thus, the twins' growth after 14 months of age

reflected in part my efforts on their behalf. Their growth data are included in the summary statistics for the sample reported elsewhere. Despite the paucity of growth data, and my interventions, their case is described here because it provides a particularly clear illustration of the constraints placed on women and their children by the social structure of a patrilineal society.

The twins were born at home, so birth weights are not available. I did not measure them when I first met them at 14 months of age. At 15 months of age, during the hot season, both twins caught the measles. Fatoumata had an especially serious case, probably because she was already more severely malnourished than her twin. For two weeks neither twin ate any solid food, and both became dehydrated. I provided oral rehydration solution and tried to convince their mother to take them to the hospital, but she refused. They eventually got better, though it took several months for them to recover fully and begin eating normally again. Following their bout with measles, at 19 months of age, Fatoumata weighed 4.2 kilos, which is more than five standard deviations below the median of the NCHS standards (anything more than 3 SD below the median is considered "severely malnourished"). Her sister Oumou weighed 5.9 kilos, which is between four and five standard deviations below the median. . . .

Although I did not measure their heights, photographs reveal that Fatoumata was already several centimeters shorter than her sister. My field notes from this visit describe them as follows: "reddish hair, no tissue in buttocks or thighs, sunken eyes, sunken fontanelles, sores on their faces, vacant stares, can barely crawl." At 19 months, they could not walk or talk. They were still nursing and eating only a little food, primarily rice or millet breakfast porridge.

Oumou began to walk when she was 24 months old, and Fatoumata at 26 months. At 26 months of age, after intermittent intervention by the author, Fatoumata weighed 7.2 kilos, and Oumou 7.8 kilos. Both of these weights fall between three and four SD below the median. The children were still nursing at this time, and were eating all the adult foods, including rice and millet with various sauces. The mother requested that I stop providing formula, because she "didn't have time to give it to them." At the time, I did not understand this statement, but as the study progressed, the truth of her assertion became apparent. The twins were weaned at 28 months of age, and their mother reported that they ate more food than before being weaned.

The twins were 3 years and 4 months old at the end of the study. They could walk, but not run, could say only the words for "mother" and "water," and spent their days standing listlessly in the doorway of their house. I never measured them again, but a photograph taken at the time, which includes my own daughter, Miranda, aged 3 years and 2 months, shows that they only reach the middle of Miranda's chest, and that Fatoumata, who had been more seriously ill with the measles, was even shorter than Oumou.

What factors contributed to malnutrition in this case? At first, I was inclined to attribute it to their mother's seemingly callous indifference to their welfare. On the scale of "maternal attitude" devised for the larger study (Dettwyler 1985, 1986), she epitomized the "below average" ranking.[2] She had asked me to stop bringing formula because it took too much time to give it to the children. In addition, she said that the children were a burden to her, that she had little chance of marrying with two small children, and that she would be in a better position for getting out of the compound if they died. As I probed into the motivations underlying these statements, the reality of her position in the family and the conditions of her life became clear.

As described earlier, Aminata lived in a compound based around four adult brothers and their elderly mother. When Aminata herself was 3 years old, she had been given to her father's sister as a foster child. A common practice throughout West Africa, child fostering involves sending young children to live with relatives for a variety of reasons (e.g., to provide labor for paternal relatives, to keep an elderly grandmother company in a rural village, or to help a female relative care for a newborn baby). Foster children often have low status in the household, and they may not be accorded the same access to scarce resources as the other children in the family (Bledsoe, Ewbank, and Isiugo-Abanihe 1988; Bledsoe 1991).

After several years, Aminata was passed on again as a foster child, from her aunt to this woman's daughter (her own cousin), who was a young adult at the time. This woman, in turn, had married into the family of four brothers, as the second wife of the third brother. In this strongly patrilineal, age-conscious society, a man's status in the family depends on his birth order, with the oldest surviving brother being the head of the family. Likewise, a woman's status depends both on the status of her husband and on her position as his first, second, third, or fourth wife. Generally speaking, first wives have higher status than later wives. This meant that Aminata was the foster child of the second wife of the third brother in a compound of four adult men. Thus, Aminata was the foster child of a woman who also had low status in the household.

In addition to her low structural position in a large, patrilineal family, Aminata was several years older than any of the children in the family. During 1982 and 1983, she was responsible for the vast majority of the heavy manual labor in the compound, including virtually all of the millet pounding, firewood chopping, water hauling, and clothes washing. She also did the majority of the cooking. Even though there were five other adult women in the household, Aminata was never allowed to rest. Partly to escape the drudgery of her existence, she used to "go out at night" with a group of boys and girls her own age.

When she was 15 years old, Aminata became pregnant by one of her "friends." The adult men of the compound did not approve of this man, and her life became even worse. The birth of twins, usually viewed as a blessing, was an excessive burden for an unmarried, adolescent girl. Her work load did not change while she was pregnant or after the twins were born, and she was routinely beaten by the women of the compound for her indiscretion in becoming pregnant before marriage. Although the twins' father wanted to marry Aminata, her foster fathers would not allow it.

On a relative scale of socioeconomic status, Aminata's compound would be considered "above average" for the community. It contained four adult male wage earners, all of whom were skilled laborers. The compound itself was large, with cement-block houses, and the other children of the family were only mildly malnourished, which is typical of children in the community. Therefore, money was available in the family; Aminata, however, had no access to it. If she needed money to take her children to the doctor or to buy the food I suggested, she had to ask her cousin, who in turn had to ask her husband. These requests were seldom granted. When she had to spend the day at the river washing clothes, she used to leave the children with a friend, because no one at her own compound would watch them for her.

She felt that there was little she could do to change her situation or to improve her children's health given her lack of resources. She really *didn't* have the time to give them formula or to administer oral rehydration solution every 15 minutes when they were dehydrated from measles or diarrhea. Pryer and Crook (1988:19) have noted, "especially during illness when appetite fails, small children need to be fed frequently during the day, which is very time-consuming, and can be especially difficult for mothers from poor families who may have other domestic and economic responsibilities."

Follow-Up In 1989, I returned to Aminata's compound. She was no longer living there, but I was able to relocate her in a neighboring community. According to Aminata, the smaller of the twins, Fatoumata, died in 1984 of malaria. Shortly thereafter, Oumou was sent to live with Aminata's own parents (whom she had not seen in many years) in Mopti, a large port town on the Niger River northeast of Bamako. Once both the twins were "out of the way" (her phrase), Aminata's foster family arranged for her to be married to a man of their choosing.

Since her marriage in 1984, Aminata has had three more children, of whom two survive. The first child, a boy, is now 4 years old. The second, a girl, died in 1986 in Mopti while Aminata was visiting Oumou. According to Aminata, this child died from the measles. That was the last time Aminata saw Oumou, and she has no plans to visit her again. The third child, another boy, is now one year old. The two surviving children have weights and heights that place them in the "mildly malnourished" category.

Aminata reports that she is very happy in her marriage and content with her life. She married into a large extended family with many adult women to share the work. She is the first of two wives of one of the older brothers. The women take turns doing the domestic labor, and she only has to work two days each week. Looking back on her childhood and adolescence, she says that although she had to work very hard, she learned how to do everything well, so that now her life is comparatively easy. She says she tries not to think of Fatoumata and Oumou because it makes her sad. She feels no personal responsibility for Fatoumata's death, or for the death of her younger daughter. When I asked, "Do you think there is anything you could have done to prevent their deaths," she replied, "You can search for medicine, and give your children medicine, but if it is their time, Allah will take them no matter what you do." Aminata does not admit to any bad feelings toward her foster family, or blame them for contributing to Fatoumata's death or Oumou's separation from her.

Fatoumata and Oumou were two of the most severely malnourished children in the study. Their malnutrition, like that of Al-Hassane and Assanatu, had many contributing causes. If Aminata had not been a foster child, or if she had gotten pregnant by a man her foster fathers liked (so they could have been married), if she had had only one child instead of twins, or if the adult women of the compound had helped more with the household labor—if any one of a number of factors had been different, her children would have been healthier. The combination resulted in an impossible situation. As this case clearly illustrates, additional income for the family would not have resulted in any improvement in either her situation or the nutritional status of her children. Additional income and nutritional advice for Aminata, personally provided by the researcher, did not help either, as she had neither the time nor the energy to take care of her children.

Case Study III: Children #62, #62a, and #105

Child #105 was a boy named Umaru, and #62 and #62a were Umaru's nephews Mori and Bakari. Umaru is one of the success stories in Farimabougou, while Mori represents one of the more tragic failures. . . .

Umaru was his parents' fourteenth child, four of whom had died. Umaru contracted polio when he was about 10 months old, and had just recovered from the measles when he entered the study at 18 months of age. At that time, his weight of 8.3 kilos placed him in the "moderately malnourished" category (between 2 and 3 SD below the NCHS median for weight-for-age). His mother, Ma, reported that he had lost a lot of weight because of the measles. He was weaned at 24 months because his mother was pregnant again.

. . . , Umaru gained weight fairly steadily over the course of the study, and his last weight of 11.3 kilos at 32 months, while still below the fifth percentile of NCHS standards, placed him in the "mildly malnourished" category typical of children in the community. In the original study, Ma was classified as "above average" in terms of maternal attitude. She was very devoted to her children. Because of his polio, she regularly took Umaru to the Chinese hospital at Kati, about 15 kilometers distant, for acupuncture treatments and physical therapy, and she spent many hours working with him at home to teach him to walk. She was very upset by the death of her first grandchild (#62, below), and distraught by the stillbirth of her own fifteenth child. This child, after 10 months of gestation, died during labor and had to be removed by Caesarian section. Her doctor warned her that she should not have any more children. Even though she had given birth to 15 children, and had 10 still surviving, she was sad that she would not be having more. While Ma was recuperating from surgery, her husband took over the cooking, clothes washing, and other domestic chores, actions that are highly atypical for Malian men. Umaru's father was devoted to his children and optimistic that Umaru would recover fully from the effects of polio.

Mori (#62) was his mother's first child. His mother, Sali, was Ma's oldest daughter, so Mori was Umaru's nephew. At birth, Mori weighed 3.9 kilos, which is above the ninetieth percentile of NCHS standards. Mori was weaned at 13 months of age, which is very early for this community, because his mother was pregnant again. When he entered the study at 15 months of age, his weight was 7.9 kilos, placing him in the "moderately malnourished" category. . . .

During the next month, Mori came down with the measles and spent 18 days in the hospital in Bamako, where he was fed through a subclavicular IV. At my next visit, when he was 16 months old, he had been home from the hospital for only a few days. His mother reported that, since coming home, he had "refused to eat" and would only drink a little water. During my visits, timed to coincide with meals, she made little effort to encourage him to eat or drink. She was not particularly interested in my suggestions for helping Mori eat, preferring to talk about her current pregnancy.

At 16 months, Mori's weight had dropped to 6.7 kilos. At 17 months, it had dropped again, to 6.4 kilos, which is more than four standard deviations below the median. When I came to remeasure him at 18 months, I was told that he had died several weeks before. During my last visit, after Mori's death, I witnessed a bitter exchange between Ma and Sali. Ma, Mori's grandmother, was sharply critical of her daughter, saying that she was not a good mother, did not care about her children, and was not willing to do what was necessary to keep them alive. Sali ignored her mother, replying that she (Sali) was young and did things the "modern" way. She blamed Mori's death on the measles and his own refusal to eat. She did not see any connection between the fact that Mori had been weaned early because of her subsequent pregnancy and his death from measles/malnutrition, and she felt no responsibility for his lack of food intake after his release from the hospital.

The fact that she had weaned Mori very early because of her subsequent pregnancy indicated that she and her husband were not observing the traditional postpartum sex taboo (until the baby is weaned, or at least until he can walk well). Her husband was a recent migrant from a rural village, and the only member of his family to migrate. When I first met them, the young couple was living with her parents, since the husband had no patrilineal relatives in the community. Shortly after Mori died, the couple moved out because of "arguments" between mother and daughter and moved in with friends of the father's who lived across town. The grandmother was not informed where they had moved, and they were lost to the study for more than a year.

According to Sali's father, his son-in-law was able to "get away" with not observing the traditional taboos, as well as with misguided allocation of scarce household resources, because he had no older agnates to put pressure on him. The fact that he was a recent migrant to the city, and the sole migrant from his fam-

ily, suggests that he may have been overwhelmed by the opportunities of urban life and was not mature or responsible enough to forego personal pleasure for the health of his children. Certainly in a rural village, a young man of his age would not be in charge of his own compound and would not be allowed to make the kinds of choices he made. In addition, in a small rural village, the young couple would not have been able to simply pick up and move away, but would have had to stay under the supervision of elders with more experience. As Gokulanathan and Verghese note, "The gradual break-up of the extended family units under the influence of the wage economy and the movement of people produce changes in the family hierarchy. The authoritative person in the family may be a wage earning member, usually a younger person who may not be sufficiently informed about *either* the traditional ways *or* modern methods (Foster, 1962)" (Gokulanathan and Verghese 1969:123).

. . .

In the case of Umaru, we find very different circumstances from those of the other children described in these case studies. Umaru's mother was happily married, an experienced, older mother with 10 healthy surviving children. Her first eight children had been born in a rural village, and she was deeply suspicious of urban mores. Despite suffering from both polio and measles, Umaru has survived, even flourished. Although his family's income was only "average" for the community, and there were many other children to feed (Umaru had seven old siblings still at home), Umaru had exceptional parents. They were devoted to each other and to their children, and did not own any of the symbols of "modern" life such as a moped, a bicycle, or even a radio. If primary health care and health education in Mali had been better when Umaru was an infant, he probably would have been vaccinated against measles and polio.

By contrast, Sali's maternal attitude was defined as clearly "below average." She was inexperienced as a mother and rejected the traditional values epitomized by her parents. Her antagonism toward her mother, and the fact that her mother was recovering from a traumatic Caesarian still birth, made it unlikely that she would or could ask her mother for help or advice. Her focus was on her husband and on the acquisition of expensive symbols of modern, urban life, including a moped and multiple sets of fancy clothes. In Mori's malnutrition and subsequent death, many factors were at work. If even one had been different, he might have survived. As it was, the combination of inexperienced parents, early weaning, measles, traditional infant feeding practices, and poor maternal (and paternal) attitude were fatal.

CONCLUSIONS

Under certain circumstances, it may be possible to point to one factor as being primarily responsible for malnutrition in a community. Droughts, famines, warfare, and refugee camps garner worldwide attention and represent obvious single-cause reasons for widespread malnutrition in particular instances. For example, the relatively high rates of severe malnutrition in northern Mali following the drought of 1984–85 can be attributed to the failure of the rains and the subsequent devastation of animal herds on which the populations relied for subsistence.

Unfortunately for change agents and development agencies (and, of course, for the affected populations), the vast majority of malnutrition in Third World populations does not have one primary cause. Nor does it have a simple solution. If alleviating malnutrition were only a matter of increasing household income, providing nutrition education for all mothers, implementing family planning programs, or immunizing all children under five against the major childhood diseases, it would be difficult enough. But the widespread chronic mild and moderate malnutrition that affects Third World children under "normal" conditions is the result of an intricate web of interacting factors.

Without the constraint of poverty, Malian women such as Jeneba and Aminata would not have to stay in untenable household situations, and Sali and her husband would not have had to choose between gas for the moped and food for the children. Without the constraint of social institutions such as child fosterage, polygyny, patrilineality, and arranged marriages, girls would not find themselves in positions like Aminata's. Without traditional infant feeding practices such as weaning as soon as the mother gets pregnant again, and letting children themselves decide whether and how much they want to eat, children like Mori might not die. Without the stress of measles, compounded by the high temperatures of the hot season, or the stress of malaria during the rainy season, malnutrition by itself would not be so devastating. Without the constraint of inadequate primary health care, measles and malaria themselves would not be so serious a threat. Without the constraint of a contaminated environment due to the complete lack of sewage and garbage disposal, children would not get diarrhea so often. Without the constraints imposed by lack of running water and electricity, women would not have to spend hours every day hauling water, chopping firewood, and pounding millet, and would thus have more time and energy to devote to child care activities.

Given the conditions of life under which periurban Malian women raise children, it is surprising that

the majority of children are *only* mildly malnourished. Like the cases described here, in many instances where children are severely malnourished it is because they have fallen through the safety net of overlapping support systems that normally ensure a minimal level of nutrition and health for children in the community. Rather than be chagrined when children fall through the cracks, one must be impressed with the number of children for whom the system works.

These three case studies are typical of the histories collected during the original 1982–83 study and the 1989 follow-up study. The details of each child's situation differed, but in every case of severe malnutrition, a variety of biological, social, and cultural factors contributed to the child's poor growth. Conversely, for those children who were growing much better than the average for this population, their household situations included few or none of the constraining factors faced by the women described above.

As the case studies presented here reveal, a truly integrated, biocultural approach in nutritional anthropology, including longitudinal case histories of individual children and of populations, is necessary if we are to understand all of the interactions between culture and biology that result in observed patterns of nutritional status, growth and development, morbidity, and mortality, and to use this understanding to design successful intervention programs to improve child health. It may not be possible, or necessary, to specify the exact contribution of each strand to the web, as they will be different for every child. It *is* possible to study and describe the web of causation, made up of many different factors that affect child growth and child health. To do so, however, requires that researchers begin from a biocultural perspective and have adequate training in both quantitative and qualitative research methodologies, training that enables them to see the faces behind the numbers.

Approaches such as "rapid ethnographic assessment" (Bentley, Pelto, and Straus 1988) can provide only a limited understanding of the causes of malnutrition in any particular community. Likewise, it is of little value to attempt to reduce the complex causes of malnutrition to one or two easily measurable factors, such as "socioeconomic status," "housing type," or "maternal educational level." In particular, researchers interested in alleviating childhood malnutrition must get beyond simplistic measures of socioeconomic status, and realize that all poor people are not the same—differences in individual and family circumstances have important effects on the health, nutritional status, and survival of children. Not all family members have equal access to the household's resources, nor do all parents put children's needs first. Finally, it is misleading, and ultimately futile, to think that malnutrition can be alleviated by any one "magic bullet" such as oral rehydration solution, Vitamin A enrichment, or breastfeeding promotion campaigns. To save a child from death by diarrhea today using oral rehydration solution, so that he can die tomorrow from malaria, is not a significant improvement. To increase family income, only to have that income spent on costly consumer goods or prestigious but nutritionally inferior "Western" foods, will not improve the nutritional status of children.

Policy planners must acknowledge that malnutrition has no easy solution. Programs to improve child health must address many, if not all, of the causes of malnutrition, including the difficult issues of the status of women in patrilineal societies and the disruptive forces of modernization. At the same time that multistranded programs to eliminate risk factors are implemented, other programs must be designed that strengthen the various strands of the safety net already operating in every community to ensure that more children survive and prosper.

NOTES

1. Birth certificates are filled out at the maternity clinic at the time of birth. If a child is not born at the clinic, he or she must be taken to the clinic within three days to register the birth. Therefore, the birth certificates are assumed to be accurate. Parents occasionally forge a birth certificate to enable a child to begin school before the official age of 8 years, but this practice did not affect the young children involved in this sample.
2. The "maternal attitude" scale divides mothers into three categories of "average," "above average," and "below average." A mother with an "above average" maternal attitude is one who always makes sure her child is awake and present at meals, fixes foods that the child especially likes, buys him extra food on a regular basis, takes him to the doctor when he is sick, and purchases the prescribed medications. A mother with a "below average" maternal attitude is one who lets her child sleep or play through meals, does not cater to his food preferences or buy him extra food, and is less likely to consult medical personnel when he is sick, spend money for prescribed medicines, or administer medications consistently.

REFERENCES

Bentley, M. E., G. H. Pelto, and W. L. Straus. 1988. Rapid Ethnographic Assessment: Applications in a Diarrhea Management Program. Soc. Sci. Med. 27(1):107–116.

Bledsoe, C. 1991. The Trickle-Down Model Within Households: Foster Children and the Phenomenon of Scrounging. In The Health Transition: Methods and Measures. Health Transition Series No. 3. J. Cleland and A. G. Hill, eds. Pp. 115–131. Canberra: Australian National University Press.

Bledsoe, C. H., D. C. Ewbank, and U. C. Isiugo-Abanihe. 1988. The Effect of Child Fostering on Feeding Practices and Access to Health Services in Rural Sierra Leone. Soc. Sci. Med. 27(6):627–636.

Clairin, R., et al. 1967. L'Alimentation des Populations Rurales du Delta Vif du Niger et de l'Office du Niger. M.I.S.O.E.S. 1967 [cited in May 1968].

Daniggelis, E. 1987a. Infant Feeding Practices and Nutritional Status. Paper presented at the annual meeting of the American Anthropological Association, Chicago.

———. 1987b. Cash Fishing and Subsistence Plantations: The Impact of a Global-Economy on Samoan Children's Growth. M.A. thesis, Department of Anthropology, University of Hawaii.

Dettwyler, K. A. 1985. Breastfeeding, Weaning, and Other Infant Practices in Mali and Their Effects on Growth and Development. Ph.D. dissertation, Indiana University, Bloomington. Ann Arbor: University Microfilms.

———. 1986. Infant Feeding in Mali, West Africa: Variations in Belief and Practice. Soc. Sci. Med. 23(7):651–664.

———. 1987. Breastfeeding and Weaning in Mali: Cultural Context and Hard Data. Soc. Sci. Med. 24(8):633–644.

———. 1989a. The Interaction of Anorexia and Cultural Beliefs in Infant Malnutrition in Mali. American Journal of Human Biology 1(6):683–695.

———. 1989b. Styles of Infant Feeding: Parental/Caretaker Control of Food Consumption in Young Children. American Anthropologist 91(3):696–703.

de Vries, M. W. 1987. Cry Babies, Culture, and Catastrophe: Infant Temperament Among the Masai. In Child Survival: Anthropological Perspectives on the Treatment and Maltreatment of Children. N. Scheper-Hughes, ed. Pp. 165–185. Boston: D. Reidel Publishing Company.

Diakite, S. 1968. Nutrition in Mali. In Proceedings of the West African Conference on Nutrition and Child Feeding. Pp. 87–97. Dakar, Senegal. Washington, DC: United States Department of Health, Education, and Welfare, Public Health Service.

Gokulanathan, K. S., and K. P. Verghese. 1969. Socio-Cultural Malnutrition (Growth Failure in Children due to Socio-Cultural Factors). J. Trop. Pediatr. 15:118–124.

Guldan, G. S. 1988. Maternal Education and Child Caretaking Practices in Rural Bangladesh: Part 1, Child Feeding Practices: Part 2, Food and Personal Hygiene. Ph.D. dissertation, School of Nutrition, Tufts Univerity.

Hamill, P. V. V., T. A. Drizd, C. L. Johnson, R. B. Reed, A. F. Roche, and W. M. Moore. 1979. Physical Growth: National Center for Health Statistics Percentiles. Am J. Clin. Nutr. 32:607–629.

Hull, V., and M. Simpson, eds. 1985. Breastfeeding, Child Health and Child Spacing: Cross-cultural Perspectives. London: Croom Helm.

Imperato, J. P. 1977. African Folk Medicine: Practices and Beliefs of the Bambara and Other Peoples. Baltimore: York Press, Inc.

Marshall, L. B., ed. 1985. Infant Care and Feeding in the South Pacific. New York: Gordon and Breach.

May, J. M. 1968. The Ecology of Malnutrition in the French Speaking Countries of West Africa and Madagascar. New York: Hafner.

Mondot-Bernard, J., and M. Labonne. 1982. Satisfaction of Food Requirements in Mali to 2000 A.D. Paris: Development Centre of the Organization for Economic Co-operation and Development.

Mull, D., and D. Mull. 1987. Infanticide Among the Tarahumara of the Mexican Sierra Madre. *In* Child Survival: Anthropological Perspectives on the Treatment and Maltreatment of Children. N. Scheper-Hughes, ed. Pp. 113–132. Boston: D. Reidel Publishing Company.

N'Diaye, B. 1970. Groupes ethniques au Mali. Bamako: Edition Populaires.

Pryer, J., and N. Crook. 1988. Cities of Hunger: Urban Malnutrition in Developing Countries. Oxford: Oxfam.

Scheper-Hughes, N. 1987. Culture, Scarcity, and Maternal Thinking: Mother Love and Child Death in Northeast Brazil. *In* Child Survival: Anthropological Perspectives on the Treatment and Maltreatment of Children. N. Scheper-Hughes, ed. Pp. 187–208. Boston: D. Reidel Publishing Company.

Stini, W. A. 1985. Growth Rates and Sexual Dimorphism in Evolutionary Perspective. *In* The Analysis of Prehistoric Diets. R. I. Gilbert and J. H. Mielke, eds. Pp. 191–226. New York: Academic Press.

Stinson, S. 1985. Sex Differences in Environmental Sensitivity During Growth and Development. Yearbook of Physical Anthropology 28:123–147.

World Bank, Document of the. 1979. Report and Recommendations of the President of the International Development Association to the Executive Director on a Proposed Credit to the Republic of Mali for an Urban Development Project. June 12, 1979. Report WP-2595-MLI.

Zeitlin, M., and G. S. Guldan. 1988. Appendix IIC Bangladesh Infant Feeding Observations. *In* Maternal Education and Child Caretaking Practices in Rural Bangladesh: Part 1, Child Feeding Practices; Part 2, Food and Personal Hygiene, p. 106. Ph.D. dissertation, School of Nutrition, Tufts University.

Zeitlin, M., H. Ghassemi, and M. Monsour. 1990. Positive Deviance in Child Nutrition. Tokyo: United Nations University Press.

✤ 42

An Anthropological Perspective on Obesity

Peter J. Brown
Melvin Konner

The subject of this selection is another kind of malnutrition in sharp contrast to the undernourished children in Mali in the previous selection. Obesity is a large problem in the developed world, especially in societies like the United States. Excess fat carries with it increased risk for cardiovascular disease, stroke, and certain kinds of cancer. As we saw in earlier selections about the diet of our prehistoric ancestors (selections 2 and 7), most humans never lived with a predictable food surplus. Obesity was never a possibility for our ancestors, just as excessive fatness is not a worry for people currently living in the poorer countries of the world.

In U.S. society, fat is a major concern for many people. Weight loss is a huge industry—and a profitable one, because studies show that most weight lost through dieting is eventually regained. Fear of fatness is an important factor in a simultaneous epidemic of anorexia nervosa and other eating disorders among young women generally from afflu-

ent families (Brumberg 1988). From a psychological standpoint, obesity and anorexia might be seen as flip sides of the same cultural coin. Overweight people face stigma and discrimination, whereas others are never satisfied with their weight and are literally dying to be thin. Obviously, questions of fat and thin are much more than purely biological and medical issues. In recent years there have been a number of excellent medical anthropological and feminist studies of the questions of eating disorders in contemporary America (Bordo 1993; Condit 1990).

This selection is an example of the biocultural approach to medical anthropology. It explores the interaction of genes and culture in an evolutionary context, and it argues that many human populations are predisposed to the problem of obesity. This is because humans evolved in environments that were prone to food shortages. In such contexts, individuals who are able to store energy reserves in the form of fat might be at a selective advantage. For many people throughout the world, these food shortages still exist, as we saw in selection 41. The problem of hunger also continues to plague rich countries like the United States, but some people are hungry because they are dieting and others are hungry because their food stamps have run out. The United States is a highly stratified society with huge differences in access to resources between rich and poor. In general, however, there is food in abundance so that it is easy for even the poor to become fat. As a consequence, because status markers must by definition be difficult to achieve, being thin ironically may become a symbolic marker of wealth. This selection explores the cultural meanings of the perfect body from a cross-cultural perspective. As is often the case, an anthropological perspective allows us to view a contemporary problem in a new way.

As you read this selection, consider these questions:

- *Why is central body fatness more of a risk for chronic disease than peripheral body fatness? What are the implications of this for gender differences in obesity?*
- *How might obesity be culturally constructed?*
- *Can you think of ways that the anthropological approach to obesity might yield practical suggestions to chronic disease prevention programs?*
- *What are some similarities and differences between this analysis and the Stone Agers in the fast lane argument of selection 2?*
- *Why do you think plumpness is a marker of beauty for women in so many other cultures? What does this tell us about cross-cultural standards of beauty?*

An anthropological approach to human obesity involves both an evolutionary and a cross-cultural dimension. That is, it attempts to understand how the human predisposition to obesity so evident in modern affluent societies may have been determined during our species' long evolutionary history as hunters and gatherers, as well as the variation in obesity prevalence in different societies, social classes, or ethnic groups.

The evolutionary success of *Homo sapiens* is best understood by reference to the operation of natural selection on our dual system of inheritance; that is, on genes and culture, but also, and perhaps especially, on their interaction. Human biology and culture are the product of adaptation to environmental constraints; traits that enhance an individual's ability to survive and reproduce should become common in human societies. In this view, the health and illness of a population can be conceived as measures of biocultural adaptation to a particular ecological setting. Changing patterns of morbidity and mortality, such as the epidemiological transition from infectious to chronic diseases, are the result of historical changes in lifestyle (*i.e.* culture) that affect health.

It is valuable to view obesity from this evolutionary perspective because of its great historical scope. The first appearance of the genus *Homo* occurred over two million years ago, and the first anatomically modern humans (*Homo sapiens sapiens*) became predominant about 40,000 years ago.[1] From either prehistoric point of departure, during most of human history, the exclusive cultural pattern was one of hunting and gathering. This original human lifestyle is rare, but a few such groups have been the subject of detailed anthropological study.[2]

Culture, in an anthropological sense, entails learned patterns of behavior and belief characteristic of a particular society. This second dimension of the anthropological perspective includes variables demonstrably related to the prevalence of obesity in a particular group—material aspects of lifestyle, like diet and productive economy—as well as more idealistic variables, the relationship of which to obesity is more speculative—such as aesthetic standards of ideal body type or the symbolic meaning of fatness.

Cross-cultural comparison thus serves two purposes, one relating to each of the two dimensions. First, technologically simple or primitive societies provide ethnographic analogies to amplify our understanding of prehistoric periods, or to test hypotheses about biocultural evolution. Such societies provide useful analogies to prehistoric societies, particularly in terms of economic production and diet. Second, cross-cultural comparison allows us to see our own society's health problems and cultural beliefs about health in a new way. In a heterogeneous society like the United States, where particular social groups have markedly high prevalences of obesity, attention to cultural variation in beliefs and behaviors has practical value for medicine. Going beyond the U.S. to the numerous cultural varieties in the anthropological record gives us a fascinating range of further variation for systematic analysis. Such analysis is likely to reveal relationships that may not appear in other approaches, and attention to this wider range of cultures becomes even more relevant as obesity becomes a factor in international health.

In this paper we argue that throughout most of human history, obesity was never a common health problem, nor was it a realistic possibility for most people. This was because, despite the qualitative adequacy of their diet, most primitive societies have been regularly subjected to food shortages. Scarcity has been a powerful agent of natural selection in human biocultural evolution. Both genes and cultural traits that may have been adaptive in the context of past food scarcities today play a role in the etiology of maladaptive adult obesity in affluent societies. Following this evolutionary argument about the origins of obesity, we turn our attention to the cross-cultural range of beliefs about ideal body characteristics and the social meanings of obesity. A prerequisite for both discussions is a review of some basic facts concerning the social epidemiology of obesity.

HUMAN OBESITY: THREE SOCIAL EPIDEMIOLOGICAL FACTS

Humans are among the fattest of all mammals;[3] the proportion of fat to total body mass ranges from approximately 10 percent in the very lean to over 35 percent in the obese.[4] In other mammals, the primary function of fat deposits is insulation from cold, but in humans, it is now widely accepted that much (but not all) fat serves as an energy reserve. The social distribution of adiposity within and between human populations is not random, and that distribution provides a key to understanding obesity. Three widely recognized social epidemiological facts about obesity are particularly salient for this discussion: (1) higher levels of fatness and risk of obesity in females represents a fundamental aspect of sexual dimorphism in *Homo sapiens*; (2) obesity is rare in unacculturated primitive populations, but the prevalence often increases rapidly during modernization; and (3) the prevalence of obesity is related to social class, usually positively; but among females in affluent societies, that relationship is inverted.

Obesity and Gender

Differences in fat deposition are an important aspect of sexual dimorphism in *Homo sapiens*.[5] Sexual dimorphism is found in many primate species, and it is more pronounced in terrestrial, polygynous species. Humans are only mildly dimorphic in morphological variables like stature; a survey of human populations around the world reveals a range of dimorphism in stature from 4.7 to 9.0 percent.[6] The most significant

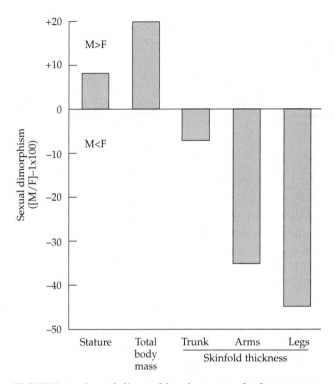

FIGURE 1   Sexual dimorphism in stature, body mass, and fat measures among white Americans aged 20 to 70 in Tecumseh, Michigan. Sexual dimorphism calculated by comparing male versus female means by ([M/F] −1 × 100); positive figures refer to greater male measures. Data are from Bailey.[4] Skinfold thicknesses are means of 4 sites (trunk) or 5 sites (arms and legs/thighs); the mean sexual dimorphism in all 17 fat measures is −19%.

aspects of sexual dimorphism reside predominantly in soft tissue. On average for young adults in an affluent society, adipose tissue constitutes approximately 15 percent of body weight in males and about 27 percent in females.[4]

Fatness, particularly peripheral or limb body fat, is the most dimorphic of the morphological variables, as shown in Figure 1. Adult men are larger than women in stature (+8%) and total body mass (+20%), whereas women have more subcutaneous fat as measured in skinfold thicknesses. Bailey's analysis of sex differences in body composition using data from white Americans in Tecumseh, Michigan show greater female skinfolds in 16 of 17 measurement sites (the exception is the suprailiac). In general, adult limb fatness was much more dimorphic than trunk fatness: trunk: −7.5% (mean of 5 measures); arms: −35.4% (mean of 4 measures); and legs/thighs: −46.7% (mean of 5 measures).[4]

It is noteworthy that peripheral body fat does not have the same close association with chronic diseases (*i.e.* Type II diabetes mellitus or hypertension) as

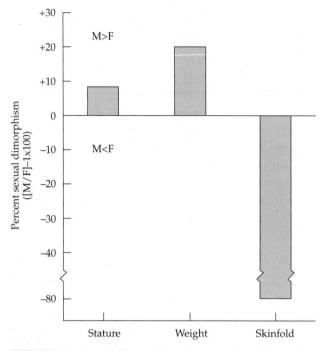

FIGURE 2   Sexual dimorphism in stature, weight, and mid-triceps skinfolds among !Kung San hunter-gatherers of Botswana. Sample includes 527 men and women, aged 10–80, all living in a traditional lifestyle. Sexual dimorphism calculated by comparing male versus female means by ([M/F]−1 × 100); positive figures refer to greater male measures. Note the larger male/female difference in fat than among white Americans shown in Figure 1.

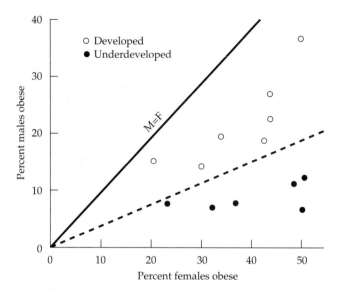

FIGURE 3   Gender differences in prevalence of obesity in 14 populations by general economic development. Only complete society prevalences were used, and underdeveloped populations were limited to groups with a significant degree of obesity. Operational definitions of obesity differ between studies. Populations include: Pukapuka, Rarotonga and New Zealand urban Maori,[13] Capetown Bantu, Guyana, Lagos (Nigeria), Puerto Rico, Germany, London,[12] U.S. Blacks, and U.S. Whites.[16] The unbroken line demarcates equal male/female obesity rates. The broken line indicates an apparent division between the proportion of gender difference in obesity between developed and underdeveloped countries.

centripetal or trunk fatness. Thus the sexual dimorphism in fat deposition may be unrelated to the dimension of obesity that most affects health. The developmental course of this dimorphism is also of interest. It is present in childhood, but increases markedly during adolescence, due to greatly increased divergence in the rate of fat gain.[7] Thus this divergence occurs at the time of reproductive maturation.

Although there is some population-specific variation in fat distribution, human sexual dimorphism in overall fat and peripheral fat appears to be universal. Although very small in stature and extremely lean by worldwide standards, the !Kung San, a hunting and gathering society of the Kalahari desert, show a similar pattern of sexual dimorphism, with a pronounced difference in measures of subcutaneous fat for women (see Figure 2). The sexual dimorphism of the !Kung San is about +6.7% for stature, +20% in weight, and −80% in midtriceps skinfolds.[8]

Sex differences are also seen in the prevalence of obesity. Despite methodological differences in the operational definition of obesity and in sampling frameworks, data from the 14 populations shown in Figure 3 show that in all of the surveys, females have a higher prevalence of obesity than males. Variations in the male/female ratio of proportions of obesity seen in this figure reveal a new regularity that remains to be explained—namely, that more affluent western populations have more equivalent male/female ratios of obesity prevalence than poor populations in the underdeveloped world.

Obesity and Modernization

The second social epidemiological fact regards culture change and the origins of obesity. It is significant that anthropometric studies of traditional hunting and gathering populations report no obesity. By contrast, numerous studies of traditional societies undergoing the process of modernization (or Westernization) report rapid increases in the prevalence of obesity.[9–12] A classic natural experiment study by Prior and colleagues compared the diet and health of Polynesian islanders at different stages of acculturation: the prevalence of obesity in the most traditional island

(Pukapuka) was 15.4%; for a rapidly modernizing population (Rarotonga), it was 29.3%; and for urban Maoris it was 35.4 percent.[13] Trowell and Burkitt, whose recent volume contains 15 case studies of societies experiencing increased obesity and associated Western diseases during modernization, conclude that obesity is the first of these diseases of civilization to appear.[14]

Change in diet appears to be a primary cause for the link between modernization and obesity. More precisely, westernization of traditional diets involves decreased intake of fiber and increased intake of fats and sugar. The seeming inevitability of this change toward a less healthy diet is impressive but not well understood. We suspect that more is involved in this dietary change than the simple imitation of prestigious western foodways: the quick shift from primitive to high fat, high sugar diets with the advent of affluence may have evolutionary roots.

Obesity and Social Class

The third and possibly most important fact concerning the social epidemiology of obesity is its association with social class and ethnicity. Research primarily by Stunkard and colleagues have shown that social class and obesity are inversely related, at least in heterogeneous and affluent societies like the United States.[15,16] The inverse correlation of social class and obesity is very strong, particularly for females. A few studies, however, have found a weak association of class and obesity for groups including men, children, and certain ethnic groups.[17] But there is no doubt that social factors play a role in the epidemiology of obesity, and that the high prevalence of obesity for lower class women reflects that, "obesity may always be unhealthy, but it is not always abnormal."[15]

The association between socioeconomic class and obesity among adult women, therefore, merits special attention. This association is not constant through the life cycle. Garn and Clark describe a pattern of growth called "the socioeconomic reversal of fatness in females": in childhood, middle and upper class girls (and boys) are consistently fatter than poorer girls; at around the time of puberty, the relative level of fatness in the two groups switches; and in adulthood, lower class women are consistently fatter than middle and upper class women.[18]

In the traditional societies typically studied by anthropologists, the social epidemiology of adult obesity is not well documented. The data indirectly suggest, however, that the relationship of obesity and social class is often a positive one. Surveys from developing countries show a positive association between social

class and obesity prevalence and, as expected, an inverse correlation between class and protein-calorie malnutrition.[19]

EVOLUTION AND OBESITY: DIET, FOOD SCARCITIES, AND ADAPTATION

Both genes and lifestyle are involved in the etiology of obesity, although the relative importance of either factor, and the ways in which they interact, are not thoroughly understood.[20] We suggest that both genetic and cultural predispositions to obesity may be products of the same evolutionary pressures, involving two related processes: first, traits that cause fatness were selected because they improved chances of survival in the face of food scarcities, particularly for pregnant and nursing women; second, fatness may have been directly selected because it is a cultural symbol of social prestige and an index of general health.

Cultural Evolution from Food Foraging to Food Production

For 95 to 99 percent of our history, humans lived exclusively as hunters and gatherers. Studies of contemporary food foragers reveal some cultural and biological commonalities despite variation in their ecological context. Food foragers live in small, socially flexible, seminomadic bands; experience slow population growth due to prolonged nursing and high childhood mortality; enjoy high quality diets and spend proportionately little time directly involved in food collection; and are generally healthier and better nourished than many contemporary third world populations relying on agriculture.

The reality of food foraging life is to be found somewhere between the Hobbesian "nasty, brutish, and short" and the "original affluent society," a phrase popularized by some anthropologists during the 1960s.[21] It is important to dispel romantic notions of food foragers, like the !Kung San of Botswana, as innocents leading a carefree existence; they suffer from a 50 percent child mortality rate, a low life expectancy at birth, and even a homicide rate that rivals that of many metropolitan areas. Yet, given the length of time that it has survived, food foraging must be considered a successful strategy of adaptation.

Approximately 12,000 years ago, some human groups shifted from a food foraging economy to one of food production. This shift required the domestication

TABLE 1   Late Paleolithic, Contemporary American, and Currently Recommended Dietary Composition[26]

	Late Paleolithic Diet	Contemporary American Diet	Current Recommendations
Total dietary energy (percent)			
Protein	34	12	12
Carbohydrate	45	46	58
Fat	21	42	30
P : S ratio[a]	1.41	0.44	1.00
Cholesterol (mg)	591	600	300
Fiber (gm)	45.7	19.7	30–60
Sodium (mg)	690	2300–6900	1100–3300
Calcium (mg)	1580	740	800–1200
Ascorbic Acid (mg)	392.3	87.7	45

[a] Polyunsaturated: saturated fat ratio.

of plants and animals, an evolutionary process in which humans acted as agents of selection for domestic phenotypes. This economic transformation, known as the neolithic revolution, may be considered the most important event in human history because it allowed population growth and the evolution of complex societies and civilization. The current consensus among archeologists is that the new economy based on agriculture was something that people were effectively forced to adopt because of ecological pressures from population growth and food scarcities.[22] Nearly everywhere it has been studied, the switch from food foraging to agriculture is associated with osteological evidence of nutritional stress, poor health, and diminished stature.[23]

It is important to note that the beginning of agriculture is linked to the emergence of social stratification. Civilization was made possible by the political, economic, and military power of urban elites over agricultural surpluses collected in the form of tribute. For members of the ruling class, social stratification has numerous advantages, the most important of which is guaranteed access to food during periods of relative food scarcity. In state level societies, nutritional stress is never evenly distributed across the social spectrum. Functionally, the poor insulate the rich from the threat of starvation.

Obesity is thus not simply a disease of civilization. It is common only in certain kinds of civilized societies—ones with an absolute level of affluence so that even the poor have access to enough food to become obese. Trowell has suggested that obesity became common in Europe, first in elites and then the rest of society, only about 200 years ago.[24]

The Adequacy of Preindustrial Diets

The adequacy of the diet of food foragers, and by close analogy that of our prehistoric ancestors, has been the subject of considerable interest. New analytical techniques now being applied to skeletal populations by archeologists are expanding our knowledge of prehistoric diet.[25] A recent analysis of the nutritional components of the Paleolithic diet,[26] shown in Table 1, suggests that the diet of prehistoric food foragers was high in protein, fiber, and vegetable carbohydrates and low in sugar and saturated fats. There are striking similarities of this reconstructed stone age diet and the daily nutritional requirements recommended by the U.S. Senate Select Committee, in all areas except cholesterol intake. With this exception, the Paleolithic diet could be considered a model preventive diet, more stringent and thus probably more healthy even than the currently recommended one. But this fact reflects limitations in the availability and choice of foods rather than some primitive wisdom about a nutritionally optimal diet. Studies of culture change have repeatedly shown that when traditional populations with healthy diets have the opportunity, they readily switch to the less healthy (except in terms of abundance) Western diets.

Another method of estimation of the adequacy of the preindustrial diet is through cross-cultural comparison. Marjorie Whiting used ethnographic data from the Human Relations Area Files (HRAF) and nutritional studies to survey some major components of diet in a representative sample of 118 nonindustrial societies with economies based on food-foraging, pastoralism, simple horticulture, and agriculture.[27] (The HRAF is a compilation of ethnographic information on over 300 of the most thoroughly studied societies in the anthropological and historical record, cross-indexed for hundreds of variables. Subsamples of societies are chosen for representativeness of world areas and economic types.) In general, the quality of nonindustrial diets is high, the mean percent of calories derived from fat and carbohydrates falling within the recommended U.S. standards, and the percentage of protein nearly twice the recommended amount.[26] For the 84% of societies where food supply is adequate or plentiful, therefore, the diet seems superior to that of the United States. The major inadequacy of preindustrial diets and productive economies, however, is their susceptibility to food shortages.

The Ubiquity of Food Shortages

Food shortages have been so common in human prehistory and history that they could be considered a virtually inevitable fact of life in the past. Whiting's cross-cultural survey found some form of food shortages for all of the societies in the sample. . . . In 28.7 percent of the societies, food shortages are rare, occurring every 10 to 15 years, whereas in 24.3 percent they happen every 2 to 3 years. Shortages occur annually or even more frequently in 47 percent of the societies. Half of these are annual shortfalls, which Whiting described as happening "a few weeks preceding harvest, anticipated and expected, recognized as temporary," and in the other 23.5 percent of the societies, shortages are more frequent than once a year. This distribution has great evolutionary significance.

. . . For the 113 societies with adequate data, 29.3 percent had severe shortages that were characterized by the exhaustion of emergency foods, many people desperate for food, and starvation deaths—in short, a famine. Moderate shortages, in which food stores were used up, where emergency foods were used, and where people lost considerable weight, were found in 34.4 percent of the societies. Finally, 36.3 percent had mild food shortages, with fewer meals than usual, some weight loss, but no great hardships.[27] Two examples, one archeological and one ethnographic, will serve to illustrate these patterns and their relationship to the relative reliance on food foraging or food production.

The southwestern United States, where we today find Native American groups like the Pima, with endemic obesity and a high prevalence of type II diabetes,[28] was in the prehistoric past the frequent site of food shortages. Tree-ring analysis has been used to calculate the frequency of ecological stresses and resulting food shortages affecting these people, the builders of the impressive kivas and cliff dwellings. The data from southern New Mexico suggest that, between 600 and 1249 A.D., every other year had inadequate rainfall for dry farming, and that there was severe stress (more than two successive years of total crop failures) at least once every 25 years.[29] The complex agricultural societies of the prehistoric southwest expanded quickly during a period of uncharacteristically good weather. Despite a variety of social adaptations to food shortages, when lower rainfall pattern resumed, the complex chiefdomships could not be maintained: the population declined, and the culture devolved back to food foraging.

Medical studies of the !Kung San hunter-gatherers have found that adults were in generally good health, but exhibited periodic mild caloric undernutrition.[30] Seasonal variation in the availability of food resulted in an annual cycle of weight loss and weight gain in both food-foraging and food-producing societies. Agriculturalists, however, experience greater seasonal swings of weight loss and gain. Seasonal weight loss among the !Kung, although it varied by ecological region and year, averaged between 1 and 2 percent of adult body weight.[8,31] Seasonal weight losses among African agriculturalists are more severe, averaging 4 to 6.5 percent of total body weight in typical years.[32]

Biological and Cultural Adaptations to Scarcity

Food shortages suggest a hypothesis of the evolution of obesity. Because shortages were ubiquitous for humans under natural conditions, selection favored individuals who could effectively store calories in times of surplus. For three-fourths of the societies, such stores would be depleted, or at least called on, every two to three years, and sometimes more frequently.

Medical data on famine victims show that, in addition to outright starvation, malnutrition from food shortages has a synergistic effect on infectious disease mortality, as well as decreasing birth weights and rates of child growth.[33] Females with greater energy reserves in fat have a selective advantage over their lean counterparts in withstanding the stress of food shortage, not only for themselves, but for their fetuses or nursing children. Humans have evolved to "save up" food energy for the inevitability of food shortages through the synthesis and storage of fat. Moreover, females, whose reproductive fitness depends upon their ability to withstand the nutritional demands of pregnancy and lactation, appear to have been selected for more slow-releasing peripheral body fat than males.

In this evolutionary context the usual range of human metabolic variation must have produced many individuals with a predisposition to become obese; yet they would, in all likelihood, never have the opportunity to do so. Furthermore, in this context there could be little or no natural selection against such a tendency. Selection could not provide for the eventuality of continuous surplus because it had simply never existed.

There is little evidence that obesity, at least moderate obesity, reduces Darwinian reproductive fitness. A follow-up study of participants to the Third Harvard Growth Study found a positive correlation between fatness and fertility when holding both social class and ethnicity constant.[34] The influence of social class is important and complex: in developed countries, fatness, lower social class, and fertility are all positively associated, whereas in underdeveloped countries, fatness and fertility are associated only in upper socioeconomic classes.[35] A minimal level of female fatness may increase lifetime reproductive success because of its association with regular cycling as well as earlier menarche. In preindustrial societies, social status is related, both symbolically and statistically, to fertility and fatness.

It is likely that under some conditions fatness is an adaptation to successful completion of pregnancy. Recommended weight gain during pregnancy is between 20 and 30 pounds, and failure to gain weight (which may be caused by inadequate caloric intake) is considered a clinically ominous sign.[36,37] Especially for women with lower gains and lower pregravid weight, weight gain is positively correlated with birth weight and negatively correlated with perinatal mortality. The energy cost of pregnancy is estimated to be 80,000 kcal (300 kcal/d), assuming no change in energy output[38]—a reasonable assumption for nonindustrial societies. Intrauterine growth retardation associated with working during pregnancy is greatest against the background of low pregravid weight and low pregnancy weight gain.[39] Failure to supplement usual intake adequately will result in a depletion of pregravid tissue reserves.

The ongoing energy cost of lactation, if milk is the sole primary infant food, is higher than that of pregnancy, and lactation in traditional societies may last up to four years and be superimposed on early pregnancy. Estimated needed supplements, converted to energy in milk with high efficiency (around 90%), range from 500 kcal/d in the early postpartum period to 1000 kcal/d by the end of the first year.[36,40] Well-fed women with high pregnancy weight gains can supplement less and safely attain a deliberately negative energy balance during lactation by drawing on prepartum fatty tissue reserves.[41] At the other extreme, experimental interventions in Gambia[42] and Guatemala[43] provided caloric supplementation to pregnant and lactating women. In the Gambian case, women readily took supplements larger than the above-mentioned estimates, and supplemented women who completed pregnancy in the lean season experienced a six-fold reduction of the proportion of low-birth-weight infants, ending up with an incidence typical of developed countries (4.7%). In both populations, supplements during lactation also increased the duration of postpartum infertility.

Using the figure 80,000 kcal for pregnancy, and a conversion rate of 9.1 kcal/g, pregnancy with no supplementation could be maintained by pregravid tissue reserves amounting to 8.8 kg of fat. Viewed from the perspective of the costs of shortage rather than the costs of pregnancy *per se*, an annual or less frequent shortage of the length and type experienced by the Gambian women, whether occurring during pregnancy or lactation, would be cushioned against by excess fat amounting to 15 to 20% of body weight. In as

much as women in traditional societies spend the great majority of their reproductive lives either pregnant or nursing, an ideal of plumpness would be adaptive throughout that period. A custom such as the fattening hut for brides-to-be (see below) might provide a critical head-start on this lifelong reproductive energy drain.

Humans have also evolved other cultural mechanisms to minimize the effects of food shortages, including economic diversification, storage of foods, knowledge of possible famine foods, conversion of surplus food into durable valuables to be exchanged for food in emergencies, and cultivation of strong social relations with individuals in other regions.[44] These mechanisms act as buffers between environmental fluctuation and biological adaptation.

THE SOCIAL MEANING OF OBESITY: CROSS-CULTURAL COMPARISONS

Fatness is symbolically linked to psychological dimensions such as self-worth and sexuality in many societies of the world, including our own, but the nature of that symbolic association is not constant. In mainstream U.S. culture, obesity is socially stigmatized[45] even to the point of abhorrence. Weight loss is a major industry in the U.S., with annual expenditures of over five billion dollars. Most cultures of the world, by contrast, view fatness as a welcome sign of health and prosperity.

In an obesity-prevention campaign in a Zulu community outside of Durban,[46] one of the health education posters depicted an obese woman and an overloaded truck with a flat tire, with a caption "Both carry too much weight." Another poster showed a slender woman easily sweeping under a table next to an obese woman who is using the table for support; it has the caption "Who do you prefer to look like?" The intended message of these posters was misinterpreted by the community because of a cultural connection between obesity and social status. The woman in the first poster was perceived to be rich and happy, since she was not only fat, but had a truck overflowing with her possessions. The second poster was perceived as a scene of an affluent mistress directing her underfed servant.

Given the rarity of obesity in unacculturated preindustrial societies, it is not surprising that many groups have no ethnomedical definition of or concern with obesity. Given the frequency of food shortages, it is equally predictable that thinness, rather than fatness, will be deemed a serious medical symptom. The Tupinamba of Brazil have no descriptive term for fat people, but are reported to fear the symptom of thinness (*angaiuare*).[47] In the preindustrial context, thin people are to be pitied; this is the case for food foragers like the !Kung San, where culturally defined thinness (*zham*) is viewed as a symptom of starvation.

It may be large body size rather than obesity *per se* that in agricultural societies becomes an admired symbol of health, prestige, prosperity, or maternity. The agricultural Tiv of Nigeria, for example, distinguish between a very positive category, too big (*kehe*), and an unpleasant condition, to grow fat (*ahon*).[48] The first is a compliment—sign of prosperity that also refers to the seasonal weight gain of the early dry season when food is plentiful. The second term refers to a rare and undesirable condition.

Even in the industrialized U.S., there is ethnic variation in definitions of obesity. Some Mexican-Americans have coined a new term, *gordura mala* (bad fatness) because the original term *gordura* continues to have positive cultural connotations.[49] There has also been historical variation in clinical standardized definitions of obesity in American medicine. Between 1943 and 1980, definitions of ideal weights declined for women but not for men; more recently, upward revision of those standards has been proposed, due to an apparent disjunction in some data sets between cosmetically ideal weights and the weights at which mortality is minimized. This, however, remains controversial.[50,51] In any case, the definition of obesity is ultimately linked to cultural conceptions of normality, beauty, and health.

Cross-Cultural Variation in Ideal Body Type

In addition to the basic association between plumpness and health, culturally defined standards of beauty may have been a factor in the sexual selection for phenotypes predisposed to obesity. In a classic example, Malcom described the custom of fattening huts for the seclusion of elite Efik pubescent girls in traditional Nigeria.[52] A girl spent up to two years in seclusion before marriage, and at the end of this rite of passage she possessed symbols of womanhood and marriageability: a three-tiered hairstyle, clitoridectomy, and fatness. This fatness was a primary criterion of beauty as it was defined by the elites, who had the economic resources to participate in this custom. Similar fattening huts were found in other parts of West Africa.

Among the Havasupai of the American Southwest, if a girl at puberty is thin, a fat woman stands (places

TABLE 2   Cross-Cultural Standards of Female Beauty

	Number of Societies	*Percent of Category*
Overall Body		
Extreme obesity	0	0
Plumpness/moderate fat	31	81
Thin/abhorence of fat	7	19
Breasts		
Large or long	9	50
Small/abhorence of large	9	50
Hips and Legs		
Large or Fat	9	90
Slender	1	10
Stature		
Tall	3	30
Moderate	6	60
Small	1	10

her foot) on the girl's back so that she will become attractively plump. In this society, fat legs, and to a lesser extent arms, are considered essential to beauty.[53] The Tarahumara of Northern Mexico, whose men are famous as long-distance runners, reportedly consider large, fat thighs as the first requisite of beauty; a good-looking woman is called a "beautiful thigh."[54] Among the Amhara of the Horn of Africa, thin hips are called "dog hips" in a typical insult.[55] A South African Bemba courting song has the following verse: "Hullo Mama, the beautiful one, let us go to town/You will be very fat, you girl, if you stay with me."[56]

But how common is such a cultural connection between beauty and fat? There has been no systematic cross-cultural survey of definitions of feminine beauty or ideal body type among the societies of the world. The lack of a survey reflects, in part, the failure of ethnographers and historians to report adequately on this cultural element. Of the 325 cultures coded by the Human Relation Area Files, only 58 have adequate data to estimate some characteristic of ideal female body type.

The data summarized in Table 2 must be considered cautiously for a number of reasons: Because of the paucity of ethnographic data, a representative sample is impossible. Although limited to sources rated good or better, there is potential ethnographer bias toward the exotic. Observations cover a wide historical time span, often characterized by substantial cultural changes. There is the problem of relative standards; given the endemic obesity in modern society, what we consider normal may be fat to members of a society where obesity is uncommon. There is no consideration of intracultural diversity. Because the unit of analysis is a culture, the HRAF data base is skewed toward demographically small and technologically simple societies; the HRAF data base does not include the U.S. or modern European societies.

Granting the weaknesses of the data base, some guarded generalizations still seem possible. Cultural standards of beauty seem to be based on the normal characteristics of the dominant group of a society; they do not refer to physical extremes. No society on record has an ideal of extreme obesity. On the other hand, the desirability of plumpness or being filled out is found in 81 percent of societies for which there is data. This standard, which probably includes the clinical categories of overweight and mild obesity, apparently refers to the desirability of subcutaneous fat deposits. For societies where data on ideal standards on hips and legs is available, it appears that plumpness in peripheral body fat is commonly preferred. Societies that favor plumpness as a standard of beauty are found in all of the major world culture areas, with the exception of Asia. There appears to be no trend in preference for breast-size or stature. Ethnographic discussion of beauty in other societies often emphasizes cultural enhancements to the body, such as scarification, clothes, body paint, jewelry, and other adornments, rather than attributes of the body itself.[57] Standards of sexual beauty are based upon images of nubile, postpubertal, young-adult years in virtually all societies.

Fatness may also be a symbol of maternity and nurturance. In traditional societies where a woman attains her proper status only through motherhood, this symbolic association increases the cultural acceptability of obesity. A fat woman, symbolically, is well taken care of, and she in turn takes good care of her children. Fellahin Arabs in Egypt describe the proper woman as an "envelope for conception," and therefore a fat woman is a desirable ideal because she has more room to bear the child, lactate abundantly, and give warmth to her children.[58]

Although there is cross-cultural variation in standards of beauty, this variation falls within a certain range. American ideals of thinness occur in a setting where it is easy to become fat, and preference for plumpness occurs in settings where it is easy to remain lean. In context, both standards require the investment of individual effort and economic resources; furthermore, each in its context involves a display of wealth. In poor societies the rich impress the poor by becoming fat, which the poor cannot do. In rich societies even the poor can become fat, and avidly do; therefore, the rich must impress by staying thin, as if to say, "We have so little doubt about where our next meal is coming from, that we don't need a single gram of fat store." Cultural relativism in feminine beauty

standards, therefore, may be limited by evolutionarily determined human universals on the one hand and by lawful cross-cultural variation on the other.

The ethnographic record concerning body preferences in males is very weak. The HRAF data base includes only 12 societies with adequate information to gauge ideal male body type. In all of these societies, the expressed preference was for a muscular physique and for tall or moderately tall stature. Other characteristics mentioned include broad shoulders and being well filled out. One extreme in this admiration of large body size would be Japanese Sumo wrestlers whose program to build large bodies is really purposeful obesity; similar patterns of fattening young male wrestlers is found in Polynesia.[59] With few exceptions (e.g. the !Kung San)[8] human societies admire large body size, but not necessarily fatness, as an attribute of attractiveness in men. All of these physical characteristics can be considered as indicators of general health and nutritional status. Large body size and even obesity, however, are desirable because they symbolize economic success, political power, and social status in some societies.

Big Men, political leaders in tribal New Guinea, are described by their constituents in terms of their size and physical well-being (as well as other attributes). A Big Man may be described as a tall forest beech tree or as a man "whose skin swells with 'grease' [or fat] underneath."[60] Large body size may, in fact, be an index of differential access to food resources. This is seen in chiefdomships, as in ancient Polynesia, where hereditary political leaders sit at the hub of a redistribution system in which chiefly families are assured a portion of each family's harvest. The spiritual power (mana) and noble breeding of a Polynesian chief is expected to be seen in his physical appearance. One ethnographer in Polynesia was asked, "Can't you see he is a chief? See how big he is?"[61] The Bemba of South Africa believe that fatness in a man demonstrates not only his economic success but also his spiritual power in fending off the sorcery attacks.[62] A similar symbolic association can be assigned to deities. The corpulence of the seated Buddha, for example, symbolizes his divinity and otherworldliness.

Cultural variation in the meaning of fatness is also found among ethnic groups in the United States. Massara's ethnographic study of the cultural meanings of weight in a Puerto Rican community in Philadelphia[63] documents the positive associations and lack of social stigma of obesity. In addition, quantitative evidence[64] suggests that there are significant differences in ideal body preferences between this ethnic community and mainstream American culture. Positive evaluations of fatness may also occur in lower class Black Americans[65] and Mexican Americans.[17] There is also heterogeneity within these ethnic groups; upwardly mobile ethnics more closely resemble mainstream American culture in attitudes about obesity and ideal body shape.

In contrast to these ethnic minorities, and most of the cultures of the world, the ideal of female body shape in dominant middle/upper class America is thin. Studies suggest that females hold this cultural value more strongly than males,[66] who tend to be more satisfied with their own current body shape. Over the past three decades cosmetic ideals of female body shape have gotten thinner,[67] even thinner than medical ideals. Cultural beliefs about attractive body shape, therefore, place pressure on females to lose weight, and appear to be involved in the etiology of anorexia and bulimia. Neither the socioeconomic reversal of fatness in females nor the social history of symbolism of thinness has been adequately examined. Thinness, like tanning, is a contemporary symbol of economic status and leisure time for women. Both may be unhealthy, and both represent reversals of previous ideals.

Finally, although we have focused on the role of food shortages in human history, they are unfortunately not limited to the past. The drought and famine in the Horn of Africa and the Sahel have justifiably received world attention. Even in the United States, arguably the richest nation in human history, an estimated 20 million people are hungry.[68] This continuing worldwide epidemic of hunger presents a powerful and tragic counterbalance to our contemplation of the new epidemic of obesity and a reminder of the sometimes harsh realities of our history.

SUMMARY

An anthropological perspective on obesity considers both its evolutionary background and cross-cultural variation. It must explain three basic facts about obesity: gender dimorphism (women > men), an increase with modernization, and a positive association with socioeconomic status. Preindustrial diets varied in quality but shared a tendency to periodic shortages. Such shortages, particularly disadvantageous to women in their reproductive years, favored individuals who for biological and cultural reasons, stored fat. Not surprisingly, the majority of the world's cultures had or have ideals of feminine beauty that include plumpness. This is consistent with the hypothesis that fat stores functioned as a cushion against food shortages during pregnancy and lactation. As obesity has increased, the traditional gap between males and females in its prevalence has narrowed. Under Western conditions of abundance, our biological tendency to regulate body weight at levels above our ideal cannot be easily controlled even with a complete reversal of the widespread cultural ideal of plumpness.

REFERENCES

1. Pilbeam, D. 1984. The descent of hominoids and hominids. Sci. Am. **250**: 84–96.
2. Lee, R. B. & I. DeVore, Eds. 1968. Man the Hunter. Aldine. Chicago, IL.
3. Pitts, G. C. & T. R. Bullard. 1968. Some interspecific aspects of body composition in mammals. *In* Body Composition in Animals and Man. National Academy of Science, Washington, D.C. Pub. No. 1598:45–70.
4. Bailey, S. M. 1982. Absolute and relative sex differences in body composition. *In* Sexual dimorphism in *Homo sapiens*. R. L. Hall, Ed. Praeger Scientific. New York.
5. Pond, C. M. 1978. Morphological aspects and the ecological and mechanical consequences of fat deposition in wild vertebrates. Ann. Rev. Ecol. Syste. **9**: 519–570.
6. Stini, W. A. 1978. Malnutrition, body size and proportion. Ecol. Food Nutr. **1**: 125–132.
7. Tanner, J. M. 1962. Growth at Adolescence. Blackwell Scientific. Oxford.
8. Lee, R. B. 1979. The !Kung San: Men, Women, and Work in a Foraging Society. Harvard University Press. Cambridge, MA.
9. Page, L. B., A. Damon & R. C. Moellering. 1974. Antecedents of cardiovascular disease in six Solomon Islands societies. Circulation **49**: 1132–1146.
10. Zimmet, P. 1979. Epidemiology of diabetes and its macrovascular manifestations in Pacific populations: the medical effects of social progress. Diabetes Care **2**: 144–153.
11. West, K. 1978. Diabetes in American Indians. *In* Advances in metabolic disorders. Academic Press. New York.
12. Christakis, G. 1973. The prevalence of adult obesity. *In* Obesity in Perspective. G. Bray, Ed. **2**: 209–213. Fogarty International Center Series on Preventive Medicine.
13. Prior, I. A. 1971. The price of civilization. Nutr. Today **6**(4): 2–11.
14. Trowell, H. C. & D. P. Burkitt. 1981. Western Diseases: Their Emergence and Prevention. Harvard University Press. Cambridge, MA.
15. Goldblatt, P. B., M. E. Moore & A. J. Stunkard. 1965. Social factors in obesity. J. Am. Med. Assoc. **192**: 1039–1044.
16. Burnight, R. G. & P. G. Marden. 1967. Social correlates of weight in an aging population. Milbank Mem. Fund. **45**: 75–92.
17. Ross, C. E. & J. Mirowsky. 1983. Social epidemiology of overweight: a substantive and methodological investigation. J. Health Soc. Behav. **24**: 288–298.

18. Garn, S. M. & D. C. Clark. 1976. Trends in fatness and the origins of obesity. Pediatrics **57**: 443–456.

19. Arteaga, P., J. E. Dos Santos & J. E. Dutra De Oliveira. 1982. Obesity among school-children of different socio-economic levels in a developing country. Int. J. Obesity **6**: 291–297.

20. Stunkard, A. J., T. I. A. Sorenson, C. Hanis, T. W. Teasdale, R. Chakaborty, W. J. Schull & F. Schulsinger. 1986. An adoption study of obesity. N. Engl. J. Med. **314**: 193–198.

21. Sahlins, M. 1972. Stone Age Economics. Aldine. Chicago, IL.

22. Wenke, R. J. 1980. Patterns in Prehistory. Oxford. New York.

23. Cohen, M. N. & G. J. Armelagos, Eds. 1984. Paleopathology at the Origins of Agriculture. Academic Press. New York.

24. Trowell, H. 1975. Obesity in the western world. Plant Foods for Man **1**: 157–165.

25. Gilbert, R. I. & J H. Mielke, Eds. 1985. The Analysis of Prehistoric Diets. Academic Press. New York.

26. Eaton, S. B. & M. Konner. 1985. Paleolithic nutrition: a consideration of its nature and current implications. N. Eng. J. Med. **312**: 283–289.

27. Whiting, M. G. 1958. A cross-cultural nutrition survey. Doctoral Thesis. Harvard School of Public Health. Cambridge, MA.

28. Knowler, W. C., D. J. Pettitt, P. J. Savage & P. H. Bennett. 1981. Diabetes incidence in Pima Indians: contribution of obesity and parental diabetes. Am. J. Epidemiol. **113**: 144–156.

29. Minnis, P. E. 1985. Social Adaptation to Food Stress: A Prehistoric Southwestern Example. University of Chicago Press. Chicago, IL.

30. Truswell, A. S. & J. D. L. Hansen. 1977. Diet and nutrition of hunter-gatherers. In Health and Disease in Tribal Societies. Ciba Foundation, Eds. 213–226. Elsevier. Amsterdam.

31. Wilmsen, E. 1978. Seasonal effects of dietary intake in the Kalahari San. Fed. Proc. Fed. Am. Soc. Exp. Bio. **37**: 65–71.

32. Hunter, J. M. 1967. Seasonal hunger in a part of the west African savanna: a survey of body weights in Nangodi, north-east Ghana. Trans. Inst. Br. Geog. **41**: 167–185.

33. Stein, Z. & M. Susser. 1975. The Dutch famine, 1944–1945, and the reproductive process. Pediatr. Res. **9**: 70–76.

34. Scott, E. C. & C. J. Bajema. 1982. Height, weight and fertility among participants of the third Harvard growth study. Hum. Biol. **54**: 501–516.

35. Garn, S. M., S. M. Bailey & I. T. T. Higgens, 1980. Effects of socioeconomic status, family life, and living together on fatness and obesity. In Childhood Prevention of Atherosclerosis and Hypertension. R. Lauer & R. Skekelle, Eds. Raven Press. New York.

36. Eastman, N. J. & E. Jackson. 1968. Weight relationships in pregnancy. Obstet. Gynecol. Surv. **23**: 1003–1025.

37. Naeye, R. L. 1979. Weight gain and outcome of pregnancy. Am. J. Obstet. Gynecol. **135**: 3–9.

38. Blackburn, M. W. & D. H. Calloway. 1976. Energy expenditure and consumption of mature, pregnant and lactating women. J. Am. Diet. Assoc. **69**: 29–37.

39. Naeye, R. L. & E. C. Peters. 1982. Working during pregnancy: effects on the fetus. Pediatrics **69**: 725–727.

40. Thomson, A. M., F. E. Hytten & W. Z. Billewicz. 1970. The energy cost of human lactation. Br. J. Nutr. **24**: 565–572.

41. Butte, N. F., C. Garza, J. E. Stuff, E. O. Smith & B. L. Nichols. 1984. Effect of maternal diet and body composition on lactational performance. Am. J. Clin. Nutr. **39**: 296–306.

42. Prentice, A. M., R. G. Whitehead, M. Watkinson, W. H. Lamb & T. J. Cole. 1983. Prenatal dietary supplementation of African women and birth-weight. Lancet **1**: 489–492.

43. Delgado, H. A. Lechug, C. Yarbrough, R. Martorell, R. E. Klein & M. Irwin. 1977. Maternal nutrition—its effect on infant growth and development and birth spacing. In Nutritional Impacts on Women. K. S. Moghissi & T. N. Evans, Eds. Harper & Row. Hagerstown, MD.

44. Colson, E. 1979. In good years and bad: food strategies of self-reliant societies. J. Anthropol. Res. **35**: 18–29.

45. Cahnman, W. J. 1968. The stigma of obesity. Sociol. Q. **9**: 294–297.

46. Gampel, B. 1962. The "Hilltops" community. In Practice of Social Medicine. S. L. Kark & G. E. Steuart, Eds. E. & S. Livingstone. London.

47. Evreux, Y. 1864. Voyage dans le Nord du Bresil Fait durant les Annees 1613 et 1614. F. Denis, Ed. A. Franch. Paris and Leipzig.

48. Bohannan, P. & L. Bohannan. 1969. A source notebook on Tiv religion (5 vol.). Human Relations Area Files. New Haven, CT.

49. Ritenbaugh, C. 1982. Obesity as a culture-bound syndrome. Cult. Med. Psychiatry **6**:347–361.

50. Metropolitan Life Foundation. 1983. Height and Weight Tables. Metropolitan Life Insurance Company.

51. Burton, B. T., W. R. Foster, J. Hirsch & T. B. Van Itallie. 1985. Health implications of obesity: an NIH consensus development conference. Intl. J. Obesity **9**: 155–169.

52. Malcom, L. W. G. 1925. Note on the seclusion of girls among the Efik at Old Calabar. Man **25**: 113–114.

53. Smithson, C. L. 1959. The Havasupai Woman. U. Utah Press. Salt Lake City, UT.

54. Bennett, W. C. & R. M. Zingg. 1935. The Tarahumara: an Indian Tribe of Northern Mexico. U. Chicago Press. Chicago, IL.

55. Messing, S. D. 1957. The Highland Plateau Amhara of Ethiopia. Doctoral Dissertation (Anthropology). U. Pennsylvania. Philadelphia, PA.

56. Powdermaker, H. 1960. An anthropological approach to the problem of obesity. Bull. N.Y. Acad. Sci. **36**: 286–295.

57. Brain, R. 1979. The Decorated Body. Harper & Row. New York.

58. Amnar, H. 1954. Growing Up in an Egyptian Village. Routledge & Kegan Paul. London.

59. Beaglehole, E. & P. Beaglehole, 1938. Ethnology of Pukapuka. Bernice P. Bishop Museum. Honolulu, HI.

60. Strahern, A. 1971. The Rope of Moka. Cambridge University Press. New York.

61. Gifford, E. W. 1929. Tongan Society. Bernice P. Bishop Mus. Bull. 61. Honolulu, HI.

62. Richards, A. I. 1939. Land, Labour and Diet in Northern Rhodesia: an Economic Study of the Bemba Tribe. Oxford University Press. London.

63. Massara, E. B. 1979. Que gordita! a study of weight among women in a Puerto Rican community. Ph.D. dissertation. Bryn Mawr College. Philadelphia, PA.

64. Massara, E. B. 1980. Obesity and cultural weight evaluations. Appetite **1**: 291–298.

65. Styles, M. H. 1980. Soul, black women and food. *In* A Woman's Conflict: The Special Relationship between Women and Food. J. R. Kaplan, Ed. Prentice Hall. Englewood Cliffs, N.J.

66. Garner, D. M., P. E. Garfinkel, D. Schwartz & M. Thompson. 1980. Cultural expectations of thinness in women. Psychol. Rep. **47**: 483–491.

67. Fallon, A. E. & P. Rozin. 1985. Sex differences in perceptions of desirable body shape. J. Abnorm. Psychol. **94**: 102–105.

68. Physician Task Force on Hunger in America. 1985. Hunger in America: the Growing Epidemic. Harvard University School of Public Health. Boston, MA.

International Health Issues and Programs

✤ CONCEPTUAL TOOLS ✤

■ *Many medical anthropologists work in the field of international health, most often as consultants to specific programs.* Since the World Health Organization's 1978 proclamation for primary health care (PHC), there have been efforts to institute basic health services and prevention programs on a worldwide basis. PHC represented a change from previous international health programs aimed at single disease eradication. The idea of PHC was to bring health *to the people,* to empower communities through health initiatives, and to decrease mortality through "horizontal" efforts—as opposed to fighting disease through "vertical" programs. PHC work requires sensitivity to local cultural beliefs and values, as well as cooperation with and empowerment of local people. Medical anthropology has made significant contributions to this field (Lane and Rubinstein 1996).

■ *Primary health care programs often center on mother and infant health.* The child survival initiatives have used relatively simple technologies—oral rehydration therapy (ORT), childhood immunizations, promotion of breast-feeding, and the use of growth charts to identify malnourished children for supplementary feeding. These programs clearly work in lowering infant and child mortality (Basch 1990; Coreil and Mull 1990).

■ *Medical anthropologists study the culture and organization of international health programs themselves.* There is a culture to international health programs and policies, just like there is a culture to clinical biomedicine. Health policies develop out of political processes, and local sociocultural contexts shape the implementation of programs. Medical anthropologists have shown that cultural factors *within the health program* are sometimes important obstacles to the success of a project (Foster 1987). An excellent example of an ethnography of a health policy and its implementation is Judith Justice's *Policies, Plans, and People* (1986).

■ *Some medical anthropologists strive to promote cooperation of traditional ethnomedical practitioners within international health programs.* Traditional healers and lay midwives are health workers who often cooperate with biomedical practitioners. For example, Edward Green (1985) has helped organize and train local traditional healers in Swaziland to use oral rehydration therapy. Another area of substantial work is the supplementary training of traditional birth attendants (TBAs) in efforts to reduce maternal mortality (Cosminsky 1986).

43

Ethnomedicine and Oral Rehydration Therapy: A Case Study of Ethnomedical Investigation and Program Planning

Carl Kendall

Dennis Foote

Reynaldo Martorell

As we have seen, the interest of medical anthropologists in the ethnomedical systems of other societies can have practical value. This selection demonstrates that preexisting ethnomedical beliefs make a difference in regard to the acceptance of a health promotion message. It is an example of the fallacy of empty vessels that may plague international health programs. In the case study presented here, the health planners did not take into account the fact that the Hondurans might have their own folk models for the causes of diarrhea that could hamper the acceptability of oral rehydration therapy. This case study is particularly interesting not only because of the role of traditional ethnomedical beliefs but also because of the effect of the anthropologists' study on the health program.

Dehydration due to diarrhea has been a major cause of childhood mortality in the developing world. On a worldwide scale, millions of dehydration deaths can be prevented if children are kept properly hydrated during diarrhea episodes with a mixture of water, salt, sugar, and other minerals; this is called oral rehydration therapy (ORT).

This intervention does not cure the diarrhea and it has no effect on the sources of infection, but there is no doubt that it is a simple, appropriate technology that can save many lives. When babies are sick with diarrhea, they often have little appetite (and ORT doesn't taste very good) so applying ORT requires work and patience by the mother.

In this case, the local ethnomedical system includes four causes of diarrhea. The researcher discovered that the public health messages about ORT were widely known in the village, but the treatment was not always used. One of the causes of the diarrhea, empacho, was thought to be significantly different from the other causes and it therefore required a different remedy. We have already read about treatments for empacho in the case of dangerous folk med-

ical treatments in Texas (selection 30). Because it is believed that there is a clogging or obstruction of the digestive tract, a traditional treatment for empacho is a purgative. This treatment is dangerous for a child sick with diarrhea because it exacerbates the problem of dehydration. In both the Texas example and the Honduras example described here, a sizable percentage of children with diarrhea were not being treated with ORT and were, in fact, being put at greater risk.

The anthropologists discovered this problem and reported it to their international health program. What should be done with this cultural information? In this case, there was a confrontation between the biomedical culture and the local ethnomedical system. This case study raises issues of cross-cultural communication, which we explored with regard to clinical medicine (selections 29 to 32). It may be that the LEARN model of cross-cultural medicine (listen, explain, acknowledge differences, recommend, and negotiate) is also applicable to international health programs.

As you read this selection, consider these questions:

- *Why did the ORT program planners include a component of ethnomedical research in their overall scheme? Why was the ethnomedical advice ignored by the central program staff?*

- *What makes empacho so different from other causes of diarrhea? Why does the purgative therapy make sense from this ethnomedical viewpoint?*

- *Did the anthropologists suggest that to circumvent the problem of empacho the ORT program actually lie to the local people? Is this ethical?*

- *How might the LEARN model (selection 32) have been applied in this case?*

INTRODUCTION

The World Health Organization (WHO) has designated diarrheal disease control a primary objective.[1] A component of this control program is the promotion of home-based oral rehydration therapy (ORT). Oral rehydration therapy has been shown, both in clinical trials and in the field to be a safe and effective therapy for dehydration. WHO promotes a dry sealed packet containing 3.5 g sodium chloride, 2.5 g potassium chloride, 2.5 g sodium bicarbonate and 20 g glucose that is added to one liter of clean water in the home. Reaching millions of rural households with this simple solution will tax existing health delivery systems, and WHO has called for operational or applied research to improve delivery of these services.

WHO and other agencies supporting oral rehydration activities acknowledge that ORT programs and promotional campaigns must be appropriate to the social and cultural context of the program.[2] Anthropologists have been encouraged to participate, and bring to the problem skills and research tools appropriate for both operational research and larger questions involved in the extension of coverage of ORT. Among these tools are ethnomedical models, such as Kleinman's explanatory models.[3] Ethnomedical models have been used principally to explain outcomes, particularly program failure.[4] Although they are often mentioned as useful for planning and for operational research, the lack of case-histories in the literature suggests their relative neglect in practice. This paper presents a case study of ethnomedicine and program planning, including a subsequent evaluation of a program that incorporates an ethnomedical perspective to promote acceptance and use of home-based ORT. Points are illustrated with current results from the Mass Media and Health Practices Evaluation, a longitudinal study of 750 families in 20 sites in Honduras, conducted concurrently with the ethnographic investigation. The paper concludes with a discussion of the need for and difficulties in the application of ethnomedical perspectives in investigation and early program planning.

THE PROGRAM

PROCOMSI (Proyecto de Comunicacion Masiva Aplicada a la Salud Infantil or Mass Communication Project Applied to Infant Health) is a health promotion project administered jointly by the Academy for Educational Development and the Division of Education of the Honduras Ministry of Health. Primary emphasis is placed on home-based ORT. The program promotes WHO authorized packets of ORS called, in Honduras, Litrosol. A number of preventive behaviors, including exclusive breast-feeding of young infants, are encouraged as well. The project has been active in Honduras for three years.

The project consists of an integrated program of radio, print materials and health worker training to teach or reinforce changes in a variety of practices and beliefs surrounding infant diarrhea. The method for using these media, with proper testing and program modification procedures, was institutionalized by the country's Ministry of Health for broader use in health education efforts.

The methods are innovative in several respects:

heavy use of research for planning;
intensive use of pretesting and formative evaluation in message and project design;
use of an integrated campaign format through multiple channels;
and concentration on a very focused set of objectives.

. . .

The study involves a sample of 750–800 families distributed over 20 communities. Each family is visited monthly over a period of two years by a fieldworker who asks survey questions, makes observations and/or measures the children. Initial findings point to high levels of exposure to campaign components, learning new information and trying the advocated behaviors. The results are being intensively evaluated by the Institute for Communication Research, Stanford University. The data on which this paper is based are drawn from that evaluation. The project has used a behavior-oriented and context appropriate promotional strategy to inform a predominantly rural population of approximately 350,000 people about the preparation and use of ORT. Radio, print materials and face-to-face instruction were the principal tools of the campaign.

THE RESEARCH

The paper reports results from several research activities associated with ORT production and evaluation in Honduras. First, in a single community, interviews were conducted on beliefs and practices related to diarrhea. Next, a pre-intervention survey was conducted in this community. During the spring of 1980 the research site was visited repeatedly. Interviews were conducted with four key informants and Ministry of Health staff. In June 1980, all households in the community were administered an interview schedule to collect baseline data on household size and composition, maternal histories, morbidity, mortality, hygiene and sanitation and other measures. Two years later, the community was restudied to measure morbidity, program campaign recall, and recognition and use of ORT. These studies served as the basis for the design of the Mass Media and Health Practices (MMHP) Evaluation discussed above. In addition, the Academy for Education Development (AED), the implementors of the project, conducted a developmental investigation, prior to program development. This investigation focused on diarrheal disease treatment, literacy, radio listening habits and household characteristics.

THE SITE OF THE EVALUATION'S ETHNOMEDICAL RESEARCH

Los Dolores (a pseudonym), the site of research, consists of five linked hamlets scattered in mountainous terrain at altitudes of 1000 and 1600 m. Wet and dry seasons are sharply demarcated. Rainfall is commonly 1000 mm per year and during winter *(invierno)* which extends from May to October, streams are high. By contrast during the dry summer *(verano)* low stream flow is only 1–2 liters/second/km.[5] A peak of diarrhea incidence is reached during the month of June, just after the start of the rainy season.

The soils support extensive stands of needleleaf and broadleaf evergreens and deciduous shrubs, as well as some deciduous broadleaf vegetation. The valley floors are most heavily farmed, but because of population pressures on these lands, some villagers must often farm plots with slopes in excess of 45 degrees. All household heads in Los Dolores possess lands, although the plots are quite small (< *5 manzanas*). Rural countrypeople grow corn, sorghum, beans, potatoes and some rice; sugar cane is grown for cash but none of the farms of Los Dolores could be considered commercial-scale.

Los Dolores is culturally representative of the 20 sites chosen for the evaluation, which share Ladino culture.

THE SOCIAL CONTEXT AND THE SITES OF THE MMHP EVALUATION

Evaluation sites are found, as in Los Dolores, in Honduras' Health Region I. In Central America, the local political-administrative unit is the *municipio* or municipality, containing a headquarters *(cabecera)* and a number of villages *(aldeas)* and hamlets *(caserios)*. The *municipios* in the evaluation sample are Sabanagrande, Yuscaran and Danli. The ethnographic evaluation site is an *aldea* in Yuscaran. Although the three municipios are ecologically distinctive, the conditions of rural life are remarkably similar.

A typical rural community is a locale with a number of town centers connected by paths. These centers are clusters of houses often no more than 50 m apart. Many of these adjacent households are connected by ties of kinship. The houses are predominantly adobe, one-story high, with tile roofs. Often they are only a single room with a cooking area attached to an exterior wall. Most floors are of dirt. The houses contain two or three beds for the seven inhabitants. The plot surrounding the house is divided into areas for play and reception of guests, areas for the drying of grains, and areas for micturation, defecation and disposal of garbage.

All *aldeas* are linked to their *cabeceras* by roads, although six of the sites included in the study become inaccessible during the rainy season. Irregular bus service is found in most of the *aldeas* of Sabanagrande and many in Danli, but not in Yuscaran. All *aldeas* have primary schools for grades 1 to 6, and all *cabeceras* have secondary schools.

Only three *aldeas* have completed piped-water systems, although others much like Los Dolores have partially completed networks. None of the *aldeas* have a.c. electric power networks, although some rural inhabitants use automobile batteries to power televisions, and an occasional household near a power line will receive electricity. Latrine programs were begun in 1980 in almost all *aldeas*. No *aldeas* have completed the program and most latrines are little used.

The 5345 people enumerated in the initial baseline sample are overwhelmingly young. 4.2% of the total population was less than a 1 year old at the time of the census, 24.8% less than 5 years of age, and 58% less than 12 years of age. Little difference is found between sites.

Rural Honduran households are predominantly organized into conjugal family households. The 747 households included in a census had a mean household size of 7.16 members. Households in Los Dolores composed mostly of the conjugal pair and offspring, have a mean size of 5.83 (SD 3.29).

Most household heads in the evaluation sample are small landowners producing subsistence crops of corn and beans. Although self reports of land ownership are notoriously unreliable, of the 521 households for which both ownership and area data are available, 85% of the sample own their own land (although few have full legal title). Ownership of land is skewed, with 5.4% of households owning 53.9% of the land. . . .

COSMOPOLITAN MEDICAL SERVICES

The physician or nurse nearest Los Dolores is located in the Ministry of Health facility in the county seat, 1$^1/_2$ hours' walk away. A Ministry of Health center there is staffed by a graduate medical student completing his or her year of obligatory rural social service, and two auxiliary nurses. Although there are no pharmacies, several stores in town stock medicines which are prescribed, often, by shopkeepers and clerks. Local, part-time curers also serve as heath care providers, prescribing and injecting medicines. The countrypeople (*campesinos*) of Los Dolores occasionally use the hospital facilities available in Tegucigalpa, the nation's capital, 1$^1/_2$ hours by bus from the county seat, when one is available. The Ministry has two local unpaid representatives in Los Dolores, a recently appointed *guardian* (village health worker) who works with the auxiliary nurses, and a *representante* who works with the health promoter in sanitation projects. Neither of these individuals, a recently married couple in their twenties, are local healers.

LOCAL MEDICAL SERVICES

There are no *injectadores* (persons who dispense medication by injection) or *purteras* (traditional or trained midwife) in Los Dolores. Several women will assist family and friends in childbirth, but refuse the vocation of midwife. Nearby communities provide these healers, however. Several men and women are *sobadores* or masseurs. A *sobador* massages the body and prescribes medicines for a number of diseases. These include *empacho*, to be described below, and *fluxion*, a flux or chill that is felt to enter the body. A large number of herbal remedies are known to older men and women. Younger householders claim not to know these remedies and appear to prefer commercially packaged medicines.

FOLK MEDICAL ATTRIBUTIONS OF CAUSE

A key goal in the promotion of ORT was to express program messages in a rural vocabulary using lay understanding of diarrhea. Both the initial evaluation and the developmental investigation demonstrated the importance for treatment decisions of folk medical attribution of disease causality. The results of these in-vestigations have been reported elsewhere,[6] but for purposes of the paper, a brief summary is provided.

Interviews with key informants concerning diarrheal etiology and treatment revealed a number of folk illnesses associated with diarrheal symptoms believed to be causes of diarrhea.[7] These are:

1. *empacho*
2. *ojo* (evil eye)
3. *caida de mollera* (fallen fontanelles)
4. *lombrices* (worms).

Episodes of diarrhea are believed to be caused by these folk illnesses when the diarrhea is especially severe and when the episode is refractive. As has been pointed out elsewhere,[8] folk diagnosis is often a pragmatic activity involving trial and error appraisal of a medicine's efficacy. These folk illnesses are the attributions of last resort. Since the effect of ORT on morbidity is small, but its impact on mortality high, these complicated diarrheas, which are diagnosed pragmatically in episodes of long duration, are important for reaching those cases of diarrhea that are likely to be fatal.

Empacho is a painful condition of the gut characterized by explosive evacuations and flatulence. Locally it is differentiated by cause; for it is believed that it can be brought on by eating the wrong kinds of food (foods that are heavy (*pesado*) or a combination of foods that are improperly balanced along the hot-cold spectrum); eating at improper times or missing a meal or eating foods that are incompletely cooked or raw. *Empacho* also produces a special skin quality that is used as a diagnostic indicator. A masseur or masseuse (*sabador* or *sabadora*) treats *empacho* by massaging the body and administering a purgative. Purgatives are considered to be any substance (most frequently oils, sometimes "salts," but also absorbents) that promotes evacuation. This evacuation serves to clean (*limpiar*) the gut of its improperly digested contents which are considered dirty (*sucio*).

Rural countrypeople are aware of the potent effect of purgatives and prescribe milder purgatives to children; nevertheless, the use of purgatives may contribute to the high mortality attributed to diarrhea which accounts for 24% of all reported infant and child deaths in Honduras.[9]

Evil eye, the result of malicious, penetrant visual rays, produces fever. A diagnostic sign is a lack of symmetry in the eyes. Local informants make a sharp distinction between *mal de ojo*, a condition of red, sore eyes and *ojo* or sometimes *mal de ojo*, produced by penetrant rays. Treatment for the latter involves bundling, as for any fever and spraying the skin with a number of liquids. Purgatives are not used since etiology does not involve contamination of the gut.

Fallen fontanelles are believed to be caused by improper maternal handling of an infant. According to local ethnoanatomy, the infant's palate is incompletely developed. Thus the tissue underlying the fontanells can fall. Treatment is specific to the ethnoanatomical effect, involving pushing up on the roof of the mouth and tapping on the heels of the inverted child and/or sucking on the fontanells.

Worms are considered a normal symbiote of the gut, but when mistreated, leave their "sack" and wander through the body causing illness. If left untreated by a purgative the worms could cause a fatal illness—worm fever (*fiebre de lombrices*). Most episodes of worm-caused diarrhea are felt to be benign, however, and are not treated by the administration of medicines. If the diarrhea continues too long, however, treatment is sought. This treatment often involves the administration of mild local purgatives. Worms, as a normal symbiote, are not the same category of calamity as the other folk illnesses mentioned above. Worm fever, on the other hand, is treated much like *empacho*, discussed below.

FOLK MEDICAL TREATMENT DECISIONS

The original study could uncover no resistance to the incorporation of ORT to cases of diarrhea attributed to *ojo* or *caidu*. However, cases of *empacho* are generally thought to require the administration of a purgative, and it was felt that parents would resist the use of ORT for the treatment of this disease, and continue to use folk remedies. Since it was felt that *empacho* would have to be addressed by the program, a convenience sample of ten mothers in Los Dolores were asked if they knew about a range of illnesses, including *empacho*. These illnesses include those attributed as primary causes of mortality in Honduras by the Ministry of Heath, and an additional group of folk illnesses. Respondents were asked if they had heard of the disease, and if it was curable. All responded "yes" to both questions. They were then read a list of healers and asked "Can healer *X* cure disease *Y*" . . .

Almost uniformly, respondents believed that although cosmopolitan medical staff could cure diarrhea and dysentery, they would be unsuccessful in treating either *empacho* or *ojo*. Since the source of ORT would be the Ministry of Health (and a fictitious physician, "Dr. Salustiano," a major campaign figure), the staff felt that program messages were unlikely to

be successful in convincing rural parents to treat episodes of diarrhea attributed to *empacho* with ORT.

No mothers interviewed in 1980 knew about dehydration. Those who recognized the word thought it was a synonym for malnutrition (*desnutrición*), this followed from the use of pre-mixed oral and intravenous solutions called *suero* that mothers were familiar with. These expensive solutions, literally translated into English as whey or serum are prescribed during *empacho*, since the gut is thought to need rest.

NON-USE OF ETHNOMEDICAL RESULTS IN PLANNING

A natural outcome of these findings could have been the promotion of ORT as a purgative, or at least as a specific treatment for *empacho*. A medical consultant to the implementation project, Dr. M. M. Levine, was among the first to suggest such a strategy. Two factors, however, militated against the promotion of ORT as a purgative or as a cure for *empacho*.

The first was the expressed resistance on the part of Ministry staff physicians to both the illness label "*empacho*" and the use of "purgative" in PROCOMSI activities. *Empacho* was not considered a disease entity and physicians did not want the program to appear to support purgative use.

The second difficulty was that the implementors' survey research activities did not often encounter *empacho* attributed as a cause of diarrhea. When questioned "what causes diarrhea?" respondents would most often reply dirty water or worms. The reasons for these attributions will be discussed later. Because of these difficulties, a resistant Ministry and inadequate survey research justification, the implementors ignored *empacho* as an impediment to ORT use. ORT was promoted then, not as a purgative but as salts that were good for diarrhea and avoided dehydration, the latter a concept unknown to rural countrypeople and laboriously taught in the campaign, which began in March 1981.

THE TWO-YEAR IMPACT SURVEY

In May of 1980 and again 2 years later (June 1982) all households were censused and standardized interviews were conducted in all households containing children under 5 years of age in Los Dolores. The 2–year impact survey measured:

1. Diarrhea morbidity and treatment, including use of ORT (2 weeks/month and 6 month recall of episodes, with "diarrhea" defined by the mother);

2. Breastfeeding and nutrition (breastfeeding and weaning practices, list of foods consumed) for children less than 3 years of age;

3. Household demographic changes, including mortality; and

4. PROCOMSI campaign exposure, recall and recognition.

. . .

RESULTS

Morbidity

The morbidity survey was conducted in June 1982. For the two week period prior to the visit to each household with a child under five, mothers reported 12 episodes of diarrhea. There 12 episodes totaled 70 days of diarrhea with a mean duration of 5.8 days (SD 2.48). No child was reported as having had more than one episode, and specific incidence of diarrhea in children less than 60 months of age for a 2 week period between 1 and 22 June was 375/1000. During the entire month (18 May–22 June) a total of 17 episodes were reported in 17 of 32 children, for a total of 122 days of diarrhea (mean duration 6.58 days, SD 3.5) for a 1 month incidence of 531/1000 in children less than 60 months of age. . . . Clearly diarrhea is a salient problem. Information was collected for episodes (three in total) that occurred as long as 6 months prior to the intervention. There are grounds for suspecting that memory effects were responsible for the low number of cases reported, although diarrhea is highly seasonal. There are no grounds for suspecting that the three cases reported between 1 and 6 months prior to the survey were in any way especially salient cases.

The evaluation has currently analyzed diarrheal morbidity for two data sweeps, the first in June and July of 1981 during the rainy season, and the second in March of 1982, during the dry season. Thirty-six per cent of the children were reported to have had diarrhea in the previous two weeks of the rainy season of 1981 while 21.5% were said to have been sick during the dry season of 1982.

. . .

Combining information on diarrhea from all appropriate questions, we have estimated that *at least* 56.0% of children in wave 1 and 45.0% in wave 2 were ill with diarrhea in the previous 6 months. We emphasize the words "at least" because of the effects of memory loss. Clearly, diarrheal diseases are a major public health problem in Honduras as they are in these other areas. . . .

The MMHP evaluation data and the data collected in Los Dolores are comparable. There were 18 children less than 3 years of age in 17 out of 44 households in Los Dolores. Of these 18 children, 7 had completed breastfeeding at the time of the survey. Mean duration of breastfeeding was 16.85 months (SD 6.2 months). Only one mother reported never breastfeeding, and only one of the mothers reported breastfeeding for less than two months. Other mothers were still breastfeeding children at 27 and even 34 months. . . . Thirteen of the 18 children less than 3 years of age were reported to have had an episode of diarrhea in the previous month, but only 3 of the 7 children still breastfeeding had reported episodes.

Although the numbers are too small to be significant and are confounded by age, diet and behavioral differences, some impact of breastfeeding on diarrheal incidence may be reflected in these data. All mothers suspended powered or cow's milk, as well as meat, eggs and many other foods during episodes of diarrhea. Breastfeeding mothers, however, continued breastfeeding during episodes.

CAMPAIGN EXPOSURE, RECALL AND RECOGNITION, JUNE 1982

. . . All families claimed awareness of the ORT packet and its use; all could name it. All families claimed to have heard about it both through radio and by word of mouth. No mothers, except mothers in those households with posters, reported the posters as a source of information about the program. Although no mother knew the word dehydration or about ORT packets before program implementation, 12 of the 24 mothers correctly defined dehydration as the loss or absence of fluids in the body. Three of the 24 mothers could correctly recall the five components stressed in the mixing messages (mix with 1 liter of water, use all of one packet, give whole liter in 1 day, shake the bottle, throw left-over away after 1 day). Fourteen other families missed only a single component: the amount of fluid to give a child per day (1 liter). It appears that the promotion campaign has been successfully conducted in Los Dolores.

A survey of mothers in the MMHP evaluation sample, conducted in April 1982 demonstrates similarly high figures for the sample. 85.3% of families reported owning a radio; 77.5% of the total sample had a working radio. Coverage of the population, expressed as the percentage of all mothers remembering hearing at least one spot on the previous day is 38.9%. The percentage of listeners who report having heard a spot between 6 a.m. and 9 p.m. by hour varies between 60.5 and 78.9%.

46.6% of the sample reported having seen a PROCOMSI health poster and could describe it, much higher than the percentage for Los Dolores. 92.5% of the total MMHP sample could identify "Litrosol" in April 1982. For preparation of ORS, 94.2% of the sample who had used Litrosol reported mixing it with one liter of water. 95.7% reported using all of one packet. 59.7% reported giving the whole liter in 1 day. 83.5% reported agitating the bottle to mix the solution. 32.6% reported throwing away the solution after 1 day.

USE

Of the 20 cases of diarrhea reported in the previous 2 weeks, 11 used ORT. Use does not imply that each and every case followed PROCOMSI's therapeutic regimen. For the most part, mothers gave less ORT than the prescribed liter per day. Nine cases did not use ORT. Eight of these diarrheal episodes were attributed to *empacho*.

Initial findings of the survey demonstrate that for March 1982 during the dry season 26.1% (55/211) of diarrheal episodes that occurred during the last 2 weeks were treated with ORT. The percentage of cases varied from *municipio* to *municipio*. . . .

This variation may have been due to the availability of Litrosol. The figures are not directly comparable with Los Dolores because of seasonal differences and the ethnographer's presence. Approximately 40% of these diarrheal episodes were treated with purgatives. Unfortunately, attributions of cause by treatment are not yet available from the evaluation.

DISCUSSION

The program appears to have been successful in providing knowledge about ORT, and in achieving its use in the home. On the other hand, over a 6-month period, 9 out of 20 diarrheal episodes in children were not treated with ORT. Although there are grounds for suspecting the quality of recall of the three episodes that were reported to have occurred prior to 1 month, only one of the episodes reported did not use Litrosol, and this was the only non-*empacho* episode in which Litrosol was not used. With this one exception, the diarrheas which were not treated with ORT were attrib-

uted to *empacho*. The initial findings from ethnographic investigation early in the program were confirmed: those episodes of diarrhea attributed to this folk illness are treated with purgatives, and not with ORT.

Two reasons were given earlier to explain why a promotional strategy for ORT appropriate to this folk illness was not approved: (1) the rejection by the Honduran cosmopolitan medical community of the public discussion of *empacho* and the promotion of ORT as a purgative in a Ministry of Health program; and (2) the relatively few mothers who reported *empacho* as a cause of diarrhea.

As reported earlier, lay treatment does not proceed directly from recognition of symptoms to diagnosis. In fact, diagnosis is negotiated among family and health specialists during the course of the illness and its treatment. *Empacho* is rarely diagnosed early in an episode and when diagnosed is considered a serious and potentially fatal illness. In addition, *empacho* is characterized by other symptoms as well as diarrhea, such as abdominal pain. These "primary" symptoms are perhaps more salient than diarrhea as evidence of *empacho*. These are among the reasons that frequency of the *empacho* response to survey items could have been low. These results blunted the urgency of both evaluators' and implementers' attempts to promote a cure for *empacho* in the program. In fact, the term *"empacho"* which can be considered a symptom or an illness, overlaps incompletely with the disease category "diarrhea." Some biomedical researchers believe that *empacho* may be characterized by an etiology different from that of most diarrheas; one suspicion is a rotaviral agent, and another food allergies or other disorders of digestion.

A detailed discussion of the first reason for rejection of a strategy for *empacho* is beyond the scope of this paper. However, it involves issues raised, for example, in Hahn and Kleinman about the truth status of ethnomedical events.[10] In contrast to biomedicine, ethnomedicine appears to offer results of dubious reliability and little precision.

In this case, however, program planners might have been willing to accept the findings of PROCOMSI's initial developmental investigation. Why did these findings not corroborate the importance of *empacho* in treatment decisions about diarrheal disease? The answer to this question briefly put, is that the validity of findings from "what if'" survey formats can be greatly challenged. Especially when laboratory findings cannot be used to corroborate assessments, only an intensive case-by-case review can control for issues of validity of disease categories and criteria for attribution.

Whatever the final results of the microbiological and metabolic investigations currently being planned for *empacho*, the findings that were significant for program planning and for interpretation of results were collected using research techniques appropriate to a subject area broadly defined here as "ethnomedicine." However, this example reinforces the results of many other ethnographic studies conducted in conjunction with social change programs; that is, that such findings are usually not accorded independent status for purposes of planning. It is hoped that the successful ethnomedical investigation in the PRO-COMSI project will not only advance diarrheal disease control and health education efforts, but will also promote ethnomedical investigation, as an independent and appropriate operational research tool.

REFERENCES

1. World Health Organization. Scientific Working Group Reports 1978–1980. Programme for Control of Diarrhoeal Diseases. Unpublished reports. World Health Organization, Geneva. The WHO diarrhoeal diseases control programme. *Wkly Epid. Rec.* **54**, No. 16, 121–123, 1979. World Health Organization. *Progamme for Control of Diarrhoeal Diseases—Training Modules,* 1980.
2. See Ref. 1, for example, WHO environmental health and diarrhoeal disease prevention. Report of a Scientific Working Group, Diarrhoeal Diseases Control Programme, Document No. R-680, p. 15 and United States Agency for International Development. *Health Sector I, Honduras,* Project Paper, Project No. 522–0153.
3. Kleinman A. International health care planning from an ethnomedical perspective: critique and recommendations for change. *Med. Anthrop.* **2**, 71–94. Kleinman A. *Patients and Healers in the Context of Culture.* University of California Press, Los Angeles, 1980.
4. cf. Wellin E. Directed culture change and health programs in Latin America. *Millbank Meml Fund Q.* **44**, 111–128.
5. Agency for International Development Resources Inventory Center. *National Inventory of Physical Resources, Central American and Panama: Honduras.* AID/RIC GIPR No. 5, 1966.
6. Kendall C., Foote D. and Martorell R. Anthropology, communications, and health: the mass media and health practices program in Honduras. *Hum. Org.* **42**, 353–360; . . .
7. A number of environmental causes are also felt to produce diarrhea, as well as a number of other conditions, states and agents, such as *lombrices.* These are described in Ref. 6. They are not discussed further in this article.
8. Young J. *Medical Choice in a Mexican Village.* Rutgers University Press, New Brunswick, 1981; and Kleinman A. *op. cit.* Ref 3.
9. Direccion General de Estadistica y Censos. *Anuario Estadistico, 1978.* Tegucigalpa, Ministerior de Economia, 1980.
10. Hahn R. A. and Kleinman A. Belief in pathogen, belief as medicine; "voodoo death" and the "placebo phenomenon." *Med. Anthrop. Q.* **4**, No. 4, 3ff., 1983.

 44

Saving the Children for the Tobacco Industry

Mark Nichter
Elizabeth Cartwright

Incorporating ethnographic studies into international health programs has required some modification of traditional anthropological methods to make fieldwork briefer and more focused. These new methodologies include protocols called focused ethnographic studies (FES) (Bentley, Pelto, and Pelto 1990; Gove and Pelto 1993). Medical anthropologists have planned a significant role for PHC including programs aimed at oral rehydration therapy (as we saw in selection 43), safe motherhood initiatives, interventions against acute respiratory infections (ARI) (Nichter 1993), and introduction of appropriate weanling foods (Dettwyler and Fishman 1992). As this selection explains, nearly all of these international health efforts have been aimed at infectious diseases in children. Two lessons are apparent when reviewing this intensive PHC work: First, cultural factors must be considered in designing successful community-based programs; second, the underlying political and economic processes that result in the disastrous health conditions of the Third World are seldom addressed by international health projects.

This selection examines a different international health problem—the proliferation of tobacco use in the poor countries of the world. As cigarette smoking has decreased in the United States, there has been an extended effort to expand the market in developing countries. Cigarette companies have long been a powerful political force in the United States; tobacco growers were given federal subsidies, and the companies were able to promote an addictive and lethal product to the American public with impunity. Only recently have these companies told the complete truth about their product. Political-economic downturns in the United States have resulted in a rapid acceleration in cigarette marketing in the Third World. Critics of these policies argue that this is tantamount to exporting chronic disease and death. The marketing strategies of multinational tobacco companies to expand international sales include saturation advertising with persuasive ads wherein cigarettes are depicted as consumables of modern, wealthy, and sophisticated people.

There are ironic contradictions between U.S. trade policy and "agricultural" development on one hand and health policies on the other. This selection is a good example of a political-economic analysis applied to an international health problem. The emphasis is on the interrelation of
macroeconomic factors (tobacco company profits), health consequences (the coming Third World epidemics of lung cancer and chronic diseases), household economic costs (the purchase of cigarettes), and American ideological models of free choice and individual responsibility. Part of the mission of medical anthropology is to remind people of the bigger picture of health problems; this selection does just that.

As you read this selection, consider these questions:

- *Why do tobacco companies need to recruit new smokers in the Third World? Does the early death of smokers hurt their business?*

- *What is meant by children being innocent and therefore more in need of international health interventions?*

- *Is this selection cynical? What steps of action and intervention does it suggest? What are some obstacles that you might anticipate?*

- *Why might people in Third World countries be attracted to U.S. products like baby formula and cigarettes?*

- *Why are local governments not inclined to regulate cigarette smoking for their own populations?*

Over the last 15 years, the United States has played a significant role in fostering child survival and safe motherhood programs on a global scale. Under these programs massive immunization and oral rehydration efforts have been initiated and have achieved impressive adoption rates in many Third World settings. At the recent World Summit on Children researchers estimated that immunization programs have saved the lives of nearly two million children and oral rehydration has saved another one million (Potts 1990; United Nations International Children's Emergency Fund [UNICEF] 1990). We juxtapose this image of success with the sobering realization that chronic ill health related to tobacco consumption is dramatically increasing among adults in Third World countries. This escalating health problem affects not only the present but future generations in both direct and indirect ways.

We argue that "primary health care" and "child survival" need to be considered within a context of pathogenic trends in life-style which accompany "defective modernization" (Simonelli 1987). In addition, we question the focus of these international programs on children, often to the neglect of households, which are, after all, the units of health production (Berman, Kendall, and Bhattacharyya 1991).[1]

We maintain that the effects of tobacco consumption need to be viewed not just in relation to the health
of smokers but also to the health and welfare of all household members. In this article, therefore, we examine how tobacco consumption negatively influences household health in three ways. First, smoking leads to and exacerbates chronic illness, which in turn reduces adults' ability to provide for their children. Smoking also daily diverts scarce household resources which might be used more productively. And third, children living with smokers are exposed to smoke inhalation and have more respiratory diseases. In short, we adopt an expanded concept of child survival that is both household-centered and diachronic. Unless such a perspective is adopted, the success in child survival that may be realized by immunizing children and keeping them rehydrated will be vitiated by a second child survival crisis arising from the chronic ill health or the death of their parents.

We maintain that the disease focus of child survival programs, like the individual responsibility focus of antismoking campaigns, diverts attention away from the political and economic dimensions of ill health.[2] Saving the children, the symbols of innocence, puts the United States in a favorable light in a turbulent world and competitive international marketplace, but it also deflects attention from other issues. One such issue is that families with young children represent a huge potential market for American products, such as tobacco, which undermine household health.

While U.S. support of child survival programs received significant positive press coverage, tobacco more quietly became the eighth largest source of export revenue for the United States in 1985–86 (Wharton Econometrics 1987). Fostering tobacco consumption in the Third World may be healthy for the U.S. trade balance but not for those populations whose health is endangered by increased tobacco accessibility and advertising.

In this article we shall document the environmental and human impact of a cash crop so appealing as an immediate source of tax revenue and profit for First and Third World governments that policy makers surreptitiously support the tobacco industry even while speaking publicly in favor of antismoking initiatives.

TOBACCO PRODUCTION, THE ECOSYSTEM, AND ENVIRONMENTAL HEALTH

Recently, Maurice King (1990) has argued that primary health care policy must be contextualized in relation to the sustainability of the environment. King largely focuses his attention on population growth and the resource capacity of local ecosystems in the context of a rapidly deteriorating environment. Sustainability must, however, be viewed even more broadly. It needs to be viewed in relation to the carrying capacity of adults and how this is impacted by a mix of life-style and environmental factors that contribute to chronic ill health and incapacitating disease.

In this light it has been estimated that throughout the globe more than 100 million people, including workers and their dependents, rely for their livelihood on tobacco-based agriculture, manufacturing, and commerce (Tobacco Journal International 1988). Economically, tobacco has become a very attractive crop in many developing countries for the taxes and export earnings it generates. For example, 47% of Malaysia's taxes (Fischer 1987:20) and 55% of Malawi's export earnings (Madeley 1983:124) derive from tobacco sales. The Brazilian government receives $100 million per month from this source (Mufson 1985).

The Third World presently accounts for 75% of the total tobacco acreage under production (Stanley 1989), with most plots averaging less than one hectare in size (Muller 1983:1304). To help small farmers participate in tobacco production, international tobacco companies, the World Bank, and the Food and Agricultural Organization (FAO) have made available loans, extension advice, seed, and pesticides to farmers (Motley 1987; Muller 1983:1304). Since 1980, the World Bank has loaned more than $1 billion (U.S.) for agricultural

projects supporting tobacco production (Stanley 1989:12).

In most cases this assistance has rendered tobacco more profitable than competing food crops. Additionally, the heavy consumption of cigarettes worldwide makes the demand for tobacco, as well as its price, more consistent than many other primary products (Muller 1983). Increasing rates of tobacco consumption in developing countries further adds to the marketability of this crop.

However, there are many long-term environmental and health costs associated with tobacco cultivation. An enormous amount of firewood is necessary to cure tobacco leaves, for example. Given an average of 2–3 hectares of forest needed to flue-cure one ton of tobacco, Madeley (1983:1310) has estimated that 2.5 million hectares of trees are cut worldwide each year for tobacco curing. This is approximately one out of every eight trees harvested on an annual basis. The absence of adequate wood for the curing process has become a major constraint on tobacco production in Southern Brazil, Pakistan, Kenya, and Nigeria (Muller 1983:1305).

In areas vulnerable to erosion, tree-felling reduces the productivity of soil needed for growing food crops. It may also increase the time and energy necessary for gathering firewood for household use. In addition, farmers and field hands may be exposed to hazardous levels of pesticides in countries where there are fewer health regulations for farmworkers pertaining to protective clothing and length of exposure (Madeley 1983:1310). Existing regulations are often also difficult to enforce, though the pesticides are usually highly toxic varieties that are banned in the United States. Since tobacco requires 8 to 16 times the number of applications of pesticides as food crops, the health risks from its cultivation both through direct exposure and contamination of drinking water are considerably greater (Madeley 1983:1310).

PREVALENCE OF TOBACCO USE

Worldwide, one billion smokers consume 5 trillion cigarettes per year or 14 cigarettes per day per smoker (Chandler 1986:39). On an international scale, it is estimated that about 50% of adult males and 10% of adult females are smokers (Stanley 1989:5). In developed countries, however, these proportions are 51% and 21% (Stanley 1989), with notable differences among national groups. For example, in Japan and the USSR rates of smoking among males are 66% and 65% respectively, while among females the rates are 14% and 11%. In the United States, on the other hand, the rates for males are considerably lower but are more nearly equal for the two sexes (32% and 27% for males and females respectively). The U.S. rates are closer to Latin American figures which, however, show almost consistently higher rates for males and lower rates for females than the U.S. rate. . . . In [some] Asian countries . . . , percentages of male smokers are 50% to 100% higher than in the United States, while percentages of women smokers are much lower.

Specific data for smoking prevalence do not exist for much of the Third World. [Data] are incomplete in that they do not differentiate type of smoker by amount of tobacco consumed, smoker's age, or duration of habit. These various lacunae make cross-national comparisons difficult.[3] For example, while rates of smoking appear particularly high among both urban and rural areas in the Pacific, the quantity of tobacco consumed may be much less than in Asia or Africa.

Regional patterns of tobacco consumption exist and are manifested in distinct public/private, gender, and age cohort smoking behavior. In China, for example, smoking prevalence among males increases sharply between the age of 20 and 24, while among females it increases after age 45.[4] . . . While urban smoking rates globally are generally higher than rural rates, this is not always the case. Higher rates of smoking have been reported among Chinese peasants than among urban dwellers. In one survey 81% of male peasants were found to smoke (Tomson and Coulter 1987) as compared to a countrywide average of 61%.

Trends in Tobacco Use

In the United States, smoking prevalence has been declining steadily since 1974 at an annual rate of approximately 2% (cf. Cohen 1981). Between 1974 and 1985, 1.3 million people per year quit smoking. The number of ex-smokers has been offset, however, by the addition of approximately one million new young American smokers a year (Pierce, Fiore, and Novotny 1989). Notably, teenage girls are the chief segment of the North American population who are increasing their consumption of tobacco (Greaves and Buist 1986:8). In 1987, U.S. consumers smoked 1.5% less than in 1986 and 10% less than in 1981.

The American tobacco industry, however, has been little affected by the decline in domestic tobacco consumption. Over this time period, U.S. cigarette exports have increased 56%, and production has increased 5% (Grise 1988). In developing countries, 54% of adult males and 8% of adult females are presently believed to smoke (Stanley 1989). This calculation includes both traditional forms of smoking and the rapidly increasing use of manufactured cigarettes.[5] Tobacco consumption worldwide is estimated to have increased by 73% over the last 20 years, particularly in the Third World. This increase represents not simply *more* people becoming smokers, but a larger *percentage* of the world's population acquiring tobacco habits. Between 1970 and 1985 increases in cigarette consumption exceeded population growth by significant amounts in Africa, Asia, and South America. . . .

Traditional uses of tobacco tend to predispose men more than women to adopt highly refined packaged cigarettes. In much of Africa, Asia, the Pacific, and Latin America, women generally start smoking later than men (Waldron et al. 1988). Social sanctions commonly prohibit young women from smoking commercial cigarettes but are often less restrictive about the consumption of locally grown tobacco products. Sanctions may reflect women's lack of access to Western goods and do not result in a sex difference in overall tobacco consumption (Waldron et al. 1988). Access to goods like tobacco is associated with women's work opportunities and their acquisition of disposable income. Cigarette companies are presently attempting to capitalize on women's enhanced income worldwide by selling cigarettes as a marker of status change (Gupta and Ball 1990).

MARKETING OF CIGARETTES

On a worldwide scale, the tobacco industry spends approximately $12.5 billion dollars annually on advertising. Not surprisingly, cigarettes rank among the top three most advertised products in the world (Jacobson 1983). In 1988 the U.S. tobacco industry spent $2.5 billion dollars for advertising and promotion, or about $6.5 million dollars a day. In contrast, the U.S. Office of Smoking and Health has a total annual budget of $3.8 million dollars (Cohen 1981). This discrepancy between expenditures for tobacco promotion versus expenditures for health through smoking cessation is not limited to the United States. In 1983, $10,000 (U.S.) was spent by the Argentinean government on antitobacco campaigns, while tobacco companies reportedly spent $40 million (U.S.) on marketing and publicity (Baragiola 1986).

Cigarette smoking is escalating rapidly among adolescents in several developed countries (Mintz 1987). It has been well documented in the West that 90% of persons who smoke cigarettes have begun by the age of 19 (Kandel and Logan 1984). This trend reflects a greater availability of cigarettes to teens, and it is associated with an increased number of misconceptions regarding the risk of addiction and individual vulnerability to smoking-related diseases (Leventhal, Glynn, and Fleming 1987:3376). Within the context of the family, researchers have found that adolescents whose parents and older siblings smoke are more likely to become smokers themselves (Chassin et al. 1984:239).

Over three-quarters of the world's young people aged 15–24 live in Third World countries. This population constitutes an immense marketing opportunity, as well as an extremely vulnerable audience for advertising campaigns. Cigarette advertising in developing countries has been largely directed toward men, but women and adolescents are being increasingly targeted as well (Taha and Ball 1985). Even when not specifically targeted, adolescents interpret cigarette advertisements in ways very similar to adults (Aitken, Leathar, and O'Hagan 1985:785). Research suggests, for example, that adolescents find it difficult to comprehend the long-term risks of smoking (Aitken et al. 1987; Amos, Hillhouse, and Robertson 1989; Charlton 1990; Roberts 1987; Stebbins 1987). Teens are also more susceptible to the images of romance, success, sophistication, popularity, and adventure which advertising suggests they could achieve through the consumption of cigarettes (McCarthy and Gritz 1987; Yankelovich et al. 1977). As two critics of this form of advertising in Kenya observe, however:

> The cruel irony is that the majority of Kenyans (like many of the target groups for Western advertisements) will never have the successful careers, the high consumption life styles or the sense of satisfaction depicted in the advertisements. Yet when they buy the attractively packaged cigarettes they are buying part of the myth. Along with their deadly products, the tobacco industry pedals the myth of the Western ideal of development. (Currie and Ray 1984:1137; see also Stebbins 1987:529)

Rather than being regarded simply as objects to consume, cigarettes become indices of social membership for adolescents who are searching for their identities or who wish to escape the immediate reality into which they have been born (Baudrillard 1981). The growing number of adolescent smokers at home and abroad suggests that the impact of these forms of tobacco promotion may be formidable.

HOUSEHOLD EXPENDITURES ON TOBACCO

How much of a drain on household income is tobacco consumption among those living at the margin? Little household-based data exist on expenditure for tobacco in relation to household income. One study in São Paolo, Brazil, found that expenditure for cigarettes in a low-income population ranged from 3.1 to 14.6% ($\bar{x} = 9.8\%$) of family income (Silveira et al. 1982). This was higher than expenditures for either transportation (5.8%) or milk (8.3%) among the same families. Brazil is the fifth largest cigarette market in the world, and cigarettes are the most heavily advertised product. Over 40% of Brazil's 120 million people are under the age of 15, 70% of its people live in urban areas, and television reaches three-quarters of all households. Sixty percent of males and 26% of females in urban areas of Brazil smoked in 1978 (Jacobson 1983:37).

A 1979 study by Nichter (1991) in South India among subsistence level agricultural households of the Shudra and Harijan castes found that tobacco was consumed in one form or another (smoking, snuff, in conjunction with betel nut) in virtually every household. Sixty-five percent of a sample of males over age 25 ($N = 100$) were smokers of "beedies" or cigarettes. Respondents smoked for relaxation, as a means of social exchange, to reduce hunger, control toothache, enhance digestion, and assist with routine defecation.

Among two convenience samples of households ($N = 50$) of male smokers (where female tobacco consumption habits were assumed to vary randomly), weekly modal expenditure on all forms of tobacco was 5 rupees (median expenditure = Rs. 4.5). In 1979, the daily wage for agricultural labor was Rs. 5–6 (U.S. $.63–.75) in this region. Among a sample of smokers ($N = 25$) having a mean estimated yearly household income of Rs. 2500 (U.S. $312), tobacco purchases were estimated to account for 10% of total household income. Among a second sample ($N = 25$) having a mean estimated annual household income of Rs. 3,600 (U.S. $450), tobacco accounted for 7% of annual income. These annual tobacco expenditures equaled annual household health care expenses in both samples (Nichter 1991).

In a study conducted in 1988–89 in Alexandria, Egypt, Marcia Inhorn (personal communication) found that 151 of 190 (79%) lower-class male heads of household had smoked cigarettes. Of the 145 regular cigarette smokers, 102 (70%) smoked between one and three packs per day at a daily cost of £1–3 (U.S. $.40–1.20) for the lowest priced, Egyptian-manufactured brand. Cigarette expenditures for most men were between £30–90 per month. Although monthly combined household incomes ranged from £40–400 per month, the majority (65%) ranged from £50–200. On a regular basis, expenditures for cigarettes thus accounted for between one-third and one-half of all disposable income in the majority of households. In nuclear family households supported by a cigarette-smoking husband, the husband's need for "pocket money" to buy cigarettes was often regarded by wives as the major reason for their inability to provide proper nourishment for their children. Although a small number of husbands had intentionally "weaned" themselves from cigarettes to less expensive water-pipe tobacco, the majority of Egyptian men in this study were addicted to cigarettes, having begun smoking in most cases during their late adolescent years.

MORBIDITY/MORTALITY

In 1989 the World Health Organization estimated that 2.5 million people die each year of tobacco-related deaths, approximately one death every 13 seconds (Ile and Kroll 1990). One-and-a-half to two million of these deaths occurred in developed countries, with the United States accounting for approximately 400,000 deaths per year (Peto 1990).[6] The two biggest tobacco producers outside the United States, China and India, also have high tobacco-induced mortality rates which are predicted to rise even higher. Peto has estimated that fewer than 100,000 Chinese people now die of tobacco-related diseases a year, but by the year 2025 two million Chinese (mostly male) will die a year. In India as in China, some 60–80% of adult males smoke. Gupta (1989) has conservatively estimated that in this decade 630,000 to one million adults will die per year from tobacco induced diseases.

Beyond the fatalities, the estimated lost productivity associated with chronic diseases related to smoking is staggering. The Office of Technology Assessment of the U.S. Congress has calculated that in 1985 the direct costs of treating smoking-related diseases in the United States was $22 billion. The indirect costs from lost income because of illness and premature deaths attributable to tobacco was $43 billion (Stanley 1989:27). These figures are rough estimates of the price one country is paying for tobacco use. It is impossible to calculate comparable costs among impoverished populations in developing countries.

Overshadowing these figures on fatalities and lost productivity among tobacco users are considerations of "significant others" indirectly affected by the inability of an adult to support them, for those directly affected by tobacco-related ill health are often responsible for the economic well-being of children, pregnant or lactating mothers, and older relatives. Expensive treatment regimens and disabilities resulting in lost wages can severely deplete family resources.

Fatal and disabling diseases either induced or exacerbated by tobacco that have been reported in the medical literature include: lung cancer, chronic ob-

structive lung disease, heart disease, myocardial infarctions, peripheral vascular disease, and hypertension. These diseases develop in a manner which is dose-dependent and increases with time of exposure (Peto 1986)—i.e., the earlier a person starts smoking and the higher the tar content of the tobacco smoked, the greater the risk of developing pathological problems (Tominaga 1986:131).

Manufactured cigarettes bearing international brand names which are sold in the Third World often have much higher tar and nicotine levels than those sold in the West. . . . The median tar level in the United States is 20 mg/cigarette, while in Indonesia it is 36 mg/cigarette (Stanley 1989:4). The use of filter-tips in Western countries has become increasingly popular, as have low-tar cigarettes. Cigarettes produced in the Third World, however, are often unfiltered, as are traditional tobacco products such as beedies. Yach (1986:286) notes a disturbing trend in which people from the lowest social classes in both Nigeria and South Africa smoke cigarettes with the highest tar and nicotine contents. Access to "safer" cigarettes varies between richer and poorer nations, as well as between social classes within individual countries.

Because there is a 20–25 year time lag before health problems related to smoking manifest themselves, current disease rates reflect the consequences of habits acquired decades ago. The Council on Scientific Affairs of the American Medical Association cites increased usage of cigarettes as the major contributing cause of increasing rates of lung cancer in the Third World (Council on Scientific Affairs 1990:3318). Further epidemiological profiles of Third World adults are sure to reflect changing trends in both active and passive smoking. An increasing number of children smoke and/or are exposed to adults who smoke (Nath 1986:33). It is estimated that approximately 200 million children now under 20 years of age will die from tobacco use (Peto and Lopez 1990:1).

Passive smoke inhalation constitutes a significant health risk by increasing susceptibility to acute respiratory tract infections. Acute lower respiratory tract infections are the second major cause of death among children in the Third World, accounting for some three to four million infant and child deaths per year, or approximately one-third of the total global infant child mortality (Berman and McIntosh 1985; Gadomski 1990; World Health Organization 1988). The cumulative incidence of acute respiratory tract infections increases significantly with the presence of a smoker in the household (Chen et al. 1988).[7] This holds true for, children of parents who do and do not have histories of asthma or wheezing. . . .

In sum, smoking directly affects the health of children either when they themselves smoke or when they are the passive recipients of their parents' smoke. Indirectly, their health is also affected by the health of their caretakers: with increased absenteeism, decreased productivity, and more money spent on illness treatments, families with members who have tobacco-related illnesses are likely to have fewer resources to spend on nutritious food and health care.

UNITED STATES POLICY AND COMPLICITY

This year the first author interviewed a U.S. marketing executive in East Africa who said,

> It is our moral duty to help educate those in the Third World and to help Third World nations become self-sufficient so they can stand on their own two feet and be full partners in international trade. Literacy is good for business and good for democracy. There are some who say that taking advantage of an illiterate population through image advertising is immoral. They may have a point. The innocence of an illiterate population is easily exploited. When that population can read, however, it's a question of free choice. Once literate, you have to respect a man's choice. They are on their own.

Notwithstanding antismoking legislation at home, the U.S. government has exerted its influence in developing the world tobacco market in several ways. In the 20 years following World War II, one billion dollars in Food for Peace (PL480) funds were spent supplying Third World countries with tobacco as a means of reducing the U.S. surplus and creating a market for cigarettes in the Third World (Motley 1987; Stebbins 1988; Taylor 1984). As Stebbins notes,

> Despite its name, the Food for Peace program's main function was not to combat hunger and malnutrition, but to develop new markets for American agricultural products, to dispose of surplus commodities and to further U.S. foreign policy. (1988:9)

More recently, U.S. trade policy has protected the American tobacco industry. Countries such as Japan, South Korea, and Thailand (to name but the most recent examples), have been pressured to open their doors to American cigarette sales and advertising or suffer trade sanctions (American Public Health Association 1988; Connolly 1988a, 1988b; Connolly and Walker 1987; U.S. Department of Agriculture 1988). When South Korea resisted American tobacco industry advertising, it was met with a retaliatory list of possible trade sanctions which would go into effect should restrictions continue (John 1988:28). Section 301 of the revised 1974 United States Trade Act protects American export industry from "discriminatory" trade restrictions, including foreign monopolies in tobacco sales, importations, and advertising. As Schmeisser has noted, the tobacco industry has used the 1974 Trade Act to enlist the services of the executive branch of the U.S. government to "arm twist offending foreign powers into a more magnanimous trade posture" (Schmeisser 1988:18). The Food and Agricultural Organization (FAO) and the World Bank have meanwhile promoted tobacco production through multimillion dollar loans to several Third World countries, including India and Pakistan.

U.S. foreign policy on health matters is inconsistent. Small children are worth saving, apparently because they are innocent, while their older brothers and sisters and their parents are fair game for the tobacco industry. The marketing executive quoted above introduced a curious variation on the theme of innocence by equating it with illiteracy. While it may be immoral to influence those unable to read through advertising, literacy renders people responsible for their actions as free agents. This argument fosters victim-blaming: the poor of the Third World who "choose" to smoke processed cigarettes, often to affiliate with a highly advertised fantasy good life (commodity fetishism), are, by this reasoning, held accountable for their own poor judgment (or Western taste?).

Several health activists interviewed by the first author in India and the Philippines expressed the opinion that antismoking campaigns need to play a greater role in primary health care programs. Immunization emerged as a metaphor which was extended to antismoking campaigns. Children need to be immunized against the false consciousness of cigarette image advertisements, just as they need to be immunized against polio and measles.[8] Emotional appeals targeted at parents who smoke were also suggested as a means of making them more aware that they were risking their ability to care for their children.

While these tactics merit consideration, polluted environments, poor occupational health conditions, and other more immediate health risks serve to minimize the impact of such messages.[9] "Immunization" programs, in the form of antismoking messages, may also divert attention from issues essential to successful antismoking programs. A national policy which fosters the accessibility of cigarettes may be masked by token policy gestures such as legislation that bans cigarette advertisements on the radio while allowing billboard advertisements in bus terminals. Such actions give the appearance of an antismoking position which is in fact not sustained for reasons related to profit and tax revenues.

Incorporating smoking education within existing primary health care programs is insufficient (Milio 1985:610). What is needed is to reduce public access to cigarettes. Such a program, however, requires political will of a different order from what is necessary to mount a mass media antismoking campaign (Stebbins 1990:233). The political will must be strong enough to withstand significant losses from tax revenues and survive a public outcry if tobacco taxes are raised.

SUMMARY AND CONCLUSIONS: LESSONS FOR INTERNATIONAL HEALTH AND MEDICAL ANTHROPOLOGY

The foregoing data suggest that it will be difficult for the many Third World countries that derive substantial revenue from internal cigarette sales (external sales are another matter) to escape the paradoxes contained in the following scenario.

1. At a time when incomes are falling in much of the Third World, increased funds are needed to maintain social welfare programs and child survival efforts.[10]

2. Significant tax revenue is generated by cigarette taxation in an environment in which tobacco consumption is increasing. (For example, 12% of Brazil's revenue comes from tobacco sales, "enough to pay all expenses for medical care in the country including drugs and hospitalization, or 40% of all social benefits of the country" [Lokshin and Barros 1983:1314].)

3. Existing consumer demand increases as a result of advertising. Advertising targets new markets and populations who are not already brand loyal. Young people and women increasingly are the targets of carefully planned campaigns.

4. The age of initiation into smoking decreases, particularly in urban areas. A younger age of initiation translates into a younger age when the negative health effects of smoking are realized. These effects are increasingly apparent in the 35–45 age range.

5. A significant number of adults are affected by chronic disease during the time when their carrying capacity for the young and the old (especially women) is high. This begins to have a noticeable impact on the household production of health.

6. Short-term assets from cigarette tax revenues are offset by the costs of long-term health care and loss of productivity. However, politicians, whose tenures in office are relatively short, look to tobacco as an immediate source of revenues which enable them to finance programs of high visibility in order to marshal public support. Child survival programs provide highly visible proof of government action which is also internationally applauded.

7. Faced with massive chronic health problems linked to smoking, in the context of poor environmental and occupational health conditions, child survival programs and adult health care programs will compete for very limited funds.

. . .

A greater awareness of U.S. complicity in propagating tobacco consumption in the Third World and the toll it is likely to take challenges our national values, our national stake in appearing to be morally right and committed to the development of "health for all." Research revealing the tobacco industry's role in the household production of ill health shifts attention from our collective public efforts to "save the children" to our support of cigarette sales in Third World countries as a means of establishing a more equitable balance of trade. Such research recontextualizes the problem as one involving serious ethical questions concerning free trade and market justice.

The concept of "market justice" ultimately lays responsibility for poor health in the hands of the consumer/citizen in the name of free trade as a democratic principle tied to individual rights. Factors that predispose and condition humans to engage in "voluntary behavior" associated with health risk need to be examined critically. So does a behavioral model of public health rooted in the "market justice/individual responsibility" paradigm of health education (McLeroy, Gottlieb, and Burdine 1987). Several questions need to be raised. Do people freely choose their own risks in an environment saturated by market images (Foege 1990)? How has a desire to engage in risky behavior been fostered? Have particular segments of a population been targeted for promotion of products associated with risky behavior? Who profits from the promotion of risk-taking behavior? To what extent have people become immune to antismoking messages? What images have been employed to reduce the impact of health education messages?

Beauchamp (1976, 1985), among others (e.g., Neubauer and Pratt 1981), has argued for the formulation of a new critical paradigm of public health that is sensitive to the production and representation of so-called voluntary risks. This paradigm challenges attempts to limit public attention to the behavior of the smoker or drinker (Beauchamp 1976:12). Central to this emergent paradigm is the critical examination of "market justice" as a means of opening dialogue about a counter ethic. Since a major American tobacco company is presently affiliating itself with the Bill of Rights in its latest marketing campaign, research exposing the household and environmental costs of a "free" international tobacco trade are timely.[11]

The case of tobacco illustrates why medical anthropologists interested in public health need to pay as much attention to the social relations of consumption and the semiotics of consumables as they do to modes of production and world systems penetration of local markets.[12] Each contributes in profound and multiple ways to international health. International health must be situated within what Baudrillard (1981:200) has termed our true environment, "the universe of communication" as well as within the market, its economic equivalent. Within this environment the illusion of freedom is fostered through objects of immediate gratification, such as cigarettes, alcohol (Singer 1986), and sugar (Mintz 1985), which establish group membership, affiliate one with the "good life," take the edge off frustrated aspirations, blur the contradictions of everyday life, and make the intolerable tolerable for the moment. At issue is the hidden cost in human suffering and ecological destruction paid for expressions of personal freedom shaped by market interest. Taking stock of this issue constitutes an agenda for international health as important as vaccine development. Pathogens come in all shapes and sizes.

NOTES

1. While progress in international health has unquestionably been made when measured in terms of reduction in mortality among infants and young children, international progress may be criticized for approaching health problems among the poor with acute-care strategies, while in actuality these problems more closely resemble chronic illnesses (Chen 1986).

2. Social scientists (Crawford 1979; Neubauer and Pratt 1981; Winkler 1987), as well as people in public health (Allegrante and Green 1981; Bush 1986; Godin and Shephard 1984), have identified the attention to the physical body as a means of diverting attention from the body politic. It has been suggested, for example, that such a tactic underlies support for the fitness movement in the United States, where responsibility for ill health is placed upon the individual rather than on those complicit in manipulating national tastes for fast driving, irresponsible sex, drinking, smoking, etc., through the media. Individuals are also held responsible for their own health in situations where illnesses result from environmental pollution and hazardous working conditions (Alexander 1988).

3. Also missing are data on the meaning of smoking in different cultures. Prevalence data must be viewed critically and in relation to the meaning of tobacco consumption and exchange (Black 1984; Marshall 1981).

4. Other countries have similar age-related tobacco consumption trends as China. For example, in the Philippines 30% of the population are smokers. Eighty percent of Philippine smokers are males aged 26–35 who consume at least half a pack a day. The majority of these smokers come from the lower socioeconomic classes (Aung-Thwin 1987).

5. The *Multinational Monitor* (Motley 1987) has published a much larger table of "smokers worldwide," summarizing data available from the World Health Organization and numerous other sources. In most cases, figures cited exceed those noted from Stanley (1989). The validity of these figures varies depending on the survey methods employed and the sample size. The figures are meant to provide some estimate of smoking prevalence.

6. In contrast to these statistics, the U.S. tobacco industry proclaimed in 1980 that "many eminent scientists hold the view that no case against smoking has been proved" (Ashton and Stepney 1983).

7. Chapman et al. (1990) argue that the risks associated with passive smoking particularly threaten the cigarette industry, because passive smoking shifts attention from the arena of individual and personal freedom to social responsibility and larger units of analysis.

8. An immunization model has been applied in U.S. smoking prevention programs. See, for example, Evans, Rozelle, and Maxwell (1981); Hurd et al. (1980); McAlister, Perry, and Maccoby (1979); and Perry, Maccoby, and McAlister (1980); as well as Duryea, Ransom, and English (1990) for a critical commentary.

9. While significant, tobacco is far from being the only factor increasing respiratory diseases. Breathing the air in Mexico City is equivalent to smoking two packs of cigarettes every day (Wayburn 1991). Poorly regulated occupational settings, as well as the larger polluted living environment, have been clearly implicated in contributing to the increased prevalence of various cancers and pulmonary disorders. Antismoking campaigns need to be situated within this wider context to weigh all causative factors appropriately. It would be a shame to see tobacco habits scapegoated at the expense of ignoring such issues as improper disposal and regulation of industrially produced toxins. On the use of smoking as a "whipping boy," see Alexander (1988), Brown et al. (1990), and Sterling (1978).

10. At a time when increases in foreign aid for child survival are unlikely and the average incomes of many Third World nations throughout much of Africa and Latin America are reported as falling 10 to 25 percent (Chernomas 1990), governments are being encouraged to explore new means of community financing (Bossert 1990; Chen 1986).

11. Those engaged in developing a critical public health paradigm may gain much from anthropological studies looking beyond the physical body to the social body, body politic, and consumer body (O'Neill 1985; Scheper-Hughes and Lock 1987). King (1990) draws attention to the deep conviction within Western civilization that we are able to control the natural world, thus

enabling all communities to develop indefinitely. This notion of progress defines modernist thinking and has been critiqued by Bateson in his discussion of *creatura* (1972) and by Toulman (1982) in his definition of a new cosmology that draws upon ecological wisdom.

12. Of course it may be argued that the mode of consumption is simply a mode of production of self-identity.

REFERENCES

Aitken, P. P., D. S. Leathar, and F. J. O'Hagan. 1985. Children's Perception of Advertisements for Cigarettes. Social Science and Medicine 21(7):785–797.

Aitken, P. P., et al. 1987. Children's Awareness of Cigarette Advertisements and Brand Imagery. British Journal of Addiction 82:615–622.

Alexander, J. 1988. Ideological Construction of Risk: An Analysis of Corporate Health Promotion Programs in the 1980s. Social Science and Medicine 26(5): 559–567.

Allegrante, J., and L. Green. 1981. When Health Policy "Becomes Victim Blaming." New England Journal of Medicine 305:1528–1529.

American Public Health Association. 1988. Limiting the Exploration of Tobacco Products. American Journal of Public Health 78(2):195–196.

Amos, A., A. Hillhouse, and G. Robertson. 1989. Tobacco Advertising and Children—The Impact of the Voluntary Agreement. Health Education Research 4:51–57.

Ashton, H., and R. Stepney. 1983. Smoking : Psychology and Pharmacology. Cambridge, England: Cambridge University Press.

Aung-Thwin, M. 1987. Insecurity Hindering Philippine Tobacco Industry. Tobacco Journal International 6:399–400.

Baragiola, A. M. 1986. Tabaquismo: Aspectos sanitorias, educativos y sociales. Revista Argentina de Analysis, Modificación y Terapía del Compartamiento 2(4):49–54.

Barthes, Roland. 1973. Mythologies. London: Paladin Press.

Bateson, Gregory. 1972. Steps to an Ecology of Mind. New York: Ballantine Books.

Baudrillard, Jean. 1981. For a Critique of the Political Economy of the Sign. St. Louis, MO: Telos Press.

Beauchamp, Dan E. 1976. Public Health as Social Justice. Inquiry 18(1):3–14.

———. 1985. Community: The Neglected Tradition of Public Health. Hastings Center Report, December:28–36.

Becker, Marshall. 1986. The Tyranny of Health Promotion. Public Health Reviews 14:15–25.

Berman, Peter, Carl Kendall, and Karabi Bhattacharyya. 1991. The Household Production of Health: Putting the People at the Center of Health Improvement. Social Science and Medicine. (In press.)

Berman, S., and K. McIntosh. 1985. Acute Respiratory Infections. Reviews of Infectious Diseases 7(5):29–46.

Black, P. 1984. The Anthropology of Tobacco Use: Tobain Data and Theoretical Issues. Journal of Anthropological Research 40(4): 475–503.

Bossert, T. 1990. Can They Get Along without Us? Sustainability of Donor Supported Health Projects in Central America and Africa. Social Science and Medicine 39(9): 1015–1023.

Brown, L. R., et al. 1990. State of the World, 1990: Worldwatch Institute Report on Progress toward a Sustainable Society. New York: W. W. Norton.

Bush, Roger. 1986. Health Promotion—An Ethical Perspective. The Western Journal of Medicine 144(1):102–103.

Chandler, William. 1986. Banishing Tobacco. Worldwatch Paper 68. Washington, DC: Worldwatch Institute.

Chapman, Simon, et al. 1990. Why the Tobacco Industry Fears the Passive Smoking Issue. International Journal of Health Sciences 20(3):417–427.

Charlton, A. 1990. Children's Advertisement Awareness Related to Their Views on Smoking. Health Education Journal 45:75–78.

Chassin, Laurie, et al. 1984. Predicting the Onset of Cigarette Smoking in Adolescents: A Longitudinal Study. Journal of Applied Social Psychology 14(3):224–243.

Chen, Lincoln. 1986. Primary Health Care in Developing Countries: Overcoming Operational, Technical and Social Barriers. Lancet 2(2):1260–1265.

Chen, Y., et al. 1988. Chang-Ning Epidemiological Study of Children's Health: Passive Smoking and Children's Respiratory Diseases. International Journal of Epidemiology 17(2):348–355.

Chernomas, Robert. 1990. The Debt-Depression of the Less Developed World and Public Health. International Journal of Health Services 20(4):537–543.

Cohen, Nicholas. 1981. Smoking, Health and Survival: Prospects in Bangladesh. Lancet 1(2):1090–1093.

Connolly, Gregory. 1988a. The American Liberation of the Japanese Cigarette Market. World Smoking and Health 13:20–25.

———. 1988b. Tobacco and United States Trade Sanctions. In Smoking and Health 1987: Proceedings of the 6th World Conference on Smoking and Health. M. Aoki, S. Hisomichi, and S. Tominaga, eds. Pp. 351–354. New York: Elsevier Science.

Connolly, Gregory, and Bailus Walker, Jr. 1987. Restrictions on Importation of Tobacco by Japan, Taiwan and South Korea. New England Journal of Medicine 316(22):1416–1417.

Council on Scientific Affairs. 1990. The Worldwide Smoking Epidemic. Journal of the American Medical Association 263(24):3312–3318.

Crawford, Robert. 1979. Individual Responsibility and Health Politics in the 1970's. In Health Care in America. S. Reverby and G. Rosner, eds. Pp. 249–268. Philadelphia: Temple University Press.

Currie, Kate, and Larry Ray. 1984. Going Up in Smoke: The Case of British American Tobacco in Kenya. Social Science and Medicine 19(11):1131–1139.

Duryea, E. J., M. V. Ransom, and G. English. 1990. Psychological Immunization: Theory, Research, and Current Health Behavior Applications. Health Education Quarterly 17(2):169–178.

Evans, R. I., R. M. Rozelle, and S. Maxwell. 1981. Social Modeling Films to Deter Smoking in Adolescents: Results of a Three-year Field Investigation. Journal of Applied Psychology 66:399–414.

Fischer, P. M. 1987. Tobacco in the Third World. Journal of the Islamic Medical Association 19:19–21.

Foege, William H. 1990. The Growing Brown Plague. Journal of the American Medical Association 264(12):1580.

Gadomiski, Anne, ed. 1990. ALRI and Child Survival in Developing Countries. Workshop Report. Baltimore, MD: Johns Hopkins Institute for International Programs.

Gallup Organization, Inc. 1988. The Incidence of Smoking in Central and Latin America. Conducted for the American Cancer Society. Princeton, NJ: Gallup Organization.

Godin, Gaston, and Roy Shephard. 1984. Physical Fitness—Individual or Societal Responsibility? Canadian Journal of Public Health 95:200–202.

Greaves, L., and M. Buist. 1986. The Tobacco Industry Weeding Women Out. Broadside 7(7):3–4.

Grise, U. N. 1988. Tobacco Situation and Outlook Optimistic for Next Several Years. Tobacco International 190(6):7–8.

Gupta, Prakash. 1989. An Assessment of Excess Mortality Caused by Tobacco Usage in India. In Tobacco and Health: The Indian Scene. L. D. Sanghvi and P. Notari, eds. Pp. 57–62. UICC Workshop. Bombay, India: Tata Memorial Centre.

Gupta, Prakash, and Keith Ball. 1990. India: Tobacco Tragedy. Lancet 334:594–595.

Hurd, P. D., et al. 1980. Prevention of Cigarette Smoking in Seventh Grade Students. Journal of Behavioral Medicine 3:15–28.

Ile, Michael L., and Laura A. Kroll. 1990. Tobacco Advertising and the First Amendment. Journal of the American Medical Association. 264(12):1593–1594.

Jacobson, Bobbie. 1983. Smoking and Health: A New Generation of Campaigners. British Medical Journal 287:483–484.

John, G. A. 1988. Section 301 Charges by CEA and the Korean Monopoly Response. Tobacco International 190:6, 28.

Kandel, D. B., and J. A. Logan. 1984. Patterns of Drug Use from Adolescence to Young Adulthood: Periods of Risk for Initiation, Continued Use and Discontinuation. American Journal of Public Health 74:660–666.

King, Maurice. 1990. Health Is a Sustainable State. Lancet 336:664–667.

Leeder, S. R., et al. 1976. Influence of Personal and Family Factors on Ventilatory Function of Children. British Journal of Preventive Social Medicine 30:219–224.

Leventhal, Howard, Kathleen Glynn, and Raymond Fleming. 1987. Is the Smoking Decision an "Informed Choice"?: Effect of Smoking Risk Factors on Smoking Beliefs. Journal of the American Medical Association 257(24):3373–3376.

Lokshin, Fernando, and Fernando Barros. 1983. Smoking or Health: The Brazilian Option. New York State Journal of Medicine 83(13):1314–1316.

Madeley, John. 1983. The Environmental Impact of Tobacco Production in Developing Countries. New York State Journal of Medicine 83(13):1310–1311.

Marshall, Mack. 1981. Tobacco Use and Abuse in Micronesia: A Preliminary Discussion. Journal of Studies on Alcohol 49:885–893.

McAlister, A., C. Perry, and N. Maccoby. 1979. Adolescent Smoking: Onset and Prevention. Pediatrics 63:659–662.

McCarthy, W. J., and E. R. Gritz. 1987. Madison Avenue as the Pied Piper: Cigarette Advertising and Teenage Smoking. Paper presented at the annual meeting of the American Psychological Association, New York City, August 13.

McLeroy, K. R., N. Gottlieb, and J. Burdine. 1987. The Business of Health Promotion: Ethical Issues and Professional Responsibilities. Health Education Quarterly 14(l):91–109.

Milio, Nancy. 1985. Health Policy and the Emerging Tobacco Reality. Social Science and Medicine 21(6):603–614.

Mintz, Morton. 1987. The Smoke Screen: Tobacco and the Press, an Unhealthy Alliance. Multinational Monitor 8(7,8):15–17.

Mintz, Sidney. 1985. Sweetness and Power: The Place of Sugar in Modern History. New York: Penguin.

Mosley, William Henry. 1984. Child Survival: Research and Policy. Population and Development Review 10:3–23.

Motley, Susan. 1987. Burning the South: U.S. Tobacco Companies in the Third World. Multinational Monitor, July/August, 8(7/8):7–10.

Mulfson, S. 1985. Cigarette Companies Develop Third World as a Growth Market. Wall Street Journal. 5 July: Al, A16.

Muller, Mike. 1983. Preventing Tomorrow's Epidemic. The Control of Smoking and Tobacco Production in Developing Countries. New York State Journal of Medicine 83(13):1304–1309.

Nath, Uma Ram. 1986. Smoking: Third World Alert. Oxford: Oxford University Press.

Neubauer, Dean, and Richard Pratt. 1981 The Second Public Health Revolution: A Critical Appraisal. Journal of Health Politics, Policy and Law 6(2):205–228.

Nichter, Mark. 1991. Anthropology's Contribution to Health Service Research in the Third World. (Unpublished manuscript in the files of the first author).

O'Neill, John. 1985. Five Bodies. The Human Shape of Modern Society. Ithaca, NY: Cornell University Press.

Peach, H. 1986. Smoking and Respiratory Disease Excluding Lung Cancer. In Tobacco: A Major International Health Hazard. D. G. Zaridze and R. Peto, eds. Pp. 61–72. Lyon, France: International Agency for Research on Cancer.

Perry, C., N. Maccoby, and A. McAlister. 1980. Adolescent Smoking Prevention: A Third Year Follow-up. World Smoking and Health 1:40–45.

Peto, Richard. 1986. Influence of Dose and Duration of Smoking on Lung Cancer Rates. In Tobacco: A Major International Health Hazard. D. G. Zaridze and R. Peto, eds. Pp. 23–33. Lyon, France: International Agency for Research on Cancer.

———. 1990. Future Worldwide Health Effects of Current Smoking Patterns. Paper presented at WHO Workshop, Perth, Australia, April 3.

Peto, Richard, and A. D. Lopez. 1990. Proceedings. Seventh World Conference on Tobacco and Health. Perth, Australia, April 3.

Pierce, J. P., M. C. Fiore, and T. E. Novotny. 1989. Trends in Cigarette Smoking in the United States. Projections to the

Year 2000. Journal of the American Medical Association 261(1):61–65.

Potts, Malcolm. 1990. Mere Survival or a World Worth Living In? The Lancet 36:866–868.

Rothwell, K., and R. Maseroni. 1988. Tendancies et effets du tabagisme dans le monde. World Health Statistics Quarterly 41:228–241.

Roberts, J. L. 1987. The Name of the Game—Selling Cigarettes on BBC TV. London: Health Education Authority.

Scheper-Hughes, Nancy, and Margaret Lock. 1987. The Mindful Body: A Prolegomenon to Future Work in Medical Anthropology. Medical Anthropology Quarterly (n.s.) 1:6 41.

Schmeisser, Peter. 1988. Pushing Cigarettes Overseas. New York Times Magazine July 10: 16–22, 62.

Silveira, Lima, et al. 1982. Implicaçóes Médicas e Socio-econômicas do Tabagismo em Familias de Baixa Renda em Sao Paulo. Jornal Pediatrico (Rio) 52:325–328.

Simonelli, Jeanne. 1987. Defective Modernization and Health in Mexico. Social Science and Medicine 24(1):23–36.

Singer, Merrill. 1986. Toward a Political-Economy of Alcoholism: The Missing Link in the Anthropology of Drinking. Social Science and Medicine 23(2):113–130.

Stanley, Kenneth. 1989. Control of Tobacco Production and Use. (Unpublished manuscript in the files of the authors.)

Stebbins, Kenyon R. 1987. Tobacco or Health in the Third World: A Political Economy Perspective with Emphasis on Mexico. International Journal of Health Services 17(3):521–536.

———. 1988. Tobacco, Politics, Economics and Health: Implications for Third World Populations. Paper presented at the annual meeting of the American Anthropological Association, Phoenix.

———. 1990. Transnational Tobacco Companies and Health in Underdeveloped Countries: Recommendations for Avoiding an Epidemic. Social Science and Medicine 30(2): 227–235.

Sterling, Theodore. 1978. Does Smoking Kill Workers or Working Kill Smokers, or the Mutual Relationship between Smoking, Occupation and Respiratory Disease. International Journal of Health Services 8(3):437–452.

Taha, Ahmed, and Keith Ball. 1985. Tobacco and the Third World: The Growing Threat. East African Medical Journal 62:735–741.

Taylor, Peter. 1984. The Smoke Ring: Tobacco, Money and Multinational Polities. New York: Pantheon Books.

Tobacco Journal International. 1988. Counting the Multitudes of the World's Tobacco People. Tobacco Journal International 3:166, 170.

Tominaga, S. 1986. Spread of Smoking to the Developing Countries. In Tobacco: A Major International Health Hazard. D. G. Zaridze and R. Peto, eds. Pp. 125–133. Lyon, France: International Agency for Research on Cancer.

Tomson, D., and A. Coulter. 1987. The Bamboo Smoke Screen: Tobacco Smoking in China. Health Promotion 2(2):95–108.

Toulman, Steven. 1982. The Return to Cosmology. Berkeley: University of California Press.

Tuomkilehto, Jaakko, et al. 1986. Smoking Rates in Pacific Islands. Bulletin of the World Health Organization 64(3): 447–456.

United Nations International Children's Emergency Fund (UNICEF). 1990. The State of the World's Children. New Delhi: UNICEF.

United States Department of Agriculture. 1988. World Tobacco Situation. Foreign Agricultural Service Report. FT 8–88.

Waldron, Ingrid, et al. 1988. Gender Differences in Tobacco Use in Asian, African and Latin American Societies. Social Science and Medicine 27:1269–1275.

Wayburn, E. 1991. Human Health and Environmental Health. Western Journal of Medicine 154:341–343.

Wharton Econometrics. 1987. The Importance of Tobacco to the United States Foreign Trade. Washington, DC: United States Department of Health and Human Services.

Winkler, Daniel. 1987. WHO Should be Blamed for Being Sick? Health Education Quarterly 14(l):11–25.

World Health Organization. 1988. Can Community Health Workers Deal with Pneumonia? World Health Forum 9:221–224.

Yach, Derek. 1986. The Impact of Smoking in Developing Countries with Special Reference to Africa. International Journal of Health Services 16(2):279–292.

Yankelovich, S., et al. 1977. A Study of Cigarette Smoking among Teenage Girls and Young Women: Summary of the Findings. Washington, DC: U.S. Government Printing Office.

Yu, Jing Jie, et al. 1990. A Comparison of Smoking Patterns in the People's Republic of China with the United States: An Impending Health Catastrophe in the Middle Kingdom. Journal of the American Medical Association 264(12):1575–1579.

45

The Epidemiology of Functional Apartheid and Human Rights Abuses

H. Kristian Heggenhougen

Medical anthropologists working in public health programs easily get caught up in the details of projects. The goals of specific projects may be to introduce bed nets against malaria, to increase ORT against diarrhea-dehydration death, to promote breast-feeding and appropriate weanling foods against malnutrition, to increase the use of condoms to prevent AIDS or promote family planning, and so forth. The list of medical anthropological activities in international health projects is quite long (Lane and Rubinstein 1996). From the viewpoint of an international health worker working within a project, it is difficult to see the bigger picture, largely because there is too much to do here and now. On the other hand, when scholars try to explain the causes of health problems on a global scale, the analysis sometimes seems unduly critical and does not point toward specific actions. Anthropologists must serve a dual role in international health. First, they must help in the design and implementation of programs that are culturally appropriate and acceptable to local populations. Second, they must explain the complexity of the health problems in an international context and demonstrate how political and economic policies, historical forces, local cultural traditions, and systems of social stratification all play roles in the genesis of health problems. The solution to these health problems must take this complex web of forces into account—health improvements require political will as well as medical and public health tools.

This selection reminds us of the sociopolitical context of international health problems. It is an editorial about the end of the official policy of apartheid in South Africa as a reason for both celebration and reflection.

William Foege, the Director of the Task Force for Child Survival, has often said that the mission of public health must be social justice. This is an important and profound message. In general, clinical medicine works on one patient at a time—and only after the patient becomes sick. People in clinical medicine work very hard; their efforts are noble and they cure many people. When people are healed, they can thank their doctor. But clinical medicine is not well equipped to be effective on a larger, social level. The tools of clinical medicine are not designed to prevent health prob-

lems from occurring in the first place. People working in preventive medicine and public health are not thanked for the diseases they prevent or the lives they prolong. These people do not work for the gratitude of patients they have helped but rather for the satisfaction of knowing that their health programs improve the lives of those whom they will never meet. As we saw in the last selection, such public health projects are often underfunded, even though health improvements are recognized as being good for our society and our economy. Health programs are justified with a logic of costs and benefits—both economic and political.

Although people working in public health receive some social recognition and compensation, in part because they are working within the system, those who question the system and work directly for social justice outside the health-care realm are often vilified by society as troublemakers. President Nelson Mandela of South Africa is an example of such a troublemaker. His work will ultimately result in improvements in the health and welfare of the citizens of South Africa; increased social justice and economic opportunity will be more effective than an army of surgeons.

Questions of social inequality are domestic issues also. Middle-aged African-American men in Harlem have lower life expectancies than middle-aged men in an impoverished village in Bangladesh, and this premature death is caused by everyday (and preventable) medical conditions, such as cardiovascular disease (McCord and Freeman 1990). Medical anthropological studies of ethnicity and health continually emphasize the role of social class (see selection 31). This selection argues that recognition of the multifactorial causes of morbidity and mortality—particularly in regard to the social epidemiological distribution of suffering among the poor—requires our attention and action.

Medical anthropologists have made, and will continue to make, important contributions to the improvement of international health programs combating specific diseases and encouraging culturally appropriate and affordable health care. Although this is important work, we must keep the wider context in mind. As citizens of a rich nation in a poor world, we have moral responsibilities to help improve the lives of our fellow human beings.

434

As you read this selection, consider these questions:

- *What does the author mean by functional apartheid? Is this a characteristic of your society and your city? What might be some of the health consequences of this functional apartheid?*

- *If people working in international health programs become politically involved in local communities—for example, in human rights abuses—they might risk getting kicked out of the country. What do you think about this dilemma?*

- *Why does the author argue that the PHC Declaration at Alma Ata in 1978 and the WHO reports about the health consequences of apartheid were radical in their orientation? What is the meaning of the adage that "politics is medicine writ large"?*

- *Is it possible to be a successful scientist (including anthropologist) or doctor and be active in political struggles? Are there complications in this? Is the author asking too much of us?*

Over the past several years we have witnessed the dismantling of apartheid in South Africa, culminating with the all race election in April, 1994. To reach this stage, the cost in human lives has been considerable, but a cost greatly overshadowed by the lives lost and maimed by apartheid itself. We can only hope that the new South Africa will be born and allowed to mature without the price of additional loss of lives, and without the replacement of one form of apartheid with another.

The world might well congratulate itself by apartheid's collapse. Yet, in countries throughout the world, the structure and practice of a functional apartheid persists—in the United States[1] and other developed countries as elsewhere. While we may share in the celebration of the collapse of apartheid in South Africa we should not be blinded to the tenacity of apartheid in its various guises and its destructive consequences throughout the world. Groups of people are marginalized, exploited and abused, as a result both of their ethnicity and of their class; for being "the Other." They are those often considered less than human—the "gooks," "trash," "Inditos" or "subversivos," supposedly not true and equal citizens in their own countries (the "others," those apartheid: set aside). Whether apartheid is official Government policy or *de facto* (functional) may be a significant distinction but the health impact on "the others" may not be obviously distinctive.

A decade ago the WHO publications, *Apartheid and Health* and *Apartheid and Mental Health*, spoke poignantly and quite "radically" of the ill health effects of apartheid.[2] The epidemiology resulting from the direct and "hidden" human rights abuses of functional apartheid point to a worldwide epidemic of pandemic proportions—to incredible human suffering and needless death. Other health "risks," albeit severe, pale in comparison. Of course, infectious diseases are important and are responsible for the majority of morbidity and mortality in the world. Thus, malaria, TB, schistosomiasis and other specific diseases do warrant our attention. But, as we seek to prevent and to treat these diseases we must recognize their disproportional prevalence among certain groups of people and that they are as much an outcome of functional apartheid, and the synergistic relationship with malnutrition, including diarrhea, as of specific vectors.

The degree to which functional apartheid occurs, and to which marginalized people are abused and suffer (as identifiable groups), does of course vary from country to country, yet its presence in one form or another is pervasive. Unfortunately, there are ample examples. In terms of so-called "ethnic cleansing" Rwanda and the former Yugoslavia are but extreme examples. The thousands of accounts of the horrendous abuses suffered by Guatemalan Maya populations—marginalized both by ethnicity and class—is another.

In 1974 Vincente Navarro spoke metaphorically and dramatically but, I believe, correctly, when he stated that the equivalent of 20 nuclear bombs explode every year in Latin America without making a single sound.[3] From all accounts, and not only in Latin America, they are more numerous today—and still quite silent. There is obvious violence in the world, of course. Civil wars, homicides, torture (whether state sponsored or not), rape and a pervasive climate of fear in the lives of all too many have been a part of recent and current world history. Cambodia, Guatemala, El Salvador, Liberia, Nicaragua, Rwanda and the former Yugoslavia come immediately to mind, and the past history of countries such as Argentina, Uruguay and Chile serve as testimony. Until recently, in a country such as Colombia, the national homicide rate was ten times that of New York City. And in the United States, where a woman is raped every six minutes, violence is also rampant.[4] These human rights abuses quite clearly explain a great deal of the epidemiological, physical and mental health, patterns for people in these countries.

But the point Navarro wanted to make is that violence is not only direct but also "hidden" and silent. It is the violence resulting from the inequitable structure of apartheid (of "otherness"). It is this violence against which the Zapatistas in Chiapas say they are, finally, openly fighting. It is a violence which, according to even PAHO and similar institutions, claims more than one million Latin American lives a year. They may not talk about it in terms of apartheid or human rights abuses as such but to state that, "more than one million children under age five are dying each year, the majority from diseases which are preventable with today's technology"[5] is not too far apart. Elsewhere it is no less drastic. And the inter-relationships between the two kinds of violence also cannot be ignored.

It may no longer be particularly fashionable to speak of "social pathologies" when discussing health patterns, especially for marginalized groups; people's eyes glaze over—they throw their hands up in despair—when "poverty" is wheeled out as the underlying, root, cause of disease. Health problems seem, then, too overwhelming, the required tasks, too difficult. But, though difficult to handle, the evidence for such a connection—for acknowledging the social and human rights roots of disease—is inescapable, and our inattention, whether from dealing (and quite meaningfully so) with the more specific and "manageable" (aspects of the) problems—with "what (we feel) we can do"—or from plainly feeling such an association irrelevant, allows the continued attack on our public health; that is, if we, as public health and social science and medicine professionals, think of it as "our" health at all and not as "just their's."

The importance of class—of poverty—and of ethnicity in terms of health risks must not be considered too simply, however. It is not enough to make the link, especially since there are ample examples of relatively poor regions and countries of the world with much better health indicators than those of much richer groups and nations. A range of interconnected stressors affecting people's lives must be considered. Albeit class and ethnic differences may exist, the degree to which basic human rights and social welfare policies exist is also important. As is people's sense of dignity—the degree to which people are able to live in dignity, whether poorer than, or of an ethnicity different from, the majority of the elite, must enter into the equation.

Within the field of international public health the PHC Declaration of Alma Ata in 1978 served as a watershed for a wider perspective in thinking about why and how people get sick and for a reformulation of efforts to improve health. However cynical we may be

of the PHC policies now professed by most countries, and though we lament the rather limited nature of presently existing vertical rather than comprehensive PHC efforts, the interconnection of human rights and socioeconomic factors and health has been legitimized and stimulated—again, brought onto center stage—by this Declaration. But, precisely because the concepts of equity and social justice—and not only the establishment of equitable health care systems—are central to the PHC philosophy, it becomes difficult to implement comprehensive PHC programs since these, ultimately, must question and try to correct inequitable social relationships. We are left with asking whether Primary Health Care will be allowed to succeed.[6]

To use Guatemala as an example, the Nutritional Institute for Central America and Panama (INCAP) established in the early 1970s that 70% of all (Mayan and Ladino) Guatemalan children were malnourished. Seventy percent! By the 1980s INCAP confirmed that the rate had increased to 80%.[7]

If health is to improve in Guatemala the root causes of malnutrition must be attacked. A 1982 PAHO study concluded that 93% of all deaths of children between 1 and 4 were avoidable. Malnutrition must be attacked, of course, not only because of its deadly synergism with disease, but because of basic humanity and the human rights of children and adults.[7]

The health of Guatemalans is not only infected as a result of the structural violence of functional apartheid but has also been deeply affected by direct violence (large scale torture and murder) and a pervasive atmosphere of fear. Doughty asserts that "only the Spanish conquest equaled [the] devastation of holocaust proportions..." which has occurred in Guatemala since 1954.[8]

By and large, medical anthropologists working within public health and in collaboration with epidemiologists have concentrated on the significance of cultural factors in explaining epidemiological patterns and in promoting successful public health interventions. In the most negative sense anthropologists have been used to finding the culturally relevant buttons to push to market preconceived "effective and necessary" public health interventions. In a more positive light, anthropologists have been interpreters and intermediaries ensuring that public health interventions are mutually agreed upon and culturally appropriate.

Other contributions have concerned the health impact of the stresses of immigrant and refugee populations, and the relationship between degrees of acculturation and health. Such work has obviously been of great significance and continues to be of importance. Cultural practices do influence disease patterns. Despite this importance, however, I urge anthropologists, and other social scientists concerned with public health to include in their work human rights and socioeconomic (class) issues to a much greater extent. It is fundamental to public health. Any understanding of epidemiological patterns—any efforts to improve the health of people showing low health indicators—must consider, and attempt to affect, human rights and inequitable socio-political and economic conditions. The recent focus of national and international public health debates on "violence and health" and "health and human rights" is a promising development (and hopefully not just a passing fad) which has re-emphasized the importance of these issues. For example, at the Harvard School of Public Health in the United States there is now a Center for Health and Human Rights, and Harvard Medical School initiated a course on "Culture, Poverty and Infectious Diseases" in 1994.

Though not to be forgotten, our gaze must examine more than specific vectors and the so-called unhealthy behaviors of people, to include the total condition of people's lives—the context in which people (have to) live their everyday lives. In Nancy Scheper-Hughes' book *Death Without Weeping*,[9] for example, the message should be clear that it is not the culturally adapted practices allowing people to cope which should be criticized—such as mothers supposedly "not weeping" when their children die since they are supposedly "glad" that God so loved their child "angelitos" that He did not want to wait to have them with Him. We should rather criticize the social conditions which make such culturally adapted coping mechanisms necessary.

Considering violence, in both its direct and indirect forms—and the human rights and health issues so powerfully affecting the lives of hundreds of millions of people throughout the world, it is clear that improved health requires interventions and involvement from the outside as well as the inside. This presents ethical dilemmas to anthropologists (and others), often considered as the danger of cultural or ethical imperialism. The problem is also seen in terms of adherence to a philosophy of cultural relativism on the one hand and an agreement about cross-cultural universals on the other. These, however, do not necessarily have to be contradictory.

I would argue that most anthropologists are cultural relativists to the extent that we celebrate (the vibrancy of) cultural differences, yet increasingly we agree that we have obligations to take an ethical stance—some would even argue that this is a sine qua non for anthropologists—even if we realize (though we hate to admit it) that our ethical norms, at least in part, may be culturally derived.

Renteln[10] claims that ethical positions may be culture bound—or culturally derived through the process of acculturation—but by suggesting there are cross-cultural universals on which people from a range of cultures agree, she suggests that our relatively culture-bound ethical positions need not be imperialist since they often over-lap with the basic ethical positions of people in other cultures.

The issue of the appropriateness of intervention is confused, of course, in that the activities of concern occur within nation states, which many hold inviolable, yet these are not necessarily discrete cultural entities. States call on "cultural relativism" for support to avoid interference for maintaining inequitable political and social relationships. A recognition of cultural differences does not absolve us from the need to make ethical stances and to speak and act against human rights abuses and social inequities. The situation in countries such as Guatemala makes this emphatic. And, in any case, outside involvement has taken place for a long, long time both in toppling progressive regimes and in keeping despots in power. This alone should make us overcome our hesitancy to "interfere." [Yeats's poem comes to mind: "Things fall apart; the centre cannot hold;/ Mere anarchy is loosed upon the world,/ The blood-dimmed tide is loosed, and everywhere/ The best lack all conviction, while the worst/ Are full of passionate intensity."]

According to Anthony Cohen the dilemma for anthropologists should not necessarily be a matter of cultural relativism or not, and whether to intervene but rather "the issue for us is how to translate concern into action; and an anthropologist without concern is no anthropologist at all."[11]

Improvement in public health requires changes. Changes in behavior and in cultural practices are frequently suggested and often relevant. But improving health in countries such as Guatemala call for more basic (socioeconomic and political) changes. It requires an attack on the persistence of a system of functional apartheid, it requires elimination of overt state sponsored violence and torture and it requires a move towards a much more equitable system of land-distribution and employment compensation. How this can be done without putting people at further and greater risk must be included in such consideration. It may also not be appropriate for foreigners to direct such interventions in Guatemala, or elsewhere, although based on a basic and universal human rights credo (i.e. the UN Charter on Human Rights) we, as outsiders, have a responsibility to voice our concern and to assist those who are, in a step by step fashion, beginning to improve the overall conditions of their lives, to improve their health. Primary Health Care and the current concern with Health and Human Rights are two sides of the same coin—namely that basic equity, social justice, human rights and human dignity are essential to achievement of health. And it is with these issues, including, of course, the provision of easily accessible (available, affordable and acceptable) curative health services, that action must be taken.

What I am calling for is by no means easy, especially since we can not look at these issues simplistically, but, as my colleague, Paul Farmer, notes, "we must play with a full deck of cards"—no matter how expert we are in our own disciplines, nor how important specific technical interventions may be, we must insist on looking at, and attempting to improve people's health, through a matrix of a range of sociocultural (including political, economic and historical) factors not least of which are the examination, and consequences, of functional apartheid and human rights abuses. As I see it, this "playing with a full deck of cards" is of course what a journal such as *Social Science & Medicine* is all about but something which, in our erudition, we sometimes neglect. To paraphrase Norman Bethune,[12] this is fundamental to public health because (functional) apartheid based on greed and the human rights abuses against the "Others" are what cause the "wounds"—they cause (and keep causing) death and human misery.

REFERENCES

1. Brooks, D. D., Smith D. R. and Anderson R. J. Medical apartheid an American perspective. *JAMA* **266**, 2746, 1993.
2. WHO. *Apartheid and Health*. WHO, Geneva, 1983; *Apartheid and Mental Health Care*. WHO, Geneva, 1984.
3. Navarro V. The economic and political determinants of human (including health) rights. In *Imperialism, Health and Medicine*, pp. 53–76. Baywood Pub. Co., Farmingdale, New York, 1974. (See also: Navarro V. The underdevelopment of health or the health of underdevelopment: an analysis of the distribution of human health resources in Latin America. In *Imperialism, Health and Medicine* (Edited by Navarro V.), pp. 15–36. Baywood Pub. Co., Farmingdale, New York, 1974.
4. Heise L. Violence against women: the missing agenda. In *The Health of Women—A Global Perspective* (Edited by Koblinsky M., Timyan J. and Gay J.), pp. 171–196. Westview Press, Boulder, 1993.
5. Knouss R. F. The health situation in Latin America and the Caribbean: an overview. In *Health and Health Care in Latin America during the Lost Decade: Insights for the 1990s* (Edited by Weil C. and Scarpaci J.), p. 13. Minnesota Latin American Series, No. 3. 1992.
6. Heggenhougen H. K. Will primary health care efforts be allowed to succeed? *Soc. Sci. Med.* **19**, 217, 1984.
7. Green L. B., Consensus and coercion: primary health care and the Guatemalan State *Med. Anthrop Q.* **3**, 301, 1989.
8. Doughty P. L. Crossroads for anthropology: human rights in Latin America. *Human Rights and Anthropology*, pp. 43–71. Cultural Survival, Cambridge, MA, 1988.
9. Scheper-Hughes N. *Death Without Weeping: The Violence of Everyday Life in Brazil*. University of California Press, Berkeley, 1992.
10. Renteln A. R. Relativism and the search for human rights. *Am. Anthrop.* **90**, 56, 1988.
11. Hastrup K. and Elsass P. Anthropological advocacy—a contradiction in terms? *Curr. Anthrop.* **31**, 246, 1990.
12. Bethune N. Wounds. In *Away with All Pests: An English Surgeon in People's China: 1954–1969* (Edited by Horn J.), pp. 184–186. Monthly Review Press, New York, 1969.

References

TO THE INSTRUCTOR

Anderson, Robert. 1996. *Magic, Science and Health: The Aims and Achievements of Medical Anthropology.* Fort Worth, TX: Harcourt Brace.

Foster, George, and Barbara Anderson. 1978. *Medical Anthropology.* New York: Wiley.

Hahn, Robert A. 1995. *Sickness and Healing: An Anthropological Perspective.* New Haven, CT: Yale University Press.

Helman, Cecil, G. 1994. *Culture, Health and Illness.* Oxford: Butterworth Heinemann.

Landy, David, ed. 1977. *Culture, Disease, and Healing: Studies in Medical Anthropology.* New York: Macmillan.

Logan, Michael, and Edward E. Hunt, eds. 1978. *Health and the Human Condition.* North Scituate, MA: Duxbury.

McElroy, Ann, and Patrcia K. Townsend. 1996. *Medical Anthropology in Ecological Perspective.* Boulder, CO: Westview Press.

Sargent, Carolyn F., and Thomas M. Johnson, eds. 1996. *Medical Anthropology: Contemporary Theory and Method.* Westport, CT: Praeger.

Todd, Harry F., Jr., and Julio L. Ruffini, eds. 1979. *Teaching Medical Anthropology.* Vol. 1. Washington, DC: Society for Medical Anthropology.

TO THE STUDENT

Anderson, Robert. 1996. *Magic, Science and Health: The Aims and Achievements of Medical Anthropology.* Fort Worth, TX: Harcourt Brace.

McElroy, Ann, and Patricia K. Townsend. 1996. *Medical Anthropology in Ecological Perspective.* Boulder, CO: Westview.

Podolefsky, Aaron, and Peter J. Brown, eds. 1997. *Applying Anthropology: An Introductory Reader.* Mountain View, CA: Mayfield.

Sargent, Carolyn F., and Thomas M. Johnson, eds. 1996. *Medical Anthropology: Contemporary Theory and Method.* Westport, CT: Praeger.

PART I. UNDERSTANDING MEDICAL ANTHROPOLOGY

Brown, Peter J., Marcia Inhorn, and Daniel Smith. 1996. Disease, Ecology, and Human Behavior. In *Medical Anthropology: Contemporary Theory and Method,* edited by Carolyn Sargent and Thomas Johnson, pp. 183–219. Westport, CT: Praeger.

Diamond, Jared. 1987. "The Worst Mistake in Human History." *Discover, May:* 64–66.

Goodman, Alan, and Thomas Leatherman, eds. In press. *Building a New Biocultural Synthesis: Political-Economic Perspectives on Human Biology.* Ann Arbor: University of Michigan Press.

Hahn, Robert A. 1995. *Sickness and Healing: An Anthropological Perspective.* New Haven, CT: Yale University Press.

Harrison, G. A., et al. 1988. *Human Biology: An Introduction to Human Evolution, Variation, Growth, and Adaptability.* Oxford: Oxford University Press.

Johnston, Francis E., and Setha Low. 1984. "Biomedical Anthropology: An Emerging Synthesis in Anthropology." *Yearbook of Physical Anthropology* 27:215–227.

Jurmain, Robert, Harry Nelson, and William Turnbaugh. 1984. *Understanding Physical Anthropology and Archaeology.* St. Paul, MN: West.

Kendall, Carl. 1990. "Public Health and the Domestic Domain: Lessons from Anthropological Research on Diarrheal Diseases." In *Anthropology and Primary Health Care,* edited by Denis Mull and Jeannine Coreils, pp. 173–195. Boulder, CO: Westview.

Lee, Richard. 1992. "Art, Science, or Politics: The Crisis in Hunter-Gatherer Studies." *American Anthropologist* 94: 31–54.

McElroy, Ann, and Patricia K. Townsend. 1996. *Medical Anthropology in Ecological Perspective.* Boulder, CO: Westview.

McKeown, Thomas. 1979. *The Role of Medicine: Dream, Mirage, or Nemesis.* Princeton, NJ: Princeton University Press.

McNeill, William H. 1976. *Plagues and Peoples.* New York: Doubleday.

Moore, Lorna, et al. 1980. *The Biocultural Basis of Health: Expanding Views of Medical Anthropology*. St. Louis, MO: Mosby.

Payer, Lynn. 1988. *Medicine and Culture*. New York: Penguin.

Singer, Merrill. 1997. "Farewell to Adaptationism: Unnatural Selection and the Politics of Biology." *Medical Anthropology Quarterly 10*: 496–515.

Turshen, Meredith. 1984. *The Political Ecology of Disease in Tanzania*. New Brunswick, NJ: Rutgers University Press.

Ware, Norma. 1992. "Suffering and the Social Construction of Illness: the Delegitimation of Illness Experience in Chronic Fatigue Syndrome." *Medical Anthropology Quarterly 6*:347–361.

Weller, Susan, and A. K. Romney. 1988. *Systematic Data Collection*. Newbury Park, CA: Sage.

Wiley, Andrea. 1992. "Adaptation and the Biocultural Paradigm in Medical Anthropology: A Critical Review." *Medical Anthropology Quarterly 6*:216–236.

Young, James. 1981. *Medical Choice in a Mexican Village*. New Brunswick, NJ: Rutgers University Press.

EVOLUTION, HEALTH, AND MEDICINE

Armelagos, George. 1997. "Disease, Darwin, and the Third Epidemiological Transition." *Journal of Human Evolution 5*:212–220.

Eaton, S. Boyd, Marjorie Shostak, and Melvin Konner. 1988. *The Paleolithic Prescription: A Program of Diet and Exercise and a Design for Living*. New York: Harper & Row.

Ewald, Paul. 1994. *Evolution of Infectious Disease*. Oxford: Oxford University Press.

Johnson, Allen, and Timothy Earle. 1987. *The Evolution of Human Societies: From Foraging Group to Agrarian State*. Palo Alto, CA: Stanford University Press.

Nesse, Randolph, and George C. Williams. 1994. *Why We Get Sick: The New Science of Darwinian Medicine*. New York: Random House.

Solway, J. S., and R. B. Lee. 1990. "Foragers, Genuine or Spurious? Situating the Kalahari San in History." *Current Anthropology 31*: 109–146.

Whitaker, Elizabeth D. 1996. "Ancient Bodies, Modern Customs, and Our Health." In *Applying Anthropology*, edited by A. Podolefsy and P. J. Brown, pp. 36–45. Mountain View, CA: Mayfield.

HUMAN BIOLOGICAL VARIATION

Armelagos, George. 1997. "Disease, Darwin, and the Third Epidemiological Transition." *Journal of Human Evolution 5*:212–220.

Boas, Franz. 1940. *Race, Language, Culture*. New York: Macmillan.

Frisancho, A. Roberto. 1993. *Human Adaptation and Accommodation*. Ann Arbor: University of Michigan Press.

Lasker, Gabriel. 1969. "Human Biological Adaptability." *Science 14*: 1480–1486.

BIOARCHAEOLOGY AND THE HISTORY OF HEALTH

Armelagos, George, and John R. Dewey. 1970. "Evolutionary Responses to Human Infectious Diseases." *BioScience 157*:638–644.

Caldwell, John. 1982. *Theory of Fertility Decline*. San Francisco: Academic Press.

Cohen, Mark N. 1989. *Health and the Rise of Civilization*. New Haven, CT: Yale University Press.

Cohen, Mark N., and George J. Armelagos, eds. 1984. *Paleopathology at the Origins of Agriculture*. New Haven, CT: Yale University Press.

Kunitz, Stephen. 1983. *Disease Change and the Role of Medicine: The Navajo Experience*. Berkeley: University of California Press.

Kunitz, Stephen J. 1994. *Disease and Social Diversity: The European Impact on the Health of Non-Europeans*. New York: Oxford University Press.

McKeown, Thomas. 1979. *The Role of Medicine: Dream, Mirage, or Nemesis?* Princeton, NJ: Princeton University Press.

McNeill, William H. 1976. *Plagues and Peoples*. Garden City, NY: Doubleday.

CULTURAL AND POLITICAL ECOLOGIES OF DISEASE

Alland, Alexander. 1970. *Adaptation in Cultural Evolution*. New York: Columbia University Press.

Baer, Hans. 1996. "Toward a Political Economy of Health in Medical Anthropology." *Medical Anthropology Quarterly 10*:451–454.

Brown, Peter J. 1986. "Socioeconomic and Demographic Effects of Malaria Eradication: A Comparison of Sri Lanka and Sardinia." *Social Science and Medicine 22*(8):847–861.

Brown, Peter J. 1997. "Culture and the Global Resurgence of Malaria." In *The Anthropology of Infectious Disease: International Health Perspectives*, edited by Marcia Inhorn and Peter Brown, pp. 119–141. Newark, NJ: Gordon and Breach.

Burnet, M., and D. O. White. 1978. *The Natural History of Infectious Disease*. Cambridge: Cambridge University Press.

Durham, William H. 1991. *Coevolution: Genes, Mind, and Culture*. Palo Alto: Stanford University Press.

Edgerton, Robert. 1992. *Sick Societies: The Myth of Primitive Harmony*. New York: Free Press.

McKeown, Thomas. 1988. *The Origins of Human Disease*. New York: Blackwell.

Moran, Emilio F., ed. 1990. *The Ecosystem Approach in Anthropology: From Concept to Practice.* Ann Arbor: University of Michigan Press.

Oaks, Stanley C., et al., eds. 1991. *Malaria: Obstacles and Opportunities.* Washington, DC: National Academy Press.

Ormerod, W. E. 1976. "Ecological Effects of Control of African Trypanosomiasis." *Science* 191:815–821.

Trostle, J. and J. Sommerfeld. 1996. "Epidemiology and Medical Anthropology." *Annual Review of Anthropology* 25: 253–274.

Wiley, Andrea. 1992. "Adaptation and the Biocultural Paradigm in Medical Anthropology: A Critical Review." *Medical Anthropology Quarterly* 6:216–236.

BELIEF AND ETHNOMEDICAL SYSTEMS

Csordas, Thomas, and Arthur Kleinman. 1996. "The Therapeutic Process." In *Medical Anthropology: Contemporary Theory and Method,* edited by Carolyn F. Sargent and Thomas F. Johnson, pp. 3–20. Westport, CT: Praeger.

Dow, James. 1986. "Universal Aspects of Symbolic Healing: A Theoretical Synthesis." *American Anthropologist* 88: 56–69.

Eisenberg, Leon. 1977. "Disease and Illness: Distinctions Between Professional and Popular Ideas of Sickness." *Culture, Medicine and Psychiatry* 1: 9–23.

Hahn, Robert A. 1995. *Sickness and Healing: An Anthropological Perspective.* New Haven, CT: Yale University Press.

Hahn, Robert A., and Arthur Kleinman. 1983. "Belief as Pathogen, Belief as Medicine." *Medical Anthropology Quarterly* 14(4): 3, 16–19.

Kleinman, Arthur. 1980. *Patients and Healers in the Context of Culture.* Berkeley: University of California Press.

Moerman, Daniel E. 1991. "Physiology and Symbols: The Anthropological Implications of the Placebo Effect." In *The Anthropology of Medicine: From Culture to Method,* edited by L. Romanucci-Ross, D. E. Moerman, and L. R. Tancredi, pp. 129–146. Westport, CT: Bergin and Garvey.

Payer, Lynn. 1988. *Medicine and Culture.* New York: Penguin.

Payer, Lynn. 1994. *The Disease Mongers.* New York: Wiley.

Rhodes, Lorna Amarasingham. 1996. "Studying Biomedicine as a Cultural System." In *Medical Anthropology: Contemporary Theory and Method,* edited by Carolyn Sargent and Thomas Johnson. Westport, CT: Praeger.

THE SOCIAL CONSTRUCTION OF ILLNESS AND THE SOCIAL PRODUCTION OF HEALTH

Berger, Peter L., and Thomas Luckmann. 1967. *The Social Construction of Reality: A Treatise in the Sociology of Knowledge.* Garden City, NY: Anchor.

Janzen, John. 1978. *The Quest for Therapy: Medical Pluralism in Lower Zaire.* Berkeley: University of California Press.

McCord, Colin, and Harold Freeman. 1990. "Excess Mortality in Harlem." *New England Journal of Medicine* 322: 173–177.

Sontag, Susan. 1978. *Illness as Metaphor.* New York: Farrar, Strauss & Giroux.

HEALERS IN CROSS-CULTURAL PERSPECTIVE

Casteneda, Carlos. 1973. *The Teachings of Don Juan.* New York: Simon & Schuster.

Chagnon, Napoleon. 1968. *Yanomamo: The Fierce People.* New York: Holt, Rinehart & Winston.

DesJarlais, Robert. 1992. *Body and Emotion: The Aesthetics of Illness and Healing in the Nepal Himalayas.* Philadelphia: University of Pennsylvania Press.

Desowitz, Robert S. 1987. *The Thorn in the Starfish: How the Human Immune System Works.* New York: Norton.

Hahn, Robert A., and Atwood D. Gaines, eds. 1985. *Physicians of Western Medicine: Anthropological Approaches to Theory and Practice.* Dordrecht: D. Reidel.

Harner, Michael. 1968. "The Sound of Rushing Water." *Natural History,* June/July.

Harner, Michael. 1990. *The Way of the Shaman.* San Francisco: Harper & Row.

Jones, David E. 1972. *Sanapia: A Comanche Medicine Woman.* New York: Holt, Rinehart & Winston.

Katz, Pearl. 1990. "Ritual in the Operating Room." In *American Culture: Essays on the Familiar and Unfamiliar,* edited by L. Ploicov, pp. 279–294. Pittsburgh: University of Pennsylvania Press.

Katz, Richard. 1982. *Boiling Energy.* Cambridge, MA: Harvard University Press.

Konner, Melvin. 1982. *The Tangled Wing: Biological Constraints on the Human Spirit.* New York: Holt, Rhinehart & Winston.

Konner, Melvin. 1987. *Becoming a Doctor: A Journey of Initiation in Medical School.* New York: Penguin.

Laderman, Carol, and Marina Roseman, eds. 1996. *The Performance of Healing.* New York: Routledge.

Shostak, Marjorie. 1981. *Nisa: The Life and Words of a !Kung Woman.* London: Allen Lane, Penguin Books Ltd.

Tylor, Edward B. 1889. *Primitive Culture: Researches in the Development of Mythology, Philosophy, Religion, Language, Art, and Custom.* New York: Holt.

CULTURE, ILLNESS, AND MENTAL HEALTH

Allen, J. S., and Sarich, V. M. 1988. "Schizophrenia in an Evolutionary Perspective." *Perspective in Biology and Medicine* 32:132–153.

DesJarlais, Robert, Arthur Kleinman, et al., eds. 1995. *World Mental Health: Problems, Priorities and Responses in Low-Income Countries.* New York: Oxford University Press.

Gaines, Atwood. 1992. *Ethnopsychiatry: The Cultural Construction of Professional and Folk Psychiatries*. Albany: State University of New York Press.

Hahn, Robert A. 1995. *Sickness and Healing: An Anthropological Perspective*. New Haven, CT: Yale University Press.

Heggenhougen, H. Kristian. 1984. "Traditional Medicine and the Treatment of Drug Addicts: Three Examples from Southeast Asia." *Medical Anthropology Quarterly* 16(os) (1): 3–7.

Johnson, Thomas. 1987. "Premenstrual Syndrome as a Culture-Specific Disorder." *Culture, Medicine and Psychiatry* 11: 337–356.

Kleinman, Arthur. 1988. *Rethinking Psychiatry*. New York: Free Press.

Kleinman, Arthur and Byron Good, eds. 1985. *Culture and Depression: Studies in the Anthropology and Cross-Cultural Psychiatry of Affect and Disorder*. Berkeley: University of California Press.

Nuckolls, Charles. 1996. *The Cultural Dialectics of Knowledge and Desire*. Madison: University of Wisconsin Press.

Ritenbaugh, Cheryl. 1978. "Obesity as a Culture Bound Syndrome." *Culture, Medicine and Psychiatry* 6: 347–361.

Rubel, Arthur J., Carl W. O'Nell, and Rolando Collado-Ardon. 1984. *Susto: A Folk Illness*. Berkeley: University of California Press.

Scheper-Hughes, Nancy. 1979. *Saints, Scholars and Schizophrenics: Mental Illness in Rural Ireland*. Berkeley: University of California Press.

Selye, Hans. 1976. *Stress in Health and Disease*. Boston: Butterworths.

Simons, Ronald. 1985. "Latah." In *The Culture-Bound Syndromes*, edited by Ronald C. Simons and Charles C. Hughes. Dordrecht and Boston: D. Reidel.

Simons, Ronald. 1996. *BOO: Culture, Experience, and the Startle Reflex*. New York: Oxford University Press.

Simons, Ronald C. and Charles C. Hughes. eds. 1985. *The Culture-Bound Syndrome*. Dordrecht and Boston: D. Reidel.

Solzhenitsyn, Aleksandr. 1973 *The Gulag Archipelago, 1918–1956*. New York: Harper & Row.

Szasz, Thomas. 1974. *The Myth of Mental Illness: Foundations of a Theory of Personal Conduct*. New York: Harper & Row.

CRITICAL MEDICAL ANTHROPOLOGY

Gordon, D., and M. Lock. 1988. *Biomedicine Examined*. Dordrecht and Boston: Kluwer Academic Publishers.

Lindenbaum, Shirley, & Margaret Lock, eds. 1993. *Knowledge, Power and Practice*. Berkeley: University of California Press.

Rosen, George. 1974. *From Medical Police to Social Medicine: Essays in the History of Health Care*. New York: Neale Watson Publishers.

Shore, Bradd. 1995. *Culture in Mind*. New York: Oxford University Press.

PART II. APPLYING MEDICAL ANTHROPOLOGY

Chambers, Erve. 1985. *Applied Anthropology: A Practical Guide*. Englewood Cliffs, NJ: Prentice-Hall.

Eddy, Elizabeth M., and William L. Partridge, eds. 1987. *Applied Anthropology in America*. New York: Columbia University Press.

Johnson, Thomas M. 1997. "Anthropology and the World of Physicians." In *Applying Cultural Anthropology*, edited by Peter J. Brown and Aaron Podolefsky, pp. 271–274. Mountain View, CA: Mayfield.

van Willigen, John. 1993. *Applied Anthropology: An Introduction*. Westport, CT: Bergin & Garvey.

van Willigen, John, Barbara Rylko-Bauer, and Ann McElroy, eds. 1989. *Making Our Research Useful: Case Studies in the Utilization of Anthropological Knowledge*. Boulder, CO: Westview Press.

Wulff, Robert M., and Shirley J. Fiske, eds. 1987. *Anthropological Praxis: Translating Knowledge into Action*. Boulder, CO: Westview Press.

CASE STUDIES IN EXPLANATORY MODELS

Blumhagen, Dan. 1980. "Hypertension: A Folk Illness with a Medical Name." *Culture, Medicine and Psychiatry* 4:197–227.

Brown, Peter J., Jessica Gregg, and Bruce Ballard. 1997. "Culture, Ethnicity, and the Practice of Medicine." In *Human Behavior for Medical Students*, edited by Alan Stoudemire. New York: Lippincott.

Foster, George M. 1994. *Hippocrates' Latin American Legacy: Humoral Medicine in the New World*. Langhorne, PA: Gordon & Breach.

Harwood, Alan. 1977. *Rx-Spiritist as Needed: A Study of a Puerto Rican Community Mental Health Resource*. New York: Wiley.

Heurtin-Roberts, Suzanne, and Efrain Reisin. 1990. "Folk Models of Hypertension among Black Women: Problems in Illness Management." In *Anthropology and Primary Health Care*, edited by J. Coreil and J. D. Mull. Boulder, CO: Westview Press.

Kleinman, Arthur. 1988. *Rethinking Psychiatry*. New York: Free Press.

Konner, Melvin. 1993. *Medicine at the Crossroads: The Crisis in Health Care*. New York: Pantheon.

Leslie, Charles M. 1972. "The Professionalization of Ayurvedic and Unani Medicine." In *Medical Men and Their Work: A Sociological Reader*, edited by E. Freidson and E. J. Lorber, pp. 39–54. Chicago: Aldine.

Leslie, Charles M. 1976. *Asian Medical Systems: A Comparative Study*. Berkeley: University of California Press.

Logan, Michael H. 1977. "Anthropological Research on the Hot-Cold Theory of Disease: Some Methodological Suggestions." *Medical Anthropology* 1: 87–108.

Mathews, Holly F. 1988. "Sweet Blood Can Give You Sugar: Black American Folk Beliefs about Diabetes." *City Medicine 2*: 12–16.

Polgar, Stephen. 1962. "Health and Human Behavior: Areas of Interest Common to the Social and Medical Sciences." *Current Anthropology 3*: 159–205.

Romanucci-Ross, Lola. 1969. "The Hierarchy of Resort in Curative Practices: The Admiralty Islands." *Journal of Health and Social Behavior 10*: 201–209.

Snow, Loudell F. 1993. *Walkin' Over Medicine*. Boulder, CO: Westview Press.

Sontag, Susan. 1978. *Illness as Metaphor*. New York: Farrar, Straus & Giroux.

Sontag, Susan. 1990. *Illness as Metaphor* and *AIDS and its Metaphors*. New York: Doubleday.

ETHNICITY AND HEALTH CARE

Barker, Judith, and Margaret Clark, eds. 1992. "Cross-Cultural Medicine: A Decade Later." *Western Journal of Medicine 157*: 247–374.

Barth, Fredrik, ed. 1969. *Ethnic Groups and Boundaries. The Social Organization of Culture Difference*. London: Allen & Unwin.

Brown, Peter J., Jessica Gregg, and Bruce Ballard. 1997. "Culture, Ethnicity, and the Practice of Medicine." In *Human Behavior for Medical Students*, edited by Alan Stoudemire. New York: Lippincott.

Clark, Margaret, ed. 1983. "Cross-Cultural Medicine." *Western Journal of Medicine 139*: 805–932.

DelVecchio Good, Mary-Jo, Paul Brodin, Byron Good, and Arthur Kleinman, eds. 1992. *Pain as Human Experience: An Anthropological Perspective*. Berkeley: University of California Press.

Goodman, Alan, and George Armelagos. 1996. "The Resurrection of Race: The Concept of Race in Physical Anthropology in the 1990s." In *Race and Other Misadventures*, edited by L. R. L. Reynolds. Dix Hills, NY: General Hall.

Harris, Marvin. 1980. *Patterns of Race in the Americas*. Westport, CT: Greenwood.

Harwood, Alan, ed. 1981. *Ethnicity and Medical Care*. Cambridge, MA: Harvard University Press.

Illich, Ivan. 1976. *Medical Nemesis: The Expropriation of Health*. New York: Pantheon Books.

Inhorn, Marcia. 1994. *Quest for Conception: Gender, Infertility, and Egyptian Medical Traditions*. Philadelphia: University of Pennsylvania Press.

Weller, Susan C., Lee M. Pachter, Robert Trotter, and Roberta Baer. 1992. "Empacho in Four Latino Groups: A Study in Intra- and Inter-Cultural Variation in Beliefs." *Medical Anthropology 15*: 109–136.

Wright, Lawrence. 1994. "One Drop of Blood." *The New Yorker 70*: 46–55.

Wulff, Robert M., and Shirley J. Fiske, eds. 1987. *Anthropological Praxis: Translating Knowledge into Action*. Boulder, CO: Westview Press.

Zborowski, Mark. 1952. "Cultural Components in Response to Pain." *Journal of Social Issues 8*: 16–30.

Zborowski, Mark. 1969. *People in Pain*. San Francisco: Jossey-Bass.

STIGMA AND COPING WITH CHRONIC ILLNESS

Ablon, Joan. 1988. *Living with Difference: Families with Dwarf Children*. New York: Praeger.

Bolton, R., and G. Orozco. 1994. *The AIDS Bibliography: Studies in Anthropology and Related Fields*. Arlington, VA: American Anthropological Association.

Eisenberg, David, et al. 1993. "Unconventional Medicine in the United States." *New England Journal of Medicine 328*: 246–252.

Farmer, Paul. 1988. *AIDS and Accusation: Haiti and the Geography of Blame*. Berkeley: University of California Press.

Farmer, Paul, Margaret Connors, and Janie Simmons. 1996. *Women, Poverty and AIDS: Sex, Drugs and Structural Violence*. Monroe, ME: Common Courage Press.

Goffman, Erving. 1963. *Stigma: Notes on the Management of Spoiled Identity*. Englewood Cliffs, NJ: Prentice-Hall.

Gregg, Charles T. 1983. *A Virus of Love and Other Tales of Medical Detection*. Albuquerque: University of New Mexico Press.

Hahn, Robert A. 1995. *Sickness and Healing: An Anthropological Perspective*. New Haven, CT: Yale University Press.

Kleinman, Arthur. 1988. *The Illness Narratives: Suffering, Healing and the Human Condition*. New York: Basic Books.

Murphy, Robert F. 1987. *The Body Silent*. New York: Holt.

Murphy, Robert F., and Buell Quain. 1955. *The Trumaí Indians of Central Brazil*. Locust Vally, NY: J. J. Augustin.

Murphy, Yolanda, and Robert Murphy. 1985. *Women of the Forest*. New York: Columbia University Press.

Price, Reynolds. 1994. *A Whole New Life*. New York: Atheneum.

Savishinsky, Joel S. 1991. *The Ends of Time: Life and Work in a Nursing Home*. Westport, CT: Bergin & Garvey.

Sokolovsky, Jay, ed. 1983. *Growing Old in Different Societies: Cross-cultural Perspectives*. Belmont, CA: Wadsworth.

Wolf, Naomi. 1992. *The Beauty Myth: How Images of Beauty Are Used Against Women*. New York: Anchor Books.

GENDER AND WOMEN'S HEALTH

Coulmas, Florian, ed. 1997. *The Handbook of Sociolinguistics*. Oxford: Blackwell Publishers.

Ginsburg, Faye D. 1989. *Contested Lives: The Abortion Debate in an American Community*. Berkeley: University of California Press.

Hahn, Robert A., ed. 1987. "Obstetrics in the United States: Woman, Physician, and Society." *Medical Anthropology Quarterly 1*: 227–320.

Hahn, Robert A., and Atwood D. Gaines, eds. 1985. *Physicians of Western Medicine: Anthropological Approaches to Theory and Practice*. Dordrecht: D. Reidel.

Latour, Bruno. 1986. *Laboratory Life: The Construction of Scientific Facts*. Princeton, NJ: Princeton University Press.

Martin, Emily. 1987. *The Woman in the Body: A Cultural Analysis of Reproduction*. New York: Beacon.

Martinez, Rebecca, Leo Chavez, and Alan Hubbell. 1997. "Purity and Passion: Risk and Morality in Latina Immigrants' and Physicans' Beliefs About Cervical Cancer." *Medical Anthropology* 17: 337–362.

Miller, Barbara D. 1987. "Female Infanticide and Child Neglect in Rural North India." In *Child Survival: Anthropological Perspectives on the Treatment and Maltreatment of Children*, edited by Nancy Scheper-Hughes, pp. 95–112. Dordrecht: D. Reidel.

Morgen, Sandra, ed. 1989. *Gender and Anthropology: Critical Reviews for Research and Teaching*. Washington, DC: American Anthropological Association.

Payer, Lynn. 1988. *Medicine and Culture*. New York: Penguin.

Sargent, Carolyn F., and Caroline B. Brettell, eds. 1996. *Gender and Health*. Upper Saddle River, NJ: Prentice Hall.

Scheper-Hughes, Nancy. 1992. *Death Without Weeping: The Violence of Everyday Life in Brazil*. Berkeley: University of California Press.

Tannen, Deborah. 1990. *You Just Don't Understand: Women and Men in Conversation*. New York: Morrow.

Turnbull, Colin M. 1972. *The Mountain People*. New York: Simon & Schuster.

CULTURE AND NUTRITION: FAT AND THIN

Bordo, Susan. 1993. *Unbearable Weight: Feminism, Western Culture, and the Body*. Berkeley: University of California Press.

Brumberg, Joan Jacobs. 1988. Fasting Girls: The Emergence of Anorexia Nervosa as a Modern Disease. Cambridge, MA: Harvard University Press.

Cassidy, Claire. 1982. "Protein-Energy Malnutrition as a Culture-Bound Syndrome." *Culture, Medicine, and Psychiatry* 6: 325–345.

Condit, Vicki Bentley. 1990. "Anorexia Nervosa: Levels of Causation." *Human Nature* 1: 391–413.

Dettwyler, Katherine A. 1994. *Dancing Skeletons: Life and Death in West Africa*. Prospect Heights, IL: Waveland.

Dettwyler, Katherine, and Claudia Fishman. 1992. "Infant Feeding Practices and Growth." *Annual Review of Anthropology* 21: 171–204.

Fernandez, Renate L. 1990. *A Simple Matter of Salt: An Ethnography of Nutritional Deficiency in Spain*. Berkeley: University of California Press.

Greene, Lawrence S., ed. 1977. *Malnutrition, Behavior, and Social Organization*. New York: Academic Press.

INTERNATIONAL HEALTH ISSUES AND PROGRAMS

Basch, Paul F. 1990. *Textbook of International Health*. New York: Oxford University Press.

Bentley, Margaret, Perti Pelto, and Gretel Pelto. 1990. "Applied Anthropological Research Methods: Diarrhea Studies as an Example." In *Anthropology and Primary Health Care*, edited by J. Coreil and J. D. Mull. Boulder: Westview Press.

Coreil, Jeannine, and J. Denis Mull, eds. 1990. *Anthropology and Primary Health Care*. Boulder, CO: Westview Press.

Cosminsky, Sheila. 1986. "Traditional Birth Practices and Pregnancy Avoidance in the Americas" In *The Potential of the Traditional Birth Attendant*, edited by A. Mangay-Maglacas and J. Simons. Vol. WHO Offset Publication No. 95. Geneva: World Health Organization.

Dettwyler, Katherine, and Claudia Fishman. 1992. "Infant Feeding Practices and Growth." *Annual Review of Anthropology* 21: 171–204.

Foster, George. 1987. "Bureaucratic Aspects of International Health Agencies." *Social Science and Medicine* 25:1039–1048.

Gove, Sandy, and Gretel H. Pelto. 1993. "Focused Ethnographic Studies in the WHO Programme for the Control of Acute Respiratory Infections." *Medical Anthropology* 15: 409–424.

Green, Edward C. 1985. "Traditional Healers, Mothers and Childhood Diarrheal Disease in Swaziland: The Interface of Anthropology and Health Education." *Social Science and Medicine* 20(3): 277–285.

Justice, Judith. 1986. *Policies, Plans, and People: Foreign Aid and Health Development*. Berkeley: University of California Press.

Lane, Sandra D., and Robert A. Rubinstein. 1996. "International Health: Problems and Programs in International Health." In *Medical Anthropology: Contemporary Theory and Method*, edited by Carolyn Sargent and Thomas Johnson, Westport, CT: Praeger.

McCord, Colin, and Harold Freeman. 1990. "Excess Mortality in Harlem." *New England Journal of Medicine* 322: 173–177.

Nichter, Mark. 1993. "Introduction: Anthropological Studies of Acute Respiratory Infection." *Medical Anthropology* 15: 319–334.

Credits

George J. Armelagos, "Health and Disease in Prehistoric Populations in Transition" from *Diseases in Populations in Transition*, Alan C. Swedlund and George Armelagos, editors, Bergin and Garvey, 1990. Copyright ©1990 Alan C. Swedlund and George Armelagos. Reproduced with permission of Greenwood Publishing Group, Inc., Westport, CT.

Maryann S. Bates and W. Thomas Edwards, "Ethnic Variations in the Chronic Pain Experience." Reprinted with permission from *Ethnicity and Disease*, 1992, 2:1, 63–83. Copyright ©1992 International Society on Hypertension in Blacks.

Gaylene Becker, "Coping with Stigma: Lifelong Adaptation of Deaf People." Reprinted with permission from *Social Science and Medicine*, Vol. 15, pp. 21–24, 1981, Elsevier Science Ltd., Oxford, England.

Elois Ann Berlin and William C. Fowkes, "A Teaching Framework for Cross-Cultural Health Care," *Western Journal of Medicine* 139:130–134. Reprinted by permission of The Western Journal of Medicine.

Marie I. Boutté, "Genetic Prophecy: Promises and Perils for Late-Onset Diseases," *Practicing Anthropology*, 1992, 4:1, 6–9. Reprinted with permission of Society for Applied Anthropology.

Michael F. Brown, "The Dark Side of Shaman." With permission from *Natural History*, November, 1989, 8–10. Copyright ©1989 American Museum of Natural History.

Peter J. Brown, "Cultural Adaptations to Endemic Malaria in Sardinia," *Medical Anthropology* 5:3, 1981. Reprinted with permission of Gordon and Breach Publishers.

Peter J. Brown and Melvin Konner, "An Anthropological Perspective on Obesity," *Annals of the New York Academy of Sciences*, 1987. Reprinted with permission of The New York Academy of Sciences.

Lauren Clark, "Gender and Generation in Poor Women's Household Production Experiences." Reproduced by permission of American Anthropological Association from *Medical Anthropology Quarterly* 7:4, December 1993. Not for further reproduction.

Robert S. Desowitz, "The Fly That Would Be King" from *New Guinea Tapeworms and Jewish Grandmothers: Tales of Parasites and People* by Robert S. Desowitz. Copyright ©1981 by Robert S. Desowitz. Reprinted by permission of W.W. Norton & Company, Inc.

Katherine A. Dettwyler, "The Biocultural Approach in Nutritional Anthropology: Case Studies of Malnutrition in Mali," *Medical Anthropology* 15:1, 17–39. Reprinted with permission of Gordon and Breach Publishers.

William W. Dressler, "Ethnomedical Beliefs and Patient Adherence to a Treatment Regimen: A St. Lucian Example," *Human Organization* 39:88–91. Reprinted with permission from Society for Applied Anthropology.

Boyd S. Eaton, Marjorie Shostak, and Melvin Konner, "Stoneagers in the Fast Lane." Reprinted with permission from *American Journal of Medicine* 84; 1988:739–749. Excerpta Medica, Inc.

Paul P. Farmer and Arthur Kleinman, "AIDS as Human Suffering." Reprinted by permission of *Daedalus*, Journal of the American Academy of Arts and Sciences, from the issue entitled "Living with AIDS," Spring 1989, Vol. 118, No. 2.

Kaja Finkler, "Sacred Healing and Biomedicine Compared." Reproduced by permission of the American Anthropological Association from *Medical Anthropology Quarterly* 8:2, June 1994. Not for further reproduction.

George M. Foster, "Disease Etiologies in Nonwestern Medical Systems." Reproduced by permission of the American Anthropological Association from *American Anthropologist* 78:4, December 1976. Not for further reproduction.

Alan Harwood, "The Hot-Cold Theory of Disease: Implications for the Treatment of Puerto-Rican Patients," Journal of the American Medical Association, 1971, Vol. 216, 1153. Copyright ©1971 American Medical Association. Used with permission.

H. Kristian Heggenhougen, "The Epidemiology of Functional Apartheid and Human Rights Abuses." Reprinted with permission from *Social Science and Medicine*, Vol. 10, No. 3, 281–284, 1995, Elsevier Science Ltd., Oxford, England.

Marcia C. Inhorn, "Genital Herpes: An Ethnographic Inquiry into Being Discreditable in American Society." Reproduced by permission of the American Anthropological Association from *Medical Anthropology Quarterly* 17:3, May 1986. Not for further reproduction.

Carl Kendall, Dennis Foote, and Reynaldo Martorell, "Ethnomedicine and Oral Rehydration Therapy." Reprinted with permission from *Social Science and Medicine*,

Index